P9-DWY-207

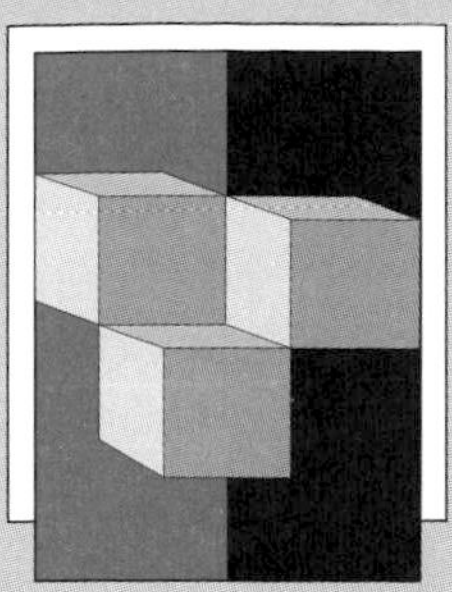

LEGAL ENVIRONMENT OF BUSINESS

IRWIN LEGAL STUDIES IN BUSINESS SERIES

Adamson
Basic Business Law
1995

Barnes/Dworkin/Richards
Law for Business
Sixth Edition, 1997

Bennett-Alexander/Pincus
Employment Law
1995

Blackburn/Klayman/Malin
The Legal Environment of Business
Fifth Edition, 1994

Bowers/Mallor/Barnes/Phillips/Langvardt
Law of Commercial Transactions and Business Associations
1995

Dworkin
Contract Law Tutorial Software
1993

Dworkin/Barnes/Richards
Essentials of Business Law and the Regulatory Environment
1995

Klayman/Bagby/Ellis
Irwin's Business Law
1994

McAdams
Law, Business and Society
Fourth Edition, 1995

McAdams/Pincus
Legal Environment of Business: Ethical and Public Policy Contexts
1997

McCarty/Bagby
Irwin's Legal and Regulatory Environment of Business
Third Edition, 1996

Metzger/Mallor/Barnes/Bowers/Phillips/Langvardt
Business Law and the Regulatory Environment: Concepts and Cases
Ninth Edition, 1995

Richards
Law for Global Business
Second Edition, 1997

Tucker/Henkel
The Legal and Ethical Environment of Business
1992

Legal Environment of Business

Ethical and Public Policy Contexts

Tony McAdams

University of Northern Iowa
Department of Management

Laura Pincus

DePaul University
Department of Management

IRWIN

Chicago · Bogotá · Boston · Buenos Aires · Caracas
London · Madrid · Mexico City · Sydney · Toronto

Irwin Book Team
Publisher: *Rob Zwettler*
Sponsoring editor: *Karen Mellon*
Editorial coordinator: *Christine Scheid*
Director of marketing: *Kurt L. Strand*
Project supervisor: *Maggie Rathke*
Production supervisor: *Pat Frederickson*
Designer: *Larry J. Cope*
Cover designer: *Stuart Paterson, Image House Inc.*
Cover illustration: *Keith D. Skeen*
Director, Prepress Purchasing: *Kimberly Meriwether David*
Compositor: *Times Mirror Higher Education Group, Inc., Imaging Group*
Typeface: *10/12 Times Roman*
Printer: *Von Hoffman Press, Inc*

Times Mirror
Higher Education Group

Library of Congress Cataloging-in-Publication Data

McAdams, Tony.
Legal environment of business:ethical and public policy contexts /Tony McAdams, Laura Pincus.
p. cm.—(Irwin legal studies in business series)
Includes bibliographical references and index.
ISBN 0-256-17051-7
1. Business law—United States. 2. Business ethics—United States. 3. Industrial policy—United States. I. Pincus, Laura B. II. Title. III. Series.
KF889.3.M39 1997
346.73'07—dc20
[347.3067]

96–28713

Printed in the United States of America
1 2 3 4 5 6 7 8 9 0 VH 3 2 1 0 9 8 7 6

To those who have offered me their consistent integrity, who have walked beside me on my path, and who have gently guided me when I couldn't find the way.

LAURA PINCUS

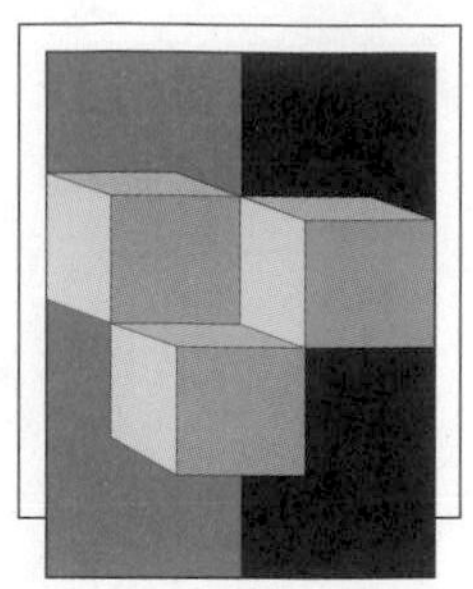

About The Authors

Laura B. Pincus

Tony McAdams

Laura B. Pincus. J.D., is the Director of DePaul University's Institute for Business & Professional Ethics, and Associate Professor of Legal Studies and Ethics at DePaul's Kellstadt Graduate School of Business (where she won the University's Excellence in Teaching award). She has also served as an adjunct professor at Northwestern's Kellogg Graduate School of Business.

Pincus graduated from the University of Chicago Law School and magna cum laude from Tufts University, and is a member of the Illinois bar. She is Co-Founder and past Chair of the Employment and Labor Law Section of the Academy of Legal Studies in Business, co-editor of the Section's newsletter, and was President of the Midwest Academy of Legal Studies in Business for the 1994–1995 term.

Pincus has done extensive research on the ethics of the employment relationship which has culminated in the publication of a textbook, *Employment Law for Managers,* and has published articles in, among other publications, *Hofstra Law Review, Columbia Business Law Journal, Harvard Journal of Law & Technology, American Business Law Journal, Journal of Business Ethics, Labor Law Journal, Journal of Individual Employment Rights,* and *Journal of Legal Studies Education.*

Tony McAdams is Professor of business law and business ethics in the Management Department of the University of Northern Iowa. He earned degrees at the University of Northern Iowa (B.A.), University of Iowa (J.D.), and Columbia University (M.B.A.).

Professor McAdams has been recognized for teaching excellence at the college, university, and national levels, including the designation Distinguished Teacher of the Year at the University of Kentucky, where he taught before moving to UNI as the Head of the Management Department. In 1996, Professor McAdams received a Regents Award for Faculty Excellence at UNI.

Professor McAdams has been published in both business and law journals including *The Harvard Business Review, The Academy of Management Review,* and *The American Business Law Journal.* His other textbook, *Law, Business, and Society,* is in its fourth edition.

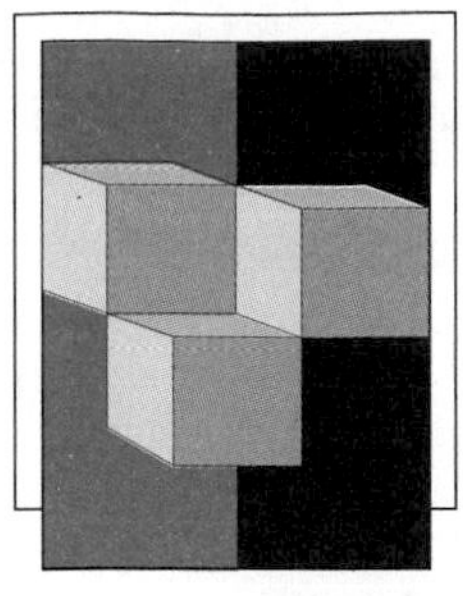

PREFACE

OVERVIEW

Legal Environment of Business: Ethical and Public Policy Contexts is a comprehensive legal environment of business text directed primarily to undergraduates at both two- and four-year institutions. We provide thorough coverage of "standard" legal environment topics including both public and private law. Our primary pedagogical strategy is to place the law in the managerial context of business; that is, we wrote the book from the perspective of the owner/manager building and operating a business. We want students to learn the law in the context of the practice of business. In addition, we place the law in the context of the ethics/social responsibility, public policy, economics, and international concerns that have such an enormous impact on business practice and on the role of law in business. In doing so, this text clearly addresses American Assembly of Collegiate Schools of Business (AACSB) ethical and environmental standards.

The theme of this book is building and managing a business. Our book represents a significant departure from almost all legal environment and business law texts in that we have tried to present the law not merely as a series of discrete topics, but rather as integrated components in the actual process of building and managing a business. That is, we ask the students to join us in thinking of themselves as owners or managers, and we take them through the principal stages of business practice demonstrating how the law affects each of those stages. We rely primarily on two mechanisms for establishing the building-and-managing-a-business theme:

1. We have organized the book's 16 chapters to mirror the general progression of building a business. We begin with two chapters introducing the law, ethics, and public policy venues that are foundations for the entire book. Then we turn to Business Organizations, Contracts, Property, Employment Law, and so on right through to the final chapter, International Business: Building and Managing a Business as It Goes Global. We have tried to place each chapter in the logical stream of development that an owner/manager would be likely to face in an evolving business. The book, in turn, is divided into four parts according to a similar logic:

Part I Setting Up the Business

Chapter 1 Law, Ethics, and Public Economic Policy: Foundations of a Business

Chapter 2 The Businessperson's Introduction to American Legal Thought and the Legal System

Chapter 3 Business Organizations: Building the Structure of the Business

Chapter 4 Contracts

Chapter 5 Property Law: Building the Business via Buying, Leasing, or Selling Property

Chapter 6 Building and Managing Human Resources from a Legal Perspective: Part I—Employment Law

Chapter 7 Building and Managing Human Resources from a Legal Perspective: Part II—Labor Law

Part II The Business's Relationship with the Government

Chapter 8 Government Regulation of Business and Administrative Law

Chapter 9 Intellectual Property and Computer Law: Protecting the Business's Ideas

Chapter 10 Securities Law: Financing the Growing Business

Chapter 11 Marketing Law: Building and Managing Sales

Part III The Business's Relationship with Customers and Clients

Chapter 12 Consumer Protection and Debtor/Creditor Law

Chapter 13 Business Torts and Crimes

Chapter 14 Product Liability

Part IV The Business's Relationship with the Community

Chapter 15 Environmental Law: Building and Managing the Firm as Part of the World

Chapter 16 International Business: Building and Managing a Business as it Goes Global

2. Each chapter is organized and written according to the building-and-managing-a-business theme. That goal is attacked in two principal ways. Beginning with Chapter 2, we start each chapter with a "business profile": in most chapters a real story involving real people who are operating a business and who, in many instances, have encountered legal difficulties. We build the chapters in the context of those stories by returning to them from time to time throughout each chapter. When not relying on the chapter profile to provide the building-and-managing-a-business narrative, we ask the students to place themselves in decision-making roles where they are facing legal dilemmas. We raise hundreds of examples of the kinds of legal problems that our students are likely to face in building and managing a business and we ask them to solve those problems.

Thus, we have tried to knit together a multidimensional "story" about the development and evolution of businesses and how the law so dramatically affects each step in that process. We should note that although the text is written in a sequential format, each chapter is a fully contained unit in and of itself and a decision to omit one or more chapters or to approach those chapters in a sequence other than the one we suggest will not cause undue confusion for students.

Beyond the building-and-managing-a-business theme, our primary teaching concern lies in demonstrating the role of law in the larger context of the public policy and global environments. Chapter 1 provides an overview of that ethics, economics, and public policy context, and we continue it in every chapter throughout the text. We do so primarily in two ways:

1. As we proceed through each chapter, we raise and ask the students to confront some of the ethics, public policy/free market, and international themes that emerge from that chapter.
2. Each chapter concludes with a three-part summary of the legal, ethics, and public policy/economics issues in that chapter. That is, we are constantly reenforcing the importance of looking at the law in its larger context.
3. To lend both authenticity and interest to the book, we provide hundreds of law cases and readings. The law cases are edited for readability, but we have made a point of retaining significant portions of the original opinions so that students will face an analytical challenge. The readings are drawn from a variety of sources, but are weighted heavily toward newspapers such as *The Wall Street Journal* and the *Los Angeles Times.*
4. Key terms are defined in a marginal glossary and at the back of the book.
5. We provide many hundreds of questions at the end of the chapters, after the law cases, in association with the chapter profiles, and elsewhere throughout the book. We are constantly asking the students to confront the law as an inquiry and critical analysis rather than as a descriptive package of facts.
6. We have tried to achieve a conversational, interactive tone that, as one reviewer said, provides "almost a quality of warmth" for the reader. Our writing is designed to put the student at the center of an evolving conversation with us about where her or his business life will be affected by legal, ethical, and public policy dilemmas.
7. Many tables, figures, boxes, and legal forms are provided to add perspective to the material and to provide a change of direction from the narrative structure of the text.

AACSB Standards

AACSB accreditation standards expect that both undergraduate and MBA curricula should provide an understanding of perspectives that form the context for business. Coverage should include:

1. Ethical and global issues
2. The influence of political, social, legal, regulatory, environmental, and technological issues, and
3. The impact of demographic diversity on organizations.

As noted, that broad, environmental context is one of the principal features and goals of this text. Chapter 1 is devoted entirely to that direction by investigating the critical relationship between law, ethics, free market economics, and public policy. Chapter 15 is directed entirely to environmental law from a public policy perspective and Chapter 16 is directed entirely to international themes with particular attention to ethics and social responsibility in the global business arena. In every other chapter we have provided readings, questions, and thought-provoking "boxes" directed to ethics, public policy, and international issues. Every chapter concludes with a summary of the ethics/public policy and economics (as well as legal issues) themes raised in that chapter. A set of ethics and public policy end-of-chapter questions is also provided. Thus, throughout the book students are constantly expected to be thinking about the law in the environmental context that the AACSB expects and that we believe to be essential to their full understanding of the legal environment of business.

Chapter Organization

Each chapter opens with a paragraph serving as a "reader's guide" which reminds the student of previous chapters, explains the direction of the instant chapter, and explains how the instant chapter fits into the larger scheme of the text; that is, building and managing a business. Then we introduce the chapter profile that provides, in most cases, an actual business situation that will serve as the backbone of the chapter and as a "storytelling" or narrative device to lend interest and continuity to the materials. We then return to the profile a number of times throughout the chapter. Law cases, readings, excerpts, and exhibits are interspersed with our examination of the law. That examination comes, in part, in straightforward descriptions of "black letter" rules, but our principal tactic is to raise real-life or hypothetical situations and put the reader in the active role of addressing the legal problems in those situations. Each chapter concludes with summaries of the legal, ethics/public policy, and economics themes in the chapter along with a series of chapter questions covering both law and ethics/public policy problems.

Supplements

To both help in understanding the thematic direction of the text and ease the burden of daily preparation, an instructor's manual and test bank accompany the text. The instructor's manual consists essentially of a summary of the text outlining the material in a manner that will serve either as an easy "refresher" for leading class discussion of the chapters or as the foundation for class lectures. The test bank includes an extensive array of both objective and essay questions.

Acknowledgements

We wish to thank all the reviewers of this text: Donald J. Boudreaux, Clemson University; James G. Frierson, East Tennessee State University; Nathan T. Garrett, NCCU School of Business; Frank Giesber, Texas Lutheran College; John Houlihan, University of Southern Maine; Deborah A. Howard, University of Evansville; Lisa L. Knight, James Madison University; Andrew W. Markley, Grove City College; Sharlene A. McEvoy, Fairfield University; Robert McMahan, Indiana State University; Kathy Sherony Roseman, Mount St. Clare College; Thomas M. Rutkowski, State University of New York—Cobleskill; Daphnie Sipes, University of Texas—San Antonio; and William Woodward, University of Alabama—Huntsville.

We also wish to thank all the survey respondents: William W. Ambrose, Jr., DeVry Institute—Pomona; Thomas M. Apke, California State University—Fullerton; Kay J. Auerbach; Del Mar College; John Bacheller, Jr., DeKalb College; Janie G. Blankenship, Del Mar College; Monique Boisvert-Guay, University of Southern Maine; Michael K. Braswell, University of North Texas; Rita Marie Cain, University of Missouri—Kansas City; Susan Clark, Westark Community College; David Culp, LaSalle University; Samuel A. DiLullo, Villanova University; Thomas Dornback, Illinois Benedictine College; Vernon P. Dorweiller, Michigan Technological University; Paul E. Fiorelli, Xavier University; Stephen Garlick, DeVry

Institute—Kansas City; Richard F. Golen, University of Massachusetts—Dartmouth; Keith Griggs, Gardner-Webb University; Marsha Hass, College of Charleston; Jack M. Hires, Valparaiso University; James E. Jump, Oakland City College; John A. Kane, Ferris State University; Lisa L. Knight, James Madison University; W. Albert Martin, Johnson & Wales University; Michael Mass, The American University; Michael O. McDonald, University of Louisville; Robert McMahan, Indiana State University; Sharlene A. McEvoy, Fairfield University; James B. Meir, Andrew College; Mary S. Murphy, Spokane Community College; Joseph M. O'Donnell, Suffolk Community College; Todd B. Piller, SUNY Ag & Tech—Cobleskill; Durga Prasad, Southern Connecticut State University; Roger W. Reinsch, Emporia State University; Alan C. Roline, University of Minnesota—Duluth; Robert M. Rowlands, Harrisburg Area Community College; Kenneth L. Schneyer, Johnson & Wales University; Mark E. Smith, University of Louisville; Jeff Stockner, Tiffin University; Larry A. Strate, University of Las Vegas; Jack A. Taylor, Birmingham—Southern College; Harold E. Tepool, Vincennes University; J. Brick Van Der Snick, Elgin Community College; Laura A. Vietzen, Elgin Community College; Michael G. Walsh, Villanova University; Darryl L. Webb, University of Alabama—Tuscaloosa; Bernard S. Winick, University of Akron; and William B. Woodward, University of Alabama—Huntsville.

Professor McAdams extends particular thanks to The College of Business Administration, Management Department, and library at the University of Northern Iowa for their understanding and generous support of this project; Professor James Freeman, University of Kentucky, for his foundation work on portions of the business organizations and securities materials; and Professor Carey Kirk, College of Business Administration, University of Northern Iowa, for his careful and able review of portions of this text.

Laura Pincus would also like to recognize the support, assistance, pure knowledge, and other gifts lent to this text by the following individuals: the intellectual and professional support of Charlie Melville (who drafted the Intellectual Property and Computers chapters) and Rocky Perkovich (who revised the Labor Law chapter); the inspiration of Karen Mellon and Craig Beytien; the patient support of Christine Scheid; the commitment of Tony McAdams; her twin lighthouses, Dawn D. Bennett-Alexander and Victoria Geguzys Fredman, y tambien K. H. She reverently honors G. D. and Tunkashila.

Final Thoughts

Laura Pincus:

"So many people play a role in the creation of a textbook, the primary of which are my students. I am drawn to classroom each quarter because of them, their enthusiasm, their motivation, and their insights. They remain critical, effective, yet compassionate judges of each effort we make, and I am privileged to be a part of their lives, if only for a short while."

Tony McAdams

Laura Pincus

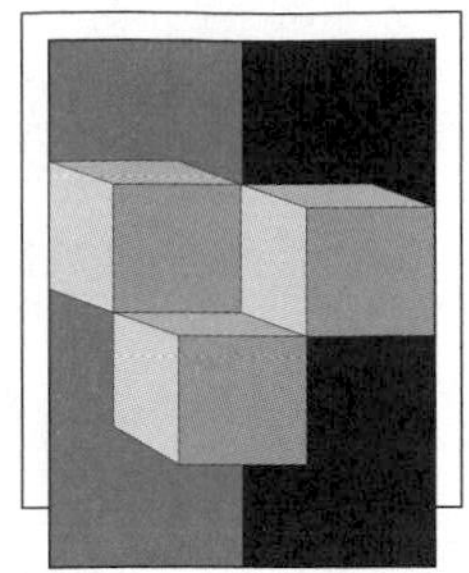

Contents in Brief

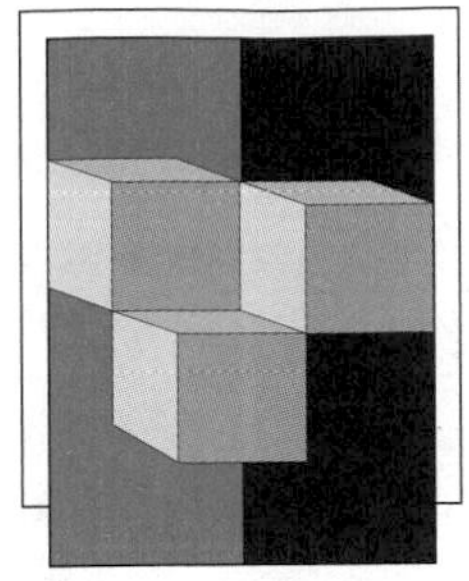

Contents

Part I

Setting Up the Business

Chapter 1

Chapter 2

CHAPTER 3

CHAPTER 4

CHAPTER 5

CHAPTER 6

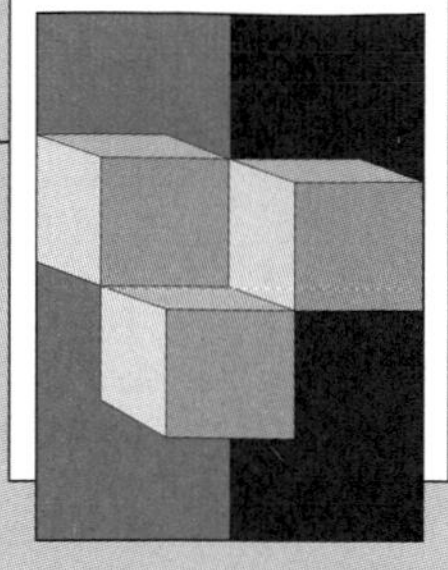

PART I

SETTING UP THE BUSINESS

CHAPTER

1

LAW, ETHICS, AND PUBLIC ECONOMIC POLICY:

FOUNDATIONS OF A BUSINESS

READER'S GUIDE

This text is built upon two themes: (1) the role of the law in the process of building a business and (2) the convergence of law, ethics, and public economic policy in each area of our legal system. To a considerable extent, our approach is one of perspective. The text asks the reader to imagine herself or himself in the process of creating, building, and expanding a business, while considering the legal, ethical, and public policy implications of each decision relevant to building that business.

I. BUILDING A BUSINESS

Chapter by chapter, the text introduces topics chronologically relevant to a businessperson's decisions. For example, among the earliest issues a businessperson may face in creating a firm or implementing an idea would be the form of organization the business should take. Therefore, after a general introduction to the concepts of law, ethics, and economic policy, the text begins with a chapter on corporate organizations.

As the reader proceeds through the text, she or he is introduced to business environment topics in a sequence that parallels the developmental pattern of a business from idea inception through growth to international expansion, while considering the many opportunities and hurdles that the law presents along the way (e.g., intellectual property protection, torts, environmental laws). Each chapter begins with a profile of an actual business dilemma, emphasizing the building-a-business theme and demonstrating the legal and ethical issues that may arise.

The building-a-business approach allows readers to view the law from a perspective of the businessperson as the business grows, rather than simply examining the law as relatively discrete packages of technical information, applicable to certain business and not others. The approach is particularly important in light of concerns of the business community regarding its need for individual decision makers able to integrate the various dimensions of business practice into a unified whole.

II. LAW, ETHICS, AND PUBLIC ECONOMIC POLICY

The second central theme requires the reader to critically question the role of law in both business practice and the life of the nation. To achieve that goal, the text joins ethics and free market reasoning in addressing legal issues raised throughout the book. For example, readers may consider whether the free market in combination with corporate/managerial ethics could be expected to effectively replace the protective functions of the Food and Drug Administration (as some critics are currently proposing). Or consider the utility of ethics and social responsibility in curbing business crime. In fact, in contemplating our entire justice system, rooted as it is in free market competitiveness, one might consider whether our nation would function more efficiently with revised rules that encourage a more cooperative view of trial practice.

This approach asks that the reader engage in precisely that public policy analysis that all citizens should employ. That is, broadly, how much law do we need in our lives? Does the market work well? Where do its imperfections lie? Can we rely on managerial or corporate ethics to supplement the "wisdom" of the market? Should we employ the law only when the market and ethics have failed to resolve the dilemma in question?

In answering these questions, the reader will acquire a clearer understanding of the businessperson's dual role of profit seeker and citizen, but the readers will also learn to reason more crisply by subjecting problem after problem to analysis by market reasoning, by ethical reasoning, and by legal reasoning. Legal reasoning and the foundations of the American legal system are discussed in detail in Chapter 2. This chapter will instead address the foundations of capitalism, public policy, and ethical reasoning.

III. Capitalism: The Roles of Government in Business and Business in Government

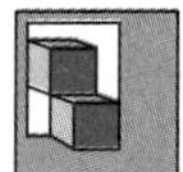

We are lucky to have been witnesses in recent years to some of the most striking political and economic adjustments in recorded history. The Berlin Wall fell. Germany is reunited. Our primary antagonist, the Soviet Union, is gone—replaced by Russia and the other struggling republics, the Commonwealth of Independent States (CIS). At this writing in 1994, only China, Cuba, North Korea, and a few other smaller nations remain even nominally committed to Marxist-Leninist doctrine, although the 1993 Russian election suggests that communism appeals to those who miss the glory and security of the former Soviet Union.

In assessing the fall of communism, former U.S. State Department policy planner Francis Fukuyama raised the provocative argument that we are approaching the end of ideological history. The fascism of the Nazis and the Marxism of the Communists have failed, and Western liberal democracy has survived as the universal expression of human government. Thus, while other approaches to government could emerge, Fukuyama says that for the foreseeable future the world will come more and more to understand that democracy, with its roots in personal freedom and capitalism, is the best method of structuring human relations.[1]

Of course, others see a more confused picture. Harvard professor and now Secretary of Labor Robert Reich sees the following:

> Human civilization is at the brink of a new era. Choose which one:
>
> (*a*) History is ending in bureaucratic corporatism . . . Key decisions are shifting away from elected politicians and legislative bodies toward multinational bureaucracies (such as the G-7) and global corporations unaccountable to any single population.
>
> (*b*) History alternates between periods of central control and chaos, and we are again entering the latter. The 40-year interval of superpower stability is giving way to tribal fragmentation and warfare with ethnic tensions flaring over Eastern Europe and the former Soviet Union, the Asian subcontinent, and even within advanced industrial nations . . .
>
> (*c*) History is ending in cultural authoritarianism. Societies like Japan and Germany, which reward group loyalty and investment, are gaining economic power over societies organized around individual liberty and personal consumption. Meanwhile, much of the Third World is succumbing to Islamic fundamentalism.

(*d*) History is ending in liberal democracy and individual liberty. Modern economies depend on educated work forces, which in turn are demanding rights and freedoms that only liberal democracies can provide (look at Latin America).

(*e*) All of the above.

The correct answer is, of course, (*e*). History is unfolding dramatically in every direction at once, spewing enough data to prove any grand historical design that the human imagination possibly can devise.[2]

These insights from Fukuyama and Reich capture the central political/economic question of the day and provide the starting point for our investigation of the role of law in the business life of America. Essentially, the purpose of this book is to ask (1) What is the proper role of business in American society? and (2) How much, if any, government regulation of business is necessary to secure that role? Fukuyama says Western liberal thought—that is, capitalist democracy—has won. Even if Fukuyama is correct, we know that most nations and peoples feel uncomfortable in turning over their fate to a free market. Hence, a key question facing all nations is: What blend of free market principles and government intervention is in the best interests of all of the people?

Free Market versus Planning. In the United States, we certainly cannot understand our system of laws without a firm appreciation for the principles of capitalism from which those laws spring, in pertinent part. We chose a capitalist, democratic approach to life. Other cultures have placed less faith in the market and more in government planning. The legal systems in those countries reflect a preference for greater central authority.

This chapter will provide an exploration into the range of the economic spectrum, moving from a laissez-faire, free market approach on the extreme right, to a brief reminder of command economy principles on the far left; but the bulk of our focus will rest where the world is at this moment—that is, we will examine the notion of the *mixed economy*. For now, at least, capitalism is the victor, but a vital question remains: How much government should be mixed with the market?

The free market approach assumes that we can operate our business structure and our society at large free of all but the most basic legal mechanisms such as contract and criminal law. The wisdom of the market—our individual judgments, in combination with our individual consciences—would serve to regulate American life. Government regulatory agencies, occupational licensure, zoning restrictions, antitrust law, and all but the most basic government services (perhaps limited to the police, the courts, and the army) would be unnecessary.

On the other hand, the collectivist alternatives (communism, socialism, and their variations) pose the notion that the business community and society at large require more expansive government intervention than that characterizing the U.S. system. Individual judgment would be supplemented with or largely supplanted by the collective will.

Of course, today's debate is no longer about capitalism versus communism but about the mixed economy—that is, about what form of capitalism best serves the world's needs. At the moment, the center of the struggle lies in the U.S., Japanese, and European versions of capitalism, but that will surely change as China's remarkable economic transformation so vividly reminds us. Capitalism has shown itself to be the stronger vehicle for productivity, efficiency, and personal freedom. Is it the stronger vehicle for building a sense of community, for improving the standard of living of all citizens, and for coping with the uncertainties of the future? Should we embrace the Japanese practice of close cooperation between government and business? Or the European model of capitalism with a heavy overlay of welfare programs? Or America's firmer commitment to market principles? Or some amalgam of the three? Or will a new direction emerge? Indeed, at this writing in 1994, the Japanese appear to be moving guardedly toward a less-managed market system.

Law? Finally, this chapter should be read as a foundation for the study of law that follows. Once a society settles on some broad political and economic principles, it pours a thin veneer or many heavy coats (depending on the system chosen) of social control on that foundation to implement the goals of the larger system. The law serves as a primary method of social control. So, to understand the law, we need to understand its roots in political economy.

A. Capitalism

Although many intellectual forces have played a role in shaping American capitalism, this discussion will be limited to a brief mention of four themes of particular historical significance.

John Locke's Natural Right of Property. Locke, the brilliant English philosopher, provided in his *Two Treatises of Government* (1690) much of the intellectual underpinning of the Declaration of Independence and, thus, the course of American life. Locke argued that the rights of life, liberty, and property were natural to all humans. Those rights predated any notion of an organized society. Hence, society's only control over those rights was to protect them. Locke's viewpoint was a powerful intellectual and moral argument for the establishment of industrial capitalism in which private ownership of property and freedom from government restraint were vital.

Adam Smith and Laissez-Faire Capitalism. Smith's *An Inquiry into the Nature and Causes of the Wealth of Nations* (1776) offered profound theoretical support to free market principles. Smith argued that the Invisible Hand of supply and demand would determine the price of goods. Competition would ensure the greatest good for the greatest number. Thus, government should not interfere in the market system. Rather, government should fulfill only those public services (defense, justice, public works, and the like) in which business cannot practically engage. He believed government interference would only disturb the natural genius of the market.

Writing about traditional philosophers and their theories about the connection between ethics and economics, economist Amertya Sen explains the impact of Smith-style capitalism.

> In one way or another, they saw economics as a branch of "practical reason," in which concepts of good, the right and the obligatory were quite central. What happened then? As the "official" story goes, all this changed with Adam Smith, who can certainly be described as the father of modern economics. He made, so it is said, economics scientific and hardheaded, and the new economics that emerged in the nineteenth and twentieth centuries was all ready to do business with no ethics to keep it tied to "morals and moralizing." That view of what happened is not only reflected in volumes of professional economics writings, but has even reached the status of getting into the English literature via a limerick by Stephen Leacock, who was both a literary writer and an economist:

Adam, Adam, Adam Smith
Listen what I charge you with!
Didn't you say
In class one day
That selfishness was bound to pay?
Of all the doctrines that was the Pith.
Wasn't it, wasn't it, wasn't it Smith?[3]

Sen later explains how this reading of Smith's work is ill placed. Smith indeed considered the values of ethics in decision making, though it is not completely clear from some of his writing, including this excerpt from *The Wealth of Nations:*

> It is not from the benevolence of the butcher, the brewer or the baker that we expect our dinner, but from their regard to their own interest. We address ourselves not to their humanity but to their self-love.

Herbert Spencer and Social Darwinism. Charles Darwin's explorations of the origins of the species led him to the theory that all of life evolved through a process of natural selection, so that the strongest and the most fit survived. Spencer applied Darwin's survival of the fittest to the development of society. He argued that the more capable individuals would inevitably rise to influential positions. Government interference would only inhibit the natural selection process. Thus, Social Darwinism provided the late-19th-century leaders of industry an ideal rationale for their positions of extreme wealth and power.

Max Weber and the Protestant Ethic. In his book *The Protestant Ethic and the Spirit of Capitalism,* Weber argued that Protestants, particularly Calvinists, were moved by a religious philosophy that demanded a lifetime of disciplined effort in pursuit of good work. Salvation demanded productivity. The accumulation of worldly goods was material evidence of that productivity, but one's success was not to be squandered. Rather, it was to be reinvested to enhance the value of goods placed in human hands via God's grace. Thus, hard work and thrift were moral responsibilities, and in turn, the accumulation and multiplication of worldly goods to be used for the benefit of all people served to measure one's success in meeting God's expectations. The Protestant ethic was a powerful spur to and justification for capitalist enterprise.

So, capitalism in America arose from rather noble, if debatable, intellectual premises, but capitalism also moved to the fore on the strength of promises to the people not

Source: Butler, Clay Cartoon, "The Glory of Capitalism" from FACT SHEET FIVE by Clay Butler. Reprinted by permission of Clay Butler.

afforded by any previous economic system. Conservative commentator Irving Kristol summarized the hope offered by capitalism:

> What did capitalism promise? First of all, it promised continued improvement in the material conditions of all its citizens, a promise without precedent in human history. Secondly, it promised an equally unprecedented measure of individual freedom for all of these same citizens. And lastly, it held out the promise that, amidst this prosperity and liberty, the individual could satisfy his instinct for self-perfection—for leading a virtuous life that satisfied the demands of his spirit (or, as one used to say, his soul)—and that the free exercise of such individual virtue would aggregate into a just society.[4]

Capitalism in Theory—Ayn Rand. Capitalism was built on a sound intellectual footing and was stimulated by the promise of unprecedented general welfare. These forces, in combination with America's natural resources and an astonishingly courageous and hardy population, led to the development of a powerful economic machine. But that machine, in the view of many Americans, ran out of control for a time. The era of the robber barons and abuses associated with them brought widespread popular sentiment for governmental restraints on capitalism. Thus, as is discussed in subsequent chapters, America's substantially free market economy was, in increasing increments, placed under government regulation. Today, ours is commonly labeled a *mixed economy.* And despite the striking rhetoric and significant deregulation strides of the Reagan free market era, America remains a nation of big government.

Our purpose now is to reconsider the merits of a purer form of capitalism. Did we turn too hastily from the market? Should we further shed our governmental role in economic affairs and restore our faith in the Invisible Hand? Or, even if the market in a substantially pure form cannot practically be achieved and relied on, may we not profit from a reminder of the nature of that system? Are at least some strides in that direction demanded? Can we, in large measure, do without regulation by law? Will a genuinely unfettered market better serve our needs than our current amalgam of business restrained by government?

> Democracy, Winston Churchill once said, is a bad system of government, except when compared with all the others. Much the same might be said of capitalism. It is not a system much celebrated by poets, nor should it be—the philosophers, the priests. From time to time it has seemed romantic to the young but not very often. Capitalism is a system that commends itself to the middle aged after they have had some experience of the way history treats the plans of man.
>
> Source: From remarks by Michael Novak, George Frederick Jewett Chair in religion and public policy at the American Enterprise institute, upon his acceptance of the Institution for World Capitalism International Prize, October 13, 1994.

To answer the questions above, we need a firm understanding of capitalism in a pure form, which has almost entirely slipped from view. The controversial philosopher and novelist Ayn Rand was an uncompromising advocate of free market principles. She believed the necessary categories of government were only three in number: the police, the armed services, and the law courts. Via her philosophy of objectivism, Rand argued that the practice of free market principles is necessary to the pursuit of a rational, moral life. Rand's viewpoint has been the subject of vigorous criticism. Its merits are for the reader to assess, but it is fair to say that she was among America's most ardent and articulate apostles of a genuine free market. Compare her arguments to those of columnist George Will, following this excerpt from Rand's *The Virtue of Selfishness.*

MAN'S RIGHTS

by Ayn Rand

If one wishes to advocate a free society—that is, capitalism—one must realize that its indispensable foundation is the principle of individual rights. If one wishes to uphold individual rights, one must realize that capitalism is the only system that can uphold and protect them. And if one wishes to gauge the relationship of freedom to the goals of today's intellectuals, one may gauge it by the fact that the concept of individual rights is evaded, distorted, perverted, and seldom discussed, most conspicuously seldom by the so-called "conservatives."

"Rights" are a moral concept—the concept that provides a logical transition from the principles guiding an individual's actions to the principles guiding his relationship with others—the concept that preserves and protects individual morality in a social context—the link between the moral code of a man and the legal code of a society, between ethics and politics. *Individual rights are the means of subordinating society to moral law.*

Every political system is based on some code of ethics. The dominant ethics of mankind's history were variants of the altruist-collectivist doctrine which subordinated the individual to some higher authority, either mystical or social. Consequently, most political systems were variants of the same statist tyranny, differing only in degree, not in basic principle, limited only by the accidents of tradition, of chaos, of bloody strife and periodic collapse. Under all such systems, morality was a code applicable to the individual, but not to society. Society was placed *outside* the moral law, as its embodiment or source or exclusive interpreter—and the inculcation of self-sacrificial devotion to social duty was regarded as the main purpose of ethics in man's earthly existence.

Since there is no such entity as "society," since society is only a number of individual men, this meant, in practice, that the rulers of society were exempt from moral law; subject only to traditional rituals, they held total power and exacted blind obedience—on the implicit principle of: "The good is that which is good for society (or for the tribe, the race, the nation), and the ruler's edicts are its voice on earth."

This was true of all statist systems, under all variants of the altruist-collectivist ethics, mystical or social. "The Divine Right of Kings" summarizes the political theory of the first—"*Vox populi, vox dei*" of the second. As witness: the theocracy of Egypt, with the Pharaoh as an embodied god—the unlimited majority rule or *democracy* of Athens—the welfare state run by the Emperors of Rome—the Inquisition of the late Middle Ages—the absolute monarchy of France—the welfare state of Bismarck's Prussia—the gas chambers of Nazi Germany—the slaughterhouse of the Soviet Union.

All these political systems were expressions of the altruist-collectivist ethics—and their common characteristic is the fact that society stood above the moral law, as an omnipotent, sovereign whim worshiper. Thus, politically, all these systems were variants of an *amoral* society.

The most profoundly revolutionary achievement of the United States of America was *the subordination of society to moral law.*

The principle of man's individual rights represented the extension of morality into the social system—as a limitation on the power of the state, as man's protection against the brute force of the collective, as the subordination of *might* to *right*. The United States was the first *moral* society in history.

All previous systems had regarded man as a sacrificial means to the ends of others, and society as an end in itself. The United States regarded man as an end in himself, and society as a means to the peaceful, orderly, *voluntary* coexistence of individuals. All previous systems had held that man's life belongs to society, that society can dispose of him in any way it pleases, and that any freedom he enjoys is his only by favor, by the *permission* of society, which may be revoked at any time. The United States held that man's life is his by *right* (which means: by moral principle and by his nature), that a right is the property of an individual, that society as such has no rights, and that the only moral purpose of a government is the protection of individual rights.

A "right" is a moral principle defining and sanctioning a man's freedom of action in a social context. There is only *one* fundamental right (all the others are its consequences or corollaries): a man's right to his own life. Life is a process of self-sustaining and

Continued

Continued

self-generated action; the right to life means the right to engage in self-sustaining and self-generated action—which means: the freedom to take all the actions required by the nature of a rational being for the support, the furtherance, the fulfillment, and the enjoyment of his own life . . .

America's inner contradiction was the altruist-collectivist ethics. Altruism is incompatible with freedom, with capitalism, and with individual rights. One cannot combine the pursuit of happiness with the moral status of a sacrificial animal.

It was the concept of individual rights that had given birth to a free society. It was with the destruction of individual rights that the destruction of freedom had to begin.

* * *

Bear clearly in mind the meaning of the concept of "*rights*" when you read the list which that [the 1960 Democratic Party] platform offers:

1. The right to a useful and remunerative job in the industries or shops or farms or mines of the nation.
2. The right to earn enough to provide adequate food and clothing and recreation.
3. The right of every farmer to raise and sell his products at a return which will give him and his family a decent living.
4. The right of every businessman, large and small, to trade in an atmosphere of freedom from unfair competition and domination by monopolies at home and abroad.
5. The right of every family to a decent home.
6. The right to adequate medical care and the opportunity to achieve and enjoy good health.
7. The right to adequate protection from the economic fears of old age, sickness, accidents, and unemployment.
8. The right to a good education.

A single question added to each of the above eight clauses would make the issue clear: *At whose expense*?

Jobs, food, clothing, recreation (!), homes, medical care, education, etc., do not grow in nature. These are man-made values—goods and services produced by men. *Who* is to provide them?

If some men are entitled *by right* to the products of the work of others, it means that those others are deprived of rights and condemned to slave labor.

Any alleged "right" of one man, which necessitates the violation of the rights of another, is not and cannot be a right.

* * *

And while people are clamoring about "economic rights," the concept of political rights is vanishing. It is forgotten that the right of free speech means the freedom to advocate one's views and to bear the possible consequences, including disagreement with others, opposition, unpopularity, and lack of support. The political function of "the right of free speech" is to protect dissenters and unpopular minorities from forcible suppression—*not* to guarantee them the support, advantages, and rewards of a popularity they have not gained . . .

Such is the state of one of today's most crucial issues: *political* rights versus "*economic* rights." It's either-or. One destroys the other. But there are, in fact, no "economic rights," no "collective rights," no "public-interest rights." The term *individual rights* is a redundancy: there is no other kind of rights and no one else to possess them.

Those who advocate laissez-faire capitalism are the only advocates of man's rights.

Questions

1. Do you believe true "altruism" can exist in a capitalist system? Does anyone do anything without any regard for their self-interest in the act? Consider whether the mere satisfaction of your own personal desire to do it equals self-interest, even in the case of an anonymous donation.
2. Does it bother you at all that Rand constantly refers to "men" and the rights of "men"? Rand was considered by some feminist scholars as a misogynist. Some contend that Rand considered women to be a lesser gender (notwithstanding the fact that she was a woman). Does this alter your reading of her work?
3. Do you agree with Rand that there is only one fundamental right, "a man's right to his own life"? Contrast this perspective to those of Locke and Smith.

Congress, the Presidency, and Government Regulation of Business: From Colonial Independence to Corporate Interference?

by George Will

Congress is symbolically and literally the epicenter of American government, being located on Breed's Hill where the four quadrants of the federal city touch. Throughout our history the President has been in abeyance more often than waxing, and the shrinkage of the presidency under Mr. Clinton is a direct consequence of the end of the Cold War.

The presidency became a national symbol of rallying point when we lived in a hair-trigger world; when Soviet missiles were six minutes away on submarines off North Carolina. As the threat recedes and as the inherent melodrama of politics in a Cold War world recedes, the presidency itself is receding. . . .

The history of American response to government is a complicated one. Our country was founded by people who regarded government as a necessary evil—evil in its potential, often evil in its impact—but a necessity. Therefore all of our political parties and participants for the first hundred and some years of our existence believed that their task was to keep government marginal in our lives. But by about the 1890s, the growth of industrial capitalism had begun to produce economic entities so large and so powerful and so threatening to many people—trusts, banks, railroads, Standard Oil, U.S. Steel—that many Americans began to think that government needed to weigh in as a countervailing force against these powerful private economic entities. . .

Well, since then we have lived a lot and learned a lot. There has been a disappointment with [Lyndon Johnson's] Great Society legislation, which is perceived to have promised much more than has been delivered. Then there came Vietnam and then there came Watergate, both giving rise to skepticism about the competence and the good motives of government. It is hard, ladies and gentlemen, to recall that, in the mid 1960s, such was the hubris of our government and such was the complacency of the political class that Washington really believed we had so mastered the management of a modern economy that the government could, in effect, outlaw the business cycle as a political problem for the foreseeable future. Then, the political class really believed that the only political problem would be the equitable allocation of those revenues, which were then pouring into the government in a gusher at constant tax rates well in excess of existing government needs. The distribution of all that revenue was going to be the only problem of politics for the foreseeable future.

Well, it hasn't worked out that way to say the very least. As a result, the American people today have ended their romance with government. There will not be in our lifetime the sentimentalizing of government that we saw under Kennedy's "Camelot."

Questions

1. Do you think that most of America regards government today as a necessary evil (as opposed to an *un*necessary evil, or a good)?
2. In his last paragraph, Will seems to be reflecting with fondness, even missing, the sentimentalizing of government. Should we yearn longingly for the Camelot years, or would you say we are better off now?
3. When companies expand to the likes of U.S. Steel and others, do you believe that government must weigh in as a countervailing force or would the market take care of any resulting problems? Is there any possible market response to these behemoths or are they too all powerful?

Capitalism in Practice—Privatization in America and Abroad. Around the globe, from Russia to Eastern Europe and from the United Kingdom to Southeast Asia, expanded faith in the free market was the singular economic message of the 1980s and 1990s. The basic point to recognize is the free market argument that virtually all services now performed by the government may be more efficiently and more equitably managed by the impersonal forces of the market.

Most commonly, privatization follows two patterns: (1) contracting out where government, in effect, turns over a portion of its duties, such as garbage collection, to a private firm; and (2) the sale of public assets, such as an airport, to a private purchaser. Chicago, under Mayor Richard M. Daley, has been particularly aggressive in pursuing privatization, resulting, for example, in annual savings of $900,000 by turning janitorial work over to private firms. In 1989, cars were being abandoned on Chicago streets faster than the city could haul them away. The government turned to private towing firms, which paid the city $25 per abandoned car and then sold them at a profit for scrap.[5] A Reason Foundation study estimates that some $227 billion in commercial airports, utilities, highways, bridges, water systems, and so on could be sold to the private sector and operated at a profit while saving money for the public.[6]

At least 14 states have privately operated prisons. Private firms are managing schools in Baltimore and Miami. New York pays a private company, America Works, to move welfare recipients to training and work. The cost? $5,300 versus the $23,000 per year that the state would otherwise pay to support the welfare client. America Works claims a 68 percent success rate.[7]

Privatization Abroad. Capitalism has swept the globe. In five years during the late 1980s and early 1990s, Mexico sold off $22 billion of state-owned companies, including the telephone system and an airline.[8] Zambia announced in 1993 that it intended to sell 150 companies that controlled 80 percent of its economy. Ironically, the companies had been nationalized in the 1970s and 1980s, and the Zambian government intends to give the former multinational owners the first opportunity to repurchase the companies.[9] Germany is thinking of turning its highway system over to private interests,[10] and even China, virtually the last bastion of communism, has created a semi-independent railway company to manage part of its vast system.[11]

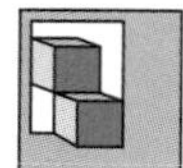

Privatization: An Assessment. Of course, privatization won't cure the world's economic problems. Critics argue that the savings from privatization result simply from paying substandard wages and cutting corners on quality. Professor Jonathan Goodrich lists these primary concerns regarding privatization:

- Unemployment of government workers because of privatization.
- Lower quality of service.
- Government loss of control and accountability.
- The government paying too much for the services done by a private company.[12]

B. *Collectivism*

The term *collectivism* embraces various economic philosophies on the left of the political-economic spectrum: principally, communism and socialism. Capitalism is characterized by economic individualism. On the other hand, communism and the various styles of socialism are characterized by economic cooperation.

Communism. Clearly, Soviet communism, the *totalitarian* version of collectivism practiced by Marxist-Leninists, has been rejected by the bulk of the world. Nonetheless, we need to briefly remind ourselves of some fundamental Marxist principles because, as *The Wall Street Journal* reminded us a few years ago, "His shadow persists: Marx can't be ignored. In his critique of capitalism the great analyst helped to shape today's agenda."[13] Lenin, not Marx, created the Communist dictatorship in Russia. Lenin and the other Communist totalitarians, most notably Stalin and Mao, cannot be defended. However, Marx, along with Freud and Einstein, are the thinkers who have most profoundly shaped the 20th century. For our purposes, Marx's central message concerns the severe abuses that can accompany unrestrained capitalism. Marx was particularly concerned about the growing imbalance between rich and poor. Moreover, he felt that the pursuit of wealth and self-interest would erode society's moral core. More broadly, Marx built an economic interpretation of history, arguing that "the mode of production in material life determines the general character of the social, political, and spiritual processes of life."[14] The power and originality of those thoughts, along with concerns about the excesses of capitalism, mean that Marx will continue to influence our lives for the foreseeable future.

Problems. Communism appears to have run its course philosophically. However, the problems that generated its appeal—poverty, oppression, political inequality, and so on—remain. Hence, the world continues to look to government intervention. The question is: How much? We will briefly remind ourselves of the *socialist* response to that question. Socialists reject Communist totalitarianism and embrace democracy while calling for aggressive government intervention to correct economic and social ills. Socialism, as an operating philosophy for a society, is largely discredited. Around the world, from Argentina to Mexico to Zambia to Great Britain and even to the "welfare states" of Scandinavia, government is getting out of the business of managing economics. At the same time, socialist concerns and principles remain highly influential.

Socialism. The distinctions between communism and socialism are not entirely clear. Historically, socialism has been associated with democratic governments and peaceful change while communism has been characterized by totalitarianism and violent revolution. Socialists aim to retain the benefits of industrialism while abolishing the social costs often accompanying the free market. Nationalization is limited to only the most vital industries, such as steel, coal mining, power generation, and transportation. While nationalization may be relatively uncommon, the government is likely to be directly involved in regulating growth, inflation, and unemployment. In the contemporary Western world, Austria, Norway, Denmark, Sweden, South Africa, and France are among the nations where socialist principles assumed a significant presence. Now those nations have grown more sympathetic to free markets.

Middle Ground? A Mixed Economy. Communism has failed. Socialist principles, to the extent that they call for central planning, bloated bureaucracies, and restraints on personal freedom, are discredited. An era has passed, but the shape of the future is unclear. Some middle ground in free market and welfare state principles seems to be the next step, but the appropriate mixture is proving elusive. For years, the Scandinavian states of Sweden, Norway, and Denmark practiced their market socialism or social democracy with such success that it was labeled a "third way" between the harsher extremes of capitalism and communism. Their welfare states provided healthy economic growth with cradle-to-grave social care for all in a system emphasizing the collective welfare over individual preferences. Scholar Robert Livingston described Germany's similar approach:

> The *social* aspects have always been as important—perhaps more important—than the profit motive. Not only is the social-welfare net essential, not only does a "social partnership" exist between employers and the employed . . . but more broadly the economic system rests upon an implicit social contract, in which employers, the employed (through their unions), the government and, less clearly, the Central Bank are all partners.[15]

Welfare. Now, in the mid-1990s, even that dream of social justice built on a capitalist foundation is foundering as the welfare states of Austria, Germany, France, Great Britain, Scandinavia, and others reluctantly acknowledge that the competitive forces of the global market are not accommodating to their generous social concerns. With deficits exploding, unemployment in the double digits, and worker absenteeism pushing toward 25 percent, even the Swedes turned away in the early 90s from the Social Democratic Labor Party that had governed for more than half a century and embraced moderates who sought to reduce government spending and reinvigorate the market. Of course, welfare state principles have not been abandoned, but in the United States and much of Europe the central question in political economy is that of the proper mixture of government and markets. The search for a stable middle ground continues.

C. America's Economic Future—Where Are We?

We have inspected the entire economic continuum. We know that communism has been discredited. Hence, the far left has little to offer. President Reagan and, to a lesser extent, President Bush gave us a 12-year view of the virtues and demerits of greater faith in the free market. Should we heed Reagan's call to place our faith in largely unrestrained capitalism, or do we need to move our present *mixed economy* a bit closer to the welfare state model, which itself is under great pressure? Or must a new model emerge? In sum, how much government do we need?

But It's the Law. Many economists contend that we are overregulated and that government intervention has gone too far. Consider the case of the nuns of the Missionaries of Charity in New York City. In 1988, Mother Theresa, the head of the order, reached an agreement with Mayor Ed Koch, allowing the nuns to turn an abandoned building into a homeless shelter for the cost of one dollar. Not much would be needed for the 64-person shelter as the order requires not only a vow of poverty, but also an avoidance of the routine use of modern conveniences, such as washing machines and elevators. The nuns found a fire-gutted building on 148th Street and, after finding a Madonna in the ashes, believed they had found their shelter.

Unfortunately, transferring the building to the order was not so easy. No city official had the actual authority to transfer the building, postponing the transfer for a year and a half. Further, after two years of struggling, the nuns were told they must comply with a city ordinance requiring that every building have an elevator. The nuns had only $500,000 for the entire renovation and could not pay the additional $100,000 to install an elevator. Recall that the nuns were forbidden by their faith from using (or allowing residents to use) the elevator, even if it were installed. The nuns eventually gave up and decided that they could use the money much more efficiently providing soup and sandwiches than paying for an elevator that no one would use.[16]

What alternatives exist? Do we have a system that overregulates but underprotects? Recently, senator and presidential candidate Robert Dole proposed an act that would require a cost–benefit analysis to be done before any further legislation is passed. In other words, Congress would have to show that the benefits of any given bill justify the costs of implementing the legislation and the possible harms that might result from it. The Environmental Protection Agency is opposed to the bill, arguing that it will have to hire as many as 1,000 additional employees to perform these cost–benefit analyses. Is this the answer, or will this simply create more red tape?

No Easy Answers. Immense problems remain in America even though the wisdom of the capitalist approach is almost universally conceded. That is, despite its remarkable productive and organizational power, the free market is not without imperfections. Nowhere are those imperfections more apparent than in Eastern Europe, where the capitalist revolutionaries who broke away from communism in 1989 have seen the free market fall tragically short of their hopes. Of course, those hopes were unrealistic; however, simply unleashing the free market probably may not be the route to a better life for all.

D. The Role of the Corporation in the American Economy

Corporate critics have long argued that the public interest has not been well served by America's big corporations. We recognize that colossal size and the economies of scale that accompany it have been critical to American competitiveness in today's unforgiving global market. At the same time, that very size, the critics say, permits continuing abuse of the American public. Of course, we recognize that big companies are a fixture of the American landscape. However, a reminder of the specifics may be useful.

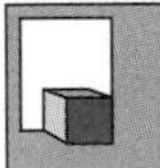

Death by Regulation

There are certain universal truths widely recognized by careful observers of the Washington scene. First, politicians want to "do something positive." This wish exists regardless of whether or not there is any real need to do anything at all, and to question the need for action is an anathema. Responses to Love Canal, Chilean grapes, and Alar indicate how often the government safety programs are launched, not on the basis of science, but on sensationalism.

Second, an important asymmetry exists between action and inaction. There are risks associated with an agency's decision to act, and there are risks associated with an agency's decision not to act. The latter risks, however, are usually much more visible than the former. For example, a program to improve automobile side impact protection will also increase retention of older, less safe cars by making new cars much more costly. But consider how much easier it is for a journalist to focus on the first story than the second—the photographs of crumpled cars, the videotapes of crash tests, the interviews with the victims' families. By comparison, how would anyone even begin to identify the accidents that result from the price effect of a new standard? In short, one photographed injury outweighs a thousand unphotographed fatalities.

Source: Sam Kazman, "Death by Regulation," Competitive Enterprise Institute PolicyFax (202/331-1010), Topic Code #72, Document #7200401 (Fall 1991), excerpted from *Regulation: The Cato Review of Business and Government.*

The Corporate State. Historically, the foundation of the critics' argument has been that giant companies hold monopoly power, permitting them to secure excess profits at the expense of the consumer. Considerable evidence supported that view; but it has been rendered somewhat passe in this era of fierce international economic competition with the giants of Japan, Germany, and the balance of the world. Further, as we discuss below, many of America's old-line titans (GM, IBM, Sears, and so on) are struggling to retain their strength, suggesting that bigness is not a guarantor of success in the contemporary market.

A litany of societal ills—pollution, discrimination, white-collar crime, misleading advertising—has long been laid at the corporate doorstep. Now the subject of intense governmental, public, and internal corporate scrutiny, those problems, while yet very real, seem no longer attributable to mere corporate size or malevolence. The bulk of this book is devoted to the governmental/corporate/public attack on those serious social ills. However, the critics say, those specific ills are only symptomatic of a more encompassing malady. Basically, the concern is that America has committed its *soul* to business values in a way that is progressively undermining our national well-being. We will briefly examine that argument in order to have it in mind as we proceed through our more detailed study of corporate social responsibility and government regulation of business.

America's Soul? Generally, the critics contend the power of the business community has become so encompassing that virtually all dimensions of American life have absorbed elements of the business ethic. Values commonly associated with businesspersons (competition, profit seeking, reliance on technology, faith in growth) have overwhelmed traditional humanist values (cooperation, individual dignity, human rights, meaningful service to society). In the name of efficiency and productivity, it is argued that the warmth, decency, and value of life have been debased. We engage in meaningless work in an artificial culture. Objects dominate our existence. We operate as replaceable cogs in a vast, bureaucratic machine. Our natural environment is shredded in the pursuit of progress. Indeed, we lose ourselves, the critics argue.

Politics. We can elaborate on the case of the corporate critics by directing our attention to some areas of special concern. We will begin with politics, where critics charge that superior resources enable the business community to unfairly slant the electoral and lawmaking processes in favor of corporate interests.

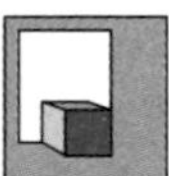

In recent years, the corporate community has taken a more direct and vigorous role in the political process. As a result, corporate critics are increasingly concerned that the financial weight of big business will prove so influential that our pluralist, democratic approach to governance may be significantly distorted. Today, money is central to the task of acquiring elective office. And following election, dollars to finance lobbying on Capitol Hill can be critical in shaping congressional opinion.

Corporate funds cannot lawfully be expended for federal campaign contributions. However, corporations can lawfully establish **political action committees** (PACs) to solicit and disburse voluntary campaign contributions. That is, corporations can solicit contributions from employees, shareholders, and others. That money is then put in a fund, carefully segregated from general corporate accounts, and disbursed by the PAC in support of a federal election campaign.

political action committees. A legally defined lobbying group that uses funds and activities to support certain political views.

The checkbook dominates politics at the national level. In the 1991–92 election cycle, PACs donated $205 million to legislators and political parties, with $189 million of that total (a 19 percent increase over 1989–90) going to congressional candidates, three-fourths of which went to incumbents. As *Newsweek* expressed it:

> The bottom line is a grubby, demeaning and never-ending quest for campaign contributions that is the bane of a political career and a blight on the political process.[17]

TABLE 1.1

TOP TEN—TOTAL PAC SPENDING 1991–92

Teamsters	$11,825,340
American Medical Association	6,263,921
National Education Association	5,817,975
National Rifle Association	5,700,114
National Association of Realtors	4,939,014
Association of Trial Lawyers of America	4,392,462
American Federation of State, County, and Municipal Employees	4,281,395
United Auto Workers	4,257,165
National Congressional Club	3,864,389
National Abortion Rights Action League	3,831,321

Source: Gregory Cerio and Kendall Hamilton, *Newsweek,* May 24, 1993, p. 6. Drawn from Federal Election Commission data.

Much of that money comes from business and labor PACs (see Table 1.1). The biggest contributor in the 1991–92 federal elections alone was the real estate PAC, totaling $3 million; the United Auto Workers gave $2.2 million.[18] But as displayed in Table 1.1, business and labor interests are only part of the PAC story. Many special interest groups spend a great deal of money in hopes of influencing the political process. For example, the Association of Trial Lawyers of America raised their contribution by 55 percent over the previous election cycle as it sought particularly to stop tort-reform legislation.[19] Naturally, PAC money is largely directed to those politicians who can be most useful to PAC interests.

Reform? At this writing in 1994, both the House and Senate have approved bills reforming election finance. The Senate bill bans PACs; the House bill puts a $200,000 cap on aggregate contributions by a PAC. To offset the limitations on PAC money, the House bill calls for partial public funding of federal campaigns and the Senate bill relies largely on a tax on campaigns that violate spending limits.[20] A House–Senate compromise is expected. Of course, many politicians and analysts are unconvinced of the need for reform. In Robert Samuelson's view, special interest efforts are merely an expression of democracy, and he argues that those efforts do not dominate the political process in any case:

> PACs remain a minority of all contributions. In 1986 they were 21 percent for the Senate (up from 17 percent in 1984) and 34 percent for the House (level with 1984).
>
> The diversity of the 4,157 PACs dilutes their power. There are business PACs, labor PACs, pro-abortion PACs, anti-abortion PACs, importer PACs, and protectionist PACs. Contributions are fairly evenly split between Democrats ($74.6 million in 1986) and Republicans ($57.5 million). . .
>
> Of course special interests mob Congress. That's democracy. One person's special interest is another's crusade or livelihood. To be influential, people organize.[21]

Lobbying. Those who criticize corporate influence on the legislative process are not concerned with PACs alone. Sophisticated and expensive lobbying is a staple of the business community's efforts to implement its legislative agenda. Of course, lobbying is defended as an efficient method of better acquainting busy politicians with the subtleties of the diverse issues they must address, and lobbying is not confined to the big spenders of the business community—witness the many consumer lobbies. An estimated 20,000 lobbyists annually spend perhaps $1.5 billion (including campaign contributions) attempting to influence officials in Washington.[22]

Congress is considering legislation to curb lobbying influence. One bill includes stronger lobby registration requirements and limits on gifts to legislators. President Clinton urged repeal of the corporate tax deduction for lobbying expenses, and he argued for new rules preventing lobbyists from making or soliciting campaign contributions. Also at issue are methods to stop the so-called revolving door, where former lawmakers become lobbyists and return to Washington to lobby. One proposal would bar former legislators from lobbying sitting legislators for two years, bar them from lobbying their former congressional committees for five years, and permanently bar them from lobbying for foreign clients.[23]

Business Values. The corporation is arguably the central institution in contemporary America. In every dimension of American life, business values are increasingly pervasive. To those who criticize the corporation, that near-blanket adoption of the business ethic signals a dangerous distortion of the nation's priorities. In an editorial, the *Des Moines Register* commented that commercials have become so interwoven with our total existence that they cannot effectively be separated out:

> The insinuation of commercials into American life is everywhere. On Saturday mornings, the cartoon character the kids are watching may be for sale at the toy store. On prime-time shows and in movies, the brand-name product that is used as a stage prop probably isn't there by accident.
>
> No one seems to mind. In an ad-saturated society, people willingly pay a premium price for a shirt that is adorned with an advertising logo. By choice, people wear commercial messages.
>
> It's the triumph of hucksterism in America.[24]

IV. Foundations of Business Ethics

No effort will be made in this text to *teach ethics.* The purpose here is not to improve the reader's ethical quotient. Rather, the goal is to sensitize the reader to the ethical component of business life. From a decision-making perspective, business ethics is one form of decision making, the same as shareholder wealth, legal regulation, or religious beliefs. Some sense of the ethical climate of business—some glimpse of the specific ethical problems facing the businessperson—should be useful in assessing the role of ethics in the business decision-making equation and in evaluating the utility of ethics as a regulator of business behavior.

A. Ethical Theories: Roads to Decisions

Volumes of literature are devoted in general terms to the question of defining ethics. We cannot hope to advance that discussion here. Ethics, of course, involves judgments as to good and bad, right and wrong, and what ought to be. We seek to use reason in discovering how individuals ought to act. Business ethics refers to the measurement of business behavior based on standards of right and wrong, rather than relying entirely on principles of accounting and management. (In this discussion, morals will be treated as synonymous with ethics. Distinctions certainly are drawn between the two, but those distinctions are not vital for our purposes.)

Finding and following the moral course is not easy for any of us, but the difficulty may be particularly acute for the businessperson. The bottom line is necessarily unforgiving. Hence, the pressure to produce is intense and the temptation to cheat may be very great. Although the law provides useful guideposts for minimum comportment, no clear moral guidelines have emerged. Therefore, when the businessperson is faced with a difficult decision, a common tactic is simply to do what he or she takes to be correct at any given moment. Indeed, in one survey of ethical views in business, 50 percent of the respondents indicated that the word *ethical* meant "what my feelings tell me is right."[25]

Philosophers have provided powerful intellectual support for that approach. Existentialists, led by the famed Jean-Paul Sartre, believe standards of conduct cannot be rationally justified and no actions are inherently right or wrong. Thus, each person may reach his or her own choice about ethical principles. That view finds its roots in the notion that humans are only what we will ourselves to be. If God does not exist, there can be no human nature, because there is no one to conceive that nature.

In Sartre's famous interpretation, existence precedes essence. First humans exist; then we individually define what we are—our essence. Therefore, each of us is free, with no rules to turn to for guidance. Just as we all choose our own natures, so must we choose our own ethical precepts. Moral responsibility belongs to each of us individually.

Universal Truths? Have we then no rules or universal standards by which to distinguish right from wrong? Have we no absolutes? Philosophers seek to provide guidance beyond the uncertainties of ethical relativism. We will survey two ethical perspectives, teleology and deontology, which form the core of ethical analysis. Before proceeding to those theories, we will note the important role of religion in ethics and take a brief look at three additional formulations—libertarianism, distributive justice, and virtue ethics—that have been increasingly influential in contemporary moral analysis.

Religion. Judeo-Christian beliefs, the Moslem faith, Confucianism, Buddhism, and so on are powerful ethical voices in contemporary life. They often feature efforts such as the Golden Rule to build absolute and universal standards. Scholarly studies indicate that most American managers believe in the Golden Rule and take it to be their most meaningful moral guidepost. From a religious point of view, the deity's laws are absolutes that must shape the whole of one's life, including work. Faith, rather than reason, intuition, or secular knowledge, provides the foundation for a moral life built on religion.

Libertarianism. Contemporary philosopher Robert Nozick has built an ethical theory rooted in the notion of personal liberty. For him, morality springs from the maximization of personal freedom. Justice and fairness, right and wrong are measured not by equality of results (e.g., wealth) for all, but from ensuring equal opportunity for all to engage in informed choices about their own welfare. Hence, Nozick takes essentially a free market stance toward ethics.

Distributive Justice. Harvard philosopher John Rawls calls for maximizing justice, which in turn implies an equitable distribution of goods and services. Although his position is quite complex, in essence Rawls seeks to identify that social contract under which free, rational people would choose to order their affairs if they were situated behind a "veil of ignorance" that prevented them from knowing their status in society (intelligence, appearance, wealth). He argues that they would build a cooperative system in which benefits (e.g., income) would be distributed unequally only where doing so would be to the benefit of all, particularly the least advantaged. All those behind the veil would agree to that standard because they could not know whether they would be among the advantaged or disadvantaged. From this system of distributive economic justice, it would seem to follow that ethical justice would be measured by the capacity of the act in question to enhance cooperation among members of society.

Virtue Ethics. In recent years, an increasing number of philosophers have argued that the key to good ethics lies not in rules, rights, and responsibilities but in the classic notion of character. As Plato and Aristotle argued, our attention should be given to strategies for encouraging desirable character traits such as honesty, fairness, compassion, and generosity. Aristotle believed that virtue could be taught much as any other skill. Virtue ethics applauds the person who is motivated to do the right thing and who cultivates that motivation in daily conduct. A part of the argument is that such persons are more morally reliable than those who simply follow the rules but fail to inspect, strengthen, and preserve their own personal virtues.

Teleology or Deontology—An Overview. **Teleological ethical systems** emphasize the end, the product, the consequences of a decision. The morality of a decision is determined by measuring the probable outcome. A morally correct decision is one that produces the greatest good. The teleological approach calls for reaching moral decisions by weighing the nonmoral consequences of an action. For the teleologist, the end is primary.

telelogical ethical systems. Systems that assume that everything has a purpose. These theories are interested in the outcome or consequence of an action.

To the deontologist, principle is primary and consequence is secondary or even irrelevant. Maximizing right rather than good is the deontological standard. The deontologist might well refuse to lie even if doing so would maximize good. **Deontology,** derived from the Greek word meaning *duty,* is directed toward what ought to be, toward what is right. Relationships among people are important because they give rise to duties. A father may be morally committed to saving his son from a burning building, rather than saving another person who might well do more total good for society. Similarly, deontology considers motives. For example, why a crime was committed may be more important than the actual consequences of the crime.

deontology. Deontological theories disregard consequences and focus on the act itself.

The distinction here is critical. Are we to guide our behavior in terms of rational evaluations of the consequences of our acts, or are we to shape our conduct in terms of duty and principle—that which ought to be? Let's take a closer look at **utilitarianism,** the principle teleological ethical theory, and **formalism,** the principle deontological ethical theory.

utilitarianism. An ethical theory that deems an action right if it provides the greatest good to the greatest number.

formalism. An ethical theory that contends that there are rules or principles that should govern behavior.

Teleology-Utilitarianism. In reaching an ethical decision, good is to be weighed against evil. A decision that maximizes the ratio of good over evil for all those concerned is the ethical course. Jeremy Bentham (1748–1832) and John Stuart Mill (1806–1873) were the chief intellectual forces in the development of utilitarianism. Their views and those of other utilitarian philosophers were not entirely consistent. As a result, at least two branches of utilitarianism have developed. According to **act-utilitarianism,** one's goal is to identify the consequences of a particular act to determine whether it is right or wrong. **Rule-utilitarianism** requires one to adhere to all the rules of conduct by which society reaps the greatest value. Thus, the rule-utilitarian may be forced to shun a particular act that would result in greater immediate good (punishing a guilty person whose constitutional rights have been violated) in favor of upholding a broader rule that results in the greater total good over time (maintaining constitutional principles by freeing the guilty person). In sum, the principle to be followed for the utilitarian is the greatest good for the greatest number.

act-utilitarianism. Act-utilitarianism contends that one should look to the consequences of an act to determine whether it is right or wrong.

rule-utilitarianism. Rule-utilarianism contends that one should adhere to rules of conduct that offer society the greatest value.

Deontology-Formalism. The German philosopher Immanuel Kant (1724–1804) developed perhaps the most persuasive and fully articulated vision of ethics as measured not by consequence (teleological) but by the rightness of rules. In this formalistic view of ethics, the rightness of an act depends little (or, in Kant's view, not at all) on the results of the act. Kant believed in the key moral concept of goodwill. The moral person is a person of goodwill, and that person renders ethical decisions based on what is right, regardless of the consequences of the decision. Moral worth springs from one's decision to discharge one's duty. Thus, the student who refuses to cheat on exams is morally worthy if his or her decision springs from duty, but morally unworthy if the decision is merely one born of self-interest, such as fear of being caught.

categorical imperative. Kant's theory that a rule is right where it can be applied universally.

How does the person of goodwill know what is right? Here, Kant propounded the **categorical imperative,** the notion that every person should act on only those principles that he or she, as a rational person, would prescribe as universal laws to be applied to the whole of humankind. A moral rule is categorical rather than hypothetical in that its prescriptive force is independent of its consequences. The rule guides us independent of the ends we seek. Kant believed that every rational creature can act according to his or her categorical imperative, because all such persons have "autonomous, self-legislating wills" that permit them to formulate and act on their own systems of rules. To Kant, what is right for one is right for all, and each of us can discover that "right" by exercising our rational faculties.

Theory Applied to Reality. Theory must face the test of reality. The bulk of that testing will be left to the reader. However, let's apply the two dominant ethical theories to the case of Bubba Smith. Charles "Bubba" Smith, a massive and successful football lineman for Michigan State University and three professional teams, worked for several years after his football career in commercials for a brewing company. He loved making the commercials and they were very successful, but he decided to remove himself from beer advertising because he felt he was promoting alchol consumption.

Utilitarianism. Does the collective harm in Smith's work outweigh the collective benefit? Under this analysis, Smith must seek to maximize pleasure and reduce pain, not merely for himself, but for all. Employing a cost–benefit analysis, is the societywide pain produced by alcohol consumption exceeded by the societywide pleasure? Does Smith bear any responsibility for either?

Formalism. Would we want to universally apply a rule that all those situated similarly to Smith should do as he did and desist from working in support of the consumption of beer? Remember that our concern is with intentions rather than consequences. Hence, rather than engaging in a cost–benefit analysis, we would decide whether we prefer a universal standard under which all would decline to promote activities that might be harmful to others. Or would we prefer a universal standard holding that all adults who consume beer are personally and fully responsible for the consequences of doing so?

Obviously, no ethical theory provides easy answers to life's most difficult questions. However, those theories are useful in identifying and sorting the issues that lead to better decision making.

B. Managerial Ethics: Evidence and Analysis

Steiner and Steiner: The Roots of Business Ethics. Scholars George and John Steiner help to clarify this muddy picture by identifying six primary sources of the business ethics construct in America.[26]

Genetic Inheritance. Although the view remains theoretical, sociobiologists have in recent years amassed persuasive evidence and arguments suggesting that the evolutionary forces of natural selection influence the development of traits such as cooperation and altruism that lie at the core of our ethical systems. Those qualities of goodness often associated with ethical conduct may, in some measure, be a product of genetic traits strengthened over time by the evolutionary process.

Religion. Via a rule orientation exemplified by the Golden Rule (or its variations in many religions) and the Ten Commandments, religious morality is clearly a primary force in shaping our societal ethics. The question here concerns the applicability of religious ethics to the business community. Could the Golden Rule serve as a universal, practical, helpful standard for the businessperson's conduct?

Philosophical Systems. To the Epicureans, the quality of pleasure to be derived from an act was the essential measure of its goodness. The Stoics, like the Puritans and many contemporary Americans, advocated a disciplined, hardworking, thrifty lifestyle. These philosophies and others, like those cited earlier, have been instrumental in our society's moral development.

Cultural Experience. Here, the Steiners refer to the rules, customs, and standards transmitted from generation to generation as guidelines for appropriate conduct. Individual values are shaped in large measure by the norms of the society.

The Legal System. Laws represent a rough approximation of society's ethical standards. Thus, the law serves to educate us about the ethical course in life. The law does not and, most would agree, should not be treated as a vehicle for expressing all of society's ethical preferences. Rather, the law is an ever-changing approximation of current perceptions of right and wrong.

Codes of Conduct. Steiner and Steiner identify three primary categories of such codes. Company codes, ordinarily brief and highly generalized, express broad expectations about fit conduct. Second, company operating policies often contain an ethical dimension. Express policy as to gifts, customer complaints, hiring policy, and the like serves as a guide to conduct and a shield by which the employee can avoid unethical advances from those outside the company. Third, many professional and industry associations have developed codes of ethics, such as the Affirmative Ethical Principles of the American Institute of Certified Public Accountants. In sum, codes of conduct seem to be a growing expression of the business community's sincere concern about ethics. However, the utility of such codes remains unsettled.

Why Do Some Managers Cheat? *Values.* We may begin to answer that question by examining the value structures of those who manage. The German philosopher Edward Spranger identified six fundamental value orientations for all humans.[27] On the basis of Spranger's classification, William Guth and Renato Tagiuri surveyed a group of top-level executives and arrived at the ranking of average value scores shown at the top of page 22.[28]

Thus, managers appear to value more strongly the features of the pragmatic person than the sensitivities often associated with the lower three items. By contrast, ministers, for example, ranked the values in the following order: religious, social, aesthetic, political, theoretical, and economic.[29] In the same vein, Professor George England of the University of Minnesota found that 91 percent of 1,072 managers he surveyed believed trust

Value	*Score*
Economic	45
Theoretical	44
Political	44
Religious	39
Aesthetic	35
Social	33

Source: Reprinted by permission of the *Harvard Business Review*. Excerpt from "Personal Values and Corporate Strategy" by William D. Guth and Renato Tagiuri (September–October 1965).

to be important, but only 12 percent felt trust would help them in their careers. On the other hand, 75 percent of the managers thought ambition was important, and 73 percent thought it would help them become successful.[30]

Psychological Forces. An array of personal needs and preferences clearly play an important role in why managers, and humans generally, engage in wrongdoing. *Business Week* took an interesting look at the motivations behind the Wall Street insider trading scandals of the late 1980s.[31] Young, often Ivy League–educated, highly paid traders crossed the line in order to earn yet more money. *Business Week* asked, "Why wasn't $1 million a year enough?" Of course, no one has definitive answers, but *Business Week*'s interviews with traders, academics, and psychologists produced the important conclusion that the conventional response—greed—was only a partial explanation. Other influential forces included (1) a predisposition to cut corners, (2) compulsive drives, (3) a yearning to maintain the emotional high that accompanied success, (4) the stimulation in danger, (5) a craving for recognition, (6) inexperience, and (7) intellectual excitement.

Moral Development. Scholars argue that some individuals are simply better prepared to make ethical judgments than are others. Psychologist Lawrence Kohlberg built and empirically tested a comprehensive theory of moral development in which he claimed that moral judgment evolves and improves primarily as a function of age and education.

Kohlberg, via interviews with children as they aged, was able to identify moral development as movement through distinct stages, with the later stages being improvements on the earlier ones. Kohlberg identified six universal stages grouped into three levels:

1. Preconventional level
   - Stage 1: Obey rules to avoid punishment.
   - Stage 2: Follow rules only if it is in own interest, but let others do the same. Conform to secure rewards.
2. Conventional level
   - Stage 3: Conform to meet the expectations of others. Please others. Adhere to stereotypical images.
   - Stage 4: Doing right is one's duty. Obey the law. Uphold the social order.
3. Postconventional or principled level
   - Stage 5: Current laws and values are relative. Laws and duty are obeyed on rational calculations to serve the greatest number.

Stage 6: Follow self-chosen universal ethical principles. In the event of conflicts, principles override laws.[32]

At Level 3, the individual is able to reach independent moral judgments that may or may not be in conformity with conventional societal wisdom. Thus, the Level 2 manager might refrain from sexual harassment because it constitutes a violation of company policy and the law. A manager at Level 3 might reach the same conclusion, but his or her decision would have been based on independently defined, universal principles of justice.

Kohlberg found that many adults never pass beyond Level 2. Consequently, if Kohlberg was correct, many managers may behave unethically simply because they have not reached the upper stages of moral maturity.

Kohlberg's model is based on very extensive longitudinal and cross-cultural studies over a period of more than three decades. For example, one set of Chicago-area boys was interviewed at 3-year intervals for a period of 20 years. Thus, the stages of moral growth exhibit "definite empirical characteristics" such that Kohlberg was able to claim that his model had been scientifically validated.[33] While many critics remain, the evidence, in sum, is supportive of Kohlberg's general proposition.

Feminine Voice? One of those lines of criticism requires a brief inspection. Carol Gilligan, a colleague of Kohlberg, contends that our conceptions of morality are, in substantial part, gender-based.[34] She claims that men typically approach morality as a function of justice, impartiality, and rights while women are more likely to build a morality based on care, support, and responsiveness. Men, she says, tend to take an impersonal, universal view of morality as contrasted with the feminine "voice" that rises more commonly from relationships and concern for the specific needs of others. Gilligan then criticizes Kohlberg because his highest stages, 5 and 6, are structured in terms of the male approach to morality while the feminine voice falls at stage 3. Further, Kohlberg's initial experimental subjects were limited to young males. The result, in Gilligan's view, is that women are underscored.

Organizational Forces. Values, psychological factors, and moral decision-making skills undoubtedly all play a role in managerial misdeeds. However, a considerable body of evidence suggests that forces external to the manager can also be quite influential. In three extensive surveys from 1961 through 1984, managers were asked to rank six factors "in order of their influence or contribution to unethical behaviors or actions by managers" (see Table 1.2).

Clearly, managers share the perception that the boss's behavior is the critical ingredient (among the six studied) in maintaining an ethical workplace. The influence of one's co-workers and one's industry or profession is likewise thought to be significant, but society's moral climate and the presence or absence of formal company policy (such as a code of conduct) are generally not perceived to be highly influential. Finally, these managers uniformly dismiss the importance of personal financial need in cheating. Of course, these studies address a limited array of issues, and it may be that these managers are merely passing the buck. In your personal experience, if any, with unethical behavior, were any of these six factors influential in your conduct? Or does the blame lie with you—your values, your personal preferences, or your moral decision-making system? Or some combination of all of those and more?

Cheating—Other Pressures. Many factors clearly are at work, and that in itself is an important lesson. We are often inclined to attribute cheating merely to the desire for personal advancement. But that force, important though it is, does not fully explain cheating. Most of us wish to advance, but some of us are not willing to cheat. Perhaps we are all

TABLE 1.2

FACTORS INFLUENCING UNETHICAL MANAGERIAL BEHAVIOR

	1984 Study	*1977 Study*	*1961 Study*
Behavior of superiors	1*	1	1
Behavior of one's peers in the organization	2	4	3
Ethical practices of ones' industry or profession	3	3	2
Society's moral climate	4	5	—†
Formal organizational policy (or lack thereof)	5	2	4
Personal financial need	6	6	5

*1 is most influential; 6 is least influential.
†Factor not included.

Note: Suggested by similar table in Archie B. Carroll, *Business and Society* (Cincinnati: South-Western Publishing Co., 1989) p. 120.

Sources: 1984 study—Barry Posner and Warren Schmidt, "Values and the American Manager: An Update," *California Management Review* 26, no. 3 (Spring 1984), p. 202; 1977 study—Steve Brenner and Earl Molander, "Is the Ethics of Business Changing?" *Harvard Business Review* 55, no. 1 (January–February 1977), p. 57; 1961 study—Raymond Baumhart, "How Ethical Are Businessmen?" *Harvard Business Review* 39, no. 4 (July–August 1961), p. 6.

genetically predisposed to cheat in order to survive. Perhaps we are actually taught to cheat. Perhaps we simply have not fully understood the fundamental moral truths. Perhaps we all too willingly submit to the unethical example and wishes of others. Perhaps, as Karl Menninger suggested, we have lost our sense of sin.[35]

The Corporation as a Moral Person. We have given a good deal of attention to the moral dilemma of the individual manager. At this point, an alternative conception should be considered. Many philosophers and commentators have now embraced the notion of the corporation as a person in the fullest sense of the word. Of course, the corporation has long been treated as a person of sorts in the eyes of the law. We can legitimately hold the corporation legally blameworthy for employee wrongs. But can we attribute moral responsibility to the corporation? Ordinarily, we consider an individual morally responsible for act or event X only (1) if the person did X or caused X to occur and (2) if the person's conduct was intentional. Does a corporation ever do or cause any event, or are all so-called corporate acts really the decisions of an individual or individuals? And even if a corporation could act, could it do so intentionally? In a sense, can a corporation think?

How might a corporation be thought of as a fully functioning moral being? Philosopher Peter French is perhaps the leading proponent of the corporate moral personhood notion.[36] For our purposes, the theory begins with what French calls the Corporate Internal Decision Structure (CID Structure), by which he means (1) an organizational system of decision making—the organizational chart—and (2) a set of procedural and policy rules. Via the CID Structure, the judgments and actions of the individual managers, officers, and directors are "processed," and those actions and judgments become the will of the corporation. Thus, the corporate action process parallels that of humans. To French, the corporation displays the characteristics necessary for intentional conduct—hence, his view of the corporation as a moral person. (French's argument goes on in a much more detailed and sophisticated fashion, but this glimpse will suffice here.) Many philosophers support French's position; many differ. The critics' arguments are multiple, but at bottom the corporation, to them, does not appear to be a person. That is, even though a corporation may be *analogous* to a person, it is not necessarily *identical* to a person. For example, do corporations possess all of the rights of a person (e.g., the right to life)?[37]

Even if a corporation can be treated as a moral person, should we want to do so? We might answer yes because, in the event of wrongdoing, we could avoid the nearly impossible task of finding the guilty party within the corporate maze. Why not simply place the blame (or at least part of it) on the organization? But if we were to do so, would we somehow depreciate perhaps the central moral precept in our society—the notion that each of us must accept responsibility for our actions?

Moral World? Or perhaps, as Professor Jeffrey Nesteruk suggests, we need to move beyond the person/property debate and recognize that existing legal categories don't adequately express the nature of corporations.[38] Nesteruk sees the corporation as a "moral world," not merely a legal construct or a passive framework to expedite managerial action but a persuasive moral environment actively influencing the nature of ethical decision making within it. Hence, Nesteruk calls for a third legal category, reaching beyond person or property to label the corporation an *organizational actor.* Such an approach would highlight the influential role of the organization itself in the ethical choices made by individuals within that organization. The corporation, he argues, is *both* a moral person (and thus morally responsible) and a moral world in which individuals make decisions (and thus are morally responsible.)

C. Business Ethics in Practice

Having established a general ethical foundation, we now turn to the pragmatics of dealing with specific ethical problems. As noted, when questioned regarding the forces that contribute to unethical decision making in working life, managers point to the behavior of their superiors and the nature of company policy regarding wrongdoing. Hence, we assume that the organization committed to ethical quality can institute some structures and procedures to encourage decency. Codes of conduct are a common corporate ethics tool. The codes vary from rather specific lists of dos and don'ts to general statements of company aspirations. The Johnson & Johnson credo (p. 27) is the most frequently cited corporate ethics statement.

Financial World: What is your definition of an ethical business?

Elaine Sternberg, author of Just Business: It's one that seeks to maximize long-term owner value while respecting distributive justice and ordinary decency. Distributive justice exists when rewards are proportional to contributions—properly structured performance-related pay and promotions based on merit, for example. Ordinary decency requires honesty, fairness, refraining from coercion, and legality. When something violates distributive justice or ordinary decency, the ethical business will not do it even if it appears to maximize owner value.

Do you agree with this definition?

Source: "Just Business," *Financial World,* Fall 1994, p. 66. Reprinted with permission.

TABLE 1.3

WHAT COMPANY CODES OF CONDUCT STRESS

A study of 202 corporate codes of conduct found these subjects included at least 75 percent of the time and, similarly, found these subjects not mentioned at least 75 percent of the time.

Included	*Frequency*	*Not Included*	*Frequency*
Relations with U.S. government	86.6%	Personal character matters	93.6%
Customer/supplier relations	86.1	Product safety	91.0
Political contributions	84.7	Environmental affairs	87.1
Conflicts of interest	75.3	Product quality	78.7
Honest books or records	75.3	Civic and community affairs	75.2

Sources: William Frederick and James Weber, University of Pittsburgh; Marilynn Cash Matthews, Washington State University.

Codes of Conduct. Over 80 percent of the respondents to a 1991 survey of American corporations indicated that they use an employee code of conduct, while European (71 percent) and Canadian firms (68 percent) were slightly less likely to do so.[39] The most commonly prohibited behaviors are set out in Table 1.3. We should note that some evidence suggests that the codes may actually contribute to ethical problems. Professor William Frederick of the University of Pittsburgh argues that the "culprit is not personal values but corporate culture."[40] Frederick points to studies demonstrating that corporations with codes of ethics are actually cited by federal agencies more frequently than those without such codes. And he argues that the codes themselves characteristically emphasize conduct that strengthens the company's profit picture. As exhibited in Table 1.3, company codes normally ignore the firm's role in a variety of pressing social issues.[41] In sum, Frederick's important, data-based study lends scientific support to the view that company goals often have the effect of submerging personal values.

At the same time, corporate efforts to attack ethics problems continue to grow. A 1992 survey of Fortune 1000 companies found over 40 percent of them holding ethics seminars while one-third have established ethics committees. And some 200 firms have recently appointed ethics officers to act as ombudspersons.[42]

Although there exist competing, real-life forces that cloud managers' ethics landscape, what do you think about the J C Penney buyer who supplemented his $56,000 annual income with about $1.5 million in bribes and kickbacks over four years? The buyer offered promises of large orders or crucial competitive information in exchange for cash payments. A *Wall Street Journal* article explains that "unlike kickbacks to government buyers, retail bribery hurts customers, not taxpayers. Because customers can shop around, it doesn't stir much outrage. Indeed, some in the retail industry don't even realize it's illegal."[43] Do you believe this claim? Could someone not believe that these kickbacks are illegal?

Business Crime—Managerial Liability. While business itself is the victim of shoplifting, employee theft, fraud, and so on, reaching tens of billions of dollars annually, our concern is with white-collar crime in which the criminals are themselves corporations or managers. Regrettably, we have extensive evidence of widespread business crime. Professor Amitai Etzioni summarized some of that evidence is his 1990 criminal justice testimony to Congress:

> What do we know about the scope of corporate crime and who the actual perpetrators are? The Inspector General's office in the Department of Defense reports that 20

Our Credo

We believe our first responsibility is to the doctors, nurses and patients,
to mothers and fathers and all others who use our products and services.
In meeting their needs everything we do must be of high quality.
We must constantly strive to reduce our costs
in order to maintain reasonable prices.
Customers' orders must be serviced promptly and accurately.
Our suppliers and distributors must have an opportunity
to make a fair profit.

We are responsible to our employees,
the men and women who work with us throughout the world.
Everyone must be considered as an individual.
We must respect their dignity and recognize their merit.
They must have a sense of security in their jobs.
Compensation must be fair and adequate,
and working conditions clean, orderly and safe.
We must be mindful of ways to help our employees fulfill
their family responsibilities.
Employees must feel free to make suggestions and complaints.
There must be equal opportunity for employment, development
and advancement for those qualified.
We must provide competent management,
and their actions must be just and ethical.

We are responsible to the communities in which we live and work
and to the world community as well.
We must be good citizens—support good works and charities
and bear our fair share of taxes.
We must encourage civic improvements and better health and education.
We must maintain in good order
the property we are priviledged to use,
protecting the environment and natural resources.

Our final responsibility is to our stockholders.
Business must make a sound profit.
We must experiment with new ideas.
Research must be carried on, innovative programs developed
and mistakes paid for.
New equipment must be purchased, new facilities provided
and new products launched.
Reserves must be created to provide for adverse times.
When we operate according to these principles,
the stockholders should realize a fair return.

of the 100 largest defense contractors have been convicted in criminal cases since 1983. A study by the Department of Justice that looked at almost 600 of the largest U.S. publicly owned manufacturing, wholesale, retail, and service corporations with annual sales of $300 million or more, showed that during 1975 and 1976 "over 60 percent had at least one enforcement action initiated against them . . . more than 40 percent of the manufacturing corporations engaged in repeated violations." The Resolution Trust Corporation, established to manage the savings and loan bail-out, reports that criminal fraud was discovered in 60 percent of the savings institutions seized by the government in 1989. My own study of the Fortune 500 found that

> 62 percent were involved in one or more incidents of corrupt behavior, including price fixing, environmental and anti-trust violations, bribery and fraud, during the period between 1975 and 1984. VSI Corporation, the largest aircraft fastener manufacturer and a subsidiary of Fairchild Industries, Inc., pleaded guilty this month to scheming to falsify test reports on parts for 15 years. A recent General Accounting Office report found that about 52 percent of the gasoline it sampled was labeled with a higher octane level than it actually contained. The report estimates that such misbranding costs American motorists as much as $150 million per year. Researchers at Rutgers University studied 1,000 people convicted of federal white-collar crime and found that 43 percent had previous arrest records leading to our conclusion that past penalties were not deterring continued criminal behavior. (*U.S. News & World Report*, May 7, 1990, p. 24.) From oil spills to laundering drug money, from tax evasion to price fixing, corporate crime is far from rare.[44]

Punishment. Anger over corporate crime itself has been magnified for many years by the widespread sense that business criminals are not meaningfully punished even when caught. In November 1991, to supplement earlier sentencing standards for individuals, the federal government imposed new guidelines on punishments for organizations. The basic idea was to achieve similar punishments for similar offenses. The new guidelines dramatically boost the potential size of fines, corporations may be placed on probation, and management is required to report criminal conduct. Under a complicated formula, fines are assessed based on both the seriousness of the offense and the company's role in the offense. Penalties may go up depending on senior management's role in the crime, the firm's criminal history, the firm's cooperation with authorities, and the strength of the company's compliance effort.[45]

Whistle-Blowing. Today, employees seem increasingly inclined to follow the dictates of conscience in speaking out—publicly, if necessary—against wrongdoing by their employers. Historically, complaints were taken to management and resolved there. "Going public" was considered an act of disloyalty. Americans continue to maintain a strong tradition against "squealing." Indeed, management has good reason to discourage irresponsible, precipitous whistle-blowing that might disclose legitimate trade secrets, cause unnecessary conflict among employees, unfairly tarnish the company image, and so on.

However, increased respect for whistle-blowing has provoked expanded legislative and judicial protection for whistle-blowers. Congress and President Bush agreed on the Whistleblower Protection Act of 1989, which, in brief, makes it easier for federal employees to get their jobs back if they have been demoted or fired after revealing mismanagement. More than 20 other federal laws provide some form of whistle-blower protection and most apply to both public and private employees.

Some 34 states now also have whistle-blower protection statutes for public sector employees. About half of those also offer protection to private sector employees discharged for complaining about a company action believed to violate a law or regulation. In some instances, those state whistle-blower laws apply only if the employee first gave management a chance to resolve the alleged difficulty.

Finally, some court decisions have afforded protection to whistle-blowers by denying employers the right to fire at-will employees (those not working under contract) because of their decision to blow the whistle. Traditionally, at-will employees could be fired for any reason (see Chapter 12), but courts have begun to restrict that right, particularly when the firing is deemed to violate public policy (as in the case of a legitimate whistle-blowing complaint).

Federal Judge Awards Ex-GE Staffer Record Amount in Whistle-Blower Case

by Amal Kumar Naj

A federal judge awarded $13.4 million [subsequently set at $11.5 million] to a former General Electric Co. employee for exposing a defense-contract fraud at the company, sending a strong message of encouragement to corporate whistle-blowers.

The award is the highest ever in a whistle-blower case. In deciding in favor of the GE employee, the judge also harshly criticized GE and the U.S. Justice Department for their conduct toward employees who try to uncover wrongdoings at their companies.

The case in the Cincinnati court was closely watched because the Department of Justice, which is charged with assisting and aiding whistle-blowers, had joined GE in contending that the employee had "manipulated" the federal False Claims Act for his personal gains.

After GE pleaded guilty and paid $69 million in fines and penalties in July to settle the civil and criminal charges, the government argued that the GE employee shouldn't receive any more than $4.5 million for his role.

Responding to the award, GE said it "strongly disagrees" with the judge's decision to offer a "bounty" to Chester Walsh, the employee. Under the Whistleblower Protection Act, GE cannot challenge the award. But it said it will appeal the court's award of $2.5 million in attorney fees to Mr. Walsh's lawyers from GE's pocket.

Under the Whistleblower Protection Act, Mr. Walsh was entitled to as much as $14.9 million, or 25 percent of the $59.5 million GE paid to settle the civil portion of the charges. The fraud involved diversion of U.S. funds by high-level company employees and an Israeli general, Rami Dotan, in connection with Israel's acquisition of GE jet engines. The scheme was orchestrated by employees at GE's Aircraft Engine unit in Cincinnati and at the company's offices in Israel.

Mr. Walsh, who was based in Tel Aviv, gathered evidence for more than four years and then sued GE in Cincinnati in November 1990 under the act. The statute allows private citizens to bring such action in behalf of the government and then collect a portion of the federal fines or assessments against the company.

GE had maintained that Mr. Walsh had violated the company's self-policing policies by not bringing the matter to the attention of the company. The Justice Department had joined GE in arguing that Mr. Walsh deliberately waited before filing his suit in order to collect a large reward. The government asked for a smaller award in order to "send a strong message" that whistle-blowers shouldn't get "large windfalls" for preparing their case "in a dilatory fashion."

But in his written order, Judge Carl B. Rubin said that there's "no dispute" that without the documents Mr. Walsh had to "smuggle" out of Israel "it would have been difficult, if not impossible, to sustain a case against" GE. The Justice Department had contended that much of the information Mr. Walsh provided was already known to the media and to Israeli government investigators, all of which "ultimately would have led" U.S. investigators to the fraud.

But Judge Rubin cited a secret testimony from an agent of the Federal Bureau of Investigation to discredit the government's contention. The FBI agent was quoted as saying that GE "had taken substantial measures to cover [the fraud] up for a space of two years. I have no reason to believe that anyone within GE would have ever told us besides Mr. Walsh, [who] brought us the only information that we had."

Judge Rubin, who has presided over other whistle-blower suits against GE, said the Justice Department's "pattern of behavior" in whistle-blower cases "has always been a mystery." "This is not the first case where this court has noted antagonism of the Justice Department to a whistle-blower," he said. Whistle-blowing "should be encouraged by monetary rewards," he added.

* * *

The judge also took GE to task for maintaining that it would have put a stop to the fraud if Mr. Walsh had immediately reported to the company. He cited the example of a GE employee, Alaric Fine, who was reassigned after he reported his suspicions to the company . . .

Continued

Continued

Mr. Walsh said half of his award will go to Taxpayers Against Fraud, a Washington, DC, group that was a co-plaintiff in his suit.

Questions

1. Why is the role of "squealer" or whistle-blower so repugnant to many Americans? Do you consider it ethical or unethical?
2. How would you feel about a classmate who blew the whistle on you for cheating on an examination? Would you report cheating by a classmate if it came to your attention? Explain.
3. Assume an employee of an American corporation speaks out to warn the public against a danger in one of the employer's products. The employee is fired.
   a. Can the employee successfully argue that the First Amendment guarantee of freedom of speech protects him or her from dismissal? Explain.
   b. Would it make a difference if the firm operated a nuclear reactor for generating electricity? Explain. (You can refer to Chapter 5 for discussion of the First Amendment.)

Source: *The Wall Street Journal,* December 7, 1992, p. A5. Reprinted by permission of *The Wall Street Journal.*

Bribery Abroad. Multinational business firms face a special and complex ethical dilemma. In many cultures, the payment of bribes—*baksheesh* (Middle East), *mordida* (South America), or *dash* (Africa)—is accepted as necessary and, in some cases, lawful ways of doing business. American firms and officers wishing to succeed abroad have faced great pressure to engage in practices that are, of course, illegal and unethical in the American culture. In recent years, some 370 firms, including such respected names as Gulf Oil, Lockheed, Exxon, and 3M, have confessed to questionable payments abroad totaling perhaps $745 million. For example, Lockheed expended $12.6 million in Japan alone in seeking aircraft sales. Disclosure of widespread bribery by American firms, including government officials at the highest levels, led to the 1977 enactment of the Foreign Corrupt Practices Act (FCPA). The act was amended in 1988 in an attempt to deal with complaints that it put U.S. companies at too great a competitive disadvantage with foreign companies and that the act imposed an excessive compliance burden on U.S. firms.[46]

In brief, American corporations and managers are engaging in criminal conduct under the act if they offer or provide bribes to foreign government officials to obtain or retain business. And new accounting standards were imposed to eliminate slush funds and other devices useful in facilitating bribes. The act does not forbid "grease" payments to foreign officials or political parties where the purpose of the payments is "to expedite or to secure the performance of a routine governmental action,"[47] such as processing papers (e.g., visas), providing police protection, and securing phone service. And those accused may offer the affirmative defense that the alleged payoff was lawful in the host country or was a normal, reasonable business expenditure directed to specific marketing and contract performance activities. Criminal penalties include fines of up to $2 million for companies, and individuals may be fined $10,000 and imprisoned for as long as five years if they either participate in a violation, know of a violation, or are "aware of the high probability of the existence" of a bribery situation "unless the person actually believes that such circumstance does not exist."[48] That is, corporations and individuals cannot use head-in-sand tactics to avoid knowledge of wrongdoing.

Controversy. The FCPA has been controversial from the outset. Some businesspeople see it as a blessing both because it is an honorable attempt at a firm moral stance and because it is often useful for an American businessperson abroad to say, "No, our laws forbid me from doing that." On the other hand, some see the act as damaging to our competitiveness. When the FCPA was enacted originally, we had hoped that other nations would join us. None has done so.

> "It hurts us," says an executive of a Fortune 500 company's subsidiary that is trying to build a presence in China. He complains that foreign competitors often entertain prospective customers far more lavishly than his company would ever judge reasonable under the act. To get around the law, he says, some American companies enlist middlemen to take care of "local business practices"—while Japanese companies take care of such matters by themselves, without paying middlemen.[49]

And one's attitude toward the act depends a great deal on one's heritage and customs. In many nations, payments to public officials are simply a staple of commerce, a routine part of doing business. Indeed, in Denmark those payments are not only legal, they are tax deductible. Danish companies trying to make deals in Eastern Europe and Africa are advised to report bribes on their tax returns as "consultant fees," which will be treated as tax deductible so long as they are necessary to make a sale.[50] Some critics have argued that the FCPA is "the highwater mark of American paternalism."[51] What do they mean?

The article that follows details the practice of *quanxi* (influence peddling) and the legal and cultural conflicts that American businesspeople face as they try to conform to the requirements of the FCPA, company codes, and personal ethics while seeking a profit in the potentially immense Chinese market.

If You Don't Play the Game You Don't Stand to Gain

by Karl Wilson

Whichever way you look at it, more and more businessmen are finding it impossible to clinch deals in China without offering what is euphemistically termed "financial assistance."

Safely back in Hong Kong after his first foray into China on business, the young American executive looked exhausted.

"I can't believe the amount of corruption that goes on in that place," he said. "It is impossible to get anything done unless you bribe someone . . . simply impossible."

Last week China's state-run television reported the biggest crackdown on corruption since the communists came to power in 1949: Four businessmen from Haikou, the capital of Hainan province, were arrested and charged with the misappropriation of $35 million between January and August last year.

* * *

Talk to anyone who has done business in China and you will be told a dozen stories about corruption. To many mainlanders, however, it is not corruption but simple business etiquette. It is not a bribe but a "gift" or a "favor."

When it comes to corruption or "favors," foreign businessmen agree it is worse in the south of China than in the north.

Veteran China traders point out living standards in China have outpaced income by so much in recent years that more people are soliciting "favors" from foreigners.

* * *

A national crackdown on official corruption earlier in the year netted 64,000 offenders throughout

Continued

Continued

the country. But one businessman with many years of doing business in China said: "That is just a drop in the bucket."

Whether it be a senior government official or factory worker, corruption has become an ingrained part of China's business ethic.

One businessman said: "If you don't play the game you don't stand to gain. Only a fool refuses to play the game. Who would turn his back on such a market?"

Another businessman said: "Doing business anywhere in the world costs you something . . . only in China it costs you a bit more.

"I will never understand why foreign businessmen take such a sanctimonious stand towards China. You mean to tell me there isn't corruption in Australia, the U.K., or the United States?

"Try dealing with the Teamsters union in America or Australia's trade unions."

* * *

One businessman explained the process: "When you arrive you give the family gifts, obviously the more important the official or businessman the more expensive the gifts. But you give him nothing because that would be corruption. There is nothing wrong, however, with giving gifts to his family . . .

"But there is no guarantee a deal will be struck. That is something foreigners don't quite understand."

* * *

Businessmen with many years' experience in doing business in China say it does not pay to be up-front with a "favor."

One recent example of a botched "favor" was when a Hong Kong broker tried to get a licence to sell B-shares in Shenzhen.

The Canadian Chinese broker, who had little experience in doing business in China, was told to bribe an official to get the licence.

Putting $100,000 into a brown envelope, the young broker took the train to Shenzhen and his designated meeting with a senior official at the People's Bank of China.

Fifteen minutes later, the young broker handed over the envelope and grasped the banker's hand saying, "I can leave this in your capable hands." The banker threw the broker out of his office along with the $100,000.

"He should have suggested meeting him at home and taken a few expensive gifts with him for the family. I know many Chinese officials are starting to get very concerned about the level of up-front favors. The government says it is cracking down but it is the government which houses the worst offenders," one Hong Kong businessman said.

"The point is, no matter how expensive the gift, it is no guarantee that you will sign a contract."

What has become popular among Chinese businessmen and officials is the invitation by their counterparts in Hong Kong to visit the territory on "business."

"When they arrive it is important to give them 'pocket money' which can be anything from $2,000 upwards depending on how important the person is."

A Hong Kong industrialist said: "Also, you are required to cover air fares, hotel accommodation and meals. That is considered the polite thing to do. . . We call it corruption and it comes out of our marketing budget. In China, it is part of legitimate business practice."

Questions

1. Carl Kaufmann of Du Pont raised the following bribery issue: As the head of a multinational corporation, you learn that one of your plant managers has been arrested in a distant republic. His alleged crime is that goods found in your warehouse lack the proper customs stamp and papers. But the truth is more complicated. For years, "grease" has been a way of life in this country's bureaucracy, and your plant manager has been paying gratuities to the customs officers. But he knows it is against home office policy, and so he stops. Their inspection follows. The price for dropping all charges: $18,000. Would you pay up? Or let your man be put in jail? Explain.
2. Which alternative is more ethical?[52] Explain.

Source: Abridgement of "The Hard Graft Business in China" by Karl Wilson, South China Morning Post, January 10, 1993, p. 4. Reprinted by permission of the South China Morning Post Publishers, Ltd.

A Dissent. To this point, this chapter has been directed, rather conventionally, to the notion that the cause of decency in the corporate community will be enhanced if we achieve a sufficient understanding of ethical dilemmas and the decision systems necessary to deal with them. Therefore, it is fitting to look at an aggressively cynical viewpoint that rejects ideals in favor of a pragmatism often considered more in keeping with today's business reality.

Nothing Succeeds Like an S.O.B.

by R. H. Morrison

The real key to all success is perseverance. The willingness to hang in there, take the lumps that come, and get up off the floor more than once, is the attribute that you must have.

You will also have to become a dedicated, single-minded S.O.B. You have to change your thinking, your attitude toward reality, and develop what could be described as a Machiavellian outlook on the world.

1. First, you cannot be overconcerned with morality in the conventional sense. You must become convinced there is nothing essentially wrong with exploiting people and situations. The game of business is like the game of football. If the quarterback on the offensive team discovers that a defensive halfback simply cannot cover one of his pass receivers, he will use that weakness to his maximum advantage. The defender may wind up losing his job, but this is of no concern to the quarterback. The name of the game is winning, and exploiting situations and people is part of that game.

2. You have to learn to become cool and detached in dealing with other people. You never get emotionally involved with people or situations. Essentially you view everything in terms of objects and situations. You do not suffer with intellectual analysis of the results of your actions.

3. You actually enjoy the game. You enjoy the exploitation, you derive the satisfaction from using people, things, and situations to achieve your goal. You do not do this for amusement or self-aggrandizement, but simply to get that which you are after.

4. Above all you have a rational view of society as it exists. You are neither impressed nor bothered by philosophical viewpoints that stress that the greatest goals in life are serving your fellow man.

5. In short you are not a nice guy, you are an S.O.B., dedicated to success, and having convinced yourself you need that success, it will be achieved. As for money, that's the way you keep score.

If this attitude puts some strain on your psyche, and you feel it is overly cynical or outright debasing, I would like to engage in a brief, philosophical dissertation concerning the reality of such things as truth and morals.

In point of fact, *there is no such thing as real truth in human affairs.* Let's examine the most often quoted rule of behavior, the so-called golden rule: "Do unto others as you would have others do unto you." This sounds as though it is the perfect philosophical solution

Continued

Continued

to human action. However, all humans are not the same, and there are aberrations in the human psyche. If, for example, a masochist were to apply the golden rule to everybody he came in contact with, there would be many unhappy people in the vicinity.

So even the most likely sounding philosophy has holes in it. The plain truth is, that truth is a point of view.

For example, let's take a common happening that affects everybody in the vicinity. Rain! Rain falls universally on everybody in an area. The farmer says the rain is good because it makes his crops grow, and this is the truth. The roadbuilder, the owner of the baseball team, and the people going on a picnic say the rain is bad because it stops them from doing what they need to do. And that, too, is the truth. So we have several people with exactly opposing opinions about an event, and all are telling the truth. So, in fact, the truth is little more than a point of view, and it depends on whose moccasins you are standing in as to whether good or bad.

The problem with things of this nature is that people tend to take extreme viewpoints. Thus, the farmer who demands that it always rain is advocating flood. The roadbuilder who advocates that it never rain is advocating drought. The truth has to be a reasonable compromise between these points of view. And so it is with all affairs of mankind—there has to be a compromise from the extremes in order to arrive at a livable situation. But those moralists who set down rules carved in stone and hand them down as the great truth from above are little more than con men attempting to force people to live in a society that advocates a single truth or a single point of view. It very seldom works.

Morals are nothing more than social customs. They change with time, generations, and societies. For example, a cannibal is moral in a cannibalistic society. He is obviously immoral in a noncannibalistic society.

In this country we have had great changes in moral attitudes over the years, and they change every day. In the Old West, horse stealing was a hanging offense. Today it is a misdemeanor. In the early days of this country, political corruption, prostitution, slavery, and other moral outrages were common coin. Yet we had a higher percentage of people going to church in those days than we do today . . .

Such is the continuous hold of morality on a society. Therefore, the small businessman who is stepping out into the business world can be little concerned with the changing fads of human morals, or philosophical opinions about what is or is not truth.

* * *

When you have made it up the mountain, reached the pinnacle, you can then do what the rest of those successful entrepreneurs have done before you. You can write a code of ethics, make speeches about morality to business and civic groups, and look down with a cold smile on all the scrambling, scratching little bastards below, trying to find their path to the top. You can even do what some of the rest of them have done—roll rocks down on them just for the hell of it, and make the road a little tougher.

I like to think of the small businessman as an eagle. A high-flying loner, whose only morality is to get that which he deems is his right. He flies alone, finds what he needs himself, and lives where and as he chooses.

I think of corporations, government bureaucracies, and others as vultures. Vultures operate in groups, picking the bones of the dead and defenseless, and are simply put here to demonstrate Machiavelli's rule that only the fittest survive. Start now!

Questions

1. Is truth merely a point of view? Evaluate the author's argument.
2. William Starr, director of the Center for Ethics Studies, explains problems of ethical relativism:

   Surely we believe that there are ethical standards below which we should not accept. This would lead us into a crass ethical relativism based on different ethical standards which different societies possess. So, if a

Continued

given society requires us to do something which is morally abhorrent in order to do business in that society, we ought to refuse. Yet we do not wish to unilaterally impose our ethical standards on the rest of the world. This can show disrespect toward other countries and cultures, can have the United States be called dogmatic and intolerant of ethical standards other than its own, and perpetuate the stereotype of the ugly American.[53]

Are morals merely relative or situational, changing according to time, place, and circumstances? In other words, when in Rome, should one always do as the Romans do?

3. Assume a businessperson's goal is success and that issues of morality are of insignificant concern. Is Morrison's formula the best route to success? Explain.
4. In some eras and cultures, spiritual success has been preferable to material success. Is that the case in contemporary America? Explain.

Source: *Business and Society Review* 28 (Winter 1978–79), pp. 69–70. Reprinted by permission from the *Business and Society Review*.

V. Corporate Social Responsibility

As illustrated above, the business community has been the subject of intense criticism even as the influence of business values in American life has grown more dominant. That increasing business influence, in conjunction with the perception of serious business misdeeds, has led in recent decades to the development of the notion of *corporate social responsibility*.

The issue is as follows: Must business decision making include consideration not merely of the welfare of the firm but of society as well? For most contemporary readers, the answer is self-evident — of course business bears a social responsibility. Business has enjoyed a central and favored role in American life. As such, it must assume a measure of the burden for the welfare of the total society. Problems such as discrimination, pollution, and poverty require the full strength of the nation, including the vast resources of business. Professors Steven Brenner and Earl Molander's survey of *Harvard Business Review* readers revealed that:

> Most respondents have overcome the traditional ideological barriers to the concept of social responsibility and have embraced its practice as a legitimate and achievable goal for business.[54]

Only 28 percent of the respondents endorsed the free market view, popularly associated with Milton Friedman, that "the social responsibility of business is to 'stick to business,' " and 69 percent agreed with the idea that " 'profit' is really a somewhat ineffective measure of business's social effectiveness." Indeed, the respondents seemed to hold a rather optimistic, activist view of business's role in society. Of those responding, 77 percent disagreed with the position that "every business is in effect 'trapped' in the business system it helped create, and can do remarkably little about the social problems of our times."[55]

Corporate acceptance of social responsibility, as manifested in that 1976 survey, seems to have matured and expanded to the point that today's businesspeople feel willing to directly tackle some of our most challenging social issues. A 1990 *Business Week* Harris Poll shows that contemporary executives and graduate business students firmly endorse business's responsibility to help solve society's problems.[56]

A New Ideology. The ascendance of the social responsibility concept represents one of the most striking ideological shifts in American history. From the settling of the nation until roughly 1950, business was expected to concentrate on one goal—the production and distribution of the best products at the lowest possible prices. Of course, social responsibility arguments were raised, but business was largely exempt from any affirmative duty for the resolution of social problems. Rendered practical perhaps by increasing prosperity, the public, led by business scholars and critics, began in the 1950s to consider a larger role for corporate America. In four decades, the role of business in society has been radically altered. Profit seeking remains central and essential, but for most businesspersons, the new and rather unwieldy ingredient of social responsibility must be added to the equation.

Doubts Remain. But skepticism remains. Actual performance may or may not measure up to the business community's expressions of commitment. And mighty though their resources are, how much progress can we expect businesspeople to make in solving huge social dilemmas? As economics correspondent Robert Kuttner sees it, "Despite recent ballyhoo, supporters of improved public education, worker training, and national health care won't be rescued by the white knight of Corporate America."[57]

A. What Is Social Responsibility?

Many definitions of social responsibility (SR) have been offered, and a broad consensus seems to have emerged, but no single expression has successfully embraced the full spectrum of views. For example, Davis and Blomstrom put it this way: "The idea of social responsibility is that decision makers are obligated to take actions which protect and improve the welfare of society as a whole along with their own interests."[58]

Kenneth Andrews suggests the same tone but offers some additional dimensions:

> By "social responsibility" we mean the intelligent and objective concern for the welfare of society that restrains individual and corporate behavior from ultimately destructive activities, no matter how immediately profitable, and leads in the direction of positive contributions to human betterment, variously as the latter may be defined.[59]

Social Responsibility Pyramid. Figure 1.1, developed by Professor Archie Carroll, depicts social responsibility as much more than a form of corporate charity. Social responsibility begins with making a profit, the foundation on which all other social contributions necessarily rest. At the same time, the honorable corporation complies with those legal and ethical obligations that all citizens must meet. Having fulfilled those duties, the firm that seeks to be a good citizen and contribute to its own long-term best interests may also choose to engage in voluntary philanthropic efforts (in the form of money, facilities, management time, etc.) to build a better community.

Profit Maximization. Although social responsibility, framed in terms of business's duty to society, appears broadly accepted in business and among the general public, recall that a significant body of sentiment adheres to the free market view alluded to previously and perhaps best expressed by Milton Friedman:

THE PYRAMID OF CORPORATE SOCIAL RESPONSIBILITY **FIGURE 1.1**

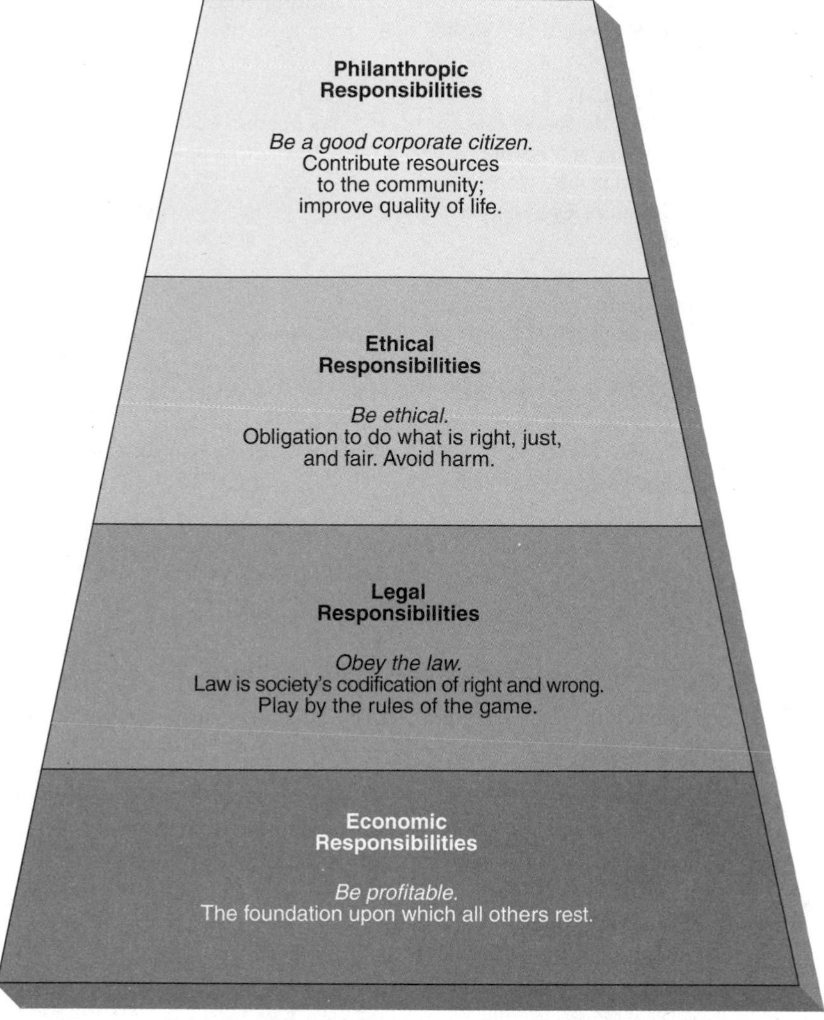

Source: Archie B. Carroll, "The Pyramid of Corporate Social Responsiblity: Toward the Moral Management of Organizational Stakeholders." Reprinted from *Business Horizons* 34, no. 4 (July –August 1991), pp. 39, 42. Copyright © 1991 by the Foundation for the School of Business at Indiana University. Used with permission.

> [In a free economy] there is one and only one social responsibility of business—to use its resources and engage in activities designed to increase its profits, so long as it stays within the rules of the game, which is to say, engages in open and free competition, without deception or fraud.[60]

Friedman believes the firm, maximizing its profits, is necessarily maximizing its contribution to society. He believes social responsibility is both unworkable and unjust. He asks how selected private individuals can know what the public interest is. He also argues that any dilution of the profit-maximizing mode—such as charitable contributions—is a misuse of the stockholders' resources. The individual stockholder, he contends, should dispose of assets according to her or his own wishes.

TABLE 1.4 A CORPORATE REPORT CARD

Socially responsible companies got stars from the Council on Economic Priorities. Other corporations with less than stellar records received dishonorable mentions.

Good Grades

Pitney Bowes: For its affirmative-action, profit-sharing, and child-care-leave practices.

Xerox: For allowing employees with three years of service to take a leave with full pay to do community work.

Cummins Engine: Gets high marks for giving 5 percent of its domestic pretax profits to charity.

Bad Grades

Perdue Farms: For its unsafe facilities and for allegedly firing workers with job-related injuries.

USX: Recently settled federal charges for workplace health and safety violations, paying $3.3 million in fines.

Exxon: For its poor handling of the 1989 Alaskan oil spill and for the explosion of an oil pipe near Staten Island.

Source: Council on Economic Priorities. In Karen Springen and Annetta Miller, "Doing the Right Thing," *Newsweek*, January 7, 1991, p.42.

B. SOCIAL RESPONSIBILITY IN PRACTICE

> Faced with increased public scrutiny, businesses are scrambling to become socially responsible.[61]

That observation by *Newsweek* suggests what has so clearly come to pass. The debate is over. The corporate community, perhaps reluctantly, now acknowledges its increased responsibility to the larger society. Today, the question is one of what to do and how to do it. The accompanying "Corporate Report Card" (Table 1.4) suggests some of the activities that companies are doing (or failing to do) to make a contribution to society beyond providing quality products and services.

Ben & Jerry's. The unorthodox but highly successful East Coast ice-cream company has integrated social responsibility into the heart of the company's approach to business. Each year, 7.5 percent of pretax profits goes to worthy causes. Ben & Jerry's supports an entrepreneurial fund to encourage new businesses. Employees are urged to volunteer for community service, for which they are paid their normal salaries by the company. Founder Ben Cohen says, "Business has a responsibility to give back to the community."[62]

But Is Corporate Social Responsibility Good Business? The empirical evidence is mixed. Many studies show highly responsible firms with very favorable economic returns.[63] Others show little or no relationship between social responsibility and performance.[64] In some sense, the question is moot because the public has spoken so clearly:

> Studies have shown that the public is paying ever-closer attention to corporate behavior. A recent Roper poll of 1,496 U.S. consumers found that 52 percent said they would pay 10 percent more for a so-called socially responsible product and 67 percent said they are concerned about a company's social performance when they shop.

Remember Ayn Rand? Rand is consistently criticized for her theory that individuals *should* be selfish and that we all act only in our own self-interest. When asked about social responsibility to others in our communities, she responds,

> The moral purpose of one's life is the achievement of happiness. This does not mean that he is indifferent to all men, that human life is of no value to him, and that he has no reason to help others in an emergency—but it does mean that he does not subordinate his life to the welfare of others, that he does not sacrifice himself to their needs, that the relief of their suffering is not his primary concern, that any help he gives is an act of generosity, not of moral duty.

Source: From Ayn Rand, *The Virtue of Selfishness,* p. 49.

Loblaws, a Canadian grocery chain, reports it sees a 10 to 60 percent increase in sales of products after they are labeled with the company's environmental seal. Ethical mutual funds are also paying off. In a test that compared the return of [Domini Social Index] listed companies and the S&P 500 from 1986 to 1990, the DSI's total return was 80 percent, almost identical to the S&P's.[65]

C. Corporate Public Policy

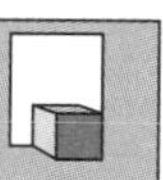

Social Responsiveness. As the principle of social responsibility became increasingly acceptable to the corporate community, the nature of the debate shifted a bit to whether corporate *performance* conformed to those principles. The idea of *corporate social responsiveness* then emerged. The movement was away from the moral theme of responsibility, obligation, and duty to the more practical notion of how best to manage the firm's response to social issues. However, social responsiveness, being reactive in character, proved inadequate to the demands of an increasingly complicated corporate-societal compact. Mere responsiveness to social problems in this era cannot meet the needs of the business community nor the demands of the larger society.

Public Policy. Hence, in recent years, we have witnessed the evolution of *corporate public policy,* wherein business takes a more activist stance in addressing contemporary social issues. Public policy refers to the process by which the total society identifies and manages its problems and goals. The corporate public policy approach calls for the business community to recognize that it should play a part in setting the larger public policy agenda and dealing with it. Hence, business, rather than taking a responsive role, must be an active player in social themes. Business now must be closely attuned not merely to market signals but to government signals and to the larger society's preferences. All of this, of course, requires the contemporary manager to learn about a much broader range of issues than was the case historically. Profit now rests not merely in providing the best product or service at the lowest price but in understanding and dealing with the very complex interplay between the corporation, government, and society. Thus, today's socially responsible firm is likely to be even more involved in identifying and attempting to manage social issues. To do so, many corporations have now built the public policy process into their management structure and systems.

Recently the Department of Commerce issued the following ethics guidelines for companies. Companies are not at all required to abide by these recommendations but those that make exceptional efforts will be held up as models of American business.

U.S. Department of Commerce Model Business Principles

Recognizing the positive role of U.S. business in upholding and promoting adherence to universal standards of human rights, the administration encourages all businesses to adopt and implement voluntary codes of conduct for doing business around the world that cover at least the following areas:

- Provision of a safe and healthy workplace.
- Fair employment practices, including avoidance of child and forced labor and avoidance of discrimination based on race, gender, national origin, or religious beliefs; and respect for the right of association and the right to organize and bargain collectively.
- Responsible environmental protection and environmental practices.
- Compliance with U.S. and local laws promoting good business practices, including laws prohibiting illicit payments and ensuring fair competition.
- Maintenance, through leadership at all levels, of a corporate culture that respects free expression consistent with legitimate business concerns, and does not condone political coercion in the workplace; that encourages good corporate citizenship and makes a positive contribution to the communities in which the company operates; and where ethical conduct is recognized, valued, and exemplified by all employees.

In adopting voluntary codes of conduct that reflect these principles, U.S. companies should serve as models, encouraging similar behavior by their partners, suppliers, and subcontractors.

Adoption of codes of conduct reflecting these principles is voluntary. Companies are encouraged to develop their own codes of conduct appropriate to their particular circumstances. Many companies already apply statements or codes that incorporate these principles. Companies should find appropriate means to inform their shareholders and the public of actions undertaken in connection with these principles. Nothing in the principles is intended to require a company to act in violation of host country or U.S. law. This statement of principles is not intended for legislation.

Model Business Principles: Procedures

When President Clinton announced his decision to renew China's MFN status last year, he also announced a commitment to work with the business community to develop a voluntary statement of business principles relating to corporate conduct abroad. The president made it clear that U.S. business can and does play a positive and important role in promoting the openness of societies, respect for individual rights, free markets and prosperity, environmental protection, and the setting of high standards for business practices generally.

The Clinton administration today is offering an update on our efforts to follow-through on the president's commitment to promote the Model Business Principles and best practices among U.S. companies. The principles already have gained the support of some U.S. companies. A process is ongoing to elicit additional support for these principles and to continue to examine issues related to them. The elements of this process are as follows:

Voluntary Statement of Business Principles

The administration, in extensive consultations with business and labor leaders and members of the nongovernmental

Continued

Continued

organization (NGO) community, developed these model principles, which were reported widely in the press earlier this spring. This model statement is to be used by companies as a reference point in framing their own codes of conduct. It is based on a wide variety of similar sets of principles U.S. companies and business organizations already have put into global practice. The administration encourages all businesses everywhere to support the model principles. (Copies of the model statement are available by calling the U.S. Department of Commerce Trade Information Center, 1-800-USA-TRADE.)

Efforts by U.S. Business

As part of the ongoing effort, U.S. businesses will engage in the following activities:

Conferences on best practices issues. In conjunction with Business for Social Responsibility, a nonprofit business organization dedicated to promoting laudable corporate practices, or other appropriate organizations, the administration will work to encourage conferences concerning issues relating to the practices contained in the Model Business Principles. Such conferences can provide a forum for information-sharing on new approaches for the evolving global context in which best practices are implemented. [For further information on Business for Social Responsibility, contact Bob Dunn, president, (415) 865-2500.]

Best practices information clearinghouse and support services. One or more nonprofits will work with the U.S. business community to develop a clearinghouse of information regarding business practices globally. The clearinghouse will establish a library of codes of conduct adopted by U.S. and international companies and organizations, to be cataloged and made available to companies seeking to develop their own codes. The clearinghouse would be available to provide advice to companies seeking to develop or improve their codes, advice based on the accumulated experience of other companies. Business for Social Responsibility (described above) is highly respected and is one resource that businesses and NGOs alike can turn to for information on best business practices.

Efforts by the U.S. Government

The U.S. government also will undertake a number of activities to generate support for the Model Business Principles:

Promote multilateral adoption of best practices. The administration has begun and will continue its effort to seek multilateral support for the Model Business Principles. Senior U.S. government officials already have met with U.S. company officials and U.S. organizations operating abroad as well as with foreign corporate officials to seek support for the principles. For example, the American Chambers of Commerce in the Asia Pacific recently adopted a resolution by which their members agreed to work with their local counterparts in the countries in which they operate to seek development of similar best practices among their members. The United States also will present the Model Business Principles at the Organization for Economic Cooperation and Development (OECD) and the International Labor Organization (ILO) as part of these organizations' ongoing behavior. Therefore, on an annual basis, the administration will offer a series of awards to companies for specific activities that reflect best practices in the areas covered by the Model Business Principles. The awards will be granted pursuant

Continued

Continued

to applications by interested companies. NGOs and private citizens will be encouraged to call attention to activities they believe are worthy of consideration. [For further information on the Best Practices Awards Program, contact Melinda Yee, U.S. Department of Commerce, (202) 482-1051.]

Presidential-business discussions. The President's Export Council (PEC), a high-level advisory group of chief executive officers, provides a forum for the president to meet regularly with U.S. business leaders to discuss issues relating to U.S. industries' exports and operations abroad. The administration will put the Model Business Principles on appropriate PEC meeting agendas to provide high exposure.

Summary

Consider business decision making and the pressures that come to bear on the process. First, the decision maker must consider the facts of the situation. Next there are legal constraints that must be reviewed and complied with. Third, the decision maker must contemplate the economics of the decision and the public policy issues that may be presented by these facts. Finally, the decision must be subject to ethical concerns and constraints.

Some might argue that an economic or free market approach to many of these issues ignores morality in favor of efficiency. To the contrary, Judge Richard Posner of the Seventh Circuit Court of Appeals and noted law and economics scholar explains:

> But is there really a fundamental inconsistency between morality and efficiency? . . . Honesty, trustworthiness, and love reduce the costs of transactions. Forswearing coercion promotes the voluntary exchange of goods. Neighborliness and other forms of selflessness reduce external costs and increase external benefits. Charity reduces the demand for costly public welfare programs. Care reduces social waste.[66]

Efficiency in a moral society is therefore achieved through ethical transactions. Law, ethics, and economics converge in any given transaction to produce the most efficient and effective result.

The purpose of this text is to walk with the decision maker from the first steps in choosing to run a business, through the operations of the business, to internationalization and expansion. Throughout this process, the text presents the relevant issues that might face the decision maker at each stage. Although answers are not always readily available or even offered in the text, considering the questions is the critical activity.

CHAPTER QUESTIONS

1. Can the realistic businessperson expect to be both ethical and successful? Explain.
2. Resolve this ethical dilemma posed by Carl Kaufmann of Du Pont:[67]

   Assume that federal health investigators are pursuing a report that one of your manufacturing plants has a higher-than-average incidence of cancer among its employees. The plant happens to keep excellent medical records on all its employees, stretching back for decades, which might help identify the source of the problem. The government demands the files. But if the company turns them over, it might be accused of violating the privacy of all those workers who had submitted to private medical exams. The company offers an abstract of the records, but the government insists on the complete files, with employee names. Then the company tries to obtain releases from all the workers, but some of them refuse. If you give the records to the feds, the company has broken its commitment of confidentiality. What would you do?
3. *a.* Among your classmates, would you expect to find a difference between males and females in the incidence of cheating? Explain.
   b. In her book *Lying*, Sissela Bok argues that lying by professionals is commonplace. For example, she takes the position that prescribing placebos for experimental purposes is a lie and immoral. Do you agree with her position? Explain.
   c. Is the use of an unmarked police car an immoral deception? Explain.
   d. One study estimates that Americans average 200 lies per day if one includes white lies and inaccurate excuses. On balance, do you believe Americans approve of lying? Explain.
4. *Tonight Show* host Jay Leno performed in commercials encouraging his audience to "eat your body weight in Doritos."[68] He says that he turned down alcohol ads at twice the money. "I don't drink . . . And I don't like to sell it. You don't see dead teenagers on the highway with bags of Doritos scattered around them."[69]
   a. Are you in agreement with the moral distinction that Leno draws between encouraging the consumption of alcohol and encouraging the consumption of Doritos? Explain.
   b. Given the influence of television and of stars, is all television advertising by celebrities inherently unethical? Explain.
5. A pharmacist in Lexington, Kentucky, refused to stock over-the-counter weight reducers. His reasons were (1) the active ingredient is the same as that in nasal decongestants; (2) he feared their side effects, such as high blood pressure; and (3) he felt weight reduction should be achieved via self-discipline.[70] Assume the pharmacist manages the store for a group of owners who have given him complete authority about the products stocked. Was his decision ethical? Explain.
6. When *Business and Society Review* surveyed the presidents of 500 large U.S. companies, 51 responded with their reactions to hypothetical moral dilemmas. One question was:

   Assume that you are president of a firm which provides a substantial portion of the market of one of your suppliers. You find out that this supplier discriminates illegally against minorities, although no legal action has been taken. Assume further that this supplier gives you the best price for the material you require, but that the field is competitive. Do you feel that it is proper to use your economic power over this supplier to make him stop discriminating?[71]

Respond to this question.

7. In general, does the American value system favor cheaters who win in life's various competitions over virtuous individuals who lose with regularity? Explain.
8. *a.* Rank the following occupations as to your perception of their ethical quality: businesspersons, lawyers, doctors, teachers, farmers, engineers, carpenters, librarians, scientists, professional athletes, letter carriers, secretaries, journalists.
   b. In general, do you find educated professionals to be more ethical than skilled but generally less-educated laborers? Explain.
   c. Can you justify accepting an occupation that is not at or near the top of your ethical ranking? Explain how your ranking affects your career choices.
9. Comment on the following quotes from Albert Z. Carr:

   [M]ost bluffing in business might be regarded simply as game strategy—much like bluffing in poker, which does not reflect on the morality of the bluffer. I quoted Henry Taylor, the British statesman who pointed out that "falsehood ceases to be falsehood when it is understood on all sides that the truth is not expected to be spoken"—an exact description of bluffing in poker, diplomacy, and business.

   [T]he ethics of business are game ethics, different from the ethics of religion.

   An executive's family life can easily be dislocated if he fails to make a sharp distinction between the ethical systems of the home and the office—or if his wife does not grasp that distinction.
10. Assume that you are working as manager of women's clothing in a large department store. You observe that the manager of equivalent rank to you in men's clothing is performing poorly in that she arrives late for work, she keeps her records ineptly, and she is rude to customers. However, her work has no direct impact on your department.
   a. Do you have any responsibility either to help her or to report her poor performance? Explain.
   b. If the store as a whole performs poorly, but you have performed well, do you bear any degree of personal responsibility for the store's failure when you confined your efforts exclusively to your own department even though you witnessed mismanagement in other departments? Explain.
11. We are often confronted with questions about the boundaries of our personal responsibilities.
   a. How much money, if any, must you give to satisfy your moral responsibility in the event of a famine in a foreign country? Explain.
   b. Would your responsibility be greater if the famine were in America? Explain.
12. In November 1980, a fire in the Las Vegas MGM Grand Hotel resulted in 84 deaths and 500 injuries. Prior to the fire, Las Vegas fire chief Roy Parrish said fire officials and building inspectors had met with hotel officials to urge the expansion of the sprinkler system, even though the change was not required under existing law. The hotel did not undertake the expansion. (At the time of the fire, sprinklers were installed in the basement and the 1st and 26th floors.)
   a. In this case, is the legal standard also the proper ethical standard? Explain.
   b. Safety is purchased. Is the failure to make that purchase unethical? Explain.
   c. How can you decide when the cost of doing right is too high?

Notes

1. Francis Fukuyama, "Are We at the End of History?" *Fortune,* January 15, 1990, p. 75.
2. Robert Reich, "Is Liberal Democracy the Hallmark of Our Era?" *The Wall Street Journal,* February 6, 1992, p. A12. Reprinted by permission of *The Wall Street Journal,* © 1992 Dow Jones and Company, Inc. All rights reserved worldwide.
3. Amertya Sen, "Does Business Ethics Make Economic Sense?" in *The Ethics of Business in a Global Economy,* ed. Paul Minus (Boston: Kluwer Academic Publishers, 1993).
4. Irving Kristol, "When Virtue Loses All Her Loveliness—Some Reflections on Capitalism and 'The Free Society,'" in *Capitalism Today,* ed. Daniel Bell and Irving Kristol (New York: New American Library, 1971), p. 15.
5. Richard Worsnop, "Privatization," *CQ Researcher* 2, no. 42 (November 13, 1992), p. 979.
6. Ibid., p. 980.
7. Jay Matthews, "Taking Welfare Private," *Newsweek,* June 29, 1992, p. 44.
8. Matt Moffett, "Jacques Rogozinski, Mexico's $22 Billion Man, Spreads the Gospel as an Apostle of Privatization," *The Wall Street Journal,* March 16, 1993, p. A16.
9. Richard Holman, "Zambia's Privatization Program," *The Wall Street Journal,* March 8, 1993, p. A6.
10. Richard Holman, "Germany May Privatize Roads," *The Wall Street Journal,* February 10, 1993, p. A8.
11. Richard Holman, "China Deregulates a Railway," *The Wall Street Journal* February 10, 1993, p. A8.
12. Jonathan N. Goodrich, "Privatization in America," *Business Horizons* 31, no. 1 (January–February 1988), pp. 11, 16.
13. Henry Myers, "His Statutes Topple, His Shadow Persists: Marx Can't Be Ignored," *The Wall Street Journal,* November 25, 1991, p. A1.
14. Ibid.
15. Robert Livingston, "A Social-Conscience Driven Economy," *The Wall Street Journal,* February 19, 1992, p. A19.
16. Philip Howard, "The Worst of Both Worlds," *Across the Board,* May 1995, p. 41.
17. Tom Morganthau, "Checkbook Politics," *Newsweek,* April 2, 1990, p. 32.
18. Associated Press, "Incumbents Got 70% of PAC Money," *Waterloo Courier,* April 30, 1992, p. C2.
19. Glenn Simpson, "Study: PAC Spending Jumps 18% in 1992," *Roll Call,* June 3, 1993, p. 1.
20. "Inside Congress," *Congressional Quarterly,* December 11, 1993, p. 3357.
21. Robert Samuelson, "The Campaign Reform Fraud," *Newsweek,* July 13, 1987, p. 43.
22. Evan Thomas, "Peddling Influence," *Time,* March 3, 1986, pp. 26–27.
23. Jeffrey Birnbaum and John Harwood, "Campaign-Finance, Lobbying Overhaul Picks Up Steam after Years of Hot Air," *The Wall Street Journal,* May 7, 1993, p. A4.
24. Editorial, "Triumph of Hucksterism," *Des Moines Register,* May 29, 1989, p. 8A.
25. Raymond Baumhart, *Ethics in Business* (New York: Holt, Rinehart & Winston, 1968), p. 10.
26. George Steiner and John Steiner, *Business, Government, and Society: A Managerial Perspective,* 5th ed. (New York: Random House, 1988), pp. 329–40.
27. Edward Spranger, *Types of Men,* trans. P. Pigors (Halle, Germany: Niemeyer, 1928).
28. William D. Guth and Renato Tagiuri, "Personal Values and Corporate Strategy," *Harvard Business Review* 43, no. 5 (September–October 1965), p. 123.
29. Adapted from G. W. Allport, P. E. Vernon, and G. Lindzey, *Manual for the Study of Values* (Boston: Houghton Mifflin, 1960), p. 14, as reported in Archie B. Carroll, *Business and Society* (Boston: Little, Brown, 1981), p. 70.
30. Reported in Rick Wartzman, "Nature or Nurture? Study Blames Ethical Lapses on Corporate Goals," *The Wall Street Journal,* October 9, 1987, p. 27.
31. William Glaberson, "Why Wasn't $1 Million a Year Enough?" *Business Week,* August 25, 1986, p. 72.
32. For an elaboration of Kohlberg's stages, see, e.g., W. D. Boyce and L. C. Jensen, *Moral Reasoning* (Lincoln, NE: University of Nebraska Press, 1978), pp. 98–109.

33. L. Kohlberg, "The Cognitive-Developmental Approach to Moral Education," *Phi Delta Kappan* 56 (June 1975), p. 670.
34. C. Gilligan, "In a Different Voice: Women's Conceptions of Self and Morality," *Harvard Educational Review* 47, no. 4 (November 1977), p. 481. And see, e.g., C. Gilligan, *In a Different Voice* (Cambridge, MA: Harvard University Press, 1982); L. Blum, "Gilligan and Kohlberg: Implications for Moral Theory," *Ethics* 98, no. 3 (April 1988), p. 472; and O. Flanagan and K. Jackson, "Justice, Care and Gender: The Kohlberg-Gilligan Debate Revisited," *Ethics* 97, no. 3 (April 1987), p. 622.
35. Karl Menninger, *Whatever Became of Sin?* (New York: Hawthorn Books, 1973).
36. For an overview, see Peter French, "The Corporation as a Moral Person," *American Philosophical Quarterly* 16, no. 3 (July 1979), pp. 297–317.
37. For one critic's view, see John Ladd, "Persons and Responsibility: Ethical Concepts and Impertinent Analogies," in *Shame, Responsibility and the Corporation,* ed. Hugh Curtler (New York: Haven Publishing, 1986), pp. 77.
38. Jeffrey Nesteruk, "Legal Persons and Moral Worlds: Ethical Choices within the Corporate Environment," *American Business Law Journal* 29, no. 1 (Spring 1991), p. 75.
39. Ronald E. Berenbeim, *Corporate Ethics Practices* (New York: The Conference Board, 1992), p. 11.
40. Wartzman, "Nature or Nurture?" p. 21.
41. Ibid.
42. Kenneth Labich, "The New Crisis in Business Ethics," *Fortune* 125, no. 8 (April 20, 1992), p. 168.
43. Andrea Gerlin, "How a Penney Buyer Made up to $1.5 Million on Vendors' Kickbacks," *The Wall Street Journal,* February 7, 1995, p. 1.
44. "Oversight on the U.S. Sentencing Commission and Guidelines for Organizational Sanctions," Hearings before the Subcommittee on Criminal Justice of the Committee on the Judiciary, House of Representatives, 101st Congress, March 7 and May 24, 1990, serial no. 112 (Washington, DC: U.S. Government Printing Office, 1990), pp. 235–36.
45. U.S. Sentencing Commission: 1991, "Sentencing Guidelines for Organizational Defendants," *Federal Register* 56(95), p. 22786.
46. Amended by certain provisions of the Omnibus Trade and Competitiveness Act of 1988.
47. 15 U.S.C. 78dd-1(b),-2(b) (1982), as amended by 1988 Trade Act 5003(a), (c).
48. Foreign Corrupt Practices Act Amendments of 1988, 15 U.S.C. 78dd-1A(f)(2)(A)(B).
49. Ford Worthy, "When Somebody Wants a Payoff," *Fortune,* Pacific Rim, 1989, pp. 117, 118.
50. "Bribes Are Tax Deductible for Danes," *The Reuter Asia–Pacific Business Report,* June 4, 1993, BC cycle.
51. Hirschhorn, "Foreign Corrupt Practices Act: Narrowed, Significantly Clarified," *The National Law Journal,* December 26, 1988–January 2, 1989, p. 16. Reported in Beverley Earle, "Foreign Corrupt Practices Act Amendments" *Selected Papers of the ABLA National Proceedings,* ed. William Elliot, vol. 18, pp. 193, 198.
52. Carl Kaufmann, "A Five-Part Quiz on Corporate Ethics," *Washington Post,* July 1, 1979, p. C-4.
53. William Starr, "When in Rome, Should We Do as the Romans Do?" Unpublished manuscript, in possession of the authors, p. 1.
54. Steven N. Brenner and Earl A. Molander, "Is the Ethics of Business Changing?" *Harvard Business Review* 55, no. 1 (January–February 1977), pp. 57, 59.
55. Ibid., p. 68.
56. Kevin Gudridge and John Byrne, "A Kinder, Gentler Generation of Executives?" *Business Week,* April 23, 1990, p. 86.
57. Robert Kuttner, "U.S. Business Isn't About to Be Society's Savior," *Business Week,* November 6, 1989, p. 29.
58. Keith Davis and Robert L. Blomstrom, *Business and Society: Environmental and Responsibility,* 3rd ed. (New York: McGraw-Hill, 1975), p. 6.
59. Kenneth R. Andrews, *The Concept of Corporate Strategy* (Homewood, IL: Dow Jones-Irwin, 1971), p. 120.
60. Milton Friedman, *Capitalism and Freedom* (Chicago: University of Chicago Press, 1962), p. 133.

61. Karen Springen and Annetta Miller, "Doing the Right Thing," *Newsweek,* January 7, 1991, p. 42.
62. Jennifer Laabs, "Ben & Jerry's Caring Capitalism," *Personnel Journal* 71, no. 11 (November 1992), pp. 50, 55.
63. See Phillip I. Cochran and Robert Wood, "Corporate Responsibility and Financial Performance," *Academy of Management Journal* 27, no. 1 (March 1984), p. 42, for an excellent study of the issue and a survey of previous research.
64. For a summary of some of these studies, see Alfred A. Marcus, Phillip Bromiley, and Robert Goodman, "Preventing Corporate Crises: Stock Market Losses as a Deterrent to the Production of Hazardous Products," *Columbia Journal of World Business* 22, no. 1 (Spring 1987), p. 33.
65. Springen and Miller, "Doing the Right Thing," pp. 42, 43.
66. Richard Posner, *Economic Analysis of Law* (Boston: Little Brown & Co., 1986), p. 239.
67. Kaufmann, "Five-Part Quiz," p. C-4.
68. "Short Takes," *The Des Moines Register,* February 5, 1990, p. 2T.
69. Ibid.
70. Reported on WKYT TV, Channel 27, "Evening News," Lexington, Kentucky, May 12, 1980.
71. "Business Executives and Moral Dilemmas," *Business and Society Review,* no. 13 (Spring 1975), p. 51.

CHAPTER

2

The Businessperson's Introduction to American Legal Thought and the Legal System

Reader's Guide

As a starting point for understanding the law as it applies to building and managing a business, it is critical to grasp fundamental concepts of the legal process. This chapter highlights those elements of the legal process that impact business decisions.

PROFILE

James Pierce owns a company that manufactures, markets, and distributes a super-premium ice cream under the brand name "al Gelato." Many of his clients are restaurant owners who have the ice cream on their menus. Restaurants in Chicago are a seasonal business, and James finds that, although his customers pay quite well and on time in the summer months, they are not so quick with the checks during the winter and spring. It is

now April and he is specifically frustrated by the lag time of one of his clients. James would like to file a lawsuit for $750 past due on an ice-cream delivery from January, yet has never filed a lawsuit and doesn't quite know where to start.

QUESTIONS

1. What is the first step in filing a lawsuit?
2. How will Pierce know in which court to file the suit?
3. Does he need a lawyer for this action?

I. Legal Thought: Critical Legal Analysis

Have you ever heard the expression, someone is "thinking like a lawyer"? Would you take this to be a compliment or an insult? What does it mean to think like a lawyer? Although they sometimes get a bad reputation for filing lawsuits at the drop of a hat, lawyers are also the ones who are most familiar with the complicated legal procedures warranted by our law's original intent.

Critical analysis of a case also requires the evaluation of any analogies presented to the court. In many legal arguments, opponents will locate previous cases that they argue apply to the present case. Inevitably, parties can find cases where the court reaches *their* desired conclusion. The question is, Should the judge's decision in the prior case dictate the decision in this case? The answer depends on how similar the key facts and circumstances are in the two cases. Just because two cases are similar in one way does not mean that the same conclusion should be reached. Search the facts of the analogized case to determine if there are critical differences.

Finally, consider that, like it or not, most judges are white, middle-aged males. Do you always agree with the opinions of this group, or even the way they reach their opinions? Judges are not always right. You may disagree with them, and your opinions may be just as carefully reasoned as theirs. Who is to say that they are right and you are wrong?

Table 2.1 presents an approach to critical thinking, proposed by legal scholars Klayman, Bagby, and Ellis, that can help to ensure appropriate analysis of arguments and conclusions.[1]

II. The American Legal System

Presumably, we can agree that some business practices have unfavorable consequences for society. Thus, the issue becomes: What should be done, if anything, to change those consequences? The fundamental options in the United States have been threefold: let the market regulate the behavior; leave the problem to the individual decision maker's own ethical dictates; or pass a law. Throughout this text, the impact of the law, the market, and ethics will be addressed in connection with each business issue or decision. However, to understand the relevance of the market and of ethics to business decisions, it is critical to understand the rules of the game under which all businesspeople play.

This chapter, then, begins the discussion of the legal regulation of business with a brief outline of the American legal system and how it functions. This chapter will also introduce alternatives for resolving business/society conflicts without resorting to the legal system, such as negotiation, mediation, and arbitration. Although these alternatives are not new, they have been receiving much more attention in recent years.

TABLE 2.1 CRITICAL THINKING

Critical Thinking Inquiry	*Definition*	*Function in Critical Analysis*	*Critical Thinking Tips*
Issue	Subject or controversy addressed in author's expression	Essential to understanding points under discussion	May be obscured in complex or poorly composed expression or author's sophistry
Conclusion	Author's answer to the issue under controversy	Summary of author's slant or logical direction; the precise point advocated for audience's acceptance	Look for indicator words: *therefore, thus, as a result, it follows that*
Reasons	Statements of facts, evidence, analogies, or beliefs used to support a conclusion	Answers why audience should accept author's conclusion; relationship of reasons to conclusion is focus of critical thinking inquiry	Look for indicator words: *because, the fact is, as a result of, by reason of, due to, in view of, on account of, thanks to*
Ambiguities	Words or phrases susceptible to alternate meanings	Often inevitable given the imprecision of language; good authors prevent much ambiguity; sophists use them to manipulate opinon	Evaluate key terms in issue, conclusion, and reasons; examine context meaning; request author clarification; substitute alternate meaning to test whether conclusion changes
Statistical flaws	Failure in rigor of scientific method; nonrepresentative or biased sample; uncontrolled conditions; research method not replicable; deceptive but impressive large numbers; misleading percentages; ambiguous averages; unknown variance	Factual-based claims misleading if statistical flaws in empirical evidence; sampling often a practical necessity	Demand author "show me"; use personal experience or others' studies as benchmark for comparison; examine controlled conditions; search for sample bias

CRITICAL THINKING

TABLE 2.1 (continued)

Critical Thinking Inquiry	*Definition*	*Function in Critical Analysis*	*Critical Thinking Tips*
Rival hypotheses and conclusion	Alternate hypotheses consistent with author's reasons or conclusion; alternate conclusion consistent with author's reasons or hypothesis	Author's reasoning weakened by rival hypotheses or conclusions; generated easily because rivals may be more accurate than author's reasoning	Initially ignore author's hypothesis, then author's conclusion; use personal experience to search for alternate explanations consistent with author's conclusion, then generate alternate conclusions consistent with author's reasons
Analogies	Similarities between different things, suggesting that other similarities exist	Can provide convincing reasons, particularly when scientifically gathered evidence is missing or difficult to collect; law uses analogy significantly; most people accept anaolgy; however, weak analogies can be misleading	Carefully examine both the similarities and differences between two things compared: analogy is weak reason if differences predominate; may be good reason if similarities predominate; generate competing yet plausible analogies to weaken author's analogies
Reasoning errors and logical fallacies	Analytical flaws that weaken or contradict author's reasoning:	Fallacious argument misleads the reader	Be vigilant; always look for all these fallacies
	• *Diversions* lure reader from critical thinking • *Glittering generalities* divert and evoke emotion	Diversions and glittering generalities obscure reasons, assumptions, and analogies or evoke emotion	
	• *Appeals to authority* urge acceptance of accepted person's views	Appeals to authority are fallacious if unrelated to authority's expertise	
	• *Ad hominem abusive* attacks person or group	Ad hominem is invalid reason unless person attacked is biased	

Table 2.3 (*continued*) Critical Thinking

Critical Thinking Inquiry	*Definition*	*Function in Critical Analysis*	*Critical Thinking Tips*
	• *Circular reasoning* simply restates conclusion as evidence	Circular reasoning disguises conclusion as reasons by begging the question	
	• *False dilemma* raises conflict between reasoning of author and author's opposition	False dilemma incorrectly forces misbelief that there are only two choices	
Value assumptions	Unstated fundamental normative beliefs—honesty, excellence, tradition, self-reliance—implicit in author's reasoning	Some value assumptions are inevitable; they appear to strengthen conclusions with weak factual support; usually not clearly stated but hidden in value-laden terms	Look for value-laden phrases and normative tone of author's reasons or how author moves from incomplete or unconvincing reasons to partially unsupported conclusion; confront hidden value assumptions explicitly
Descriptive assumptions	Unstated factual beliefs implicit in author's reasoning	Some descriptive assumptions inevitable, so expression has to make the writing or speech manageable in size; seem to strengthen conclusions until confronted by reader	Look for hidden descriptive assumptions used as missing links in logic; identify author's background or bias to suggest any type of hidden assumption

Source: Elliot Klayman, John Bagby, and Nan Ellis, *Business Law* (Burr Ridge, IL: Richard D. Irwin, 1994), p. 1.

A debtor fails to remain current on his car and insurance payments; without authorization, the bank buys an expensive policy to cover its interest in the car, then seeks reimbursement from the debtor; and a jury awards the debtor $38 million in damages to correct the "injustice." A movie theater must pay a large jury award to a man who was denied entrance to the movies because he was accompanied by his two-year-old son. He claimed the action was age discrimination. A school district in Georgia was ordered by the courts to pay for an autistic child to attend school in Japan because the child's parents were not satisfied with the services offered the child in Georgia.

Are these fair legal decisions? Would you feel differently if you were the parent of the autistic child seeking adequate education? On the other hand, are courts and the American legal system too hard on business? Do the courts make big business pay for all that is ailing society? After all, Motorola's defense costs against a large pollution suit recently hit $15.2 million, using the resources of 180 lawyers and assistants![2]

Are these fair legal decisions? Would you feel differently if you were the parent of the autistic child seeking adequate education? On the other hand, are courts and the American legal system too hard on business? Do the courts make big business pay for all that is ailing society?

The American Legal System Is Flawed. Not many would disagree with this statement, though the majority would also add that it's the most effective, efficient, and fair system we know. As a business owner, how can you protect yourself and your business? On the other hand, how can you use the legal system to protect yourself from the strength wielded by big business today?

Before turning to our detailed examination of the technical dimensions of the law, we should remind ourselves of the central purpose of our legal system: the pursuit of justice. As you read this chapter, ask yourself repeatedly, Does this rule (this procedure, this case) contribute to the search for justice?

A 1994 poll by the American Bar Association showed that 65 percent of Americans believed that equal justice existed under our legal system. In fact, 26 percent of respondents believed that it existed "most of the time" and 57 percent believed that it was somewhat likely that it would be achieved in the future.[3] While, at first blush, these numbers may seem promising, they also mean that a full 35 percent of the American public did not believe that equal justice existed at the time of the poll. Indeed, 22 percent actually claimed that they had little confidence that the system met society's needs.

Although not our primary concern, criminal law is a vivid vehicle for addressing the notion of justice. In a separate national survey of 2,512 adult Americans, 87 percent said that our criminal justice system did not treat people equally. Among those who doubted the fairness of the system, 93 percent believed that rich people received special treatment, 61 percent said minorities weren't treated fairly, and 77 percent said the same of poor people. Eighty-five percent of whites and 64 percent of black and Hispanic-Americans had a "positive attitude" toward the police. Overall, 57 percent expressed faith in the criminal justice system.[4]

Of course, the issue of justice was at the forefront of our thoughts in 1992–93 with the Rodney King beating, the resulting police officers' trials, and the devastating riot in South Central Los Angeles. King, a black man, was struck more than 50 times by police officers' batons during his arrest after a high-speed chase in Los Angeles. The beating happened to be recorded on videotape by a civilian onlooker. The officers' acquittal in their initial trial led to the April 1992 riot in which 52 people were killed, perhaps 2,300 were injured, and property damage was estimated at $1 billion.

The confusion mounted when two black men accused of attacking truck driver Reginald Denny (a white man) during the L.A. riots were acquitted of the most serious charges against them. Prosecutors used a television videotape of the Denny beating to link the suspects to the crimes. The jury found the suspects guilty of some mayhem and assault charges but did not find sufficient evidence of attempted murder or aggravated mayhem, both of which required evidence of "specific intent."

A. Legal Foundations of Common and Statutory Law

Trying to Define Law. Just as this text investigates how business fits into society, we should begin our look at the legal system by considering how law fits into our society—from the perspectives of both those intimately associated with the law and outsiders looking at law as a social phenomenon. We begin by asking, what exactly is law?

Judges' Interpretations. The great jurists Oliver Wendell Holmes and Benjamin Cardozo held similarly pragmatic visions of the meaning of law: "The prophecies of what the courts will do in fact, and nothing more pretentious, are what I mean by the law," said Holmes.[5] To Cardozo, the law was "a principle or rule of conduct so established as to justify a prediction with reasonable certainty that it will be enforced by the courts if its authority is challenged."[6]

The notion of law as rules of conduct enforced by courts will form our working definition for much of the remainder of the text. These rules, however, are not static; they are changing and changeable by both court and legislative action.

Sociologist's Interpretation. The influential thinker Max Weber emphasized the role of external force in explaining the meaning of law.

> An order will be called law if it is externally guaranteed by the probability that coercion (physical or psychological), to bring about conformity or avenge volition, will be applied by a staff of people holding themselves specially ready for that purpose.[7]

Anthropologist's Interpretation. Bronislaw Malinowski, the respected scholar of primitive law, seemed to regard the law as the natural product of cooperative, reciprocal human relationships:

> The rules of law stand out from the rest in that they are felt and regarded as the obligations of one person and the rightful claims of another. They are sanctioned not by mere psychological motive, but by a definite social machinery of binding force, based . . . upon mutual dependence, and realized in the equivalent arrangement of reciprocal services.[8]

Thus, under this approach, binding social custom is appropriately referred to as law.

Philosophers' Interpretations. To Plato, law was one method of social control; Cicero found the heart of the law in the distinction between the just and the unjust. Perhaps the most influential legal philosopher, Roscoe Pound, built on the social control theme to argue that the law is a mechanism for ordering private interests for the good of the whole society:

> Looked at functionally, the law is an attempt to satisfy, to reconcile, to harmonize, to adjust these overlapped and often conflicting claims and demands . . . so as to give effect to the greatest total of interests or to the interests that weigh most in our civilization, with the least sacrifice of the scheme of interests as a whole.[9]

A Dissenting Opinion. To the critics of the American legal system, including those in the critical legal studies movement, the foregoing explanations fail to capture the reality of the law as an instrument of repression. For example, radical sociologist Richard

Quinney argues that we should be freed from "the dead hand of the legalistic mentality." Quinney asks us to imagine a life without law because, to him, law as practiced in America is the unjust product of the power of special interests.

> While law is to protect all citizens, it starts as a tool of the dominant class and ends by maintaining the dominance of that class. Law serves the powerful over the weak . . . Moreover, law is used by the state (and its elitist government) to promote and protect itself . . . We are indoctrinated with the ideology that it is our law, to be obeyed because we are all citizens of a single nation. Until law is the law of the people, law can be nothing other than official oppression.[10]

B. Objectives of the Law

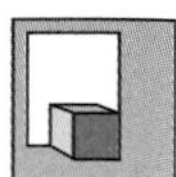

Law is shaped by social forces. The values, history, ideas, and goals of society are among the forces that determine the nature of a society's legal system. The diverse character of American society leads inevitably to differences of opinion regarding the proper direction for our legal system. However, certain broad goals can be identified.

Maintain Order. The law is instrumental in imposing necessary structure on America's diverse and rapidly changing society. Whether with stop signs, zoning ordinances, marriage licenses, or homicide statutes, the legal system seeks to prevent harm by imposing certain established codes of conduct on the mass of persons. Immediate self-interest is muted in favor of long-term general welfare. The problem then becomes one of how far to go in seeking to preserve a valuable but potentially oppressive commodity. Should the law require all motorcyclists to wear helmets? Or all businesses to close on Sunday? Or all motorists to limit their speed to 55 miles per hour?

Resolve Conflict. Because society cannot and would not wish to successfully regulate all dimensions of human conduct, a system for solving differences is required. An effort is made to substitute enlightened dispute resolution for the barbarism that might otherwise attend inevitable differences of opinion. With the law of contracts, for example, we have developed a sophisticated, generally accepted, and largely successful system for both imposing order and resolving conflict. Nevertheless, enormous problems remain, and new ones always arise.

One test of the vitality and merit of a legal system is its ability to adapt to change. Consider the 1992 case of 12-year-old Gregory Kingsley, who was granted a divorce from his parents. Gregory's parents were separated. He lived rather unhappily with each of them for a time, but after his mother said that she wanted to put him up for adoption, he was placed with a foster family. He initiated his divorce action in a Florida trial court to permit himself to be adopted by his foster family. His mother then resisted the divorce. Gregory won at the lower court, and he won on appeal on abandonment grounds, although the appeals court overturned the lower court's judgment that he had the right (the *standing,* as it is labeled in the law) to sue on his own. The decision is a good example of our legal system struggling to maintain order and resolve new varieties of conflicts born of stunning societal change. Should children be able to bring lawsuits on their own? Will this decision lead to frivolous claims by other children?

Preserve Dominant Values. Americans have reached general accord regarding many values and beliefs, and the law has been put to work in preserving those standards. For example, in the Bill of Rights we have set out those fundamental freedoms that must be protected to preserve the character of the nation. Of course, in many instances societal opinion is divided. What happens when no clear consensus emerges about an issue? What if the issue involves a conflict between two values long clutched firmly to the American breast? Freedom of speech is central to a meaningful life, but what if that speech consists of anti-Semitic parades and demonstrations organized by the Ku Klux Klan?

Guarantee Freedom. That Americans are free and wish to remain so is the nation's most revered social value. It is, in a sense, a subset of the third goal in this list, but because of its preeminence, it properly stands alone. The problem, of course, is that freedom must be limited. Drawing the line often gives rise to severe societal conflict.

In general, you are free to do as you like so long as you do not violate the rights of others. But what are those rights? Do I have a right to smoke-free air, or do you have a right to smoke wherever you wish? Even if the rights of others are not directly violated, personal freedom is limited. The so-called victimless crimes—vagrancy, gambling, pornography, prostitution—are examples of instances where the law retards freedom in the absence of immediate injury to the rights of others. Should each citizen be free to do as he or she likes so long as harm does not befall others? Or does pornography, for example, inevitably give rise to societal harm? Should homosexuals and lesbians be permitted to serve in America's armed services?

Preserve Justice. In sum, justice, is the goal of the American legal system. Professor Franz Schurmann traces a bit of the evolution of the notion of justice.

> Since ancient times, great sprawling empires with many diverse peoples were held together not only by armies but by common systems of justice. The first such system was that of the Babylonian ruler Hammurabi at the end of the third millennium B.C. While most Americans would view his rigid "eye for an eye and tooth for a tooth" with horror, in his time it represented a great step forward for humankind. It announced that Babylon would treat all its subjects according to the same system of justice.
>
> * * *
>
> Rome, as a republic and then an empire, inspired America's founding fathers. Rome's grandeur lasted a millennium. If the "great American experiment" is to last well into the next century, history indicates that, besides strength, it will need justice—the guarantee that every member of the polity will be treated fairly and equitably.
>
> * * *
>
> Roman law took a long time evolving but reached its fullest development when Rome became a great empire ruling over a vast human diversity. After it started freeing its slaves, its core practical principle became encapsulated in the phrase *suum cuique,* "to each his own," meaning that everyone has a legitimate place in the realm and a right to expect fair and equal treatment from the state.[11]

More than any other, the issue of justice should be at the forefront of all legal studies. A number of cultural and procedural problems sometimes stand in the way of justice in a **criminal action.** Those problems and others also trouble our system of **civil action.**

criminal action. The law extracted from decided cases.
civil action. An action brought to enforce a civil right, in contrast to a criminal action.

Profile Perspective: If James Pierce pursues his claim against the slow-paying restaurant owner in court, which of the above purposes would be served?

C. Locating and Analyzing Case Law

To prepare for law cases in this text, a bit of practical guidance may be useful. The study of law is founded primarily on the analysis of judicial opinion. Except for the federal level and a few states, trial court decisions are filed locally for public inspection rather than being published. Appellate opinions, on the other hand, are generally published in volumes called **reports.** State court opinions are found in the reports of that state, as well as a regional reporter published by West Publishing Company that divides the United States into units, such as Southeastern (SE) and Pacific (P).

reports. Published volumes of judicial decisions.

Within the appropriate reporter, the cases are arranged in a workable fashion and are *cited* by case name, volume, reporter name, and page number. For example, Royce Graff, Debra Graff, Bobby Hausmon and Betty Hausmon v. Brett Beard and Dorothy Beard, 858 S.W.2d 918 (Texas S.Ct. 1993), means that the opinion will be found in volume 858 of the Southwestern Reporter, 2d series, at page 918 and that the decision was reached in 1993 by the Texas Supreme Court. Federal court decisions are found in several reporters, including the *Federal Reporter* and the *United States Supreme Court Reports.*

Profile Perspective: Who would be the parties in a case filed by James Pierce? Who is the plaintiff and who is the defendant? What do you think would be the primary issue to be decided by the court and what do you believe would be its decision?

D. Additional Classifications of Law

Some elementary distinctions will make the role of law clearer.

Substantive and Procedural Law.

Substantive law creates, defines, and regulates legal rights and obligations. Thus, in terms of the topics of this course, the Sherman Act forbids restraints of trade. By judicial interpretation, price-fixing between competitors is a restraint of trade.

Procedural law embraces the systems and methods available to enforce the rights specified in the substantive law. So, procedural law includes the judicial system and the rules by which it operates. Questions of where to hear a case, what evidence to admit, and which decisions can be appealed fall within the procedural domain.

substantive law. The body of law setting out rights and duties that affect how people behave in organized social life.

procedural law. The body of law controlling public bodies such as courts, as they create and enforce rules of substantive law.

Law by Judicial Decision and Law by Enactment.

In general, American rules of law are promulgated by court decisions **case law** or via enactments by constitutional assemblies, legislatures, administrative agencies, chief executives, and local government authorities. Enactments include constitutions, statutes, treaties, administrative rules, executive orders, and local ordinances.

case law. The law extracted from decided cases.

Case Law (Judicial Decisions). Our case law has its roots in the early English king's courts, where rules of law gradually developed out of a series of individual dispute resolutions. In addition, in the 18th century, Lord Mansfield incorporated into the king's courts many of the decisions of the courts of the law merchants—private courts operated by merchants throughout Europe. This source of law was imported to America and is now known as the **common law.** (This term may be confusing because it is frequently used to designate not just the law imported from England of old but also all judge-made or case law.)

common law. Judge-made law. To be distinguished from statutory law as created by legislative bodies.

stare decisis. "Let the decision stand." A doctrine of judicial procedure expecting a court to follow precedent in all cases involving substantially similar issues unless extremely compelling circumstances dictate a change in judicial direction.

The development of English common law rules and American judicial decisions into a just, ordered package is attributable in large measure to reliance on the doctrine of ***stare decisis*** ("let the decision stand"). That is, judges endeavor to follow the precedents established by previous decisions. Subordinate courts are required to follow precedent established by the decisions of their superior courts. Federal district courts have to follow decisions of their courts of appeals and the Supreme Court. However, the Supreme Court may ignore its own precedent.

As societal beliefs change, so does the law. For example, a Supreme Court decision approving racially separate but equal education was eventually overruled by a Supreme Court decision mandating integrated schools. However, the principle of *stare decisis* is generally adhered to because of its beneficial effect. It offers the wisdom of the past and enhances efficiency by eliminating the need for resolving every case as though it were the first of its kind. *Stare decisis* affords stability and predictability to the law. It promotes justice by, for example, reducing "judge-shopping" and neutralizing judges' personal prejudices.

Statutes (Enactments). In this section, our primary concern is with the laws that have been adopted by the many legislative bodies—Congress, the state legislatures, city councils, and the like. These enactments are labeled **statutory law.** Some areas of law, such as torts, continue to be governed primarily by common law rules, but the direction of American law lies largely in the hands of legislators. Of course, legislators are not free of constraints. Federal legislation cannot conflict with the U.S. Constitution, and state legislation cannot violate either federal law or the constitutions of that state and the nation.

statutory law. Laws enacted by legislative bodies.

Law and Equity. Following the Norman conquest of England in 1066, a system of king's courts was established in which the king's representatives settled disputes. Those representatives were empowered to provide remedies of land, money, or personal property. The king's courts became known as *courts of law,* and the remedies were labeled *remedies of law.* However, some litigants sought compensation other than the three provided. They took their pleas to the king.

Typically, the chancellor, an aide to the king, would hear these petitions and, guided by the standard of fairness, could grant a remedy (such as an injunction or specific performance) specifically appropriate to the case. The chancellors' decisions, as well as those from ecclesiastical courts, accumulated over time such that a new body of remedies—and with it a new court system, known as *courts of equity*—evolved. Both court systems were adopted in the United States following the American Revolution, but today actions at law and equity are typically heard in the same court.

public law. Laws regulating the relationship between the government and its citizens.

private law. The law regulating the relationships between individuals or entities.

Public Law and Private Law. **Public law** deals with the relationship between government and the citizens. Constitutional, criminal, and administrative law (relating to such bodies as the Federal Trade Commission) fall in the public law category. **Private law** regulates the legal relationship between individuals. Contracts, agency, and commercial paper are traditional business law topics in the private law category.

Civil Law and Criminal Law. The legislature or other lawmaking body normally specifies that new legislation is either *civil* or *criminal* or both. Broadly, all legislation not specifically labeled criminal law falls in the civil law category. Civil law addresses the legal rights and duties arising among individuals, organizations such as corporations, and governments. Thus, for example, a person might sue a company raising a civil law claim of breach of contract. Criminal law, on the other hand, involves wrongs against the general welfare as formulated in specific criminal statutes. Murder and theft are, of course, criminal wrongs because society has forbidden those acts in specific legislative enactments. Hence, wearing your hat backwards would be a crime if such a statute were enacted and if that statute met constitutional requirements.

Crimes. Crimes are of three kinds. In general, *felonies* are more serious crimes, such as murder, rape, and robbery. They are typically punishable by death or by imprisonment in a federal or state penitentiary for more than one year. In general, *misdemeanors* are less serious crimes, such as petty theft, disorderly conduct, and traffic offenses. They are typically punishable by fine or by imprisonment for no more than one year. *Treason* is the special situation in which one levies war against the United States or gives aid and comfort to its enemies.

Elements of a Crime. In a broad sense, crimes consist of two elements: (1) a wrongful act or omission **(actus reus)** and (2) evil intent **(mens rea)**. Both elements must be present for a crime to exist. Thus, an individual who pockets a ballpoint pen and leaves the store without paying for it may be charged with petty theft. However, the accused may defend by arguing that he or she merely absentmindedly and unintentionally slipped the pen in a pocket after picking it off the shelf to consider its merits. Intent is a state of mind, so the jury or judge must reach a determination from the objective facts as to what the accused's state of mind must have been.

actus reus. Wrongful act or omission.

mens rea. Evil intent

Criminal Defenses. The law recognizes certain defenses to criminal prosecution. Infancy, intoxication, insanity, and self-defense are some of the arguments available to the defendant. Precise standards for each of these and other defenses differ from state to state, depending on the relevant statutory and case law. The federal Constitution and the various state constitutions also afford protections to the accused.

The Fourth Amendment to the federal Constitution prevents unreasonable searches and seizures; the Fifth Amendment requires a grand jury indictment for capital crimes, forbids double jeopardy and compulsory self-incrimination, and mandates due process of law; the Sixth Amendment guarantees a speedy and public trial by jury, the right to confront and obtain witnesses, and the right to a competent lawyer; and the Eighth Amendment prohibits excessive bail or fines and cruel and unusual punishment.

Profile Perspective: Would James Pierce's suit be classified as a civil suit or a criminal suit?

III. The Judicial Process

One of the functions of the law, as mentioned above, is the resolution of conflicts. Most disputes are, in fact, settled without resort to litigation; but when agreement cannot be reached, the citizenry can turn to the courts, a highly technical and sophisticated dispute resolution mechanism.

FIGURE 2.1 **STATE AND FEDERAL COURT SYSTEMS**

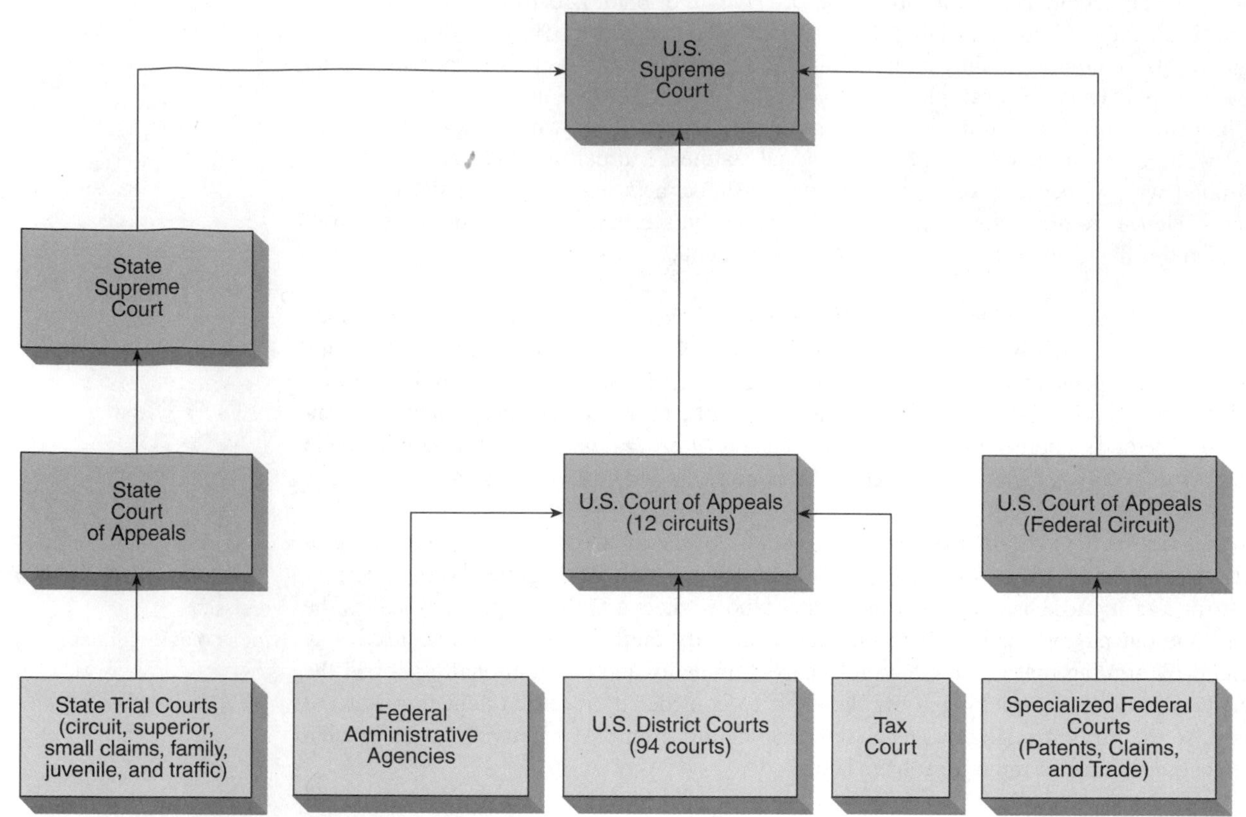

A. STATE COURT SYSTEM

Although state court systems vary substantially, a general pattern can be summarized. At the heart of the court pyramid in most states is a *trial court of general jurisdiction,* commonly labeled a *district court* or a *superior court.* It is here that most trials—both civil and criminal—arising out of state law would be heard, but certain classes of cases are reserved to courts of limited subject matter jurisdiction or to various state administrative agencies (such as the state public utilities commission and the workers' compensation board). Family, small claims, juvenile, and traffic courts are examples of trial courts with limited jurisdiction. At the top of the judicial pyramid in all states is a court of appeals, ordinarily labeled the *supreme court.* A number of states also provide for an intermediate court of appeals located in the hierarchy between the trial courts and the highest appeals court (see Figure 2.1).

B. FEDERAL COURT SYSTEM

District Courts. The district courts provide the foundation of the federal judicial system. The Constitution provides for a Supreme Court and such inferior courts as Congress shall authorize. Pursuant to that authority, Congress has established at least one district court for each state and territory. These are trial courts where witnesses are heard and questions of law and fact are resolved. More populous areas with heavier case loads have additional district courts. As circumstances demand, Congress adds courts at the district level. Most federal cases begin in the district courts or in a federal administrative agency (such as the Interstate Commerce Commission or the Federal Communications Commission). Congress has also provided for several courts of limited jurisdiction, including a tax court and a U.S. Claims Court.

Court of Appeals. Congress has divided the United States geographically into 11 judicial circuits and the District of Columbia and has established a court of appeals for each. Those courts hear appeals from the district courts within their circuit and review decisions and enforce orders of the various federal administrative agencies.

In 1982, Congress created the U.S. Court of Appeals for the Federal Circuit. That court hears, among others, all patent appeals and all appeals from the U.S. Claims Court (monetary claims against the United States).

Supreme Court. The Supreme Court consists of nine justices appointed for life by the president and confirmed by the Senate. The number of justices on the Supreme Court is determined by Congress. In limited instances, the Supreme Court serves as an original or trial court. However, almost all of the Supreme Court's work consists of reviewing lower court decisions, principally from the courts of appeals and from state high courts. Recent congressional legislation has dramatically limited the number of mandatory appeals that come to the Court "as a matter of right." Now, virtually all parties seeking Supreme Court review must petition the Court for a ***writ of certiorari,*** which commands the lower court to forward the trial records to the Court. Decisions regarding those petitions are entirely discretionary with the Court. Typically it will hear those cases that will assist in resolving conflicting courts of appeals decisions, as well as those that raise questions of special significance about the Constitution or the national welfare. The Court annually receives more than 5,000 cases but agrees to a full hearing for approximately 100 of those.

writ of certiorari. An order of a court to an inferior court to forward the record of a case for reexamination by the superior court.

C. Jurisdiction

A plaintiff may not simply proceed to trial at the court of his or her preference. The plaintiff must go to a court with **jurisdiction**—that is, a court with the necessary power and authority to hear the dispute. The court must have jurisdiction over both the subject matter and the persons (or in some instances, the property) involved in the case.

jurisdiction. The power of a judicial body to adjudicate a dispute. Also the geographical area within which that judicial body has authority to operate.

Subject-Matter Jurisdiction. Subject-matter jurisdiction imposes bounds on the classes of cases a court may hear. The legislation or constitution creating the court will normally specify that court's jurisdictional authority. For example, state courts of general jurisdiction may hear most types of cases, but a criminal court or probate court is limited in the subject matter it may hear (see Figure 2.2).

The outer bounds of federal jurisdiction are specified in the Constitution, while Congress has further particularized that issue by statute. Essentially, the federal district courts may hear two types of cases: (1) those involving a federal question and (2) those involving diversity of citizenship and more than $50,000. Diversity of citizenship exists where parties are from two different states or from one state and a foreign country, or between a citizen of one state and a foreign country.

Federal question jurisdiction exists in any suit where the plaintiff's claim is based on the U.S. Constitution, a U.S. treaty, or a federal statute. Thus, litigants can bring to the federal courts cases involving, for example, the federal antitrust statutes, federal criminal laws, constitutional issues such as freedom of the press, and federal tax questions. Federal question jurisdiction does not require an amount in controversy exceeding $50,000. Fur-

FIGURE 2.2 SUBJECT-MATTER JURISDICTION

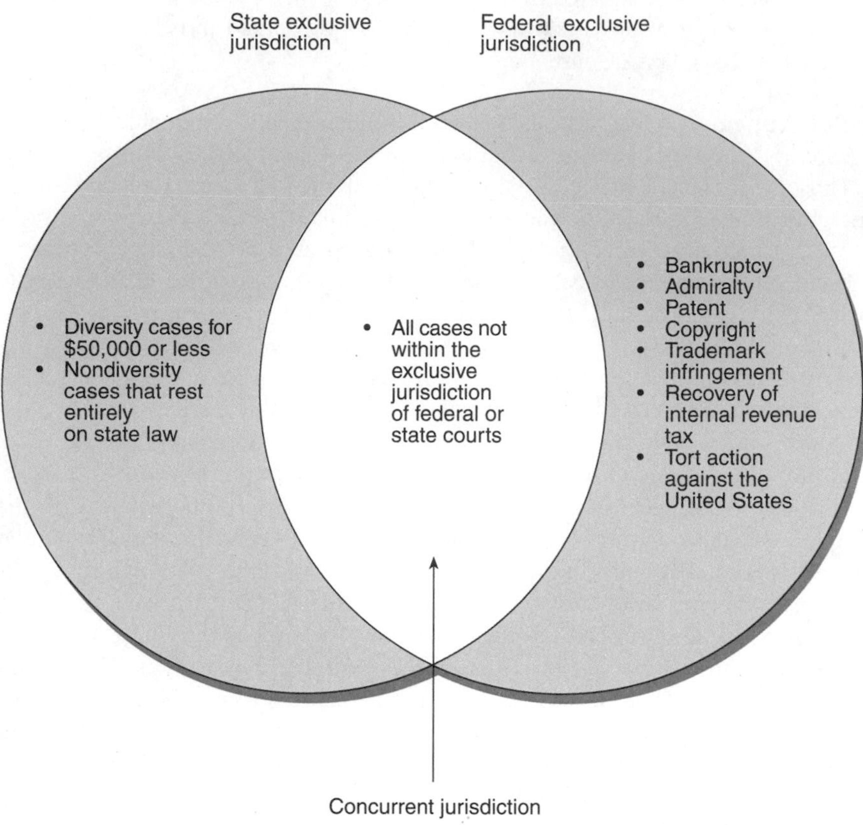

ther, federal and state courts have *concurrent jurisdiction* for some federal questions. Thus, some federal question cases are decided in state courts applying federal law. Congress has accorded the federal courts exclusive jurisdiction over certain subjects, including federal criminal laws, bankruptcy, and copyrights. Under *diversity jurisdiction,* federal district courts may hear cases involving more than $50,000 where the plaintiff(s) and the defendant(s) are citizens of different states. (Corporations are treated as citizens both of their state of incorporation and the state in which their principal place of business is located.) Diversity cases may also be heard in state courts, but plaintiffs frequently prefer to bring their actions in federal courts. The quality of the federal judiciary is generally believed to be superior to that of the states, and the federal courts are considered less likely to be influenced by local bias. Federal court action may also have procedural advantages, such as greater capacity to secure witnesses' testimony.

long-arm statutes. State enactments that accord the courts of that state the authority to claim jurisdiction over people and property beyond the borders of the state so long as certain "minimum contracts" exist between the state and the people or property.

Personal Jurisdiction. Judicial authority over the person is known as *in personam jurisdiction.* In general, a state court's powers are limited to the bounds of the state. While the matter is fraught with complexities, it is fair to say that state court jurisdiction can be established in three ways: (1) When the defendant is a resident of the state, a summons may be served at that residence. (2) When the defendant is not a resident, a summons may be personally served should he or she be physically present in the state. (3) All states have legislated **long-arm statutes** that allow a court to secure jurisdiction against an out-of-state party where the defendant has committed a tort in the state or where the defendant is conducting business in the state. Hence, in an auto accident in Iowa involv-

STAGES OF A LAWSUIT

FIGURE 2.3

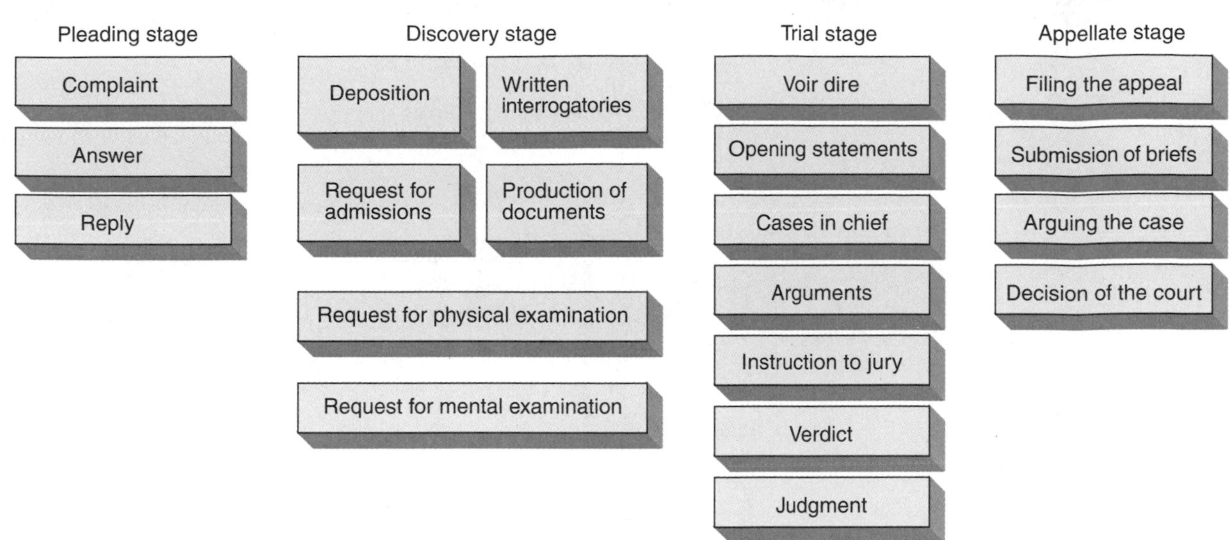

ing both an Iowa resident and an Illinois resident, the Iowan may sue in Iowa and achieve service of process over the Illinois defendant as a consequence of the jurisdictional authority afforded by the long-arm statute.

A state court may also acquire jurisdiction via an *in rem action,* an action based on a *rem,* or "thing." In that instance the defendant may be a nonresident, but his or her property, which must be the subject of the suit, must be located within the state.

Profile Perspective: In which court should James Pierce file his suit? Federal court or state court? Do you need additional facts to reach this decision? Explain.

D. STANDING

Resorting to the courts is frequently an undesirable method of problem solving. Therefore, all who wish to bring a claim before a court may not be permitted to do so. To receive the court's attention, the litigant must demonstrate that she or he has **standing** to sue. That is, the person must show that her or his interest in the outcome of the controversy is sufficiently direct and substantial to justify the court's consideration. The litigant must show that she or he personally is suffering, or will be suffering, injury. Mere interest in the problem at hand is insufficient to grant standing to sue.

standing. A stake in a dispute sufficient to afford a party the legal right to bring or join a litigation exploring the subject of the dispute.

pleadings. The formal entry of written statements by which the parties to a lawsuit set out their contentions and thereby formulate the issues on which the litigation will be based.

complaint. The first pleading filed by the plaintiff in a civil lawsuit.

E. THE CIVIL TRIAL PROCESS

Civil procedure varies by jurisdiction. The following generalizations merely typify the process (see Figure 2.3).

Pleadings. **Pleadings** are the documents by which each party sets his or her initial case before the court. A civil action begins when the plaintiff files his or her first pleading, which is labeled a **complaint.** The complaint specifies (1) the parties to the suit, (2) evidence as to the court's jurisdiction in the case, (3) a statement of the facts, and (4) a prayer for relief (a remedy).

2120 - Served **2220 - Not Served** **2620 - Sec. of State** **(Rev. 8/5/93) CCM1-12D**
2121 - Alias Served **2121 - Alias Not Served** **2621 - Alias Sec. of State**

Returnable in
ROOM No. 602, RICHARD J. DALEY CENTER
9:30 A. M. Sharp
In the Circuit Court of Cook County, Illinois

Name All Parties

plaintiff-	**No.**..................................
v.	**Amount Claimed $**......................
defendant-	**Return Date**..........................

SUMMONS

To each defendant:

YOU ARE SUMMONED and required:

1. To file your written appearance by yourself or your attorney and pay the required fee in Room 602, Richard J. Daley Center, Chicago, Illinois, at or before 9:30 a.m. on* ...., **19**....

2. To file your answer to the complaint in Room 602 as required by Par. 3(c) in the Notice to Defendant.

IF YOU FAIL TO DO SO, A JUDGMENT BY DEFAULT MAY BE TAKEN AGAINST YOU FOR THE RELIEF ASKED IN THE COMPLAINT, A COPY OF WHICH IS HERETO ATTACHED.

To the Officer:

This summons must be returned by the officer or other person to whom it was given for service, with endorsement of service and fees, if any, immediately after service, and not less than 3 days before the day for appearance. If service cannot be made, this summons shall be returned so endorsed.

This summons may not be served later than 3 days before the day of appearance.

THERE WILL BE A FEE TO FILE YOUR APPEARANCE, IF CLAIM IS $1,500.00 OR LESS, FEE WILL BE $69.00 OVER $1,500.00 THE FEE WILL BE $89.00 OVER $15,000.00 THE FEE WILL BE $104.00

WITNESS...................................

Aurelia Pucinski
....
Clerk of Court

Date of Service:......................,**19**....
(To be inserted by officer on copy left with defendant or other person)

Name
Attorney for
Address
Telephone
Atty. No.
**** Service by Facsimile Transmission will be accepted at:**..
(Area Code) (Facsimile Telephone Number)

OVER

Complaint Verified (Revised 6/14/93) CCMD 8A

IN THE CIRCUIT COURT OF COOK, COUNTY, ILLINOIS

Plaintiff...	No. ....
v.	Contract ....
	Amount Claimed $ ....
Defendant ...	Return Date ....

COMPLAINT

The plaintiff ... claim ... as follows:

I, ... certify that I am the .... plaintiff in the above entitled action. The allegations in this complaint are true.

...., 19.....

Name
Attorney for
Address
City
Telephone
Atty. No.

....

[ ] Under penalties as provided by law pursuant to 735 ILCS 5/1-109 the abovesigned certifies that the statement set forth herein are true correct.

printed on recycled paper

AURELIA PUCINSKI, CLERK OF THE CIRCUIT COURT OF COOK COUNTY, ILLINOIS

summons. A document originating in a court and delivered to a party or organization indicating that a lawsuit has been commenced against him, her, or it. The summons constitutes notice that the defendant is expected to appear in court to answer the plaintiff's allegations.

motion to dismiss. A motion made by the defendant in a civil case to defeat the plaintiff's case, usually after the complaint or all the pleadings have been completed.

answer. The defendant's first pleading in a lawsuit, in which the defendant responds to the allegations raised in the plaintiff's complaint.

counterclaim. A cause of legal action filed by the defendant in a lawsuit against the plaintiff in the same suit.

cross-claim or cross-complaint. Defendant's assertion of a claim of action against a codefendant.

The complaint is filed with the clerk of court and a **summons** is issued, directing the defendant to appear in court to answer the claims alleged against him or her. A sheriff or some other official attempts to personally deliver the summons to the defendant. If personal delivery cannot be achieved, the summons may be left with a responsible party at the defendant's residence. Failing that, other modes of delivery are permissible, including a mailing. Publication of a notice in a newspaper will, in some instances, constitute good service of process. Ordinarily, a copy of the complaint accompanies the summons, so the defendant is apprised of the nature of the claim.

The defendant has several options. He or she may do nothing, but failure to respond may result in a default judgment in favor of the plaintiff (an automatic result in favor of the plaintiff). The defendant may choose to respond by filing a **motion to dismiss,** the essence of which is to argue that even if the plaintiff's recitation of the facts is accurate, a claim on which relief can be granted has not been stated. For example, a student may be offended by a teacher's bizarre manner of dress; but, barring unusual circumstances, the student could not, as a matter of law, successfully challenge the teacher's costume.

Alternatively, the defendant may file with the court an initial pleading, called an **answer,** wherein the defendant enters a denial by setting out his or her version of the facts and law, or in which the defendant simply concedes the validity of the plaintiff's position. The answer may also contain an *affirmative defense* that would bar the plaintiff's claim. For example, the defendant might assert the statute of limitations or the statute of frauds. The defendant's answer might include a counterclaim or cross-claim. A **counterclaim** is the defendant's assertion of a claim of action against the plaintiff. A **cross-claim** is the defendant's assertion of a claim of action against a codefendant. In some states, this would be labeled a **cross-complaint.** In the event of a counterclaim or the assertion of new facts in the answer, the plaintiff will respond with a reply. The complaint, answer, reply, and their components are the pleadings that serve to give notice, to clarify the issues, and to limit the dimensions of the litigation.

Motions. As necessary during and after the filing of the pleadings, either party may file motions with the court. For example, a party may move to clarify a pleading or to strike a portion deemed unnecessary. Of special importance is a motion for a judgment on the pleadings or a motion for summary judgment. In a *motion for a judgment on the pleadings,* either party simply asks the judge to reach a decision based on the information in the pleadings. However, the judge will do so only if the defendant's answer constitutes an admission of the accuracy of the plaintiff's claim or if the plaintiff's claim clearly has no foundation in law.

In a *motion for a summary judgment,* the party filing the motion is claiming that no facts are in dispute. Therefore, the judge may make a ruling about the law after the discovery stage without taking the case to trial. In a summary judgment hearing, the court can look beyond the pleadings to hear evidence from affidavits, depositions, and so on. These motions serve to avoid the time and expense of trial. The following case is an example of the use of a summary judgment motion.

discovery. Legal procedures by which one party to a litigation may obtain information from the other party. Depositions and interrogatories are examples of discovery procedures.

Discovery. Justice is the goal of the legal system. Information is central to reaching a just result. **Discovery** is the primary information-gathering stage in the trial process. Discovery (1) preserves the testimony of witnesses who may not be available for trial, (2) reduces the likelihood of perjury, (3) aids in defining and narrowing the facts and issues, (4) promotes pretrial settlements, (5) increases the likelihood of concluding the case with a summary judgment, and (6) helps prevent surprises at the trial. In general, five discovery techniques are provided.

CASE

Woodruff v. Georgia State University et al.

304 S. E.2d 697 (Ga 1983)

Justice Weltner

Woodruff brought this action against the Board of Regents, Georgia State University and certain Georgia State University professors alleging state and federal constitutional violations, tort, and breach of contract claims. The trial court granted summary judgment and Woodruff appeals.

Woodruff was admitted to a master's degree program in the music department of Georgia State University in 1972. In the fall of 1973, she received an "F" on the basis of plagiarism and appealed that grade to an appeals committee within the university. The committee changed the grade to an "incomplete." She alleges that thereafter her professors were "hostile and sarcastic" to her, refusing to help her with course work and thesis preparation, changing course requirements prior to graduation, placing damaging information about her in an open file, and giving her undeservedly low grades in an attempt to block her graduation.

In 1979, after seven years in a program which normally takes two or three years to complete, Woodruff was awarded the degree of Master of Arts in Music. She then applied for admittance into a doctoral program at the University of Georgia in Athens, which required recommendations from former professors. Woodruff's former professors either refused or ignored her request for recommendations. In their depositions, several professors testified that Woodruff was an "argumentative and troublesome" student who was erratic in her studies and not academically qualified to proceed to a doctoral program. They offered academic reasons for withholding their recommendations.

Woodruff filed suit in January 1982, alleging libel and slander, intentional infliction of mental distress, conspiracy in withholding recommendations, negligent supervision of her graduate studies, breach of contract, and constitutional violations.

* * *

[T]he central issue is whether or not a dispute concerning academic decisions of a public education institution is a justiciable controversy.

In the general realm of educational institutions, we have reviewed standards of dismissals and student discipline. We have examined the denial of student eligibility to participate in sports, and we have refused to permit the judiciary to referee high school football games. The Court of Appeals has upheld the authority of a local board of education to impose proficiency requirements as a prerequisite to graduation from high school.

We have not thus far, however, entertained an individual student's complaint seeking money damages for alleged impropriety in academic assessment of her work.

* * *

We now decline to review a teacher's academic assessment of a student's work.

This is clearly consistent with the authorities we have mentioned. It is restraint which stems from confidence that school authorities are able to discharge their academic duties in fairness and with competence. It is born alike of the necessity for shielding the courts from an incalculable new potential for lawsuits, testing every Latin grade and every selection for the Safety Patrol.

It protects every teacher from the cost and agony of litigation initiated by pupils and their parents who would rely upon the legal process rather than the learning process.

Continued

Continued

It protects every school system—all of them laboring under pressures of financing, personnel problems and student discipline, academic performance, taxpayer revolt and patron unrest, and a rising tide of recalls—from an added and unbearable burden of continuous legal turmoil.

Judgment affirmed.

Questions

1. *Woodruff* is the decision of what court?
2. Who were the defendants in *Woodruff* and why did they move for a summary judgment?
3. What was the legal issue facing the appellate court in *Woodruff?* Do you agree with its decision? Explain.

Depositions. A party or a witness may be required to appear before a court officer to give recorded, sworn testimony in response to questions raised by the attorneys for both sides of the controversy. Testimony is much like that at trial. Depositions are particularly helpful in trial preparation.

Although necessary to the preparation of an effective legal case, depositions (oral questions to a witness) are time consuming and sometimes considered "fishing expeditions" by which the questioning lawyer attempts to determine the scope of a witness's knowledge or whether the witness knows anything not yet uncovered. Due to the nature of a deposition, attorneys sometimes use the procedure to encourage settlements; settle and the depositions are no longer needed. At the top of the list of burdensome procedures for a company, the deposition of the chief executive is one that is usually sought to be avoided.

Interrogatories. Written questions calling for written answers signed under oath may be required. Unlike depositions, interrogatories may only be directed to parties, and they can call for information outside the party's personal knowledge, requiring the party to peruse her or his records.

Discovery of Documents and Property. Either party may request access to documents, as well as real and personal property, for the purpose of inspection relevant to the trial.

Physical and Mental Examinations. When the physical or mental state of a party is at issue, the court may be asked to enter an order calling for an examination. Good cause must be shown, and the court must be satisfied that the need for information outweighs the party's constitutional right to privacy.

Admissions. Either party may make written request of the other, seeking an admission as to the truth of a specified issue of fact or law. If the receiving party agrees to or fails to deny the truth of the admission, that issue of fact or law is conclusively established for trial purposes. For example, in a suit alleging a defective transmission in a recently purchased automobile, the auto dealer might be asked to agree that the auto was sold under a warranty and that the warranty included the transmission.

Profile Perspective: What discovery would be beneficial in James Pierce's case against his slow-paying restaurant owner?

Changes? Because of widespread concerns about delays and expenses associated with litigation, the federal rules governing trials were changed in 1993. Basically, the new rules require the parties to voluntarily disclose all "reasonably available" relevant documents, data, names, and phone numbers of anyone likely to have discoverable information, insurance coverage, and so on. The new rules also limit interrogatories and depositions and require the parties to confer and develop a discovery plan and discuss settlement possibilities. At this writing in 1994, Congress is under pressure to amend the new rules, which many lawyers believe to be too sweeping in their requirements.

Pretrial Conference. Either party may request, and many courts require, a pretrial meeting involving the attorneys, the judge, and occasionally the parties. Usually following discovery, the conference is designed to plan the course of the trial in the interests of efficiency and justice. The participants seek to define and narrow the issues through informal discussion. The parties also attempt to settle the dispute in advance of trial. If no settlement is reached, a trial date is set.

The Judge and Jury. The federal Constitution and most state constitutions provide for the right to a jury trial in a civil case (excepting equity actions). Some states place dollar minimums on that guaranty. At the federal level and in most states, unless one of the parties requests a jury, the judge alone will hear the case and decide all questions of law and fact. If the case is tried before a jury, that body will resolve questions of fact.

Jurors are selected from a jury pool composed of a cross section of the community. A panel is drawn from that pool. The individuals in that panel are questioned by the judge, by the attorneys, or by all to determine if any individual is prejudiced about the case such that he or she could not reach an objective decision on the merits. The questioning process is called ***voir dire.***

voir dire. Process of questioning jury panel members by attorneys and judge prior to selection of jurors.

From an attorney's point of view, jury selection is often not so much a matter of finding jurors without bias as it is a matter of identifying those jurors who are most likely to reach a decision favorable to one's client. To that end, elaborate mechanisms and strategies have been employed, particularly in criminal trials, to identify desirable jurors. For example, sophisticated, computer-assisted surveys of the trial community have been conducted to develop objective evidence by which to identify jurors who would not admit to racial prejudice but whose profile suggests the likelihood of such prejudice. A few attorneys have taken the rather exotic tactic of employing body language experts to watch potential jurors during *voir dire* for those mannerisms said to reveal their inner views.

After questioning, the attorneys may *challenge for cause,* arguing to the judge that the individual cannot exercise the necessary objectivity of judgment. Attorneys are also afforded a limited number of **peremptory challenges,** by which the attorney can have a potential juror dismissed without the judge's concurrence and without offering a reason. However, peremptory challenges may not be used to reject jurors on the basis of race or gender.

peremptory challenges. Each attorney is allowed a specific number of preemptory challenges where she or he may dismiss a juror without offering a reason.

Jury selection and the jury system are the subject of considerable debate in the legal community. Are juries necessary to a just system? How small can a jury be and still fulfill its duty? Is the jury process too slow and expensive? Should very long and complex cases, such as those in the antitrust area, be heard only by judges?

The Trial. The trial begins with the opening statement by the plaintiff's attorney. Then the opposing attorney offers his or her statement. Each is expected to outline what he or she intends to prove. The plaintiff then presents evidence, which may include both

exhibits. Copies of written instruments on which a pleading is founded, annexed to the pleading and by reference made a part of it. Also any paper or thing offered in evidence and marked for identification.

testimony and physical evidence, such as documents and photos, called **exhibits.**

The attorney secures testimony from his or her own witness via questioning labeled *direct examination.* After the plaintiff's attorney completes direct examination of the plaintiff's own witness, the defense attorney may question that witness in a process labeled *cross-examination. Redirect* and *recross* may then follow. The plaintiff's attorney then summarizes the testimony and the exhibits and rests his or her case.

At this stage, the defense may make a motion for a judgment as a matter of law, arguing, in essence, that the plaintiff has offered insufficient evidence to justify relief, so time and expense may be saved by terminating the trial. Understandably, the judge considers the motion in the light most favorable to the plaintiff. Such motions ordinarily fail, and the trial goes forward with the defendant's presentation of evidence.

At the completion of the defendant's case, both parties may be permitted to offer *rebuttal* evidence, and either party may move for a directed verdict. Barring a directed verdict, the case goes forward, with each party making a *closing argument.* When the trial is by jury, the judge must instruct the jurors as to the law to be applied to the case. The attorneys often submit to the judge their views of the proper instructions. Because the law lacks the clarity that laypersons often attribute to it, framing the instructions is a difficult task, frequently resulting in an appeal to a higher court. Finally, the verdict of the jury is rendered and a judgment is entered by the court.

Post-Trial Motions. The losing party may seek a *judgment notwithstanding the verdict (judgment n.o.v.)* on the grounds that in light of the controlling law, insufficient evidence was offered to permit the jury to decide as it did. Such motions are rarely granted. The judge is also empowered to enter a judgment n.o.v. on his or her own initiative.

Either party may also move for a new trial. The winning party might do so on the grounds that the remedy provided was inferior to that warranted by the evidence. The losing party commonly claims an error of law to support a motion for a new trial. Other possible grounds for a new trial include jury misconduct or new evidence.

Appeals. After the judgment is rendered, either party may appeal the decision to a higher court. The winner may do so if he or she feels the remedy is inadequate. Ordinarily, of course, the losing party brings the appeal. The appealing party is the *appellant* or the *petitioner,* while the other party is the *appellee* or *respondent.* The appeals court does not try the case again. In theory, at least, its consideration is limited to mistakes of law at the trial level. For example, the appellant will argue that a jury instruction was erroneous or that the judge erred in failing to grant a motion to strike testimony alleged to have been prejudicial. The appeals court does not hear new evidence. It bases its decision on the trial record, legal briefs filed by the opposing attorneys, and, at times, oral arguments.

The appellate court announces its judgment and ordinarily explains that decision in an accompanying document labeled an *opinion.* (Most of the cases in this text are appellate court opinions.) If no error is found, the lower court decision is *affirmed.* In finding prejudicial error, the appellate court may simply *reverse* (overrule) the lower court. Or the judgment may be to *reverse and remand,* wherein the lower court is overruled and the trial court must try the case again in accordance with the law as articulated in the appeals court opinion. After the decision of the intermediate appellate court, a further appeal may be directed to the highest court of the jurisdiction. Most of those petitions are denied.

Class Actions. A class action allows a group of individuals to sue or be sued in one judicial proceeding, provided they are "similarly situated," that is, their claim or the claim against them arises out of similar or closely related grievances. For example, if hundreds of people were injured in a hotel fire, a subset of that group might file an action against the hotel on behalf of all the injured parties. The class action thus permits lawsuits that might otherwise be impractical due to the number of people involved or the small amount of each claim. The class action is also expedient; many potential causes of action can be disposed of in one suit.

Recently, a federal district court approved the use of a class action in a sexual harassment case, an area of the law where claims had previously been restricted to individual plaintiffs. In this case, the court ruled that the Eveleth Taconite Company's mines are a hostile environment for all hourly female workers.[12]

Profile Perspective: Is there any possibility that Pierce's claim could be characterized as a class action? Why or why not?

IV. The U.S. Constitution: Related to Private Sector Business?

> We the People of the United States, in Order to form a more perfect Union, establish Justice, insure domestic Tranquility, provide for the common defense, promote the general Welfare, and secure the Blessings of Liberty to ourselves and our Posterity, do ordain and establish this Constitution for the United States of America.

The Preamble to our Constitution, the words that opened this section, summarizes the Founding Fathers' lofty goals for America. The idealism embodied in the Preamble is both inspiring and touching. In reading it, we should reflect on the dream of America and the Constitution's role in molding and protecting that entirely new image of a nation. That we continue to be guided, more than 200 years later, by those rather few words is testimony to the brilliance and wisdom of its creators and to our determination to build a free, democratic, just society. Our Constitution is a remarkable document, so powerful in its ideas and images that it has reshaped the world.

A. *Structure and Purpose*

The Constitution is reprinted in Appendix A. We will now take some time to review its structure.

The Preamble identifies certain goals for our society, such as unity (among the various states), justice, domestic tranquility (peace), defense from outsiders, an increasing general welfare, and liberty. Article I sets up Congress and enumerates its powers. Article I, Section 8, Clause 3 is particularly important because it gives Congress the power to regulate commerce (the Commerce Clause). Article II sets up the executive branch, headed by the president, and Article III establishes the court system. Articles IV and VI, as well as the Fourteenth Amendment, address the relationship between the federal government and the states. Article VI provides in Clause 2 (the Supremacy Clause) for the supremacy of federal law over state law. Article V provides for amendments to the Constitution. The first 10 amendments, known as the Bill of Rights, were ratified by the states and put into effect in 1791. The remaining 17 amendments (11 through 27) were adopted at various times from 1798 through 1992.

From this review we can see that the Constitution serves a number of broad roles:

- It establishes a national government.
- It controls the relationship between the national government and the government of the states.
- It defines and preserves personal liberty.
- It contains provisions to enable the government to perpetuate itself.

The heavens will not fall, nor the seas rise up to engulf us, if Congress approves two pending amendments to the Constitution. Nonetheless the amendments are needless. They ought to be quietly buried.	Source: James Kilpatrick, "Amendments Likely to do Little Harm or Good," The Tampa Tribune, July 31, 1995, p. 7.

In establishing a national government, the Constitution sets up three branches and provides mechanisms for them to check and balance each other, as illustrated by the following article dealing with a proposed amendment prohibiting desecration of the American flag.

Flag Burning under Fire

by Jamin Raskin & Michael Anderson

The Congress and the states shall have the power to prohibit the physical desecration of the flag of the United States. Display of the Confederate flag shall be deemed to be physical desecration of the flag of the United States.

The first sentence in the above proposed constitutional amendment recently passed the House of Representatives and the Senate Judiciary Committee, but the second should be added on the Senate floor before this amendment goes any further.

The unprecedented effort to subtract liberty from the Bill of Rights represents a comic outbreak of literal-mindedness among the patriotically correct. But if we are going to start treating "The Flag" as a species of sacred living things—like flora and fauna—then let us at least confront the most prevalent insult and threat to the supremacy to Old Glory. We refer, of course, to the flag of the confederacy.

In the last few years, flames set for political reasons consumed fewer than a dozen American flags. Ever since the U.S. Supreme Court decided in 1989 that flag-burning is protected expression, members of the Revolutionary Communist Party and other sectarian performance artists found that the transgressive force of the stunt was gone. If you have a right to burn the flag, you get no attention for doing it. Flag-burnings quickly subsided. Now, in a fit of pre-election posturing, Republican leaders have revived flag wars with a constitutional amendment already perilously close to enactment. But if we are going to become self-important bores about flags and symbolic speech, can we continue to ignore the flag that gives the finger to Old Glory every day?

On an average day when no American flags are on fire, countless thousands of people display Confederate flags, wear Confederate flag baseball hats, shake Confederate pompoms, sun themselves on Confederate beach towels, or sport Confederate flag bumper stickers on their pickup trucks. Two states even incorporate the infamous Confederate design in their official state flags. In some parts of the country, you see the Stars and Bars a lot more that the Stars and Stripes.

Symbol of Treason

The Confederate battle flag symbolized secession from—and armed rebellion against—the United States. It was flown by imposter states that conspired

Continued

Continued

to bring down the U.S. government through an act of war in order to perpetuate the most shameful institution in our history. From Fort Sumter and Gettysburg in the last century to Montgomery and Selma and Little Rock in this one, the Confederate flag has advertised contempt for the Union and hostility to the nation's commitment to freedom and equality for African-American citizens.

* * *

Under the redrafted new amendment, it will be clear that Confederate flag-wavers no longer have a First Amendment defense.

Now, surely one is tempted to respond: Aren't at least some citizens who wave the Confederate flag simply expressing nontreasonous regional pride? But this sensible reasoning is obsolete in the new age of authoritarian literal-mindedness. After all, flag burners being carted off to jail will no longer be able to object that they were only protesting an illegal war, denouncing the centralization of power in Washington, or vividly demonstrating how a particular policy is disgracing the country. From now on, the government will define and control the symbolic meaning of flags for citizens. And strict constructionists know this: the original meaning of the Confederate flag was the violent replacement of the American flag and destruction of the federal government. When African-Americans see that flag, they know what is being desecrated.

* * *

Once upon a time, you had the right to make a jerk out of yourself whether you burned the flag of freedom or waved the flag of slavery. Seems now Republican Congress wants to change all that. It's a bad idea, but if amend we must, let's get our symbols straight. To become a truly sacred object, the U.S. flag cannot exist side by side with a display of the anti-flag, the historical and semiotic negation of patriotism, liberty, and justice.

Questions

1. Do you agree that flag-burning should be protected expression under the First Amendment?
2. Would you support passage of the amendment quoted at the beginning of the article? Do you agree with the coupling of the two statements; need they go together?
3. Is there any negative impact that may result from the passage of the amendment?

Source: *Connecticut Law Tribune,* July 31, 1995, p. 17.

Another role of the Constitution is to balance the central federal authority with dispersed state power. As established by the Constitution, the federal government holds only those powers granted to it by the states. The people via the states hold all of those powers not expressly denied them by the Constitution.

Recall that the Bill of Rights was enacted to protect the citizenry from the government. The Constitution does not protect the citizenry from purely private concentrations of power, such as large corporations. In fact, corporations themselves are often entitled to the protections of the Constitution.

B. The Bill of Rights and Business

The Constitution profoundly shapes the practice of American business. The Constitution embodies and supports America's belief in capitalism. Indeed, it has been argued that the economic self-interest of the framers had a persuasive impact on the principles embodied in the Constitution. Article 1, Section 8, Clause 3 of the Constitution (the Commerce Clause) affords Congress enormous authority in regulating business. Further discussion of the Commerce Clause will be deferred to Chapter 7. The bulk of this chapter will be directed to some of the key intersections between the business community and the Bill of Rights. When we think of the Bill of Rights, corporations ordinarily do not come to mind. However, extensive litigation in recent years serves notice that the relationship between the corporate "person" and the fundamental freedoms is both important and murky.

On the other hand, the Constitution *only* regulates the relationship between the government and the public; it does not regulate the actions of individual private citizens. In other words, the Constitution only dictates state action. Where the government plays no role in a transaction, the Constitution does not apply. In a question of freedom of speech, many times it is the government that will not allow the speech, so there is state action; but the answer is not quite so obvious in other situations. If a state-run university decides to conduct searches of the desks of all of its faculty, the search would have to comply with Fourth Amendment protection against unreasonable searches and seizures. However, if a private university chooses to conduct a similar search, the Constitution does not apply.

As you read this section, consider how the constitutional restrictions or protections may have some impact on private business decisions. Also try to acquire an appreciation for the complex tensions that arise as the government attempts to identify and ensure individual rights while seeking to defend and promote both U.S. commerce and the rights of American business.

C. The First Amendment

> Congress shall make no law respecting an establishment of religion, or prohibiting the free exercise thereof; or abridging the freedom of speech, or the press; or the right of the people peaceably to assemble, and to petition the Government for a redress of grievances.

These few words constitute one of the most powerful and noble utterances in history. The freedoms guaranteed in the First Amendment reflect the basic beliefs of American life. Much of the magnificence that we often associate with America is embodied in the protections of the First Amendment. After 200 years, it remains a source of wonder that our vast bureaucratic system and our approximately 250 million independent citizens continue to rely on that sentence as a cornerstone of our way of life.

Freedom of Religion. The First Amendment forbids (1) the establishment of an official state religion (the Establishment Clause) and (2) undue state interference with religious practice (the Free Exercise Clause). Government may neither encourage nor discourage the practice of religion generally, nor may it give preference to one religion over another. Broadly, the idea of the First Amendment is to maintain a separation between church and state. However, the precise boundary of that separation has become one of the more contentious social issues in contemporary life.

Blue Laws. Perhaps surprisingly, religious beliefs often become a source of dispute in business practice. Consider the so-called blue laws, those statutes and ordinances limiting or prohibiting the conduct of business on Sundays. For more than 200 years, until the 1950s, U.S. stores were rather uniformly closed for business on Sundays. Then exceptions emerged; food and newspapers, in particular. Jewish merchants began to object on discrimination grounds because they closed on Saturdays to observe their Sabbath and then were also forced to close on Sundays. Lawsuits followed. In the leading case of *McGowan* v. *Maryland,* the Supreme Court upheld the constitutionality of a blue law on the grounds that the primary purpose of the law was the furtherance of a legitimate social goal (in this case, provision of a uniform day of rest), rather than a furtherance of religious goals.[13] The Court felt that the practice of treating Sunday as a religious holiday had fallen into disuse. Now, Sunday closings are left to the states and localities to decide for themselves. Conflict remains surprisingly common. For example, in 1994 the Connecticut Supreme Court ruled that a Connecticut blue law forbidding auto sales on Sunday was an unconstitutional violation of due process because, among other reasons, it arbitrarily singled out car dealers for Sunday closing while almost all other businesses were free to operate on that day.[14] A group of auto dealers had challenged the statute claiming that it gave an unconstitutional advantage to next-door New York dealers who were free to sell seven days per week. Many Connecticut dealers opposed the Sunday openings, feeling that the extra hours would not produce additional business. Now, liquor stores are the only businesses in Connecticut that must close on Sundays.

Texaco and Sunday Closing. In the article that follows, we see the blue law issue turned on its head. Here, a gas station owner wants to close on Sunday, but Texaco says he must operate as usual.

Can Texaco Win a Battle if the Lord Is on the Other Side?

by Bill Richards

Texaco Corp. has a divinely inspired mess on its hands here [Salem, Oregon] these days.

Texaco's troubles began when Barry Davis, a devout Christian fundamentalist who runs three Texaco service stations in Oregon, says he had a talk with the Almighty. Mr. Davis, 50 years old, credits God for making him Texaco's all-time top gasoline pumper—not to mention helping him earn nearly $470,000 last year. Texaco's star says God told him to shut his stations each week for the 24-hour biblical Sabbath—sunset Friday to sunset Saturday. The closings began on January 1.

That also happens to be prime gas-pumping time, but Mr. Davis says he was sure Texaco would understand. "Texaco is the most religious oil company in the nation," he declares.

Sabbath in Texaco Red

That may be debatable. The company says Mr. Davis's uplifting gesture caused a 26 percent slide in his stations' January sales. Texaco sued Mr. Davis in federal court in Portland, Oregon, . . . demanding he pay less attention to the Almighty and more to his contract, which calls for a seven-day-a-week, 24-hour-a-day operation. The company obtained a court order directing Mr. Davis to stay open on the Sabbath.

Mr. Davis, insisting that he can easily make up lost sales during the other six days, ignored the order. Friday night, precisely at 8:17 as the sun slipped below the horizon here, he slapped four-foot-high signs in his gas station windows saying, in Texaco red, "Closed for the Sabbath."

* * *

[L]egal experts say Mr. Davis isn't covered by the 1964 federal civil rights act, which protects employees against religious discrimination by employers. The problem: Mr. Davis is not an employee. He is a

Continued

Continued

contractor, who leases the land from Texaco. "In the eyes of the law, he might as well be General Motors," says Lewis Maltby, director of the American Civil Liberties Union's workplace-rights office in New York City. "I don't think he has a legal leg to stand on."

Mr. Davis has countered that while the civil rights act may not cover Texaco, his religious freedom was violated when federal Judge Helen Frye ordered him to reopen last week. A federal court can't enforce a private agreement in a way that violates a contractor's constitutional right, says David Shannon, Mr. Davis's attorney. "We feel the federal action occurred when the judge ordered Mr. Davis to be open on the Sabbath," Mr. Shannon says.

Judge Frye rejected that argument Monday, while granting Texaco a preliminary injunction against Mr. Davis's Sabbath closing. The judge said the fight is simply a dispute between the oil company and Mr. Davis. Mr. Shannon says he will appeal.

* * *

Texaco says that while Mr. Davis has a right to his religious beliefs, the company also has a contractual right to terminate his contracts. "This is a contract dispute and has nothing to do with religious beliefs," says the company's public relations official, who adds quickly, "I'd certainly like to be talking about other things."

* * *

Texaco's uneasiness may be justified. Company officials acknowledge they have already started getting letters from customers supporting Mr. Davis's stand . . .

Mr. Davis's dealer colleagues are also lining up. Michael Sherlock, executive director of the Oregon Gasoline Dealers Association, which represents operators of 1,800 gasoline outlets in the state, says Mr. Davis's agreement with God may be a bit unusual, "but we have plenty of dealers who would like to close on Sundays because of their own religious beliefs." Mr. Davis's case could also set a precedent for other dealers who don't want to stay open all night when traffic is light, Mr. Sherlock says.

Mr. Davis seems content to stay above the fray. In his hilltop house here, with a discreet wooden cross on the door and photos of his eight children scattered through the living room, he says Texaco knows full well that God is on his side.

* * *

Afterword—In late May 1993, Texaco announced that it had terminated Mr. Davis's leases after Mr. Davis declined to follow the court order to remain open on Sundays. Mr. Davis indicated that he would be appealing the termination under the U.S. Petroleum Marketing Practices Act, which provides for 90 days' notice and reasonable grounds prior to termination.

In 1993, Congress and the president approved the Religious Freedom Restoration Act, which clearly affirms America's high regard for religious freedom. The bill says that the government can infringe on religious freedom only for the most "compelling" reasons. That had been the accepted legal standard until a 1990 Supreme Court decision had made it easier for the government to interfere with religious practice. The bill is expected to have the greatest impact for minority religions whose practices sometimes conflict with state regulations. For example, the Amish have objected to state laws requiring bright safety reflectors on their horse-drawn buggies.

Questions

1. In your view, what is the ethically proper course of action for Texaco? Explain.
2. A Seventh Day Adventist was discharged by her employer when she refused to work on Saturday. Those of her faith celebrate the Sabbath on Saturday. She sought unemployment compensation, but the South Carolina Employment Security Commission denied her petition. The commission ruled that she had failed, without good cause, "to accept available work when offered." She carried an appeal to the Supreme Court. How would you rule? Explain. [See *Sherbert* v. *Verner,* 374 U.S. 398 (1963).]
3. For purposes of applying the First Amendment, how should religion be defined? That is, how do we tell the difference between a cult and a religion, or do we?

Source: *The Wall Street Journal,* May 6, 1993, p. A1.

Freedom of Speech. As illustrated by the flag-burning case, none of the remarkable freedoms guaranteed by the Constitution receives greater respect from the judiciary than the right to free expression. And so it should be. Freedom of speech is the primary guarantor of the American approach to life. In particular, Americans believe the free expression of ideas is the most likely path to finding the best of ideas. We believe in a marketplace of ideas just as we believe in a marketplace of goods. So freedom of speech is central to self-respect, political freedom, and the maximization of wisdom.

Freedom of speech is not an absolute. Clearly, we cannot make slanderous statements about another or publicly utter obscenities at will or yell "fire" in a crowded theater. Nonetheless, in general, the state cannot tell us what we can lawfully say; that is, the state cannot, for the most part, regulate the *content* of our speech. On the other hand, the state does have greater authority to regulate the *context* of that speech; that is, the state may be able to restrict where and when we say certain things if that regulation is necessary to preserve compelling state interests. Therefore, the Ku Klux Klan clearly can express hatred for black people, but the state may restrict where and when those expressions are made if necessary for the public safety. Of course, we have no right to freedom of speech expressed on the private property of another such as our place of employment or even, most courts have ruled, the common areas of an enclosed shopping mall. Remember, the Constitution protects us from the government, not from private parties. In general, however, we can say what we wish on public property such as a park, a state-supported college campus, or a community sidewalk. Even in those places, however, the state may need to impose reasonable time and place regulations.

Sometimes, the question becomes one of what constitutes speech. As we saw in the flag-burning case, the First Amendment clearly extends to expression in forms other than actual verbiage or writing. In the leading case in this area, the Supreme Court extended First Amendment protection to the wearing of black armbands to high school as a protest against the Vietnam War where no evidence of disruption was presented.[15] Does panhandling (begging) on a public street constitute speech? [See *Loper* v. *New York City Police Dept.,* 802 F.Supp. 1029 (S.D.N.Y. 1992).]

Hate Speech and Hate Crimes. In recent years, First Amendment controversies have become a routine ingredient in daily life. The most highly publicized episodes have involved hate crimes and university speech codes. How can we stop cross burnings and other expressions of bigotry without violating free speech rights? In 1992, the Supreme Court unanimously struck down a St. Paul, Minnesota, ordinance that forbade cross burnings and bias-motivated disorderly conduct. Although governments may constitutionally regulate so-called fighting words, those regulations may not be based on the *message* conveyed by those words.[16]

Many states and localities have passed laws increasing penalties for crimes committed where discrimination motivated the behavior. For example, a Wisconsin statute imposed additional penalties against those who "intentionally" selected their criminal victim "because of the race, religion, color, disability, sexual orientation, national origin, or ancestry of that person." Todd Mitchell, a black man, was sentenced to two years in prison for aggravated assault; but because he said, "There goes a white boy; go get him," his sentence was increased by two years. The Wisconsin Supreme Court struck down the statute, but the U.S. Supreme Court reversed.[17] The Court said that a judge may properly consider a defendant's motivation so long as the crime in question involved conduct rather than expression. The Court concluded that the Wisconsin statute was directed to conduct whereas the St. Paul ordinance was directed to expression. Do you agree with the Court's treatment of cross burning as *expression* rather than *conduct?*

Speech Codes. In an effort to stop on-campus expressions of bigotry, a number of colleges and universities have established codes that forbid certain specified classes of speech. For example, a code might prohibit language that *intentionally demeans or disparages the race, religion, color, sex, national origin, creed, sexual preference, disability, height, weight, or age of the person to whom the remarks are directed.* Such codes, particularly where broadly drawn, appear to be constitutionally suspect, but the controversy continues at this writing in 1994. In the most highly publicized of these cases, the University of Pennsylvania accused a first-year student, Eben Jacobowitz, of racial harassment because he shouted the phrase "water buffalo" at a group of black women who were making noise sometime after midnight outside the dormitory where he was studying. Mr. Jacobowitz admitted making the remark but denied that it was racially motivated. A campus judicial officer concluded that the remark was a racial slur, although experts on the subject were prepared to testify that the phrase has no racial connotations whatsoever. Eventually, the women decided to drop their action, believing it was compromised by unfair publicity, but they continued to believe the remark was racially motivated and they claimed that the student's complete expression was "black water buffalo."[18]

The implementation of speech codes and subsequent cases like that at the University of Pennsylvania have been criticized for mandating so-called politically correct speech. The charge is that only language acceptable to liberals is tolerated on college campuses. Columnist Stephen Chapman put the claim this way:

> If you call someone a black SOB, you're in trouble; if you call someone a rich SOB, you're blessed. Racial minorities, women, homosexuals, and other favored blocs are allowed to use terms of abuse against other groups that other groups are not allowed to use against them.[19]

Of course, those speech codes are simply designed to stop hurtful, purposeless insults that have their roots in bigotry. Achieving that laudable goal in a constitutional manner is, however, a very difficult task in a nation that properly venerates free speech.

A Campus Dispute. The decision that follows illustrates the role of the First Amendment in campus life. In this case, a fraternity's "ugly woman contest" raised claims of racism, sexism, and general insensitivity.

Corporate Speech. Corporations, of course, are not natural persons. Instead, as expressed so eloquently by Chief Justice Marshall in the *Dartmouth College* case of 1819, the corporation is an "artificial being, invisible, intangible, and existing only in contemplation of law." Are the expressions of artificial beings accorded constitutional protection equivalent to that of a person? The question has become increasingly important in recent years as corporations have taken a much more active role in public affairs.

Advocacy advertising. Historically, corporate America had maintained a low profile in political life and public affairs. Quiet, behind-the-scenes negotiation was the preferred method of achieving the business community's public affairs agenda. Then, in the late 1960s and early 1970s, some corporations began *advocacy advertising* programs where they bought advertising space to express a point of view on public issues such as taxes, free trade, energy policy, and environmental concerns. That new, high-profile approach was spurred, in part, by the public's outrage over high oil company profits (during and following the oil shortages of 1972–73) and a rather widespread public unease with corporate America in the Vietnam War era. Now corporations, labor unions, foreign governments, and all manner of public interest organizations regularly engage in advocacy advertising in an attempt to educate and persuade the citizenry on issues of public policy.

IOTA XI Chapter v. George Mason University

CASE

993 F.2d 386 (4th Cir. 1993)

Senior Circuit Judge Sprouse

George Mason University appeals from a summary judgment granted by the district court to the IOTA XI Chapter of Sigma Chi Fraternity in its action for declaratory judgment and an injunction seeking to nullify sanctions imposed on it by the University because it conducted an "ugly woman contest" with racist and sexist overtones. We affirm.

I

Sigma Chi has for two years held an annual "Derby Days" event, planned and conducted both as entertainment and as a source of funds for donations to charity. The "ugly woman contest," held on April 4, 1991, was one of the "Derby Days" events. The Fraternity staged the contest in the cafeteria of the student union. As part of the contest, eighteen Fraternity members were assigned to one of six sorority teams cooperating in the events. The involved Fraternity members appeared in the contest dressed as caricatures of different types of women, including one member dressed as an offensive caricature of a black woman. He was painted black and wore stringy, black hair decorated with curlers, and his outfit was stuffed with pillows to exaggerate a woman's breasts and buttocks. He spoke in slang to parody African-Americans.

There is no direct evidence in the record concerning the subjective intent of the Fraternity members who conducted the contest. The Fraternity, which later apologized to the University officials for the presentation, conceded during the litigation that the contest was sophomoric and offensive.

Following the contest, a number of students protested to the University that the skit had been objectionably sexist and racist. Two hundred forty-seven students, many of them members of the foreign or minority student body, executed a petition, which stated: "[W]e are condemning the racist and sexist implications of this event in which male members dressed as women. One man in particular wore a black face, portraying a negative stereotype of black women."

On April 10, 1991, the Dean for Student Services, Kenneth Bumgarner, discussed the situation with representatives of the objecting students. That same day, Dean Bumgarner met with student representatives of Sigma Chi, including the planners of and participants in the "ugly woman contest." He then held a meeting with members of the student government and other student leaders. In this meeting, it was agreed that Sigma Chi's behavior had created a hostile learning environment for women and blacks, incompatible with the University's mission.

The Dean met again with Fraternity representatives on April 18, and the following day advised its officers of the sanctions imposed. They included suspension from all activities for the rest of the 1991 spring semester and a two-year prohibition on all social activities except pre-approved pledging events and pre-approved philanthropic events with an educational purpose directly related to gender discrimination and cultural diversity. The University's sanctions also required Sigma Chi to plan and implement an educational program addressing cultural differences, diversity, and the concerns of women. A few weeks later, the University made minor modifications to the sanctions, allowing Sigma Chi to engage in selected social activities with the University's advance approval.

On June 5, 1991, Sigma Chi brought this action under 42 U.S.C.§1983* against the University and Dean Bumgarner. It requested declaratory judgment and injunctive relief to nullify the sanctions as violative of the First and Fourteenth Amendments. Sigma Chi moved for summary judgment on its First Amendment claims on June 28, 1991, filing with its motions numerous affidavits explaining the nature of the "ugly woman contest."

* * *

Continued

*Every person who, under color of any statute, ordinance, regulation, custom or usage of any State or Territory or the District of Columbia, subjects or causes to be subjected, any citizen of the United States or any other person within its jurisdiction therof to the deprivation of any rights, priveleges, or immunities secured by the Constitution and laws, shall be liable to the party injured in an action at law, suit in equity, or other proper proceeding for redress. (42 U.S.C. §1983.)

Continued

In addition to the affidavit of Dean Bumgarner explaining his meetings with student leaders, the University submitted the affidavits of other officials, including that of University President George W. Johnson and Vice-President Earl G. Ingram. President Johnson, by his affidavit, presented the "mission statement" of the University [which stresses equality and fair treatment.]

* * *

Vice President Earl G. Ingram's affidavit represented:

(6) The University's affirmative action plan is a part of an overall state plan designed, in part, to desegregate the predominately "white" and "black" public institutions of higher education in Virginia . . . The behavior of the members of Sigma Chi that led to this lawsuit was completely antithetical to the University's mission, as expressed through its affirmative action statement and other pertinent University policies, to create a non-threatening, culturally diverse learning environment for students of all races and backgrounds, and of both sexes.

(7) While the University has progressed in attracting and retaining minority students, it cannot expect to maintain the position it has achieved, and make further progress on affirmative action and minority issues that it wishes to make, if behavior like that of Sigma Chi is perpetuated on this campus.

The district court granted summary judgment to Sigma Chi on its First Amendment claim, 773 F.Supp. 792 (E.D.Va.1991).

II

The University urges that the district court's grant of summary judgment was premature. It stresses that there remain factual issues which the district court should have weighed in its conclusion. According to the University, the Fraternity's intent in staging the contest is crucial to the issue of whether its conduct was expressive. The University also stresses that if given time it could demonstrate more completely the harm the contest caused to its educational mission. It is, of course, beyond cavil that summary judgment should not be granted while a viable issue of material fact remains. Summary judgment principles require the court to find that the evidence is such that a jury could not reasonably find for the party opposing summary judgment . . .

In our view, for the reasons that follow, the district court was correct in concluding that there was no outstanding issue of material fact.

III

We initially face the task of deciding whether Sigma Chi's "ugly woman contest" is sufficiently expressive to entitle it to First Amendment protection. From the mature advantage of looking back, it is obvious that the performance, apart from its charitable fund-raising features, was an exercise of teenage campus excess. With a longer and sobering perspective brought on by both peer and official disapproval, even the governing members of the Fraternity recognized as much. The answer to the question of whether the First Amendment protects the Fraternity's crude attempt at entertainment, however, is all the more difficult because of its obvious sophomoric nature.

A

First Amendment principles governing live entertainment are relatively clear: short of obscenity, it is generally protected.

* * *

Continued

Continued

Thus, we must determine if the skit performed by Sigma Chi comes within the constitutionally protected rubric of entertainment. Unquestionably, some forms of entertainment are so inherently expressive as to fall within the First Amendment's ambit regardless of their quality. For example, in *Ward* v. *Rock Against Racism,* 491 U.S. 781, 109 S.Ct. 2746, 105 L.Ed.2d 661 (1989), the Supreme Court flatly ruled that "[m]usic, as a form of expression and communication, is protected under the First Amendment."

* * *

Even crude street skits come within the First Amendment's reach. In . . . *Schacht* v. *United States,* 398 U.S. 58, 61–62, 90 S.Ct. 1555, 1558–59, 26 L.Ed.2d 44 (1970), . . . Justice Black [declared] that an actor participating in even a crude performance enjoys the constitutional right to freedom of speech.

Bearing on this dichotomy between low and high-grade entertainment are the Supreme Court's holdings relating to nude dancing.

[I]n [another case,] *Barnes* v. *Glen Theater, Inc.,* the Supreme Court conceded that nude dancing is expressive conduct entitled to First Amendment protection.

* * *

[I]t appears that the low quality of entertainment does not necessarily weigh in the First Amendment inquiry. It would seem, therefore, that the Fraternity's skit, even as low-grade entertainment, was inherently expressive and thus entitled to First Amendment protection.

B

The University nevertheless contends that discovery will demonstrate that the contest does not merit characterization as a skit but only as mindless fraternity fun, devoid of any artistic expression. It argues further that entitlement to First Amendment protection exists only if the production was intended to convey a message likely to be understood by a particular audience. From the summary judgment record, the University insists, it is impossible to discern the communicative intent necessary to imbue the Fraternity's conduct with a free speech component.

As indicated, we feel that the First Amendment protects the Fraternity's skit because it is inherently expressive entertainment. Even if this were not true, however, the skit, in our view, qualifies as expressive conduct under the test articulated in *Texas* v. *Johnson.* It is true that the *Johnson* test for determining the expressiveness of conduct requires "[a]n intent to convey a particularized message" and a great likelihood "that the message would be understood by those who viewed it." [T]he intent to convey a message can be inferred from the conduct and the circumstances surrounding it. Thus viewed, the University's argument is self-defeating. The affidavit from the University's Vice-President, Earl Ingram, stated that the message conveyed by the Fraternity's conduct—that racial and sexual themes should be treated lightly—was completely antithetical to the University's mission of promoting diversity and providing an educational environment free from racism and sexism.

* * *

[T]he affidavits establish that the punishment was meted out to the Fraternity because its boorish message had interfered with the described University mission. It is manifest from these circumstances that the University officials thought the Fraternity intended to convey a message. The Fraternity members' apology and post-conduct contriteness suggest that they held the same view. To be sure, no evidence suggests that the Fraternity advocated segregation or inferior

Continued

Continued

social status for women. What is evident is that the Fraternity's purposefully nonsensical treatment of sexual and racial themes was intended to impart a message that the University's concerns, in the Fraternity's view, should be treated humorously. From the Fraternity's conduct and the circumstances surrounding it, we have no difficulty in concluding that it intended to convey a message.

As to the second prong of the *Johnson* test, there was a great likelihood that at least some of the audience viewing the skit would understand the Fraternity's message of satire and humor. Some students paid to attend the performance and were entertained.

* * *

[W]e are persuaded that the Fraternity's "ugly woman contest" satisfies the *Johnson* test for expressive conduct.

* * *

The University, however, urges us to weigh Sigma Chi's conduct against the substantial interests inherent in educational endeavors. The University certainly has a substantial interest in maintaining an educational environment free of discrimination and racism, and in providing gender-neutral education. Yet it seems equally apparent that it has available numerous alternatives to imposing punishment on students based on the viewpoints they express. We agree wholeheartedly that it is the University officials' responsibility, even their obligation, to achieve the goals they have set. On the other hand, a public university has many constitutionally permissible means to protect female and minority students. We must emphasize, as have other courts, that "the manner of [its action] cannot consist of selective limitations upon speech." The University should have accomplished its goals in some fashion other than silencing speech on the basis of its viewpoint.

Affirmed.

Questions

1. *a.* Should racist/sexist remarks be forbidden in college classrooms?
   b. Are speech codes a good methodology for dealing with campus bigotry?
   c. Do we give too much attention to freedom of speech at the expense of community civility? Explain.
2. Does the First Amendment prohibit public schools from teaching moral values? Explain.[20]
3. The album "As Nasty as They Wanta Be" by rappers 2 Live Crew was described as brutal and sexually explicit.
   a. How would you defend the album from a charge of obscenity?
   b. If you have heard the album, do you consider it obscene? Explain. [See *Luke Records, Inc.* v. *Nick Navarro,* 960 F.2d 134 (1992), and *Nicholas Navarro* v. *Luke Records,* 113 S.Ct. 659 (1992).]

Corporate political speech. Corporate funds cannot lawfully be expended for federal campaign contributions. Some states likewise forbid such contributions. However, corporations can lawfully establish *political action committees* (PACs) to solicit and disburse voluntary campaign contributions. Consequently, corporations have firmly established themselves in the political process. To some, that development is as it should be. Corporations should be able to defend their stake in American life, and the marketplace of ideas profits from a more complete dialogue. To others, corporations, with their enormous resources, are a threat to the democratic process. The fear is that the corporate view, supported by extraordinary wealth and power, may drown out other opinions.

Commercial Speech. On occasion, governments seek to regulate communications of a profit-seeking nature (e.g., ads for abortion services). In 1942, the Supreme Court held that commercial speech was not entitled to the protection of the First Amendment.[21] However, a series of decisions beginning in 1975 have accorded constitutional protection to commercial speech. Governments may yet impose reasonable restrictions on commercial speech where those restrictions are necessary for the public welfare.

A 1993 Supreme Court decision affirmed First Amendment protection for commercial speech where the city of Cincinnati revoked permits to place 62 freestanding newsracks on public property. The newsracks contained free magazines designed primarily to advertise the services of a pair of businesses—one selling real estate, the other providing adult educational programs. The city labeled the magazines "commercial handbills," the distribution of which was prohibited by a city ordinance, and said that the newsracks raised aesthetic and safety concerns. Distribution of newspapers on public property, however, was explicitly authorized under the city code. The businesses filed suit, claiming a First Amendment violation, and ultimately the U.S. Supreme Court, by a 6–3 vote, affirmed their claim. The city had failed to make clear the distinction between commercial circulars and conventional newspapers, and it had failed to show a clear connection between its safety/aesthetic goals and the removal of 62 racks out of some 1,500 to 2,000 on public property. In general, the case has the effect of affirming the court's shield for commercial speech, although the majority was careful to say that the case applied to the particular Cincinnati facts and that commercial speech generally deserves a lesser degree of protection than not-for-profit expression.[22]

The case that follows illustrates the application of the commercial speech doctrine to professionals. This instance concerns a certified public accountant's personal solicitation of new clients.

Consider the powerful debate raging regarding the issue of pornography and free speech. One side contends that pornography is protected speech and cannot be restricted by law; the other side claims that pornography leads to ill treatment against women (either through actual physical abuse or through negative perceptions of women). Well-known pornography critic and law school professor Catherine MacKinnon explains her concerns:

> Pornography . . . is a political practice, a practice of power and powerlessness . . . Sex forced on real women so that it can be sold at a profit to be forced on other real women; women's bodies trussed and maimed and raped and made into things to be hurt and obtained and accessed and this presented as the nature of women in a way that is acted on and acted out over and over; the coercion that is visible and the coercion that has become invisible—this and more bothers [sic] feminists about pornography . . . Pornography is integral to attitudes and behaviors of violence and discrimination which define the treatment and status of half the population.[23]

In 1985, the District Court of the Southern District of New York decided *G & A Books, Inc. v. Stern,*[24] a case in which the restriction of the sale of pornography was questioned on First Amendment grounds. In this case, the plaintiffs operated a bookstore in Times Square where they sold sexually explicit materials. The Times Square Redevelopment Corporation (defendant, a government organization) tried to condemn the property, and the bookstore filed suit to prevent this from happening. The bookstore claimed that

CASE

Justice Kennedy

Edenfield v. Fane

113 S.Ct. 1792 (1993)

In previous cases we have considered the constitutionality of state laws prohibiting lawyers from engaging in direct, personal solicitation of prospective clients. In the case now before us, we consider a solicitation ban applicable to certified public accountants (CPAs) enacted by the State of Florida. We hold that, as applied to CPA solicitation in the business context, Florida's prohibition is inconsistent with the free speech guarantees of the First and Fourteenth Amendments.

I

Respondent Scott Fane is a CPA licensed to practice in the State of Florida by the Florida Board of Accountancy. Before moving to Florida in 1985, Fane had his own accounting CPA practice in New Jersey, specializing in providing tax advice to small and medium-sized businesses. He often obtained business clients by making unsolicited telephone calls to their executives and arranging meetings to explain his services and expertise. This direct, personal, uninvited solicitation was permitted under New Jersey law.

When he moved to Florida, Fane wished to build a practice similar to his solo practice in New Jersey but was unable to do so because the Board of Accountancy had a comprehensive rule prohibiting CPAs from engaging in the direct, personal solicitation he had found most effective in the past. The Board's rules provide that a CPA "shall not by any direct, in-person, uninvited solicitation solicit an engagement to perform public accounting services . . . where the engagement would be for a person or entity not already a client of [the CPA], unless such person or entity has invited such a communication." "[D]irect, in-person, uninvited solicitation" means "any communication which directly or implicitly requests an immediate oral response from the recipient," which, under the Board's rules, includes all "[u]ninvited in-person visits or conversations or telephone calls to a specific potential client."

The rule, according to Fane's uncontradicted submissions, presented a serious obstacle, because most businesses are willing to rely for advice on the accountants or CPAs already serving them. In Fane's experience, persuading a business to sever its existing accounting relations or alter them to include a new CPA on particular assignments requires the new CPA to contact the business and explain the advantages of a change. This entails a detailed discussion of the client's needs and the CPA's expertise, services and fees.

Fane sued the Board in the United States District Court for the Northern District of Florida, seeking declaratory and injunctive relief on the ground that the Board's antisolicitation rule violated the First and Fourteenth Amendments. Fane alleged that but for the prohibition he would seek clients through personal solicitation and would offer fees below prevailing rates.

In response to Fane's submissions, the Board relied on the affidavit of Louis Dooner, one of its former chairmen. Dooner concluded that the solicitation ban was necessary to preserve the independence of CPAs performing the attest function, which involves the rendering of opinions on a firm's financial statements. His premise was that a CPA who solicits clients "is obviously in need of business and may be willing to bend the rules." In Dooner's view, "[i]f [a CPA] has solicited the client he will be beholden to him." Dooner also suggested that the ban was needed to prevent "overreaching and vexatious conduct by the CPA."

The District Court gave summary judgment to Fane . . . [T]he Court of Appeals for the Eleventh Circuit affirmed.

We granted certiorari.

Continued

Continued

II

In soliciting potential clients, Fane seeks to communicate no more than truthful, non-deceptive information proposing a lawful commercial transaction . . .

[I]t is clear that this type of personal solicitation is commercial expression to which the protections of the First Amendment apply . . . There are, no doubt, detrimental aspects to personal commercial solicitation in certain circumstances, but these detriments are not so inherent or ubiquitous that solicitation of this sort is removed from the ambit of First Amendment protection.

In the commercial context, solicitation may have considerable value. Unlike many other forms of commercial expression, solicitation allows direct and spontaneous communication between buyer and seller. A seller has a strong financial incentive to educate the market and stimulate demand for his product or service, so solicitation produces more personal interchange between buyer and seller than would occur if only buyers were permitted to initiate contact. Personal interchange enables a potential buyer to meet and evaluate the person offering the product or service, and allows both parties to discuss and negotiate the desired form for the transaction or professional relation. Solicitation also enables the seller to direct his proposals toward those consumers whom he has a reason to believe would be most interested in what he has to sell. For the buyer, it provides an opportunity to explore in detail the way in which a particular product or service compares to its alternatives in the market. In particular, with respect to nonstandard products like the professional services offered by CPAs, these benefits are significant.

In denying CPAs and their clients these advantages, Florida's law threatens societal interests in broad access to complete and accurate commercial information that First Amendment coverage of commercial speech is designed to safeguard. The commercial marketplace, like other spheres of our social and cultural life, provides a forum where ideas and information flourish. Some of the ideas and information are vital, some of slight worth. But the general rule is that the speaker and the audience, not the government, assess the value of the information presented. Thus, even a communication that does no more than propose a commercial transaction is entitled to the coverage of the First Amendment.

III

To determine whether personal solicitation by CPAs may be proscribed under the test set forth in *Central Hudson,* we must ask whether the State's interests in proscribing it are substantial; whether the challenged regulation advances these interests in a direct and material way; and whether the extent of the restriction on protected speech is in reasonable proportion to the interests served. Though we conclude that the Board's asserted interests are substantial, the Board has failed to demonstrate that its solicitation ban advances those interests.

A

To justify its ban on personal solicitation by CPAs, the Board proffers two interests. First, the Board asserts an interest in protecting consumers from fraud or overreaching by CPAs. Second, the Board claims that its ban is necessary to maintain both the fact and appearance of CPA independence in auditing a business and attesting to its financial statements.

The State's first interest encompasses two distinct purposes: to prevent fraud and other forms of deception, and to protect privacy . . . [T]here is no question that Florida's interest in ensuring the accuracy of commercial information in the marketplace is substantial.

Likewise, the protection of potential clients' privacy is a substantial state interest. Even solicitation that is neither fraudulent nor deceptive may be pressed with such frequency or vehemence as to intimidate, vex, or harass the recipient . . .

Continued

Continued

The Board's second justification for its ban—the need to maintain the fact and appearance of CPA independence and to guard against conflicts of interest—is related to the audit and attest functions of a CPA. In the course of rendering these professional services, a CPA reviews financial statements and attests that they have been prepared in accordance with generally accepted accounting principles and present a fair and accurate picture of the firm's financial condition. In the Board's view, solicitation compromises the independence necessary to perform the audit and attest functions, because a CPA who needs business enough to solicit clients will be prone to ethical lapses. The Board claims that even if actual misconduct does not occur, the public perception of CPA independence will be undermined if CPAs behave like ordinary commercial actors.

B

That the Board's asserted interests are substantial in the abstract does not mean, however, that its blanket prohibition on solicitation serves them . . . [T]he *Central Hudson* test requires that a regulation impinging upon commercial expression "directly advance the state interest involved" . . . We agree with the Court of Appeals that the Board's ban on CPA solicitation as applied to the solicitation of business clients fails to satisfy this requirement.

* * *

The Board has not demonstrated that, as applied in the business context, the ban on CPA solicitation advances its asserted interests in any direct and material way. It presents no studies that suggest personal solicitation of prospective business clients by CPAs creates the dangers of fraud, overreaching, or compromised independence that the Board claims to fear. The record does not disclose any anecdotal evidence, either from Florida or another State, that validates the Board's suppositions . . .

In contrast to the Board's anxiety over uninvited solicitation, the literature on the accounting profession suggests that the main dangers of compromised independence occur when a CPA firm is too dependent upon or involved with a long-standing client . . .

* * *

Even under the First Amendment's somewhat more forgiving standards for restrictions on commercial speech, a State may not curb protected expression without advancing a substantial governmental interest. Here, the ends sought by the State are not advanced by the speech restriction, and legitimate commercial speech is suppressed. For this reason, the Board's rule infringes upon Fane's right to speak, as guaranteed by the Constitution.

Affirmed.

Questions

1. Do you believe, as Justice O'Connor argues in a dissent not reproduced here, that commercial speech of this kind is damaging to the accounting profession and to society at large? Explain.
2. Hornell Brewing Co. marketed a malt liquor labeled Crazy Horse. The name brought protests on the grounds that it amounted to targeting Native Americans and because it was considered disrespectful to the memory of the highly respected Sioux leader.

Continued

Continued

Responding to that criticism, Congress attached a rider to an appropriations bill that forbade the use of the name Crazy Horse on an alcoholic beverage label. Hornell then challenged the constitutionality of the federal law.

a. What is the nature of that challenge?

b. How would you rule on it? Explain. [See *Hornell Brewing Co.* v. *Nicholas Brady,* 819 F. Supp. 1227 (E.D.N.Y. 1993), and Laura Bird, "Makers of a Brew Called `Crazy Horse,'" *The Wall Street Journal,* April 14, 1993, p. B8.]

3. A U.S. statute forbade the mailing of unsolicited advertisements for contraceptives. Youngs, which sold contraceptives, mailed contraceptive ads to the public at large. The ads included information regarding the public health benefits of contraceptives (e.g., family planning and prevention of venereal disease).

a. Do the ads constitute commercial speech? Explain.

b. Does the government have a "substantial interest" in preventing the mailings where the statute shields citizens from material that they are likely to find offensive and where the statute helps parents control their children's access to birth control information? Explain. [See *Bolger* v. *Youngs Drug Products Corp.,* 463 U.S. 60 (1983).]

the defendant tried to condemn the property just because they sold pornographic material, whereas the defendant claimed that the bookstore, along with 400 other businesses, must be condemned to make way for a new hotel, theaters, an office building, and a mall.

The issue for the court was whether the defendant's attempt to restrict the sale of pornography, though this was not the main motivation behind the condemnation, was an unlawful restriction on free speech. To be an acceptable and lawful restriction, the defendant had to show that its interest in condemning the property was "unrelated to the suppression of free expression," in other words, that it wasn't condemning the property *just because of the pornography.* The court determined that the project's goals were "in and of themselves substantial, important, and unrelated to the suppression of free speech."[25] The court explained that "only the legitimate, non-speech goals of fighting blight and crime will be factored into the balance . . . [Illegitimate] justifications for the project must be discounted."[26] Therefore, the court held that simply because some of the members of the defendant's board supported the project in order to get rid of pornography, this did not render the restriction unacceptable.

What do we learn from this case? Pornography, or publication of any sort, may be restricted through condemnation as long as four requirements are met:

1. The restricting party has the right to conduct the condemnation.
2. The government has a substantial interest in the property condemned.
3. The government interest is unrelated to the suppression of free expression.
4. The government employs the least restrictive means available to achieve its goal.[27]

The same four factors may be applied to more basic issues of pornography and free speech. Where a restriction is imposed, it must be shown that the purpose of the restriction is not simply to keep pornography from enquiring minds, but instead to further some separate, legitimate goal.

D. The Fourth Amendment

In an increasingly complex and interdependent society, the right of the individual to be free of unjustified governmental intrusions has taken on new significance. The Fourth Amendment provides that:

> The right of the people to be secure in their persons, houses, papers, and effects, against unreasonable searches and seizures, shall not be violated, and no Warrants shall issue, but upon probable cause. . . .

Some constitutional limitations on the police powers of government officials are a necessity. However, the boundaries of freedom from unreasonable search and seizure are the subject of continuing dispute. The police are under great pressure to cope with America's horrific crime problems, but they must do so within the confines of the Constitution, which is designed to protect us all—including criminals—from the power of an unfair, overreaching government.

exclusionary rule. Fourth Amendment rule that prohibits the introduction of evidence at a trial that has been obtained in violation of the Fourth Amendment.

Certainly, the most controversial dimension of Fourth Amendment interpretation is the **exclusionary rule,** which provides that, as a matter of due process, no evidence secured in violation of the Fourth Amendment may be admitted as evidence in a court of law. The rule has been extended to encompass any and all evidence that was located or discovered as a result of an unlawful search (considered "fruit of the poisonous tree"). It was ultimately applied to all courts by the 1961 U.S. Supreme Court decision in *Mapp* v. *Ohio.*[28] The exclusionary rule is a very effective device for discouraging illegal searches, seizures, and arrests; however, from time to time it has the effect of freeing guilty criminals.

Drugs. Of course, search and seizure rules are often at issue in the government's efforts to stop illegal drug distribution. In general, a search warrant issued by a judge is necessary to comply with the Constitution in making a narcotics search. However, a warrantless search is permissible where reasonable, as in association with an arrest or where probable cause exists to believe a drug-related crime has been committed but circumstances make securing a warrant impracticable.

As part of an arrest, a search may lawfully include the person, a car, and the immediate vicinity of the arrest. Further, a police officer may lawfully secure drugs that have been abandoned or that are in plain view even though a warrant has not been obtained. For example, a juvenile, Hodari, fled after spotting some police officers in an unmarked car. Just as he was about to be apprehended by one of the pursuing officers, Hodari tossed aside what looked like a rock but turned out to be crack cocaine. In the subsequent prosecution, the State conceded that the officer did not have the "reasonable suspicion" necessary to justify pursuing Hodari. Therefore, the question became whether the officer had, in fact, "seized" Hodari at the moment the youth saw the officer on the verge of apprehending him. To constitute either the arrest or seizure of a person, physical force must be applied or the subject must have submitted to the officer's "show of authority." Neither had happened in this case at the time Hodari threw away the cocaine. Therefore, the Supreme Court ruled, Hodari had not been seized, and the cocaine did not need to be suppressed as the "fruit of an illegal seizure."[29]

Business Searches. We know that the Fourth Amendment has been the subject of dispute in criminal cases; but it may come as a surprise to learn that the contentious issues surrounding search and seizure have also been of importance in civil actions involving the government's efforts to regulate the conduct of business.

Privacy. Though the word *privacy* is not mentioned in the Constitution, some jurists consider the Fourth Amendment's protections to extend to personal privacy. An invasion of one's privacy may constitute an *unreasonable* search. As mentioned before, the Supreme Court has liberally interpreted search to include the retrieval of blood samples and other bodily invasions, including urinalyses. Search may also include a search of or for personal information from one's self or others about one's self. So, if an employer asks a job applicant a personal question that is not related to the performance of her or his job, that question may be considered a wrongful search.

To violate the Fourth Amendment, a search must be deemed *unreasonable, unjustified at its inception, and impermissible in scope.* A search is permissible in scope where it is done in such a way as to retrieve business-related information and where it is not excessively intrusive in light of the nature of the misconduct being investigated.

Prior to any search of employer-owned property, such as desks or lockers, employees should be given formal, written notice of the intent to search without their consent. Where the employer intends to search personal effects such as purses or wallets, employees should be forewarned, consent should be obtained prior to the search, and employees should be made well aware of the procedures involved. Consent is recommended under these circumstances because an employee has a greater expectation of privacy in those personal areas. As explained above, these rights are significantly diminished where the employer is not in the public sector.

E. The Fifth and Fourteenth Amendments

Takings. The Fifth Amendment prohibits the taking of private property for a public purpose without just compensation to the owner. Thus, the Fifth Amendment imposes bounds on the eminent domain processes commonly used by governments to condemn property for such projects as new highways.

For instance, assume that your business owns a plant and property in the Indiana Dunes National Lakeshore Park District. The federal government is interested in developing the property along the beach in the dunes to be used by the public for beach access. The Fifth Amendment requires that the government pay to you the fair market value of the property taken to be used for this purpose. Of course, you and the government may disagree on the actual value of the property, and this may be the basis for a claim, but you lose the property nevertheless.

One important issue under the Takings Clause is exactly what amounts to a taking. Obviously, if property is transferred to a new owner, a taking has occurred. The harder question is when regulation, such as requiring a developer to set aside land for a park area, amounts to a taking. In spite of recent Supreme Court cases, considerable uncertainty remains.[30]

Due Process. The Due Process Clauses of both the Fifth Amendment (applying to the federal government) and the Fourteenth Amendment (applying to the states) forbid the government to deprive citizens of life, liberty, or property without due process of law.

Substantive Due Process. Laws that arbitrarily and unfairly infringe on fundamental personal rights and liberties such as privacy, voting, and the various freedoms specified in the Bill of Rights may be challenged on due process grounds. Basically, the purpose of the law must be so compelling as to outweigh the intrusion on personal liberty or the law will be struck down. For example, the U.S. Supreme Court ruled that a Connecticut statute forbidding the use of contraceptives violated the constitutional right to privacy (although the word *privacy* itself does not appear in the U.S. Constitution).[31] By judicial interpretation, the Fourteenth Amendment Due Process Clause "absorbs" the fundamental liberties of the *federal* Constitution and prohibits *state* laws (in this case, the Connecticut contraceptive ban) that abridge those fundamental liberties such as privacy.

Procedural Due Process. Basically, procedural due process means that the government must provide a fair hearing before taking an action affecting a citizen's life, liberty, or property. A fair hearing might require, among others, notice of the hearing, the right to present evidence, the right to a decision maker free of bias, and the right to appeal. However, the precise nature of procedural due process depends on the situation. A murder trial requires meticulous attention to procedural fairness; an administrative hearing to appeal a housing officer's decision to banish a student from a dormitory, while required to meet minimal constitutional standards, can be more forgiving in its procedural niceties.

Equal Protection. The Fourteenth Amendment provides that no state shall "deny to any person within its jurisdiction the equal protection of the laws." This does not mean that everyone is to be treated equally. The Due Process Clause of the Fifth Amendment has been interpreted to provide that same protection from the federal government. Fundamentally, these provisions forbid a government from treating one person differently than another where there is no rational basis for doing so. In short, the equal protection provisions forbid discrimination by the government.

V. Criticisms and Alternatives

A. Criticisms

To many Americans, our system of justice is neither systematic nor just, and in recent years our court system has come under increasing criticism. Broadly, the concerns are twofold: (1) our society too readily turns to litigation to solve disputes and (2) the justice system is unfair.

Too Many Lawyers and Lawsuits? In 1991, Vice President Dan Quayle generated enormous, generally favorable, publicity in a speech to the American Bar Association when he said, among other things:

> Let's ask ourselves: Does America really need 70 percent of the world's lawyers? Is it healthy for our economy to have 18 million new lawsuits coursing through the system annually? Is it right that people with disputes come up against staggering expense and delay?

In fact, most countries do not collect reliable data regarding lawyer numbers, and definitions about what actually constitutes a lawyer vary widely. However, based on United Nations data regarding individuals receiving law degrees (most of whom become law providers, in some fashion), a recent study concluded that the United States ranks 35th in the world in lawyers per 10,000 population.[32]

On the other hand, another recent scholarly study claims that the United States is so overpopulated with lawyers that our total economic productivity has been reduced by more than 10 percent. On an individual basis, the study finds that the average worker's pay is reduced about $2,500 annually because we have an estimated 40 percent more lawyers than would be best for maximum economic productivity.[33] That study, in turn, is challenged by another suggesting that a higher ratio of lawyers to white-collar workers, generally, was associated with *faster* economic growth in the 1980s.[34]

Clearly, we do not have definitive evidence about the impact of lawyers on the American economy. However, we can be sure that litigation has become a favorite American pastime. For example, in 1992, state courts received over 100 million new cases.[35] And we know the system is expensive. The cost of dealing with civil injuries (torts) alone is estimated at $132 billion annually.[36] The bill is split as follows: insurance industry administrative costs (24 percent), payments for economic loss (22 percent), payments for pain and suffering (21 percent), defense lawyers (18 percent), and plaintiffs' lawyers (15 percent). Note that victims, in the end, receive less than 50 percent of the total payout. On a comparative basis, the bill for justice in the United States also appears high. Tort litigation in this country consumes 2.3 percent of the GNP, compared to fairly crude estimates of 0.6 percent in Britain, 1.2 percent in West Germany, and 0.7 percent in Japan.[37]

At the same time, the widely embraced notion that the tort system has run wild does not seem fully supported by the more careful evidence. A recent, very extensive inquiry found, for example, that (1) plaintiffs, on the average, are undercompensated in tort cases, (2) only 5 percent of total civil grievances ever become lawsuits, and (3) only one in six of those seriously injured by medical malpractice actually file suits.[38]

Is the System Unfair? We can confidently say that Quayle's charges were overstated, but we can also say that our justice system is flawed.

On the Other Hand. Even as we reflect on its weaknesses, we should not forget why our legal system has been so important in building America. We are the envy of the oppressed people of the world in our efforts to maximize freedom, fairness, and democracy for all. Furthermore, laws and lawyers are central to economic efficiency. Lawyers devise the rules, processes, and structures that permit capitalism to operate effectively. Former communist states in Eastern Europe are clamoring for American legal expertise to help them put together governments founded in constitutional principles along with the legal infrastructures necessary for smoothly functioning free markets. Even the People's Republic of China, where law practice was actually forbidden prior to 1979, has now recognized the importance of lawyers in building a strong economy:

> Beijing expects the number of lawyers in China to double to 100,000 by the year 2000, which the government hopes will strengthen the legal system and expedite judicial reforms. The increase is an integral part of China's economic modernization program, which has prompted a rapid rise in litigation, arbitration and contract negotiations, straining the country's young legal system.[39]

B. Alternative Dispute Resolution (ADR)

> More and more businesses and individuals are seeking alternatives to the mainstream judicial process.

In response to problems like those cited in the previous section (particularly expense and delay), we are witnessing the advance stages of what may prove to be a revolution in dispute resolution. More and more businesses and individuals are seeking alternatives to the mainstream judicial process. Some examples follow.

Small Claims Courts. Small claims courts (e.g., Judge Wapner's *People's Court*) have proven so successful and efficient that smaller businesses, in particular, are encouraging legislatures to increase the maximum recovery limits (currently $1,000 to $4,000 in most states) in order to permit more cases to avoid the full-blown judicial process. Small claims courts typically have relaxed procedural requirements, lawyers are actually forbidden in some states, and cases can be resolved in a few weeks rather than the years sometimes required in conventional courts.[40]

In 1993, New York state established a new all-business court designed eventually to handle the bulk of all commercial disputes (contracts, sales, securities) arising in New York City. To increase efficiency, judges for the new court will specialize in commercial matters and will be permitted to develop some special procedures for expediting cases and reaching settlements.[41]

About 500 larger companies now employ ombudsmen (or ombudswomen) as informal problem solvers who can receive workplace complaints and endeavor to resolve them before bigger problems emerge. Ombudsmen take a neutral perspective rather than acting as management representatives, and conversations with ombudsmen are confidential unless the employee says otherwise.[42]

Of course, the heart of the alternate dispute resolution movement lies in *mediation and arbitration.* A 1993 Deloitte and Touche survey of 246 attorneys found nearly three-quarters of them had some experience with ADR and most of that three-quarters expected to make greater use of it in the future. Sixty-five percent of those with ADR experience said they had saved money, ranging typically from 11 to 50 percent of the expected litigation costs.[43]

Mediation. Mediation introduces a neutral third party into the resolution process. Ideally, the parties devise their own solution, with the mediator as a facilitator, not a decision maker. Even if the mediator does propose a solution, its character will be in the nature of a compromise, not a determination of right and wrong. The bottom line is that only the disputing parties can adopt any particular outcome. The mediator may aid the parties in a number of ways, such as opening up communication between them.

The following article depicts the extraordinary expansion of interest in mediation.

Mediation Firms Alter the Legal Landscape

by Ellen Joan Pollock

Imagine a legal system in which companies could put their disputes before judges of their choice, get speedy decisions, avoid the uncertainty of jury verdicts, and keep legal bills to a minimum.

This is the system that hundreds of corporations are, in fact, choosing . . . Instead of going to court, such companies are letting a burgeoning industry of private mediation and arbitration firms resolve their legal disputes, ranging from auto-accident cases to the biggest antitrust suits.

Last year alone, more than 40,000 civil cases that once would have been handled in the nation's courts were resolved by four major firms that sell quicker, less costly, less procedurally complex dispute resolution. And every week, it seems, key players in another industry—from banking to food to insurance—announce that they will submit a major area of litigation to some form of mediation or arbitration.

Tremendous Savings

The savings for companies so far have been tremendous. Since 1990, 406 companies tracked by the Center for Public Resources, a nonprofit group that pro-

Continued

Continued

vides mediators and arbitrators, saved more than $150 million in legal fees and expert-witness costs by using litigation alternatives. The cases involved disputes with more than $5 billion at stake.

"I think that we're witnessing the emergence of a [free] market in dispute resolution which is challenging the traditional state-owned monopoly in dispute resolution—which, of course, is the courts," says Howard V. Golub, general counsel of Pacific Gas & Electric Co.

With the help of a mediator, Pacific Gas & Electric recently settled six disputes stemming from the crash of a helicopter that hit one of the utility's electrical lines. Such a case typically would have taken two years to wind its way through court. PG&E estimates that it would have cost $300,000 to $500,000 to litigate if the case settled just before trial, double that if it was tried to a verdict. Instead, the case was brought to a close within 10 months of the accident, and litigation costs were about $20,000. Terms of the settlement were confidential—another reason companies like mediation.

* * *

It was the reluctance of law firms that made mediation a fringe movement of the legal profession for so long. Quite simply, there was no financial incentive for lawyers to give up endless court battles for which they billed at hourly rates.

But now companies are taking the lead in pushing for litigation alternatives . . . At the same time, litigation alternatives have become easier to use . . .

Customized Proceedings

The new mediation firms were the answer. They customize mediation or arbitration proceedings to fit the needs of the disputing parties. Mediators can engage in shuttle diplomacy or express their opinion on the value of a case. Lawyers can be banned from the conference room. And most significantly, the pretrial fact-finding stage known as discovery, which can last years, can be streamlined to the simple exchange of a few documents.

* * *

Going private also allows businesses to circumvent the lottery systems by which courts assign judges. Michael J. Dontzin, a former New York state judge now with Endispute, sums up the attractions of mediation this way: "Here you write your own rules and pick your own judge."

* * *

Critics warn that the growth of private mediation firms is draining the public court system of some of its best judges and removing some important civil cases from the courts' domain—and thus from the public's view. If the trend continues, they say, the nation could end up with a dual system in which the rich buy high-quality justice on the private market and the poor get what's left over.

Many lawyers and judges worry in particular that the move to private dispute resolution will rob the public of the legal precedents that are the foundation of the justice system. Even Matthew Crosson, chief administrator of New York's overburdened courts and a supporter of litigation alternatives, believes that secret arbitration and mediation decisions may be bad for the public in some cases. The secret resolution of a product-liability case, he notes, means "the product defect may go uncorrected because the dispute was resolved in a private setting."

Looking for Alternatives

But the corporate world finds the advantages of mediation hard to resist . . .

General Motors Corp. launched an arbitration and mediation program for its dealers about two years ago with the help of Endispute. So far 78 cases have gone through, or are going through, the program. The cases generally settle, according to H. Richard Elmquist, a GM in-house lawyer. Disputes, he says, typically are resolved in a day.

William Coulter, whose Phoenix Cadillac dealership generates $55 million in revenues a year, settled a dispute with GM over charges for repair work

Continued

he did on cars under warranty. GM claimed it had over-reimbursed him by $100,000. After a mediation that lasted less than a day, Mr. Coulter agreed to pay GM $25,000. Mr. Coulter felt that he could have pushed GM harder but decided not to "quibble." "It was more important for me to resolve the problem and have a good working relationship with the factory," he says.

Questions

1. The article cites some problems associated with mediation.
   a. List them and any other problems you find with ADR.
   b. In your opinion, is justice as likely to be achieved via ADR as through the judicial system? Explain.
2. In an effort to reduce legal expenses, some major American banks have announced that all complaints by depositors and credit-card customers will be subject to arbitration. Some of those banks limit arbitration to claims involving large sums of money, and some permit judicial appeal of the arbitration decision. Is mandatory arbitration fair to consumers? Explain. (See Ralph King, "Banks Force Griping Customers to Forgo Courts for Arbitration," *The Wall Street Journal,* January 20, 1993, p. B1.)

Source: *The Wall Street Journal,* March 22, 1993, p. B1. Reprinted by permission of *The Wall Street Journal.*

Arbitration. Arbitration is a process in which a neutral third party is given the power to determine a binding resolution of the dispute. Depending on the situation, the resolution may be either a compromise solution or a determination of the rights of the parties and a win/lose solution. Even in the latter case, however, it may be quicker and less costly than a trial, and the arbitrator may be an expert in the subject area of the dispute instead of a generalist, as a judge would be. It is procedurally more formal than mediation, with the presentation of proofs and arguments by the parties, but less formal than court adjudication.

The EEOC is considering an ADR program in which claimants would obtain a quicker response through a less burdensome process. Such a program would potentially provide a better, less-disrupted working environment. Though no formal program has yet been proposed, the EEOC Task Force on ADR has formulated a set of principles on which to build a system with ADR as an option at various stages of the EEOC charge process, not just at the beginning; parties to an EEOC dispute would be told of all possible forms of dispute resolution available to them; and the ADR available would be flexible, voluntary, and determined by a neutral decision-maker.[45]

Jury Awards or Rewards?

In Kansas, a jury awarded an employee $250,000 in actual damages plus $1 million in punitive damages for retaliatory discharge after he filed a workers' compensation claim. When a bank employee refused to provide the bank's parent corporation confidential information about bank customers, the jury awarded him over $6 million in damages. An airline flight service manager was awarded $7 million based on an evidently successful claim of age, gender, and disability discrimination.[44]

In 1995, the Supreme Court cleared the way for nationwide enforcement and reliability of arbitration awards in its case, *Allied-Bruce Terminix Cos., Inc. et al.* v. *Dobson.*[46] The court determined that states are not allowed to refuse enforcement of an agreement that affects or involves interstate commerce.

Profile Perspective: Assuming that James Pierce did not have an arbitration clause in his contracts with the slow-paying restaurant, what alternatives does he have to a traditional court suit? Would you recommend that Pierce begin to put an arbitration clause in his contracts?

VI. Comparative Law

Having surveyed the American legal system, we should conclude by reminding ourselves that our approaches to life, including our methods of finding justice, are increasingly intertwined with the cultures of the other nations of the world. In a shrinking and increasingly competitive economic environment, we cannot afford to be ignorant about the balance of the globe. Therefore, let's take a look at one example of a justice system abroad, the law of China.

From the founding of the People's Republic of China (PRC) in 1949 to the death of Mao and the fall of the Gang of Four in 1976, the official Chinese position was one of hostility to law. Statutes were few and almost no one studied law. Indeed, law had played a limited role in the entire history of China. But today the Chinese are rapidly adding statutes dealing with all dimensions of their lives. Officials enroll in short courses in the law, and press coverage of legal issues is prominent.[47]

In 1986, China approved its *General Principles of Civil Law,* a code modeled not on Oriental traditions but on Roman and German law. Fundamentally, the Chinese leaders came to understand that a strong, rational legal system would be instrumental for commercial growth. Foreign investment in China, export business, and a stronger domestic market would all require a dependable, workable legal system. So to the Chinese, the law became, in part, an economic development vehicle. Of course, ultimate authority remains in the central government, and bureaucrats perform many functions left to civil law in this country.[48]

Also, economic change has been accompanied by some problems. Crime is increasing at an annual rate of nearly 8 percent despite a system where defendants seldom go free. Similarly, the filing of civil lawsuits has grown about 10 percent annually since 1988, reflecting, in part, the move toward capitalism.[49]

So Chinese law is beginning to take on some of the dimensions of Western systems, but fundamental differences in attitudes remain:

> Most Chinese persons engage in a large variety of economic and social activities and resolve disputes involved in those activities without coming in contact with the formal legal system. As in Japan, litigation in a court of law is not considered a normal way to resolve a dispute. Custom and extrajudicial dispute settling mechanisms are utilized not only by private parties but by public entities. Decisions declaring someone right and someone wrong are not a desirable goal. Settlements and compromises are preferable. Even in court, Chinese litigants generally do not obtain a clear defeat or victory.[50]

Although you may believe that the American legal system has benefits, would you design a similar system for a recently democratized country, such as the former Soviet Union?

Summary

Legal Review. The United States has a complex set of rules that govern transactions between the government and individuals, and among individuals or firms. The rules are based on the Constitution, which protects individuals from wrongful state action. In addition, both individuals and firms may be governed by statutes that are enforceable either by the state or by other parties. Conflicts are settled either through the American judicial process, which is based on a theory of *stare decisis* (precedent) or through alternative means of dispute resolution such as mediation or arbitration.

Ethics Review. The central issue relating to the legal system in America is fairness. The Constitution, most statutes, and constitutional amendments are all guided by a concept of fairness that, in turn, permeates business transactions. However, the jury is still out regarding whether equality of opportunity is the road to fairness or justice. Consider recent arguments for and against affirmative action. Although Title VII (prohibiting employment discrimination) was enacted over 30 years ago, there are still inequities in the workplace. Is affirmative action the answer? Can legislation enact fairness and fair treatment?

Economics Review. Although the American legal system is complicated and burdensome, few would argue that *no system* is a better alternative. Without a specific list of rules and procedures for our society, interactions between individuals and firms would be arbitrary and perhaps unfair. For example, if there were no rules regarding the final settlement of disputes (such as lawsuits), individuals may agree to settle, receive the money or other settlement, then still fight for the rest. [While theorists might say that "this person" would then never be trusted again during a settlement, this might not be the result since there exist both poor information exchanges and deception.] As a consequence, when your opponent says, "I'll see you in court," you know what that means; and when she says, "a deal's a deal," you also know what that means.

Chapter Questions

1. According to Warren Avis, founder of Avis Rent-a-Car: "We've reached a point in this country where, in many instances, power has become more important than justice—not a matter of who is right, but of who has the most money, time, and the largest battery of lawyers to drag a case through the courts." [51]
   a. Should the rich be entitled to better legal representation, just as they have access to better food, better medical care, better education, and so on? Explain.
   b. Should we employ a nationwide legal services program sufficient to guarantee competent legal aid to all? Explain.
2. Maintenance of our adversary system of justice sometimes compels lawyers to engage in practices that some consider unethical. Anne Strick relates one such situation.

   Once upon a time, Williston, called by a colleague "one of the most distinguished and conscientious lawyers I or any man have ever known," was defending a client in a civil suit. In the course of the trial, Williston discovered in his client's letter file material potentially damaging to the man's case. The opposition failed to demand the file; nor did Williston offer it. His client won. But, recounts Williston in his autobiography, the judge in announcing his decision made clear that his ruling was based in part on his belief in one critical fact: a fact Williston, through a letter from the file in his possession, knew to be unfounded.

Did Williston, that " most contientious lawyer," speak up? Did he correct the Courts unfounded belief, the better to serve both truth and justice? He did not.

"Though," he wrote, I had in front of me a letter which showed his [Honor's] error," Williston kept silent. Nor did he question the propriety of his behavior. For, said he, the lawyer "is not only not obliged to disclose unfavorable evidence, but it is a violation of his duty to his client if he does so."[52]

a. Did Williston act properly? Explain.

b. Should we turn to more cooperative, less combative, approaches to dispute resolution? Explain.

3. On July 5, 1884, four sailors were cast away from their ship in a storm 1,600 miles from the Cape of Good Hope. Their lifeboat contained neither water nor much food. On the 20th day of their ordeal, Dudley and Stevens, without the assistance or agreement of Brooks, cut the throat of the fourth sailor, a 17- or 18-year-old boy. They had not eaten since day 12. Water had been available only occasionally. At the time of the death, the men were probably about 1,000 miles from land. Prior to his death, the boy was lying helplessly in the bottom of the boat. The three surviving sailors ate the boy's remains for four days, at which point they were rescued by a passing boat. They were in a seriously weakened condition.
   a. Were Dudley and Stevens guilty of murder? Explain.
   b. Should Brooks have been charged with a crime for eating the boy's flesh? Explain.
   [See *The Queen* v. *Dudley and Stephens,* 14 Queen's Bench Division 273 (1884).]
4. Tompkins was a citizen of Pennsylvania. While walking on a railroad footpath in that state, he was struck by an object protruding from a passing freight train owned by the Erie Railroad Company, a New York corporation. Tompkins, by virtue of diversity of citizenship, filed a negligence suit against Erie in a New York federal court. Erie argued for the application of Pennsylvania common law, in which case Tompkins would have been treated as a trespasser. Tompkins argued that the absence of a Pennsylvania statute addressing the topic meant that federal common law had to be applied to the case. Should the court apply the relevant Pennsylvania state law, or should the federal court be free to exercise its independent judgment about what the common law of the state is or should be? [See *Erie Railroad* v. *Tompkins,* 304 U.S. 64 (1938).]
5. Does equality always equal justice? If it does, can minorities secure justice in America? Explain. [See Ellen Pollock and Stephen Adler, "Legal System Struggles to Reflect Diversity," *The Wall Street Journal,* May 8, 1992, p. A1.]
6. Robert Malott, CEO of FMC, argued that Americans, more than Europeans and Japanese, are willing to turn to the courts to resolve disputes. Assuming Malott is correct, what would explain that condition?
7. As explained in the readings, alternate dispute resolution offers many advantages in resolving business conflicts. However, some cases do not lend themselves well to ADR. Can you list some of the considerations a company should evaluate in deciding between ADR and litigation? [See Campbell Killefer, "Some Disputes Still Deserve Their Day in Court," *The Wall Street Journal,* October 12, 1992, p. A10.]
8. Lawyers have recently begun pursuing two new damage claims. One is labeled "fear of death," which typically arises in air crashes where the severe stress of the accident, including the fear of dying, gives rise to flashbacks and continuing anguish after the accident. The second is a suit for loss of joy or loss of pleasure, as in the case of an accident victim who is in a coma and cannot receive the pleasures of a normal life. Historically, damages in these situations have been limited to economic loss and perhaps some narrowly defined emotional losses (e.g., pain and suffering).

a. What problems for the court do you see in these causes of action?

b. Would you permit those claims were you the judge? Explain.

9. Judicial reform advocates often argue that the United States should adopt the English rule providing that the winner in a lawsuit is entitled to recover its reasonable litigation expenses from the loser.

   a. In brief, what are the strengths and weaknesses of the English rule?

   b. Would you favor it? Explain.

   [See Herbert Kritzer, "Searching for Winners in the Loser Pays Rule," *ABA Journal,* November 1992, p. 55.]

10. In deciding whether to confirm a president's nominee for the Supreme Court, policy analyst Terry Eastland suggests that senators ask, among others, the following question: "[I]f there is an injustice in society, and Congress or the states have failed to act, should the Supreme Court fill the void?" Answer Eastland's question. [See Terry Eastland, "What Republicans Should Ask the Supreme Court Nominee," *The Wall Street Journal,* April 14, 1993, p. A15.]

11. American Bar Association rules seek to discourage lawyers from aggressive pursuit of clients in an ambulance-chasing fashion. In-person solicitation of clients is entirely forbidden. General mass mailings not directed to individuals known to be in need of legal assistance are permissible under the bar's guidelines. Some attorneys have used targeted mailings to potential clients known to be facing legal difficulties. For example, attorneys have offered their legal assistance via express mail messages to families whose relatives have been killed or injured in crashes or other disasters. ABA rules discourage targeted advertising, and many states have followed the ABA's advice by adopting guidelines restraining that type of advertising by lawyers.

    A Kentucky lawyer sought to mail letters to individuals against whom home foreclosure proceedings had been instituted. He offered "free information on how you can keep your home." Kentucky rules forbade targeted mailings. The attorney claimed a First Amendment violation. How would you rule? Explain. [See *Shapero* v. *Kentucky Bar Association,* 486 U.S. 466 (1988).]

12. *a.* Could the federal government lawfully ban all tobacco advertising? Explain.

    b. Should it do so? Explain.

Notes

1. Elliot Klayman, John Bagby, and Nan Ellis, *Business Law* (Burr Ridge, IL: Richard D. Irwin, 1994), p. 1.
2. Milo Geyelin, "Soaring Legal Expense: Motorola Bemoans It, but Runs a Big Tab," *The Wall Street Journal,* October 5, 1994, p. A1.
3. Steven Keeva, "Demanding More Justice," *ABA Journal,* August 1994, p. 46.
4. Mark Clements, "Findings from *Parade*'s National Survey on Law and Order," *Parade Magazine,* April 18, 1993, p. 4.
5. Oliver Wendell Holmes, *Collected Legal Papers* (New York: Harcourt Brace Jovanovich, 1920), p. 173.
6. Benjamin Cardozo, *The Growth of Law* (New Haven, Conn.: Yale University Press, 1924), p. 52.
7. Max Weber, *Law in Economy and Society,* ed. Max Rheinstein (Cambridge, MA: Harvard University Press, 1954), p. 5.
8. Bronislaw Malinowski, *Crime and Custom in Savage Society* (Patterson, NJ: Littlefield, 1959), p. 55. Originally published in 1926.
9. Roscoe Pound, "A Survey of Social Interest," *Harvard Law Review* 57 (1943), pp. 1, 39.
10. Richard Quinney, "The Ideology of Law: Notes for a Radical Alternative to Legal Oppression," *Issues in Criminology* 7 (1972), p. 1, as reported in

The Sociology of Law: A Conflict Perspective, ed. Charles E. Reasons and Robert M. Rich (Toronto: Butterworth, 1978), p. 42.
11. Franz Schurmann, "Justice for All Is a Fragile Ideal," *Des Moines Register,* p. 1C.
12. *Lois E. Jenson, et al.* v. *Eveleth Taconite Co.,* U.S. District Court, Minnesota, Third Division, Civil No. 5–88–163 (1993), reported in Milo Geyelin, "Sex-Harassment Ruling," *The Wall Street Journal,* May 17, 1993, p. B2.
13. 366 U.S. 420 (1961).
14. *Fair Cadillac* v. *Bailey,* 229 Conn. 312 (Conn. S.Ct. 1994).
15. *Tinker* v. *Des Moines School District,* 393 U.S. 503 (1969).
16. *R. A. V.* v. *St. Paul,* 112 S.Ct. 2538 (1992).
17. *Wisconsin* v. *Todd Mitchell,* 113 S.Ct. 2194 (1993).
18. Editorial, "Buffaloed at Penn," *The Wall Street Journal,* April 26, 1993, p. A14; and Associated Press, "Case Dropped in University 'Race' Incident," *Des Moines Register,* May 25, 1993, p. 4A.
19. Stephen Chapman, "Speech Codes on the Way Out," *Waterloo Courier,* July 9, 1992, p. B7.
20. This question was suggested by a reviewer, Professor Cynthia Srstka, Augustana College (South Dakota).
21. *Valentine* v. *Chrestensen,* 316 U.S. 52 (1942).
22. *City of Cincinnati* v. *Discovery Network,* 113 S.Ct. 1505 (1993).
23. Catherine MacKinnon, "Pornography, Civil Rights and Speech," 20 *Harvard C.R.–C.T.L. Rev.* 1, 21–22 (1985).
24. 770 F.2d 288 (2d Cir. 1985), *aff'g* 604 F.Supp. 898 (S.D.N.Y.).
25. 604 F.Supp. at 910.
26. Ibid.
27. Ibid. at 911
28. 367 U.S. 643.
29. *California* v. *Hodari,* 111 S.Ct. 1547 (1991).
30. See, for example, *Keystone Bituminous Coal Association* v. *DeBendictis,* 107 S.Ct. 1232 (1987); *Nollan* v. *California Coastal Commission,* 107 S.Ct. 3141 (1987); and *Lucas* v. *South Carolina Coastal Council,* 112 S.Ct. 2886 (1992).
31. *Griswold* v. *Connecticut,* 381 U.S. 479 (1965).
32. August, "Mythical Kingdom," p. 72.
33. Magee, "How Many Lawyers?" p. 417.
34. Epp, "Let's Not Kill All the Lawyers," p. A13.
35. "Today."
36. Woo and Geyelin, "Cost of Civil Justice," p. B10.
37. Ibid.
38. Saks, "Do We Really Know Anything," p. 1147.
39. Holman, "China Sees Doubling of Lawyers," p. A10.
40. Felsenthal, "Expansions of Small-Claims," p. B14.
41. Edward Felsenthal, "Its All Business for Novel Court Now in Session," *The Wall Street Journal,* January 5, 1993.
42. Junda Woo, "Ombudsmen Proliferate in the Workplace," *The Wall Street Journal,* February 19, 1993.
43. Arthur Hays, "Litigation Alternatives," *The Wall Street Journal,* May 6, 1993, p. B10.
44. Littler, Mendelson, Fastiff, Tichy, and Mathiason, *Alternate Dispute Resolution Alert,* March 1995, p. 1.
45. Ibid. 46. S.Ct. 834 (1995).
46. 46. 115 S.Ct. 834 (1995).
47. William Jones, "Sources of Chinese Obligation Law," *Law and Contemporary Problems* 52, no. 3 (Spring 1989), p. 69.
48. Percy Luney, "Traditions and Foreign Influences: Systems of Law in China and Japan," *Law and Contemporary Problems* 52, no. 3 (Spring 1989), p. 129.
49. Richard Holman, "Crime in China Rises Steadily," *The Wall Street Journal,* March 23, 1993, p. A11.
50. Luney, "Traditions and Foreign Influences," p. 136.
51. Warren Avis, "Court before Justice," *New York Times,* July 21, 1978, p. 25.
52. Anne Strick, *Injustice for All* (New York: Penguin Books, 1978), p. 123.

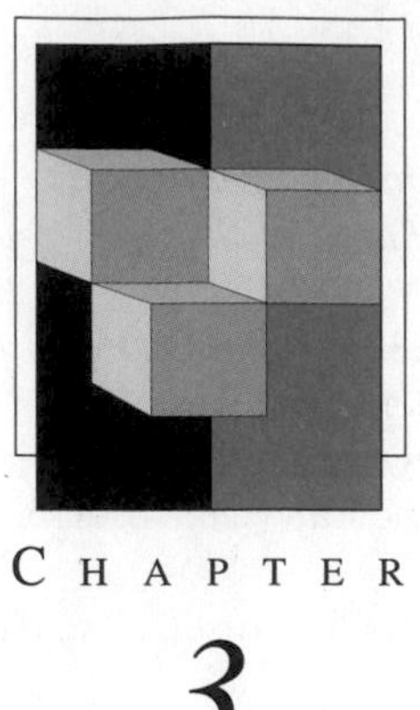

CHAPTER

3

Business Organizations: Building the Structure of the Business

Reader's Guide

Having read Chapters 1 and 2, you understand the overall goals of this book and the context (the free market, ethics, and public policy) in which we are going to examine the law; also, you have been introduced to our legal system—lawyers, courts, and the Constitution. Throughout this text we are employing the theme *the role of the law in building and managing a business* as a path for you to follow. Increasingly, the law affects every aspect of owning or managing a business, so students, whether anticipating a career working for others or on their own as entrepreneurs, need to understand the rudiments of the legal environment of business. In this chapter we will look at the process of setting up a business structure (partnership, corporation, etc.), a process that normally would be among the first steps in building and managing a successful enterprise.

Profile

The following account of a small business start-up is intended to put you as a student in the position of an owner/manager struggling with the practical hurdles of entrepreneurship. Important among those hurdles are the legal formalities that necessarily accompany business practice. Read this article. Then we will return to it from time to time throughout the chapter as we examine the many legal questions that accompany the process of building the legal structure (e.g., sole proprietorship) within which the business will operate.

Couple Wearing Multitude of Hats—and Aprons

by Jennifer Jacobs

Two years ago, Larry and Barbara LaPlume quit their Colorado jobs, sold their home overlooking Pike's Peak, paid all their bills, and moved to Cedar Falls, Iowa. They were unemployed with no prospects for work.

"We just came here cold turkey," said Barb, a native of Cedar Falls who has family here. Barb wanted to move back to a smaller town.

On a whim, the couple started a push cart business selling holograms at the local College Square Mall.

They made enough money to buy the Copper Kettle caramel corn shop and then bought Little King Deli, another food court shop just across the plaza.

"People say, 'Boy you must be rolling in the bucks. Boy you're lucky,' " said Larry, taking a

Continued

Continued

break during a hectic afternoon at an umbrella-covered table in the food court. "Well no, not really."

The LaPlumes know what it takes—and how difficult it is—for a couple to run their own business.

Business*es,* in their case.

As well as managing the snack shop, the deli and about 13 employees between the two, they own a leather goods pushcart that sells purses, wallets and bags. On November 15, they will reopen their seasonal fudge shop at which they'll peddle chocolates during Christmastime.

Away from the mall, they run a lawn mowing service that includes 13 properties a week, and also do property management for 60 Waterloo and Cedar Falls rental units.

"We work eight days a week and pretty much nine nights," said Larry, 32, who was born in Boston and has a background in manufacturing.

* * *

The LaPlumes had no idea how to start a mall business until they contacted the mall office. They learned that pushcarts can be rented by the week or month, as long as the entrepreneur proves the sales idea and maintains a professional look.

* * *

"We took all the money we had in that picture business . . . and we lumped it into (buying the Copper Kettle)," Larry said.

* * *

Larry met a Little King developer while on the board of directors for the mall. He told the contact he'd like to have the first bid on the deli if it ever went up for sale. When the out-of-town owner decided to give it up, Larry was there.

* * *

After working 9 AM to 9:30 PM for months, neither has taken a paycheck from the Copper Kettle or Little King. They continually roll over their profits to reinvest in their stores and live on income from their other businesses.

"It's been an experience," said Larry, who thinks their biggest headache is finding dependable employees.

"It took a lot of sacrifice to get here," he said. "At this level of work, I don't think I could do it for a long time."

But it's worth it, said Barb. "We couldn't see ourselves doing anything else."

Questions

1. What considerations would be involved in the LaPlumes' decision about the best form of business association for their needs?
2. What form of business association is likely to be most useful to the LaPlumes?

(As we proceed through the chapter, think about these themes.)

Source: *Waterloo Courier,* October 22, 1995, p. D1. Courtesy of *Waterloo Courier.*

I. Choosing and Creating a Structure

The success of a business, from a one-person start-up to a giant corporation, depends in good part on understanding the law governing the structure and operation of that organization. Whether you take a job as a management trainee in a big company or decide immediately to build your own business, you need to be familiar with the legal structures, principally sole proprietorships, partnerships and corporations, and, increasingly, limited liability companies, that we have developed for doing business and the rules that have emerged for operating those structures.

TABLE 3.1

COMPARING PRINCIPAL BUSINESS FORMS

Form	*Primary Advantages*	*Primary Disadvantages*
Sole proprietorship	Easily and inexpensively created and operated. Owner independence in decision making. All profits to owner. Profits taxed as personal income.	Capital accumulation limited to resources of proprietor. Owner personally liable for debts of business. Terminates on death or withdrawal of proprietor.
General partnership	Allows pooling of individuals' talents and resources. Easily organized and operated. Taxes paid on partners' personal returns.	Partners personally liable for business debts. Terminates on death or withdrawal of partner. Shared management authority (may also be an advantage, depending upon circumstances).
Corporation	Investors' risk of loss limited to capital invested. Effective structure for raising capital. Easy transferability of shares. Separate legal entity that can own property, enter contracts, and sue or be sued. Can have perpetual life.	Double taxation: corporate income taxes and individual income taxes on distributed dividends. May be expensive to create. States often require variety of reports.
Limited liability company (LLC)	Limited liability in the manner of corporations. Taxed in the manner of partnerships. Separate legal entity that can hold property, enter contracts, and sue or be sued. Easily dissolved.	Must conform to state LLC statute. Terminates on death or withdrawal of member (barring unanimous vote to continue). Not yet available in all states. Some lingering questions about tax treatment as partnership.

In general, smaller businesses with few employees and little likelihood of dramatic expansion (and accompanying capital needs) may be best suited for a sole proprietorship. A partnership may be more suitable if greater capital is required and a group of individuals want to pool their various resources and skills. As capital requirements, complexity, and the diversified nature of the operation increase, the corporate form may be the best route to take. Recently, most state legislatures have been willing to carve out new, hybrid forms, labeled limited liability companies, which combine some of the advantages of partnerships and corporations. The accompanying Table 3.1 summarizes the advantages and disadvantages of four of the principal forms of organizing a business.

Now we will turn to a closer look at a number of business organization forms and examine some of the strengths and weaknesses of each. When determining which legal form a business will adopt, most thoughtful promoters focus on five factors: cost, continuity, control, liability, and taxes. The order of importance of these considerations will vary from business to business, but all five certainly merit serious analysis. Cost reflects the initial and subsequent expenses (direct and indirect) associated with a particular form of organization. Continuity refers to the consequences of an owner dying or otherwise withdrawing from participation in the firm, or a new owner joining the business. Control focuses on who will set firm policy and run the business. Liability concerns what assets of the owners may be used to pay firm debts; tax considerations are based on maximizing the share of corporate resources available to the owner and minimizing those due the government.

A. Sole Proprietorships

The least complex and most common form of business organization in the United States is a **sole proprietorship,** a situation in which one person, the owner, is in fact the business.

The least complex and most common form of business organization in the United States is a sole proprietorship.

Cost. Few, if any, legal forms are required to organize a business. A sole proprietorship is not a separate legal entity. Any lawsuit against the business would be directed to its owner, although the business probably would be mentioned; for example, defendants Larry and Barbara LaPlume, doing business as (d/b/a) Copper Kettle.

sole proprietorship. A form of business under which one person owns and controls the business.

Continuity. A sole proprietorship terminates upon the death or withdrawal of the owner.

Control. A sole proprietorship offers enormous independence of operation. All decisions and directions lie with the owner and all profits return to the owner.

Liability. The biggest problem is that the owner is personally responsible for all losses and liabilities (as contrasted with the **limited liability** features of some other business organizations). Thus, if your sole proprietorship's liabilities exceeded its assets, you, as the owner, might be forced to pay your business debts with your personal assets.

limited liability. Maximum loss normally limited to the amount invested in the firm.

Taxes. Taxes are levied at the owner's personal tax rate, so they would often be lower in a corporate structure, for example.

Sole proprietorships are desirable in that they are easily and inexpensively created, they provide the owner great flexibility and independence, all profits go to the owner, and tax treatment would normally be more advantageous than that offered by the corporate form. Thus, if you were entering business on your own—particularly a relatively small, uncomplicated enterprise—a sole proprietorship might make good sense. Of course, it also carries the personal liability and termination disadvantages noted above; and perhaps a bigger problem is that in a sole proprietorship you would have no way of raising capital beyond your own assets and any loans you can secure.

B. Partnerships

Our discussion will begin with an overview of general partnerships and will proceed to some specialized forms labeled limited partnerships and limited liability partnerships.

A partnership can be defined as two or more persons carrying on as co-owners of a business for profit. A group of persons who agree to form a partnership or who act like partners have done just that—created a partnership. Normally, no written agreement, filings at the courthouse, or other legal notice must be given in advance for a legal partnership to exist. Of course, a written partnership agreement is advisable to set forth rights and responsibilities and to limit confusion. Furthermore, the partners' agreement, whether written or oral, can be changed at any time with their consent.

Uniform Partnership Act (UPA). Original uniform act for creation and operation of partnerships.

In those situations in which a partnership is formed without the partners agreeing to the terms under which it will operate, state laws supply the operating conditions for the partnership. Most jurisdictions have, in essence, adopted the **Uniform Partnership Act of 1914 (UPA),** which sets forth a traditional allocation of powers and responsibilities for partnerships. Some of its provisions are:

1. All partners share equally in partnership profits and losses.
2. All partners are expected to devote their full time and energies to partnership business, without compensation, and to act in the best interests of the partnership at all times.
3. An agreement made by any partner may bind the entire partnership to the terms of the agreement.
4. Unanimous consent is necessary to admit a new partner.
5. The partnership can be terminated at any time for any reason by any partner.

A partnership is free to tailor the provisions of its agreement to the particular needs of the partners. Many times, profits and losses are not shared equally, or one partner receives a salary in addition to his or her share of profits, but such variances from the UPA must be spelled out and agreed to. Failure to do so automatically triggers the UPA's provisions and may have costly and perhaps fatal consequences when disputes arise.

Revised Uniform Partnership Act. The Uniform Partnership Act was adopted in all states but Louisiana. In 1994, the National Conference of Commissioners on Uniform State Laws approved a Revised Uniform Partnership Act (RUPA). At this writing, RUPA has been adopted in only a handful of states. Hence, the UPA will provide the foundation for our partnership work in this chapter. However, it is worth noting that RUPA does include some important changes that may eventually find their way into the mainstream of partnership law. For example, RUPA relaxes, but does not eliminate, the **fiduciary** duties of partners and allows them greater flexibility in pursuing self-interested goals. Further, RUPA gives greater stability to partnerships than does the UPA because RUPA rejects the UPA rule that a partnership is dissolved whenever a partner leaves.

fiduciary. One who holds a relationship of trust with another and has an obligation to act in the best interests of the other; as one who manages property on behalf of another.

Cost. The costs in establishing a partnership are minimal. Normally, state law imposes no legal requirements, other than obtaining local business licenses and permission to operate under the proposed partnership name.

Continuity. Continuity is a problem for many partnerships that were not set up to last for a fixed period of time. Every time a partner leaves for any reason (e.g., death, insanity, voluntary or involuntary withdrawal, or personal bankruptcy) or a new partner joins, the partnership must be legally dissolved and a new one created. While under most circumstances the partnership continues to operate during the process, dissolution requires all firm creditors to be notified and appropriate arrangements made. The value of the partnership must be determined, and the withdrawing partner must be given his or her appropriate share. If the partners cannot reach an agreement, the dissatisfied partner may be able to force the partnership to sell all of its assets and give each partner his or her appropriate share. From a business point of view, it can be disastrous if partnership assets must be sold quickly to pay off a withdrawing partner. A good partnership agreement can reduce these problems.

Control. Control in a partnership is relatively simple. Either each partner has an equal say in partnership policy, or the partnership agreement sets forth an alternative scheme under which some partners have a greater voice than others. On most issues, unless otherwise agreed to by the partners, a majority vote is necessary to approve a course of action.

Other than benefiting or protecting individual partners, the most critical issue that must be addressed concerning control is making certain that tie votes among the partners do not occur continually. Many small partnerships fail because the partners are not able to muster a majority to approve a policy (typically 1–1 or 2–2 votes on a crucial issue) and have not established procedures to prevent the deadlock from becoming a permanent pitfall capable of stifling any partnership action.

Liability. Liability is often the issue that forces promoters to choose the corporate form over a partnership. All members of a partnership are personally liable to the full extent of their assets for all partnership debts. If, for instance, the partnership employee were to lose money and be unable to pay a bank loan on time, or if a partnership employee were to cause environmental damage, the partners might be forced to sell their stocks, bonds, and other personal possessions to meet the demands of various creditors. If the business is likely to be sued regularly or face catastrophic losses from accidents or other tort liability, a partnership probably would not be appropriate. On the other hand, if the partners are judgment proof (i.e., have no unencumbered assets) or the risks they face are insurable, the penalty associated with the unlimited personal liability for partnership debts is largely illusory.

Profile Perspective: Think about the LaPlumes and their small business ventures. How would their choice of business associations affect their legal liabilities if, for example, a customer choked on a bone while eating at their Little King Deli?

Taxes. Taxation is the reason many small businesses are established as partnerships. Partnerships merely serve as conduits for profits flowing from the business directly to the partners. The partners then report partnership profits or losses on their tax returns and pay the appropriate taxes at the ordinary personal income tax rate. The partnership itself merely reports the amount of income to appropriate taxing agencies and does not actually pay any income tax. Many states levy a yearly tax against the authorized shares of corporations chartered in their states. Partnerships typically escape such taxes.

C. Corporations

Partnerships and sole proprietorships make economic sense for people who are essentially selling their own and their partners' labor, expertise, or experience (e.g., three doctors, eight attorneys, or five radio repairers). Businesses that utilize many different factors in production, need large amounts of capital, and expect to continue unabated after the founding owners have departed often find partnerships unwieldy and economically unfeasible. For these businesses, organizing as a **corporation** may be more appropriate.

corporation. A form of business organization that is owned by shareholders who have no inherent right to manage the business, and is managed by a board of directors elected by the shareholders.

Creation. Broadly, the creation of a corporation involves two phases: (1) organization and (2) incorporation. During the organization phase, prior to the legal emergence of the new business, the **promoter** of the corporation typically develops an idea, raises capital, enters contracts, and so forth to get the idea off the ground. The promoter is liable for those

promoter. A person who incorporates a business, organizes its initial management, and raises its initial capital.

contracts (such as lawyer fees, money borrowed, and equipment purchased) at least until the corporation adopts the contracts. If the corporation never comes into being or it declines to assume the promoter's liabilities, those liabilities normally remain with the promoter.

In the incorporation phase, the new business achieves legal status. Requirements vary from state to state, but normally the process is initiated by filing the articles of incorporation with the secretary of state. The articles must include the name of the corporation, the number of authorized shares to be issued, the address of the corporation's initial registered office, the name of the initial registered agent, and the names and addresses of the **incorporators.** Other information such as the purpose and duration of the corporation and the corporation's initial capitalization may also be included in the articles. Once the articles of incorporation are filed and the necessary fees are paid, the secretary of state, in many states, issues a **certificate of incorporation,** also labeled a **charter.**

incorporators. Those who initiate a new corporation.

certificate of incorporation or charter. An instrument from the state bestowing the right to do business under the corporate form of organization.

For a promoter, a particularly important decision in creating a new corporation lies in deciding which state should be its legal home. A corporation doing most of its business in one state is likely to save money by incorporating in that state. Corporations engaged in interstate business should consider a variety of factors in deciding about the state of incorporation, including (1) the differences in taxes and fees among the states; (2) the degree of management decision-making discretion permitted under the statutes and court decisions of the state (e.g., state law is often a decisive factor in the success of corporate mergers and takeovers); and (3) the record-keeping requirements of the state. Delaware is a particularly popular choice for incorporation because of its low fees and favorable legal climate.

Cost. The cost of setting up a corporation is often higher than that associated with a partnership. Obtaining a charter typically requires an attorney and the completion of numerous forms and procedures dictated by the state. Taxes and license fees often have to be paid. The corporation must also undertake similar obligations in other states in which it plans to do business. After the corporation is chartered, it must file regular reports with the state, pay taxes and fees, maintain an agent for service of process, and generally comply with the state's corporate laws. This might require election of a board of directors, regular audits, shareholder meetings, and any number of items thought necessary by the state to ensure the corporation is run fairly for the benefit of all shareholders.

Continuity. As long as all state requirements are met, a corporation may enjoy a perpetual existence, thus eliminating continuity problems (such as those occurring in a partnership when an important partner decides to withdraw at an inopportune time). Ownership of stock in a corporation does not connote a personal, fiduciary duty like that existing between partners, who must always act in the best interests of the partnership, even if it is not personally advantageous. Shares typically may be transferred freely to anyone without corporate approval, and the corporation is usually under no obligation to buy back the shares of a disgruntled or departing shareholder. Likewise, on the death of a shareholder, the shares simply transfer to his or her heirs, and the corporate structure remains unchanged.

Control. Control is usually much easier to maintain in a corporation than in a partnership. Shares of stock are often sold to widely diverse groups of people who have no connection with each other and no interest in being involved in corporate dealings. For publicly traded companies, large blocks of shares are controlled by banks, mutual funds, or insurance companies, which tend to vote for the continuation of current management except in the most unusual situations. The groups that control major corporations often own or control very small percentages of the company's stock but are able to maintain their positions as board members or top corporate officers. Corporations sometimes issue nonvoting as well as **voting stock.** This **nonvoting stock** participates in firm profits and dividends but does not vote at shareholder meetings. Through this technique, existing owners can raise additional capital for the firm without risking loss of control.

voting stock. Owners of voting stock have the right to vote at shareholder meetings.

nonvoting stock. Owners of nonvoting stock participate in firm profits and dividends but may not vote at shareholder meetings.

Liability. Shareholder liability is much more limited than partner liability. Because a corporation is a separate entity, it can sue and be sued. Corporate debts are the sole obligations of the corporation and must be paid from corporate assets. In other words, a party aggrieved by an action of a corporation (e.g., an unpaid debt or an automobile accident), but unable to recoup adequate damages from the corporation cannot expect to recover its losses from the personal assets of the individual shareholders. Except in the most egregious or unusual circumstances, shareholders' losses are limited to their original investment in the corporation (limited liability).

This inability of creditors to use personal shareholder assets to satisfy corporate debts or obligations is often a powerful incentive to incorporate. By incorporating, a person starting a small business can rest at night with the assurance that a business reverse will not cause the owner's automobiles, jewelry, and so on to be sold to pay corporate debts.

Taxes. The issue of taxation presents the major drawback for choosing a corporate existence. Because a corporation is a separate economic entity, it is also a separate taxable entity. As such, corporations must pay a corporate income tax to the federal government as well as to most states in which they conduct business. Joint state and federal income taxes can approach 40 percent of profits. Furthermore, an individual receiving dividends from a corporation must pay income tax on the dividends to state and federal authorities. Thus, corporate profits are said to be subject to double taxation—first when the corporation reports a profit, and later when those profits are distributed to owners in the form of dividends.

D. *Hybrid Organizations*

Because corporations and general partnerships have various shortcomings, businesses have sought alternatives. State legislatures and Congress have responded by authorizing four other forms of organization: limited partnerships, limited liability partnerships, Sub S corporations, and limited liability companies.

Limited Partnerships. A **limited partnership** is like a partnership in many respects: It is not a taxable entity, and all losses or gains are passed through to the partners. The principal difference is that there are two classes of partners. One class, typically investors, is referred to as limited partners. They are not allowed to participate in management decision making, but they are granted limited liability so that their maximum liability in case of failure is their original investment in the project. The other class, typically the promoters, is referred to as general partners. They manage the business and are personally liable for all losses. A corporation can be the general partner in many instances, thus offering the actual general partners (the owners of the corporation) the equivalent of limited liability. Limited partnerships are particularly suitable for (1) raising capital for single-project alliances among diverse groups of investors (e.g., developing an office building or shopping mall) and (2) sheltering other income from taxation.

limited partnership. A form of business organization that has one or more general partners who manage the business and have unlimited liability for the obligations of the business and one or more limited partners who do not manage and have limited liability.

In a limited partnership, the shares or interests of the limited partners may be sold or transferred freely. Death, bankruptcy, insanity, and so on have no effect on the partnership. The general partners, on the other hand, are subject to roughly the same restrictions as in a regular partnership. However, provision is usually made in the limited partnership agreement for an alternate general partner so that the project can continue unabated should a general partner be forced to withdraw. Limited partnerships are often more complicated than corporations to form. Failure to comply with all the requirements may subject the limited partners to unlimited liability just as if they were general partners.

limited liability partnership. A special partnership form providing some of the advantages of limited liability.

Limited Liability Partnerships (LLPs). Many states, in the early and mid-90s passed legislation permitting the creation of a new business form, the **limited liability partnership.** That new structure is largely a response to increasing liability concerns in professional partnerships such as those for accountants and lawyers. LLPs are created according to the terms of the state enabling legislation. Normally the partners must register with the state; pay a fee (perhaps $200 per partner); include some language such as "limited" in their partnership name, thus indicating LLP status; and maintain sufficient professional liability insurance.

Broadly, the point of an LLP is to allow those who want to operate in a partnership framework to enjoy some of the benefits of limited liability. LLP legislation eliminates a partner's personal liability for another partner's mistakes, misconduct, negligence, and wrongful acts. That is, a partner's liability for the negligence or malpractice of another partner is limited to the partnership's assets. On the other hand, LLP status leaves the partnership itself fully liable for partners' malpractice and negligence; partners remain liable for their own torts, supervising partners may be liable for the wrongdoing of subordinates, and partnerships retain liability for all other debts such as loans. Thus, an LLP offers less powerful liability protection than an LLC (see below), but for those seeking the flexibility of the partnership along with reduced liability concerns, an LLP clearly is a desirable option.

Sub S corporation. A close corporation whose shareholders have elected to be taxed essentially like partners are taxed under federal income tax law.

Sub S Corporations. Some business projects call for the formation of a **Sub S corporation.** This creation of federal tax law allows, in certain situations, an incorporated business to escape most corporate income tax. The owners of the business then have the best of both worlds—limited liability without double taxation. To qualify, a corporation must have no more than 35 shareholders, over 80 percent of its income must be earned income (i.e., not derived from dividends, interest, royalties, and other passive sources), and almost all of its income or losses must be distributed to the owners each year. The shareholders then pay the appropriate personal income tax on their earnings just as partners would. Because of these restrictions, Sub S corporations are suitable only for smaller projects that do not need to retain capital for growth purposes. A typical situation might be eight individuals who decide to develop 100 acres of land into 200 lots, which will then be sold over a period of years. The early losses generated from building roads, sewers, parks, and so on will be passed through to the individual shareholders to reduce their current income tax, and the taxable gains will be deferred to later years. Furthermore, no additional capital will be needed by the business. When all the lots have been sold, the deal will end and the corporation will simply cease operations.

limited liability company. Hybrid of limited partnership and corporation receiving partnership tax treatment with the operating advantages of a corporation.

Limited Liability Companies (LLCs). Most states have now passed statutes authorizing what are known as **limited liability companies,** structures designed to combine the tax advantages of a partnership with the operating advantages of a corporation. Because of a 1988 IRS ruling, LLCs retain the limited liability of corporations but are treated as partnerships for tax purposes and thus do not pay federal income tax. Rather, LLC members are taxed on profits and losses as part of their individual federal tax returns. An LLC is created by filing articles of organization with the secretary of state. Many states require an annual financial report with the state.

Typically, an LLC will operate according to an agreement among the members. An LLC operates like a corporation as a separate entity and may sue, be sued, enter contracts, hold property, and so on. An LLC may be managed by the members themselves or by a management team agreed upon by the members. LLC members have no personal liability for LLC obligations. Ordinarily, LLCs may be easily dissolved by death, bankruptcy, or retirement of any member, among other things, although the remaining members can continue to operate the business by their unanimous agreement. In many states, LLCs are limited by statute to a lifetime of 30 years.

Advantages. LLCs have considerable advantages over other business forms. LLCs tend to be easier to create than limited partnerships and have no restrictions on the maximum number of investors, as do Sub S corporations. Furthermore, unlike a limited partnership, in which the general partners have unlimited liability, an LLC protects its members from personal liability, except for fraud. Currently, tax consequences sometimes make it difficult for existing, profitable businesses to become LLCs, but new businesses do not face that issue. Remember that much of the utility of an LLC is attributable to the aforementioned IRS ruling that could be modified or voided if LLC abuses become significant.

E. Franchises

In building a new business, some may seek to reduce the risk of failure by engaging in a **franchise** agreement. A franchise is essentially a distribution system in which the **franchisor** (e.g., McDonald's) holds a trade name, trade mark, copyright, or the like and uses it to build a national system and image. The **franchisee,** on the other hand, pays a fee to the franchisor and has the right to use the franchisor's name and business system to sell goods or services. Legally, a franchise may operate as a partnership, corporation, or other business organization structure.

The franchisee benefits from the experience, name exposure, and goodwill of the franchisor, and the franchisor finds benefits in shifting investment risk to franchisees and in adding the zeal and initiative of those franchisees. Franchisees are in a subordinate role in these arrangements and sometimes have been abused. As a result, most states as well as the Federal Trade Commission have instituted rules requiring franchisors to extensively disclose their operating requirements and protecting franchisees from arbitrary franchisor decisions, especially those involving termination of the franchise agreement.

franchise. A marketing arrangement in which the franchisor permits the franchisee to produce, distribute, or sell the franchisor's product using the franchisor's name or trademark.

franchisor. A party granting a franchise.

franchisee. A holder of a franchise.

F. International/Public Policy: The European Union

The member-states of the European Union have been working since 1970 to establish a European Company Statute that would provide uniform rules for setting up and operating businesses across the EU. As of this writing, each nation continues to have its own business association rules. The creation of the single market in Europe has opened enormous new commercial opportunities, but the lack of harmony in business organization law results in roadblocks to full efficiency. European companies often must conduct their business through a series of subsidiaries incorporated under the laws of each of the countries in which they seek to do business. Further, the current prohibition against cross-border mergers of subsidiaries makes productivity gains more difficult.

> The United Kingdom favors a very restricted role for workers in management, whereas Germany continues to support its longtime system of codetermination.

The chief impediment to the adoption of the European Company Statute has been the question of how deeply involved employees are to be in company decision making. The United Kingdom favors a very restricted role for workers

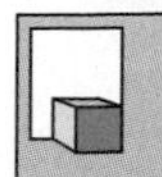

codetermination. German corporate governance and labor law system in which board representation by labor unions is required.

in management, whereas Germany continues to support its longtime system of **codetermination** (*mitbestimmung*), which affords workers and labor unions a large consultative voice in company affairs. Under codetermination, depending on the size and nature of the company, up to one-half of the members of the company's board of supervisors will consist of employee representatives. That board of supervisors appoints the company's board of directors, examines the company's profit/loss situation, checks the books, and may otherwise involve itself in critical company decisions.

Question

Should American law require that our workers, like their German counterparts, have a large consultative voice in managing company affairs? Explain.

II. Dealing with Government

Profile Perspective: If we think back for a moment to the LaPlumes and their several small businesses, including two food services, we can immediately recognize the very large role of government in the process of building and managing a business. The LaPlumes must be concerned about an array of government interventions, including state health inspections, federal OSHA safety inspections, federal wage and hour inspections, tax regulations, trademark protections, and many more.

To businesspeople, extensive government oversight is expensive and often annoying. On the other hand, the market functions imperfectly, so we have turned to government in an effort to correct those imperfections. The quarrel, of course, is about how far the government should reach. Regardless of one's philosophical position, the fact is that government, at all three levels, is a major partner in starting and operating a business.

A. Names

The choice of a name for your enterprise can be crucial to its commercial success. Beyond that, if you incorporate, your name must be acceptable to your secretary of state. If you choose a name already in use by another, you may lose its use. If you plan on doing business across state lines or even if you plan a large statewide business, you may want to do a careful name search. You may also choose to protect your name by registering it as a **trademark** or **service mark** under state and federal laws. A trademark is a word, mark, symbol, design, picture, or combination thereof that identifies a product (e.g., Nike). A service mark is the same for a provider of a service (e.g., Blockbuster—video rentals). The general idea is that the first user of a distinctive mark should be able to retain exclusive use of that potentially valuable mark. Registry with the federal government greatly aids in protecting that mark.[1]

trademark. A word, name, or other distinctive symbol registered with the government and used exclusively by the owner to identify its product.

service mark. A word, mark, symbol, design, picture, or combination thereof that identifies a service provider.

B. Licenses, Permits, and Government Oversight

Local Government. Of course, rules vary widely from community to community, but in building a business you are likely to be required to comply with a series of local government requirements. Many businesses and occupations require specific government permissions in the form of **licenses** or **permits** before business may proceed. Those licenses and permits have two purposes: (1) to raise revenue and (2) to protect public health, safety, and aesthetics.

licenses or permits. Government-granted privileges to do some act or series of acts. Authorization to do what, without a license, would be unlawful.

Zoning ordinances divide the community into geographical segments and specify the purposes (e.g., residential or commercial property) to which land and buildings in each segment may be applied. A new business must conform to the zoning code. Obviously, you ordinarily cannot open a business in a residential neighborhood, but more subtly, the sign you put on the front of your new business may be required to conform to local rules about dimensions, materials, and so forth. Similarly, most communities have building codes that require securing building permits from the community before proceeding with building or remodeling projects of anything more than a trivial nature. Building codes are designed to assure safety and stability and to maintain minimal aesthetic standards. Health and environmental permits will be required for some kinds of businesses, most notably in the case of restaurants.

zoning ordinances. Dividing a city or a county into geographical areas of restriction—for example, an area zoned R would only permit residential housing.

State Government. Not surprisingly, if you seek to practice accounting, law, medicine, or the like, you must be licensed by your state; but the requirement for a license is not limited to highly educated professionals. The range of required licenses and permits at the state or local level can be extensive and surprising. Each of the following activities and more may require government permission: selling insurance, selling real estate, cutting hair, repairing automobiles, making sewer connections, conducting auctions, operating vending machines, performing electrical installations, selling gasoline, selling cars, driving a bus, providing day care, selling hearing aids, and hauling stone.

Depending on the nature of the business, an increasingly important concern at the state level is in meeting environmental and health regulations. If your business deals with hazardous waste, waste water, or air pollutants, you will need to be concerned with state, as well as federal, standards. In any business involving food preparation, a state license or permit will be required and regular inspections will follow. If you employ others in your business, you will need to be concerned with state regulations, if any, dealing with minimum wages, hours, child labor, safety, and so forth.

Federal Government. Most small business activities do not require federal licenses or permits of any kind. However, some exceptions should be noted. Business involving investment advice, television, radio, meat products, drugs, tobacco, alcohol, and firearms all require federal government permission. Of course, the federal government's regulatory role in business is enormous and ranges from environmental protection to labor laws to job safety. Other portions of this text are devoted to those matters.

C. *Taxes*

Local. Many communities and counties impose property taxes on buildings, land, and, in some instances, the fixtures, equipment, and furniture used in businesses. Many also impose a local sales tax, and some, especially larger cities, have levied income taxes.

State. Taxes at the state level on businesses can take many forms, but new businesses involved in retailing will need to seek a state sales tax permit. Thus, businesses serve as collection agents for acquiring state revenue. In most states a new business will also need to register to pay state income taxes.

use taxes. Normally, taxes imposed on the use, storage, or consumption of tangible personal property bought outside of the state imposing the taxes.
excise taxes. Taxes imposed at both the state and federal levels on the sale of particular commodities; especially, alcohol, tobacco, and gasoline.
unemployment taxes. Federal and state (most) taxes paid by employers as a percentage of the total payroll for the purpose of funding benefits for those who have lost their jobs.
workers' compensation. State statutory system providing fixed recoveries for injuries and illnesses sustained in the course of employment. Under the system, workers need not establish fault on the part of the employer.
Employer Identification Number. Number issued to employer by federal and state governments for the purpose of record keeping associated with income and social security tax collections.
self-employment tax. A social security tax on people who are self-employed.

In addition, **use taxes, excise taxes,** alcohol/cigarette taxes, fuel taxes, and property taxes are often imposed at the state level. Businesses are also required to assist in collecting a variety of personnel taxes. In general, employers must withhold state income taxes from employees' wages. To assist workers who have lost their jobs, employers must pay **unemployment taxes** based on the business's payroll. In almost all states, businesses must make a financial contribution, usually in the form of payments to an insurance policy, by which workers are paid (**workers' compensation**) if injured on the job.

Federal. In starting a new business, you must secure an **Employer Identification Number** (EIN) from the Internal Revenue Service. Three categories of federal taxes will apply to your new business: (1) income tax, (2) self-employment tax, and (3) employment taxes. Some income tax issues were discussed earlier in this chapter. As noted, the choice of business structure (proprietorship, partnership, corporation, or hybrid) depends in considerable part on tax considerations. The **self-employment tax** is paid by sole proprietors and partners and serves as a social security tax on people who are self-employed.

For those operating businesses with employees, a trio of additional employment taxes must be addressed. The employer must withhold federal income taxes from employees' pay. The employer must both withhold the employee's share of social security taxes and pay the employer's share of those social security taxes as provided for under the Federal Insurance Contributions Act (FICA). Finally, the employer must pay the federal unemployment tax (FUTA) as part of the federal/state system of unemployment compensation for those laid off from work.[2]

III. Operating a Partnership

Having examined the primary options in structuring your new business, let's turn now to a closer look at partnership law and the actual operation of a partnership.

A critical initial step lies in providing for the partners' rights and obligations. If those are not specified in the partnership agreement, the general provisions of the UPA will control. The controlling principle is that the partners owe each other and the partnership the utmost in good faith and loyalty. Theirs is a *fiduciary* relationship and, as such, a variety of rights and duties emerge.

Management Authority. Broadly, each partner acts as a general manager for the enterprise. Absent an understanding to the contrary, each shares equally in decision making. Normally, the majority rules, but special decisions such as admitting a new partner or changing the nature of the business require unanimous consent.

Partners always have right of access to the books and the right to copy them, and under the UPA, they can demand a formal *accounting* in which, if need be, a court will supervise a review of the partnership records and books. This situation might arise, for example, when one of the partners has been wrongfully excluded from partnership business. Finally, each partner has the right to assign her or his partnership interest to another. The **assignee** is entitled to a share of the profits but does not become a partner without consent of the other partners.

assignee. A person to whom an assignment is made.

Management Obligations. Each partner has a variety of duties that are to be fulfilled within the spirit of the fiduciary relationship including:

1. A general duty to serve the partnership.
2. A duty to reveal information pertinent to the operation of the partnership.

3. A duty to exercise reasonable skill and prudence.
4. A duty to maintain confidentiality.
5. A duty to pay other partners for expenditures made on behalf of the partnership and for liabilities other partners incurred while working for the partnership.
6. A duty not to exceed the authority granted by the partnership.

A partner's duties extend beyond the six listed here. For example, what happens if you have entered an accounting partnership with some old pals from school, but you decide to serve some clients on your own outside the partnership framework? In fact, you have a duty not to compete against the partnership. Have you done so? The case that follows examines the complexities of the duty not to compete.

What happens if you have entered an accounting partnership with some old pals from school, but you decide to serve some clients on your own outside the partnership framework?

CASE

Veale v. Rose

657 S.W.2d 834
(Texas Ct. of App. 1983)

Facts

Paul Veale, Sr., Paul Veale, Jr., Gary Gibson, James Parker, and Larry Rose were partners in an accounting firm. The written partnership agreement listed the general duties of the partners and expressly recognized that Veale, Sr., and Rose had other business commitments. All the partners could pursue other business so long as those activities did not conflict with the partnership practice or materially interfere with the partners' duties. While a partner with Veale et al., Rose performed accounting work for Right Away Foods and Ed Payne and, in both instances, was personally compensated for that work. Rose's partners claimed that he owed them a share of that compensation in that he had competed with the firm in violation of the partnership agreement. The jury concluded that Rose had not competed with the partnership. The partners appealed.

* * *

Chief Justice Nye

The partnership agreement between Rose and the appellants provided in part:

> "Except with the expressed approval of the other partners as to each specific instance, no partner shall perform any public accounting services or engage in the practice of public accounting other than for and on behalf of this partnership."

Partners may be said to occupy a fiduciary relationship toward one another which requires of them the utmost degree of good faith and honesty in dealing with one another. Breaches of a partner's duty not to compete with the partnership are compensable at law by awarding to the injured partners their proportionate shares of the profits wrongfully acquired by the offending partner.

It is undisputed that while a partner of Paul G. Veale and Company, Rose rendered accounting services for Right Away Foods for which he billed and received payment personally. It is also undisputed that the partnership did not share in the proceeds of these private billings. It was

Continued

Continued

established that Rose was an officer and shareholder in Right Away, but that the compensation Rose received for his accounting services was not received in that capacity. There was some testimony from which the jury could have inferred that the work which Rose did for Right Away Foods for which he was paid (personally) was of a type which did not require the services of a CPA. However, Rose himself admitted as such on his letterhead. He also admitted that there was no reason why he could not have rendered the same services to Right Away Foods as a partner in the accounting firm. At least one of the other partners, Parker, testified that he knew of other public accounting firms which performed the types of services in question. In fact, in regard to services in connection with mergers and acquisitions, he indicated that he was unaware of any required forms that are not prepared by public accounting firms. The preponderance of all of the evidence clearly establishes that Rose had, in fact, performed accounting services for Right Away Foods while a partner of Paul G. Veale and Company, in competition with the partnership. The jury's answer in this respect was in error.

The record reveals that Rose also admitted that he performed accounting services for various enterprises owned by Mr. Ed Payne during his tenure as a partner at Veale for which he billed and received payment personally. There is no question that those services were public accounting services. His later testimony that he performed these services, in effect, after hours, or in addition to his duties to the partnership, is of no value in light of the obligations imposed by the partnership agreement and by the common understaning of the term "competition."

Reversed and remanded.

Questions

1. *a.* Why was Rose's work for Right Away Foods and Payne considered a violation of the partnership agreement?
   b. Does a partner not have "after hours" time, the time that Rose says he used in working for Payne?
2. Could Rose operate a gas station, for instance without violating the partnership agreement?

principal. In agency law, one under whose direction an agent acts and for whose benefit that agent acts.

agent. A person entrusted by a principal to act on behalf of that principal; one who is authorized to carry out the business of another.

joint liability. Liability of a group of persons in which, if one of these persons is sued, he can insist that the other liable parties be joined to the suit as codefendants, so that all must be sued collectively.

A. Third Parties and the Partnership

Technically, a partnership produces a **principal–agent** relationship (see Chapter 6), the partnership being the principal, the partners the agents. Therefore, each partner's interactions with third parties (people outside the partnership) can have important implications for the partnership. Broadly, those implications can be discussed in the context of contracts, torts, and crimes.

Contracts. Where a partner had *actual or apparent authority* to enter a contract, the partnership becomes responsible for that contract. Under the Uniform Partnership Act, partners are **jointly liable** for the contractual obligations of the partnership. Thus, for a third party to successfully sue a partnership on a breach of contract claim, each of the partners must be joined to the suit. Otherwise, neither the individual partners nor the partnership can be held responsible. Since it is often difficult to sue every partner, particularly when more than one state is involved, some states have modified that joint liability rule in various ways.

Torts. Ordinarily, where a negligent **tort** is committed in the scope of partnership business, the partnership and the partners are **jointly and severally liable** for the harm to third parties. That means the injured party may sue all of the partners jointly or one or more of the partners severally for the entire amount. The partner who was actually responsible for the tort is required to **indemnify** the partners and partnership for whatever damages they may have paid. Normally, the partnership is not responsible for the intentional torts of partners.

tort. A civil wrong not arising from a contract.

joint and several liability. Liability of a group of persons in which the plaintiff may sue all members of the group collectively or one or more individually for the entire amount.

indemnify. Reimburse one who has suffered a loss.

Crimes. In general, partners are not liable for the criminal conduct of their copartners. Unless partners participate in a crime or authorize it, they do not manifest the intent that is required for the finding of criminal conduct. Historically, a partnership itself could not be liable for a crime because it was not considered to be a legal entity; however, many states have passed legislation treating partnerships as persons in the eyes of the law, thus opening them to the possibility of being responsible for criminal conduct when a partner commits a crime.

Ethics/Public Policy Questions

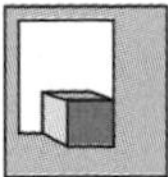

As noted, partnerships are now sometimes held criminally liable. The same can be the case for corporations. Philosopher Peter French argues that corporations are more than "legal persons," they are "moral persons" with all the moral responsibilities and duties that attend personhood. More specifically, he says that corporations have an internal decision-making system that permits them to form the intent that is necessary to hold persons responsible for criminal conduct. Could we say the same of a partnership? Is a partnership a moral person whom we should hold morally responsible in the event of criminal conduct? Should we differentiate between the moral responsibilities of partnerships and corporations? Can a partnership commit manslaughter or murder? Explain.

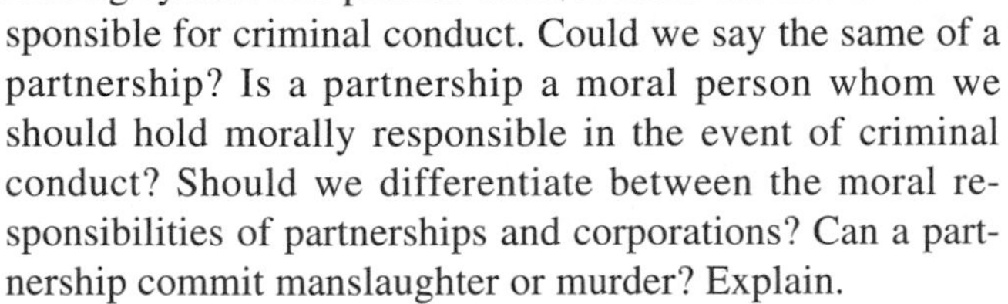

Is a partnership a moral person whom we should hold morally responsible in the event of criminal conduct?

B. Termination

The termination of a partnership consists of two steps: dissolution and winding up. **Dissolution** occurs when a partner, due to death, bankruptcy, retirement, and so forth, ceases to be a part of the conduct of the partnership's business. **Winding up** involves the collection and distribution of the partnership's assets; that is, the liquidation of the partnership's assets.

dissolution. In partnership law, the change in the relation of the partners caused by any partner ceasing to be associated with the carrying on of the business.

winding up. In partnership and corporation law, the orderly liquidation of the business's assets.

Profile Perspective: Let's return to Larry and Barbara LaPlume, the couple who opened several small businesses in their local shopping mall. What happens if they established a partnership to operate their various businesses only to find that though their marriage was sound, their working relationship was ineffectual?

Dissolution. The terms of a wisely prepared partnership agreement can dictate the course of action in a business. For example, the agreement might provide that the partnership would continue for 10 years or until $500,000 in assets had been accumulated or until either party chose to withdraw. On the other hand, regardless of what the agreement says, a partnership can be dissolved at any time if the partners concur. Alternatively, any partner could unilaterally withdraw from the partnership even if doing so would violate the partnership agreement. The withdrawing partner remains entitled to his or her share of the value of the partnership minus any damages caused.

Profile Perspective: Could one of the LaPlumes force the other out of the partnership?

If the partnership agreement includes an expulsion clause and other partners, if any, agree, a partner can be expelled based upon negligence, poor productivity, or even incompatibility. In the absence of an expulsion clause, a court order would be required. Broadly, the court would require evidence that the party to be expelled is incapable of performance (e.g., adjudicated insanity), is guilty of misconduct, or is rendering the partnership commercially impractical. Normally, something more concrete than a mere allegation of laziness, for example, would be necessary.

Profile Perspective: What happens if one of the LaPlumes should die or retire?

Since a deceased or retired partner can no longer carry out the business, a dissolution has occurred, but often it is only technical in nature (see "Continuation" below). A partnership is also dissolved when a partner is declared bankrupt or when it becomes unlawful for the partnership or a partner to continue in business (as where the partners own a bar, the liquor license is issued to the partnership, and one of the partners commits a crime that disqualifies him from eligibility for a liquor license).

In most cases, upon dissolution all affected third parties must be notified. If a third person has extended credit to the partnership, that person must receive actual notice of the dissolution. All other third persons may be notified by newspaper announcement or other reasonable means. Failure to provide notice might leave the partnership liable for unauthorized contracts or debts.

Winding Up. A partnership agreement may specify which partners have the right to commence the winding-up process. Otherwise, with limited exceptions, each partner has equal winding-up rights. During winding up, the partnership's assets are liquidated, debts are paid, accounts are collected, and all other business is completed. The proceeds from the liquidation are then distributed according to the following order:

1. Claims of creditors who are not members of the partnership.
2. Claims of creditors who are themselves partners (that is, partners who loaned money to the partnership).
3. Claims of partners who had made contributions to the partnership's working capital.
4. Profits to the partners.

If the partnership has suffered a loss, each partner must bear the loss according to the terms of their agreement or, if no agreement, in the same ratio as profit sharing. However, many complications may arise in this area.

Conflict in Winding Up. In those instances in which a partnership's assets are distributed, termination occurs automatically, but the winding-up process sometimes leads to conflict before termination is achieved. The case that follows demonstrates those problems as well as some of the practical strategies a court may employ to wind up a troubled partnership.

CASE

Paciaroni and Cassidy v. Crane

408 A.2d 946 (Del. Ct. Chan. 1979)

Facts

Richard Paciaroni (50 percent), James Cassidy (25 percent), and James Crane (25 percent) were partners in a harness-racing horse, Black Ace, which was considered the 4th- to 6th-best pacer in the United States in 1979. No formal partnership agreement existed, but it was understood that Crane would train the horse and that the other partners would be consulted on all major decisions although their practice was to accept Crane's judgment because of his acknowledged expertise as a successful trainer.

In 1979, Black Ace had won nearly $97,000 with seven races remaining, including two prestigious, large-purse events. Black Ace had developed a ringbone injury. An expert veterinarian examined the horse and recommended a treatment that Crane refused to implement. An alternate treatment was employed, and in subsequent races Black Ace became difficult to control and actually fell in one of those races. The partnership became strained as Paciaroni and Cassidy apparently blamed Crane's refusal to impose the advised treatment as the cause of the horse's problem. Crane then indicated that the partnership should cease, but he continued to operate as trainer. Paciaroni and Cassidy then directed Crane to turn the horse over to another trainer. He did so, but kept the eligibility papers without which Black Ace could not be raced. Paciaroni and Cassidy sued Crane and asked the court to appoint a receiver to handle the partnership's affairs including racing decisions for the remainder of the season, at which point the horse was to be sold. Before the court entered a decision, Black Ace raced three more times and won nearly $50,000.

* * *

[Judge] Brown

I think it is clear that a dissolution has been accomplished by the express will of the partners. As noted, the partnership was for no definite term and it was not confined to any particular undertaking. As such, it could be dissolved by the express will of any partner.

Following their meeting in July after Black Ace fell in the Meadowlands race, Crane made it clear that he wanted their partnership relation as owners of the horse to be terminated. Shortly thereafter, Paciaroni and Cassidy responded with their July 26 telegram to Crane, the content of which was as follows:

> Mr. and Mrs. J. Cassidy and Mr. and Mrs. R. Paciaroni together representing 75 percent ownership of the 3-year-old colt Black Ace hereby notify you that you are relieved of your employment as trainer of Black Ace effective immediately following the Gaines Pace at Vernon Downs, Saturday, July 28, 1979, and you are to turn over custody of said colt in good and sound condition at that time along with all necessary papers and equipment to person or persons representing Cassidy and Paciaroni.

While it might seem that the telegram was carefully worded so as to appear to relieve Crane of his duties as trainer, the fact that it also says that he is to surrender the horse to persons representing Paciaroni and Cassidy clearly indicates, I think, that Paciaroni and Cassidy had decided to go their separate way, without Crane. To the extent that there could be any doubt, it was certainly

Continued

Continued

resolved as of the time that Crane petitioned this Court for the appointment of a receiver to sell the horse. However, I am of the view that the partnership was placed in a state of dissolution by the express will of the partners at least by July 26, 1979.

Having reached this conclusion, where does it leave matters? Obviously, the partnership is now in the winding up stage. But, how is it to be accomplished here, given the unusual nature of the primary partnership asset?

All three partners agree that the horse must be sold in order to wind up partnership affairs. The only dispute is as to when he must be sold and what is to be done with him in the meantime.

* * *

[Crane argues] that there is a prevailing custom in the harness racing business that a trainer who also owns an interest in a horse, even though it be less than a majority interest, has the right to train and control the racing of the horse so long as his ownership interest continues.

* * *

However, when the basis for the testimony offered by all of [Crane's] witnesses is examined closely, it reveals a common flaw. All state, in one form or another, that such an industry custom exists because they can recall of no situation where the majority owners have taken a horse away from a trainer-minority owner and given it to another trainer without the trainer-owner's consent.

While this may be completely accurate as a matter of fact, it does not necessarily establish a custom or usage that the majority owners could not make such a change over the trainer-owners's objection should they want to do so. . . Thus, I hold that for the purpose of this proceeding, it has not been established by the evidence presented here.

Having thus disposed of Crane's contention that he has an absolute right to control Black Ace during the winding up process by virtue of the partnership agreement, I turn to the argument of Paciaroni and Cassidy that they have a similar right by virtue of constituting the majority interests. This argument I also reject. I do so because [Delaware Code] §1518(8) permits a majority vote to decide any "difference arising as to ordinary matters connected with the partnership business." Under the exceptional circumstances of this case I do not view the difference between the parties to be one which has arisen in the ordinary course of partnership business. Quite the contrary. . . Accordingly, I conclude that Paciaroni and Cassidy have no statutory right to wind up affairs simply because they can out vote Crane.

Thus, if neither side has right to control the winding-up process under the positions they have taken, where does this leave us? . . . I conclude that both sides to this controversy have sought a winding up of partnership affairs by the Court: Crane by asking for a receiver to control the horse and to bring about his sale, and Paciaroni and Cassidy by seeking authority to race the horse in the remaining seven stake races for which he is eligible in an effort to accumulate additional winnings for the partnership and to hopefully increase his value for purposes of sale in the fall. This being so, what authority does the Court possess?

To begin with, there is no power to compel one side to the controversy to buy out the interests of the other. . .

Moreover, it is generally accepted that once dissolution occurs, the partnership continues only to the extent necessary to close out affairs and complete transactions begun but not then finished. It is not generally contemplated that new business will be generated. . . However, in Delaware, there have been exceptions to this.

* * *

Continued

Continued

[W]here, because of the nature of the partnership business, a better price upon final liquidation is likely to be obtained by the temporary continuation of the business, it is permissible, during the winding up process, to have the business continue to the degree necessary to preserve or enhance its value upon liquidation, provided that such continuation is done in good faith. . . .

The business purpose of the partnership was to own and race Black Ace for profit. . . He has the ability to be competitive with the top pacers in the country. He is currently "racing fit" according to the evidence. He has at best only seven more races to go over a period of the next six weeks, after which time there are established horse sales at which he can be disposed of to the highest bidder. The purse money for these remaining stake races is substantial. The fact that he could possibly sustain a disabling injury during the six-week period appears to be no greater than it was when the season commenced. . . And the remaining stake races are races in which all three partners originally intended that he would compete, if able.

The alternative to racing on through the remaining stakes would be to turn Black Ace out to pasture until he can be placed in a suitable sale . . .

Under these circumstances, I conclude that the winding up of the partnership affairs should include the right to race Black Ace in some or all of the remaining 1979 stake races for which he is now eligible. The final question, then, is who shall be in charge of racing him.

On this point, I rule in favor of Paciaroni and Cassidy. They may, on behalf of the partnership, continue to race the horse . . .

[Crane] does have a monetary interest in the partnership assets which must be protected . . . Accordingly, I make the following ruling.

(1) As a part of winding up the affairs of the partnership, Paciaroni and Cassidy may act as the liquidating partners and may cause Black Ace to race in some or all of the seven remaining stake races, provided, however, that they shall first post security or corporate surety in the sum of $100,000 so as to secure to Crane his share of the value of the partnership asset . . .

(2) If Paciaroni and Cassidy are unable or unwilling to meet this condition, then they shall forego the right to act as liquidating partners. In that event, each party, within seven days, shall submit to the Court the names of two persons who they feel qualified, and who they know to be willing, to act as receiver for the winding up of partnership affairs . . .

(3) In the event no suitable person can be found to act as receiver, or in the event that the Court should deem it unwise to appoint any person from the names so submitted, then the Court reserves the power to terminate any further racing by the horse and to require that he simply be maintained and cared for until such time as he can be sold as a part of the final liquidation of the partnership.

Judgment for Paciaroni and Cassidy.

Questions

1. Explain the court's reasoning in ruling that none of the partners had the authority to control the horse during the winding up of the affairs of the partnership.
2. *a.* In your view, did the court intrude unnecessarily into the affairs of the partnership? Explain.
   b. In your view, did the court achieve justice in this case? Explain.
3. Yoder and Hooper manufactured and sold frozen yogurt under a formal partnership. They converted the partnership to a corporation. Yoder claimed that Hooper caused all of the corporate stock to be issued to Hooper and that Hooper received a salary from the business, all without Yoder's consent. Yoder sued and a trial court found for him. The Colorado Supreme Court ruled that the effect of incorporation was to dissolve the partnership.
   a. Was the partnership terminated?
   b. Did Hooper breach his fiduciary duties with respect to Yoder and the partnership? Explain. [See *Hooper* v. *Yoder,* 737 P.2d 852 (Col. S.Ct. 1987).]

Continuation. Following dissolution, the partners may want to capitalize on accrued goodwill and continue the partnership rather than proceeding to termination. The partnership agreement or a separate agreement may provide continuation rules including methods for settling accounts. If not, the process continues according to the UPA. Most commonly when a partner has died or retired, the remaining partners must expeditiously settle with the estate or the departing partner in an amount equal to the value of that partner's interest in the partnership. Then bookkeeping changes are entered, and a new partnership emerges. To ensure ease of continuity in the event of a partner's death, the partnership may purchase insurance on the lives of all of the partners, or the individual partners may buy insurance on each other. Upon death, those insurance funds can then be used to pay for the deceased partner's interest in the firm.

IV. Operating a Corporation

Profile Perspective: Refer again to Larry and Barbara LaPlume. We earlier considered the possibility that they would want to structure their several businesses in a partnership framework. Now think about the possibility that incorporation would be the better vehicle for their purposes. Why might that be the case? Refer back to those considerations that we offered earlier in the chapter regarding the advantages and disadvantages of the various business forms. Then turn your attention to the materials in this section that describe the actual operation of a corporation. Think about whether the operating requirements noted hereafter would make sense for the LaPlumes as they do for larger enterprises.

A. Directors

shareholders. Those owning stock in a corporation.

The **shareholders,** the owners of the corporation, elect the members of the *board of directors.* Directors who are employees of the corporation, usually officers, are *inside directors.* Boards also commonly include so-called *outside directors* who have no employment relationship with the corporation, and are chosen for the board because of their expertise, influence, and other reasons. Ordinarily, the board—especially in larger firms—does not directly engage in the day-to-day management of the corporation. Rather, it appoints *officers* (discussed below) for that purpose. Broadly, the directors are responsible for setting corporate policy and, so far as possible, ensuring the success and integrity of the operation. Consequently, they may establish a strategic plan, confer with top management, monitor the CEO, and so forth. They are also responsible for such critical decisions as issuing stock, setting dividends, removing officers, and amending bylaws. Typically, the directors establish committees, from among their number, to more efficiently manage the corporation's affairs. For example, a compensation committee would review and set pay, stock options, and the like for top officers, and an executive committee would act for the board when it is not in session.

Directors are elected for the period of time specified in the bylaws, often one year. They meet regularly, although that may vary from once per year to once per month to some other schedule entirely. Each director has one vote and a quorum is required before action can be taken. In over half the states and under the terms of the **Model Business Corporation Act (MBCA),** boards may take action without actually meeting if all of the directors agree in writing to that action.

Model Business Corporation Act (MBCA). Drafted by legal experts, the MBCA is designed to improve corporate law and to serve as a model for state legislatures in drafting their corporate laws.

B. Officers

The MBCA requires that a corporation include at least one officer who is responsible for those duties that would normally fall to a corporate secretary. Officers ordinarily are appointed by the board in accord with the bylaws, and they commonly consist of a president, one or more vice presidents, a secretary, and a treasurer. They are responsible for carrying out the policies mandated by the board and for overseeing the day-to-day business of the corporation. Officers can be removed from their positions by vote of the board.

Unlike directors, officers are agents of the corporation and are subject to agency law (see Chapter 6), which means that the corporation is bound by the actions of its officers when they are acting within the scope of their authority. Broadly, officers have **express authority** as conferred by the bylaws or by the Board of Directors, and **implied authority** that allows those actions reasonably necessary to accomplish their express duties. Normally, the officers have no personal liability on contracts properly entered on behalf of the corporation, but as we will see below, both directors and officers are liable for their own torts and crimes even if committed on behalf of the corporation.

express authority. Corporate officers' powers as expressed in the by-laws or conferred by the Board of Directors.

implied authority. Corporate officers' powers to take actions that are reasonably necessary to achieve their express duties.

C. Duties of Directors and Officers

The MBCA, state legislatures, and the courts have build an array of expectations for those who govern corporations. Broadly, directors and officers have a fiduciary duty to the corporation requiring them generally to operate with due care and loyalty.

Due Care. Directors and officers must operate prudently and honestly. Failure to do so makes them liable for losses to the corporation. The general standard of **due care and diligence** requires that officers and directors act in good faith and in the manner that a reasonably prudent person, similarly situated, would employ (see accompanying box, "MBCA Section 8.30").

due care and diligence. Corporate officers and directors must act in good faith and in a prudent manner.

Perhaps you aspire someday to be an officer or director in a corporation. In that role, you would seek, as we have discussed, to build that business. Suppose in making that effort you made a bad decision; perhaps you purchased a smaller company that proved not to be a wise investment or you allowed a subordinate a great deal of latitude in operating part of the business, and he or she hurt company performance. Have you violated the duty of due care and diligence?

The courts and the framers of the MBCA have recognized the uncertainties and risks involved in corporate decision making, and they have understood that most of us would not want to occupy roles of authority if we were subject to liability for every error. As a result, the **business judgment rule** was developed. It protects officers and directors from second-guessing in the courts so long as those officers and directors have acted in a reasonably prudent manner, that is, no bad faith, fraud, or breach of duty was involved. Bad judgment, in and of itself, would not hold a director or officer liable for a decision. That liability is possible, however. The Delaware Supreme Court, in the very influential 1985 *Van Gorkom* case, held directors liable for approving a corporate acquisition at $55 per share when they did so after a meeting of only two hours with little evidence offered and little effort made to establish the market value of the company. Thus, the directors had failed to satisfy the standards of the business judgment rule.[3] The famous case that follows demonstrates the deference the courts have shown to the judgment of officers and directors.

business judgment rule. A rule protecting business managers from liability for making bad decisions when they have acted prudently and in good faith.

MBCA Section 8.30

(*a*) A director shall discharge his duties as a director, including his duties as a member of a committee:

(1) in good faith;

(2) with the care an ordinarily prudent person in a like position would exercise under similar circumstances; and

(3) in a manner he reasonably believes to be in the best interests of the corporation.

CASE

Shlensky v. Wrigley

237 N.E.2d 776 (Ill. App. Ct. 1968)

Facts

Plaintiff Shlensky, a minority stockholder in the Chicago Cubs major league baseball team, sued the corporation's directors on the grounds of mismanagement and negligence because of their refusal to install lights at Wrigley Field, then the only major league stadium without lights. One of the defendant directors, Philip K. Wrigley, owner of 80 percent of the stock, allegedly objected to lights because of his personal opinion that "baseball is a 'daytime sport' and that the installation of lights and night baseball games will have a deteriorating effect upon the surrounding neighborhood." Allegedly, Wrigley also said that he was not interested in whether the Cubs would benefit financially from lights. Allegedly, the other members of the board of directors deferred to Wrigley on this matter and allowed him to dominate the board.

Shlensky claimed that lights would maximize attendance and revenue. The Cubs, in the years 1961–65, lost money from direct baseball operations. Shlensky attributed those losses to poor attendance and argued that without lights the losses would continue. Shlensky's evidence indicated that the Cubs drew greater attendance on the road than at home and that Chicago White Sox night games during the week drew better than the Cubs' daytime games. Shlensky sought damages and an order requiring the installation of lights and the scheduling of night games. He lost at the trial level and appealed to the Illinois Appellate Court.

* * *

Justice Sullivan

The question on appeal is whether plaintiff's amended complaint states a cause of action. It is plaintiff's position that fraud, illegality, and conflict of interest are not the only bases for a stockholder's derivative action against the directors. Contrariwise, defendants argue that the courts will not step in and interfere with honest business judgment of the directors unless there is a showing of fraud, illegality, or conflict of interest.

The cases in this area are numerous . . . However, the courts have pronounced certain ground rules . . . The court in *Wheeler* v. *The Pullman Iron & Steel Co.,* said:

> It is, however, fundamental in the law of corporations that the majority of its stockholders shall control the policy of the corporation, and regulate and govern the lawful exercise of its franchise and business. . . Every one purchasing or subscribing for stock in a corporation impliedly agrees that he will be bound by the acts and proceedings done or sanctioned by a majority of the shareholders, or by the agents of the corporation duly chosen by such majority, within the scope of the powers conferred by the charter, and courts of equity will not undertake to control the policy or business methods of a corporation, although it may be seen that a wiser policy might be adopted and the business more successful if other methods were pursued. The majority of shares of its stock, or the agents by the holders thereof lawfully chosen, must be permitted to control the business of the corporation in their discretion, when not in violation of its charter or some public law, or corruptly and fraudulently subversive of the rights and interests of the corporation or of a shareholder.

* * *

Continued

Continued

Plaintiff in the instant case argues that the directors are acting for reasons unrelated to the financial interest and welfare of the Cubs. However, we are not satisfied that the motives assigned to Philip K. Wrigley, and through him to the other directors, are contrary to the best interests of the corporation and the stockholders. For example, it appears to us that the effect on the surrounding neighborhood might well be considered by a director who was considering the patrons who would or would not attend the games if the park were in a poor neighborhood. Furthermore, the long-run interest of the corporation in its property value at Wrigley Field might demand all efforts to keep the neighborhood from deteriorating. By these thoughts we do not mean to say that we have decided that the decision of the directors was a correct one. That is beyond our jurisdiction and ability. We are merely saying that the decision is one properly before directors and the motives alleged in the amended complaint showed no fraud, illegality, or conflict of interest in their making of that decision.

While all the courts do not insist that one or more of the three elements must be present for a stockholder's derivative action to lie, nevertheless we feel that unless the conduct of the defendants at least borders on one of the elements, the courts should not interfere. The trial court in the instant case acted properly in dismissing plaintiff's amended complaint.

We feel that plantiff's amended complaint was also defective in failing to allege damage to the corporation. . . There is no allegation that the night games played by the other nineteen teams enhanced their financial position or that the profits, if any, of those teams were directly related to the number of night games scheduled. There is an allegation that the installation of lights and scheduling of night games in Wrigley Field would have resulted in large amounts of additional revenues and incomes from increased attendance and related sources of income. Further, the cost of installation of lights, funds for which are allegedly readily available by financing, would be more than offset and recaptured by increased revenues. However, no allegation is made that there will be a net benefit to the corporation from such action, considering all increased costs.

Plaintiff claims that the losses of defendant corporation are due to poor attendance at home games. However, it appears from the amended complaint, taken as a whole, that factors other than attendance affect the net earnings or losses. For example, in 1962, attendance at home and road games decreased appreciably as compared with 1961, and yet the loss from direct baseball operation and of the whole corporation was considerably less.

The record shows that plaintiff did not feel he could allege that the increased revenues would be sufficient to cure the corporate deficit. The only cost plaintiff was at all concerned with was that of installation of lights. No mention was made of operation and maintenance of the lights or other possible increases in operating costs of night games and we cannot speculate as to what other factors might influence the increase or decrease of profits if the Cubs were to play night home games.

* * *

Finally, we do not agree with plaintiff's contention that failure to follow the example of the other major league clubs in scheduling night games constituted negligence. Plaintiff made no allegation that these teams' night schedules were profitable or that the purpose for which night baseball had been undertaken was fulfilled. Furthermore, it cannot be said that directors, even those of corporations that are losing money, must follow the lead of the other corporations in the field. Directors are elected for their business capabilities and judgment and the courts cannot require them to forego their judgment because of the decisions of directors of other companies. Courts may not decide these questions in the absence of a clear showing of dereliction of duty on the part of the specific directors and mere failure to "follow the crowd" is not such a dereliction.

Affirmed.

* * *

Continued

Continued

Afterword—Duty of Care

The aforementioned *Van Gorkom* decision and an increasing reluctance by insurance companies to insure officers and directors caused some worried outside directors to leave corporate boards. As a result, some states have changed their duty of care standard such that proof of *intentional misconduct* or *gross negligence* would be required to establish a breach.

Questions

1. What was the issue in the Chicago Cubs case?
2. The Chicago Cubs added lights in 1988. How is it that the board of directors was meeting its duty of due care in the 60s by not erecting lights and was also meeting its duty of care in the 80s by doing so?
3. As noted, some states have changed their laws to offer more protection to corporate directors by requiring a showing of broadly, intentional misconduct or gross negligence. Do you favor that move toward enhanced protection? Explain.
4. Charles Pritchard, Sr., was CEO and director of Pritchard & Baird Intermediaries Corporation. His wife, Lillian, and his two sons, Charles, Jr., and William, also served on the board of directors. Pritchard & Baird was a successful company although Pritchard, Sr., had engaged in questionable business practices. Charles, Jr., and William began running the company in the late 60s. Charles, Sr., died in 1973. Lillian was never involved in oversight of the corporation. Charles, Jr., and William drained the corporation of over $12 million in what were labeled "shareholder loans" that were never repaid. The corporation went bankrupt. Lillian died in 1978. Creditors of the bankrupt firm sued Lillian's personal estate seeking $10 million and claiming that she was negligent in performing her directorial duties. It was argued that Lillian had been "a simple housewife who served as a director as an accommodation to her husband and sons." Decide this case. Explain. [See *Francis* v. *United Jersey Bank,* 432 A.2d 814 (N.J.S.Ct. 1981).]

Assume you take a job as a purchasing manager for a large manufacturing firm. Would you be breaching your duty of loyalty if you accepted a weekend golfing vacation from a supplier?

Loyalty. Directors and officers owe a fiduciary duty of loyalty to the corporation. The relationship is one of trust and all parties are required by law to act in good faith. Clearly, for example, a corporate officer cannot lawfully sell confidential corporate information or use corporate funds for personal purposes. Assume you take a job as a purchasing manager for a large manufacturing firm. Would you be breaching your duty of loyalty if you accepted a weekend golfing vacation from a supplier? Or what if your role as purchasing manager makes you aware of an extraordinarily good buy on a piece of equipment that you then purchase with your own money and resell at a substantial profit? Or what if you leave the manufacturing firm and set up your own competing business, making use of your former employer's client lists?

Each of these instances seems to suggest a breach of the duty of loyalty and a breach of commonly accepted ethical standards. The golfing vacation raises a *conflict of interest* problem for both you and the supplier. The machinery purchase raises the doctrine of **corporate opportunity,** which generally prohibits managers from taking advantage of business opportunities that should go to their employers. The manager or director should not personally benefit from an opportunity that is closely associated with the employer's line of business. Establishing a competing business, depending upon your contractual

corporate opportunity. A doctrine that prevents corporate officials from personally appropriating an opportunity that belongs to the corporation.

obligations to your former employer, is not in and of itself a breach of the duty of loyalty, but the expropriation of client lists clearly involves the improper use of confidential information and breaches the duty of loyalty.

Liability. Both the corporation itself and its employees are potentially liable for the torts and crimes committed by those employees while conducting corporate business. Under the doctrine of **respondeat superior** (see Chapter 6), the corporation itself is ordinarily responsible for torts committed by its employees so long as the acts in question were performed in the **scope of employment.** Of course, directors, officers, and employees will also bear personal liability for their torts and crimes committed within the scope of employment. However, directors and officers are often indemnified for the cost of any civil or criminal litigation against them; that is, the company chooses to pay attorney fees, settlement costs, judgments, and so forth. Indeed, under the MBCA, directors, officers, and employees must be indemnified when they are fully successful in their litigation. Many corporations purchase liability insurance to cover the litigation costs of directors and officers. The justification for these protective measures is to encourage able people to serve as directors and officers.

respondeat superior. "Let the master respond." Doctrine holding the employer liable for negligent acts committed by an employee while in the course of employment.

scope of employment. Limitation on master's liability to only those torts that a servant commits while "about the master's business."

D. SHAREHOLDERS

Most of us think of shares of corporate stock as investment vehicles, but remember that the purchase of a share makes us an owner of a portion of that company. With that ownership comes certain rights and responsibilities that are broadly outlined in state law and the articles of incorporation. Shares take a variety of forms, but the most common classes are labeled **preferred** and **common shares.** A fundamental difference between the two is that preferred shareholders ordinarily have first claim to dividends and assets upon dissolution (see below). A **dividend,** typically paid in cash or stock, is a distribution of corporate profits to shareholders. Dividends are paid by order of the board of directors and need not be paid each year or on a regular basis. Decisions regarding the payment of dividends are protected by the business judgment rule, although shareholders have occasionally been successful in suing to require a dividend payment.

Shareholder Duties. Broadly, shareholders fulfill three important roles: (1) electing and removing directors, (2) amending the articles of incorporation, and (3) voting on fundamental changes such as mergers with other corporations or selling most of the corporation's assets.

Voting. Shareholder duties are accomplished largely through annual and special meetings. The former are used to conduct ongoing shareholder business, including the election of directors and changes in the articles of incorporation. Special meetings may be needed to accomplish urgent business that cannot wait until the next annual meeting. Urgent business would ordinarily involve a fundamental change such as a board of directors' proposal to buy out another firm. In most cases, only holders of common stocks have voting rights, which normally consist of one vote per share (labeled **straight voting**). To strengthen minority shareholders' voices on the board of directors, **cumulative voting** is either permitted or required in many states. Each shareholder is entitled to one vote times the number of shares held times the number of directors to be elected. Thus, if you own 100 shares in a company and three directors are to be elected, you could cast all of your 300 votes for one candidate or you could split your votes as you wish.

preferred shares. Shares having dividend and liquidation preferences over other classes of shares.

common shares. Most universal type of corporate stock.

dividend. A shareholder's earnings from his or her stock in a corporation.

straight voting. A form of voting for directors that ordinarily permits a shareholder to cast a number of votes equal to the number of shares he or she owns for as many nominees as there are directors to be elected.

cumulative voting. A procedure for voting for directors that permits a shareholder to multiply the number of shares he or she owns by the number of directors to be elected and to cast the resulting total of votes for one or more directors.

As a practical matter, most shareholders, at least in large corporations, do not attend corporate meetings. Rather, they direct another person, via a written authorization labeled a **proxy,** to vote their shares. Often proxies are arranged by management, which writes to shareholders asking them to authorize a particular director or other designated party to serve as the shareholders' proxy. That approach aids management in its efforts to control the direction of the corporation.

proxy. Written permission from a shareholder to others to vote his or her share at a stockholders' meeting.

Shareholder Rights. Given a legitimate purpose, shareholders have the right to inspect the corporation's books and records. In most states, if provided for by the articles of incorporation, a shareholder may have a **preemptive right** to buy a fraction of any new shares issued equal to the fraction of existing shares held by that shareholder. The idea here is to protect existing shareholders if new shares are issued at a price less than the current market price (thus diluting the value of the existing shares) and to permit shareholders to maintain the degree of control in voting and the like that they enjoyed prior to the issuance of the new shares.

preemptive right. A shareholder's option to purchase new issuances of shares in proportion to the shareholder's current ownership of the corporation.

Shareholders also have the right to sue the corporation. They may do so individually or as part of a class action with other shareholders when they believe they have been wronged by the corporation (e.g., a dividend was declared but not paid). The most important form of shareholder litigation is the **derivative suit** when the corporation has been wronged either by outsiders or insiders (directors, officers, managers), but the directors refuse to act. Here shareholders are allowed to sue on behalf of the corporation and any recovery ordinarily goes to the corporation. The *Shlensky* case that we looked at earlier, in which the Chicago Cubs board of directors was sued for failing to install lights at Wrigley Field, is an example of a derivative action.

derivative suit. A lawsuit by a stockholder on behalf of the corporation where the corporation declines to act to protect the organization's rights against the conduct of an officer, director, or outsider.

Shareholder Liability. As mentioned, a great virtue of the corporate form is the idea of limited liability, meaning that in the event of corporate failure the financial responsibility lies with the corporation and the investors' losses are limited to the amount invested in the corporation. Investors' personal assets cannot be reached. Some exceptions, however, can be of importance. For example, the business may never have been properly incorporated, or its stock may have been sold for inadequate consideration **(watered stock)**. But the most important exception to the limited liability doctrine is the notion of **piercing the corporate veil;** that is, under some circumstances, the shareholders can be held personally liable when the corporation is unable to pay its obligations. For instance, the corporate veil of limited liability can be pierced if a business is started with so little capital that it is obvious to the courts that the sole purpose of incorporating was for the shareholders to escape liability for their actions.

watered stock. Inadequate consideration received for stock.

piercing the corporate veil. Holding a shareholder responsible for acts of a corporation due to a shareholder's domination and improper use of the corporation.

Suppose a corporation with little or no capital was established to supply propane gas to civic arenas, theaters, and so on. This business kept no insurance, had no assets, and would have nothing to lose should a tank explode, killing or injuring numerous people. Although its owners might think themselves to be insulated from liability and the corporation to be **judgment proof,** a court might pierce the corporate veil and hold the owners personally liable on the theory that the gross undercapitalization of their business so abused the corporate privileges granted them in their charter that they should be denied limited liability.

judgment proof. Describes those against whom money judgments will have no effect because they are insolvent or their assets are beyond the reach of the court.

The case that follows examines whether a bar's corporate veil should be pierced following a traffic accident involving an intoxicated driver.

CASE

Baatz v. Arrow Bar

452 N.W.2d 138 (S.D. 1990)

Facts

Kenny and Peggy Baatz were seriously injured in 1982 when Roland McBride negligently drove his car across the centerline and struck them on their motorcycle. McBride was uninsured and apparently was judgment proof. Baatz claims that the Arrow Bar served alcohol to McBride prior to the accident while he was already intoxicated. Edmond and LaVella Neuroth incorporated the bar and were its shareholders. The bar was uninsured. Baatz sought to pierce the corporate veil and hold the Neuroths personally liable. The trial court found for the defendants. Baatz appealed to the South Dakota Supreme Court.

* * *

Justice Sabers

Baatz claims that . . . the corporate veil should be pierced, leaving the Neuroths, as the shareholders of the corporation, individually liable. A corporation shall be considered a separate legal entity until there is *sufficient reason* to the contrary. When continued recognition of a corporation as a separate legal entity would "produce injustices and inequitable consequences," then a court has sufficient reason to pierce the corporate veil. Factors that indicate injustices and inequitable consequences and allow a court to pierce the corporate veil are:

1. fraudulent representation by corporation directors;
2. undercapitalization;
3. failure to observe corporate formalities;
4. absence of corporate records;
5. payment by the corporation of individual obligations; or
6. use of the corporation to promote fraud, injustice, and illegalities.

When the court deems it appropriate to pierce the corporate veil, the corporation and its stockholders will be treated identically.

Baatz advances several arguments to support his claim that the corporate veil of Arrow Bar, Inc., should be pierced, but fails to support them with facts, or misconstrues the facts.

First, Baatz claims that since Edmond and LaVella personally guaranteed corporate obligations, they should also be personally liable to Baatz. However, the personal guarantee of a loan is a contractual agreement and cannot be enlarged to impose tort liability. . .

Baatz also argues that the corporation is simply the alter ego of the Neuroths, and . . . the corporate veil should be pierced. Baatz' discussion of the law is adequate, but he fails to present evidence that would support a decision in his favor in accordance with that law. When an individual treats a corporation "as an instrumentality through which he [is] conducting his personal business," a court may disregard the corporate entity. Baatz fails to demonstrate how the Neuroths were transacting personal business through the corporation. In fact, the evidence indicates the Neuroths treated the corporation separately from their individual affairs.

Baatz next argues that the corporation is undercapitalized. Shareholders must equip a corporation with a reasonable amount of capital for the nature of the business involved. Baatz claims the corporation was started with only $5,000 in borrowed capital, but does not explain how that

Continued

Continued

amount failed to equip the corporation with a reasonable amount of capital. In addition, Baatz fails to consider the personal guarantees to pay off the purchase contract in the amount of $150,000, and the $50,000 stock subscription agreement. There simply is no evidence that the corporation's capital in whatever amount was inadequate for the operation of the business.

* * *

Finally, Baatz argues that Arrow Bar, Inc., failed to observe corporate formalities because none of the business' signs or advertising indicated that the business was a corporation. Baatz cites SDCL 47–2–36 [a South Dakota statute] as requiring the name of any corporation to contain the word corporation, company, incorporated, or limited, or an abbreviation for such a word. In spite of Baatz' contentions, the corporation is in compliance with the statute because its corporate name—Arrow Bar, Inc.—includes the abbreviation of the word incorporated. Furthermore, the "mere failure upon occasion to follow all the forms prescribed by law for the conduct of corporate activities will not justify" disregarding the corporate entity. Even if the corporation is improperly using its name, that alone is not a sufficient reason to pierce the corporate veil. This is especially so where, as here, there is no relationship between the claimed defect and the resulting harm.

* * *

Therefore, we affirm summary judgment dismissing the Neuroths as individual defendants.

Justice Henderson (dissenting)

This corporation has no separate existence. It is the instrumentality of three shareholders, officers, and employees. Here, the corporate fiction should be disregarded.

* * *

Peggy Baatz, a young mother, lost her left leg; she wears an artificial limb; Kenny Baatz, a young father, has had most of his left foot amputated; he has been unable to work since this tragic accident. Peggy uses a cane. Kenny uses crutches. Years have gone by since they were injured and their lives have been torn asunder.

Uninsured motorist was drunk, and had a reputation of being a habitual drunkard; Arrow Bar had a reputation of serving intoxicated persons. (Supported by depositions on file). An eyewitness saw uninsured motorist in an extremely intoxicated condition, shortly before the accident, being served by Arrow Bar. Therefore, a question of fact exists as to liability being violated.

* * *

Are the Neuroths subject to personal liability? It is undisputed, by the record, that the dismissed defendants (Neuroths) are immediate family members and stockholders of Arrow Bar. By pleadings, it is expressed that the dismissed defendants are employees of Arrow Bar. Seller of the Arrow Bar would not accept Arrow Bar, Inc., as buyer. Seller insisted that the individual incorporators, in their individual capacity be equally responsible for the selling price. Thus, the individuals are the real party in interest and the corporate entity. Arrow Bar, Inc., is being used to justify any wrongs perpetrated by the incorporators in their individual capacity. Conclusion: Fraud is

Continued

Continued

perpetrated upon the public. At a deposition of Edmond Neuroth, this "President" of "the corporation" was asked why the Neuroth family incorporated. His answer: "Upon advice of counsel, as a shield against individual liability." The corporation was undercapitalized (Neuroths borrowed $5,000 in capital) . . .

Therefore, I respectfully dissent.

Questions

1. Why did the court decline to pierce the corporate veil in this case?
2. In reciting the facts, what did the court mean when it said McBride "apparently is judgment proof"?
3. Why does the dissenting judge view this case differently than the majority?
4. Plaintiff Walkovsky was injured when negligently run down by a taxi owned by Seon Cab Corporation. The defendant, Carlton, is claimed to be a stockholder of 10 corporations, including Seon; each corporation consists of two cabs carrying the statutory minimum of $10,000 in liability insurance. Walkovsky sought to pierce the corporate veil and hold Carlton personally liable for damages exceeding the insurance coverage. Decide. Explain. [See *Walkovsky* v. *Carlton,* 223 N.E.2d 6 (N.Y. 1966).]

Dissolution. Theoretically, a corporation can "live" forever, but it need not do so. *Dissolution,* that is, the termination of a corporation's legal existence, can occur both voluntarily and involuntarily. Normally, a voluntary dissolution transpires either because the incorporators failed to get the corporation underway or because it proved to be unprofitable in its operation. Articles of dissolution are filed with the state, and the state in turn issues a certificate of dissolution, officially signaling the end of the corporation.

The state can involuntarily dissolve a corporation under some circumstances, including failure to meet administrative requirements such as filing forms or paying taxes. Shareholders can file suit seeking the involuntary dissolution of a corporation under circumstances of gross mismanagement, deadlock that is preventing the corporation from acting, or oppression of minority shareholders by those in control.

Winding Up. Normally, in a voluntary dissolution the directors act as trustees and are responsible for completing contracts, liquidating corporate assets, and distributing the proceeds to creditors and shareholders. A court-appointed receiver takes care of the winding-up duties in an involuntary dissolution.

Summary

Legal Review. The sole proprietorship, the partnership, and the corporation are the core forms of doing business in the United States. Variations on those forms, including limited partnerships and limited liability companies, have evolved over the years to facilitate business practice. With the exception of sole proprietorships, detailed and often complex rules have developed governing the creation, operation, and demise of each form of business. From the beginning to the end, government plays an important role in business practice, setting rules that control everything from naming the business, to incorporation, to safety inspections, to taxes. In building and managing a business, a key ingredient to success is a sound understanding of the various business forms, their advantages and disadvantages, and the legal requirements that accompany each.

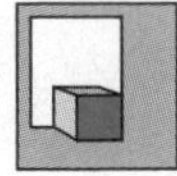

Ethics/Public Policy Review. Many of the ethical themes that arise from business organization law are addressed in Chapter 13, "Business Torts and Crimes." However, we looked briefly in this chapter at two important ethics/public policy questions: (1) Do fairness and good business practice require a change in American law that would mandate a large consultative voice for workers in managing the company? (2) Is a corporation or partnership, in some sense, a "person" that should be held morally accountable for its acts as we would hold a human accountable for his or her acts?

Economics Review. Remember that our legal system is rooted in capitalist, free market principles. The various business forms that we employ and the rules that govern them are designed to achieve fairness, but they are also designed to provide room for efficiency in the market. Features such as limited liability for shareholders and the growth of hybrid organizations with their favorable tax and liability treatments clearly are efforts to develop business organization law in a way that endeavors to maximize productivity while maintaining reasonable order and justice. An unfettered free market without legal requirements for business organizations probably would not be workable. On the other hand, excessive government oversight can dramatically reduce efficiency and personal freedom. The law of business organizations is designed to produce, among other goals, a favorable balance between market forces and regulatory/judicial commands.

Chapter Questions—Law

1. Partners Carroll and Fulton operated C&F Trucking. Carroll spent $4,600 of his personal money to buy a trailer for C&F Trucking. Both the sales invoice and the certificate of title for the trailer listed C&F Trucking as the owner. Fulton filed for bankruptcy and claimed the trailer among his assets. Does the trailer belong to the partnership or to Carroll? Explain. [See *In Re Fulton,* 43 B.R. 273 (M.D. Tenn. 1984).]
2. Mr. and Mrs. Patel, owners of the City Center Motel in Eureka, California, formed a partnership with their son, Raj, under which all three parties owned and operated the motel. However, the real estate records were not changed, so the recorded ownership remained in the parents' names. The partnership agreement included a clause according Raj the right to approve before the property could be sold. Mr. and Mrs. Patel then sold the motel without telling Raj and without notifying the buyers of Raj's right of refusal. Raj learned of the deal and refused to sell. The buyers sought a court order compelling the sale. Decide. Explain. [See *Patel* v. *Patel,* 260 Cal. Rptr. 255 (Cal. Ct. App. 1989).]
3. Stephen Vrabel and a companion were drinking in the Acri Cafe in Youngstown, Ohio, in 1947. Without provocation, Michael Acri shot Vrabel and his companion. Vrabel was seriously injured, and his friend died. Michael Acri and his wife owned the Cafe. Michael had a history of mental problems from the time of his marriage to Florence in 1931 through 1946 when they separated. Florence claimed that Michael

had beaten her, but he had never acted violently toward others prior to the shootings. During their years together, Florence played a limited role in operating the cafe, and following their separation Michael had exclusive control of the operations. Vrabel sued Florence Acri and won a court order for $7,500. Florence appealed. Decide. Explain. [See *Vrabel* v. *Acri,* 103 N.E.2d 564 (Ohio S.Ct. 1952).]

4. James Cates and others formed two partnerships to sell insurance. The partnerships contracted with insurance providers including Lloyds of London and ITT Life Insurance. Cates sued Lloyds and ITT alleging, among other things, failure to pay claims promptly. The partnerships were dissolved, but during the winding-up process, Cates died. His wife then intervened in his lawsuit against Lloyds and ITT saying that, as Cates' heir, she was entitled to an interest in partnership assets, including a share of any damages that might be awarded in the lawsuit. ITT and Lloyds won at trial. Mrs. Cates appealed. Decide. Explain. [See *Cates* v. *International Telephone and Telegraph Corp.,* 756 F.2d 1161 (5th Cir. 1985).]
5. Sylvester and Balvik formed an electrical contracting partnership. They then decided to incorporate. Each was a director, officer, and employee of the new corporation. Sylvester had 70 percent of the voting stock and Balvik 30 percent. They quarreled, and Balvik was fired, allegedly for poor performance. Balvik sought a dissolution of the corporation on the grounds that he was the victim of "oppression" and had been squeezed out. Decide. Explain. [See *Balvik* v. *Sylvester,* 411 N.W.2d 383 (N.D. 1987).]
6. Morad, Thomson, and Coupounas were shareholders in Bio-Lab, Inc., of Birmingham, Alabama. Morad and Thomson were also officers and directors. After some disputes, Morad and Thomson incorporated and operated Med-Lab, Inc., a competing business in Tuscaloosa, Alabama. Morad served as president of both companies. Coupounas filed a derivative suit on behalf of Bio-Lab claiming that Morad and Thomson, through Med-Lab, had taken a corporate opportunity that belonged to Bio-Lab. The trial court found for Coupounas. Morad and Thomson appealed. Decide. Explain. [See *Morad* v. *Coupounas,* 361 So.2d 6 (Ala. S.Ct. 1978).]
7. In 1971, Koch and Dahlbeck incorporated Viking Construction, Inc., to develop real estate. Viking was initially capitalized with $3,000, and Dahlbeck extended a $7,000 loan to the corporation. Viking began developing two Omaha, Nebraska, subdivisions with 65 lots and a total value of $430,000. Business went well for four years and then declined sharply. Dahlbeck and Koch initially received $15,000 annual salaries from Viking, but as sales declined the salaries declined and finally stopped entirely. Viking's initial capitalization of $3,000 was never expanded. Throughout its existence, Viking's average liabilities exceeded its average assets. In 1978 Viking began to liquidate and transferred all of its $11,000 in net worth to Dahlbeck to satisfy his loans to Viking. Viking dissolved in 1980, but still owed money to various creditors, including a $16,000 debt to J. L. Brock Builders. Brock sued Dahlbeck personally. Should Brock be able to pierce Viking's corporate veil and reach Dahlbeck's personal assets? Explain. [See *J. L. Brock Builders, Inc.* v. *Dahlbeck,* 391 N.W.2d 110 (Neb. S.Ct. 1986).]
8. In 1969, upon learning that Honeywell, Inc., was manufacturing antipersonnel fragmentation bombs for use in the Vietnam War, Pillsbury bought shares in Honeywell. Pillsbury testified that his motivation for buying the shares was to lobby Honeywell management and stockholders in order to convince Honeywell to stop producing munitions. Pillsbury sought to inspect Honeywell's shareholder ledgers and all corporate records dealing with weapons and munitions manufacture. Must Honeywell open its records to its shareholder, Pillsbury? Explain. [See *State Ex Rel. Pillsbury* v. *Honeywell, Inc.,* 191 N.W.2d 406 (Minn. S.Ct. 1971).]

9. Art Modell owned 80 percent of the stock of the Cleveland Stadium Corporation (CSC) and 53 percent of the stock of the Cleveland Browns pro football team. Modell was president of CSC and served on the board of directors of the Browns. Several other Browns' board members also served on the CSC board. In 1982 the Browns' board voted to buy all of the CSC stock for $6,000,000. Robert Gries, a Browns' board member, and his business, Gries Sports Enterprises, Inc., owned 43 percent of the Browns. CSC had been appraised at no more than $2 million, and Gries objected to the purchase on the grounds that the Browns' debt load was unnecessarily increased and that Modell unfairly benefited from the purchase. The other Browns directors outvoted Gries, so he filed a derivative suit seeking to rescind the CSC purchase. In addition to Modell and Gries, the Browns' board consisted of Modell's wife, three Browns employees, and Richard Cole. Decide Gries's claim. Explain. [See *Gries Sports Enterprises, Inc.* v. *Cleveland Browns Football Co.,* 496 N.E.2d 959 (Ohio S.Ct. 1986).]
10. In 1968, the Democratic National Committee ran up a phone bill of $1.5 million. Shareholders in American Telephone & Telegraph sued AT&T and its directors, claiming the company had not made a good faith effort to collect and thus had, in effect, made a political contribution to the Democratic party, an illegal contribution under federal law. The lower court cited the business judgment rule and dismissed the claim. The shareholders appealed. Decide. Explain. [See *Miller* v. *American Telephone & Telegraph Co.,* 507 F.2d 759 (3d Cir. 1974).]

Chapter Questions—Public Policy

1. Does corporate law—especially the concepts of limited liability and the business judgment rule—unfairly favor the wealthy and powerful? Explain.
2. Historically, the maximization of shareholder profit was, at least theoretically, the standard for measuring corporate success. Today, in many organizations, the profit maximization goal has been amended by concern for corporate social responsibilities. Should the corporate world return to its singular focus on profit maximization? Explain.

Notes

1. The material in this section draws, in part, from Fred Steingold, *The Legal Guide for Starting and Running a Small Business* (Berkeley: Nolo Press, 1992).
2. Ibid.
3. *Smith* v. *Van Gorkom,* 488 A.2d 858 (Del. S.Ct. 1985).

CONTRACTS

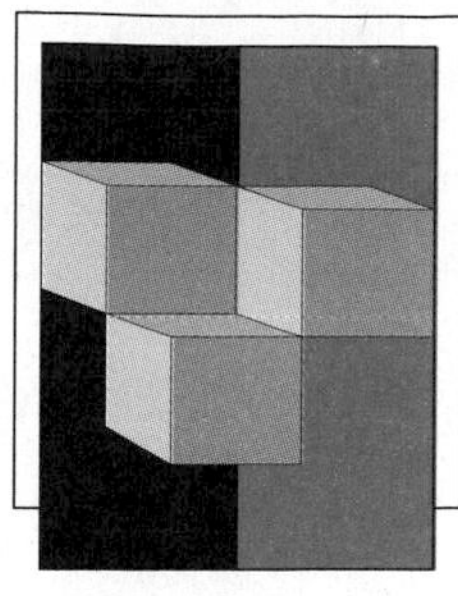

CHAPTER

4

READER'S GUIDE

In Chapter 3, we looked at the various legal structures (partnerships, corporations, etc.) that may be employed in organizing a business. In this chapter, we will survey the branch of law—contracts—that imposes order on the endless string of transactions required to build and manage a business. From beginning to end (from buying office supplies, to hiring workers, to renting production space, to selling finished products or services, and beyond) every element of the business enterprise is, of course, rooted in contract law.

PROFILE

Suppose you are paying your way through college by providing entertainment for parties as Alan Herzig does in the story that follows. Contract law provides the means for you to build stable business relationships and to achieve satisfaction if problems emerge.

LEGAL SYSTEM TESTED BY SKIRMISH OVER A DISPUTED BAT MITZVAH BILL

by Alan Abrahamson

Beverly Hills [Cal.] Municipal Court Judge Elden Fox and his wife, Janet, a senior county prosecutor, spent a year planning the dinner-dance celebrating their daughter's bat mitzvah. But so much went wrong.

The fog machine never got going. There were not enough party streamers. There were no games for the kids. And then, on top of everything else, their daughter's grand entrance—to the tune of the classic rocker by the Doors, "Twentieth Century Fox"—was marred when the master of ceremonies cut off the sound.

"If looks could kill," Janet Fox said of the look she shot emcee Alan Herzig, "he would have been dead."

What ensued was not homicide but, predictably, litigation. The Van Nuys couple refused to pay Herzig the $1,692 he billed them. So Herzig sued in Van Nuys small claims court.

* * *

At a bat mitzvah—or, for boys, a bar mitzvah—a 13-year-old is recognized by the Jewish community as an adult. The event is solemn in a synagogue but also an occasion for great joy and a gathering of family and friends, and Janet wanted to throw a memorable party for 160 guests.

* * *

Herzig's company, the Dancing Machine, has been in business since 1977. The Foxes agreed to pay

Continued

Continued

him $3,300—half before the party and the balance on the day of the party. In exchange, he promised to provide a seven-piece band, various emcee and deejay services, and party favors.

The party went off last August 13, . . . but the fog-making machine had to be scrubbed. There were not enough streamers and there were no games . . . As for the games, Herzig said he was prepared to begin playing them at one point when a fire-eater appeared.

"He was a magician, not a fire-eater," who entertained during the salad course only, leaving ample time for games, Janet Fox retorted.

Herzig does not dispute that he interrupted the song "Twentieth Century Fox." But that was good professional judgment, he said, because guests had heard the chorus several times—establishing the play on the Fox family name—and "I needed to pump the party up."

After all was said and done, Herzig still wanted the original balance due, $1,692. The Foxes offered $800.

Herzig refused and said in a letter: "I'm ready. My people are ready. If necessary, we'll rumble in small claims court!"

On August 30, Herzig sued. The rumble was on.

At an October 19 hearing before Kirkland Nyby, who has been a small claims commissioner for 15 years, Fox appeared by himself and asked for a change of venue, to the Westside. Nyby denied the request.

Fox asked for a continuance, saying his wife and daughter were unavailable and he was due back in Beverly Hills, in his own courtroom. The motion was denied.

Fox moved to disqualify Nyby, saying he was prejudiced. Denied.

* * *

Nyby stressed that he bore no animosity toward either Fox: "All I did was rule on the facts that were presented to me."

Fox walked out, but "in hindsight, I should have stayed."

In fact, he came back into the courtroom. But when Nyby said the judge was expected to participate if he stayed, Fox . . . left again.

Nyby entered a default judgment in Herzig's favor, awarding him $1,692 plus $185 in court costs.

Two months later, the Foxes were back, asking Nyby to set aside his ruling. He refused.

The Foxes appealed to Superior Court. Last Monday just a few minutes before the hearing was to begin before a temporary judge assigned to the case, Encino attorney Raoul Roth, Fox served Herzig with a 12-page brief.

At the hearing, Roth ruled that Nyby should have given the Foxes a continuance and a change of venue.

Both asked, however, to go to trial right then and there. The next day, Roth issued a ruling: Herzig was due $725 and $100 in court costs, or about what the Foxes had offered him last August.

"I thought, well, this is what they should pay for what they got," Roth said, since the Foxes did receive some services but not all they had contracted for.

"Technically, I won," Herzig said. "But I got nothing more than they were going to give me originally . . . so big deal."

"I'm not saying anybody is right or wrong," Elden Fox said, "but in light of the fact that the motions were granted and the case litigated, I feel vindicated."

"Actually," said Roth, "I think they both lost."

Questions

1. Did Herzig's performance constitute a breach of contract? Explain.
2. Assuming a breach of contract by Herzig, how would you compute the proper measure of damages for the Fox family?
3. Did either Herzig or the Fox family (*a*) achieve justice or (*b*) abuse the legal system? Explain.

Source: *Los Angeles Times,* February 13, 1995, p. B1.

I. Building a Binding Contract

A. Introduction

Mechanics. We all make promises routinely in our lives. Some of those create binding contracts; some do not. Thus, the central question in this chapter is the following: Under what circumstances do promises become enforceable contracts? In building and managing his entertainment business, if Alan Herzig promised music and games for the Fox bat mitzvah, and they promised to pay him an agreed-upon sum, those promises begin to take on a contractual character. If Herzig, on the other hand, promised that the bat mitzvah would be a great success, his words probably would not create a legally enforceable contract. Most of this chapter is devoted to explaining the well-settled principles that convert a promise to a legally enforceable contract.

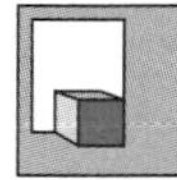

Public Policy. The mechanics of contract law can only be understood in the larger context of the goals of a capitalist society. Dependable, predictable contract law is essential to capitalism and essential to prosperity. What businessperson would agree to ship goods across America or around the world if she could not be satisfied that she would be paid and that if she were not paid she would have a mechanism for securing justice? Contract law provides the security that capitalism requires. Further, contract law memorializes our respect for personal freedom. We believe that contracts should be enforced by the courts since contracts reflect the freely expressed will of the parties. Our common law (judge-made law) of contracts has emerged from hundreds of years of court decisions here and in England. Those decisions served to particularize most rules that would govern the largely face-to-face bargains of pre-industrial England and America; but as commercial practice became increasingly complex, contract law necessarily evolved.

Dependable, predictable contract law is essential to capitalism and essential to prosperity.

The Uniform Commercial Code. The individual states had passed a wide variety of laws to clarify contract law. Then in 1941, the National Conference of Commissioners on Uniform State Laws and the American Law Institute began the process of writing the Uniform Commercial Code (UCC), a body of rules designed to render commercial law consistent across the 50 states. The UCC has been adopted in 49 states, and Louisiana has adopted portions of it. With a set of uniform, predictable rules, business can be practiced with confidence and minimal legal confusion.

The UCC is divided into 11 articles addressing the multitude of potential problems that arise in complex commercial practice. For our purposes the most important of those articles is Number 2, Sales, (see Appendix B), which governs all transactions involving the sale of **goods.** Considerable confusion surrounds the key question: What objects constitute goods and are therefore subject to the UCC? The UCC section 2-105 definition of goods has been interpreted to mean tangible, movable, personal property. Hence, cars, clothing, appliances, and the like are covered. Real estate, stocks, bonds, and so forth are not covered. Nor are contracts for *services* governed by the UCC. Of course, many transactions involve both goods and services. Characteristically, in determining whether the UCC applies, the courts have asked whether the dominant purpose of the contract is to provide a service to sell a good.

goods. All things that are movable at the time of identification to the contract for sale except the money in which the price is to be paid, investment securities, and so forth.

The first question, then, in contract disputes is whether the UCC or the common law governs the situation. Throughout this chapter, you should remember that the UCC is *always* controlling if (1) the transaction is addressed by the UCC, that is, it involves a contract for the sale of goods, and (2) if a UCC rule applies to the issue in question. On the other hand, the judge-made, common law of contracts continues to govern transactions (1) not involving the sale of goods or (2) involving the sale of goods but where no specific UCC provision applies. Increasingly, in non-UCC cases, the courts are analogizing to UCC reasoning to render their judgments; that is, the common law is borrowing or absorbing UCC principles. This chapter, while focusing primarily on the common law of contracts, will introduce the role of the sales article in the practice of business. (At this writing, revisions to the sales articles are being considered by the National Conference of Commissioners on Uniform State Laws.)

lease. A contract for the possession and use of land on one side, and a recompense of rent or other income on the other.

Note, also, that Article 2A of the UCC governs **leases** of goods. In essence, Article 2A mimics the sales article except that it governs leases of goods rather than sales. Because of space constraints, Article 2A will not receive further attention in this chapter.

Restatement of Contracts. A collection of the rules of contract law created by the American Law Institute to provide guidance to lawyers and judges.

Restatement. In an effort to bring some structure to the thousands of contract decisions that had been handed down over the years, a group of leading legal scholars produced what is known as a **Restatement of Contracts.** The Restatement does not have the force of law, but is accorded high respect by judges. The first Restatement appeared in 1932 and the Restatement (Second) of Contracts was issued in 1979. Many portions of the Restatement closely parallel UCC provisions, so we are seeing some harmonizing of the common law/UCC approaches. Certainly the Restatement and the UCC have been influential forces in moving contract law away from its earlier rules orientation to a reliance on broader principles reflecting the realities of commercial practice.

agreement. A meeting of the minds based upon offer by one party and acceptance by another.
offer. A proposal by one person to another that is intended to create legal relations on acceptance by the person to whom it is made.
acceptance. The actual or implied receipt and retention of that which is tendered or offered.
consideration. In contract law the legal value, bargained for and given in exchange for an act or promise.
capacity. The ability to incur legal obligations and acquire legal rights.
genuineness of assent. In contract law, the parties knowingly agreed to the same thing.
legality of purpose. The object of the contract does not violate law or public policy.

B. What Is a Contract?

Legally enforceable contracts must exhibit all of the following features:

1. **Agreement.** A meeting of the minds of the parties based upon an **offer** by one and an **acceptance** by the other. The determination as to whether the parties have actually reached agreement is based upon the *objective* evidence (the parties' acts, words, etc.) as a "reasonable person" would interpret it rather than upon an effort to ascertain the subjective or personal intent of the parties.
2. **Consideration.** The bargained-for legal value that one party agrees to pay or provide in order to secure the promise of another.
3. **Capacity.** The parties must have the legal ability to enter the contract; that is, they must be sane, sober, and of legal age.
4. **Genuineness of assent.** The parties must knowingly agree to the same thing. As noted above, their minds must meet as evidenced by the objective evidence. If that meeting does not occur because of mistake, fraud, or so forth, a contract does not exist because the parties' assent was not real.
5. **Legality of purpose.** The object of the contract must not violate the law or public policy.

Contracts embracing those five features are enforceable by law and hence are distinguishable from unenforceable promises.

C. Classification of Contracts

Contracts fall into a series of sometimes overlapping categories. Understanding those categories helps in revealing the rather well-ordered logic of our contract system (see Table 4.1).

TABLE 4.1

CLASSIFICATION OF CONTRACTS

Contract Formation
1. Bilateral/unilateral
   a. Bilateral contract—a promise for a promise.
   b. Unilateral contract—a promise for an act.
2. Express/implied
   a. Express contract—explicitly stated in writing or orally.
   b. Implied-in-fact contract—inferred from the conduct of the parties.
   c. Quasi-contract—implied contract created by court to prevent unjust enrichment.

Contract Performance
1. Executory contract—not yet fully performed.
2. Executed contract—fully performed by all parties.

Contract Enforceability
1. Valid contract—includes all of the necessary ingredients of a binding contract.
2. Unenforceable contract—contract exists, but a legal defense prevents enforcement.
3. Void contract—no contract at all.
4. Voidable contract—one party has the option of either enforcing or voiding the contract.

Contract Formation.

1. Bilateral and Unilateral Contracts. A **bilateral contract** emerges from a situation in which *both* parties make promises. A **unilateral contract** ordinarily involves a situation in which one party makes a promise and the other *acts* in response to that promise. For example, in beginning to establish your new restaurant business, you promise a college friend that if he completes his degree, you will hire him. He can accept your offer/promise by the act of completing college.

2. Express and Implied Contracts. When parties overtly and explicitly manifest their intention to enter an agreement, either in writing or orally, the result (if other requirements are fulfilled) is an **express contract.** For example, in managing your department at an insurance firm, you sign a form contract with a local computer store ordering a new computer. In turn, the supplier's signature on the form creates an express, bilateral agreement.

If, on the other hand, you ask your local computer service to take a look at a machine that is down and one of the service's technicians does so, you have probably entered an **implied-in-fact contract.** A court would infer a promise by you to pay a reasonable price in return for the service's promise to make a commercially reasonable effort to repair the computer. The contract is inferred on the basis of the facts, that is, on the behavior of the parties.

Suppose in managing your insurance department you have received payment for insurance that was, in fact, issued by a rival firm. In these circumstances, it would be unfair for you to be able to keep the unearned money so the courts construct an implied-in-law or **quasi-contract** permitting the actual insurer to collect the money. This unusual situation in which the court infers the existence of a contract is employed only when necessary to prevent **unjust enrichment** (as would have been the case if you were to collect an insurance premium without having issued a policy).

bilateral contract. A contract formed by an offer requiring a reciprocal promise.

unilateral contract. A contract wherein the only acceptance of the offer that is necessary is the performance of the act.

express contract. Contract whose terms are clear from the language.

implied-in-fact contract. Contract whose terms are implicitly understood based on the behavior of the parties.

quasi-contract. The doctrine by which courts imply, as a matter of law, a promise to pay the reasonable value of goods or services when the party receiving such goods or services has knowingly done so under circumstances that make it unfair to retain them without paying for them.

unjust enrichment. An unearned benefit knowingly accepted.

Contract Performance.

executory contract. Not yet fully performed or completed.

executed contract. Performances are complete.

1. Executory Contracts. A contract is labeled **executory** until all parties fully perform.

2. Executed Contracts. When all parties have completed their performances, the contract is **executed.**

Contract Enforceability.

valid contract. Effective; sufficient in law.

1. Valid Contracts. A **valid contract** meets all of the established legal requirements and thus is enforceable in court.

unenforceable contract. Meets basic requirements, but remains faulty.

2. Unenforceable Contracts. An **unenforceable contract** meets the basic contractual requirements but remains faulty because it fails to fulfill some other legal rule. For example, an oral contract may be unenforceable if it falls in one of those categories of contracts, such as the sale of land, that must be in writing (see the Statute of Frauds later in this chapter).

void contract. Entirely null; no contract at all.

3. Void Contracts. A **void contract** is, in fact, no contract at all since a critical legal requirement is missing; usually, either it is an agreement to accomplish an illegal purpose (e.g., commit a crime) or it is an agreement involving an incompetent (e.g., an individual adjudged by a court to be insane). In either case what is otherwise an enforceable contract is in fact void and hence, no contract at all.

voidable contract. Capable of bieng made void; enforceable but can be canceled.

4. Voidable Contracts. A **voidable contract** is enforceable but can be canceled by one or more of the parties. The most common voidable contracts are those entered by minors who have the option, under the law, of either disaffirming or fulfilling most contracts (explained later).

D. The Agreement: Offer

Characteristically, an offer consists of a promise to do something or to refrain from doing something in the future. A valid offer must include all of these elements:

a. Present *intent* to enter a contract.
b. Reasonable *definiteness* in the terms of the offer.
c. *Communication* of the offer to the offeree.

Intent. Assume that you are the purchasing manager for a trucking firm, and you need a small, used van to do some local, light hauling. Because time is of the essence, you decide to bypass the normal bidding process and go directly to the local dealers to make a quick purchase. At the first lot, you find a suitable van and in discussing it, the sales manager says, "Well, we don't usually do this, but since you've been such a good customer, I'll tell you, we paid $6,000 for this one so I guess we are gonna need about $8,000 to deal with you." You say, "Fine. That's reasonable. I'll take it." The manager then says, "Now wait a minute, I was just talking off the top of my head. I'll have to punch up the numbers to be sure."

Do you have a deal at that point? The core question is whether the sales manager made an offer. Normally, language of that kind has been treated by the courts as preliminary

Offer?
An at-will employee (can be fired at any time) asks you, his manager, about job security. You respond, "Good employees are taken care of. You are a good employee." Does that language amount to an offer of permanent employment?

negotiation lacking the necessary **intent** to constitute an offer. Of course, if no offer exists, you cannot accept, and no contract can emerge absent further negotiation.

intent. A conscious and purposeful state of mind.

Advertisements. The question of intent sometimes arises with advertisements. In buying the van for your business, suppose you were responding to an ad that said, "1993 full-size Ford cargo van, $8,000." Is that ad language an offer such that you can accept by promising to pay $8,000? Ordinarily, ads do not constitute offers, but rather are treated by the courts as invitations to deal. Were an ad actually treated as an offer, it would put the seller in the commercially impracticable position of being required to provide the advertised product at the advertised price to everyone who sought one, regardless of available supply. Presumably, that open-ended duty was not the seller's intent when issuing the ad. It follows then that the buyer, in responding to an ad, is technically making an offer, with the seller free to accept or decline.

Suppose you were responding to an ad that said, "1993 full-size Ford cargo van, $8,000." Is that ad language an offer such that you can accept by promising to pay $8,000?

On the other hand, courts have held that some ads do manifest a present intent to make an offer. The critical terms in those ads must be highly specific and complete, leaving nothing open for negotiation.

Definiteness. Suppose you have completed a management training program for a large warehouse appliance chain. In your first assignment as an assistant manager, your boss asks you to seek bids and make the other arrangements (subject to her approval) to resurface the store's large asphalt parking lot. You secure bids, and the lowest bidder offers to complete the work "later this summer" for $98,000. You briefly explain the offer to your boss, who tells you to take care of all the details. You are busy with other matters and you put off the parking lot project for a couple of weeks. When you get back to the contractor, he says, "Sorry, man, we hadn't heard from you, and we got another deal." Can you hold that contractor to his initial offer?

One of the requirements of a binding offer is that all of its critical terms must be sufficiently clear that a court can determine both the intentions of the parties and their duties. Clearly, in the asphalt case, many critical details—such as precisely when the work would be done, the quality of the surfacing material, its thickness, and the like—had not been established. Consequently, no offer existed. In a contract for the sale of goods, UCC 2-204 relaxes the definiteness standard by providing that "one or more terms" may be missing but the court can find a contract, nonetheless, where (1) "the parties have intended to make a contract" and (2) "there is a reasonably certain basis for giving an appropriate remedy." Under the UCC, the courts can actually fill in missing terms such as specifying a reasonable price where the contract had omitted a stipulation. The following case involving Mariah Carey, the pop music star, demonstrates some of the problems that can arise when an understanding is indefinite.

CASE

Vian v. Carey

1993 U.S. Dist. LEXIS 5460
(U.S. Dist. Ct. S. D. N. Y., 1993)

Facts

The defendant, Mariah Carey, is a famous, successful, and apparently wealthy pop musician. The plaintiff, Joseph Vian, was Carey's stepfather. He claims that he had an oral contract with Carey providing that he would hold a license to market dolls in her likeness that would play her most popular songs. Vian claims that he was accorded the license in return for his financial and emotional support of Carey, including picking her up from late-night recording sessions, providing her with the use of a car, and so forth. Vian claims that the oral contract arose from at least three occasions when Vian said, "Don't forget the Mariah dolls" and "I get the Mariah dolls." Vian claimed that Carey said, "OK" on one of those occasions and smiled and nodded on others. Carey thought those references to the dolls were merely jokes. Vian sued for breach of contract; Carey sought a summary judgment.

* * *

Judge Mukasey

Plaintiff claims that he had an oral contract with defendant. Although it is not clear from the evidence the parties have submitted, it will be assumed that the alleged contract was formed after defendant turned 18. Under New York law, an oral agreement can form a binding contract . . . In determining whether a contract exists, what matters are the parties' expressed intentions, the words and deeds which constitute objective signs in a given set of circumstances.

Therefore, the issue is whether the objective circumstances indicate that the parties intended to form a contract. Without such an intent, neither a contract nor a preliminary agreement to negotiate in good faith can exist. In making such a determination, a court may look at "whether the terms of the contract have been finally resolved." In addition, a court may consider "the context of the negotiations." Plaintiff has adduced no evidence that defendant ever intended by a nod of her head or the expression "okay" to enter into a complex commercial licensing agreement involving dolls in her likeness playing her copyrighted songs. The context in which this contract between an 18-year-old girl and her stepfather allegedly was made was an informal family setting, either in the car or on plaintiff's boat, while others were present. Vian's own version of events leads to the conclusion that there was no reason for Carey to think Vian was entirely serious, let alone that he intended to bind her to an agreement at that time. He admits he never told her he was serious. The objective circumstances do not indicate that Carey intended to form a contract with plaintiff. Although plaintiff's five-page memorandum of law fails to raise the possibility, plaintiff also has not shown that Carey intended to be bound to negotiate with plaintiff at some later date over the licensing of "Mariah dolls."

There can be no meeting of the minds, required for the formation of a contract, where essential material terms are missing. Thus, even if the parties both believe themselves to be bound, there is no contract when "the terms of the agreement are so vague and indefinite that there is no basis or standard for deciding whether the agreement had been kept or broken, or to fashion a remedy, and no means by which such terms may be made certain."

. . . The word "license" was not even used. As defendant points out, no price or royalty term was mentioned, nor was the duration or geographic scope of the license, nor was Carey's right to approve the dolls. Plaintiff admits he would not have gone ahead without defendant's approval, thus conceding the materiality of that term.

* * *

Continued

Continued

In sum, plaintiff has not raised a triable issue of fact as to the existence of a contract. Defendant's motion for summary judgment is granted.

Questions

1. Why did the court find for Carey?
2. As noted in the text, in UCC cases judges fill in contract terms where the parties clearly intended a deal. Should the court here fill in the missing terms to provide the necessary definiteness? Explain.
3. Pilgrim Village Company had employed Petersen as a construction manager at a specified annual salary and "a share of the profits." Petersen worked at salary for several years and then asked for a 10 percent share of the profits. The company refused and Peterson sued seeking "some share of the profits." How should the court rule on Peterson's claim? Explain. [See *Peterson* v. *Pilgrim Village,* 42 N.W. 2d 273 (1950).]

Communication. As explained, an effective offer must be the product of a present intent, it must be definite, and it must be communicated to the offeree. Communication of an offer expresses the offeror's intent to make that offer. Therefore, suppose a friend tells you that your neighbor has offered to sell his classic jukebox for $10,000. You call your neighbor and say, "I accept. I'll be right over with the $10,000." Do you have a deal? No. The owner did not communicate the offer to you. The fact that it was not communicated to you may suggest that your neighbor does not want to sell or does not want to sell to you.

Duration of an Offer. Communication of an offer affords the offeree the opportunity to create a contract by accepting that offer, but how long does that opportunity last? Some general rules:

1. The offeror may revoke the offer anytime prior to acceptance. (Some exceptions are explained below.) Normally, revocation is effective upon receipt by the offeree. Under the common law the offeror has the right to revoke at any time prior to acceptance, even if he expressly promised to keep the offer open for a specified period of time.
2. The offer may specify that it is open for an express period (e.g., 10 days).
3. Where a time limit is not specified in the offer it will be presumed to be open for a "reasonable period of time."
4. An offer expires if rejected or upon receipt of a counteroffer.

Irrevocable Offers. Some kinds of offers may not be revoked. We will note three of them.

1. *Option contracts.* When an offeror promises to keep an offer open for a specified period of time and, in return, the offeree pays consideration (usually money), the parties have created an **option contract,** which is a separate agreement and is enforceable by its terms. For example, a friend has offered to sell to you his customized car that you have long cherished, but you want to think about it for a few days. You might enter an option contract with your friend under which you pay $50 for the seller's promise to keep the offer open for a period of seven days. You are under no obligation to buy the car, but the seller is under a binding obligation not to withdraw the offer during the seven days.

option contract. A separate contract in which an offeror agrees not to revoke her or his offer for a stated period of time in exchange for some valuable consideration.

2. *Firm offers.* Under the UCC, if the owner of that customized car is a dealer (a merchant) and he made a written, signed offer to sell that car (a good) to you, indicating that his offer would remain open for seven days, he is bound to that promise whether you paid consideration for it or not. That situation is labeled a **firm offer** as specified in UCC 2-205, which also provides that such offers will be kept open for a reasonable period of time if the agreement does not mention a time, but that period cannot exceed three months.

firm offer. Under the Uniform Commercial Code, a signed, written offer by a merchant containing assurances that it will be held open, and which is not revocable for the time stated in the offer, or for a reasonable time if no such time is stated.

3. *Offers for unilateral contracts.* A problem sometimes arises when the offeror attempts to revoke a unilateral offer after the offeree has begun to perform. For example, your neighbor invites you to rake her leaves for $5, and then, when you are virtually done, she yells from the doorway: "Oh, sorry, I changed my mind. You go home now." Historically, the offeror (the neighbor, in this case) was free to revoke at any time; but the modern position holds that the offeror normally cannot revoke if the offeree (you) has commenced performance. If that performance is then completed (you ignore your neighbor's admonition to go home, and you finish the raking), the offeror (your neighbor) is bound to perform fully; that is, the neighbor must pay the $5.

E. THE AGREEMENT: ACCEPTANCE

Suppose you are in training with a large real estate firm and your boss has authorized you to enter negotiations to buy a parcel of farmland that your company hopes to develop for housing. After preliminary discussions, you extend a written offer to the owner indicating, among other terms, that your company is willing to pay $4,000 per acre for a 10-acre parcel. Assume the owner responds by writing: "I accept your offer at $4,000 per acre, but I need to keep the two-acre homesite." The offeree has used the word accept, but does the response constitute a legally binding acceptance?

The general rule is that an effective acceptance must be a mirror image of the offer; that is, ordinarily its terms must be the same as those in the offer. Here the offeree has changed the terms of the offer and in so doing has issued a **counteroffer,** thus extinguishing the original offer.

counteroffer. Response by the offeree that, in its legal effect, constitutes a rejection of the original offer and proposes a new offer to the offeror.

Communication of Acceptance. An offer may be accepted only by the offeree, that is, the person to whom the offer was directed. Since unilateral offers are accepted by performance, no communication of acceptance beyond that performance ordinarily is necessary. In the case of a bilateral contract (a promise for a promise), acceptance is not effective until communicated. Broadly, acceptance can be accomplished by a "yes" communicated face to face, by a nod of the head or some other appropriate signal, by telephone, or by other unwritten means, unless the law of the state requires a writing in that particular kind of transaction.

Mail Box. Confusion sometimes arises when the parties are not dealing face to face. In general, acceptance is effective upon dispatch by whatever mode of communication has been explicitly or implicitly authorized by the offeror. This well-settled position is labeled the **mail box rule** and means, among other things, that an acceptance is effective when sent even if never received.

mail box rule. Rule holding that the mailing of an acceptance is effective upon mailing when the offeror has used the mail to invite acceptance; the rule has been expanded to include the use of any reasonable manner of acceptance.

Authorization. The offeror controls the acceptance process and may specify an exclusive manner in which an acceptance must be communicated. If so, a contract is not created if the acceptance is communicated in anything other than the stipulated fashion.

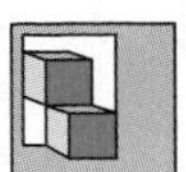

International Implications of the "Battle of the Forms"

Contract law plays a critical role in efficient international trade. Assume you are trying to open sales of your American lawn mowers in emerging Eastern European markets. You and the buyer are likely to exchange form contracts that differ somewhat in their terms. Often the sale simply goes through without reference to the conflicting terms. But what happens if market conditions change abruptly or performance is incomplete? Can you get out of the deal? Professors Dan Ostas and Burt Leete explained the rule that generally applies around the world and noted the continuing impact of socialist thinking in the former centrally planned Eastern European nations, including Hungary:

> Most nations follow the mirror image rule. . . If there is a material variance, then no contract is formed and the acceptance constitutes a counteroffer terminating the offer. The Hungarian Civil Code currently reflects this rule. Paragraph 213(2) states: "An acceptance deviating from the offer shall be considered a new offer." This language is not surprising considering that prior to break up of the Soviet bloc, the socialist countries took a rules-oriented approach to the problem of acceptances that deviated from the offer. Because of the requirements of a planned economy, the socialist legal systems took the strict view that a contract could not be concluded even if the acceptance deviates in unimportant ways from the offer.

Likewise, the United Nations Convention on the International Sale of Goods appears, in practice, to be a mirror image approach. On the other hand, German law, according to Ostas and Leete, rejects the mirror image stance in favor of the flexible position (like our UCC 2-207) that a contract emerges from conflicting terms so long as the key terms are in agreement.

Source: Daniel Ostas and Burt Leete, "Economic Analysis of Law as a Guide to Post-Communist Legal Reforms: The Case of Hungarian Contract Law," *American Business Law Journal* 32, no. 3 (1995), pp. 355, 377, 380.

Traditionally, if the offeror did not give an **express authorization** to a means of communication, an acceptance by the same or faster means than that used by the offeror was implied. **Implied authorization** might also arise from such factors as prior dealings between the parties and custom in their industry.

express authorization. In contract law, where the offeror specifies a means of communication by which the offeree can accept.

implied authorization. In contract law, where the offeror's behavior or previous dealings with the offeree suggest an agreeable means of communicating an acceptance.

Modern View. Under the UCC and the Restatement (Second) of Contracts, the rules have relaxed a bit. If no specific instructions for acceptance are included in the offer, the offeree is free to accept in any reasonable manner within a reasonable period of time, and acceptance is effective upon dispatch. Even when the means chosen are "unreasonable," acceptance is effective on dispatch under the UCC 1-201(38) and the Restatement if it is actually received in a timely manner.

F. CONSIDERATION

Earlier we identified the five key ingredients in an enforceable contract: agreement, consideration, capacity, genuineness of assent, and legality of purpose. Having examined the offer/acceptance process, we turn now to consideration. As noted earlier, consideration is the bargained-for legal value that one party agrees to pay or provide in order to secure the promise of another. It is what the promisor demands and receives in exchange for his or her promise. Consideration is used by the courts to distinguish a contract (enforceable) from a gratuitous promise (unenforceable). The **promisee** must suffer a **legal detriment;** that is, the promisee must give up something of value (an act or a promise) or must refrain from doing something that she or he has a legal right to do in order to enforce the promise offered by the **promisor.** Each party, then, must pay a "price" for a contract to be enforceable. In sum, consideration consists of (1) a detriment to the promisee (2) that is bargained for by the promisor.

promisee. The person to whom a promise is made.

legal detriment. Any act or forbearance by a promisee.

promisor. A person who makes a promise to another.

Profile Perspective: In building and managing businesses you are likely to enter a multitude of contracts, all of which must be supported by consideration (or its substitute, as explained below). Think back to Alan Herzig, who was under contract to provide entertainment for the Foxes' bat mitzvah. Formally, the arrangement was straightforward: Herzig's services in exchange for the Foxes' money. Consideration was provided in that Herzig, the promisee/entertainment provider, has suffered a detriment (promise to complete his duties) that was bargained for and given in exchange for the Foxes' promise to pay. Of course, the Fox family argued that Herzig did not complete his portion of the bargain.

The classic case that follows explores the idea of consideration and demonstrates that consideration can have legal value without involving monetary loss to the promisee.

CASE

Hamer v. Sidway

27 N.E. 256 (N.Y. 1891)

Facts

In 1869, William E. Story, Sr., promised his nephew, W. E. Story II, that he would pay the nephew $5,000 upon his 21st birthday if the nephew would refrain from drinking liquor, using tobacco, swearing, and playing cards or billiards for money until he reached that 21st birthday. The nephew agreed and performed his promise, but the uncle died in 1887 without paying the money, and the administrator of the estate, Sidway, declined to pay the $5,000 plus interest. The nephew had assigned (sold) his rights to the money to Louisa Hamer, who sued W. E. Story, Sr.'s estate. Hamer, the plaintiff, won at the trial level, lost on appeal, and then appealed to the New York Court of Appeals.

* * *

Judge Parker

When the nephew arrived at the age of twenty-one years and on the 31st day of January 1875, he wrote to his uncle informing him that he had performed his part of the agreement and had thereby become entitled to the sum of $5,000. The uncle received the letter and a few days later and on the sixth of February, he wrote and mailed to his nephew the following letter:

Continued

Continued

Buffalo, February 6, 1875
W. E. Story, Jr.
Dear Nephew:
Your letter of the 31st came to hand all right, saying that you had lived up to the promise made to me several years ago. I have no doubt but you have, for which you shall have five thousand dollars as I promised you. I had the money in the bank the day you was 21 years old that I intend for you, and you shall have the money certain. Now, Willie I do not intend to interfere with this money in any way till I think you are capable of taking care of it and the sooner that time comes the better it will please me. I would hate very much to have you start out in some adventure that you thought all right and lose this money in one year. The first five thousand dollars that I got together cost me a heap of hard work. You would hardly believe me when I tell you that to obtain this I shoved a jackplane many a day, butchered three or four years, then came to this city, and after three months' perseverance I obtained a situation in a grocery store. I opened this store early, closed late, slept in the fourth story of the building in a room 30 by 40 feet and not a human being in the building but myself. All this I done to live as cheap as I could to save something. I don't want you to take up with this kind of fare. I was here in the cholera season ´49 and ´52 and the deaths averaged 80 to 125 daily and plenty of smallpox. I wanted to go home, but Mr. Fisk, the gentleman I was working for, told me if I left then, after it got healthy he probably would not want me. I stayed. All the money I have saved I know just how I got it. It did not come to me in any mysterious way, and the reason I speak of this is that money got in this way stops longer with a fellow that gets it with hard knocks than it does when he finds it. Willie, you are 21 and you have many a thing to learn yet. This money you have earned much easier than I did besides acquiring good habits at the same time and you are quite welcome to the money; hope you will make good use of it. I was 10 long years getting this together after I was your age. Now, hoping this will be satisfactory, I stop . . .
Truly Yours,
W. E. STORY
P.S.—You can consider this money on interest.

The nephew received the letter and thereafter consented that the money should remain with his uncle in accordance with the terms and conditions of the letter. The uncle died on the 29th day of January 1887, without having paid over to his nephew any portion of the said $5,000 and interest.

* * *

The defendant contends that the contract was without consideration to support it, and, therefore, invalid. He asserts that the promisee by refraining from the use of liquor and tobacco was not harmed but benefited; that that which he did was best for him to do independently of his uncle's promise, and insists that it follows that unless the promisor was benefited, the contract was without consideration. A contention, which if well founded, would seem to leave open for controversy in many cases whether that which the promisee did or omitted to do was, in fact, of such benefit to him as to leave no consideration to support the enforcement of the promisor's agreement. Such a rule could not be tolerated, and is without foundation in the law.

* * *

"In general a waiver of any legal right at the request of another party is a sufficient consideration for a promise" (Parsons on Contracts).

Pollock, in his work on contracts, says, ". . . Consideration means not so much that one party is profiting as that the other abandons some legal right in the present or limits his legal freedom of action in the future as an inducement for the promise of the first."

Continued

Continued

Now, applying this rule to the facts before us, the promisee used tobacco, occasionally drank liquor, and he had a legal right to do so. That right he abandoned for a period of years upon the strength of the promise of the testator that for such forbearance he would give him $5,000. We need not speculate on the effort which may have been required to give up the use of those stimulants. It is sufficient that he restricted his lawful freedom of action within certain prescribed limits upon the faith of his uncle's agreement, and now having fully performed the conditions imposed, it is of no moment whether such performance actually proved a benefit to the promisor, and the court will not inquire into it, but were it a proper subject of inquiry, we see nothing in this record that would permit a determination that the uncle was not benefited in a legal sense.

* * *

Judgment reversed. Trial court decision reinstated.

Questions

1. *a.* What detriment, if any, was sustained by the nephew?
   b. What benefit, if any, was secured by the uncle?
   c. As a matter of law, do we need to inquire into the uncle's benefit? Explain.
2. Lampley began work as an at-will (can be dismissed or can quit at any time) employee of Celebrity Homes in Denver, Colorado, in May 1975. On July 29, 1975, Celebrity announced a profit-sharing plan for all employees if the company reached its goals for the fiscal year, April 1, 1975, to March 31, 1976. Lampley was dismissed in January 1976. Celebrity distributed its profits in May 1976. Lampley sued when she did not receive a share of the profits. Celebrity argued that its promise to share its profits was a gratuity, unsupported by consideration. Decide. Explain. [See *Lampley* v. *Celebrity Homes,* 594 P.2d 605 (Col 1979).]

Adequacy of Consideration. With certain exceptions, the courts do not, as Judge Parker indicated in the *Hamer* case, inquire into the economic value of the consideration in question. Legal sufficiency depends not on the value of the consideration but on whether the promisee suffered a detriment in some way. To hold otherwise would put the courts in the place of the market in deciding the value of transactions. We are all free to make both good and bad bargains.

On the other hand, the courts will rule that consideration is found wanting in situations of pretense or sham where the parties have clearly agreed on token or nominal consideration in an effort to present the transaction as a contract rather than a gift. Likewise, an extreme inadequacy of consideration will sometimes cause the court to question a contract on the grounds of *fraud, duress,* or *unconscionability* (all are discussed later in this chapter). In these instances, the agreements would be unenforceable because of a failure of consideration. However, remember these cases are uncommon, and the courts rarely inquire into the adequacy of consideration.

preexisting duty. Prior legal obligation or commitment, performance of which does not constitute consideration for a new agreement.

Appearance of Consideration. Some agreements appear to be accompanied by consideration, but in fact, that appearance turns out to be an illusion. Hence, if one agrees to perform a **preexisting duty,** consideration would be found wanting. For example, if you were to pay your neighbor $50 to keep his dog chained when outdoors and a city ordinance already requires dogs to be chained if outdoors, your promise would be unenforceable because your neighbor already had a preexisting duty under the law to keep his dog chained. So performance of a preexisting legal duty does not constitute consideration since no legal detriment or benefit has arisen.

Similarly, preexisting duties sometimes arise from contracts. Suppose you hire a contractor to resurface the parking lot at your real estate office. You agree on a price of $12,000. With a portion of the work completed, the contractor asks you to amend the agreement to add $2,000 because the project is requiring more time than anticipated. You agree. The work is completed. Could you then legally refuse to pay the additional $2,000? The answer is yes, because the contractor failed to provide consideration for the modification of your contract. He was under a preexisting duty to finish the contract; hence, he did not sustain a legal detriment in the modified agreement. Note, however, that UCC section 2-209(1) provides that "an agreement modifying a contract within this Article needs no consideration to be binding."

Suppose you learn from your neighbor that your friend, Ames, wants to sell his house. You, as a realtor, find a buyer for the house and make all of the necessary arrangements for the sale out of regard for your friendship with Ames. Then when the transaction is complete, Ames says, "Well, this has been great of you, but I don't feel right about it. When I get my check for the sale, I'll pay you $2,000 for your hard work. I really appreciate it." What if Ames does not then pay the $2,000? Do you have recourse? No. This is a situation of **past consideration,** where the performance—arranging the sale of your friend's house—was not bargained for and was not given in exchange for the promise and thus cannot constitute consideration. In effect, the performance was a gift. Of course, past consideration is really not consideration at all. In some states, courts enforce promises to pay for benefits already received where doing so amounts to a *moral obligation* that must be enforced to prevent injustice.

past consideration. Performance that is not bargained for and was not given in exchange for the promise.

Substitutes for Consideration. When necessary to achieve justice, the courts sometimes conclude that a contract exists even though consideration is clearly lacking. Moral obligation and quasi-contract (discussed earlier) are two such instances; but the most prominent of these substitutes for consideration is the doctrine of **promissory estoppel** in which the promisor is "stopped" from denying the existence of a contract where the promisee has detrimentally relied on that promise. Promissory estoppel requires:

1. A promise on which the promisor should expect the promisee to rely.
2. The promisee did justifiably rely on the promise.
3. Injustice can be avoided only by enforcing the promise.

promissory estoppel. An equitable doctrine that protects those who foreseeably and reasonably rely on the promises of others by enforcing such promises when enforcement is necessary to avoid injustice.

Consider the following. You have been a part-time employee of a small fast-food chain restaurant while attending college. Upon graduation, you tell the manager of the restaurant that you think you could handle your own franchise. He says you need to get more experience and advises you to take a full-time position with the company. You do so. Everything goes well, and when you next approach the manager, he says, "If you can come up with the $20,000 and a good location we will get you in a franchise right away. But you've gotta move on this. Maybe you better quit your job with us and concentrate on this thing." You take his advice and quit your job to devote your time to making the necessary financial arrangements and finding a vacant building to rent in a good location for a franchise. You show the building to the manager, and he agrees that it looks like a favorable location and one that can easily be converted to the company's needs. He says, "Looks like you have everything in place. If you can come up with $5,000 more we will make this thing happen." You refuse and decide to bring suit against the fast-food chain for breach of contract. The chain defends by saying that you did not provide consideration for its promise. No formal financing arrangement was ever agreed to and you had not committed yourself to any franchising obligations. Under these circumstances you would probably prevail using a promissory estoppel claim. In brief, you would argue that you had changed your position in reliance on the franchisor's promises and that relief is necessary to prevent injustice. [For a similar case, see *Hoffman* v. *Red Owl Stores,* 133 N.W. 2d 267 (1965).]

G. Capacity

Having examined two of the required ingredients in an enforceable contract, agreement and consideration, we turn now to a third, capacity to contract. To enter a binding agreement, one must have the legal ability to do so; that is, one's mental condition and maturity must be such that the agreement was entered with understanding and in recognition of one's own interests. The three primary areas of concern are intoxication, mental impairment, and minority (infancy/youthfulness), with minority being much the more common area of dispute.

Intoxication. Assume you have been drinking to celebrate your 21st birthday. You enter a contract with a friend to sell him your autographed Michael Jordan basketball card for $200. You receive the money and turn over the card. Later, when sober, you regret the deal. Will a court nullify that contract on the grounds of your intoxication? That decision depends on whether you were sufficiently intoxicated that you did not understand the nature and purpose of the contract. If the objective evidence suggests that you did not understand the transaction, the contract would be considered voidable, in which case you could probably disaffirm the contract and demand the return of the card, although courts are often not sympathetic with people who attempt to escape contracts made while intoxicated. In most states, if you recovered the card, you would be required to return the $200 to your friend.

If on recovering your sobriety, your friend argued that the contract was invalid because of your intoxication, and he demanded the return of his $200 in exchange for the card, you could then **ratify** (affirm) the contract and hold him to it. If the contract had been for one of life's **necessaries** (food, shelter, clothing, medical care, tools of one's trade, etc.), you would have been liable for the reasonable value of that necessary.

ratify. Adopting or affirming a prior nonbinding act.

necessaries. That which is reasonably necessary for a minor's proper and suitable maintenance.

Mental Incompetence. In most cases, an agreement involving a mentally incompetent person is either void or voidable. The transaction would be void, that is, no contract would exist, where the impaired party had been *adjudged* insane. If the impaired party was unable to understand the purpose and effect of the contract but had not been legally adjudged insane, the contract would be voidable (void in some states) at the option of the impaired party. The competent party cannot void the contract, and the impaired party would have to pay the reasonable value of any necessaries received under the contract.

Profile Perspective: Let's return to Alan Herzig and the bat mitzvah. Suppose the Fox parents had simply given their daughter the $3,300 in question and told her to make her own party arrangements or to keep the money as she saw fit. Assume that the 13-year-old daughter had paid the 50 percent advance ($1,650) to Herzig and then had been disappointed, as her parents were, with the quality of the party. If the Fox daughter then declined to pay the remaining $1,650, could Herzig successfully sue the daughter? Could the daughter force Herzig to return the $1,650 advance?

Minority. Minors may complete their contracts if they wish, but they also have an absolute right to rescind most of those contracts. They may rescind until they reach adulthood and for a reasonable time thereafter. (Many states have enacted statutes forbidding minors from disaffirming some classes of contracts such as those for marriage, student loans, and life insurance.) The minor has a right of recovery for everything given up in meeting the terms of the contract. Similarly, the minor must return everything that remains in her or his possession that was received from the contract. In many states, if nothing of the bargained-for consideration remains or if its value has been depreciated, the minor has no duty to replace it but can still recover whatever she or he put into the contract. If not disaffirmed in a reasonable time after reaching the age of majority, the contract is considered to be ratified, and the minor is bound to its terms. The minor is also liable for the reasonable value (not necessarily the contract price) of necessaries purchased from an adult. That is, a minor must pay the adult the reasonable value of contracted-for items such as food, clothing, shelter, medical care, basic education, and tools of the minor's trade.

Minors may complete their contracts if they wish, but they also have an absolute right to rescind most of those contracts.

Despite the flexibility accorded to minors entering contracts, the adults who are parties to those contracts are bound to them and do not have the power to disaffirm. Hence, adults put themselves at risk when they choose to bargain with minors. As noted, in many states, a minor need not make restitution if the consideration is lost, destroyed, or depreciated. On the other hand, the case that follows illustrates the growing view that minors do have some monetary obligation after disaffirming a contract.

CASE

Dodson v. Shrader

824 S.W.2d 545 (Tenn. S. Ct. 1992)

Facts

In 1987, then 16-year-old Joseph Dodson bought a used 1984 pick-up truck for $4,900 in cash from Burns and Mary Shrader, owners of Shrader's Auto Sales. Mr. Shrader later testified that he believed Dodson to be 18 or 19 years of age but that the Shrader's did not ask Dodson his age; nor did Dodson misrepresent his age to the Shraders. Nine months after the purchase, the truck developed motor troubles that a mechanic believed to be a burned valve. Dodson did not have the money for repairs. He kept driving the truck, and the engine "blew up" one month later. Dodson parked the truck in his parents' front yard. He sought a full refund from the Shraders. They refused to do so and refused to accept the return of the truck. Dodson then sued to rescind the contract and recover the purchase price.

Prior to trial, the truck was struck by a hit-and-run driver. Mr. Shrader testified that the value of the truck had then declined to $500. The Shraders argued that Dodson was responsible for the difference between the purchase price of the truck and its value at the time of trial. The trial court found for Dodson and ordered the Shraders to refund the $4,900 upon return of the truck. The Court of Appeals affirmed, and the Shraders appealed to the Tennessee Supreme Court.

* * *

Continued

Continued

Justice O'Brien

[T]he rule in Tennessee is in accord with the majority rule on the issue among our sister states. This rule is based upon the underlying purpose of the "infancy doctrine" which is to protect minors from their lack of judgment and "from squandering their wealth through improvident contracts with crafty adults who would take advantage of them in the market-place."

There is, however, a modern trend among the states, either by judicial action or by statute, in the approach to the problem of balancing the rights of minors against those of innocent merchants. As a result, two minority rules have developed which allow the other party to a contract with a minor to refund less than the full consideration paid in the event of rescission.

The first of these minority rules is called the "Benefit Rule." The rule holds that, upon rescission, recovery of the full purchase price is subject to a deduction for the minor's use of the merchandise. This rule recognizes that the traditional rule in regard to necessaries has been extended so far as to hold an infant bound by his contracts, where he failed to restore what he has received under them to the extent of the benefit actually derived by him from what he has received from the other party to the transaction.

The other minority rule holds that the minor's recovery of the full purchase price is subject to a deduction for the minor's "use" of the consideration he or she received under the contract, or for the "depreciation" or "deterioration" of the consideration in his or her possession.

We are impressed by the statement made by the Court of Appeals of Ohio:

> At a time when we see young persons between 18 and 21 years of age demanding and assuming more responsibilities in their daily lives; when we see such persons emancipated, married, and raising families; when we see such persons charged with the responsibility for committing crimes; when we see such persons being sued in tort claims for acts of negligence; when we see such persons subject to military service; when we see such persons engaged in business and acting in almost all other respects as an adult, it seems timely to re-examine the case law pertaining to contractual rights and responsibilities of infants to see if the law as pronounced and applied by the courts should be redefined.

* * *

We state the rule to be followed hereafter, in reference to a contract of a minor, to be where the minor has not been overreached in any way, and there has been no undue influence, and the contract is a fair and reasonable one, and the minor has actually paid money on the purchase price, and taken and used the article purchased, that he ought not to be permitted to recover the amount actually paid, without allowing the vendor of the goods reasonable compensation for the use of, depreciation, and willful or negligent damage to the article purchased, while in his hands. If there has been any fraud or imposition on the part of the seller or if the contract is unfair, or any unfair advantage has been taken of the minor inducing him to make the purchase, then the rule does not apply. Whether there has been such an overreaching on the part of the seller, and the fair market value of the property returned, would always, in any case, be a question for the trier of fact . . .

This rule is best adapted to modern conditions under which minors are permitted to, and do in fact, transact a great deal of business for themselves, long before they have reached the age of legal majority. Many young people work and earn money and collect it and spend it oftentimes without any oversight or restriction. The law does not question their right to buy if they have the money to pay for their purchases. It seems intolerably burdensome for everyone concerned if merchants and business people cannot deal with them safely, in a fair and reasonable way.

* * *

Continued

Continued

We note that in this case, some nine months after the date of purchase, the truck purchased by the plaintiff began to develop mechanical problems. Plaintiff was informed of the probable nature of the difficulty which apparently involved internal problems in the engine. He continued to drive the vehicle until the engine "blew up" and the truck became inoperable. Whether or not this involved gross negligence or intentional conduct on his part is a matter for determination at the trial level. It is not possible to determine from this record whether a counterclaim for tortious damage to the vehicle was asserted. After the first tender of the vehicle was made by plaintiff, and refused by the defendant, the truck was damaged by a hit-and-run driver while parked on plaintiff's property. The amount of that damage and the liability for that amount between the purchaser and the vendor, as well as the fair market value of the vehicle at the time of tender, is also an issue for the jury.

[Reversed and remanded.]

Questions

1. What was the issue in this case?
2. Distinguish the two minority rules that are summarized in this case.
3. To achieve justice in contract cases involving a minor and an adult, what would you want to know about the adult's behavior toward the minor?
4. White, a 17-year-old high school sophomore, operated a trucking business, including hiring drivers, securing jobs, and so forth. He lived with his parents and received his food, clothing, and shelter from them. Valencia operated a garage and repaired White's equipment until they had a disagreement over replacement of a motor. White then disaffirmed his contract with Valencia and refused to pay what he owed. At trial the jury found that White had caused the damage to the motor, but the court held that White could disaffirm the contract and required Valencia to refund any money paid to White under the contract. Valencia appealed.
   a. Is the fact that White was in business for himself in any way relevant to the outcome of this case? Explain.
   b. Decide the case. Explain. [See *Valencia* v. *White,* 654 P.2d 287 (Ariz. Ct. App. 1982).]

H. Genuineness of Assent

Sometimes parties appear to have concluded a binding contract, but the courts will allow them to escape that obligation because they had not, in fact, achieved an agreement. They had achieved the appearance of agreement, but not the reality. That situation arises when the contract is the product of misrepresentation, fraud, duress, undue influence, or mistake. Ordinarily, such agreements are voidable and may be rescinded because of the absence of genuine of assent, the fourth of five ingredients in a binding contract.

Profile Perspective: Returning once again to our chapter profile involving Alan Herzig, and the Fox bat mitzvah, how would the courts have dealt with their dispute had it been the product of a mistake on the part of one of the parties? Suppose that Alan Herzig, who provided the entertainment, had understood that the party was to be August 14 when, in fact, the Fox family had specified August 13. Would Herzig be responsible for fulfilling the deal even though he had another party scheduled for August 13?

---

misrepresentation. The innocent assertion of a fact that is not in accord with the truth.

fraud. An intentional misrepresentation of a material fact with intent to deceive where the misrepresentation is justifiably relied on by another and damages result.

Misrepresentation and Fraud. An innocent untruth is a **misrepresentation.** Intentional untruths constitute **fraud.** In either case, a party to a contract who has been deceived may rescind the deal, and restitution may be secured if benefits were extended to the party issuing the untruth. The test for fraud is as follows:

1. Misrepresentation of a material fact.
2. The misrepresentation was intentional.
3. The injured party justifiably relied on the misrepresentation.
4. Injury resulted.

Note that the test requires a misrepresented fact. In general, misrepresented opinions are not grounds for action; but many courts are now recognizing exceptions to that rule, especially when the innocent party has relied on opinion coming from an expert.

duress. Overpowering of the will of a person by force or fear.

Duress. Sometimes genuine assent is not secured and a contract may be rescinded because one of the parties was forced to agree. Fear lies at the heart of a **duress** claim. The party seeking to escape the contract would have to establish that a wrongful act was threatened or had occurred causing the party to enter the contract out of fear of harm such that free will was precluded. Increasingly, courts are also setting aside contracts on the grounds of economic duress. For example, suppose you know that one of your regular customers depends on your timely delivery of steel to his factory and that he cannot expeditiously find an alternative source of supply. Therefore, you tell your customer that delivery will be delayed until he agrees to pay a higher price for the steel. If he agrees, the resulting contract probably could be rescinded on the grounds of economic duress.

undue influence. Dominion that results in a right to rescind a contract.

Undue Influence. Under some circumstances, the first party to an apparent contract can escape its terms by demonstrating that the second party so dominated her will that she (the first party) did not act independently. These claims are most common in cases involving those who are old or infirm and who lose their independence of thought and action to the **undue influence** of a caregiver or advisor.

Mistake. Most of us, upon taking a new job, operate at least for a time in fear that we will make a mistake. Assume you are new to your job and are preparing a bid that your company will submit in hopes of securing the general maintenance contract for a large office building. In preparing the bid, you inadvertently submit a final price of $50,000 rather than $500,000. What happens? Do you lose your job?

mutual mistake. Where both parties to the contract are in error about a material fact.

unilateral mistake. Where one party to a contract is in error about a material fact.

In some cases, mistakes involving critical facts can be grounds for rescinding contracts. A **mutual mistake** is one in which both parties to the contract are in error about some critical fact. With exceptions, either party can rescind those contracts because genuine assent was not achieved. Your erroneous bid, however, is a **unilateral mistake,** that is, only one party to the contract made an error. The general rule is that those contracts cannot be rescinded. However, if you are able to show that the other party to the contract knew or should have known about your mistake, many courts would allow you to rescind. Certainly you would make that argument in this instance since the $50,000 bid is presumably dramatically out of line with the other bids and at odds with reasonable business expectations about the value of the contract. In cases where an error is made in *drafting* a contract, and both parties are unaware of the error (a mutual mistake), the courts will reform the contract rather than void it. That is, the contract will be rewritten to reflect what the parties actually intended.

FIGURE 4.1

FIVE REQUIREMENTS OF A BINDING CONTRACT
1. Agreement 2. Consideration 3. Capacity 4. Geniuneness of assent 5. Legality of purpose

I. Legality of Purpose

Having examined agreement, consideration, capacity, and genuineness of assent, we turn now to the final requirement for the creation of a binding contract: legality of purpose (see Figure 4.1). Illegality refers to bargains to commit a crime or a tort (e.g., a deal with a coworker to embezzle funds from one's employer); but more broadly, illegality involves bargains that are forbidden by statute or violate public policy. We can identify three general categories of illegal agreements: (1) contracts that violate statutes, (2) contracts that are **unconscionable,** and (3) contracts that violate **public policy.** In general, the effect of an`illegal contract is that it cannot be enforced, and the courts will not provide a remedy if its terms are unfulfilled. With exceptions, the parties to illegal deals are left where the courts find them.

unconscionable. A contract so one-sided and oppressive as to be unfair.

public policy. That which is good for the general public, as gleaned from a state's constitution, statutes, and case law.

1. *Contracts violating statutes.* As noted, a contract to commit a crime or a tort is illegal and unenforceable. The states have also specified certain other agreements that are illegal. Those provisions vary from state to state, but they commonly include antigambling laws, laws forbidding the conduct of certain kinds of business on Sundays (**blue laws**), laws forbidding **usury,** and laws forbidding the practice of certain professions (law, real estate, hair care, etc.) without a license.

blue laws. Laws forbidding certain kinds of business on Sundays.

usury. Interest in excess of the rate allowed by law.

2. *Unconscionable.* We address this notion in greater detail in Chapter 12, "Consumer Protection and Debtor/Credit or Law," but the idea is that certain agreements are so thoroughly one-sided that fairness precludes enforcing them. Problems of

Can Prince Escape?

According to 1996 news reports, the pop star who was once named Prince demanded that he be released from his long-term contract with Warner Music Group. He claimed that management turnover (seven top executives were removed in an 18-month period) made it impossible for the company to succeed in its marketing responsibilities. Standard recording contracts usually require at least six albums before the possibility of changing companies can be considered. Should we feel sorry for Prince? Are such contracts unconscionable?

unconscionability often arise in situations in which the bargaining power of one of the parties is much superior to the other, where one can, in effect, "twist the arm" or otherwise take advantage of the other. Both the common law of contracts and UCC 2-302 give the courts the power to modify or refuse to enforce such deals.

3. *Public policy.* The courts have wide latitude to act in the best interest of the populace. Public policy reflects the will of the people. The courts are obliged to do what the general welfare calls for. Therefore, the courts may decline to enforce certain otherwise binding contracts because to do so would not be in the best interest of the public. For example, an agreement in restraint of trade, such as a deal not to open a Ford automobile dealership in your hometown because your brother already operates one such business, might well violate public policy as well as the antitrust laws (see Chapter 11).

noncompetition clause. Employee agrees not to go into business in competition with employer.

In the same vein, businesses commonly impose **noncompetition clauses** on their employees. Thus, if as hypothesized above, your employees must sign an agreement not to compete with you so that you can protect trade secrets, prevent free-riding, and so forth, that agreement may be unenforceable as a violation of public policy. In making that decision, the court would particularly examine the reasonableness of both the geographic and time restraints that the agreement imposes on your employees. How big a circle are you drawing around your business, and for how long are you keeping your employees out of that circle? More generally, how expansive must the restriction be in order to protect your legitimate interests?

exculpatory clause or release. Portion of a contract that seeks to relieve one of the parties to the contract from any liability for breach of a duty under that contract.

Another commonplace public policy concern is the **exculpatory clause,** or **release.** If you own or manage a potentially hazardous activity such as a water slide, bungee tower, or even a health spa, you may try to protect yourself from litigation should a customer be hurt by including a release in the customer agreement. Theoretically, such agreements are enforceable in the manner of any other contractual provision. However, the courts tend to disfavor them. The result is that sometimes they are enforced, and sometimes they are not. Many factors can influence that decision, including how sweeping the exculpation is, whether it was knowingly entered, and the relative bargaining power of the parties. The case that follows examines releases in greater detail.

If you own or manage a potentially hazardous activity such as a water slide, bungee tower, or even a health spa, you may try to protect yourself from litigation should a customer be hurt by including a release in the customer agreement.

CASE

Milligan v. Big Valley Corp.

754 P.2d 1063 (Wyo. S.Ct. 1988)

Facts

Dean Griffin entered an ironman decathlon at the Grand Targhee Ski Resort in Alta, Wyoming, on April 13, 1985. The resort was owned and operated by Big Valley Corporation. The decathlon consisted of several events, including swimming five laps of the pool, bowling one line, drinking a quart of beer, throwing darts, and both downhill and cross-country ski races. The

Continued

Continued

downhill ski race, the first event, was conducted early in the morning before the resort was opened to the public. The snow was hard and icy. Prior to the race all participants, in consideration of being allowed to enter, were required to sign a "general release of claim." On April 13, 1984, Griffin signed the release, which in part stated:

> In consideration of my being allowed to participate in IRONMAN DECATLON [sic] at Targhee Resort, Alta, Wyoming, I irrevocably and forever hereby release and discharge Targhee Resort and the other sponsors of and any and all of the employees, agents or servants and owners of Targhee Resort and the other sponsors of IRONMAN DECATLON [sic] officially connected with this event of and from any and all legal claims or legal liability of any kind, nature and description involving or relating to bodily injury or death suffered or sustained by me, or any property damage of mine, during my stay at Targhee Resort.
>
> I hereby personally assume all risks in connection with said event and I further release the aforementioned resort, its agents, and operators, including but not limited to persons not mentioned, for any harm, injury or damage which might befall me as a participant in this event including all risks connected therewith, whether foreseen or unforeseen and further save and hold harmless said resort and persons from any claim by me or my family, estate, heirs or assigns.

About 10 minutes after the race began, Griffin, an experienced, expert skier, was found unconscious about three-quarters of the way down the hill. He died a few hours later. No one witnessed the incident, but it was speculated that he lost control and struck a tree.

Elizabeth Milligan, administratrix of Griffin's estate, commenced a wrongful death action alleging negligence and misconduct by Big Valley. The trial court granted a summary judgment for Big Valley based on the release signed by Griffin. Milligan appealed.

* * *

Justice Cardine

Exculpatory agreements, releasing parties from negligence liability for damages or injury, are valid and enforceable in Wyoming if they do not violate public policy. Generally, specific agreements absolving participants and proprietors from negligence liability during hazardous recreational activities are enforceable, subject to willful misconduct limitations.

This court recently addressed the issue of the validity and enforceability of a release in *Schutkowski* v. *Carey*. In *Schutkowski,* a skydiving student brought a negligence action against her instructors after being injured during her first jump. This court held that a release signed by the student prior to her injuries excused her instructors from any liability for negligence. In reaching this holding, we adopted the four-part test found in *Jones* v. *Dressel,* Colo., 623 P.2d 370 (1981), to determine whether this type of release is valid and enforceable. This four-part test is applicable here. Thus, we consider: "(1) Whether there exists a duty to the public; (2) the nature of the service performed; (3) whether the contract was fairly entered into; and (4) whether the intention of the parties is expressed in clear and unambiguous language."

A duty to the public exists if the nature of the business or service affects the public interest and the service performed is considered an essential service. Thus, our first inquiry is whether sponsoring, coordinating, and organizing a ski race is a business or service affecting the public interest and is considered an essential service demanding a public duty.

A release agreement affecting the public interest, giving rise to a public duty, has been described as one that "concerns a business of a type generally thought suitable for public regulation. The party seeking exculpation is engaged in performing a service of great importance to the public, which is often a matter of practical necessity for some members of the public. The

Continued

Continued

party holds himself out as willing to perform this service for any member of the public who seeks it. As a result of the essential nature of the service, in the economic setting of the transaction, the party invoking exculpation possesses a decisive advantage of bargaining strength against any member of the public who seeks his services."

Types of services thought to be subject to public regulation, and therefore demanding a public duty or considered essential, have included common carriers, hospitals and doctors, public utilities, innkeepers, public warehousemen, employers, and services involving extra-hazardous activities. Generally, a private recreational business does not qualify as a service demanding a special duty to the public, nor are its services of a special, highly necessary or essential nature.

The Ironman Decathlon can best be labeled a recreational type of activity of no great public import.

The agreement in question does not involve severe disparity of bargaining power . . . A disparity of bargaining power will be found when a contracting party with little or no bargaining strength has no reasonable alternative to entering the contract at the mercy of the other's negligence. For example, a member of the public contracting with a public utility, common carrier, hospital, or employer often has no real choice or alternative and is, therefore, at the mercy of the other party. Such is not the case here. . . . Skiing in the race was not a matter of practical necessity for the public, and putting on the race was not an essential service. Nor was skiing in the race the only reasonable alternative. Thus, no decisive bargaining advantage or disadvantage existed. Further, no evidence suggests that the decedent was unfairly pressured into signing the agreement or that he was deprived of an opportunity to understand its implications.

Milligan argues that the release was entered into unfairly because it contained boiler plate language prepared solely by the resort and was an adhesive contract. The argument is without merit. The mere fact that a contract is on a printed form prepared by one party and offered on a "take it or leave it" basis does not automatically establish it as an adhesive contract. There must be a showing that the parties were greatly disparate in bargaining power and that there was no opportunity for negotiation for services which could not be obtained elsewhere. Here no such showing was made . . .

The final factor requires us to determine whether the release agreement evidences the parties' intent to release Big Valley from liability for negligent acts in clear and unambiguous language . . .

Milligan first argues that the release is ambiguous in not specifically naming appellee Big Valley Corporation in the document. An ambiguous contract is one "capable of being understood in more ways than one. It is an agreement which is obscure in its meaning, because of indefiniteness of expression, or because a double meaning is present."

* * *

The language could not be clearer. Examining the release in light of the purpose of the contract, it is clear that the parties intended to release the ski resort and all those involved in the Ironman Decathlon from liability . . .

Milligan also argues that the language of the release is too broad and ambiguous to release Big Valley Corporation . . . The release specifically and repeatedly exempts Big Valley from any responsibility for potential "legal claims or legal liability of any kind whether foreseen or unforeseen." Although the release does not contain the word "negligence," we held in *Schutkowski* that "the absence of the word 'negligence' is not fatal to an exculpatory clause if the terms of the contract clearly show intent to extinguish liability." . . .

Milligan's second argument is that there exists a genuine issue of material fact as to whether Big Valley was guilty of willful and wanton misconduct.

* * *

Continued

Continued

Big Valley Corporation is guilty of willful and wanton misconduct only if it deliberately acted, or failed to act, in reckless disregard of the consequences or in a manner that evidenced a high degree of probability that harm would result to others. Here it is clear that Big Valley did not act in utter disregard of consequences but was concerned for the safety of the participants. Big Valley attempted to protect the racers from danger by inspecting the course, . . . by grooming the course, by allowing the race at a time when the public would not be present on the mountain, by having someone ski the course to assess the snow conditions, and by announcing warnings regarding the conditions to all of the racers prior to the race. Milligan states that there were no safety nets or speed gates used. No marked course was set up. The racers were started in a group rather than in timed intervals, and no helmets were provided or required. True, the race was not down a marked course; thus there were no speed gates, safety nets, or timed intervals. Nothing is presented that indicates a requirement that the race must be down a marked course or timed. The participants knew that the race was not down a marked course, that it was a "La Mans" start, and that they might be disqualified if they did other than just ski down the hill for fun.

. . . The undisputed facts show that safety was of concern to Big Valley and that specific steps were taken for the safety of the racers . . .

We conclude that the release is not void as a matter of public policy . . . We affirm the judgment for Big Valley.

Questions

1. Milligan's argument consisted essentially of two claims. Explain them and their resolution by the court.
2. Why did the court enforce Big Valley's release, which had the effect of excusing the ski resort from any negligence for which it may have been responsible?
3. *a.* Would a release like that in this case be enforceable if it involved a school district excusing itself from liability for any injury that might befall students on a class field trip?
   b. What if the school release sought to excuse the school not from its own negligence, but merely from events beyond the school's control? Explain.

II. Interpreting and Enforcing Contracts

We have examined the five ingredients in a binding contract: agreement, consideration, capacity, genuineness of assent, and legality of purpose. Having established those conditions, a contract may have been created, but the door to contract problems has not been closed. Contracts often must fulfill writing formalities to be enforceable. Third parties may have claims against some contracts. And what happens when a party to a contract does not perform as called for by the agreement? This portion of Chapter 4 explores those dilemmas.

We have examined the five ingredients in a binding contract: agreement, consideration, capacity, genuineness of assent, and legality of purpose.

A. Writing

Suppose that you manage your business affairs and your life on the theory that your word is your bond and that a handshake seals a deal. Ordinarily, you have not felt it necessary to put your agreements in writing; you have been satisfied with oral understandings. Are you foolish? Perhaps.

Suppose that you manage your business affairs and your life on the theory that your word is your bond and that a handshake seals a deal. Ordinarily, you have not felt it necessary to put your agreements in writing; you have been satisfied with oral understandings. Are you foolish? Perhaps.

Profile Perspective: Let's return to Alan Herzig and the bat mitzvah contract. If Herzig and the Fox family had not bothered to reduce their understanding to writing, would Herzig have lost his claim simply because he was unable to produce written confirmation of their deal?

Statute of Frauds. A statute specifying that certain contracts must be in writing to be enforceable.

suretyship. A third party agrees to answer for the debt of another.

Certainly, the common belief is that agreements must be in writing to be enforceable, but, in most cases, oral contracts are fully enforceable. However, the exceptions are important. Oral contracts are subject to misunderstanding or to being forgotten, and fraudulent claims can readily arise from oral understandings. Consequently, our states have drawn upon the English **Statute of Frauds** in requiring the following kinds of contracts to be in writing in order to be enforceable:

1. Answering for the obligations of another (**suretyship**).
2. The sale of land.
3. Promises that cannot be performed within one year.
4. Contracts for the sale of goods at a price of $500 or more.
5. A promise made in consideration of marriage.
6. An executor/administrator of an estate promising to pay the decedent's debts from the executor/administrator's *own* funds.

Failure to Comply. A fully performed oral contract, even though not in compliance with the Statute of Frauds, will not be rescinded by the courts. However, incomplete oral contracts that fail to comply with the Statute are unenforceable. If a party to an unenforceable oral contract has provided partial performance in reliance on the contract, the courts will ordinarily provide compensation under quasi-contract principles for the reasonable value of that performance. Now let's consider each of the six contract categories in some detail.

1. Suretyship. Assume you have just graduated from college and a longtime family friend, Jacobs, wants to help you get started in a small printing business. You secure a bank loan on the condition that you find a credit-worthy third party as a guarantor for the loan. Jacobs agrees with the bank to pay the debt if you fail to do so. Jacobs's promise to pay the debt must be in writing to be enforceable.

Under the "main purpose" exception, a promise guaranteeing to pay the debt of another need *not* be in writing if the leading object of the promise is a monetary benefit for the guarantor. Assume Black's Drugs is threatened with bankruptcy and owes money to both Higgins and Spencer. Spencer orally promises to pay Black's debt to Higgins if Black's does not do so itself. That promise is enforceable even though not in writing if its main purpose/leading object is to benefit Spencer financially by keeping Black's Drugs in business long enough to pay its debts.

2. The sale of land. Broadly, land is interpreted to include the surface itself, that which is in the soil (e.g., minerals) or permanently attached to it (e.g., buildings), and growing crops when accompanying the transfer of land. Thus, if a building was permanently attached to a lot you seek for the aforementioned printing business, that building would need to be included in the written contract; but if you contracted to have a building constructed on your lot, you would not need (at least for the purposes of the Statute of Frauds) to execute a writing with the building contractor since you would not be contracting for an interest in land. A long-term lease (normally more than one year) for that land and building would, in most states, need to be in writing. All of these principles simply reflect the special role of land in our view of wealth and freedom.

3. Promises that cannot be performed within one year. This requirement springs from a concern about faulty memories, deaths, and other impediments to the satisfactory conclusion of long-term contracts. The courts have interpreted this provision narrowly, in effect saying that such a contract need not be in writing if it is *possible,* according to its terms, to perform it within one year from the day of its creation. It follows then that a contract for an indefinite period of time (e.g., an employment contract "for the balance of the employee's life") need not be in writing to be enforceable. (It is possible that the employee will die within one year.)

4. Contracts for the sale of goods at a price of $500 or more. With exceptions, under both the English-derived Statute of Frauds and the UCC (section 2-201), contracts for the sale of goods (having a value of $500 or more under the UCC) must be in writing to be enforceable. Under the UCC, an informal writing will suffice so long as it indicates that a contract was made, it contains a quantity term, and it was signed "by the party against whom enforcement is sought." Section 2-201 provides exceptions for certain transactions of $500 or more in goods in which a contract will be enforceable even though not in writing.

5. Contracts in consideration of marriage. The mutual exchange of marriage promises need not be in writing, but any contract that uses marriage as the consideration to support the contract must be in writing to be enforceable. Such contracts would include, for example, prenuptial agreements that are entered prior to marriage and serve the purpose, among others, of specifying how the couple's property will be divided in the event of a divorce. Those contracts must be in writing to be enforceable.

6. Executor/administrator's promise. When an individual dies, a representative is appointed to oversee the estate. A promise by that executor/administrator to pay the estate's debts must be in writing if the payment will be made from the executor/administrator's personal funds. Thus, where the executor of an estate contracts with an auctioneer to dispose of the decedent's personal property, the executor's promise to pay the auctioneer must be in writing if the funds are to come from the executor's personal resources; the promise need not be in writing if the payment is to come from the estate.

The Parol Evidence Rule. Suppose you are the purchasing manager for a large manufacturer. You entered a written contract for 50 new personal computers. During negotiations, the seller's agent said they would "throw in" 10 new printers if they got the computer order; but you failed to include a provision for the printers in the contract. Is your boss about to have a fit? Perhaps, because you probably will not be able to introduce evidence of that oral understanding to alter the terms of the written contract. In general, whenever a contract has been reduced to writing with the intent that the writing represents a complete and final integration of the parties' intentions, none of the parties can introduce **parol evidence** (oral or written words outside the "four corners" of the agreement) to add to, change, or contradict that contract when that evidence was expressed/created at the time of or prior to the writing. The idea is that the written agreement is presumed to be the best evidence of the parties' intentions at the time they entered the contract. (The parol evidence rule under UCC section 2-202 is essentially the same as the common law provisions discussed here.)

parol evidence rule. When the written document is intended as the parties' final expression of their contract, parole evidence of prior agreements or representations cannot be used to vary the terms of the document.

Exceptions. The parol evidence rule can sometimes stand in the way of achieving the purposes of the parties and the courts. Thus, certain exceptions have been identified where parol evidence is admissible. Among them:

1. To add missing terms to an incomplete written contract.

FIGURE 4.2 **ASSIGNMENT OF RIGHTS**

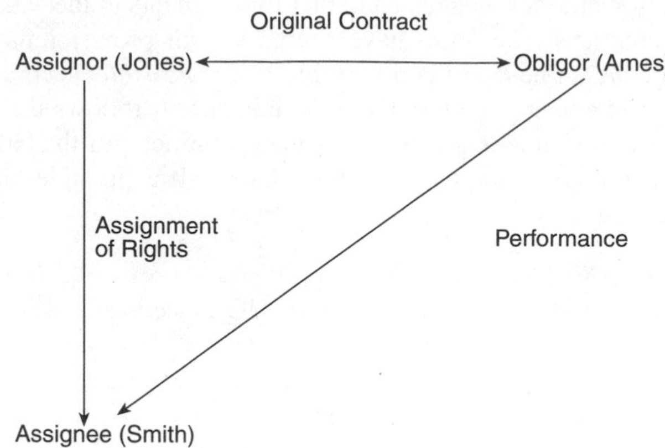

2. To explain ambiguities in a written contract.
3. To prove circumstances that would invalidate a written contract; that is, to establish one of the grounds of mistake, fraud, illegality, and so forth explained earlier in this chapter.

B. *Third Parties*

We turn now to the rights and duties of those who are not parties to a contract but are holders of legally recognizable interests in that contract. Those interests arise when (1) contract rights are assigned to others, (2) contract duties are delegated to others, or (3) contracts have third-party beneficiary provisions.

assignment. A transfer of property or some right or interest therein, from one person to another.
assignor. The maker of an assignment.
assignee. A person to whom an assignment is made.
obligor. A person who is bound by a promise or other obligation; a promisor.

Assignment of Rights. Ordinarily, a party to a contract is free to transfer her or his rights under the contract to a third party. Thus, if Ames owes Jones $500 for work performed, Jones can *assign* that right to Smith, who can now assert her right to collect against Ames. That transfer of rights is labeled an **assignment** (see Figure 4.2). Jones, the party making the transfer, is the **assignor;** Smith, the one receiving the right, is the **assignee;** and Ames, the party who must perform, is the **obligor.** Ames, the obligor, must now perform the contract for the benefit of the assignee; that is, Ames must pay the $500 to Smith. The completed assignment then extinguishes the assignor's rights under the contract.

Some contracts are not assignable without consent of the obligor. That would be the case where the obligor's duties are materially altered by the assignment. For example, if you have a contract to serve as a personal fitness trainer for a busy chief executive officer, your contract could not be assigned without your consent to another CEO, or movie star, or the like because the highly personal and specific obligations under the contract would necessarily be materially altered with a different client.

delegatee. The one to whom a duty is delegated.
delegator. The one who delegates a duty.
obligee. A person to whom another is bound by a promise or other obligation; a promisee.

Delegation of Duties. The parties to a contract may also delegate their *duties* under the contract to one or more third parties. Assume Allen has secured a contract to install windows in Boyd's new office building (see Figure 4.3). Allen could delegate that duty to another contractor, Harms (although Allen would more commonly simply enter a subcontracting arrangement without actually transferring the underlying contract). A delegation of duty leaves the **delegatee** (the one to whom the duty is delegated, Harms, in our example) primarily responsible for performance; but the *obligor*/**delegator** (the one who made the delegation, Allen) remains secondarily liable in case the delegatee fails to fulfill the duty to the **obligee** (the one to whom the duty is owed under both the original contract

DELEGATION OF DUTIES — FIGURE 4.3

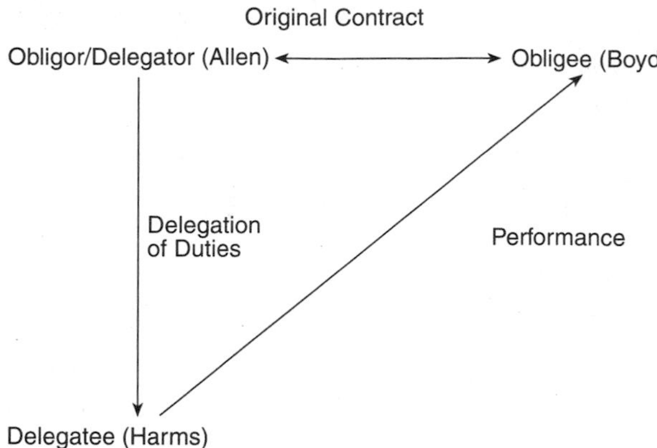

and the delegation, Boyd). As with the assignment of rights, some contractual duties, particularly those of a personal service nature, cannot be delegated without consent.

Third-Party Beneficiary Contracts.

Normally, those not a party to a contract have no rights with respect to it. However, we have seen that third parties may be assigned rights or delegated duties under a contract. A third party may also enforce a contract where that contract was expressly intended to benefit the third party. An agreement of that nature is a third-party beneficiary contract. **Third-party beneficiaries** are of three kinds: creditor, donee, and incidental. In general, creditor and donee beneficiaries can enforce contracts made by others for their benefit; incidental beneficiaries cannot do so.

third-party beneficiaries. People who are not parties to a contract but who have the right to enforce it because the contract was made with the intent to benefit them.

Creditor Beneficiary. Assume you decide to expand your used car business by advertising on television. Your ads appear on TV, and you owe the local station $2,000. Rather than paying the bill directly, you transfer a used car to Gleason with the understanding that he will pay off your bill with the television station. Thus, the station becomes the **creditor beneficiary** of the contract between you and Gleason, and the station can sue Gleason for that money if necessary while you remain secondarily responsible for the payment.

creditor beneficiary. Person who has given consideration, who is an intended beneficiary of a contract though not a party, and thus is entitled to enforce the contract.

Donee Beneficiary. When the promisee's primary purpose in entering a contract was to make a gift to another, that third party is a **donee beneficiary** of the contract. The most common of these situations involves an ordinary life insurance policy of which the owner (the promisee) pays premiums to the life insurance company (the promisor), which is obliged to pay benefits to the third party upon the death of the promisee/policy owner. If necessary, the third-party beneficiary can sue the insurance company for payment.

donee beneficiary. Person who has not given consideration, but is an intended beneficiary of a contract, though not a party, and is entitled to enforce the contract.

Incidental Beneficiary. Often a third party receives benefit from a contract although that was not the contracting parties' primary purpose or intent. For example, assume a General Motors car dealer enters into a contract to buy land adjacent to your used car lot for the purpose of opening a large dealership. You would benefit immensely from the spillover effect of the large, adjacent dealership. In such a situation, you would be an **incidental beneficiary** of the land-sale contract because that contract was not intended for your benefit. If the landowner or the GM dealer failed to perform, you, as an incidental beneficiary, would have no legal rights against either of them.

incidental beneficiary. Person who is not a party to a contract, who benefits indirectly from the contract, who was not contemplated by the parties, and who may not enforce the contract.

The case that follows illustrates third-party beneficiary reasoning in the colorful, factual context of a college basketball referee whose game calls incensed University of Iowa fans.

CASE

Bain v. Gillispie

357 N.W.2d 47 (Ia. Ct. App. 1984)

Facts

James C. Bain referees college basketball games. On March 6, 1982, he called a foul on a University of Iowa player, which permitted a Purdue player to shoot free throws leading to a last-minute victory. Iowa fans thought the call was clearly erroneous. Soon after the game, John and Karen Gillispie, operators of a novelty store in Iowa City, Iowa, began marketing a T-shirt depicting a man with a rope around his neck and the caption "Jim Bain Fan Club." Bain then sued the Gillispies. The Gillispies counterclaimed, arguing that Bain's officiating was below the level of competence required of a professional referee and thus amounted to malpractice. They sought $175,000 in damages from Bain because, they argued, Iowa's loss to Purdue eliminated the Hawkeyes from the championship of the Big 10 Conference, which, in turn, destroyed a potential market for Gillispies' memorabilia relating to Iowa's conference title. At trial, the Gillispies raised the negligence claim "referee malpractice," which was rejected. The Gillispies also claimed that they were third-party beneficiaries of an employment contract between Bain and the Big 10 Conference. The trial court granted Bain's motion for summary judgment. The Gillispies appealed.

* * *

Judge Snell

[The appeals court affirmed the trial court's judgment that Bain was not negligent in that he did not owe a legal duty to the Gillispies.]

The trial court found that there was no issue of material fact on the Gillispies' claim that they were beneficiaries under Bain's contract with the Big 10. Gillispies argue that until the contract is produced, there exists a question of whether they are beneficiaries. There is some question of whether there is a contract between Bain and the Big 10. In his response to interrogatories, Bain stated that he had no written contract with the Big 10, but that there was a letter which defined "working relationship." Although this letter was never produced and ordinarily we would not decide an issue without the benefit of examining the letter's contents, we nevertheless find the issue presently capable of determination. By deposition Gillispies answered that there was no contract between them and Bain, the Big 10 Athletic Conference, the University of Iowa, the players, coaches, or with any body regarding this issue. Thus, even if the letter were considered a contract, Gillispies would be considered third-party beneficiaries. Because Gillispies would not be privy to the contract, they must be direct beneficiaries to maintain a cause of action, and not merely incidental beneficiaries.

A direct beneficiary is either a donee beneficiary or a creditor beneficiary.

* * *

Gillispies make no claim that they are creditor beneficiaries of Bain, the Big 10 Athletic Conference, or the University of Iowa. "The real test is said to be whether the contracting parties intended that a third person should receive a benefit which might be enforced in the courts." It is clear that the purpose of any promise which Bain might have made was not to confer a gift on Gillispies. Likewise, the Big 10 did not owe any duty to the Gillispies such that they would have

Continued

Continued

been creditor beneficiaries. If a contract did exist between Bain and the Big 10, Gillispies can be considered nothing more than incidental beneficiaries and as such are unable to maintain a cause of action.

Consequently, there was no genuine issue for trial which could result in Gillispies obtaining a judgment under a contract theory of recovery. The ruling of the trial court sustaining the summary judgment motion and dismissing the counterclaim is affirmed.

Questions

1. What was the issue in the third-party beneficiary portion of this case?
2. What public policy problems would have emerged if the court had held in favor of the Gillispies on their third-party beneficiary claim?
3. Jay Andreson was shopping for a diamond engagement ring at Monahan Beaches Jewelry Center. Andreson told Monahan that the ring was intended for his fiancee, Laneya Warren. Later, Monahan sold a ring, which he represented to be a diamond, to Andreson for $3,974.25. Andreson gave the ring to Warren, who later discovered that the purported diamond was, in fact, cut glass or cubic zirconia. Warren sued Monahan on several counts, including breach of contract. Decide that claim. Explain. [See *Warren* v. *Monahan Beaches Jewelry Center, Inc.*, 548 So. 2d 870 (Fla. Ct. App. 1989).]

Profile Perspective: At the beginning of this chapter and from time to time thereafter we have considered the implications of a rather conventional, but bitterly contested contract dispute between Alan Herzig and Elden and Janet Fox, who had contracted with Herzig to provide entertainment for their daughter's bat mitzvah. Eventually all contracts come to an end. That point arrives when the duties raised by the contract are **discharged,** that is, terminated. Most contract obligations are discharged by full performance; but sometimes problems arise including an unexcused failure to perform fully, which may then constitute a **breach of contract.** The Herzig/Fox dispute was of that character with the court concluding that Herzig had provided only part performance of his contractual duties.

---

discharged. Released from liability.

breach of contract. Failure, without legal excuse, to perform any promise that forms the whole or part of a contract.

C. DISCHARGE

In this section we will examine some of the methods of contract discharge. Discharge can occur in many ways, but the most important of these are (1) conditions, (2) performance or breach, (3) lawful excuses, (4) agreement, and (5) operation of law.

Discharge by Conditions. Sometimes a contract is useful to one or more of the contracting parties only if some future event occurs or fails to occur. Under those circumstances, the parties may write into the contract a clause providing that performance is required only if the specified condition occurs or fails to occur. Otherwise, the duty to perform is discharged. Those conditions take three forms: conditions precedent, conditions subsequent, and conditions concurrent.

conditions precedent. Conditions that operate to give rise to a contracting party's duty to perform.

Conditions Precedent. A **conditions precedent** clause specifies that an event must occur before the parties to the contract are obliged to perform. Assume you are attempting to establish a business booking rock-and-roll acts for performances. You sign a deal with the alternative rock group Pearl Jam, providing for a performance "contingent upon obtaining satisfactory lease arrangements for the university fieldhouse within 14 days." If you are unable to achieve an acceptable lease, both parties are discharged from performance requirements under the contract.

conditions subsequent. Conditions that operate to discharge one from an obligation under a contract.

Conditions Subsequent. A **conditions subsequent** clause excuses performance if a future event transpires. Thus, in the Pearl Jam example, the band might include a clause providing that the agreement will be null and void if any member of the band is ill or otherwise unable to perform on the contracted evening. Hence, in a contract with a condition subsequent the parties have bound themselves to perform *unless* a specified event occurs; whereas in a contract with a condition precedent the parties have no binding duties *until* the specified event occurs.

conditions concurrent. When each party's obligation to perform under a contract is dependent on the other party's performance.

Conditions Concurrent. Here the contract simply specifies that the parties are to perform their duties at the same time. Each performance is dependent upon the other. So if Pearl Jam performs as contracted, you have a simultaneous duty to pay them for their performance. Your duty to pay is conditioned on Pearl Jam's performance and vice versa.

express conditions. Conditions within contracts that are clear from the language.

implied-in-fact conditions. Conditions derived from the parties' conduct and the circumstances of the bargain.

implied-in-law conditions or constructive conditions. Conditions imposed by the court to avoid unfairness.

Express or Implied Conditions. Another way of classifying the aforementioned conditions is to treat them either as express or implied. **Express conditions** are those explicitly agreed to by the parties, like in the situation above, where you, a concert promoter, expressly conditioned performance on your ability to secure the university fieldhouse for the concert. Express conditions are often prefaced by words such as *when, if, provided,* and so forth.

Implied-in-fact conditions are not explicitly stated in the contract but are derived by the court from the conduct of the parties and the circumstances surrounding the bargain. Suppose you contract to remove snow from your neighbor's driveway during the winter. An implied-in-fact condition of your neighbor's duty to pay would be that you would complete the work within a reasonable period of time.

Implied-in-law conditions (also called **constructive conditions**) are those that, although not expressly provided for in the contract or not able to be reasonably inferred from the facts, the court imposes on the contract in order to avoid unfairness. Hence, if you contracted to put a new roof on your neighbor's house but your written contract did not include a date for payment, the court would imply a contract clause providing that your neighbor need not pay you until the job is complete.

Discharge by Performance or Breach of Contract. Complete performance is, of course, the normal way of discharging a contract. Failure to fully perform without a lawful excuse for that failure results in a breach of contract. The consequences of both full performance and breach of contract can be described in four parts.

executed. In contract law, full performance of the terms of the bargain.

substantial performance. Performance with minor, unimportant, and unintentional deviation.

Complete Performance—No Breach of Contract. Here we find the statistically normal situation in which the parties simply do precisely what the contract calls for: pay $500, provide a particular product, present the deed for a piece of land, and so on. When fully performed a contract has been **executed.**

Substantial Performance—Nonmaterial Breach of Contract. In some cases, complete performance is not achieved because of minor deviations from the agreed-upon performance. Most notably in construction contracts and in many personal/professional service contracts, the courts have recognized the doctrine of **substantial performance.** For example, assume a contractor painted a house as agreed, except that he replaced the Sears exterior paint called for in the contract with a Sherwin-Williams paint of comparable quality. Assuming the variation has not materially altered the end product and assuming that the variation was not the result of bad faith, the court will enforce the contract as written, but require a deduction for any damages sustained as a consequence of the imperfect performance.

Unacceptable Performance—Material Breach of Contract. When a party falls beneath substantial performance and does not have a lawful excuse for that failure, a **material breach** of contract has occurred. No clear line separates substantial performance (a nonmaterial breach) from unacceptable performance (a material breach). Such decisions must be made on a case-by-case basis. We can say that material breaches are those that fall short of what the nonbreaching party should reasonably expect, that is, full performance in some cases and substantial performance in others. A material breach discharges the nonbreaching party's duties and permits that party to sue for damages or rescind the contract and seek restitution.

material breach. In contract law, performance that falls beneath substantial performance and does not have a lawful excuse.

Advance Refusal to Perform—Anticipatory Breach of Contract. Sometimes, one of the parties, before performance is due, indicates by word or deed that she or he will not perform. Normally, an **anticipatory breach** (also called **anticipatory repudiation**) is the equivalent of a material breach discharging the nonbreaching party from any further obligations and allowing the nonbreaching party to sue for damages, if any.

anticipatory breach. A contracting party's indication before the time for performance that he cannot or will not perform the contract. Same as *anticipatory repudiation.*

Discharge by Lawful Excuses (for Nonperformance). Sometimes contracts are discharged lawfully even in the event of nonperformance. This can occur when performance is either impossible or impractical.

Impossibility. After agreement is reached but performance is not yet due, circumstances may be so altered that performance is a **legal impossibility.** In such situations, nonperformance is excused. Impossibility here refers not simply to extreme difficulty but to objective impossibility; that is, the contracted-for performance cannot be accomplished by anyone. Notable examples of such situations are a personal service contract where the promisor has died or is incapacitated by illness, a contract where the subject of the agreement was rendered illegal by a change in the law subsequent to the agreement but prior to its performance, and a contract where an ingredient essential to performance has been destroyed and no reasonable substitutes are available.

legal impossibility. A party to a contract is relieved of his or her duty to perform when that performance has become objectively impossible because of the occurrence of an event unforeseen at the time of contracting.

Commercial Impracticability. Akin to the doctrine of impossibility is the situation in which duties are discharged because of unforeseen events that render performance exorbitantly expensive or thoroughly impractical. **Commercial impracticability** is specifically provided for in UCC 2-615, which reads: "Delay in delivery or nondelivery in whole or in part by a seller . . . is not a breach of his duty under a contract for sale if performance as agreed has been made impracticable by the occurrence of a contingency the nonoccurrence of which was a basic assumption on which the contract was made."

The UCC's commercial impracticability standard is more easily established than the impossibility doctrine of the common law, but note that only exceptional and unforeseeable events fall within the impracticability excuse for nonperformance. Mere changes in market conditions do not give rise to commercial impracticability. Historically, the commercial impracticability doctrine had been applied only to transactions involving the sale of goods, but now we see courts increasingly willing to apply it to other kinds of contracts as well. The *Luminous Neon* case that follows examines a commercial impracticability claim.

commercial impracticability. The standard used by the UCC to relieve a party of his or her contract obligations because of the occurrence of unforeseeable, external events beyond his or her control.

CASE

Luminous Neon, Inc. v. Parscale

836 P.2d 1201 (Ct.App.Kan.1992)

Facts

Parscale leased two custom-designed outdoor advertising signs from Luminous Neon. Parscale used the signs for her recently opened restaurant business in Topeka. Under the terms of the lease, Parscale paid $191.75 plus tax per month. The lease expired after five years. Sometime after Parscale leased the signs, the City of Topeka commenced construction on 21st Street that limited access to Parscale's business. That construction had an adverse effect on Parscale's business, and the enterprise was subsequently closed. Parscale stopped making payments on the signs after making a total of 19 payments. Luminous Neon sued for damages, and the trial court entered a summary judgment for Neon. Parscale appealed.

* * *

Judge Brazil

Parscale contends that the doctrine of impracticability of performance applies to this case and she should be excused from her obligations under the lease because the City of Topeka closed 21st Street for construction, which made access to Parscale's business difficult. Her business suffered as a consequence, and she was eventually forced to close the establishment.

* * *

This court has held: "To excuse performance, impracticability must be objective as opposed to subjective. When one agrees to perform an act possible in itself he will be liable for a breach thereof although contingencies not foreseen by him arise which make it difficult, or even beyond his power, to perform and which might have been foreseen and provided against in the contract."

This court has also noted that a distinction exists between impracticability that is subjective and that which is objective: subjective impracticability being, "I cannot do it"; objective impracticability being, "the thing cannot be done." Only objective impracticability may serve to relieve a party of his or her obligation.

The present case is one of subjective impracticability. Parscale could no longer afford to operate her business due to road construction or some other reason. It is not sufficient merely that the business suffered.

In addition, it cannot be said that road construction within Topeka is an unforeseeable event. Certainly, Parscale was aware that such an eventuality might take place. It was incumbent upon Parscale to safeguard her position in the terms of the lease.

If impossibility existed in this case, it was subjective only . . .

Affirmed.

Questions

1. Why did the court deny Parscale's commercial impracticability claim?
2. In November 1959, Ryland Parker, a 37-year-old, college-educated bachelor, went to the Arthur Murray Dance Studio for three free lessons. While there, he was told that he had "exceptional potential to become an accomplished dancer." Parker signed a contract for lessons at the bottom of which was the phrase "NONCANCELLABLE NEGOTIABLE CONTRACT"

Continued

Continued

in boldface type. Parker subsequently entered and prepaid additional contracts totaling 2,734 hours of lessons and $24,812. All of those contracts had similar language boldly displayed. Parker was severely injured in a 1961 auto accident rendering him incapable of continuing the lessons. His repeated requests for a refund were denied, and he sued Arthur Murray. The trial court found for Parker and ordered a refund for the unused lessons on the grounds of impossibility of performance. Arthur Murray appealed. Decide. Explain. [See *Parker* v. *Arthur Murray, Inc.*, 295 N.E.2d 487 (1973).]

Ethics/Public Policy Question

1. Is the trial court's decision in *Parker* v. *Arthur Murray* supportable on ethical grounds? Explain.

Discharge by Agreement. A contractual discharge is sometimes achieved by a new agreement arrived at after entering the original contract. These agreements take a variety of forms, but one—**accord and satisfaction**—will serve here to illustrate the general category. Parties reach an accord when they agree to a performance different from the one provided for in their contract. Performance of the accord is called satisfaction, at which point the original contract is discharged. A binding accord and satisfaction must spring from a genuine dispute between the parties, and it must include consideration as well as all of the other ingredients in a binding contract.

accord and satisfaction. A legally binding agreement to settle a disputed claim for a definite amount.

Assume you agree to prepare a computer program for Cabinets, Inc. Having worked comfortably with Cabinets in the past, you do not insist on an understanding about price prior to doing the work. You submit the program along with a bill for $2,000; but Cabinets refuses to pay, claiming that your price is too high. You could go to court to settle this matter, but instead Cabinets agrees to pay $1,000 for the program and hire you at a desirable fee to do yet another program for them. You have reached an accord and satisfaction, thus discharging the original contract.

Discharge by Operation of Law. Under some circumstances, contractual duties are discharged by the legal system itself. Among those possibilities: (1) Ordinarily, the contractual responsibilities of a debtor are discharged by a bankruptcy decree. (2) Each state has a **statute of limitations** that specifies the time period within which a performing party can initiate a lawsuit against a nonperforming party. That period ordinarily begins on the date of breach and extends for a number of years, which varies from state to state. UCC 2-725 provides a maximum four-year statute of limitations that, by agreement of the parties, can be reduced to not less than one year. If litigation is not commenced within the period provided by statute, the contractual duties are discharged.

statute of limitations. A statute requiring that certain classes of lawsuits must be brought within defined limits of time after the right to begin them accrued or the right is lost.

D. Remedies

An important ingredient in successful business practice is a rudimentary understanding of your rights in the event you are the victim of a breach of contract. We have looked at the elements of a binding contract and at those circumstances that discharge a party's duties under a contract. Now our

An important ingredient in successful business practice is a rudimentary understanding of your rights in the event you are the victim of a breach of contract.

The Kingsmen Get the Word: "Louie, Louie" Officially Theirs

Twenty-two years later, the Kingsmen can truly call "Louie, Louie" their own.

A federal judge in Los Angeles took ownership of the group's more than 100 recordings away from Sceptor-Wand Records and awarded it to The Kingsmen.

The record company breached its contract by not giving The Kingsmen past royalties, the June 20 decision said. The judge also ruled that the Kingsmen are entitled to all future royalties.

The Kingsmen recorded "Louie, Louie," their one big hit, in 1963.

Source: Associated Press, *Waterloo Courier*, June 27, 1995, p. B1.

concern is with what happens when one of the parties does not fulfill his or her contractual duties, that is, when the contract is breached. Remedies are provided in both law and in **equity.**

equity. Fairness; a system of courts that developed in England. A chancellor presided to mete out fairness in cases that were not traditionally assigned to the law courts headed by the king.

Remedies in Law. In general, a breach of contract allows the nonbreaching party to sue for money damages. The general goal of remedies law is to put the parties in the position they would have occupied had the contract been fulfilled. Normally, the best available substitute for actual performance is monetary damages.

> If you contract for a well-known local band to play for the grand opening of your new bar and dance club, you may be able to recover damages for any lost profits that you can attribute to the band's failure to appear.

Compensatory Damages. Fundamentally, the plaintiff in a breach of contract action is entitled to recover a sum equal to the actual damages suffered. The plaintiff is compensated for her losses by receiving a sum designed to "make her whole," to put her where she would have been had the contract not been breached. Suppose you contract with Heinz to serve as golf pro at your country club for one year at a salary of $40,000. Bad weather and other problems put your club in a bind, and you decide you have to let her go after six months. Your club is in breach, and Heinz would be entitled to $20,000 in **compensatory** or actual **damages,** among other possibilities.

compensatory damages. Damages that will compensate a party for actual losses due to an injury suffered.

Sale of goods. A breach involving a sale of goods would be governed by the UCC. Typically, the measure of compensatory damages would be the difference between the contract price and the market price of the goods at the time and place the goods were to be delivered (see UCC 2-708 and 2-713). Suppose you are working for a newly established computer manufacturer, and you have contracted with the Internal Revenue Service to deliver 1,000 basic laptop computers at $1,500 each, although the current market price is $1,600. If you fail to make that delivery, damages could be assessed in the amount of $100,000 ($100 × 1,000), which is the additional amount the IRS would need to pay to make the substitute purchase.

consequential damages. Damages that do not flow directly and immediately from an act but rather flow from the results of the act.

Consequential Damages. The victim of a breach may be able to recover not just the direct losses from the breach but also any indirect losses that were incurred as a consequence of that breach. Such **consequential damages** are recoverable only if they were foreseen or were reasonably foreseeable by the breaching party. For example, if you contract for a well-known local band to play for the grand opening of your new bar and dance club, you may be able to recover damages for any lost profits that you can attribute to the band's failure to appear. Those lost profits are a *consequence* of the breach. Of course, you will have some difficulty in specifying the profits lost and in proving that the loss was attributable to the band's failure to perform.

Incidental Damages. The costs incurred by the nonbreaching party in arranging a substitute performance or otherwise reducing the damages sustained because of the breach are recoverable as **incidental damages.** They would include such items as phone calls and transportation expenses.

incidental damages. Collateral damages that are incurred because of a breach; damages that compensate a person injured by a breach of contract for reasonable costs incurred in an attempt to avoid further loss.

Nominal Damages. In some cases of breach, the court will award only an insignificant sum, perhaps $1, because the nonbreaching party has suffered no actual damages. The point of **nominal damages** is to illustrate the wrongfulness of the breach. In these cases, the court costs are ordinarily imposed on the breaching party.

nominal damages. Small damages, oftentimes $1, awarded to show that there was a legal wrong even though the damages were very slight or nonexistent.

Punitive Damages. Sometimes when the breaching party's conduct is particularly reprehensible, the court will penalize that party by awarding **punitive damages** to the injured party. The idea is to deter such conduct in the future. Normally, punitive damages cannot be awarded in breach of contract cases except when provided for by statute or when the breach is accompanied by a tort such as fraud (as where one buys a defective car having reasonably relied on the falsehoods of a salesperson).

punitive damages. Damages designed to punish flagrant wrongdoers and to deter them and others from engaging in similar conduct in the future.

Rescission and Restitution. In some instances, including a material breach, mistake, fraud, undue influence, and duress, the wronged party may rescind (undo) the contract. The effect of a contract **rescission** is to return the parties to the positions they occupied before they entered the agreement. Generally, both parties must then make **restitution** to each other by returning whatever goods, property, and so forth were transferred under the contract or an equivalent amount of money. If the breaching party does not agree to the rescission, the wronged party would then need to secure a court order requiring the rescission.

rescission. Canceling a contract; its effect is to restore the parties to their original position.

restitution. A remedy whereby one is able to obtain the return of that which he has given the other party, or an equivalent amount of money.

Mitigation. Obviously, the law should penalize a breaching party, as we have discussed, but you may be surprised to learn that the law also imposes expectations on the victim (the nonbreaching party). Specifically, the nonbreaching party is required to take reasonable steps toward **mitigation,** that is, to minimize her or his damages. What happens, for example, if you are wrongfully dismissed from your first job after college? You are required to mitigate your damages by seeking another job. You need not take an inferior job, nor must you disturb your life by moving to another state or community, but you must take reasonable measures to minimize your claim against your former employer.

mitigation. Obligation of a person who has been injured by a breach of a contract to attempt to reduce the damages.

Liquidated Damages. We have reviewed the legal penalties for breach and the duty to mitigate. The law also offers you the opportunity to provide some control over the penalty for breach by including in your contract a **liquidated damages** clause. Here you and the other party to the contract agree in advance about the measure of damages should either of you default on your duties. That clause is fully enforceable so long as it is not designed to be a penalty but rather a good faith effort to assess in advance an accurate measure of damages. A valid liquidated damages clause limits the nonbreaching party to recovery of the amount provided for in that clause.

liquidated damages. Damages made certain by the prior agreement of the parties.

Remedies in Equity. Where justice cannot be achieved via money damages alone, the courts will sometimes impose **equitable remedies** (equity is discussed in Chapter 2). The chief forms of equitable remedy in contract cases are specific performance, injunction, reformation, and quasi-contract.

equitable remedies. Injunction, specific performance, restraining orders, and the like, as opposed to money damages.

Specific Performance. In unusual circumstances, the court may order the breaching party to remedy its wrong by performing its obligations precisely as provided for in the contract. Normally, that **specific performance** is required only where the subject matter of the contract is unique and thus cannot be adequately compensated with money. Examples of such subject matter might include a particular piece of land, an art work, or a family heirloom. By contrast, specific performance would not be available in contracts involving conventional personal property such as a television or a car unless those items were unique (e.g., a one-of-a-kind Rolls Royce).

specific performance. A contract remedy whereby the defendant is ordered to perform precisely according to the terms of his contract.

Normally, the courts will not grant a specific performance remedy in personal service contracts (e.g., an agreement by a cosmetic surgeon to perform a face-lift). If the surgeon refused to perform, specific performance probably would not be ordered. The quality of the surgery likely would not be equal to what had been bargained for; courts do not want to be in the position of supervising the completion of contracts and as a matter of public policy, we do not want to put parties, in this case, the surgeon, in a position that amounts to involuntary servitude.

Injunction. An **injunction** is a court order that may either require or forbid a party to perform a specified act. Injunctions are granted only under exceptional circumstances. Perhaps the most common of those are the noncompetition clauses in employment contracts discussed earlier in this chapter. For example, you take a computer programming job that will afford you access to company secrets. To protect itself, the company includes a clause in your employment contract specifying that you will not take employment with a competing firm for a period of one year after departure from your employer. If you should quit and seek to work for a competitor within one year, your former employer might be able to secure an injunction preventing you from doing so until the year had passed.

injunction. An equitable remedy whereby the defendant is ordered to perform certain acts or to desist from certain acts.

Reformation. **Reformation** is an equitable remedy that permits the court to rewrite the contract where it imperfectly expressed the parties' true intentions. Typically, such situations involve mutual mistake or fraud. Thus, if the parties sign a contract to sell a lot in a housing development, but the contract is written with an incorrect street address for the lot, an equity court could simply correct the error in the contract.

reformation. An equitable remedy in which a court effectively rewrites the terms of a contract.

Quasi-Contract. What happens if one party has conferred a benefit on another, but a contract has not been created because of a failure of consideration, the application of the statute of frauds, or something of the sort? To prevent unjust enrichment, the court might then imply a contract as a matter of law. For example, assume a lawn service mistakenly trims your shrubs and you watch them do so, knowing that they are supposed to be caring for your neighbor's lawn. You have not entered a contract with the lawn service, but a court might well require you to pay the reasonable value of trimming your shrubs. To do otherwise would unjustly enrich you.

Summary

Legal Review. Contracts impose order on the infinite number of transactions that are involved in building and managing a business. As we learned, a legally enforceable contract must exhibit each of the following features: (1) agreement (offer and acceptance), (2) consideration, (3) capacity, (4) genuineness of assent, and (5) legality of purpose. Proof of those five ingredients establishes a contract, but further formalities often remain. Many contracts must be in writing to be enforceable. Often, third parties, though not direct participants in the contract, may have claims against it. Those claims arise in the form of assignments of rights, delegation of duties, and third-party beneficiary provisions.

Contracts come to an end when the duties created by the contract are discharged (terminated). Discharge can occur in a variety of ways, but five of those are of particular importance: (1) conditions, (2) performance or breach, (3) lawful excuses, (4) agreement, and (5) operation of law. In the event of a breach of contract, the nonbreaching party may seek various remedies at law including: compensatory, consequential, incidental, nominal, and punitive damages along with rescission and restitution. Equitable remedies include: specific performance, injunction, reformation, and quasi-contract.

Ethics/Public Policy Review. Contract law provides not only a roadmap for business practice but what amounts to a set of ethical guidelines embodying our historic perception of commercial fairness and our respect for personal freedom. We seek commercial fairness by rules providing that contracts must not violate law or public policy, that the parties must have the legal capacity to enter an agreement, that the parties must have had an objectively defined meeting of the minds, and so on. Personal freedom, as federal court of appeals judge Alex Kozinski reminds us, is rooted in and depends on a system that guarantees contractual freedom:

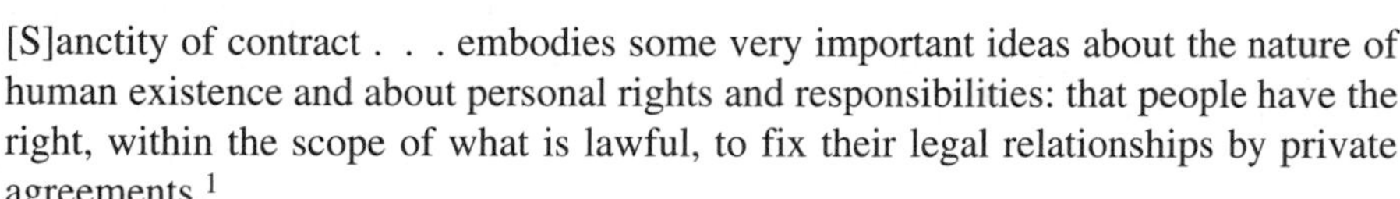

> [S]anctity of contract . . . embodies some very important ideas about the nature of human existence and about personal rights and responsibilities: that people have the right, within the scope of what is lawful, to fix their legal relationships by private agreements.[1]

Economics Review. Capitalism could not operate efficiently without a well-settled body of contract law whose stability, predictability, and common sense are key elements in America's prosperity. Obviously, contract law represents an aggressive intervention by both the judiciary and legislators into the details of contract formation and compliance. That initial intervention, however, set comprehensive ground rules that subsequently allowed government to step back and permit the market to work its will largely unfettered. Contract law has contributed enormously to the material wealth of America by providing assurance to investors and builders that they can confidently put their resources in new ventures. Similarly, we are now able to trade around the world, including even government-dominated China, with substantial certainty that contract law will protect our interests.

Chapter Questions—Law

1. Allen M. Campbell Co. sought a contract to build houses for the United States Navy. Approximately one-half hour before the housing bids were due, Virginia Metal Industries quoted Campbell Co. a price of $193,121 to supply the necessary doors and frames. Campbell, using the Virginia Metal quote, entered a bid and won the contract. Virginia Metal refused to supply the necessary doors, and Campbell had to secure an

alternate source of supply at a price $45,562 higher than Virginia Metal's quote. Campbell sued. Explain Campbell's claim. Defend Virginia Metal. Decide. [See *Allen M. Campbell Co. Inc.* v. *Virginia Metal Industries,* 708 F.2d 930 (4th Cir. 1983).]

2. The Great Minneapolis Surplus Store placed a newspaper ad saying: "Saturday 9:00 AM sharp. 3 Brand New Fur Coats. Worth $100.00. First Come. First Served. $1 each." Lefkowitz was the first customer at the store that Saturday. He demanded a coat and indicated his readiness to pay the dollar, but the store refused saying it was a "house rule" that the coats were intended for women customers only. Lefkowitz sued. Express the issue(s) in this case. Defend Great Minneapolis. Decide. Explain. [See *Lefkowitz* v. *Great Minneapolis Surplus Store,* 86 N.W.2d 689 (1957).]
3. Rose Elsten and Donald Cook lived together in Tucson, Arizona, from 1969 to 1981. They were not married, but Rose used Donald's last name, and they represented themselves as husband and wife. They had two joint bank accounts. They jointly owned a house, two cars, and some shares of stock. When Rose left Donald in 1981 she received a few hundred dollars and one car, and Donald retained the balance of the property. She sued Donald on the grounds that he had breached their agreement to share their assets equally. She argued: "[E]verything we did and purchased . . . was together as husband and wife. It was just something that we agreed on." If an agreement existed, did it violate public policy? Decide Rose's lawsuit. Explain. [See *Cook* v. *Cook,* 691 P.2d 664 (Ariz. S.Ct. 1984).]
4. Sherwood agreed to purchase a cow, Rose 2d of Aberlone, from Walker at a price of 5½ cents per pound (about $80). The parties believed the cow to be barren. Sherwood came to Walker's farm to collect the cow, but at that point it was obvious that Rose was pregnant. Walker refused to give over the cow, which was then worth $750–1,000. Sherwood sued. Does he get the cow? Explain. [See *Sherwood* v. *Walker,* 33 N.W. 919 (1887).]
5. Weaver leased a service station from American Oil. The lease included a clause providing that Weaver would hold American Oil harmless for any negligence by American on the premises. Weaver and an employee were burned when an American Oil employee accidentally sprayed gasoline at Weaver's station. Weaver had one and one-half years of high school education. The trial record provides no evidence that Weaver read the lease, that American's agent asked him to read it, or that Weaver's attention was drawn to the "hold harmless" clause. The clause was in fine print and contained no title heading. Is the contract enforceable against Weaver? Explain. [See *Weaver* v. *American Oil Co.,* 276 N.E.2d 144 (Ind. 1971).]
6. Edward Sherman wanted to sell his business, Adgraphics. He retained V. R. Brokers as an agent for the sale. On December 5, 1985, William Lyon offered $75,000 for the business. Later that day, Sherman signed a counteroffer to sell for $80,000. On December 7 at 11:35 AM Lyon signed the counteroffer and around noon he took it to Brokers. At about 9 AM that same day, Sherman told Brokers' principal, Robert Renault, that he had decided to cancel his counteroffer. Renault told Lyon of that decision immediately before Lyon handed the signed counteroffer to Renault. Lyon then sued for breach of contract. Decide. Explain. [See *Lyon* v. *Adgraphics,* 540 A.2d 398 (Conn. Ct. App. 1988).]
7. A building was rented "for use as a saloon" under an eight-year lease. Five years thereafter the state passed a law making the sale of liquor illegal. The renter, a brewery, argued that it no longer had any duties under the contract. Was the brewery correct? Explain. [See *Heart* v. *East Tennessee Brewing Co.,* 113 S.W. 364 (1908).]
8. The La Gasse Company contracted with the City of Fort Lauderdale to renovate one of the city's swimming pools. When the job was nearly complete, vandals severely damaged the pool and most of the work had to be redone. La Gasse sought additional compensation, which the City refused. La Gasse sued, claiming that the subject matter of the

contract had been destroyed, thus discharging it from responsibility. Therefore, when it repeated the work, additional compensation was warranted. Decide. Explain. [See *La Gasse Pool Construction Co.* v. *City of Fort Lauderdale,* 288 So. 2d 273 (1974).]

9. After 10 PM some grocery stores in Iowa City, Iowa, refuse to sell mustard, eggs, or toilet paper to younger customers. The concern is that the goods will be used by pranksters for "decorating" cars and houses rather than for more conventional consumption. Are the stores guilty of breach of contract when they decline to sell? Explain.
10. Patricia Niehaus, an employee of Delaware Valley Medical Center, requested and was granted a nine-month leave. The Medical Center employee handbook provided that any employee granted a leave could return to the same, or similar, job. The handbook also said that either party could terminate the employment relationship at any time and that the handbook did not constitute a contract. Upon completing her leave, Niehaus was denied a job of any kind with the Medical Center. Niehaus sued for breach of contract. Explain the Medical Center's defense. Decide. Explain. [See *Niehaus* v. *Delaware Valley Medical Center,* 631 A.2d 1314 (Super. Ct. Pa. 1993), and *Delaware Valley Medical Center* v. *Niehaus,* 649 A.2d 433 (Pa. S.Ct. 1994).]

Chapter Questions—Public Policy

1. In 1995, the Maytag Corporation reached a $16.5 million settlement with former employees at its closed Ranson, West Virginia, vending machine plant. Eight hundred former workers had filed a class-action lawsuit claiming that Maytag had lied to them before stopping operations at its Dixie-Narco vending machine plant in 1991. The Dixie-Narco employees were nonunion and were not working under written contracts; however, they claimed that Maytag had repeatedly lied to them about its plans to keep the plant open. The false promises, the lawsuit claimed, added up to an oral contract that the workers relied on to their detriment.

   Maytag had spent $37 million renovating a Williston, South Carolina, factory to build soft-drink vending machines. Maytag told Ranson workers that the South Carolina plant (where wages were $6 per hour lower) would supplement their work and would not result in a plant closure. Then, according to Maytag, declining business conditions forced the Ranson closing. Lawyers for the plaintiffs displayed in court an internal Maytag document that, according to published reports, showed that as early as 1989 the company had expected to phase out the Ranson operation.

   a. Maytag admitted no ethical or legal violations when the settlement was reached. Do you agree that Maytag was free of wrongdoing in this episode? Explain.

   b. Based upon what we know of the facts prior to the settlement, do you think that Maytag breached a contract with its employees?

   c. How might Maytag have been able to close the plant and yet avoid the subsequent litigation?

   [For a detailed account of the Ranson/Maytag story see Barry Bearak, "Lost in America: Jobs, Trust," *Los Angeles Times,* November 26, 1995, p. A1.]
2. In what sense does our system of contract law operate as an ethical system?

Notes

1. David B. Rivkin, Jr., and Lee A. Casey, "How Binding Are Contracts?" *The American Enterprise* 4, no. 6 (November–December 1993), pp. 58, 60.

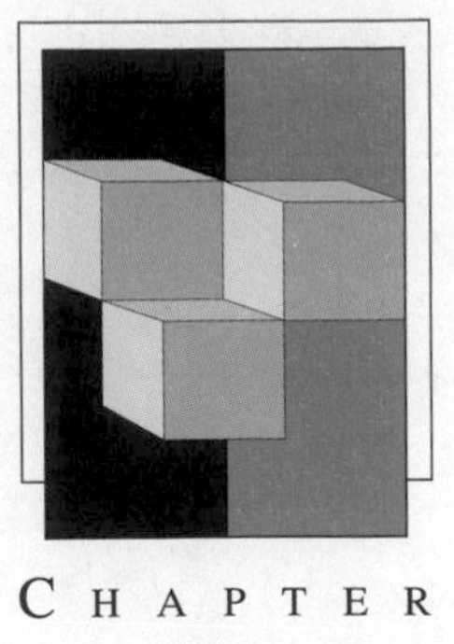

CHAPTER

5

PROPERTY LAW: BUILDING THE BUSINESS VIA BUYING, LEASING, OR SELLING PROPERTY

READER'S GUIDE

You have established your company and have begun your business negotiations or operations. Where will you conduct your business? In general, the next step in building a business would be to locate and purchase or lease space for offices, manufacturing, production, or other operations. This chapter delineates the issues involved in meeting and managing the property needs of a firm.

PROFILE

Emma recently rented an apartment in a large complex owned by Roger. She signed a standard lease that called for a payment of $800 per month for a period of one year. The lease also stated that Roger is not liable for any damage that results to anything in the apartment as a result of any cause whatsoever. Three months after she moved into the apartment, she noticed sparks coming from a fuse box in the garage and notified Roger. Roger brought in an electrician and thought the problem was fixed. Two weeks after the repairs were made, the fuse box caught on fire and started a large blaze that destroyed Emma's apartment and belongings, as well as those of her brother, who was visiting her.

QUESTIONS

1. What legal question is at issue here? To whom does Roger owe a duty? Emma? Her brother?
2. Has Roger violated the lease warranty of habitability?
3. If Roger is liable at all, how could he have better protected himself from liability?

I. NATURE OF REAL PROPERTY

real property or real estate. The earth's crust and all things firmly attached to it.

personal property. All objects and rights, other than real property, that can be owned.

When you think of property, you generally think of either a piece of property, like an immovable plot of land, or personal property, like clothes or books. The first type of property is considered **real property** or **real estate;** tangible, movable items are considered **personal property.**

In fact, real property includes not only land but also anything that is attached or fixed to it, above it, or below it. For instance, consider the land under your home or apartment. When you talk about the real property at that address, you are referring to the actual land, the building on that land, the oil beneath the land, and to some extent, even the airspace above it.

Private Property Rights

Property rights to a resource, whether a tract of land, a coal mine, or a spring creek, consist of having control over the resource. Such rights are most valuable when ownership is outright and when property can be easily exchanged for other goods and services. Although an important feature of a property right is the power to exclude others from using it, even limited command over access to a resource confers status and power to the holder.

Source: Richard Stroup and Jane Shaw, "Environment: Private Property Rights," Heartland Institute PolicyFax Datafile doc. no. 2366001.

* * *

In societies that enforce general rules of property, individuals pursuing their self-interest must serve the need of others.

Private property is essential for the preservation of liberty because the economic power which accompanies it is required to check and restrain political power.

Source: From "Property Rights Essential to Wealth and Freedom" by Felix R. Livingston, World Capitalism Review, October, 1993, pp. 12–13. Reprinted by permission of Center for World Capitalism.

When an item of personal property becomes so attached to real property that it would be unreasonable to conceive of the real property without it, that item is called a **fixture** and is considered to be part of the real property. To determine whether an item of personal property has become a fixture, consider (1) whether it has been attached by its roots or otherwise permanently attached to the real property by plaster, cement, bolts, or other lasting means (like a light post), (2) whether it was specifically adapted for this piece of realty (like custom window shades), or (3) the relationship of the parties (law favors sellers and tenants over buyers and landowners). If the real property is transferred, all fixtures are transferred with it. That is why a building located on real property is considered part of the real property; it is permanently fixed to the property.

fixture. A thing that was originally personal property and that has been actually or constructively affixed to the soil itself or to some structure legally a part of the land.

The law relating to real property is complicated as a result of its long history. Historically, land was a means of survival. The person with the most real property had the most power, food, or money (through farming, other agricultural ventures, or natural minerals like oil); disagreements over land were numerous. Although our society has become through the years more focused on service and technology, property battles are still waged. The purpose of this chapter is to identify some of the battles that continue and discuss the legal resolutions to those conflicts.

II. Types of Interest in Real Property

We use the word **estate** to designate the type of interest that you might have in a piece of property. If a person's interest in real property is only a right to use it for a period of time, that interest may be called a **leasehold estate.** On the other hand, if a person has the full right to a piece of property during her lifetime, but not beyond her death, her estate is called a **life estate** in the property. And if someone transfers an entire interest in real property, the estate transferred would be a **fee simple.**

An interest in real property may be transferred to someone else through a variety of means. Property may be transferred permanently through a sale, temporarily through a lease, or partially through an easement. So, the type of estate you have is determined by

estate. An interest in land or property owned by a decedent at the time of her or his death.

leasehold estate. A right to occupy and to use land pursuant to a lease or contract.

life estate. A property interest that gives a person the right to possess and to use property for a time that is measured by her or his lifetime or that of another person.

fee simple. A form of land ownership that gives the owner the right to possess and to use the land for an unlimited period of time, subject only to governmental or private restrictions, and unconditional power to dispose of the property during her lifetime or upon her death.

looking to the duration and nature of the interest or right to possess. The following sections discuss the nature of each type of interest, including the real estate lease, sales of property, and easements to use property.

III. Leasehold Interests

lease. A contract for the possession and use of land or other property, including goods, on one side, and a recompense of rent or other income on the other.

tenant/lessee. A party to a lease contract who pays rent in return for the right to possess and to use property.

landlord/lessor. A party to a lease contract who allows a tenant to possess and to use her or his property in return for rent payments.

At one point or another, most people rent an apartment or lease a building. To transfer the right to use the space or building for a specific period of time, the property owner enters into a written contract with the renter called a **lease,** which must satisfy all of the requirements of any other contract. The renter, or person using the property under the lease, is called the **tenant** or **lessee,** and the owner of the property is called the **landlord** or **lessor.** A leasehold interest is created by agreement of the parties through the lease.

A lease transfers only the *possession* of the property, not the ownership interest, and generally provides for some limits on the use of the property. For instance, the lessor generally reserves the right to enter the property for inspection or to show the apartment to prospective renters at the end of the lease. In addition, the lease may provide that the lessee may only use the property for a specific purpose or may identify those purposes for which the property may not be used.

For example, assume that Karen, Shefali, and Vicki decide that they want to get an apartment together. They find the perfect place and are given a lease to sign to rent the apartment. The lease provides that the women do not disturb other tenants with unreasonable noise levels. Since Karen is a rock guitarist, the women ask that this clause be removed and the landlord refuses. In this example, the landlord is allowed to impose this restriction on the women's use of the apartment. If they are concerned that they cannot abide by the restriction, they should not rent the apartment.

A. Types of Leases

There are several types of leases or tenancies, each of which describes the duration or term of the right to possess the property. Usually, you can look to the type of lease to determine the type of tenancy agreed to. A lease is subject to the common law of contracts and is therefore generally valid whether written or oral. However, a lease must be in writing if it is subject to the Statute of Frauds, such as a lease for more than one year in duration.

Table 5.1 summarizes the types of tenancies.

term tenancy. The tenancy that exists where a landlord and tenant have agreed to the term of the lease period and a specific termination date for the lease.

Term Tenancy. A **term tenancy** is also called *an estate for years.* This type of leasehold interest refers to a standard lease contract that has a specific starting date and a specific termination date. Where a lessee and a lessor have agreed to a term tenancy, the lease automatically expires on the termination date. When you rent an apartment, typically you sign a year lease, though term tenancies can exist for any period of time. A term tenancy is created by the words, "to lessee for [length of term]."

Table 5.1

Types of Tenancies

Type of Tenancies	*How Terminated*
Term tenancy	Terminated according to lease term
Periodic tenancy	Terminated upon sufficient notice of either side
Tenancy at will	Terminated at any time by either side
Tenancy at sufferance	Already terminated but tenant refuses to leave

APARTMENT LEASE — UNFURNISHED
(For Use In Illinois)

GEORGE E. COLE®
LEGAL FORMS

NO. L-17
SEPTEMBER 1994

CAUTION: Consult a lawyer before using or acting under this form. *Neither the publisher nor the seller of this form makes any warranty with respect thereto, including any warranty of merchantability or fitness for a particular purpose.*

IF UNHEATED, CHECK HERE: ____
(SEE PARAGRAPH 11)

APARTMENT LEASE
UNFURNISHED

DATE OF LEASE	TERM OF LEASE		MONTHLY RENT	SECURITY DEPOSIT*
	BEGINNING	ENDING		

**IF NONE, WRITE "NONE". Paragraph 2 of this Lease then INAPPLICABLE.*

LESSEE
NAME •
APT. NO. •
ADDRESS OF PREMISES •

LESSOR
NAME •
BUSINESS ADDRESS •

In consideration of the mutual covenants and agreements herein stated, Lessor hereby leases to Lessee and Lessee hereby leases from Lessor for a private dwelling the apartment designated above (the "Premises"), together with the appurtenances thereto, for the above Term.

ADDITIONAL COVENANTS AND AGREEMENTS *(if any)*

LEASE COVENANTS AND AGREEMENTS

RENT

1. Lessee shall pay Lessor or Lessor's agent as rent for the Premises the sum stated above in the box designated "MONTHLY RENT", monthly in advance, until termination of this lease, at the Lessor's address stated above or such other address as Lessor may designate in writing. The first payment is due on or before ______________, 19 _____, and subsequent payments on the _______ day of each succeeding month.

SECURITY DEPOSIT

2. Lessee has deposited with Lessor the Security Deposit stated above for the performance of all covenants and agreements of Lessee hereunder. Lessor may apply all or any portion thereof in payment of any amounts due Lessor from Lessee, and upon Lessor's demand Lessee shall in such case during the term of the lease promptly deposit with Lessor such additional amounts as may then be required to bring the Security Deposit up to the full amount stated above. Upon termination of the lease and full performance of all matters and payment of all amounts due by Lessee, so much of the Security Deposit as remains unapplied shall be returned to Lessee. This deposit does not bear interest unless and except as required by law. Where all or a portion of the Security Deposit is applied by Lessor as compensation for property damage, Lessor when and as required by law shall provide to Lessee an itemized statement of such damage and of the estimated or actual cost of repairing same. If Lessor utilizes his or her own labor to repair any damage caused by the Lessee, the Lessor may include the reasonable cost of his or her labor to repair such damage. If the building in which Premises are located (the "Building") is sold or otherwise transferred, Lessor may transfer or assign the Security Deposit to the purchaser or transferee of the Building, who shall thereupon be liable to Lessee for all of Lessor's obligations hereunder, and Lessee shall look thereafter solely to such purchaser or transferee for return of the Security Deposit and for other matters (including any interest or accounting) relating thereto.

CONDITION OF PREMISES; REDELIVERY TO LESSOR

3. Lessee has examined and knows the condition of Premises and has received the same in good order and repair except as herein otherwise specified, and no representations as to the condition or repair thereof have been made by Lessor or his agent prior to, or at the execution of this lease, that are not herein expressed or endorsed hereon; and upon the termination of this lease in any way, Lessee will immediately yield up Premises to Lessor in as good condition as when the same were entered upon by Lessee, ordinary wear and tear only excepted, and shall then return all keys to Lessor.

LIMITATION OF LIABILITY

4. Except as provided by Illinois statute, Lessor shall not be liable for any damage occasioned by failure to keep Premises in repair, and shall not be liable for any damage done or occasioned by or from plumbing, gas, water, steam or other pipes, or sewerage, or the bursting, leaking or running of any cistern, tank, wash-stand, water-closet, or waste-pipe, in, above, upon or about the Building or Premises, nor for damage occasioned by water, snow or ice being upon or coming through the roof, skylight, trap-door or otherwise, nor for damages to Lessee or others claiming through Lessee for any loss or damage of or to property wherever located in or about the Building or Premises, nor for any damage arising from acts or neglect of co-tenants or other occupants of the Building, or of any owners or occupants of adjacent or contiguous property.

USE; SUBLET; ASSIGNMENT

5. Lessee will not allow Premises to be used for any purpose that will increase the rate of insurance thereon, nor for any purpose other than that hereinbefore specified, nor to be occupied in whole or in part by any other persons, and will not sublet the same, nor any part thereof, nor assign this lease, without in each case the written consent of the Lessor first had, and will not permit any transfer, by operation of law, of the interest in Premises acquired through this lease, and will not permit Premises to be used for any unlawful purpose or purpose that will injure the reputation of the same or of the Building or disturb the tenants of the Building or the neighborhood.

USE AND REPAIR

6. Lessee will take good care of the apartment demised and the fixtures therein, and will commit and suffer no waste therein; no changes or alterations of the Premises shall be made, nor partitions erected, nor walls papered, nor locks on doors installed or changed, without the consent in writing of Lessor; Lessee will make all repairs required to the walls, ceilings, paint, plastering, plumbing work, pipes and fixtures belonging to Premises, whenever damage or injury to the same shall have resulted from misuse or neglect; no furniture filled or to be filled wholly or partially with liquids shall be placed in the Premises without the consent in writing of Lessor; the Premises shall not be used as a "boarding" or "lodging" house, nor for a school, nor to give instructions in music, dancing or singing, and none of the rooms shall be offered for lease by placing notices on any door, window or wall of the Building, nor by advertising the same directly or indirectly, in any newspaper or otherwise, nor shall any signs be exhibited on or at any windows or exterior portions of the Premises or of the Building without the consent in writing of Lessor; there shall be no lounging, sitting upon, or unnecessary tarrying in or upon the front steps, the sidewalk, railing, stairways, halls, landing or other public places of the Building by Lessee, members of the family or others persons connected with the occupancy of Premises; no provisions, milk, ice, marketing, groceries, furniture, packages or merchandise shall be taken into the Premises through the front door of the Building except where there is no rear or service entrance; cooking shall be done only in the kitchen and in no event on porches or other exterior appurtenances; Lessee, and those occupying under Lessee, shall not interfere with the heating apparatus, or with the lights, electricity, gas, water or other utilities of the Building which are not within the apartment hereby demised, nor with the control of any of the public portions of the Building; use of any master television antenna hookup shall be strictly in accordance with regulations of Lessor or Lessor's agent; Lessee and those occupying under Lessee shall comply with and conform to all reasonable rules and regulations that Lessor or Lessor's agent may make for the protection of the Building or the general welfare and the comfort of the occupants thereof, and shall also comply with and conform to all applicable laws and governmental rules and regulations affecting the Premises and the use and occupancy thereof.

ACCESS

7. Lessee grants Lessor free access to the Premises at all reasonable hours for the purpose of examining the same or to make any needful repairs which Lessor may deem fit to make for the benefit of or related to any part of the Building. Lessee also hereby grants permission to Lessor to show, and to new rental applicants to inspect, the apartment at reasonable hours of the day, within ______________ of the expiration of the term of this lease. Lessee will allow Lessor to have placed upon the Premises, at all times, notice of "For Sale" and "To Rent" and will not interfere with the same.

RIGHT TO RELET

8. If Lessee shall abandon or vacate the Premises, the same may be re-let by Lessor for such rent and upon such terms as Lessor may see fit, subject to Illinois statute, and if a sufficient sum shall not thus be realized, after paying the expenses of such reletting and collecting, to satisfy the rent hereby reserved, Lessee agrees to satisfy and pay all deficiency.

HOLDING OVER

9. If the Lessee retains possession of the Premises or any part thereof after the termination of the term by lapse of time or otherwise, then the Lessor may at Lessor's option within thirty days after the termination of the term serve written notice upon Lessee that such holding over constitutes either (a) renewal of this lease for one year, and from month tenancy, upon the terms of this lease except at double the monthly rental specified under Section 1, or (c) creation of a tenancy at sufferance, at a rental of ____________________ dollars per day for the time Lessee remains in possession. If no such written notice is served then a tenancy at sufferance with rental as stated at (c) shall have been created, and in such case if specific per diem rental shall not have been inserted herein at (c), such per diem rental shall be one-fifteenth of the monthly rental specified under Section 1 of this lease. Lessee shall also pay to Lessor all damages sustained by Lessor resulting from retention of possession by Lessee.

RESTRICTIONS ON USE

10. Lessee will not permit anything to be thrown out of the windows, or down the courts or light shafts in the Building; nothing shall be hung from the outside of the windows or placed on the outside window sills of any window in the Building; no parrot, dog or other animal shall be kept within or about the Premises; the front halls and stairways and the back porches shall not be used for the storage of carriages, furniture or other articles.

WATER AND HEAT

11. The provisions of subsection (a) only hereof shall be applicable and shall form a part of this lease unless this lease is made on an unheated basis and that fact is so indicated on the first page of this lease, in which case the provisions of subsection (b) only hereof shall be applicable and form a part of this lease.

(a) Lessor will supply hot and cold water to the Premises for the use of Lessee at all faucets and fixtures provided by Lessor therefor. Lessor will also supply heat, by means of the heating system and fixtures provided by Lessor, in reasonable amounts and at reasonable hours, when necessary, from October 1 to April 30, or otherwise as required by applicable municipal ordinance. Lessor shall not be liable or responsible to Lessee for failure to furnish water or heat when such failure shall result from causes beyond Lessor's control, nor during periods when the water and heating systems in the Building or any portion thereof are under repair.

(b) Lessor will supply cold water to the Premises for the use of Lessee at all faucets and fixtures provided by Lessor therefor. Lessor shall not be liable or responsible to Lessee for failure to furnish water when such failure shall result from causes beyond Lessor's control, nor during periods when the water system in the Building or any portion thereof is under repair. All water heating and all heating of the Premises shall be at the sole expense of Lessee. Any equipment provided by Lessee therefor shall comply with applicable municipal ordinances.

STORE ROOM

12. Lessor shall not be liable for any loss or damage of or to any property placed in any store room or any storage place in the Building, such store room or storage place being furnished gratuitously and not as part of the obligations of this lease.

DEFAULT BY LESSEE

13. If default be made in the payment of the above rent, or any part thereof, or in any of the covenants herein contained to be kept by the Lessee, Lessor may at any time thereafter at his election declare said term ended and reenter the Premises or any part thereof, with or (to the extent permitted by law) without notice or process of law, and remove Lessee or any persons occupying the same, without prejudice to any remedies which might otherwise be used for arrears of rent, and Lessor shall have at all times the right to distrain for rent due, and shall have a valid and first lien upon all personal property which Lessee now owns, or may hereafter acquire or have an interest in, which is by law subject to such distraint, as security for payment of the rent herein reserved.

NO RENT DEDUCTION OF SET OFF

14. Lessee's covenant to pay rent is and shall be independent of each and every other covenant of this lease. Lessee agrees that any claim by Lessee against Lessor shall not be deducted from rent nor set off against any claim for rent in any action.

RENT AFTER NOTICE OR SUIT

15. It is further agreed, by the parties hereto, that after the service of notice or the commencement of a suit or after final judgment for possession of the Premises, Lessor may receive and collect any rent due, and the payment of said rent shall not waive or affect said notice, said suit, or said judgment.

PAYMENT OF COSTS

16. Except as provided by Illinois law, Lessee will pay and discharge all reasonable costs, attorney's fees and expenses that shall be made and incurred by Lessor in enforcing the covenants and agreements of this lease.

RIGHTS CUMULATIVE

17. The rights and remedies of Lessor under this lease are cumulative. The exercise or use of any one or more thereof shall not bar Lessor from exercise or use of any other right or remedy provided herein or otherwise provided by law, nor shall exercise nor use of any right or remedy by Lessor waive any other right or remedy.

FIRE AND CASUALTY

18. In case the Premises shall be rendered untenantable during the term of this lease by fire or other casualty, Lessor at his option may terminate the lease or repair the Premises within 60 days thereafter. If Lessor elects to repair, this lease shall remain in effect provided such repairs are completed within said time. If Lessor shall not have repaired the Premises within said time, then at the end of such time the term hereby created shall terminate. If this lease is terminated by reason of fire or casualty as herein specified, rent shall be apportioned and paid to the day of such fire or other casualty.

SUBORDINATION

19. This lease is subordinate to all mortgages which may now or hereafter affect the real property of which Premises form a part.

PLURALS; SUCCESSORS

20. The words "Lessor" and "Lessee" wherever herein occurring and used shall be construed to mean "Lessors" and "Lessees" in case more than one person constitutes either party to this lease; and all the covenants and agreements herein contained shall be binding upon, and inure to, their respective successors, heirs, executors, administrators and assigns and be exercised by his or their attorney or agent.

SEVERABILITY

21. Wherever possible each provision of this lease shall be interpreted in such manner as to be effective and valid under applicable law, but if any provision of this lease shall be prohibited by or invalid under applicable law, such provision shall be ineffective to the extent of such prohibition or invalidity, without invalidating the remainder of such provision or the remaining provisions of this lease.

COMPLIANCE WITH LAWS, STATUTES AND ORDINANCES

22. The parties to this lease acknowledge that the terms of this lease may be inconsistent with the laws, statutes or ordinances of the jurisdiction in which the Premises are located, and where inconsistent, those terms may be superseded by the provisions of such laws, statutes or ordinances. To the extent the provisions of such laws, statutes or ordinances supersede the terms of this lease, such provisions are hereby incorporated into the terms of this lease by this reference, and the parties to this lease agree to refer to such provisions and to be bound thereby. With respect to Premises located in the City of Chicago, the parties agree to refer to and, to the extent provided above, be bound by the provisions of the City of Chicago Residential Landlord and Tenant Ordinance, Chapter 193.1, Municipal Code of Chicago, as amended from time to time. A summary of such Ordinance is attached to this lease.

WITNESS the hands and seals of the parties hereto, as of the Date of Lease stated above.

LESSEE:	LESSOR:
________________________________ (seal)	________________________________ (seal)
________________________________ (seal)	________________________________ (seal)

ASSIGNMENT BY LESSOR

On this ____________________, 19 ____, for value received, Lessor hereby transfers, assigns and sets over to ________________________________, all right, title and interest in and to the above lease and the rent thereby reserved, except rent due and payable prior to ____________________, 19 ____.

________________________ (seal)

________________________ (seal)

GUARANTEE

On this ____________________, 19 ____, in consideration of Ten Dollars ($10.00) and other goods and valuable consideration, the receipt and sufficiency of which is hereby acknowledged, the undersigned Guarantor hereby guarantees the payment of rent and performance by Lessee, Lessee's heirs, executors, administrators, successors or assigns of all covenants and agreements of the above lease.

________________________ (seal)

________________________ (seal)

FORM No. 79
June, 1994

CONTRACT, REAL ESTATE SALE
(Illinois)

THIS MEMORANDUM WITNESSETH, THAT purchaser, ____________________
____________________, hereby agrees to purchase at the price of
____________________ Dollars,
the following described real estate, situated in the County of __________ and State of Illinois:

Permanent Real Estate Index Number(s): ____________________

Address(es) of real estate: ____________________

and seller, ____________________
agrees to sell said premises at said price, and to convey to purchaser a good and merchantable title thereto; by __________ general Warranty Deed, with release of homestead rights, but subject to: (1) existing leases, expiring ____________________ the purchaser to be entitled to the rents from ____________________; (2) all taxes and assessments levied after the year 19_____; (3) any unpaid special taxes or special assessments levied for improvements not yet completed and to unpaid installments of special assessments which fall due after ____________________ levied for improvements completed; also subject to any party wall agreements of record; to building line restrictions and building restrictions of record, and to

Premiums on insurance policies held by Mortgagees shall be paid for by purchaser pro rata for the unexpired time.
Purchaser has paid ____________________ Dollars, as earnest money, to be applied on such purchase when consummated, and agrees to pay within five days after the title has been examined and found good, or accepted by him, said insurance premiums and the further sum of ____________________ Dollars, at the office of ____________________,
provided a good and sufficient __________ general Warranty Deed, conveying to said purchaser a good and merchantable title to said premises (subject as aforesaid), shall then be ready for delivery. The balance to be paid as follows:

with interest from the date hereof at the rate of _____ per cent per annum, payable semi-annually, to be secured by the purchaser's notes and mortgage, or trust deed, of even date herewith, on said premises, in the form known as ____________________

A Certificate of Title issued by the Registrar of Titles of Cook County, or complete merchantable abstract of title or merchantable copy brought down to date hereof, or merchantable title insurance policy of ____________________ shall be furnished by the seller within a reasonable time, which abstract shall, upon the consummation of this sale remain with the seller, or his assigns, as part of his security, until the deferred installments are fully paid. The purchaser or his attorney if an abstract or copy be furnished shall, within ten days after receiving such abstract, deliver to the seller or his agent (together with the abstract), a note or memorandum in writing, signed by him or his attorney, specifying in detail the objections he makes to the title, if any; or if none, then stating in substance that the same is satisfactory. In case material defects be found in said title, and so reported, then, if such defects be not cured within sixty days after such notice thereof, this contract shall, at the purchaser's option become absolutely null and void, and said earnest money shall be returned; notice of such election to be given to the seller but the purchaser may nevertheless elect to take such title as it then is, and in such case the seller shall convey, as above agreed, provided, however, that purchaser shall have first given a written notice of such election, within ten days after the expiration of the said sixty days, and tendered performance hereof on his part. In default of such notice of election to perform, and accompanying tender, within the time so limited, the purchaser shall, without further action by either party, be deemed to have abandoned his claim upon said premises, and thereupon this contract shall cease to have any force or effect as against said premises, or the title thereto, or any right or interest therein, but not otherwise, and said earnest money shall be returned.

Should purchaser fail to perform this contract promptly on his part, at the time and in the manner herein specified, the earnest money paid as above, shall, at the option of the seller be retained by the seller as liquidated damages, and this contract shall thereupon become and be null and void. Time is the essence of this contract, and of all the conditions hereof.

The notices required to be given by the terms of this agreement shall in all cases be construed to mean notices in writing, signed by or on behalf of the party giving the same, and the same may be served either upon the other party or his agent.

If the taxes and assessments to be paid by the seller cannot be paid at time this contract is to be closed then the seller is to pay same on or before ____________________ next ensuing.

This contract and the said earnest money shall be held by ____________________ for the mutual benefit of the parties concerned, and after the consummation of the sale___he___ shall be at liberty to retain the canceled contract permanently; and it shall be the duty of said ____________________ in case said earnest money be retained as herein provided, to apply the same, first to the payment of any expenses incurred for the seller by his agent in said matter, and second, to the payment to seller's broker of a commission of _______ per cent on the selling price herein mentioned, for his services in procuring this contract rendering the overplus to the seller.

Seller warrants to purchaser that no notice from any city, village or other governmental authority of a dwelling code violation which existed in the dwelling structure before the execution of this contract has been received by the seller, his principal or his agent within 10 years of the date of execution of the contract.

WITNESS the hands of the parties hereto, this ____________________ day of ____________________ 19_____

____________________(SEAL)

____________________(SEAL)

____________________(SEAL)

periodic tenancy. The tenancy that exists when the landlord and tenant agree that the rent will be paid in regular successive intervals until notice to terminate is given but do not agree on a specific duration of the lease.

Periodic Tenancy. A **periodic tenancy** is a leasehold interest similar to a term tenancy, except that it continues until either side gives notice to terminate the lease. Periodic tenancies can be transferred through express terms or by implication. An express leasehold transfer of a periodic tenancy would be created by the words, "to lessee from month to month [or some other period], beginning ———."

An implied periodic tenancy would be created if a tenant paid rent on a regular periodic basis with no agreement as to a termination date. The implication would be that the lease would be periodic for successive periods of time equal to the rent payments. For example, assume that Charlie leases garage space for his car from Kerry, paying $60 each month. There has been no agreement as to a termination date for this lease. In this example, Charlie has a periodic tenancy for successive one-month periods.

holdover lease. The tenancy that exists where a tenant subject to a term lease is allowed to remain on the premises after the term has expired.

Periodic leases may also exist when a tenant has been allowed to remain on the premises of the property after a term lease has expired; this is also called a **holdover lease.** There is no longer a term lease (because it has automatically expired at the end of the term); instead, the lease has become a periodic tenancy. The period is, again, determined by how often rent is due (monthly, weekly, or some other period). In the above example, assume that Charlie and Kerry had first agreed to a term lease for six months, with rent paid monthly. The lease expires at the end of the six-month period, but Kerry lets Charlie continue to use the garage. Charlie now has a month-to-month periodic lease.

If a lease continues month to month, how is it ever terminated? Periodic leases are terminable at will by either party as long as proper notice is given at least one period in advance. Therefore, if the period of the lease is month to month, at least a one-month notice must be given. If the lease is week to week, only a one-week notice must be given. The Uniform Residential Landlord and Tenant Act, which has been adopted in a minority of states, provides for at least a 10-day notice on a week-to-week lease and a 60-day notice on a month-to-month lease.

tenancy at will. A leasehold interest that occurs when a property is leased for an indefinite period of time and is terminable at the will of either party to the lease.

Tenancy at Will. A **tenancy at will** is a tenancy that may be terminated at any time by either party. A tenancy at will may arise where the parties agree not to agree. That is to say, the parties agree not to have a termination date for the contract for some reason or another. For example, perhaps the property owner is planning to sell the property but does not yet have a purchaser. The owner may lease the property with the provision that the lessee must vacate the apartment whenever the owner finds a purchaser for the building.

Though two parties may expressly enter into a tenancy at will, such a tenancy may also occur by implication where there has been some failure to comply with the law for a term tenancy. For instance, two parties agree to enter into a lease contract, but no formal lease nor any formal agreement has ever been reached. The tenant still has the right to be on the property, but either party may end the lease at his or her whim.

Although a literal tenancy at will at common law provides that no notice need be given to end the lease, many states statutorily require that notice of a minimum period be given. Death, sale, or subsequent lease of the property may also terminate the interest.

tenancy at sufferance. The leasehold interest that occurs when a tenant remains in possession of property after the expiration of a lease.

Tenancy at Sufferance. A **tenancy at sufferance** exists when a tenant who originally lawfully entered and took possession of the property now unlawfully occupies it. The most likely such situation occurs when a tenant refuses to leave the property upon termination of the lease. Under a tenancy at sufferance, the landlord owes the tenant no duty other than not to hurt her or him. The landlord can choose to treat the tenant as a periodic tenancy, as discussed above, but is not required to do so. If not, the landlord may begin proceedings to legally evict or remove the tenant from the premises.

Profile Perspective: What type of lease agreement did Emma and Roger enter into? If Emma's apartment was not destroyed and she remained longer than one year without signing a new lease, what type of lease arrangement would that be considered?

B. Rights and Duties of the Parties to a Lease

The lessor and lessee owe each other certain obligations according to the common law of contracts, state statutes, or the lease agreement itself. The lease may contain a number of clauses defining the relationship; these generally provide for the transfer of interest as of a certain date, a reversion of interest to the landlord on a certain date, a description of the property (usually by its address), and the amount of rent. Most of the rights or obligations of the parties may be modified by the lease contract. The generally accepted terms found in most leases are discussed below.

Rights of the Lessor/Duties of the Lessee. The lessor has the right to receive compensation in exchange for allowing the lessee to use the property, usually called **rent,** and has the right to inspect the property and to make repairs. The lessee has a duty to pay the rent, to maintain the property in a reasonable manner (or to pay for any misuse), and to be responsible for individuals invited onto the property. These rights are usually enumerated in the lease agreement, and you can imagine how much easier it makes any conflict if they *are* included in a well-drafted lease.

rent. The consideration paid by a lessee to a lessor in exchange for the right to possess and to use property.

The right of a lessee to use the property is contingent on the lessor's receipt of the rent payment. Failure to pay the rent may result in termination of the lease agreement. The rent may be determined through a variety of methods. In a residential lease, a specific rent amount is usually specified in the lease. However, in commercial leases, a different method is used to calculate the amount of rent due.

Net Leases. A net lease specifies that the lessee is responsible not only for the rent due on the property, but also for the costs of maintaining the property, including taxes and insurance. The lessee and lessor may agree that the lessee pays all of the costs, including heat, water, and any other, of taking care of the property.

Percentage Rental Agreements. The lessor generally knows less about the tenant's business than the tenant. So, to ensure that the risk of the business venture is on the tenant (who should know the nature of the risk), a landlord may set a minimum rent amount that may escalate as the tenant's profits increase. For instance, a lease may provide that the tenant will pay a certain percentage of his or her gross sales, but at a minimum, $500 per month. In this way, the lessor is protected in case the business does not do well but is also able to take advantage of a profitable tenant.

Appraisal Leases. As protection against inflation, a landlord may demand an appraisal lease. An appraisal lease requires that the property value, and therefore the rent amount, be reevaluated at certain times during the lease term. In this way, the landlord can protect against a situation in which he or she has a relatively low-priced lease at an address that has gone way up in value. The parties agree to the term of the lease, the times for appraisals, and the method by which the rent will be calculated based on the appraisals.

The right to receive rent is freely assignable by the landlord. In addition, if the lessor transfers her or his entire interest in the property to someone else (for instance, sells the property), this transfer would include the lessor's rights in the lease. The new property owner becomes the lessor. For example, Donna owns a building that contains several apartments, one of which is rented by Shelly for $300 per month. Donna just bought a car and owes $300 each month to a financing company. Donna may assign her right to receive Shelly's rent to the financing company to pay for her car loan.

To protect the value and nature of her or his property, a lessor may periodically, and with due notice, make inspections of the property. If repairs are necessary to protect the integrity of the property, the landlord has the right to enter the premises to make these repairs. If the property or a part of it is destroyed by an unreasonable act of the tenant, the tenant may be obligated to either make or pay for the repairs.

The owner also may have the right, through the lease contract, to show the property to prospective purchasers or tenants. Although the common law requires that the parties have agreed to this in advance, most form residential leases today contain some provision for limited or restricted access.

eviction. Depriving the tenant of the possession of the leased premises.

lockout. Where the landlord deprives the tenant of the possession of the premises by changing the locks on the property.

constructive eviction. A breach of duty by the landlord that makes the property uninhabitable or otherwise deprives the tenant of the benefit of the lease and gives rise to the tenant's right to vacate the property and to terminate the lease.

If the lessee breaches any of the terms of the contract, the lessor may begin **eviction** proceedings. These proceedings require that the lessee and lessor appear before a judge to determine whether a breach actually took place. If it did, the judge may grant the lessee sufficient time to find alternate lodging. Some state statutes provide that a landlord may not evict a tenant in any other way, such as changing the locks (a **lock-out).** A landlord's locking out of a tenant or otherwise forcing the tenant to move without a court eviction, such as by turning off utilities like heat or water, is called a **constructive eviction.** Where constructive evictions are prohibited by statute, the lessor may be liable for any harm or damage that results.

Duties of the Lessor/Rights of the Lessee. Additional duties of the lessor may be listed in the lease agreement, but there are several that are imposed universally. Some of these duties appear rather broad, including the duty to allow "quiet enjoyment" of the property by the lessee. A residential lessee has the right to use the property for any purpose, except those that are illegal, are against public policy, or in such a way would permanently harm the premises. A landlord's interference with this right to quiet enjoyment of the property may constitute a breach of the lease.

implied warranty of habitability. Implied warranty arising in lease or sale of residential real estate that the property will be fit for human habitation.

Owners are also required to make whatever repairs are necessary to maintain the property (both common areas and tenant's area) in a habitable, safe, and secure manner. Most states have specific statutory requirements for safety measures that must be taken to protect tenants. For instance, a landlord may be required by state statute to provide a fire extinguisher and smoke detector in every apartment. In fact, there is a common law **implied warranty of habitability** that requires the landlord to make sure that the leased property is in proper condition for its intended use. (A lessor of a commercial property would not have to provide the same facilities as a lessor of a residential property.)

rent-strike statutes. Legislation that allows a tenant to deduct from the rent payment the cost of property repairs that are otherwise the responsibility of the landlord.

In states in which the weather becomes cold during the winter, the statute may provide for heat-on and heat-off deadlines for the landlord. The landlord would be required to turn on the heat by a certain date and to maintain reasonable temperatures during the inclement weather. If the owner fails to satisfy these obligations, many states allow the tenant to make the necessary purchases or repairs and to deduct their cost from the rent payment (allowed through **rent-strike statutes).**

The right of a commercial lessee to use the property may be further restricted. For example, the lease may provide that the commercial lessee is not allowed to run a liquor store on the site nor operate an adult book store, even though these functions may be allowed by law. This type of restriction is acceptable and lawful.

The lease may provide that the lessee has the right to transfer her or his *entire* lease interest to a third party through a lease **assignment.** A transfer of only a portion of the lease interest (such as for just the summer, with the lessee returning in the fall) is called a **sublease.** Because the third party would now be a party to the lease, many leases provide that an assignment may only be made with the consent of the landlord. But by knowingly accepting payment of the rent by the third party, the landlord may be deemed to have **ratified** the lease assignment.

assignment. A transfer of property or some right or interest.

sublease. A transfer of some but not all of a tenant's remaining right to possess property under a lease.

ratified. The adoption or affirmance by a person of a prior act that did not previously bind her or him.

A lessee's assignment of a lease is viewed merely as an assignment of the lessee's rights under the lease, not the duties. So, without any other agreement, the lessee remains liable for the rent and all of the other duties under the lease. The lessee may be relieved of this responsibility if (1) the landlord agrees to terminate the lease and to begin a new lease with the third party or (2) the landlord grants the lessee a **novation,** accepting the third party as solely responsible for the lease duties.

novation. A mutual agreement between all parties concerned for the discharge of a valid existing obligation by the substitution of a new valid obligation on the part of the debtor or another, or a like agreement for the discharge of a lessee to a landlord by the substitution of a new lessee.

Consider the following example: Jenna rents an apartment from Lily; but she recently found an apartment she prefers because she can also work out of it. Wendy is willing to rent Jenna's apartment as a sublessee and to finish out Jenna's lease term. Lily agrees to the assignment but not to a novation. Jenna remains liable on the lease, and if Wendy doesn't pay the rent, Jenna will be responsible to Lily.

Profile Perspective: What duty does Roger owe to Emma in connection with her losses and on what basis?

Duties of the Landlord to Third Parties. At common law, the duty of an owner of leased property to someone who is injured on the property depended on that person's classification as an invitee, licensee, or trespasser. An **invitee** is someone who has been invited onto the property by the owner for the owner's benefit, such as a customer. A **licensee** is someone who has been invited onto the property for the licensee's benefit, such as a lessee or employee. A **trespasser** is someone who has not been invited onto the property and who has no rights in the property.

invitee. A person who is on private premises for a purpose connected with the business interests of the possessor of those premises, or a member of the public who is lawfully on land open to the public.

licensee. A person lawfully on land in possession of another for purposes unconnected with the business interests of the possessor.

trespasser. One who enters the property of another without permission or authority.

At common law, a landowner had different obligations to each of these types of individuals and a different duty of care would be applied depending on the classification of the injured party. In present law, the duty generally depends on who actually has control of that area where the injury occurred. A landowner has a basic duty of reasonable care in connection with all areas of the property. If no reasonable care is exercised and someone gets hurt, that person is likely to recover.

If the injury occurs in a lessee's apartment as a result of the condition of that apartment, the lessee may be held liable in place of the landlord. The court may look to the landlord's duty to repair under the lease to determine whether the landlord or the tenant should have fixed the dangerous situation or maintained that area. For example, assume Josephine, a landlord, has agreed to repair cracked areas of tile in the kitchen of a rented apartment but has not yet had a chance to do it. Carl invites his friend Beatrice to his apartment and she injures herself on the unfixed cracked tiles. The court would probably find that Josephine has assumed responsibility for the condition of the tiles.

Some states allow a landlord to delegate the responsibility to maintain the property in a safe manner to the lessee by contract, but only for harm resulting to the lessee, not third parties. The landlord will remain responsible to third parties for any resulting damage. For example, a lease may read: "lessee assumes full responsibility for the condition of the premises and will be liable for injury resulting from any defect on the property."

Lawsuits Plaster Apartment Complex

by Charlie Brennan

Susan Murray picked up the phone a week ago and heard the chilling words.

"If you testify, you can kiss your dog goodbye," an unidentified caller said.

Death threats are almost routine in murder or drug cases. They're not so routine in landlord-tenant disputes.

But there's nothing routine about the firestorm swirling around the 450-unit Park Preserve at Cherry Creek in southeast Denver.

Tenants have alleged that they sign a lease for one unit but end up in a worse apartment, that repair requests are ignored, and that security is inadequate.

Owner Andrew Grossman of Minneapolis says that claims are exaggerated, but the legal landslide in Denver includes:

- A 39-count lawsuit by the Colorado attorney general alleging consumer fraud and seeking up to $125,000 in damages. The attorney general launched an investigation into possible witness tampering in the wake of the threat against Murray.
- Two lawsuits sparked by unsolved slayings. Survivors of 22-year-old Leonard Howard—including his four children—filed suit in Denver District Court claiming a broken lock on his apartment door went unrepaired, allowing Howard's killer to ambush him.
- Four cases in which former tenants charge deception and negligence. Two of those Denver District Court cases are countersuits by tenants who were sued for back rent or eviction after they withheld rent in protest.
- As many as 11 pending cases in Denver County Court, brought by city attorney's office, alleging unsafe conditions and building-code violations.

* * *

"I think that the claims are exaggerated," Grossman said. "When this is tried [in court], we will be vindicated."

Grossman blames some of the complaints on a Denver management team he's since replaced.

"Employees at the site did not perform up to our expectations, and frankly we were quite surprised by the problems that arose," he said.

* * *

Changes have come too late for Murray, who's moving out. She had not decided whether to sue Park Preserve until she received the threat against Sassy, her 14-year-old poodle on February 10.

Murray, 33, is an epileptic and she suffered stress-induced seizures after the threat.

And she plans to sue.

Questions

1. Do you feel that landlords generally have greater power in negotiations and after the lease has been signed than tenants? Consider that many landlords need occupants in order to meet their mortgage payments and thus may not be in as safe a position as many believe.
2. Consider the case of Leonard Howard. Do you believe that the court should find Grossman responsible for Howard's death because the door lock was not fixed? If yes, what sentence or fine would you impose?
3. Shouldn't a tenant who is dissatisfied with an apartment or complex simply move out? Why or why not?

Source: *Rocky Mountain News,* February 18, 1995, p. 5A.

When property is leased for commercial purposes, the landlord remains liable for injuries occurring in that part of the premises that is open to the public, as long as the injuries are not due to the tenant's negligence. This would exclude areas that are marked as "staff only" or places where the public is not expected to go, like kitchens in restaurants.

Profile Perspective: Does Roger owe any duty to Emma's brother? Is he liable for losses as a result of destruction to her brother's personal property?

Prohibited Lease Terms. Although certain rights and duties of the lessee and lessor may be negotiated, as stated above, other terms are either nonnegotiable or may not be in the lease at all. These prohibited lease clauses are regulated by state law, but similarities across state lines often exist.

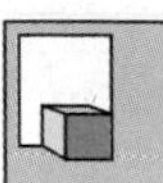

For example, some states prohibit a **confession of judgment clause** in residential leases. This clause says that the tenant "authorizes any attorney to appear in court and waive the tenant's right to notice and trial by jury and to confess judgment in favor of the landlord for any rent due." In fact, beneath the legal jargon this clause really states that the tenant would allow the landlord to go into court and obtain a judgment against the tenant with no notice to the tenant that the court is hearing the case, nor any opportunity to defend.

confession of judgment clause. A clause stipulating that the lessee grants judgment in any action on the contract to the landlord without the formality of an ordinary proceeding.

Other residential lease clauses prohibited in various states include:

- **Limitation of liability or exculpatory clause**—limits the landlord's liabilities arising from the lease. Unenforceable where tenant was compelled to agree by unequal bargaining position, or where landlord knew of dangerous condition but did not warn tenant.
- **Waiver of notice clause**—the tenant agrees to waive notice of termination of the lease.
- **Jury trial waiver clause**—the tenant waives the right to a jury trial in an eviction action.
- **Attorney's fees clause**—the tenant agrees to pay the attorney's fees of the landlord in any dispute arising from the lease.
- **Waiver of statutory rights clause**—if a state has a landlord-tenant ordinance, there can be no waiver of the rights guaranteed by that statute.
- **Excessive late fee clause**—if a fee is charged for the tardy payment of rent, it must be reasonable and not excessive.

Profile Perspective: Is the exculpatory clause in Emma's lease valid and enforceable? Explain.

Discrimination. Pursuant to the Fair Housing Act[1] and the common law, a lessor is not allowed to discriminate against potential or present tenants on the basis of their race, color, gender, national origin, or religion. For example, a landlord may not refuse to lease an apartment to a prospective tenant simply because that tenant is a Hare Krishna (a religion based in Hinduism) and makes the landlord uncomfortable. Similarly, a landlord may not decide that only Jewish people are welcome as tenants.

Assume, for example, that Joseph owns a building that has a storefront unit. Prashant, an Indian and an accountant, wants to lease the storefront as his office space. Joseph says that he won't lease it to Prashant because the neighborhood is primarily African-American and Joseph is concerned about racial tensions that might result. Joseph would be discriminating on the basis of Prashant's national origin. He would be required to lease the space to Prashant.

CASE

Justice Kelly

Honce v. Vigil

1 F.3d 1085 (1993)

In August 1990, Ms. Honce arranged to rent a lot in Mr. Vigil's mobile home park. Ms. Honce placed a mobile home on the property in mid-September and moved in at the beginning of October. Mr. Vigil invited Ms. Honce to accompany him socially on three occasions in September, prior to her moving in. . . [After the third attempt] she responded that she did not want to go out with him at any time. He told her that he had only wanted to be friends and did not ask her out again. . .

After Ms. Honce moved in, she and Mr. Vigil had a series of disputes over the property. The first involved a plumbing problem, which Mr. Vigil refused to pay for because he claimed that the problem was not in his part of the line. The next arose over the building of a fence for Ms. Honce's dog. Mr. Vigil required all tenants with dogs to erect fenced dog-runs. He prohibited the use of cement and preferred that his own fencing materials be used. . .

[The court describes the nature of the disputes.]

Mr. Vigil testified that he believes there is a "conspiracy" against him, led by his former girlfriend and the sheriff's department. Relationships with most of his tenants quickly break down because of this conspiracy and the problems are often with women. He has evicted between 10 and 25 tenants in the past, both male and female, including his own nephew.

Ms. Honce's neighbors testified that they had similar problems with Mr. Vigil. Rose and Russell Haenner stated that he bothered Mrs. Haenner almost daily. . .

Ms. Honce alleges that Mr. Vigil's actions amount to sexual discrimination and harassment, which forced her to leave the trailer park. The district court granted judgment as a matter of law for Mr. Vigil, following the conclusion of plaintiff's evidence. The court found no disparate treatment in Mr. Vigil's equally poor treatment of all of his tenants, and no evidence of sexual harassment. As for constructive eviction, the court found that the sheriff's advice, not the landlord's actions, caused her to vacate.

* * *

I. The Fair Housing Act

The Fair Housing Act prohibits gender-based discrimination in the rental of a dwelling or in the provision of services in connection with a rental. Discrimination may occur by treating one gender less favorably (disparate treatment) or by sexual harassment.

A. Disparate Treatment

The district court determined that there was insufficient evidence of disparate treatment because Mr. Vigil was "equally nasty" to all of his tenants. Ms. Honce argues that Mr. Vigil was more hostile to women, pointing to the evidence of his past problems with women and the supposed "conspiracy" against him by law enforcement. . .

Here the landlord did not refuse to rent to Ms. Honce, nor did he actually evict her. Ms. Honce offers no evidence of a discrepency in services provided. The landlord offered the same materials for property improvements to Ms. Honce as to her neighbors, and insisted on compliance with the rental agreement. The fact that Mr. Vigil believed that there was a conspiracy against him is not actionable unless he refused to rent to women with the same rental services as men. Such was not the case.

Continued

Continued

B. Sexual Harassment

Few courts have addressed sexual harassment in the context of fair housing. In *Shellhammer* v. *Lewallen,* the landlord requested that Mrs. Shellhammer pose nude for pictures, and she refused. One month later, he offered her money for sex, which she also rejected. Three months later, the landlord evicted her. The district court found that the eviction was in response to the tenant's rejection and awarded damages.

* * *

Although Mr. Vigil may not be the most rational actor, Title VIII does not make irrational rental policies illegal. Ms. Honce failed to present evidence of a causal connection, and a conclusional allegation is insufficient to create a question of fact. We agree that no reasonable jury could find quid pro quo harassment here.

Affirmed.

* * *

Dissent: Circuit Judge Seymour

I must respectfully dissent from the majority's affirmance of the directed verdict in this case. My examination of the record reveals that, under the standards governing review of directed verdict rulings, Ms. Honce offered sufficient evidence to raise a jury issue on each of her claims.

* * *

I turn first to the issue of disparate treatment. To raise a jury issue on this claim, Ms. Honce was required to present evidence from which the jury could reasonably infer that Mr. Vigil, as a landlord, treated tenants who were women more harshly than tenants who were men. Although the majority refers to the testimony of Mr. and Mrs. Haenner, it fails to draw the inference from their evidence that is most favorable to Ms. Honce [required by a review of a directed verdict] or to recognize that this favorable inference supports Ms. Honce's assertion of disparate treatment. Mr. and Mrs. Haenner both testified that Mr. Vigil harassed Mrs. Haenner almost daily about tenancy matters while refusing to deal with Mr. Haenner on those problems even when Mr. Haenner asked him to do so. Mrs. Haenner told her husband that the situation was so unbearable that she was moving out of the trailer park with or without him. . . .

Moreover, Mr. Vigil himself testified that the problems he had as a landlord primarily involved tenants who were women. The court specifically asked Mr. Vigil: "Do you have the same problems with males in your mobile home subdivision as you do the females?" Mr. Vigil responded:

> On the accusations, normally they've been with women. It's a routine situation. Somebody gets evicted; they plan to go make a report at the police station and include sex. But they're not bright enough to even come up with it themselves. I'm the one that told them years ago that that's what I'm going to be accused of, that someday I was going to be sitting in a court because they can't get to me through money, through law. The only way that they can get to me is through false sexual accusations.

Apparently, Mr. Vigil believed that women tenants were constantly attempting to take advantage of him and his money using sex. . . This evidence also supports an inference that Mr. Vigil was selectively hostile to women.

Continued

Continued

Questions

1. Since men cannot make a sexual harassment claim against Mr. Vigil based on the above behavior, isn't it likely that the only claims filed would be by women? If the behavior is annoying to both men and women, but only women could file an action against Mr. Vigil based on gender, you would expect to find claims primarily by women. Does this mean that sexual harassment or discrimination occurred?
2. Are you persuaded by the majority or the dissent? By Mr. Vigil's statement repeated in the dissenting opinion?

unconscionability. A contract so one-sided and oppressive as to be unfair.

Unconscionability. The **unconscionability** concept that was first created in the UCC applies to leases as well. This concept provides that a clause in a contract may be deemed invalid where the contract term is patently unfair to one of the parties and therefore unenforceable. This concept is usually applied in favor of the tenant and against the landlord due to their unequal bargaining positions. The court does not allow the landlord to take advantage of the tenant just because the tenant signed the lease. For example, the prohibited lease terms mentioned in the previous section might be considered unconscionable if they were not already prohibited by statute.

An example of unconscionability may exist where Peter rents an apartment from Whitney by a lease that states that Whitney has the right to enter the apartment whenever necessary to make standard repairs. However, after Peter moves in, Whitney repeatedly enters the apartment at 2:00 A.M. to repair problems. The court would find that the lease clause allowing her to enter without notice and at unreasonable hours would be unconscionable.

IV. Ownership Interests in Real Property

A leasehold estate transfers only the right to possess, inhabit, or use property. Ownership is not transferred through a lease. The following sections identify the nature of ownership interests.

A. Fee Simple Estate

A *fee simple absolute* is the most common form of ownership interest in real property. The owner of the fee has the greatest possible rights in connection with the property; that is, the owner is the sole owner and there are no conditions attached to the ownership or use of the property, except those imposed by law. A fee simple absolute is transferred by a deed that states, "to [name of grantee]." No other words are necessary.

defeasible fee simple. A title to property that is open to attack, that might be defeated by the performance of some act, or that is subject to conditions.

restrictive covenants. An agreement restricting the use of real property.

The owner has exclusive possession of the property and has the right to transfer it either through a sale or a will. The owner also has the right to carve smaller interests out of the absolute fee. For instance, the owner of an apartment building may hold a fee simple absolute, yet the tenants of the building own leases that the owner has carved out.

Where a fee simple is transferred with conditions, the interest is considered a **defeasible fee simple.** The conditions may provide that the ownership interest continue until certain events occur (such as "transferred until the property is zoned for commercial units") or as long as certain events occur (such as "transferred as long as a member of the Lustig family lives on the premises"). These conditions are also called **restrictive covenants.**

Assume Keith transfers real property to Max through an instrument that states: "to Max, as long as he is in the real estate investment business, then to Lucy." In this example, Max will receive a defeasible fee simple, and Lucy will receive a fee simple absolute if Max changes professions. Lucy may never receive an interest if Richard remains in the real estate investment business. However, if she does receive an interest, it will be a fee simple absolute. Lucy's interest is considered a **possibility of reverter,** since she may never receive it.

possibility of reverter. An interest that is uncertain or may arise only upon the occurrence of a condition.

Consider a transfer by Ned of land and a stable to the park district through an instrument that states: "to the park district as long as horseback riding remains a park district–sponsored activity." Three years later, the park district discontinues its horseback riding instruction. The land and stable will then revert to Ned or his heirs.

In the first example, Keith retains no interest because either Max will retain the property or Lucy will get it. In the second example, Ned does retain an interest in the property because there was always the chance that the condition would occur and the land would revert to him or his heirs. Ned's interest is considered a **partial ownership interest.**

partial ownership interest. An interest that may revert back to the original grantor.

B. Life Estate

A life estate is an interest in property that is measured by the life of the grantee or some other person. A life estate is transferred using such words as: "to Juan for life" or "to Juan for the life of Rachel." The first transfers possessory rights in the property to Juan until he dies; the second transfers possessory rights in the property to Juan until Rachel dies. This second transfer of a life estate is called an **estate per *autre vie.***

estate per *autre vie*. A life estate that is measured by the life of someone other than the possessor.

life tenant. The possessor of a life estate interest.

The person holding the estate, the **life tenant,** has the right to use the property, sell or mortgage his or her interest, harvest crops or modify the fixtures on the property, or otherwise change the property. The life tenant may only convey the extent of her or his interest, nothing more. So, a life tenant cannot convey a fee simple to someone else, because the life tenant's rights stop at the end of the stated life (the tenant's or another's).

A life interest may be the only interest conveyed in the grant of the property, such as, "to Juan for life." In that case, the property will revert back to the original owner at the death of the life tenant. The grant of the life estate may also specify another recipient to take a fee simple at the end of the life estate. This would be transferred through words such as, "to Juan for life, then to Barbara." In this example, Barbara receives a fee simple absolute upon Juan's death and is considered a **remainderman** (or remainderperson may be the appropriate terminology today, though no court has yet used it!). Where there is a remainderman, the future interest created by the grantor is called a **nonreversionary interest.** Where there is no remainderman, the future interest back to the grantor is called a *reversionary interest.*

remainderman. One who is entitled to the remainder of the estate after a particular estate carved out of it has expired.

nonreversionary interest. The interest held by a remainderman. It is called nonreversionary because it does not revert to the original grantor.

The life tenant is not allowed to commit waste of the property through abuse or neglect because that would damage the rights of those who received the property after her or him. If the life tenant commits waste of the property, the remainderman has the right to sue the life tenant. For example, the life tenant on a property that has tremendous natural beauty may not destroy that beauty and build a shopping mall without the consent of the remaindermen.

Additional Forms of Life Interests. The common law created two forms of life estates for the purpose of providing financial security to someone after the death of his or her spouse. For instance, when a husband dies, a wife had a right to a life estate in one-third of her husband's real property that he owned while they were married. This right is called a **dower interest.** A **curtesy interest** is a similar life interest granted to husbands when their wives die, but instead allows the husband a life interest in the full amount of the deceased wife's real property *if* a child had been born between him and his wife.

dower interest. The right of a wife upon the death of her husband to receive a life estate in one-third of her husband's real property.

curtesy interest. The right of a husband upon the death of his wife to receive all of the wife's real property *as long as* the two had a child between them.

elective share. Legislative mandate that a spouse receive a specific percentage interest in a deceased spouse's estate.

These provisions still exist in some states, but many states have discontinued or modified the practice by statutes. In their place, some states have **elective share** statutes, which allow a spouse to receive a specific percentage of the deceased's estate (both real and personal property), not merely a life estate. The share is considered elective because the spouse has the choice of receiving the statutory share or receiving any amount left through a will, if in fact the spouse received anything.

Assume Matthew died and left a wife, Sarah. In his will, Matthew provided that Sarah would receive only the house in which they lived. The remainder of his large estate was given to his best friend, Bob. The state in which they all lived had an elective share statute allowing the spouse 30 percent of the deceased's property by election. Sarah may elect to receive 30 percent of Matthew's estate if that amount would be of greater value than the house.

C. Concurrent Ownership

More than one person may own a piece of property at the same time. These owners may each share a percentage of the property or may own different segments of a larger piece of property. The following sections describe different ways in which people may share ownership of real estate.

tenants in common. Co-owners of real property who have undivided interests in the property and equal rights to possess it.

undivided share. A share of the interest in property that is not subject to division into parts.

Tenancy in Common. Where two or more people own the same real property, and no other form of ownership is stated, the ownership is presumed to be as **tenants in common.** (The owners are called tenants even though they own the property and do not lease it.) Common tenancy means that each owner owns an **undivided share** in the entire property, whether owned in equal shares or not. For example, if you and your brother each own a 50 percent undivided share in a piece of property, the property cannot be split without selling it. There would be no way to divide it because each of you owns 50 percent of each part of the property.

Where the property is not owned in equal shares, the tenants in common still retain an equal right to use the property. However, the income is shared in relation to their ownership interests. Assume that Vincent, Greg, and Luis own property in unequal shares. Vincent and Greg each owns 40 percent of the interest, and Luis owns 20 percent. Each man has an equal right to enter and to use the property, but they would share in relation to these unequal percentages if they sold the property.

partition. A legal proceeding that enables joint tenants or tenants in common to put an end to the tenancy and to vest in each tenant a sole estate in specific property or an allotment of the lands and buildings. If division is impossible, the estate may have to be sold and the proceeds divided.

A transfer of common tenancy may occur with the death of a tenant or by sale or gift. If a tenant in common dies, the interest of that tenant passes to his or her heirs, not to the other tenants. These heirs now take the place of the deceased as tenants in common with the other tenants. A tenant in common has the right to sell or give her or his right in the property to a third party *without* the consent of the other tenants.

A tenant in common may form a **partition** when that owner wants to take her or his portion of the property interest and leave the common tenancy. When this happens, the property may be independently valued or the owners may agree to the value of the property, and the departing owner will receive her or his percentage interest in the property. This may occur through a sale of the property or the other owners may purchase the departing owner's share.

Joint Tenancy. **Joint tenancy** is similar to tenancy in common in that each owner has an undivided right to use the property, but it also includes the **right of survivorship.** A right of survivorship exists where a deceased owner's right in the property passes not to her or his heirs but instead to the other owners. In the above example, assume that Vincent, Greg, and Luis own real property as joint tenants. Vincent dies. Vincent's interest in the property is transferred to Greg and Luis in equal shares.

There are four requirements to forming a joint tenancy, called unities. First, unity of possession requires that each tenant be given an undivided interest in the property. Unity of interest requires that the undivided shares be equal. Unity of title requires that each owner take the property by the same instrument. Unity of time requires that each owner take title to the property at the same time.

If any of these unities is violated, the tenancy is considered to be a tenancy in common. Therefore, if one owner sells her or his interest (thus violating the unities of time and title), the joint tenancy is broken and the owners are considered tenants in common.

joint tenancy. An estate held by two or more jointly with an equal right in all to share in the enjoyments of the land during their lives.

right of survivorship. A feature of a joint tenancy that causes a co-owner's interest in property to be transferred on her or his death to the surviving co-owner(s).

Tenancy by the Entirety. Although **tenancy by the entirety** is only recognized in about half of the states, it is one of the most restrictive types of ownership. A tenancy by the entirety is based on a legal fiction that a husband and wife are one legal unit. A husband and wife therefore own property as one and may not divide it. The effect of this fiction is that a husband and wife owning property in the entirety may not divide the property without the other's consent, except in the case of death or divorce.

In the case of divorce, the parties are treated as tenants in common, who share undivided one-half interests in the property. Tenancy by the entirety has a right of survivorship, so in the case of death, the deceased's share passes to the surviving spouse.

Tenancy by the entirety has fallen out of use in many states because a creditor of either the husband or the wife cannot use the property to satisfy a debt. So, even though one of the spouses actually has a financial interest in a valuable piece of property, that individual may escape paying a debt because the creditor cannot attach it. Some states, to avoid this perceived unfairness, allow the attachment. The creditor is then able to force a sale of the debtor's share. Other states, in a throwback to historical times, allow the attachment only to creditors of the husband but not to creditors of the wife. A creditor who is owed a debt by both the husband and the wife may attach the property.

tenancy by the entirety. A form of co-ownership of property by a married couple that gives the owners a right of survivorship and cannot be severed during life by the act of only one of the parties.

Community Property. Some states, including Arizona, California, Idaho, Louisiana, Nevada, New Mexico, Texas, and Washington, recognize a form of co-ownership called **community property.** It is defined as property acquired during a marriage through the labor or skill of either spouse. Each spouse owns one-half of all community property, even if the property is held in the name of just one spouse.

Community property does not include property held by either spouse at the time she or he entered into the marriage or property received during the marriage as a gift or inheritance. This property is instead called **separate property.** In some states, real property purchased during the marriage with separate property funds is considered separate property. The difficulty in this rule, however, is proving that the funds came from the separate property area rather than community property.

community property. Property acquired during a marriage through the labor or skill of either spouse.

separate property. Property held by either spouse at the time of the marriage or property received by either spouse through a gift or inheritance.

CASE

Justice Ferguson

Snover v. Snover

502 N.W.2d 370 (1993)

On December 29, 1977, Mayland Snover executed a quitclaim deed to property in Alpena County to "Mayland Snover, a single man, . . . and William Snover and Nancy Snover, husband and wife, . . . as joint tenants with full rights of survivorship and not as tenants in common." William and Nancy (plaintiffs) were Mayland's son and daughter-in-law. Some years later, Mayland married Gladys Snover (defendant). On June 30, 1988, Mayland signed a quitclaim deed, conveying the premises to "Mayland Snover and Gladys Snover, husband and wife." On September 3, 1988, Mayland died, survived by plaintiffs and defendant.

Plaintiffs originally brought this action in district court seeking to evict defendant from the premises. Defendant removed the action to circuit court and counterclaimed with a quiet-title action. Plaintiffs moved for summary judgment, contending that by the first deed, Mayland created an indestructible joint tenancy and that, upon his death, plaintiffs acquired a fee simple absolute title to the property. Defendant contended that the first deed created only a tenancy in common, with Mayland holding an undivided one-half interest. Defendant further contended that the second deed therefore created a tenancy by the entireties in Mayland Snover and defendant in Mayland's undivided one-half interest.

The trial court denied plaintiffs' motion for summary disposition and held that the first deed created a "simple joint tenancy"; that Mayland, in conveying an interest to the defendant, destroyed the survivorship interest created in the simple joint tenancy; and that when Mayland Snover died, defendant then held a one-half interest, with plaintiffs holding the other one-half interest as tenants in common. On November 8, 1989, a judgment quieting title was entered pursuant to the trial court's opinion. We reverse.

The language in the original deed in this case has been consistently held to create an indestructible joint tenancy among all of the grantees, whose interest in the property thereafter is limited to a personal life estate with a contingent remainder. A conveyance by any of the grantees does not operate to convey more than that interest or in any way diminish the contingent remainder of the named joint tenants. . . Defendant's contention that such a construction should be altered when two of the grantees are married has no basis in our case law. Indeed, such a construction, however reasonable under certain family circumstances, would create chaos among property rights that the courts must avoid.

The trial court's judgment quieting title in defendant is reversed and the case is remanded to the trial court for entry of an order granting summary disposition to plaintiffs.

Questions

1. Explain the basis of Gladys's argument that the law should have a different effect where two of the grantees are married, such as she and Mayland. Do you agree?
2. Explain the court's description of one's interest in an indestructible joint tenancy: "a personal life estate with a contingent remainder."
3. What do you think are the additional facts beneath this court case? Does it appear that William and Nancy were fond of Mayland's new wife?

If the parties divorce, each maintains her or his right to the separate property and they will split community property equally. Upon death of a spouse, the spouse's one-half interest is passed to her or his heirs, not to the other spouse (unless she or he is an heir).

Tenancy in Partnership. The Uniform Partnership Act has created a new form of tenancy called **tenancy in partnership,** in which partners are allowed to hold, buy, or sell real property in the name of the partnership. The partners own the property only in their roles as partners, so if one dies, the partnership has a right of survivorship and that partner's share reverts to the firm. A partner may sell her or his interest, but the sale is viewed as if the partner were acting as an agent of the firm.

tenancy in partnership. The manner in which partners co-own partnership property, much like a tenancy in common, except that partners have a right of survivorship.

Combination Ownership. In recent years, a form of co-ownership has developed that blends some of the qualities of several ownership forms: **condominium and cooperative ownership.** The law relating to these types of ownership varies from state to state. Owners retain individual control and specific ownership over a precise segment of the real estate (such as their apartment), but own common areas (such as a rooftop deck) as tenants in common.

In a condominium, owners are bound by a condominium **declaration,** which describes the real estate and the rights and obligations of owners. The condominium may also have **bylaws** that govern the maintenance and operation of the building. These documents act as contracts between all of the owners.

In a cooperative, one corporate entity (the cooperative) owns all of the property and individual tenants own shares of the cooperative. So, an individual apartment dweller does not own her or his apartment outright, but instead owns a share in the cooperative equivalent to the size of the apartment. The apartment is then leased from the cooperative. The bylaws of the corporation detail the rights and obligations of the tenants and regulate the expenses shared by each tenant.

Because a tenant owns only shares in the entity that owns the building, as opposed to owning the actual apartment, financing is sometimes difficult to obtain, so transferring or selling the property interest may be harder. Bylaws may also restrict the right of a tenant to transfer the property or may require that the cooperative association approve any new shareholder/owner.

Table 5.2 summarizes the types of ownership estate and Table 5.3 summarizes the types of ownership interest.

condominium or cooperative ownership. An interest in property where owners retain individual control and specific ownership over a precise segment of real estate, but own common areas as tenants in common.

declaration. A document that defines the rights, responsibilities, and powers of property owners in a condominium.

bylaws. A document that governs the maintenance and operation of a condominium building.

V. Nonpossessory Interests and Restrictions

Someone may have an interest in land that does not amount to an ownership or possessory interest but does affect the property. These are called **nonpossessory interests.**

An **easement** is the right to use someone's property without taking anything away from the property. Usually, an easement describes someone's right to cross another's property without causing any harm to the property. A **profit,** also called a **profit à prendre,** grants someone the right to enter another's property, not just to cross it, but to take something away from it.

nonpossessory interest. An interest in real property that is not sufficient to be an ownership or possessory interest.

easement. The right to use property without taking anything away from the property.

profit or profit à prendre. The right to enter property and to take something away from it, such as crops.

A. *Licenses*

A **license** creates a contractual right to use real property in a certain manner, similar to a right that a profit grants to take something away from it. Contrary to a profit, however, a

license. A contractual right to use property in a certain manner.

TABLE 5.2 TYPES OF OWNERSHIP ESTATES

Type	*Form*	*Features*
Fee simple absolute	"to Whitney"	▪ Absolute ownership without restrictions
Fee simple defeasible	"to Whitney, as long as . . ." or "to Whitney, until . . ."	▪ May be terminated by an action or the end of an action ▪ The individual to whom the property goes at the end of the defeasible fee has a "possibility of reverter" and may be the grantor or another ("to Whitney, as long as . . ., then to Clara")
Life estate	"to Whitney for life" or "to Whitney for life, then to Clara"	▪ The term of the estate is measured by Whitney's life ▪ The individual who owns the interest at the end of the life estate is called the remainderman ▪ If there is no remainderman, the future interest is called a reversion to the grantor

license does not create an interest in the real property. A license may therefore be revoked at any time by the property owner, unless the license is coupled with an interest in the land. In fact, tickets to a Cubs game at Wrigley Field are really licenses that allow ticket holders to use the property to view a baseball game. If a ticket holder becomes unruly, Wrigley Field owners have the right to revoke the license, even though the ticket holder has paid for the right to be there. This revocation is based on the ticket holder's failure to use the property in an acceptable manner.

easement or profit appurtenant. The right of an owner of adjacent land to enter or to enter and take away from property next to it.

right-of-way. Where an easement appurtenant refers to the right to physically cross property.

implied easement. Also called *easement by prescription* or *way of necessity.* An interest created where someone has openly used an adjoining piece of property for access with no complaint from the owner for a statutorily determined period of time.

B. Easements and Profits Appurtenant

There are two types of easements and profits: appurtenant and in gross. The **easement appurtenant** or **profit appurtenant** refers to the right of an owner of *adjacent land* to enter or take away from property next to it. An easement appurtenant referring to the right to cross a property may also be called a **right-of-way.**

An easement appurtenant may be created through a contract, in other words, sold to the user, or may be created by implication. If someone has openly used an adjoining piece of property for access with no complaint by the owner of that property for a period of time (specified by statute), there may be an **implied easement,** also called an **easement by prescription** or a **way of necessity.** Also, an easement is implied if a piece of real property is landlocked and there is no way to access it other than across another property. Assume that Susie has property right next to Jack's. The only way that Susie can get to her property

TABLE 5.3

TYPES OF OWNERSHIP INTEREST

Type	*Form*	*Features*
Concurrent tenancy	"to Whitney and Clara as tenants in common"	▪ Owners do not have to hold equal interest ▪ Upon the death of a concurrent tenant, the tenant's interest is passed to her or his heirs, not to the other tenant(s)
Joint tenancy	"to Whitney and Clara as joint tenants"	▪ Owners must hold equal, undivided interests, granted by the same instruments at the same time ▪ Upon the death of a joint tenant, that tenant's share is passed to remaining tenants, not to her or his heirs (called right of survivorship)
Tenancy by the entirety	"to Whitney and Sam, as husband and wife"	▪ Husband and wife may not divide interest without consent, except in death or divorce ▪ Includes right of survivorship, so upon death, interest passes to remaining spouse

from the road is to drive across Jack's land using his driveway. Jack sells to Susie an easement appurtenant that allows her to use the driveway to access her land. Susie's land is considered the **dominant estate,** and Jack's land is the **servient estate** (see Figure 5.1). Easements or profits appurtenant run with the land of both estates, meaning that they are transferred as part of the real property upon sale or other transfer.

However, if the owner of a servient estate decides to sell the property, the easement or profit appurtenant runs with the land *only* if the new owner knew or should have known

dominant estate. The property accessed through an easement appurtenant or implied easement.

servient estate. The property subject to an easement appurtenant or implied easement.

EASEMENT APPURTENANT

FIGURE 5.1

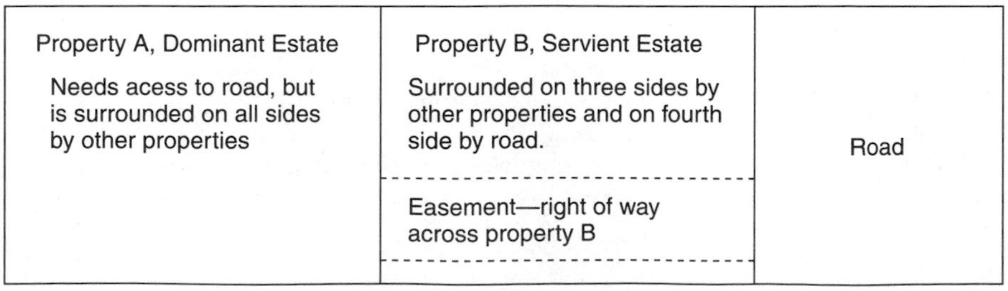

CASE

Justice Najam

Bauer v. Harris

617 N.E.2d 923 (Ind. Ct. App. 1993)

Since 1883, the Bauer family has owned a one-and-three-quarters-acre tract of land in Vandenburgh County, which lies adjacent and contiguous to property presently owned and acquired by the Harrises in March of 1989. Since the early 1990s, the Bauers have used a 12-foot-wide path or driveway which crossed the extreme southern tip of the Harris property to gain access to the Bauer property from Darmstadt Road east of the Harris property. During that time, the Bauers have constructed agricultural buildings on their property and used their property for a number of personal and business purposes, including boarding horses, operating a granary, and gardening and farming.

From 1904 to approximately 1940, the Evansville-Princeton traction line was in service along the east/west boundary between the Bauer/Harris properties and members of the public used the driveway for access to the railroad. Until approximately 1921, the Bauers operated a granary business, and their customers would use the driveway for access to the granary. While the driveway was not the only means of ingress and egress to the Bauer property, the Bauers, their customers and lessees used the driveway primarily because it provided more convenient access.

In 1987, the Bauers leased their property to Peyronnin Construction Company. Peyronnin's vehicles also used the driveway across the Harris property in order to gain access to the Bauer property. While using the Bauer property, Peyronnin placed gravel on the driveway to facilitate construction traffic. In early May of 1989, after the Harrises had acquired title to their property but before taking possession, Peyronnin complied with the Harris's request that it remove the gravel and plant grass over the driveway.

Also in early May of 1989, the Bauers decided to sell their property at public auction. A representative of the Bauers placed a sign advertising the auction near the Darmstadt Road in the driveway area. The Harrises protested and the sign was relocated off Darmstadt Road on the Bauers' property. That sign apparently awakened the Harrises, because shortly thereafter the Harrises erected a fence which obstructed the driveway, declaring that the Bauers had no right to cross their property. The Bauers filed suit on August 2, 1989, claiming an easement over the Harris property and the Harrises counterclaimed to quiet title to the disputed area. The trial court entered judgment for the Harrises and the Bauers appealed.

* * *

The primary dispute between the parties concerns the proper interpretation to be given our decision in *DeShields* v. *Joest,* where we discussed what constitutes exclusive use of a prescriptive easement:

> By exclusive, the law does not mean that the right of way must be used by one person only, because two or more persons may be entitled to the use of the same way, but simply *the right should not depend for its enjoyment upon a similar right in others,* and that the party claiming it exercises it under some claim existing in his favor, independent of all others. *It must be exclusive as against the right of the community at large.*

The Harrises contend that the trial court's interpretation of *DeShields* is correct, apparently reasoning that *DeShields* means that the use of an easement cannot be exclusive for the required period if the general public also uses the easement. The Bauers, however, urge that the mere fact that the general public also used the easement does not render the Bauers' use nonexclusive. We hold that the trial court misapplied the *DeShields* decision to the facts of

Continued

Continued

this case. The trial court's conclusion that the Bauers' use was not exclusive is contrary to law because the Bauers did not rely upon the general public's use of the driveway but instead relied upon their own use of the driveway for personal and business purposes to establish their claim.

Public use of an easement does not per se deprive a claimant of exclusive use of an easement. Rather, *DeShields* provides only that, "the right should not depend for its enjoyment upon a similar right in others."

* * *

The trial court's findings disclosed that, but for the use by the public and by a utility company to gain access to the railroad, only the Bauers, their customers and lessees used the easement. The railroad ceased service in 1940 and the court found that the utility company vehicles crossed the Harris property only from time to time. However, whether the Bauers' use of the driveway was exclusive during the period the railroad was in service is not dispositive. If we determine from the court's findings that the Bauers maintained exclusive use for *any* 20-year period, the Bauers acquired a prescriptive easement over the Harris's property by operation of law at the conclusion of that period.

The court's findings show, in fact, that the Bauers continued using the driveway for both personal access to their property and for use by their customers and lessees after 1940 and until 1989 when the Harrises constructed a fence blocking the driveway. Use by the Bauers' customers and lessees was not use by the general public but was derivative of the Bauers' claim of right to use the driveway. . .

Thus, in the context of a prescriptive easement, the term "exclusive use" means an independent claim of right, a use which does not depend upon the use by others; it does not mean a use which excludes others entirely.

[The court finds the use continuous and adverse, in satisfaction of the requirements for a prescriptive easement.]

Questions

1. What could the Harrises have done to avoid this result?
2. Do you agree with the court's explanation of exclusive use? Does it make sense to you?
3. Do you believe that prescriptive easements are fair to both sides?

of the nonpossessory interest. But how do you know if the purchaser "should have known" of the interest? A purchaser should have known of the interest if that interest was recorded in the appropriate office in that county. Consider that Susie now decides to sell the property to Keith. When Keith buys the property, he is also purchasing the right to use Jack's driveway. In this example, Jack may not deny Keith this right, since it runs with the land. However, Jack now decides to sell his property to Sophie. If Susie or Jack has recorded the easement in the proper office, or if someone informs Sophie of the existence of the easement, the easement runs with the land and is valid.

C. Easements and Profits in Gross

Easements or profits in gross allow persons to enter or take away from property but do not rely on the ownership of adjacent property. For example, a township may obtain an easement in gross from a property owner that allows the township to construct a road across the property. The township may not actually own property adjacent to that particular property. A profit in gross may occur where someone is allowed to enter a property and to remove assets from it, such as soil or timber.

Assume Theo owns a house in the Indiana Dunes area, across the street from a public beach. Although the beach is public, there is no actual access to it except through the private property of those with beachfront property. In this example, there is an implied easement in gross across the private property to the public beach area.

D. Termination of Easements and Profits

An easement or profit may be terminated in three ways. First, the contract may specify termination of the right; for example, a contract term might allow the easement for three years or only to a certain owner. Second, the easement or profit holder may deed the right back to the owner of the property. Third, the holder of the right may simply relinquish the right by abandoning it and showing the property owner that she or he has no further intent to use it. It is not enough for the right holder to simply stop using it; there must be evidence of intent to relinquish the right.

E. Liens

lien. The financial interest of the lienholder in the property as a result of a debt or other obligation of the landowner.

A **lien** (pronounced *lean*) is similar to a secured interest in real property. A lien represents the financial interest of the lienholder in a property as a result of a debt or other agreement. For example, assume a painter paints your dining room walls and has charged you $500. You don't have the money to pay her at the moment, though she has a contractual right to be paid upon completion of the job. The painter may record a *mechanic's lien* against the property in the amount of the debt. Anyone purchasing the property would make the purchase subject to the lien.

mortgage. A specific type of lien. A conveyance of property to secure the performance of some obligation (usually, the payment of a loan) that expires at the end of the performance.

One of the most familiar types of liens is a **mortgage.** A mortgage is a loan from one party, usually a bank, to a property owner that is secured by a lien on the property itself. If the owner fails to make payments on the loan, the bank can pursue the lien through selling the property and taking what it is owed from the proceeds.

F. Nonpossessory Restrictions on Property

Nuisance. Although landowners usually have the right to do whatever they want with real property they own, that right may be restricted by someone who has no actual interest in the property. One nonpossessory restriction on real property use is through the law of nuisance. **Nuisance** is unreasonable interference with someone else's enjoyment of their own land. So, if you use your property in a way that interferes with your neighbor's use of her property, you may be committing nuisance.

nuisance. Unreasonable interference with someone's enjoyment of their land.

Consider that Jeffers owns an apartment in a loft building that was recently renovated from its original purpose as a metalworks factory. The walls are rather thin, since the building was not originally built for residential use. Caterina lives in the unit above Jeffers and constantly plays loud music, disturbing him. It might be reasonably expected to hear a bit of Caterina's music in the middle of the afternoon, but loud music at 11:00 P.M. may be considered a nuisance. Nuisances reported in newspapers may concern air or water pollution from industrial property to neighboring residential property, or perhaps noise pollution from an airport to surrounding neighborhoods.

Zoning. Another nonpossessory restriction on the use of real property comes from public regulation of land use, called **zoning.** A municipality may dictate the types of activities that may take place on private property by creating various zones. Property parcels are usually broken up into residential, industrial, and commercial zones that restrict the size of the land parcel, the size of buildings that may be built, and types of businesses that may be conducted there.

zoning. Restriction on the use of land as a result of public land use regulation.

One example of zoning involves a city's restriction on the sale of pornographic materials. Often, a city chooses to restrict the sale of these types of items to specific areas that are not family-based or are not frequented by minors. Note that some private property owners (as opposed to cities) have tried to impose these restrictions themselves through claims of nuisance. The private owners claim that the pornography stores prevent them from quietly enjoying their own property.

Eminent Domain. The government may actually enter private property and not only restrict its use, but begin to use the property for a public purpose. This taking of property by the government is called **eminent domain** or **condemning.** Eminent domain may also refer to actions of the government that impair a property's value. As long as fair compensation is paid for the government's use or possession of the property, eminent domain is allowed. Where land is partially taken, most states provide that the owner will receive the difference in the value of the land prior to the taking and the value of the land after the taking (as opposed to the actual value of the land taken).

eminent domain. A governmental power whereby the government can take or condemn private property for a public purpose on the payment of just compensation.

condemning. To appropriate land for public use.

A Modest Proposal

by Richard A. Posner

"Just compensation," in the words of the Fifth Amendment, must be paid to an owner whose property is taken from him under the eminent domain power. Why? The answer may seem transparent: otherwise there would be a hideous loss to the owner of the property that was taken. But people insure against the destruction of their homes by fire, why not from government taking? Then the only uncompensated taking, besides the subjective or nonmarket values that just compensation excludes, would be the cost of the insurance premium. The existence of well-developed insurance markets casts doubt on a recent effort to explain the requirement of just compensation by reference to risk aversion and on the slightly older view that failure to compensate would "demoralize" condemnees and lead them to use resources less efficiently in the future, for example by always renting rather than buying property that might be condemned. As long as a rule of not paying compensation was well known, no one would be surprised or demoralized. Indeed, people who bought property after the rule was announced would not be hurt at all, for the risk of a government taking (a risk measured by the cost of insurance against such a taking) would be reflected in a lower price for the property; the buyer would be fully compensated. If the point is that the risk of a government taking would be less readily insurable than that of a natural disaster, because it would be less predictable, one is entitled to be skeptical. The government's eminent domain takings probably do not vary more from year to year than the losses from, say, earthquakes; and insurance can be bought against expropriation of property by foreign governments. If the concern is that the government

Continued

Continued

might use the power of eminent domain to oppress its political enemies or vulnerable minority groups, a partial answer at least is that such conduct would violate such constitutional guarantees as free speech and equal protection of the laws.

Questions

1. Do you believe in Posner's incentives argument, that potential condemnees would rather rent than own if condemnation is a possibility? Are there any benefits that cannot be obtained by renting property?
2. *a.* Is it possible to determine, with any degree of probability, what property might be condemned and what property is not at risk?

   b. Which is more predictable, condemnation or earthquakes?
3. *a.* Does insurance adequately take care of the compensation issue? What would encourage the government to be careful (or not arbitrary) with its choices of property to condemn when it does not have to pay for such property?

   b. Isn't this a windfall for the government, which does not have to pay when it appropriates property?

Source: *Economic Analysis of Law,* 3rd ed. (Boston: Little, Brown & Co., 1986).

Property may be taken or used through eminent domain when a municipality is constructing a highway and needs the property to accommodate the direction of the road or when a municipal airport must allow its planes to fly low over homes neighboring it. The property owner subject to this taking of airspace may receive fair compensation. A municipality's declaration of certain land as wetlands or its provision that no trees may be cut from land in order to preserve its natural state may also decrease the property value and therefore constitute a taking that must be compensated. In addition, if only a portion of a parcel of property is taken, the landowner will receive the difference in the value of the property before and after the taking, but not damages that are considered remote or speculative.

> "Since property is a sacred and inviolable right, no one may be deprived thereof unless a legally established public necessity obviously requires it."
>
> *Declaration of the Rights of Man and Citizen* (1789)

Property Rights and Wrongs

by Jonathan Tolman

Over the last decade the environmental movement has undergone a subtle but profound shift. Originally, environmental laws were designed to curb the pollution of large corporations. But as Congress and federal agencies have expanded the scope of these laws, they have begun to reach far beyond big industry polluters.

Russell Jacobs, for example, is not a tycoon. Married, he lives in Raymond, Wisconsin, and works for the post office. His wife, Gail, provides day care for neighborhood children while their own three children are in

Continued

Continued

school. In 1990, Mr. Jacobs did what many middle-class Americans dream of—he bought a plot of land in the suburbs to build his family a home. Before buying the lot, he checked with the Racine County government, which assured him that he could build his house.

Unfortunately for Mr. Jacobs, the federal government considered his small plot of land in the suburbs a "calcareous fen." For those unfamiliar with bureaucratic jargon, a fen is an area not quite wet enough to be a marsh, but still wet enough to qualify as a wetland. Calcareous only means that it sits on top of limestone, typical of much of Wisconsin.

The Army Corps of Engineers told Mr. Jacobs that he needed a permit in order to build on his calcareous fen. He applied for his permit and received a letter, 242 days later, informing him that his permit had been denied. Richard W. Craig of the Corps of Engineers wrote, "The purpose of the project is to facilitate the construction of a single-family home. I have determined that the issuance of the requested permit would be contrary to the public interest."

Why the federal government concluded that Mr. Jacobs's half an acre of calcareous fen was ecologically vital remains a mystery. Nonetheless, the government decided that the public should continue to enjoy benefits from the calcareous fen. With the stroke of a pen, the federal government effectively stripped Mr. Jacobs of the right to use his property. Mr. Jacobs's case represents a glaring violation of the Takings Clause of the Fifth Amendment, which reads, "no property shall be taken for public use without just compensation."

* * *

When a landowner is forced to provide a portion of his or her land for public purposes this principle should apply.

This is the fundamental reason why the government must compensate when it prohibits people like the Jacobses from building their house. A house does not infringe upon anyone else's property rights. The government prohibition did not seek to protect the property rights of others; rather it sought to benefit the "public interest." Hundreds of other government actions are also designed to benefit the public interest.

Whether a government builds a school, park, or a military base, the government must compensate when it takes the property of landowners, regardless of how important the activity is to the public interest. The case is no different with regulations, even when they protect "public interests" as important as calcareous fens.

Source: *The Wall Street Journal.*

Babbitt Blasts 1872 Law Giving Firm Land Windfall

by Tom Kenworthy

Interior Secretary Bruce Babbitt, lamenting what he called a "tawdry process" required by a 19th century mining law, Wednesday handed over federal lands containing more than $1 billion worth of minerals to a Danish mining company for $275.

Using props dating from the administration of Ulysses S. Grant—who signed the 1872 Mining Act that still allows miners to take title to government land for as little as $2.50 an acre and to pay no mineral royalties—Babbitt called upon Congress to end what he called a "flagrant abuse of the public interest."

"You might reasonably ask, how can a public official give away a billion dollars without going to jail?" Babbitt said at a news conference in the Interior Department's main building, where he displayed a Matthew Brady photograph of Grant and signed the deed with a pen made in the 1870s. Babbitt also held

Continued

Continued

up two dimes minted in 1872 to illustrate the bargain the company was receiving. The $275 purchase price is the same fee that would have been charged for the land in 1872.

Questions

1. If the law has not yet been changed, is it unethical in any way for the Danish firm to take advantage of it?
2. The law exists to this day and Congress has refused to make any changes except to include a temporary moratorium on further deals in several pieces of pending legislation. Can you imagine a reason why the act will remain? Why might Congress not repeal it?
3. What message does this send to the public?

Source: As appeared in *Chicago Sun Times,* September 6, 1995, p. 24.

Environmental Regulations. Finally, some land use may be restricted by environmental regulations. For instance, in certain areas, no further industrial pollution is allowed, but other areas may allow small amounts. Environmental regulations are discussed in greater detail in Chapter 15.

VI. Transfer of Interests in Real Property

Real property may be transferred or conveyed through four different methods: sale, gift, bequest, or adverse possession.

A. Transfer by Sale

deed. An instrument transferring title to property.

Where a property is transferred through a sale, a contract is formed between the parties. The instrument transferring title to the property is called a **deed.** To be a valid and enforceable deed, the instrument must satisfy the following requirements:

1. It must identify the name of the buyer and the property owner.
2. It must contain a description of the property that is legally sufficient to prevent any confusion between the property sold and another.
3. It must contain words that evidence an intent to convey the property, such as "I hereby sell, grant, transfer . . . this property to . . . ," and that specify the type of interest being transferred (fee simple, life estate, or other).
4. It must be signed by the property owner (or owners). If the owner is married, the document is usually signed by both spouses.
5. It must then be delivered to the buyer in order for the transfer to be complete.
6. Each state has different statutory requirements for recording a deed; some may require that the deed be witnessed and notarized.

general warranty deed. A deed that carries with it certain warranties or guarantees.

There are several different forms of deeds. An ordinary deed transferring real estate between two private contracting parties is called a **general warranty deed.** It provides a warranty or contractual promise that:

1. The person granting the deed owns the property (known as a *covenant of seizin).*
2. She or he has sufficient title to the property (so a life estate holder could not convey a fee simple) *(covenant of the right to convey).*
3. The property does not have any encumbrances, such as outstanding liens (*covenant against encumbrances).*

4. The grantor will defend the deed against anyone who claims to have a superior title, that is, against anyone who claims that promise 2 is incorrect *(covenant of quiet enjoyment).*

If a deed contains the above promises, it is automatically considered to be a warranty deed. If it fails to do so, it is considered a **grant deed.** A **quitclaim deed** makes no such promises. The grantor of a quitclaim deed simply says, "you now have whatever interest I had, though I make no claim as to the nature of my interest." If the grantor had a life estate, the recipient gets a life estate; if the grantor had a fee simple, the recipient gets a fee simple.

grant deed. A deed that does not have the warranties contained in a warranty deed.

quitclaim deed. A deed conveying only the right, title, and interest of the grantor in the property described, as distinguished from a deed conveying the property itself.

closing date. The date on which a transfer of property is made.

Risk of Loss. Where real property is supposed to be transferred by a contract, whether it results in a quitclaim or warranty deed, a question arises about the risk of loss before the sale goes through. For instance, what happens if two parties agree to transfer land, but before the **closing date** (the date on which the sale is to be completed) the land is entirely damaged by a flood? The land still exists; should the buyer have to pay the same price? Or any price at all?

The *Uniform Vendor and Purchaser Risk Act* is a statute relating to this very issue and has been adopted by 12 states. The act provides that a purchaser does not have to go through with the sale if the land is all or partially destroyed or taken by eminent domain *before either transfer of legal title or the possession of the property has taken place.* If legal title has been transferred or the purchaser has taken possession of the property, the purchaser must pay the seller the full contract price.

The act was intended to specify the risk of loss when a fire, earthquake, or other calamity occurs in connection with the sale of property. Problems arise when deciding whether the purchaser has actually taken possession. For instance, in one case, the purchaser entered the premises, made substantial alterations, began to conduct his business, and kept others out. When a subsequent fire destroyed much of the property, the court held that the purchaser still had to pay the full purchase price.[2]

B. Transfer by Will or Gift

A testator (decedent with a will) may transfer property through a will effective upon his or her death. A will may devise a testator's property to one or several persons through precise language. For example, Pierrot dies leaving a will that states: "I hereby devise all of my interest in my Parisian property and residence to my wife, Clarice." Clarice will receive whatever interest Pierrot has in the property, whether it is a life estate, fee simple, or other.

A transfer of real property by gift is effected through a written instrument evidencing a donative intent, that is, the intent to give away an interest in the property. Any transfer of an interest in land must be in writing and signed by the grantor pursuant to the Statute of Frauds. A quitclaim deed is usually used for gift transfers of land interest so that the grantor retains no responsibility for the property.

C. Adverse Possession

It is possible to obtain title to real property even though the property owner had no intention to transfer it; this occurs in the case of **adverse possession.** If someone possesses property for a specified period of time and satisfies certain other requirements, he or she may actually acquire title to the property similar to when an actual sale has occurred. Adverse possession is defined in each state by a statute that stipulates the exact requirements for transfer.

adverse possession. Open and notorious possession of real property over a given length of time that denies ownership in any other claimant.

Quit Claim Deed
TENANCY BY THE ENTIRETY
(Individual to Individual)

CAUTION: Consult a lawyer before using or acting under this form. *Neither the publisher nor the seller of this form makes any warranty with respect thereto, including any warranty of merchantability or fitness for a particular purpose.*

THE GRANTOR(S) (NAME AND ADDRESS)

(The Above Space For Recorder's Use Only)

of the ______ of ______ County of ______, State of ______ for and in consideration of ______ DOLLARS, ______ in hand paid, CONVEY(S) and QUIT CLAIM(S) to

(NAMES AND ADDRESS OF GRANTEES)

husband and wife as TENANTS BY THE ENTIRETY and not as joint tenants with a right of survivorship, or tenants in common, of the ______ of ______ County of ______ State of ______ all interest in the following described Real Estate situated in the County of ______ in the State of Illinois, to wit: (See reverse side for legal description.) hereby releasing and waiving all rights under and by virtue of the Homestead Exemption Laws of the State of Illinois.* TO HAVE AND TO HOLD said premises not as tenancy in common, not in joint tenancy, but as TENANTS BY THE ENTIRETY, FOREVER.

Permanent Index Number (PIN): ______

Address(es) of Real Estate: ______

DATED this ______ day of ______ 19___

PLEASE PRINT OR TYPE NAME(S) BELOW SIGNATURE(S)

______(SEAL) ______(SEAL)

______(SEAL) ______(SEAL)

State of Illinois, County of ______ ss. I, the undersigned, a Notary Public in and for said County, in the State aforesaid, DO HEREBY CERTIFY that

personally known to me to be the same person___ whose name______ subscribed to the foregoing instrument, appeared before me this day in person, and acknowledged that ___ h ___ signed, sealed and delivered the said instrument as ______free and voluntary act, for the uses and purposes therein set forth, including the release and waiver of the right of homestead.

IMPRESS SEAL HERE

Given under my hand and official seal, this ______ day of ______ 19___

Commission expires ______ 19___ ______
NOTARY PUBLIC

This instrument was prepared by ______
(NAME AND ADDRESS)

*If Grantor is also Grantee you may want to strike Release and Waiver of Homestead Rights.

PAGE 1

SEE REVERSE SIDE ►

Legal Description

of premises commonly known as ____________________

____

SEND SUBSEQUENT TAX BILLS TO:

MAIL TO:	____________________ (Name)	____________________ (Name)
	____________________ (Address)	____________________ (Address)
	____________________ (City, State and Zip)	____________________ (City, State and Zip)

OR RECORDER'S OFFICE BOX NO. ________

PAGE 2

Warranty Deed
TENANCY BY THE ENTIRETY
Statutory (ILLINOIS)
(Individual to Individual)

CAUTION: Consult a lawyer before using or acting under this form. *Neither the publisher nor the seller of this form makes any warranty with respect thereto, including any warranty of merchantability or fitness for a particular purpose.*

THE GRANTOR (NAME AND ADDRESS)

(The Above Space For Recorder's Use Only)

of the ______________________ of ______________________ County
of ______________________, State of ______________
for and in consideration of ______________ DOLLARS, ______________
in hand paid, CONVEY___ and WARRANT ___ to

(NAMES AND ADDRESS OF GRANTEES)

as husband and wife, not as Joint Tenants with rights of survivorship, nor as Tenants in Common, but as TENANTS BY THE ENTIRETY, the following described Real Estate situated in the County of ______________ in the State of Illinois, to wit: (See reverse side for legal description.) hereby releasing and waiving all rights under and by virtue of the Homestead Exemption Laws of the State of Illinois.* TO HAVE AND TO HOLD said premises as husband and wife, not as Joint Tenants nor as Tenants in Common but as TENANTS BY THE ENTIRETY forever. SUBJECT TO: General taxes for __________ and subsequent years and

Permanent Index Number (PIN): ______________________

Address(es) of Real Estate: ______________________

DATED this __________ day of ______________ 19___

PLEASE PRINT OR TYPE NAME(S) BELOW SIGNATURE(S)

______________________(SEAL) ______________________(SEAL)

______________________ ______________________

______________________(SEAL) ______________________(SEAL)

______________________ ______________________

State of Illinois, County of ______________________ ss. I, the undersigned, a Notary Public in and for said County, in the State aforesaid, DO HEREBY CERTIFY that

personally known to me to be the same person___ whose name_______ subscribed to the foregoing instrument, appeared before me this day in person, and acknowledged that ____ h ____ signed, sealed and delivered the said instrument as _________free and voluntary act, for the uses and purposes therein set forth, including the release and waiver of the right of homestead.

IMPRESS SEAL HERE

Given under my hand and official seal, this ______________ day of ______________ 19_____

Commission expires ______________ 19___ ______________________
NOTARY PUBLIC

This instrument was prepared by ______________________
(NAME AND ADDRESS)

*If Grantor is also Grantee you may wish to strike Release and Waiver of Homestead Rights.

PAGE 1

SEE REVERSE SIDE ►

Legal Description

of premises commonly known as ______________________________

____

SEND SUBSEQUENT TAX BILLS TO:

MAIL TO:	______________________ (Name)	______________________ (Name)
	______________________ (Address)	______________________ (Address)
	______________________ (City, State and Zip)	______________________ (City, State and Zip)

OR RECORDER'S OFFICE BOX NO. ________

PAGE 2

CASE

Justice Spindler

Walter v. Balogh

619 N.E.2d 566 (Ind. 1993)

Martin Walter died in 1983. At that time, his wife Alwilda was 79 years of age . . . Barry Hoeppner became a tenant farmer of the Walters in 1974. Over time, Barry and his business partner, Mark Balogh, became responsible for farming approximately 600 acres of the Walters' land. They also became close friends of the Walters and did many favors for them. After Martin Walter died, both Barry and Mark did considerable favors for Alwilda.

The Walters also had other tenants, Bruce and Minnie Provine, who since 1957 had operated another tract of land of 285 acres for the Walters. In 1984, Alwilda Walter decided to make gifts to both the Provines and to Barry and Mark. She stated her desire to give each of them the farms which they had been tending. For the purpose of drafting the necessary papers, she contacted attorney Jeanne Miller of New Haven, Indiana. Mrs. Miller advised Alwilda that if she reported the gift as being made *instanter* she would incur a sizeable gift tax liability. To lessen that liability, Mrs. Miller set up contracts whereby the possession of the farms would be delivered and the responsibility of operation would be solely in the hands of the donees. For tax purposes, they set up a payment schedule to be made over a period of years and each time a payment became due, Alwilda would forgive the due payment as a gift, thus taking advantage of annual gift tax allowances.

* * *

In June of 1988, Alwilda, who was then 84 years of age, started to become confused and forgetful. Her niece, Ellen Bates, became involved in Alwilda's financial affairs. Alwilda appointed Bates as her attorney-in-fact. . . Alwilda also executed another codicil to her will which in part revoked the provision forgiving the debts of the appellees. In August 1988, the bank was appointed as her guardian. . .

As Alwilda's guardian, the bank issued a notice of default to the appellees with respect to their obligations under the 1985 mortgages. [Alwilda and the bank claimed that the debt forgiveness was the result of duress, undue influence, and failure of consideration.] . . .

We believe the trial judge to be correct in his observation that Alwilda was interested in, and in fact did give, a gift to the appellees in 1984. . .

The evidence is clear in this case that Mrs. Walter at all times wanted to make an outright gift of the property to the appellees and that Mrs. Miller formulated the contract to accomplish that purpose.

It also has been stated that "equity looks to the substance and not to the form." When one looks solely to the technical form of the papers drafted in this case, the opinion of the court of appeals is right on target. However, in this case, the form was no more than that. We hold the technical form used to accomplish the inheritance tax purposes should not be used to defeat the express desire of Alwilda, which in fact was the substance of the entire transaction. The trial court was correct when it held that Alwilda's intent [to give a gift to the appellees] should prevail.

Questions

1. If you were the bank in this case, what would be your strongest argument? And do you personally agree with that argument?
2. Does it sway your decision knowing that the issue arose simply because Mrs. Walter tried to avoid having to pay the entire inheritance tax?
3. How could this situation have been avoided?

CASE

Mary Moody Northen, Inc., v. Bailey

418 S.E.2d 882 (1992)

Justice Lacy

This is an adverse possession case involving 100 acres of mountainous land in Giles County. The 100 acres are part of a 2,475-acre parcel on which Mountain Lake Hotel is situated. Since the early 1900s, the Moody family has owned the hotel and surrounding property. W. L. Moody, Jr., was actively involved with the operation of the hotel during his lifetime. His daughter, Mary Moody Northen, bought the property and hotel in 1968. Upon her death, the present legal title holder, Mary Moody Northen, Inc., a charitable foundation, succeeded to her interest.

The claimants are the children of Jim Bailey. For most of his 71 years, Bailey lived in a four-room log house located in a clearing on the south slope of John's Creek Mountain. The site is within the 2,475-acre parcel now owned by the foundation. Although the house itself was destroyed by fire in 1971, his children periodically return to the land on which it was located.

In 1989, six of the nine Bailey children filed this suit against Mary Moody Northen, Inc., seeking to establish that their father acquired an ownership interest in the land through adverse possession and that that interest passed to them upon his death.

* * *

During the relevant time period, not only were the legal title holder and Bailey aware of each other's occupancy on the parcel, but they communicated on a number of occasions. . .

The legal title holder had a number of surveys made of the entire parcel; none was performed for the 100 acres in dispute here, and there are no monuments or markings delineating the boundaries of the 100 acres claimed. Beginning in 1940, the hotel's caretaker marked the boundary of the entire parcel by marking the trees with white paint. Although the land occupied by Bailey was within those boundaries, he did not question the markings. . .

The resident caretaker of the hotel from 1944 to 1984, the manager of the hotel from 1946 to 1961, and the manager's wife testified that Bailey lived on the land with Mr. Moody's permission.

* * *

Here, the record reveals continuing occupancy; it supports a finding that the occupant told his children that he owned the land; and it supports a finding that the occupant engaged in certain activities that were consistent with ownership. However, the record does not support even an inference that this claim of ownership was relayed to the true owner. . . The legal title holder took affirmative steps to exercise his dominion and control over his property on more than one occasion; yet, Bailey objected only once. . .

For these reasons, we conclude that the trial court erred in holding that the claimant established ownership through adverse possession of the land titled of record in the name of the foundation. Accordingly, the decree of the trial court will be reversed, and we will enter final judgment for the foundation.

Questions

1. What can a potential adverse possessor do to more easily prove her or his title?
2. How could the legal title holder have better protected himself from this type of claim?
3. Is it fair, given the circumstances, to deny the children the right to the property?

Generally, to obtain land through adverse possession, the following requirements must be met:

1. Possession of the property must be actual and exclusive—The adverse possessor must actually be inhabiting the property (in other words, not just walk across it to work each day) and must be the only person who does occupy the property.
2. The possession must be open, visible, and notorious—The owner of the property must be able to see that another possesses or occupies the land. The adverse possessor may not acquire possession if the occupancy is secret to others.
3. The possession must be continuous for the period of time specified in the statute (often some time between 5 to 30 years)—Possession is not continuous if the owner or the courts interrupt possession during the specified time.
4. Possession must be hostile and adverse to the interests of the owner—Possession is not hostile where the adverse possessor either has permission of the owner or could possess the property alongside the possession of the owner.

Adverse possession exists to settle boundary disputes or to promote equitable settlement of conflicting possession claims. The doctrine also serves to encourage property owners to make use of their property or to transfer it to someone who might.

For example, Rocky and Thelma own properties next to each other. Many years ago, Thelma erected a wooden fence separating the properties. Unintentionally, Thelma placed the fence so that it infringed on Rocky's property by three feet. Forty-one years after the fence was built, Rocky decided to pave his driveway and learned that the fence was infringing. The occupancy satisfies the requirements for adverse possession (as long as the time period is sufficient according to the state statute) and Thelma now owns that part of Rocky's property.

VII. International Ownership of Real Property

The legal protection of real property described above is applicable to the United States. Other countries may have varying forms of property protection that do not recognize the same rights in land as the U.S. form. Our form of protecting property is not "inevitable."

For instance, the Basic Law of the Federal Republic of Germany (1949) states that "[property's] content and limits shall be determined by law . . . property imposes duties. Its use should also serve the commonwealth." To the contrary, this obligation to the state is not represented in American law, except in specific circumstances of eminent domain.

In southern Africa, personal property is considered as individual and those who take property without the owner's permission are subject to punishment. On the other hand, the rights of someone to real property must coexist with the rights of the group or the community. Consequently, land rights in Africa are comparable to our theory of common tenancy.

Where the public/private property lines are blurred, businesses have a greater risk of government involvement and control over their operations. For instance, assume a company plans to build a large plant in a country in which the government has a right to enter and take over the plant as soon as it is built; the company would likely reduce its investment in the plant because of the risk of losing it to this **expropriation.**

expropriation. A government's taking of a business's assets, such as a manufacturing facility, usually without just compensation.

Property Rights Essential to Wealth and Freedom—Summary of Felix Livingston's New Book

In *Preserving Property in Russia: The Great and Chief End of Government,* Dr. Livingston suggests that former communist countries now embracing democratic capitalism must allow private property rights to flourish if they are to achieve and sustain prosperity.

He says that nations in transition to democratic capitalism will be more successful if they understand three important aspects of the connection between property rights and greater wealth and freedom:

(1) Given what David Hume called "the selfishness and confined generosity of man along with the scanty provision nature has made for his wants," property rights enforced by law motivate people to pursue their self-interest in a way which helps others.
(2) Private economic rights are essential to political liberty, in part because they insulate people from the coercive acts of public officials.
(3) The competitive market system, of which property rights are an indispensable feature, is the only way nations have been able to improve their material well-being over time.

As the Russian people prepare for democratic elections and constitutional reforms, Livingston concludes, they would do well to heed the observation of John Locke that the preservation of property is the "great and chief end" of government.

Questions

1. Can you identify an act that one might do that is not in her or his self-interest?
2. Consider the following: "If we all act rationally in a system designed for efficiency (like capitalism), and we act with integrity (don't expect something for nothing, etc.), there will be no conflict of interests if everyone acts in their own self-interest. Integrity here is defined as living according to one's convictions and values—acting consistently." (Adapted from Ayn Rand, *The Virtue of Selfishness.*) Do you agree? Explain.
3. Do you agree with Locke's statement in the final sentence, "the preservation of property is the 'great and chief end' of government"?

Source: *World Capitalism Review,* October 1993, p. 11. Reprinted by permission of the Center for World Capitalism.

What is the effect of these differences in the concepts of real property on the ownership of property in different countries? That depends on the country. A business owner may challenge a government expropriation of its real property in order to obtain adequate compensation for its loss. The business may pursue a claim for compensation in the country where the expropriation took place, or it may pursue assets of the country that reside in other countries. Finally, the business may seek assistance from its own government in the form of diplomatic intervention.

Although the issue of private versus public property may affect the risk involved in foreign investments, many countries, including the United States, also have restrictions on the foreign ownership of property. In the United States, the Secretary of the Interior may only lease deposits of coal, oil, gas, and other nonfuel minerals located on federal land to U.S. citizens. Foreign investors may not lease that federal land. There are similar regulations for grazing and lumbering permits on U.S. lands.

In addition, public lands may only be owned or transferred to people who are or who intend to be U.S. citizens, and those intended citizens may not be from a country with which the United States is at war. Similar restrictions exist in many countries and must be investigated before a business decides to set up shop there.

Summary

Legal Review. A lessee may lease real property through a term tenancy, a periodic tenancy, a tenancy at will, or a tenancy at sufferance. The lessee and lessor have several rights and obligations as the result of any of these leases. The lessor has the right to receive rent for the use of the property, to protect the property from damages, to enter and to make repairs, and to show the property to prospective buyers. Many of these rights may be assigned. The tenant has the right to use the property for any purpose, except those that are illegal, against public policy, or permanently harmful to the premises. The tenant may also have the right to assign the lease, to have a habitable environment, and to be free from unreasonable intrusions.

An ownership interest in property may take several forms: fee simple absolute, defeasible fee simple, possibility of reverter, life estate, or remainder. An ownership interest may also take the form of a joint tenancy, tenancy in common, tenancy by the entirety, tenancy in partnership, or some type of combination ownership interest.

Public Policy Review. There are several ways in which public policy may be implemented through property law. Through the laws of nuisance or zoning, a municipality may regulate the types of activities that may occur on a given piece of property, subject to constitutional restrictions. Consider that the U.S. form of property ownership is not the only form. In many countries, the right to land is considered a shared right by the community, whereas the treatment of personal property may be the same as in the United States.

Ethics Review. Understanding property rights requires an understanding of the effect of our actions and decisions on others. Given the nature of real property, when we make a change to our property (such as cutting down an area of trees), we are affecting those surrounding us (such as our neighbors). We are part of a communal society that depends on communication and compliance for an ordered social system. Issues such as nuisance, zoning, property uses, adverse possession, and restrictive covenants raise ethical issues of our rights to free activity and movement, the right to freely contract, and our freedom of association.

Chapter Questions

1. The roof of a commercial building collapsed during a severe rainstorm and two shoppers in the building were injured.
   a. Who is liable for the injuries: the landlord/present owner, the tenant who owned the store in which the injury occurred, or the previous landowner, who had knowledge of the weak roof but failed to warn the new owner?
   b. How does a new landlord protect him- or herself from liability for this type of event?
   [In *Haskel Co.* v. *Lane Co.,* 612 So. 2d 669 (Fl. Ct. Ap. 1993).]
2. Dance bought parcel A from an architect who also designed Dance's car dealership on the same property. The architect designed the property so that it drained onto parcel B, owned by the architect, though Dance never actually acquired an easement from the architect to do this. Parcel B was later sold to Tatum, who was aware of the drainage onto the property from parcel A.
   a. Does parcel A have an easement over parcel B?
   b. Is Tatum required to honor this easement?
   [In *Tatum* v. *Dance,* 605 So. 2d 110 (Fl. Ct. App. 1992).]

3. Stam did not tell Bovsky, the buyer of her house, that the house was riddled with ghosts. Bovsky purchased the house under a warranty deed; but when he later tried to sell it, he was not able to do so at a reasonable price because everyone seemed to have heard Stam's earlier stories. Did Stam violate any terms of the warranty deed?
4. Samuels purchased a parcel of land for his home, bordered by a lot owned by McAllister. Between the two parcels was a fence that Samuels wanted to remove and replace with a new fence on a new fence line. McAllister wanted the fence built along the same fence line. The parties had the property surveyed and found that the old fence line was actually nine inches inside Samuels's property, not on the line between the two. When Samuels tried to build a fence along the newly discovered boundary, McAllister claimed that he had acquired the additional nine inches by adverse possession.
   a. Is McAllister's claim true?
   b. How could McAllister have made a stronger claim for adverse possession?
   [In *McAllister* v. *Samuels,* 857 S.W.2d 768 (Tx. App. 1993).]
5. Menefee owned two tracts of land, one behind the other. The first tract has access to a public road; but to reach the road from the second tract required crossing the first. Menefee sold the rear tract to her brother along with an access license granted in the deed. Menefee's brother used a strip of land along Menefee's border to access the road for seven years. Menefee became annoyed with this constant use, so she constructed a fence and gate, requiring her brother to access the road by crossing through a cesspool. To open the gate, in fact, he had to actually walk through the cesspool. Upset by these changes, Menefee's brother sued Menefee to establish an easement by necessity (in addition to the license) along the original border of the property. Did Menefee's brother establish an easement by necessity? [In *Samuelson* v. *Alvarado,* 847 S.W.2d 319 (Tx. App. 1993).]
6. The Town of Rocky Mount sought to condemn over 38 acres of farmland to allow it to erect a waste-water treatment plant. James Elwood Hudson was the legal owner of the land in question, which was attached to another Hudson parcel by an easement over property in between the two pieces of property (shown below). A hearing was held to determine the value of the property to be taken and the commissioners awarded Hudson $92,512 plus $10,000 representing the damage to the value of the rest of Hudson's parcel. Hudson had leased the two parcels, both as a pair and separately, for use as a dairy farm, but had not operated the farm nor leased it out for the past three years. The town therefore claimed that the value of the loss was speculative and remote. On the other hand, Hudson claimed that he could no longer use the land that remained because it was "worthless" without the second parcel of land.

Parcel taken by eminent domain (previously owned by Hudson)	Parcel owned by a third party Easement	Parcel still owned by Hudson

   a. Is a determination that the remaining land held by Hudson was damaged by the removal of the second parcel incorrect, too speculative, or remote? Should Hudson receive anything in addition to the actual value of the land taken?
   b. Assume there was a river on the far side of the land taken (the left side of the diagram). What other evidence could Hudson have shown or arguments could he have made to prove that his second parcel was damaged by the loss under these facts?

   [In *Town of Rocky Mount* v. *Hudson,* 421 S.E.2d 407 (1992).]

7. BPS Co. was a self-storage company that leased space to Liberty Moving and Storage. Liberty later discovered that some of the items stored in the space were damaged by water. Liberty sued for breach of the implied warranties in the lease agreement. BPS claimed, however, that the issue was taken care of by a lease term that read:

   > Lessor is not liable for any damage to property of lessee arising from any cause whatsoever including, without limitation, any acts of negligence, improper construction, or failure to repair any building or improvement on the premises.

   Is this exculpatory clause valid and sufficient to relieve the lessor of any liability for the damage? [In *Fireman's Fund Ins. Co.* v. *BPS Co.,* 491 N.E.2d 365 (Ohio 1985).]
8. City of Detroit initiated condemnation proceedings to acquire various parcels of land for expansion of the Cobo Hall convention center. Van Wald leased a building that was to be condemned across the street from Cobo to run his furniture business. In fact, part of the building was to be condemned and Van Wald was going to be able to continue operations in a modified format. Van Wald claimed that, in addition to actual losses sustained, he should receive amounts to compensate him for both lost profits and the interruption of his business.
   a. Should Van Wald receive amounts for his lost profits and business interruption?
   b. What will Van Wald need to show to prove the amounts of his lost profits (so that they are not considered too speculative and remote)?

   [In *Detroit* v. *Larned Associates,* 501 N.W.2d 189 (Mich. 1993).]
9. A landlord hired a security guard to patrol a ramp in the apartment building's parking lot. The guard was hurt during a fight with a trespasser and did not return. The landlord then installed a camera system that monitored the parking lot ramp doors from the doorman's desk in the lobby. Six months later, an assailant abducted and assaulted a woman after following her up the parking ramp. She sued the landlord. Is the landlord liable? If yes, was the liability increased or decreased because he took steps to protect the tenants? [In *Holland* v. *Leidel,* 494 N.W.2d 772 (Mich. 1992).]
10. Lessor inspects an apartment after the previous tenant leaves and notices a rotted staircase. Before fixing the staircase, the lessor rents the apartment to a new lessee. Three weeks into the lease term and after the lessee has fully moved into the apartment, the lessee falls through the stairs and sustains injuries. The landlord contends that the staircase area is fully within the control of the lessee and, therefore, the landlord is not liable for the harm. The lessee claims that the landlord's previous knowledge gives rise to the liability.
    a. Who is right here?
    b. If the landlord was not going to have time to fix the staircase prior to the tenant's moving-in date, what could the landlord have done to prevent its liability?

    [In *Dickison* v. *Hargitt,* 611 N.E.2d 691 (Ind. Ct. App. 1993).]

NOTES

1. 42 U.S.C. 3604(b).
2. *Kings Ridge Electrical Corp.* v. *LaBella,* 298 N.Y.S.2d 12, 31 A.D.2d 821 (1969).

Building and Managing Human Resources from a Legal Perspective: Part I—Employment Law

Chapter 6

Reader's Guide

Your business is up and running, and you have found a site for your operations. Who will conduct your business? Under many circumstances, you will choose to hire additional individuals to assist you in your operations. On what terms will you hire these people and will you need contracts? How does the law affect your decisions in this area?

Profile

Hooters Guys?

Men don't high kick with Radio City Rockettes or shake pompons with the Dallas Cowboy cheerleaders.

Hooters restaurants, therefore, should be given the same leeway when it comes to gender-based hiring, the chain's parent company argues.

Hooters of America Inc. is fighting to continue hiring only women waitresses, who wear skimpy orange shorts and tight white T-shirts or tank tops while serving up chicken wings and burgers.

The Equal Employment Opportunity Commission said Hooters should hire men to work alongside the women, a recommendation the company said it would ignore.

Hooters bought full-page ads in Wednesday's *USA Today* and *The Washington Post,* featuring a burly mustachioed man wearing a blond wig and Hooters uniform, holding a plate of chicken wings and exclaiming: "Come on, Washington. Get a grip."

Executives of the Atlanta-based chain say their customers expect to see sexy, All-American women at their restaurants, which built a reputation on their perky Hooters Girls.

* * *

Duncan Fisher, a manager at the restaurant, said many of the women would lose their jobs if the company were forced to hire male servers. While construction workers who eat at Hooters several times a week guffawed at the ads, waitresses wore orange pins saying "Save Our Jobs."

The EEOC has been investigating the 170-restaurant chain for the past four years and said several months ago that Hooters' policy of hiring only female waitresses amounts to sex discrimination.

Four Chicago men who sued Hooters also filed a complaint with the EEOC, prompting the investigation. Their lawsuit claiming discrimination is pending.

* * *

The Rockettes and the Dallas Cowboys are allowed to hire all-female troupes and Playboy is allowed to hire all-female bunnies, Mike McNeil, a Hooters vice president, noted at a news conference in Washington.

David Larson, a professor of labor and employment law at Creighton University in Omaha, Nebraska, said there's no comparison.

Continued

Continued

"The distinction is that there was never any question that Playboy was selling sex, not in the sense of prostitution, but the image of the club had a very heavy sexual aspect to it," said Larson, a former professor-in-residence at the EEOC. "I don't think Hooters is doing the same thing. They've made it clear publicly that they're selling food."

Questions

1. Is Hooters in violation of Title VII?
2. If you were to redraft Title VII to ensure that your response to question 1 is addressed clearly, how would you rewrite its language?
3. Whether or not Hooters is in violation of Title VII, do you believe it *should* be allowed to discriminate in favor of women in its hiring practices?

Source: " Hooters guys? I don't think so, say customer restaurant chain, "*Waterloo Courier,* November 16, 1995, p. 36. Reprinted by permission of the Associated Press.

Employee suits against employers are turning the workplace into a legal combat zone.

Employee suits against employers are turning the workplace into a legal combat zone.[1] In 1960, about one-third of the American workforce was represented by unions. Today, that figure is about 11 percent. Collective bargaining (see Chapter 7), established to protect the interests of workers, has proven inadequate to the task.[2] Not surprisingly, federal and state regulations governing work practices have exploded. The variety of protections is prodigious: antidiscrimination laws, wage and hour laws, worker safety laws, unemployment compensation, workers' compensation, and social security, to name a few. All managers should have at least an introductory sense of this web of rules that now profoundly influences business conduct.

The first part of this chapter will introduce Title VII of the Civil Rights Act of 1964 and discuss its antidiscrimination provisions. The second part will focus on other statutes that govern the employment relationship. Be wary, however, as this area of law is not only extremely complicated but also subject to probable modifications and explosive. Judges have been known to find small particularities in statutes and rule one way, only to find that Congress later jumps in to overrule the case precedent with a new statute, in which the judges find an opening . . . and so on and so on. Accordingly, this chapter will provide only an overview to the enigmatic structure of the law of human resource management, highlighting issues rather than providing answers.

I. Regulating Equality and Fairness?

A. *Legal Foundations of Antidiscrimination Protections*

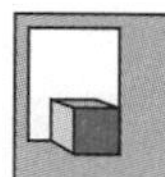

History. In 1941, A. Philip Randolph, president of the predominantly black Brotherhood of Sleeping Car Porters, organized black leaders and threatened a massive protest march in Washington, DC. In response, President Franklin Roosevelt issued Executive Order 8802 (such orders have the force and effect of law), which created a Fair Employment Practice Committee. Congress was hostile to the order and limited the committee's budget, but Roosevelt's action was a critical first step for the federal government in addressing racial discrimination. Likewise, during the 1940s, several states enacted their own fair employment laws.

The next striking step toward racial equality was the landmark *Brown* v. *Board of Education*[3] decision in 1954, in which the Supreme Court forbade "separate but equal" schools. *Brown* repudiated the doctrine enunciated in an 1896 Supreme Court case, *Plessy* v. *Ferguson,*[4] in which the Court held that a Louisiana statute requiring equal but separate accommodations for whites and blacks on trains was not unconstitutional. (The history of *Plessy* and *Brown* is a particularly apt illustration of the living, changing character of the law. Although stability and hence predictability in the law are important, they must not stand in the way of achieving justice in a changing society.) A period of intense activism followed *Brown,* as citizens engaged in sit-ins, freedom rides, boycotts, and the like to press claims for racial equality in housing, public transportation, employment, and so on. It was a turbulent, sometimes violent, era, but those activities were critical ingredients in subsequent advances for the black population.

Then, in 1964, the National Labor Relations Board asserted its jurisdiction over racial discrimination where it constitutes an unfair labor practice. With the passage of the 1964 Civil Rights Act, the campaign against discrimination solidified as one of the most energetic and successful social movements in American history.[5]

Constitutional Provisions. The Fourteenth Amendment to the federal Constitution provides that no state shall deny to any person life, liberty, or property without *due process of law* or deny him or her the *equal protection of the laws.* Thus, citizens are protected from discrimination at the instigation of a state government. Then, by Supreme Court decision in 1954, the Due Process Clause of the Fifth Amendment ("nor shall any person . . . be deprived of life, liberty, or property, without due process of law") was interpreted to forbid invidious discrimination by the federal government. Thus, the Fifth and Fourteenth Amendments have been useful tools against government discrimination.

Civil Rights Act of 1866. Of course, the constitutional provisions are broadly drawn and thus open to variation in interpretation. The Constitution protects the citizenry from the government but not from private-sector abuse. Therefore, statutes and executive orders were necessary to attack discrimination more explicitly and to reach private-sector problems. The Civil Rights Act of 1866, as amended in 1991, forbids all forms of racial bias arising out of contract. Employment relationships are, of course, founded in contract. Thus, when a black person is discriminated against by a private employer or by a labor union, the act has been violated.

Executive Orders. Although a number of executive orders (EO) address discrimination issues, one is of special importance here. EO 11246 requires each government agency to include an "equal opportunity" clause in its agreements with federal contractors. Thus, firms doing business with the federal government must agree, in a broad sense, not to discriminate because of race, color, religion, sex, or national origin and to take affirmative action to avoid and correct underutilization of minorities and women. The Office of Federal Contract Compliance (OFCCP) uses the government's enormous leverage as a purchaser to enforce EO 11246. Noncompliance may result in contract termination or in rendering firms ineligible for future federal business.

Civil Rights Act of 1964. Relying on its authority to regulate interstate commerce, Congress forbade (in Title VII of the Civil Rights Act of 1964) discrimination in employment because of race, color, religion, sex, or national origin. The act applies to private-sector employers with 15 or more employees, employment agencies, and labor unions operating a hiring hall. The Equal Employment Opportunity Act of 1972 amended the 1964 Act to extend coverage to all state and local governments. The Civil Rights Act forbids employment discrimination in most units of the federal government, but Congress itself and those judicial and legislative positions not subject to competitive civil service standards are exempt. Private clubs are exempt from the act, and religious organizations may discriminate in employment on the basis of religion.

The act, as interpreted, prohibits discrimination in hiring, discharge, and general conditions of employment. Although the act forbids employment discrimination against the specified protected classes (race, color, religion, sex, national origin), a number of exceptions are recognized. The more important exceptions are those regarding seniority, employee testing, bona fide occupational qualifications, and veterans' preferences.

Civil Rights Act of 1991. After two years of bickering, political posturing, and sometimes sincere debate about racial quotas, Congress and President Bush agreed on new legislation designed primarily to reverse parts of seven recent Supreme Court decisions. The practical effect of those decisions had been to add difficulty to plaintiffs' efforts to redress perceived civil rights violations. The bill was a rebuff to the conservative direction that the Supreme Court had taken in those cases, and it serves as a useful reminder of the importance of the balance-of-powers notion in our approach to federal governance. The Civil Rights Act of 1991, while creating some new law, primarily serves to return the law more nearly to where it had been prior to those Supreme Court decisions. The substance of that law is discussed throughout this chapter.

Other Federal Statutes. Several more federal statutes, including the Equal Pay Act, the Age Discrimination in Employment Act, and the Americans with Disabilities Act, offer protection against discrimination. The impact of those statutes is discussed later in this chapter.

Pre-Title VII Newspaper Want Ad for Females

The exhibit below is typical of want ads from the classified section found in newspapers in the United States before Title VII was passed in 1964. For publication purposes, all names and phone numbers have been omitted.

FEMALE EMPLOYMENT

Female Help Wanted 23

ATTRACTIVE, NEAT APPEARING, RELIABLE YOUNG LADIES
FOR permanent employment as food waitresses. Interesting work in beautiful surroundings. Good salary plus tips. UNIFORMS FURNISHED. Vacation with pay. Age 21–35 years. For interview appointment phone...

SETTLED white woman who needs home to live in.

LADY to run used furniture store on...

GIRL FRIDAY
If your are a qualified executive secretary, dependable, and would like a solid connection with a growing corporation, write me your qualification in confidence...

A REFRESHING CHANGE
FROM your household chores! Use those old talents of yours and become a part-time secretary. You can earn that extra money you have been needing by working when you want. XXX has temporary positions open in all locations in town and you can choose what and where you want. TOP HOURLY RATES...NO FEE

Opening Soon...WAITRESSES...NO EXPERIENCE NECESSARY
Will train neat, trim, and alert applicants to be coffee house and cocktail waitresses. Apply at once.

CLERK FOR HOTEL
CLERK for medium-size, unusually nice motor hotel. 6-day wk. Hours 3–11. Experience not necessary. Must be mature, neat, and refined. Call...

B. ENFORCEMENT

The Equal Employment Opportunity Commission (EEOC), a federal agency created under the terms of the Civil Rights Act of 1964, is primarily responsible for enforcing the provisions of the act. The commission imposes record-keeping requirements on businesses, unions, and employment agencies in order to build a record should a discrimination issue emerge. The EEOC also investigates discrimination claims, attempts to resolve disputes via *conciliation,* and, if necessary, engages in litigation. Most complaints are settled through the conciliation process.

In essence, Title VII of the 1964 Act established two methods of enforcement: individual actions and pattern or practice suits.

[EEOC seal] **U.S. EQUAL EMPLOYMENT OPPORTUNITY COMMISSION**

Chicago District Office 500 W. Madison Street, Suite 2800
Chicago, IL 60661–2511
PH: (312) 353–2713
TDD: (312) 353–2421
FAX: (312) 353–7355

ARE YOU IN THE RIGHT PLACE?

The Equal Employment Opportunity Commission **(EEOC)** was created by Congress to investigate charges of employment discrimination against employers (including state or local government, but ***not*** Federal government), labor unions and employment agencies.

THE LAWS ENFORCED BY THE EEOC ARE:

Title VII of the **Civil Rights Act of 1964,** which prohibits employment discrimination based on race, color, religion, sex or national origin. The employer must employ 15 or more employees and a charge must be filed within **300 days** of the alleged discriminatory act.

Title I of the **AMERICANS WITH DISABILITIES ACT OF 1990** which prohibits employment discrimination against qualified individuals with disabilities. A qualified individual is a person who satisfies the skill, experience, education, and other job-related requirements of the position held or desired, and who, with or without reasonable accommodation, can perform the essential functions of that position. The employer must employ 25 or more employees (15 or more after July 26, 1994) and a charge must be filed within **300 days** of the alleged discriminatory act.

The **AGE DISCRIMINATION IN EMPLOYMENT ACT OF 1967,** which prohibits employment discrimination against persons who are **40** years of age or older. The employer must employ 20 or more employees and a charge should be filed within **300 days** of the alleged discriminatory act.

The **EQUAL PAY ACT OF 1963,** which prohibits discrimination in the payment of wages to men and women performing substantially equal work. A lawsuit must be filed within **two years** of the alleged discriminatory act. A charge may be filed within this same two year period, but is ***not*** required.

EACH OF THE LAWS ABOVE ALSO PROHIBIT A COVERED EMPLOYER FROM TAKING ADVERSE EMPLOYMENT ACTION AGAINST A PERSON WHO FILES A CHARGE OF EMPLOYMENT DISCRIMINATION, PARTICIPATES IN AN INVESTIGATION OR OPPOSES AN UNLAWFUL EMPLOYMENT PRACTICE.

Continued

ARE YOU IN THE RIGHT PLACE? (continued)

WHAT THE EEOC DOES NOT DO

The EEOC does not investigate complaints of discrimination based on political affiliation or the denial of housing or credit. The EEOC also does not investigate unfair employment action other than those that are alleged to be discriminatory under laws described above.

THE EEOC CANNOT ACCEPT A CHARGE CONCERNING FEDERAL GOVERNMENT EMPLOYMENT; SUCH A CHARGE CAN ONLY BE FILED WITH THE EEOC OFFICE OF THE AGENCY ALLEGED TO HAVE DISCRIMINATED.

* * *

IF YOU BELIEVE THAT YOU MAY BE IN THE WRONG PLACE, PLEASE NOTIFY THE RECEPTIONIST.

Individual Actions. Normally, a private party seeking redress under Title VII must satisfy a series of administrative requirements before litigation is permitted. A job applicant or employee with a discrimination grievance must begin by filing a complaint with the appropriate local or state fair employment practices agency, where provided for by state law. After 60 days, the grievant may turn to the EEOC for aid. Charges must be filed with the EEOC within 180 days of the discriminatory act, or 300 days if preceded by a local or state filing.

Going forward with an EEOC action is often frustrating because the agency is always burdened with a backlog of cases. When a charge is filed, the commission must investigate. The commission may decide that the complaint does not appear to raise a violation, in which case the charges will be dismissed and a right-to-sue letter will be issued releasing the grievant to file his or her own lawsuit. If reasonable cause is found to believe that a violation has occurred, the EEOC will attempt to conciliate the dispute. That failing, the commission may file a civil suit or issue a right-to-sue letter to the grievant. Thus, several years may pass before the administrative process and any subsequent lawsuits have run their course.

Pattern or Practice Suits. In brief, the commission has the authority to investigate and take action on charges of a pattern or practice of discrimination. Pattern or practice claims seek to prove a general policy of discrimination rather than a specific instance of bias. Pattern or practice suits are based primarily on a statistically significant deficiency in the percentage of minority employees in the employer's workforce, as compared with the percentage of minority employees in the relevant labor pool. The employer may be able to rebut the discriminatory inference in a variety of ways. For example, it might be demonstrated that the relevant labor market was improperly drawn or that the statistical disparity is the result of nondiscriminatory conditions.

Remedies. Remedies under Title VII of the Civil Rights Act of 1964 include granting back pay, affording seniority relief, imposing reporting requirements, and so on. One of the more contentious portions of the Civil Rights Act of 1991 greatly expands employers' potential financial liability for civil rights violations. Victims of *intentional* discrimination based on sex, religion, or disability may seek compensatory and punitive damages that had previously been available only in discrimination cases based on race or ethnicity. Such damages are capped at $50,000 to $300,000, depending on the size of the employer's workforce. The Civil Rights Act of 1866 provides for the possibility of unlimited damages in race discrimination cases arising out of all aspects of the employment contract relationship. The 1991 Act also provides that plaintiffs suing under Title VII or the Americans with Disabilities Act may seek jury trials. Since juries often award large recoveries, employment discrimination claims now raise very worrisome financial risks for the employer.

Arbitration. Given the potential damages, attorneys' fees, and so on, employers quite naturally try to avoid litigation. Recent court decisions suggest that a sound, fair arbitration system can be a legally permissible route for reducing reliance on litigation of discrimination claims.

Settlements. Of course, many cases are simply resolved among the parties. For example, in 1991, the Marriott hotel chain, while not admitting wrongdoing, settled a sex discrimination suit regarding promotion policies.[6] The class action involved about 3,000 women and claimed that Marriott engaged in discrimination by systematically excluding women from managerial roles in the chain's food and beverage division. In the settlement, Marriott adopted specific promotion goals, placed $3 million in a settlement fund, and agreed to revise its promotion system.

Profile Perspective: What is the procedural posture of the Hooters case, as identified in the profile?

II. Protecting Employees from Wrongful Discrimination

A. Background: The American Condition

Title VII of the 1964 Act places race, color, and national origin among those protected classes against which discrimination is forbidden. The act was directed primarily to improving the employment opportunities of blacks, but it applies to all races and colors, including whites and Native Americans. The national origin proviso forbids discrimination based on one's nation of birth, ancestry, or heritage. Therefore, an employment office sign reading "Mexicans need not apply" would clearly be unlawful.

The Education Gap. In 1968, black men earned 45 percent less than white men, but by 1977 that gap had narrowed to 29 percent.[7] Then, in the 1980s, that closure stopped. Why? Clearly, racism remains a wearing burden in America; but the more specific cause here appears to be a want of education. Because of declining financial aid and other forces, the gap in education between black and white males, which closed dramatically in the 1970s, did not change in the 1980s.[8]

Median Income of U.S. Families (1991) dollars)

	Black	*White*	*Ratio*
1970	19,144	31,209	61.3
1978	19,739	33,327	59.2
1988	19,329	33,915	57.0
1991	21,548	37,783	57.0

Source: Census Bureau and Urban League, *The State of Black America* (1993).

CHARGE QUESTIONNAIRE This form is affected by the Privacy Act of 1974; see Privacy Act Statement on back before completing this form.	EEOC Use Only Name (Intake Officer)

Please answer the following questions, telling us briefly why you believe you have been discriminated against in employment. An officer of the EEOC will talk with you after you complete this form.

Social Security Number ____ – ____ – ____

(Please Print)

NAME ______________________________ DATE ________
(First) (Middle Name or Initial) (Last)

ADDRESS ________________ TELEPHONE NO. (Include area code) ________

CITY ________ STATE ________ ZIP ________ COUNTY ________

Please provide the name of an individual at a different address in your local area who would know how to reach you.

NAME ________ RELATIONSHIP ________ PHONE ________

ADDRESS ________ CITY ________ STATE ________ ZIP ________

I believe I was discriminated against by: (Check thost that apply)

☐ EMPLOYER ☐ UNION (Give Local No.) ☐ EMPLOYMENT AGENCY ☐ OTHER (Specify)

APPROX. NO. EMPLOYED BY THIS EMPLOYER

________ ________ ________

NAME ________ ADDRESS ________ ________ CITY, STATE, ZIP ________	NAME ________ ADDRESS ________ ________ CITY, STATE, ZIP ________

If you checked "Employer" above, are you now employed by the Employer that you believed discriminated against you?

YES: From ________ (date) ________ (current position)	NO: I applied for ________ (position) on ________ (date)	OR: I was employed as ________ (position) until ________ (date) I was ________

Cause of discrimination based on (Check appropriate box(es)):

☐ Race ☐ Color ☐ Sex ☐ Age ☐ Other - Explain briefly:

☐ National Origin ☐ Disability ☐ Religion ☐ Retaliation ________________

What action was taken against you that you believe to be discrimatory? What harm, if any, was caused to you or others in your work situation as a result of that action? (if more space is required, use reverse.)

____

____

____

____

____

____

____

WHAT WAS THE MOST RECENT DATE THE HARM YOU ALLEGED TOOK PLACE? ________________

EEOC Form 283 (Test: 10/94)

Why do you believe this action was taken against you?

____

Normally your identity as a complainant will be disclosed to the organization which aliegedly discriminated against you.

Do you ☐ consent or ☐ not consent to such disclosures?

Have you sought assistance about the action you think was discriminatory from any agency, from your union, an attorney, or from any other source? ☐ No ☐ Yes (If answer is yes, complete below.)

NAME OF SOURCE ASSISTANCE ______________ DATE ______

RESULTS IF ANY: ______________

Have you filed a complaint about the action you think was discriminatory with any other Federal, State, or Local Government Anti-discrimination agency? ☐ No ☐ Yes (If answer is yes, complete below.)

NAME OF SOURCE ASSISTANCE ______________ DATE ______

RESULTS IF ANY: ______________

Have you filed an EEOC Charge in the past? ☐ No ☐ Yes (If answer is yes, complete below.)

APPROX. DATE FILED	ORGANIZATION CHARGED	CHARGE NUMBER (IF KNOWN)

I declare under penalty of perjury that the foregoing is true and correct.

SIGNATURE DATE

PRIVACY ACT STATEMENT: This form is covered by the Privacy Act of 1974: Public Law 93–579. Authority for requesting personal data and the uses thereof are:

1. FORM NUMBER TITLE/DATE. EEOC Form 283, Charge Questionnaire (12/93).
2. AUTHORITY. 42 U.S.C. § 2000e-5(b); 29 U.S.C. § 211, 29 U.S.C. § 626. 42 U.S.C. § 12117(a)
3. PRINCIPAL PURPOSE. The purpose of this questionnaire is to solicit information in an acceptable form consistent with statutory requirements to enable the Commission to act on matters within its jurisdiction. When this form constitutes the only timely written statement of allegations of employment discrimination, the Commission will, consistent with 29 CFR 1601.12(b) and 29 CRF 1626.8(b), consider it to be a sufficient charge of discrimination under the relevant statute(s).
4. ROUTINE USES. Information provided on this form will be used by Commission employees to determine the existence of facts relevant to a decision as to whether the Commission has jurisdiction over allegations of employment discrimination and to provide such charge filing counselling as is appropriate. Information provided on this form may be disclosed to other State, local and federal agencies as may be appropriate or necessary to carrying out the Commission's functions. Information may also be disclosed to charging parties in consideration of or in connection with litigation.
5. WHETHER DISCLOSURE IS MANDATORY OR VOLUNTARY AND EFFECT ON INDIVIDUAL FOR NOT PROVIDING INFORMATION. The providing of this information is voluntary but the failure to do so may hamper the Commission's investigation of a charge of discrimination. It is not mandatory that this form be used to provide the requested information.

Reverse Side of Form 283 (Test 10/94)

Attachment to Form 283

What makes you believe that the action(s) occurred because of your (race, sex, national origin, religion, color, age, disability, as applicable or because of retaliation)____________________

—and how will discrimination be proved?

Witnesses to action(s)? yes [ ] no [ ]

Comparators? Are there others of same (race, sex, national origin, religion, color, age, disability as applicable) treated more favorably than you under similar circumstances?

yes [ ] no [ ]

Are there others of same (race, sex, national origin, religion, color, age, disability, as applicable) treated more favorably than you under similar circumstances?

yes [ ] no [ ]

Biased remarks, gestures, etc. (describe) ____________________

Other proof of discrimination?____________________

[EEOC seal] **U.S. EQUAL EMPLOYMENT OPPORTUNITY COMMISSION**

Chicago District Office 500 W. Madison Street, Suite 2800
Chicago, IL 60661–2511
PH: (312) 353–2713
TDD: (312) 353–2421
FAX: (312) 353–7355

YOU MAY FILE A CHARGE

The Equal Employment Opportunity Commission enforces certain employment discrimination laws. During the time that you are in our office a member of our staff will interview you to see if your problem falls within the laws that we enforce.

We will ask you questions about the size of the organization with whom you have the problem, about what happened to you and when it happened to you, about why you think it happened to you and about how others were treated. What you tell us is very important.

We will use your information to determine whether the organization can be investigated by us. If we believe that we have no authority to investigate the organization, we will explain this to you.

If we believe what happened to you is not likely to be a violation of any of our laws, we will explain this to you.

Sometimes we can't tell whether what happened or may happen to you is something that we should investigate. We may ask you to get additional information or wait until it is clear as to what has happened and then to return to our office.

Regardless of what we believe, you may file a charge with us. This is your decision to make. If you do file a charge under these circumstances, we may still dismiss your charge because we have no authority to investigate or because we believe that no violation of the law has occurred. Filing a charge gives you an independent right to sue the organization. Whether you would win your lawsuit would be a matter for the court to determine.

My signature acknowledges that I have read this notice.

SIGNATURE:______________________ DATE:__________________________

A recent study, the first of its kind, shows that Hispanic-Americans are three times more likely to live in poverty than are non-Hispanic whites. Nine percent of non-Hispanic whites live in poverty, but 29 percent of America's Hispanics fall below the poverty line.[9] These figures, in concert with America's rapidly changing demographic makeup, suggest that our view of race-based problems, including discrimination, will need to be broadened in the coming years.

Changing Demographics. Of course, the disadvantages of minority life in America are not limited to blacks.

A 1993 Census Bureau study projects a rather dramatic new picture of America's racial balance (percentages are rounded to nearest whole number):

- Hispanics in 2010 will replace blacks as the nation's largest minority group.
- Non-Hispanic whites' share of the population will drop from 76 percent now to 68 percent in 2010 and 53 percent in 2050.
- Blacks, with 12 percent of the population today, will rise to 13 percent in 2010 and to 16 percent in 2050.
- Asian-Americans, the fastest growing portion of the population, will rise from today's 3 percent share to 10 percent by 2050.
- Hispanics, now at 9 percent of the population, will rise to 14 percent in 2010 and 23 percent in 2050.
- Our Native American population will nearly double to 4.3 million by mid-century, but the percentage share will rise only slightly to about 1 percent.[10]

In fairness, we should note that U.S. discrimination problems are by no means unique. Throughout the 1990s, Germany has been dealing with right-wing extremist attacks against the more than 6 million Turks, Slavs, Romanians, and other foreigners who came to Germany seeking work and asylum. Those attacks, which resulted in 17 deaths in 1992, are the product of both racism and a difficult job market following German reunification. France, in recent years, has absorbed some 5 million (mostly North African) immigrants. The result has been greatly increased tension: A survey on race relations, ordered by the Socialist government in Paris, disclosed that 76 percent of the French people believed there were too many Arabs in their country, 46 percent declared there were too many blacks, 40 percent said there were too many Asians, and 24 percent complained that there were too many Jews.[11]

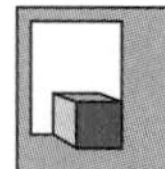

Can the Market Fix Discrimination? If the market were left to its own devices, wouldn't you expect firms that discriminate to fall by the wayside? That is, if a firm hires its employees based on prejudices and discriminatory views (such as women can't do a certain job), then it is limiting its pool of possible employees. Another firm that does not discriminate can choose from the larger pool and is more likely to obtain the *most* qualified individual for the job. Judge Richard Posner explained the economic impact of this theory in terms of race discrimination:

> In a market of many sellers, the intensity of the prejudice against blacks will vary considerably. Some sellers will have only a mild prejudice against them. These sellers will not forgo as many advantageous transactions with blacks as their more prejudiced competitors (unless the law interferes). Their costs will therefore be lower, and this will enable them to increase their share of the market. The least prejudiced

> sellers will come to dominate the market in much the same way as people who are least afraid of heights come to dominate occupations that require working at heights: they demand a smaller premium.[12]

Under what circumstances would Posner's argument fail? Consider the implications if the discriminating firm held a monopoly on its good or service. What is the effect of regulation such as Title VII on Posner's argument?

B. *Don't We All Discriminate? Theories of Discrimination*

The fact is, when any employment decision is made, discrimination exists. Does that surprise you? Isn't it appropriate for an employer to discriminate for some jobs on the basis of actual qualifications such as education and experience? In fact, employers can, should, and do discriminate based on perfectly acceptable grounds. You wouldn't find it strange or wrong for a business to require a human resources degree for applicants to a position as vice president of human resources. American law merely forbids discrimination on a *few, specific, non-job-related* factors (such as religion and race), as you will see below.

The Civil Rights Act of 1964 as amended by the Civil Rights Act of 1991 is the primary vehicle for pursuing employment discrimination claims. However, keep in mind the other constitutional, statutory, and executive order protections mentioned above. Title VII of the 1964 Act provides two primary theories of liability: disparate treatment and disparate impact. (A third theory of liability, perpetuation of past intentional discrimination, will not be discussed here.)

Disparate Treatment. The basic elements of disparate treatment exist where an employer *intentionally* treats some people less favorably than others because of their race, color, religion, sex, or national origin. Intent ordinarily is established by circumstantial evidence. In a simplified form, a claim under disparate treatment analysis would proceed as follows:

1. *Plaintiff's (employee's) prima facie case* (sufficient to be presumed true unless proved otherwise). Optimally the plaintiff would present direct, explicit evidence of intentional disparate treatment. For example, that evidence might take the form of a letter from an employer to an employment agency indicating that "women would not be welcome as applicants for this physically taxing job." Because direct evidence of that nature is ordinarily unavailable, the plaintiff must then build the following prima facie case from which intent and, hence, disparate treatment may be inferred:

   a. Plaintiff belongs to a protected class.
   b. Plaintiff applied for a job for which the defendant was seeking applicants.
   c. Plaintiff was qualified for the job.
   d. Plaintiff was denied the job.
   e. The position remained open, and the employer continued to seek applications.

2. *Defendant's (employer's) case.* If the plaintiff builds a successful prima facie case, the burden shifts to the defendant to do one of two things. First, the employer may show that the employment decision was based on a **legitimate, nondiscriminatory reason (LNDR),** for example, greater work experience or education. However, the defendant need not *prove* its decision not to hire the plaintiff was, in fact, based on that legitimate, nondiscriminatory reason. The defendant simply must raise a legitimate issue of fact disputing the plaintiff's discrimination claim.

legitimate nondiscriminatory reason (LNDR). An employer's justification for taking adverse action against an employee or applicant where the basis for the action is something other than the individual's membership in a protected class (such as termination for dishonesty or theft).

bona fide occupational qualification (BFOQ). A defense in a discrimination claim where the employer argues that a particular religion, sex, or national origin is a necessary qualification for a particular job.

Second, the employer may defend its actions by showing that the decision was based on a **bona fide occupational qualification (BFOQ).** Discrimination is lawful where sex, religion, or national origin is a BFOQ reasonably necessary to the normal operation of that business. The exclusion of race and color from the list suggests Congress thought those categories always unacceptable as bona fide occupational qualifications. The judicially created defense of business necessity is applicable to racial classifications. The BFOQ was meant to be a very limited exception applicable to situations in which specific inherent characteristics are necessary to the job (e.g., wet nurse) and where authenticity is required (e.g., actors).

For instance, in certain positions, a certain gender may be a bona fide qualification for that position. Consider the position of locker room attendant; it is arguable that being a woman is a qualification of the position of a locker room attendant for a female locker room. An easy way to remember the appropriateness of BFOQs is to consider the job of a priest; it would be a BFOQ to require that the priest be of a certain religion, even though this is actually discriminating against those who are not of that religion.

In connection with gender, many employers have simply assumed that women could not perform certain tasks. Women were thought to be insufficiently aggressive for sales roles, and women were denied employment because they were assumed to have a higher turnover rate due to the desire to marry and have children. Those stereotypes are at the heart of sex discrimination litigation generally and sex as a BFOQ particularly.

Dothard v. *Rawlinson,* a 1977 Supreme Court case, offers a good example of the BFOQ analysis.[13] Dianne Rawlinson sought employment as a prison guard in Alabama. She was a 22-year-old college graduate with a degree in correctional psychology. She was denied employment because she failed to meet the 120-pound weight requirement for the job. The state also required such employees to be at least five feet, two inches tall. Alabama operated four all-male, maximum security prisons. The district court characterized the Alabama prison system as one of "rampant violence" and having a "jungle atmosphere." Rawlinson sued, claiming employment discrimination. Resolve this case under the BFOQ analysis, including the defenses that would be raised by the state.

3. Plaintiff's response or rebuttal. Assuming the defendant was successful in presenting a legitimate, nondiscriminatory reason for its action, the burden of proof shifts back to the plaintiff to show that:

a. The reason offered by the defendant was not the true reason but was, in fact, merely a **pretext** to hide discrimination.
b. Discrimination was the real reason for the defendant employer's action.[14]

pretext. After an employee has established a prima facie case of discrimination and the employer has articulated a BFOQ or LNDR, the employee must show that the proffered defense is pretextual, that is, that the BFOQ is not actually bona fide (or not applied in all situations) or that the LNDR has been applied differently to this individual compared to another.

Profile Perspective: In the Hooters case, identify the prima facie case that could be made by the four male plaintiffs. What would be Hooters' response? Would gender qualify as a BFOQ? If Hooters is successful in establishing its defense, would the men have a claim of pretext?

Disparate Impact. Disparate impact analysis arose out of situations in which employers used legitimate or neutral employment standards that, despite their apparent neutrality, had a greater or different impact on a protected class than on other employees. For example, a preemployment test, offered with the best of intentions and constructed to be a fair measurement device, may disproportionately exclude members of a protected class and thus be unacceptable, barring an effective defense. Alternatively, an employer surreptitiously seeking to discriminate may establish an apparently neutral, superficially valid employment test that has the effect of achieving the employer's discrimination goal.

For example, a tavern might require its bouncer to be at least six feet, two inches tall and weigh at least 180 pounds. Such a standard disproportionately excludes women, Asians, and Hispanics from consideration and probably is impermissible, barring an effective defense. Disparate impact analysis is similar to that of disparate treatment, but critical distinctions mark the two approaches. In particular, note that disparate treatment requires proof of intent, whereas disparate impact does not.

1991 Act. A 1989 Supreme Court decision in the *Wards Cove* case had greatly increased the plaintiff's (employee's) burden in winning a disparate impact case. The Civil Rights Act of 1991 directly addressed that case by significantly increasing the demands of proof on the defendant (employer). Because the 1991 Act is new and little tested in court, we cannot yet be sure of its ultimate meaning. However, the best evidence at this writing in 1994 is that the law returns at least generally to the direction that the Court elaborated in the *Griggs* case that follows shortly. Disparate impact following the 1991 Act appears to require the following:

1. *Plaintiff's (employee's) prima facie case.* There are two elements to the plaintiff's prima facie case. First, the plaintiff must prove (often with statistical evidence) that a protected class is suffering an **disparate impact** in the workplace in question. For example, the statistical analysis to establish disparate impact against black applicants must be based on a comparison of the racial composition of the group of persons actually holding the jobs in question versus the racial composition of the *job-qualified* population in the relevant labor market.

   Second, the plaintiff must identify the *specific employment practice or policy* (e.g., test score, skill, or height) that caused the disparate impact on the protected class. However, if the employer's decision-making process cannot be divided into pieces for analysis, the plaintiff may allege that a combination of practices and policies was responsible for the disparate impact.

2. *Defendant's (employer's) case.* Assuming the plaintiff/employee establishes a prima facie case, the burden of proof shifts to the employer to demonstrate that the employment practice/policy is (*a*) job related and (*b*) consistent with business necessity.

3. *Plaintiff's response.* If the employer succeeds in demonstrating job relatedness and consistency with business necessity, the plaintiff/employee may yet prevail by demonstrating that *an alternate, less discriminatory business practice is available and that the employer refuses to adopt it.*

disparate impact. An employee may make a prima facie case for adverse impact where the employer's facially neutral rule results in a different impact on one protected group than on another (also known as adverse impact).

Profile Perspective: Does the Hooters case involve disparate impact or disparate treatment?

Statutory Defenses. In a broad sense, business necessity, as explained above, is the principle defense to discrimination charges. However, as mentioned previously, Title VII affords four specific exemptions or defenses of particular note: (1) seniority, (2) employee testing, (3) bona fide occupational qualification (mentioned above), and (4) veterans' preferences.

CASE

Chief Justice Burger

Griggs v. Duke Power Co.

401 U.S. 424 (1971)

We granted the writ in this case to resolve the question whether an employer is prohibited by the Civil Rights Act of 1964, Title VII, from requiring a high school education or passing of a standardized general intelligence test as a condition of employment in or transfer to jobs when (*a*) neither standard is shown to be significantly related to successful job performance, (*b*) both requirements operate to disqualify Negroes at a substantially higher rate than white applicants, and (*c*) the jobs in question formerly had been filled only by white employees as part of a long-standing practice of giving preference to whites.

Congress provided, in Title VII of the Civil Rights Act of 1964, for class actions for enforcement of provisions of the Act and this proceeding was brought by a group of incumbent Negro employees against Duke Power Company . . .

The District Court found that prior to July 2, 1965, the effective date of the Civil Rights Act of 1964, the company openly discriminated on the basis of race in the hiring and assigning of employees at its Dan River plant. The plant was organized into five operating departments: (1) Labor, (2) Coal Handling, (3) Operations, (4) Maintenance, and (5) Laboratory and Test. Negroes were employed only in the Labor Department where the highest-paying jobs paid less than the lowest-paying jobs in the other four "operating" departments in which only whites were employed. Promotions were normally made within each department on the basis of job seniority. Transferees into a department usually began in the lowest position.

In 1955 the company instituted a policy of requiring a high school education for initial assignment to any department except Labor, and for transfer from the Coal Handling to any "inside" department (Operations, Maintenance, or Laboratory). When the company abandoned its policy of restricting Negroes to the Labor Department in 1965, completion of high school also was made a prerequisite to transfer from Labor to any other department. From the time the high school requirement was instituted to the time of trial, however, white employees hired before the time of the high school education requirement continued to perform satisfactorily and achieve promotions in the "operating" departments. Findings on this score are not challenged.

The company added a further requirement for new employees on July 2, 1965, the date on which Title VII became effective. To qualify for placement in any but the Labor Department it became necessary to register satisfactory scores on two professionally prepared aptitude tests, as well as to have a high school education. Completion of high school alone continued to render employees eligible for transfer to the four desirable departments from which Negroes had been excluded if the incumbent had been employed prior to the time of the new requirement. In September 1965 the company began to permit incumbent employees who lacked a high school education to qualify for transfer from Labor or Coal Handling to an "inside" job by passing two tests—the Wonderlic Personnel Test, which purports to measure general intelligence, and the Bennett Mechanical Comprehension Test. Neither was directed or intended to measure the ability to learn to perform a particular job or category of jobs. The requisite scores used for both initial hiring and transfer approximated the national median for high school graduates.

The District Court had found that while the company previously followed a policy of overt racial discrimination in a period prior to the Act, such conduct had ceased. The District Court also concluded that Title VII was intended to be prospective only and, consequently, the impact of prior inequities was beyond the reach of corrective action authorized by the Act . . .

The Court of Appeals concluded there was no violation of the Act.

* * *

Continued

Continued

The objective of Congress in the enactment of Title VII is plain from the language of the statute. It was to achieve equality of employment opportunities and remove barriers that have operated in the past to favor an identifiable group of white employees over other employees. Under the Act, practices, procedures, or tests neutral on their face, and even neutral in terms of intent, cannot be maintained if they operate to "freeze" the status quo of prior discriminatory employment practices.

The Court of Appeals' opinion, and the partial dissent, agreed that, on the record in the present case, "whites register far better on the company's alternative requirements" than Negroes. This consequence would appear to be directly traceable to race. Basic intelligence must have the means of articulation to manifest itself fairly in a testing process. Because they are Negroes, petitioners have long received inferior education in segregated schools . . .

Congress did not intend by Title VII, however, to guarantee a job to every person regardless of qualifications. In short, the Act does not command that any person be hired simply because he was formerly the subject of discrimination, or because he is a member of a minority group. Discriminatory preference for any group, minority or majority, is precisely and only what Congress has proscribed . . .

The Act proscribes not only overt discrimination but also practices that are fair in form, but discriminatory in operation. The touchstone is business necessity. If an employment practice which operates to exclude Negroes cannot be shown to be related to job performance, the practice is prohibited.

On the record before us, neither the high school completion requirement nor the general intelligence test is shown to bear a demonstrable relationship to successful performance of the jobs for which it was used. Both were adopted, as the Court of Appeals noted, without meaningful study of their relationship to job-performance ability. Rather, a vice president of the company testified, the requirements were instituted on the company's judgment that they generally would improve the overall quality of the workforce.

The evidence, however, shows that employees who have not completed high school or taken the tests have continued to perform satisfactorily and make progress in departments for which the high school and test criteria are not used . . .

The Court of Appeals held that the company had adopted the diploma and test requirements without any "intention to discriminate against Negro employees." We do not suggest that either the District Court or the Court of Appeals erred in examining the employer's intent; but good intent or absence of discriminatory intent does not redeem employment procedures or testing mechanisms that operate as "built-in headwinds" for minority groups and are unrelated to measuring job capability.

* * *

Nothing in the Act precludes the use of testing or measuring procedures; obviously they are useful. What Congress has forbidden is giving these devices and mechanisms controlling force unless they are demonstrably a reasonable measure of job performance. Congress has not commanded that the less qualified be preferred over the better qualified simply because of minority origins. Far from disparaging job qualifications as such, Congress has made such qualifications the controlling factor, so that race, religion, nationality, and sex become irrelevant. What Congress has commanded is that any tests used must measure the person for the job and not the person in the abstract.

The judgment of the Court of Appeals is . . . reversed.

Questions

1. According to the Supreme Court, what was Congress's objective in enacting Title VII?
2. Had Duke Power been able to establish that its reasons for adopting the diploma and test standards were entirely without discriminatory intent, would the Supreme Court have ruled differently? Explain.

Continued

Continued

3. Statistical evidence showed that 35 percent of new hires in grocery and produce at Lucky Stores, a retail grocery chain, were women, and 84 percent of new hires in deli, bakery, and general merchandise were women. Statistical evidence also showed that 31 percent of those promoted into apprentice jobs in grocery and produce were women, and 75 percent of those promoted into apprentice jobs in deli, bakery, and general merchandise were women. Grocery and produce jobs generally were higher paying jobs than those in deli, bakery, and general merchandise. Women received significantly fewer overtime hours. Do these facts regarding Lucky Stores suggest discrimination? Explain. [See *Stender* v. *Lucky Stores, Inc.*, 803 F. Supp. 259 (DC Cal. 1992).]

Seniority. Section 703(h) of the Civil Rights Act of 1964 provides that an employer may lawfully apply different standards of compensation or different conditions of employment pursuant to a bona fide (good faith) seniority system, provided such differences are not the product of an intent to discriminate. That is, the seniority system must not have been created for a discriminatory or other illegal purpose, and the seniority provisions must apply equally to all.

Employee Testing. Testing is, of course, central to professional personnel practice and to maximizing employee productivity; but testing has often been, both intentionally and unintentionally, a primary vehicle in perpetuating discrimination. Recall that only job-related tests supported by detailed, statistical evidence as to their scientific validity are lawful.

III. Gender Discrimination

To understand the application of Title VII, we will consider the issues surrounding gender discrimination; after all, we all have a gender and may have been subject to discrimination at some point no matter which gender we are.

A. *Background: The American Condition*

By most measures, even after years of struggle, women continue to occupy a distinctly secondary role in American life. More than 30 years after the passage of the 1963 Equal Pay Act, women earn from 70 to 74 cents (depending on the study) for every dollar earned by men.[15] The figures are even more dispiriting for minority women. In 1991, black women earned 62 cents and Hispanic women earned 54 cents for every dollar earned by white men.[16] The female/male pay gap was 59 cents on the dollar in 1977, so we have made progress; but the bulk of that progress is actually attributable to a decline in men's wages in recent years.[17]

Depends on the Job. As displayed in Figure 6.1, in certain specific occupations, particularly those paying by the hour, women's pay much more closely equals that of men; but in white-collar roles, women's pay sometimes sinks, on the average, to as low as half that of men.[18] Claims that the disparity is due to differences in credentials by sex were challenged in a recent scholarly study finding that in a sample of 800 corporate managers, "if women were men with the same credentials, they would earn about 18 percent more."[19]

ACROSS-THE-BOARD DOLLAR DISPARITY

FIGURE 6.1

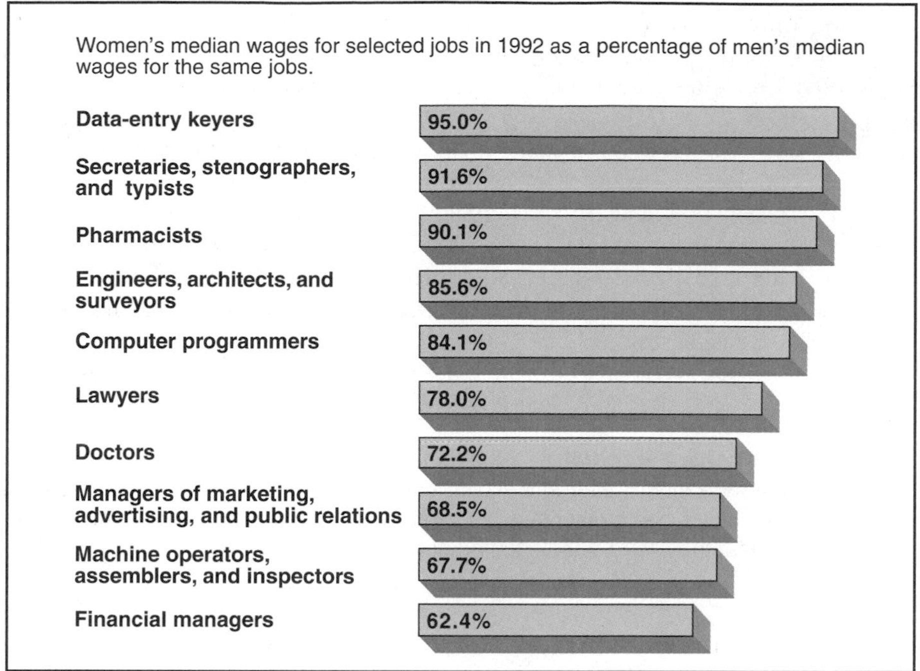

Source: Bureau of Labor Statistics.

Indeed, Americans generally agree that women are not treated fairly. A 1992 Gallup poll of 684 adults found only 36 percent of those responding believed that women and men are treated equally in seeking promotions.[20]

Abroad. Women's frustration over the disparities noted here will not be allayed by a look around the balance of the world. In Japan, on the average, women earn only about half of what men earn, but in all other industrialized countries, the United States ranks on the low end of the scale. According to a University of Illinois study using data from the late 1980s:

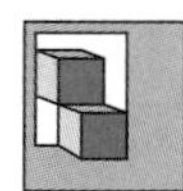

> [T]he ratio of female-to-male weekly wages ranged from 80 percent to 90 percent in Australia, Denmark, France, New Zealand, Norway, and Sweden. Other countries in western Europe, and the United States, had ratios of roughly 65 percent to 75 percent, with the United States on the low side.[21]

Glass Ceilings, and Walls. In 1992, *Fortune* asked: "When Will Women Get to the Top?"[22] Not for a long time, according to a poll of CEOs of 201 of the nation's largest companies:

> [O]nly 16 percent believe it is "very likely" or "somewhat likely" that they could be succeeded by a female CEO within the next decade. And only 18 percent think it's "very likely" that even after 20 years a woman would be picked to run their companies.[23]

> Not only do women confront a glass ceiling as they seek promotion, but recent studies suggest that many women are unable to move laterally out of traditional female roles (e.g., communications and staff support) and into power roles such as sales and production.

Not only do women confront a **glass ceiling** as they seek promotion, but recent studies suggest that many women are unable to move laterally out of traditional female roles (e.g., communications and staff support) and into power roles such as sales and production.[24]

Of course, women have made important strides in recent years. The percentage of women officers in Fortune 50 firms more than doubled—from 2.2 to 5.1 percent—between 1990 and 1992.[25] Furthermore, in the early 1990s some 6.1 million women occupied managerial roles, as opposed to about 3.5 million in 1983.[26] Another very encouraging sign is that women now own some 5.4 million businesses and are starting new businesses at twice the rate of men.[27] And in professional life, generally, the changes have been striking. During the 1980s, the number of female doctors doubled, and women lawyers and dentists tripled. Indeed, in 1990 one in four lawyers was a woman.[28]

glass ceiling. An artificial barrier to advancement in the workplace usually used in connection with women.

Profile Perspective: If the female waitresses in the Hooters case were paid above the average male waiter in a similar establishment, would the women still have any claim that they were being discriminated against, that they were being kept to demeaning positions, or that they were unable to find better positions?

Parent *and* Manager? Many of the most trying and poignant sex discrimination issues are those arising out of the increasing conflicts (particularly for women but increasingly for men) between being a parent and pursuing a career. Historically, an employed woman who became pregnant faced a serious threat to her professional future. In 1978, Congress amended the Civil Rights Act of 1964 with the Pregnancy Discrimination Act, which treats pregnancy discrimination as a form of sex discrimination. Table 6.1 summarizes some of the circumstances of pregnant employees and outlines the protections of the Pregnancy Discrimination Act.

In 1983, the Supreme Court interpreted the act to apply to employees' pregnant spouses. By a 7-to-2 vote the Court ruled that pregnancy-related expense benefits for the spouses of male employees must be equal to the pregnancy-related expense benefits accorded to married female employees.[29] Then, in 1987 the Court upheld a California law giving pregnant women a four-month leave from work and guaranteeing them their job back after the leave.[30] The Family and Medical Leave Act provides further relief.

Discrimination to a Different Drummer

Joseph Egan worked for Jenny Craig, Inc., weight-loss company. Although at first he was flattered from his female coworkers' "oohs" and "ahs" over his biceps and his "tight buns," he became concerned when a female supervisor asked him to fix her car. The women at the office also asked him to lift heavy boxes, carry trash, start their cars, or shovel snow. Mr. Egan claims that he felt like a token pair of biceps. Another supervisor (female) told him that she had dreamed about him naked. "If a man had said that, it would be on talk shows all over the place," Mr. Egan, 28 years old, believes. "But when it happens to men, it's no big deal."

Continued

TABLE 6.1

PREGNANT WOMEN IN THE WORKFORCE

- 71 percent of all women who become pregnant are working at the time.
- 38 percent are in the workforce by the time their children are three months old.
- 58 percent are working by the time their children reach one year of age.

Among women who are working when they become pregnant:

- 50 percent are back in the labor force by the time their children are three months old.
- About 75 percent of those women return to the same job that they had before.
- 72 percent have returned to the labor force by the time their children are a year old.

Of the women who work sometime during their pregnancy:

- 50 percent work into their third trimester.
- Of those who work into their third trimester, 59 percent are back at work within three months of their children's births.

Source: "Work around Childbirth," Rand Corp.

The Pregnancy Discrimination Act makes it illegal for an employer with more than 15 employees to:

- Fire an employee for becoming pregnant.
- Refuse to hire a worker because she is pregnant.
- Demote or penalize a worker because she is pregnant.
- Refuse to promote a worker because she is pregnant.
- Deny disability leave if such a leave is available to other disabled workers.
- Deny health insurance for pregnancy if there is insurance available for other medical conditions.
- Deny fringe benefits, such as the crediting of vacation days, seniority, or pay increases, while a woman is on leave for childbirth if other disabled employees continue to accrue such benefits.

Source: Reported in Kathleen Hughes, "Pregnant Professionals Face Pressures at Work as Attitudes toward Them Shift," *The Wall Street Journal,* February 6, 1991, p. B1. Reprinted by permission of *The Wall Street Journal,*

Continued

Other men who worked for Jenny Craig claimed that they were dissuaded from even taking the jobs because the clientele was about 85 percent women. They were told that it was improbable that a man would be able to relate to women with low self-esteem and other problems associated with being overweight.

After working for four years as a salesperson and manager for Jenny Craig, Inc., Mr. Egan quit his job and joined seven other male ex-employees who sued or complained about treatment at Jenny Craig. Jenny Craig called the claims "frivolous." In November 1994, the Massachusetts Commission Against Discrimination found that he and two other men had probable cause of gender bias.

Is this any different than a woman working at a male body-building salon? Why?

Adapted from *The Wall Street Journal.*

B. Fetal Protection

In 1991, the Supreme Court decided perhaps the most significant civil rights case in two decades. The *Johnson Controls* decision addresses the dilemma of whether fertile women may lawfully be denied jobs involving exposure to substances that may cause harm to their fetuses.

Profile Perspective: Assume that Hooters instituted a policy that no pregnant woman was allowed to act as a waitress for two reasons. First, as a woman progresses through her pregnancy and begins to show, she no longer has the "look" that Hooters is shooting for. Second, given the hustle and bustle of waitressing, Hooters believes that it will be unsafe for the woman and her unborn child. Would Hooters be allowed to institute this policy? Why or why not?

C. Sexual Harassment

Broadly, sexual harassment consists of unwelcome sexual advances, requests for sexual favors, and other verbal or physical conduct of a sexual nature. That conduct in a work setting constitutes sex discrimination in violation of Title VII.

Well-settled case law and federal guidelines have established two categories of sexual harassment:

1. *Quid pro quo sexual harassment.* In these cases, continued employment or an employment benefit such as a promotion are conditioned by a manager or a supervisor on the employee's willingness to engage in sexual conduct; that is, a boss expects a sexual opportunity in trade for a job benefit.
2. *Hostile environment sexual harassment.* In these cases, no employment benefit need be lost or gained. Rather, the question is one of whether the work environment has become offensive and abusive because of the pervasive presence of, for example, sexual aggression, sexual jokes, pornographic pictures, sexually derogatory comments, and so on. That hostile environment may be the product of conduct by managers, supervisors, coworkers, or even those not actually employed by the firm in question.

The evidence suggests that sexual harassment at work is widespread. Thirty-one percent of the women and 7 percent of the men surveyed in a 1994 nationwide Harris poll indicated that they had been the victims of sexual harassment at work. However, 63 percent of those surveyed said there was no sexual harassment in their workplace.[31] A 1992 survey of *Working Woman* readers reported a 60 percent rate of harassment.[32]

Sexual harassment charges filed at the federal level fell under 5,000 in 1989. Then Anita Hill's dramatic sexual harassment allegations against now U.S. Supreme Court Justice Clarence Thomas in his Senate confirmation hearings apparently spurred a new surge in filings, as these totaled 10,608 in 1992.[33]

What Is It? The Problem with Defining Sexual Harassment. Not surprisingly, a continuing difficulty in dealing with sexual harassment lies in identifying it. At the workplace level, the confusion can be considerable. A 1992 Roper poll summarized 22 situations and asked the respondents which of them constituted sexual harassment. Clear majorities found sexual harassment in only three of the situations.

UAW v. Johnson Controls, Inc.

CASE

499 U.S. 187 (1991)

Justice Blackmun

In this case we are concerned with an employer's gender-based fetal-protection policy. May an employer exclude a fertile female employee from certain jobs because of its concern for the health of the fetus the woman might conceive?

I

Respondent Johnson Controls, Inc., manufactures batteries. In the manufacturing process, the element lead is a primary ingredient. Occupational exposure to lead entails health risks, including the risk of harm to any fetus carried by a female employee.

Before the Civil Rights Act of 1964 . . . became law, Johnson Controls did not employ any woman in a battery-manufacturing job. In June 1977, however, it announced its first official policy concerning its employment of women in lead-exposure work:

> [P]rotection of the health of the unborn child is the immediate and direct responsibility of the prospective parents. While the medical profession and the company can support them in the exercise of this responsibility, it cannot assume it for them without simultaneously infringing their rights as persons. . . .
>
> Since not all women who can become mothers wish to become mothers (or will become mothers), it would appear to be illegal discrimination to treat all who are capable of pregnancy as though they will become pregnant.

Consistent with that view, Johnson Controls "stopped short of excluding women capable of bearing children from lead exposure" . . . but emphasized that a woman who expected to have a child should not choose a job in which she would have such exposure. The company also required a woman who wished to be considered for employment to sign a statement that she had been advised of the risk of having a child while she was exposed to lead . . .

Five years later, in 1982, Johnson Controls shifted from a policy of warning to a policy of exclusion. Between 1979 and 1983, eight employees became pregnant while maintaining blood lead levels in excess of 30 micrograms per deciliter . . . This appeared to be the critical level noted by the Occupational Health and Safety Administration [sic] (OSHA) for a worker who was planning to have a family . . . The company responded by announcing a broad exclusion of women from jobs that exposed them to lead: ". . . [I]t is [Johnson Controls'] policy that women who are pregnant or who are capable of bearing children will not be placed into jobs involving lead exposure or which could expose them to lead through the exercise of job bidding, bumping, transfer or promotion rights."

The policy defined "women . . . capable of bearing children" as "[a]ll women except those whose inability to bear children is medically documented." . . . It further stated that an unacceptable work station was one where, "over the past year," an employee had recorded a blood lead level of more than 30 micrograms per deciliter or the work site had yielded an air sample containing a lead level in excess of 30 micrograms per cubic meter . . .

II

In April 1984, petitioners filed . . . a class action challenging Johnson Controls' fetal-protection policy as sex discrimination . . . Among the individual plaintiffs were petitioners Mary Craig, who had chosen to be sterilized in order to avoid losing her job, Elsie Nason, a 50-year-

Continued

Continued

old divorcee, who had suffered a loss in compensation when she was transferred out of a job where she was exposed to lead, and Donald Penney, who had been denied a request for a leave of absence for the purpose of lowering his lead level because he intended to become a father . . . The District Court certified a class [action.]

The District Court granted summary judgment for defendant-respondent Johnson Controls . . .

The Court of Appeals . . . affirmed the summary judgment by a 7-to-4 vote . . . Specifically, the court concluded that there was no genuine issue of material fact about the substantial health-risk factor because the parties agreed that there was a substantial risk to a fetus from lead exposure . . . The Court of Appeals also concluded that, unlike the evidence of risk to the fetus from the mother's exposure, the evidence of risk from the father's exposure, which petitioners presented, "is, at best, speculative and unconvincing."

* * *

III

The bias in Johnson Controls' policy is obvious. Fertile men, but not fertile women, are given a choice as to whether they wish to risk their reproductive health for a particular job.

* * *

Respondent does not seek to protect the unconceived children of all its employees. Despite evidence in the record about the debilitating effect of lead exposure on the male reproductive system, Johnson Controls is concerned only with the harms that may befall the unborn offspring of its female employees.

* * *

We hold that Johnson Controls' fetal-protection policy is sex discrimination forbidden under Title VII unless respondent can establish that sex is a "bona fide occupational qualification."

IV

We therefore turn to the question whether Johnson Controls' fetal-protection policy is one of those "certain instances" that come within the BFOQ exception.

* * *

Johnson Controls argues that its fetal-protection policy falls within the so-called safety exception to the BFOQ. Our cases have stressed that discrimination on the basis of sex because of safety concerns is allowed only in narrow circumstances. In *Dothard* v. *Rawlinson,* this Court indicated that danger to a woman herself does not justify discrimination . . . We there allowed the employer to hire only male guards in contact areas of maximum-security male penitentiaries only because more was at stake than the "individual woman's decision to weigh and accept the risks of employment" . . .

The concurrence [not reprinted here] ignores the "essence of the business" test and so concludes that "the safety to fetuses in carrying out the duties of battery manufacturing is as much a legitimate concern as is safety to third parties in guarding prisons (*Dothard*) or flying airplanes (*Criswell*)" . . . By limiting its discussion to cost and safety concerns and rejecting the "essence of the business" test that our case law has established, the concurrence seeks to expand

Continued

Continued

what is now the narrow BFOQ defense. Third-party safety considerations properly entered into the BFOQ analysis in *Dothard* and *Criswell* because they went to the core of the employee's job performance. Moreover, that performance involved the central purpose of the enterprise . . . The concurrence attempts to transform this case into one of customer safety. The unconceived fetuses of Johnson Controls' female employees, however, are neither customers nor third parties whose safety is essential to the business of battery manufacturing. No one can disregard the possibility of injury to future children; the BFOQ, however, is not so broad that it transforms this deep social concern into an essential aspect of batterymaking.

Our case law, therefore, makes clear that the safety exception is limited to instances in which sex or pregnancy actually interferes with the employee's ability to perform the job . . .

The [Pregnancy Discrimination Act's] amendment to Title VII contains a BFOQ standard of its own: unless pregnant employees differ from others "in their ability or inability to work," they must be "treated the same" as other employees "for all employment-related purposes" . . . In other words, women as capable of doing their jobs as their male counterparts may not be forced to choose between having a child and having a job.

V

We have no difficulty concluding that Johnson Controls cannot establish a BFOQ. Fertile women, as far as appears in the record, participate in the manufacture of batteries as efficiently as anyone else. Johnson Controls' professed moral and ethical concerns about the welfare of the next generation do not suffice to establish a BFOQ of female sterility. Decisions about the welfare of future children must be left to the parents who conceive, bear, support, and raise them rather than to the employers who hire those parents . . . Title VII and the PDA simply do not allow a woman's dismissal because of her failure to submit to sterilization.

Nor can concerns about the welfare of the next generation be considered a part of the "essence" of Johnson Controls' business. Judge Easterbrook in this case pertinently observed: "It is word play to say that 'the job' at Johnson [Controls] is to make batteries without risk to fetuses in the same way 'the job' at Western Air Lines is to fly planes without crashing" . . .

VII

It is no more appropriate for the courts than it is for individual employers to decide whether a woman's reproductive role is more important to herself and her family than her economic role. Congress has left this choice to the woman as hers to make.

Reversed and remanded.

Questions

1. *a.* What reasoning supported the Supreme Court's judgment that sex was not a BFOQ in this case?
   b. What reasoning supported the Supreme Court's judgment that employer liability for a prenatal injury "seems remote at best"?
   c. Do you agree with the Court's reasoning on the liability issue? Explain.
2. Make the argument that the *Johnson Controls* decision will result in job losses in American industry and a reduced ability for American business to compete in the international market.
3. As a businessperson, what steps would you take in an effort to cope with the implications of the *Johnson Controls* decision?

Those involved direct questions about sexual practices and being required to sleep with the boss in exchange for a raise. Strong majorities rejected a finding of sexual harassment in such situations as:

- A compliment about a coworker's appearance.
- Asking a coworker for a date.
- A woman looking "up and down" a man as he walks by.
- Referring to women as "girls."

A middle ground of great confusion included such situations as:

- A male boss calling a female "honey."
- A man looking "up and down" a woman as she walks by.
- Men in the office repeatedly discussing the appearance of female coworkers.[34]

In the case that follows, the Supreme Court addressed the question of when mere sexist behavior in the workplace crosses over to become actionable sexual harassment.

Profile Perspective: Assume that the female waitresses at Hooters are constantly subject to touching and groping by male customers. The male customers claim that they are encouraged to do so by the nature of the attire the women are required to wear. Could the women sustain a suit for sexual harassment against the company, claiming that the requirement that they wear these scant uniforms encourages sexual harassment by patrons?

CASE

HARRIS V. FORKLIFT SYSTEMS, INC.

114 S.Ct. 367 (1993)

Justice O'Connor

In this case we consider the definition of a discriminatorily "abusive work environment" (also known as a "hostile work environment") under Title VII of the Civil Rights Act of 1964.

I

Teresa Harris worked as a manager at Forklift Systems, Inc., an equipment rental company, from April 1985 until October 1987. Charles Hardy was Forklift's president.

The Magistrate found that, throughout Harris' time at Forklift, Hardy often insulted her because of her gender and often made her the target of unwanted sexual innuendos. Hardy told Harris on several occasions, in the presence of other employees, "You're a woman, what do you know" and "We need a man as the rental manager"; at least once, he told her she was "a dumb ass woman." Again in front of others, he suggested that the two of them "go to the Holiday Inn to negotiate [Harris's] raise." Hardy occasionally asked Harris and other female employees to get coins from his front pants pocket. He threw objects on the ground in front of Harris and other women, and asked them to pick the objects up. He made sexual innuendos about Harris's and other women's clothing.

In mid-August 1987, Harris complained to Hardy about his conduct. Hardy said he was surprised that Harris was offended, claimed he was only joking, and apologized. He also promised he would stop, and based on this assurance Harris stayed on the job. But in early September,

Continued

Continued

Hardy began anew: While Harris was arranging a deal with one of Forklift's customers, he asked her, again in front of other employees, "What did you do, promise the guy . . . some [sex] Saturday night?" On October 1, Harris collected her paycheck and quit.

Harris then sued Forklift, claiming that Hardy's conduct had created an abusive work environment for her because of her gender. The United States District Court for the Middle District of Tennessee, adopting the report and recommendation of the Magistrate, found this to be "a close case," but held that Hardy's conduct did not create an abusive environment. The court found that some of Hardy's comments "offended [Harris], and would offend the reasonable woman," but that they were not

> so severe as to be expected to seriously affect [Harris's] psychological well-being. A reasonable woman manager under like circumstances would have been offended by Hardy, but his conduct would not have risen to the level of interfering with that person's work performance.
>
> Neither do I believe that [Harris] was subjectively so offended that she suffered injury . . . Although Hardy may at times have genuinely offended [Harris], I do not believe that he created a working environment so poisoned as to be intimidating or abusive to [Harris].

* * *

We granted certiorari to resolve a conflict among the Circuits on whether conduct, to be actionable as "abusive work environment" harassment (no *quid pro quo* harassment issue is present here), must "seriously affect [an employee's] psychological well-being" or lead the plaintiff to "suffe[r] injury."

II

Title VII of the Civil Rights Act of 1964 makes it "an unlawful employment practice for an employer . . . to discriminate against any individual with respect to his compensation, terms, conditions, or privileges of employment, because of such individual's race, color, religion, sex, or national origin." As we made clear in *Meritor Savings Bank* v. *Vinson,* 477 U. S. 57 (1986), this language "is not limited to 'economic' or 'tangible' discrimination. The phrase 'terms, conditions, or privileges of employment' evinces a congressional intent 'to strike at the entire spectrum of disparate treatment of men and women' in employment," which includes requiring people to work in a discriminatorily hostile or abusive environment. When the workplace is permeated with "discriminatory intimidation, ridicule, and insult," that is "sufficiently severe or pervasive to alter the conditions of the victim's employment and create an abusive working environment," Title VII is violated.

This standard, which we reaffirm today, takes a middle path between making actionable any conduct that is merely offensive and requiring the conduct to cause a tangible psychological injury. As we pointed out in *Meritor,* "mere utterance of an . . . epithet which engenders offensive feelings in a employee" does not sufficiently affect the conditions of employment to implicate Title VII. Conduct that is not severe or pervasive enough to create an objectively hostile or abusive work environment—an environment that a reasonable person would find hostile or abusive—is beyond Title VII's purview. Likewise, if the victim does not subjectively perceive the environment to be abusive, the conduct has not actually altered the conditions of the victim's employment, and there is no Title VII violation.

But Title VII comes into play before the harassing conduct leads to a nervous breakdown. A discriminatorily abusive work environment, even one that does not seriously affect employees' psychological well-being, can and often will detract from employees' job performance, discourage employees from remaining on the job, or keep them from advancing in their careers. Moreover, even without regard to these tangible effects, the very fact that the discriminatory conduct was so

Continued

Continued

Justice Scalia, concurring

Meritor Savings Bank v. *Vinson* held that Title VII prohibits sexual harassment that takes the form of a hostile work environment. The Court stated that sexual harassment is actionable if it is "sufficiently severe or pervasive 'to alter the conditions of [the victim's] employment and create an abusive work environment.' " Today's opinion elaborates that the challenged conduct must be severe or pervasive enough "to create an objectively hostile or abusive work environment—an environment that a reasonable person would find hostile or abusive."

"Abusive" (or "hostile," which in this context I take to mean the same thing) does not seem to me a very clear standard—and I do not think clarity is at all increased by adding the adverb "objectively" or by appealing to a "reasonable person's" notion of what the vague word means. Today's opinion does list a number of factors that contribute to abusiveness, but since it neither says how much of each is necessary (an impossible task) nor identifies any single factor as determinative, it thereby adds little certitude. As a practical matter, today's holding lets virtually unguided juries decide whether sex-related conduct engaged in (or permitted by) an employer is egregious enough to warrant an award of damages. One might say that what constitutes "negligence" (a traditional jury question) is not much more clear and certain than what constitutes "abusiveness." Perhaps so. But the class of plaintiffs seeking to recover for negligence is limited to those who have suffered harm, whereas under this statute "abusiveness" is to be the test of whether legal harm has been suffered, opening more expansive vistas of litigation.

Be that as it may, I know of no alternative to the course the Court today has taken. One of the factors mentioned in the Court's nonexhaustive list—whether the conduct unreasonably interferes with an employee's work performance—would, if it were made an absolute test, provide greater guidance to juries and employers. But I see no basis for such a limitation in the language of the statute. Accepting *Meritor*'s interpretation of the term "conditions of employment" as the law, the test is not whether work has been impaired, but whether working conditions have been discriminatorily altered. I know of no test more faithful to the inherently vague statutory language than the one the Court today adopts. For these reasons, I join the opinion of the Court.

Justice Ginsburg, concurring

Today the Court reaffirms the holding of *Meritor Savings Bank* v. *Vinson:* "[A] plaintiff may establish a violation of Title VII by proving that discrimination based on sex has created a hostile or abusive work environment." The critical issue, Title VII's text indicates, is whether members of one sex are exposed to disadvantageous terms or conditions of employment to which members of the other sex are not exposed. As the Equal Employment Opportunity Commission emphasized, the adjudicator's inquiry should center, dominantly, on whether the discriminatory conduct has unreasonably interfered with the plaintiff's work performance. To show such interference, "the plaintiff need not prove that his or her tangible productivity has declined as a result of the harassment." [*Davis* v. *Monsanto Chemical Co.,* 858 F. 2d 345, 349 (CA6 1988)]. It suffices to prove that a reasonable person subjected to the discriminatory conduct would find, as the plaintiff did, that the harassment so altered working conditions as to "ma[k]e it more difficult to do the job."

Questions

1. Justice Scalia (in his concurring opinion) is clearly uncomfortable with what he takes to be the vague standard set down by the majority. Why, then, did he vote with the majority?
2. Summarize Justice Ginsburg's suggested test for establishing a hostile or abusive work environment.
3. *a.* What test did the majority settle on to define sexual harassment of the kind in the *Harris* case?
   b. What constitutional challenge might be raised to that test? Explain.
   c. Are you comfortable with the majority's test in *Harris?*

D. Sexual Stereotypes

Ann B. Hopkins, a Price Waterhouse manager, was hoping in 1982 to be promoted to partner. She had earned at least $34 million in consulting contracts for the firm, a record exceeding that of the 87 other candidates for partner, all of whom were male. Despite her success, Hopkins was denied partnership. She left the firm and filed a sex discrimination claim. The firm says she was an "overbearing, arrogant, and abrasive manager."[35] She argued that her occasional cursing and her sometimes brusque manner would have been overlooked had she been a male.

At trial, she introduced the partners' written evaluations, which included such words and phrases as "macho," "lady partner," and "charm school." One mentioned that "she may have overcompensated for being a woman." Hopkins testified that a chief partner suggested she wear makeup, have her hair styled, walk more femininely, and so on. Based on that evidence and expert testimony, Hopkins claimed she was a victim of sexual stereotyping. The firm offered evidence in support of its contention that Hopkins's personality and interpersonal skills were the issue in the case. One consultant said he left the firm in part because of what he perceived to be the difficulty in working with Hopkins, whom he accused of once "screaming obscenities over the phone at him for 'up to' 45 minutes."[36]

Hopkins won at the district court level, where the court found that Price Waterhouse was guilty of sex discrimination.[37] The District of Columbia Court of Appeals affirmed, finding "ample support for the district court's finding that the partnership selection process was impermissibly infected by stereotypical attitudes toward women."[38] The court went on to hold that Price Waterhouse had to show that bias as a consequence of sexual stereotyping was not the decisive factor in the decision to deny promotion. The case then went to the U.S. Supreme Court. How would you rule on this claim of sexual stereotyping as sex discrimination? [See *Price Waterhouse* v. *Hopkins,* 109 S.Ct. 1775 (1989).] If you find for Hopkins, would you order Price Waterhouse to offer her the partnership she sought? Explain.

E. Equal Pay

Title VII affords protection from discrimination in pay because of sex. The **Equal Pay Act of 1963** directly forbids discrimination on the basis of sex by paying wages to employees of one sex at a rate less than the rate paid to employees of the opposite sex for equal work on jobs requiring equal skill, effort, and responsibility and performed under similar working conditions (*equal* has been interpreted to mean "substantially equal").

Equal Pay Act of 1963. The Act requires equal pay to individuals of either gender.

The act provides for certain exceptions. Unequal wage payments are lawful if paid pursuant to (1) a seniority system, (2) a merit system, (3) a system that measures earnings by quantity or quality of production, or (4) a differential based on "any other factor other than sex." An employer seeking to avoid a violation of the Equal Pay Act can adjust its wage structure by raising the pay of the disfavored sex. Lowering the pay of the favored sex violates the act.

Paying women and men the same amount for the same work is simple enough in principle, but the legal issues have proved slippery, indeed. For example:

- Is travel reimbursement a wage? Maternity payments?[39] [According to the federal government, no.]
- Must the plaintiff establish a pattern of sex-based wage discrimination?[40] [According to the federal government, no.]
- Are jobs unequal in effort, and thus "unequal work," when a part of one job includes tasks that females are physically unable to perform?[41] [No, if those tasks do not constitute a substantial part of the job.]

In the leading case of *Corning Glass Works* v. *Brennan,* the Supreme Court was faced with the question of whether different shifts constituted differing working conditions.[42] Women had been engaged in glass inspection on the day shift. Corning added a night shift of inspectors, which, due to state protective laws, was composed entirely of males. The night shift demanded and received higher wages than the female day inspectors. The Supreme Court held that the time of day in and of itself is not a working condition. That term, the Court said, refers to "surroundings" and "hazards." However, shift differentials could lawfully constitute a "factor other than sex" if established by the employer.

F. Comparable Worth

Equal pay for equal work is hardly a radical notion, but equal pay for work of comparable value would, if fully realized, dramatically alter the nature of the American labor market. **Comparable worth** calls for determining the compensation to be paid for a position based on the job's intrinsic value in comparison to wages being paid for other jobs requiring comparable skills, effort, and responsibility and having comparable worth to the organization.

comparable worth. The legal theory that all employees should be paid the same wages for work requiring comparable skills, effort, and responsibility and having comparable worth to the employer.

The argument is that the dollar value assigned to jobs held predominantly by men is higher than the value assigned to jobs held predominantly by women. To proponents of comparable worth, such disparities cannot be explained by market forces. They argue that women are the continuing victims of sex discrimination in violation of Title VII of the Civil Rights Act of 1964.

A variety of studies have contrasted pay scales in traditionally female jobs with those in traditionally male jobs where the jobs are judged to be of comparable worth. For example, licensed practical nurses in Illinois in 1983 earned an average of $1,298 per month, whereas electricians earned an average of $2,826.[43] A 1987 Child Welfare League study fixed the median salary of garbage collectors at $14,872 annually, as compared with $12,800 for child care workers.[44] The same study found social workers with master's degrees earned about $21,800 per year, whereas auto salespeople averaged $22,048.[45]

There may be market explanations for the inequality between wages in occupations that are traditionally male-dominated as opposed to those jobs that are traditionally female-dominated. Economist and jurist, Judge Richard Posner, explained:

> [While] irrational or exploitive discrimination is one possibility[,] another is that male wages include a compensatory wage premium for the dirty, disagreeable, and often strenuous jobs that men dominate presumably because their aversion to such work is less than women's. Another (these are not mutually exclusive of course) is differences in investments in market-related human capital (earning capacity). If a woman allocates a substantial part of her working life to household production, including child care, she will obtain a substantially lower return on her market human capital than a man planning to devote much less time to household production, and she will therefore invest less in that human capital. Since earnings are in part a return on one's human capital investments (including education), women's earnings will be lower than men's. In part this will show up in the choice of occupations: Women will be attracted to occupations that don't require much human capital. Of course the amount of time women are devoting to household production is declining, so we can expect the wage gap to shrink if the economic model is correct.[46]

Posner concluded by qualifying his comments with "if the economic model is correct." Why might you believe that this model would not be correct or that the wage gap may not shrink completely? If actual prejudice (i.e., prejudging) exists, that is, women are *believed* to be less valuable as workers than men, regardless of their *actual* abilities, then employers may continue to hire men at higher wages. In other words, even though women are actually spending less time at home and the household and child care duties are more likely to be split, employers may still *believe* that women will get pregnant and quit. Given this prejudice, employers will not pay women commensurate with men, notwithstanding market influences. Do you agree?

A number of companies, state governments, and foreign countries practice some form of comparable worth, but most continue to rely on the market as the best measure of worth. The U.S. Supreme Court has yet to directly explore the substance of the comparable worth debate. In the *Gunther*[47] case, the Court held, in effect, that Title VII does not forbid the comparable worth theory. However, federal appeals court decisions to date have rejected the comparable worth theory in the context of Title VII sex discrimination.[48]

IV. Affirmative Action

The struggle for civil rights in the workplace sometimes cannot be achieved, in the short run, simply by avoiding discriminatory practices. Obviously, obeying the law is expected of all. However, as a matter of social policy, we have decided that mere compliance with the civil rights laws, guaranteeing equal opportunity in the workplace, is not always adequate to correct the wrongs of discrimination. Among other problems, a great deal of time ordinarily would need to pass before the lingering effects of past discrimination would no longer be felt if we were to do nothing more than not practice discrimination. Therefore, we have decided as a society to implement the policy that we label **affirmative action** as a means of remedying past wrongs and preventing the same in the future. In following an affirmative action plan, employers consciously take positive steps to seek out minorities and women for hiring and promotion opportunities, and they often employ goals and timetables to measure progress toward a workforce that is representative of the qualified labor pool.

affirmative action. A government/private sector program, springing from the civil rights movement, designed to *actively promote* the employment and educational opportunities of protected classes rather than merely forbidding discrimination.

Affirmative action efforts arise in two ways: (1) courts may order the implementation of affirmative action after a finding of wrongful discrimination, and (2) employers may voluntarily adopt affirmative action plans. Some may do so because they believe it is a wise management strategy or because they approve of affirmative action as a matter of social policy, or both. Others may adopt affirmative action because they wish to do business with the federal government. All government contractors must meet the affirmative action standards of the Office of Federal Contract Compliance Programs. As discussed above, those standards consist essentially of established goals and timetables for strengthening the representation of "underutilized" minorities and women.

Good Policy? Affirmative action is one of the most hotly disputed social issues in contemporary life. Minorities and women have been the victims of discrimination. Should white males "pay" for those wrongs? Critics decry affirmative action as reverse discrimination. They argue that affirmative action is paternalistic and encourages the view that minorities and women can progress only with the aid of white males.[49] Studies confirm that affirmative action plans stigmatize minorities and women in the minds of coworkers. Minorities and women are often assumed to have achieved their positions via quotas and not as the result of their efforts and abilities.[50]

Now, many white males feel that they are surrounded and under siege by the forces of affirmative action and multiculturalism. Even if so, *Newsweek* argues that being a white man is still a very comfortable role in contemporary America:

> But is the white male truly an endangered species, or is he just being a jerk? It's still a statistical piece of cake being a white man, at least in comparison with being anything else. White males make up just 39.2 percent of the population, yet they account for 82.5 percent of the Forbes 400 (folks worth at least $265 million), 77 percent of Congress, 92 percent of state governors, 70 percent of tenured college faculty, almost 90 percent of daily-newspaper editors, 77 percent of TV news directors. They dominate just about everything but NOW and the NAACP.[51]

Affirmative Action in Practice. *United Steelworkers of America* v. *Weber* is perhaps the clearest Supreme Court statement to date about the permissible boundaries of affirmative action.[52] Weber, a white male, challenged the legality of an affirmative action plan that set aside for black employees 50 percent of the openings in a training program until the percentage of black craft workers in the plant equaled the percentage of blacks in the local labor market. Weber was denied entry to the training program. The federal district court and the federal court of appeals held for Weber, but the U.S. Supreme Court reversed. Therefore, under *Weber,* race-conscious affirmative action remedies *can* be permissible. Several qualities of the Steelworkers' plan were instrumental in the Court's favorable ruling:

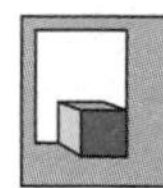

1. The affirmative action was part of a plan.
2. The plan was designed to "open employment opportunities for Negroes in occupations which have been traditionally closed to them."
3. The plan was temporary.
4. The plan did not unnecessarily harm the rights of white employees. That is, (*a*) it did not require the discharge of white employees; (*b*) it did not create an absolute bar to the advancement of white employees.

Therefore, affirmative action in situations like that in *Weber* does not constitute unlawful reverse discrimination.

The Supreme Court clarified the law's affirmative action commands a bit further in the *Burdine* case, in which the Court asserted that Title VII does not require the employer to hire a minority or female applicant whenever that person's objective qualifications were equal to those of a white male applicant. Therefore, "the employer has discretion to choose among equally qualified candidates, provided the decision is not based upon unlawful criteria."[53]

Profile Perspective: If the male plaintiffs are successful in the Hooters case, what type of affirmative action plan might the court encourage?

Recent Developments. In 1995, the Supreme Court ruled that any contracting or hiring practice based on race must meet an extremely high legal standard to be lawful. The following article addresses the implications of this decision.

Supreme Court Ruling Imperils U.S. Programs of Racial Preference

by Paul M. Barrett

The Supreme Court joined the assault on affirmative action, attacking the foundations of the vast federal network of programs providing preferential treatment to minorities.

In a 5–4 decision, the high court ruled that Congress must meet an extremely tough legal standard to justify any contracting or hiring practice based on race.

The court's conservative majority stopped short of striking down any particular program. But yesterday's decision is sure to provoke a raft of court challenges against government minority-preference programs and to fuel the growing political backlash against affirmative action.

"This signals the beginning of the end for the era of racial preferences," said Clint Bolick of the Institute for Justice in Washington, a conservative activist who is helping to lead the charge against affirmative action. Lawyer William Coleman, a former transportation secretary and longtime advocate of affirmative action, called the ruling "a very dishonest and shocking opinion."

Justice Sandra Day O'Connor wrote the majority opinion, declaring that "strict scrutiny of all governmental racial classifications is essential" to distinguish between legitimate programs that redress past discrimination and programs that "are in fact motivated by illegitimate notions of racial inferiority or simple racial politics." As a practical matter, this "strict scrutiny" test will be very hard for the government to meet, although Justice O'Connor added that it needn't be seen as "fatal" for all affirmative action programs.

Justices Antonin Scalia and Clarence Thomas said in separate concurring opinions that they would have gone much further, wiping out all government race preferences. "These programs stamp minorities with a badge of inferiority and may cause them to develop dependencies or to adopt an attitude that they are 'entitled' to preferences," wrote Justice Thomas, the only minority-group member on the high court.

Filling out the majority were Chief Justice William Rehnquist and Justice Anthony Kennedy. Justices John Paul Stevens, David Souter, Ruth Bader Ginsburg and Stephen Breyer dissented.

* * *

Effect on Contractors

The decision's most immediate effects are likely to be felt among the tens of thousands of small companies that do business with the federal government. Last year, the government set aside $6.4 billion of contracts for minority businesses, in industries ranging from construction to computer services. In addition, the government provided incentives and set goals that helped bring the total amount of federal contracts going to minority-owned firms to $14.4 billion, or 8.3 percent of federal procurement—a sharp increase from 3.6 percent a decade earlier.

Those programs have changed the face of American small business, helping many minority-owned firms to get their start but also provoking a wave of resentment among white-owned firms that lost business as a result.

* * *

Smaller employers subject to this regulation have had more trouble complying with it and would be more likely to try to use yesterday's ruling to attack it in court, according to Stephen Bokat, general counsel of the U.S. Chamber of Commerce. But it is unlikely that large companies will drop special minority hiring efforts in the immediate future, Mr. Bokat thinks. "The AT&Ts and IBMS have well-entrenched programs and have the resources to get through the regulatory maze that affirmative action can create, and they would just as soon not see it undone," he predicts.

* * *

Overturning Precedent

The Supreme Court majority took the unusual step yesterday of formally overruling one of its two major precedents upholding federal affirmative action and thoroughly eviscerating the other one. Justice O'Connor wrote that the court had simply gone astray in 1990 when it upheld Federal Communications Com-

Continued

Continued

mission preferences for minorities seeking broadcast licenses. That 5–4 ruling "undermined important principles of this Court's equal protection jurisprudence," she maintained. Four members of the 1990 majority have left the court.

* * *

Not "Fatal"

Justice O'Connor went out of her way to "dispel the notion that strict scrutiny is strict in theory, but fatal in fact." She held out the possibility that some federal programs could be sustained under the high court's tougher new standard. Yesterday's decision "alters the playing field in some important respects," she said, but the best course would be to leave it to lower courts to take the first crack at applying the new standard for federal affirmative action.

Questions

1. Do you agree with the Court's ruling? Why or why not? What are the implications of your decision?
2. Should racial preferences be allowed to rectify an imbalance in workplace racial representation?
3. Assume that economists can prove that discriminating firms will die out in the long run because decisions in those firms are not based on true qualifications but instead on race. Would you still support affirmative action? If not, are you not concerned that the effect of this "market correction" might take an awfully long time? What is to remedy the situation of workers *today?*

Source: *The Wall Street Journal,* June 13, 1995; p. A1.

V. Additional Discrimination Topics

A. The Americans with Disabilities Act

In 1990, Congress and President Bush approved the Americans with Disabilities Act (ADA), among the most far-reaching pieces of protective legislation in the nation's history. The ADA forbids discrimination in employment, public accommodations, public services, transportation, and telecommunications against the 43 million Americans who are disabled. The act seeks to remove barriers to a full, productive life for disabled Americans while eliminating humiliations, such as the following, that have often accompanied impairments:

- The Kentucky woman who was dismissed from a job because her AIDS-stricken son moved back home.
- The blind Harvard Law School graduate who wrote to 600 corporations three times over without receiving a single job offer.
- The college that refused to hire a severely arthritic woman because trustees thought "normal students shouldn't see her."
- The paralyzed Vietnam veteran who must use the service entrance to restaurants because the regular doorways are too narrow for his wheelchair.[54]

Although the act guarantees access to public transportation, shopping malls, restaurants, doctors' offices, and all public accommodations and services, as well as telephone access for 24 million hearing-impaired and 3 million speech-impaired Americans, we will limit our exploration to the employment provisions of the new legislation.

Prior to the passage of the ADA, disabled individuals were protected by federal law (the Rehabilitation Act of 1973) against employment discrimination only in public-sector jobs and those jobs in the private sector for which employers received federal grants or contracts. The ADA both forbids private-sector employment discrimination against disabled workers and applicants and amends and updates the Rehabilitation Act, affirming broad protection in public-sector and publicly funded employment. Small businesses with fewer than 15 employees are exempted from the employment elements of the act.

A disabled person is an individual who (1) has a physical or mental impairment that substantially limits one or more major life activities, (2) has a record of such an impairment, or (3) is regarded as having such an impairment. Major life activities include caring for oneself, seeing, hearing, learning, and working, for example. One who has a history of cancer, for example, might have a record of such an impairment. And one might be viewed by others as impaired because of, for example, a physical deformity when, in fact, that condition does not impair job performance in any material way.

Defining Disability. Blindness, hearing loss, mental retardation, cosmetic disfigurement, anatomical loss, and disfiguring scars are examples of **covered disabilities.** Alcoholism, drug abuse, and AIDS are covered. However, the ADA specifically excludes job applicants and employees who *currently* use illegal drugs when the employer acts on the basis of such use. Thus, the act covers those who are rehabilitated and no longer using illegal drugs, those in rehabilitation and no longer using illegal drugs, and those erroneously regarded as using illegal drugs. Employers may expect the same performance and behavior from alcoholics and drug abusers as from all other employees. In sum, the ADA treats alcoholism and drug addiction as medical problems and protects those who are overcoming their impairments.

Specifically excluded as disabilities are homosexuality, bisexuality, exhibitionism, gambling, kleptomania, and pyromania, among others. Questions regarding which conditions constitute disabilities will continue to require litigation. For example, in interpreting the federal Rehabilitation Act and state disability laws, some courts have treated obesity as a disability while others have not.

Reasonable Accommodation. An employer may not discriminate in hiring or employment against a **qualified person with a disability.** A qualified person is one who can perform the **essential functions** of the job. The ADA requires employers to make

covered disabilities. A physical or mental impairment that substantially limits one or more major life activities of an individual; a record of such impairment or being regarded as having such impairment.

qualified person with a disability. An individual with a covered disability who can perform the essential functions of her or his position, with or without reasonable accommodation.

essential functions of a position. Those tasks that are fundamental, as opposed to marginal or unnecessary, to the fulfillment of the position's objectives.

DISCRIMINATING QUESTIONS

Legal and illegal versions of similar job-interview questions:

Legal	*Illegal*
Do you have 20-20 corrected vision?	What is your corrected vision?
How well can you handle stress?	Does stress ever affect your ability to be productive?
Can you perform this function with or without reasonable accommodation?	Would you need reasonable accommodation to perform this job?
How many days were you absent from work last year?	How many days were you sick last year?
Are you currently using illegal drugs?	What medications are you currently taking?
Do you regularly eat three meals a day?	Do you need to eat a number of small meals at regular intervals throughout the day to maintain your energy level?
Do you drink alcohol?	How much alcohol do you drink per week?

Source: EEOC's "Enforcement Guidance on Pre-employment Disability-Related Inquiries," May 1994, cited in *The Wall Street Journal,* July 15, 1994, p. B1. Reprinted by permission of *The Wall Street Journal.*

reasonable accommodation. An accommodation to an individual's disability or religion that does not place an undue burden on the employer, which may be determined by looking to the size of the employer, the cost to the employer, the type of employer, and the impact of the accommodation on the employer's operations.

undue hardship. A burden imposed on an employer by accommodating an individual's disability or religion that would be too onerous for the employer to bear.

reasonable accommodations for disabled employees and applicants. Reasonable accommodations might include such things as structural changes in the workplace, job reassignment, job restructuring, or new equipment.

Hardship. An employer's primary defense is that of **undue hardship.** An employer need not make an accommodation to a disabled person if that adjustment would be unduly expensive, substantial, or disruptive. An employer can call on the hardship defense only after an appropriate accommodation has been identified. All new facilities must be accessible to disabled parties unless structurally impractical, but Congress appears to have intended that changes to existing facilities should not be required if they would involve large expense.

The ADA does not require affirmative action plans or quotas. Unqualified applicants need not be hired, and one who cannot perform the essential functions of the job after reasonable accommodations may be discharged.

Compliance Costs. The EEOC has estimated that the average cost per disabled employee for a company complying with the ADA will be $261.[55] A *Wall Street Journal* survey of 79 companies found that 61 percent of the respondents felt that compliance with the law would be easy; 28 percent thought it would be difficult.[56] The Principal Financial Group explained its compliance experience in accommodating the needs of a hearing-impaired employee:

> The Principal made accommodations for a deaf pension-department employee for less than $300. This involved hiring an interpreter for the job evaluation (approximately $40 for two hours/once per year), restructuring the job (no cost), purchasing a telecommunicative device (TDD) to enable the employee to use the telephone ($239), and educating other employees in the department (no cost).[57]

As the following article suggests, not every accommodation is so low-cost or effective.

Unreasonable Accommodation: The Case Against the Americans with Disabilities Act

by Brian Doherty

Though only five years ago, 1990 was a different political era. A kinder, gentler Republican president was in the White House, the Democrats controlled Congress, and Sen. Edward Kennedy praised Senate Minority Leader Bob Dole for his key role in passing a new antidiscrimination law.

Any sweeping regulatory package in civil rights wrappings that wins the enthusiastic support of those two is bound to mean trouble. The law was the Americans with Disabilities Act, and it gives the feds veto rights over such issues as whether a prospective employer can ask a would-be trucker if he has epilepsy; how far grab bars must be from the back walls of toilet stalls; what surfaces are permitted for subway platforms; how restaurant seating must be arranged; and dozens of other aspects of running businesses and city governments.

* * *

Once the bill was in motion, a disabled person from every member's district was sent to lobby for the ADA. "You'd look out into the hall and see 50 people in wheelchairs and people climbing out of

Continued

Continued

wheelchairs trying to crawl up the Capitol steps, and logic and rationality go out the window," reminisces Lori Eisner, a staffer for Rep. Tom DeLay (R-TX), one of the few congressmen to vote against the ADA. "The ADA is filled with lack of definition, everything's open-ended, but the attitude was, this is a good-feeling thing, let the courts decide."

The "good-feeling thing" is now reality, and it doesn't feel nearly as good as promised. The ADA has emerged as a prime example of congressional irresponsibility. While many of its specific results surely could not have been intended, the law's vague prescriptions and wide reach guaranteed it would become, and will remain, an expensive headache to millions without necessarily improving the lives of its supposed beneficiaries.

* * *

[Restaurateur Blair Taylor] owns the Barolo Grill in Denver—"a very high profile, upscale, Jags-and-Rolls-Royces type of Italian restaurant in an expensive shopping district called Cherry Creek" . . .

Taylor is "a 40-year-old yuppieish kind of white guy. I'm a safe, wonderful target for these things." "These things" for Taylor mean nearly two years of legal conflicts with both the Justice Department and the City of Denver that ended up costing around $100,000 in construction and legal fees.

Taylor's troubles started in December 1992, just after opening the Grill, with a phone call from the DOJ . . . "They told me they were investigating complaints for noncompliance," he says. He wasn't immediately responsive: "The first week of running a new restaurant isn't when you have a lot of free time." Taylor insists that he could take a walk from his restaurant and find 40 businesses in worse ADA shape than his was . . . "[The DOJ] will just say, 'No, Mr. Taylor was a horrible person.' "

Not exactly a horrible person, but DOJ civil rights lawyer Kate Nicholson, who worked on the Barolo case, does call Taylor "very difficult." She denies any malice or example-making, stressing that Taylor made continual promises to make changes by given dates and missed them all. DOJ isn't generally quick to sue, she says.

DOJ was unhappy with the four-inch step up to the door of the Barolo Grill, even though parking valets would always be available to help the wheelchair users over the hump. Justice Department enforcers also didn't like the 11-inch raised platform in the back of the Barolo, with 9 tables, in addition to the 17 on the main floor.

A ramp to the platform was built, destroyed, then rebuilt in response to Justice's complaints. The first time the ramp wasn't long enough for DOJ's very detailed building standards. The ramp is now the requisite 11 feet long and 41 inches wide to navigate an 11-inch rise, costing Taylor three tables' worth of space in his usually sold-out restaurant.

The front ramp created a whole new set of problems, since it violated Denver city ordinances and required variances. "I said, 'I promised the federal government I'd do this ASAP, and city law won't let me do it?' " says Taylor. "It was an eight-and-a-half month process through various city boards.

* * *

By February 1994, Taylor had city permits for his ramps, bathrooms, fire alarm, roof drainage, sanitary water waste management tests, new air systems, and strobe lighting— "a tremendous number of irrelevant things that were at the bottom about putting in two ramps." The DOJ went ahead and sued anyway in April, since they still had complaints.

* * *

Its complaints included: The handrails on the entrance ramp had two more inches between them and the restaurant's window than the law allows; the restroom grab bar was mounted two and a half inches too far from the back wall; carpeting ended two inches before the patio door; and the wine storage room didn't have a ramp to its door (which was also not wide enough).

* * *

The suit was settled with a $16,000 fine. Six thousand dollars of it went to protestors from Atlantis/ADAPT, a local handicapped-activist group that picketed the Barolo Grill.

The federal government flew two attorneys for every meeting, gave them hotels, rental cars, meals. "They came in from DC seven times," says Taylor. "We figure at least $250,000 was spent to force a restaurant in Denver to comply." He says the restaurant

Continued

Continued

continues to average about one wheelchair-using patron a month—the same as before the case: "nor have we ever once had a customer's wheel touch the ramp to the upper platform."

* * *

Sitting in the handicapped-accessible restaurant that cost him more months and more thousands of dollars and more grief than he could have imagined, Blair Taylor says, "I want to be helpful because I'm a nice person. I don't want to be forced to do something to help you to the detriment of my own well-being."

Questions

1. *a.* If the DOJ had "very detailed building standards," how could Taylor allow the ramp to the platform be built the first time *not* according to those standards? What do you think happened?

   b. Consider some of the DOJ's later concerns. If the restroom's grab bar was not mounted correctly, wheelchair-using patrons may not be able to use it at all. Do you believe the DOJ's concerns were trivial?
2. When you first read this account, for whom did you feel sympathy? Was it the poor restaurateur who believes that he was just used as a scapegoat to set an example? Or do you feel more for the DOJ, which was repeatedly ignored, and the disabled patrons who really couldn't use a ramp (or other accommodations) unless it *did* comply with the regulations?
3. On whose shoulders should the burden of these types of public accommodation fall? Could you argue that perhaps the government should allow a subsidy to those businesses that are required to modify their environments to more fully serve the public? Do you agree with Taylor's last sentence?

Source: Reprinted with permission from the August–September issue of *Reason Magazine*. Copyright © 1995 by the Reason Foundation, 3415 S.Sepulveda Blvd., Suite 400, Los Angeles CA 90034.

Profile Perspective: Assume that Sara applies for a position as a Hooters waitress. Sara is qualified for the position. Unfortunately, she lost the use of her right eye in an accident several years ago and must wear a patch on that eye at all times. The patch does not interfere with any of her waitressing abilities. Hooters refuses to hire her because she does not have the right "look" for the restaurant. Is Hooters in violation of the ADA?

B. Age Discrimination

America has a culture in which youth is valued. It must be very strange indeed to people in other cultures, like the Japanese, who revere age and believe that with it comes wisdom and insight unobtainable by the young. In our culture, the general perception is that with youth comes energy, imagination, and innovation. With age comes decreasing interest, lack of innovation and imagination, and a lessening of the quality of the person.

Older employees suffer from these perceptions in the workplace, subtle and unconscious though they may be. Although statistics show that older workers are more reliable, harder working, more committed, and less prone to absenteeism than younger workers—all characteristics that employers say they value—the general perception of them as employees is exactly the opposite. This adversely affects older workers, who may not be treated as well because they are perceived as less desirable employees.

Many employers feel older employees may be more expensive to retain because they have greater experience and seniority. Each year they may receive a raise until their salary becomes a burden on the firm. Management realizes that it could reduce costs by terminating older employees, who may have more experience than necessary to perform the requirements of the position, and hiring younger, less experienced employees.

This may seem to be a realistic and legitimate business decision, but once terminated, older workers are disadvantaged in the search for new employment. Either they are viewed as overqualified or employers express concern about their ability to adequately perform. The concerns are usually based on preconceived, stereotypical notions about the deterioration of an older worker's senses, physical capabilities, response time, and competence. Although some generalizations may be grounded in fact, the act of generalizing rather than making individualized conclusions constitutes wrongful discrimination.

As a result of these stereotypes, the Age Discrimination in Employment Act (ADEA) was enacted to prohibit employers (including state and local governments), employment agencies, and labor organizations from discriminating because of age against employees 40 years of age or older, thus eliminating mandatory retirement for most occupations. The ADEA permits both private lawsuits and action by the EEOC.

Age discrimination is established under disparate treatment/disparate impact analysis similar to that for race and sex, although three Supreme Court justices recently, and pointedly, noted that no *high court* decision has incorporated disparate impact into ADEA law.[58]

BFOQ. The chief defense available to an employer-defendant is the bona fide occupational qualification. In essence, an employer must demonstrate that only employees of a certain age can safely or efficiently complete the work in question. Thus, in *Hodgson* v. *Greyhound Lines,*[59] the bus company defended its policy of hiring intercity drivers 34 years of age or younger. Greyhound demonstrated that its safest drivers were those 50 to 55 years of age with 16 to 20 years of driving experience with Greyhound—two qualifications that those 40 years of age or older (the protected class) could not attain. Given that evidence, the company was able to lawfully maintain its policy.

Cases. In recent years, we have seen an explosion of age discrimination complaints. Nearly 23,000 claims were filed with the federal and state governments in the first half of 1992, a total equaling that for all of 1985.[60] Most complaints do not reach court: Many result in dismissals, but those that are settled can be very expensive, ranging typically from \$50,000 to \$400,000 per worker.[61] Claims often arise simply from ill-advised remarks:

> Claims vary from allegations that managers spoke of getting "new blood" or told older people they were "slowing down" to charges that workers were coerced into retirement. A 41-year-old former claims representative for Allstate Insurance Co., who said a company official told her that Allstate wanted a "younger and cuter" image, won a \$2.8 million award.[62]

Allstate planned to appeal.

Layoffs. The huge layoffs of the early 1990s have hit hard at older workers. In 1993, McDonnell Douglas agreed to pay \$20.1 million to settle EEOC charges of age discrimination in laying off or forcing retirement for 10,000 St. Louis employees.[63] Nine hundred were at least 55 years old, and the EEOC argued that 370 fewer workers should have been cut from that group.[64] McDonnell Douglas contends it did not discriminate.

Although the case law has been split in instances in which older, higher-paid employees were laid off to reduce costs, a 1993 Supreme Court decision appears to have settled some of those cases in which disparate treatment is at issue. In *Hazen Paper*[65] (see question 3 at end of next article), the Court held that no disparate treatment exists when the motivating factor in the decision is something other than the employee's age (such as salary, pension status, years of service, or seniority), even though that factor may be correlated to age.

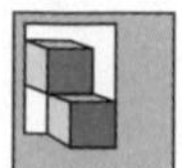

Europe. As the next article reveals, the United States has a much firmer age discrimination policy than do most European nations.

Profile Perspective: Assume that Barbara has applied for a position as a Hooters waitress. Barbara is 53 years old and in excellent condition. Hooters does not hire her, saying that its customers prefer younger females as waitresses and that the restaurant would lose business if all of its waitresses were over 50. Is Hooters in violation of the ADEA?

Forty-Somethings Face Greater Job Discrimination in Europe Than Here

by Chris Conte

Age discrimination is illegal in the United States, but European employers legally can—and often do—refuse to consider job applications from older people, reports the Wyatt Co. The consulting firm says many Europeans who lose jobs after age 45 can only find short-term contracts or temporary work. A lawsuit recently forced the British Civil Service to modify its practice of only recruiting people who are under 30, though.

Employers in most European countries also can force employees to retire when they reach the normal age of eligibility for pensions—between 55 and 67, depending on the country. But some countries require advance notice for such layoffs, and others require extended jobless benefits for workers who don't have pensions or some other source of retirement income.

Questions

1. Metz alleges that he was fired in violation of the ADEA. He had been a plant manager for a company that was experiencing financial problems. His employer notified him that the plant would be closed and he would be laid off. The company then sent the assistant manager of another plant, Burzloff, to Metz's plant to inspect it and make repairs. Burzloff requested that he be allowed to manage Metz's plant; the employer approved this request and discharged Metz. At the time of his layoff, the 54-year-old Metz had a salary of $15.75 an hour; when the 43-year-old Burzloff replaced Metz, his salary was $8.05 per hour.[66]

   Metz had worked for Transit for 27 years. He had received raises each year, even though the company was not profitable during some of those years. The company decided its poor financial performance did not justify retaining Metz, whose salary was comparatively high. Metz was not asked to take a pay cut before he was dismissed. The court framed the issue in the case in this manner:

   > The sole issue on appeal is whether the salary savings that can be realized by replacing a single employee in the ADEA age-protected range with a younger, lower-salaried employee constitutes a permissible, nondiscriminatory justification for the replacement.[67]

   Resolve that issue. Explain.

2. Assume you own a clothing store designed to appeal primarily to the "young adult" market. Should the law permit you to hire only young adults as salespersons? Explain.

3. Walter Biggins, a then-62-year-old chemist, believed he deserved a raise from $44,000 to $100,000 annually from his small, family-owned Holyoke, Massachusetts, employer, Hazen Paper Co.[68] Initially courteous discussions descended to rancor, and Biggins was fired weeks before his pension was to vest. He was entitled to damages under ERISA, but Biggins also claimed age discrimination. A jury found a willful violation of the ADEA. The federal district court overruled the jury on the willfulness issue. The court of appeals reversed, giving considerable weight to evidence of pension interference, including testimony that Hazen had offered to keep Biggins as a consultant, in which capacity he would not have received his pension.

   As mentioned earlier, the Supreme Court ruled that an employer does not violate the ADEA by firing an older employee to prevent pension benefits from vesting. Why did the Court reach that decision? [See *Hazen Paper Company* v. *Walter F. Biggins,* 113 S.Ct. 1701 (1993).]

Source: *The Wall Street Journal,* July 27, 1993, p. A1. Reprinted by permission of *The Wall Street Journal.*

C. Religious Discrimination

In general terms, discrimination on the basis of religion is to be analyzed in the manner of the other protected classes specified by Title VII. Religion is not limited to orthodox faiths, but it does exclude mere shams designed to legitimize otherwise impermissible conduct. The Supreme Court has defined the necessary faith as a "sincere and meaningful belief occupying in the life of its possessor a place parallel to that filled by the God of those admittedly qualified."[69]

In the absence of an appropriate defense (for example, BFOQ), an employer cannot decline to hire or otherwise discriminate against an individual or group on the grounds of religion. The plaintiff's problem in such cases is to prove that religious bias was the motivation for the disputed employment practice. Discrimination on the grounds of religion is permissible if "an employer demonstrates that he is unable to reasonably accommodate an employee's or prospective employee's religious observance or practice without undue hardship on the conduct of the employer's business." Thus, the primary issue in the area of religious discrimination has come to be that of determining reasonable accommodation in varying factual settings.

The leading case is *Trans World Airlines, Inc.* v. *Hardison,* in which the Sabbatarian plaintiff worked in a parts warehouse that operated around the clock, seven days a week.[70] Because of a transfer, Hardison was at the bottom of the departmental seniority list and was unable to take his Sabbath off. The company conferred with Hardison and permitted the union to seek a swap of shifts or a change in jobs, but the efforts were unsuccessful. A seniority modification could not be agreed on, and the company rejected Hardison's request for a four-day week because the solution would have required the use of another employee at premium pay.

The Supreme Court's opinion in the case reduced the employer's duty to a very modest standard: "To require TWA to bear more than a de minimis cost in order to give Hardison Saturdays off is an undue hardship." Saturdays off for Hardison would have imposed extra costs on TWA and would have constituted religious discrimination against other employees who would have sought Saturday off for reasons not grounded in religion. The *Hardison* court also took the position that the collective bargaining agreement's seniority provisions need not give way to accommodate religious observance. The Court found sufficient accommodation in TWA's reducing weekend shift sizes and allowing voluntary trading of shifts.

By contrast, the Supreme Court declined to review a federal court of appeals decision holding that an employer failed to reasonably accommodate an employee who declined to work on Sundays when the employer made no effort to find substitutes, did not permit employees to post bulletin-board notices seeking substitutes, and did not itself use the bulletin board to seek volunteers to replace the employee.[71]

VI. Employer Liability

Respondeat Superior. Employers increasingly bear civil liability both for their employees' job-related mistakes and misconduct and for rather new forms of negligence claims against the employers for their decisions in hiring, retaining, training, and supervising employees. Under the doctrine of ***respondeat superior*** (let the master respond), employers have long been held vicariously (indirectly) liable for harm to third parties caused by the intentional or negligent acts of their employees. Of course, those acts must have occurred in the scope of employment.

respondeat superior. "Let the master respond." A doctrine that allows a third party to sue an employer for the acts of its employees.

Believe It!
A Florida employer that allowed a drunk sales representative to drive home after a social function was held liable for the resulting accident in which another motorist was killed. The employee ran a stop sign after having 13 alcoholic beverages.

The Test. Of course, finding the employer liable does not excuse the employee from liability. But the *respondeat superior* doctrine does have the potential effect of opening the employer's deeper pockets to the plaintiff. The general trend in these cases has been to expand the definition of the scope of employment. Presently, the standard requires all of the following ingredients:

1. The employee was subject to the employer's supervision.
2. The employee was motivated, at least in part, by desire to serve the employer's business interests.
3. The problem arose substantially within normal working hours and in a work location.
4. The act in question was of the general kind the employee had been hired to perform.

Who's an Employee? This might seem to be one of the easier questions presented in this text; unfortunately, that's not the case. Many people who we consider employees are actually **independent contractors.** Employers do not owe the same duties to independent contractors as they do to their employees. Similarly, an employer may not be liable for the acts of its independent contractors under *respondeat superior.*

independent contractor. A person who contracts with a principal to perform some task according to his or her own methods, and who is not under the principal's control regarding the physical details of the work.

Courts have offered varied interpretations of whether or not someone is an employee. Generally, the interpretation used depends on the factual circumstances presented by each case and the law that is at issue. Although many laws refer to similar definitions of "employee" or "independent contractor," other laws or regulations may rely on entirely different tests to answer the issue. Congress has responded by stating that employees are those who are not classified as independent contractors. The House has further explained that an employee is "one who works for another." The National Labor Relations Act states that "the term 'employee' shall not include . . . any individual having the status of an independent contractor" but does not define independent contractor.

A persuasive indicator of independent contractor status is the ability to control the manner in which the work is performed. The employer need not actually control the work, but must merely have the *right or ability to control the work.* The distinction made is whether the employment agreement is merely to perform, or to perform in a certain manner and under certain circumstances.

On the other hand, a number of other considerations may also be analyzed in reaching determinations. For example, it has been held that an employee is one who works for wages or salary and is under direct supervision. An independent contractor has been defined as one who does a job for a price, decides how the work will be done, usually hires others to do the work, and depends for income not upon wages, but upon the difference between what he or she pays for goods, materials, and labor and what he or she receives for the end result, that is, upon profits.

Once an employer determines who is and who is not an employee, one final issue exists. Many statutes and regulations apply only if the employer has a requisite number of employees. How are employees counted? As of what date? Do part-time workers count? What if an employer hires a large number of employees, but only a few report to work on any given day?

For example, Title VII provides that an employer is covered by the proscriptions of the statute if it employs 15 or more employees for each working day in each of 20 or more calendar weeks in the current or preceding calendar year. But what is a "working day"? It is generally held that this number should be computed by counting the number of employees maintained on the payroll in a given week, as opposed to the number of employees who work on any one day.

However, this form of calculation is merely the majority approach; other courts have found that part-time employees who work for any part of each day of the workweek should be counted, and part-time employees who work full days for only a portion of the workweek should not be counted.

VII. Cautious Hiring

Negligent Hiring. In recent years, employers' potential liability for employee wrongdoing has been significantly expanded by a line of cases finding employers liable for negligence in hiring an employee or retaining an employee who subsequently causes harm to a third party. Typically, the employer is liable on negligence grounds for hiring or retaining an employee whom the employer knew or should have known to be dangerous, incompetent, dishonest, or the like where that information was directly related to the injury suffered by the plaintiff.

For example, an International House of Pancakes restaurant in Georgia was sued when DeLima, a waitress, became upset with two patrons, Jackson and Odom, whom DeLima believed to be intoxicated and excessively boisterous. DeLima "manhandled" Jackson. Then she grabbed Odom by the hair, punched her face several times, and poured coffee down her back (after Odom had thrown a cup of coffee at DeLima). The patrons sued IHOP for negligent hiring, among other claims, but the court dismissed that claim because the restaurant had no knowledge of prior violent behavior by the waitress, and she had denied having had any such problems when completing her employment application.[72]

Discrimination/Privacy. Employers' interests in avoiding negligent hiring problems sometimes conflict with the state's duty to erase employment discrimination. Equal employment opportunity laws and privacy considerations limit employers' permissible lines of inquiry in employment interviews (see also "Testing and Employee Privacy"). For some time, employers have been cautioned against inquiring into applicants' arrest/conviction records in the absence of clear job relatedness. Similarly, questions about sexual preference and marital status raise discrimination concerns. Now, with the passage of the Americans with Disabilities Act, questions regarding medical history and impairments must be carefully constructed. Further, such seemingly reasonable questions as how the applicant would meet child care duties or whether the applicant could be available on weekends might raise concerns about discrimination based on gender and religion.[73]

Recently, the Target chain of discount stores, without admitting fault, agreed to pay $1.3 million to settle the claims of an estimated 2,500 applicants for security positions who took the Rodgers Condensed CPI-MMPI "psychscreen" test in California. The true-false questions that follow illustrate those that raised discrimination and privacy concerns:

- I have never been in trouble because of my sex behavior.
- I have not had difficulty starting or holding my bowel movement.
- I am fascinated by fire.

- I believe there is a God.
- I would like to be a florist.[74]

Understand that lawsuits based on wrongful interview questions are uncommon and difficult to prove. Further, if the interview is restricted to job-related questions, no legal problems are likely.

References. Similarly, a sharp growth in defamation claims against employers has limited the usefulness of checking references when undertaking a hiring decision. Approximately 40 percent of larger American corporations have written policies declining to comment on employees without their permission.[75] Of course, the truth is a complete defense in these cases, and firms that avoid secondhand information, personal issues, and potential discrimination themes such as age are very likely not to have problems. However, a mistake can be expensive.

> As an example of how costly it can be to violate somebody's rights when giving a job reference, a salesman was awarded $1.9 million when his former employer told a prospective employer that the salesman was a "classical sociopath," a "zero," and was disliked by office personnel.
>
> In another case, four dental-claim adjusters for an insurance company were fired for gross insubordination following a dispute over filling out an expense report. Although the company did not inform any prospective employer of the reasons for the firing, the former employees had to list the reason for their termination on new job applications.
>
> The court awarded the workers $570,000 on grounds that when they were forced to tell a new employer the reason for their firings, it was the same as the insurance company's offering the damaging reason.[76]

Broadly, a successful defamation suit requires:

1. A false and defamatory statement.
2. The statement must be "published" to a third party.
3. The employer must be responsible for the publication.
4. Damages must occur.

Misleading Letter of Recommendation May Result in Liability

by Wayne Barlow

Families of office workers killed and wounded by a former coworker may seek punitive damages against the assailant's former employer, Allstate Insurance Co., in a lawsuit that alleges that Allstate failed to disclose in a letter of recommendation to the victim's employer, Fireman's Fund, that the gunman had been fired several years earlier for carrying a pistol in his briefcase.

Paul Calden had left Allstate in November 1989 for allegedly violating company policy by frequently carrying a firearm and was subsequently hired by Fireman's Fund in 1990. He was fired by Fireman's Fund in 1992 for being absent from work without a doctor's note.

Continued

Continued

The lawsuit alleges, among other things, that Allstate (1) provided Calden with a letter of recommendation that stated that his departure was not related to job performance; (2) knew of Calden's mental instability and dangerous propensity for violence but failed to disclose fully and truthfully this information; and (3) was aware of Calden's acts described as devil worship on his personal computer, bizarre stories, and threatening behavior toward Allstate female staff members. *Jerner* v. *Allsate Insurance Co.,* Fla.Cir. Ct., No. 93-09472 (8/10/95).

Questions

1. Given the situation alleged in *Jerner,* what type of rule would you institute in your workplace regarding references?
2. How would you rule in *Jerner?*
3. Should there be a law protecting employers that give true references or recommendations, whether positive or negative?

Source: From "Recent Legal Decisions Affect You" by Wayne E. Barlow, D. Diane Hatch and Betty Scutnard Murphy. Used with permission of Personnel Journal, copyright © November 1995. All rights reserved.

Truth in Hiring. Some courts have recently begun to look favorably on employee causes of action alleging employer misrepresentations during the hiring process.[77] Typically, the employee claims that promises made during the hiring process were not fulfilled or that the employee was fraudulently induced to take the job because of falsehoods during the hiring process. In the leading case, a lawyer, Victoria Stewart, convinced a federal court of appeals that she should be able to take to trial her claim that her New York City law firm, Jackson & Nash, had enticed her to work with them with representations that they had secured a major environmental law client and needed her to head their new environmental law department. That work never materialized, and eventually she was dismissed from the firm.[78]

VIII. The Regulatory Environment beyond Antidiscrimination Statutes

A. *Fair Labor Standards Act*

The Great Depression of the 1930s shattered many Americans' faith in an unfettered free market and led, among other things, to extensive government regulation of employment relations. The Fair Labor Standards Act (FLSA), passed in 1938 and later amended, is directed to these major objectives:

1. The establishment of a minimum wage that provides at least a modest standard of living for employees.
2. A flexible ceiling on hours worked weekly, the purpose of which is to increase the number of employed Americans.
3. Child labor protection.
4. Equal pay for equal work regardless of gender.

Wages and Hours. The FLSA requires covered employees to be paid a specified minimum wage and to be paid time and a half for any work in excess of 40 hours per week.

Generally speaking, employees and enterprises are covered by the FLSA if they are engaged in producing goods for interstate commerce. A number of occupations are exempt from some or all of the act. Professional, administrative, and executive employees as well as outside salespersons are exempt from the minimum wage and overtime provisions. The

FLSA applies to state and local government workers as well as those in the private sector. And every state has its own wage and hour laws, which often reach workers not covered by the federal act.

Problems. A variety of problems arise under the FLSA wage and hour provisions. For example, must an employer pay employees for required activities (such as putting on protective gear) before proceeding to workstations and after leaving them? Yes, according to one recent decision.[79] If the federal minimum wage were raised from its current $4.25 per hour, would unemployment increase in low-wage jobs? Yes, according to most studies.[80] Should on-call workers be paid overtime wages for the hours spent waiting to be paged? Federal appeals court decisions are split, but the weight of opinion at this writing in 1994 suggests that some on-call workers may be able to collect overtime pay if the employer's rules effectively prevent the employee from using the on-call time for personal purposes.[81]

In 1993, Food Lion, the supermarket chain, reached a $16.2 million settlement with the Labor Department to resolve allegations of overtime violations. The settlement was the largest of its kind in history, but will provide workers with only about $330 each in back pay. Food Lion had set time limits for its employees to complete various tasks. The Labor Department contended that the time limits were inadequate, thus effectively forcing the employees to work overtime without pay in order to complete their work.

Child Labor. Under federal law, with certain exceptions (principally agriculture), children under 14 years of age may not be employed. Those aged 14 and 15 may engage in sales and certain other jobs outside school hours for a limited time. At age 16, children may engage in any nonhazardous work. Then at 18, young adults may enter certain jobs (such as mining) that the government deems to be hazardous.

A shrinking labor pool, shifting immigration patterns, and difficult economic conditions for many have led to a concern that young workers may be threatened in the workplace. In the late 19th century, we were worried about eight-year-old children who were employed for 12-hour days in sweatshops or who lost fingers in textile milling machines. Now, new concerns about safety are being raised, both in underdeveloped nations that export goods to us and in the United States itself.

Exploitation in America? Ironically, as American companies are taking steps to improve child labor conditions abroad, we find those problems emerging more seriously and poignantly in the United States than has been the case in many years. As *Fortune* reported in 1993:

> Like tuberculosis and measles, child labor is making a comeback in the United States. From New York to California, employers are breaking the law by hiring children of 7 to 17 who put in long, hard hours and often work in dangerous conditions.[82]

Enforcement. A big part of the problem lies in our inability or unwillingness to enforce the child labor laws:

> Child labor laws . . . rarely are enforced. In 1980 the U.S. Labor Department had 1,059 investigators. Today, after several budget cuts, it deploys only 833 agents to enforce not only the child labor laws but a dozen other major regulations, among them the minimum wage laws. According to the National Safe Workplace Institute . . . a business can expect a visit by a federal labor inspector once every 50 years.[83]

Values? Of course, for some families, child labor may be an important income supplement. Further, a safe job at a fair wage for a youngster can be a valuable tool in personal maturation. However, the reemergence of child labor problems suggests the possibility that we are not significantly concerned about child labor abuses. Do Americans most value education or income? Do we most value cheap clothing for ourselves or safe working conditions for Third World children? On the other hand, is child labor simply a necessity for economic subsistence and subsequent progress in portions of America as well as the Third World?

B. *Health and Safety at Work*

Deaths. Recent government studies of workplace deaths provide a mixed picture of occupational safety in the United States:

- Workplace deaths decreased from 7,405 in 1980 to 5,714 in 1989.
- The fatality rate also fell from 8.9 deaths per 100,000 workers in 1980 to 5.6 in 1989.
- From 1980 through 1989, a total of 62,289 civilians died on the job, or an average of about 17 per day.
- The riskiest occupation was mining, followed by construction.
- Workplace homicides had declined 24 percent, from 914 murders in 1980 to 694 in 1989; but by 1992, workplace murders had risen to 1,004.
- In 1992, for all workers, homicide was the second leading cause of job-related deaths, trailing vehicle crashes. For women, in 1992, homicide was the number one cause of on-the-job death.[84]

OSHA. In 1970, Congress approved the Occupational Safety and Health Act (OSHA) in response to increasing concerns that workplaces were unnecessarily hazardous. Broadly, OSHA imposes a **general duty** on employers to provide a workplace free of "recognized hazards causing or likely to cause death or serious physical harm to employees." Employers have an absolute duty to remove any serious and preventable workplace hazards that are generally recognized in the industry and are known to the employer or should be known to the employer. That general duty is then supplemented with numerous, detailed, and demanding specific *standards.* A federal agency, the Occupational Safety and Health Administration (also labeled OSHA), is responsible for ensuring safe workplaces.

general duty. An OSHA provision requiring that employers furnish to each employee employment and a place of employment free from recognized hazards that cause or are likely to cause death or serious physical harm to the employee.

OSHA also requires that employers maintain complete records listing and summarizing injuries, illnesses, and deaths on the job. Notice of any OSHA citations or of any imminent dangers on the job must also be posted at the job site. Fatalities as well as injuries requiring the hospitalization of five or more workers (a pending rule change would reduce that to three or more) must be reported to the area OSHA office within 48 hours (which would be reduced to eight hours under the pending rule).

Enforcement. OSHA's most publicized enforcement mechanism is the unannounced on-site inspection. Inspections arise at the initiative of the agency itself or at the request of employees or their representatives. The inspections must be conducted in a reasonable manner during working hours or other reasonable times, and ordinarily they must not be announced in advance. An employer can insist that the inspector produce a warrant prior to undertaking an inspection. Employer and employee representatives may accompany the inspector.

If violations are discovered, citations may be issued. Immediate, serious threats can be restrained with a court order. Uncorrected violations may lead to significant fines or imprisonment.

In one well-publicized example of OSHA violations, a North Carolina poultry plant owner pleaded guilty in 1992 to involuntary manslaughter for the deaths of 25 workers in a fire at his processing plant. The plant had no sprinkler system or fire alarms, and inspectors said that many exits were locked or blocked. Some doors had been locked, allegedly to keep insects out, to keep employees in during breaks, and to prevent theft.[85] The owner was sentenced to nearly 20 years in prison, but he will probably be eligible for release after two to three years. The plant had never been inspected by North Carolina OSHA officials during its 11 years of operation.[86] Indeed, records indicated that only 40 of North Carolina's 83 chicken-processing plants had been inspected in the past 20 years.[87]

Currently, OSHA inspections are targeted to industries in which injuries are more likely, and inspections may be limited to perusal of company safety records. If those records reveal problems in excess of national industry norms, full inspections may follow. Less dangerous locations, such as retailers, are unlikely to be inspected at all without an employee complaint.

C. Workers' Compensation

Historically, when a worker was injured on the job, his or her recourse was to sue the employer. Typically, the employee would bring a negligence claim, and commonly the employer would assert one of three defenses: (1) *contributory negligence,* meaning the employee was at least partially responsible for his or her own harm; (2) *assumption of the risk,* meaning the employee recognized or should have recognized a potentially harmful workplace situation but proceeded voluntarily to engage in his or her duties; and (3) *fellow servant rule,* meaning the harm to the employee was the result of a coworker's conduct. Proof of any of these defenses acted as a complete bar to recovery for the injured employee. The burden of overcoming these defenses and combating the superior resources of the employer meant that employees often could not secure compensation for workplace injuries.

Believe It!
An exotic dancer who was drunk when she left her job one evening was hurt in a car accident. The Iowa Supreme Court held that she is entitled to workers' compensation for the injuries she suffered since drinking was encouraged as part of her job.

Then, early in this century, the states began enacting workers' compensation laws to provide an administrative remedy for those injured or killed on the job. Now all states provide some form of protection. Rather than filing a lawsuit, workers or their families simply apply for compensation based on illness, injury, or death. Typically, the system is governed by a state board or commission. Most decisions are routine and are accomplished by completing the necessary forms. Often, a claims examiner will check to verify the nature and severity of the injury. Commission decisions can be appealed to the courts.

In all but three states (Texas, New Jersey, and South Carolina), employers are compelled to participate in workers' compensation, depending on state law, either by purchasing insurance privately, contributing to a state-managed fund, or being self-insured (paying claims directly from their own funds). Of course, firms with good safety records are rewarded with lower premium payments.

Benefits. The amount of recovery for injury or death is determined by a benefits schedule, which specifies the sum to be awarded for the injury in question. The amount of the award is normally a percentage of the worker's salary either for a specified period of time or indefinitely, depending on the severity of the injury. Injury benefits normally amount to one-half to two-thirds of regular wages. Death benefits ordinarily are tied to the wages of the deceased and range from enough to pay funeral arrangements to approximately $100,000 (depending on the number of dependents) in California. Weekly maximum benefits for workers with total but temporary disabilities range from just over $200 in some states to over $700 in others.

Coverage. Certain employment classifications, such as agriculture, may be excluded from workers' compensation; but about 90 percent of the labor force is covered, and some of those not covered are shielded by other statutes such as the Federal Employer's Liability Act.

In general, injuries, illnesses, and deaths are compensable if (1) the occurrence was accidental and (2) it arose in the course of employment. Thus, workers' compensation provides a form of no-fault protection in the workplace. In brief, workers give up the right to sue and the burdens that accompany that course, and employers participate in an insurance system that recognizes the inevitability of injury and death on the job. All states provide that the workers' compensation recovery is the exclusive remedy available for workplace injury, illness, or death. However, recent court decisions have begun to find limited exceptions that, in certain jurisdictions, permit employees to sue for damages beyond the often inadequate recoveries permitted under workers' compensation.

Litigation. Notwithstanding its no-fault character, workers' compensation has generated extensive litigation. For example, one court found an employee's "chronic anxiety" to be work-related and not the result of normal "bodily wear and tear."[88] And a 16-year-old employed as a "gas jockey" was covered by workers' compensation for injuries sustained when, during a slow time at work, he showed a friend a "trick" in which a match might be tossed into oil, gasoline, and grease without causing an explosion. On this occasion, an explosion did result, but the Workers' Compensation Board ruled and the court agreed that this "horseplay" was covered by the New York statute since it was "related to his employment."[89] On the other hand, a United Parcel Service driver who sustained a back injury while bending over to tie his shoe while on the job was excluded from compensation because, among other reasons, the injury did not arise from activity that was peculiar to the work setting.[90]

Economic Growth. In assessing the value of government programs such as workers' compensation, we must balance the evident value to society of our relatively efficient, fair system of caring for workers and their families against the market's insistence on economic efficiency. During its recession from the late 1980s through the early 1990s, California lost more than a million jobs, many of which moved to other states.[91] Management often cited uncompetitive workers' compensation costs as a reason for leaving California. Reportedly, Intel, a large California computer microchip firm, chose New Mexico for a new plant, in part because its workers' compensation costs would have been $80 million higher in California.[92]

IX. Testing and Employee Privacy

Perhaps the most explosive employment issue of the 1990s is privacy on the job. Increasingly, employers are engaging in an array of testing and monitoring procedures both before and after hiring. Drug testing, integrity tests, personality tests, AIDS tests, spying, television and computer monitoring of work performance, and so forth are routine personnel practices in many firms. Employers have a legitimate interest in these strategies not only to hire better employees and improve productivity but to protect coworkers, reduce insurance claims, and protect consumers from poor products and service. On the other hand, job applicants and employees often feel the intrusive presence of Big Brother in their lives.

A. Background: The American Condition

American Management Association (AMA) annual survey results suggest that drug use among American workers has declined dramatically. As demonstrated in the following table, positive results on drug tests have fallen significantly for both applicants and employees.

	Job Applicants Testing Positive	*Employees Testing Positive*
1989	11.4%	8.1%
1990	5.8	4.2
1991	4.6	2.7
1992	4.3	2.5

Source: "Fewer People Fail as Workplace Drug Testing Increases," *HR Focus* 70, no. 6 (June 1993), p. 24.

In 1993, 84 percent of the firms in the AMA survey engaged in drug testing.[93] Only 3 out of 503 companies responding to the survey indicated that they would hire on a probationary basis an individual who tested positive. Fifty-seven percent of the companies reported that employees who test positive are referred for counseling and treatment, 15 percent immediately dismiss those people, 20 percent apply a suspension or some other discipline, and 3 percent assign them to other duties. Eighty-seven percent of the firms use urinalysis for drug testing, 14.4 percent took blood samples, and 1.3 percent used hair samples.

B. The Drug-Free Workplace

Congress encouraged the effort against drug abuse by passing the Drug-Free Workplace Act of 1988. The act applies to employers that do business with ($25,000 or more) or receive aid from the federal government. They are required to develop an antidrug policy for employees, provide drug-free awareness programs for them, acquaint them with available assistance for those with drug problems, and warn them of the penalties that accompany violation of the policy. The act requires employees to adhere to the company policy and to inform the company within five days if they are convicted of or plead no contest to a drug-related offense in the workplace. Of course, in the event of a violation, company policy might include a mandatory rehabilitation program or termination.

C. Legal Arguments against Alcohol and Drug Testing

Notwithstanding the seriousness of the drug problem in America, critics are concerned that personal rights may be trampled in the zeal to attack substance abuse. Some of the concerns are that the tests (1) are often unreliable, (2) invade employee privacy, and (3) do not measure actual job impairment.

Challenges to drug testing are rooted primarily in the following legal claims/defenses.

Federal Constitution. As explained in Chapter 2, the Fourth Amendment to the U.S. Constitution forbids unreasonable searches and seizures. Drug tests, depending on the circumstances, arguably violate those constitutional rights. But remember that the Constitution, in general, protects us from the government, not from private-sector employers.

State Constitutions. Many state constitutions offer protection similar to that at the federal level, and some strengthen that protection. For example, California's constitutional right to privacy extends to both private- and public-sector employees.

Common Law Claims. Judge-made (common law) claims that might provide a challenge to drug testing, depending on the circumstances, include privacy, defamation (dissemination of erroneous information about an employee), negligence (in testing or selecting a test provider), and wrongful discharge (discussed later in this chapter).

State and Local Laws. A number of states and communities have enacted drug testing laws. In general, those laws place limits on testing. For example, Connecticut forbids private employers from requiring drug tests of job applicants unless written notice of the test is provided, the applicant receives a copy of any positive test report, and other procedural requirements are met.[94] On the other hand, Utah specifically permits testing both for prospective and current employees.[95]

D. *Legal Alcohol and Drug Testing*

Broadly, employment-based alcohol and drug testing occurs in four circumstances: preemployment screening, routine physical examinations, reasonable suspicion testing, and random testing.[96]

1. Preemployment testing is commonplace. Ordinarily it is lawful, but some state and local laws impose restrictions.
2. Assuming proper standards are met, drug testing as a part of periodic physical examinations is lawful in most states.
3. Reasonable suspicion is something less than probable cause and means that the employer has evidence, such as lapses in performance, that would justify a drug test. Such tests, given a sound factual foundation, probably are permissible.
4. Random drug testing raises particularly difficult legal issues. The Supreme Court has upheld such testing for public-sector employees where public safety was involved (police and transportation workers) and for those having access to particularly sensitive information.[97] In the limited number of private-sector cases addressing random testing, the courts are split.[98]

E. *Other Tests and Surveillance*

In 1988, President Reagan approved legislation banning most uses of polygraph tests by private employers. The law forbids the use of lie detector tests in screening job applicants and in random testing of employees, but it does permit the test in special security situations involving, for example, pharmaceutical companies or where the employer has sound evidence tying an employee to theft or other wrongdoing.[99]

Integrity Tests. Now that lie detectors are normally not permissible, employers have turned to paper-and-pencil integrity tests to accomplish similar goals. In general, such tests are lawful and, according to recent research, surprisingly useful. The tests have been shown to be rather effective in identifying those who are more likely to cheat in some way at work. Furthermore, some intriguing evidence suggests that those tests are also helpful in measuring general conscientiousness. One study that statistically evaluated the results of 40 other studies and data involving more than 500,000 test subjects found that the tests are useful in identifying those who are likely to be tardy, absent, and generally disruptive on the job.[100] Of course, such tests often raise privacy concerns.

Spying. Testing is only one of a broad array of employer strategies that raise invasion-of-privacy concerns in applicants and employees but are viewed as necessary efficiency measures by management. An estimated 20 million Americans are subject to electronic monitoring on the job.[101] Snooping is practiced by tabulating keystrokes, searching computer files, reviewing e-mail, and so on. Some companies keep tabs on how many times an employee goes to the bathroom or talks on the telephone, and some use video cameras to watch over work areas. One southern California medical company even requires that workers with visible "hickeys" be sent home without pay.[102] That policy was instituted in response to complaints from both patients and other workers. Monitoring is chiefly an effort to increase productivity or to investigate thefts and espionage.[103]

Some companies notify their employees about surveillance policies, but many believe their goals cannot be accomplished without secrecy. In any case, the law at this point is decidedly supportive of employer spying. In particular, if a company announces a reasonable policy of searches and surveillance where reasonably justified by work circumstances, such measures are lawful even if they include such tactics as searching desks, lockers, and offices.

Smoking. Facing surging health insurance costs, many companies now require employees to take measures to improve their health. Workers are rewarded for losing weight, reducing cholesterol counts, curbing high blood pressure, and so forth; others are penalized when they fail to do so or even when they choose to engage in dangerous activities such as skiing or sky diving. In recent years, many firms have moved to bar smoking, in response to the Indoor Smoking Act, discussed in Chapter 15.

X. Employee Benefits and Income Maintenance

What were once fringe benefits—health insurance, life insurance, pensions, and so forth—are now central ingredients in employee compensation. Employers pay 37 cents to the average employee in benefit payments for every dollar paid in wages.[104] And those costs are escalating. A recent nationwide survey showed per employee expenses for health and dental coverage rising from an average of $2,354 per year in 1988 to an estimated $3,200 per year in 1990.[105] And demands for expanded benefits, particularly child care, are growing. Consequently, many employers are reducing benefits, increasing deductibles, instituting copayment requirements, or offering "cafeteria" benefit plans.

A. Family and Medical Leave

The 1993 Family and Medical Leave Act provides up to 12 weeks of unpaid leave in any 12-month period for family needs such as birth or adoption of a child, caring for a child or parent, or an employee's own serious illness. Employees taking leave are entitled to reinstatement to the same or an equivalent job. The bill applies to all companies employing 50 or more workers and is expected to cover about 40 percent of the workforce. In practice, the impact of the bill may prove to be modest. Many workers simply cannot afford

TABLE 6.2

FAMILY LEAVE POLICIES AROUND THE WORLD

Country	*Duration of Leave (weeks)*	*Number of Paid Weeks and Percent of Normal Pay (paid by government and/or employer)*
Canada	17–41	15 weeks/60%
France	18	16 weeks/90%
Germany	14–26	14–19 weeks/100%
Japan	12	12 weeks/60%
Sweden	12–52	38 weeks/90%

Source: Women at Work, International Labor Office, Global Survey. Reprinted in Karen Mathes, "Is Family Leave Legislation Necessary?" *HR Focus,* 69, no. 3 (March 1992), p. 3.

to take unpaid leave. Further, many large companies already had such rules in place and at least 12 states had previously imposed rules as strong as the new federal standard. In any case, as Table 6.2 illustrates, the new U.S. standard is quite modest in comparison with those of our competitors abroad. But have those countries been too generous?

B. AIDS

Expenses for chronic, serious illnesses have skyrocketed. The average treatment for an AIDS patient is estimated to cost something over $100,000.[106] As a consequence, many employees who most desperately need health care are threatened with the loss of their employer-provided coverage. John McGann, a Texas employee of H&H Music Company, was diagnosed with AIDS. H&H's insurance plan had a $1 million lifetime cap, and at least in that sense, McGann felt secure. Then, when his bills began to mount, the company changed to a new plan that had an AIDS cap of $5,000. McGann died in 1991, and that same year a federal court ruled that H&H had been within its rights in *retroactively* changing its insurance plan.[107] McGann's executor took the case to the U.S. Supreme Court, which declined to hear it. H&H had switched to a self-insured plan in which the company pays its own insurance claims. Such plans are governed by ERISA, the federal benefits law (discussed later in this chapter), under the terms of which H&H's change was lawful. About 40 percent of American workers are covered by self-insured plans. Many company insurance plans, self-insured and otherwise, limit or exclude coverage for such things as psychiatric care and infertility treatments.

The Americans with Disabilities Act (ADA) (discussed earlier) forbids discrimination in insurance plans, although the language of the statute is unclear.[108] McGann may have been able to use the ADA to block the H&H action under recently released Equal Employment Opportunity Commission guidelines interpreting the act. However, disease-specific insurance caps are permissible where they are not simply a "subterfuge" to avoid the ADA—that is, where the distinction in treatment is the result not of discrimination but of legitimate actuarial/financial/risk classification considerations. Several years of litigation will likely be necessary to resolve this issue.

C. COBRA

Also of note in the area of health insurance is the Consolidated Budget Reconciliation Act of 1985 (COBRA), which, among other provisions, requires most employers to permit employees to retain group health coverage at their own expense when they leave the company unless they were fired for gross misconduct. That option also extends to the spouse and children of an employee, even if the employee dies or is divorced. Coverage must be available to the employee and family for a period of 18 to 36 months, depending on the circumstances.

D. Unemployment Compensation/WARN

The tragedy of the Great Depression, when up to 25 percent of the workforce was unemployed, led in 1935 to the passage of the Social Security Act, one portion of which provided for an unemployment insurance program. Today, all 50 states and the federal government are engaged in a cooperative system that helps to protect the temporarily jobless. The system is financed through a payroll tax paid by employers.

The actual state tax rate for each employer varies, depending on the employer's *experience* ratings—the number of layoffs in its workforce. Thus, employers have an incentive to retain employees. In 1992, combined federal and state unemployment taxes per employee ranged from a high of about $630 in Rhode Island to a low of just over $90 in South Dakota.

Rules vary by state, but in general, employees qualify for unemployment benefits by reaching a specified total of annual wages. Those losing their jobs must apply to a state agency for unemployment compensation, which varies by state and ranges from approximately $150 per week to over $400. Benefits may be collected up to a specified maximum period, usually 26 weeks. During that time, those collecting compensation must be ready to work and must make an effort to find suitable work. Workers may be disqualified from unemployment coverage for a variety of reasons, including quitting work or being fired for misconduct. Because of disqualifications, failure to reach the necessary wage total for eligibility, and a variety of other reasons, only about one-third of those losing their jobs subsequently collect unemployment compensation.

WARN. In 1988, Congress sought to ease some job-loss situations by enacting the Worker Adjustment and Retraining Notification Act (WARN), which requires firms to provide 60 days' notice if they plan to lay off one-third or more of their workers at any site employing at least 150 workers, drop 500 employees at any site, or close a plant employing at least 50 workers. However, a 1993 General Accounting Office study concluded that the law had been ineffectual, with half of plant closings not covered by the law and many firms simply remaining ignorant of the law's requirements. Congress is considering stiffer requirements, although critics fear that any change will simply encourage increased use of contract and part-time employees.

E. Social Security

The 1935 Social Security Act, as amended, protects those retired workers who qualified for the program by paying taxes to the social security fund for a specified number of quarters. The act also provides payments for disability, hospital insurance (Medicare for the aged), and survivors of deceased workers. About 90 percent of the workforce is covered by social security. With some exceptions, workers are required to pay a tax, which is deducted from payroll checks by employers. That sum is then matched by the employers and forwarded to the federal government.

Crisis? Serious problems are on the horizon. Happily, average life expectancies continue to climb, but that means the ratio of employed workers to those retired is falling. In 1935, 10 adults were working to support each retiree; today, there are 5 or so; and by the year 2035, only 2 adults will be working for every adult who is retired.[109]

F. Pensions

As early as the late 1800s, some employers began to adopt pension plans for their employees. In 1974, Congress approved the Employee Retirement Income Security Act (ERISA), under which the government regulates pension funds to help ensure their long-term financial security by reducing fraud and mismanagement. ERISA requires that fund managers keep detailed records, engage in prudent investments, and provide an annual report that has been certified by qualified, impartial third parties.

ERISA also establishes strict **vesting rights** (the point at which the employee has a nonforfeitable right to the funds) to ensure that employees actually receive the pensions to which they are entitled. ERISA requires that employee contributions must vest fully and immediately. Employer contributions typically vest after 10 years of work, but other options are available. Furthermore, those vested funds are not lost should the employee change jobs.

vesting rights. The right of an individual to a present or future fixed benefit.

ERISA also included provisions for establishing the Pension Benefit Guaranty Corporation (PBGC) to protect retirees in the event of the failure of a pension fund. The PBGC guarantees that vested persons will be paid up to a specified maximum, even if the pension fund does not have sufficient resources to meet its obligations. PBGC funding is provided by company contributions.

Problems? Despite the PBGC, ERISA, union efforts, and many well-meaning companies, millions of employees in retirement and more to come cannot be assured of the security that we have come to expect in old age. The basic problem, of course, is money. The rocky course of our economy in recent years is now being felt by retirees:

1. A recent survey found that two-thirds of the major American corporations have reduced retiree health plans or intend to do so.[110] Under ERISA, those benefits can be reduced or eliminated, as established in the *McGann* case, discussed earlier in this chapter.
2. About 15 percent of the PBGC-backed pension funds (representing 41 million Americans) are not fully funded. For example, General Motors agreed in 1990 to add $3 billion to its employees' pension benefits, even though its existing plan was underfunded by many billions of dollars. In 1992, GM remained about $12 billion short of full funding in its pension fund, but it hopes to be fully funded by the end of the century.[111]

XI. Terminations: Protection from Wrongful Discharge

Most Americans work without benefit of an employment contract for a specified period of time. They are labeled **at-will employees** in that they may be fired at any time, but they may also quit at any time. One study estimates that 150,000 U.S. workers are *unjustly* discharged annually.[112] During the 1970s, wrongful discharge suits totaled fewer than 200, but in 1989 alone more than 20,000 such suits were litigated in some fashion.[113]

at-will employees. An individual not under contract for a specified term and therefore, under the general rule, subject to discharge by the employer at any time for any reason.

Historically, the at-will worker in the United States could be discharged at any time for good reasons, bad reasons, or no reason at all. Harsh though it may seem, the employment-at-will doctrine is merely an extension of well-settled contract principles: Employer and employee both freely entered the bargain understanding its terms, and thus the court should, in general, enforce those terms, including the right of dismissal and the right of the employee to quit at any time. Critics argue that the doctrine ignores the obvious inequality of bargaining power between employers and employees.

Nonetheless, the general rule remains that employees without a contract for a specified term are presumed to be working at will and thus may be dismissed for any reason.

However, in recent decades the at-will rule has been softened by certain legislative and judicially imposed limitations. For instance, as covered earlier, Title VII provides that an employee may be terminated for any reason *other* than on the basis of the employee's gender, religion, race, color, or national origin. Other statutory exceptions to the at-will rule include our labor laws protecting union workers and OSHA, which prohibits firings based on retaliation for reporting an OSHA violation. Although the law varies greatly from state to state, state-based limitations are also increasingly common.

A. Judicial Limitations on At-Will Principles

Recent court decisions have provided new grounds for dismissed at-will employees to claim that they have been wronged. Those judicial decisions were often provoked by transparently unjust dismissals, including, for example, whistle-blowers who exposed their employers' misdeeds and employees who declined to commit perjury on behalf of their employers. Those judicial limitations to the at-will doctrine fall into four categories: (1) express or implied contracts, (2) implied covenant of good faith and fair dealing, (3) public policy, and (4) tort claims.

Express or Implied Employment Contracts. A number of states have recognized a contract protection for at-will employees that arises, typically, either from the employee handbook or from employer conduct and oral representations. The notion here is that the courts will imply a contract based on either language in the handbook or assurances of continued employment such as routine promotions, no notice of poor performance, longevity, and oral communications.

Implied Covenant of Good Faith and Fair Dealing. A few state courts, most emphatically those in California, have held that neither party to a contract may *act in bad faith* to deprive the other of the benefits of the contract. For example, a California court held that a newly hired, at-will employee who quit his former job, moved across country, and set up an office and was then dismissed before actually beginning work was damaged by his employer's breach of the implied covenant.[114]

Public Policy. The majority of the states have now adopted some form of public policy (the general preference of the citizenry) exception providing that a dismissal is wrongful if it results from employee conduct that is consistent with the will of the people as expressed in statutes, constitutions, and so on. Those exceptions are established on a case-by-case basis, and they differ from state to state. In addition to those noted above, the exception often protects, for example, those fired for pursuing a lawful claim (e.g., workers' compensation) and those fired for fulfilling a civic responsibility (e.g., jury duty).

Tort Claims. An influential California decision in the *Foley* case[115] and other similar cases around the country have limited dismissed at-will employees' rights to recover damages in actions for breach of contract and breach of the implied warranty of good faith and fair dealing to *economic losses* (out-of-pocket costs and lost wages). One of the consequences is that dismissed employees are increasingly turning to various kinds of tort actions (often labeled *tag-along torts*) where the potential financial recovery, including punitive damages, is much greater than for contract claims alone. Those tort possibilities include, among others, defamation, intentional infliction of emotional distress, interference with contract, and invasion of privacy.[116]

The following case addresses the public policy limitation on the at-will rule.

CASE

Wagenseller v. Scottsdale Memorial Hospital

710 P.2d 1025 (Arizona S.Ct. 1985)

Facts

Catherine Wagenseller was employed by Scottsdale Memorial Hospital as a staff nurse on an at-will basis. After two promotions over the next few years, she was terminated after a fateful rafting trip with some employees from the hospital. Wagenseller had refused to participate in the group's staging of a parody of the song "Moon River," which allegedly concluded with members of the group "mooning" the audience. The employees had performed the skit twice at the hospital following their return from the river, but Wagenseller continued to decline to participate. Following her continued refusals, her relationship with her supervisor (who was also on the trip) began to deteriorate and Wagenseller experienced harassment, abusive language, and humiliation from the supervisor. After meeting to discuss some problems with her department, Wagenseller was terminated. Wagenseller claims that her termination was proximately caused by her failure to participate in the skit, in violation of public policy.

* * *

Justice Feldman

[The court discusses the general rule that public policy is defined in state constitutions and statutes, as well as judicial decisions.] We do not believe, however, that expressions of public policy are contained only in the statutory and constitutional law, nor do we believe that all statements made in either a statute or the Constitution are expressions of public policy. Thus we will look to the pronouncements of our founders, our legislature, and our courts to discern the public policy of this state.

All such pronouncements, however, will not provide the basis for a claim of wrongful discharge. Only those which have a singularly public purpose will have such force. "Chaos would result if a single doctor engaged in research were allowed to determine, according to his or her individual conscience, whether a project should continue. An employee does not have a right to continued employment when he or she refuses to conduct research simply because it would contravene his or her personal morals. An employee at will who refuses to work in answer to a call of conscience should recognize that other employees and their employer might heed a different call." Although an employee facing such a quandry may refuse to do the work believed to violate her moral philosophy, she may not also claim a right to continued employment.

In the case before us, Wagenseller refused to participate in activities which arguably would have violated our indecent exposure statute. She claims that she was fired because of this refusal. While this statute may not embody a policy which "strikes at the heart of a citizen's social rights, duties, and responsibilities" as clearly and forcefully as a statute prohibiting perjury, we believe it was enacted to preserve and protect the commonly recognized sense of public privacy and decency. The statute does, therefore, recognize bodily privacy as a "citizen's social right" . . . We thus uphold this state's public policy by holding that termination for refusal to commit an act which might violate [the statute] may provide the basis of a claim for wrongful discharge.

Questions

1. In reading *Wagenseller,* did you have the sense that the Arizona Supreme Court was stretching the law in some sense in order to achieve justice? Explain.

Continued

Continued

2. An employer provided medical insurance, a pension, and a profit-sharing plan for its at-will employees. After successfully completing the company's probationary period, an at-will employee was dismissed. The employee sued.
   a. Based on these facts, build an argument for the plaintiff's wrongful discharge claim.
   b. Decide. Explain. [See *Luedtke* v. *Nabors Alaska Drilling, Inc.*, 768 P.2d 1123 (1989).]
3. An applicant received a job offer, which was confirmed in a letter stating that his annual salary would be $80,000. He was terminated seven months into his first year of work. Was the dismissal a breach of contract? Explain. [See *Bernard* v. *IMI Sys., Inc.*, 618 A.2d 338 (N.J. S.Ct. 1993).]

B. Termination: Handle with Care

Remember that employment at will remains overwhelmingly the law of the land. We have been looking at *limitations* on that doctrine. Those limitations have become increasingly prevalent. Nonetheless, in most instances, an at-will employee can be dismissed without fear of the courts. How, then, do we actually go about the practice of termination in a manner designed to maximize fairness to all parties and to minimize legal fallout? Consider three potential pitfalls: (1) employee handbooks, (2) employer conduct, and (3) defamation.

Employee Handbooks. Employee handbooks are important to establish a code of conduct for a business and to outline the employer's responsibilities along with the employee's rights and benefits. Unfortunately, sloppy handbooks often lead to legal problems. The handbook should include unambiguous language, uncontradicted by provisions elsewhere in the handbook, indicating that the employee is serving at will.

Employer Conduct. At the actual moment of termination, the language and procedures employed are important both for the dignity of the employee and to prevent subsequent legal problems. Table 6.3 presents advice for employers to follow in terminating employees.

Defamation. Errors in the firing process can become very expensive, as Procter & Gamble learned in 1993 when a Texas jury awarded a dismissed P&G employee $15.6 million. Don Hagler had worked for P & G for 41 years when he was publicly accused of stealing a $35 phone and was fired. Hagler said the phone was his, and he accused P&G of libel because notices accusing him of theft were posted on company bulletin boards and included in the company e-mail system. Procter & Gamble may appeal the decision.[117] Table 6.4 provides advice for avoiding defamation in the firing process.

C. Reform?

Wrongful discharge suits can be very expensive for employers and often not particularly remunerative for fired employees. A study by the Rand Institute for Civil Justice found a median verdict of $177,000. After appeals, settlements, and lawyer fees, the median net recovery was $74,500.[118] From both sides of the fence, the system seems not to make a lot of sense. Furthermore, the greater cost from wrongful discharge litigation may lie in workers not hired. Another Rand study estimated that employment may drop as much as 5 percent in some states because of fear of wrongful discharge suits. Companies simply turn to temporaries, retain poor performers, and engage in elaborate screening measures as strategies for avoiding lawsuits.[119]

TABLE 6.3

ADVICE ON TERMINATION

Interviews with consulting firms indicate various methods to be followed when employees must be let go. Some of this advice is as follows:

Dos	*Don'ts*
▪ Give as much warning as possible for mass layoffs. ▪ Sit down one-on-one with the individual, in a private office. ▪ Complete a firing session within 15 minutes. ▪ Provide written explanations of severance benefits. ▪ Provide outplacement services away from company headquarters. ▪ Be sure the employee hears about his termination from a manager, not a colleague. ▪ Express appreciation for what the employee has contributed, if appropriate.	▪ Don't leave room for confusion when firing. Tell the individual in the first sentence he is terminated. ▪ Don't allow time for debate during a firing session. ▪ Don't make personal comments when firing someone; keep the conversation professional. ▪ Don't rush a fired employee off-site unless security is really an issue. ▪ Don't fire people on significant dates, like the 25th anniversary of their employment or the day their mother died. ▪ Don't fire employees when they are on vacation or have just returned.

Source: Suzanne Alexander, "Firms Get Plenty of Practice at Layoffs, but They Often Bungle the Firing Process," *The Wall Street Journal,* October 14, 1991, p. B1. Reprinted by permission of *The Wall Street Journal.*

TABLE 6.4

SOME DOS AND DON'TS OF FIRING

- **Be certain of the facts** when firing someone. Conduct a thorough investigation and bring in experts in employment law and labor relations either from corporate headquarters or from the outside.
- **Be factual and avoid innuendo** when discussing a firing with other people or when recording what happened. Such caution should extend to personnel files as well.
- **Tell only those who need to know** the details of a worker's firing. Limiting the number of people who know gives the fired employee less ammunition for suing for defamation of character. It shows professionalism and good faith on the part of the company.
- **Avoid making examples** of fired employees. Let the fired employee's behavior and the facts speak for themselves. The details of a firing often seep out in the workplace and indirectly serve as a deterrent.
- **If an example must be made** of someone to prevent similar actions, be extremely careful in the wording of any announcement. Accuse someone of something as serious as theft or sexual harassment only if you're sure of the facts.

Source: Gabriella Stern, "Companies Discover that Some Firings Backfire into Costly Defamation Suits," *The Wall Street Journal,* May 5, 1993, p. B1. Reprinted by permission of *The Wall Street Journal.*

Avoid Litigation. Because of the problems terminations can cause, employers and lawyers alike are looking to methods of avoiding wrongful discharge suits. In some instances, workers waive the right to sue in exchange for mandatory arbitration of disputes.[120] Other companies have given up the right to dismissal at will. For example, Federal Express lets employees appeal discharges to appeals panels composed of five members, three of whom are chosen from a pool by the employee.[121] Finally, the National Conference of Commissioners on Uniform State Laws has drafted a "Model Employment Termination Act" for possible adoption by the states. The model act has three key ingredients:

1. Termination for good cause only.
2. Arbitration as the preferred method of settling termination cases.
3. Strict limits on employer liability for wrongful discharge.[122]

XII. Additional Issues

A. Immigration

Given that America is a nation founded on immigration and proudly open to the "huddled masses" of the globe for more than 200 years, it now comes as something of a jolt that immigration policy has become one of the most hotly disputed issues in American life.

Part of the unease lies simply in the numbers. From 1980 to 1990, approximately 9.5 million legal and illegal immigrants entered the United States, the most in any decade since we became a nation.[123] Those immense numbers in a time of economic distress, of course, cause alarm. Further, many Americans, but particularly those in southern California and Texas, are troubled that we are unable to stop the influx of illegal aliens. Others worry that we won't be able to assimilate the new immigrants in a manner that respects multiculturalism but maintains a nation basically of one language, political tradition, and will. Finally, some say the current distress is really just another manifestation of racism, in that most of the newer immigrants are not European Caucasians.

In any case, a 1993 *USA Today* poll found that nearly two-thirds of Americans wanted a reduction in immigration.[124] Likewise, nearly two-thirds thought that immigrants hurt the economy (by holding down wages) more than they help it. Seventy-five percent believed that Irish immigrants benefit America and 65 percent thought the same of Poles; but only 19 percent shared that sentiment about Haitians and 20 percent about Iranians. We have responded to this situation with legislation.

Immigration Reform and Control Act (IRCA). Enacted by Congress, IRCA's purpose is to eliminate work opportunities that attract illegal aliens to the United States. The Act requires that most employers determine the eligibility of employees for work, but prohibits discrimination against an individual on the basis of her or his national origin or citizenship.

The 1986 **Immigration Reform and Control Act (IRCA)** sought to slow the entry of illegal aliens by subjecting employers to criminal and civil penalties for knowingly hiring unauthorized aliens. The IRCA also contained an amnesty provision that permitted illegal aliens already in the United States to come forward and secure permanent resident status. Nearly 3 million formerly illegal aliens have secured permanent resident status under the act, but illegal entry continues to flourish.[125]

In an effort to boost our economy, legislation was approved in 1990 to triple the number of visas annually allotted to highly skilled workers such as scientists, engineers, artists, athletes, and managers to about 140,000. Additional visas were set aside for investor-immigrants who can create jobs in America. However the new investor program is off to a slow start.

B. Benefits for Homosexual Partners

Should the partners and dependents of unmarried homosexual employees receive employment benefits such as those accorded to the spouses and dependents of married employees? The following article explains that a small but growing number of American companies are taking that direction.

Gays Make Gains in Health Care

by Julia Lawlor

Software giant Microsoft is the latest and the largest company to extend health benefits to partners and dependents of its gay employees.

Could GM, GE, and IBM be next? Not likely, say benefits experts. At least in the foreseeable future.

While Digital Equipment and Du Pont are studying it, most large companies have been slow to add these benefits. AT&T has angered gay employees for refusing to pay death benefits to the partner of a gay employee who died.

Most of the 27 firms and groups that now offer unmarried-partner health benefits are either small, progressive companies like Ben & Jerry's; cities like Berkeley, California; or high-tech firms that have younger management and enlightened policies. Apple Computer, Silicon Graphics, and Borland International added gay-partner benefits to recruit and keep good employees, says Mark Wagoner of Foster Higgins consultants.

The companies are "definitely younger, definitely hipper," says Alan Emery, a corporate consultant from San Francisco.

Only about 75 companies offer any kind of benefit to employees' unmarried partners—gay or heterosexual. Those benefits can range from access to the company gym to full health benefits. Lotus Development lets gay partners withdraw funds from employees' 401(k) retirement plans.

Despite the high cost of AIDS treatment, companies that give gay-partner health benefits say added costs have been low. That's because only 1 percent to 4 percent of eligible employees sign up. Microsoft estimates its health care costs will rise only 1 percent as a result of the change.

Why do so few employees sign up for these benefits?

For one, they have to pay taxes on them. The IRS doesn't recognize unmarried partners as dependents.

And to get the benefits, you have to admit that you're gay. That's a big problem. Says Paula Ettelbrick, a former official of a gay-rights group: "The fear of discrimination at work is so widespread that most people remain closeted."

Questions

1. List the nonfinancial issues that a company should consider in deciding whether to follow the direction taken by Microsoft and others.
2. In your mind, is this issue akin to race and gender discrimination? Explain.
3. Would you offer these benefits, as Microsoft decided to do? Explain.

Summary

Legal Review. You hear employers saying it all of the time: "There are too many laws! We can't hire whom we want anymore!" On the other hand, the law specifically states that an employer can hire whomever it chooses, as long as that decision is not made based on certain prohibited grounds (gender, national origin, race, color, age, disability, or religion). An employee who believes that she or he is subject to discrimination has two options to proving a case: disparate treatment and disparate impact.

Disparate treatment exists where there is some intent to discriminate on prohibited grounds. The employer's defense is that those grounds constitute some bona fide occupational qualification for the position. Disparate impact occurs where there is facially neutral policy that has a different effect on a protected group than on other employees. The employer may defend the policy by proving that it is justified by business reasons. The employee may then show that the same business justification could be accomplished through a less discriminatory alternative.

Employers are legally restricted in other ways as well. For instance, employers must comply with, among other statutes, the Occupational Safety and Health Act, the Fair Labor Standards Act, and the Immigration Reform and Control Act. Further, an employer may not terminate an employee in retaliation for the employee's exercising rights under any of these acts.

Although employers may feel that their hands are often tied, that they cannot run their businesses the way they would like as a result of the myriad of laws to which they are subject, in fact, the purpose of the regulation is merely to even the playing field between employees and employers, ensuring that each acts in a fair, equitable manner.

Ethics Review. The previous paragraph explains that a fair and equitable balance is sought. Is this so easy to define? Several of the chapter readings showed how complying with statutes can be a grave burden for an employer (e.g. "Unreasonable Accommodation," p. 251). Is the law more concerned with fairness to the employee or the employer? Is there such an imbalance in the bargaining positions of the two that laws are necessary? Or instead, would you agree with legal economists like Posner, who argue that law is merely an imposition that ruins true market decisions? Others would argue that we simply do not treat each other fairly if we don't have to. The workplace is where most Americans spend most of their lives. What obligations do we owe each other in this environment?

Economics Review. Recalling again Posner's argument against law-based discrimination prohibitions, consider what the nation would be like if there were no employment regulations. Actually, this shouldn't be too difficult. In each area, simply take a look at what the nation was like before the regulation went into effect. Before 1964, it was not unheard of to see advertisements for "colored maids" or "white businessmen," or which stated that "women need not apply." Are you uncomfortable returning to an environment in which these ads are commonplace? Consider the workplace before the enactment of OSHA. Workers had to protect themselves because their employers did not impose many safety precautions. Workers who refused to work in unsafe environments were simply fired; there were other workers who would be willing to take the open job. Does a market really work in a world in which unemployment among both professionals and blue-collar workers is constant?

Chapter Questions

1. In general, employers are forced to bear, or at least share, the legal burden for their employees' negligent conduct on the job.
   a. Why do we force employers to bear that responsibility?
   b. Should we do so? Explain.
2. Many companies refer to credit reports when investigating job applicants. The Fair Credit Reporting Act requires employers to notify applicants if they are rejected because of information in a credit report.
   a. In your judgment, does evidence of failure to pay debts constitute useful information in the job selection process? Explain.

b. Is the use of that information an invasion of privacy as you understand it? Is it unethical? Explain.

3. In Iowa, a waitress was dismissed from Maid-Rite Cafe for misconduct after she told others that the cafe was going to be closed. She had received that information from another employee. She learned that the original source of the story was an individual who was not associated with the cafe. Later, four people asked the waitress if the business was closing and she said that she had heard that to be the case. She lost her job, and she sought unemployment compensation. About 20 people in the community signed a petition saying that she was a good waitress and not the kind to start a rumor. How would you rule on her unemployment compensation claim? Explain. [See Gene Raffensperger, "Woman Fired for Passing Rumor," *Des Moines Register,* April 29, 1989, p. 2A.]
4. Stephen Bokat, vice president and general counsel of the U.S. Chamber of Commerce, said, "You fully expect that every time you discharge an employee, or don't promote an employee, or demote an employee, you're going to get a lawsuit. That was not true even 10 years ago."[126]
   a. Why are we experiencing an expansion in employee lawsuits?
   b. In general, is that trend toward litigation a necessary response to a historical abuse of power by employers? Explain.
   c. Can you suggest means other than litigation for settling workplace disputes?
5. As discussed in this chapter, many recent judicial decisions have afforded at-will employees much-improved protection against unfair dismissals. A special area of concern is whether at-will employees can be dismissed for off-duty conduct. The decisions are split, but the trend seems to be toward greater respect and protection for employee privacy. Nonetheless, companies still retain broad latitude to dismiss. For example, an employee convicted of selling drugs would most likely not be protected by the courts from a company dismissal.

   Virginia Rulon-Miller, an IBM salesperson, had been dating another IBM employee, Matt Blum, for several years. Her superiors were aware of the relationship. Blum left IBM to join a competitor, QYX, and he moved from San Francisco to Philadelphia. QYX transferred him back to San Francisco, and he and Rulon-Miller resumed dating. Again, her superiors were aware of the relationship, and one mentioned that he didn't "have any problem" with her romance. Rulon-Miller did well in her sales role and was promoted to a management position, where she continued to do well, as evidenced by a $4,000 raise. Nonetheless, one week after receiving notice of the raise, Rulon-Miller was either dismissed (her version) or transferred (the company's version). IBM felt her romance and her concern for the success of Blum created a conflict of interest. Despite being an at-will employee, Rulon-Miller argued that she was protected by IBM's written policies that detail those circumstances under which an employee's private life can become a company issue. She filed suit, claiming wrongful discharge. Decide. Explain. [See *Rulon-Miller* v. *IBM,* 1 BNA IER Cases 405, 162 Cal. App. 3d 241 (1984).]
6. On the average, European workers enjoy very much better job benefits than their American counterparts. For example, if we include Social Security, the typical American worker will receive a pension providing about one-third of his or her preretirement income; that average ranges from 50 to 90 percent in other industrialized nations.[127]
   a. Do we need to provide more generous pension provisions in the United States? Explain.
   b. If so, should the money come from employees, employers, the government, or some combination of all? Explain.

7. As discussed in this chapter, American law forbids a variety of forms of discrimination. At the same time, we revere personal freedom. For example, we protect the First Amendment rights of neo-Nazi groups and the Ku Klux Klan, notwithstanding their racist goals. Do you favor recent legislation banning hate speech? Should we pass laws forbidding group defamation, malicious and degrading remarks directed to a racial or ethnic group? Explain.
8. Pan American Airways, Inc., maintained a policy of excluding men from positions as flight attendants. The policy was challenged on sex discrimination grounds. Pan American defended its policy with a survey showing that 79 percent of all passengers preferred being served by females. Then Pan Am offered expert testimony to show that the passenger preference was attributable to "feminine" qualities possessed by few males. The district court ruled for Pan Am on the grounds that "all or substantially all" [the test articulated in *Weeks* v. *Southern Bell Telephone,* 408 F.2d 228 (5th Cir. 1969)] men were unable to successfully fulfill the duties of flight attendants. The decision was appealed. Decide. Explain. [See *Diaz* v. *Pan American Airways, Inc.,* 311 F. Supp. 559 (S.D. Fla. 1970), 442 F.2d 385 (5th Cir.), cert. denied, 404 U.S. 950 (1971).]
9. The accompanying ad for foreign exchange dealers appeared in the December 11, 1987, issue (p. 22) of *The Nation,* an English-language newspaper published in Bangkok, Thailand.
   a. Analyze the legality of the ad based on American law.
   b. Should American firms abroad adhere to American antidiscrimination policies even if those policies might put the American firms at a competitive disadvantage or offend the values and mores of the host country? Explain.

An American Bank
invites applications for
CORPORATE FOREIGN EXCHANGE DEALERS
for its Bangkok branch

Qualifications:

- Thai national
- Age 23–30 years, preferably male
- University graduate in Finance, Economics or related field
- 1–2 years dealing experience
- Good command of both spoken and written English

Salary is negotiable and attractive benefits will be provided for the successful candidates. The bank offers excellent opportunities for career advancement.

Send application stating details of qualifications and experience, present salary, and a recent photo to

The Nation
Class 1191
GPO Box 594
Bangkok 10501

10. Would a readily visible office wall display of nude and seminude female figures located in a common work area (e.g., one poster, on display for eight years, depicted a "woman with a golf ball on her breasts and a man standing over her, golf club in hand, yelling 'fore.' ") in combination with obscene comments about women on a routine basis (e.g., "whores," "all that bitch needs is a good lay") give rise to an intimidating, hostile, or offensive working environment within the meaning of the sex-

ual harassment law? Explain. [See *Rabidue* v. *Osceola Refining Co.,* 805 F.2d 611 (6th Cir. 1986). But see *Robinson* v. *Jacksonville Shipyards,* 760 F. Supp. 1486 (M.D. Fla. 1991).]

11. A woman sought a freightyard job. Her application was denied because she failed to meet the company's requirement of two years' truck-driving experience or training. The woman believed she was a victim of sex discrimination.
    a. Build a case on her behalf.
    b. Build a case for the trucking company.
    c. Decide the case. Explain.
    [See *Chrisner* v. *Complete Auto Transit, Inc.,* 645 F.2d 1251 (1981).]
12. The author of a *Harvard Law Review* article argues for discrimination claims based on appearance:

    > The most physically unattractive members of our society face severe discrimination . . . The unattractive ("those individuals who depart so significantly from the most commonly held notions of beauty that they incur employment discrimination") are poorly treated in such diverse contexts as employment decisions, criminal sentencing, and apartment renting. Although appearance discrimination can have a devastating economic, psychological, and social impact on individuals, its victims have not yet found a legal recourse.

    Should we treat some aspects of appearance (for example, shortness, obesity, and unattractive facial characteristics) as disabilities, thus forbidding discrimination based on those characteristics? Explain. [See note, "Facial Discrimination: Extending Handicap Law to Employment Discrimination on the Basis of Physical Appearance," *Harvard Law Review* 100, no. 8 (June 1987), p. 2035.]

NOTES

1. Donald C. Bacon, "See You in Court," *Nation's Business* 77, no. 7 (July 1989), p. 17.
2. Clyde Summers, "Effective Remedies for Employment Rights: Preliminary Guidelines and Proposals," *University of Pennsylvania Law Review* 141, no. 2 (December 1992), p. 457.
3. 347 U.S. 483 (1954).
4. 163 U.S. 537 (1896).
5. A portion of the material in this paragraph is drawn from William P. Murphy, Julius G. Getman, and James E. Jones, Jr., *Discrimination in Employment,* 4th ed. (Washington: Bureau of National Affairs, 1979), pp. 1–4.
6. Ann Hagedorn and Thomas F. O'Boyle, "Marriott Stettles," *The Wall Street Journal,* March 7, 1991, p. B8.
7. Christopher Conte, "More Schooling Is the Key to Improving Wages of Black Workers," *The Wall Street Journal,* May 11, 1993, p. A1.
8. Ibid.
9. Associated Press, "Census Report Shows Hispanics Still Struggling," *Waterloo Courier,* August 23, 1993, p. A10.
10. Associated Press, "Racial, Ethnic U.S. Balance Faces Change," *Waterloo Courier,* September 29, 1993, p. A1.
11. "Hate Rises," *Parade,* May 13, 1990, p. 15.
12. Richard Posner, *Economic Analysis of Law* (Boston: Little Brown & Co., 1986), p. 616.
13. 97 S.Ct. 2720.
14. See *St. Mary's Honor Center* v. *Hicks,* 113 S.Ct. 2742 (1993).
15. Joan Rigdon, "Three Decades after the Equal Pay Act, Women's Wages Remain Far from Parity," *The Wall Street Journal,* June 9, 1993, p. B1.
16. Ibid.
17. Ibid.
18. Ibid.
19. Ibid.

20. Gallup poll for Accountants on Call, "Profiles of the American Worker." Reported in *HR Focus* 69, no. 8 (August 1992), p. 13.
21. Lindley Clark, "The Pay Gap Narrows—Slowly," *The Wall Street Journal,* July 2, 1993, p. A6.
22. Anne Fisher, "When Will Women Get to the Top?" *Fortune* 126, no. 6 (September 21, 1992), p. 44.
23. Ibid.
24. Julie Lopez, "Study Says Women Face Glass Walls as Well as Ceilings," *The Wall Street Journal,* March 3, 1992, p. B1.
25. Fisher, "When Will Women Get to the Top?" p. 44.
26. Al Neuharth, "Risk-Taking Women Create Own Ceilings," *USA Today,* August 14, 1992, p. 15A.
27. Ibid.
28. Alan Otten, "Male Professions Are Much Less So," *The Wall Street Journal,* November 15, 1993, p. B1.
29. *Newport News Shipbuilding & Dry Dock Co.* v. *EEOC,* 462 U.S. 669 (1983).
30. *California Federal Savings and Loan Association* v. *Mark Guerra, Director, Department of Fair Employment and Housing,* 479 U.S. 272 (1987).
31. Gannett News Service, "Poll Gauges Workplace Harassment," *Des Moines Register,* March 28, 1994, p. 3A.
32. Ronni Sandroff, "Sexual Harassment—The Inside Story," *Working Woman,* June 1992, p. 47.
33. Barbara Jorgensen, "Warning: Sexual Harassment Can Be Dangerous to Your Company's Health," *Electronic Business,* May 1993, p. 1.
34. Alan Otten, "Uncertainty Persists on Sexual Harassment," *The Wall Street Journal,* July 29, 1992, p. B1.
35. Michael J. McCarthy, "Supreme Court to Rule on Sex-Bias Case," *The Wall Street Journal,* June 14, 1988, p. 33.
36. Ibid.
37. *Hopkins* v. *Price Waterhouse,* 618 F.Supp. 1109 (1985).
38. *Hopkins* v. *Price Waterhouse,* 825 F.2d 458, 468 (1987).
39. Refer to the Department of Labor's Interpretive Bulletin, as reported in Charles A. Sullivan, Michael Zimmer, and Richard Richards, *Federal Statutory Law,* (Indianapolis: Michie Publ., 1980) p. 596.
40. Ibid., pp. 598–601.
41. Ibid., p. 608, reporting *Shultz* v. *American Can Co.—Dixie Prods.,* 424 F.2d 356 (8th Cir. 1970).
42. 417 U.S. 188 (1974).
43. Council on the Economic Status of Women, State of Minnesota, "Men's, Women's Comparable Jobs," *Des Moines Sunday Register,* January 8, 1984, p. 3C.
44. "Child Care Workers Near Pay Bottom," *Waterloo Courier,* January 3, 1988, p. A8.
45. Ibid.
46. Posner, pp. 313–14.
47. *County of Washington* v. *Gunther,* 452 U.S. 161 (1981).
48. See, for example, *Spaulding* v. *The University of Washington,* 740 F.2d 686 (1984).
49. Clint Bolick, "The Great Racial Divide," *The Wall Street Journal,* November 30, 1992, p. A10.
50. Gannett News Service, "Affirmative Action Brands Workers, Qualified or Not," *Des Moines Register,* August 31, 1992, p. 6A.
51. David Gates, "White Male Paranoia," *Newsweek,* March 29, 1993, pp. 48, 49.
52. 99 S.Ct. 2721 (1979).
53. *Texas Department of Community Affairs* v. *Burdine,* 450 U.S. 248 (1981).
54. Associated Press, "Congress on Verge of Passing Landmark Disabilities Bill," *Waterloo Courier,* December 3, 1989, p. B1.
55. Gary Coulton and Roger Wolters, "Employee and Management Rights and Responsibilities under the Americans with Disabilities Act (ADA): An Overview," *Employee Responsibilities and Rights Journal* 6, no. 1 (March 1993), p. 55. Citing Equal Employment Opportunity Commission, "Equal Employment Opportunity for Individuals with Disabilities," *Federal Register* 56, no. 40 (1991), pp. 8577–603.
56. Albert Karr, "Compliance Costs Are Often Modest under the New Disability Law," *The Wall Street Journal,* August 4, 1992, p. A1.
57. Catherine Bennett and Max Johnson, "Complying with Disability Act Isn't Costly," *Des Moines Register,* July 29, 1992, p. 7A.
58. *Hazen Paper Company* v. *Walter F. Biggins,* 113 S.Ct. 1701 (1993).
59. 499 F.2d 859 (7th Cir. 1974).
60. Junda Woo, "Ex-Workers Hit Back with Age-Bias Suits," *The Wall Street Journal,* December 8, 1992, p. B1.
61. Ibid.
62. Ibid.
63. Kevin Salwen, "EEOC Warns against Layoffs Based on Age," *The Wall Street Journal,* March 2, 1993, p. A4.

64. Ibid.
65. 113 S.Ct. 1701 (1993).
66. "Age Discrimination," 56 U.S.L.W. 2155 (1987), summarizing *Metz* v. *Transit Mix, Inc.*
67. *Metz* v. *Transit Mix, Inc.,* 828 F.2d 1202, 1205 (7th Cir. 1987).
68. See Paul M. Barrett, "How One Man's Fight for a Raise Became a Major Age-Bias Case," *The Wall Street Journal,* January 7, 1993, p. A1.
69. *United States* v. *Seeger,* 380 U.S. 163 (1965).
70. 432 U.S. 63 (1977).
71. *EEOC* v. *Ithaca Industries,* 849 F.2d 116 (4th Cir. 1988), cert. denied, 109 S.Ct. 306 (1988).
72. *Odom* v. *Hubeny, Inc.,* 345 S.E.2d 886 (Ga. Ct. App. 1986).
73. Junda Woo, "Job Interviews Pose Rising Risk to Employers," *The Wall Street Journal,* March 11, 1992, p. B5.
74. Associated Press, "Strange Questions Cost Target $11.3 Million," *Waterloo Courier,* July 11, 1993, p. A3.
75. Ted Shelsby, "Lawsuits Curtail Checking References of Job Applicants," *Waterloo Courier,* January 29, 1990, p. B5.
76. Ted Shelsby, "Rules Change for Personnel Managers," *Waterloo Courier,* January 29, 1990, p. B5.
77. Jonathan Moses, "Employers Face New Liability: Truth in Hiring," *The Wall Street Journal,* July 9, 1993, p. B1.
78. *Stewart* v. *Jackson & Nash,* 976 F.2d 86 (2d Cir. 1992).
79. *Reich* v. *IBP, Inc.,* 820 F. Supp. 1315 (D. Kan. 1993).
80. See Daniel Seligman, "A Minimal Debate," *Fortune,* March 22, 1993, p. 180.
81. Junda Woo, "More 'On-Call' Workers Sue for Overtime," *The Wall Street Journal,* July 13, 1992, p. B6.
82. Brian Dumaine, "Illegal Child Labor Comes Back," *Fortune,* April 5, 1993, p. 86.
83. Ibid., pp. 86, 87.
84. Associated Press, "Murder Is Top Workplace Killer in Five States," *Des Moines Register,* November 29, 1993, p. 1A; and Stuart Silverstein, "Safety in the Workplace Is Becoming a Growing Concern," *Waterloo Courier,* March 18, 1994, p. C1.
85. Laurie Grossman, "Owner Sentenced to Nearly 20 Years over Plant Fire," *The Wall Street Journal,* September 15, 1992, p. C12.
86. Associated Press, "More than Half of Poultry Plants Never Checked in North Carolina," *Waterloo Courier,* November 12, 1991, p. B4.
87. Ibid.
88. *Joseph Albanese's Case,* 389 N.E.2d 83 (Mass. 1979).
89. *Lubrano* v. *Malinet,* 480 N.E.2d 737 (N.Y. 1985).
90. *United Parcel Service* v. *Fetterman,* 336 S.E.2d 892 (Va. 1985).
91. Jim Carlton, "California Law Alters Workers' Compensation," *The Wall Street Journal,* July 19, 1993, p. A2.
92. Ibid.
93. "Fewer People Fail as Workplace Drug Testing Increases," *HR Focus* 70, no. 6 (June 1993), p. 24.
94. Littler, Mendelson, Fastiff, and Tichy, *The 1990 Employer,* (Chicago: Tort & Insurance Practice Section, ABA, 1990 vol. I, p. Q11.
95. Ibid.
96. Ibid., p. Q13.
97. See, e.g., *National Treasury Employees Union* v. *Von Raab,* 109 S.Ct. 1385 (1989).
98. See *Luck* v. *Southern Pacific Transportation Company,* 218 Cal. App. 3d 1 (1990). But see *Luedtke* v. *Nabors Alaska Drilling Co.,* 768 P.2d 1123 (Alaska 1989).
99. "Ban on Most Uses of Polygraph Tests Clears Congress," *The Wall Street Journal,* June 10, 1988, p. 40.
100. Daniel Seligman, "Searching for Integrity," *Fortune* 127, no. 5 (March 8, 1993), p. 140.
101. Wire Reports, "Bosses Peek at E-Mail," *USA Today,* May 24, 1993, p. B1.
102. Associated Press, "Company Cracking Down on Workers with Hickeys," *Waterloo Courier,* January 21, 1993, p. A6.
103. "Bosses Peek at E-Mail," p. B1.
104. Littler et al., *The 1990 Employer,* p. K1.
105. Dan Dundon, "Explosive Costs Could Rewrite Company-Employee 'Contract,' " *Waterloo Courier,* February 4, 1990, p. A1.
106. Bruce Shenitz, "Patients Left Out in the Cold," *Newsweek,* November 23, 1992, p. 48.
107. *McGann* v. *H&H Music Co.,* 946 F.2d 401 (5th Cir. 1991).
108. Shenitz, "Patients Left Out in the Cold," p. 48.
109. Editorial, "Avoiding a Social Security Crisis," *Des Moines Register,* December 26, 1992, p. 8A.
110. Melinda Beck, "Big Costs, Broken Promises," *Newsweek,* January 11, 1993, p. 59.

111. Albert Karr, "Risk to Retirees Rises as Firms Fall to Fund Pensions They Offer," *The Wall Street Journal,* February 4, 1993, p. A1.
112. Jack Stieber, "Recent Developments in Employment-at-Will," *Labor Law Journal* 36, no. 8 (August 1985), p. 557.
113. John Skipper, "Employer's Right to Make Choices Erodes," *Des Moines Register,* July 5, 1990, p. 8A.
114. *Sheppard* v. *Morgan Keegan & Co.,* 218 Cal. App. 3d 61 (1990).
115. *Foley* v. *Interactive Data Corp.,* 47 Cal. 3d 654 (1988).
116. This discussion of judicial limitations on the at-will doctrine relies heavily on Littler et al., *The 1990 Employer,* Section E.
117. Gabriella Stern, "Companies Discover that Some Firings Backfire into Costly Defamation Suits," *The Wall Street Journal,* May 5, 1993, p. B1.
118. Summers, "Effective Remedies for Employment Rights," p. 457.
119. Milo Geyelin and Jonathan Moses, "Rulings on Wrongful Firing Curb Hiring," *The Wall Street Journal,* April 7, 1992, p. B3.
120. Wade Lambert, "Employee Pacts to Avoid Suits Sought by Firms," *The Wall Street Journal,* October 22, 1992, p. B1.
121. Christopher Conte, "Who Fires? Some Companies Give Up the Right to Dismiss Employees at Will," *The Wall Street Journal,* May 12, 1992, p. A1.
122. Jeremy Fox and Hugh Hindman, "The Model Employment Termination Act: Provisions and Discussion," *Employee Responsibilities and Rights Journal* 6, no. 1 (March 1993), p. 33.
123. Maria Puente, "Sentiment Sours as Rate of Arrival Rises," *USA Today,* July 14, 1993, p. 1A.
124. Ibid.
125. Harry Bernstein, "How Immigration Reform Law Helps U.S. Workers," *Los Angeles Times,* January 30, 1990. p. D3.
126. Bacon, "See You in Court," p. 17.
127. Associated Press, "Specialists Sound Warnings about 'Strong' Pension System," *Waterloo Courier,* August 5, 1992, p. B6.

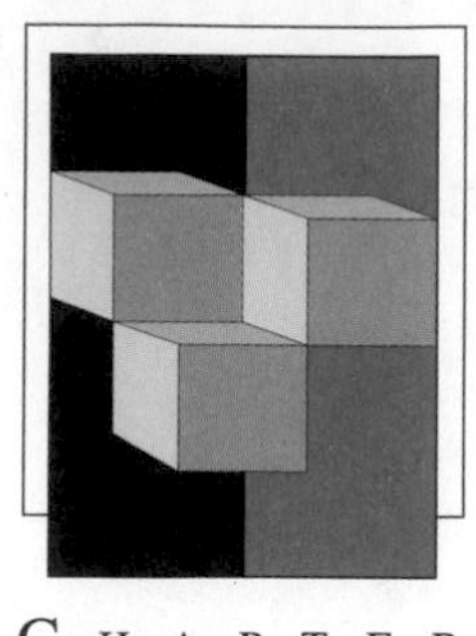

CHAPTER

7

MANAGING HUMAN RESOURCES FROM A LEGAL PERSPECTIVE: PART II—LABOR LAW

READER'S GUIDE

You have learned about how businesses are organized and the law governing their relationships with other businesses, customers, and employees. However, what law governs business decisions if employees are represented by a union or they try to organize into a union? This chapter examines labor-management relations.

PROFILE

Karen Lustig is the founder and owner of a small computer consulting firm that is two years old and is located in Chicago, Illinois. The firm consists of a secretary and two systems analysts in addition to Lustig. Lustig performs solely managerial and executive tasks as the firm's chief officer. The two systems analysts trouble shoot and advise clients regarding their computer systems, and each has a bachelor's degree and industry experience. The secretary serves as secretary to Lustig and the analysts and as such performs routine clerical tasks. The firm's clients are located solely in Illinois, and they have paid fees to the firm during the past 12 months in the amount of approximately $100,000. As a result, the firm is struggling financially and its future is in doubt.

The systems analysts and the secretary believe that Lustig pays inadequate wages and that their benefit package is inadequate. They contact a local union, and after meeting with a representative, they join the union. Subsequently, the union representative informs Lustig that her employees have joined the union and that the union now wishes to bargain collectively with Lustig on their behalf. Lustig declines to do so, and after the union representative leaves the building, she discharges the two systems analysts claiming that one has had a poor attendance record and that the other has been the subject of client complaints.

The union then files unfair labor practice charges with the National Labor Relations Board claiming that the two employees were fired unlawfully and should be reinstated with back pay. The union also files with the NLRB a petition for an election so that Lustig's employees can choose the union as their bargaining representative.

Assume that ultimately the union wins the election and Lustig begins to negotiate with it for a collective bargaining agreement. After months of bargaining, she and the union have reached tentative agreement on many issues; the only remaining unresolved issues relate to wage increases. The final offer from the union is for a wage increase of 5 percent, but Lustig is only willing to raise wages by 3 percent.

QUESTIONS

1. Can the law regulate the relations between a small business such as Lustig's and its employees and the union? On what basis?
2. Can the NLRB order Lustig to reinstate and pay two employees when one was guilty of misconduct and the other had a poor attendance record?
3. Is it ethical for employees to join a union to demand more money and benefits when they know that the company is struggling financially and its future is in doubt?
4. Can Lustig implement her offer of a 3 percent wage increase? Why or why not?

Union membership has declined dramatically in recent years. Only about 15.5 percent of private-sector workers belong to unions.[1] The causes are many:

> Stagnant incomes, a declining manufacturing sector, foreign competition, high unemployment, deregulation, a changing workforce, and a high-tech workplace have all meant trouble in the union hall.[2]

Strikes have declined to the lowest levels since World War II.[3] Demographic changes in the workplace, increased use of economic weapons by employers (e.g., strike replacements), and unresponsiveness by union leaders, among other factors, have led to the current state of unions.[4] Broadly, unions simply do not have the power today that they enjoyed in the past. Nonetheless, because fairness and sound employee relations are necessary to maintaining workplace productivity, labor law remains very important. In addition, the rate of union penetration in the public sector is much higher than in the private sector. Thus, labor law is also an important pat of managing government employees.

I. History

During a relatively short period of time, the United States moved from an agrarian to an industrial society.[5] Goods formerly produced in the home or in small shops by a craftsman and a few apprentices suddenly became the products of factories employing hundreds of people. Then, because of the large number of workers, intermediaries were necessary to supervise and manage the operation of the workplace. The personal relationship that had once existed between workers and their employer disappeared.[6]

Competition among these developing firms in the late 1800s was fierce. Increases in demand often caused firms throughout an industry to expand their operations to keep pace with the growing market. However, since the firms within a given industry all increased output at the same time, production often exceeded the demand for goods.[7] To stay in business, companies had to cut production costs. Faced with fixed costs for raw materials and overhead expenses, companies found that one production cost could be reduced: the cost of labor. By paying workers as little as possible and making them work 14- or 18-hour days, employers could lower their total production costs. Thus, employers had an economic incentive for ignoring the human needs of the workers. The presence of an economic incentive to abuse workers, combined with the absence of the personal relationship between employer and worker, led to a severe deterioration of working conditions.[8]

Farmers and Immigrants. At the same time, two other situations had a significant influence on the development of labor conflict. The first was that workers often left farms and moved to cities to be near their jobs. Unfortunately, that movement destroyed an important safety net. That is, if wages did not provide the full measure of living expenses, farm families still had their gardens, chickens, and cows to use for food. Once these families moved to the cities, all expenses had to be covered by whatever wages were paid, no matter how meager an amount that might be.[9]

A second major factor generating labor conflict was foreign immigrants' influx into northern and midwestern industrial centers. The availability of people anxious to work meant competition for jobs was fierce and employers could fill jobs easily, regardless of low wages and deplorable working conditions.[10] In addition, some highly educated immigrants were escaping political and religious persecution in their homelands. Immigrants brought to the United States ideas, philosophies, and experiences in class struggle and labor conflict, which presumably exacerbated a struggle that was coming to a head in any case.[11]

Immigrants brought to the United States ideas, philosophies, and experiences in class struggle and labor conflict, which presumably exacerbated a struggle that was coming to a head in any case.

A Grim Picture. To say that working conditions for many people at this time were unpleasant or even dismal would be a vast understatement. The term *desperate* better describes the problem. Children were impressed into service as soon as they were big enough to do a job and then made to work 12- and 14-hour days.[12] In fact, small children were employed in coal mines for 10–12 hours each day, and at a rate of $1–3 per week, because they were small enough to fit in the confined spaces.[13] Textile companies would send men called *slavers* to New England and southern farm communities to gather young women to work in the mills.[14] Employers built factory and mining towns where workers would be forced to rent company-owned tenements and buy provisions from company stores at exorbitant rates.[15]

These conditions enable us to better understand the sense of injustice felt by many workers and the belief of many that a redistribution of wealth might provide the only solution to the class conflict.

A. Organizing Labor

The Knights of Labor, initially a secret society, was the first major labor organization in the United States. The Knights of Labor, led first by Uriah Stephens and then by Terence V. Powderly, had a large following during the 1870s and 1880s.[16] The order admitted any workers to its ranks, regardless of occupation, gender, or nationality; in fact, the only people excluded from the group were gamblers, bankers, stockbrokers, and liquor dealers.[17] The Knights of Labor dedicated itself to principles of social reform. For example, the group sought the protection of wage and hour laws, improved health care systems, and mandatory education.[18] However, the goals of the Knights of Labor were perhaps too broad and far-reaching to bring workers any relief from their immediate problems. Great philosophical divisions within the Knights of Labor brought about its rapid decline.[19]

Skilled Workers. Samuel Gompers, who built and developed the American Federation of Labor (AFL), had more practical, attainable goals in mind for his organization. Gompers, a worker in the cigar industry, saw the need to organize workers along craft lines so that each craft group could seek higher wages and better working conditions for its own workers, all of whom had the same type of skills and, presumably, shared the same occupational goals.[20] This approach, a national association of local unions directed to workers' pragmatic needs rather than the more politically motivated activities of the Knights of Labor, proved to be a successful formula for union organization.

Laborers. The Congress of Industrial Organizations (CIO) was organized in response to the need of an entire segment of the working population to which the AFL was virtually unresponsive.[21] The AFL consisted of unions of craft labor. By the 1930s, however, millions of workers were employed in highly compartmentalized jobs requiring very little skill. Assembly-line production required repetitive tasks that could be performed by untrained workers.[22] The interests of these unskilled workers differed greatly from those of skilled workers, and ordinarily the unskilled workers did not qualify for membership in most craft unions. Initially, the AFL considered organizing these employees under the umbrella of its Committee of Industrial Organizations.[23] However, funneling these workers into the craft unions was not a particularly practical solution to their need for organization, and the members of the AFL were not willing to accept the idea of unions set up along industry, rather than craft, lines. John L. Lewis, Sidney Hillman, David Dubinsky, and a number of others saw the need for industrywide unionization in mass-production industries. When their suggestions were rejected out of hand at the 1935 international meeting of the AFL, these people started the CIO.[24]

A great deal of competition existed between the AFL and the CIO through the 1930s and 1940s. The AFL remained attached to traditional notions of labor-management struggle, trying to achieve gains through intrafirm improvements. The CIO was less conventional (in its day) in its approach. It strove for industrywide improvements coupled with political solutions, such as price controls, low-cost housing, and foreign trade policies that would minimize competition from low-cost foreign labor.[25] After years of bitter conflict, the organizations agreed to stop raiding one another for members, and in 1955, the two groups united forces. They function together today as the AFL–CIO.[26]

B. Unions and the Developing Law

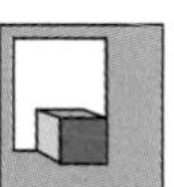

Through the late 19th and early 20th centuries, employers had been very successful in discouraging union organizing. Three devices used by employers to inhibit union formations were "yellow dog" contracts, blacklists, and the American Plan. A **yellow dog contract** was an employment agreement under which the employee was bound by the contract's terms not to become a member of a union. **Blacklists** were simply lists of union organizers or sometimes even participants in labor activities circulated among all the companies in an industry or geographic locale; employers were told not to hire the people named on the lists because they were union instigators.[27] The third strategy, the American Plan, associated the union movement with foreign subversives and involved the use of company unions, organizations ostensibly representing employees but controlled and dominated by the employers themselves.[28]

yellow dog contract. An employment agreement by an employee not to become a member of a union.

blacklists. Lists of union organizers or participants in labor activities circulated to companies in order to dissuade the companies from hiring the listed individuals.

The most effective legal means to halt a union in its incipiency was a curt injunction. If a group of workers began picketing a factory, for example, an employer could easily obtain from a state or federal court an order forbidding the workers to continue such activities because such efforts were considered either a civil or criminal conspiracy.[29]

Responding to mounting public pressure, in 1932 Congress passed the Norris-LaGuardia Act. Designed primarily to prevent antitrust problems, the act withdrew from the federal courts the right to issue injunctions against labor activities and made clear that the terminology "restraint of trade," which was the heart of the 1890 Sherman Antitrust Act, was not meant to include the organization or activities of labor. The Norris-LaGuardia Act also specifically outlawed the use of yellow dog contracts. Even the Norris-LaGuardia Act proved ineffectual, however, because employers were still able to go into state courts to obtain injunctive relief.[30]

Labor Protection. From 1932 to 1935, labor tensions continued to mount. The nation was still caught in the Great Depression. Believing that one element essential to economic recovery was stability in the workforce, Congress addressed the labor question with the Wagner Act of 1935. This legislation, patterned after the Railway Labor Act of 1926, gave workers for the first time the unequivocal right to organize and engage in concerted activities for their mutual aid and benefit. To protect this right, Congress identified and made illegal a number of unfair labor practices. These unfair labor practices were all activities that Congress feared employers might use to thwart workers' attempts to unionize and to undermine the economic power that would come from the workers' new-found rights.[31] Through the Wagner Act, Congress also established the National Labor Relations Board, an administrative agency charged with the responsibility of overseeing and ensuring fair union representation elections and investigating, prosecuting, and trying employers accused of unfair labor practices.[32]

Management Protection. Unions grew rapidly with the passage of the Wagner Act, and by 1947, Congress decided labor no longer needed such a protective watchdog.[33] In fact, Congress thought management might need a little help in coping with ever-growing labor organizations.[34] Thus, Congress decided to neutralize its position vis-à-vis labor organizations by imposing some responsibilities on these organizations. Congress did so by enacting the Taft-Hartley Act, a series of amendments to the Wagner Act that identified as unfair labor practices certain activities unions used to exercise economic leverage over employers as part of the collective bargaining process. The Taft-Hartley Act also added a provision to the existing labor legislation that ensured employers' right to speak out in opposition to union organizing—in effect, protecting their First Amendment right to freedom of speech. Thus, the Taft-Hartley Act signaled a move by the government away from unconditional support for labor toward a balance of rights between labor and management.[35]

Corrupt Union Leaders. Congressional hearings in the 1950s uncovered another source of concern in the area of labor relations. This time, the problems were not between labor and management, although certainly friction between the two continued to exist. Attention now was focused on union leaders who were abusing their power. Once in power, some union leaders had prevented others from challenging that power by not holding meetings of the union's rank and file, not scheduling elections, and using union funds to promote their own election campaigns. Stories came to light accusing some union officials of accepting collective bargaining agreements with terms that were against the interest of their constituencies, in exchange for bribes paid to them by corporate management. These agreements were aptly called *sweetheart deals*. Evidence indicated certain union officials had looted their unions' treasuries.[36]

In response to the growing evidence that union leaders were benefiting at the expense of the membership, Congress in 1959 enacted the Labor-Management Reporting and Disclosure Act (LMRDA), also known as the Landrum-Griffin Act. This act contains provisions requiring unions to keep records of their funds, including statements of their assets, liabilities, salaries paid, and all other expenditures. It also prohibits unions from loaning money except under specified circumstances and in conformity with certain procedural rules. These financial statements and transactions must all be reported annually to the government.

Members' Rights. The Landrum-Griffin Act also contains a set of provisions often referred to as the "Bill of Rights" for the individual union members. These provisions are designed to protect union members by requiring that union meetings be held, that members be permitted to speak and vote at these meetings, that every employee covered by a collective bargaining agreement have the right to see a copy of that agreement, and that a union member be informed of the reasons and given a chance for a hearing if the union wishes to suspend or take disciplinary action against that member, unless he or she is being suspended for nonpayment of dues.[37] Although these provisions had the potential for eliminating internal union problems, court decisions have done much to emasculate the protections provided in Landrum-Griffin.

The law has also regulated the manner in which unions represent employees in the collective bargaining process. Because a union serves as employees' exclusive bargaining representative, the courts have devised a *duty of fair representation.*[38] To fulfill this duty, a union must represent employees, both in negotiating and enforcing the collective bargaining agreement, "without hostility or discrimination . . . [and] . . . with complete good faith and honesty [so as to] avoid arbitrary conduct."[39]

C. Labor Unions Today

The decades of the 1960s, 1970s, and the 1980s were marked by the decline of unions with respect to the percentage of the workforce they represented and to their power to influence the work environment.

During the 70s, unions made concessions at the bargaining table in response to a deteriorating economy,[40] and employers increased the use of illegal tactics.[41] At the end of the decade, an attempt to reform labor law failed. The 1980s commenced with the permanent replacement of striking air traffic controllers by President Ronald Reagan, which, although the dispute did not arise under the National Labor Relations Act, prefaced the increased use of strike replacements by private-sector employers. However, the decline in union penetration in the private sector has at the current time leveled off.[42] Moreover, this three-decade period has seen tremendous growth of unions in the public sector.[43] Therefore, the role and influence of unions remain as an important consideration for all managers.

Profile Perspective: Recall that all of Lustig's clients are in Illinois. Does Congress's constitutional power to regulate interstate commerce apply? What if Lustig purchases material from out of state? Or if her clients were themselves engaged in interstate commerce? Would the NLRB have jurisdiction in any of these cases? Why or why not?

This historical progression—from labor's helplessness, to active union organizing following passage of the Wagner Act in 1935, to restoration of balance between labor and management in 1947, to a recognition of the powerlessness of the individual within the union, to the current state of unionization today—sounds very smooth and logical. The entire process has been likened by many to the swinging of a pendulum. Don't forget, however, that labor conflicts in the United States have often been attended by severe violence; have driven apart towns, factories, and even families;[44] and have raised emotions to higher pitches than perhaps any other social or political issue. Labor law must be understood within this context.

II. Labor Legislation Today

A. The Statutory Scheme of Labor Law and Its Goals

Today, labor-management relations are governed by the National Labor Relations Act (NLRA), as enforced by the NLRB.[45] This act includes within it the Wagner Act, the Taft-Hartley Act, and portions of the Landrum-Griffin Act. The remaining provisions of the Landrum-Griffin Act make up the Labor-Management Reporting and Disclosure Act (mentioned earlier) and the Bill of Rights of Members of Labor Organizations. These provisions deal with the internal operations of labor organizations and the relationship between individual union members and the union itself rather than with the relationship between the union and the employer.

Given its constitutional authority to regulate interstate commerce, the congressional basis for labor legislation is the elimination of obstructions to the free flow of commerce caused by labor conflicts. Congress contends that labor conflict is due, in large part, to a lack of bargaining power on the part of individual employees and, thus, sets out to correct the problem by protecting union and **concerted activity** by employees and by regulating collective bargaining between labor organizations and management. Keep these ideas in mind as you examine the choices made by Congress in regulating labor-management relations and the decisions made by the NLRB and the courts in interpreting and applying these statutory mandates.[46]

concerted activity. Organizing, forming, joining, or assisting labor organizations, bargaining collectively through representatives of the employees' choosing, or other activities taken for the purpose of collective bargaining or other mutual aid or protection.

The National Labor Relations Act, Section 1, sets out the following policy statement:

> It is declared to be the policy of the United States to eliminate the causes of certain substantial obstructions to the free flow of commerce and to mitigate these obstructions when they have occurred by encouraging the practice and procedure of collective bargaining and by protecting the exercise by workers of full freedom of association, self-organization, and designation of representatives of their own choosing, for the purpose of negotiating the terms and conditions of their employment or other mutual aid or protection.

Thus, the NLRA has two goals: employee free choice and stable collective bargaining. In the absence of labor-management legislation such as that contained in the NLRA, what restraints are there to ensure that these two goals can be attained? Were those restraints effective in the early part of this century?

Profile Perspective: Is Karen Lustig covered by the NLRA? Could this be true even though her firm is so small?

Right to Organize. First, the NLRA gives employees the right to engage in concerted activity, known for the most part as strikes and collective bargaining. Section 7 of the NLRA states:

> Employees shall have the right to self-organization, to form, join or assist labor organizations, to bargain collectively through representatives of their own choosing, and to engage in other concerted activities for the purpose of collective bargaining or other mutual aid or protection, and shall also have the right to refrain from any and all of such activities except to the extent that such right may be affected by an agreement requiring membership in a labor organization as a condition of employment.

Unfair Labor Practices by Management. Second, as previously mentioned, the act describes and outlaws certain activities by employers that would hamper or discourage employees from exercising the rights granted to them in Section 7. Thus, Section 8(a) of the act makes it an **unfair labor practice** for an employer to:

unfair labor practice. Activities identified by Congress that employees might use to thwart workers' attempts to unionize and to undermine the economic power that would come from the workers' right to concerted activities and to unionize.

1. Interfere with, restrain, or coerce employees in the exercise of the rights given to them by Section 7.
2. Dominate, interfere, or assist with the formation of any labor organization, including contributing financial support to it.
3. Encourage or discourage membership in any labor organization by discrimination in regard to hiring, tenure of employment, promotion, salary, or any other term of employment.
4. Discharge or take any other action against an employee because he or she has filed charges or given testimony under the act.
5. Refuse to bargain collectively with a duly certified representative of the employees.

These five provisions are designed to allow employees to organize in an atmosphere free from intimidation by the employer, with minds clear of the fear that the employer might be able to affect their jobs adversely because of their choice to participate in a labor organization and to continue their participation in the union. In addition, if employees have chosen a union as their exclusive collective bargaining representative, Section 8(a) regulates the bargaining between the employer and the union. The provisions also ensure that the employer, through his or her position of authority, will not be able to interfere with union activities by either seizing control of the union or rendering it impotent by refusing to bargain collectively.

Unfair Labor Practices by Union. Section 8(b) lists activities constituting unfair labor practices by a labor organization. Some of these provisions mirror some of the activities prohibited to employers. Moreover, at least since the enactment of the Taft-Hartley Act, the law is not sympathetic to labor organizations that try to use certain coercive tactics, threats of the loss of livelihood, or any other strong-arm methods. Finally, Section 8(b) also regulates the union's collective bargaining practices, including economic action. Thus, a labor organization is not permitted to:

1. Restrain or coerce any employee in the exercise of his or her rights as granted by Section 7.
2. Cause or attempt to cause an employer to discriminate against an employee who has chosen not to join a particular labor organization or has been denied membership in such an organization.
3. Refuse to bargain collectively with an employer on behalf of the bargaining unit it is certified to represent.
4. Induce or attempt to induce an employer to engage in secondary boycott activities.
5. Require employees to become union members and then charge them excessive or discriminatory dues.
6. Try to make an employer compensate workers for services not performed.
7. Picket or threaten to picket an employer in an attempt to force the employer to recognize or bargain with a labor organization that is not the duly certified representative of a bargaining unit.

The remaining subparts of Section 8 cover a variety of problems: Section 8(c) protects the First Amendment rights of people involved in labor disputes and spells out limitations on those rights. Section 8(d) describes and defines the duties of employers and labor organizations to bargain collectively over certain mandatory subjects. This section also sets up a cooling-off process under which a party that wishes to renegotiate a collective bargaining agreement must serve notice of its desire to do so 60 days in advance of the agreement's expiration date. Sections 8(e) and (f) describe situations in which it is impermissible for both employers and labor organizations to extend their disputes beyond the confines of their own internal conflict.

Representation Matters. Section 9 of the act also sets forth the procedures by which employees may choose, usually through a secret ballot election, whether to be represented by a particular union or no union at all.

B. National Labor Relations Board

The NLRB is an administrative agency instrumental in regulating labor-management relations. Its primary tasks are designating appropriate bargaining units of workers (deciding which workers have a sufficient community of interest so that their needs can be best acknowledged and so collective bargaining is efficient for the employer and the union); conducting elections for union representation within the chosen bargaining unit; certifying the results of such elections; and investigating, prosecuting, and adjudicating charges of unfair labor practices.[47]

Although the congressional mandate by which the NLRB was formed gives the agency jurisdiction theoretically to the full extent of the interstate commerce powers vested in Congress, the agency has neither the funding nor the staff to administer its duties to all of American industry. Moreover, the act and the NLRB recognize that certain categories of employees should be excluded from the act, either because they play no role in commerce or because they are more closely aligned with management. Thus, some limitations have been placed on the board by both statute and the agency's own decisions.

These restrictions on jurisdiction take two basic forms. (1) Employers: The NLRB itself requires the portion of an employer's business involved in interstate commerce to exceed certain dollar amounts, which differ depending on the nature of the industry. Labor disputes involving firms falling beneath the minimum are assumed not to significantly affect commerce. (2) Employees: Entire groups of employees are excluded from coverage. For example, government employees, railroad and airline workers covered by the Railway Labor Act, agricultural workers, domestic workers, independent contractors, and supervisors and other managerial employees are not protected by the board.[48]

C. Choosing a Bargaining Representative—Elections

Representation elections are the process by which the NLRB achieves the first of the two statutory goals under the act: employee freedom of choice. However, as we shall see, in doing so there is sometimes a conflict between that goal and the other statutory goal, stable collective bargaining. The NLRB has devised certain rules to resolve such conflicts.

Election Petition. A union, employee, or employer initiates the formal organizing process by filing an election petition with the NLRB. The petition is sent to the employer, thus providing notice of union activity. Also, the employer must post notices supplied by the NLRB so that employees are aware of the petition. The NLRB then assumes its authority to closely oversee the conduct of employer and union. Of course at that point, the employer is free to simply recognize its employees' interest in joining a particular union and to engage in bargaining with that union, commonly called *voluntary recognition.* However, this process is uncommon. Failing voluntary recognition, the process proceeds through the NLRB. To conserve its resources for serious matters, the NLRB will accept only those petitions supported by a substantial showing of interest, which has been interpreted to mean the signatures of at least 30 percent of the employees in the bargaining unit the union seeks to represent. (In practice today, most unions will not proceed toward an election without 50 to 65 percent of the employees' signatures.) Those signatures accompany the petition, or they may appear on authorization cards, which unions may provide to workers to affirm their interest in an election or in union representation.

Procedure. The NLRB ordinarily will first attempt to settle certain issues such as whether a union contract already covers the employees or whether the election should be delayed either by agreement or by order of the board after a hearing. In determining the timing of the election, the two statutory goals of employee free choice and stable collective bargaining may conflict. For example, if the employees are already covered by a collective bargaining agreement, should they be able to choose again during the term of the agreement? Surely, to do so would provide for employee free choice. But what of stable collective bargaining? Should not the collective bargaining agreement be recognized? Similarly, if the employees have rejected a union in an election, can they be prohibited from voting again in the name of stable collective bargaining? If so, what of their right to freedom of choice? Alternatively, what if the employees choose to unionize in an election, but reconsider before a collective bargaining agreement is reached? Can they have another election?

To resolve these conflicts the NLRB has devised bars to an election. In the first instance set forth above, the board will prohibit an election during the term of a collective bargaining agreement, but only for a period not to exceed three years. This is known as the **contract bar rule.** An **election year** or **certification year bar** prohibits an election for 12 months following a prior election so that the employer can enjoy stable collective bargaining without negating the employees' freedom of choice.

contract bar rule. The NLRB prohibits an election during the term of a collective bargaining agreement, for a maximum of three years.

election year or certification year bar. NLRB prohibits an election for 12 months following a prior election.

However, the crucial issue to be addressed at this point is normally whether the proposed bargaining unit (the designated employee group, for example, all hourly workers, all welders, or all craftspersons) is appropriate for the election.

Appropriate Bargaining Unit. The key consideration in establishing an appropriate employee bargaining unit is the community of interest among the employees. The NLRB searches for an appropriate bargaining unit because collective bargaining will not be stable and efficient (the second statutory goal) if it involves employees with diverse interests. Therefore, the bargaining unit may range from a portion of a plant to multiple employers in multiple plants. Plants may have more than one appropriate bargaining unit, depending on the composition of the workforce. The NLRB makes the decision regarding the appropriate bargaining unit on the basis of such considerations as physical location of the plants, physical contact among employees, similarity of wages, benefits, working conditions, differences in skill requirements among job categories, and common supervision.

Profile Perspective: Recall that Lustig employs two systems analysts and one secretary and that all three of them wish to be represented by the union. Do the two categories of employees share the same community of interests? Should they both be placed in one appropriate bargaining unit? Why or why not?

Unit Exclusions. Certain classes of employees, such as supervisors, are excluded from the bargaining unit. Obviously, supervisors are excluded because they act on behalf of the employer and through their power to direct and assign work and to discipline and discharge employees, exert control over their subordinates who are or may be in the bargaining unit. However, the treatment of other types of employees may not be so clear.

Some employees determine and implement employer policies without assigning work or disciplining other employees, for example, fiscal officers who allocate financial resources on behalf of employers. Should these people be permitted to join other employees in an appropriate bargaining unit? In *NLRB* v. *Bell Aerospace Co., Division of Textron, Inc.,*[49] the Supreme Court faced this issue with respect to employees who were buyers responsible for purchasing materials to be used in the employer's manufacturing facility. The Supreme Court held that these employees, referred to as "managerial employees," could be excluded from the bargaining unit if they "formulated, determined, and effectuated" employer policy and did so with sufficient discretion so that they did not simply conform to a policy already established.

Another dilemma is posed by those employees who work in an employer's business office and as such have access to employer files and other business data, for example, executive secretaries. On the other hand, however, the actual tasks that they perform are no different than those performed by other secretaries. Should they also be excluded? The NLRB has ruled that these "confidential employees" can be excluded only if they assist in a confidential capacity individuals who formulate, determine, and effectuate employee or labor relations policies on behalf of the employer.

The Election for Union Representative. After the parties have agreed to conduct an election, or alternatively, the NLRB has directed that an election be conducted following a hearing, the board will require that the employer post notices and conduct the election (see Figures 7.1 and 7.2). The union representative may be selected only by a majority of the votes cast by the employees. The NLRB oversees the election to ensure the process is carried on under "laboratory conditions."[50] In other words, elections must be held under circumstances that, to the extent possible, are free from undue or unfair influence by either the employer or by unions vying for the right to represent the bargaining unit.

To determine if an election was conducted under the necessary "laboratory conditions," the NLRB has the power to review the conduct of the employer or the union during the period between the filing of the election petition and the election itself. The board will also, if called upon, monitor the polling place itself, including the conduct of its own agents, because "the final minutes before an employee casts his vote should be his own, as free from interference as possible."[51] If the NLRB determines that objectionable conduct has taken place, it will invalidate the results of the election and another will be held.

For both employers and employees, the circulation of racist propaganda designed to engender racial antipathy is grounds for setting aside an election. Historically, the NLRB took a similarly firm stance regarding all manner of propaganda and misrepresentation. Frequently, the board has set aside elections tainted by trickery such as falsehoods, allegations, misstatements, and the like. However, its position in this area has changed; its current position is that misrepresentation alone will not constitute grounds for overturning an election. The burden is on the parties to correct misrepresentations and sort out the truth via the marketplace of ideas. The board would intervene only if the deceptive manner of the misrepresentation (e.g., a forged document) made it impossible for the parties themselves to discern the truth. Some courts have endorsed the NLRB view; others have not. The NLRB may once again change its position. Hence, "most parties remain cautious regarding possible misrepresentations, particularly in the very late stages of a campaign, when the other side will not have time to reply."[52]

PETITION NOTICE

FIGURE 7.1

NOTICE TO EMPLOYEES

FROM THE

National Labor Relations Board

A PETITION has been filed with this Federal agency seeking an election to determine whether certain employees want to be represented by a union.

The case is being investigated and NO DETERMINATION HAS BEEN MADE AT THIS TIME by the National Labor Relations Board. IF an election is held Notices of Election will be posted giving complete details for voting.

It was suggested that your employer post this notice so the National Labor Relations Board could inform you of your basic rights under the National Labor Relations Act.

YOU HAVE THE RIGHT under Federal Law

- **To self-organization**
- **To form, join, or assist labor organizations**
- **To bargain collectively through representatives of your own choosing**
- **To act together for the purposes of collective bargaining or other mutual aid or protection**
- **To refuse to do any or all of these things unless the union and employer, in a state where such agreements are permitted, enter into a lawful union-security agreement requiring employees to pay periodic dues and initiation fees. Nonmembers who inform the union that they object to the use of their payments for nonrepresentational purposes may be required to pay only their share of the union's costs of representational activities *(such as collective bargaining, contract administration, and grievance adjustments).***

It is possible that some of you will be voting in an employee representation election as a result of the request for an election having been filed. While NO DETERMINATION HAS BEEN MADE AT THIS TIME, in the event an election is held, the NATIONAL LABOR RELATIONS BOARD wants all eligible voters to be familiar with their rights under the law IF it holds an election.

The Board applies rules that are intended to keep its elections fair and honest and that result in a free choice. If agents of either unions or employers act in such a way as to interfere with your right to a free election, the election can be set aside by the Board. Where appropriate the Board provides other remedies, such as reinstatement for employees fired for exercising their rights, including backpay from the party responsible for their discharge.

NOTE:

The following are examples of conduct that interfere with the rights of employees and may result in the setting aside of the election.

- **Threatening loss of jobs or benefits by an employer or a union**
- **Promising or granting promotions, pay raises, or other benefits to influence an employee's vote by a party capable of carrying out such promises**
- **An employer firing employees to discourage or encourage union activity or a union causing them to be fired to encourage union activity**
- **Making campaign speeches to assembled groups of employees on company time within the 24-hour period before the election**
- **Incitement by either an employer or a union of racial or religious prejudice by inflammatory appeals**
- **Threatening physical force or violence to employees by a union or an employer to influence their votes**

Please be assured that IF AN ELECTION IS HELD every effort will be made to protect your right to a free choice under the law. Improper conduct will not be permitted. All parties are expected to cooperate fully with this Agency in maintaining basic principles of a fair election as required by law. The National Labor Relations Board, as an agency of the United States Government, does not endorse any choice in the election.

NATIONAL LABOR RELATIONS BOARD
an agency of the
UNITED STATES GOVERNMENT

THIS IS AN OFFICIAL GOVERNMENT NOTICE AND MUST NOT BE DEFACED BY ANYONE

FORM NLRB-666 (5-90) ☆U.S. GOVERNMENT PRINTING OFFICE: 1991-312-471/51356

FIGURE 7.2 ELECTION NOTICE

GENERAL

PURPOSE OF THIS ELECTION — This election is to determine the representative, if any, desired by the eligible Employees for purposes of collective bargaining with their Employer. (See VOTING UNIT in this Notice of Election for description of eligible employees.) A majority of the valid ballots cast will determine the results of the election.

SECRET BALLOT — The election will be by SECRET ballot under the supervision of the Regional Director of the National Labor Relations Board. Voters will be allowed to vote without interference, restraint, or coercion. Electioneering will not be permitted at or near the polling place. Violations of these rules should be reported immediately to the Regional Director or the agent in charge of the election. Your attention is called to Section 12 of the National Labor Relations Act:

> **ANY PERSON WHO SHALL WILLFULLY RESIST, PREVENT, IMPEDE, OR INTERFERE WITH ANY MEMBER OF THE BOARD OR ANY OF ITS AGENTS OR AGENCIES IN THE PERFORMANCE OF DUTIES PURSUANT TO THIS ACT SHALL BE PUNISHED BY A FINE OF NOT MORE THAN $5,000 OR BY IMPRISONMENT FOR NOT MORE THAN ONE YEAR, OR BOTH.**

Upon arrival at the voting place, voters should proceed to the Board agent and identify themselves by stating their name. The Board agent will hand a ballot to each eligible voter. Voters will enter the voting booth and mark their ballot in secret. DO NOT SIGN YOUR BALLOT. Fold the ballot before leaving the voting booth, then personally deposit it in a ballot box under the supervision of the Board agent and leave the polling area.

A sample of the official ballot is shown at the center of this Notice.

ELIGIBILITY RULES — Employees eligible to vote are those described under VOTING UNIT in this Notice of Election, including employees who did not work during the designated payroll period because they were ill or on vacation or temporarily laid off, and also including employees in the military service of the United States who appear in person at the polls. Employees who have quit or been discharged for cause since the designated payroll period and who have not been rehired or reinstated prior to the date of this election are not eligible to vote.

SPECIAL ASSISTANCE — Any employee or other participant in this election who has a handicap, and who in order to participate in this election needs special assistance, such as a sign language interpreter, should notify the Regional Director as soon as possible and request the necessary assistance.

CHALLENGE OF VOTERS — If your eligibility to vote is challenged, you will be allowed to vote a challenged ballot. Although you may believe you are eligible to vote, the polling area is not the place to resolve the issue. Give the Board agent your name and any other information you are asked to provide. After you receive a ballot, proceed to the voting booth, mark your ballot and fold it so as to keep the mark secret. DO NOT SIGN YOUR BALLOT. Return to the Board agent who will ask you to place your ballot in a challenged envelope, seal the envelope, place it in the ballot box, and leave the polling area. Your eligibility will be resolved later.

AUTHORIZED OBSERVERS — Each of the interested parties may designate an equal number of observers, this number to be determined by the Regional Director or agent in charge of the election. These observers (a) act as checkers at the voting place and at the counting of ballots; (b) assist in the identification of voters; (c) challenge voters and ballots; and (d) otherwise assist the Regional Director or agent.

INFORMATION CONCERNING ELECTION — The Act provides that only one valid representation election may be held in a 12-month period. Any employee who desires to obtain any further information concerning the terms and conditions under which this election is to be held, or who desires to raise any question concerning the holding of an election, the voting unit, or eligibility rules, may do so by communicating with the Regional Director or agent in charge of the election.

(*Continued*) **FIGURE 7.2**

VOTING UNIT

Those eligible to vote are all full-time and regular part-time production and maintenance employees, including flex graphic press operators, rewinder operators, slitter operators, coater operators, forklift operators, typesetting and graphics employees, plant shipping clerk, and offset employees, employed by the Employer at its facility currently located at 3400 W. 43rd Place, Chicago, IL, during the payroll period ending December 15, 1994; excluding all office clerical employees, guards and supervisors as defined in the Act.

DATE AND TIME OF ELECTION

DATE: Thursday, January 12, 1995 TIME: 3:00 p.m. to 4:00 p.m.

PLACE: New Building/Lunch Area

Employees are free to vote at any time during the scheduled polling period.

UNITED STATES OF AMERICA

National Labor Relations Board

FORM NLRB-707N2 *(RC, RM, RD CASES)* (4-84)

OFFICIAL SECRET BALLOT

For certain employees of

LABELS UNLIMITED COMPANY

SAMPLE

Do you wish to be represented for purposes of collective bargaining by -

MISCELLANEOUS WAREHOUSEMEN, AIRLINE, AUTOMOTIVE PARTS, SERVICE, TIRE AND RENTAL, CHEMICAL AND PETROLEUM, ICE, PAPER, AND RELATED CLERICAL AND PRODUCTION EMPLOYEES UNION, LOCAL NO. 781, Affiliated with INTERNATIONAL BROTHERHOOD OF TEAMSTERS, AFL-CIO

MARK AN "X" IN THE SQUARE OF YOUR CHOICE

YES	NO
☐	☐

DO NOT SIGN THIS BALLOT. Fold and drop in ballot box.
If you spoil this ballot return it to the Board Agent for a new one.

FIGURE 7.2 *(Continued)*

RIGHTS OF EMPLOYEES

Under the National Labor Relations Act, employees have the right

- To self-organization
- To form, join, or assist labor organizations
- To bargain collectively through representatives of their own choosing
- To act together for the purpose of collective bargaining or other mutual aid or protection
- To refuse to do any or all of these things unless the Union and Employer, in a State where such agreements are permitted, enter into a lawful union-security agreement requiring employees to pay periodic dues and initiation fees. Nonmembers who inform the union that they object to the use of their payments for nonrepresentational purposes may be required to pay only their share of the union's costs. of representational activities (such as collective bargaining, contract administration, and grievance adjustment).

It is the responsibility of the National Labor Relations Board to protect employees in the exercise of these rights.

The Board wants all eligible voters to be fully informed about their rights under Federal law and wants both Employers and Unions to know what is expected of them when it holds an election.

If agents of either Unions or Employer interfere with your right to a free, fair, and honest election, the election can be set aside by the Board. When appropriate, the Board provides other remedies, such as reinstatement for employees fired for exercising their rights, including backpay from the party responsible for their discharge.

The following are examples of conduct that interfere with the rights of employees and may result in the setting aside of the election:

- Threatening loss of jobs or benefits by an Employer or a Union
- Promising or granting promotions, pay raises, or other benefits to influence an employee's vote by a party capable of carrying out such promises
- An Employer firing employees to discourage or encourage union activity or a Union causing them to be fired to encourage union activity
- Making campaign speeches to assembled groups of employees on company time within the 24-hour period before the election
- Incitement by either an Employer or a Union of racial or religious prejudice by inflammatory appeals
- Threatening physical force or violence to employees by a Union or an Employer to influence their votes.

The National Labor Relations Board protects your right to a free choice

Improper conduct will not be permitted. All parties are expected to cooperate fully with this Agency in maintaining basic principles of a fair election as required by law. The National Labor Relations Board as an agency of the United States Government does not endorse any choice in the election.

NATIONAL LABOR RELATIONS BOARD ★

NATIONAL LABOR RELATIONS BOARD

an agency of the

UNITED STATES GOVERNMENT

Elizabeth Kinney, Regional Director
National Labor Relations Board
Region - 13
200 W. Adams Street, Suite 800
Chicago, Illinois 60606
Phone: (312) 353-7570

CASE

General Shoe Corp.

77 NLRB 124 (1948)

Facts

In this case, the NLRB was called upon to determine if conduct that did not constitute a violation of the sections of the NLRA prohibiting certain practices could still be relied upon to invalidate an election under its Section 9 authority for holding representation elections. During the campaign, the employer brought groups of 20–25 employees to his office and spoke to them in order to persuade to vote against the union. The employer also sent supervisors to the employees' homes for the same purpose. However, at no time during these conversations did the employer or his supervisors say or do anything that would be an unfair labor practice.

* * *

When we are asked to invalidate elections held under our auspices, our only consideration derives from the Act which calls for freedom of choice by employees . . . Conduct that creates an atmosphere which renders improbable a free choice will sometimes warrant invalidating an election, even though that conduct may not constitute an unfair labor practice. An election can serve its true purpose only if the surrounding conditions enable employees to register a free and untrammeled choice for or against a bargaining representative . . .

We do not subscribe to the view . . . that the criteria applied by the Board in a representation proceeding to determine whether certain alleged misconduct interfered with an election need necessarily be identical to those employed in testing whether an unfair labor practice was committed . . . In election proceedings, it is the Board's function to provide a laboratory in which an experiment may be conducted, under conditions as nearly ideal as possible, to determine the uninhibited desires of the employees. It is our duty to establish those conditions; it is our duty to determine whether they have been fulfilled.

Union Activity on Company Property and Time. In these cases, the NLRB is called upon to balance the competing rights of the employer as the property owner and the Section 7 rights of employees. Thus, the Supreme Court has decided that the establishment and enforcement of a rule prohibiting union solicitation by employees outside working time, although on company property, "is an unreasonable impediment to self-organization." This ruling is based on the board's rationale that "working time is for work" but that time outside of work is "an employee's time to use as he wishes without unreasonable restraint although the employee is on company property."[53] However, a distinction must be made between the activity of employees and nonemployees. Accordingly, an employer may restrict union activity by nonemployee union organizers on company property and time so long as other alternative channels of communication are available to the union and the employer does not permit other nonemployees to solicit employees or distribute material.[54] If the solicitor is an off-duty employee, the employer may limit his or her access to nonworking areas so long as the prohibition is made known and is not applied in a discriminatory fashion.[55]

Although unfair labor practices may occur at any point, they are frequently committed at this juncture by employers anxious to prevent their plants from becoming organized. This is not meant to suggest that overzealous unions never commit unfair labor practices or that employers always do. However, employers who are resistant to unions have a great many natural advantages in the struggle against them. An employer could distribute written arguments and objections to unions along with paychecks and thereby ensure that every employee sees the document. (Such an action, by itself, is *not* an unfair labor practice.)[56] The employer effectively has a captive audience and generally is in better financial shape to stage a battle than the union is. Finally, and perhaps most important, the employer is the one who, in the final analysis, doles out or withholds benefits to the employees and provides them with jobs in the first place.

Protection of Free Speech. In addition to these considerable inherent advantages, employers also have the right to speak out against unions in the form of ads, speeches, and the like. Section 8(c) of the Taft-Hartley Act is designed to ensure employers' and labor organizations' traditional First Amendment rights so long as they do not overstep certain bounds:

> The expressing of any views, argument or opinion, or the dissemination thereof, whether in written, printed, graphic or visual form, shall not constitute or be evidence of an unfair labor practice . . . if such expression contains no threat of reprisal or force or promise of benefit.

Threats of Reprisal or Force. Clearly, when an employer tells employees that, for example, they will all be discharged if they engage in union activity, there has been interference with their rights. Similarly, if an employer interrogates them about their activities or spies on them while they attend union meetings, there has been unlawful interference. However, problems often arise in determining whether antiunion arguments put forth by an employer are legitimate or whether they contain veiled threats. Suppose, for instance, that a company owner warns her employees that if she has to pay higher wages, she will be forced to go out of business and the employees will all lose their jobs. Such statements of economic forecast by employers have been the subject of a great deal of litigation. The following case explains the issues involved.

CASE

NLRB v. Gissel Packaging Co.

395 U.S. 575 (1969)

Facts

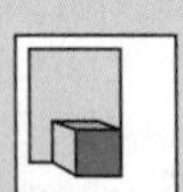

The president of Sinclair Company, one of four companies whose actions were being examined in this case, tried to dissuade his employees from joining a union. To that end, he informed them that, if the union won the election, it was bound to call a strike because the Teamsters were a "strike-happy" outfit. He told the employees on more than one occasion that the company's financial position was precarious and that a strike would likely force the plant to close. He suggested that the out-of-work employees would have a difficult time finding new jobs because of their age and lack of education. The union lost the election by a vote of 7 to 6 and filed objections to the election with the NLRB.

Both the NLRB and later the Court of Appeals agreed that the election should be set aside, despite the company's claim that it had merely been exercising its First Amendment rights to express its views to employees. The Supreme Court affirmed the Court of Appeals decision.

* * *

Continued

Continued

Chief Justice Warren

We note that an employer's free speech right to communicate his views to his employees is firmly established and cannot be infringed by a union or the board. Thus, § 8(c) [29 U.S.C. § 158(c)] merely implements the First Amendment by requiring that the expression of "any views, arguments, or opinion," shall not be "evidence of an unfair labor practice," so long as such expression contains "no threat of reprisal or force or promise of benefit" in violation of § 8(a)(1). Section 8(a)(1), in turn, prohibits interference, restraint, or coercion of employees in the exercise of their right to self-organization.

Any assessment of the precise scope of employer expression, of course, must be made in the context of its labor relations setting. Thus, an employer's rights cannot outweigh the equal rights of the employees to associate freely, as those rights are embodied in § 7 and protected by § 8(a)(1) and the proviso to § 8(c). And any balancing of those rights must take into account the economic dependence of the employees on their employers, and the necessary tendency of the former, because of that relationship, to pick up intended implications of the latter that might be more readily dismissed by a more disinterested ear. Stating these obvious principles is but another way of recognizing that what is basically at stake is the establishment of a nonpermanent, limited relationship between the employer, his economically dependent employee, and his union agent, not the election of legislators or the enactment of legislation whereby that relationship is ultimately defined and where the independent voter may be freer to listen more objectively and employers as a class freer to talk.

Within this framework, we must reject the company's challenge . . . Thus, an employer is free to communicate to his employees any of his general views about unionism or any of his specific views about a particular union, so long as the communications do not contain a "threat of reprisal or force or promise of benefit." He may even make a prediction as to the precise effects he believes unionization will have on his company. In such a case, however, the prediction must be carefully phrased on the basis of objective fact to convey an employer's belief as to demonstrably probable consequences beyond his control or to convey a management decision already arrived at to close the plant in case of unionization. If there is any implication that an employer may or may not take action solely on his own initiative for reasons unrelated to economic necessities and known only to him, the statement is no longer a reasonable prediction based on available facts but a threat of retaliation based on misrepresentation and coercion, and as such without the protection of the First Amendment.

* * *

Equally valid was the finding by the court and the board that petitioner's statements and communications were not cast as a prediction of "demonstrable 'economic consequences,' " but rather as a threat of retaliatory action. The board found that petitioner's speeches, pamphlets, leaflets, and letters conveyed the following message: that the company was in a precarious financial condition; that the "strike-happy" union would in all likelihood have to obtain its potentially unreasonable demands by striking, the probable result of which would be a plant shutdown, as the past history of labor relations in the area indicated; and that the employees in such a case would have great difficulty finding employment elsewhere. In carrying out its duty to focus on the question "[W]hat did the speaker intend and the listener understand?" the board could reasonably conclude that the intended and understood import of that message was not to predict that unionization would inevitably cause the plant to close but to threaten to throw employees out of work regardless of the economic realities. In this connection, we need go no further than to point out (1) that petitioner had no support for its basic assumption that the union, which had not yet even presented any demands, would have to strike to be heard, and that it

Continued

Continued

admitted at the hearing that it had no basis for attributing other plant closings in the area to unionism; and (2) that the board has often found that employees, who are particularly sensitive to rumors of plant closings, take such hints as coercive threats rather than honest forecasts.

Affirmed.

Questions

1. *a.* Why does the Court suggest the NLRB has a duty to determine what the speaker intended and what the listener understood?
   b. How does that differ from merely looking at what they actually said?
   c. Why is that difference important?
2. The Court notes that employees are economically dependent on their employers. Aren't employers similarly economically dependent on their employees? Why or why not?
3. Suppose the employees of Steno Office Supply, Inc., a large manufacturing firm, have petitioned the NLRB for an election. Company management personnel begin inviting workers to lunch to discuss the upcoming election and the likely consequences of unionization. These lunches are held at the local country club. During these discussions, at which employee comments are encouraged although not forced, managers make allusions to the union organizer's sexual orientation. The comments, made in the form of jokes, suggest that homosexual favors may be required in lieu of dues.
   a. If the union loses the election, should the NLRB set the election aside because of the tactics used? Explain.
   b. Which, if any, of these tactics seem problematic?
   c. Would any one of the tactics by itself be enough to set aside the election? Explain.
   d. What standard should the board use in making its determination?
   e. What additional information might you want to have before making a decision in this particular case?

   [See *General Knit of California,* 239 NLRB 619 (1978), 99 LRRM 1687, for a discussion of the historical standard. But see *Midland National Life Insurance,* 263 NLRB No. 24 (1982) for the current view.]

Promise of Benefit. Although threats of force or reprisal are clearly unlawful in union campaigns, the rationale behind the prohibition against promises of benefit is not as intuitively obvious. In the case of *NLRB* v. *Exchange Parts Co.,* 375 U.S. 409 (1964), Exchange Parts sent its employees a letter shortly before a representation election that spoke of "the empty promises of the union" and "the fact that it is the company that puts things in your envelope." After mentioning a number of benefits, the letter said: "The Union can't put any of those things in your envelope—only the company can do that." Further on, the letter stated, "It didn't take a Union to get any of those things and . . . it won't take a Union to get additional improvements in the future." Accompanying the letter was a detailed statement of the benefits granted by the company since 1949 and an estimate of the monetary value of such benefits to the employees.

In addition, the letter outlined further benefits, such as additional vacation days and overtime pay, that the company had recently decided to institute. In the representation election two weeks later, the union lost. The Court of Appeals did not think the employer's actions constituted an unfair labor practice. The Supreme Court disagreed, reversing the decision. Justice Harlan stated:

We think the Court of Appeals was mistaken in concluding that the conferral of employee benefits while a representation election is pending, for the purpose of inducing employees to vote against the union, does not "interfere with" the protected right to organize.

The broad purpose of § 8(a)(1) is to establish "the right of employees to organize for mutual aid without employer interference." We have no doubt that it prohibits not only intrusive threats and promises but also conduct immediately favorable to employees which is undertaken with the express purpose of impinging upon their freedom of choice for or against unionization and is reasonably calculated to have that effect. In *Medo Photo Supply Corp.* v. *NLRB,* this Court said: "The action of employees with respect to the choice of their bargaining agents may be induced by favors bestowed by the employer as well as by his threats or domination" . . . The danger inherent in well-timed increases in benefits is the suggestion of a *fist inside the velvet glove* [emphasis added]. Employees are not likely to miss the inference that the source of benefits now conferred is also the source from which future benefits must flow and which may dry up if it is not obliged.

Union Persuasion. Employers, of course, are not the only parties affected by Section 8(c). Unions are also restricted in the type of preelection persuasion they employ. In cases involving promises of benefits made by the union, the board has been more reluctant to set aside elections than it has when such promises have been made by management. The board's reasoning is that employees realize that union preelection promises are merely expressions of a union platform, so to speak. Employees recognize that these are benefits for which the union intends to fight. Employers, on the other hand, really do hold within their power the ability to confer or withdraw benefits. Nonetheless, occasionally a union does promise a benefit in a manner that violates Section 8(c).

Discipline and Discharge of Employees. Section 8(a)(3) of the NLRA prohibits "discrimination with regard to hire or tenure of employment in order to encourage or discourage union membership." Clearly then, if an employee joins a union, or refuses to join a union, he or she cannot be discharged or disciplined. But what if that employee engages in some other form of union activity, such as filing grievances, wearing union buttons, or serving in an elected union office? The Supreme Court has decided that employer retaliation might discourage employees from union membership. The Court has given this expansive interpretation to the term "union membership" because the policy of the act "is to insulate employees' jobs from their organizational rights" set forth in Section 7.[57]

But remember, the act provides that the employer's action must be "in order to" achieve that purpose. Thus, to violate Section 8(a)(3) there must be proof of the employer's state of mind when it discharged or disciplined the employee in question. However, there are few if any cases in which an employer has stated that it has taken action against an employee because of his or her union activity. How then, can such a state of mind, or intent, be shown?

The following excerpt from *Radio Officers* v. *NLRB* addresses that issue:

But it is also clear that specific evidence of intent . . . is not an indispensable element of proof of violation of Section 8(a)(3) . . . [That] specific intent is unnecessary where employer conduct inherently encourages or discourages union membership is but an application of the common-law rule that a man is held to intend the foreseeable consequences of his conduct . . . [When] encouragement or discouragement will result, it is presumed that he intended such consequence . . .

> Obviously, it would be gross inconsistency to hold that an inherent effect of certain discrimination is encouragement (or discouragement) of union membership, but that the Board may not reasonably infer such encouragement.[58]

Upon what factors may the NLRB rely to infer the necessary motive? Among those commonly used are the timing of the employer action relative to the union activity; whether other employees who have not engaged in union activity were guilty of the same misconduct but not treated in the same fashion; and whether the alleged misconduct was condoned or tolerated before the union activity.

Questions

1. What if instead of discharging employees active in the union, the employer, following a union victory in a representation election, closes the plant and relocates elsewhere with new employees and without the union?
2. What if instead of closing and relocating, the employer closes the plant and does not reopen and admittedly does so because of the employees' selection of the union? [See *Textile Workers Union* v. *Darlington Mfg. Co.,* 380 U.S. 263 (1965).]

Profile Perspective: Recall that Lustig discharged the systems analysts immediately after the union demanded that she bargain with it as the representative of her employees. Now that the union has filed unfair labor practice charges, how can it prove Lustig discharged the employees because of their union activity? How do you account for the fact that the two employees were also guilty of misconduct? Can that be ignored just because they also engaged in union activity? How should the NLRB handle these cases in which there is a dual motive?

Mt. Healthy City School District Bd. of Education v. Doyle

CASE

429 U.S. 274 (1977)

Justice Rehnquist

A rule . . . which focuses solely on whether protected conduct played a part, "substantial" or otherwise, in a decision . . . could place an employee in a better position as a result of the exercise of . . . protected conduct than he would have occupied had he done nothing. The difficulty with [that] rule . . . is that it would require reinstatement in cases where a dramatic and perhaps abrasive incident is inevitably on the minds of those responsible for the decision . . . even if the same decision would have been reached had the incident not occurred . . . [The employee] ought not to be able, by engaging in [protected] conduct, to prevent his employer from assessing his performance record and reaching a decision not to rehire on the basis of that record, simply because the protected conduct makes the employer more certain of the correctness of its decision.

* * *

Initially, in this case the burden was properly placed upon [the employee] to show that his conduct was . . . protected, and that this conduct was a "substantial factor" . . . in the [employer's] decision . . . [H]aving carried that burden, however, the District Court should have gone on to determine whether the [employer] had shown by a preponderance of the evidence that it would have reached the same decision [to take action] even in the absence of the protected conduct.

The Union as Exclusive Bargaining Agent. Once a union has been elected and certified as the representative of a bargaining unit, it becomes the exclusive agent for all of the employees within that bargaining unit, whether they voted for the union or not. The exclusivity of the union's authority has a number of implications, but one is particularly relevant in determining whether an employer has failed to demonstrate good faith at the bargaining table. Specifically, the employer must deal with the certified representative who acts on behalf of all employees in the bargaining unit. The employer commits an unfair labor practice if she or he attempts to deal directly with the employees or recognizes someone other than the workers' chosen representative. In both instances, the issue is fairly straightforward. The employer is undermining the position of the representative by ignoring him or her.

D. Collective Bargaining

Section 8(a)(5) of the NLRA requires an employer to engage in good faith collective bargaining with a representative of the employees, and Section 8(b)(3) imposes the same duty on labor organizations. Failure to bargain by either an employer or representative of the employees constitutes an unfair labor practice.

What is collective bargaining? What must one do to discharge the duty imposed? According to Section 8(d) of the NRLA:

> To bargain collectively is the performance of the mutual obligation of the employer and the representatives of the employees to meet at reasonable times and confer in good faith with respect to wages, hours, and other terms and conditions of employment . . . but such obligation does not compel either party to agree to a proposal or require the making of a concession.

Note what is *not* included. The duty to bargain in good faith does not require that the parties reach agreement. The NLRB and the courts recognize that collective bargaining, like any negotiations, is consensual. Thus, the act governs only the process, not the result, of collective bargaining. Three distinct questions are raised by Sections 8(a)(5), 8(b)(3), and 8(d):

1. What constitutes good faith?
2. About which subjects must the parties bargain?
3. What conduct constitutes bargaining in good faith?

Bargaining in Good Faith. Good faith is a murky area with no definitive answers. The NLRB and the courts look at the totality of the objective evidence in the negotiations to secure a sense of whether the parties intend to engage in serious negotiations. Over the years, various factors (none of which is conclusive in and of itself) have been identified by the board and the courts as being suggestive of good faith bargaining. Some of these include the following:[59]

1. The employer must make a serious attempt to adjust differences and to reach an acceptable common ground, that is, one must bargain with an open mind and a sincere desire to reach agreement.
2. Counterproposals must be offered when another party's proposal is rejected. This must involve the give and take of an auction system.[60]
3. A position with regard to contract terms may not be constantly changed.[61]
4. The employee must be willing to incorporate oral agreements into a written contract.[62]

Surface Bargaining. The NLRA itself specifies that a mere inability to reach an agreement or the failure to make a concession does not mean the parties have failed to bargain collectively in good faith. But the NLRB and the courts have rejected so-called surface bargaining, in which a party is merely going through the motions without manifesting a sincere intent to reach an understanding. In identifying surface bargaining, which indicates an absence of good faith, the NLRB and the courts consider the total bargaining picture. This includes, but is not limited to, factors such as the four noted above and other considerations such as the number of times the parties have met, whether meetings were prematurely ended or canceled, and whether a party has reneged on a tentative agreement.[63]

However, an employer that faithfully attends bargaining sessions, makes some concessions, submits counterproposals, and "fulfills its procedural obligations" will not be found guilty of surface bargaining regardless of its other conduct in negotiations.[64] The fact that a party engages in "hard bargaining" by failing to yield on a major issue while conceding other issues does not result in a finding of surface bargaining.[65]

Take-It-or-Leave-It Bargaining. In the 1960s General Electric made a "fair, firm offer" to its union and refused to budge unless the union could prove to GE's satisfaction that a change was appropriate. At the same time, GE built a massive publicity campaign to persuade the public and its employees that the union should accept GE's offer. This approach has come to be labeled Boulwarism after GE vice president Lemuel Boulware, who created it. During the subsequent strike, the case went to court, where GE's tactics were struck down. The court did not explicitly reject take-it-or-leave-it bargaining, but rather rejected the total package as showing a lack of good faith bargaining. The inflexible position in combination with the marketing campaign effectively left GE without room to bargain meaningfully.[66]

Per Se Breach. The NLRB and the courts have struggled with the question of whether there are any actions that, if taken by one of the bargaining parties, would constitute a per se breach of the duty to bargain in good faith. Are there actions so detrimental to the bargaining process that use of them is enough to justify a finding of bad faith, irrespective of the other party's conduct?

Suppose a union was in the midst of bargaining with management over terms of a new collective bargaining agreement and began using economic weapons against the employer while negotiations were proceeding. In the case of *NLRB* v. *Insurance Agents' International Union,* Insurance Agents' International Union was negotiating a collective bargaining agreement with Prudential Insurance Company of America.[67] The union decided to use its economic power to harass the company during these negotiations. The union's tactics included:

> [R]efusal for a time to solicit new business, and refusal [after the writing of new business was resumed] to comply with the company's reporting procedures; refusal to participate in the company's "May Policyholders' Month Campaign"; reporting late at district offices the days the agents were scheduled to attend them, and refusing to perform customary duties at the offices, instead engaging there in "sit-in-mornings," "doing what comes naturally," and leaving at noon as a group; absenting themselves from special business conferences arranged by the company; picketing and distributing leaflets outside the various offices of the company on specified days and hours as directed by the union; distributing leaflets

> each day to policyholders and others; and soliciting policyholders' signatures on petitions directed to the company; and presenting the signed policyholders' petitions to the company at its home office while simultaneously engaging in mass demonstrations there.[68]

The NLRB thought the union's use of economic weapons against the company during a time when negotiations were not at an impasse showed bad faith on the part of the union, even though no evidence had been presented indicating the union had refused to cooperate at the bargaining table. The board's reasoning was that:

> The respondent's [union's] reliance upon harassing tactics during the course of negotiations for the avowed purpose of compelling the company to capitulate to its terms is the antithesis of reasoned discussion it was duty-bound to follow. Indeed, it clearly revealed an unwillingness to submit its demands to the consideration of the bargaining table where argument, persuasion, and the free interchange of views could take place. In such circumstances, the fact that the respondent continued to confer with the company and was desirous of concluding an agreement does not alone establish that it fulfilled its obligation to bargain in good faith.[69]

Justice Brennan, writing the opinion for the Supreme Court, disagreed with the NLRB, saying that:

> It is apparent from the legislative history of the whole act that the policy of Congress is to impose a mutual duty upon the parties to confer in good faith with a desire to reach agreement, in the belief that such an approach from both sides of the table promotes the overall design of achieving industrial peace. Discussion conducted under that standard of good faith may narrow the issues, making the real demands of the parties clearer to each other, and perhaps to themselves, and may encourage an attitude of settlement through give and take . . . But apart from this essential standard of conduct, Congress intended that the parties should have wide latitude in their negotiations . . .
>
> It must be realized that collective bargaining, under a system where the government does not attempt to control the results of negotiations, cannot be equated with an academic collective search for truth—or even with what might be thought to be the ideal of one . . .
>
> The system has not reached the ideal of the philosophic notion that perfect understanding among people would lead to perfect agreement among them on values. The presence of economic weapons in reserve, and their actual exercise on occasion by the parties, is part and parcel of the system that the Wagner and Taft-Hartley Acts have recognized. Abstract logical analysis might find inconsistency between the command of the statute to negotiate toward an agreement in good faith and the legitimacy of the use of economic weapons, frequently having the most serious effect upon individual workers and productive enterprises, to induce one party to come to the terms desired by the other. But the truth of the matter is that at the present statutory stage of our national labor relations policy, the two factors—necessity for good-faith bargaining between parties, and the availability of economic pressure devices to each to make the other party incline to agree on one's term—exist side by side. One writer recognizes this by describing economic force as "a prime motive power for agreements in free collective bargaining" . . .

> [W]e think the board's approach involves an intrusion into the substantive aspects of the bargaining process . . .
>
> The use of economic pressure, as we have indicated, is of itself not at all inconsistent with the duty of bargaining in good faith.[70]

If using economic weapons during the negotiating process is not an exercise of bad faith and if the NLRB must close the door of the bargaining room, so to speak, and not judge what goes on behind it, can you think of any activities short of a complete refusal to bargain that would constitute lack of good faith?

Similarly, if a union requests an employer to provide information relating to an allegation that the employer has violated the collective bargaining agreement or to negotiations for such an agreement, the employer will violate section 8(a)(5) if it fails to provide the information. However, the NLRB will find a violation only if the information sought is relevant to the claim or negotiations and it is not confidential.

Two practices have provided the major source of "bad faith" findings by the Supreme Court. The first arises when a company, during negotiations, announces that it cannot accede to higher wage demands, for example, without sending the company into bankruptcy. The union is willing to accept that limitation because, after all, it will do the employees no good to have high wages if they then lose their jobs as a result. The union, however, asks to see the company's books to verify that the company is, indeed, in the financial straits it claims. A company's refusal to disclose such information to the union is a refusal to bargain in good faith.[71]

The second set of circumstances involves a situation in which a company institutes a change unilaterally during the bargaining period that affects one of the subjects of collective bargaining or offers better terms directly to the employees than the company has ever proposed to the union. Assume, for example, that at the bargaining table, an employer is only willing to offer one week's paid vacation to employees of two years or less. It then announces (not at the bargaining table but directly to the employees themselves) that effective immediately, all employees who have worked for six months or more are entitled to two weeks' paid vacation. According to the Supreme Court, such action taken by the company would be strong evidence of bad faith.[72]

Mandatory Bargaining Subjects. Although employers and labor representatives are free to discuss whatever lawful subjects they mutually choose to discuss, Section 8(d) of the NLRA clearly sets out some mandatory subjects over which the parties must bargain. These are wages, hours, and "other terms and conditions of employment." Although these topics for mandatory bargaining seem simple enough, questions still arise frequently. For example, suppose the union and employer bargain over wages and agree to institute merit increases for employees. Must the employer also bargain over which employees are entitled to receive these increases or who will make the decision at the time they are to be given? Does the question of bringing in subcontractors to perform certain jobs fall within the scope of wages, hours, and terms and conditions of employment since the use of subcontractors may reduce the amount of work available to regular employees? Or does that subject belong more directly to the management of the firm? What about a decision to close a plant?

Generally, the board and the courts will balance three factors. First, they look to the effect of a particular decision on the workers—how direct is it and to what extent is the effect felt? Second, they consider the degree to which bargaining would constitute an intrusion into entrepreneurial interest or, from the opposite side, intrusion into union affairs. Third, they examine the practice historically in the industry or the company itself.[73]

Permissive and Prohibited Bargaining Subjects. In the *Borg-Warner* case,[74] the Supreme Court approved and clarified the distinction between mandatory and permissive bargaining subjects. Those matters not directly related to wages, hours, and terms and conditions of employment and not falling within the category of prohibited subjects are considered permissive. Either party may raise permissive subjects during the bargaining process, but neither may pursue them to the point of a bargaining impasse. Refusal to bargain over a permissive subject does not constitute an NLRA violation, and permissive subjects must simply be dropped if the parties do not reach agreement. Permissive subjects ordinarily would include such items as alteration of a defined bargaining unit, internal union affairs, and strike settlement agreements. Prohibited bargaining subjects are those that are illegal under the NLRA or other laws.

Unilateral Change. A similar violation occurs if an employer, during the course of negotiations, institutes a unilateral change in employee benefits. For example, in the 1962 Supreme Court case of *NLRB* v. *Katz,* an employer made three unilateral changes.[75] He granted merit increases, changed the sick leave policy, and instituted a new system of automatic wage increases. This strategy was considered a failure to bargain in good faith because the employer's actions tended to obstruct the process and to make the negotiations more difficult. Therefore, the employer clearly demonstrated a lack of good faith when it unilaterally granted better benefits than any offered at the bargaining table.

Profile Perspective: After bargaining for several months and exchanging numerous proposals and counterproposals, Lustig and the union agreed on all issues but wages. If Lustig had bargained in good faith to this point of impasse before implementing a wage increase, would she have violated her duty to bargain in good faith when she implemented the changes? Why or why not? What if she implemented a wage increase that differed from her last proposal made to the union at impasse? Would this change your answer to the previous question?

E. STRIKES

For many, the initial image of labor conflict is one of employees on strike, picketing a store or factory. Striking is, however, an extremely drastic measure under which employees must bear an immediate loss of wages and, in many instances, risk job loss. Similarly, employers bear the loss of a disruption to continued operations.

Strikes are at a post–World War II low in the United States, although they remain a significant feature of the industrial scene.[76] A Deutsche Bank research study of strikes during the 1980s found:

Nation	*Average Workdays Lost During 1980s per 1,000 Employees*
Spain	631
Great Britain	309
United States	118
Germany	27
Japan	9

Source: Christopher Conte, "Lost Labor," *The Wall Street Journal,* July 21, 1992, p. A1. Reprinted by permission of *The Wall Street Journal.*

Strikes are of two kinds:

1. Those used purely as economic weapons to persuade an employer to provide more favorable employee benefits or better working conditions. These are known a economic strikes.
2. Those instituted by workers in response to the employer's commission of an unfair labor practice such as interfering with legitimate union activities or its failure to bargain in good faith. These are known as unfair labor practice strikes.

Economic Strikes. All strikes not involving unfair labor practices fall into this category. In what has been labeled "the most significant change in collective bargaining to occur since the passage of the Wagner Act in 1934," employers are now increasingly willing to permanently replace economic strikers.[77] Employers had enjoyed that right where necessary "in an effort to carry on the business" since a 1938 Supreme Court decision, but for practical reasons they had rarely exercised it.[78] Later decisions had imposed some limitations on that right. For example, any striker who is permanently replaced is put on a preferential hiring list and will have priority to be selected to fill subsequent vacancies. However, President Reagan's 1981 dismissal of 11,300 striking air traffic controllers effectively crushed their union (PATCO) and caused private-sector employers to reassess their long-standing reluctance to use replacements during and after strikes.[79] Thus, recent years have seen some major employers like Hormel, Caterpillar, Greyhound Bus Lines, Firestone/Bridgestone, the National Football League, and Major League Baseball use, or threaten to use, strike replacements.

Unfair Labor Practice Strikes. In general, these strikers cannot be fired for their legitimate strike-related conduct. They may be replaced by temporary workers, but they are entitled to have their jobs back at the conclusion of the strike even if the replacements must be fired to provide openings.

The *TWA* decision that follows greatly strengthened management's hand in employing permanent replacements for economic strikes. The Democratic majority in Congress forwarded legislation that would prohibit hiring permanent replacements for striking workers. However, with the new Republican majorities in the House and the Senate, prospects for passage have dimmed even more.[80]

CASE

Justice O'Connor

TWA, Inc. v. Flight Attendants

489 U.S. 426 (1989)

We decide today whether, at the end of a strike, an employer is required by the Railway Labor Act (RLA or Act) . . . to displace employees who worked during the strike in order to reinstate striking employees with greater seniority.

I

In March 1984, Trans World Airlines, Inc. (TWA) and the Independent Federation of Flight Attendants (IFFA or Union) began negotiations . . . on a new collective bargaining agreement . . .

For two years TWA and the Union unsuccessfully bargained over wages and working conditions . . . [O]n March 7, 1986, the Union went out on strike.

Continued

Continued

TWA informed its flight attendants before and during the strike that it would continue operations by hiring permanent replacements for striking flight attendants, by continuing to employ any flight attendant who chose not to strike, and by rehiring any striker who abandoned the strike and made an unconditional offer to return to any available vacancies. TWA also informed its flight attendants that any vacancies created as a result of the strike would be filled by application of the seniority bidding system to all working flight attendants and that such job and domicile assignments would remain effective after the strike ended . . . Thus, at the conclusion of the strike, senior full-term strikers would not be permitted to displace permanent replacements or junior nonstriking flight attendants and could be left without an opportunity to return to work. TWA's promise not to displace working flight attendants after the strike created two incentives specifically linked to the seniority bidding system: it gave senior flight attendants an incentive to remain at or return to work in order to retain their prior jobs and domicile assignments; it gave junior flight attendants an incentive to remain at or return to work in order to obtain job and domicile assignments that were previously occupied by more senior, striking flight attendants.

As promised, TWA continued its operations during the 72-day strike by utilizing . . . flight attendants who either did not strike or returned to work before the end of the strike and by hiring and fully training new flight attendants . . . The Union made an unconditional offer to TWA . . . to return to work. TWA accepted the offer but refused the Union's May 27th demand that TWA displace those prestrike employees who were working. . . . Accordingly, TWA initially recalled only the 197 most senior full-term strikers to fill available job and domicile vacancies. By the terms of a poststrike arbitral agreement, these strikers and all subsequently reinstated full-term strikers returned to work as vacancies arose and with precisely the seniority they would have had if no strike had occurred. In May 1988, more than 1,100 full-term strikers had been reinstated with full seniority.

In an effort to reinstate all the full-term strikers by displacing the newly hired flight attendants and less senior crossover employees, the union . . . filed the instant action contending that, even assuming the strike was economic, the full-term strikers were entitled to reinstatement either under the terms of the prestrike collective bargaining agreement or under the RLA itself. On cross motions for partial summary judgment, the district court held that the full-term strikers were not entitled to displace either the junior crossovers or the 1,220 new hires employed by TWA immediately after the strike commenced. (The motions did not require the district court to rule on the status of the remaining new hires.) The district court also held that 463 new hires not fully trained by the end of the strike could be displaced by full-term strikers.

* * *

The Court of Appeals . . . affirmed the district court's ruling that full-term strikers could not displace the 1,220 fully trained new hires but could displace the 463 untrained new hires . . . The Court of Appeals, however, reversed the district court's ruling that more senior full-term strikers could not displace junior crossovers . . .

Today, we reverse the Court of Appeals . . . and hold that an employer is not required by the RLA to lay off junior crossovers in order to reinstate more senior full-term strikers at the conclusion of a strike.

II

We have observed in the past that carefully drawn analogies from the federal common labor law developed under the NLRA may be helpful in deciding cases under the RLA.

* * *

Both the RLA and the NLRA protect an employee's right to choose not to strike . . . and, thereby, protect employees' rights to "the benefit of their individual decisions not to strike."

Continued

Continued

* * *

The positions occupied by newly hired replacements, employees who refused to strike, and employees who abandoned the strike, are simply not "available positions" to be filled. As noted above, those positions that were available at the conclusion of the strike were filled "according to some principle, such as seniority, that is neutral . . ." That the prospect of a reduction in available positions may divide employees and create incentives among them to remain at work or abandon a strike before its conclusion is a secondary effect fairly within the arsenal of economic weapons available to employers . . .

While the employer and union in many circumstances may reach a back-to-work agreement that would displace crossovers and new hires or an employer may unilaterally decide to permit such displacement, nothing in the NLRA or the federal common law we have developed under that statute requires such a result.

* * *

[RLA discussion omitted.]

IV

Neither the RLA itself nor any analogies to the NLRA indicate that the crossover policy adopted by TWA . . . was unlawful. Rather, the decision to guarantee to crossovers the same protections lawfully applied to new hires was a simple decision to apply the preexisting seniority terms of the collective bargaining agreement uniformly to all working employees. That this decision had the effect of encouraging prestrike workers to remain on the job during the strike or to abandon the strike and return to work before all vacancies were filled was an effect of the exercise of TWA's peaceful economic power, a power that the company was legally free to deploy once the parties had exhausted the private dispute resolution mechanisms of the RLA . . .

Reversed.

Questions

1. Why should an employer be permitted to replace strikers? Would a strike be one of employees' Section 7 rights?
2. *a.* How would you vote on the proposed federal legislation banning the practice of permanently replacing economic strikers? Explain.

   b. Is there any reason to distinguish between economic strikers and unfair labor practice strikers? Any reason not to do so?
3. Assume Mary Wills, a bottle inspector for Pop Soda Inc. and a member of a certified bargaining unit, struck along with other bottle inspectors to protest an allegedly unfair labor practice committed by the employer. The bottle inspectors offered to return to work after a one-week strike, and, although their positions were not filled, Pop Soda offered them entirely different positions as bottle sorters, telling the employees that they would shortly thereafter be returned to their regular inspector jobs. Wills was the only one who accepted this offer; the other employees insisted that they were legally entitled to their former jobs. Wills made subsequent inquiries, attempting to get her inspecting job back, but the company at no time made a proper offer for that position. After three and a half months of working as a bottle sorter, Wills resigned because of physical problems with her hand. She then made a claim to the NLRB that Pop Soda had committed an unfair labor practice by not reinstating her to her inspecting position. She asked for reinstatement and back pay.

   Do you think she is entitled to either or both of these remedies? [See *The Coca-Cola Bottling Company of Memphis and International Brotherhood of Teamsters, et al.,* 269 NLRB No. 160 (1983–84 CCH NLRB ¶ 16,259), decided April 23, 1984.]

Because a replaced striker can be effectively discharged, and because strike replacements often undermine the solidarity unions must maintain, the use of strike replacements is a highly emotional issue.[81] One famous American author vividly described these feelings:

What Is a Scab?

After God had finished the rattlesnake, the toad, and the vampire, he had some awful substance left with which He made a scab. A scab is a two-legged animal with a corkscrew soul, a water-logged brain, and a combination backbone made of jelly and glue. Where others have hearts, he carries a tumor of rotten principles.

When a scab comes down the street, men turn their backs, and angels weep in heaven, and the devil shuts the gates of hell to keep him out. No man has a right to scab as long as there is a pool of water deep enough to drown his body in, or a rope long enough to hang his carcass with. Judas Iscariot was a gentleman compared with a scab. For betraying his Master, he had character enough to hang himself. A scab hasn't!

Esau sold his birthright for a mess of pottage. Judas Iscariot sold his Savior for 30 pieces of silver. Benedict Arnold sold his country for a promise of a commission in the British army. The modern strikebreaker sells his birthright, his country, his wife, his children, and his fellow men for an unfulfilled promise from his employer, trust or corporation.

Esau was a traitor to himself. Judas Iscariot was a traitor to his God. Benedict Arnold was a traitor to his country.

A strikebreaker is a traitor to his God, his country, his family, and his class!

Source: P. S. Foner, *Jack London, American Rebel* (New York, Citadel Press, 1947), pp. 57–58.

Notification of the Intent to Strike. Congressional desire to maintain industrial peace is manifested, in part, through the conditions imposed by Section 8(d) of the NLRA. These provisions are designed to prevent ill-conceived strikes by requiring that any party desiring to terminate or renegotiate a collective bargaining agreement must serve written notice on the other party at least 60 days prior to the expiration of the agreement then in force. Within 30 days of notifying the other party of its desires, the moving party must also notify the Federal Mediation and Conciliation Service and any state or local conciliation boards set up for the purpose of resolving that type of dispute. Failure to give this notice is considered a refusal to bargain in good faith. Moreover, any worker who goes on strike during this cooling-off period loses his or her status as an employee for purposes of being protected by the NLRA. Such an employee may be discharged by the employer without any repercussions from the act.

The 60-day notification period allows both parties some leeway during which they can discuss and, ideally, resolve their contract disputes before the old contract terminates. The notification provision ensures that neither employers nor employees are left in the lurch, unprepared for or unaware of the other party's dissatisfaction with the present bargaining agreement. Perhaps more important, the public is protected to a great extent. A strike in any sector of industry tends to have a ripple effect, creating disturbances throughout the economy.

Lockouts. Work stoppages sometimes take the form of **lockouts,** in which management shuts the door on some or all employees. Lockouts have become more common since the *TWA* decision. Lockouts take two forms:

lockouts. Where employees are kept from the workplace by the employer.

1. *Defensive*—The company says it must keep employees out to protect itself against violence or sabotage.
2. *Offensive*—The company uses the lockout as a strategy to persuade the workers to accept its position.

Lockouts can be very potent weapons, since workers are not paid and many states do not offer unemployment compensation for those locked out. Since the *TWA* decision, workers have become more reluctant to strike when a contract expires, but management may now force the issue by ordering a lockout to persuade the union to accept company terms. For example:

> Warehouse workers at Hasbro, Inc., headquarters in Pawtucket, RI, were locked out for two months. Hasbro executives argued they needed to cut costs and workers' salaries to remain competitive. The lockout ended after Teamsters Local 251 signed a three-year contract.[82]

Picketing and Boycotts. There are two types of picketing or boycotting: primary and secondary.

Primary Picketing. In addition to striking, unions often engage in picketing or boycotting in an effort to pressure an employer with which it is negotiating and to broadly publicize their concerns. Picketing is the familiar process of union members gathering and sometimes marching, placards in hand, at a place of business. Peaceful, informational picketing for a lawful purpose is protected by the NLRA. However, some kinds of picketing are forbidden, and all picketing can be regulated by the government to ensure the public safety. Primary picketing is expressed directly to the employer with whom the picketers have a dispute. Primary picketing enjoys broad constitutional and statutory protection.

Secondary Picketing/Boycotts. Secondary picketing or boycotting is directed to a business other than the primary employer, and ordinarily it is unlawful. That is, unions are engaging in an unfair labor practice if they threaten or coerce a third party with whom they are not engaged in a dispute in order to cause that third party to cease doing business with the firm that is the real target of the union's concern. Assume union A has a dispute with company B. Direct, primary picketing, a strike, and the like against company B would normally be permissible. But if A were to impose pressure via picketing, for example, on company C, a supplier of company B, that pressure would ordinarily constitute unlawful behavior. Thus, secondary picketing, secondary boycotts, and other forms of coercion against parties not the principals in a labor dispute are, with some exceptions, unlawful labor practices.

F. Employees' Rights within or against the Union

The Union's Duty of Fair Representation. As you have seen in previous sections of this chapter, the union is given statutory authority to be the exclusive bargaining agent for the employees in the designated bargaining unit. This means that even if an individual employee in the bargaining unit does not agree with the union policies or is not a member of the union, he or she cannot bargain individually with the employer. Such an employee will still be bound by the terms of the collective bargaining agreement.

Because employees are placed in that position with respect to their union, the Supreme Court has ruled that unions have a duty to fairly represent all members of the bargaining unit, whether or not they become members of the union. Sometimes the task is difficult because of divergent interests within the unit (one of the reasons for taking great care in choosing an appropriate bargaining unit). For example, if a company is in difficult financial circumstances, it may tell union negotiators that the company must do one of two things to stay viable—lay off workers or give all employees a cut in salary. The workers who have seniority and would not lose their jobs in a layoff are likely to push for the former; workers with less seniority, who would normally be let go during a layoff, will prefer in most instances to retain their jobs even if they are forced to take a cut in wages.

This type of situation, however, is a far cry from those in which a union has arbitrarily or with purposeful intent discriminated against some segment of its rank-and-file membership. In addition to the racial discrimination found in many unions, sex discrimination was also rampant. Unions were notorious for negotiating contracts in which women were excluded from certain jobs and paid lower wages for performing work identical to their male counterparts. In recognition of the discrimination being practiced by many unions, Congress built special provisions into the Equal Pay Act of 1963 and the Civil Rights Act of 1964, making it illegal for unions to discriminate on the basis of race, color, creed, national origin, or sex.

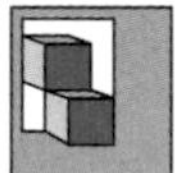

The Bill of Rights of Labor Organization Members. The Bill of Rights for members of labor organizations is contained in Title 1, Section 101 of the Labor-Management Reporting and Disclosure Act (LMRDA or Landrum-Griffin Act). The Bill of Rights was designed to ensure equal voting rights, the right to sue the union, and the rights of free speech and assembly. These rights of union members are tempered by the union's right to enact and enforce "reasonable rules governing the responsibilities of its members."[83]

Many people are extremely skeptical about the union leaders' ability or desire to be responsive to the interests of the membership rather than to their own needs for power or money. For some, this skepticism is a function of the transformation that employees go through when they assume positions of authority.[84] This skepticism is also due to the information brought to light in congressional hearings in the late 1950s.

> Prior to the enactment of the LMRDA in 1959, the Select Senate Committee discovered widespread corruption, dictatorship, and racketeering in a number of large international unions. The committee found that the president of the Bakery and Confectionery Workers' International Union of America had "railroaded through changes in the union constitution which destroyed any vestigial pretenses of union democracy . . ." The committee likewise found Teamster officials joining with others to take over illegal gambling operations with an "underworld combine," and the top officers of the United Textile Workers of America avariciously misappropriating union funds. "Democracy [was] virtually nonexistent" in the International Union of Operating Engineers because the union was ruthlessly dominated through "violence, intimidation, and other dictatorial practices."[85]

Even though union members are guaranteed the rights of free speech and assembly, federal court cases, at both the district and circuit court levels, have made clear that unions are not obligated to provide space in union newspapers for articles containing viewpoints opposed to those of union leadership, nor are they obligated to hold meetings at the behest of their membership even when the union constitution provides a procedural means for calling such a meeting. Moreover, the union ,meeting agenda can be set by the union leadership in such a way as to preclude discussion of particular issues. The union is permitted to establish reasonable rules to govern such situations.

Other federal court decisions have come down equally firmly in interpreting other rights guaranteed by the workers' Bill of Rights. Thus, although union members are entitled to vote in union elections, they do not have the right to demand a vote on a decision of whether to strike. Likewise, the union is not required to submit a proposed collective bargaining agreement to the membership for ratification or approval, although the Bill of Rights gives members the right to see a copy of the agreement under which they are working.[86]

As a result of these court rulings, one could make a tenable argument that employees are now caught in a double bind: Not only is the employer a potential source of trouble for the employee; so may be the very union that was supposed to be his or her vehicle for relief.

The NLRB and Worker Participation. Spurred by Japanese success and methods, American companies have been experimenting with a variety of strategies to improve productivity. Among them is increased worker participation in management decision making as a part of the more general effort at total quality management (TQM). President Clinton and Labor Secretary Robert Reich are strong advocates of quality circles and TQM. However, as we have seen, the NLRA, Sections 2(5) and 8(a)(2), provides that employer domination or interference with the formation or administration of any labor organization is an unfair labor practice. Broadly, the law is designed to prevent sham unions that, in fact, are dominated by management. Hence, in 1992 and 1993 the NLRB was called on to decide two cases involving the legality of some company-created labor-management committees designed to strengthen production quality. The article that follows describes the NLRB decisions and examines some of the political and industrial policy implications of preserving legitimate union interests on the one hand, while striving for quality improvement via employee involvement on the other.

DuPont Is Told It Must Disband Nonunion Panels

by Kevin G. Salwen

In a major blow to corporate worker-management teams, the National Labor Relations Board ordered DuPont Co. to disband seven such panels and to deal instead with the company's chemical workers union.

At the same time, the board attempted to lay out how companies can set up the increasingly popular labor-management teams.

The decision has been eagerly awaited by U.S. companies because it is the first major case to address the issue of safety committees in corporations where a union is present. Late last year, the NLRB ruled that worker-management teams at Electromation Inc. of Elkhart, Ind., were illegal "sham unions" because they set up "action committees" at a time when the Teamsters union was trying to organize the plant.

Legislative Hurdles

The DuPont ruling is a blow to the philosophy of Labor Secretary Robert Reich, who is a strong advocate of worker-management teams as a way of solving workplace problems. Mr. Reich has said repeatedly that he would seek legislation protecting the sanctity of worker-management teams if the NLRB's rulings have the effect of stifling such groups.

Such legislation wouldn't be easy to enact. Labor unions would fight efforts to curtail their already dwindling muscle within corporations, and they still hold much sway within the Democratic party.

Continued

Continued

The NLRB was unanimous in deciding that the DuPont safety and fitness committees were illegal "labor organizations" under the National Labor Relations Act of 1935. The panels made decisions concerning safety in DuPont's Deepwater, NJ, facility, but those determinations were subject to the approval of management members on the teams, the board said. The union has several thousand members, all at the Deepwater facility.

Company Control

DuPont management dominated the committees in other ways as well, the NLRB decided. For example, the Wilmington, Delaware–based chemical company set the size of each panel, and determined which employees would staff the committee if more than the required number volunteered. It also reserved the right to set up or disband any of the committees. Cumulatively, the board said, that meant the committees' administration was dominated by DuPont, rather than being an equal labor-management team.

Moreover, "some committees dealt with issues which were identical to those dealt with" by the Chemical Workers Association—and with even greater success, the board said. For example, the Antiknocks Area Safety Committee got a new welding shop for a worker who had complained of poor ventilation, while the union's attempt to resolve the same problem had failed.

Similarly, the committees decided on incentives and awards for workers, areas the NLRB said were "mandatory subjects of bargaining."

Guidelines Are Suggested

Still, the board attempted to create an outline from which companies could set up teams. For instance, such committees would need to avoid "dealing" with management as a union might. Specifically, the board indicated that the committees should exist "for the sole purpose of imparting information . . . or planning educational programs."

In addition, the board suggested that management not dominate the panels, but rather be a participant with a commensurate number of votes—notably a minority.

Meanwhile, the board singled out as being legal the quarterly safety conferences that DuPont began in 1989. At those conferences, the board said, it was announced that bargainable matters couldn't be dealt with and that "the conference wasn't a 'union issue.' "

* * *

The board's decision upheld an administrative ruling issued last May. DuPont disbanded the seven committees soon after that administrative ruling. Now the company and union agree in advance on issues such as committee makeup and procedure before establishing a safety committee, company officials said.

Source: *The Wall Street Journal,* June 7, 1993, p. A2. Reprinted by permission of *The Wall Street Journal,*

CASE

Electromation, Inc.

309 NLRB No. 163 (1992)

Member Raudabaugh, concurring

I believe that [Section 8(a)(2)] is to be understood in the context of the Wagner Act of 1935. The theory underlying the Wagner Act was that employees and employer were locked in an adversarial struggle . . . [and that] . . . the economic power of the employer completely overmatched the power of the individual employee. However, if the employees were permitted to combine their strength and form a labor organization, they could more effectively confront the economic power of the employer.

Continued

Continued

* * *

[This] adversarial model . . . is at odds with a cooperative model of labor relations.

* * *

By 1947, the labor-management world had undergone major change. The Taft-Hartley amendments of that year were enacted [because] . . . economic warfare . . . was no longer seen as a prudent means of settling disputes.

* * *

In light of the Taft-Hartley Act and the socio-economic changes on which it was based, I believe that there is substantial doubt that the Supreme Court would now [interpret Section 8(a)(2)] as the Court decided it in 1938 . . . Today, if employees freely choose to participate in an employee participation program, that would seem consistent with their Taft-Hartley right to refrain from choosing traditional union representation. Similarly, if employers and employees can amicably resolve their differences through cooperation, that would seem consistent with Taft-Hartley's encouragement of peaceful methods of resolving disputes.

* * *

Of course, this is not to say that all employee participation programs are lawful . . . The question before me is how to interpret these words in a way that will accommodate labor-management cooperation and the Section 7 rights of employees . . . [which] turns on the following factors: (1) the extent of the employer's involvement in the structure and operation of the committees; (2) whether the employees, from an objective standpoint, reasonably perceive the employee participation program as a substitute for full collective bargaining through a traditional union; (3) whether employees have been assured of their Section 7 right to choose to be represented by a traditional union under a system of full collective bargaining, and (4) the employer's motives in establishing the employee participation program.

Questions

1. Does the *DuPont* decision forbid worker-management cooperative decision-making efforts? Explain.
2. In your view, do the *DuPont* and *Electromation* decisions harm American industrial competitiveness? Explain.
3. Since Section 8(a)(2) was passed to prevent sham unions, should it be construed to prohibit various employer-employee plans intended to improve quality, morale, and so forth, but which also deal with conditions of employment? Under these circumstances, is Section 8(a)(2) obsolete and outdated? [See "Study Commends Worker Participation but Says Labor Laws May Be Limiting," *The Wall Street Journal,* June 3, 1994, p. A2.]

G. Union Security Agreements and Right-to-Work Laws

To maintain their membership, unions typically seek a collective bargaining clause requiring all employees to become union members after they have been employed for some period of time—generally 30 days (union shop agreements)—or, at the least, requiring them to pay union dues and fees (agency shop agreements). These arrangements are lawful under the NLRA.

Twenty-one states have enacted so-called right-to-work laws, which prohibit union security arrangements in collective bargaining agreements. In these states, nonmembers receive all the benefits of having union representation. Needless to say, unionized plants are far less common in right-to-work states than in states without those laws.

Finally, at one time, unions with a great deal of bargaining leverage would insist on clauses in collective bargaining agreements that restricted employers from hiring anyone not already a union member. These closed-shop agreements are now prohibited by the NLRA.

CASE

Abood v. Detroit Board of Education

431 U.S. 209 (1977)

Justice Stewart

A Union and a local government employer are specifically permitted to agree to an "agency shop" arrangement, whereby every employer represented by a union—even though not a union member—must pay to the union, as a condition of employment, a service fee equal in amount to union dues. The issue before us is whether this arrangement violates the . . . rights of . . . employees who object to . . . unions as such or to various union activities financed by the compulsory service fees.

* * *

[I]t is Congress that is charged with identifying "[t]he ingredients of industrial peace and stabilized labor-management relations" . . . Congress determined that it would promote peaceful labor relations to permit a union and an employer to conclude an agreement requiring employees who obtain the benefit of union representation to share its cost, and that legislative judgment was surely an allowable one.

* * *

The principle of exclusive union representation . . . is a central element in the congressional structuring of industrial relations. The designation of single representative avoids the confusion that would result from attempting to enforce two or more agreements specifying different terms and conditions of employment. It prevents interunion rivalries from creating dissension within the workforce and eliminating the advantages to the employee of collectivization. It also frees the employer from the possibility of facing conflicting demands from different unions, and permits the employer and a single union to reach agreements and settlements that are not subject to attach from rival labor organizations.

The designation of union as exclusive representative carries with it great responsibilities. The tasks of negotiating and administering a collective bargaining agreement and representing the interest of employees in settling disputes and processing grievances are continuing and difficult ones. They often entail expenditure of much time and money . . . The services of lawyers, expert negotiators, economists, and a research staff, as well as general administrative personnel, may be required. Moreover, in carrying out these duties, the union is obligated to "fairly and equitably to represent all employees . . . union and nonunion," within the relevant unit . . . A union-shop arrangement has been thought to distribute fairly the cost of these activities among those who benefit, and it counteracts the incentive that employees might otherwise have to become "free riders"—to refuse to contribute to the union while obtaining benefits of union representation that necessarily accrue to all employees.

Continued

Continued

. . . An employee may very well have ideological objections to a wide variety of activities undertaken by the union in its role as exclusive representative. [For example] his moral or religious views about the desirability of abortion may not square with the union's policy in negotiating a medical benefits plan . . . The examples could be multiplied. To be required to help finance the union as a collective bargaining agent might well be thought, therefore, to interfere in some way with an employee's freedom to associate for the advancement of ideas, or to refrain from doing so, as he sees fit. But the judgment that such interference as exists is . . . justified by the legislative assessment of the important contribution of the union shop to the system of labor relations established by Congress.

Administering the Agreement. One of the great virtues of collective bargaining agreements is that they ordinarily provide for a system by which labor management disputes may be resolved. To avoid turning to the courts, the agreement ordinarily will spell out a series of steps for settling problems. If a difficulty arises that cannot be settled informally, the dissatisfied employee typically files a written complaint (grievance) with the union, which then discusses the matter with the company.

Failing a settlement, the dispute proceeds up the chain of authority in the company and the union. If all of these efforts fail, the dispute moves to binding arbitration, which often may be provided for in the collective bargaining agreement. An arbitrator is a neutral third party (or parties) who is mutually agreed on by labor and management. The arbitrator holds a hearing to receive each party's version of the facts. The arbitrator issues an opinion called an award, which is binding on all the parties except for a very limited basis for review by the courts.

Public-Sector Unions. The degree of union organization in the public sector accounts for much of the recent growth in union membership. Legal regulation of public-sector labor-management relations is a matter of state law. Although the specific provisions of those laws therefore vary from state to state, many of the concepts discussed earlier arising under the NLRA are applicable. However, some fundamental policies and doctrines are quite different. Two of these doctrines applicable uniquely to the public sector are the nondelegability doctrine, which bears on the constitutionality of public-sector labor laws, and the ability of public-sector employees to strike.

The nondelegability doctrine is based on the fact that public-sector employees are, either directly or indirectly, held accountable to the electorate via the ballot box. Thus, a mayor or governor, or his or her employees as their representatives, have certain powers and responsibilities that cannot be given to, or delegated to, an individual or entity that is not accountable to the voters, such as a union or an arbitrator.[87]

With regard to public employee strikes, some states prohibit them and others permit them under restricted conditions. In either case, the basis for treating public employees different than private-sector employees on this point is against the role of public employees as servants of the voters. In the minds of some, as public servants these employees have a higher duty or responsibility than private employees. In addition, certain public employees, for example, police officers and fire fighters, work in positions that clearly involve public safety and to permit them to strike might endanger the citizenry.

H. The Future of Unions

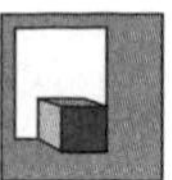

We began this chapter with a look at the declining fortunes of the American union movement. Our central concern remains the future of unions. The following article presents one point of view.

Unions Display a Revival of Militancy

Dana Milbank and Wendy Bounds

Workers used to solve their disputes with companies by marching off the job. But when flight attendants at Alaska Airlines got into a tiff with the company over scheduling and work rules, they selected a more effective weapon: a "Campaign for Chaos."

"We are going into work every day," says Gail Bigelow of the Association of Flight Attendants. "But at any given time we could call a work stoppage. It could last a day or a half-hour, but the company will have no idea when it's coming."

In response, the unit of Alaska Air Group has ordered at least three managers and supervisors from headquarters to ride on every flight in case of a work stoppage, producing a slowdown at the upper levels. "It's been a long couple of weeks," says an Alaska Airlines spokesman.

After more than a decade of retreat, union militancy appears to be surging. Unions are taking on employers with publicity campaigns, creative strikes and shows of solidarity in the workplace. Some see the new spirit as a backlash against the 1980s that will reinvigorate labor.

'More Anger and Militancy'

"There's been more militancy at the rank-and-file level," says Jeff Faux, president of the Economic Policy Institute in Washington. "There's more stress on the job, and that means more anger and militancy."

He attributes the rise in activism to a decline in real wages and benefits and an assault on job security that includes the use of anti-union consultants and permanent replacements for strikers. At the same time, workers have found their upward mobility blocked, creating an overeducated and restless work force.

The new activism may, of course, amount to no more than a last stand for labor. Although U.S. Union membership has shown small gains, it continues to shrink as a proportion of the work force. . . Work stoppages, meanwhile, fell to the lowest level in 45 years in 1992, according to the Bureau of Labor Statistics. A labor-backed bill banning permanent replacements for striking workers faces bleak prospects. And recent contract negotiations have brought unions little improvement in pay and benefits.

Sar Levitan, director of George Washington University's Center for Social Policy, believes unions are more concerned with defending health and pension benefits for an aging membership than with winning new benefits or expanding their membership. "I don't see much of an offensive," he says.

But at the same time, union victories in representation elections reached 50% last year, the highest rate since 1984, according to an analysis by the Bureau of National Affairs . . .

The new militancy has some important differences from the past; unions these days are more likely to use boycotts and town meetings than picket lines and baseball bats. In the old days, the activism would have meant more strikes. But in today's promanagement labor landscape fostered by the Reagan and Bush administrations, workers realize that walking

Continued

Continued

off the job often means getting fired. And in a weak economy, union workers are in no mood to lose their jobs to replacement workers.

Unions have been flocking to a variety of creative tactics . . . At American Telephone & Telegraph Co. last year, the Communications Workers set up an "electronic picket line" in which 70,000 people pledged to boycott AT&T if the union didn't get its way. The CWA estimates the threatened boycott would have cost AT&T $3 million to $5 million a week in lost revenue. An AT&T spokesman said the threat "sounds like a weapon" but denies that it had an impact.

Boycott of State Farm

In an ongoing dispute at A. E. Staley Manufacturing Co., in Decatur, Ill., the Allied Industrial Workers have pressured Staley representatives to resign from two bank boards and have launched a boycott of State Farm insurance, an indirect owner of the company, a unit of Britain's Tate & Lyle PLC.

The union also marched on Staley and State Farm offices and the state capitol. Instead of a strike, the union has been able to slow down work by scrupulously following safety rules workers had ignored before. Apparently frustrated by the union's tactics, the company locked out the workers. "Here was an accumulated frustration built up in the '80s, one defeat after another," says Philip Mattera, research director for Corporate Campaign Inc., a New York consulting firm advising the union. "They're tired of being pushed around."

But there are limits to the effectiveness of this new spirit. Workers striking three plants owned by PPG Industries Inc. recently organized a display of interunion solidarity. The workers, represented by the Aluminum, Brick and Glass Workers, organized a rally in downtown Pittsburgh at which hundreds of union faithful from five different unions circled PPG's glass headquarters. The protesters, some in camouflage suits, yelled slogans, waved flags and brandished banners that said things like "I'd rather die on my feet than live on my knees."

"I'm starting to see a lot of progress in the movement," said Mike Davin, a Teamster at the rally. "It's coming back."

Not so fast. PPG has declared that it will close two of the three plants on strike—claiming the closures are unrelated to the dispute.

The Mine Workers, meanwhile, are hoping to boost their fortunes by discarding their violent image in their selective strikes against coal companies. "We're no radicals here," says Mike Thomas, a worker at Ashland Coal Inc.'s Hobet No. 21 mine picketing along Highway 119 just up from Madison, W.Va. "We know the companies would like nothing more than to see us agitated, but we'll sit tight."

Violence during the strikes has been limited to companies' charges of rock-throwing, shooting at power equipment and igniting fires "of suspicious origin." Strikers from Mr. Thomas's Local 2286 trapped company supervisors for three hours in a school parking lot but didn't hurt anyone.

The Mine Workers' relatively peaceful solidarity has had some impact. As the union's selective strikes enter a third month, idling 14,000 workers, four coal producers have abandoned the 12-member Bituminous Coal Operators' Association and reached their own deals with the union.

But even an all-out victory for the Mine Workers would do little more than keep them from slipping further; their core demand is security in the few jobs they still have rather than improvements in pay and perks. "You'll never hear us mention wages," says John Ghiz, 48-year-old miner on strike. "We have to be concerned that we'll even have a job."

Source: *The Wall Street Journal*, July 8, 1993, p. A2. Reprinted by permission of *The Wall Street Journal*,

Summary

Legal Review. Clearly, unions do not enjoy the same status that they once did. However, the employer-employee relationship continues, and as part of that relationship the danger will always be present that employees will need protection from arbitrary employer and union conduct and employers will need protection from abusive union practices. Perhaps the very nature and dynamic of the employment relationship create these needs. Thus, the labor laws remain, and will remain, an important facet in managing any enterprise.

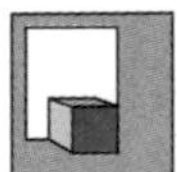

Ethics and Public Policy Review. Whether they will remain or not, should individuals be represented by unions, or should individuals be left to bargain on their own? You have read a great deal about the unethical conduct of unions and of employers—would we be better off without such group negotiations? On the other hand, it does appear that employers have the upper hand in negotiations and, perhaps, there is no way to ensure fairness without group bargaining. Most labor advocates would argue that unions are the only answer and, without them, employers' unethical conduct would run rampant.

Chapter Questions

1. *a.* In your opinion, what are the average blue-collar worker's biggest sources of job dissatisfaction? Can they be eliminated through collective bargaining? Explain.
   b. In your opinion, what are the average white-collar worker's biggest sources of job dissatisfaction? What means do such workers have for eliminating those sources of dissatisfaction? Explain.
2. *a.* Imagine what the world will be like 50 years from now. In what ways do you picture the work life of the average American to have changed? Explain.
   b. Imagine the ideal work world. How close does that picture come to the one you conjured up in response to the previous question? What types, if any, of labor or other legislation would bring society closer to that ideal? Explain.
3. You are the human resource manager for a manufacturing firm that is presently the subject of an organizing campaign by a union that has filed an election petition with the NLRB just 30 days ago. Your plant manager has come to you and said that he wishes to discharge one of her employees. She further explains that the employee in question has worked for the company for three years and throughout that time has had a terrible attendance record. She adds that up to this point the employee has not received any discipline for his attendance. Upon inquiry, the plant manager tells you that the employee has been seen on the plant floor wearing a button that says "Union Yes!" In addition the plant manager tells you that she knows that the employee is an outspoken union activist. What would you advise the plant manager to do? Why?
4. A union representing a bargaining unit comprising both men and women and multiple racial and ethnic groups demands to see detailed information that the employer keeps on wages paid to women and minorities, as well as hiring statistics about these members of the workforce.
   a. Should the employer be required to let employees see these data? Explain.
   b. What circumstances might affect your decision? [See *Westinghouse Electric Corp.*, 239 NLRB No. 18 (1978).]

c. Suppose that, instead of asking for wage information, the union asked to see the questions, answers, and individual scores achieved by employees on psychological aptitude tests that the employer requires them to take. If the employer refuses to turn these scores over, has it committed an unfair labor practice? Explain.

d. Does this situation differ significantly from the previous situation? [See *Detroit Edison Co.* v. *NLRB,* 440 U.S. 301 (1979).]

5. United Plant Guard Workers of America (UPGWA) sought union certification at Arbitron Services, Inc. The union and the company stipulated certain election procedures to be followed, including, among other things, the hours, date, and location at which balloting would be held and the posting of notices of the election. Several days before the election, the company posted notices of the election in several conspicuous locations. Two days before the election, the union mailed notices to employees listed on sheets supplied to the union by the company. The election was held on a regular payday. Out of 314 employees eligible to vote, a total of only 64 valid votes (26 of them for the union) were cast. the UPGWA petitioned the NLRB following the union's defeat, claiming that the low voter turnout resulted in the defeat, which led to the inference that notice of the election to the employees had been inadequate and that the election results should be set aside. What do you think the NLRB's response is likely to be? Explain. [See *Iona Security Services, Inc.,* and *National Union, United Plant Guard Workers of America,* 269 NLRB No. 53 (1983–84 CCH NLRB ¶ 16,145), March 21, 1984.]

6. A bargaining unit, consisting of 56 employees at the time of a union representation election, voted in favor of unionization by a vote of 29 to 23. The employer sought to have the election results nullified, alleging that six days prior to the election, a union official meeting with 20 employees had referred to a company vice president as a "stingy Jew." The company had witnesses to substantiate this claim, and the union did not deny it.

   a. Do you think the election results should be set aside? Explain. [See *NLRB* v. *Silverman's Men's Wear, Inc.,* 656 F.2d 53 (3d Cir. 1981).]

   b. Suppose, instead, union officers came to campaign meetings for a Japanese-owned company wearing T-shirts that said, "Remember Pearl Harbor" and "Japs speak with forked tongue and slant eyes." Do you think the result would be any different? Explain. [See *YKK (USA) Inc.* and *Sandra M. Collins et al.,* 296 NLRB No. 8 (1983–84 CCH NLRB ¶ 16,158), March 8, 1984.]

7. The Clayton Act exempts union wage negotiations from the antitrust laws. Workers in many different and competing companies may lawfully join together to form a single bargaining unit (for example, the Teamsters' union). Of course, the antitrust laws forbid competing companies from joining together in the manner workers are allowed to do. Economist Gary Becker of the University of Chicago argued that the time had come to treat union conspiracies in the same manner as those of management. He argued for replacing traditional trade unions with company unions (unions limited in membership to a single company), such as those used in Japan. He said union shop laws and other protections could be strengthened so management could not dominate the union. He noted the general decline of union membership in the United States: "In 1955, one of every three members of the U.S. labor force belonged to a union, compared with 17 percent in 1987." Becker argued that these declines were largely due to the growth of such protections as unemployment compensation, social security, medicare, and new barriers against unfair dismissals. Should labor unions be fully subject to the antitrust laws? Explain. [See Gary Becker, "It's Time to Scrap a Few Outmoded Labor Laws," *Business Week,* March 7, 1988, p. 18.]

8. Consider the following account of a contrast in labor-management relations in the United States and Japan.

   By 1989, Nippon Steel planned to reduce jobs in steel by 19,000 (41 percent of the work force). However, Nippn did not intend to dismiss "surplus personnel" or to offer voluntary retirement. Those workers were to be reemployed elsewhere in the steel division, or they were to be retrained for new jobs in other divisions. On the other hand, USX (the American leader in steel) released some 87,000 workers from 1980 to 1987. Of course, those workers received many benefits, such as jobless pay, insurance, and early retirements. Nonetheless, USX officials explained that company health took priority over worker welfare. Executive Vice President Bruce Johnson remarked that "it would have been futile to devise a human relations strategy ahead of a business strategy" during the massive cutbacks in steel.

   Do you support the Nippon approach or the USX approach, or are the situations simply not comparable? Explain. [See Associated Press, "Japanese Job Traditions under Attack," *Des Moines Register,* October 8, 1987, p. 9S.]
9. Section 8(a)(3) of the National Labor Relations Act permits a labor-management agreement requiring all employees to pay a sum equivalent to union dues even though they may not choose to become members of the union (an agency shop). Some employees who had chosen not to join the union but who were paying the equivalent of dues claimed that their money had been misused because the union allegedly spent funds on such activities as organizing the employees of other companies, lobbying, and participating in social, charitable, and political events. May a union lawfully expend nonmember dues in support of activities unrelated to collective bargaining? [See *Communications Workers of America* v. *Beck,* 487 U.S. 735 (1988).]
10. A union-management dispute led to an economic strike, at which point the employer hired replacement workers. At the end of the strike, the workforce consisted of 25 former strikers and 69 replacement workers. The agreement settling the strike provided that strikers would be recalled as vacancies arose. However, the employer did not follow the agreement when it recalled four workers (three of whom were replacements) and failed to consider any of 28 strikers who remained out of work.

    Well-settled labor law provides that "economic strikers who have been permanently replaced but who have unconditionally offered to return to work are entitled to reinstatement upon the departure of the replacements." The NLRB found a violation of the National Labor Relations Act, and framed the issue as follows: "How should the layoff of the permanent replacement worker—who has a contractual right to recall—affect the reinstatement rights of unreinstated strikers?" The NLRB ruled that it would require a showing that the laid-off replacements had no "reasonable expectancy of recall." Then the burden of proof would shift to the employer to justify its failure to recall strikers when vacancies arose. The NLRB decision was appealed. Decide. Explain. [See *Aqua-Chem, Inc.* v. *NLRB,* 910 F.2d 1487 (7th Cir., 1990), cert. denied., 111 S.Ct. 2871 (1991).]
11. Some employees were transferred from a unionized plant to a new location.
    a. Are the employees who were transferred to the new location still members of their original bargaining unit? Explain.
    b. What test should the National Labor Relations Board employ in deciding whether the employer must recognize and bargain with the union in the new location? [See *Gitano Group, Inc.,* 308 *NLRB* No. 173 (1992).]

12. A field organizer for the International Brotherhood of Electrical Workers (IBEW) sought work with a nonunion electrical firm. In applying for a job as an electrician, the organizer told the company that he would use his time during lunch and after work in an effort to organize employees. Indeed, while his application was being processed, he organized a picket line at the company to protest low wages. The foreman then told the organizer that he would not be hired because "it's kind of hard to hire you when you're out there on the other side picketing." Had he been hired, the organizer acknowledged that he would have maintained some relationship with the union, and he would likely have later returned to full-time employment with the union. Was the organizer unlawfully denied employment? Explain. [See *Willmar Electric Service, Inc.* v. *National Labor Relations Board,* 968 F.2d 1327 (D.C. Cir., 1992), cert. denied, 113 S.Ct. 1252 (1993).]

Notes

1. "Standing Firm in the New Workplace," *Los Angeles Times,* March 16, 1995, p. E1.
2. Louis Rukeyser, ed., *Louis Rukeyser's Business Almanac* (New York: Simon & Schuster, 1988), p. 60.
3. "As Caterpiller Lures Picket Line Crossers, a Strike Settlement Is Put to a Severe Test," *The Wall Street Journal,* July 6, 1994, p. B1.
4. See Alan Glassman, Naomi Berger Davidson, and Thomas Cummings, *Labor Relations: Reports from the Firing Line* (New York: Business Publications, Inc., 1988), pp. 114–57.
5. The historical and political background information used in this chapter was drawn from a number of sources and amalgamated in such a way that precise footnoting was difficult. For example, many of the sociological trends described are discussed in three or four sources. We would, therefore, like to acknowledge the works of the following people, whose research and insights proved to be invaluable resources: Richard S. Belous, Hyman Berman, Angela Y. Davis, Richard Edwards, John J. Flagler, Eli Ginzberg, J. David Greenstone, Isaac A. Hourwich, and Sar A. Levitan.

   Amy Gershenfeld Donnella, the author of this chapter (first edition), would like especially to acknowledge and thank Professor Archibald Cox, from whom she took a course in labor law in 1978, and whose textbook and class lectures provided the cornerstone of her understanding of the subject. She hopes that her own good fortune at having had the opportunity to study labor law under Professor Cox will translate into a richer educational experience for students using this textbook.
6. Archibald Cox, with Derek Bok and Robert A. Gorman, *Cases and Materials on Labor Law,* 8th ed. (Mineola, NY: Foundation Press, 1977), pp. 7–8.
7. Richard Edwards, *Contested Terrain: The Transformation of the Workplace in the Twentieth Century* (New York: Basic Books, 1979), pp. 40–41.
8. John J. Flagler, *The Labor Movement in the United States* (Minneapolis: Lerner Publications, 1972), pp. 26–33.
9. Cox, *Labor Law,* p. 8.
10. Isaac A. Hourwich, *Immigration and Labor* (New York: Arno Press, 1969), pp. 125–45.
11. Cox, *Labor Law,* p. 9.
12. Flagler, *Labor Movement,* pp. 26–28.
13. Glassman et al., *Firing Line,* pp. 5–6.
14. Flagler, *Labor Movement,* pp. 26–28.
15. Hourwich, *Immigration and Labor,* pp. 232–49.
16. Flagler, *Labor Movement,* p. 47.
17. J. David Greenstone, *Labor in American Politics* (New York: Alfred A. Knopf, 1969), p. 21.
18. Cox, *Labor Law,* p. 11.
19. Greenstone, *Labor in American Politics,* p. 22.
20. Ibid., p. 23.
21. Flagler, *Labor Movement,* pp. 81–83.
22. Greenstone, *Labor in American Politics,* pp. 41–42.

23. John Fossum, *Labor Relations—Development, Structure, Process,* 6th ed. (Burr Ridge, IL: Richard D. Irwin, 1995), p. 38.
24. Cox, *Labor Law,* pp. 86–87.
25. Ibid., pp. 87–88.
26. Ibid., p. 88.
27. Flagler, *Labor Movement,* pp. 54–56.
28. Fossum, *Labor Relations,* p. 36.
29. See *Vegelahn* v. *Guntner,* 167 Mass. 92, 44 N.E. 1077 (1896).
30. Cox, *Labor Law,* pp. 60–66.
31. Greenstone, *Labor in American Politics,* p. 83.
32. Ibid., p. 47.
33. Cox, *Labor Law,* p. 91.
34. Patrick Hardin, *The Developing Labor Law* (Washington, DC: Bureau of National Affairs, 1992), pp. 31–32.
35. Ibid., p. 94.
36. Ibid., pp. 1, 107–8,
37. Ibid., pp. 1, 108.
38. *Steele* v. *Louisville and Nashville Railroad,* 323 U.S. 192 (1944).
39. *Vaca* v. *Sipes,* 386 U.S. 171 (1967); *Miranda Fuel Co.,* 140 NLRB 181 (1962).
40. Paul Weiler, *Governing the Workplace: The Future of Labor and Employment Law* (Cambridge, MA: Harvard University Press, 1990), pp. 9–10.
41. "Promises to Keep: Securing Workers' Rights to Self-Organization under the National Labor Relations Act," *Harvard Law Review* 96 (1983), p. 1769.
42. See "Uncle Sam Gompers," *The Wall Street Journal,* October 25, 1995, p. A26; "Chief AFL–CIO Organizer to Try Civil Rights Tactics," *The Wall Street Journal,* February 8, 1996, p. B10; "Signs of Revival," *The Wall Street Journal,* September 1, 1995, p. A1.
43. Benjamin Aaron, Joyce Najita, and James Stern, eds., *Public Sector Bargaining* (Washington, DC: Bureau of National Affairs, 1988), p. 1.
44. See Dave Hage and Paul Klauda, *No Retreat, No Surrender: Labor's War at Hormel* (Boston, MA: Morrow & Co., 1989).
45. The National Labor Relations Act is found in Title 29 U.S.C. § 151 et seq.
46. *U.S.* v. *Lopez,* 115 S. Ct. 1624 (1995).
47. Cox, *Labor Law,* pp. 113–22.
48. Ibid., pp. 99–101.
49. 416 U.S. 267 (1974).
50. See *Sewell Mfg. Co.,* 138 NLRB 66 (1962), stating that the board's goal is to conduct elections "in a laboratory under conditions as nearly ideal as possible to determine the uninhibited desires of employees" and "to provide an atmosphere conducive to the sober and informed exercise of the franchise free from . . . elements which prevent or impede reasonable choice."
51. *Milchem, Inc.,* 170 NLRB 362 (1968).
52. Littler, Mendelson, Fastiff and Tichy, *The 1990 Employer* (Chicago: Tort & Insurance Practice Section, ABA, 1990), vol. 2, p. U17.
53. *Republic Aviation Corp.* v. *NLRB,* 324 U.S. 793 (1945).
54. *NLRB* v. *Babcock & Wilcox,* 351 U.S. 105 (1956).
55. *Tri-County Medical Center,* 222 NLRB 1089 (1976).
56. See Section 8(q) of the Taft-Hartley Act.
57. *Radio Officers* v. *NLRB,* 347 U.S. 17 (1954).
58. Ibid.
59. Benjamin J. Taylor and Fred Whitney, *Labor Relations Law,* 4th ed. (Englewood Cliffs, NJ: Prentice Hall, 1983), p. 406.
60. *Majure Transport Co.* v. *NLRB,* 199 F.2d 735 (1952).
61. *NLRB* v. *Norfolk Shipbuilding & Drydock Corp.,* 172 F.2d 813 (1949).
62. *Southern Saddlery Co.,* 90 NLRB 1205 (1950).
63. Hardin, *Developing Labor Law,* pp. 616–20.
64. Littler et al., *The 1990 Employer,* p. V13, citing *Reichhold Chemicals, Inc.,* 288 NLRB No. 8 (1988).
65. Ibid., citing *NLRB* v. *Crockett-Bradley, Inc.,* 598 F.2d 971 (5th Cir. 1979).
66. *NLRB* v. *General Electric Company,* 418 F.2d 736 (1969).
67. *NLRB* v. *Insurance Agents' International Union,* 361 U.S. 477 (1960).
68. Ibid., at 480–81.
69. Ibid., at 482, citing 119 NLRB 769–71.
70. Ibid., at 488.
71. *NLRB* v. *Truitt Mfg. Co.,* 351 U.S. 149 (1956).
72. *NLRB* v. *Katz,* 369 U.S. 736 (1962).
73. See *First National Maintenance Corporation* v. *NLRB,* 101 S.Ct. 2573 (1981).
74. 356 U.S. 342 (1958).
75. 369 U.S. 736 (1962).

76. Daniel Seligman, "Unions and Strikers: A Huge Nonproblem," *Fortune,* May 31, 1993, p. 175.
77. Littler et al., *The 1990 Employer,* p. V6.
78. *NLRB* v. *Mackay Radio & Tel. Co.,* 304 U.S. 333 (1938).
79. Littler et al., *The 1990 Employer,* p. V6.
80. "Clinton and the Strikers," *Des Moines Register,* January 29, 1995, p. B14.
81. "As Caterpillar Lures Picket-Line Crossers, a Striker's Mettle Is Put to a Severe Test," *The Wall Street Journal,* July 6, 1994, p. B1.
82. Cliff Edwards, "Companies Turn Up Pressure by Locking Out Protesting Workers," *Waterloo Courier,* July 4, 1993, p. C3.
83. *United Steelworkers of America* v. *Sadlowski,* 457 U.S. 102 (1982).
84. Thomas Goeghegan, *Which Side Are You On?* (New York: Farrar, Straus & Giroux, 1991), p. 196.
85. *Sadlowski* v. *United Steelworkers of America,* 645 F.2d 1114, 1124 (D.C. Cir. 1981).
86. Zech and Khun, "National Labor Policy: Is It Truly Designed to Protect the Worker?" *Selected Papers of the American Business Law Association: National Proceedings,* 1982, pp. 442–43.
87. Robert Perkovich and Mark Stein, "Challenges to Arbitration under Illinois Public Sector Labor Relations Statutes," *Hofstra Labor Law Journal* 7, no. 1 (Fall 1989), p. 197.

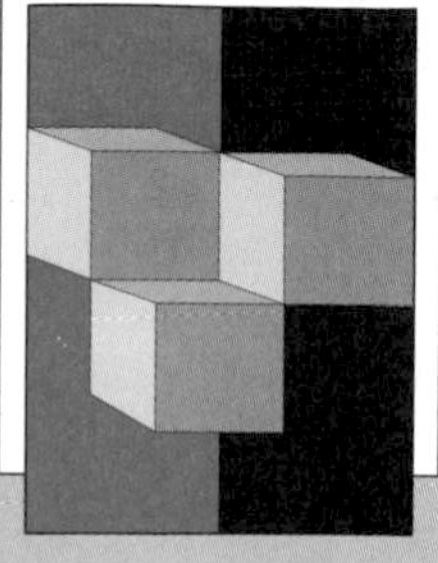

PART II

THE BUSINESS'S RELATIONSHIP WITH THE GOVERNMENT

Government Regulation of Business and Administrative Law

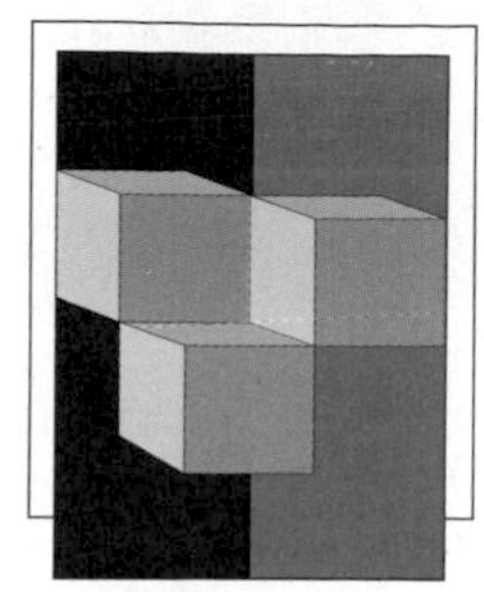

Chapter 8

Reader's Guide

The first part of this text led us through the legal dimensions of setting up a business: the choice of formal structures (corporations, partnerships, etc.), contracts, property, and some features of hiring and managing employees, including employment and labor law. Now we turn to managing the growing business's relationship with government.

Successfully building and managing a business in America requires skill in dealing with the many regulatory demands of local, state, and federal governments. In this chapter, we will summarize the regulatory process. Our fundamental concerns are (1) Why did we decide, as a society, to embrace extensive government regulation of business? (2) What is the nature and role of the powerful federal administrative agencies in our business lives? and (3) perhaps the central question in this book, Should we reduce the power of government in business?

> A woman speaking to the *Des Moines Register*'s 24-hour phone line for anonymous callers: "I prefer big government to big business; government is for the people, corporations are for the money."
>
> Do you agree?
>
> Source: "Your 2¢ Worth," *Des Moines Register,* March 16, 1996, p. 4T.

Profile

Mark McDonald founded Miami Air Charter, a freight and passenger business, in 1987. By March 1995, McDonald had expanded his successful charter company into Nations Air, a jet passenger airline offering discounted fares between Boston, Pittsburgh, and Philadelphia. McDonald's basic idea was to offer very cheap fares (sometimes as low as $39 between Pittsburgh and Philadelphia) to expand the number of people who choose to fly.

Competing with giants such as USAir was daunting. From 1990 to 1995, 76 companies asked the government for permission to fly jets with more than 60 passengers. Only 30 of those continued in operation in 1995.[1] So McDonald had to satisfy the Department of Transportation (DOT) to begin service. At that point, he ran into trouble. Among other things the DOT demanded assurance of the financial stability of the operation, which in this case meant having in hand $4.2 million for start-up costs and three months of operation. He secured government permission and began flying in March 1995, but in July 1995 the Federal Aviation Administration (FAA) found alleged safety problems. Nations Air was flying two Boeing 737-200s but voluntarily grounded them and contracted replacement service. McDonald labeled the problems "paperwork and documentation," but the FAA said the airline had failed to fully train all of its pilots, among other shortcomings.[2] McDonald was able to restore service after a few days of corrective measures, but at the time of this writing, Nations Air had temporarily returned one of its two jets to charter service in order to pick up much-needed revenue.

Presumably, McDonald has been frustrated by the government's role in his struggle, but most of us would probably agree that some oversight in the air industry is wise.

I. Too Much Government?

Certainly Mark McDonald's frustration with government is broadly shared. A 1995 public opinion poll showed 76 percent of Americans rarely or never trust "government to do what is right," the highest level of distrust since the polling began in the late 1950s.[3] Of course, much of that frustration lies with the enormous expense of government programs. As of 1995, total annual government spending (local, state, and national) surpassed $2.5 trillion (12 zeroes) or $23,000 per household, which would be sufficient to purchase all of the U.S. farmland as well as all of the stock of the 100 most profitable American corporations.[4] For the business community, paying the bill for big government may be less annoying than the sometimes suffocating presence of government rules, many of which, to the critics, have few redeeming values. Nonetheless, the American people clearly are not prepared to scrap the government's protective authority. Why, with our extraordinary heritage of individualism, freedom, and capitalism, have we turned significant segments of our lives over to government?

A. Market Failure

market failure. Economic theory arguing that the free market works imperfectly because of certain allegedly inherent defects such as monopoly, public goods, and so forth.

The core of our support for government regulation of business rests in the notion of **market failure,** the unsurprising but quite powerful view that the market works imperfectly. In theory, government intervention in a free enterprise economy is justified only when the market is unable to maximize the public interest—that is, in instances of market failure.

Market failure is attributed to certain inherent imperfections in the market itself.

Inadequate Information. Can consumers choose the best pain reliever in the absence of complete information about the virtues of the competing products? An efficient free market presumes reasoned decisions about production and consumption. Reasoned decisions require adequate information. Because we cannot have perfect information and often will not have adequate information, the government, it is argued, may impose regulations to either improve the available information or diminish the unfavorable effect of inadequate information. Hence we have, for example, labeling mandates for consumer goods, licensure requirements for many occupations, and health standards for the processing and sale of goods.

monopoly. Market power permitting the holder to fix prices or exclude competition.

Monopoly. Of course, the government intervenes to thwart anticompetitive monopolies and oligopolies throughout the marketplace. (That process is addressed in Chapter 11.) Of immediate interest here is the so-called natural **monopoly.** Telephone and electrical services are classic examples of a decline in per unit production costs as the firm becomes larger. Thus, a single large firm is more efficient than several small ones, and a natural monopoly results. In such situations, the government has commonly intervened (in the form of public service commissions) to preserve the efficiencies of the large firm while preventing that firm from taking unfair advantage of the consumer.

Negative Externalities. When all the costs of a good or service are not fully internalized or absorbed by the producer, they fall elsewhere as what economists have labeled *externalities, neighborhood effects,* or *spillovers.* Pollution is a characteristic example of a **negative externality.** The environment is used without charge as an ingredient in the production process (commonly as a receptacle for waste). Consequently, the product is underpriced. The consumer does not pay the full social cost of the product, so those remaining costs are thrust on parties external to the transaction. Government regulation is sometimes considered necessary to place the full cost burden on those who generated it, which in turn is expected to result in less wasteful use of resources.

negative externality. A spillover where all the costs of a good or service are not fully absorbed by the producer and thus fall on others.

Public Goods. Some goods and services cannot be provided through the pricing system because we have no method for excluding those who choose not to pay. For such **public goods,** the added cost of benefiting one person is zero or nearly so, and in any case, no one can effectively be denied the benefits of the activity. National defense, insect eradication, and pollution control are examples of this phenomenon. Presumably most individuals would refuse to voluntarily pay for what others would receive free. Thus, in the absence of government regulations, public goods would not be produced in adequate quantities.

public goods. Goods or services usually provided by government when underproduced by markets.

B. Philosophy and Politics

The correction of market failure could explain the full range of government regulation of business, but an alternative or perhaps supplemental explanation lies in the political process. Three general arguments have emerged.

1. One view is that regulation is considered necessary for the protection and general welfare of the public. We find the government engaging in regulatory efforts designed to achieve a more equitable distribution of income and wealth. Many believe government intervention in the market is necessary to stabilize the economy, thus curbing the problems of recession, inflation, and unemployment. Affirmative action programs seek to compensate for the racism and sexism of the past. We even find the government protecting us from ourselves, both for our benefit and for the well-being of the larger society. For example, cigarette advertising is restricted, and seatbelts are required in many states.
2. Another view is that regulation is developed at the behest of industry and is operated primarily for the benefit of industry. Here, the various subsidies and tax advantages afforded to business might be cited. In numerous instances, government regulation has been effective in reducing or entirely eliminating the entry of competitors. Antitrust law has been instrumental in sheltering small businesses. Government regulation has also permitted legalized price-fixing in some industries. Of course, it may be that although regulation is often initiated primarily for the public welfare, industry eventually "captures" the regulatory process and ensures its continuation for the benefit of the industry. Further, some corporations seek government standards so they can do what is best for society without being undercut by their less socially responsible competitors.
3. Finally, bureaucrats who perform government regulation are themselves a powerful force in maintaining and expanding that regulation.

II. History of Government Regulation of Business

Government has always played some role in American commerce. In the early years of the republic, tariffs were imposed to protect manufacturers, subsidies were provided to stimulate commerce, and a few agencies were established (e.g., the Patent and Trademark Office in 1836).

Prior to the Civil War, the major, if weak, link between government and business was the national bank, which possessed very limited authority. Banking remained a fundamentally private enterprise restrained only by weak state statutes. A meaningful federal banking system simply did not exist. Indeed, it is estimated that by 1860 "some 1,500 banks were issuing about 10,000 different types of bank notes."[5] Then the need for a centralized approach to the Civil War forced Congress to pass the National Banking Act of 1864, which laid the foundation for the dual system of extensive federal and state banking regulation that we know today. Following the Civil War, the "Robber Barons" (Carnegie, Rockefeller, and their colleagues) came to the fore. Philosopher Herbert Spencer adapted Darwin's survival of the fittest theory to the world of commerce, thereby giving the business community an intellectual foundation for asserting its leadership. Extraordinary industrial growth followed.

By the late 1880s, anger over the conduct of the rail and industrial trusts manifested itself in the Populist movement, which embodied the struggle of the common people against the predatory acts of the moneyed interests. The railroads, in particular, were bent on growth and seemed unconcerned with the general welfare.

Several states enacted railroad regulatory legislation, and Congress passed the Interstate Commerce Commission Act of 1887, which banned rate discrimination against short hauls and the practice of keeping rates secret until the day of shipment.

As explained in Chapter 11, the development of giant trusts and holding companies (e.g., Standard Oil) led to extraordinary commercial advances but also to widespread abuse in the form of price-fixing, price-slashing to drive out competitors, market sharing, and the like. Blacklists and other antilabor tactics were common. At the same time, small merchants and wholesalers were being squeezed by the weight of big manufacturing interests such as American Tobacco, Quaker Oats, Heinz, Swift, and Anheuser Busch. Similarly, retail giants (such as Sears and Woolworth) were applying extreme competitive pressure on smaller businesses. The passage of the Sherman Antitrust Act in 1890 had relatively little immediate impact; however, presidents Roosevelt, Taft, and Wilson all took up the regulatory cause, and with the passage in 1914 of the Clayton and Federal Trade Commission acts, antitrust law became an important ingredient in American business life.

The Depression compelled many archconservatives to surrender to the need for government intervention. President Roosevelt took office in 1933, and the first 100 days of his term saw the passage of 15 major pieces of legislation. In all, Roosevelt secured approval of 93 major bills during his first two terms in office. The federal government became the biggest voice in America as the administration sought to correct the tragedy of the Depression. The legislation literally changed the character of American life. Congress established the Civilian Conservation Corps to place the unemployed in public works projects. The Federal Emergency Relief Act funded state-operated welfare programs. The Glass-Steagall Act divided investment and commercial banking and provided for insurance on bank deposits. The list went on and on, and the result was a new view of the business-government relationship. Effectively, the government and the citizenry conceded that the old view of an automatically self-correcting economy was invalid.[6]

Distrust of the market provoked further government regulation in the decades subsequent to the Depression, and that regulation has followed a much broader path. Rather than regulating single industries (transportation, banking, communication), the government interventions of more recent years have swept across the entire economy to address such issues as discrimination, pollution, and worker safety. In the 1960s and the bulk of the 1970s, no social problem seemed too daunting for the government's regulatory efforts.[7] But the late 1970s to the present have been a period of resistance to government intervention resulting in significant *deregulation* of some dimensions of the economy.

Public Policy Questions

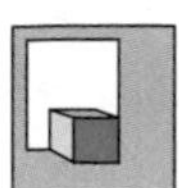

1. After decades of growth in government, why are many Americans increasingly ambivalent, or actively hostile, toward that system?
2. One of the discouraging features of the mid-90s job market is that so many companies are increasing employment by hiring temporaries, part-timers, and outside contractors. How might expanding government rules be influencing that trend away from full-time employment?

III. The Constitutional Foundation of Government Regulation

As you think about how you will deal with government in the process of building and managing a business, you may be surprised to learn that the core of government's power over business lies in a few words in the U.S. Constitution. The Commerce Clause, Article I, Section 8 of the Constitution, provides that: "The Congress shall have Power . . . To regulate Commerce with foreign Nations, and among the several States, and with the Indian Tribes." State authority to regulate commerce resides in the police power reserved to the states by the Constitution. **Police power** refers to the right of the state governments to promote the public health, safety, morals, and general welfare by regulating persons and property within each state's jurisdiction. The states have, in turn, delegated portions of the police power to local government units.

police power. The government's inherent authority to enact rules to provide for the health, safety, and general welfare of the citizenry.

A. Supremacy Clause

Sometimes state or local law conflicts with federal law. Such situations are resolved by the **Supremacy Clause** of the Constitution, which provides that, "This Constitution and the Laws of the United States . . . shall be the Supreme Law of the Land."

Supremacy Clause. An element of the U.S. Constitution providing that all constitutionally valid federal laws are the paramount law of the land and, as such, are superior to any conflicting state and local laws.

Ours is a federalist form of government wherein we divide authority between federal, state, and local units of government. Conflicts between the preferences of each level are inevitable. However, the Supremacy Clause, as interpreted by the Supreme Court, establishes that, in the event of an irreconcilable conflict, federal law will prevail and the state or local law will be ruled unconstitutional. Were it not so, we would have great difficulty in achieving a unified national policy on any issue.

At the same time, the Supreme Court recently affirmed the states' strong role in our dual system of government by announcing that "it will read federal law to preempt state governmental functions only if Congress plainly states its intent to do so."[8]

B. Commerce Clause

The **Commerce Clause,** as interpreted by the judiciary, affords Congress exclusive jurisdiction over foreign commerce. States and localities, nevertheless, sometimes seek in various ways to regulate foreign commerce. For example, a state may seek, directly or indirectly, to impose a tax on foreign goods that compete with those locally grown or manufactured. Such efforts violate the Commerce Clause.

Commerce Clause. That portion of the U.S. Constitution that permits federal regulation of foreign and interstate trade.

Federal control over interstate commerce was designed to create a free market throughout the United States, wherein goods would move among the states, unencumbered by state and local tariffs and duties. Not surprisingly, that profoundly sensible policy has been the source of extensive conflict and litigation. As with foreign commerce, the states and localities have tried to influence the course of interstate commerce. The judiciary has not been sympathetic with those efforts. In the famous *Wickard* v. *Filburn* case,[9] the U.S. Supreme Court found that a farmer's 23 acres of homegrown and largely home-consumed wheat were subject to federal regulation because the home consumption reduced the demand for wheat, thus affecting interstate commerce in the crop. So intrastate activities *affecting* interstate commerce in some way are subject to federal rules. Then in 1996, the Supreme Court appeared to begin to rethink the federal government's sweeping authority under the Commerce Clause.

New Direction? Perhaps reflecting the current conservative tide, the Supreme Court in 1995 surprised most observers by striking a blow for states' rights. In 1990, the federal government approved the Gun-Free School Zones Act, which forbade "any individual knowingly to possess a firearm at a place that [he] knows . . . is a school zone."[10] A 12th grade San Antonio, Texas, student carried an unloaded, concealed gun into his high school and was charged with violating the act. His case reached the Supreme Court, where he claimed and the Court agreed that Congress did not have the constitutional authority to regulate the matter. By a 5–4 vote the Court held that Congress exceeded its powers by defining the possession of a gun as economic activity that, through repetition elsewhere, would have a substantial effect on interstate commerce.[11] The Court, in substance, said that the federal government was trying to regulate a *local* matter, a subject left by the Constitution to local or state government. The decision upset no existing precedents, but it clearly signaled the Court's willingness to examine congressional power over our lives, power that has expanded essentially without question since the New Deal of the 1930s.

By a 5–4 vote the Court held that Congress exceeded its powers by defining the possession of a gun as economic activity.

In Practice. Think about the practical impact of Commerce Clause reasoning on your efforts to build a business career. Suppose your professional life takes an entrepreneurial direction, and you decide to open a neighborhood cafe. After you have been in business for a time, a federal civil rights official says that the government has received a complaint that you violated the Americans with Disabilities Act by dismissing an obese employee. Without reaching the merits of the claim, you contend in court that the federal government has no authority over your business because your restaurant is local in character. Although your business has grown to the point that you have 25 employees, the government is unable to produce evidence that you have ever served an out-of-state customer. Does the federal government have constitutional authority to regulate your business? Should it have that authority? [For a similar case, see *Katzenbach* v. *McClung,* 379 U.S. 294 (1964).]

The historically crucial decision that follows sets out reasoning of the kind that has guided the courts in this area over the past 30 years.

CASE

Justice Clark

Heart of Atlanta Motel v. United States

379 U.S. 241 (1964)

This is a declaratory judgment action, attacking the constitutionality of Title II of the Civil Rights Act of 1964 . . . [The lower court found for the United States.]

Continued

Continued

1. The Factual Background and Contentions of the Parties

. . . Appellant owns and operates the Heart of Atlanta Motel, which has 216 rooms available to transient guests. The motel is located on Courtland Street, two blocks from downtown Peachtree Street. It is readily accessible to interstate highways 75 and 85 and state highways 23 and 41. Appellant solicits patronage from outside the State of Georgia through various national advertising media, including magazines of national circulation; it maintains over 50 billboards and highway signs within the state, soliciting patronage for the motel; it accepts convention trade from outside Georgia and approximately 75 percent of its registered guests are from out of state. Prior to passage of the act the motel had followed a practice of refusing to rent rooms to Negroes, and it alleged that it intended to continue to do so. In an effort to perpetuate that policy this suit was filed.

The appellant contends that Congress in passing this act exceeded its power to regulate commerce under [Article I] of the Constitution of the United States; that the act violates the Fifth Amendment because appellant is deprived of the right to choose its customers and operate its business as it wishes, resulting in a taking of its liberty and property without due process of law and a taking of its property without just compensation; and, finally, that by requiring appellant to rent available rooms to Negroes against its will, Congress is subjecting it to involuntary servitude in contravention of the Thirteenth Amendment.

The appellees counter that the unavailability to Negroes of adequate accommodations interferes significantly with interstate travel, and that Congress, under the Commerce Clause, has power to remove such obstructions and restraints; that the Fifth Amendment does not forbid reasonable regulation and that consequential damage does not constitute a "taking" within the meaning of that amendment; that the Thirteenth Amendment claim fails because it is entirely frivolous to say that an amendment directed to the abolition of human bondage and the removal of widespread disabilities associated with slavery places discrimination in public accommodations beyond the reach of both federal and state law . . .

[A]ppellees proved the refusal of the motel to accept Negro transients after the passage of the act. The district court sustained the constitutionality of the sections of the act under attack and issued a permanent injunction . . . It restrained the appellant from "[r]efusing to accept Negroes as guests in the motel by reason of their race or color" and from "[m]aking any distinction whatever upon the basis of race or color in the availability of the goods, services, facilities, privileges, advantages, or accommodations offered or made available to the guests of the motel, or to the general public, within or upon any of the premises of the Heart of Atlanta Motel, Inc."

2. The History of the Act

. . . The act as finally adopted was most comprehensive, undertaking to prevent through peaceful and voluntary settlement discrimination in voting, as well as in places of accommodation and public facilities, federally secured programs and in employment. Since Title II is the only portion under attack here, we confine our consideration to those public accommodation provisions.

3. Title II of the Act

This Title is divided into seven sections beginning with § 201(a) which provides that: "All persons shall be entitled to the full and equal enjoyment of the goods, services, facilities, privileges, advantages, and accommodations of any place of public accommodation, as defined in this section, without discrimination or segregation on the ground of race, color, religion, or national origin."

4. Application of Title II to Heart of Atlanta Motel

It is admitted that the operation of the motel brings it within the provisions of § 201(a) of the act and that appellant refused to provide lodging for transient Negroes because of their race or color and that it intends to continue that policy unless restrained.

Continued

Continued

The sole question posed is, therefore, the constitutionality of the Civil Rights Act of 1964 as applied to these facts. The legislative history of the act indicates that Congress based the act on § 5 and the Equal Protection Clause of the Fourteenth Amendment as well as its power to regulate interstate commerce . . .

[Part 5 omitted.]

6. The Basis of Congressional Action

While the act as adopted carried no congressional findings the record of its passage through each house is replete with evidence of the burdens that discrimination by race or color places upon interstate commerce . . . This testimony included the fact that our people have become increasingly mobile with millions of people of all races traveling from state to state; that Negroes in particular have been the subject of discrimination in transient accommodations, having to travel great distances to secure the same; that often they have been unable to obtain accommodations and have had to call upon friends to put them up overnight, and that these conditions have become so acute as to require the listing of available lodging for Negroes in a special guidebook which was itself "dramatic testimony to the difficulties" Negroes encounter in travel. These exclusionary practices were found to be nationwide, the Under Secretary of Commerce testifying that there is "no question that this discrimination in the North still exists to a large degree" and in the West and Midwest as well. This testimony indicated a qualitative as well as quantitative effect on interstate travel by Negroes. The former was the obvious impairment of the Negro traveler's pleasure and convenience that resulted when he continually was uncertain of finding lodging. As for the latter, there was evidence that this uncertainty stemming from racial discrimination had the effect of discouraging travel on the part of a substantial portion of the Negro community. This was the conclusion not only of the Under Secretary of Commerce but also of the Administrator of the Federal Aviation Agency, who wrote the Chairman of the Senate Commerce Committee that it was his "belief that air commerce is adversely affected by the denial to a substantial segment of the traveling public of adequate and desegregated public accommodations." We shall not burden this opinion with further details since the voluminous testimony presents overwhelming evidence that discrimination by hotels and motels impedes interstate travel.

7. The Power of Congress over Interstate Travel

The power of Congress to deal with these obstructions depends on the meaning of the Commerce Clause.

* * *

In short, the determinative test of the exercise of power by the Congress under the Commerce Clause is simply whether the activity sought to be regulated is "commerce which concerns more States than one" and has a real and substantial relation to the national interest. Let us now turn to this facet of the problem.

* * *

The same interest in protecting interstate commerce which led Congress to deal with segregation in interstate carriers and the white-slave traffic has prompted it to extend the exercise of its power to gambling, to criminal enterprises, to deceptive practices in the sale of products, to fraudulent security transactions, and to racial discrimination by owners and managers of terminal restaurants . . .

That Congress was legislating against moral wrongs in many of these areas rendered its enactments no less valid. In framing Title II of this act Congress was also dealing with what it considered a moral problem. But that fact does not detract from the overwhelming evidence of the disruptive effect that racial discrimination has had on commercial intercourse. It was this

Continued

Continued

burden which empowered Congress to enact appropriate legislation, and, given this basis for the exercise of its power, Congress was not restricted by the fact that the particular obstruction to interstate commerce with which it was dealing was also deemed a moral and social wrong.

It is said that the operation of the motel here is of a purely local character. But, assuming this to be true, "[i]f it is interstate commerce that feels the pinch, it does not matter how local the operation which applies the squeeze."

* * *

Thus the power of Congress to promote interstate commerce also includes the power to regulate the local incidents thereof, including local activities in both the states of origin and destination, which might have a substantial and harmful effect upon that commerce. One need only examine the evidence which we have discussed above to see that Congress may—as it has—prohibit racial discrimination by motels serving travelers, however "local" their operations may appear.

Nor does the act deprive appellant of liberty or property under the Fifth Amendment. The commerce power invoked here by the Congress is a specific and plenary one authorized by the Constitution itself. The only questions are: (1) whether Congress had a rational basis for finding that racial discrimination by motels affected commerce, and (2) if it had such a basis, whether the means it selected to eliminate that evil are reasonable and appropriate. If they are, appellant has no "right" to select its guests as it sees fit, free from governmental regulation.

There is nothing novel about such legislation. Thirty-two states now have it on their books either by statute or executive order and many cities provide such regulation. Some of these acts go back four-score years. It has been repeatedly held by this Court that such laws do not violate the Due Process Clause of the Fourteenth Amendment.

* * *

It is doubtful if in the long run appellant will suffer economic loss as a result of the act. Experience is to the contrary where discrimination is completely obliterated as to all public accommodations. But whether this be true or not is of no consequence since this Court has specifically held that the fact that a "member of the class which is regulated may suffer economic losses not shared by others . . . has never been a barrier" to such legislation . . . Likewise in a long line of cases this Court has rejected the claim that the prohibition of racial discrimination in public accommodations interferes with personal liberty . . . Neither do we find any merit in the claim that the act is a taking of property without just compensation. The cases are to the contrary . . .

We find no merit in the remainder of the appellant's contentions including that of "involuntary servitude." . . . We could not say that the requirements of the act in this regard are in any way "akin to African slavery" . . .

We, therefore, conclude that the action of the Congress in the adoption of the act as applied here to a motel which concededly serves interstate travelers is within the power granted it by the Commerce Clause of the Constitution, as interpreted by this Court for 140 years.

Affirmed.

Questions—Law

1. What government arguments supported the claim that the Heart of Atlanta racial policy affected interstate commerce?
2. What test did the Court articulate to determine when Congress has the power to pass legislation based on the Commerce Clause?

Continued

Continued

3. Juan Paul Robertson was charged with various narcotics offenses and with violating the federal Racketeer Influenced and Corrupt Organizations Act (RICO) by investing the proceeds from his unlawful activities in an Alaskan gold mine. He paid for some mining equipment in Los Angeles and had it shipped to Alaska. He hired seven out-of-state employees to work in the Alaskan mine. Most of the resulting gold was sold in Alaska, although Robertson transported $30,000 in gold out of the state. He was convicted on the RICO charge, but appealed claiming that the gold mine was not engaged in or affecting interstate commerce. Was Robertson's gold mine engaged in or affecting interstate commerce? Explain. [See *United States* v. *Juan Paul Robertson,* 115 S.Ct. 1732 (1995).]
4. In the San Antonio case in which a 12th grade student brought a concealed gun to school, how would you argue that the possession of a gun in a school zone substantially affects interstate commerce?

Question—Ethics/Public Policy

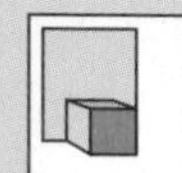

1. *Should* the federal government regulate an essentially local business to further the cause of racial equity? Explain.

IV. State and Local Regulation of Interstate Commerce

Inevitably, your business career in America will involve products or services that move in interstate commerce and thus are subject to federal regulation. Suppose you manage a trucking firm devoted exclusively to shipping manufactured goods from Ohio to New York. Clearly, the federal government has authority to regulate that interstate trade, but can Ohio and New York do the same? As noted, the states via their constitutional police power have the authority to regulate commerce within their jurisdictions for the purpose of enhancing the general welfare. That is, to assist in maintaining the public health, safety, and morals, states must be able to control persons and property within their jurisdictional authority. However, we have seen that the Commerce Clause, as interpreted, accords the federal government broad authority over commerce. As explained, the federal government has exclusive authority over foreign commerce. Purely intrastate commerce, having no significant effect on interstate commerce, is within the exclusive regulatory jurisdiction of the states. The confusion arises in the middle ground of interstate commerce where regulation by the federal government or state governments or both may be permissible.

Although federal government regulation of interstate commerce is pervasive, it is not exclusive. Indeed, the Commerce Clause itself does not explicitly limit the states' authority to interfere with commerce. However, our interest in maintaining an open market across America, that is, in preventing local economic protectionism, has caused the courts to hand down many decisions limiting states' powers to restrain the free flow of interstate commerce. As we see in the *Carbone* case that follows, a state regulation unconstitutionally interferes with interstate commerce if (1) the ordinance *discriminates* against interstate commerce or (2) it *burdens* interstate commerce to a substantially greater extent than it provides local benefits.

CASE

Carbone v. Town of Clarkstown

114 S.Ct. 1677 (1994)

Facts

In an agreement with the New York State Department of Environmental Conservation, Clarkstown agreed to close its landfill and build a solid waste transfer station that would separate recyclable from nonrecyclable items. A local contractor agreed to build the $1.4 million facility and operate it for five years at which time Clarkstown would purchase it at a price of $1.00. During those five years, the town guaranteed a minimum waste flow of 120,000 tons per year, for which the contractor could charge the hauler a "tipping" fee of $81 per ton. If the station received less than 120,000 tons in a year, the town agreed to make up the tipping fee deficit. Hence, Clarkstown hoped to finance its new facility with income generated by the tipping fees. The $81 per ton fee exceeded the disposal cost of unsorted solid waste on the private market. To assure sufficient use of the facility, Clarkstown adopted a flow-control ordinance requiring all nonhazardous solid waste within the town to be deposited at the new transfer station.

C. A. Carbone, Inc., operated a recycling center in Clarkstown. Under the ordinance, Carbone could continue to receive solid waste for recycling, but any nonrecyclable residue had to go to the new transfer station for which Carbone had to pay the $81 fee. Clarkstown discovered that Carbone was shipping nonrecyclable waste to out-of-state disposal sites. Clarkstown sought a court order requiring Carbone to adhere to the flow-control ordinance. Two New York state courts upheld the ordinance. The U.S. Supreme Court granted certiorari.

* * *

Justice Kennedy

At the outset we confirm that the flow control ordinance does regulate interstate commerce, despite the town's position to the contrary . . .

While the immediate effect of the ordinance is to direct local transport of solid waste to a designated site within the local jurisdiction, its economic effects are interstate in reach. The Carbone facility in Clarkstown receives and processes waste from places other than Clarkstown, including from out of State. By requiring Carbone to send the nonrecyclable portion of this waste to the Route 303 transfer station at an additional cost, the flow control ordinance drives up the cost for out-of-state interests to dispose of their solid waste. Furthermore, even as to waste originant in Clarkstown, the ordinance prevents everyone except the favored local operator from performing the initial processing step. The ordinance thus deprives out-of-state businesses of access to a local market . . . It is well settled that actions are within the domain of the Commerce Clause if they burden interstate commerce or impede its free flow.

The real question is whether the flow control ordinance is valid despite its undoubted effect on interstate commerce. For this inquiry, our case law yields two lines of analysis: first, whether the ordinance discriminates against interstate commerce, and second, whether the ordinance imposes a burden on interstate commerce that is "clearly excessive in relation to the putative local benefits." As we find that the ordinance discriminates against interstate commerce, we need not resort to the [second] test.

The central rationale for the rule against discrimination is to prohibit state or municipal laws whose object is local economic protectionism . . .We have interpreted the Commerce Clause to invalidate local laws that impose commercial barriers or discriminate against an article of commerce by reason of its origin or destination out of State.

Clarkstown protests that its ordinance does not discriminate because it does not differentiate solid waste on the basis of its geographic origin. All solid waste, regardless of origin, must be

Continued

Continued

processed at the designated transfer station before it leaves the town. [T]he ordinance erects no barrier to the import or export of any solid waste but requires only that the waste be channeled through the designated facility . . .

With respect to this stream of commerce, the flow control ordinance discriminates, for it allows only the favored operator to process waste that is within the limits of the town. The ordinance is no less discriminatory because in-state or in-town processors are also covered by the prohibition . . .

In this light, the flow control ordinance is just one more instance of local processing requirements that we long have held invalid. See *Minnesota* v. *Barber,* 136 U.S. 313 (1890) (striking down a Minnesota statute that required any meat sold within the state, whether originating within or without the State, to be examined by an inspector within the State); *Foster-Fountain Packing Co.* v. *Haydel,* 278 U.S. 1 (1928) (striking down a Louisiana statute that forbade shrimp to be exported unless the heads and hulls had first been removed within the State).

* * *

The essential vice in laws of this sort is that they bar the import of the processing service. Out-of-state meat inspectors, or shrimp hullers . . .are deprived of access to local demand for their services . . .

The flow control ordinance has the same design and effect. It hoards solid waste, and the demand to get rid of it, for the benefit of the preferred processing facility.

* * *

The flow control ordinance at issue here squelches competition in the waste-processing service altogether, leaving no room for investment from outside.

Discrimination against interstate commerce in favor of local business or investment is *per se* invalid, save in a narrow class of cases in which the municipality can demonstrate, under rigorous scrutiny, that it has no other means to advance a legitimate local interest. A number of *amici* contend that the flow control ordinance fits into this narrow class. They suggest that as landfill space diminishes and environmental cleanup costs escalate, measures like flow control become necessary to ensure the safe handling and proper treatment of solid waste.

The teaching of our cases is that these arguments must be rejected absent the clearest showing that the unobstructed flow of interstate commerce itself is unable to solve the local problem. The Commerce Clause presumes a national market free from local legislation that discriminates in favor of local interests. Here Clarkstown has any number of nondiscriminatory alternatives for addressing the health and environmental problems alleged to justify the ordinance in question. The most obvious would be uniform safety regulations enacted without the object to discriminate. These regulations would ensure that competitors like Carbone do not underprice the market by cutting corners on environmental safety.

* * *

The flow control ordinance does serve a central purpose that a nonprotectionist regulation would not: It ensures that the town-sponsored facility will be profitable, so that the local contractor can build it and Clarkstown can buy it back at nominal cost in five years. In other words . . . , the flow control ordinance is a financing measure. By itself, of course, revenue generation is not a local interest that can justify discrimination against interstate commerce.

* * *

Continued

Continued

Clarkstown maintains that special financing is necessary to ensure the long-term survival of the designated facility. If so, the town may subsidize the facility through general taxes or municipal bonds. But having elected to use the open market to earn revenues for its project, the town may not employ discriminatory regulation to give that project an advantage over rival businesses from out of State.

* * *

State and local governments may not use their regulatory power to favor local enterprise by prohibiting patronage of out-of-state competitors or their facilities. We reverse the judgment and remand the case . . .

Questions

1. Explain the Court's reasoning in concluding that the transportation and processing of local garbage actually was a matter of interstate commerce.
2. What was Clarkstown's motive in creating the flow-control ordinance?
3. An Indiana statute prohibited the practice of backhauling municipal waste. Indiana was trying to prevent truckers from hauling trash on the homeward-bound leg of a trip after having delivered other goods on the outbound leg. On its face, the statute applied evenly to intrastate and interstate carriers. Most in-state waste was hauled in dedicated garbage trucks (those used exclusively for garbage). The Indiana statute was challenged by two companies engaged in brokering waste disposal.
   a. What constitutional challenge was raised by the plaintiffs?
   b. What defense was raised by Indiana?
   c. Decide.
   [See *Government Suppliers Consolidating Services and Jack Castenova* v. *Evan Bayh and Kathy Prosser,* 975 F.2d 1267 (1992); cert. denied., 113 S.Ct. 977 (1993).]

A. Overview of State and Local Regulation

Profile Perspective: Because he operates an interstate carrier, Mark McDonald of Nations Air must be primarily concerned with federal laws, but for many businesses, addressing the requirements of state and local rules is also an important ingredient in business success. For example, Shawn M. Miller, an enterprising Californian, sought, in 1995, to renovate an existing laundromat located in a historic building near the University of Southern California campus. Two weeks before he was scheduled to open for business, a Los Angeles Bureau of Sanitation inspector reportedly told him that a new Bureau policy required the installation of a lint trap in his sewer line to protect the city's waste water collection and treatment facilities. The problem, according to Miller, was that the only city-approved lint collector, which cost several thousand dollars and weighed over 3,000 pounds, would require an industrial crane for installation and the crane would not fit through the door. The Preservation Society then refused to allow Miller to tear down a wall in the historic building in order to allow room for the crane. Miller wrote to the Los Angeles Bureau of Sanitation: "These inordinate levels of bureaucratic runaround and delay for the installation of eight washing machines are wholly unacceptable."[12] Belying bureaucrats'

"These inordinate levels of bureaucratic runaround and delay for the installation of eight washing machines are wholly unacceptable."

reputation for foot-dragging, the Bureau of Sanitation responded to Miller's protest in one week by waiving the lint screen requirement and issuing his industrial waste permit.

Expanding Government. The magnitude and visibility of federal regulation of business has obscured our bountiful web of state and local rules. Indeed, as measured by jobs, local government is growing more rapidly than state government and state government is growing more rapidly than the federal government. In May 1992, state and local government employment had reached 4,368,000,[13] a new record, and one that substantially exceeds the federal total of about three million.[14] Of course, part of that growth is attributable to population increase, particularly in Sun Belt states. However:

In May 1992, state and government employment had reached 4,368,000, a new record.

> By 1988, there were 147 "fulltime equivalent" (FTE) positions in state government for every 10,000 Americans, against only 61 in 1952. At the local level, the comparable figures were 358 versus 195.[15]

Just as state and local employee rolls have grown, so have the rules that some of those employees enforce. Many of those rules are designed to regulate business behavior. Those regulations fall into three broad categories: (1) controlling entry into business, (2) regulating competition, and (3) preventing consumer fraud. We need to remember that this upward spiral in rules, however lamentable in some ways, often springs from our demands for a better life.

The states are primarily responsible for regulating the insurance industry and are heavily involved in regulating banking, securities, and liquor sales. Many businesses and professions—from funeral preparations to barbering to the practice of medicine—require a license from the state. Public utilities (e.g., gas, electricity, and sewage disposal) are the subject of extensive regulation governing entry, rates, customer service, and virtually the fullness of the companies' activities. Many states have passed laws forbidding monopoly, usury, false advertising, stock fraud, and other practices harmful to the consumer. Furthermore, Congress in the mid-90s appears to be committed to pushing federal activities such as welfare and highway safety rules back to the states, suggesting that state government growth is unlikely to abate.

Local regulation is much less economically significant than state regulation. Local government intervention in business typically involves various licensure requirements. For example, businesses like bars and theaters are often required to obtain a local permit to operate. Certain tradespeople (such as plumbers, electricians, and builders) may be required to gain local or state occupational licensure to legally engage in their craft. Licensure protects the public from unsafe, unhealthy, and substandard goods and services, but critics contend that the benefits of licensure are exceeded by its costs in increased prices, decreased services, and administrative overhead.

Case for Discussion—Motorcycle Helmets. Having taken an introductory look at government regulation of business, we turn now to a real-life situation in which rules were imposed and then removed. Your task is to evaluate this situation and make a judgment: Was the government correct the first time in intervening or the second time in withdrawing its oversight?

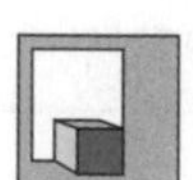

In 1995, the federal government lifted its rules imposing financial penalties on states that did not require motorcycle riders to wear helmets. Twenty-five states continue to require helmets.[16] A number of states are debating repeal of their helmet laws. In 1996, the

California Assembly voted to repeal that state's helmet law, but at this writing the state Senate has not taken up the measure and Governor Pete Wilson has indicated that he would veto it if passed. The competing arguments are set out in the following debate that accompanied California's decision to pass its helmet law.

Motorcycle Helmet Laws Help Protect Everybody

USA Today Editorial

Our Views: Laws Requiring Motorcyclists to Wear Helmets Make Sense—for Riders and Taxpayers

The motorcycle helmet controversy is on the road again in California.

It revved up . . . when a new law ordered all motorcyclists—youths and adults—to wear helmets.

Outraged cyclists scrambled to revive the national debate on this travel-weary topic. But they haven't realized—or won't acknowledge—that the dialogue shifted long ago from personal freedom to public responsibility.

Wayne Thomas of the California Motorcyclist Association argues against helmet laws by citing lower accident and death rates in the three states without such laws—Colorado, Illinois, and Iowa. He says those rates indicate that helmets reduce cyclists' caution and actually restrict their driving ability.

More persuasive arguments appear on the other side of the debate.

Of 474 motorcycle-accident victims treated during almost four years in Orange County, California, only six of the 20 who died wore helmets—just one from a head injury. The 238 wearing helmets had no serious neck injuries, had fewer and less-serious head injuries, spent less time on respirators and suffered less permanent physical and mental damage.

And their hospital bills averaged $16,000, compared to $30,000 for those who crashed without helmets.

When cyclists who don't wear helmets run up hospital bills almost twice as costly as those of riders with helmets, everyone's insurance costs go up.

That—not death rates—may have been the most telling consideration for the 22 states that make minors wear helmets and the 24, plus the District of Columbia, that mandate them for all riders.

Add other factors—disability and unemployment payments, rehabilitation costs—and states with helmet laws have 43 percent lower societal costs from motorcycle accidents, says California assemblyman Richard Floyd's office.

That takes the issue far beyond whether motorcyclists should be protected from themselves.

With soaring costs driving even basic health care beyond many families' reach, it's time for cyclists to give this road show rerun a rest.

These Laws Mock Freedom

by Paul Lax

Opposing View: Mandatory Helmet Laws Don't Work and Are a Precedent for Taking Away Other Freedoms

Last March, I was in Sacramento lobbying against the proposed California helmet law. A large yellow bow was tied around the Capitol dome and Governor Pete Wilson made a speech about the debt we all owed to those fighting against Iraq for the cause of freedom.

Continued

Continued

Freedom. The word trips effortlessly from the lips of politicians, but lip service is all it got in California.

What's wrong with helmet laws? One, they don't work. Two, they destroy individual freedom.

In California, we put evidence of the ineffectiveness of helmet laws before the legislature. Fatality rates in states that require everyone to wear helmets are higher, per 100 accidents, than in free states. Helmet laws are a placebo.

The second reason should worry everyone, even if you never go near a motorcycle. The helmet law was passed on the claim that freedom was costing the state money. Proponents blamed unhelmeted riders for avoidable medical costs. The numbers used to pass the law were false, it's now been acknowledged.

But even if they had been correct, what sort of precedent does this establish?

Whether I wear a helmet or not, who is affected? Obviously, only me. To the best of my knowledge, no one is yet claiming that a head injury can result from being near a person who isn't wearing a helmet.

If cost is the prime factor, then there is no activity the state cannot regulate. The reasoning used to pass this law could be used to outlaw smoking or require us all to eat a good breakfast.

Is liberty still an inalienable right, or can you yell "costs" at our legislators and have them trample freedom like so many frightened sheep? If so, one of your most cherished freedoms may be next.

Questions

1. Has the market failed such that regulation is required to compel riders to wear motorcycle helmets? Explain.
2. List the competing considerations in this debate.
3. Should bicycle riders be required to wear helmets? Explain.
4. How would you vote on laws requiring the use of motorcycle helmets? Explain.

Source: *USA Today,* January 3, 1992, p. 10A.

V. Administrative Law

A. The Agencies

administrative law. That branch of public law addressing the operation of the government's various agencies and commissions. Also the rules and regulations established by those agencies and commissions.

administrative agency. An agency of the government charged with administering particular legislation.

No matter what direction your managerial or entrepreneurial career takes you, the activities of the federal government's administrative agencies are likely to closely affect your business practice. The Equal Employment Opportunity Commission (EEOC) probably will shape your hiring practices; the Environmental Protection Agency (EPA) probably will shape your ecological consciousness; the Occupational Safety and Health Administration (OSHA) probably will shape safety guidelines in your work area; and so on. **Administrative law** is the label applied to the rules governing the administrative operations of government. The federal Administrative Procedure Act (APA) defines an **administrative agency** as any government unit other than the legislature and the courts. However, our attention will be limited to the prominent regulatory agencies (Federal Trade Commission, Federal Communications Commission, Securities and Exchange Commission, etc.) rather than the various executive departments (Agriculture, Defense, etc.) and nonregulatory, welfare agencies (Social Security Administration, Veterans Administration, and the Public Health Service). Although our fundamental concern lies at the federal level, administrative law principles are fully applicable to the conduct of state and local governments. At the local level, planning and zoning boards and property tax assessments appeals boards are examples of administrative agencies.

At the state level, examples include public utility commissions and the various state licensure boards for law, medicine, architecture, and the like.

History. Congress established the Interstate Commerce Commission (ICC), the first federal regulatory agency, in 1887 for the purpose of regulating railroad routes and rates. The Food and Drug Administration (FDA, 1907) and the Federal Trade Commission (FTC, 1914) followed, but federal regulation became pervasive only in response to the Great Depression of the 1930s. Congress created the Securities and Exchange Commission (SEC), the Federal Communications Commission (FCC), the Civil Aeronautics Board (CAB), and the National Labor Relations Board (NLRB), among others, as a response to the widely shared belief that the stock market crash and the Depression were evidence of the failure of the free market.

The next major burst of regulatory activity arrived in the 1960s and 1970s when Congress created such agencies as the EEOC (1965), the EPA (1970), the OSHA (1970), and the Consumer Product Safety Commission (CPSC, 1972).

Note that the work of most of the early agencies was directed to controlling entire industries such as transportation or communications and that the primary purpose of most of those agencies was to address economic concerns. Then with the arrival of the prosperity and social turbulence of the 1960s and 1970s, Congress built a rather massive array of new agencies directed not to economic issues but to social reform in such areas as discrimination, the environment, job safety, and product safety.

As we explore later in the chapter, the free market enthusiasm of the 1980s resulted in strenuous efforts to deregulate the economy and reduce the influence of the federal agencies and the government generally. Now, with the 1994 Republican revolution in Congress, government downsizing and further deregulation of business seem inevitable, although federal rules will continue to shape business practices.

Creating the Agencies. The so-called independent agencies (e.g., FTC, FCC, NLRB, and SEC) are created by Congress via statutes labeled **enabling legislation.** For example, the FTC is empowered to pursue unfair trade practices by the authority of its enabling legislation, excerpts of which follow:

enabling legislation. Law that establishes an administrative agency and grants power to that agency.

> Section 1: A commission is created and established, to be known as the Federal Trade Commission, which shall be composed of five commissioners, who shall be appointed by the President, by and with the advice and consent of the Senate . . .
>
> Section 5: Unfair methods of competition in or affecting commerce, and unfair or deceptive acts or practices in or affecting commerce, are hereby declared unlawful.

In creating an agency, Congress delegates a portion of its authority to that body. Congress acknowledges the existence of a problem and recognizes that it is not the appropriate body to address the specific elements of that problem—hence, the agency. The president, ordinarily with the advice and consent of the Senate, appoints the administrator or the several commissioners who direct each agency's affairs. Commissioners are appointed in staggered terms, typically of seven years' duration. The appointment of commissioners for most of the independent agencies must reflect an approximate political balance between the two major parties.

In effect, Congress has created a fourth branch of government. Recognizing that it possesses neither the time nor the expertise to handle problems arising from nuclear power, product safety, racial discrimination, labor unions, and much more, Congress wisely established "minigovernments" with the necessary technical resources and day-to-day authority to address those problems.

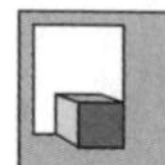

Too Much Power? The legitimacy of the entire agency system has often been challenged on the grounds that (1) the agencies have exceeded their authority under their congressional enabling legislation, (2) Congress has forsaken its constitutional duties by delegating lawmaking authority to appointed bureaucrats, and (3) the agencies, as minigovernments, violate the constitutional separation-of-powers doctrine in that executive, legislative, and judicial authority are vested in a single body. For decades, however, those challenges have routinely failed. Congress deliberately drew the pieces of enabling legislation so broadly that courts have readily rejected challenges that the agencies have gone further in influencing American commerce than Congress intended. As discussed below, both legal and political forces work to prevent these minigovernments from abusing their authority. Recently, however, the attack on agency authority has been renewed. Congress is reconsidering the delegation-of-duty theme by studying legislation providing that a new agency regulation would not be effective until Congress voted for it. Of course, that legislation would force Congress and the president to speak directly to the wisdom of all new federal rules.

VI. The Administrative Process

As we have noted, the administrative agencies act as minigovernments, performing quasi-executive, quasi-legislative (rule making), and quasi-judicial (adjudicatory) roles broadly involving control of supply, rates, and conduct in large segments of American life. Whether you are a manager or an entrepreneur, those agencies will profoundly affect your business practices.

A. *Operating the Agencies*

Executive Functions. The basic executive duty of the various agencies is to implement the policy provided for in the enabling legislation and in the agencies' own rules and regulations. A large part of agency activity consists of performing mundane, repetitive tasks that are necessary for a smoothly operating society but that do not merit the day-to-day attention of Congress or the courts. Thus, agencies enter into contracts, lease federal lands, register security offerings, award grants, resolve tax disputes, settle workers' compensation claims, administer government benefits to the citizenry, and so on. Most agencies offer informal advice, both in response to requests and on their own initiative, to explain agency policy and positions. Of course, a big part of the agencies' executive duties is the protection of the public in one way or another by ensuring compliance with laws and regulations. Therefore, most agencies spend a great deal of time conducting inspections and investigations and collecting information.

Legislative Functions. The agencies create *rules* that, in effect, are laws. These rules provide the details necessary to carry out the intentions of the enabling legislation. In day-to-day business practice, the rules are likely to be much more important than the original congressional legislation. The Occupational Safety and Health Act calls for a safe and healthy workplace, but the rules necessary for interpreting and enforcing that general mandate come, not from Congress, but from OSHA.

The Rule-Making Process. The Administrative Procedure Act provides for both *informal* and *formal* rule-making processes for legislative rules (see Table 8.1). Under both

TABLE 8.1

AGENCY RULE-MAKING PROCESS

Informal Agency Rule Making (legislative in character)	***Formal Agency Rule Making (legislative/judicial in character)***
Public notice in *Federal Register*	Public notice in *Federal Register*
Public comment (informal)	Public comment (formal)
Final rule in *Federal Register*	Final rule in *Federal Register*

approaches, the process begins with the publication of a Notice of Proposed Rule Making in the ***Federal Register*** (a daily publication of all federal rules, regulations, and orders). Thereafter, in the case of informal rule making, the agency must permit written comments on the proposal and may hold open hearings. Having received public comments, the agency either discontinues the process or prepares the final rule.

Federal Register. A federal publication providing notice of federal rule making by federal agencies.

In the case of formal rule making, after providing notice, the agency must hold a public hearing that must be conducted with most of the procedural safeguards of a trial, where all interested parties may call witnesses, challenge the agency evidence, and so on.

Final agency rules are published in the *Federal Register* and later compiled in the ***Code of Federal Regulations.*** Informal rule making is the standard approach. It provides an efficient mechanism for agency action; however, it does so at some cost in procedural safeguards and opportunities for public input.

Code of Federal Regulations. A compilation of final federal agency rules.

Judicial Functions. Informal procedures such as settlements are the preferred method of resolving disputes between the administrative agencies and business. Thus, in 1995, the BBDO Worldwide advertising agency promised the FTC that it would not mislead the public about the amount of fat, calories, or cholesterol in the Häagen-Dazs frozen yogurt it tries to sell.[17] Commonly, however, agencies must turn to judicial proceedings to enforce agency rules. Thus, as a manager you could be called before the National Labor Relations Board for a hearing to determine whether you wrongfully dismissed an employee for engaging in protected union activities, or the Consumer Product Safety Commission may hold a hearing to decide whether your company's new baby stroller is unsafe. Adjudicatory administrative hearings are equal in significance and much superior in number to all federal court trials each year.

Administrative Hearing. Typically, after an investigation, a violation of a statute or rule may be alleged. Affected parties are notified. An effort is made to reach a settlement via a **consent order,** in which the party being investigated agrees to steps suitable to the agency but under which the respondent makes no admission of guilt, thus retarding the likelihood of subsequent civil liability. Federal law also encourages the use of alternate dispute resolution methods such as arbitration.

consent order. The order administrative agencies issue when approving the settlement of an administrative action against some party.

administrative law judge (ALJ). An officer who presides at the initial hearing on matters litigated before an administrative agency. He or she is independent of the agency staff.

Administrative Law Judge. Failing a settlement, the parties proceed much as in a civil trial. Ordinarily, the case is heard by an **administrative law judge (ALJ).** The respondent may be represented by counsel. Parties have the right to present their cases, cross-examine, file motions, raise objections, and so on. However, they do not have the right to a jury trial. An ALJ resolves all questions of law and fact and then issues a decision (order). That order must be based on "substantial evidence in the record." In general, that decision is final unless appealed to the agency or commission. After exhausting opportunities for review within the agency, appeal may be taken to the appropriate federal court, usually a court of appeals.

B. Controlling the Agencies

We recognize that agency influence in business practice and in American life in general is enormous. What is to keep the agencies from abusing their authority? Of course, we can lobby the agencies, and Congress has passed some pieces of legislation in an effort to make the agencies more accountable to the public. For example, the federal Freedom of Information Act requires government agencies to turn over records (with certain exceptions) to the public on request; the Sunshine Act, or "open meetings" law, requires agencies to admit the public to their meetings (with certain exceptions); and the Regulatory Flexibility Act requires federal agencies to give particular attention to the impact of regulations on small businesses. In 1996, Congress was considering legislation to toughen small business protection by allowing those businesses to sue federal agencies that fail to meet the Regulatory Flexibility Act's guidelines. However, the public's direct input and these pieces of legislation are probably much less influential in controlling agency behavior than our system of checks and balances between the branches of government.

Executive Constraints. As noted, the president appoints the top administrators for the various agencies, thus significantly influencing the conservative or liberal slant of the agency's agenda. Further, the president obviously has great influence in the budget process. Proposed rules judged to be major are reviewed by the White House budget office. In 1993, President Clinton issued an executive order requiring a cost-benefit review for all rules costing the economy more than $100 million.

Congressional Constraints. Congress creates and can dissolve the agencies. Congress controls agency budgets and thus can encourage or discourage particular agency action. Broadly, Congress oversees agency action, and agencies often check with Congress before undertaking major initiatives. Congress can directly intervene by amending the enabling legislation or by passing laws that require agencies to take specific directions.

Judicial Review. Agency rules and orders may be challenged in court, and the threat of judicial review is probably the chief constraint on agency power. However, the sheer bulk of agency activities means only a very small portion of those activities will receive judicial scrutiny. Historically, the courts have taken a rather narrow approach to judicial review. Two commonsense considerations support that restrained judicial stance. The first is deference to the presumed expertise of the administrative agencies. Jurists, being generalists in the field of law, have been reluctant to overrule the judgment of specialists specifically chosen to regulate within their area of expertise. Second, very crowded judicial calendars act as a natural brake on activist judicial review. For those reasons, judges have traditionally disposed of administrative law cases in an expeditious manner, by readily sustaining the judgment of the agency. Of course, the courts have overruled the agencies when appropriate.

Not surprisingly, judicial review of agency decisions raises a variety of technical, esoteric issues of law. The nature of those issues depends, in part, on whether the court is reviewing an agency's rule-making function or its adjudicatory function. Cases turn on questions like these:

1. Does the legislature's delegation of authority meet constitutional requirements?
2. Has the agency exceeded the authority granted by the enabling legislation?
3. Has the appealing party exhausted all the available administrative remedies?
4. Are the agency's findings of fact supported by substantial evidence in the record as a whole?

These issues are close to the heart of the administrative law practitioner, but their exploration is not necessary to the layperson's understanding of the larger regulatory process.

In building or helping manage a business in America, you cannot escape the eye of the federal administrative agencies. Normally, your interaction with them will involve simply filling out forms or engaging in quiet negotiation; but what happens if an agency order is issued, you believe it to be wrong, and no amount of negotiation can produce a satisfactory (from your point of view) resolution? Perhaps you or your employer will need to sue, or perhaps the government will sue you to secure compliance. For example, an OSHA inspection may have resulted in a fine or an instruction to install new safety devices, or the Consumer Product Safety Commission may have ordered you to redesign a product, or the SEC may have blocked your new public stock offering. What can you do? As the next case so colorfully depicts, these disputes sometimes must be settled in court.

CASE

F.C.C. v. Pacifica Foundation

98 S.Ct. 3026 (1978)

Facts

A satiric humorist named George Carlin recorded a 12-minute monologue entitled "Filthy Words" before a live audience in a California theater. He began by referring to his thoughts about "the words you can't say on the public, ah, airwaves, um, the ones you definitely wouldn't say, ever." He proceeded to list those words and repeat them over and over again in a variety of colloquialisms. The transcript of the recording . . . indicates frequent laughter from the audience.

At about 2 o'clock in the afternoon on Tuesday, October 30, 1973, a New York radio station, owned by Pacifica Foundation, broadcast the "Filthy Words" monologue. A few weeks later a man, who stated that he had heard the broadcast while driving with his young son, wrote a letter complaining to the Federal Communications Commission. He stated that, although he could perhaps understand the "record's being sold for private use, I certainly cannot understand the broadcast of same over the air that, supposedly, you control."

The complaint was forwarded to the station for comment. In its response, Pacifica explained that the monologue had been played during a program about contemporary society's attitude toward language and that, immediately before its broadcast, listeners had been advised that it included "sensitive language which might be regarded as offensive to some." Pacifica characterized George Carlin as a "significant social satirist" who "like Twain and Sahl before him,

Continued

Continued

examines the language of ordinary people . . . Carlin is not mouthing obscenities, he is merely using words to satirize as harmless and essentially silly our attitudes toward those words." Pacifica stated that it was not aware of any other complaints about the broadcast.

On February 21, 1975, the FCC issued a declaratory order granting the complaint and holding that Pacifica "could have been the subject of administrative sanctions" . . . The commission did not impose formal sanctions, but it did state that the order would be "associated with the station's license file, and in the event that subsequent complaints are received, the commission will then decide whether it should utilize any of the available sanctions it has been granted by Congress."

* * *

[T]he commission concluded that certain words depicted sexual and excretory activities in a patently offensive manner, noted that they "were broadcast at a time when children were undoubtedly in the audiences (i.e., in the early afternoon)" and that the prerecorded language, with these offensive words "repeated over and over," was "deliberately broadcast" . . .

In summary, the commission stated: "We therefore hold that the language as broadcast was indecent and prohibited" . . .

The United States Court of Appeals for the District of Columbia Circuit reversed . . .

Justice Stevens

This case requires that we decide whether the Federal Communications Commission has any power to regulate a radio broadcast that is indecent but not obscene. [At the Court of Appeals] Judge Tamm concluded that the order represented censorship and was expressly prohibited by ¶ 326 of the Communications Act. Alternatively, Judge Tamm read the commission opinion as the functional equivalent of a rule and concluded that it was "overbroad" . . .

Chief Judge Bazelon's concurrence rested on the Constitution. He was persuaded that ¶ 326's prohibition against censorship is inapplicable to broadcasts forbidden by ¶ 1464 (prohibiting "obscene, indecent, or profane language by means of radio communications"). However, he concluded that ¶ 1464 must be narrowly construed to cover only language that is obscene or otherwise unprotected by the First Amendment . . .

Judge Leventhal, in dissent, stated that the only issue was whether the commission could regulate the language "as broadcast" . . .

Emphasizing the interest in protecting children, not only from exposure to indecent language, but also from exposure to the idea that such language has official approval . . . he concluded that the commission had correctly condemned the daytime broadcast as indecent.

Having granted the commission's petition for certiorari . . . we must decide: (1) whether the scope of judicial review encompasses more than the commission's determination that the monologue was indecent "as broadcast"; (2) whether the commission's order was a form of censorship forbidden by ¶ 326; (3) whether the broadcast was indecent within the meaning of ¶ 1464; and (4) whether the order violates the First Amendment of the United States Constitution.

I

The general statements in the commission's memorandum opinion do not change the character of its order. Its action was an adjudication . . . It did not purport to engage in formal rule making or in the promulgation of any regulations. The order "was issued in a specific factual context"; questions concerning possible action in other contexts were expressly reserved for the future. The specific holding was carefully confined to the monologue "as broadcast" . . .

Continued

Continued

II

The relevant statutory questions are whether the commission's action is forbidden "censorship" within the meaning of ¶ 326 and whether speech that concededly is not obscene may be restricted as "indecent" under the authority of ¶ 1464.

* * *

The prohibition against censorship unequivocally denies the commission any power to edit proposed broadcasts in advance and to excise material considered inappropriate for the airwaves. The prohibition, however, has never been construed to deny the commission the power to review the content of completed broadcasts in the performance of its regulatory duties.

* * *

Entirely apart from the fact that the subsequent review of program content is not the sort of censorship at which the statute was directed, its history makes it perfectly clear that it was not intended to limit the commission's power to regulate the broadcast of obscene, indecent, or profane language. A single section of the [Radio Act of 1927] is the source of both the anticensorship provision and the commission's authority to impose sanctions for the broadcast of indecent or obscene language. Quite plainly, Congress intended to give meaning to both provisions. Respect for that intent requires that the censorship language be read as inapplicable to the prohibition on broadcasting obscene, indecent, or profane language.

We conclude, therefore, that ¶ 326 does not limit the commission's authority to impose sanctions on licensees who engage in obscene, indecent, or profane broadcasting.

III

The only other statutory question presented by this case is whether the afternoon broadcast of the "Filthy Words" monologue was indecent within the meaning of ¶ 1464 . . .

The commission identified several words that referred to excretory or sexual activities or organs, stated that the repetitive, deliberate use of those words in an afternoon broadcast when children are in the audience was patently offensive and held that the broadcast was indecent. Pacifica takes issue with the commission's definition of indecency, but does not dispute the commission's preliminary determination that each of the components of its definition was present. Specifically, Pacifica does not quarrel with the conclusion that this afternoon broadcast was patently offensive. Pacifica's claim that the broadcast was not indecent within the meaning of the statute rests entirely on the absence of prurient appeal.

The plain language of the statute does not support Pacifica's argument. The words "obscene, indecent, or profane" are written in the disjunctive, implying that each has a separate meaning. Prurient appeal is an element of the obscene, but the normal definition of "indecent" merely refers to nonconformance with accepted standards of morality.

* * *

Because neither our prior decisions nor the language or history of ¶ 1464 supports the conclusion that prurient appeal is an essential component of indecent language, we reject Pacifica's construction of the statute. When that construction is put to one side, there is no basis for disagreeing with the commission's conclusion that indecent language was used in this broadcast.

IV

Pacifica makes two constitutional attacks on the commission's order. First, it argues that the commission's construction of the statutory language broadly encompasses so much constitutionally protected speech that reversal is required even if Pacifica's broadcast of the "Filthy Words"

Continued

Continued

monologue is not itself protected by the First Amendment. Second, Pacifica argues that inasmuch as the recording is not obscene, the Constitution forbids any abridgement of the right to broadcast it on the radio.

A

The first argument fails because our review is limited to the question of whether the commission has the authority to proscribe this particular broadcast. As the commission itself emphasized, its order was "issued in a specific factual context" . . .

That approach is appropriate for courts as well as the commission when regulation of indecency is at stake, for indecency is largely a function of context—it cannot be adequately judged in the abstract.

* * *

It is true that the commission's order may lead some broadcasters to censor themselves. At most, however, the commission's definition of indecency will deter only the broadcasting of patently offensive references to excretory and sexual organs and activities. While some of these references may be protected, they surely lie at the periphery of First Amendment concern . . .

B

When the issue is narrowed to the facts of this case, the question is whether the First Amendment denies government any power to restrict the public broadcast of indecent language in any circumstances. For if the government has any such power, this was an appropriate occasion for its exercise.

The words of the Carlin monologue are unquestionably "speech" within the meaning of the First Amendment. It is equally clear that the commission's objections to the broadcast were based in part on its content. The order must therefore fall if, as Pacifica argues, the First Amendment prohibits all governmental regulation that depends on the content of speech. Our past cases demonstrate, however, that no such absolute rule is mandated by the Constitution.

The classic exposition of the proposition that both the content and the context of speech are critical elements of First Amendment analysis is Mr. Justice Holmes's statement . . .

> We admit that in many places and in ordinary times the defendants in saying all that was said in the circular would have been within their constitutional rights. But the character of every act depends upon the circumstances in which it was done . . . The most stringent protection of free speech would not protect a man in falsely shouting fire in a theatre and causing a panic. It does not even protect a man from an injunction against uttering words that may have all the effect of force . . . The question in every case is whether the words used are used in such circumstances and are of such a nature as to create a clear and present danger that they will bring about the substantive evils that congress has a right to prevent.

Other distinctions based on content have been approved . . . The government may forbid speech calculated to provoke a fight . . . It may pay heed to the "commonsense differences between commercial speech and other varieties" . . . It may treat libels against private citizens more severely than libels against public officials . . . Obscenity may be wholly prohibited . . .

The question in this case is whether a broadcast of patently offensive words dealing with sex and excretion may be regulated because of its content. Obscene materials have been denied the protection of the First Amendment because their content is so offensive to contemporary moral standards . . . But the fact that society may find speech offensive is not a sufficient reason for suppressing it. Indeed, if it is the speaker's opinion that gives offense, that consequence is a reason

Continued

Continued

for according it constitutional protection. For it is a central tenet of the First Amendment that the government must remain neutral in the marketplace of ideas. If there were any reason to believe that the commission's characterization of the Carlin monologue as offensive could be traced to its political content—or even to the fact that it satirized contemporary attitudes about four-letter words—First Amendment protection might be required. But that is simply not this case. These words offend for the same reasons that obscenity offends . . .

* * *

In this case it is undisputed that the content of Pacifica's broadcast was "vulgar," "offensive," and "shocking." Because content of that character is not entitled to absolute constitutional protection under all circumstances, we must consider its context in order to determine whether the commission's action was constitutionally permissible.

C

We have long recognized that each medium of expression presents special First Amendment problems . . . And of all forms of communication, it is broadcasting that has received the most limited First Amendment protection . . . The reasons for [that distinction] are complex, but two have relevance to the present case. First, the broadcast media have established a uniquely pervasive presence in the lives of all Americans. Patently offensive, indecent material presented over the airwaves confronts the citizen, not only in public, but also in the privacy of the home, where the individual's right to be left alone plainly outweighs the First Amendment rights of an intruder . . . Because the broadcast audience is constantly tuning in and out, prior warnings cannot completely protect the listener or viewer from unexpected program content . . .

Second, broadcasting is uniquely accessible to children, even those too young to read . . .

It is appropriate, in conclusion, to emphasize the narrowness of our holding. This case does not involve a two-way radio conversation between a cab driver and a dispatcher, or a telecast of an Elizabethan comedy. We have not decided that an occasional expletive in either setting would justify any sanction or, indeed, that this broadcast would justify a criminal prosecution. The commission's decision rested entirely on a nuisance rationale under which context is all-important. The concept requires consideration of a host of variables. The time of day was emphasized by the commission. The content of the program in which the language is used will also affect the composition of the audience, and differences between radio, television, and perhaps closed-circuit transmissions, may also be relevant . . .

The judgment of the court of appeals is reversed.

[Omitted are the appendix containing a transcript of the "Filthy Words" monologue, as well as the concurring opinions of Justices Powell and Blackmun and the dissenting opinions of Justices Brennan, Marshall, Stewart, and White.]

Afterword

The George Carlin case, in a sense, lives on 17 years after it was heard. Its most recent spasm was a Supreme Court decision[18] declining to review a 7–4 federal appeals court decision in the *Action for Children's Television* case,[19] which ordered a 10 PM to 6 AM "safe harbor" for indecent radio and television programming. The tortured history of the government's regulation of indecency is illuminating. All was well for a few years after the Carlin case until broadcasters began pushing the boundaries by talking about sex without using the seven dirty words; then Geraldo and Sally Jessy and other talk show hosts began to intimately examine topics like cross-dressing, and complaints began to clutter the FCC mailbox.

In 1987, the FCC wrote new rules to expand its conception of indecency to include describing sexual topics in a "patently offensive way." Those rules were struck down in 1989 by a federal court of appeals, which ordered a safe harbor during which adults would be able to hear

Continued

Continued

or see indecent programming. Congress responded by legislating a 24-hour ban on indecent programming. Those rules were struck down by the appeals court in 1991. Congress passed a second law in 1992 allowing a midnight to 6 AM safe harbor and the FCC established conforming regulations.[20] Those rules were challenged in the *Action for Children's Television* case, in which the court ordered a safe harbor from 10 PM to 6 AM, although the majority made it clear that, in their view, indecent programming could be banned until midnight.

Questions—Law

1. *a.* Why was the question of whether the FCC's decision constituted adjudication or rule making significant to the subsequent judicial appeals?
   b. Explain the Supreme Court's resolution of that issue.
2. Why is the two-letter word "or" critical to the outcome of this case?
3. Why was the FCC's action not considered censorship?

Questions—Public Policy

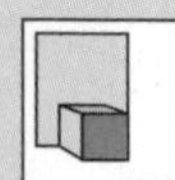

1. Would the Court's ruling in the *Action for Children's Television* decision affect television shows like the hit *NYPD Blue,* which periodically includes profane language and nudity, if it were telecast outside the safe harbor?
2. This continuing First Amendment struggle is well illustrated by the FCC's pursuit of radio shock jock Howard Stern. From 1988 through 1994, the FCC proposed nearly $2 million in fines on Stern's employer, Infinity Broadcasting. Stern's 6 to 11 morning program held the number one rating in both New York City and Los Angeles. For an extended period of time, much of Stern's programming was devoted to sexual matters. He and celebrities discussed sexual fantasies, he invited women to disrobe in his studio, and he described the process over the radio. He talked at length about masturbation and "spewing evil gunk all over everybody"; he discussed anal intercourse and rectal bleeding and remarked that two of his critics might be stranded at sea and "be forced to drink their own urine."

   Responding to the FCC decision, columnist James Kilpatrick said: "By any standard known to the law, the broadcasts were in fact indecent, and the fine was appropriate to the offense."[21]

   a. Do you agree?
   b. Do you see any risk to society in curbing Stern's speech?
3. Employ free market reasoning to examine the FCC's indecency stance.

VII. Reduce Regulation?

Profile Perspective: Return your attention to Mark McDonald and Nations Air. The company struggled to meet the government's financial, safety, and paperwork expectations. Would McDonald, his company, and the American public be better off in a more lightly regulated environment? Fewer rules would almost certainly increase short-term efficiency, but would Nations Air and the public be well served in the long term by less government intervention? Could we count on the pressure of free market forces to assure the safe, fair, efficient operation of Nations Air? Think about those questions as we turn now to an examination of the pluses and minuses of government regulation of business.

The world has voted resoundingly for the free market. From eastern Europe to the Soviet Union, Great Britain, and China, the market has been embraced and government intervention has been depreciated. America has led the revival of free market principles, but critics of government say we have some distance to go yet. Those critics believe government continues to be overly involved in American business practice.

A. CRITICISMS

Excessive Regulation. In brief, the argument is that government regulations reduce business efficiency, curb freedom, and unjustly redistribute resources. Whether those criticisms are fair or not, an important ingredient in building your own business or successfully managing the business of another is anticipating and minimizing the overhead costs associated with meeting government standards. Consider some specific costs:

- *Total bill.* One comprehensive study put the total cost of federal government regulation in 1990 at about $400 billion, or $4,000 per household.[22] Another revealing way of looking at regulatory expense is that small businesses (fewer than 500 employees) in 1992 spent, according to a recent study, about $5,400 per employee in meeting federal regulatory requirements. Big companies spent about $3,000 per employee.[23] (Note that those figures do not reflect the benefits derived from those regulations.)
- *Personnel and paper.* According to the Center for the Study of American Business, the total number of federal regulators rose from 102,192 in 1985 to 128,566 in 1994 and then to 130,929 in 1995.[24] On the other hand, according to the U.S. Office of Personnel Management, the total number of federal civilian employees actually declined to its lowest level in 30 years in 1996, with 204,530 fewer workers on the payroll than when President Clinton took office and with 11.2 federal employees per thousand Americans as opposed to 13.6 per thousand in 1966.[25]
- *Jobs.* Economist Robert Hahn reminds us that direct costs are only the most visible regulatory "tax":

  > The measurable costs of regulation pale against the distortions that sap the economy's dynamism. The public never sees the factories that weren't built, the new products that didn't appear, or the entrepreneurial idea that drowned in a cumbersome regulatory process.[26]

  Indeed, some estimates place the regulatory cost to the economy in unrealized growth at $500 billion annually.[27]

Summary. In addition to the expense of the regulations, the business community's primary complaints can be summarized as follows:

1. Overlap and conflict among agencies.
2. Overextension of agency authority, not merely in setting goals but in dictating how those goals are to be met.
3. Adversarial attitudes toward business.
4. Agency delay in issuing required permits, rules, and standards.
5. Escalating reporting requirements.

Insufficient Regulation. Our society is rapidly changing, complex, and, in many ways, troubled. Consequently, calls for new government regulations and more money for existing regulatory efforts are routine. Advocates of increased regulation point to the many successes of government intervention: legal equality for minorities and women; prevention of the sale of dangerous food and drugs; the Auto Safety Act, which, by some estimates, saves 12,000 lives per year; child labor laws; increasingly safe workplaces; cleaner air; and on and on. Indeed, one recent study's best guess is that social regulation (environment, health, and safety), unlike economic regulation, generated *net benefits* to society of about $2 billion in 1988.[28]

Excessive Industry Influence. As we have noted, the industries to be regulated were often instrumental in spawning the various federal agencies. Noted economist George Stigler summarized the argument: "[R]egulation is acquired by the industry and is designed and operated primarily for its benefit."[29] Stigler further contended that, where possible, firms will encourage government regulations restricting entry (licensing), thus limiting competition: "Every industry or occupation that has enough political power to utilize the state will seek to control entry."[30]

As evidence of industry influence in agency affairs, critics argue that agency employees who leave federal service frequently turn to jobs in the industry they were formerly charged with regulating. Similarly, agency recruits are often drawn from the industry being regulated. Industry influence over the regulatory process is considerable. Industry expertise is invaluable, and the industry voice should be heard. The question is one of the volume of the voice.

The Ethics Reform Act of 1989 seeks to reduce some of these problems. Among other provisions, the act bars high government officials from lobbying the executive branch of government for one year after leaving their government posts.

Underrepresentation of Public Opinion. Agency critics also charge that the diffuse voice of public opinion does not receive the attention accorded the pleas of special interests. It is generally acknowledged that public sentiment, being largely unorganized, is greatly underrepresented in regulatory matters, whereas well-financed, skillfully organized special interests carry political weight far beyond the numbers they represent.

Mechanics. These complaints are not meant to represent the full range of criticisms of the federal regulatory process. In particular, the mechanics of agency conduct are frequently assailed. Allegations of inefficiency, incompetence, and arbitrariness are commonplace. The pace of work is said to be slow, and enforcement of policy often appears weak and ineffectual.

B. Deregulation

deregulation. Returning authority to the free market by shrinking government bureaucracies and reducing government rules.

In response to those criticisms, both Democrats and Republicans, beginning in the late 1970s, began to reduce the quantity of federal regulatory intervention. Primarily, the **deregulation** movement consisted of shrinking the federal bureaucracy, eliminating as many government rules as possible, and expediting the process of complying with those rules that could not be removed.

In those cases where a government role continued to be considered necessary, the deregulation advocates argued for applying free market incentives and reasoning to the achievement of regulatory goals. Thus, rather than *forbidding* undesirable conduct (such as pollution), the government might *impose a tax* on those behaviors society wants to discourage. In effect, a business would purchase the right to engage in conduct society considers injurious or inefficient. Similarly, rather than rationing the right to land at airports at peak times, the government might auction those rights to the highest bidder. Market incen-

HOW COSTS VARY

TABLE 8.2

Regulation	*Agency*	*Annual Number of Deaths (per 100,000 of exposed population)*	*Cost Per Life Saved*
Mandatory seat belts for cars	National Highway Traffic Safety Administration	9.1	$390,000
Prohibitions on alcohol and drug use by railroad employees	Federal Railroad Administration	0.2	$650,000
Control and disposal standards for benzene	Environmental Protection Agency	2.1	$4,000,000
Disposal standards for uranium mine wastes	Environmental Protection Agency	43.0	$69,000,000
Restrictions on worker exposure to asbestos	Occupational Safety and Health Administration	6.7	$117,000,000
Restrictions on worker exposure to formaldehyde	Occupational Safety and Health Administration	0.1	$94,000,000,000

Source: Louis Richman, "Bringing Reason to Regulation," *Fortune,* October 19, 1992, pp. 94, 96.

tives would (1) encourage companies to use cost-effective compliance means and (2) raise the price of dangerous products, thus discouraging their use. However, monitoring difficulties, particularly in the case of pollution, render the taxing or auction methods inexact at best. Some object to the idea of allowing businesses to engage in undesirable conduct or highly prized conduct merely because they have the resources to pay for those privileges.

Similarly, cost-benefit analysis would be applied to all significant regulations. Regulations would be imposed only if added benefits equaled or exceeded added costs. Table 8.2, based on data by Professor Kip Viscusi, illustrates that some regulations are, in a cost-benefit sense, much more sensible than others.

Ethics/Public Policy Questions

Cost-benefit analysis, though clearly a useful, if inexact, tool, cannot accurately capture all of the considerations involved in tough public policy choices. Professor Kip Viscusi showed, for example, that smoking is not necessarily the economic drain on society that we have come to assume. Since smokers often die younger than would otherwise be the case, they may actually save us money:

Smoking is not necessarily the economic drain on society that we have come to assume.

> Lung cancer and heart disease caused by smoking require extra medical care, costing an average of 55 cents per pack of cigarettes sold, and they drive up life-insurance premiums by 14 cents a pack. But on the other side of the ledger, Viscusi finds that each pack smoked saves America $1.19 in pension and social security payments, and 22 cents in nursing-home expenses.[31]

1. Given these data, should we desist from our efforts to discourage adult smoking?
2. Would it be ethical to do so? Explain.

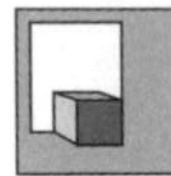

C. Further Deregulation?

Throughout this text, we have been asking you to think about the impact of law in building and managing a business. Recently, the federal government approved new legislation, the Telecommunications Act of 1996, that will significantly affect your professional future, offering enormous new business opportunities and challenges. In a resounding affirmation of deregulation policy, Congress and President Clinton were able to agree on the new bill, which will alter the course of commerce and culture in America and, inevitably, around the world. The legislation evidences our faith in a substantially free market as the best means of addressing the coming global telecommunications revolution. The bill's core provisions address the following:

- *Competition*—Frees the telephone, television, and computer industries from laws that had prevented them from competing in each other's businesses.
- *Expansion*—Allows television companies to own stations reaching up to 35 percent of viewers (had been a 25 percent maximum).
- *Cable TV*—Immediately deregulates rates for customers of small systems; deregulates all rates by 1999 (or sooner if competition is present in the market); makes it harder for cable customers to contest rates with the FCC.
- *Long-distance phone service*—Allows the seven regional Bell companies (Baby Bells) to provide long-distance service.
- *Local phone service*—Preempts state and local laws, thus easing entry for big competitors such as AT&T, MCI, and cable TV companies.
- *Sex/violence issues*—Makes it a crime for online computer services or users to transmit indecent material over the Internet without restricting minors' access. Mandates TV manufacturers to include V-chips in new sets, which allow customers to automatically block objectionable programming.
- *Guaranteed phone service*—Guarantees phone service everywhere, but lets states and the FCC decide how to pay for it.[32]

Pros and Cons. No one can more than dimly project the impact of the telecommunications bill other than to say that it will change our lives. Supporters of the bill expect dramatic new product breakthroughs, many new jobs, U.S. worldwide telecommunications superiority, expanded consumer choice, and lower prices. Critics think the bill is essentially a prescription for consolidation and monopoly in the telecommunications industry. They envision more jobs lost than gained, shrinking consumer choices, and higher rates. Arguably, new technologies such as powerful satellites and compression of movies over phone lines will reduce the threat of consolidation and monopoly. The measures to curb children's access to sex and violence are being tested in court, largely on First Amendment grounds.

Years may pass before we will have a reasonably clear picture of whether Congress's faith in the free market has served us well in the telecommunications industry. However, we can now make some assessment of the success of other deregulation initiatives.

Profile Perspectives: If Nations Air were to use small planes (10–30 seats) for commuter flights, it would be required to contend with new FAA rules requiring commuter lines to meet the same safety standards that have long been in place for the major carriers. Should McDonald seek to enter an alliance with a foreign carrier, he would find that a number of those carriers are either forbidden to fly into America or must endure closer scrutiny because of FAA safety concerns. Whatever strategic direction he takes, McDonald may need to decide whether he will allow certain child-restraint seats on his planes. Some of those seats, although approved for airline use, in fact, do not work well for very young children, according to an FAA study. So at every turn, the government's presence is felt. Would Nations Air and America be better off without this close oversight?

The Good News. In the key deregulated industries of transportation and communications, productivity is up and prices are down. According to a 1992 Interstate Commerce Commission study, productivity in those industries, except for telephones, improved (or declined at a slower rate) after deregulation than before. Furthermore, the data show that productivity gains were greatest where deregulation was most thorough (railroads, trucking, and airlines). Similarly, prices fell in all deregulated industries, although in the telephone business the price decline was greater before deregulation than after.[33]

In a similar vein:

- *New businesses.* The number of new businesses increased by 12.3 percent in the deregulated industries of transportation and financial services, compared to 8.2 percent for the whole economy.[34]
- *Airlines.* According to one study, airfares fell about 29 percent following deregulation.[35] Many more people are now able to fly.
- *Shipping.* One expert calculated that transportation costs were 6.2 percent of our gross domestic product in 1993. In 1979, prior to deregulation, transportation accounted for 8.0 percent of our GDP. That decline in costs frees a great deal of money for making things rather than moving them around.[36]

Japan. Perhaps the strongest support for deregulation is that others around the world have looked at the American experience and are beginning to do the same. The following article notes that even the Japanese, so long and successfully committed to government/private-sector cooperation, are struggling with deregulation.

Japan's Big Problem: Freeing Its Economy from Over-Regulation

by David P. Hamilton, Michael Williams, and Norihiko Shirouzu

Despite Japan's proclamations about tackling its economic malaise, it is still struggling to deal with the biggest drag on its growth: over-regulation . . .

By one estimate, regulation-inflated prices in areas ranging from air travel to agriculture cost Japanese consumers about $250 billion a year, or $2,000 per

Continued

Continued

person. Unleashing that spending power could revive the economy, increase imports and narrow Japan's huge trade surplus with the United States and other nations. In the few areas Japan has already opened up, consumers and companies are benefiting.

Growth in Cellular Phones

Take cellular communications, an industry Japan pioneered but then regulated so heavily the United States and Europe soon surpassed it. A year ago, the government finally permitted people to buy cellular phones instead of just renting them. Phone prices have dropped by more than half, and even to zero, as companies woo subscribers with cut-rate sets. Service fees also are falling. And sales are exploding. From last April through this January, consumers snapped up 1.6 million cellular phones, almost four times the number of new rentals the entire previous year.

* * *

Discounters' Gains

Rule changes have also fueled a boom in discount stores specializing in everything from clothing to liquor. Last May, the Ministry of International Trade and Industry (MITI) exempted stores with floor space of less than about 1,200 square yards from the lengthy application process required of larger stores. Small-store openings doubled, while openings of larger ones increased 41 percent. Now, Japanese can buy a can of beer for as little as $1.20, less than half the price of a few years ago.

In some cases, the mere prospect of deregulation is shaking things up. Service stations are fighting price wars fueled by rule changes that next year will allow unrestricted imports of cheap gasoline.

"It's share, share, share. Everybody's vying for a bigger share ahead of next year's deregulation," complains Naritoshi Fukumoto, who runs a gasoline station on the outskirts of Tokyo. "It's a war that we don't really want, but when people start slashing prices all around me, I have no choice but to respond."

Once a week, Mr. Fukumoto sheds his oil-stained uniform for street clothes and checks out competitors' pumps to get a handle on prices. Reluctantly, he has reduced his price to 103 yen a liter (about $4.60 a gallon) from 120 yen six months ago. More cuts are likely: A nearby rival has just gone down to 95 yen a liter.

. . . Although the economy is highly advanced, it is still run, in many ways, like a developing one. For years, regulations and tax laws hindered imports, suppressed consumption, encouraged consumers to save—and enabled Japan to finance the export machine that made it rich. Not long ago, Japan's system of "mercantile capitalism" aroused envy in the West.

These days, that brand of capitalism seems to do more harm than good. Japan's trade surpluses drive up the yen's value as foreigners buy yen to pay for Japanese goods. So far this year alone, the yen has soared 22 percent against the dollar. The strong yen makes exports more expensive and imports cheaper. And that, in turn, erodes the earnings of Japan's exporters and threatens to trigger another downturn.

* * *

Comprehensive deregulation could add half a percentage point to Japan's economic growth even without counting the new industries likely to crop up, Hidehiro Iwaki of the Nomura Research Institute estimates. The alternative may be a long, chaotic economic workout, forced by the high yen. "We must deregulate or die," says one pro-reform MITI bureaucrat.

Japanese businessmen talk about a long list of regulations they want axed. One is the Large-Scale Retail Store Law, which limits big retailers' operating hours and makes them wait months for permission to open a new outlet. Other rules rig brokerage commissions and limit stock listings, and are partly to blame for Japan's stock-market slump. Restrictions on domestic air travel make it cheaper for Tokyoites to fly to Seoul than to Sapporo.

Some Odd Rules

Many bureaucratic dictates defy common sense. Health rules make it illegal to sell aspirin or cold medicine without a pharmacist present. The government keeps a monopoly on the production and sale of ordinary table salt.

Despite some deregulatory successes, Japan hasn't shown much will to tackle the red-tape monster . . .

Four times in the past 20 months, officials have churned out deregulation packages. These have typically run hundreds of pages and listed reams of rules—but have targeted most rules for future study rather than the trash heap.

Continued

Continued

* * *

Falling Prices Painful

Not just bureaucratic intransigence is involved. Cutting red tape now would intensify the pain of falling prices just when the economy is weak. And because deregulation would slash employment in trucking, agriculture, and other inefficient industries, many Japanese are understandably reluctant. As many as 12 million jobs could vanish in the initial rush of deregulation, Haruo Shimada of Keio University estimates. He sees net job growth as the eventual result of reform, but only after brutal short-term dislocation.

Already, employment in laggard areas such as retailing is dropping as large stores undermine weak ones. Small shops, restaurants, and distributors cut 210,000 workers, 5 percent of their work force, during the past three years. Future reforms could accelerate the cutbacks. John Chanoki, an analyst at James Capel Pacific Ltd., believes the advent of self-service gasoline stations could doom the jobs of nearly 100,000 workers—a quarter of the current total.

Questions

1. What do the authors mean in describing the Japanese economy as one of "mercantile capitalism"?
2. Why does Japan seem to fear deregulation; that is, what losses may accompany a deregulated economy?

Source: *The Wall Street Journal,* April 25, 1995. Reprinted by permission of *The Wall Street Journal.*

The Bad News. Deregulation has not been a painless process. In the short term, bankruptcies were common in the airline and trucking industries. Cable television rates increased dramatically in many markets to the point that Congress decided to reregulate those rates (only to substantially deregulate them again with the 1996 Telecommunications Act). Critics place part of the blame for the savings and loan failures of the 1980s (costing taxpayers $400 billion in bailout funds and interest) on weakened government oversight of the industry. Beyond the industry-specific concerns, the bigger doubt about deregulation is what it says about America's future. Government intervention was often designed, in part, to provide some shelter to groups, locales, and industries that likely would suffer in an open market. We guaranteed plane and bus service to smaller communities and profits to some carriers. We subsidized rural phone service with funds from larger markets. These strategies arguably were useful in preserving small town, rural life and in providing a cushion for economically disadvantaged Americans. Of course, from a free market perspective, those efforts actually harmed those they were designed to benefit and imposed a penalty on all others.

On balance? The United States remains the least regulated of all the industrialized nations. America is not committed to government regulation as a matter of political policy. Rather, regulation has resulted, in most cases, from an effort to correct evident wrongs. Much-maligned agencies such as the EPA, OSHA, and FDA were not borne of a desire for big government and central planning. Pollution, industrial accidents, and dangerous food and drugs clearly were the impetus for the creation of those agencies. Now we are asking whether the free market, on balance, provides the best solution to some of those problems.

SUMMARY

Legal Review. This chapter began by examining the question of why we decided, as a society, to embrace extensive government regulation of business. We looked at the notion of market failure and at a bit of the history of government intervention in business affairs. The Commerce Clause, which provides the constitutional authority for federal regulation of business, was analyzed, and an overview of state and local regulation of business followed. Essentially, the chapter posed questions about the wisdom of expanded government oversight.

The Administrative Law portion of the chapter began with a discussion of the history and duties of federal agencies (Federal Trade Commission, Occupational Safety and Health Administration, Food and Drug Administration, etc.). We considered certain court challenges of agency action. The chapter closed with a detailed evaluation of the federal regulatory process, the pluses and minuses of the federal deregulation initiative, and the broad, public policy question of whether we should trim the role of government rules in the practice of business. That is, should we place greater faith in the free market?

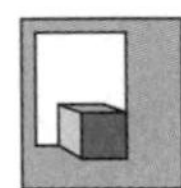

Ethics/Public Policy Review. This chapter examined the core question in this entire text: How much government regulation of business do we need? Put another way, to what extent can we rely on the business community's sense of ethics/social responsibility combined with the force of the free market to assure good corporate conduct? Clearly, the dominant sentiment in the mid-90s is to get the government off our backs. And perhaps with good reason. Commentator Cal Thomas noted that "the Environmental Protection Agency alone now has 18,000 staff members and an operating budget of $4.5 billion, quadruple its original size in 1970."[37] Sounding a familiar theme, Indiana businesswoman Jean Ann Harcourt complained about seemingly pointless rules:

> Harcourt said it makes sense for her workers to wear protective head gear while making pencils. But why, she asked, must she keep track of the amount of fumes her company emits when the paints and lacquers are nontoxic?[38]

Of course, those rules are more than annoying; they can be devastating to productivity. After the severe 1994 California earthquake, Governor Pete Wilson suspended the normal rules for rebuilding devastated freeways in Los Angeles. The Santa Monica Freeway was back in business in 64 days, a project that reportedly would have required two and one-half years under the normal rules.[39]

Economics Review. We looked at evidence showing that deregulation appears, on balance, to have been good for America. The new Telecommunications Reform Act reflects Washington's confidence in the market. Nonetheless, the public seems of two minds. On the one hand, the surveys show overwhelming sentiment for less government; on the other hand, when the questions become more specific, the answers become more divided. In a 1993 Gallup poll, 37 percent of the respondents said we have too much regulation of business, 30 percent said we have the right amount, and 28 percent said we need more.[40] Similarly, a 1991 Roper poll found 75 percent of those surveyed saying we should not postpone stronger air pollution rules, 76 percent opposed postponing stronger clean water standards, and 68 percent said that we should not eliminate air-bag requirements.[41]

Clearly, we do not want to fully entrust our welfare to the market, nor do we want to continue to be frustrated by foolish rules. We want what author James Champy has called for: A government that is "easy to do business with."[42]

CHAPTER QUESTIONS—LAW

1. The Federal Communications Commission received a pair of complaints from viewers about allegedly indecent television and radio programming. In one case, a Seattle television station showed graphic scenes in a sex-education class. In another, a St. Louis radio station broadcast a reading of a *Playboy* interview with Jessica Hahn, who alleged that she was raped by evangelist Jim Bakker. Sheep sounds were played in the background during the reading.

   Does either case violate the indecency standards for broadcasting as you understand them? Explain. [See Daniel Pearl, "Hot Career of the Future: Indecency Screener," *The Wall Street Journal,* July 13, 1995, p. B1.]
2. As a safety measure, Arizona enacted a statute that limited the length of passenger trains to 14 cars and freight trains to 70 cars. Trains of those lengths and greater were common throughout the United States. The Southern Pacific Railroad challenged the Arizona statute.
   a. What was the legal foundation of the Southern Pacific claim?
   b. Decide the case. Explain.
   [See *Southern Pacific Railroad* v. *Arizona,* 325 U.S. 761 (1945).]
3. A provision of the Airline Deregulation Act of 1978 prohibits states from enforcing any law "relating to rates, routes, or services" of any air carrier. In 1987, the National Association of Attorneys General (representing all 50 states) passed guidelines designed to regulate fare advertisements in order to prevent deception. A specific concern was ads that displayed reduced fares in large print, with taxes and add-ons in small print. Several airlines filed suit to block the guidelines.
   a. What constitutional argument did they raise?
   b. Decide. Explain.
   [See *Morales* v. *Trans World Airlines,* 112 S.Ct. 2031 (1992).]
4. Alabama's legislature imposed a higher tax on out-of-state insurance companies than on in-state firms. Out-of-state companies could reduce, but not eliminate, the differential by investing in Alabama.
   a. What constitutional objection was raised by the out-of-state firms?
   b. What defense was raised by the state?
   c. Decide. Explain.
   [See *Metropolitan Life Ins. Co.* v. *Ward,* 470 U.S. 869 (1985)].
5. The Pennsylvania legislature passed legislation requiring all trucks over a specified weight to display an identification marker and pay a $25 annual fee for that marker. Trucks registered in Pennsylvania were exempted from the marker fee on the grounds that the $25 would be treated as a part of the general state vehicle registration fee. Later, the Pennsylvania legislature reduced the $25 fee to $5 and imposed a $36-per-axle fee on all trucks over a specified weight. At the same time, the legislature reduced the fee for registering trucks (of the specified weight class) in Pennsylvania by the amount of the axle tax. The American Trucking Associations challenged the Pennsylvania laws.
   a. Identify the central constitutional issue in this case.
   b. Decide the case. Explain.
   [See *American Trucking Associations, Inc.* v. *Scheiner,* 483 U.S. 266 (1987)].
6. In the interest of safety, an Iowa statute prohibited the use of 65-foot double-trailer trucks within its borders. Scientific studies revealed that 65-foot doubles were as safe as 55-foot singles (permissible under Iowa law). The State of Iowa argued that the statute promoted safety and reduced road wear by diverting much truck traffic to

other states. Consolidated Freightways challenged the statute. Decide. [See *Raymond Kassel et al.* v. *Consolidated Freightways Corporation of Delaware,* 101 S.Ct. 1309 (1981).]

Chapter Questions—Economics/Public Policy

1. Pulitzer Prize–winning author and presidential advisor, Arthur Schlesinger:

> The assault on the national government is represented as a disinterested movement to "return" power to the people. But the withdrawal of the national government does not transfer power to the people. It transfers power to the historical rival of the national government and the prime cause of its enlargement—the great corporate interests.[43]

   a. Using 19th and 20th century American economic history, explain Schlesinger's claim that corporate interests are the primary cause of big government.
   b. Do you agree with Schlesinger that we continue to need big government to counteract corporate interests and achieve fairness for all in American life? Explain.
2. Transportation deregulation has resulted in an immediate loss of service to some smaller communities. Some of that loss has been compensated for with the entry of smaller, independent firms.
   a. Has deregulation endangered small-town America? Explain.
   b. Should we apply free market principles to the postal service, thus, among other consequences, compelling those in small and remote communities to pay the full cost of service rather than the subsidized cost now paid? Explain.
3. The expense of government regulation is not limited to the direct cost of administering the various agencies. Explain and offer examples of the other expenses produced by regulation.
4. To the extent the federal government achieves deregulation, what substitutes will citizens find for protection?
5. A major issue facing the Federal Aviation Administration is that of congestion in the airways caused by too many planes seeking to take off or land at peak times at high-demand airports. How might we solve that problem while maintaining reasonable service?
6. In calculating the costs and benefits of a new rule, make the argument that added regulation normally slows the economy and leads to increased deaths.

Notes

1. Associated Press, "Another Start-up Airline Sputters," *Des Moines Register,* August 5, 1995, p. 8S.
2. "Nations Air Grounds Itself after FAA Finds Training Deficiencies," *Air Safety Week* 9, no. 28 (July 24, 1995)
3. Associated Press, "76% Distrust Government, Survey Says," *Des Moines Register,* August 1, 1995, p. 1A.
4. Stephen Moore, "If You Bought 2 Trillion Copies of This Paper . . . ," *The Wall Street Journal,* February 6, 1995, p. A14.

5. Karl Schriftgiesser, *Business and the American Government* (Washington, DC: Robert B. Luce, 1964), p. 14.
6. The remarks in this paragraph were drawn, in part, from "Interventionist Government Came to Stay," *Business Week,* September 3, 1979, p. 39.
7. Ibid.
8. See "Federalism—Clear Congressional Mandate Required to Preempt State Law," *Harvard Law Review* 105, no. 1 (November 1991), p. 196; and *Gregory* v. *Ashcroft,* 111 S.Ct. 2395 (1991).
9. 317 U.S. 111 (1942).
10. 18 U.S.C. § 922(q)(1)(A).
11. *United States* v. *Lopez,* 115 S.Ct. 1624 (1995).
12. Shawn M. Miller, "A Laundry Squeezed by the City's Bureaucratic Wringer," *Los Angeles Times,* February 4, 1995, p. B7.
13. Christopher Conte, "What Shakeout?" *The Wall Street Journal,* July 21, 1992, p. A1.
14. Timothy Noah, "Fiscal Crisis or No, States' Bureaucracies Just Keep Swelling," *The Wall Street Journal,* July 1, 1991, p. A1.
15. Editorial, "Punched In," *The Wall Street Journal,* March 25, 1991, p. A10.
16. "Three of Five Unbelted Motorists in Fatal Crashes Would Have Survived," *PR Newswire,* February 15, 1996.
17. "Agency Settles with FTC over Yogurt Ads," *Waterloo Courier,* October 20, 1995, p. D5.
18. *Action for Children's Television* v. *Federal Communications Commission,* 116 S.Ct. 701 (1996).
19. *Action for Children's Television* v. *FCC,* 58 F.3d 654 (1995).
20. This historical overview of the indecency issue is drawn from Edmund Andrews, "Court Upholds a Ban on 'Indecent' Broadcast Programming," *The New York Times,* July 1, 1995, sec. 1, p. 7.
21. James Kilpatrick, "Indecent Radio Broadcasts Deserve Fine," *Des Moines Register,* December 27, 1992, p. 3C.
22. William Niskanen, "The Costs of Regulation (Continued)," *Regulation* 15, no. 2 (Spring 1992), p. 25.
23. Michael Selz, "Costs of Complying with Federal Rules Weigh More Heavily on Small Firms," *The Wall Street Journal,* November 1, 1995, p. B2.
24. Murray Weidenbaum, "Everywhere You Look There's a Regulator," *The Wall Street Journal,* September 12, 1995, p. A23.
25. "The Shrinking Government," *Des Moines Register,* February 2, 1996, p. 8A.
26. Louis Richman, "Bringing Reason to Regulation," *Fortune,* October 19, 1992, p. 94.
27. Miles Pomper, "Rush to Change Federal Safety Regulations Worries Some," *Waterloo Courier,* January 17, 1995, p. A1.
28. William Niskanen, "The Total Cost of Regulation?" *Regulation* 14, no. 3 (Summer 1991), p. 23.
29. George Stigler, "The Theory of Economic Regulation," *Bell Journal of Economics and Management Science* 2 (Spring 1971), p. 3.
30. Ibid., p. 5.
31. Periscope, "Puff Price," *Newsweek,* December 12, 1994, p. 6.
32. Drawn from Associated Press, *Des Moines Register,* and *The Wall Street Journal* reports.
33. Niskanen, "The Costs of Regulation," p. 26.
34. Louis Rukeyser, ed., *Louis Rukeyser's Business Almanac* (New York: Simon & Schuster, 1988), p. 165.
35. Associated Press, "Deregulation of American Business Had a Price," *Des Moines Register,* December 20, 1989, p. 5S.
36. David Nicklaus reporting the findings of Robert V. Delaney of Cass Informations Systems, St. Louis, in "Time to Let Business Keep on Truckin'," *St. Louis Post-Dispatch,* October 9, 1994, p. 1E.
37. "Cutting Red Tape," *Indianapolis News,* May 25, 1995, p. A8.
38. Ibid.
39. Ibid.
40. "The Regulatory Muddle," *The American Enterprise* 4, no. 6 (November–December 1993), p. 85.
41. Ibid.
42. Tom Richman, "Government Should Be Easy to Do Business with," *The State of Small Business,* May 1995, p. 98.
43. Arthur Schlesinger, Jr., "In Defense of Government," *The Wall Street Journal,* June 7, 1995, p. A14.

CHAPTER 9

Intellectual Property and Computer Law: Protecting the Business's Ideas

Reader's Guide

Many new and start up businesses are based on the owner's idea for a new product, design, or service. The law of intellectual property deals with the ways a business can protect its own version of those new ideas.

Profile

Jerry Irwin started his own company, BOS, Inc., in the office supply business. The company achieved extraordinary service with a brand new concept: an online catalog and order-entry system. This system gave customers a full description of each item in the catalog, and wherever practical, an on-screen picture of the item, along with the current price. The system also included a very user-friendly search index system for rapid location of any desired item, and ordering was interactive. New customers could use an interactive system for opening new accounts.

Jerry hired an independent consulting firm for $50,000 to do the actual programming for the system. Charlie Costens, an employee of the independent consulting firm, worked closely with Jerry's staff during the entire project (six months), and delivered the finished project essentially on time and within budget.

This new system has been so successful for BOS, Inc., that Jerry's business has grown dramatically.

Questions

1. Does Jerry "own" anything in the new system he developed?
2. What steps should Jerry take to protect his new concept?
3. What can Jerry do to exploit the concept?

intellectual property. intangible personal property.
personal property. Property that is not real estate, though owned by an individual or entity.
real property. "Real estate" or land.

I. Introduction

Let's start by trying to get our arms around the idea and meaning of "intellectual property." Just what is it?

To lawyers, **intellectual property** refers to intangible **personal property** (as opposed to **real property**). It is personal property because it is not real estate, and it is intangible because you can't touch it or feel it. Interestingly enough, the Chinese during the recent GATT negotiations often referred to intellectual property as "invisible property."

There are many sorts of intangible personal property, including such things as stock or bonds (stock or bonds represent the right to receive dividends or interest from the issuer). However, one essential characteristic sets intellectual property apart from other forms of personal property.

The fundamental characteristic of intellectual property is that it is the *product of the human mind.* It can be a new machine, a new medicine, a new song, play, or novel, or a new computer program. These are specific examples of intellectual property.

Suppose you write a story and generate a hard copy from a word processor. You give a copy of the story to a friend for review and comment. After a very heated but unrelated argument, he shreds the hard copy of the story. Has the friend destroyed your intellectual property? No. He has destroyed the hard copy, but the hard copy is an item of *tangible* personal property. The intellectual property is the story itself, and that has been unaffected by your friend's action.

Alternatively, suppose your friend returns the manuscript to you. Then, after changing the names of the characters, he submits the story under his own name for publication. This time, the friend has stolen your intellectual property.

Protecting property rights in intellectual property is not universal. Many civilizations and cultures simply do not recognize such rights, and this conflict in cultures has been and still is a major stumbling block in the globalization of business. This conflict will be discussed under "Emerging Issues" later in this chapter.

There is hardly a field of business today that does not face significant intellectual property issues. The entertainment business, everything from writers and performers to recorded music and movies, is totally founded on the concepts of intellectual property. The same is true for the publishing business. Computers and technology are moving at warp speed as we enter the 21st century, and the issues of how to protect your own technology and avoid infringing someone else's are paramount to success in business. As you proceed through this chapter, the scenario of Jerry Irwin will help you focus on several practical and current intellectual property issues.

A. *Public Policy Issues*

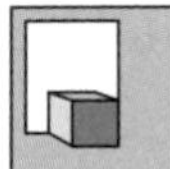

From the public policy standpoint, we must consider several competing public interests. First, there is a public interest in encouraging the development of technology. As set forth in the Constitution, our Founding Fathers determined that this could best be accomplished by granting exclusive rights to the creators of technology for a limited time. How do we justify government-sponsored monopolies (exclusive rights) in the face of a competing public interest in free competition as defined in our antitrust (antimonopoly) laws? Finally, there is a public interest in providing the widest possible access to ideas. Where do we draw the line between what is covered by the exclusive rights and what is not covered and hence is available to the public?

The Monopoly for Disclosure Bargain. Article I, Section 8 of the U.S. Constitution provides that, "The Congress shall have Power . . . To promote the Progress of Science and useful Arts, by securing for limited Times to Authors and Inventors the exclusive Right to their respective Writings and Discoveries." Notice several very key points in this short grant of power. First, the fundamental objective is promotion of progress in science and the useful arts. Second, this objective is to be attained by securing exclusive rights (monopolies), and finally, the exclusive rights are for a limited time. The *Bonito Boat* case that follows includes an effective and recent analysis of this constitutional provision by the U.S. Supreme Court.

The underlying concept is that anyone who discovers some new advance in technology has the right to keep his or her discovery secret. This would mean that the public at large would not know about nor reap benefits from the discovery. Absent some form of property right and protection, people would have no economic incentive to develop new technology if anyone else was free to copy it as soon as it was introduced to the public. So the *patent system* was designed to encourage public disclosure of the technology by granting an exclusive right (monopoly) for a limited time in return for the full public disclosure of the technology.

Protection of Ideas and Thoughts. A second public policy issue is how to draw the line between a new technology that is protectible, fundamental ideas or laws of nature that should be freely accessible to everyone, and advances or improvements that are so insignificant that they do not merit protection. In other words, at one end of the spectrum there are certain very fundamental laws of nature or ideas that should not be subject to exclusive appropriation by anyone; at the other end are minor improvements that are not really worthy of protection. In between lie those advances in technology that represent a significant step forward and for which exclusive rights in return for disclosure is a fair bargain. This technology should be made available to the public as building blocks for development of further technology. The public learns of the new technology when the patent is issued, but has no right to use it until the patent expires.

The constitutional provision also speaks to granting exclusive rights to authors for their writings, and the same public policy issue arises here. At the one end of the spectrum, all *words* must be in the public domain, free for all to use, whether for personal communication or for artistic expression in the form of books, plays, poetry, or advertisements. Imagine if someone claimed to have created the word *cyberspace* and that individual was given the rights to that word. Anyone who wanted to use the word in a sentence would have to pay the creator a fee. This would not only be unmanageable, but also excessively restrictive and proprietary. Therefore, protection in the form of exclusive rights must, at the very least, be for a certain combination of words.

At the other end of the spectrum, however, is the issue that if a competitor can simply change the order of words or substitute synonyms, the exclusive right is not worth very much. In practical terms, can the creators of the currently popular TV series *ER* acquire the exclusive rights to a show based upon the events and staff in a large Chicago hospital emergency room? If they cannot protect the concept, what if anything can they protect? (Consider that a competing network began airing a new show, *Chicago Hope,* at the very same time *ER* hit the airwaves. Both shows featured medical personnel in Chicago hospitals.)

Federal Preemption by Patent and Copyright Laws. A final public policy issue is the balance of power between the states and the federal government with respect to protecting intellectual property rights. The *Bonito Boat* case that follows discusses all of these public policy issues and is resolved on the basis of federal preemption of state laws relating to exclusive rights in technology. In this case, Bonito Boats, Inc. (Bonito), developed a hull design for a fiberglass recreational boat that it marketed under the trade name Bonito Boat Model 5VBR. Designing the boat hull required substantial effort on the part of Bonito. A set of engineering drawings was prepared, from which a hardwood model was created. The hardwood model was then sprayed with fiberglass to create a mold, which then served to produce the finished fiberglass boats for sale. Bonito made no attempt to patent its new design. The Model 5VBR was extremely popular with the boating public, becoming one of the top sellers in its class.

The Florida legislature enacted a statute that makes it unlawful for any person to use the direct molding process—a form of reverse engineering—to duplicate unpatented boat hulls and forbids the sale of any hulls duplicated by this method.

Bonito filed a lawsuit alleging that Thunder Craft Boats, Inc. (Thunder Craft), had violated the Florida statute by using the direct molding process to duplicate the Bonito 5VBR fiberglass hull and had knowingly sold such duplications in violation of the Florida statute.

Thunder Craft filed a motion to dismiss, arguing that the Florida statute conflicted with the federal patent law and was therefore invalid under the Supremacy Clause of the federal Constitution.

CASE

Bonito Boats, Inc. v. Thunder Craft Boats, Inc.

489 U.S. 141 (1989)

Justice O'Connor

Article 1 §8, cl. 8 of the Constitution gives Congress the power "[t]o promote the Progress of Science and useful Arts, by securing for limited Times to Authors and Inventors the exclusive Right to their respective Writings and Discoveries." The Patent Clause itself reflects a balance between the need to encourage innovation and the avoidance of monopolies which stifle competition without any concomitant advance in the "Progress of Science and useful Arts." As we have noted in the past, the Clause contains both a grant of power and certain limitations upon the exercise of that power. Congress may not create patent monopolies of unlimited duration, nor may it "authorize the issuance of patents whose effects are to remove existent knowledge from the public domain, or to restrict free access to materials already available" . . .

From their inception, the federal patent laws have embodied a careful balance between the need to promote innovation and the recognition that imitation and refinement through imitation are both necessary to invention itself and the very lifeblood of a competitive economy.

* * *

Section 102(b) of [the patent statute] provides: "A person shall be entitled to a patent unless . . . (*b*) the invention was . . . in public use or on sale in this country more than one year prior to the date of application for patent in the United States" . . .

[T]he federal patent scheme creates a limited opportunity to obtain a property right in an idea. Once an inventor has decided to lift the veil of secrecy from his work, he must choose the protection of a federal patent or the dedication of his idea to the public at large. As Judge Learned Hand once put it: "[I]t is a condition upon the inventor's right to a patent that he shall not exploit his discovery competitively after it is ready for patenting; he must content himself with either secrecy or legal monopoly."

* * *

[T]he federal patent system thus embodies a carefully crafted bargain for encouraging the creation and disclosure of new, useful, and nonobvious advances in technology and design in return for the exclusive right to practice the invention for a period of years. "[The inventor] may keep his invention secret and reap its fruits indefinitely. In consideration of its disclosure and the consequent

Continued

Continued

benefit to the community, the patent is granted. An exclusive enjoyment is guaranteed him for 17 years, but upon expiration of that period, the knowledge of the invention inures to the people, who are thus enabled without restriction to practice it and profit by its use . . .

The attractiveness of such a bargain and its effectiveness in inducing creative effort and disclosure of the results of that effort, depend almost entirely on a backdrop of free competition in the exploitation of unpatented designs and innovations . . . [F]ree exploitation of ideas will be the rule, to which protection of a federal patent is the exception . . . State law protection for techniques and designs whose disclosure has already been induced by market rewards may conflict with the very purpose of the patent laws by decreasing the range of ideas available as the building blocks of further innovation. The offer of federal protection from competitive exploitation of intellectual property would be rendered meaningless in a world where substantially similar state law protections were readily available. To a limited extent, the federal patent laws must determine not only what is protected, but also what is free for all to use . . .

Thus our past decisions have made clear that state regulation of intellectual property must yield to the extent that it clashes with the balance struck by Congress in our patent laws.

* * *

In this case, the Bonito 5VBR fiberglass hull has been freely exposed to the public for a period in excess of six years. For purposes of federal law, it stands in the same stead as an item for which a patent has expired or been denied; it is unpatented and unpatentable . . . [P]etitioner chose to expose its hull design to the public in the marketplace, eschewing the bargain held out by the federal patent system of disclosure in exchange for exclusive use. Yet the Florida statute allows petitioner to reassert a substantial property right in the idea, thereby constricting the spectrum of useful public knowledge . . . We think it clear that such protection conflicts with the federal policy "that all ideas in general circulation be dedicated to the common good unless they are protected by a valid patent."

* * *

The Florida statute is aimed directly at the promotion of intellectual creation by substantially restricting the public's ability to exploit ideas that the patent system mandates shall be free for all to use.

* * *

We therefore agree with the majority of the Florida Supreme Court that the Florida statute is preempted by the Supremacy Clause, and the judgment of that court is hereby affirmed.

Questions

1. The Court says that an inventor "must choose the protection of a federal patent or the dedication of his idea to the public at large." What happens if the idea or product is not patentable?
2. Do you approve of the actions of Thunder Craft?
3. Consider that the design and production of boats is much more important in Florida than in Iowa. Under these circumstances, why is a unified national policy important?

II. Types of Protection

The law of intellectual property is subdivided into four distinct areas, each of which will be discussed in detail in this section. The areas are patents, trade secrets, copyrights, and trademarks.

A. Patents

As discussed above, a patent grants to its owner the exclusive right to make, use, and sell her or his invention for a limited period of time, currently 20 years. In the following section, we will explore what kinds of things are patentable, the procedure involved in getting a patent, and the rights of a patent owner.

Patentable Subject Matter. Patents are obtainable on an invention that is new and useful and that falls under one or more classes listed in the statute. Specifically, the statute authorizes patents for any new and useful process, machine, manufacture, composition of matter, or improvement on one of these classes. Separate and very specific provisions authorize patents on designs[1] and asexually reproduced plants.[2] The *Diamond* v. *Chakrabarty* case discusses and illustrates the breadth of the definition of statutory subject matter. In this case, a microbiologist (respondent) filed an application for a patent relating to his invention of human-made, genetically engineered bacteria capable of breaking down multiple components of crude oil. Because of this property, which is possessed by no naturally occurring bacteria, Chakrabarty's invention is believed to have significant value for the treatment of oil spills.

The United States Patent Office held that live, human-made microorganisms were not patentable subject matter under the statute. The Court of Customs and Patent Appeals (now the Court of Appeals for the Federal Circuit) reversed, holding that the fact that the microorganisms are alive is without significance for application of the law. The Supreme Court affirmed the Court of Customs and Patent Appeals.

CASE

Diamond v. Chakrabarty

447 US 303 (1980)

Chief Justice Burger

The question before us in this case is a narrow one of statutory interpretation requiring us to construe 35 U.S.C. §101, which provides: "Whoever invents or discovers any new and useful . . . manufacture, or composition of matter . . . may obtain a patent therefor. . ."

* * *

[T]his Court has read the term "manufacture" . . . in accordance with its dictionary definition to mean "the production of articles for use from raw or prepared materials by giving to these materials new forms, qualities, properties, or combinations, whether by hand-labor or by machinery"

Continued

Continued

. . . Similarly, "composition of matter" has been construed consistent with its common usage to include "all compositions of two or more substances and . . . all composite articles, whether they be the results of gases, fluids, powders or solids" . . . In choosing such expansive terms a "manufacture" and "composition of matter," modified by the comprehensive "any," Congress plainly contemplated that the patent laws would be given wide scope.

* * *

The Committee reports accompanying the 1952 Act inform us that Congress intended statutory subject matter to "include any thing under the sun that is made by man" . . .

This is not to suggest that §101 has no limits or that it embraces every discovery. The laws of nature, physical phenomena, and abstract ideas have been held not patentable . . . Thus, a new mineral discovered in the earth or a new plant found in the wild is not patentable subject matter. Likewise, Einstein could not patent his celebrated law that $E = mc^2$; nor could Newton have patented the law of gravity. Such discoveries are "manifestations of . . . nature, free to all men and reserved exclusively to none."

Judged in this light, respondent's micro-organism plainly qualifies as patentable subject matter. His claim is not to a hitherto unknown natural phenomenon, but to a nonnaturally occurring manufacture or composition of matter . . . a new bacterium with markedly different characteristics from any found in nature and one having the potential for significant utility. His discovery is not nature's handiwork, but his own; accordingly it is patentable subject matter under §101.

* * *

The petitioner's second argument is that micro-organisms cannot qualify as patentable subject matter until Congress expressly authorizes such protection . . . The briefs present a gruesome parade of horribles. Scientists, among them Nobel laureates, are quoted suggesting that genetic research may pose a serious threat to the human race. . .

It is argued that this Court should weigh these potential hazards in considering whether respondent's invention is patentable subject matter under §101. We disagree. The grant or denial of patents on micro-organisms is not likely to put an end to genetic research or to its attendant risks . . .

What is more important is that we are without competence to entertain these arguments—either to brush them aside as fantasies generated by fear of the unknown, or to act on them . . . Congress is free to amend §101 so as to exclude from patent protection organisms produced by genetic engineering . . . Or it may choose to craft a statute specifically designed for such living things. But, until Congress takes such action, this Court must construe the language of §101 as it is. The language of that section fairly embraces respondent's invention.

Questions

1. Isuzu, in developing its sport utility vehicle, the "Trooper," considered the conventional alternatives for the rear door. One was a single door opening upward, a second was a single door hinged on either the left or right side, and the third was a split rear door. After noting the drawbacks of each existing alternative, the Isuzu engineers hit upon the idea of a split rear door, with one door much larger than the other. That is, the line between the doors was not centered on the vehicle. The idea was widely acclaimed by industry experts. Is this design patentable?

Continued

Continued

2. Presumably the organism developed by Chakrabarty is self-propagating. If a user acquires some quantity of the microorganism from the patent owner, what is to stop the user from allowing the organism to reproduce to provide an ongoing supply without purchasing additional organisms from the patent owner? Stated another way, did the patent owner get the true benefit of the exclusive right granted by the patent? What alternatives do you suggest?
3. As of 1992, the organism patented by Chakrabarty had not been used in a commercial application. Although it is "new" and "made by man," and hence, according to the Court, patentable, it is still a living organism, and its impact on the delicate balance of nature is not known. What kind of public policy or government regulation is necessary to control the biotechnology industry?

Procedure to Obtain a Patent. The process for obtaining a patent can be long and expensive. Once you decide to proceed, you must prepare and file an application (usually including one or more detailed drawings) with the United States Patent and Trademark Office. To comply with the constitutional mandate, your application must fully describe the invention.[3] That is, the description must have sufficient detail that the full extent of the invention is available to the public upon expiration of the inventor's limited monopoly.

Figure 9.1 shows the cover page of a U.S. patent for a computerized lottery wagering system. It identifies the name of the inventor, the assignee of the patent, information on the filing and prosecution of the application, one schematic drawing illustrating the invention, and an abstract.

The Patent Office examines the application to be sure that it is new and useful and that it falls within one of the statutory classes discussed above. Not every development by an inventor rises to the level of an invention. The Patent Office, over the years, has developed an objective **test of nonobviousness.** It attempts to determine if the development described in the application would have been obvious to the ordinarily skilled worker in the art at the time the invention was made.[4] If it would have been obvious, the development is not patentable. Only those developments that represent a real step forward—those that would *not* have been obvious—are considered inventions.

test of nonobviousness. Determines whether the development described in the patent application would have been obvious to an ordinary skilled worker in the art at the time the invention was made.

Once the Patent Office satisfies itself that all conditions for patentability have been met, it will issue the official patent.

The Patent Office is an administrative agency under the Department of Commerce. An applicant dissatisfied with any decision by the patent examiner is entitled to appeal within the agency to the Patent Office Board of Appeals; if dissatisfied with the decision of the Board, the applicant may appeal to the Court of Appeals for the Federal Circuit, a special appellate level federal court with jurisdiction in all patent matters.

Patent Owner's Rights. The patent statutes give the owner of a patent the exclusive right to make, use, and sell the invention. The application for a patent must be filed by the individual(s) who made the invention. However, the inventor can assign all or any part of his or her patent rights to another individual or entity (transfer ownership). Technical people employed by a corporation generally sign, at the time of employment, an agreement giving their employer all rights to any inventions made during the course of their employment.

FIGURE 9.1 COVER PAGE OF A U.S. PATENT

US005415416A

United States Patent [19]

Scagnelli et al.

[11] Patent Number: **5,415,416**

[45] Date of Patent: **May 16, 1995**

[54] **COMPUTERIZED LOTTERY WAGERING SYSTEM**

[75] Inventors: **John B. Scagnelli**, Holmdel; **Joseph A. Fiscella**, Maywood, both of N.J.

[73] Assignee: **Lottotron Inc.**, Hackensack, N.J.

[21] Appl. No.: **181,361**

[22] Filed: **Jan. 13, 1994**

Related U.S. Application Data

[63] Continuation of Ser. No. 4,633, Jan. 12, 1993, abandoned, which is a continuation of Ser. No. 489,814, Mar. 6, 1990, abandoned.

[51] **Int. Cl.**[6] **A63F 9/22**

[52] **U.S. Cl.** .... **273/439**; 273/138 A; 379/95

[58] **Field of Search** .... 273/439, 138 R, 138 A, 273/269, 237, 85 G; 379/90, 91, 93, 95

[56] **References Cited**

U.S. PATENT DOCUMENTS

4,669,730	6/1987	Small	273/138 A
4,713,837	12/1987	Gordon	379/93
4,792,968	12/1988	Katz	379/92
4,815,741	3/1989	Small	273/138 A
4,842,278	6/1989	Markowicz	273/138 A
4,845,739	7/1989	Katz	379/92
4,922,522	5/1990	Scanlon	273/138 A
4,969,183	11/1990	Reese	273/138 A

FOREIGN PATENT DOCUMENTS

1162336	2/1984	Canada	379/93

Primary Examiner—Jessica J. Harrison
Attorney, Agent, or Firm—Weingram & Zall

[57] **ABSTRACT**

A wagering system for accepting wagers over the telephone comprising: (a) automatic call director means (ACD) for receiving incoming calls from subscribers who wish to wager on the system; b) voice responsive means (wagering VRU) connected thereto for receiving the incoming calls routed from the ACD, and for playing a series of recorded audio messages requesting subscriber wager information to be input via telecommunication means; and (c) host processor means having storage means and being connected to the wagering VRU for receiving the subscriber wager information, storing it in a master subscriber wager file in the storage means, and assigning an associated ticket number to the wager.

34 Claims, 18 Drawing Sheets

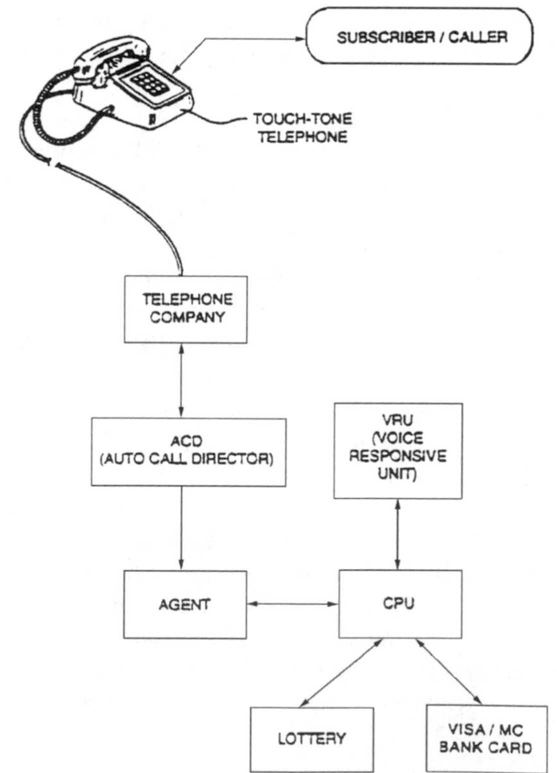

The owner of a patent can license a company to manufacture the patented product but still retain the exclusive right to sell the product. A **license** involves the transfer of rights under a patent, without transferring ownership. Or, in the reverse, the inventor can manufacture the product, license someone else to sell the product, and license the customer to use it.

license. The transfer rights under a patent, without transferring ownership.

Licenses can be either exclusive or nonexclusive. Under an exclusive license, only a single person or entity has the exclusive right; not even the inventor or patent owner retains any rights under the patent. A nonexclusive license, on the other hand, assumes that other entities possess similar rights under the patent.

The owner of a patent enforces these exclusive rights through a suit for patent infringement filed in the federal courts. If successful, the patent owner is entitled to statutory damages that include actual damages (at least in the amount of a reasonable royalty).[5] The statute specifies that damages may be trebled and provides for recovery of attorney fees and an injunction ordering the infringing party to stop the infringing activity.

Profile Perspective: Consider Jerry Irwin's method of doing business. Would you contend that it is patentable? Is the idea of an online catalog and order-entry system patentable? If not, do you think that the computer program that makes the online catalog work is patentable? Finally, who owns the intellectual property rights in the computer program developed by Costens? (Revisit this question after the discussion of the *CCNV* case, later in the chapter.)

B. Trade Secrets

For many businesses, particularly small and new ones, the expense and risk involved in obtaining a patent pose a significant obstacle. What happens if the Patent Office decides your invention is unpatentable and turns down the application? What can you do while waiting for your patent to be issued? How can you prevent an employee from taking your intellectual property and either competing with you or delivering it to a competitor? All of these issues have led to the development of a significant body of business law involving the concept of trade secrets.

In a sense, trade secret law is a statement of minimum standards of commercial ethics, balancing the claims of the owner of the trade secret with others, including employees, suppliers, and competitors, who may wish to use that information.

Subject Matter of Trade Secrets. Trade secret law in the United States developed through the common law; hence, it was originally different in each jurisdiction. In an effort to unify the law, the Uniform Trade Secrets Act (UTSA) was developed in 1979 and has been passed with very minor variations by some 35 states. The UTSA defines a trade secret as:

> Information, including a formula, pattern compilation, program, device, method, technique, or process, that (i) derives independent economic value, actual or potential, from not being generally known to and not being readily ascertainable by proper means by other persons who can obtain economic value from its disclosure or use, and (ii) is the subject of efforts that are reasonable under the circumstances to maintain its secrecy.

Procedure to Protect a Trade Secret. A trade secret is simply defined as information that is valuable and not known to others. As such, a trade secret is merely information acquired by a business through its own hard work.

The key to protection of a trade secret is keeping it secret. Obviously, once the information is known, it is no longer secret. A business must therefore take reasonable steps to maintain the security of its information. Suitable steps usually include restrictions on access to the information (i.e., only certain employees are permitted access to the information) and reasonable measures for physical security (e.g., a confidential formulation is always kept in a locked cabinet).

Typically, a business will advise all employees as to specific information that it regards as confidential or a trade secret; it often will enter into agreements with those employees having access to the information, restricting them from using the information should they ever leave employment with the company.

The following article examines one such case with a high-profile company and shows some of the competing issues.

IBM Sues to Silence Former Employee

Michael W. Miller

Peter Bonyhard was one of IBM's star engineers when disk-drive maker Seagate Technology, Inc., hired him away last year. Seagate instantly gave him a high-stakes assignment: develop its next generation of "heads"—the delicate parts that read and record computer disks' data.

Today IBM and Peter Bonyhard are embroiled in a fierce legal battle, one that raises sweeping questions about job-hopping in the computer industry. IBM says Seagate lured Mr. Bonyhard to steal its secret formula for MR heads. In December, IBM won an injunction in the U.S. District Court barring Mr. Bonyhard from working on Seagate's MR project. In the same court last month, IBM filed additional allegations against Seagate's chief technical officer, another ex-IBMer, and accused Seagate of a scheme to raid IBM's talent.

In an unusually aggressive move, IBM launched its suit against Mr. Bonyhard without even claiming to have any evidence that he had actually leaked secrets. Instead, IBM declared that there would simply be no way for Mr. Bonyhard to do his new job at Seagate without disclosing confidential IBM information.

The suit has escalated into angry warfare between IBM and Seagate, the disk-drive industry's biggest independent player. Seagate, Mr. Bonyhard, and Seagate's chief technical officer, Brendan Hegarty, deny all IBM's charges. As they see it, IBM's suit is a thinly disguised tactic to intimidate its employees into not working for the competition.

IBM wants its top technical people "to remain in lifetime servitude to IBM" or "accept a menial position with a competitor," Seagate alleged in a countersuit accusing IBM of unfair competition.

Mr. Bonyhard, who fled his native Hungary during the Soviet invasion of 1956, has filed his own countersuit accusing IBM of interfering with his right to work wherever he pleases. "In Hungary, when you graduated from college you were assigned a job and you had very little choice about it," he says. "I think if IBM had its way there would be a somewhat reminiscent lack of freedom."

Mr. Bonyhard, who is 55 years old, was known at IBM for a brilliant mind, a healthy ego, and a disdain for rules and red tape. Managers considered him a "wild duck," IBM jargon for a maverick who causes headaches but also sparks unconventional new ideas.

Continued

Continued

In April, an appeals court lifted the injunction that had forced Seagate to reassign Mr. Bonyhard, so he is back at work on the MR project. He says the field, which several other companies are pursuing, is broad enough for him to maneuver without violating any IBM confidences.

IBM insists it sued Mr. Bonyhard only because he posed an egregious threat to its trade secrets—not to discourage job-hopping in any way. "If that were the intent, you'd have a lot more lawsuits," says Mr. Chesler. "Look at all the people who left IBM in the last year and a half—we brought one suit."

He says Mr. Bonyhard presented a rare case of an employee loaded with IBM secrets who took a "mirror image" job at a direct competitor. Moreover, even though IBM at first charged only that it was "inevitable" that Mr. Bonyhard would leak trade secrets, IBM now says it has evidence of actual leaks.

In an amended complaint, IBM says Mr. Bonyhard has told Seagate "some of IBM's most innovative trade secrets" in MR head design. Just as important, IBM says, Mr. Bonyhard has steered Seagate away from possible approaches that he knew from his work at IBM would turn out to be expensive dead ends.

Questions

1. Assume that Mr. Bonyhard had been hired as president of Seagate, and was hired for his managerial expertise rather than his technical background and knowledge. Would IBM have sued? Would they have been successful?
2. When a manager changes jobs, does she or he have any ethical obligations toward her or his former employer?
3. Does a covenant not to compete that effectively prevents a person from earning a living by using his or her business expertise amount to involuntary servitude?

Source: *The Wall Street Journal,* July 15, 1992. Reprinted by permission of *The Wall Street Journal.*

A related issue occurs when confidential or trade secret information must be disclosed to outsiders. The most common example happens when the owner of a business tries to franchise, sell, or merge the business. If, in fact, an important aspect of the success of the business is the existence of a trade secret, the franchisee or purchaser will insist on disclosure. The owner must protect the trade secret by means of a confidential nondisclosure agreement, under which the party receiving the information (the purchaser or franchisor) acknowledges that the information received is proprietary and agrees not to use any information disclosed for his or her own purposes.

Trade Secret Owner's Rights. The owner of a trade secret has the right to use the trade secret information in his or her business forever. However, the information remains proprietary or valuable only if it remains secret. If the same information is developed by a competitor independently, there is absolutely nothing that the original owner can do. For example, a customer list containing names of contacts and projects as well as pricing and other data is often considered a trade secret. Any other competitor has the full right to put together the identical information derived from public sources.

Generally, the trade secret owner's rights are to take action against misappropriation of the information. The term **misappropriation** covers the acquisition of trade secret information by improper means. For example, if a competitor bribes one of your employees to obtain a proprietary computer program or a file with customer and pricing information, the information has clearly been obtained by improper means.

misappropriation. Acquisition of trade secret information by improper means.

Misappropriation also includes use of information in a way that breaches a duty of confidentiality. Thus, if an employee or outsider has a duty of confidentiality by virtue of an agreement of the type described earlier, any breach of the agreement is actionable. Particularly in the case of high-level employees, the duty of confidentiality can arise by implication based on the dealings of the parties.

Profile Perspective: Consider whether the computer program developed by BOS, Inc., is a legitimate trade secret. Are any other aspects of the system pioneered by BOS, Inc., protectible as trade secrets? What steps should Jerry take to protect his trade secret rights, if any?

C. *Copyrights*

copyright. A limited monopoly in an article of copyrightable work.

A **copyright,** like a patent, is a limited monopoly (currently life of the author plus 50 years), which is based on Article I, Section 8 of the U.S. Constitution. Although the Constitution speaks in terms of "writings" and "authors," copyright protection today spans a very broad spectrum of business and the creative arts. Copyright law, like patent law, is governed exclusively by federal statute, the Copyright Act of 1976.[6]

Subject Matter of Copyrights. The statute lists eight specific classes of copyrightable works: literary works; musical works, including any accompanying words; dramatic works, including any accompanying music; choreographic works; pictorial, graphic, and sculptural works; motion pictures and other audiovisual works; sound recordings; and architectural works.[7] At the same time, the statute expressly precludes copyright protection for any idea, procedure, system, method of operation concept, principle, or discovery.[8]

Ownership of Copyrights. Historically, the copyright laws of the United States were based on the idea that the creator (originally, authors, musicians, and artists) had a property right in his or her creation. So, the copyright statutes, like the patent statutes, have always provided that the copyright belongs to the creator of the work. Typically, employers require their employees, particularly those in technical or creative fields, to agree to assign any patents or copyrights they may create during employment to the employer.

Complications arise when the creation is done by an individual who is not an employee in the traditional sense, as in the case of creation of a computer program or advertising program by an outside consultant.

In *Community for Creative Non-Violence* v. *Reid,*[9] the U.S. Supreme Court squarely addressed this issue. CCNV, a nonprofit association dedicated to eliminating homelessness in America, in 1985 decided to sponsor a sculpture to dramatize the plight of the homeless. James Reid worked with the group to create a suitable sculpture. Ultimately, they decided on a modern nativity scene in which the traditional holy-family members appear as contemporary homeless people huddled on a steam grate. The parties agreed that the project should cost no more than $15,000, not including Reid's services, which he agreed to donate. No mention was made of copyright or ownership.

For two months, Reid worked on the sculpture, sometimes with the assistance of personnel from CCNV.

After a public display of the work for about two months, the work was returned to Reid's studio for minor repairs, after which CCNV had plans for an extensive tour. Reid refused, and CCNV sued, demanding return of the work, and a determination of ownership of the copyright.

The Supreme Court ordered Reid to return the work, stating that CCNV had in fact bought and paid for the work itself. However, on the ownership of copyright issue, the Court held that in the case of an individual who is not an employee, and absent any contrary agreement between the parties, the creator owned the copyright. The Court did remand the case to the District Court for a determination as to whether or not CCNV personnel made sufficient contribution to the project that there would be co-ownership of the work.

In many situations, the act of violating a copyright is called by another name: plagiarism. Consider the events that led to the following article.

An Explanation and an Apology

by Mark N. Hornung

Today . . . is my last day as editorial page editor. I owe all of you an explanation.

The morning of February 23, I sat down to write a column I had been researching on the balanced budget amendment. Unfortunately, I had writer's block.

So I walked around, attended the regularly scheduled editorial board meeting, and later tried again. Still, no results. I notified colleagues I would probably miss filing a column that day and attended my other duties.

A short time later, I came across an editorial on the very subject I had researched in the morning's *Washington Post.* With deadline pressures mounting, I began typing the editorial into my computer queue as notes. I then started to write over and around the notes. Determined to meet deadlines and to attend to other responsibilities, I was not mindful that I was breaking the rules of my craft.

That realization came two weeks later. On Tuesday, my editor showed me copies of my column and the *Washington Post* editorial. After retracing my steps, I understood that I had plagiarized.

Horrified and heartbroken that I had put the *Sun-Times* at risk, I immediately offered to resign. I also phoned the editorial page editor of the *Washington Post.* She graciously accepted my apology.

I was born, raised, and educated in Chicago. I have a deep and abiding love for the city and its people. For the last 12 years as a journalist in Chicago, I have been privileged to chronicle the events and people that are vital to our city and our state.

I did so because I enjoyed it and because I have faith in the people of the city and state to improve our communities. My faith remains strong. And I intend to continue my commitments in different but significant ways.

Larry Perrotto, chief executive officer of the *Sun-Times* parent American Publishing Co., has graciously invited me to remain in another capacity outside the editorial department. I don't know what I will do.

* * *

I am very sorry about what I did. In this case, that's not enough.

Continued

Continued

Questions

1. Do you sympathize with Hornung's story? Have you ever found yourself in a similar circumstance?
2. *a.* Do you believe Hornung's story ("Determined to meet deadlines and to attend to other responsibilities, I was not mindful that I was breaking the rules of my craft")?

   b. Do you believe that Hornung should have been fired? What other alternatives did the *Sun-Times* have?
3. How does one prevent this from happening?

Source: "An Explanation and an Apology?" by Mark N. Hornung, *Chicago Sun-Times,* March 10, 1995, p. 29. Reprinted by permission, *Chicago Sun-Times,* copyright © 1995.

Procedure to Obtain a Copyright. The procedure for obtaining a copyright is very different from the procedure involved in patenting an invention. Copyright protection is obtained simply by publication of the work (the actual statutory phrase is "fixed in a tangible medium of expression"[10]), preferably with the statutory notice, which is the word *copyright,* its abbreviation *copr.,* or the international copyright symbol ©, followed by the year of first publication and the name of the owner of the copyright. The copyright is *perfected* by filing an application to register the copyright, along with copies of the work in the Copyright Office in Washington, DC. The Copyright Office is one of the functions of the Library of Congress.

Figure 9.2 is a sample of the first page of copyright "Form VA," which must be filled out and filed to register a copyright in works of the visual arts.

Copyright Owner's Rights. The statute provides that the copyright owner has the exclusive right to do and to authorize reproduction of the copyrighted work, distribution of copies or recordings of the work to the public, and public performance or display of the work.[11]

fair use. A doctrine that permits the use of copyrighted works for purposes such as criticism, news reporting, training, or research.

The major limitation upon the exclusive rights discussed above is the doctrine of **fair use,**[12] which permits use of the copyrighted work for purposes such as criticism, news reporting, teaching, or research. It has been incorporated into the copyright statutes and is discussed in some detail in the case that follows. In *Sony Corp* v. *Universal City Studios, Inc.,* Universal City Studios (respondent) owned the copyrights on a variety of television programs that were broadcast over the public airwaves and brought suit against Sony (petitioner) for copyright infringement. Sony manufactured and sold the Betamax home videotape recorders, called at the time *VTRs.*

Universal argued that customers who had purchased the VTRs had used them to unlawfully record copyrighted programs, and that Sony, because of its marketing of the device, was liable for copyright infringement.

Both parties conducted surveys that showed that the primary use of the machine for most owners was "time-shifting," the practice of recording a program to view it once at a later time and thereafter erasing it. Both surveys also showed, however, that a substantial number of interviewees had accumulated libraries of tapes.

The District Court denied all relief and entered judgment for petitioner. The Court of Appeals for the Ninth Circuit reversed, holding the petitioner liable, and remanded the case to the District Court for determination of appropriate relief. The Supreme Court reversed the Ninth Circuit.

COPYRIGHT FORM VA **FIGURE 9.2**

Filling Out Application Form VA

Detach and read these instructions before completing this form.
Make sure all applicable spaces have been filled in before you return this form.

BASIC INFORMATION

When to Use This Form: Use Form VA for copyright registration of published or unpublished works of the visual arts. This category consists of "pictorial, graphic, or sculptural works," including two-dimensional and three-dimensional works of fine, graphic, and applied art, photographs, prints and art reproductions, maps, globes, charts, technical drawings, diagrams, and models.

What Does Copyright Protect? Copyright in a work of the visual arts protects those pictorial, graphic, or sculptural elements that, either alone or in combination, represent an "original work of authorship." The statute declares: "In no case does copyright protection for an original work of authorship extend to any idea, procedure, process, system, method of operation, concept, principle, or discovery, regardless of the form in which it is described, explained, illustrated, or embodied in such work."

Works of Artistic Craftsmanship and Designs: "Works of artistic craftsmanship" are registrable on Form VA, but the statute makes clear that protection extends to "their form" and not to "their mechanical or utilitarian aspects." The "design of a useful article" is considered copyrightable "only if, and only to the extent that, such design incorporates pictorial, graphic, or sculptural features that can be identified separately from, and are capable of existing independently of, the utilitarian aspects of the article."

Labels and Advertisements: Works prepared for use in connection with the sale or advertisement of goods and services are registrable if they contain "original work of authorship." Use Form VA if the copyrightable material in the work you are registering is mainly pictorial or graphic; use Form TX if it consists mainly of text. **NOTE:** Words and short phrases such as names, titles, and slogans cannot be protected by copyright, and the same is true of standard symbols, emblems, and other commonly used graphic designs that are in the public domain. When used commercially, material of that sort can sometimes be protected under state laws of unfair competition or under the Federal trademark laws. For information about trademark registration, write to the Commissioner of Patents and Trademarks, Washington, D.C. 20231.

Architectural Works: Copyright protection extends to the design of buildings created for the use of human beings. Architectural works created on or after December 1, 1990, or that on December 1, 1990, were unconstructed and embodied only in unpublished plans or drawings are eligible. Request Circular 41 for more information.

Deposit to Accompany Application: An application for copyright registration must be accompanied by a deposit consisting of copies representing the entire work for which registration is to be made.

Unpublished Work: Deposit one complete copy.

Published Work: Deposit two complete copies of the best edition.

Work First Published Outside the United States: Deposit one complete copy of the first foreign edition.

Contribution to a Collective Work: Deposit one complete copy of the best edition of the collective work.

The Copyright Notice: For works first published on or after March 1, 1989, the law provides that a copyright notice in a specified form "may be placed on all publicly distributed copies from which the work can be visually perceived." Use of the copyright notice is the responsibility of the copyright owner and does not require advance permission from the Copyright Office. The required form of the notice for copies generally consists of three elements: (1) the symbol "©", or the word "Copyright," or the abbreviation "Copr."; (2) the year of first publication; and (3) the name of the owner of copyright. For example: "© 1991 Jane Cole." The notice is to be affixed to the copies "in such manner and location as to give reasonable notice of the claim of copyright." Works first published prior to March 1, 1989, **must** carry the notice or risk loss of copyright protection.

For information about notice requirements for works published before March 1, 1989, or other copyright information, write: Information Section, LM-401, Copyright Office, Library of Congress, Washington, D.C. 20559-6000.

LINE-BY-LINE INSTRUCTIONS

Please type or print using black ink.

1 SPACE 1: Title

Title of This Work: Every work submitted for copyright registration must be given a title to identify that particular work. If the copies of the work bear a title (or an identifying phrase that could serve as a title), transcribe that wording *completely* and *exactly* on the application. Indexing of the registration and future identification of the work will depend on the information you give here. For an architectural work that has been constructed, add the date of construction after the title; if unconstructed at this time, add "not yet constructed."

Previous or Alternative Titles: Complete this space if there are any additional titles for the work under which someone searching for the registration might be likely to look, or under which a document pertaining to the work might be recorded.

Publication as a Contribution: If the work being registered is a contribution to a periodical, serial, or collection, give the title of the contribution in the "Title of This Work" space. Then, in the line headed "Publication as a Contribution," give information about the collective work in which the contribution appeared.

Nature of This Work: Briefly describe the general nature or character of the pictorial, graphic, or sculptural work being registered for copyright. Examples: "Oil Painting"; "Charcoal Drawing"; "Etching"; "Sculpture"; "Map"; "Photograph"; "Scale Model"; "Lithographic Print"; "Jewelry Design"; "Fabric Design."

2 SPACE 2: Author(s)

General Instruction: After reading these instructions, decide who are the "authors" of this work for copyright purposes. Then, unless the work is a "collective work," give the requested information about every "author" who contributed any appreciable amount of copyrightable matter to this version of the work. If you need further space, request Continuation Sheets. In the case of a collective work, such as a catalog of paintings or collection of cartoons by various authors, give information about the author of the collective work as a whole.

Name of Author: The fullest form of the author's name should be given. Unless the work was "made for hire," the individual who actually created the work is its "author." In the case of a work made for hire, the statute provides that "the employer or other person for whom the work was prepared is considered the author."

What is a "Work Made for Hire"? A "work made for hire" is defined as: (1) "a work prepared by an employee within the scope of his or her employment"; or (2) " a work specially ordered or commissioned for use as a contribution to a collective work, as a part of a motion picture or other audiovisual work, as a translation, as a supplementary work, as a compilation, as an instructional text, as a test, as answer material for a test, or as an atlas, if the parties expressly agree in a written instrument signed by them that the work shall be considered a work made for hire." If you have checked "Yes" to indicate that the work was "made for hire," you must give the full legal name of the employer (or other person for whom the work was prepared). You may also include the name of the employee along with the name of the employer (for example: "Elster Publishing Co., employer for hire of John Ferguson").

"Anonymous" or "Pseudonymous" Work: An author's contribution to a work is "anonymous" if that author is not identified on the copies or phonorecords of the work. An author's contribution to a work is "pseudonymous" if that author is identified on the copies or phonorecords under a fictitious name. If the work is "anonymous" you may: (1) leave the line blank; or (2) state "anonymous" on the line; or (3) reveal the author's identity. If the work is "pseudonymous" you may: (1) leave the line blank; or (2) give the pseudonym and identify it as such (for example: "Huntley Haverstock, pseudonym"); or (3) reveal the author's name, making clear which is the real name and which is the pseudonym (for example: "Henry Leek, whose pseudonym is Priam Farrel"). However, the citizenship or domicile of the author **must** be given in all cases.

Dates of Birth and Death: If the author is dead, the statute requires that the year of death be included in the application unless the work is anonymous or pseudonymous. The author's birth date is optional but is useful as a form of identification. Leave this space blank if the author's contribution was a "work made for hire."

Author's Nationality or Domicile: Give the country of which the author is a citizen or the country in which the author is domiciled. Nationality or domicile **must** be given in all cases.

FIGURE 9.2 (CONTINUED)

Nature of Authorship: Catagories of pictorial, graphic, and sculptural authorship are listed below. Check the box(es) that best describe(s) each author's contribution to the work.

3-Dimensional sculptures: fine art sculptures, toys, dolls, scale models, and sculptural designs applied to useful articles.

2-Dimensional artwork: watercolor and oil paintings; pen and ink drawings; logo illustrations; greeting cards; collages; stencils; patterns; computer graphics; graphics appearing in screen displays; artwork appearing on posters, calendars, games, commercial prints and labels, and packaging, as well as 2-dimensional artwork applied to useful articles.

Reproductions of works of art: reproductions of preexisting artwork made by, for example, lithography, photoengraving, or etching.

Maps: cartographic representations of an area such as state and county maps, atlases, marine charts, relief maps, and globes.

Photographs: pictorial photographic prints and slides and holograms.

Jewelry designs: 3-dimensional designs applied to rings, pendants, earrings, necklaces, and the like.

Designs on sheetlike materials: designs reproduced on textiles, lace, and other fabrics; wallpaper; carpeting; floor tile; wrapping paper; and clothing.

Technical drawings: diagrams illustrating scientific or technical information in linear form such as architectural blueprints or mechanical drawings.

Text: textual material that accompanies pictorial, graphic, or sculptural works such as comic strips, greeting cards, games rules, commercial prints or labels, and maps.

Architectural works: designs of buildings, including the overall form as well as the arrangement and composition of spaces and elements of the design. **NOTE:** Any registration for the underlying architectural plans must be applied for on a separate Form VA, checking the box "Technical drawing."

3 SPACE 3: Creation and Publication

General Instructions: Do not confuse "creation" with "publication." Every application for copyright registration must state "the year in which creation of the work was completed." Give the date and nation of first publication only if the work has been published.

Creation: Under the statute, a work is "created" when it is fixed in a copy or phonorecord for the first time. Where a work has been prepared over a period of time, the part of the work existing in fixed form on a particular date constitutes the created work on that date. The date you give here should be the year in which the author completed the particular version for which registration is now being sought, even if other versions exist or if further changes or additions are planned.

Publication: The statute defines "publication" as "the distribution of copies or phonorecords of a work to the public by sale or other transfer of ownership, or by rental, lease, or lending"; a work is also "published" if there has been an "offering to distribute copies or phonorecords to a group of persons for purposes of further distribution, public performance, or public display." Give the full date (month, day, year) when, and the country where, publication first occurred. If first publication took place simultaneously in the United States and other countries, it is sufficient to state "U.S.A."

4 SPACE 4: Claimant(s)

Name(s) and Address(es) of Copyright Claimant(s): Give the name(s) and address(es) of the copyright claimant(s) in this work even if the claimant is the same as the author. Copyright in a work belongs initially to the author of the work (including, in the case of a work make for hire, the employer or other person for whom the work was prepared). The copyright claimant is either the author of the work or a person or organization to whom the copyright initially belonging to the author has been transferred.

Transfer: The statute provides that, if the copyright claimant is not the author, the application for registration must contain "a brief statement of how the claimant obtained ownership of the copyright." If any copyright claimant named in space 4 is not an author named in space 2, give a brief statement explaining how the claimant(s) obtained ownership of the copyright. Examples: "By written contract"; "Transfer of all rights by author"; "Assignment"; "By will." Do not attach transfer documents or other attachments or riders.

5 SPACE 5: Previous Registration

General Instructions: The questions in space 5 are intended to find out whether an earlier registration has been made for this work and, if so, whether there is any basis for a new registration. As a rule, only one basic copyright registration can be made for the same version of a particular work.

Same Version: If this version is substantially the same as the work covered by a previous registration, a second registration is not generally possible unless: (1) the work has been registered in unpublished form and a second registration is now being sought to cover this first published edition; or (2) someone other than the author is identified as a copyright claimant in the earlier registration, and the author is now seeking registration in his or her own name. If either of these two exceptions apply, check the appropriate box and give the earlier registration number and date. Otherwise, do not submit Form VA; instead, write the Copyright Office for information about supplementary registration or recordation of transfers of copyright ownership.

Changed Version: If the work has been changed and you are now seeking registration to cover the additions or revisions, check the last box in space 5, give the earlier registration number and date, and complete both parts of space 6 in accordance with the instruction below.

Previous Registration Number and Date: If more than one previous registration has been made for the work, give the number and date of the latest registration.

6 SPACE 6: Derivative Work or Compilation

General Instructions: Complete space 6 if this work is a "changed version," "compilation," or "derivative work," and if it incorporates one or more earlier works that have already been published or registered for copyright, or that have fallen into the public domain. A "compilation" is defined as "a work formed by the collection and assembling of preexisting materials or of data that are selected, coordinated, or arranged in such a way that the resulting work as a whole constitutes an original work of authorship." A "derivative work" is "a work based on one or more preexisting works." Examples of derivative works include reproductions of works of art, sculptures based on drawings, lithographs based on paintings, maps based on previously published sources, or "any other form in which a work may be recast, transformed, or adapted." Derivative works also include works "consisting of editorial revisions, annotations, or other modifications" if these changes, as a whole, represent an original work of authorship.

Preexisting Material (space 6a): Complete this space **and** space 6b for derivative works. In this space identify the preexisting work that has been recast, transformed, or adapted. Examples of preexisting material might be "Grunewald Altarpiece" or "19th century quilt design." Do not complete this space for compilations.

Material Added to This Work (space 6b): Give a brief, general statement of the **additional** new material covered by the copyright claim for which registration is sought. In the case of a derivative work, identify this new material. Examples: "Adaptation of design and additional artistic work"; "Reproduction of painting by photolithography"; "Additional cartographic material"; "Compilation of photographs." If the work is a compilation, give a brief, general statement describing both the material that has been compiled **and** the compilation itself. Example: "Compilation of 19th century political cartoons."

7,8,9 SPACE 7,8,9: Fee, Correspondence, Certification, Return Address

Fee: The Copyright Office has the authority to adjust fees at 5-year intervals, based on changes in the Consumer Price Index. The next adjustment is due in 1996. Please contact the Copyright Office after July 1995 to determine the actual fee schedule.

Deposit Account: If you maintain a Deposit Account in the Copyright Office, identify it in space 7. Otherwise leave the space blank and send the fee of $20 with your application and deposit.

Correspondence (space 7): This space should contain the name, address, area code, and telephone number of the person to be consulted if correspondence about this application becomes necessary.

Certification (space 8): The application cannot be accepted unless it bears the date and the **handwritten signature** of the author or other copyright claimant, or of the owner of exclusive right(s), or of the duly authorized agent of the author, claimant, or owner of exclusive right(s).

Address for Return of Certificate (space 9): The address box must be completed legibly since the certificate will be returned in a window envelope.

PRIVACY ACT ADVISORY STATEMENT Required by the Privacy Act of 1974 (P.L. 93 - 579)
The authority for requesting this information is title 17, U.S.C., secs. 409 and 410. Furnishing the requested information is voluntary. But if the information is not furnished, it may be necessary to delay or refuse registration and you may not be entitled to certain relief, remedies, and benefits provided in chapters 4 and 5 of title 17, U.S.C.
The principal uses of the requested information are the establishment and maintenance of a public record and the examination of the application for compliance with legal requirements.
Other routine uses include public inspection and copying, preparation of public indexes, preparation of public catalogs of copyright registrations, and preparation of search reports upon request.
NOTE: No other advisory statement will be given in connection with this application. Please keep this statement and refer to it if we communicate with you regarding this application.

(CONTINUED) FIGURE 9.2

FORM VA
For a Work of the Visual Arts
UNITED STATES COPYRIGHT OFFICE

REGISTRATION NUMBER

VA VAU

EFFECTIVE DATE OF REGISTRATION

Month Day Year

DO NOT WRITE ABOVE THIS LINE. IF YOU NEED MORE SPACE, USE A SEPARATE CONTINUATION SHEET.

1

TITLE OF THIS WORK ▼ **NATURE OF THIS WORK ▼** See instructions

PREVIOUS OR ALTERNATIVE TITLES ▼

PUBLICATION AS A CONTRIBUTION If this work was published as a contribution to a periodical, serial, or collection, give information about the collective work in which the contribution appeared. **Title of Collective Work ▼**

If published in a periodical or serial give: **Volume ▼** **Number ▼** **Issue Date ▼** **On Pages ▼**

2 a

NAME OF AUTHOR ▼ **DATES OF BIRTH AND DEATH** Year Born ▼ Year Died ▼

Was this contribution to the work a "work made for hire"? ☐ Yes ☐ No

AUTHOR'S NATIONALITY OR DOMICILE Name of Country OR { Citizen of ▶ / Domiciled in ▶

WAS THIS AUTHOR'S CONTRIBUTION TO THE WORK Anonymous? ☐ Yes ☐ No Pseudonymous? ☐ Yes ☐ No — If the answer to either of these questions is "Yes," see detailed instructions.

NATURE OF AUTHORSHIP Check appropriate box(es). **See instructions**
☐ 3-Dimensional sculpture ☐ Map ☐ Technical drawing
☐ 2-Dimensional artwork ☐ Photograph ☐ Text
☐ Reproduction of work of art ☐ Jewelry design ☐ Architectural work
☐ Design on sheetlike material

NOTE
Under the law, the "author" of a "work made for hire" is generally the employer, not the employee (see instructions). For any part of this work that was "made for hire" check "Yes" in the space provided, give the employer (or other person for whom the work was prepared) as "Author" of that part, and leave the space for dates of birth and death blank.

b

NAME OF AUTHOR ▼ **DATES OF BIRTH AND DEATH** Year Born ▼ Year Died ▼

Was this contribution to the work a "work made for hire"? ☐ Yes ☐ No

AUTHOR'S NATIONALITY OR DOMICILE Name of Country OR { Citizen of ▶ / Domiciled in ▶

WAS THIS AUTHOR'S CONTRIBUTION TO THE WORK Anonymous? ☐ Yes ☐ No Pseudonymous? ☐ Yes ☐ No — If the answer to either of these questions is "Yes," see detailed instructions.

NATURE OF AUTHORSHIP Check appropriate box(es). **See instructions**
☐ 3-Dimensional sculpture ☐ Map ☐ Technical drawing
☐ 2-Dimensional artwork ☐ Photograph ☐ Text
☐ Reproduction of work of art ☐ Jewelry design ☐ Architectural work
☐ Design on sheetlike material

3 a

YEAR IN WHICH CREATION OF THIS WORK WAS COMPLETED ◀ Year — **This information must be given in all cases.**

b **DATE AND NATION OF FIRST PUBLICATION OF THIS PARTICULAR WORK** — **Complete this information ONLY if this work has been published.** Month ▶ Day ▶ Year ▶ ◀ Nation

4

COPYRIGHT CLAIMANT(S) Name and address must be given even if the claimant is the same as the author given in space 2. ▼

See instructions before completing this space.

TRANSFER If the claimant(s) named here in space 4 is (are) different from the author(s) named in space 2, give a brief statement of how the claimant(s) obtained ownership of the copyright. ▼

DO NOT WRITE HERE OFFICE USE ONLY
APPLICATION RECEIVED
ONE DEPOSIT RECEIVED
TWO DEPOSITS RECEIVED
FUNDS RECEIVED

MORE ON BACK ▶
• Complete all applicable spaces (numbers 5-9) on the reverse side of this page.
• See detailed instructions. • Sign the form at line 8.

DO NOT WRITE HERE

Page 1 of ______ pages

FIGURE 9.2 **(CONTINUED)**

EXAMINED BY

FORM VA

CHECKED BY

☐ CORRESPONDENCE Yes

FOR COPYRIGHT OFFICE USE ONLY

DO NOT WRITE ABOVE THIS LINE. IF YOU NEED MORE SPACE, USE A SEPARATE CONTINUATION SHEET.

5

PREVIOUS REGISTRATION Has registration for this work, or for an earlier version of this work, already been made in the Copyright Office?

☐ **Yes** ☐ **No** If your answer is "Yes," why is another registration being sought? (Check appropriate box) ▼

a. ☐ This is the first published edition of a work previously registered in unpublished form.

b. ☐ This is the first application submitted by this author as copyright claimant.

c. ☐ This is a changed version of the work, as shown by space 6 on this application.

If your answer is "Yes," give: **Previous Registration Number** ▼ **Year of Registration** ▼

6

DERIVATIVE WORK OR COMPILATION Complete both space 6a and 6b for a derivative work; complete only 6b for a compilation.

a. Preexisting Material Identify any preexisting work or works that this work is based on or incorporates. ▼

See instructions before completing this space.

b. Material Added to This Work Give a brief, general statement of the material that has been added to this work and in which copyright is claimed. ▼

7

DEPOSIT ACCOUNT If the registration fee is to be charged to a Deposit Account established in the Copyright Office, give name and number of Account.

Name ▼ **Account Number** ▼

CORRESPONDENCE Give name and address to which correspondence about this application should be sent. Name/Address/Apt/City/State/ZIP ▼

Area Code and Telephone Number ▶

Be sure to give your daytime phone ◀ number

8

CERTIFICATION* I, the undersigned, hereby certify that I am the

check only one ▼

☐ author

☐ other copyright claimant

☐ owner of exclusive right(s)

☐ authorized agent of ________________

Name of author or other copyright claimant, or owner of exclusive right(s) ▲

of the work identified in this application and that the statements made by me in this application are correct to the best of my knowledge.

Typed or printed name and date ▼ If this application gives a date of publication in space 3, do not sign and submit it before that date.

Date▶

Handwritten signature (X) ▼

9

MAIL CERTIFICATE TO

Name ▼

Number/Street/Apt ▼

City/State/ZIP ▼

Certificate will be mailed in window envelope

YOU MUST:
- Complete all necessary spaces
- Sign your application in space 8

SEND ALL 3 ELEMENTS IN THE SAME PACKAGE:
1. Application form
2. Nonrefundable $20 filing fee in check or money order payable to *Register of Copyrights*
3. Deposit material

MAIL TO:
Register of Copyrights
Library of Congress
Washington, D.C. 20559-6000

The Copyright Office has the authority to adjust fees at 5-year intervals, based on changes in the Consumer Price Index. The next adjustment is due in 1996. Please contact the Copyright Office after July 1995 to determine the actual fee schedule.

*17 U.S.C. § 506(e): Any person who knowingly makes a false representation of a material fact in the application for copyright registration provided for by section 409, or in any written statement filed in connection with the application, shall be fined not more than $2,500.

July 1993—300,000 PRINTED ON RECYCLED PAPER ☆U.S. GOVERNMENT PRINTING OFFICE: 1993-342-582/80,021

CASE

Sony Corp v. Universal City Studios, Inc.

464 U.S. 417 (1984)

Justice Stevens (joined by Justices Burger, Brennan, White, and O'Connor)

Copyright protection "subsists . . . in original works of authorship fixed in any tangible medium of expression" . . . This protection has never accorded the copyright owner complete control over all possible uses of his work. Rather, the copyright act grants the copyright holder "exclusive" rights to use and to authorize the use of his work in five qualified ways, including reproduction of the copyrighted work in copies . . . All reproductions of the work, however, are not within the exclusive domain of the copyright owner; some are in the public domain.

* * *

Even unauthorized uses of a copyrighted work are not necessarily infringing . . . Sections 107 through 118 . . . describe a variety of uses of copyrighted material that "are not infringements of copyright" . . . The most pertinent in this case is §107, the legislative endorsement of the doctrine of "fair use."

That section identifies various factors that enable a court to apply an "equitable rule of reason" analysis to particular claims of infringement. Although not conclusive, the first factor requires that "the commercial or nonprofit character of an activity" be weighed in any fair use decision. If the Betamax were used to make copies for commercial or profitmaking purpose, such use would presumptively be unfair. The contrary presumption is appropriate here, however, because the District Court's findings plainly establish that time-shifting for private home use must be characterized as a noncommercial nonprofit activity. Moreover, when one considers the nature of a televised copyrighted audiovisual work, . . . time-shifting merely enable[s] a viewer to see such a work which he had been invited to witness in its entirety free of charge . . .

This is not, however, the end of the inquiry because Congress has also directed us to consider "the effect of the use upon the potential market for or value of the copyrighted work" . . . The purpose of copyright is to create incentives for creative effort. Even copying for noncommercial purposes may impair the copyright holder's ability to obtain the rewards that Congress intended him to have. But a use that has no demonstrable effect upon the potential market for, or the value of, the copyrighted work need not be prohibited in order to protect the author's incentive to create.

Thus, although every commercial use of copyrighted material is presumptively an unfair exploitation of the monopoly privilege that belongs to the owner of the copyright, noncommercial uses are a different matter . . . What is necessary is a showing by a preponderance of the evidence that *some* meaningful likelihood of future harm exists. If the intended use is for commercial gain, that likelihood may be presumed. But if it is for a noncommercial purpose, the likelihood must be demonstrated.

In this case, respondents failed to carry their burden with regard to home time-shifting.

* * *

Justice Blackmun, dissenting (joined by Justices Marshall, Powell, and Rehnquist)

The doctrine of fair use has been called, with some justification, "the most troublesome in the whole law of copyright" . . . Despite the absence of clear standards, the fair use doctrine plays a crucial role in the law of copyright. The purpose of copyright protection, in the words of the

Continued

Continued

Constitution, is to "promote the Progress of Science and the useful Arts." Copyright is based on the belief that by granting authors the exclusive rights to reproduce their works, they are given an incentive to create, and that "encouragement of individual effort by personal gain is the best way to advance public welfare through the talents of authors and inventors in 'Science and the useful Arts' " . . .

There are situations, nevertheless, in which strict enforcement of this monopoly would inhibit the very "Progress of Science and the useful Arts" that copyright is intended to promote. An obvious example is the researcher or scholar whose own work depends on the ability to refer to and to quote the work of prior scholars. . . But there is a crucial difference between the scholar and the ordinary user. When the scholar forgoes the use of a prior work, not only does his own work suffer, but the public is deprived of his contribution to knowledge. The scholar's work, in other words, produces external benefits from which everyone profits.

* * *

The making of a videotape recording for home viewing is an ordinary rather than a productive use of the Studios' copyrighted works . . . Copyright gives the author a right to limit or even to cut off access to his work . . . A VTR recording creates no public benefit sufficient to justify limiting this right . . .

It may be tempting . . . to stretch the doctrine of fair use so as to permit unfettered use of this new technology in order to increase access to television programming. But such an extension risks eroding the very basis of copyright law, by depriving authors of control over their works and consequently of their incentive to create.

Questions

1. As a dedicated fan of professional football in general, you have taped the last 10 Super Bowls. A friend is planning a Super Bowl party and has offered you $50 for the use of those tapes at the party. Have you infringed the NFL's copyright?
2. Go Video, Inc., has developed and offers for sale a two-cassette VCR intended for professional editors and studios that makes it easier for them to edit their productions. It just so happens that this machine makes it awfully easy to copy from one videotape to another. A friend has proposed that the two of you purchase a unit, and pay for it by duplicating and selling rented videos to your classmates. Is this legal? Would you participate?
3. How would your world be different today if Sony had won this case?

Assignment and licensing of copyrights is very much like assignment and licensing of patents. An assignment transfers ownership, and a license grants rights to use. Like patents, the various exclusive rights granted by the statute may be divided up in licensing arrangements. For example, to include in this book a number of articles and excerpts from articles, it was necessary for the publisher to obtain a license to use these writings. Sometimes in exchange for a citation, other times for a small monetary payment, the copyright owners were willing to license the right to publish the writing to the publisher of this text. That license includes the right to publish in this text and this text alone.

The copyright statute provides one major exception to the general rules of licensing. Its "compulsory licensing provisions" state that if the owner of a music copyright permits a recording to be made and distributed, then anyone is free to make his or her own recording, provided the copier pays the royalty specified by statute.[13]

The statutory remedies for copyright infringement include actual damages to the copyright holder, profits of the infringer, temporary and permanent injunctive relief, and impoundment and disposition (usually destruction) of the infringing articles.[14]

Profile Perspective: While the outside consulting firm was developing the computer program, Jerry's own marketing staff at BOS, Inc., developed a marketing program. Marketing brochures were designed, created, and mailed to all existing customers, and more than 10,000 additional copies were mailed to prospective accounts. What, if any, of the work done by Jerry's organization can be copyrighted? Consider specifically the computer program and marketing materials. Who owns the copyright in the computer program?

D. Trademarks and Service Marks

Subject Matter of Trademarks. Although patents and copyrights have their origin in the U.S. Constitution and both remain in the exclusive domain of federal statutory law, trademarks are different in that they originated in the common law and involve both federal and state law. Federal involvement with trademarks is, however, limited to cases involving or affecting interstate commerce. (Note that, in today's technologically advanced world, almost all businesses affect interstate commerce. As long as a company has an e-mail account or uses the Internet to market its goods or services, it may be considered to affect interstate commerce. Courts have yet to rule on this recent development.)

The federal law of trademarks is codified in the Lanham Act,[15] which defines a **trademark** as "any word, name, symbol, or device or any combination thereof adopted and used by a manufacturer or merchant to identify his goods and distinguish them from those manufactured or sold by others." For example, consider the following list of trademarks: Old Spice®, Kool-Aid®, Tylenol®, Kleenex®, Q-tips®, and Listerine®. In all likelihood, you recognize all of them immediately and probably can identify the specific product or product line on which they appear. Can you name the company that produces each of them?[16]

trademark. Any word, name, symbol, or device or any combination of these items that has been adopted and used by a merchant or manufacturer to identify its goods.

These trademarks are identifiable and carry with them some concept of quality and performance. Even if you do not know the specific manufacturer, you buy the brand because of its known reputation for quality. Thus, the trademark is the basis for the purchase decision.

A trademark is typically a word or symbol applied to or used in association with a product; a service mark is a word or symbol applied to or used in association with a service. For example, FTD is a registered service mark for the service of providing flowers by wire in another city. It is common to use the word *trademark* for both trademarks and service marks.

At the state level, trademark laws vary rather widely. Many states offer broad protection, whereas others offer much more limited protection. State protection is operative only within the bounds of a given state; hence, all but local companies opt for federal trademark protection. The balance of our discussion of trademarks will be limited to the Lanham Act and the federal law of trademarks.

Classification of Trademarks. Trademarks can be categorized in several ways: by form (word marks, symbol or design marks, or composite marks), by use (on a product, on a service, or as a certification), or by relative strength. It is this last classification that is most important to the businessperson in understanding the nature and scope of trademark protection.

generic mark. A trademark employing a common descriptive name for a product.

A **generic mark** is one employing the common descriptive name for a product. For example, the term *carbonated* is the generic term for a beverage having carbonation. We know what carbonated means because everyone uses it to mean the same thing. Although a company could also use the descriptive term *contains carbonation,* carbonated is still protected. No one is permitted to have exclusive rights to a generic term.

descriptive mark. A trademark that is merely descriptive of the product or its qualities.

A **descriptive mark** is one that is merely descriptive of the product or qualities of the product to which it is applied. For example, a bakery might employ the trademark "oven-fresh" on its goods. Because the term *oven-fresh* is simply descriptive of the qualities of baked goods, it would be unfair to permit any one merchant to develop exclusive rights in the mark. Thus, anyone in the bakery business is free to use this descriptive term. A merchant can use such a phrase as a trademark, but will be unable to develop any exclusive rights in the mark.

suggestive mark. A trademark that suggests the product or its qualities, more than merely descriptive.

A **suggestive mark** is one that may suggest the product or the qualities of the product to which it is applied, but yet is not merely descriptive of that product. The courts say that if a term requires imagination, thought, or perception to reach a conclusion as to the nature of the goods, it is suggestive. For example, the Second Circuit Court of Appeals held that "Roach Motel" was a suggestive mark when used on an insect trap.[17]

arbitrary trademark. A trademark that is a new word or a common word that bears no relation to the product to which it is applied.

A trademark is considered **arbitrary** if it is a new word, or if it is a common word that has no relation whatsoever to the product to which it is applied. For example, the well-known trademark Kodak® is arbitrary. It is a combination of five letters that has no independent meaning at all. A more subtle example would be Ivory®. You can look in any dictionary and find a number of standard definitions for the word *ivory.* However, as applied to soap, the mark is considered arbitrary. In the trademark sense, arbitrary trademarks are the strongest.

The trademark statute provides that a mark that is not arbitrary may be registered only if it can be shown that "the mark has become distinctive of applicant's goods in commerce."[18] Such a showing is called *secondary meaning.* In reality, it means that through widespread, continuous, and exclusive use, a particular mark has developed a new or secondary meaning, which serves to identify the specific goods of a particular merchant. The Owens-Corning case later in this chapter discusses secondary meaning.

There is a unique and fascinating marketing/legal problem associated with extensive (and successful) advertising of a trademark. That is, the advertising program can be too successful, and the trademark can become so well known that it becomes the generic name for a product or service. For instance, Xerox was a totally arbitrary name for a new copying process. Because they were so successful, Xerox Corporation became extremely concerned that other copier companies would begin to use the term *xerox* as a generic term to describe a copying machine. We use the word sometimes even to actually describe the act of copying. (Have you ever said, "I need to xerox this paper"?) In an effort to avoid this genericizing of its brand name, Xerox began to use the words "Xerox brand copiers" in all of its marketing materials rather than simply Xerox.

This concern has not yet abated, as evidenced by these Internet queries sent on August 28, 1995, to an Internet list-server that focuses on economics and the law:

> I've been reading a draft of the new Cooter and Ulen law and economics text. They have a good discussion of intellectual property, and one thing they mention is that Coca Cola protects its trademark by sending agents to restaurants and asking for "a Coke." If they are served Pepsi, they threaten to sue, and often do sue.
>
> Xerox, Kleenex, and so forth are also products whose brand names are really product names by now. The problem is that nobody has incentive to pay to win the test case for opening up the name to free use.

QUESTION: Could such a suit be launched by entrepreneurial lawyers as a class action suit, on behalf of (*a*) customers, (*b*) potential competitors, or (*c*) the restaurants serving cola drinks? Would this be profitable?

Professor ________________, Bloomington, Indiana

I am troubled by ________'s latest . . . Regarding a class action suit to "open up" a trademark, I have a problem with that. We grant trademarks because we believe they serve a valid purpose. Imagine that I trademark "ggffgg" for my product. Now, if public lawsuits to "open up" the trademark are likely to win, then a competitor has an interest in converting "ggffgg" into a common noun, and might do so by inducing writers, and others, to so use it. Would you then permit a suit to open it up to succeed—I don't think so.

Associate Professor ________________, The Law Center,
University of Southern California

Coke, Xerox, Kleenex, and other companies put a lot of effort into trying to keep their trademarked names from falling into public domain usage. Is there some reason why this causes harm—do people really have trouble realizing that Canon makes copiers, or Pepsi makes cola, or Curad makes adhesive bandages, or that Novell offers a DOS that competes with MS-DOS? I see no evident harm, and am therefore puzzled as to why ______________ is interested in suing people?

Unidentified professor, Columbia University Law School

I had occasion to do some training at Xerox's Palo Alto Research Center. When one of the participants (not a Xerox employee) suggested that we could get something Xeroxed, the Xerox employees rebuked him . . . I would have thought they would be happy to have their name be a synonym for a much-purchased product.

Professor ________________, Director, Willamette
University Center for Dispute Resolution

Questions

1. Also consider such generic-type brand names as Band-Aid®, Kleenex®, and Kool-Aid®. Do you use these terms only to describe the branded products that they represent or to describe the generic items?
2. What are the appropriate answers to the questions posed by the first e-mail above?
3. Consider the final point above. Should a company be pleased that individuals use its brand name, such as Xerox, as a household name? Explain.

Federal Registration. Under common law, trademark rights were acquired by adopting a mark and applying it to goods sold in the trade. As originally codified in the Lanham Act, use of the mark in commerce was required before an application could be filed to register the mark.

The Lanham Act provided for registration of trademarks in the United States Patent Office. Once an application for registration is filed, the Patent Office examines it to be sure that all statutory conditions are met. Specifically, the Patent Office ensures that generic marks are not registered and that nonarbitrary marks are registered only if an appropriate showing of secondary meaning is provided.

A federal registration of a trademark is valid for 10 years, but it is renewable indefinitely, so long as the owner continues to use the mark and files the appropriate application for renewal.

The following case is interesting, both for its discussion of the concept of secondary meaning and for the public policy implications of the ability of a specific entity to register and acquire exclusive rights in a color as a trademark.

CASE

In re Owens-Corning Fiberglas Corp.

774 F.2d 1116 (Fed. Cir. 1985)

Owens-Corning filed an application to register the color "pink" as a trademark for the company's fibrous glass residential insulation. The Examiner's denial of registration was affirmed by the Trademark Trial and Appeal Board, and Owens-Corning appealed to the Court of Appeals for the Federal Circuit. Reversed.

* * *

Newman, Circuit Judge

The principal purpose of the Lanham Act was the modernization of trademark law, to facilitate commerce and to protect the consumer . . . Section 45 of the Act defines "trademark" to include "any word, name, symbol, or device or any combination thereof adopted and used by a manufacturer or merchant to identify his goods and distinguish them from those manufactured or sold by others."

* * *

Registration has been granted, for example, for containers, product configurations, packaging, . . . slogans, sounds, ornamental labels, and goods which take the form of the mark itself. The jurisprudence under the Lanham Act developed in accordance with the statutory principle that if a mark is capable of being or becoming distinctive of applicant's goods in commerce, then it is capable of serving as a trademark.

* * *

The Supreme Court has stated "a product feature is functional if it is essential to the use or purpose of the article or it affects the cost or quality of the article . . . The court looked at the following factors to determine functionality: (1) whether a particular design yields a utilitarian advantage, (2) whether alternative designs are available in order to avoid hindering competition, and (3) whether the design achieves economies in manufacture or use.

No argument has been raised that the color "pink" for OCF's fibrous glass residential insulation violates any of these factors, or that alternative, equally arbitrary designs are not available to other producers of fibrous glass insulation.

* * *

Continued

Continued

We conclude that OCF's use of the color "pink" performs no non-trademark function, and is consistent with the commercial and public purposes of trademarks. A pink color mark registered for fibrous glass insulation does not confer a "monopoly" or act as a barrier to entry in the market. It has no relationship to production of fibrous glass insulation. It serves the classical trademark function of indicating the origin of the goods, and thereby protects the public . . .

That a trademark confers no monopoly was settled by the Supreme Court . . . "[T]he right to a particular mark grows out of its use, not its mere adoption; its function is simply to designate the goods as the product of a particular trader and to protect his good will against the sale of another's product as his . . .

"In truth, a trademark confers no monopoly whatever in the proper sense, but is merely a convenient means for facilitating the protection of one's goodwill in trade by placing a distinguishing mark or symbol—a commercial signature—upon the merchandise or the package in which it is sold."

OCF's "pink" color mark performs this role. It gives "the public a reliable indication of source and thus facilitates responsible marketplace competition."

* * *

II

OCF argues that the color "pink" has become distinctive of its insulation by virtue of exclusive and continuous use since 1956, and has acquired a secondary meaning in the marketplace.

* * *

An evidentiary showing of secondary meaning, adequate to show that a mark has acquired distinctiveness indicating the origin of the goods, includes evidence of the trademark owner's method of using the mark, supplemented by evidence of the effectiveness of such use to cause the purchasing public to identify the mark with the source of the product.

* * *

OCF submitted extensive affidavit, and documentary evidence. Joseph Doherty, OCF's Vice President of Marketing Communications, averred that OCF has advertised the "pink" color mark as applied to fibrous glass residential insulation since 1956; that OCF spent approximately $42,000,000 on consumer advertising in the media of television, radio, newspapers, and consumer magazines during the period of 1972 through 1981, with an estimated expenditure of $11,400,000 in 1981 alone.

* * *

The record contains detailed storyboards for two different commercials aired during this time period featuring the "Pink Panther," a pink cartoon character promoting the use of "pink" Owens-Corning Fiberglas insulation. The narration for these commercials discusses how homeowners can cut the high cost of fuel if they would only "[a]dd another layer of pink" in their attics. The scenes emphasize the distinctive "pink" color of OCF's product and reinforce the image with the slogan "Put your house in the pink."

* * *

In addition, the record contains consumer survey evidence. This survey was conducted to enable OCF to evaluate an advertising program, but its data are pertinent to the issue. In June 1980, male homeowners were asked the question "To the best of your knowledge, what manufacturer makes pink insulation?" Forty-one percent responded with applicant's name . . . A similar survey in January 1981, after the first Pink Panther television commercial blitz, showed that applicant's recognition rate had increased to 50 percent.

Continued

Continued

* * *

The requirements of the statute having been met, OCF is entitled to register its mark.

Questions

1. Harley-Davidson, alleging that its 45-degree V-twin single crankpin motorcycle engine has a very distinctive sound, has filed an application to register the sound, pure and simple, as a trademark. What action would you expect the Trademark Office to take on this application? (See following article.)
2. As a competitor to Owens-Corning, you have decided to enter the residential fiberglass insulation market. Is it ethical for you to select a pink for your product, which while clearly pink is equally clearly a different pink from that used by Owens-Corning? Would your answer be different if your product were sold strictly to the commercial insulation market?
3. Why is functionality, or nonfunctionality, an important aspect of this case?

Afterword

The U.S. Supreme Court has recently confirmed the rule that use of a color, pure and simple, can function as a trademark. [*Qualitex* v. *Jacobson Products Co., Inc.,* 115 S. Ct. 1300, 131 L.Ed.2d 248 (1995).]

When the examiner is satisfied with the application, the mark is published for opposition in the *Official Gazette.* The *Official Gazette,* a publication of the U.S. Patent and Trademark Office, in one section lists all marks that have been passed by the trademark examiners, and anyone who sees potential damage by registration of the mark is entitled to file an opposition. This is a contested administrative proceeding, adjudicated by the Trademark Trial and Appeal Board (TTAB) within the Patent and Trademark Office. Appeals from the TTAB are to the federal court system.

The amendments to the Lanham Act in 1988 provided, for the first time, an opportunity to register a mark based upon a bona fide "intent to use."[19] This provision had been widely sought by major corporations that wished to establish their trademark position prior to actually putting a product on the market with a new trademark.

Figure 9.3 is a sample of the written application to register a hypothetical trademark based upon intent to use. Figures 9.4 and 9.5 are attachments to that application.

Trademark Owner's Rights. Registration provides many major advantages to the trademark owner. First, it provides constructive notice to the entire country of the trademark user's claim to rights in the mark.[20] In other words, if a small firm starts operations in the Pacific Northwest, registration will give the firm nationwide protection for its mark. Second, upon the user's filing of certain affidavits after six years of continuous use following registration, the mark becomes incontestable, which gives the owner significant procedural advantages in enforcing rights in the mark. And finally, the statutory remedies become available in enforcement.

Under the Lanham Act, the trademark owner can bring an action for infringement seeking the statutory remedies of treble damages, attorney fees, and destruction of infringing labels.[21]

SAMPLE WRITTEN APPLICATION BASED ON INTENT TO USE IN COMMERCE (ONE CLASS) **FIGURE 9.3**

TRADEMARK/SERVICE MARK APPLICATION, PRINCIPAL REGISTER, WITH DECLARATION	MARK (Word(s) and/or Design) 1 THEORYTEC	CLASS NO. 2 (If known) 9

TO THE ASSISTANT SECRETARY AND COMMISSIONER OF PATENTS AND TRADEMARKS:

APPLICANT'S NAME: A-OK Software Development Group 3

APPLICANT'S BUSINESS ADDRESS: 100 Main Street 4
(Display address exactly as it should appear on registration) Anytown, Missouri 12345

APPLICANT'S ENTITY TYPE: (Check one and supply requested information)

	Individual - Citizen of (Country): 5a
X	Partnership - State where organized (Country, if appropriate): Missouri 5b Names and Citizenship (Country) of General Partners: Mary Baker, citizen of the USA; Harry Parker, citizen of the USA; and Jane Witlow, citizen of the USA
	Corporation - State (Country, if appropriate) of Incorporation: 5c
	Other (Specify Nature of Entity and Domicile): 5d

GOODS AND/OR SERVICES:

Applicant requests registration of the trademark/service mark shown in the accompanying drawing in the United States Patent and Trademark Office on the Principal Register established by the Act of July 5, 1946 (15 U.S.C. 1051 et. seq., as amended) for the following goods/services (SPECIFIC GOODS AND/OR SERVICES MUST BE INSERTED HERE):
Computer software for analyzing statistics 6

BASIS FOR APPLICATION: (Check boxes which apply, but never both the first AND second boxes, and supply requested information related to each box checked.)

[ ] 7(a)	Applicant is using the mark in commerce on or in connection with the above identified goods/services. (15 U.S.C. 1051(a), as amended.) Three specimens showing the mark as used in commerce are submitted with this application. •Date of first use of the mark in commerce which the U.S. Congress may regulate (for example, interstate or between the U.S. and a foreign country): •Specify the type of commerce: (for example, interstate or between the U.S. and a specified foreign country) •Date of first use anywhere (the same as or before use in commerce date): •Specify manner or mode of use of mark on or in connection with the goods/services: (for example, trademark is applied to labels, service mark is used in advertisements)
[X] 7(b)	Applicant has a bona fide intention to use the mark in commerce on or in connection with the above identified goods/services. (15 U.S.C. 1051(b), as amended.) •Specify intended manner or mode of use of mark on or in connection with the goods/services: On labels affixed to the software (for example, trademark will be applied to labels, service mark will be used in advertisements)
[ ] 7(c)	Applicant has a bona fide intention to use the mark in commerce on or in connection with the above identified goods/services, and asserts a claim of priority based upon a foreign application in accordance with 15 U.S.C. 1126(d), as amended. • Country of foreign filing: • Date of foreign filing:
[ ] 7(d)	Applicant has a bona fide intention to use the mark in commerce on or in connection with the above identified goods/services and, accompanying this application, submits a certification or certified copy of a foreign registration in accordance with 15 U.S.C. 1126(e), as amended. • Country of registration: • Registration number:

NOTE: Declaration, on Reverse Side, MUST be Signed

...ents and the like so made are
...001, and that such willful false
...resulting registration, declares
...behalf of the applicant:
.../service mark sought to be
...1051(b), he/she believes
...best of his/her knowledge and
...right to use the above
...of or in such near resemblance
...goods/services of such other
person, to cause confusion, or to cause mistake, or to deceive; and that all statements made of his/her own knowledge are true and that all statements made on information and belief are believed to be true.

February 2, 1992 DATE	Mary Baker 8 SIGNATURE
(123) 456-7890 TELEPHONE NUMBER	Mary Baker, General Partner PRINT OR TYPE NAME AND POSITION

13

FIGURE 9.4 **SAMPLE DRAWING—TYPEWRITTEN**

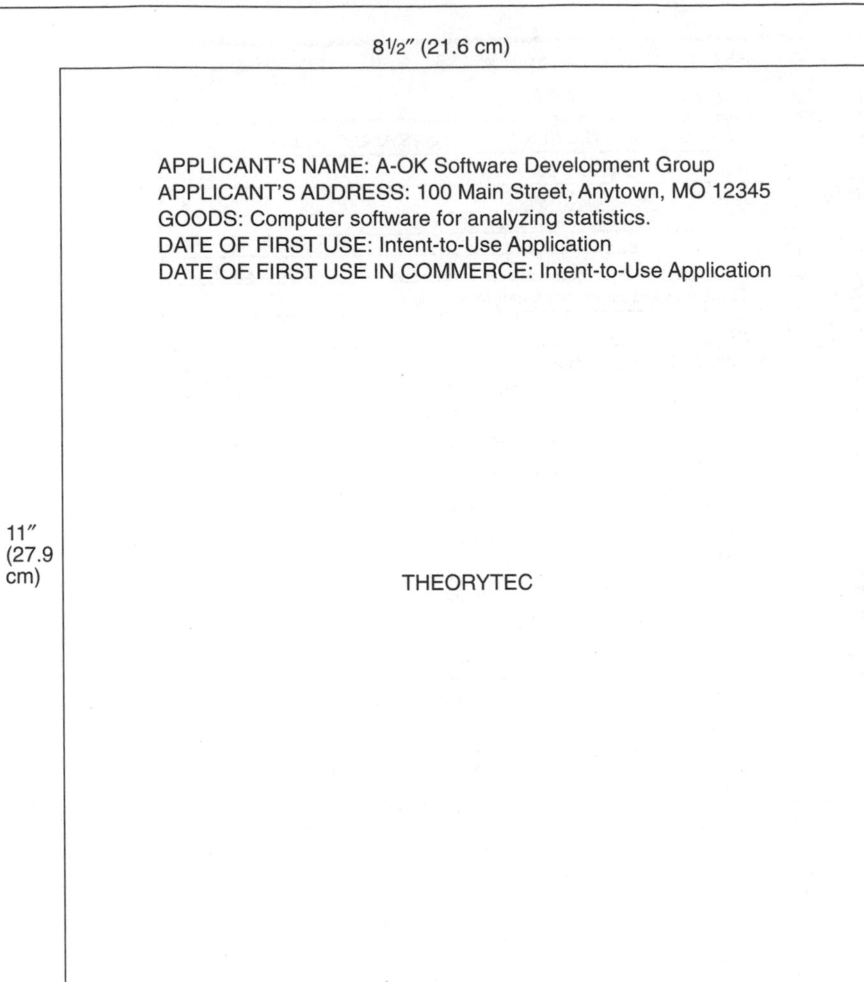

The fundamental issue in a trademark infringement action is *likelihood of confusion.* Where the marks are the same, and the goods on which they are used are the same, the issue is clear. However, when either the marks or the goods are different, the issue becomes much more difficult, and taken into account are the strength of the mark, the similarity of the marks, the similarity of the goods upon which the marks are used, the similarity of the channels of distribution, and evidence, if any, of actual confusion. For example, Coca-Cola was able to stop a competitor from using the mark "LeCoq" on soft drinks.[22] Even though the marks look different, they sound very similar, and Coke® is a very strong mark. The owner of the mark Johnny Walker® for whiskey was able to stop use of the identical mark on cigars.[23] Again, the court found the mark to be very strong and accorded protection, even though the goods were very dissimilar.

Rights under a trademark can be licensed or assigned, but the process is more difficult than simply licensing or assigning a patent or copyright. You will recall that a trademark is the commercial signature of the owner. Therefore, in the case of a licensing transaction, the owner must maintain absolute control of the specification and

SAMPLE SPECIMENS FOR GOODS (LABEL AFFIXED TO COMPUTER DISK) FIGURE 9.5

quality of the licensed product or service. In the case of an assignment of rights under a trademark, the assignment document must also assign all the goodwill of the business associated with the mark.

Profile Perspective: Jerry's marketing staff decided to call their online catalog and ordering system "Supplies on Call" and adopted the slogan "A whole warehouse on your Desk." Can BOS, Inc., register the name "Supplies on Call" as a trademark? Can BOS, Inc., register the slogan "A whole warehouse on your desk" as a trademark? What protection will BOS, Inc., have if it does not apply for or obtain federal registration of either or both the name and slogan?

III. Emerging Issues

A. Protection of Computer Programs

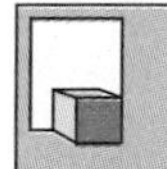

As we have seen, the idea of property rights in intellectual property, at least in the United States, dates from our Constitution. Technology at that time was pretty simple by current standards, and writings meant just that. How do we adapt the classical concepts of patents and copyrights to the tremendous advances in technology that are taking place at an ever-increasing rate? One of the most interesting questions revolves around the protection of computer programs. Should they be protectible? If so, what form of intellectual property protection makes for the best fit? And finally, just what is protected?

> Kevin D. Mitnick, 31 years old, stands accused of breaking into dozens of corporate computers, pilfering thousands of credit-card records, and stealing a fortune in software. Yet to his fans on the Internet, Mr. Mitnick is a "legend," a "technology-wielding genius," and a "hero."[24]

A computer program is nothing more than a series of instructions, telling a computer what to do. Computer experts talk in terms of *source code* (a series of instructions written in a form that can be read by a human being) and *object code,* those same instructions as they exist within the computer. Typically, programming languages (such as BASIC, COBOL, or FORTRAN) use words and symbols that are similar to English and clearly understandable to a programmer. A *compiler* is a very sophisticated program that takes the source code written in BASIC and translates it into object code or instructions as to settings of the switches in the computer.

A computer program could be patented if it met the requirements set out earlier in this chapter. That is, it must be related to patentable subject matter, and then it must be new and nonobvious. Under the language of the *Chakrabarty* case, a person can patent "anything under the sun made by man." It seems pretty clear that computer programs are patentable subject matter. Recent cases have indeed held that computer programs are patentable.[25]

However, the questions of newness and nonobviousness are much more difficult. To the extent that a computer program contains, for example, a series of instructions for alphabetizing a series of names in a database, what is new? In a word-processing program, setting margins or line spacing is nothing more than what has been done on a manual typewriter for many years. Thus, the only computer programs that are patentable are those that, like any other application for patent, are based upon something truly new and would not have been obvious to the skilled worker in the art.

The difficulties in obtaining patent protection have led software companies to explore the use of copyright as a vehicle for protecting their software. The source code could be copyrighted as a writing. But when you go to the computer store and buy a new program, you do not get the source code. Typically, you get a diskette that contains the object code. If the producer has copyrighted the source code, does that cover the object code?

To many in the field, the most important issue is the scope of the resulting copyright. If the copyright protects only the exact words of the source code, it would be extremely easy for a competitor to make minor modifications and get around the grant of exclusivity of the owner. However, the statute expressly provides that ideas and concepts cannot be appropriated exclusively.

B. Intellectual Property and the Internet

One of the biggest new frontiers in the arena of intellectual property is the Internet. The following short piece lays out the fundamental problem:

> Throughout the time I've been groping around cyberspace, an immense, unsolved conundrum has remained at the root of nearly every legal, ethical, governmental,

> and social vexation to be found in the virtual world. I refer to the problem of digitized property. The enigma is this: If our property can be infinitely reproduced and instantaneously distributed all over the planet without cost, without our knowledge, without its even leaving our possession, how can we protect it? How are we going to get paid for the work we do with our minds? And, if we can't get paid, what will assure the continued creation and distribution of such work?
>
> Since we don't have a solution to what is a profoundly new kind of challenge, and are apparently unable to delay the galloping digitization of everything not obstinately physical, we are sailing into the future on a sinking ship.[26]

This describes the emergence of the World Wide Web and the explosion of communication on the Internet. As pointed out above, a work on the Internet can be reproduced forever, with no control or even knowledge by the author. All kinds of proposals have been suggested, but the problem is so new and has arisen so quickly that it is impossible to predict at this time just what way the law will go.

C. International Protection of Intellectual Property and GATT

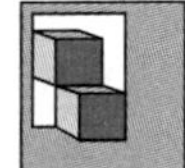

At the outset of this chapter, we noted that the concept of property rights in intellectual property is much stronger in our Western civilization. The following article briefly describes the magnitude of the business problem the differing views of intellectual property create.

Modern-Day Pirates Steal U.S. Ideas

Pirates still sail the waters of the South China Sea, but the most profitable piracy is on land.

Last year, American companies lost an estimated $3.1 billion in Asian business because of intellectual piracy, patent violations, and counterfeiting of American products.

Worldwide, the United States' loss is estimated at $8.1 billion, according to the Washington-based International Intellectual Property Alliance.

By far the biggest American losers in Asia are computer software makers, who lost an estimated $2 billion in 1993. Asian pirating of U.S. music tapes and CDs totaled $478 million last year, and Hollywood lost $357 million to illegal videotape sales.

But stopping intellectual property violations—or even defining the problem—is not easy, warned Charles McManis, Washington University law professor. Citing industry figures, McManis said U.S. companies estimate about a quarter of their exports involve intellectual property. But he warned the figures are soft.

Experts said the problem of intellectual theft varies greatly from country to country. But most said China posed a growing problem. "The Chinese actually have some nice-looking laws," said William P. Alford, director of East Asian Legal Studies at Harvard Law School. "But the problem comes in enforcement," he said. "In my view, the [Chinese officials] lack a respect for the rule of law, lack a consciousness about the rights of people and have a weak court system." Alford said many of China's

Continued

...retired army sergeants who have no legal ...g. Corruption—at all levels of government, ...iness, and the legal system—is pandemic in China. This works against strong patent and copyright laws and enforcement.

But McManis does see slow progress in other Asian nations. "Taiwan is the most advanced—since they started implementing the changes in about 1986. South Korea is about three or four years behind."

Alford agrees. He said South Korea, Taiwan, and Singapore seem more serious about protecting patents and copyrights. "The U.S. Trade Representative Office will tell you this is because we have been beating them over the head," he said. "But these nations have their own reasons . . . Their economies have opened up to the point where they have a self-interest to protect intellectual property."

Questions

1. What does the author mean when he states, "Their economies have opened up to the point where they have a self-interest to protect intellectual property"?
2. On a visit to Mexico, you run across a street vendor with a table full of the very latest CDs by American artists. Everything from the plastic cases to the labels and graphics are exactly like the ones in the U.S. stores, and to your ear, the sound quality is exactly the same. He offers them for sale for $1.99 each.
   a. Would you buy as many as you could afford? Explain.
   b. How could the original producer prevent this reselling?
3. This article suggests that some of the Asian nations may have adequate intellectual property laws on the books, but the fact is that they do not, or cannot, properly enforce them. What should be the U.S. government's policy toward trade with such nations?

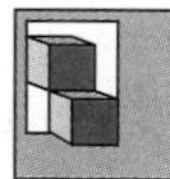

The issue of tariffs and other barriers to international business and trade has been the focus of international negotiations for many years. In recent years, the focus of these discussions has shifted to include unification of laws and enforcement of intellectual property rights, and significant progress in this area has been made in the last few years.

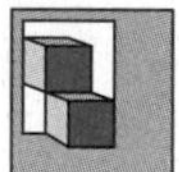

Profile Perspective: Suppose Jerry Irwin successfully obtains a federal registration of the mark "Supplies on Call." In the countries of the Pacific Rim, is his trademark protection limited to the words as they appear in English, or is he entitled to exclusive rights in the words as they appear in Chinese or Japanese characters?

D. Right of Publicity

The right of publicity is a relatively new form of intellectual property created at the state law level. It is derived from and carries bits and pieces from the law of defamation, trademark, false advertising, and the right of privacy.

Digital Audio Recording Raises Copycat Fears in Music Industry

Digital audio tape recording—the home taping enthusiast's dream and the music industry's worst nightmare—finally is here.

The recording industry, aware of statistics showing that 4 of 10 people over the age of 10 have taped recorded music in the last year, is holding its breath. In DAT, the big guns in the hardware industry are unleashing a product that threatens to do to the audiocassette what tapes and compact discs did to the once-mighty vinyl LP.

* * *

How well the expensive DAT machines fare with consumers is an open question, but some analysts predict that, like CD players, the prices will come down sharply when the new format gains popularity. A disturbing blip on the horizon for DAT manufacturers, however, is the prospect of recordable-erasable CDs, which Tandy Corp., for one, is developing.

The imminent arrival of these digital technologies has revived the debate over home taping and whether artists should be reimbursed for potential lost sales. The money most likely would come from royalty fees on blank tapes or recorders.

A recent study by the congressional Office of Technology Assessment said home taping may be causing as much as a 22 percent loss in prerecorded music sales. The office said its fall 1988 survey showed that 42 percent of people over age 10 had taped recorded music in the previous year.

Songwriters, composers, and music publishers claim that with DAT they'll lose even more royalties as listeners make virtually perfect tape copies of their favorite CDs.

But a bill pending in Congress to limit the number of copies that DAT machines can make has eased concerns of record manufacturers and cleared the way for introduction of the machines. The bill codifies an agreement reached last summer in Athens between the recording and manufacturing industries.

But the artists who create the songs aren't satisfied. They question whether the new anticopying technology is tamper-proof and say that even limited copying cuts into their business and will lead, ultimately, to fewer recordings being made.

* * *

To the recording industry, the scary part about DAT, which uses the 1s and 0s of computer language to make exact duplicates of the source material, is that as many as 20 generations of digital copies can be made without discernible loss of quality.

Faced with the threat of runaway home copying, which copyright law generally has declared to be legal "personal use," the recording industry association in 1987 threatened to sue any manufacturer that introduced a consumer DAT model before copyright issues could be addressed.

The Athens agreement settled the legal question—for now—by instituting the Serial Copy Management System. SCMS will allow one DAT copy to be made from a copyrighted CD, but the user cannot make a copy from the DAT copy. It would allow a CD to be copied indefinitely onto different blank DAT tapes.

The system also limits to two the number of generations of copies that can be made from a nondigital source, such as today's "analog" audiocassettes, LPs, or radio broadcasts. One copy of a copy could be made from analog sources.

SCMS uses a silicon chip that will be able to detect an electronic antipiracy "flag" that is placed on copyrighted digital material such as music CDs. The chip will "write" this flag onto the first DAT copy made from the CD. If a DAT recorder detects this flag, its record function will not operate.

Continued

Continued

Questions

1. Is the issue presented by DATs different from the issues presented in the Sony case? That is, what do you think the outcome would be if the producers of DATs were sued for contributory infringement of copyrighted music?
2. What is the justification for the arrangement everyone seems to have agreed to, allowing one or two copies to be made from a CD, but prohibiting additional copies?
3. If I buy a CD, shouldn't I have the right to do whatever I want with it?

Source: *Chicago Tribune,* April 8, 1990.

The right of publicity can be broadly defined as the inherent right of every person to control the commercial use of his or her identity. For example, the Tennessee statute reads:

> §47-25-1103 (a) Every individual has a property right in the use of his name, photograph or likeness in any medium in any manner. (b) The individual rights provided for in subsection (a) shall constitute property rights and shall be freely assignable and licensable, and shall not expire upon the death of the individual so protected, whether or not such rights were commercially exploited by the individual during the individual's lifetime. . .
>
> §47-25-1105 (a) Any person who knowingly uses or infringes upon the use of another individual's name, photograph, or likeness in any medium, in any manner . . . as an item of commerce for purposes of advertising products, merchandise, goods or services . . . without such individual's prior consent . . . shall be liable in a civil action.

Summary

Legal/Public Policy Review. Intellectual property is the intangible product of a human mind, and the concept that one can acquire rights to intellectual property is fundamental to our culture. From the legal standpoint, intellectual property covers several widely diverse kinds of property, each of which has its own separate characteristics.

Patents are a limited monopoly granted by the government in exchange for a full public disclosure of an invention. As a matter of public policy, the patent system represents a determination by the government that to encourage disclosure of technology by granting a limited period of exclusive rights, all society will reap the benefits of innovation. To obtain a patent, the invention must be new, useful, and nonobvious to a skilled worker in the art at the time the invention was made. These standards are intended to ensure that the reward of exclusivity is granted only for a significant contribution to technology.

A trade secret can be any form of information acquired by a business that has value because it is not known by others. A trade secret has value so long as it can be maintained in secret. If a business maintains reasonable security precautions, it will have a claim against anyone who obtains the information by wrongful means or who violates a duty of confidentiality.

Copyrights, originally intended to protect literary and artistic creations, are now widely used to protect commercial creations. Like patents, copyrights are a limited-time monopoly granted by the government in return for disclosure. Copyrights are the most popular way to protect proprietary computer programs. The standard for copyrightability is simply originality. So long as the work represents the original work by the person who developed it, it can be copyrighted.

Trademarks are names or symbols that become the commercial signature of the producer. The law of trademarks has developed through the common law and, like other intellectual property, gives the owner the right to prevent others from using the mark on similar goods. Trademarks present a particularly vexing public policy issue to the extent that a producer tries to acquire exclusive rights in ordinary words or phrases (or colors).

Several contemporary intellectual property problems exist. The first is protection of computer programs. Computers were not contemplated at the time the original statutes for protecting intellectual property were developed. Computer software is a truly dynamic part of business today, in terms of both software developed for widespread commercialization and programs developed (and paid for) to meet the specific needs of a particular business. Most programs do not meet the rigorous standards for patentability, and hence copyright protection has become the favored approach. The fundamental issue is, Just what does the copyright protect? If the protection is limited to the specific program, it will be very easy to get around, and the value of exclusivity granted by the copyright statute will be of little value. On the other hand, if the program is given a very broad scope of protection, it may tend to stifle innovation. The look-and-feel issue is an example of a possible middle ground.

Economics Review. The globalization of business has brought to the fore the conflict between our culture, which recognizes property rights in intellectual property, and the cultures of other parts of the world, particularly Asia, which have not traditionally recognized such rights. GATT negotiations and agreements have focused on bringing the rest of the word generally into conformity with our views. Enforcement now becomes the central issue.

Still another side of innovation is presented by the unique ability of DAT recorders to make copies that cannot be distinguished from the original. A large part of the entertainment business survives on royalties generated from recordings, and if perfect copies can be made, the door is wide open to piracy.

Finally, the right of publicity presents a new and completely different form of intellectual property, made possible by the trend to use individuals, particularly well-known figures, to promote the commercialization of various products.

Chapter Questions

1. Define the following terms and concepts:
   a. Patent
   b. Trade secret
   c. Copyright
   d. Trademark
   e. Secondary meaning
   f. Fair use
   g. Nonobviousness
   h. Intellectual property
   i. Right of publicity

2. Kinko photocopied excerpts of several copyrighted books, without permission and without payment, compiled the excerpts into course packets, and sold the packets to college students. The owner of the copyright sued for copyright infringement. Kinko defended by asserting that its copying was a fair use of the copyrighted material for educational purposes. Argue the case for the copyright owner. Who do you think should prevail, and why? [See *Basic Books Inc.* v. *Kinko Graphic Corp.,* 758 S. Supp. 1522 (S.D.N.Y. 1991).]
3. Professor of English I. B. Wright always dreamed of a career as a writer of fiction. He generated his first attempt at a novel on a word processor and sent copies to about a dozen publishers and several friends and acquaintances. None of the copies contained the copyright notice. Four years later, a new novel by an unknown author suddenly appeared on a best-seller list. To Wright's great surprise, it was his novel with a new title and the names of all the characters completely changed. Does Professor Wright have a claim against the publisher? Against the author? Explain.
4. Rolls Royce, a British company that has a worldwide reputation as a producer of luxury automobiles and jet engines, obtained a U.S. registration of the words "Rolls Royce" as a trademark for its products.
   a. Alexander Knockoff formed a small company and began producing a low-cost reproduction of a roll-top desk that he called "The Rolls Royce." What action, if any, would you recommend that Rolls Royce take? Explain.
   b. Would your answer be any different if Alexander Knockoff's company were one with a potentially negative public image, as for example, a cigarette company that promoted its brand as "The Rolls Royce"?
5. All modern digital computers perform their operations on the basis of numbers in the binary system. Samuel Benson, a mathematician employed in research by IBM, developed a mathematical formula that could be used to translate any number from the standard decimal system to the binary system. IBM, as Benson's assignee, filed an application to patent the formula. What action would you expect the Patent Office to take on this application and why? [See *Gottschalk* v. *Benson,* 409 U.S. 63 (1972).]
6. Can the developer of a computer program secure Design Patent protection on its screen icons as an additional protection for the look and feel of its computer programs? [See *Ex parte Strijland,* 26 U.S.P.Q.2d 1259 (Bd. Pat. App. 1992).]
7. Modern Electronics ran a series of humorous print advertisements set in the 21st century. They all showed one of Modern Electronics' products delivering the message that their products would still be around. One of the ads showed a Modern Electronics boombox next to a robot, dressed in a blond wig, gown, and jewelry, all carefully selected to resemble Vanna White. The robot was in the process of turning a letter on a game board, instantly recognizable as part of *Wheel of Fortune.* The caption to the ad said, "Longest running game show. 2012 A.D." Vanna White sued Modern Electronics for violation of her right of publicity. Decide the case. [See *White* v. *Samsung Electronics Corp.,* 971 F.2d 1395 (9th Cir. 1992).]
8. Sally Suma had always been a large woman and was terribly upset at her inability to find casual clothes, particularly jeans that fit properly. She finally decided to go into business herself and established a company called Hogg Wyld. Her first product was a line of jeans tailored for larger women. She wanted a name that was striking and, working with her advertising agency, came up with the name Lardashe. Jordache didn't think the name was a bit funny and promptly brought suit for infringement of its registered and widely known trademark, Jordache. Decide the case. [See *Jordache Enterprises, Inc.,* v. *Hogg Wyld, Ltd.,* 828 F.2d 1482 (10th Cir. 1987).]

9. Fujitec America, Inc., is a new American subsidiary of an old-line Japanese manufacturer of elevators. Fujitec is a major player throughout the world market, but has only recently decided to enter the U.S. market. As the elevator business has developed in this country, the major profit nucleus is long-term (five years) service contracts to repair and maintain existing elevator systems. Fujitec has decided as a part of its entry strategy to actively seek service business on elevator systems manufactured by others. Is it ethical for Fujitec to hire a core staff of service technicians from their competitors?
10. While surfing the Internet, you find an article on intellectual property that is particularly interesting. If you download the article onto your hard drive and then later read it from the screen, have you infringed the owner's copyright? Would it make a difference if you printed out a hard copy of the article?
11. The Software Publishers Association is the principal trade association of the personal computer software industry, representing over 1,100 members. One of their primary concerns is software piracy—they use the phrase "softlifting"—which is the unauthorized reproduction of copyrighted software. The estimate is that software piracy results in the loss of $8 billion annually to software developers. They have established a hotline and actively encourage people to report instances of unauthorized duplication of software. In effect, they are soliciting whistle-blowers.
    a. How do you feel about this approach?
    b. Is this a vehicle for vengeance by a disgruntled employee?
    c. Is this good or bad?
12. Is it fair or right for the United States to force its view on intellectual property on the rest of the world as part of the GATT or NAFTA negotiations?

NOTES

1. 35 U.S.C. §171.
2. 35 U.S.C. §161.
3. 35 U.S.C. §112.
4. 35 U.S.C. §103.
5. 35 U.S.C. §284.
6. Title 17, United States Code.
7. 17 U.S.C. §102.
8. 17 U.S.C. §102(b).
9. 490 U.S. 730 (1989).
10. 17 U.S.C. §102.
11. 17 U.S.C. §106.
12. 17 U.S.C. §107.
13. 17 U.S.C. §§115–16.
14. 17 U.S.C. §501 et seq.
15. 15 U.S.C. §1051 et seq.
16. Old Spice—Shulton (now Procter & Gamble); Kool-Aid—General Foods; Tylenol—McNeil PPC; Kleenex—Kimberly-Clark; Q-tips—Chesbrough Ponds; Listerine—Warner Lambert.
17. *American Home Products Corp.* v. *Johnson Chemical Co., Inc.,* 589 F.2d 103 (2d Cir. 1978).
18. 15 U.S.C. §1052(f).
19. 15 U.S.C. §1051(b).
20. 15 U.S.C. §1065.
21. 15 U.S.C. §1117.
22. *Coca Cola Co.* v. *Christopher,* 37 F. Supp. 216 (E.D. Mich. 1941).
23. *John Walker & Sons, Ltd.* v. *Tampa Cigar Co.,* 105 U.S.P.Q. 351 (5th Cir. 1955).
24. Jared Sandberg, "Immorality Play: Acclaiming Hackers as Heroes," *The Wall Street Journal,* February 27, 1995, p. B1.
25. See, for example, *Diamond* v. *Diehr,* 450 U.S. 175 (1981); *In re Abele,* 684 F.2d 902 (CCPA 1982); and *Arrhythmia Research Technology, Inc.* v. *Corazonix Corp.,* 22 U.S.P.Q.2d 1033 (Fed. Cir. 1992).
26. John Perry Barlow, "The Economy of Ideas: A Framework for Rethinking Patents and Copyrights in the Digital Age," Internet publication. © Wired Online, Wired Ventures.

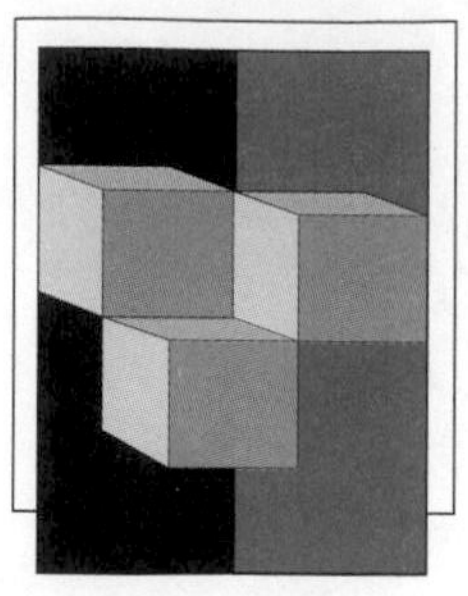

CHAPTER

10

SECURITIES LAW: FINANCING THE GROWING BUSINESS

READER'S GUIDE

In this chapter, we turn to the rules imposed by federal and state governments on the process of raising money in financial markets to build a business. Suppose you had a clever idea, you worked, and you built a new business. Perhaps you incorporated your firm, entered into contracts, bought a site, hired employees, and began to learn the ins and outs of complying with government regulations. Now everything is healthy for your firm except that you need more money to expand and remain competitive. This chapter examines the rules governing the process of raising money, giving particular attention to federal oversight designed to prevent fraud, insider trading, and the like.

PROFILE

going public. Selling shares in a company on the open market.

initial public offering (IPO). A security offered for sale to the public for the first time.

In August 1995, Netscape Communications Corporation, maker of the dominant software for browsing the World Wide Web, **went public;** that is, in an effort to raise capital, the company began selling shares to the public through what is known as an **initial public offering (IPO).** In one of the most riotous entries in stock market history, 13.8 million shares traded hands the first day, giving the then 15-month-old company a market value of $1.9 billion even though it had not yet turned a profit. The stock opened the day at $28.00 per share and at times that first day rose as high as $74.75 before closing at $58.25.[1]

Netscape's internet browsing software, Navigator, was created by Marc Andreessen and fellow graduate students at the University of Illinois. Silicon Graphics founder James Clark persuaded Andreessen and his team to leave school and start the new company with funding from Clark and other investors.[2]

QUESTIONS

1. What rules govern the IPO?
2. What are "private placements" and other capital-raising strategies often employed by expanding businesses like Netscape?
3. What federal securities rules govern the behavior of publicly traded firms like Netscape?

I. CAPITAL MARKETS: AN OVERVIEW

Historically, the American investment/capital market process operated largely under laissez-faire principles; but with the stock market crash of 1929, we turned to government oversight to smooth volatility in the market and strengthen integrity in buying and selling securities. The securities market operates through a system of stock exchanges, investment bankers, and stock brokers who organize the selling and buying of securities. The more influential exchanges include the New York Stock Exchange (NYSE), where shares in the most prominent American, and some foreign firms, are traded; the National Association of Securities Dealers Automated Quotation System (NASDAQ), the over-the-counter (OTC) market of both large and small firms; and the American Stock Exchange (AMEX). Other markets operate in the United States and many of the major cities around the world.

Futures. Commodities such as grain, precious metals, livestock, and financial futures (based on foreign currency prices, Treasury bonds, etc.) are traded as investments in the commodities futures market. The futures market basically involves deals to buy or sell commodities in the future at a price specified today. Thus the dealers are taking an educated gamble about the direction of the price of that commodity. Those trades are conducted on such prominent exchanges as the Chicago Board of Trade (CBOT) and the Chicago Mercantile Exchange (MERC). The **Commodity Futures Trading Commission (CFTC)** regulates futures trading.

futures. Contracts to deliver or take delivery of specified quantities of commodities at a previously specified price.

Commodity Futures Trading Commission (CFTC). Federal regulatory agency responsible for overseeing futures trading.

Topless Bar Goes Public

Rick's Cabaret, the posh Houston topless bar . . ., now is publicly traded on the NASDAQ Small Cap Market.

Club owner Robert Watters achieved his dream of taking Rick's public on October 13, 1995. The stock opened at $3 a share, and proceeds of the offering totaled $5.6 million. The stock closed at $3.81.

NASDAQ at first denied Watters' request to be traded, but Watters appealed and won the chance to put his company's name on the exchange.

"We took a long, hard look at Rick's because of the nature of the business," NASDAQ spokesman Mark Beauchamp said. "We concluded it was a legitimate, licensed business that met listing requirements."

The money flowing into the Rick's coffers will go toward expansion of Watters' nightlife interests.

Question

1. As a matter of ethics, did NASDAQ make the proper decision in listing Rick's Cabaret? Explain.

Source: Associated Press, *Des Moines Register,* November 24, 1995, p. 6S.

II. Introduction to Federal and State Securities Laws

The *Securities Act of 1933* regulates the initial issuance to the public of *new, nonexempt* securities and prohibits their sale until they have been properly registered with the **Securities and Exchange Commission (SEC).** The act requires issuers of new stocks to make extensive disclosures about operational and financial matters and bars fraudulent and deceptive practices. The *Securities Exchange Act of 1934* controls the resale of securities on the *secondary market* through exchanges and brokers. The 1934 act requires issuers of publicly traded securities to make regular reports to their shareholders. It established the SEC and set standards for the industry, including requiring the registration of brokers and dealers and prohibiting deceptive practices. Many other federal laws and SEC rules regulate the securities markets, but our primary concern will be with the 1933 and 1934 acts.

Securities and Exchange Commission (SEC). Federal regulatory agency responsible for overseeing the securities markets.

The Securities and Exchange Commission. The SEC administers the various federal securities statutes. The agency creates specific rules and regulations to implement those general statutory guidelines. The SEC has primary responsibility for investigating securities law violations and securing compliance with the law. The SEC also serves in a judicial capacity in that administrative law judges hold hearings to determine whether securities laws have been violated. If so, the SEC can issue **cease and desist orders,** instructing the defendant to stop its violations, and it can impose civil fines. The SEC does not have the authority to impose criminal penalties, although it can ask the Justice Department to do so.

cease and desist orders. Orders, often from an agency, instructing a party to refrain from a specified act.

State Laws. Some states turned to protective securities legislation even before the 1933 and 1934 federal statutes were enacted. State **blue sky laws** are based on the theory that a state has a duty to protect its citizens from unwise, fraudulent, or excessively speculative investments. Most states have adopted the Uniform Securities Act of 1956 as drafted by the National Conference of Commissioners on Uniform State Laws, but many of those states have amended the act so that blue sky laws differ somewhat from state to state. In general, the blue sky laws provide for registration of securities, registration of brokers, and various measures to prevent fraud.

blue sky laws. State statutes regulating the sale of securities to prevent consumer fraud.

Self-Regulation. The SEC is the primary federal agency responsible for regulating the securities industry, but it cannot do the entire job itself. The securities industry has been a leader in building self-regulation programs. With Supreme Court approval,[3] since 1987 most brokerage firms have required clients to agree to take disputes about their investments to arbitration rather than to court. Unfortunately, the arbitration process took on the characteristics of the paper wars it was designed to replace, and the results generally appear to have been particularly favorable to the industry. Basically, the system permits the securities industry to set the rules and pick the pool of arbitrators. Arbitrators do not need to know the law and often cannot secure access to necessary documents. So in 1996, a blue-ribbon panel proposed reforms to streamline the process, including measures to assure better document production, an expansion of the current six-year statute of limitations on bringing an arbitration claim, an expanded pool of arbitrators, expanded use of **mediation,** and a $750,000 cap on punitive damages.[4] At this writing, those reforms are under consideration by the SEC.

mediation. An extrajudicial proceeding in which a third party (the mediator) attempts to assist disputing parties to reach an agreeable, voluntary resolution of their differences.

derivatives. Specialized trading contracts tied to underlying assets such as bonds or currencies.

Derivatives. In another self-regulation initiative, six of Wall Street's biggest securities firms agreed, in 1995, to self-imposed rules to more closely control the largely unregulated, $12.1 trillion **derivatives** industry. Derivatives are contracts linked to underlying assets, where the derivative purchaser in essence makes a bet on whether the value of that underlying asset, such as stock indexes, bonds, and currencies, will rise or fall. The highly speculative nature of some derivatives trading and the resulting spectacular losses, including bankruptcies for the Orange County government in southern California and Barings, the British merchant bank, have led some legislators to believe government intervention is necessary. The rules, developed jointly with the SEC and the CFTC, are designed to head off new regulatory oversight. The rules provide for such measures as written disclosure to customers about the risks of trading in derivatives.[5]

The highly speculative nature of some derivatives trading and the resulting spectacular losses, including bankruptcies for the Orange County government in southern California and Barings, the British merchant bank, have led some legislators to believe government intervention is necessary.

The New York Stock Exchange, with SEC approval and oversight, has established many regulations for its members and is active in investigating insider abuses and manipulations. The National Association of Securities Dealers plays a similar role for dealers in over-the-counter securities.

A. What Is a Security?

The Securities Act of 1933 defines a security as:

> any note, stock, treasury stock, bond, debenture, evidence of indebtedness, certificate of interest or participation in any profit-sharing agreement, collateral-trust certificate, preorganizational certificate or subscription, transferable share, investment contract, voting-trust certificate, certificate of deposit for a security, fractional undivided interest in oil, gas, or other mineral rights, or, in general, any interest or instrument commonly known as a "security," or any certificate of interest or participation in, temporary or interim certificate for, receipt for, guarantee of, or warrant or right to subscribe to or purchase, any of the foregoing.

Any instrument called a *bond, stock, debenture, share,* and so on will almost certainly be considered a security. Often, disputes over the applicability of securities laws involve attempts by promoters to raise money for various schemes in which investors pool their money with the expectation of future returns, but no pieces of paper that look like securities are involved. In *SEC* v. *W. J. Howey Co.,* set out below, orange groves were held to be securities according to the following test: "the person invests his money in a common enterprise and is led to expect profits solely from the efforts of the promoter or a third party."

CASE

Securities & Exchange Commission v. W. J. Howey Co.

328 U.S. 293 (1946)

Justice Murphy

This case involves the application of § 2(1) of the Securities Act of 1933 to an offering of units of a citrus grove development coupled with a contract for cultivating, marketing and remitting the net proceeds to the investor.

* * *

Most of the facts are stipulated. The respondents, W. J. Howey Company and Howey-in-the-Hills Service, Inc., are Florida corporations under direct common control and management. The Howey Company owns large tracts of citrus acreage in Lake County, Florida. During the past several years it has planted about 500 acres annually, keeping half of the groves itself and offering the other half to the public "to help us finance additional development." Howey-in-the-Hills Service, Inc., is a service company engaged in cultivating and developing many of these groves, including the harvesting and marketing of the crops.

Each prospective customer is offered both a land sales contract and a service contract, after having been told that it is not feasible to invest in a grove unless service arrangements are made. While the purchaser is free to make arrangements with other service companies, the superiority of Howey-in-the-Hills Service, Inc., is stressed. Indeed, 85 percent of the acreage sold during the three-year period ending May 31, 1943, was covered by service contracts with Howey-in-the-Hills Service, Inc.

Continued

Continued

The land sales contract with the Howey Company provide for a uniform purchase price per acre or fraction thereof, varying in amount only in accordance with the number of years the particular plot has been planted with citrus trees. Upon full payment of the purchase price the land is conveyed to the purchaser by warranty deed. Purchases are usually made in narrow strips of land arranged so that an acre consists of a row of 48 trees. During the period between February 1, 1941, and May 31, 1943, 31 of the 42 persons making purchases bought less than five acres each. The average holding of these 31 persons was 1.33 acres and sales of as little as 0.65, 0.7, and 0.73 of an acre were made. These tracts are not separately fenced and the sole indication of several ownership is found in small land marks intelligible only through a plat book record.

The service contract, generally of a 10-year duration without option of cancellation, gives Howey-in-the-Hills Service, Inc., a leasehold interest and "full and complete" possession of the acreage. For a specified fee plus the cost of labor and materials, the company is given full discretion and authority over the cultivation of the groves and the harvest and marketing of the crops. The company is well established in the citrus business and maintains a large force of skilled personnel and a great deal of equipment, including 75 tractors, sprayer wagons, fertilizer trucks and the like. Without the consent of the company, the land owner or purchaser has no right of entry to market the crop; thus there is ordinarily no right to specific fruit. The company is accountable only for an allocation of the net profits based upon a check made at the time of picking. All the produce is pooled by the respondent companies, which do business under their own names.

The purchasers for the most part are nonresidents of Florida. They are predominantly business and professional people who lack the knowledge, skill, and equipment necessary for the care and cultivation of citrus trees. They are attracted by the expectation of substantial profits. It was represented, for example, that profits during the 1943–1944 season amounted to 20 percent and that even greater profits might be expected during the 1944–1945 season, although only a 10 percent annual return was to be expected over a 10-year period. Many of these purchasers are patrons of a resort hotel owned and operated by the Howey Company in a scenic section adjacent to the groves. The hotel's advertising mentions the fine groves in the vicinity and the attention of the patrons is drawn to the groves as they are being escorted about the surrounding countryside. They are told that the groves are for sale; if they indicate an interest in the matter they are then given a sales talk.

It is admitted that the mails and instrumentalities of interstate commerce are used in the sale of the land and service contracts and that no registration statement or letter of notification has ever been filed with the commission in accordance with the Securities Act of 1933 and the rules and regulations thereunder.

Section 2(1) of the act defines the term "security" to include the commonly known documents traded for speculation or investment. This definition also includes "securities" of a more variable character, designated by such descriptive terms as "certificate of interest or participation in any profit-sharing agreement," "investment contract" and "in general, any interest or instrument commonly known as a 'security.' " The legal issue in this case turns upon a determination of whether, under the circumstances, the land sales contract, the warranty deed and the service contract together constitute an "investment contract" within the meaning of § 2(1). An affirmative answer brings into operation the registration requirements of § 5(a), unless the security is granted an exemption under § 3(b). The lower courts, in reaching a negative answer to this problem, treated the contracts and deeds as separate transactions involving no more than an ordinary real estate sale and an agreement by the seller to manage the property for the buyer.

. . . [A]n investment contract for purposes of the Securities Act means a contract, transaction or scheme whereby a person invests his money in a common enterprise and is led to expect profits solely from the efforts of the promoter or a third party, it being immaterial whether the shares in the enterprise are evidenced by formal certificates or by nominal interests in the physical assets employed in the enterprise. Such a definition necessarily underlies this Court's decision in *S.E.C.* v. *Joiner Corp.* and has been enunciated and applied many times by lower federal courts. It permits the fulfillment of the statutory purpose of compelling full and fair disclosure

Continued

Continued

relative to the issuance of "the many types of instruments that in our commercial world fall within the ordinary concept of a security." H. Rep: No. 85, 73d Cong., 1st Sess., p. 11. It embodies a flexible rather than a static principle, one that is capable of adaptation to meet the countless and variable schemes devised by those who seek the use of the money of others on the promise of profits.

The transactions in this case clearly involve investment contracts as so defined. The respondent companies are offering something more than fee simple interests in land, something different from a farm or orchard coupled with management services. They are offering an opportunity to contribute money and to share in the profits of a large citrus fruit enterprise managed and partly owned by respondents. They are offering this opportunity to persons who reside in distant localities and who lack the equipment and experience requisite to the cultivation, harvesting, and marketing of the citrus products. Such persons have no desire to occupy the land or to develop it themselves; they are attracted solely by the prospects of a return on their investment. Indeed, individual development of the plots of land that are offered and sold would seldom be economically feasible due to their small size. Such tracts gain utility as citrus groves only when cultivated and developed as component parts of a larger area. A common enterprise managed by respondents or third parties with adequate personnel and equipment is therefore essential if the investors are to achieve their paramount aim of a return on their investments. Their respective shares in this enterprise are evidenced by land sales contracts and warranty deeds, which serve as a convenient method of determining the investors' allocable shares of the profits. The resulting transfer of rights in land is purely incidental.

Thus all the elements of a profit-seeking business venture are present here. The investors provide the capital and share in the earnings and profits; the promoters manage, control and operate the enterprise. It follows that the arrangements whereby the investors' interests are made manifest involve investment contracts, regardless of the legal terminology in which such contracts are clothed. The investment contracts in this instance take the form of land sales contracts, warranty deeds and service contracts which respondents offer to prospective investors. And respondents' failure to abide by the statutory and administrative rules in making such offerings, even though the failure results from a bona fide mistake as to the law, cannot be sanctioned under the act.

This conclusion is unaffected by the fact that some purchasers choose not to accept the full offer of an investment contract by declining to enter into a service contract with the respondents. The Securities Act prohibits the offer as well as the sale of unregistered, nonexempt securities. Hence it is enough that the respondents merely offer the essential ingredients of an investment contract.

We reject the suggestion of the Circuit Court of Appeals, that an investment contract is necessarily missing where the enterprise is not speculative or promotional in character and where the tangible asset which is sold has intrinsic value independent of the success of the enterprise as a whole. The test is whether the scheme involves an investment of money in a common enterprise with profits to come solely from the efforts of others. If that test be satisfied, it is immaterial whether the enterprise is speculative or nonspeculative or whether there is a sale of property with or without intrinsic value. The statutory policy of affording broad protection to investors is not to be thwarted by unrealistic and irrelevant formulae.

Reversed.

Questions

1. List the key ingredients in identifying whether an enterprise is a security.
2. Why do we care whether a particular enterprise should be classified as a security?
3. Fifty-seven residents of Co-op City, a cooperative housing project in New York City, purchased contracts labeled *stocks* that permitted them to acquire apartments. Should those stocks be treated as securities for the purpose of applying federal law when the tenants bought the stocks not for investment, but to secure living space, and when stocks did not give dividend rights, could not appreciate in value, and were not negotiable? Explain. [See *United Housing Foundation, Inc.,* v. *Forman,* 421 U.S. 837 (1975).]

III. Raising Money/Selling Securities: The 1933 Act

Profile Perspective: Marc Andreessen and his graduate student colleagues developed Navigator as a commercial product with the aid of Silicon Graphics founder James Clark and other investors. At that time, Netscape was not publicly traded. Andreessen and his colleagues, because of their extraordinarily promising product, were able to find the backing they needed to bring their product into full development and proceed with an IPO.

Businesses rarely begin with an IPO. Rather, they are built step-by-step with other financing strategies until some reach the point at which an IPO is desirable. Often, inventors like Andreessen and other small business developers initially scramble for resources. They may rely on sweat equity; their own, probably limited funds; family loans; government aid, such as Small Business Administration (SBA)–backed loans; bank loans; and other sources. Start-ups or growth also may be funded by individual, private investors who are simply looking for ways to make money. These "angels" are estimated to provide tens of billions in risk capital each year. Particularly promising new businesses may be able to secure capital from **venture capital funds,** which are partnerships, corporations, investment banks, and other organizations designed to make money by investing in new, growing and often risky enterprises. However, few businesses are so fortunate. Even if they secure the necessary initial funding and have some success, they likely will never reach the financial heights necessary to mount an IPO. Rather, the next stage in capital formation for those who are beginning to prosper and want to grow often would be to issue some form of **exempt security.**

venture capital funds. Organizations designed to invest in new and often risky business enterprises.

exempt security. Certain kinds of securities and certain transactions involving securities are not required to meet federal registration requirements under the 1933 Act.

A. *Exemptions*

The 1933 act provides that every securities offering, unless exempt, must be registered with the SEC prior to sale. The legal, accounting, and professional fees involved in registering a *nonexempt* security can be very large, as are the printing and underwriting costs. Mistakes, along with delays in getting approval from regulatory bodies, can generate enormous expense. The cost of floating a $10 million initial public offering can easily exceed $1 million. Further, if the issuer is successful in bringing the new security to the market, heavy additional expenses are encountered each year thereafter. Annual audits, SEC reports, and quarterly financial reports must be prepared and distributed. Shareholder meetings must be held. As noted, few entrepreneurs can expect to be so well favored as the Netscape team. Hence, your most promising strategy in building your business and looking for money—particularly if you are seeking a relatively small sum—may be to qualify your security for one of the registration exemptions provided by the law. Broadly, the law offers two kinds of exemptions from the 1933 act's registration requirements: *securities exemptions* and *transaction exemptions.* Note that these exemptions apply to registration requirements but do not provide protection from the liability/antifraud provisions of the law.

Securities Exemptions. Securities exempt from registration include those issued or guaranteed by federal, state, or local governments, as well as those of banks and savings and loans, charitable and religious institutions, and common carriers such as motor carriers and railroads (for certain types of offerings). Most insurance and annuity contracts are similarly exempt.

Transaction Exemptions. Transactions in securities that are exempt from registration requirements take three primary forms: private placements, intrastate offerings, and small issues.

Private Placements. These are securities sold without a public offering, thus excusing them from registration requirements. **Private placement** sales generally may be made to an unlimited number of **accredited investors** (institutional investors such as banks and pension funds, wealthy individuals, larger businesses, and upper-level insiders of the issuer). Private placements may be sold to no more than 35 nonaccredited investors, and those investors must either be financially sophisticated themselves or be represented by those who are sophisticated about investment matters. No general public selling of private placement securities is permitted. Broadly, all private placement purchasers must either receive or have access to all the information necessary to make an informed decision. SEC rules also include more specific information disclosure requirements depending on the nature of the party issuing the security. The general theory of private placement law is that sophisticated investors do not need extensive government protection.

private placements. Securities sold without a public offering, thus excusing them from SEC registration requirements.

accredited investors. Financially sophisticated and/or wealthy individuals and institutions who understand and can withstand the risk associated with securities investments.

Intrastate Offerings. **Intrastate offerings** are those sold only in a single state to residents of that state. Even if this requirement is met, the issuer must demonstrate that 80 percent of its business (revenues, assets, and so on) and 80 percent of the proceeds from the issue are to be used in that state. Further, no resale to nonresidents may be made for nine months after the offering is complete. This exemption is designed to aid purely local businesspeople in obtaining funds without meeting costly SEC registration requirements.

intrastate offerings. Registration exemption for securities sold only to residents of the state in which the issuer is organized and doing business.

Small Issues. Congress has been concerned about easing access to capital for small businesses. To lower costs for **small issues,** the SEC has provided a variety of exemptions from registration requirements for securities offerings not exceeding $5 million. For example, SEC Regulation A allows an issuer to sell up to $5 million in securities in a 12-month period under simplified registration procedures. Regulation A has no limit on the number of purchasers, and those purchasers need not be sophisticated investors. An offering statement must be filed with the SEC, but that statement does not require the detail of a registration statement and is substantially less expensive to prepare. No restrictions are placed on resale of these securities.

small issues. Registration exemption for securities issued in small amounts.

Although an issue may qualify for a total or partial exemption from SEC rules, state blue sky laws may not offer the same exemptions. In that case, issuers would still have to comply with those state laws.

B. Registration Requirements

Profile Perspective: Netscape's extraordinary prospects and the very strong climate for technology issues left the market unusually well suited for James Clark, Mark Andreessen, and others to seek more capital and in the process earn millions for themselves. Successful, growing firms whose needs do not fit within the exemptions noted above may pursue an IPO. At this point a professional **underwriter,** a key to IPO success, would be hired to manage the sale of the new securities, to assist in preparing the necessary documents, and to confer with lawyers, accountants, and SEC officials. Remember, however, that relatively few firms can afford to undertake an IPO and almost none are so

underwriter. Professional who helps sell new securities or buys those securities for the purpose of resale.

well positioned to enter the market as was Netscape. Those that do pursue an IPO must comply with the very complex and expensive registration process required under both state blue sky laws and the 1933 federal act.

Blue Sky Laws. Most states require registration of securities issued or traded in that state. In many states, registration requirements specify disclosure of certain information and operate on the premise that informed investors can digest that information and substantially protect themselves. In those states, securities meeting federal registration requirements can routinely fulfill the state's requirements. Other states believe that more activist intervention is required to protect investors. In those states the securities regulator must be convinced that the issue actually has investment merit and is likely to produce a reasonable return. For example, Massachusetts initially denied its residents the opportunity to buy Apple Computer stock because it was considered too risky and too expensive. The clamor was so great and so many residents simply decided to have brokers in other states purchase the stock for them that Massachusetts was finally forced to relent.

registration statement. Document filed with the SEC upon issuance of a new security detailing the information investors need to evaluate that security.

prospectus. A communication, usually in the form of a pamphlet, offering a security for sale and summarizing the information needed for a prospective buyer to evaluate the security.

The 1933 Act. Unlike state protective statutes, the Securities Act of 1933 is not concerned with the value or speculative nature of an issue; rather, it focuses on full disclosure of all the material facts. Before an offering can be sold, a detailed **registration statement** must be submitted to the SEC. The statement will include audited financial records, a description of the business, an overview of the management of the firm, and other information necessary for the SEC to determine that the registration contains all the data investors need to evaluate the security. Additionally, a **prospectus** must be given to every person to whom the security is offered for sale. The prospectus, which contains much the same information as the registration statement, is the primary sales document for the offering and is designed to disclose the information necessary for an offeree to make an informed decision. In 1995, the SEC issued new rules intended to speed up the stock-trading process. As part of that effort, the rules increase flexibility in security registration procedures. For example, preliminary prospectus information can now be delivered in several pieces and in stages, and prospectuses can be rearranged to allow pricing information to be printed earlier than other materials.[6]

Ethics/Public Policy Questions

The new prospectus rules and the entire registration process are intended to carefully inform consumers about the security in question. However, *The Wall Street Journal* recently observed:

> [T]he SEC's new rule doesn't address a more fundamental investor problem with prospectuses: clarity. Currently, most prospectuses are written in legalese that most investors find difficult to decipher. "The most important thing we as an industry can do for customers is to stop using our jargon and put things in plain English," says Joseph Grano (a PaineWebber executive).[7]

1. Why does the securities industry rely on legalese in prospectuses intended to inform the purchasing public?
2. In your view, do the legalese-filled prospectuses constitute a breach of the securities industry's ethical duties to its customers?

C. The Registration Process

The 1933 act divides the IPO registration process into well-defined periods with strict rules for each.

Prefiling Period. This is the time before the registration is filed. All offers to buy or sell the security are forbidden prior to registration. Publicity designed to condition the market, to encourage interest in the new issue or having that effect, is forbidden during the prefiling period.

Waiting Period. This is the time between the filing and the declaration by the SEC that the registration is effective. Technically, the registration is effective 20 days after receipt by the SEC. However, if the SEC review discloses deficiencies, the issuer receives a new 20-day period in which to make changes. Although the SEC cannot reject an offering based on its perception of the likelihood of the offering's success, it can lengthen the approval process and increase accompanying expenses; thus, offerings the SEC deems undesirable or misleading become practically impossible to market.

During this period, sales are not permitted, but the new issue can be publicized by a preliminary prospectus called a **red herring** and by a **tombstone ad.** A red herring summarizes the information in the registration statement and specifies that both sales and offers to buy must await registration approval. A tombstone ad is limited to setting forth what is being offered, when it is available, and from whom a prospectus may be obtained. The tombstone ad must specify that it does not constitute an offer to sell.

red herring. A preliminary securities prospectus that provides information but does not constitute an offer to sell.

tombstone ad. A securities advertisement that does not constitute an offer and that usually appears in the financial press set inside heavy black borders suggestive of a tombstone.

Thus, the general point of the waiting period is to allow buyers to calmly reflect on the wisdom of buying the new issue while it is being scrutinized by the SEC. Of course, many do not do so. Instead, they may rely on their brokers, their own intuition, or other evidence, but they will have received a prospectus. Thus, the SEC does not protect investors from their own foolishness, but it does ensure that all have access to adequate information.

Post-Effective Period. This is the period after the SEC has declared the registration to be effective. Once the registration is effective, sales may begin; but a final prospectus must accompany or precede delivery of the security. Normally, the IPO issuer and underwriter are expected to sell out the issue as soon as possible; however, under a procedure labeled a **shelf registration,** large, reliable issuers may file a registration with the SEC and hold the securities "on the shelf" to await more favorable market conditions before selling. This approach offers considerable cost savings in the registration process.

shelf registration. IPO registration that permits the issuer to hold the securities for sale until favorable market conditions emerge or the issuer needs the proceeds.

IV. Liability and Remedies: The 1933 Act

Defects, both intentional and negligent, in the registration process can lead to significant penalties under the 1933 act. Criminal liability may be imposed for willful violations of the act. The act also imposes civil liability for all material misstatements, misleading data, or omissions in the prospectus and other registration material filed with the SEC. Quite simply, anyone who purchases an initial public offering[8] that is subject to registration requirements and contains errors, omissions, or misleading statements or for which no registration material is filed may be able to recover damages in an amount up to the original purchase price for all money lost as a result of the investment. No proof of reliance and causation is necessary. The mere fact that the error was made and that the investor lost money (the price of the security fell) is enough to entitle the investor to a recovery if the error or omission is deemed to be material. This means an investor can be perfectly satisfied with a purchase, but if the investment goes bad within the three-year statute of limitations, the purchaser can scan the prospectus for the error, misstatement, or omission. Finding such a problem with the prospectus can lead to the recovery of the total damages resulting from the decline in price of the original purchase.

The company; any officer or director of the company; its accountants, attorneys, real estate appraisers, and other experts who helped develop the offering and registration; the underwriters; and anyone who signed the registration statement may be liable for damages suffered by purchasers of the security (explained below).

A. Due Diligence

due diligence. A defense against a securities violation claim where the defendant used ordinary prudence and still failed to find an error or omission in the registration statement.

The primary defense to a false registration claim is to establish **due diligence,** which, oversimplified, means that the party being sued was not guilty of negligence. All defendants except the issuer can employ the due diligence defense. The precise standards of the due diligence defense depend on the role of the defendant in the registration process and the portion of the registration statement that is faulty. In general, one displays due diligence by conducting a reasonable investigation to establish reasonable grounds to believe and, in fact, believing that the registration statement is both true and free of material omissions. The famous case that follows illustrates the application of the due diligence defense to alleged violations of the Securities Act of 1933.

CASE

Escott v. BarChris Construction Corp.

283 F. Supp. 643 (S.D.N.Y. 1968)

Facts

BarChris constructed bowling "centers" consisting of bowling alleys and, often, restaurants and bars. Business boomed with the introduction of automatic pin setters in 1952. In 1961, BarChris decided to raise money by selling debentures. A registration statement was filed with the SEC. However, by 1962 the bowling industry was saturated, new orders declined, and existing customers were unable to pay. BarChris itself went bankrupt in 1962 and was unable to make its interest payments on the debentures. Escott and others who had bought debentures sued BarChris, its officers, directors, auditors, the debenture underwriters, and others under Section 11 of the Securities Act of 1933. They claimed that BarChris's registration statement contained significant errors regarding sales, assets, liabilities, earnings, and so on.

* * *

District Judge McLean

I turn . . . to the question of whether defendants have proved their due diligence defenses. The position of each defendant will be separately considered.

Continued

Continued

Russo

Russo was, to all intents and purposes, the chief executive officer of BarChris. He was a member of the executive committee. He was familiar with all aspects of the business. . . .

It was Russo who arranged for the temporary increase in BarChris's cash in banks on December 31, 1960, a transaction which borders on the fraudulent. He was thoroughly aware of BarChris's stringent financial condition in May 1961. He had personally advanced large sums to BarChris of which $175,000 remained unpaid as of May 16.

In short, Russo knew all the relevant facts. He could not have believed that there were no untrue statements or material omissions in the prospectus. Russo has no due diligence defenses.

* * *

Trilling

Trilling . . . was BarChris's controller. He signed the registration statement in that capacity, although he was not a director . . .

Trilling was not a member of the executive committee. He was a comparatively minor figure in BarChris. The description of BarChris's "management" on page 9 of the prospectus does not mention him . . .

Trilling may well have been unaware of several of the inaccuracies in the prospectus. But he must have known of some of them. As a financial officer, he was familiar with BarChris's finances and with its books of account. He knew that part of the cash on deposit on December 31, 1960 had been procured temporarily by Russo for window dressing purposes. He knew that BarChris was operating Capitol Lanes in 1960. He should have known, although perhaps through carelessness he did not know at the time, that BarChris's contingent liability on Type B lease transactions was greater than the prospectus stated. In the light of these facts, I cannot find that Trilling believed the entire prospectus to be true.

But even if he did, he still did not establish his due diligence defenses. He did not prove that as to the parts of the prospectus expertised by Peat, Marwick he had no reasonable ground to believe that it was untrue. He also failed to prove, as to the parts of the prospectus not expertised by Peat, Marwick, that he made a reasonable investigation which afforded him a reasonable ground to believe that it was true. As far as appears, he made no investigation. He did what was asked of him and assumed that others would properly take care of supplying accurate data as to the other aspects of the company's business. This would have been well enough but for the fact that he signed the registration statement. As a signer, he could not avoid responsibility by leaving it up to others to make it accurate. Trilling did not sustain the burden of proving his due diligence defenses.

Birnbaum

Birnbaum was a young lawyer, admitted to the bar in 1957, who, after brief periods of employment by two different law firms and an equally brief period of practicing in his own firm, was employed by BarChris as house counsel and assistant secretary in October 1960. Unfortunately for him, he became secretary and a director of BarChris on April 17, 1961, after the first version of the registration statement had been filed with the Securities and Exchange Commission. He signed the later amendments, thereby becoming responsible for the accuracy of the prospectus in its final form.

Although the prospectus, in its description of "management," lists Birnbaum among the "executive officers" and devotes several sentences to a recital of his career, the fact seems to be that he was not an executive officer in any real sense. He did not participate in the management of the company. As house counsel, he attended to legal matters of a routine nature.

Continued

Continued

* * *

It seems probable that Birnbaum did not know of many of the inaccuracies in the prospectus. He must, however, have appreciated some of them. In any case, he made no investigation and relied on the others to get it right . . . As a lawyer, he should have known his obligations under the statute. He should have known that he was required to make a reasonable investigation of the truth of all the statements in the unexpertised portion of the document which he signed. Having failed to make such an investigation, he did not have reasonable ground to believe that all these statements were true. Birnbaum has not established his due diligence defenses except as to the audited 1960 figures.

Auslander

Auslander was an "outside" director, i.e., one who was not an officer of BarChris. He was chairman of the board of Valley Stream National Bank in Valley Stream, Long Island . . .

In February and early March 1961, before accepting Vitolo's invitation, Auslander made some investigation of BarChris. He obtained Dun & Bradstreet reports which contained sales and earnings figures for periods earlier than December 31, 1960. He caused inquiry to be made of certain of BarChris's banks and was advised that they regarded BarChris favorably.

* * *

Auslander was elected a director on April 17, 1961. The registration statement in its original form had already been filed, of course without his signature. On May 10, 1961, he signed a signature page for the first amendment to the registration statement which was filed on May 11, 1961. This was a separate sheet without any document attached. Auslander did not know that it was a signature page for a registration statement. He vaguely understood that it was something "for the SEC."

Auslander attended a meeting of BarChris's directors on May 15, 1961. At that meeting he, along with the other directors, signed the signature sheet for the second amendment which constituted the registration statement in its final form. Again, this was only a separate sheet without any document attached. Auslander never saw a copy of the registration statement in its final form.

At the May 15 directors' meeting, however, Auslander did realize that what he was signing was a signature sheet to a registration statement. This was the first time that he had appreciated that fact. A copy of the registration statement in its earlier form as amended on May 11, 1961 was passed around at the meeting. Auslander glanced at it briefly. He did not read it thoroughly.

* * *

In considering Auslander's due diligence defenses, a distinction is to be drawn between the expertised and non-expertised portions of the prospectus. As to the former, Auslander knew that Peat, Marwick had audited the 1960 figures. He believed them to be correct because he had confidence in Peat, Marwick. He had no reasonable ground to believe otherwise.

As to the non-expertised portions, however, Auslander is in a different position. He seems to have been under the impression that Peat, Marwick was responsible for all the figures. This impression was not correct, as he would have realized if he had read the prospectus carefully. Auslander made no investigation of the accuracy of the prospectus. He relied on the assurance of Vitolo and Russo, and upon the information he had received in answer to his inquiries back in February and early March. These inquiries were general ones, in the nature of a credit check. The information which he received in answer to them was also general, without specific reference to the statements in the prospectus, which was not prepared until some time thereafter.

Continued

Continued

It is true that Auslander became a director on the eve of the financing. He had little opportunity to familiarize himself with the company's affairs. The question is whether, under such circumstances, Auslander did enough to establish his due diligence defense with respect to the non-expertised portions of the prospectus.

* * *

Section 11 imposes liability in the first instance upon a director, no matter how new he is. He is presumed to know his responsibility when he becomes a director. He can escape liability only by using that reasonable care to investigate the facts which a prudent man would employ in the management of his own property. In my opinion, a prudent man would not act in an important matter without any knowledge of the relevant facts, in sole reliance upon representations of persons who are comparative strangers and upon general information which does not purport to cover the particular case. To say that such minimal conduct measures up to the statutory standard would, to all intents and purposes, absolve new directors from responsibility merely because they are new. This is not a sensible construction of Section 11, when one bears in mind its fundamental purpose of requiring full and truthful disclosure for the protection of investors.

I find and conclude that Auslander has not established his due diligence defense with respect to the misstatements and omissions in those portions of the prospectus other than the audited 1960 figures.

* * *

Peat, Marwick

The part of the registration statement purporting to be made upon the authority of Peat, Marwick as an expert was . . . the 1960 figures . . . [T]he question is whether . . . Peat, Marwick . . . had reasonable ground to believe and did believe that the 1960 figures were true and that no material fact had been omitted from the registration statement which should have been included in order to make the 1960 figures not misleading.

* * *

The 1960 Audit

Peat, Marwick's work was in general charge of a member of the firm, Cummings, and more immediately in charge of Peat, Marwick's manager, Logan. Most of the actual work was performed by a senior accountant, Berardi . . .

Berardi was then about thirty years old. He was not yet a C.P.A. He had had no previous experience with the bowling industry. This was his first job as a senior accountant. He could hardly have been given a more difficult assignment.

* * *

It is unnecessary to recount everything that Berardi did in the course of the audit. We are concerned only with the evidence relating to what Berardi did or did not do with respect to those items which I have found to have been incorrectly reported in the 1960 figures in the prospectus . . .

Capitol Lanes

First and foremost is Berardi's failure to discover that Capitol Lanes had not been sold. This error affected both the sales figure and the liability side of the balance sheet.

* * *

Continued

Continued

Berardi did become aware that there were references here and there in BarChris's records to something called Capitol Lanes. He also knew that there were indications that at some time BarChris might operate an alley of that name. He read the minutes of the board of directors' meeting of November 22, 1960 which recited that: "* * * the Chairman recommended that the Corporation operate Capitol Lanes, 271 Main Street, East Haven, Connecticut, through a corporation which would be a subsidiary of Sanpark Realty Corp."

* * *

Berardi testified that he inquired of Russo about Capitol Lanes and that Russo told him that Capitol Lanes, Inc. was going to operate an alley some day but as yet it had no alley. Berardi testified that he understood that the alley had not been built and that he believed that the rental payments were on vacant land.

I am not satisfied with this testimony. If Berardi did hold this belief, he should not have held it. The entries as to insurance and as to "operation of alley" should have alerted him to the fact that an alley existed. He should have made further inquiry on the subject. It is apparent that Berardi did not understand this transaction.

* * *

The S-1 Review

The purpose of reviewing events subsequent to the date of a certified balance sheet (referred to as an S-1 review when made with reference to a registration statement) is to ascertain whether any material change has occurred in the company's financial position which should be disclosed in order to prevent the balance sheet figures from being misleading. The scope of such a review, under generally accepted auditing standards, is limited. It does not amount to a complete audit.

* * *

Berardi made the S-1 review in May 1961. He devoted a little over two days to it, a total of 20 ½ hours. He did not discover any of the errors or omissions pertaining to the state of affairs in 1961 . . . The question is whether, despite his failure to find out anything, his investigation was reasonable within the meaning of the statute.

What Berardi did was to look at a consolidating trial balance as of March 31, 1961 which had been prepared by BarChris, compare it with the audited December 31, 1960 figures, discuss with Trilling certain unfavorable developments which the comparison disclosed, and read certain minutes. He did not examine any "important financial records" other than the trial balance . . .

In substance, . . . Berardi . . . asked questions, he got answers which he considered satisfactory, and he did nothing to verify them.

* * *

Berardi had no conception of how tight the cash position was. He did not discover that BarChris was holding up checks in substantial amounts because there was no money in the bank to cover them. He did not know of the loan from Manufacturers Trust Company or of the officers' loans. Since he never read the prospectus, he was not even aware that there had ever been any problem about loans from officers.

* * *

Continued

Continued

There had been a material change for the worse in BarChris's financial position. That change was sufficiently serious so that the failure to disclose it made the 1960 figures misleading. Berardi did not discover it. As far as results were concerned, his S-1 review was useless.

* * *

Here again, the burden of proof is on Peat, Marwick. I find that that burden has not been satisfied. I conclude that Peat, Marwick has not established its due diligence defense.

* * *

[Judgment for Escott and other debenture buyers.]

Questions

1. Why was the Court willing to find the director, Auslander, liable even though he was "new" to the corporation and "had little opportunity to familiarize himself with the company's affairs"?
2. What is an S-1 review?
3. In March 1976, Holiday Inn filed a registration statement with the SEC with respect to the issuance of public stock. In reliance on the prospectus published on March 23, Strauss bought 100 shares of Holiday Inn stock. The value of Straus's stock declined, and she sued Holiday Inn under Section 11 of the 1933 act, claiming that the prospectus contained misleading statements and omissions in that it failed to disclose a decline in profits. Specifically, Straus argued that Holiday Inn suffered a financial decline in the first two months of 1976 as compared with the first two months of 1975 and that Holiday Inn was aware of that decline on March 23. She said that if Holiday Inn's foreign currency translation losses (due to a decline in the value of the dollar) were excluded, Holiday Inn suffered a seven-cents-per-share decline in profits for the first two months of 1976 as compared to the first two months of 1975 and that the decline should have been disclosed in the prospectus. Including the translation losses as provided for under generally accepted accounting principles resulted in a one-cent-per-share decline in profits for January–February 1976 as compared to January–February 1975. Did Holiday Inn violate Section 11? Explain. [See *Straus* v. *Holiday Inn,* 460 F. Supp. 729 (S.D.N.Y. 1978).]
4. Rule 144a allows approximately 4,000 large institutions to trade privately placed securities that may not be offered to or traded by small (or many) individual investors.
   a. As these securities make up approximately 35 percent of all recent offerings, what problems will the ruling cause small investors?
   b. Is the volume of private placements likely to rise or fall? Explain.
   c. What are the implications for a regulatory system in which investors are willing to commit billions of dollars to investments that may not have complied with all the requirements of SEC regulation?
   d. Is it possible that SEC rules are counterproductive in some situations? List some examples of this problem.

V. Regulating the Resale of Securities: The 1934 Act

Profile Perspective: The Netscape IPO was extraordinarily successful and Netscape shares moved into vigorous trading. The IPO portion of Netscape's movement to the open market was regulated by the provisions of the 1933 act.

The subsequent *resale* of securities after an IPO—buying and selling of shares on the open market—is regulated by the 1934 Securities Exchange Act. Thus, the 1933 act has, in the main, a onetime impact commanding detailed registration requirements as securities pass from the issuer to the market; whereas the 1934 act is primarily directed to all trading subsequent to that IPO stage and requires all securities issuers to engage in regular information disclosures. Indeed, the general purpose of the 1934 act is to ensure the steady flow of reliable information to investors.

A. *Disclosure*

The 1934 act regulates many aspects of the financial dealings of publicly held companies. Any company with more than $5 million in assets and 500 shareholders may be subject to some provisions of the act, as are any businesses that have issued a class of securities traded on a national securities exchange. All companies required to register with the SEC must file annual and quarterly reports with the SEC, as well as monthly reports if certain specified occurrences take place. Investment companies, banks, insurance companies, and various other industries are exempt from these disclosure requirements, but over 10,000 firms must disclose the specified data to the SEC and the public on a regular basis. Not only does the prompt dissemination of information limit the possibilities for insider trading, but it also allows the financial markets to operate more efficiently. To the extent that information is public, the financial markets can process that information and trade the underlying securities so that their market values reflect that new data.

In addition, the 1934 act sets up the SEC and gives markets like the New York Stock Exchange some power of self-regulation to be exercised with SEC oversight. Furthermore, the SEC is authorized to regulate the extension of credit used to buy securities, trading by members of the exchanges, and manipulative practices by members. It may also suspend trading of securities if it becomes necessary. The SEC also regulates brokers and dealers, municipal securities dealers, and others dealing in securities information. The SEC also has the power to establish accounting rules for listed securities that ordinarily is accomplished by deferring to the expertise of the Financial Accounting Standards Board (FASB).

B. *Day-to-Day Oversight*

Besides registration and submission of various reports, publicly held companies are regulated concerning their recordkeeping, repurchases of securities, proxy solicitations, director changes, corrupt foreign practices, and many other areas of day-to-day activities. Stockholders who are officers or directors of a company or who own large blocks of the stock are required to report their transactions involving the company's securities to the SEC and are prohibited from engaging in certain stock transactions in which their position could give them an unfair advantage over the uninformed public. It is also a violation for anyone to trade shares on the basis of inside information—information not available to the investing public at the time. Restrictions also are placed on tender offers (explained below), purchases of substantial blocks of stock, and institutional investment managers. Misleading statements in proxy solicitations or about the purchase or sale of a security, along with other unfair or deceptive practices, can result in criminal or civil liability under the 1934 act.

VI. Tender Offers

So far, this chapter has focused on how to build your business beyond the limits of straightforward loans and your own personal financial resources, that is, by encouraging others to buy a piece of your success in the manner of the Netscape IPO. Now let's imagine that yet bigger possibilities are on the horizon. Perhaps you see value for your business and your shareholders in acquiring another business. Perhaps you can work out a friendly merger (see Chapter 11) or takeover, or perhaps a **hostile takeover** will be required. Or perhaps your firm is the *target* of a takeover or merger. In the 1980s, takeovers became a primary weapon in big business strategy as colorful figures like corporate raider T. Boone Pickens captured front-page attention with their bold and often hostile attempts to buy out desirable targets. Commonly, a takeover is accomplished via a **tender offer,** which is a public bid to the shareholders of the target firm offering to buy shares at a specified price for a defined period of time. A tender offer thus goes past management and directly to the shareholders. When management objects, the takeover is considered hostile.

In the 1980s, takeovers became a primary weapon in big business strategy as colorful figures like corporate raider T. Boone Pickens captured front-page attention with their bold and often hostile attempts to buy out desirable targets.

hostile takeover. The acquisition of a formerly independent business where the acquired business resists the union.

tender offer. A public bid to the shareholders of a firm offering to buy shares at a specified price for a defined period of time.

A. SEC Takeover Rules

When one company attempts to take over another, SEC rules can often be crucial. All tender offers must be registered with the SEC. Furthermore, certain disclosure rules are triggered when groups purchase more than 5 percent of a company's outstanding stock.

B. Takeover Defenses

In recent years, as hostile takeover attempts have become more frequent, many strategies have been developed to limit their success. Typically, management uses state requirements to slow down or eliminate the possibility of a hostile takeover. Takeover candidates use their political clout to convince legislators of the harmful effects a takeover could have for the state in which the business is incorporated or has a major presence. Such economic issues as plant closings, wholesale transfers, or moving the headquarters often strike a responsive chord. From the standpoint of investors, regulators, and raiders, such tactics are troublesome, and they may turn to SEC standards to advance their cause.

Bidders for a company can rely on amendments to the 1934 act to get more information about a target company and to shorten the period of time during which shareholders can decide whether to accept the offer. These amendments also have placed additional restrictions on a company's ability to use state law to fend off a takeover. For instance, in the Mobil-Marathon takeover battle, the **lockout defense** was rejected by the courts. In this maneuver, the target's board opposed a "totally inadequate" offer by giving another friendly corporation **(white knight)** the right to purchase 10 million authorized but unis-

lockout defense. Takeover defense where the target company manipulates its assets, shares, etc. in order to make the company unattractive as a takeover candidate.

white knight. In a takeover battle, a friendly company that rescues the target company from a hostile takeover. Often the rescue is accomplished by a merger between the target and the white knight.

sued shares and a contingent option to purchase a major oil field in the event of a hostile takeover. The purpose of this transaction was to make the takeover candidate more expensive and financially unattractive to the raider. The court held this practice to be manipulative in that it set an artificial ceiling on what the shareholders could expect to receive should the company or its assets be sold. In effect, the shareholders were being harmed in order to keep the company from being sold and to keep existing management in power.

Other Defenses. Additional defensive strategies include selling large blocks of stock to employees, issuing much new debt, attempting to take over the hostile bidder, requiring that the same sale or exchange terms be offered to all shareholders, mandating that the board or a supermajority of all shareholders must approve takeover bids, selling off the most attractive corporate assets, finding another purchaser, or buying out the bidder at a profit **(greenmail).** Clearly, some of these techniques are more desirable than others from the standpoint of the target, and many, such as taking on substantial new debt or selling off attractive corporate assets **(scorched earth defense),** can seriously damage the long-run prospects of the business.

greenmail. Takeover defense involving the target corporation's repurchase of a takeover raider's stock at a premium not offered to other shareholders.

scorched earth defense. Takeover defense where the target corporation takes on new debt, sells assets, and so on in an effort to make itself a less attractive target.

VII. Securities Fraud

As you are raising money in the open market to expand your business, you must, of course, avoid running afoul of the penalties under the securities laws and endeavor to hire honorable accountants, underwriters, lawyers, and others to see that they too do not engage in securities fraud. Section 10(b) of the 1934 act and SEC Rule 10b-5 [implementing the policy Congress established in section 10(b)] are the principal securities law antifraud weapons. Rule 10b-5 prohibits misstatements or omissions of material fact. Although the precise boundaries are not fully clear, the plaintiff ordinarily must show (1) the misstatement or omission was *material,* that is, it was likely to affect the price of the security; (2) the defendant acted with **scienter,** that is, the fraud was intentional or, according to many courts, the product of gross recklessness; or (3) the plaintiff *relied on* the defendant's fraud. When the SEC brings a fraud claim using Rule 10b-5, it need not prove reliance.

scienter. Intent to commit a legal wrong. Guilty knowledge.

In an interesting example of the influence of free market financial reasoning on the law, some courts have adopted the **fraud-on-the-market theory** allowing investors to demonstrate reliance merely by showing they bought shares and in so doing assumed the integrity of the price set by the market. The fraud-on-the-market hypothesis is that in an open and developed securities market the price of a stock will reflect all of the available material information about that stock. The market absorbs all of that material information and transforms it into the market price. Thus, when buying stock one automatically relies on its price as an accurate measure of its value given the available information.

fraud-on-the-market theory. Misleading statements distort the market and thus defraud a securities buyer whether the buyer actually relies on the misstatement or not. Based on the assumption that the price of a stock reflects all of the available information about that stock.

A. Fraud Limits

In December 1995, Congress overrode President Clinton's veto to enact the Private Securities Litigation Reform Act, which is designed to stop groundless fraud claims, especially class actions, by angry investors whose stock purchases went awry. Critics say the bill provides too much protection for the investment community and effectively closes the courthouse door for many wronged investors. The bill, which imposes substantial limitations on private fraud actions under the 1933 and 1934 acts, will be clarified by judicial interpretation, but its primary ingredients include significant protections for the financial community:

- It creates a safe harbor from legal liability for forward-looking statements about company prospects. Those forecasts must, however, be accompanied by warnings about risks. This provision allows companies to more safely publicize earnings and new product projections.
- It requires a plaintiff's fraud pleading (the complaint initiating the case) to include facts showing that the defendant intentionally engaged in misleading behavior. Failure to provide that proof would prevent moving to the discovery stage of a trial, in which the plaintiff can search for damaging evidence.
- It protects accountants and securities underwriters whose clients have engaged in fraud. The bill abolishes **joint and several liability** for those secondary defendants who audited the books or did the underwriting for a firm that engaged in fraud but subsequently went broke. Traditionally, under joint and several liability each participant in a tortious act like fraud can be held fully liable for damages, which made the deep pockets of the secondary defendants particularly desirable and vulnerable. Now, with very limited exceptions, those accountants and underwriters can be liable only for the portion of the harm they actually caused as well as a 50 percent premium in cases where the principal defendant is insolvent.
- It gives the SEC authority to sue those who aid and abet the commission of fraud.[9] (Private investors do not have that power. See the *Central Bank of Denver* case that follows.)

joint and several liability. Liability of a group of persons in which the plaintiff may sue all members of the group collectively, or one or more individually for the entire amount.

Even if the new reform law proves to sharply inhibit investor protections, we should remember that many other avenues of recovery remain. The SEC itself, the self-regulatory bodies within the investment industry, and state securities regulators are all empowered to pursue securities fraud, and private plaintiffs can still pursue claims under state securities laws, other federal laws, and the common law of the states.

Ethics/Public Policy Question

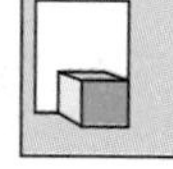

Accounting firms paid an estimated $1.6 billion in fraud claims arising out of the 1980s savings and loan crisis, in large part because the savings and loan operations audited by the accounting firms often were insolvent. As noted, the Private Securities Litigation Reform Act permits liability only for the portion of the fraud that is directly attributable to the responsible accountants. Is it fair to substantially deprive defrauded investors of the deep pockets of large public accounting firms? Explain.

Is it fair to substantially deprive defrauded investors of the deep pockets of large public accounting firms?

B. Secondary Parties

Clearly, all those (including secondary parties such as accountants and lawyers) who *directly* participate in securities fraud have violated the law; but what about the liability of secondary parties who merely *aid and abet* that fraud? Since the 1940s, many federal court decisions have upheld private lawsuits against secondary parties. Large accounting firms with deep pockets have been particularly attractive targets since crooked or incompetent investment promoters are often penniless or hard to reach. As noted above, the recent securities reform law specifically permits the SEC to sue secondary parties who aid and abet a fraud; but in the surprising decision that follows, the Supreme Court overturned decades of precedent and held that secondary parties who aid and abet a stock fraud may *not* be sued by *private parties* under the 1934 act.

CASE

Central Bank of Denver v. First Interstate Bank of Denver

114 S.Ct. 1439, 128 L.Ed. 2d 119 (1994)

Facts

In 1986 and 1988, a Colorado Springs, Colorado, public housing authority issued $26 million in bonds with Central Bank serving as *indenture trustee* for the bond issues. The bonds were secured by landowner assessment *liens* requiring that (1) the land subject to the liens was to be worth at least 160 percent of the bonds' outstanding principal and interest and that (2) the land developer, AmWest Development, was to give Central Bank annual reports assuring that the 160 percent goal was being met. After questions were raised about the accuracy of the 1988 *appraisal* showing steady land values from 1986 to 1988, and noting that Colorado Springs property values were declining and that Central Bank was operating with an appraisal that was almost 16 months old, the bond underwriter expressed concern that the 160 percent test was not being met. Central Bank asked its in-house appraiser to review the 1988 appraisal. He thought the appraisal was optimistic and suggested that Central hire an outside appraiser to review the 1988 appraisal. Central, however, decided to delay the review until the end of the year, six months after the June 1988 closing on the bond issues. Before that review was complete, the Housing Authority defaulted on the 1988 bonds. Bond purchasers sued the Housing Authority, the underwriter, and an AmWest director claiming violations of section 10(b) of the Securities Act of 1934. Central Bank was also sued on the grounds that it was secondarily liable under section 10(b) for aiding and abetting the other defendants' fraud. The District Court granted summary judgment for Central Bank, but the Tenth Circuit Court of Appeals reversed. The United States Supreme Court granted certiorari to review the question of aiding and abetting liability under section 10(b).

* * *

Justice Kennedy

As we have interpreted it, § 10(b) of the Securities Exchange Act of 1934 imposes private civil liability on those who commit a manipulative or deceptive act in connection with the purchase or sale of securities. In this case, we must answer a question reserved in two earlier decisions: whether private civil liability under § 10(b) extends as well to those who do not engage in the manipulative or deceptive practice but who aid and abet the violation.

* * *

The 1933 and 1934 Acts create an extensive scheme of civil liability. The Securities and Exchange Commission (SEC) may bring administrative actions and injunctive proceedings to enforce a variety of statutory prohibitions. Private plaintiffs may sue under the express private rights of action contained in the Acts. They may also sue under private rights of action we have found to be implied by the terms of § 10(b) and § 14(a) of the 1934 Act. This case concerns the most familiar private cause of action: the one we have found to be implied by § 10(b), the general antifraud provision of the 1934 Act. Section 10(b) states:

Continued

Continued

> It shall be unlawful for any person, directly or indirectly, by the use of any means or instrumentality of interstate commerce or of the mails, or of any facility of any national securities exchange . . .
>
> (b) To use or employ, in connection with the purchase or sale of any security registered on a national securities exchange or any security not so registered, any manipulative or deceptive device or contrivance in contravention of such rules and regulations as the [SEC] may prescribe.

Rule 10b-5, adopted by the SEC in 1942, casts the proscription in similar terms.

* * *

With respect . . . to . . . the scope of conduct prohibited by § 10(b), the text of the statute controls our decision. In § 10(b), Congress prohibited manipulative or deceptive acts in connection with the purchase or sale of securities. It envisioned that the SEC would enforce the statutory prohibition through administrative and injunctive actions. Of course, a private plaintiff now may bring suit against violators of § 10(b). But the private plaintiff may not bring a 10b-5 suit against a defendant for acts not prohibited by the text of § 10(b). To the contrary, our cases considering the scope of conduct prohibited by § 10(b) in private suits have emphasized adherence to the statutory language, " '[t]he starting point in every case involving construction of a statute.' "

* * *

Adherence to the text in defining the conduct covered by § 10(b) is [also] consistent with our decisions interpreting other provisions of the securities Acts.

* * *

Our consideration of statutory duties, especially in cases interpreting § 10(b), establishes that the statutory text controls the definition of conduct covered by § 10(b). That bodes ill for [First Interstate] for "the language of Section 10(b) does not in terms mention aiding and abetting." To overcome this problem, respondents and the SEC suggest (or hint at) the novel argument that the use of the phrase "directly or indirectly" in the text of § 10(b) covers aiding and abetting.

* * *

The federal courts have not relied on the "directly or indirectly" language when imposing aiding and abetting liability under § 10(b), and with good reason. There is a basic flaw with this interpretation. According to respondents and the SEC, the "directly or indirectly" language shows that "Congress . . . intended to reach all persons who engage, even if only indirectly, in proscribed activities connected with securities transactions." The problem, of course, is that aiding and abetting liability extends beyond persons who engage, even indirectly, in a proscribed activity; aiding and abetting liability reaches persons who do not engage in the proscribed activities at all, but who give a degree of aid to those who do.

* * *

Congress knew how to impose aiding and abetting liability when it chose to do so . . . If, as respondents seem to say, Congress intended to impose aiding and abetting liability, we presume it would have used the words "aid" and "abet" in the statutory text. But it did not . . .

We reach the uncontroversial conclusion, accepted even by those courts recognizing a § 10(b) aiding and abetting cause of action, that the text of the 1934 Act does not itself reach

Continued

Continued

those who aid and abet a § 10(b) violation. Unlike those courts, however, we think that conclusion resolves the case. It is inconsistent with settled methodology in § 10(b) cases to extend liability beyond the scope of conduct prohibited by the statutory text. To be sure, aiding and abetting a wrongdoer ought to be actionable in certain instances. The issue, however, is not whether imposing private civil liability on aiders and abettors is good policy but whether aiding and abetting is covered by the statute.

As in earlier cases considering conduct prohibited by § 10(b), we again conclude that the statute prohibits only the making of a material misstatement (or omission) or the commission of a manipulative act . . . The proscription does not include giving aid to a person who commits a manipulative or deceptive act. We cannot amend the statute to create liability for acts that are not themselves manipulative or deceptive within the meaning of the statute.

* * *

Because the text of § 10(b) does not prohibit aiding and abetting, we hold that a private plaintiff may not maintain an aiding and abetting suit under § 10(b). The absence of § 10(b) aiding and abetting liability does not mean that secondary actors in the securities markets are always free from liability under the securities Acts. Any person or entity, including a lawyer, accountant, or bank, who employs a manipulative device or makes a material misstatement (or omission) on which a purchaser or seller of securities relies may be liable as a primary violator under 10b-5, assuming *all* of the requirements for primary liability under Rule 10b-5 are met. . . .

[First Interstate concedes] that Central Bank did not commit a manipulative or deceptive act within the meaning of § 10(b). Instead, in the words of the complaint, Central Bank was "secondarily liable under § 10(b) for its conduct in aiding and abetting the fraud." Because of our conclusion that there is no private aiding and abetting liability under § 10(b), Central Bank may not be held liable as an aider and abettor. The District Court's grant of summary judgment to Central Bank was proper, and the judgment of the Court of Appeals is *reversed.*

* * *

Justice Stevens, with whom Justice Blackmun, Justice Souter, and Justice Ginsburg join, dissenting

The main themes of the Court's opinion are that the text of § 10(b) of the Securities Exchange Act of 1934 does not expressly mention aiding and abetting liability, and that Congress knows how to legislate. Both propositions are unexceptionable, but neither is reason to eliminate the private right of action against aiders and abettors of violations of § 10(b) and the Securities and Exchange Commission's Rule 10b-5 . . .

In *hundreds* of judicial and administrative proceedings in every circuit in the federal system, the courts and the SEC have concluded that aiders and abettors are subject to liability under § 10(b) and Rule 10b-5 . . . [A]ll 11 Courts of Appeals to have considered the question have recognized a private cause of action against aiders and abettors under § 10(b) and Rule 10b-5.

* * *

Even had § 10(b) not been enacted against a backdrop of liberal construction of remedial statutes and judicial favor toward implied rights of action, I would still disagree with the majority for the simple reason that a "settled construction of an important federal statute should not be disturbed unless and until Congress so decides" . . . A policy of respect for consistent judicial and administrative interpretations leaves it to elected representatives to assess settled law and to

Continued

Continued

evaluate the merits and demerits of changing it. Even when there is no affirmative evidence of ratification, the Legislature's failure to reject a consistent judicial or administrative construction counsels hesitation from a court asked to invalidate it. Here, however, the available evidence suggests congressional *approval* of aider and abettor liability in private § 10(b) actions.

* * *

As a general principle, I agree, "the creation of new rights ought to be left to legislatures, not courts" . . . While we are now properly reluctant to recognize private rights of action without an instruction from Congress, we should also be reluctant to lop off rights of action that have been recognized for decades, even if the judicial methodology that gave them birth is now out of favor . . .

I respectfully dissent.

Questions

1. Explain the issue and the holding in the *Central Bank* case.
2. Contrast the majority and dissenting opinions in the *Central Bank* case.
3. Explain the practical implications of the *Central Bank* decision for accountants, lawyers, banks, and other secondary parties.
4. Discuss the wisdom of the *Central Bank* decision.

C. RICO

The 1970 Racketeer Influenced and Corrupt Organizations Act (**RICO**) (see Chapter 13), which was originally designed to stop organized crime activities, has often been used to pursue securities fraud. However, the 1995 Private Securities Litigation Reform Act (discussed above prior to the *Central Bank* case) amends RICO to explicitly preclude its use for securities fraud claims except where a criminal fraud conviction has been obtained. Clearly, the point of the amendment was to force plaintiffs to use the securities laws rather than RICO (with its appealing treble damages provision), although the precise implications of the amendment will not be clear until tested in court.[10]

RICO. Federal organized crime law making it illegal to acquire or operate an enterprise by a pattern of racketeering behavior.

D. Insider Trading

Profile Perspective: Let's return to Marc Andreessen and the Netscape story. Assume he learns from a team of Netscape programmers that the advanced Internet browser they have been working on is nearing completion. Clearly, marketing the new program will drive the value of Netscape stock rapidly upward. Should Andreessen immediately collect all of the money he can to buy more shares in Netscape? Of course, the answer is no.

The use of insider information for financial profit in securities trading is called **insider trading** and might be subject to civil, criminal, and regulatory liability. Congress and the SEC have taken the position that fairness as well as confidence in our securities markets requires that insiders be forbidden from trading on information not available to the general

insider trading. Trading securities while in possession of material nonpublic information, in violation of a fiduciary duty.

public. Various laws forbid insider trading, but it is most commonly pursued as a form of fraud in violation of SEC Rule 10b-5. Unfortunately, we have no official definition of insider trading. Further, we have a great debate about who should be treated as an insider. Much of the world only tepidly restricts insider trading and wonders why we in America find it so troublesome. Many critics argue that much insider trading is actually beneficial and the problem, if there is one, should be left to the market. Nonetheless, after a period of relative quiet, in the mid-90s we are seeing a significant increase in SEC insider investigations. Much of the activity appears to be triggered by the recent wave of mergers and acquisitions that provide insiders with privileged information about impending deals and present a very big temptation to trade (illegally) on that information.

The Law. The philosophical debate aside, once a person is determined to have inside information the rules on insider trading appear to be very simple—anyone who has access to nonpublic information of a material nature (such as a recent oil strike, results of a major lawsuit, huge earnings increases, an impending takeover bid) must (1) refrain from trading in the stock and telling friends, relatives, and others to trade in the stock or (2) release the information to the public, wait a reasonable period of time, and then trade as desired.

Not surprisingly, the simplicity of those rules turns out to be deceptive. In practice, insider trading is an area of enormous uncertainty, as evidenced by the following discussion of short-swing profits, Rule 10b-5, and temporary insiders.

E. Short-Swing Profits

One of the earliest SEC concerns was that insiders would use access to financial reports and other data to buy (or sell) shares just prior to releasing positive (negative) information about the company and then almost immediately sell (or buy) back the shares at a profit when the market price of the stock had responded to this new information. In an attempt to limit the ability of major participants in corporate affairs to gain a short-term economic advantage due to their early access to earnings reports and other inside, nonpublic information that might cause a change in stock prices when made public, the 1934 act prohibits officers, directors, and 10 percent beneficial owners of a corporation from receiving **short-swing profits.** These are any profits made on company stock held for less than six months. Any such profits must be returned to the company whether or not inside information was used to secure that profit. In 1996, the SEC altered short-swing rules to exempt many routine transactions such as moving assets in and out of company stock funds where the transactions are at least six months apart. The changes are expected to significantly reduce the cost of complying with the short-swing rules.

short-swing profits. Profits made by an insider through sale/purchase of company stock within six months of acquisition.

F. Rule 10b-5

The prohibition against short-swing profits leaves open the possibility that an **insider** could still profit by buying (selling) shares just prior to the release of positive (negative) information but then refraining from trading for at least six months. While the trade would not trigger the short-swing profits provision, it would still be insider trading under Rule 10b-5, and the insider could be prosecuted. Although the short-swing profits restriction spells out exactly who is an insider and what transactions are forbidden, the persons and behavior covered by Rule 10b-5 can be much less clear. In recent years, the question of who is an insider under Rule 10b-5 and the conditions under which someone can be held liable for dealing in insider information have been in a

insider. In securities law, anyone who has knowledge of facts not available to the general public.

state of flux. Clearly, corporate officers, directors, and attorneys may have access to inside information; in particular instances, engineers in an oil field also could—but so could brokers, analysts, printers, and journalists.

G. Temporary Insiders and Outsiders

Insider trading is rooted, generally, in the notion of breach of **fiduciary duty;** that is, insiders should not seek to profit in ways that violate their responsibilities to the firm and its shareholders. That same responsibility can also extend to those who are not technically insiders, but nonetheless are in possession of inside information. Temporary insiders such as consultants, accountants, engineers, and lawyers would breach their fiduciary duty if they traded personally on information they acquired in their inside work or if they tipped others for their trading advantage.

fiduciary duty. The responsibility of one in a position of trust with another to act in the best interests of the other.

Outsiders are all those people who might indirectly receive inside information. Although the subject of great controversy, recent court decisions have increasingly found some outsiders to be guilty of insider trading. That guilt springs generally from two theories: the tipper/tippee theory and the misappropriation theory.

Tipper/Tippee Theory. A **tipper** (one who conveys inside information to another) violates the law if (1) the tip is used in trading, (2) the tip constitutes a breach of the tipper's fiduciary duty, and (3) the tipper receives a personal benefit of some kind from the disclosure. The recipient of that information (the **tippee**) even though an outsider—commonly a friend or relative—likewise may not lawfully trade on inside information if he or she knew or should have known that the tipper was violating a fiduciary duty in disclosing the information.

tipper. In securities law, one who conveys inside information to another.

tippee. In securities law, one who receives inside information from another.

For example, in 1995 two former AT&T officials (tippers) pleaded guilty to criminal charges of passing tips to friends (tippees) about forthcoming AT&T acquisition plans. Some of the profit from the illegal trading had been funneled back to one of the AT&T officials. Two of the people who received those tips and traded on them also pleaded guilty. The SEC alleged that the inside traders earned illegal profits of $2.3 million based on early information about one of those deals, AT&T's prospective acquisition of NCR.[11]

Misappropriation Theory. Outsiders may also be guilty of violating Rule 10b-5 if they wrongfully secure material, nonpublic information and tip or trade on it for personal gain—this is known as **misappropriation.** The outsider might be a lawyer, underwriter, a printer who distributes SEC-required documents, or even a therapist. In effect, the outsider has stolen the information. In doing so, if the outsider has breached a fiduciary duty (e.g., to his employer), a misappropriation claim may be raised. In an unusually egregious breach of trust, a California psychotherapist used information secured in an August 1994 therapy session and employed it to earn trading profits (with a partner) of over $177,000. The psychotherapist, a veteran of 35 years in practice, was engaging in marriage counseling with an executive who mentioned that his employer, Lockheed, was approaching a major financial deal. The therapist immediately traded on that information and profited when Lockheed and Martin Marietta merged a few days after the counseling session. In 1995, the therapist pleaded guilty to one criminal count of insider trading and settled SEC civil charges for $110,000. As a matter of law, the therapist misappropriated the information that he had received in confidence, thus breaching his fiduciary relationship with the executive.[12]

misappropriation. In securities law, taking material, nonpublic information and engaging in insider trading in violation of a fiduciary duty.

Misappropriation theory is a powerful weapon against insider trading, but the law remains unsettled. In the *Carpenter* case that follows, a federal Court of Appeals endorsed the misappropriation theory as applied to a *Wall Street Journal* reporter.

CASE

UNITED STATES V. CARPENTER

791 F.2d 1024 (2nd Cir. 1986)

Facts

R. Foster Winans, a *Wall Street Journal* reporter, co-authored a daily investment advice column, "Heard on the Street," which, upon publication, often had an impact on the market price of stocks discussed in the column. As Winans knew, the *Journal*'s rule was that the column's contents were the newspaper's confidential information prior to publication. Winans schemed with Felis and another stockbroker to give them advance information about what he would be saying in the column. The stockbrokers bought and sold stocks based on the likely impact of Winans's column on market prices. Carpenter, a *Journal* news clerk, participated in the scheme, largely as a messenger. After an SEC investigation, Winans and Felis were convicted of insider trading and wire and mail fraud. Carpenter was convicted of aiding and abetting. (Contrast with the *private action* decision in the *Central Bank* case, p. 426). Winans, Felis, and Carpenter appealed, claiming that they could not have violated SEC Rule 10b-5 because they were not corporate insiders nor had they misappropriated (taken or stolen) information from insiders.

* * *

Judge Pierce

[We must] assess whether this case falls within the purview of the "misappropriation" theory of section 10(b) and Rule 10b-5 thereunder.* . . . It is clear that defendant Winans, as an employee of the *Wall Street Journal,* breached a duty of confidentiality to his employer by misappropriating from the *Journal* confidential prepublication information, regarding the timing and content of certain newspaper columns, about which he learned in the course of his employment.

* * *

[A]ppellants argue, the misappropriation theory may be applied only where the information is misappropriated by corporate insiders or so-called quasi-insiders, who owe to the corporation and its shareholders a fiduciary duty of abstention or disclosure. Thus, appellants would have us hold that it was not enough that Winans breached a duty of confidentiality to his employer, the *Wall Street Journal,* in misappropriating and trading on material nonpublic information; he would have to have breached a duty to the corporations or shareholders thereof whose stock they purchased or sold on the basis of that information.

Continued

*Section 10(b), prohibits the use "in connection with the purchase or sale of any security . . . [of] any manipulative or deceptive device or contrivance in contravention of such rules and regulations as the Commission may prescribe . . ."

Rule 10b-5 states:

It shall be unlawful for any person, directly or indirectly, by use of any means or instrumentality of interstate commerce, or of the mails or of any facility of any national securities exchange,

(*a*) To employ any device, scheme, or artifice to defraud,

(*b*) To make any untrue statement of a material fact or to omit to state a material fact necessary in order to make the statements made, in the light of the circumstances under which they were made, not misleading, or

(*c*) To engage in any act, practice, or course of business which operates or would operate as a fraud or deceit upon any person, in connection with the purchase or sale of any security.

Continued

Appellants . . . interpret the misappropriation theory too narrowly . . . [T]he misappropriation theory . . . broadly proscribes the conversion by "insiders" *or others* of material non-public information in connection with the purchase or sale of securities.

* * *

Further, we think that the application of the misappropriation theory herein promotes the purposes and policies underlying section 10(b) and Rule 10b-5. In construing the Rule's meaning, we must begin with its language. The Rule prohibits "*any* person," acting "directly or indirectly," from employing "*any* device, scheme or artifice to defraud." It equally prohibits "*any* act, practice, or course of business which operates as a fraud or deceit upon *any* person." This repeated use of the word "any" evidences Congress' intention to draft the Rule broadly.

* * *

The legislative intent of the 1934 Act is similarly broad-reaching. As this Court has noted in applying the misappropriation theory, "the antifraud provision was intended to be broad in scope, encompassing all 'manipulative and deceptive practices which have been demonstrated to fulfill no useful function.' " We perceive nothing "useful" about defendants' scheme. Nor, in our view, could any purported function of the scheme be considered protected given Congress' stated concern for the perception of fairness and integrity in the securities markets.

* * *

In enacting the Insider Trading Sanctions Act of 1984, Congress noted that the intent of the 1934 Act was to condemn all manipulative or deceptive trading "whether the information about a corporation or its securities originates from inside or outside the corporation." Further, the reason for this view was clearly stated: "the abuses sought to be remedied [by section 10(b)] were not limited to actions of corporate insiders and large shareholders." Clearly, Congress has understood its predecessors to have delineated illegal conduct along the lines not simply of relationships to corporations and duties arising thereunder . . . Rather, Congress apparently has sought to proscribe as well trading on material, nonpublic information obtained not through skill but through a variety of "deceptive" practices, unlawful acts which we term "misappropriation."

We do not say that merely using information not available or accessible to others gives rise to a violation of Rule 10b-5. That theory of 10b-5 liability has been rejected. There are disparities in knowledge and the availability thereof at many levels of market functioning that the law does not presume to address. However, the critical issue is found in the district judge's careful distinction between "information" and "conduct" . . . Obviously, one may gain a competitive advantage in the marketplace through conduct constituting skill, foresight, industry and the like . . . But one may not gain such advantage by conduct constituting secreting, stealing, purloining or otherwise misappropriating material nonpublic information in breach of an employer-imposed fiduciary duty of confidentiality. Such conduct constitutes chicanery, not competition; foul play, not fair play.

* * *

Winans "misappropriated—stole, to put it bluntly—valuable nonpublic information entrusted to him in the utmost confidence." The information misappropriated here was the *Journal*'s own confidential schedule of forthcoming publications. It was the advance knowledge of the timing and content of these publications, upon which appellants, acting secretively, reasonably expected to and did realize profits in securities transactions. Since section 10(b) has been found to proscribe

Continued

Continued

fraudulent trading by insiders or outsiders, such conduct constituted fraud and deceit, as it would had Winans stolen material nonpublic information from traditional corporate insiders or quasi-insiders. Felis' liability as a tippee derives from Winans' liability . . .

Nor is there any doubt that this "fraud and deceit" was perpetrated "upon a[ny] person" under section 10(b) and Rule 10b-5 . . . Appellants Winans, and Felis and Carpenter by their complicity, perpetrated their fraud "upon" the *Wall Street Journal,* sullying its reputation and thereby defrauding it "as surely as if they took [its] money."

* * *

Although not every breach of an employee's fiduciary duty to his employer constitutes mail or wire fraud, it is clear that "the concealment by a fiduciary of material information which he is under a duty to disclose to another under circumstances where the non-disclosure could or does result in harm to another is a violation of the [mail fraud] statute." In the present case, the scheme to misappropriate material nonpublic information regarding the *Journal*'s forthcoming publications in breach of the employee's duty of confidentiality to the *Journal* in connection with securities transactions . . . threatened to harm the *Journal*'s reputation for professionalism and integrity.

* * *

Miner, Circuit Judge, dissenting in part

Since I am of the opinion that the misappropriation theory cannot be interpreted so expansively as to encompass the activities of these defendants, I respectfully dissent from so much of the majority opinion as affirms the convictions for securities fraud.

Until today, the misappropriation theory of criminal liability for securities fraud was applied only in those cases involving the taking and use of non-public, confidential, *securities-related* information by those who obtain that information through special relationships with their sources of knowledge . . .

No confidential securities information imparted by reason of any special relationship was purloined by these defendants. The "Heard" columns written by Winans consisted of high quality, accurate articles dealing with the strengths and weaknesses of various securities, and the research data upon which the columns were based were fully available to the public.

* * *

While the proscription of fraudulent and deceptive practices in connection with the purchase and sale of securities is a broad one, it never was intended to protect the reputation, or enforce the ethical standards, of a financial newspaper . . . Harm to reputation, rather than to securities markets or market participants, never has been recognized as a proper subject for redress under section 10(b) or rule 10b-5.

* * *

Continued

Continued

Afterword

The U.S. Supreme Court later reviewed the *Carpenter* decision and left the status of the misappropriation theory in some doubt. The Court's vote on the misappropriation argument was split 4–4, thus letting stand the Court of Appeals decision, but clearly not providing a ringing endorsement of misappropriation reasoning. The Court did unanimously approve the wire and mail fraud convictions. [See *Carpenter* v. *United States,* 484 U.S. 19 (1987).]

Questions—Law

1. Based upon your reading of the appeals court decision in the *Carpenter* case, should the misappropriation theory be applied to outsiders? Explain.
2. *a.* Could *The Wall Street Journal* itself or its parent, Dow Jones, lawfully trade in the stock of companies to be discussed in forthcoming articles?
   b. Would they be likely to do so? Explain.
3. Financial printers are paid large sums of money to prepare documents for tender offers, registration statements, and so on. Advance knowledge of the data contained in these documents could be very valuable, and thus careful steps are taken to stop any premature leaks. The printing may be divided up among many printers, or the printers may even be sequestered for a period of time. If a printer were to use information in a document for his or her own benefit, would this constitute insider trading? Explain. [See *Chiarella* v. *United States,* 445 U.S. 222 (1980).]

Question—Public Policy

From a free market point of view, restraints on insider trading do not make a great deal of sense. Explain that view. Do you agree with the free market position? Explain.

VIII. Securities Regulation around the Globe

Historically, European and Asian governments chose not to look closely at insider trading, viewing it largely as one of the perks of a managerial role and, in any case, a problem best left to industry self-regulation. Even where officially forbidden, as in Japan, enforcement has been much less than aggressive. Now the fall of Soviet communism, the emergence of independent states in Eastern Europe, and newfound global faith in free markets have led to worldwide reconsideration of securities regulation policy. For example, in 1995 India altered its securities laws to give greater power to the Securities and Exchange Board of India, including broader investigative authority and the power to issue fines.[13]

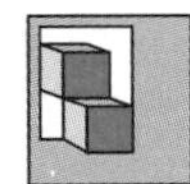

In 1994, Germany became the last of the major financial trading centers to outlaw insider trading. Then in 1995, German authorities secured their first conviction under the law, imposing a $1.3 million fine on the son of the owner of a machinery company, Krones AG. According to investigators, the son had early information about big losses for the company's South American subsidiaries. He sold about $800,000 in shares and averted a $250,000 loss.[14] Germany is trying to encourage more outside investment by making its trading fairer and more open. However, its insider trading law remains relatively benign, as reported by *The Wall Street Journal:*

> Germany has no automatic notification by companies or stock exchanges that substantial changes in stock prices have occurred . . . In the United States, if a company's stock begins trading at double the normal value, stock exchange officials

automatically make inquiries to company officials about the volatility. In Germany, though, federal authorities possess no oversight powers over fiercely independent regional stock exchanges. Further, the supervisory office—with 100 people—is tiny compared with the U.S. Securities and Exchange Commission, which has over 850 enforcement officers.[15]

In the face of serious financial scandals, Russia is relying on self-regulation, believing it to be cheaper and more effective than government intervention. The Russian SEC has a vigorous free market orientation and, at this writing, is encouraging new legislation that would license self-regulation in the investment industry. This in a nation where: "False advertising, pyramid schemes, and broken contracts have been the hallmarks of the Russian securities industry."[16]

"False advertising, pyramid schemes, and broken contracts have been the hallmarks of the Russian securities industry."

Summary

Legal Review. In this chapter, our goal was to understand the general pattern of federal rules and policies governing the U.S. securities industry. We began by identifying the nature of a security. Thereafter, we turned to the Securities Act of 1933 and its provisions to encourage full disclosure of all facts relevant to the *initial* sale of securities. The Securities Exchange Act of 1934 endeavors to assure honesty in all dimensions of the *resale* of securities by providing for close oversight of the securities industry. The 1934 act established the Securities and Exchange Commission to provide that oversight.

Having set out the foundational material in the 1933 and 1934 acts, we turned to a trio of problem areas—tender offers/takeovers, fraud, and insider trading—that have been well-publicized and significant elements of SEC business in recent years. The chapter provided an examination of the interplay between ethics, that is, self-regulation, the force of the free market, and SEC rules. Our purpose was to consider the effectiveness of each of those constraints in assuring an honest and efficient securities industry.

Ethics/Public Policy Review. Few segments of the American economy are more dependent on an image of honor and integrity than the securities industry. And yet, few segments of the American economy are currently more troubled by allegations of fraud and manipulation. Consequently, securities regulation in the 1990s is a public policy war zone. On the one hand, the Orange County and Barings bankruptcies, memories of the famous trading scandals of the 1980s (do you recognize the name Michael Milken?), and ongoing allegations of fraud from small-time, local investment advisors to the biggest firms on Wall Street cause critics and many government officials to feel that our regulatory structure should be strengthened and more rigorously enforced. On the other hand, in 1995 Congress was able to pass, over President Clinton's veto, new legislation that makes it more difficult for investors to bring securities fraud lawsuits. The general sentiment in Congress seems to be that we need to put more faith in self-regulation (ethics) and the market and rely less on government intervention and lawsuits.

Do you recognize the name Michael Milken?

Economics Review. The health of the American and global economies depends on efficient investment markets in which capital formation is easily accomplished so that growth and jobs can follow. Thus, many Republicans in Congress and free market advocates believe we need to drastically reduce our reliance on government oversight in the securities markets. Stephen Blumenthal, Republican counsel to the House Commerce Committee, says, "[I]t's frighteningly expensive to raise capital. If you're a couple of engineers making disk drives, you want to sell stock in five or six states and 6 percent will go to legal and compliance. That could have been used to build more disk drives."[17] Many politicians, investment brokers, and even regulators themselves think that the process can be streamlined. The idea would be to allow the market a chance to more efficiently work its will. At the same time, many other Wall Street executives, politicians, and securities regulators are not convinced that the securities law system is broken. They favor reasonable government oversight to preserve the integrity of the industry and thus retain the faith of the investing public.

Chapter Questions—Law

1. Define (*a*) security, (*b*) private placements, (*c*) blue sky laws, (*d*) fraud, (*e*) short-swing profits, (*f*) tender offers, (*g*) registration, and (*h*) prospectus.
2. Discuss the exemptions available for certain types of securities.
3. Explain how federal securities laws attempt to make provisions for small businesses.
4. Ivan Landreth and his sons owned all of the stock in a lumber business they operated in Tonasket, Washington. The owners offered the stock for sale. During that time a fire severely damaged the business, but the owners made assurances of rebuilding and modernization. The stock was sold to Dennis and Bolten, and a new organization, Landreth Timber Company, was formed with the senior Landreth remaining as a consultant on the side. The new firm was unsuccessful and was sold at a loss. The Landreth Timber Company then filed suit against Ivan Landreth and his son seeking rescission of the first sale, alleging, among other arguments, that Landreth and sons had widely offered and then sold their stock without registering it as required by the Securities Act of 1933. The district court acknowledged that *stocks* fit within the definition of a *security,* and that the stock in question "possessed all of the characteristics of conventional stock." However, it held that the federal securities laws do not apply to the sale of 100 percent of the stock of a closely held corporation. Here, the district court found that the purchasers had not entered into the sale with the expectation of earnings secured via the labor of others. Managerial control resided with the purchasers. Thus, the sale was a commercial venture rather than a typical investment. The Court of Appeals affirmed, and the case reached the Supreme Court. Decide. [See *Landreth Timber Co.* v. *Landreth,* 471 U.S. 681 (1985).]
5. For two years, representatives of Basic Incorporated and Combustion Engineering, Inc., had engaged in various meetings and conversations regarding the possibility of a merger. During that time, Basic issued three public statements indicating that no merger talks were in progress. Then, in 1978 the two firms merged. Some Basic shareholders had sold their stock between the first public denial of merger talks and the time when the merger was announced. Those stockholders filed a class action claiming Basic had made false and misleading statements in violation of Section 10(b) of the 1934 Securities Act and SEC Rule 10b-5. The plaintiff stockholders claimed they had suffered injury by selling their stocks at prices artificially depressed by the allegedly false statements. They argued that they would not have sold their stocks had they been truthfully informed of the merger talks. The trial court, in finding for Basic, took the position that preliminary merger discussions are immaterial. But the lower court certified (approved) the stockholders' class action, saying that reliance by the plaintiffs on Basic's statements could be presumed (and thus reliance need not be proved by each

plaintiff in turn). In certifying the class action, the lower court embraced the efficient-market theory or the fraud-on-the-market theory. The court of appeals agreed with the lower court's class action certification based on efficient-market reasoning, but the appeals court reversed the immateriality finding regarding preliminary discussions. The case went to the Supreme Court.

a. Explain the efficient-market theory and its role in this case.

b. Decide the materiality issue. Explain.

[See *Basic, Inc.* v. *Max L. Levinson,* 485 U.S. 224 (1988).]

Chapter Questions—Economics/Public Policy

1. Christopher Farrell commented in *Business Week* regarding the 1987 stock market crash, which resulted in an immediate 23 percent "devaluation of corporate America":

   > Economists will argue for years over what caused the crash of 1987. But it's already clear that the October 19 cataclysm marks the failure of the most pervasive belief in economics today: an unquestioning faith in the wisdom of free markets.

   Do you agree? Explain. [See "Where Was the Invisible Hand?" *Business Week,* April 18, 1988, p. 65.]
2. This chapter addresses insider trading and other suspect practices in the securities markets. Commentator George Will thinks those, and similar, problems, as popularized in the movie *Wall Street,* are "draining capitalism of its legitimacy":

   > A moral vulnerability of capitalism today is the belief that too much wealth is allocated capriciously, not only by the randomness of luck but by morally tainted shortcuts around a level playing field for all competitors. The legitimacy of the economic order depends on a consensus that, on balance, rewards are rationally related to the social value of the effort involved.

   Do you agree? Explain. [See "Capitalist Flaws Should Worry GOP," *Des Moines Register,* December 30, 1987, p. 6A.]
3. New York securities lawyer Saul Cohen recently argued in *The Wall Street Journal* that securities regulation as we have known it for several decades is becoming irrelevant. Cohen points to the large-scale departure of individual, small investors from the market. Those people, presumably recognizing the complexity of stock trading, have removed themselves as direct investors in favor of putting their money with professional managers of mutual funds and pension plans. Cohen says: "With the individual investor fleeing the market, regulation in his interest will be seen even by regulators to be a huge waste of the public's money." Cohen sees a market composed of big institutional investors and individual rich investors who will be operating under many fewer rules than is now the case. Efficiency will be the watchword as the wastefulness of regulations designed to protect little people who are no longer in the market becomes apparent. Cohen expects state securities commissions to stay in business but with much less work to do. The SEC will retrench but will continue to have an important role, among others, in keeping an eye on money managers and mutual funds. Given declining rules, Cohen expects renewed attention to the ethical duties of investment managers. Comment. [See Saul S. Cohen, "The Death of Securities Regulation," *The Wall Street Journal,* January 17, 1991, p. A10.]

4. In early 1991, SEC Chair Richard Breeden, testifying before the Senate Securities Subcommittee, indicated that he might propose a "shareholder bill of rights" to counteract what he sees as extreme measures by state legislatures and courts to protect companies against unwanted takeovers. Breeden said, "We have a problem we can't solve fully with disclosure: The extent to which state laws have become tolerant of management cementing themselves in." Breeden believes that the antitakeover measures offer excessive protection for corporate management, thus, in some instances, diminishing shareholders' capacity to maximize their pecuniary interests. Breeden is particularly disturbed with a Pennsylvania law that requires management to consider the interests of groups such as employees in making major corporate decisions, thus arguably harming shareholder (owner) interests. Comment. [See Kevin Salwen, "SEC Chairman Considers Holders' 'Bill of Rights,' " *The Wall Street Journal,* February 25, 1991, p. C19.]

Notes

1. Julie Pitta, "Investors Get Caught Up in the Netscape," *Los Angeles Times,* August 10, 1995, p. D1.
2. Ibid.
3. *Shearson/American Express* v. *McMahon,* 482 U.S. 220 (1987).
4. Michael Siconolfi, "New Arbitration Rules: Mixed Bag for Investors," *The Wall Street Journal,* January 23, 1996, p. C1.
5. Robert Rosenblatt and Michael Hiltzik, "Derivatives Sellers Agree to Police Themselves," *Los Angeles Times,* March 10, 1995, p. D2.
6. Michael Siconolfi, "SEC to Issue Prospectus Rules Allowing Fast Trade Settlement," *The Wall Street Journal,* May 10, 1995, p. C1.
7. Ibid.
8. A 1995 Supreme Court decision, directed to any person who "offers or sells a security . . . by means of a prospectus or oral communication," ruled that liability for omissions or misstatements under section 12(2) of the 1933 Act is limited in its reach to the initial public offering and thus does not apply to later purchases of that stock. [See *Gustafson* v. *Alloyd Company,* 63 *Law Week* 4165 (1995).]
9. For journalistic interpretations of the new bill, see Jeffrey Taylor, "Congress Sends Business a Christmas Gift," *The Wall Street Journal,* December 26, 1995, p. A2; and Kathy Kristof, "New Law for Wronged Investors," *Los Angeles Times,* December 23, 1995, p. D1.
10. See "Congress Passes Bill Removing Securities Fraud from RICO's List of Predicate Acts," *Civil RICO Report* 11, no. 16 (February 5, 1996).
11. Francis McMorris, "More Plead Guilty in AT&T Insider Case," *The Wall Street Journal,* August 21, 1995, p. B5.
12. Ralph Vartabedian, "Therapist Pleads Guilty to Insider Lockheed Deal," *The Wall Street Journal,* December 14, 1995, p. D1.
13. Richard Holman, "India Amends Securities Laws," *The Wall Street Journal,* January 30, 1995, p. A20.
14. Matt Marshall, "Germany's Law on Inside Trading Brings a Conviction," *The Wall Street Journal,* August 21, 1995, p. A5.
15. Ibid.
16. Neela Banerjee, "Russian Securities Trading, a Business with a Past, Bets Future on Regulation," *The Wall Street Journal,* February 8, 1995, p. A15.
17. Roger Lowenstein, "House Aims to Fix Securities Laws, but, Indeed, Is the System Broken?" *The Wall Street Journal,* August 10, 1995, p. C1.

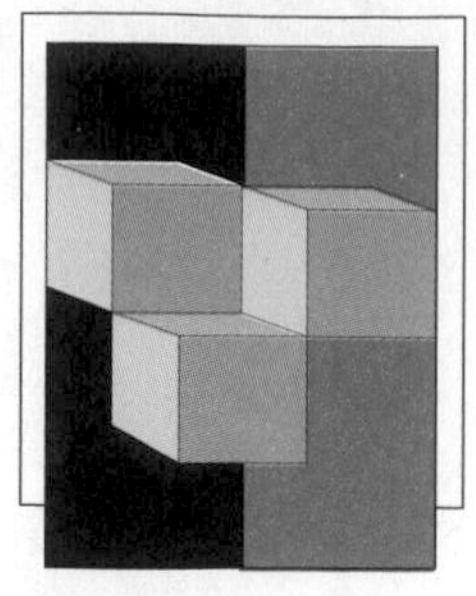

CHAPTER

11

Marketing Law: Building and Managing Sales

Reader's Guide

In Chapter 10, we surveyed federal and state regulation of the process of raising money for business expansion. We will assume the business you are building or managing is financially solid. Now your task is to begin to sell like crazy. You must convince the public that your product or service will add value to their lives. Not surprisingly, the law rather closely scrutinizes the marketing process. In this chapter, we will examine marketing law in its two primary dimensions. We will begin with advertising and its regulations broadly forbidding falsehoods and deceptions. Then we will turn to antitrust law and its restraints on marketing practices such as price-fixing and price discrimination, which might help you build your business in the short term but are anticompetitive and illegal.

I. Advertising and Sales: Deception?

PROFILE I

In 1996, Bass Beers Worldwide began test-marketing Hooper's Hooch, an "alcoholic lemonade" (4.7 percent alcohol) in Miami, Florida, and San Diego, California. If broadly marketed in the United States, Hooch is expected to sell for about $5 per six-pack. The new "alco-pop" was introduced in Britain in 1995 and sold at the phenomenal rate of 6 million cases annually. Critics in Britain say Hooch has been targeted to underage drinkers. Hooch's advertising logo is a grinning cartoon of a lemon, and its slogan is, "One taste, and you're hooched." The liquor industry there has agreed to self-policing measures to avoid overt appeals to teens and to avoid linking drinking with drugs, violence, aggression, or sexual prowess. The word *alcoholic* will be prominently displayed on all labeling, and Bass itself agreed to use the phrase "alcoholic lemon" rather than "alcoholic lemonade" in marketing Hooch. In 1995, Bass Beers announced that its profits had jumped by 9 percent, citing the popularity of Hooper's Hooch as one of the reasons.

Should the profitability of a product affect our judgment about the ethics of marketing that product? Explain.

Profile Perspective: As has been our practice in this text, let's consider your future in building and managing a business. Suppose you have joined an advertising firm following graduation. One of its clients is a major brewery that competes with Bass Beers. The client wants to develop an ad campaign to introduce an alco-pop designed to compete with Hooch. You suggest meeting the competition head on by building a new ad campaign around a cartoon-like "Hip Kat" who goes to great parties, does well with the girl cats, and drinks. On hearing your suggestion, your boss asks, "But what about the trouble R. J.

Reynolds is having right now with Joe Camel? Everyone, including the law, is after them for trying to sell smokes to kids."

Is your Hip Kat cartoon-like campaign lawful? We will examine some of the constraints that the law imposes on advertising and sales strategies. Is your Hip Kat idea honorable? Obviously, ethics plays a big role in constraining unfair marketing. We will return to that issue from time to time. Could we do with less regulation in this highly contentious area; that is, could we rely more completely on the market itself to police deception?

A. Advertising Regulation

The question of the legality of the Hip Kat campaign or any other advertising practice is not readily resolved, in part, because so many branches of law must be considered. Among numerous possibilities, we will examine the common law (judge-made law); state statutory law, including the Uniform Commercial Code; and federal statutory law, including the Federal Trade Commission Act and the Lanham Act. Remember that the First Amendment affords freedom of speech protection to advertising, although that protection is narrower than for political speech. Of course, false and deceptive advertising is not protected. (See Chapter 2 for an examination of the First Amendment and commercial speech.)

The Common Law—Deceit. The common-law remedy for false or misleading advertising is the tort action of **deceit,** which embraces what we often label *fraud* or *misrepresentation.* As discussed in Chapter 4, Contracts, and Chapter 12, Consumer Protection and Debtor/Creditor Law, the general test for deceit is as follows:

deceit. A tort involving intentional misrepresentation to deceive or trick another.

1. Misrepresentation of a material fact.
2. The misrepresentation was intentional.
3. The injured party justifiably relied on the misrepresentation.
4. Injury resulted.

Here the critical question often is whether we are dealing with fact or opinion. In advertising, we ordinarily apply the label **puffing** to a seller's statement of opinion, for example, "This is the healthiest food you can put in your mouth." What if your Hip Kat says, "Man, this is the smoothest drink going"? That kind of sales talk has not generally constituted grounds for legal action. (See Chapter 14, Product Liability, for a more thorough discussion.)

puffing. An expression of opinion by a seller not made as a representation of fact.

State Statutory Law. All of the states seek to prevent deception and unfairness in advertising. As explained in Chapter 14, the Uniform Commercial Code provides a cause of action for breach of an express warranty if, for example, the seller directly promises a cookie with 25 calories when, in fact, the total is 50. Some states, such as California, broadly forbid "any unlawful, unfair, or fraudulent business act or practice." At this writing, R. J. Reynolds is in fact facing a suit claiming that its Joe Camel campaign targets children and thus violates California's unfair advertising statute. The idea is that the advertising is unfair because it helps merchants in the sale of cigarettes to children, a practice forbidden by California law.[1] So under California law, your Hip Kat campaign might be unlawful. Furthermore, as part of two 1996 settlements of smoking-related lawsuits, the Liggett Group, smallest of the top five American tobacco companies, agreed to abandon the use of cartoon-like characters in its promotion activities.

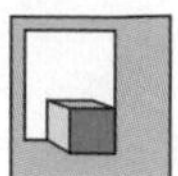

Ethics/Public Policy Questions

1. How would you vote in California's Joe Camel case? Explain.
2. Has the market operated effectively to protect children from smoking, or do we need to intervene yet more? Explain.

B. The Federal Trade Commission Act

Profile Perspective: We return now to your new job in advertising. Your Hip Kat campaign may be in some trouble, but your boss was impressed with your imagination nonetheless and asks you to develop a brief, catchy, attention-grabbing phrase for an important client, one of the nation's leading discount chains. After much reflection, you suggest the words: "Always the low price. Always." Your boss compliments you for your cleverness and just when you are feeling pretty good about yourself, says, "But we can't use it. We'll get sued." Is he correct?

> "Always the low price. Always."

Federal Trade Commission. Agency of the federal government responsible for promoting fair trade practices in interstate commerce.

To help answer that question, let's examine the Federal Trade Commission Act, which with the **Federal Trade Commission (FTC)** itself, is the primary federal weapon against fraud and misrepresentation. The FTC was created in 1914 for the purpose, broadly, of preventing unfair business practices. The FTC's regulatory efforts span a broad range of consumer activity. Much of that material will be found in Chapter 12, Consumer Protection and Debtor/Creditor Law. Here we will restrict our attention to the FTC role in advertising.

deception. Trade claim that is either false or likely to mislead the reasonable consumer and that is material to the consumer's decision making.

Unfair and deceptive trade practices, including those in advertising, are forbidden under section 5 of the Federal Trade Commission Act. The term *unfair* has been only loosely defined. We will focus our attention on **deception.** The FTC test for deception requires that the claim is (1) false or is likely to mislead the reasonable consumer and (2) the claim is material to the consumer's decision making. Proof of actual deception is not necessary; rather, a showing of some probability of deception is sufficient. The words in an ad must be examined in their total context, and the FTC may consider evidence regarding consumers' actual interpretations. Reasonable consumers are something like "ordinary people." "Materiality" refers to whether the claim affects consumer choice.

Deception can take many forms, including, for example, testimonials by celebrities who do not use the endorsed product or do not have sufficient expertise to evaluate its quality. The primary areas of dispute involve quality and price.

ad substantiation. Under Federal Trade Commission policy, product claims for which reasonable evidentiary support does not exist constitute unfair and deceptive trade practices.

Quality Claims. "Fewer calories," "faster acting," "more effective" are the kinds of claims that may lead to allegations of deception unless they are factually supportable. Under the FTC's **ad substantiation** program, advertisers are engaging in unfair and deceptive practices if they make product claims without some reasonable foundation for those claims. For example, credible survey evidence must be in hand if an advertiser says, "Consumers prefer our brand two to one."

When is a sale truly not a sale?

Pricing. Deception in price advertising sometimes takes the form of the so-called **bait and switch** practice, where a product is advertised at a very low price to attract customers although the seller actually has no intention of selling at that price. Once the customer is in the door (having taken the bait) the strategy is to switch the customer's attention to another, higher-priced product.

bait and switch. An unlawful sales tactic in which the seller advertises a product at a dramatically reduced price with no intention of selling at that price. The seller then disparages the "bait" and "switches" the buyer's attention to a higher-priced product.

Sale pricing also sometimes leads to claims of deception. When is a sale truly not a sale? Do some retailers offer phony markdowns based on inflated "original" or "regular" prices? In 1964, the FTC issued guidelines for proving that a former price was genuine. However, since 1970 the agency has largely ignored price advertising cases, thus leaving the issue to the states.

C. The Lanham Act

Profile Perspective: Let's return to your advertising career. Your boss comes to you now to bat around a problem the agency is having. The agency's major client is upset because its chief competitor (both make antacid products) is using the phrase "strongest antacid there is" in its ads. No scientific evidence has been produced to confirm that one antacid is stronger than the other in actually relieving the symptoms of acid indigestion; but your agency's client wants to know why you aren't making the same kind of claim. Can you do so lawfully? Could your client sue its competitor for false advertising?

This situation is likely to be addressed under Section 43(a) of the Lanham Act, which, among other things, forbids the use of false or misleading descriptions or representations in commercial advertising and permits *competitors* to sue each other on those grounds. Under the Lanham Act, your client could use the "strongest antacid" language if the claim were true, and your client could sue if its competitor's claim was not true.

In 1994, Johnson & Johnson–Merck Consumer Pharmaceuticals, makers of Mylanta Double-Strength antacid, sued Rhone-Poulenc Rorer Pharmaceuticals, maker of Extra Strength Maalox Plus (ESMP) antacid for false advertising in violation of Lanham in that Rorer used the language "strongest antacid there is." The court found that ESMP was, in fact, stronger in certain laboratory tests. Thus, the ad was not literally false, but was it misleading in causing consumers to think that the "strongest antacid" language meant ESMP provided the strongest relief in the human body: Remember—no credible evidence had been developed to demonstrate that one antacid was stronger than the other in actually relieving symptoms. The court found that Johnson & Johnson's survey evidence failed to show that a substantial number of consumers had actually been misled by the ESMP words, so the claim was ruled neither false nor misleading.[2]

The brief case that follows provides another example of Lanham in practice, but also raises interesting questions about corporate power and a sense of humor.

CASE

Polar Corp. v. Coca-Cola Co.

871 F. Supp. 1520 (D. Mass. 1994)

Facts

Since 1902, Polar Corporation, a Massachusetts regional producer of soft drinks and seltzer, had used Orson, a polar bear, as a marketing symbol. In 1993, Coke began using polar bears in an enormous advertising campaign. Polar felt that its customers were being confused by the Coke campaign and decided to fight back with humor rather than a lawsuit. For about a week in December 1994, Polar ran a 30-second television commercial in which a computer-generated polar bear examines a Coke can, makes an unhappy sound, and flips the can over his shoulder into a trash bin. A sign over the bin reads "Keep the Arctic pure." The polar bear then reaches down into the freezing Arctic water and pulls out a can of Polar Seltzer. The bear then drinks the Polar soda and smiles contentedly. A Coca-Cola spokesperson labeled the Polar ad "unbearable." Coca-Cola filed suit seeking an order enjoining Polar from further broadcasting the commercial.

* * *

District Judge Gorton

Coca-Cola argues that Polar's commercial violates the Lanham Act by disparaging the purity and the quality of Coke. Section 43(a) of the Lanham Act provides, in pertinent part:

> Any person who . . . uses in commerce any word, term, name, symbol, or device, or any combination thereof, or any false designation of origin, false or misleading description of fact, or false or misleading representation of fact, which . . . *in commercial advertising or promotion, misrepresents the nature, characteristics, qualities, or geographic origin of his or her or another person's goods,* services or commercial activities, shall be liable in a civil action by any person who believes that he or she is or is likely to be damaged by such an act.

This Court finds that, by causing the polar bear to throw the can of Coke into a trash bin labeled "Keep the Arctic Pure," Polar has implied that Coke is not pure. Because there is no evidence suggesting that Coke is not "pure," the Court concludes that Polar has misrepresented the nature and quality of Coke . . .

The Court further finds that Coca-Cola, engaged in an industry that relies heavily on the consumer's perception of quality and purity, has shown a potential for irreparable harm if the injunction is not granted. Moreover, that harm outweighs any injury that Polar would suffer as a result of the injunction, especially because Polar, in effect, would be enjoined only from misrepresenting the nature and quality of Coke. Finally, the public interest would not be adversely affected by the issuance of an injunction.

* * *

Therefore, Coca-Cola's motion for a preliminary injunction is allowed and this Court orders that:

> Polar, its officers, agents, servants, employees and attorneys, and those persons in active concert or participation with Polar during the pendency of this action are enjoined from broadcasting, causing to be broadcast, publishing, disseminating or distributing, in any way, directly or indirectly, the television commercial for Polar brand soft drinks that features a polar bear discarding a Coke can into a trash barrel.

* * *

Continued

Continued

Afterword

Polar was deluged with letters of support, including many $1 bills for an Orson defense fund. Polar subsequently modified the ad.

Questions

1. How do you argue that Polar's ad does not misrepresent the purity of Coke?
2. Would you have handled this situation differently than Coke did? Explain.
3. In an ad for Tropicana Products' Premium Pack orange juice, Olympic decathalon champion Bruce Jenner squeezed an orange while saying, "It's pure, pasteurized juice as it comes from the orange," and then shows Jenner pouring the fresh-squeezed juice into a Tropicana carton while the audio says, "It's the only leading brand not made with concentrate and water." Coca-Cola sued Tropicana for false advertising in violation of the Lanham Act because the ad represented that Premium Pack contained unprocessed, fresh-squeezed juice when in fact the juice was pasteurized (heated) and sometimes frozen prior to packaging. Coke sought an injunction to stop the ad. Decide. Explain. [See *Coca-Cola Co.* v. *Tropicana Products, Inc.,* 690 F.2d 312 (2d Cir. 1982).]
4. Some Kraft, Inc., advertisements claimed its Kraft Singles cheese slices contained the same amount of calcium as 5 ounces of milk and more calcium than most brands of imitation cheese. Kraft argued that at least some of its ad claims were true because the slices were made from 5 ounces of milk and thus have a high calcium content. The government pointed out that about 30 percent of that calcium is lost in the process of converting milk to cheese, such that the ads resulted in an exaggeration of the actual calcium content. Are those ads deceptive? Explain. [See *Kraft Inc.* v. *F.T.C.,* 970 F.2d 311 (1992), cert. denied, 113 S.Ct. 1254 (1993).]

II. Antitrust Law and Marketing

the highly publicized quarrel between Ticketmaster and Pearl Jam

We have looked at some of those advertising and sales practices that raise legal problems. Now we turn our attention to antitrust law as a referee of sorts endeavoring to assure a level playing field in business practice. We will begin to examine the impact of antitrust in building and managing a business by reviewing the highly publicized quarrel between Ticketmaster, the nation's dominant ticket distribution service, and the rock group Pearl Jam.

PROFILE II

In 1994, Pearl Jam filed a civil complaint with the U.S. Justice Department claiming that Ticketmaster was violating antitrust laws resulting in unfairly high service charges for tickets. Ticketmaster service fees range, generally, from $3 to $15 per ticket. Ticketmaster provides ticket service for more than 50 major sports teams and exclusively controls ticketing for about two-thirds of the major stadiums, amphitheaters, and arenas in America. Other companies offer ticket service, primarily on a regional basis.

In 1995, Ticketmaster bid for but failed to secure the ticket contract for the 1996 Summer Olympics in Atlanta, Georgia. Ticketmaster's clients seem very happy with the company's work. Those clients argue that exclusive ticketing arrangements are necessary to maintain quality control and to prevent customers and advertisers from being confused by multiple ticket sources.

In July 1995, the Justice Department announced that it would not pursue an antitrust action against Ticketmaster, but that competitive developments in the industry would continue to be monitored. Attorney General Janet Reno pointed to the entry of new competition into the ticket service market. A class action suit was also dismissed in a California state court, but other private class actions, an antitrust claim by a competitor, MovieFone, and a New York state inquiry remain in process at this writing.

QUESTIONS

1. On the basis of these facts, what antitrust claims might be raised against Ticketmaster?
2. Why did the Justice Department point to the entry of new firms when it announced its decision against pursuing Ticketmaster?
3. Is the Ticketmaster dispute best left to the force of the market?

A. ANTITRUST AND BUSINESS PRACTICE

Imagine that you take a sales job with a large national firm. You are out on the road, calling on clients, learning the business, trying to make some money, and trying to impress your boss. As it turns out, antitrust law is an important consideration in what you can and cannot do on your sales rounds. Sales personnel and managers must take antitrust law seriously, as Du Pont illustrated by handing out to its employees a small plastic card, like a credit card, on which were printed the following Ten Don'ts of Antitrust:

1. Don't discuss prices with competitors.
2. Don't divide customers, markets, or territories with competitors.
3. Don't agree upon or attempt to control a customer's resale price.
4. Don't attempt to restrict a customer's resale activity.
5. Don't offer a customer prices or terms more favorable than those offered competing customers.
6. Don't require a customer to buy a product only from you.
7. Don't use one product as bait to sell another.
8. Don't disparage a competitor's product unless the statements are true.
9. Don't make sales or purchases conditional on reciprocal purchases or sales.
10. Don't hesitate to consult with your legal counsel.

B. ANTITRUST AND THE AMERICAN CHARACTER

Antitrust law not only affects business practice and our day-to-day personal lives, but also is a powerful force in shaping the character and direction of American life. Broadly, antitrust law was designed to preserve the advantages of a free market. Today in the federal courts, conservative Reagan/Bush judges are dominant and antitrust is certainly not being used aggressively as a lever for social change. We no longer subscribe to the simplistic notion that "bigness (in business) is bad." Nonetheless, antitrust continues to be an important public policy tool.

Public Policy Question

What core American values are we trying to preserve when the government employs antitrust law to intervene in the market and attack monopoly, price-fixing, and so on, that is, what were we trying to preserve about America when we adopted our antitrust laws?

C. Roots of Antitrust Law

Personal freedom is the essence of America. We fear excessive concentrations of power both in government and business. Following the Civil War and up to World War I, Americans felt that big businesses, symbolized most notably by John D. Rockefeller and Standard Oil, would abuse workers, consumers, and competitors in order to increase their own wealth and power. Furthermore, monopoly grew from an economic issue to become, in the late 1800s, the dominant domestic political theme of the day. Bigness was perceived to be a threat to democracy. Consequently, we lost some of our faith in the free market and turned to government rules, including in 1887 the Interstate Commerce Commission Act, to stop discriminatory rates. Then in 1911, the United States won the Supreme Court victory that broke the Standard Oil monopoly.[3] That new view that market forces must be tempered by government intervention has, of course, profoundly altered American life.

D. Antitrust Statutes

A brief look at the various antitrust statutes will serve to place them in historical context. A further examination will accompany the case materials.

Sherman Antitrust Act, 1890. Section 1 of the Sherman Antitrust Act forbids restraints of trade, and Section 2 forbids monopolization, attempts to monopolize, and conspiracies to monopolize. Several enforcement options are available to the federal government.

1. Violation of the Sherman Act opens participants to criminal penalties. The maximum corporate fine is $10 million per violation; individuals may be fined $350,000 and imprisoned for three years. Sherman Act violations are classified as felonies.
2. Injunctive relief is provided under the civil law. The government or a private party may secure a court order preventing continuing violations of the act and affording appropriate relief (such as dissolution or divestiture).

Perhaps the most important remedy is that available to private parties. An individual or organization harmed by a violation of the act may bring a civil action seeking three times the damages (treble damages) actually sustained. Thus, the victim is compensated, and the wrongdoer is punished.

Clayton Act, 1914. Sherman forbade the continued practice of specified anticompetitive conduct, but it did not forbid conduct that was *likely to lead to* anticompetitive behavior. Furthermore, many felt that judicial interpretations of Sherman had seriously weakened that legislation. Hence, the 1914 approval of the Clayton Act. The Clayton Act forbids price discrimination, exclusive dealing, tying arrangements, requirements contracts, mergers restraining commerce or tending to create a monopoly, and interlocking directorates.

Civil enforcement of the Clayton Act is similar to the Sherman Act in that the government may sue for injunctive relief, and private parties may seek treble damages. Injunctive relief was also extended to private parties under both the Clayton and Sherman acts. In general, criminal law remedies are not available under the Clayton Act.

Federal Trade Commission Act. The Federal Trade Commission Act created a powerful, independent agency designed to devote its full attention to the elimination of anticompetitive practices in American commerce. The FTC proceeds under the Sherman Act, the Clayton Act, and Section 5 of the FTC Act itself, which declares unlawful "unfair methods of competition" and "unfair or deceptive acts or practices in or affecting commerce." The commission's primary enforcement device is the cease and desist order, but fines may be imposed.

E. Exemptions from Federal Antitrust Laws

For practical and political reasons, selected industries and enterprises have been excused by Congress from the antitrust laws. Unions enjoy a partial exemption. Baseball is exempt, but the other professional sports are subject to the antitrust laws. Closely regulated industries (e.g., insurance, shipping, banking, and securities) historically have been largely free of antitrust oversight, although the Supreme Court, in 1992, made it clear that this **state action** exemption is available only in instances of "active supervision."[4] Of course, trademarks, patents, and copyrights constitute limited, government-granted monopolies. Historically, professional services (accounting, law, medicine, etc.) were not threatened by antitrust action. A series of Supreme Court decisions have altered that immunity, but the Court clearly believes that regulation of the professions is a matter best addressed at the state level.

state action. Situation of a sufficiently close relationship between the state and the action in question that the action can reasonably be treated as that of the state itself.

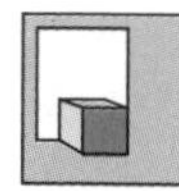

Public Policy Questions

1. Why have unions been partially shielded from federal antitrust laws?
2. Should unions be fully subject to market forces?

State Law. Most states, through legislation and judicial decisions, have developed their own antitrust laws and, in recent years, have been more aggressively asserting their authority. In *California* v. *American Stores,*[5] a 1990 decision, the U.S. Supreme Court unanimously upheld the right of states and others to use the federal Clayton Act to require divestiture of assets as a remedy in harmful mergers. In that case, California had challenged the merger of two large supermarket chains. The Court's conclusion was particularly striking in that it permits states and private citizens to raise the divestiture threat in challenging mergers even though those mergers have already received approval from the Federal Trade Commission or the U.S. Justice Department.

III. Monopolies and Marketing

Suppose that you have been successful in your marketing career and while yet a young person, you decide to take a big risk and go into business for yourself. You open a six-screen movie theatre in Las Vegas. You are so successful and competitive that you are able to buy out all of your competitors except for Roberts, who is a small exhibitor of mostly second-run films. Then Roberts decides to fight back by opening new theatres. Soon Roberts has 28 screens and is showing many first-run movies while you are operating 23 first-run screens. At its high point, your share of the first-run market box office receipts reaches 93 percent, but three years thereafter it has fallen to 75 percent and your share of exclusive exhibition rights to first-run movies has fallen from 91 to 39 percent. Nonetheless, you are successful beyond your dreams when the federal Justice Department notifies you that it is beginning an inquiry into your business practices. They are threatening to sue to force you to sell some of the theatres you have acquired.

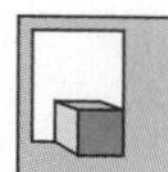

Public Policy Questions

1. What harm are you accused of causing?
2. What violation of the law is the government alleging?
3. Defend yourself based upon free market reasoning.

[See *United States* v. *Syufy Enterprises,* 903 F.2d 659 (9th Cir. 1990).]

A. MONOPOLY ANALYSIS

Let's examine how the courts evaluate a situation like the one just described. The principal legislation is found in the Sherman Act, Section 2:

> Every person who shall monopolize, or attempt to monopolize, or combine or conspire with any other person or persons, to monopolize any part of the trade or commerce among the several States, or with foreign nations, shall be deemed guilty of a felony punishable by a fine.

From an economic viewpoint, a **monopoly** is a situation in which one firm holds the power to control prices or exclude competition in a particular market. By contrast, an **oligopoly** is the situation in which a few firms share monopoly power.

monopoly. Market power permitting the holder to fix prices and/or exclude competition.

oligopoly. An economic condition in which the market for a particular good or service is controlled by a small number of producers or distributors.

Thus, the critical inquiries are the percentage of the market held by the alleged monopolist and the behavior that produced or maintained that market share. The Sherman Act does not, as interpreted, punish efficient companies who legitimately earn and maintain large market shares.

It is important to note that a considerable debate rages in the legal community about whether *conduct* or *structure* (or, indeed, several other possibilities) constitutes the best test of anticompetitive conditions. Should we concern ourselves with a firm's behavior, or should we focus on those industries in which a few firms control a large percentage of the market? Is a concentrated market undesirable in and of itself, or should we challenge market concentration only when it has been acquired or maintained via abusive conduct? In this free market era, the conduct view predominates, but you are advised to consider the implications of each policy.

Although the case law is not a model of clarity, a rather straightforward framework for monopoly analysis has emerged:

1. Define the relevant *product market.*
2. Define the relevant *geographic market.*
3. Compute the defendant's *market power.*
4. Assess the defendant's *intent.*
5. Raise any available *defenses.*

Product Market. Here, the court seeks, effectively, to draw a circle that encompasses categories of goods in which the defendant's products or services compete and excludes those not in the same competitive arena. The fundamental test is that of interchangeability, as determined primarily by the price, use, and quality of the product in question.

An analysis of cross elasticity of demand is a key ingredient in defining the product market. Assume that two products, X and Y, appear to be competitors. Assume that the price of X doubled and Y's sales volume was unchanged. What does that tell us about whether X and Y are, in fact, in the same product market?

Defining the product market is really the process we all go through in routine purchasing decisions. Let us assume that you feel a rather undefined hunger for salty snack food. You proceed to the nearby convenience store. Many options confront you, but for simplicity, let's confine them to chips, nuts, and popcorn. Of course, each of those food types is composed of variations. As you sort through the choices—corn chips, cheese curls, Spanish peanuts, rippled potato chips, and so on—you employ the criteria of price, use, and quality in focusing your decision. In so doing, you are defining the product market for "salty junk food." Products closely matched in price, use, and quality are interchangeable; thus they are competitors in the same product market. But, for example, an imported salty cheese at $10 per quarter pound presumably is not in the same product market as salted sunflower seeds.

Expressed as a matter of elasticity, the critical question becomes something like the following: If the price of potato chips, for example, falls by 10 percent, does the sales volume of salted nuts likewise fall? If so, we have a strong indication that potato chips and salted nuts lie in the same product market and thus are competitors.

Profile Perspective: If one of the antitrust claims against Ticketmaster goes to trial, the case could well turn on the question of defining the product market. On the basis of what you have read here, express the product market from both the plaintiff's point of view and that of the defendant, Ticketmaster.

Geographic Market. Once the product market has been defined, we still must determine where the product can be purchased. The judicial decisions to date offer no definitive explanation of the geographic market concept. A working definition might be "any section of the country where the product is sold in commercially significant quantities." From an economic perspective, the geographic market is defined by elasticity. If prices rise or supplies are reduced within the geographic area in question (e.g., New England) and demand remains steady, will products from other areas enter the market in quantity sufficient to affect price or supply? If so, the geographic market must be broadened to embrace those new sources of supply. If not, the geographic market is not larger than the area in question (New England).

Market Power. Market share is a primary indicator of market power, although we have no firm guidelines about what percentage of the market must be controlled to create a monopoly. In the *Alcoa* case, Judge Hand found a monopoly where Alcoa had 90 percent of the virgin ingot aluminum market.[6] The Fifth Circuit Court of Appeals once indicated that "something more than 50 percent of the market is a prerequisite to a finding of monopoly."[7] The complexity of the market share decision is well illustrated by a recent federal appeals court ruling that freed Kodak from a pair of decades-old government restraints on its marketing practices. The government had imposed those restraints and sought to retain them because of Kodak's market dominance. Kodak continues to control 70 percent of the domestic film market, but the appeals court felt that Kodak's 36 percent global share did not represent market power and that foreign competition would restrain Kodak's ability to raise prices.[8]

Additional Factors. Market share alone cannot be determinative of monopoly power. The courts are interested in other features of the market, including **barriers to entry,** the strength of the competition, **economies of scale,** trends in the market, and pricing patterns. The point of these inquiries is to determine whether the market in question remains competitive even though one firm has a large market share.

barriers to entry. Economic or technological conditions in a market making entry by a new competitor very difficult.

economies of scale. Expansion of a firm or industry's productive capacity resulting in a decline in long-run average costs of production.

Intent. Assuming the market share is of threatening proportions, the next test element is proof of an intent to monopolize. A monopoly finding requires both a showing of monopoly power and evidence of the willful acquisition or maintenance of that power. A showing of intent does not demand, for example, an internal memo, setting out a plan to acquire monopoly power. Rather, a showing of purposeful or deliberate acts that are predatory or unfair (such as price-fixing) will normally suffice to establish the requisite intent.

Defenses. The defendant may yet prevail if the evidence demonstrates that the monopoly was **thrust upon** the firm, rather than that the firm affirmatively sought its monopoly posture. The thrust-upon defense had its genesis in Judge Learned Hand's opinion in the aforementioned *Alcoa* case, where that most aptly named jurist suggested the Sherman Act would not be violated if monopoly power were innocently acquired via superior skill, foresight, or industry or by failure of the competition as a consequence of changes in costs or consumer preference. Depending on the circumstances, other defenses (e.g., possession of a patent) may be persuasive.

thrust upon. Company holds a monopoly innocently because of superior performance, the failure of competition, or changing market conditions.

B. A Monopoly Case

In the Las Vegas theatre story, you were an aggressive, successful entrepreneur and the courts protected you from an arguably overreaching government. Now let's turn the tables a bit and imagine that you are a successful entrepreneur being squeezed by a yet more successful competitor. Will the law protect you or will it allow the market to work its will, in which case you are likely to be crushed? The *Aspen Skiing* case that follows illustrates that dilemma while demonstrating that ample vitality remains in antimonopoly law. The controlling position in the late-90s is likely to be a centrist view, where monopoly law is enforced but not used as an instrument for social change, and the virtues of the free market are respected but market failure is acknowledged and addressed in the courts.

CASE

Aspen Skiing Company v. Aspen Highlands Skiing Corporation

472 U.S. 585 (1985)

Facts

Aspen is a destination ski resort with a reputation for "super powder," a wide range of runs, and an active night life . . . Between 1945 and 1960, private investors independently developed three major facilities for downhill skiing: Aspen Mountain (Ajax) [owned by Ski Co.], Aspen Highlands (Highlands), and Buttermilk. A fourth mountain, Snowmass [owned by Ski Co.], opened in 1967.

The development of any major additional facilities is hindered by practical considerations and regulatory obstacles . . .

Between 1958 and 1964, three independent companies operated Ajax, Highlands, and Buttermilk. In the early years, each company offered its own day or half-day tickets for use of its mountain. In 1962, however, the three competitors also introduced an interchangeable ticket. The six-day, all-Aspen ticket provided convenience to the vast majority of skiers . . . The revenues from the sale of the three-area coupon books were distributed in accordance with the number of coupons collected at each mountain.

In 1964, Buttermilk was purchased by Ski Co., but the interchangeable ticket program continued. Thus, by 1967 when Snowmass opened, Ski Co. owned three areas: Ajax, Buttermilk and Snowmass with Aspen Highlands remaining a separate company.

In the 1971–1972 season, the coupon booklets were discontinued and an "around the neck" all-Aspen ticket was developed . . .

Continued

Continued

A random-sample survey was commissioned to determine how many skiers with the four-area ticket used each mountain, and the parties allocated revenues from the ticket sales in accordance with the survey's results.

* * *

In the 1970s the management of Ski Co. increasingly expressed their dislike for the all-Aspen ticket. They complained that a coupon method of monitoring usage was administratively cumbersome. They doubted the accuracy of the survey and decried the "appearance, deportment, [and] attitude" of the college students who were conducting it. In addition, Ski Co.'s president had expressed the view that the four-area ticket was siphoning off revenues that could be recaptured by Ski Co. if the ticket was discontinued . . .

In March 1978, the Ski Co . . . board decided to offer Highlands a four-area ticket provided that Highlands would agree to receive a 12.5 percent fixed percentage of the revenue—considerably below Highland's historical average based on usage. Later in the 1978–1979 season, a member of Ski Co.'s board of directors candidly informed a Highland's official that he had advocated making Highlands "an offer that [it] could not accept."

Finding the proposal unacceptable, Highlands suggested a distribution of the revenues based on usage to be monitored by coupons, electronic counting, or random sample surveys. If Ski Co. was concerned about who was to conduct the survey, Highlands proposed to hire disinterested ticket counters at its own expense—"somebody like Price Waterhouse"—to count or survey usage of the four-area ticket at Highlands. Ski Co. refused to consider any counterproposals, and Highlands finally rejected the offer of the fixed percentage.

As far as Ski Co. was concerned, the all-Aspen ticket was dead. In its place Ski Co. offered the three-area, six-day ticket featuring only its mountains. In an effort to promote this ticket, Ski Co. embarked on a national advertising campaign that strongly implied to people who were unfamiliar with Aspen that Ajax, Buttermilk, and Snowmass were the only ski mountains in the area. For example, Ski Co. had a sign changed in the Aspen Airways waiting room at Stapleton Airport in Denver. The old sign had a picture of the four mountains in Aspen touting "Four Big Mountains" whereas the new sign retained the picture but referred only to three.

Ski Co. took additional actions that made it extremely difficult for Highlands to market its own multi-area package to replace the joint offering . . .

Without a convenient all-Aspen ticket, Highlands basically "becomes a day ski area in a destination resort." Highlands' share of the market for downhill skiing services in Aspen declined steadily after the four-area ticket based on usage was abolished in 1977: from 20.5 percent in 1976–1977, to 15.7 percent in 1977–1978, to 13.1 percent in 1978–1979, to 12.5 percent in 1979–1980, to 11 percent in 1980–1981.

* * *

Justice Stevens

II

In 1979, Highlands filed a complaint in the United States District Court for the District of Colorado naming Ski Co. as a defendant. Among various claims, the complaint alleged that Ski Co. had monopolized the market for downhill skiing services at Aspen in violation of §2 of the Sherman Act . . . The case was tried to a jury which rendered a verdict finding Ski Co. guilty of the §2 violation and calculating Highlands' actual damages at $2.5 million.

Continued

Continued

In her instructions to the jury, the District Judge explained that the offense of monopolization under §2 of the Sherman Act has two elements: (1) the possession of monopoly power in a relevant market, and (2) the willful acquisition, maintenance, or use of that power by anticompetitive or exclusionary means or for anticompetitive or exclusionary purposes. . . . Ski Co. does not challenge the jury's special verdict finding that it possessed monopoly power. Nor does Ski Co. criticize the trial court's instructions to the jury concerning the second element of the §2 offense.

On this element, the jury was instructed that it had to consider whether "Aspen Skiing Corporation willfully acquired, maintained, or used that power by anticompetitive or exclusionary means or for anticompetitive or exclusionary purposes."

* * *

III

Ski Co. is surely correct in submitting that even a firm with monopoly power has no general duty to engage in a joint marketing program with a competitor. Ski Co. is quite wrong, however, in suggesting that the judgment in this case rests on any such proposition of law. For the trial court unambiguously instructed the jury that a firm possessing monopoly power had no duty to cooperate with its business rivals.

The absence of an unqualified duty to cooperate does not mean that every time a firm declines to participate in a particular cooperative venture, that decision may not have evidentiary significance, or that it may not give rise to liability in certain circumstances . . . The high value that we have placed on the right to refuse to deal with other firms does not mean that the right is unqualified.

* * *

IV

The question whether Ski Co.'s conduct may properly be characterized as exclusionary cannot be answered by simply considering its effect on Highlands. In addition, it is relevant to consider its impact on consumers and whether it has impaired competition in an unnecessarily restrictive way. If a firm has been "attempting to exclude rivals on some basis other than efficiency," it is fair to characterize its behavior as predatory. It is, accordingly, appropriate to examine the effect of the challenged pattern of conduct on consumers, on Ski Co.'s smaller rival, and on Ski Co. itself.

Superior Quality of the All-Aspen Ticket

The average Aspen visitor "is a well-educated, relatively affluent, experienced skier who has skied a number of times in the past . . ." Over 80 percent of the skiers visiting the resort each year have been there before—40 percent of these repeat visitors have skied Aspen at least five times. Over the years, they developed a strong demand for the six-day, all-Aspen ticket in its various refinements. Most experienced skiers quite logically prefer to purchase their tickets at once for the whole period that they will spend at the resort; they can then spend more time on the slopes and enjoying apres-ski amenities and less time standing in ticket lines. The four-area attribute of the ticket allowed the skier to purchase his six-day ticket in advance while reserving the right to decide in his own time and for his own reasons which mountain he would ski on each day. It provided convenience and flexibility, and expanded the vistas and the number of challenging runs available to him during the week's vacation.

Continued

Continued

While the three-area, six-day ticket offered by Ski Co. possessed some of these attributes, the evidence supports a conclusion that consumers were adversely affected by the elimination of the four-area ticket. In the first place, the actual record of competition between a three-area ticket and the all-Aspen ticket in the years after 1967 indicated that skiers demonstrably preferred four mountains to three . . .

Highlands' Ability to Compete

The adverse impact of Ski Co.'s pattern of conduct on Highlands is not disputed in this Court. Expert testimony described the extent of its pecuniary injury. The evidence concerning its attempt to develop a substitute product either by buying Ski Co.'s daily tickets in bulk, or by marketing its own Adventure Pack, demonstrates that it tried to protect itself from the loss of its share of the patrons of the all-Aspen ticket . . .

Ski Co.'s Business Justification

Perhaps most significant, however, is the evidence relating to Ski Co. itself, for Ski Co. did not persuade the jury that its conduct was justified by any normal business purpose. Ski Co. was apparently willing to forgo daily ticket sales both to skiers who sought to exchange the coupons contained in Highlands' Adventure Pack, and to those who would have purchased Ski Co. daily lift tickets from Highlands if Highlands had been permitted to purchase them in bulk. The jury may well have concluded that Ski Co. elected to forgo these short-run benefits because it was more interested in reducing competition in the Aspen market over the long run by harming its smaller competitor.

That conclusion is strongly supported by Ski Co.'s failure to offer any efficiency justification whatever for its pattern of conduct. In defending the decision to terminate the jointly offered ticket, Ski Co. claimed that usage could not be properly monitored. The evidence, however, established that Ski Co. itself monitored the use of the three-area passes based on a count taken by lift operators, and distributed the revenues among its mountains on that basis. Ski Co. contended that coupons were administratively cumbersome, and that the survey takers had been disruptive and their work inaccurate. Coupons, however, were no more burdensome than the credit cards accepted at Ski Co. ticket windows. Moreover, in other markets Ski Co. itself participated in interchangeable lift tickets using coupons. As for the survey, its own manager testified that the problems were much overemphasized by Ski Co. officials, and were mostly resolved as they arose. Ski Co.'s explanation for the rejection of Highlands' offer to hire—at its own expense—a reputable national accounting firm to audit usage of the four-area tickets at Highlands' mountain, was that there was no way to "control" the audit.

In the end, Ski Co. was pressed to justify its pattern of conduct on a desire to disassociate itself from—what it considered—the inferior skiing services offered at Highlands. The all-Aspen ticket based on usage, however, allowed consumers to make their own choice on these matters of quality. Ski Co.'s purported concern for the relative quality of Highlands' product was supported in the record by little more than vague insinuations, and was sharply contested by numerous witnesses. Moreover, Ski Co. admitted that it was willing to associate with what it considered to be inferior products in other markets.

. . . [T]he record in this case comfortably supports an inference that the monopolist made a deliberate effort to discourage its customers from doing business with its smaller rival. The sale of its three-area, six-day ticket, particulary when it was discounted below the daily ticket price, deterred the ticket holders from skiing at Highlands. The refusal to accept the Adventure Pack coupons in exchange for daily tickets was apparently motivated entirely by a decision to avoid providing any benefit to Highlands even though accepting the coupons would have entailed no cost to Ski Co. itself, would have provided it with immediate benefits, and would have satisfied

Continued

Continued

its potential customers. Thus the evidence supports an inference that Ski Co. was not motivated by efficiency concerns and that it was willing to sacrifice short-run benefits and consumer goodwill in exchange for a perceived long-run impact on its smaller rival . . .

Affirmed.

Questions

1. Summarize the fundamental lessons of *Aspen.*
2. Write a brief dissenting opinion for the *Aspen* case.
3. As the *Aspen* Court says, "Aspen Skiing Company (Ski Co.) had monopolized the market for downhill skiing services in Aspen, Colorado." That being the case, why didn't the government challenge Aspen Skiing Company's market dominance?
4. Kodak dominated the American market for provision of amateur photographic films, cameras, and film-processing services. Berkey was a much smaller, but still significant, competitor in that market. In some markets, Kodak served as Berkey's supplier. In the "amateur conventional still camera" market (consisting primarily of 110 and 126 instant loading cameras), Kodak's share of the sales volume between 1954 and 1973 ranged from 64 to 90 percent. Kodak invented both the 126 and 110 cameras. The introduction of the 110 Pocket Instamatic and the companion Kodacolor II film in 1972 resulted in a dramatic Kodak camera sales increase of from 6.2 million units in 1971 to 8.2 million in 1972. Rivals were unable to bring competitive units into the market until nearly one year later. Even then, Kodak retained a strong lead. Thereafter, Berkey filed suit claiming that the introduction of the 110 system was an illegal monopolization of the camera market. The essence of the Berkey argument was as follows:

   > Kodak, a film and camera monopolist, was in a position to set industry standards. Rivals could not compete effectively without offering products similar to Kodak's. Moreover, Kodak persistently refused to make film available for most formats other than those in which it made cameras. Since cameras are worthless without film, the policy effectively prevented other manufacturers from introducing cameras in new formats. Because of its dominant position astride two markets, and by use of its film monopoly to distort the camera market, Kodak forfeited its own right to reap profits from such innovations without providing its rivals with sufficient advance information to enable them to enter the market with copies of the new product on the day of Kodak's introduction.

   On appeal, the Court noted "little doubt that . . . Kodak had monopoly power in cameras" and observed that Kodak had sometimes "predisclosed" its innovations to its rivals, and sometimes it had not done so.

   a. Was Kodak under a legal duty to predisclose innovations to rivals?

   b. What defense would you offer to counter Berkey's monopolization claim?

   c. Decide the case, and explain the reasons for your decision.

   [See *Berkey Photo,* Inc. v. *Eastman Kodak Company,* 603 F.2d 263 (2nd Cir. 1979), cert. denied, 444 U.S. 1093 (1980).]

IV. Mergers and Marketing

Profile Perspective: Let's return to the Ticketmaster story. Clearly, Ticketmaster has a very large share of the ticket service market, however it might be defined. Ticketmaster secured much of that share by buying at least 12 competitors, including mighty Ticketron. How does the law view a giant that secured its position in considerable part by purchasing its competitors?

A. *Law of Mergers*

The principal legislation dealing with mergers is found in the Sherman Act, Section 1, and the Clayton Act, Section 7:

> That no person engaged in commerce shall acquire the whole or any part of the stock or the assets of another person engaged also in commerce where the effect of such acquisition may be substantially to lessen competition, or to tend to create a monopoly.
>
> No person shall acquire the whole or any part of the stock or the assets of one or more persons engaged in commerce where in any line of commerce the effect of such acquisition or of the use of such stock by the voting or granting of proxies or otherwise, may be substantially to lessen competition, or to tend to create a monopoly.

merger. Union of two or more enterprises wherein the property of all is transferred to the one remaining firm.

Technically, a **merger** involves the union of two or more enterprises wherein the property of all is transferred to the one remaining firm. However, antitrust law embraces all those situations wherein previously independent business entities are united—whether by acquisition of stock, purchase of physical assets, creation of holding companies, consolidation, or merger.

Mergers fall, somewhat awkwardly, into three categories:

horizontal merger. Acquisition by one company of another company competing in the same product and geographic markets.

vertical merger. Union of two firms at different levels of the same channel of distribution.

conglomerate merger. Union of companies dealing in unrelated lines of commerce and thus not competing with each other or supplying each other.

1. A **horizontal merger** involves firms that are in direct competition and occupy the same product and geographic markets. A merger of two vodka producers in the same geographic market would clearly fall in the horizontal category. Would the merger of a vodka producer and a gin producer constitute a horizontal merger?
2. A **vertical merger** involves two or more firms at different levels of the same channel of distribution, such as a furniture manufacturer and a fabric supplier.
3. A **conglomerate merger** involves firms dealing in unrelated products. Thus, the conglomerate category embraces all mergers that are neither horizontal nor vertical. An example of such a merger would be the acquisition of a pet food manufacturer by a book publisher. (Conglomerate mergers currently receive little attention from the government, and we will not be examining them further.)

Merger Data. Mergers occur in waves. In the 1980s, corporate raiders acquired bad names gobbling up appealing targets, sometimes with little evident thought for either long-term performance or immediate social consequences. The early 90s were a quiet time. Then in 1994 and 1995, new records were set. In 1995, total deals reached $458 billion, up 32 percent from the 1994 record of $347 billion. The 1995 deals included Walt Disney Company's $19 billion purchase of Capital Cities/ABC.[9]

In 1995, total deals reached $458 billion, up 32 percent from the 1994 record of $347 billion.

Merger Problems. Naturally, some acquisitions prove to have been sensible; some do not. Scholar Michael Porter's examination of the merger record of 33 major American firms from 1950 to 1986 showed that more than half of their acquisitions failed and were sold off.[10] The result, the critics say, is poor economic performance, wasted stockholder funds, and lumbering corporate giants often unsuited to the competitive demands of the day. More broadly, merger excesses are accused of exacerbating the problems of bigness. Political and economic power will reside in fewer hands. Barriers to entry may increase. Absentee owners, ignorant of local needs, will alter community lifestyles. Lives will be disrupted by plant closings, changes in management, and relocations.

Merger Virtues. Nevertheless, many mergers are clearly beneficial. Some of the potential virtues of mergers include the following:

1. Mergers permit the replacement of inefficient management. Similarly, the threat of replacement disciplines managers to achieve greater efficiency.
2. Mergers may permit stronger competition with formerly larger rivals.
3. Mergers may improve credit access.
4. Mergers may produce efficiencies and economies of scale.
5. Mergers frequently offer a pool of liquid assets for use in expansion.
6. Very often, mergers offer tax advantages to at least one of the participants.
7. Growth by merger is often less expensive than internal growth.
8. Mergers help to satisfy the personal ambitions and needs of management.

A recent *Business Week* study of the mergers, acquisitions, and takeovers of the 1980s found "evidence of many more failures than successes." But the *Business Week* study reported a division of opinion among academics:

A recent *Business Week* study of the mergers, acquisitions, and takeovers of the 1980s found "evidence of many more failures than successes."

> [S]cholars such as Northwestern University's Alfred Rappaport argue that the U.S. companies are leaner than they were at the start of the decade. The threat of a takeover has forced many managers to work their companies into fighting trim. Moreover, shareholders saw enormous gains through acquisitions, leveraged buyouts, and recapitalizations. Leverage, says Rappaport, "was a fantastically good tool to make management become more shareholder-value oriented."
>
> But even Rappaport admits that merger mania was "a two-edged sword." As companies took on more leverage to feed increasing shareholder expectations, the U.S. economy was put at risk . . . In the end, it seems, neither side can make a convincing case.[11]

For America's managers, these deals have profound professional and personal consequences. They are part of a thorough restructuring of the American economy, a corporate housecleaning of sorts, that hit high gear in the 1980s and continues today. How are we to compete in a fierce world market if we fail to become "lean and mean?" Probably, we cannot. At the same time, the human consequences are staggering. Job losses are a particularly poignant product of America's industrial consolidation: "Between 1980 and 1990, more than 10 million Americans were laid off due to buyouts, mergers and company restructuring."[12] Mergers and acquisitions have become a strategic tool in this overall restructuring process, and the consequences, while personally very painful, may be necessary to the reinvigoration of a somewhat flabby American economy.

Between 1980 and 1990, more than 10 million Americans were laid off due to buyouts, mergers and company restructuring.

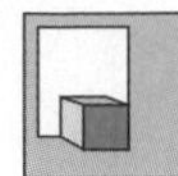

Ethics/Public Policy Question

Would you consider it a moral wrong if two *healthy, profitable* companies were to merge with the result that several thousand people lost their jobs? Explain.

B. Merger Analysis

Premerger. Mergers involving firms of significant size (as defined by government rules) must be reported to the FTC and the Justice Department. That premerger notification gives the government time to decide whether to challenge the merger before it takes place. In 1996, Sara Lee paid a $3.1 million civil fine to settle (without admitting guilt) a federal claim that the company hid the real value of a shoe-polish firm it was acquiring in order to keep the acquisition beneath the government's disclosure threshold.

Horizontal Analysis. The government's concern with horizontal mergers rests on the presumed decline in competition when one firm buys another in the same market. The analysis is much like that for monopolies and is outlined by the FTC/Justice Department 1992 horizontal merger guidelines. (Justice Department policy in recent years has not regarded most vertical and conglomerate mergers as threatening—hence the focus on horizontal mergers.)

Market Power. The guidelines are designed to identify mergers that may result in market power, defined as the ability of a seller "profitably to maintain prices above competitive levels for a significant period of time." The guidelines set out a five-step methodology for analyzing horizontal mergers:

1. Market definition.
2. Measurement of market concentration.
3. Identification of potential adverse effects.
4. Appraisal of ease of entry into the market.
5. Appraisal of possible defenses.[13]

Market The market will be defined as the smallest product and geographic market in which a hypothetical monopolist could raise prices a "small but significant and nontransitory" amount (usually set at 5 percent) above current prices.[14]

Herfindahl–Hirschman Index (HHI). Calculation used by the Justice Department to determine the degree of economic concentration in a particular market and to determine the degree to which a proposed horizontal merger would further concentrate that market. Computed by squaring the market share of each firm in a market and summing those totals.

Market concentration The **Herfindahl–Hirschman Index (HHI)** is employed to measure market concentration. Notwithstanding the formidable-sounding title, the index is computed quite easily. The market share of each firm in a market is squared and the results are summed. Thus, if five companies each had 20 percent of a market, the index for that market would be 2,000. The HHI is useful because it measures both concentration and dispersion of market share between big and small firms. If 10 firms each have 10 percent of the market, the resulting HHI is 1,000. The larger the HHI, the more concentrated the market. The new guidelines establish "safe harbors" for mergers that are considered unlikely to produce anticompetitive effects. Hence, a postmerger HHI of 1,000 or less ordinarily would not be challenged.

On the other hand, a postmerger concentration of more than 1,800 accompanied by a change in the HHI above 50 (from the premerger HHI) is *presumed* to be threatening. The presumption can be overcome by showing that market harm is unlikely, which could be established by reference to such other factors in the guidelines as adverse effects, ease of entry, efficiencies, and so on. In the middle ground involving postmerger HHI figures of 1,000 to 1,800 accompanied by changes in the HHI above 100, the guidelines find the *potential* for competitive concerns depending on the analysis of the other factors. To illustrate, consider again a market composed of five companies, each with 20 percent of the market. If two of them merge, the HHI would rise from 2,000 to 2,800, and the merger would be presumed threatening pending consideration of the other factors in the guidelines. Thus, the government's new guidelines reject the older notion of market size *alone* as a threat to the welfare of the economy.

Adverse effects Although the guidelines provide highly complex instructions about conditions likely to raise adverse competitive effects, the basic point is that the government is worried that the merger may permit cartel-like behavior in the merged firm's market.

Ease of entry The idea here is that the newly merged firm cannot arbitrarily raise prices or otherwise abuse the market if entry by competitors is timely, likely, and sufficient, since those new competitors will force the existing firms to charge competitive prices and otherwise conform to the discipline of the market.

Defenses An otherwise unacceptable merger may be saved by certain defenses. Most prominent among these are **efficiencies** and the **failing company doctrine.** Efficiencies include such desirable economic results as economies of scale or reduced transportation costs as a result of the merger. The failing company doctrine permits a merger in order to preserve the assets of a firm that would otherwise be lost to the market.

Vertical Analysis. A vertical merger involves an alliance between a supplier and a purchaser. The primary threat thus arising is that of **market foreclosure.** As illustrated in Figure 11.1, a vertical merger may deny a source of supply to a purchaser or an outlet for sale to a seller, which might then threaten competition so as to violate the Clayton Act.

The following *Brown Shoe* case illustrates both horizontal and vertical analysis.

efficiencies. A defense to an otherwise unlawful merger in which costs of production are reduced because of the merger.

failing company doctrine. A defense to an otherwise unlawful merger in which the acquired firm is going out of business and no other purchaser is available.

market foreclosure. In vertical mergers, the concern that the newly combined firm will close its doors to potential suppliers and purchasers such that competition will be harmed.

FIGURE 11.1 VERTICAL MERGER

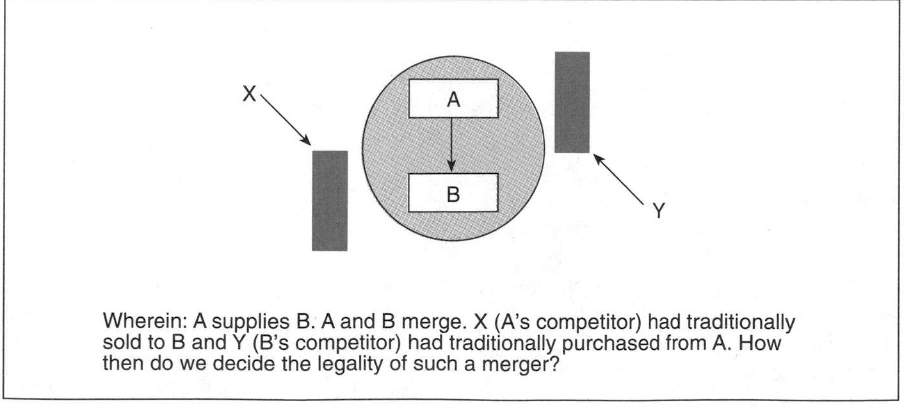

Wherein: A supplies B. A and B merge. X (A's competitor) had traditionally sold to B and Y (B's competitor) had traditionally purchased from A. How then do we decide the legality of such a merger?

CASE

Brown Shoe Co. v. United States

370 U.S. 294 (1961)

Facts

This suit was initiated in November 1955 when the Government filed a civil action alleging that a contemplated merger between the G. R. Kinney Company, Inc. (Kinney), and the Brown Shoe Company, Inc. (Brown) . . . would violate Sec. 7 of the Clayton Act . . .

Brown [was] the third largest seller of shoes by dollar volume in the United States, a leading manufacturer of men's, women's, and children's shoes, and a retailer with over 1,230 owned, operated or controlled retail outlets . . . Kinney, the eighth largest company by dollar volume, [was] itself a large manufacturer of shoes and a retailer with over 350 retail outlets . . .

The Industry

The district court found that although domestic shoe production was scattered among a large number of manufacturers, a small number of large companies occupied a commanding position. Thus, while the 24 largest manufacturers produced about 35 percent of the Nation's shoes, the top 4—International, Endicott-Johnson, Brown (including Kinney), and General Shoe—alone produced approximately 23 percent of the Nation's shoes or 65 percent of the production of the top 24 . . .

The public buys these shoes through about 70,000 retail outlets, only 22,000 of which, however, derive 50 percent or more of their gross receipts from the sale of shoes and are classified as "shoe stores" by the Census Bureau. These 22,000 shoe stores were found generally to sell (1) men's shoes only, (2) women's shoes only, (3) women's and children's shoes, or (4) men's, women's, and children's shoes.

The district court found a "definite trend" among shoe manufacturers to acquire retail outlets . . . Between 1950 and 1956 nine independent shoe store chains, operating 1,114 retail shoe stores, were found to have become subsidiaries of these large firms and to have ceased their independent operations.

And once the manufacturers acquired retail outlets, the district court found there was a "definite trend" for the parent-manufacturers to supply an ever-increasing percentage of the retail outlets' needs, thereby foreclosing other manufacturers from effectively competing for the retail accounts. Manufacturer-dominated stores were found to be "drying up" the available outlets for independent producers.

Another "definite trend" found to exist in the shoe industry was a decrease in the number of plants manufacturing shoes . . . In 1947, there were 1,077 independent manufacturers of shoes, but by 1954 their number had decreased about 10 percent to 970.

Brown Shoe

. . . In 1951, Brown [acquired] the Nation's largest operator of leased shoe departments, Wohl Shoe Company (Wohl), which operated 250 shoe departments in department stores throughout the United States. Between 1952 and 1955 Brown made a number of smaller acquisitions . . .

The acquisition of these corporations was found to lead to increased sales by Brown to the acquired companies . . .

During the same period of time, Brown also acquired the stock or assets of seven companies engaged solely in shoe manufacturing. As a result, in 1955, Brown was the fourth largest shoe manufacturer in the country, producing about 25.6 million pairs of shoes or about 4 percent of the Nation's total footwear production.

Continued

Continued

Kinney

Kinney is principally engaged in operating the largest family-style shoe store chain in the United States. At the time of trial, Kinney was found to be operating over 400 such stores in more than 270 cities. These stores were found to make about 1.2 percent of all national retail shoe sales by dollar volume . . .

In addition to this extensive retail activity, Kinney owned and operated four plants which manufactured men's, women's, and children's shoes and whose combined output was 0.5 percent of the national shoe production in 1955, making Kinney the 12th largest shoe manufacturer in the United States.

Kinney stores were found to obtain about 20 percent of their shoes from Kinney's own manufacturing plants. At the time of the merger, Kinney bought no shoes from Brown; however, in line with Brown's conceded reasons for acquiring Kinney, Brown had, by 1957, become the largest outside supplier of Kinney's shoes, supplying 7.9 percent of all Kinney's needs.

It is in this setting that the merger was considered and held to violate § 7 of the Clayton Act.

* * *

Chief Justice Warren

Legislative History

The dominant theme pervading congressional consideration of the 1950 amendments [to the Clayton Act, Section 7] was a fear of what was considered to be a rising tide of economic concentration in the American economy . . .

Other considerations cited in support of the bill were the desirability of retaining "local control" over industry and the protection of small businesses. Throughout the recorded discussion may be found examples of Congress' fear not only of accelerated concentration of economic power on economic grounds, but also of the threat to other values a trend toward concentration was thought to pose.

The Vertical Aspects of the Merger

. . . The primary vice of a vertical merger or other arrangement tying a customer to a supplier is that, by foreclosing the competitors of either party from a segment of the market otherwise open to them, the arrangement may act as a "clog on competition." . . .

The Product Market

The outer boundaries of a product market are determined by the reasonable interchangeability of use or the cross-elasticity of demand between the product itself and substitutes for it. However, within this broad market, well-defined submarkets may exist which, in themselves, constitute product markets for antitrust purposes . . . The boundaries of such a submarket may be determined by examining such practical indicia as industry or public recognition of the submarket as a separate economic entity, the product's peculiar characteristics and uses, unique production facilities, distinct customers, distinct prices, sensitivity to price changes, and specialized vendors. . . .

Continued

Continued

Applying these considerations to the present case, we conclude that the record supports the district court's finding that the relevant lines of commerce are men's, women's, and children's shoes. These product lines are recognized by the public; each line is manufactured in separate plants; each has characteristics peculiar to itself rendering it generally noncompetitive with the others; and each is, of course, directed toward a distinct class of customers . . .

The Geographic Market

We agree with the parties and the district court that insofar as the vertical aspect of this merger is concerned, the relevant geographic market is the entire nation. The relationships of product value, bulk, weight and consumer demand enable manufacturers to distribute their shoes on a nationwide basis, as Brown and Kinney, in fact, do . . .

The Probable Effect of the Merger

Once the area of effective competition affected by a vertical arrangement has been defined, an analysis must be made to determine if the effect of the arrangement "may be substantially to lessen competition, or to tend to create a monopoly" in this market.

Since the diminution of the vigor of competition which may stem from a vertical arrangement results primarily from a foreclosure of a share of the market otherwise open to competitors, an important consideration in determining whether the effect of a vertical arrangement "may be substantially to lessen competition, or to tend to create a monopoly" is the size of the share of the market foreclosed. However, this factor will seldom be determinative.

* * *

[I]t is apparent both from past behavior of Brown and from the testimony of Brown's President, that Brown used its ownership of Kinney to force Brown shoes into Kinney stores . . .

Another important factor to consider is the trend toward concentration in the industry . . .

The existence of a trend toward vertical integration, which the district court found, is well substantiated by the record. Moreover, the court found a tendency of the acquiring manufacturers to become increasingly important sources of supply for their acquired outlets. The necessary corollary of these trends is the foreclosure of independent manufacturers from markets otherwise open to them . . .

Brown argues, however, that the shoe industry is at present composed of a large number of manufacturers and retailers, and that the industry is dynamically competitive. But remaining vigor cannot immunize a merger if the trend in that industry is toward oligopoly. It is the probable effect of the merger upon the future as well as the present which the Clayton Act commands the courts and the commission to examine.

Moreover, as we have remarked above, not only must we consider the probable effects of the merger upon the economics of the particular markets affected but also we must consider its probable effects upon the economic way of life sought to be preserved by Congress. Congress was desirous of preventing the formation of further oligopolies with their attendant adverse effects upon local control of industry and upon small business. Where an industry was composed of numerous independent units, Congress appeared anxious to preserve this structure . . .

The Horizontal Aspects of the Merger

. . . The acquisition of Kinney by Brown resulted in a horizontal combination at both the manufacturing and retailing levels of their businesses. Although the district court found that the merger of Brown's and Kinney's *manufacturing* facilities was economically too insignificant to come within the prohibitions of the Clayton Act, the government has not appealed from this por-

Continued

Continued

tion of the lower court's decision. Therefore, we have no occasion to express our views with respect to that finding. On the other hand, appellant does contest the district court's finding that the merger of the companies' *retail* outlets may tend substantially to lessen competition.

The Product Market

. . . In . . . this opinion we hold that the district court correctly defined men's, women's, and children's shoes as the relevant lines of commerce in which to analyze the vertical aspects of the merger. For the reasons there stated we also hold that the same lines of commerce are appropriate for considering the horizontal aspects of the merger.

The Geographic Market

The criteria to be used in determining the appropriate geographic market are essentially similar to those used to determine the relevant product market. Moreover, just as a product submarket may have § 7 significance as the proper "line of commerce," so may a geographic submarket be considered the appropriate "section of the country." Congress prescribed a pragmatic, factual approach to the definition of the relevant market and not a formal, legalistic one. The geographic market selected must, therefore, both "correspond to the commercial realities" of the industry and be economically significant. Thus, although the geographic market in some instances may encompass the entire nation, under other circumstances it may be as small as a single metropolitan area.

* * *

We agree that the district court properly defined the relevant geographic markets in which to analyze this merger as those cities with a population exceeding 10,000 and their environs in which both Brown and Kinney retailed shoes through their own outlets. Such markets are large enough to include the downtown shops and suburban shopping centers in areas contiguous to the city, which are the important competitive factors, and yet are small enough to exclude stores beyond the immediate environs of the city, which are of little competitive significance.

The Probable Effect of the Merger

. . . The market share which companies may control by merging is one of the most important factors to be considered when determining the probable effects of the combination on effective competition in the relevant market. In an industry as fragmented as shoe retailing, the control of substantial shares of the trade in a city may have important effects on competition. If a merger achieving 5 percent control were now approved, we might be required to approve future merger efforts by Brown's competitors seeking similar market shares.

* * *

At the same time appellant has presented no mitigating factors, such as the business failure or the inadequate resources of one of the parties that may have prevented it from maintaining its competitive position, nor a demonstrated need for combination to enable small companies to enter into a more meaningful competition with those dominating the relevant markets. . .

The judgment is affirmed.

Continued

Continued

Questions

1. As to the vertical element of *Brown Shoe,* what potential harm did the Court identify?
2. In *Brown Shoe,* why did the Supreme Court settle on different geographic markets for the horizontal and vertical elements of the merger?
3. How did the Supreme Court justify its prohibition of the merger in light of the rather small market shares involved (e.g., Brown produced 4 percent of the nation's shoes, while Kinney sold about 1.2 percent of the nation's total)?
4. In 1958, Pabst Brewing Company acquired Blatz Brewing Company. Pabst was America's 10th-largest brewer, and Blatz was the 18th largest. After the merger, Pabst had 4.49 percent of the nationwide beer market and was the fifth-largest brewer. In the regional market of Wisconsin, Michigan, and Illinois, the merger gave Pabst 11.32 percent of the sales. After the merger, Pabst led beer sales in Wisconsin with 23.95 percent of that statewide market. The beer market was becoming increasingly concentrated, with the total number of brewers declining from 206 to 162 during the years 1957 to 1961. In *United States* v. *Pabst Brewing Co.,* 384 U.S. 546 (1966), the Supreme Court found the merger violated the Clayton Act, Section 7. The Court did not choose among the three geographic market configurations, saying that the crucial inquiry is whether a merger may substantially lessen competition *anywhere* in the United States. Thus, the Court held that, under these facts, a 4.49 percent share of the market was too large.

   Respected scholar and jurist Richard Posner labeled the *Pabst* decision an "atrocity" and the product of a "fit of nonsense" on the part of the Supreme Court.[15] What economic arguments would support Posner's colorful complaint?

V. American Antitrust Laws and the International Market

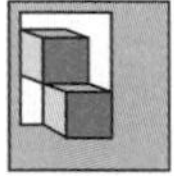

America's commercial market now very clearly embraces the entire globe. Multinational corporations dominate international business. Antitrust questions can become extremely complex in transactions involving multiple companies, in multiple nations, where those transactions are potentially governed by U.S. and foreign antitrust laws. U.S. antitrust laws are, of course, applicable to foreign firms doing business here. The Sherman, Clayton, and FTC acts, among others, are all potentially applicable to American business abroad.

A. *Foreign Antitrust Laws*

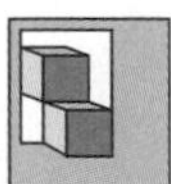

The United States historically has taken a much more aggressive attitude toward antitrust policy and enforcement than have the nations of Western Europe and Japan. Indeed, those nations generally regard cooperative economic arrangements and concentrations of industrial power as necessary and desirable components of economic success. Of course, Japan and the European Union historically have practiced economic policies involving government quite directly in regulating and managing commercial practice for the general good.

Antitrust Rules. The European Union has now put in place a set of competition rules that roughly parallel our treatment of antitrust problems. Like Sherman Section 1, the EU rules forbid concerted practices that harm competition. Abuse of market dominance (monopoly) is also forbidden, and in that instance, the EU law appears to be more aggressive than ours because, to be considered threatening, a market share in the EU need not be so large as what we would require for a challenge here in the United States.[16] Further, the

EU rules are more aggressive than ours in the sense that charging excessive prices is considered abusive and may be attacked under the antitrust laws.

Mergers in the EU are regulated like those in the United States, with premerger notification requirements and the European Union Commission to review those proposed mergers. In addition to the EU antitrust rules, each nation can continue to enforce its own national laws in those cases not exhibiting EU implications.

VI. Horizontal Restraints of Trade and Marketing

Profile Perspective: Clearly, Ticketmaster dominates the ticket distribution business. How then should the legal system respond if Ticketmaster's smaller competitors decide to cooperate with each other to better compete with Ticketmaster? Perhaps they agree to share computer resources or to divide the market among themselves on a geographical basis.

To what extent can competitors legally cooperate with each other? Such agreements between competitors are analyzed as *horizontal restraints of trade.* Those horizontal agreements, such as price-fixing, involve businesses in the same market (e.g., two neighborhood hardware retailers) that want to avoid competing with each other.

Let's examine horizontal restraints by turning our attention to a series of common managerial encounters with antitrust law. Assume that you are managing a convenience store/gas station in a small city. At the annual gasoline dealers association meeting, you and the other gas station managers are instructed by the owners to implement the following agreement: (1) both major brands (such as Shell, Exxon, and Texaco) and independents (lesser known, private labels) will not give any kind of gifts, discounts, or other premiums in association with the sale of gas; (2) the majors agree not to advertise their prices (except as they appear on the pumps). Is this arrangement permissible under the antitrust laws? Why would the owners arrive at such an agreement? [See *U.S.* v. *Gasoline Retailers Association,* 285 F.2d 688 (1961).]

A. *Rule of Reason*

Cooperation among competitors would nullify much of the virtue of the open market; therefore, our legal system casts a particularly unforgiving eye on horizontal restraints of trade. Horizontal restraints are governed by Section 1 of the Sherman Act, which forbids every contract, combination, or conspiracy in restraint of trade. However, in the *Standard Oil* decision of 1911,[17] the U.S. Supreme Court articulated what has come to be known as the **rule of reason,** which provides, in essence, that the Sherman Act forbids only unreasonable restraints of trade. After all, every contract is, in some sense, a restraint of trade. If I agree to sell my car to you, I am, in effect, declining to sell it to others. Therefore, the key inquiry is whether the restraint is harmful to competition. In answering that question, the court would look at such factors as both the pro- and anticompetitive effects of the restraint, the market power of the parties involved, the history of the restraint, and the competitive structure of the industry.

rule of reason. For antitrust purposes, reviewing an agreement in its specific factual setting, considering its pro- and anticompetitive features, to determine if it is harmful to competition.

B. *Per Se Violations*

Some antitrust violations such as horizontal price-fixing are perceived to be so injurious to competition that their mere existence constitutes unlawful conduct. Plaintiffs must prove that the violation in question occurred, but they need not prove that the violation caused, or is likely to cause, harm. Such violations are simply unreasonable on their face.

per se doctrine. Certain antitrust violations are considered so harmful to competition that they are always unlawful and no proof of actual harm is required.

However, in recent years, the use of the **per se doctrine** has declined. The economics-based notions of efficiency and consumer welfare are increasingly causing jurists to insist on a showing of the defendant's economic abuse before finding an antitrust violation.[18]

C. Horizontal Price-Fixing

The principal legislation addressing price-fixing is the Sherman Act, Section 1:

> Every contract, combination in the form of trust or otherwise, or conspiracy, in restraint of trade or commerce, among the several States, or with foreign nations, is hereby declared to be illegal.

Historically, a contract, combination, or conspiracy among competitors that reduced price competition was an unreasonable restraint of trade and per se unlawful. An inquiry into the reasonableness of the price or proof of a harmful effect was unnecessary. However, as noted, recent decisions demonstrate that the judiciary is questioning the per se rule in some instances.

price-fixing. An agreement among competitors to charge a specified price for a particular product or service. Also any agreement that prevents a seller from independently setting a price or from independently establishing the quantity to be produced.

Proof. The major dilemma in **price-fixing** and all other Sherman Act, Section 1 violations is what measure of proof satisfies the requirement of a contract, combination, or conspiracy? Evidence of collusion arises in a variety of ways. Broadly, a showing of cooperative action amounting to an agreement must be established. In general, that showing may be developed by any of the following four methods of proof:

1. *Agreement with direct evidence.* In the easiest case, the government can produce direct evidence such as writings or testimony from participants proving the existence of collusion.
2. *Agreement without direct evidence.* Here, the defendants directly but covertly agree, and circumstantial evidence such as firm behavior must be employed to draw an inference of collusion.
3. *Agreement based on a tacit understanding.* In this situation, no direct exchange of assurances occurs, but the parties employ tactics that act as surrogates for direct assurances and thus "tell" each other that they are, in fact, in agreement.
4. *Agreement based on mutual observation.* These defendants have simply observed each others' pricing behavior over time, and they are able therefore to anticipate each others' future conduct and act accordingly without any direct collusion but with results akin to those that would have resulted from a direct agreement.[19]

conscious parallelism. Conduct by competitors that is very similar or identical but that is not the product of a conspiracy and thus is not, in and of itself, illegal.

Parallel Conduct. An unlawful conspiracy is to be distinguished from independent but parallel business behavior by competitors. So-called **conscious parallelism** is fully lawful because the competitors have not agreed either explicitly or by implication to follow the same course of action. Rather, their business judgment has led each to independently follow parallel paths.

Contemporary Cases. Price-fixing is regrettably common:

- *Airlines*—In 1993, the nation's biggest airlines agreed to a $458 million settlement of a class action suit by consumers claiming price-fixing by the airlines. The claim was that the airlines used their jointly owned computerized fare database to unlawfully signal each other about prices. Most of the settlement ($408 million) was to be paid in the form of discount coupons to be applied to future flights.[20]
- *Universities*—An unusual price-fixing claim was litigated in 1992, when the Massachusetts Institute of Technology was found guilty of price-fixing with other schools

in the so-called Ivy Overlap Group. The schools shared financial information about applicants who applied to more than one of the schools. The schools limited price competition by agreeing on aid to each student. The purpose of the arrangement was to avoid bidding wars over students.

The price-fixing decision was subsequently overturned on appeal, whereupon the government and MIT reached a settlement permitting sharing of student financial aid information with other schools but forbidding discussions of individual grants to specific students.[21]

- *International cases*—Price-fixing is not confined to America. In 1994, the European Union Commission fined 19 carton-board (packaging materials) manufacturers a record $164.9 million for price-fixing.[22]

Attempted Price-Fixing. Let's say you are a convenience store manager. Assume that you simply go across the street and talk to the manager of a competing convenience store and say something like: "Heh, are you getting killed like we are on the price of milk? You know if we could just quietly both raise our prices—maybe just a dime more a gallon—we could do fine and the public still will be getting a good buy." Do those words violate the law? Perhaps not, but you are certainly moving in that direction. Consider the following February 1982 conversation between Robert L. Crandall, chief executive officer of American Airlines, and Howard Putnam, then president of Braniff. The conversation became a matter of public record after it was submitted to a federal court.

Mr. Crandall

I think it's dumb as hell for Christ's sake, all right, to sit here and pound the [expletive] out of each other and neither one of us making a [expletive] dime.

Mt. Putnam

Well . . .

Mr. Crandall

I mean, you know, goddamn, what the [expletive] is the point of it?

Mr. Putnam

Do you have a suggestion for me?

Mr. Crandall

Yes I have a suggestion for you. Raise your goddamn fares 20 percent. I'll raise mine the next morning.

Mr. Putnam

Robert, we . . .

Mr. Crandall

You'll make more money and I will too.

Mr. Putnam

We can't talk about pricing.

Mr. Crandall

Oh [expletive], Howard. We can talk about any goddamn thing we want to talk about.[23]

Business Week later commented editorially on the Crandall affair:

> Most businessmen would interpret Crandall's remarks as an illegal invitation to fix prices. So did the Justice Department . . . In February 1983, Justice filed a complaint in federal court charging American and Crandall with trying to fix prices and asking the court to bar Crandall for two years from any airline job with authority

over prices. Then followed two years' negotiations with American and Crandall. On July 14, 1985, Justice allowed American and Crandall to sign a consent decree without admitting any guilt in the Braniff affair. Deterrence, anyone?[24]

D. Refusals to Deal

The principal legislation addressing refusals to deal is the Sherman Act, Section 1, as cited in the price-fixing discussion.

group boycott. An agreement among traders to refuse to deal with one or more other traders.

A **group boycott** is yet another instance of concerted action in which a collectivity of traders jointly refuses to deal with another trader or traders. Typically, the purpose of such an arrangement is to remove or police a competitor. Depending on the facts, group boycotts may be analyzed under the rule of reason or they may be treated as per se violations.

Suppose you are doing well in your first year of on-the-job training as a convenience store manager when the district manager comes to you with a new plan that is being implemented companywide. He says the entire chain that your store is part of has reached a deal with the two largest soft-drink bottlers. They have agreed to decline to sell to the small, independent, mom-and-pop convenience stores in return for which your parent company has agreed to increase chainwide purchases from the two giants by 10 percent.

Questions

1. Does this plan constitute a group boycott/refusal to deal that would be forbidden by the Sherman Act? [For a similar set of facts, see *Klor's* v. *Broadway-Hale Stores, Inc.,* 359 U.S. 207 (1959).]
2. Would it matter if the two soft-drink giants individually and unilaterally simply decided to quit selling to the small stores?
3. Imagine that the stores involved were a full-service department store and a discount store and the products involved were televisions and appliances. How would you defend an agreement between the department store and its television and appliance suppliers to cut off the nearby discounter?

E. Horizontal Division of Markets

horizontal divisions of the market. Competitors agree to share their market geographically or to allocate customers or products among themselves.

Horizontal divisions of the market are governed by Section 1 of the Sherman Act.

After managing a convenience store in California for a couple of years and learning the business well, you receive a promotion to manager of new market development. In that role, your primary task is to do market research to decide on expansion sites for the chain. At an industry convention, you are talking with a market development manager for a competing California chain. She says, "I've heard you are thinking of moving into Washington and Oregon." You say, "Yes, we've been thinking about it." She says, "Look, we are ready to move in up there. If you go there too we'll chew each other up, just like we're doing now in California. Think about this: What if we make a deal. You get Oregon and we'll take Washington and we both promise not to later move in on each other." You say, "Well, I don't know. Can we do that? I'll talk with my boss, and get back to you."

Questions

1. Can competitors lawfully agree (*a*) to divide their market geographically or (*b*) to allocate customers among themselves?
2. Why would they wish to do so?

[See *United States* v. *Topco Associates, Inc.,* 405 U.S. 596 (1972), for an explanation of the law in this area.]

VII. Vertical Restraints and Marketing

We have been studying unfair trade practices by competitors, that is, horizontal restraints of trade. Now we turn our attention to antitrust violations on the vertical axis: restraints involving two or more members of a supply chain (e.g., a manufacturer and a retailer of that manufacturer's products).

Profile Perspective: Let's return to Ticketmaster and its new venture, *Live,* an entertainment monthly magazine that reached the market in January 1996. Assume that Ticketmaster specifies a retail price on the cover of the magazine and tells its distributors and retailers that the magazine cannot be discounted from that price. To do so, Ticketmaster argues, would be to depreciate the image of the entire company. Is Ticketmaster violating antitrust law?

A. Resale Price Maintenance/Vertical Territorial and Customer Restraints

The principal legislation involved here is found in the Sherman Act, Section 1, and the Federal Trade Commission Act, Section 5.

Manufacturers and distributors often seek to specify the price at which their customers may resell their products. Having sold its product, why should a manufacturer or distributor seek to influence the price at which the product is resold? The primary reasons are threefold: (1) to enhance the product's reputation for quality, (2) to prevent discount stores from undercutting regular retail outlets, and (3) to prevent **free riders.** [See the *B.E.C.* case below.]

free riders. Those who lawfully benefit from goods or services without paying a share of the cost of those goods or services.

resale price maintenance. An agreement between a buyer and seller specifying a minimum price beneath which or a maximum price above which the buyer cannot resell the product.

***Colgate* doctrine.** Sellers may lawfully engage in resale price maintenance if they do nothing more than specify prices at which their products are to be resold and unilaterally refuse to deal with anyone who does not adhere to those prices.

nonprice restraints. Resale limitations imposed by manufacturers on distributors or retailers in any of several forms (such as territorial or customer restraints) that do not directly affect price.

Colgate Doctrine.

An *agreement* between a seller and its buyer, specifying a minimum price beneath which or a maximum price above which is a per se violation. However, sellers may lawfully engage in **resale price maintenance** if they do nothing more than specify prices at which their products are to be resold and unilaterally refuse to deal with anyone who does not adhere to those prices. This is the so-called ***Colgate* doctrine,** announced in *United States* v. *Colgate & Co.,* 250 U.S. 300 (1919), although some legal experts believe *Colgate*'s safe harbor for sellers has been abandoned by most courts.[25]

B. Nonprice Restraints

In addition to price restraints, manufacturers commonly wish to impose restrictions on where and to whom their product may be resold. Those restrictions typically afford an exclusive sales territory to a distributor. Similarly, manufacturers may prevent distributors from selling to some classes of customers (e.g., a distributor might be forbidden to sell to an unfranchised retailer). Of course, such arrangements necessarily retard or eliminate intrabrand competition. Because price and service competition among dealers in the same brand ordinarily is of benefit to the consumer, the courts have frequently struck down such arrangements. Still, it is generally agreed that territorial and customer allocations also have merits. The *GTE Sylvania case*[26] enunciated those virtues and established the position that vertical restrictions are to be judged on a case-by-case basis, balancing interbrand and intrabrand competitive effects while recognizing that interbrand competition is the primary concern of antitrust law. Thus, the Rule of Reason is to be applied to vertical territorial and customer restraints.

At this point, you should understand the critical distinction between horizontal and vertical territorial and customer allocations. The former is per se unlawful. The latter is to be resolved under the rule of reason unless it involves an agreement on prices. *Horizontal* restrictions are those arising from an agreement among the *competitors* themselves, while *vertical* restrictions are those imposed on *buyers* by their *suppliers.* The *Business Electronics Corporation* (*B.E.C.*) case that follows offers a summary of the Supreme Court's analysis of both vertical price and nonprice restraints.

CASE

Business Electronics Corporation v. Sharp Electronics Corporation

485 U.S. 717 (1988)

Facts

Business Electronics Corporation (B.E.C.) asked the Supreme Court to review a decision of the U.S. Court of Appeals holding that a vertical restraint is per se illegal under Section 1 of the Sherman Act, only if there is an express or implied agreement to set resale prices at some level. The Supreme Court granted certiorari.

In 1968, B.E.C. became the exclusive retailer in the Houston, Texas, area of electronic calculators manufactured by Sharp Electronics Corporation. In 1972, Sharp appointed Gilbert Hartwell as a second retailer in the Houston area. Sharp published a list of suggested minimum retail prices, but its written dealership agreements with B.E.C. and Hartwell did not obligate either to observe them or to charge any other specific price. B.E.C.'s retail prices were often below Sharp's suggested retail prices and generally below Hartwell's retail prices, though Hartwell too sometimes priced below suggested retail prices. Hartwell complained to Sharp on a number of occasions about B.E.C.'s prices. In June 1973, Hartwell gave Sharp the ultimatum that he would terminate his dealership unless Sharp ended its relationship with B.E.C. within 30 days. Sharp terminated B.E.C.'s dealership in July 1973.

B.E.C. sued, alleging that Sharp and Hartwell had conspired to terminate B.E.C. and that their conspiracy was illegal per se under Section 1 of the Sherman Act. The district court submitted a question to the jury that asked whether "there was an agreement or understanding between Sharp Electronics Corporation and Hartwell to terminate Business Electronics as a Sharp dealer because of Business Electronics' price-cutting." The jury answered the question affirmatively and awarded $600,000 in damages. The Fifth Circuit reversed.

* * *

Justice Scalia

II–A

Section 1 of the Sherman Act provides that "[e]very contract, combination in the form of trust or otherwise, or conspiracy, in restraint of trade or commerce among the several States, or with foreign nations, is declared to be illegal." Since the earliest decisions of this Court interpreting this provision, we have recognized that it was intended to prohibit only unreasonable restraints of trade. Ordinarily, whether particular concerted action violates § 1 of the Sherman Act is determined through case-by-case application of the so-called rule of reason . . . Certain categories of agreements, however, have been held to be per se illegal, dispensing with the need for case-by-case evaluation.

* * *

Continued

Continued

Although vertical agreements on resale prices have been illegal per se since *Dr. Miles Medical Co.* v. *John D. Park & Sons, Co.,* we have recognized that the scope of per se illegality should be narrow in the context of vertical restraints. In *Continental T.V. Inc.* v. *GTE Sylvania Inc.,* we refused to extend per se illegality to vertical nonprice restraints, specifically to a manufacturer's termination of one dealer pursuant to an exclusive territory agreement with another. We noted that especially in the vertical restraint context "departure from the rule-of-reason standard must be based on demonstrable economic effect rather than . . . upon formalistic line drawing." We concluded that vertical nonprice restraints had not been shown to have such a "pernicious effort on competition" and to be so "lack[ing] [in] . . . redeeming value" as to justify per se illegality. Rather, we found, they had real potential to stimulate interbrand competition, "the primary concern of antitrust law":

> [N]ew manufacturers and manufacturers entering new markets can use the restrictions in order to induce competent and aggressive retailers to make the kind of investment of capital and labor that is often required in the distribution of products unknown to the consumer. Established manufacturers can use them to induce retailers to engage in promotional activities or to provide service and repair facilities necessary to the efficient marketing of their products. Service and repair are vital for many products . . . The availability and quality of such services affect a manufacturer's goodwill and the competitiveness of his product. Because of market imperfections such as the so-called free-rider effect, these services might not be provided by retailers in a purely competitive situation, despite the fact that each retailer's benefit would be greater if all provided the services than if none did.

Moreover, we observed that a rule of per se illegality for vertical nonprice restraints was not needed or effective to protect *intra*brand competition. First, so long as interbrand competition existed, that would provide a "significant check" on any attempt to exploit intrabrand market power. In fact, in order to meet that interbrand competition, a manufacturer's dominant incentive is to lower resale prices. Second, the per se illegality of vertical restraints would create a perverse incentive for manufacturers to integrate vertically into distribution, an outcome hardly conducive to fostering the creation and maintenance of small businesses.

* * *

Our approach to the question presented in the present case is guided by the premises of *GTE Sylvania:* that there is a presumption in favor of a rule-of-reason standard; that departure from that standard must be justified by demonstrable economic effect, such as the facilitation of cartelizing, rather than formalistic distinctions; that interbrand competition is the primary concern of the antitrust laws; and that rules in this area should be formulated with a view towards protecting the doctrine of *GTE Sylvania.* These premises lead us to conclude that the line drawn by the Fifth Circuit is the most appropriate one.

There has been no showing here that an agreement between a manufacturer and a dealer to terminate a "price cutter," without a further agreement on the price or price levels to be charged by the remaining dealer, almost always tends to restrict competition and reduce output. Any assistance to cartelizing that such an agreement might provide cannot be distinguished from the sort of minimal assistance that might be provided by vertical nonprice agreements like the exclusive territory agreement in *GTE Sylvania,* and is insufficient to justify a per se rule. Cartels are neither easy to form nor easy to maintain . . .

The District Court's rule on the scope of per se illegality for vertical restraints would threaten to dismantle the doctrine of *GTE Sylvania.* Any agreement between a manufacturer and a dealer to terminate another dealer who happens to have charged lower prices can be alleged to have been directed against the terminated dealer's "price cutting." In the vast majority of cases, it will be extremely difficult for the manufacturer to convince a jury that its motivation was to ensure

Continued

Continued

adequate services, since price cutting and some measure of service cutting usually go hand in hand. Accordingly, a manufacturer that agrees to give one dealer an exclusive territory and terminates another dealer pursuant to that agreement, or even a manufacturer that agrees with one dealer to terminate another for failure to provide contractually obligated services, exposes itself to the highly plausible claim that its real motivation was to terminate a price cutter. Moreover, even vertical restraints that do not result in dealer termination, such as the initial granting of an exclusive territory or the requirement that certain services be provided, can be attacked as designed to allow existing dealers to charge higher prices. Manufacturers would be likely to forgo legitimate and competitively useful conduct rather than risk treble damages and perhaps even criminal penalties.

We cannot avoid this difficulty by invalidating as illegal per se only those agreements imposing vertical restraints that contain the word "price," or that affect the "prices" charged by dealers. Such formalism was explicitly rejected in *GTE Sylvania.* As the above discussion indicates, all vertical restraints, including the exclusive territory agreement held not to be per se illegal in *GTE Sylvania,* have the potential to allow dealers to increase "prices" and can be characterized as intended to achieve just that. In fact, vertical nonprice restraints only accomplish the benefits identified in *GTE Sylvania* because they reduce intrabrand price competition to the point where the dealer's profit margin permits provision of the desired services. As we described it in *Monsanto:* "The manufacturer often will want to ensure that its distributors earn sufficient profit to pay for programs such as hiring and training additional salesmen or demonstrating the technical features of the product, and will want to see that 'free-riders' do not interfere."

* * *

Petitioner has provided no support for the proposition that vertical price agreements generally underlie agreements to terminate a price cutter. That proposition is simply incompatible with the conclusion of *GTE Sylvania* and *Monsanto* that manufacturers are often motivated by a legitimate desire to have dealers provide services, combined with the reality that price cutting is frequently made possible by "free riding" on the services provided by other dealers. The district court's per se rule would therefore discourage conduct recognized by *GTE Sylvania* and *Monsanto* as beneficial to consumers.

* * *

Affirmed.

Questions

1. Summarize the essence of the *B.E.C.* holding.
2. What practical effects would you expect the *B.E.C.* decision to have on the behavior of (*a*) manufacturers and (*b*) discounters?
3. A newspaper distributor, Albrecht, lost his distributorship because he charged a retail price in excess of that specified by the newspaper publisher, Herald Co.
   a. Is the setting of a maximum resale price illegal? Explain.
   b. Argue the case both for and against Albrecht.
   [See *Albrecht* v. *Herald Co.,* 390 U.S. 145 (1968).]

Public Policy Questions

1. Is *B.E.C.* an anticonsumer decision? Explain.
2. Assume you are managing a new-car dealership where the supplying firm (e.g., General Motors) requires you to follow a strategy of no-haggle or one-price pricing. Under the no-haggle policy, the price that all dealers must charge for particular models is set, thus eliminating customer bargaining. Many customers appreciate the elimination of haggling. Some dealers claim that the no-haggle policy reduces their profits. Could you raise an antitrust claim against your supplier based on no-haggle pricing? Explain.

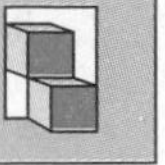

C. Tying Arrangements

The principal legislation involved here is found in the Clayton Act, Section 3; Sherman Act, Sections 1 and 2; and Federal Trade Commission Act, Section 5.

> *Clayton Act, Section 3.* That it shall be unlawful for any person engaged in commerce, in the course of such commerce, to lease or make a sale or contract for sale of goods . . . or other commodities . . . or fix a price charged therefore, or discount from or rebate upon, such price, on the condition, agreement or understanding that the lessee or purchaser thereof shall not use or deal in the goods . . . or other commodities of a competitor or competitors of the lessor or seller, where the effect of such lease, sale, or contract for sale or such condition, agreement, or understanding may be to substantially lessen competition or tend to create a monopoly in any line of commerce.

The typical **tying arrangement** permits a customer to lease or buy a desired product (the tying product) only if she or he also leases or buys another product (the tied product). Of course, such an arrangement may harm consumers, but the primary antitrust concerns are twofold: (1) a party who already enjoys market power over the tying product is able to extend that power into the tied product market; and (2) competitors in the tied product market are foreclosed from equal access to that market.

tying arrangement. Dealer agrees to sell or lease a product (the tying product) only on the condition that the buyer also purchases or leases another product (the tied product).

In brief, proof of the following conditions constitutes a per se violation:

1. Existence of a tying arrangement (that is, two products bound together, not merely one product consisting of two or more components bound together, or two entirely separate products that happen to be a part of a single transaction).
2. Market power in the tying product.
3. A substantial amount of commerce in the tied product is adversely affected.

Tunes. After many successful years in marketing with convenience stores, you have accumulated some money and some knowledge, and you decide you are ready to be your own boss. You open an audio shop called Tunes. A big part of your business is installing stereo systems in cars and trucks. Naturally, you are striving to expand your business, but you are frustrated that at least one new car manufacturer, Chrysler, includes the price of a sound system in the base price of its cars. Chrysler's share of the new car market is 10 to 12 percent. Chrysler does not reveal the subprice for the sound system itself. As you see it, Chrysler's practice simply deprives consumers of freedom of choice in the audio market and deprives you of a slice of that market.

Questions

1. Can you raise an antitrust claim against Chrysler?
2. Would that claim succeed? Explain.

[See *Town Sound and Custom Tops, Inc.* v. *Chrysler Motor Corp.*, 959 F.2d 468 (1992), cert. denied., 113 S.Ct. 196 (1992).]

D. Exclusive Dealing Contracts

exclusive dealing. Agreement to deal only with a particular buyer or a particular seller.

Profile Perspective: Ticketmaster reportedly holds exclusive ticket-selling rights at half of the nation's major arenas. Experts say that to secure those exclusive arrangements, Ticketmaster typically provides a payback to the arena; that is, Ticketmaster returns a portion of the service fee it collects on ticket sales to the arena itself.27 Are those **exclusive dealing** arrangements unlawful? Are they unfair?

(Principal legislation that addresses this subject is found in the Clayton Act, Section 3 and the Sherman Act, Section 1.)

Basically, ***exclusive dealing*** is a requirement that a buyer (e.g., Madison Square Garden) purchase only from a particular seller (e.g., Ticketmaster) or that a seller deal only with a particular buyer. The effect of these arrangements is to cut competing sellers (e.g., regional ticket services) or competing buyers (e.g., other large arenas) out of the market. After defining the relevant product and geographic markets, the test is essentially that applied to vertical mergers. What percentage of the relevant market is foreclosed by the agreement? Does the agreement foreclose a source of supply of sufficient magnitude as to substantially lessen competition? Does the agreement foreclose a market for sale of sufficient magnitude as to substantially lessen competition?

Exclusive dealing contracts are not treated as per se violations of the law. Indeed, these arrangements often have very positive features such as ensured supplies and protection against price rises for buyers and a predictable market for sellers. Those procompetitive effects are considered in weighing the legality of exclusive dealing arrangements.

E. PRICE DISCRIMINATION

price discrimination. Selling goods of like grade and quality to different buyers at different prices without justification where competitive harm results.

Historically, though not so prominently today, much of the motivation for antitrust law lay in a desire to protect small businesses from overreaching big businesses. Certainly some regional and local ticket services feel they are the victims of an overbearing Ticketmaster. Now let's imagine that you are trying to build one of those small businesses—perhaps a clothing, sporting goods, or convenience store. What happens if the big firms that supply you provide better prices to your volume competitors (big department stores, discount stores, etc.) than they do to you? At this writing, thousands of independent pharmacies in 15 states have sued the nation's largest drug manufacturers, charging them with various antitrust violations including **price discrimination.**[28] All parties agree that big buyers such as hospitals and health maintenance organizations receive steep discounts, perhaps averaging 15 percent under the prices charged to pharmacies; but the defendants believe those discounts do not violate the law.[29] Does the law of price discrimination permit these discounts? The Clayton Act, Section 2, as amended by the Robinson-Patman Act, is the principal legislation.

> That it shall be unlawful for any person engaged in commerce . . . to discriminate in price between different purchasers or commodities of like grade and quality, where either or any of the purchases involved in such discrimination are in commerce . . . and where the effect of such discrimination may be substantially to lessen competition or tend to create a monopoly in any line of commerce, or to injure, destroy, or prevent competition with any person who either grants or knowingly receives the benefit of such discrimination, or with customers of either of them . . . Provided that nothing herein contained shall prevent differentials which make only due allowance for differences in the cost of manufacture, sale, or delivery resulting from the differing methods or quantities in which such commodities are to such purchasers sold or delivered . . . And, provided further, that nothing herein

PRIMARY LINE FIGURE 11.2

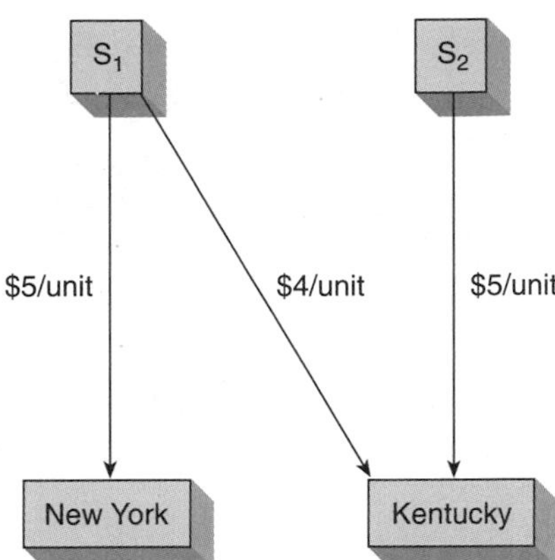

contained shall prevent price changes from time to time where in response to changing conditions affecting the market for or the marketability of the goods concerned, such as but not limited to actual or imminent deterioration of perishable goods, obsolescence of seasonal goods, distress sales under court process, or sales in good faith in discontinuance of business in the goods concerned . . . Provided, however, that nothing herein contained shall prevent a seller rebutting the prima facie case thus made by showing that his lower price or the furnishing of services or facilities to any purchaser or purchasers was made in good faith to meet an equally low price of a competitor, or the services or facilities furnished by a competitor.

In brief, price discrimination involves selling substantially identical goods (not services) at reasonably contemporaneous times to different purchasers at different prices, where the effect may be to substantially lessen competition or create a monopoly. A seller may prevail against such a charge by establishing one of the following defenses: (1) The price differential is attributable to cost savings associated with the least expensive sale. However, in practice, the difficulties in proving cost savings have made successful defenses on that ground quite uncommon. (2) The price differential is attributable to a good faith effort to meet the equally low price of a competitor. (3) Certain transactions are exempt from the act. Of special note is a price change made in response to a changing market. Thus, prices might lawfully be altered for seasonal goods or perishables. Price discrimination is perhaps best understood by reference to diagrams (see Figure 11.2).[30]

The harm here falls at the seller's level, the primary line, in that S_1's pricing policy may harm S_2. The specific fear is that S_1 will use its income from sales in New York to subsidize its lower price in Kentucky. S_1 may then be able to drive S_2 from the market. This is precisely the harm that Congress feared would be generated by the advance of chain stores across the nation. Of course, S_1 may be able to offer a defense to explain the pricing differential. For example, the price differential might be permissible if designed to allow S_1 to get a foothold in a new market. Remember that a price discrimination violation requires a showing of competitive injury.

Now consider Figure 11.3. B_1 and B_2 are direct competitors. Absent a defense, S_1 is clearly engaging in price discrimination. Here, the harm falls at the buyers' level (secondary line).

Harm may also fall on customers of customers, that is, tertiary price discrimination.

FIGURE 11.3 **SECONDARY LINE**

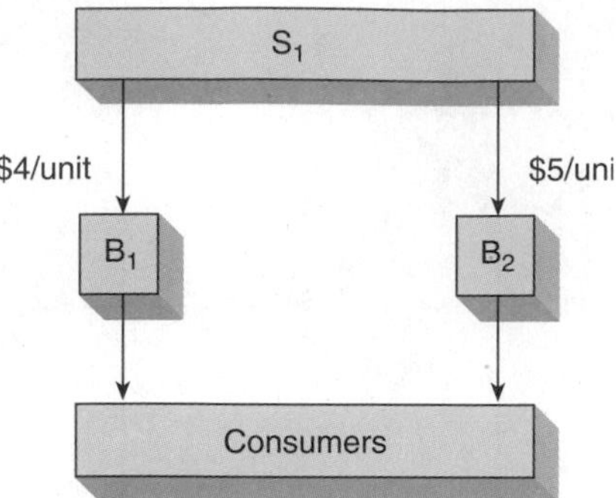

SUMMARY

Legal Review. The law limits, rather loosely, just how far a businessperson can go in trying to market a product. In this chapter, our primary concerns included advertising and sales practices, and antitrust. (Other elements of the law that affect marketing are found throughout the book, most notably in Chapter 12, Consumer Protection and Debtor/Creditor Law.) More specifically, in the first part of the chapter we gave particular attention to the provisions of the Federal Trade Commission Act and the Lanham Act, both of which forbid false and misleading advertising.

The second part of the chapter was devoted to antitrust law. We reviewed the history of antitrust law, the analysis applied to monopoly situations, and the rules regulating mergers. Then we turned to horizontal and vertical restraints of trade, looking at perhaps the most commonplace antitrust concern, price-fixing. Our review of vertical restraints addressed the considerable array of potentially unlawful marketing arrangements between suppliers and purchasers, including such problematic areas as resale price maintenance (vertical price-fixing) and tying arrangements. We concluded with price discrimination.

Ethics/Public Policy Review. This chapter sought to highlight some marketing practices that can lead to legal problems while reminding the reader of the importance of antitrust law in shaping the economic and social character of America. The underlying policy concern is a central theme in this text: How much law do we need? Think back to our discussion of Hooper's Hooch, deceptive ads, phony sale prices, and the like. Can we count on marketers to regulate their own conduct? Perhaps you are a marketing student. Are you confident that you will be consistently honest with consumers in your advertising and sales practices? Do you admire Ticketmaster's very aggressive drive to dominate its industry, or is that kind of zeal harmful both to consumers and to the nation's values?

Economics Review. Has advertising and sales law reached too far in protecting us from falsehoods and deception? In general, aren't we as consumers able to take care of ourselves, and if we aren't, doesn't the market soon force us to do so?

In the antitrust area, free market thinking was thoroughly dominant during the Republican Reagan/Bush years. Then with the advent of Democratic president Clinton and his antitrust chief Anne Bingaman, the federal Justice Department turned aggressive. Bingaman filed the first vertical merger challenge in 11 years and the first monopoly cases in a decade. She explained: "We want to keep prices down, keep markets open, and keep choices as broad as possible."[31]

Chapter Questions—Law

1. For years, American Home Products (AHP) had claimed via advertising that its product, Anacin (a painkiller), had a unique formula that was superior in effectiveness to all other nonprescription painkillers. In fact, the only active painkilling ingredient in Anacin was aspirin. The Federal Trade Commission found that American Home Products was engaging in deceptive advertising. The commission ordered AHP to stop its deceptive advertising and required it to support any future claims about the superiority of its product as a painkiller with two scientifically valid studies. AHP appealed the commission's decision. Decide. Explain. [*See American Home Products* v. *F.T.C.,* 695 F.2d 681 (3d Cir. 1982).]
2. Listerine mouthwash has been marketed since 1879 with no change in its formula. Beginning in 1921, Listerine was advertised as being effective in preventing, curing, and alleviating colds and sore throats. The Federal Trade Commission found those claims to be untrue and ordered Listerine's producer, Warner-Lambert, to desist from those claims and to include the following words in its Listerine ads for approximately one year: "Contrary to prior advertising, Listerine will not prevent colds or sore throats or lessen their severity." Warner-Lambert appealed. Decide. Explain. [See *Warner-Lambert* v. *Federal Trade Commission,* 562 F.2d 749 (D.C. Cir. 1977), cert. denied., 435 U.S. 950 (1978).]
3. Several smaller airlines sued the two giants, United and American, claiming that the two violated the Sherman Act through their computerized reservation systems (CRSs). The heart of the plaintiff's position was that United and American were monopolists that violated the law by denying other airlines reasonable access to their CRSs. American and United had the largest CRSs, but other airlines also maintained CRSs. Neither had blocked any other airline's access to its CRS, but they had charged fees (in American's case, $1.75 per booking to the airline that secured a passenger through American's CRS). United and American each controlled about 12 to 14 percent of the total air transportation market. According to the court, the plaintiffs were "unhappy" about United and American's ability to extract booking fees from them for the use of the CRSs. The U.S. Ninth Circuit Court of Appeals ruled for the defendants and the Supreme Court declined to review this case.
   a. Explain why the plaintiffs felt wronged by American and United.
   b. Explain the defendants' argument that they could not successfully charge "excessive" prices for the use of the CRSs.

   [See *Alaska Airlines* v. *United Airlines,* 948 F.2d 536 (1991), cert. denied., 112 S.Ct. 1603 (1992).]
4. Excel, a division of Cargill, was the second-largest firm in the beef-packing market. It sought to acquire Spencer Pack, a division of Land-O-Lakes, and the third-largest beef packer. After the acquisition, Excel would have remained second ranked in the business, but its market share would have been only slightly smaller than that of the leader, IBP. Monfort, the nation's fifth-largest beef packer, sought an injunction to block the acquisition, claiming a violation of Clayton, Section 7. In effect, Monfort claimed the merger would result in a dangerous concentration of economic power in the beef-packing market, with the result that Excel would pay more for cattle and charge less for its processed beef, thus placing its competitors in a destructive and illegal price-cost squeeze. Monfort claimed Excel's initial losses in this arrangement would be covered by its wealthy parent, Cargill. Then, when the competition was driven from the market, Monfort claimed, Excel would raise its processed beef prices to supracompetitive levels. Among other defenses, Excel averred that the heavy

losses Monfort claimed were merely the product of intense competition, a condition that would not constitute a violation of the antitrust laws. The district court found for Monfort and the appeals court, considering the cost-price squeeze a form of predatory pricing, affirmed. Excel appealed to the Supreme Court. Decide. Explain. [See *Cargill, Inc.* v. *Monfort of Colorado, Inc.,* 479 U.S. 104 (1986).]

5. What is the free-rider problem that frequently concerns the courts in cases involving vertical territorial restraints?
6. In 1977, Michelin failed to renew its dealership agreement with the Donald B. Rice Tire Company of Frederick, Maryland. After seven years with Michelin, approximately 80 percent of Rice's business was derived from wholesaling the tires to smaller authorized and unauthorized dealers. Other authorized dealers complained to Michelin of Rice's wholesale business. In an effort to assume primary wholesaling responsibility, Michelin chose not to renew its relationship with Rice. Rice contended that the nonrenewal was a consequence of its refusal to comply with Michelin's customer and territorial restraints, and Rice filed an antitrust action on that basis. Michelin argued that it was a new entrant into a concentrated market, and as such, restraints on intrabrand competition were necessary to induce retailers to carry Michelin tires. However, the court found frequent shortages of Michelin tires. Michelin also argued that nonrenewal was "necessary to prevent free riding by retailers on the services provided by other dealers."

   Rice had not advertised in a quantity commensurate with his sales volume. He sold to unauthorized dealers who were not bound to do any advertising and could thus reap the benefits of advertising by authorized dealers. Michelin wanted to encourage point-of-sales services and the offering of specialized services but feared authorized dealers would not invest the necessary expenditures because of their fear of being underpriced by unauthorized dealers. Decide the case. [See *Donald B. Rice Tire Company Inc.* v. *Michelin Corporation,* 483 F. Supp. 750 (D.Md., 1980), 638 F.2d 15 (1981), cert. denied., 454 U.S. 864 (1981).]
7. A board-certified anesthesiologist was denied admission to the Jefferson Parish Hospital staff because the hospital had an exclusive services contract with a firm of anesthesiologists. The contract required all surgery patients at the hospital to use that firm for their anesthesiology work. Seventy percent of the patients in the parish were served by hospitals other than Jefferson. The anesthesiologist who was denied admission sued the hospital, claiming the contract was unlawful. What antitrust violation was raised by the plaintiff? Decide. Explain. [See *Jefferson Parish Hospital District No. 2* v. *Hyde,* 466 U.S. 2 (1984).]
8. In 1990, the American Institute of Certified Public Accountants agreed to enforce a change in its ethics rules that allows its members to accept contingent fees and commissions from nonaudit clients. The agreement was the result of a consent order between the AICPA and the Federal Trade Commission. Likewise, in 1990, the American Institute of Architects signed a consent order with the Justice Department that forbids the Institute from adopting policies that would restrain architects from bidding competitively for jobs or offering discounts or doing work without compensation.
   a. What antitrust violation was the government seeking to stem in both of these cases?
   b. What defenses are offered by the professions for their policies?
9. Starter Sportswear has a license to manufacture and sell satin professional team jackets marketed as "authentic" because they are styled in the manner of jackets actually worn by the members of the various teams. Starter also sells other "nonauthentic" apparel. A Starter policy statement provides that it will sell only to retailers that carry

a representative amount of Starter's full line of apparel. Starter also has a minimum order policy specifying that it won't deal with retailers who seek quantities beneath that minimum order. Trans Sport, a retailer, began selling Starter jackets to other retailers that did not meet Starter's requirements. At that point, Starter declined to deal further with Trans Sport. Trans Sport then sued Starter.

a. List Trans Sport's claims against Starter.

b. Resolve those claims, raising all the relevant issues.

[See T*rans Sport, Inc.* v. *Starter Sportswear, Inc.,* 964 F.2d 186 (1992).]

Chapter Questions—Economics/Public Policy

1. A 1995 report from the *Los Angeles Times:*

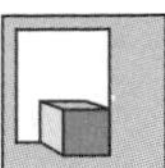

> A Paris court ordered Italian clothing giant Benetton to pay $32,000 in damages to HIV victims over an advertising campaign showing parts of the human body tatooed with the words *HIV positive.* The court said showing bare human flesh with inscriptions recalling the deadly AIDS disease "evoked Nazi barbarity or meat marking." It said the theme of the advertising campaign was an abuse of freedom of expression and a "provocative exploitation of suffering."[32]

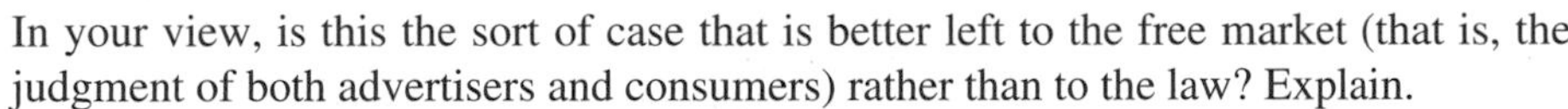

In your view, is this the sort of case that is better left to the free market (that is, the judgment of both advertisers and consumers) rather than to the law? Explain.

2. Antitrust attorney Joel Davidow says that four policy measures have been critical to the success of formerly socialist nations that are moving to a market economy: privatization, restructuring, deregulation, and adoption of competition legislation (antitrust). Now, in the 1990s, almost all of the industrial nations of the world, including Russia, Poland, Hungary, and Bulgaria, are taking all of these measures.

   a. Why is antitrust law important to the success of the new market economies in these formerly collectivist nations?

   b. Is antitrust of importance to developing nations such as India, Argentina, and Brazil? Explain.

   [See Joel Davidow, "The Relevance of Antimonopoly Policy for Developing Countries," *The Antitrust Bulletin* 37, no. 1 (Spring 1992), p. 277.]

3. In 1992, Coca-Cola controlled about 41 percent of the U.S. soft-drink market, and PepsiCo controlled just over 31 percent. Should their 72 percent combined market share be challenged by the government? Explain.

Notes

1. *Mangini* v. *R.J. Reynolds Tobacco Co.,* 875 P.2d 73 (Cal. 1994), cert. denied. 115 S.Ct. 577 (1994).
2. *Johnson & Johnson–Merck Consumer Pharmaceuticals Company* v. *Rhone-Poulenc Rorer Pharmaceuticals,* 19 F.3d 125 (1994).
3. *Standard Oil Co. of New Jersey* v. *United States,* 221 U.S. 1 (1911).
4. *Federal Trade Commission* v. *Ticor Title Insurance Co.,* 112 S.Ct. 2169 (1992).
5. *California* v. *American Stores Co.,* 495 U.S. 271 (1990).
6. *U.S.* v. *Aluminum Company of America,* 148 F.2d 416 (2d Cir. 1945).
7. *Cliff Food Stores, Inc.* v. *Kroger Co.,* 417 F.2d 203, 207 n. 2 (5th Cir. 1969).
8. For a journalistic account, see Wendy Bounds, "Court Ruling Backs Kodak on Two Decrees," *The Wall Street Journal,* August 7, 1995, p. A9.

9. Steve Lipin, "Let's Do It: Disney to Diaper Makers Push Mergers and Acquisitions to Record High," *The Wall Street Journal,* January 2, 1996, p. R8.
10. Reported in Walter Adams and James W. Brock, "The Big Business Establishment," in *Ethics, Leadership, and the Bottom Line,* ed. Charles Nelson and Robert Cavey (Croton-on-Hudson, NY: North River Press, 1991), pp. 202, 208.
11. Michael Oneal et al., "The Best and Worst Deals of the 80s," *Business Week,* January 15, 1990, pp. 52–54.
12. Jay Bookman, "Voices of Anger: Atlantans Discuss How the Country Lost Its Way," *Atlanta Journal and Constitution,* July 12, 1992, p. C3.
13. L. C. Griffiths, "Regulation of Monopolistic Methods," *Journal of Marketing* 57 (January 1993), p. 102.
14. Wayne D. Collins and Steven C. Sunshine, "Rigor and Sophistry in the New Merger Guidelines," *The American Enterprise* 4, no. 2 (March–April 1993), p. 61.
15. Richard Posner, *Antitrust Law* (Chicago: The University of Chicago Press, 1976), p. 130.
16. Margot Horspool and Valentine Korah, "Competition," *Antitrust Bulletin* 37, no. 2 (Summer 1992), p. 337.
17. *Standard Oil,* 221 U.S. 1.
18. See, for example, John DeQ. Briggs and Stephen Calkins, "Antitrust 1986–87: Power and Access (Part I)," *The Antitrust Bulletin* 32, no. 2 (Summer 1987), p. 275.
19. This analysis is drawn from William Kovacic, "The Identification and Proof of Horizontal Agreements under the Antitrust Laws," *The Antitrust Bulletin* 38, no. 1 (Spring 1993), p. 5.
20. Associated Press, "Air Travelers to Get Coupons," *Waterloo Courier,* March 23, 1993, p. A1.
21. Steve Stecklow and William Bulkeley, "Antitrust Case against MIT Is Dropped," *The Wall Street Journal,* December 23, 1993, p. A10.
22. Charles Goldsmith, "EU Fines 19 Carton-Board Companies Record $164.9 Million for Price Fixing," *The Wall Street Journal,* July 14, 1994, p. A6.
23. Russell Mokhiber, "Bigness Isn't Better," *Sloan Management Review* 28, no. 3 (Spring 1987), p. 63, reviewing Walter Adams and James W. Brock, *The Bigness Complex: Industry, Labor, and Government in the American Economy* (New York: Pantheon Books, 1986).
24. "Doesn't Anyone Give a D_ _ _?" *Business Week,* August 5, 1985, p. 92.
25. Harold Brown, "The Direction for Antitrust Law," *New York Law Journal,* November 30, 1994, p. 3.
26. *Continental T.V., Inc.* v. *GTE Sylvania Inc.,* 443 U.S. 36 (1977).
27. Deirdre Carmody, "New Mag Hypes Live Entertainment," *Rocky Mountain News,* January 27, 1996, p. 10D.
28. Anita Sharpe, "Pharmacies Sue Drug Manufacturers and Distributors over Pricing Policies," *The Wall Street Journal,* October 18, 1994, p. B9.
29. Roger Lowenstein, "Drug Pact May Be Worse than the Disease," *The Wall Street Journal,* January 25, 1996, p. C1.
30. See Earl Kintner, *A Robinson-Patman Primer* (New York: MacMillan, 1970), p. 93.
31. Associated Press, "New Antitrust Chief Opens Record Number of Inquiries," *Waterloo Courier,* July 22, 1994, p. D4.
32. "Benetton Told to Pay HIV Victims," *Los Angeles Times,* February 2, 1995, p. D2.

PART III

THE BUSINESS'S RELATIONSHIP WITH CUSTOMERS AND CLIENTS

CHAPTER

12

Consumer Protection and Debtor/ Creditor Law

Reader's Guide

Throughout this text, we have asked you to (1) imagine that you are building your own business or are employed as a manager in a business and (2) think, as an owner or manager must, about the public policy consequences of your business decisions. It can be particularly demanding to satisfy the conflicting expectations that come with those dual roles. Since we are dealing with consumer protection in this chapter, you will be looking at public policy concerns; but we will also ask you to look at those concerns from the view of ownership/management. We will review a number of consumer protection themes, including fraud, consumer product safety, debtor/creditor rules, truth-in-lending, fair debt collection, and bankruptcy.

PROFILE

Karen Melvin's 1989 Dodge Caravan leaked water into the driver's side when it rained—a problem the dealer assured her had been fixed when she bought the used minivan.[1]

"Every time I turned a corner, water would pour into my lap," the Minneapolis resident said. "I knew I had been duped."

Fed up, Melvin contacted the minivan's previous owner, Daniel Garcia of Springfield, Virginia. Garcia was surprised to learn that his former minivan was back on the road.

In 1992, he had won a lawsuit to get Chrysler Corp. to buy back the vehicle, which dripped water into his lap every time it rained. Garcia told Melvin he had the car in the shop for 36 days as mechanics tried unsuccessfully to fix the problem.

Karen Melvin's dilemma, a car that turns out to be a lemon, is all too familiar to many Americans and is merely one of a wide array of conflicts between the business community and consumers. The law offers considerable protection for wronged consumers, but it also seeks to afford reasonable latitude to well-intended merchants.

QUESTIONS

1. What are "lemon laws?"
2. Is Karen Melvin a victim of fraud?
3. Do we need to enhance the protections available to purchasers of defective cars?

I. Common Law Consumer Protection

Later in this chapter, we will explore government efforts to protect consumers from dangerous products, unfair lending practices, and the like. Before turning to that legislation, we need to appreciate the common law (judge-made law) that preceded and, in some respects, provided the foundation for the striking federal, state, and local initiatives of recent years. In addition to the product liability protection (negligence, warranties, and strict liability) discussed in Chapter 14, injured consumers can look to several common law protections, including actions for fraud, misrepresentation, and unconscionability.

A. Fraud and Innocent Misrepresentation

If the market is to operate efficiently, the buyer must be able to rely on the truth of the seller's affirmations regarding a product. Regrettably, willful untruths appear common in American commerce. A victim of **fraud** is entitled to rescind the contract in question and to seek damages, including, in cases of malice, a punitive recovery. Although fraud arises in countless situations and thus is difficult to define, the legal community has generally adopted the following elements, each of which must be proven:

fraud. An intentional misrepresentation of a material fact with intent to deceive where the misrepresentation is justifiably relied on by another and damages result.

1. There was a misrepresentation of a material fact.
2. The misrepresentation was intentional.
3. The injured party justifiably relied on the misrepresentation.
4. Injury resulted.

In identifying a fraudulent expression, the law distinguishes between statements of objective, verifiable facts and simple expressions of opinion. The latter ordinarily are not fraudulent even though they are erroneous. Thus, normal sales **puffing** ("This baby is the greatest little car you're ever gonna drive") is fully lawful, and consumers are expected to exercise good judgment in responding to such claims. However, if a misleading expression of opinion comes from an expert, and the other party does not share that expertise (e.g., the sale of a diamond engagement ring), a court probably would offer a remedy. (See Chapter 14 for further examination of puffing.)

puffing. An expression of opinion by a seller not made as a representation of fact.

Silence. In limited circumstances, silence may constitute fraud. Typically, that problem may emerge where party A misunderstands the facts of the situation and party B both knows the true facts and knows that A does not know those facts and cannot reasonably be expected to discover them. An example would be a cracked engine block, where the cracks were filled with a sealer and covered with a compound such that the crack is unlikely to be discovered even by capable inspection.[2] In such situations, the knowledgeable party may be under a duty to speak. Nonetheless, the general rule is that silence is fully permissible.

Of course, fraud can involve false conduct as well as false expression. A familiar example is the car seller who rolls back an odometer with the result that the buyer is misled.

A variation on the general theme of fraud is **innocent misrepresentation,** which differs from fraud only in that the falsehood was unintentional. The wrongdoer believed the statement or conduct in question to be true, but he or she was mistaken. In such cases, the wronged party may secure rescission of the contract, but ordinarily damages are not awarded. (See Chapters 4, 10, and 11 for examinations of fraud in other contexts.)

innocent misrepresentation. An unintentional misrepresentation of a material fact where the misrepresentation is justifiably relied on by another and damages result.

B. Unconscionable Contracts

The doctrine of **unconscionability** emerged from court decisions where jurists concluded that some contracts are so unfair or oppressive as to demand intervention. (Unconscionability is also included in state statutory laws via the Uniform Commercial Code 2-302.) The legal system intrudes on contracts only with the greatest reluctance. Mere foolishness or want of knowledge does not constitute grounds for unconscionability, nor is a contract unconscionable and hence unenforceable merely because one party is spectacularly clever and the other is not. Rather, unconscionability requires a showing that (1) the bargaining power of the parties was so unbalanced that the agreement was not truly freely entered, or (2) the clause or contract in question was so unfair as to violate societal values.

unconscionability. A contract so one-sided and oppressive as to be unfair.

Suppose you own a furniture store, and you find that your customers all too frequently are unable to make their required payments. One method you employ to better protect yourself is to provide in your standard installment sales contract that the balance due on each item purchased by a particular buyer will remain due until payments have been made on *all* items purchased by that buyer. Thus, everything an individual customer buys from you serves as collateral for all other purchases by that buyer. From a business point of view, this extra protection makes good sense; but from the consumer's point of view, is it so unfair as to be unconscionable?[3]

The case that follows illustrates the application of unconscionability reasoning in an interesting situation far afield from conventional consumer protection.

CASE

Don King Productions, Inc. v. Douglas

742 F. Supp. 778 (S.D.N.Y. 1990)

Facts

James "Buster" Douglas, a professional boxer, and his manager John P. Johnson (assisted by Johnson's lawyer, Stephen Enz) entered into a boxing promotion agreement with Don King Productions on December 31, 1988. Douglas received $25,000 at the time. The contract gave DKP exclusive promotional rights for Douglas's boxing for three years. DKP expressed its intent to promote a world championship bout for Douglas. In the event Douglas became world champion, the contract was to be automatically extended for the full period of the championship and two years thereafter. The agreement promised at least 10 bouts over three years, with purses to be negotiated but with floors of $25,000 and $10,000 in expenses for each.

Douglas participated in three bouts, the last of which was a heavyweight championship fight with Mike Tyson in Tokyo, Japan, on February 10, 1990. Douglas's contract provided for a total of $1.3 million for that fight. Douglas knocked out Tyson in round 10, thus becoming the world champion. However, King, who was also Tyson's promoter, protested the outcome, using various means including public claims of a "long count" in round 8 when Tyson had knocked Douglas to the mat.

Johnson and King met in February 1990 to discuss a Douglas match that King planned for the Trump Plaza in Atlantic City, New Jersey. At about that time, the Mirage Hotel of Las Vegas contacted Johnson seeking to schedule a bout there. On February 21, 1990, Douglas and Johnson signed a contract with Mirage. The contract provided for a reported total of $60 million for two fights but required Douglas to secure a release from the contract with King or a court order voiding the contract.

DKP then sued Douglas and Johnson for breach of contract and the Mirage for interference with contract. Douglas and Johnson asserted counterclaims for slander and intentional infliction of emotional distress based on King's claims that Tyson should have been declared the winner and that Douglas was not a deserving champion. Those claims were rejected by the court. Douglas and Johnson also claimed their contract with DKP was *unconscionable.*

* * *

Judge Sweet

The Unconscionable Contracts Defense

Douglas and Johnson plead as an affirmative defense that the contracts they entered into with DKP are unconscionable. Under New York law . . . a determination of unconscionability

> requires a showing that the contract was both procedurally and substantively unconscionable *when made*—i.e., "some showing of an 'absence of meaningful choice on the

Continued

Continued

part of one of the parties together with contract terms which are unreasonably favorable to the other party." *Gillman* v. *Chase Manhattan Bank, N.A.,* 534 N.E.2d 824, 828 (1988).

The factual contentions set forth in the Douglas/Johnson interrogatories to support the unconscionability defense—that the Tokyo conduct of King was unconscionable, that King is a powerful promoter, and that exclusive, extendable terms of the contracts are unreasonably favorable to King—are as a matter of law insufficient.

The Douglas/Johnson contention that the contracts "became unconscionable" *after* their inception owing to King's conduct during the Tokyo fight is unavailing . . . The doctrine of unconscionability implicates the circumstances and terms of a contract at the time of formation—not the parties' subsequent performance under it . . . The Tokyo performance by King . . . has . . . absolutely no bearing on the defense of unconscionability, which relates to substantive and procedural fairness of a contract "when made."

Douglas/Johnson next contend that King so dominates promotion of heavyweight fights that the Douglas-King contracts are inherently procedurally unconscionable . . . Douglas/Johnson make no allegation here that deceptive or high-pressure tactics were employed in concluding the contracts, that contract terms were concealed in fine print, or that there was a gross asymmetry in the experience and education of the parties, each of whom was represented by counsel throughout the course of their arm's-length negotiations.

. . . [T]he unconscionability defense does not here implicate its primary use as "a means with which to protect the commercially illiterate consumer beguiled into a grossly unfair bargain by a deceptive vendor or finance company." *Marvel Entertainment Group, Inc.* v. *Young Astronaut Council,* No. 88–5141, 1989 WL 129504 (S.D.N.Y. October 27, 1989). Without some definite allegation of a defect in the contract negotiation process apart from King's stature in the boxing field, which alone does not suggest "inequality so strong and manifest as to shock the conscience and confound the judgment," (quoting *Christian* v. *Christian,* 365 N.E.2d 849, 855 (1977), defendants have failed to create an issue of procedural unconscionability requiring resolution by jury.

The contention that the contracts require Douglas to fight exclusively for DKP for the extendable terms of such contracts, which could amount to the rest of the boxer's professional life, equally fails to satisfy the requirement of substantive unconscionability. Only in "exceptional cases" is "a provision of [a] contract . . . so outrageous as to warrant holding it unenforceable on the ground of substantive unconscionability alone." *Gillman,* 534 N.E.2d at 829 . . .

Douglas and Johnson . . . cite no case considering or holding an exclusive services contract unconscionable on grounds of duration . . . The court therefore declines to revisit its prior legal determinations that the contract durational terms were definite in nature and the contracts were supported by sufficiently-definite price consideration to induce Douglas' promise to fight exclusively for DKP. The unconscionability defense accordingly shall be stricken, there having been no proffer or allegation sufficient to establish either its procedural or substantive elements.

[So ordered.]

Afterword

King, Douglas, and the Mirage settled their dispute. King agreed to assign the promotion rights to the Douglas–Evander Holyfield fight to the owner of the Mirage, Steve Wynn. Douglas agreed to pay $4 million to King. Douglas lost to Holyfield but left boxing, having earned some $30 million.

Questions

1. *a.* Why did the court reject Douglas's unconscionability argument?
   b. Do you agree with the court? Explain.

Continued

Continued

2. What does the court mean by its statement that a contract must be "both procedurally and substantively unconscionable"?
3. Plaintiff Willie had listed his business in the Wichita, Kansas, Yellow Pages for 13 years. The plaintiff was expanding his business, and he entered into an agreement with the defendant phone company to include additional telephone numbers in the directory. The defendant inadvertently failed to include one of the numbers in the directory. The contract signed by the parties included a conspicuous exculpatory clause limiting the phone company's liability for errors and omissions to an amount equal to the cost of the ad. On discovering the omission, the plaintiff had begun advertising the number on television at a cost of approximately $5,000. Plaintiff contends the exculpatory clause is unconscionable, and, therefore, unenforceable. Decide. Explain. [See *Willie* v. *Southwestern Bell Telephone Company,* 549 P.2d 903 (Kan. 1976).]

II. The Consumer and Government Regulation of Business

A. State Laws

Having looked at the common law foundation of consumer protection, we now turn to some of the many governmental measures that provide shelter in the marketplace. Many states have enacted comprehensive consumer protection statutes, such as Pennsylvania's Unfair Practices and Consumer Protection Law. States also have specific statutes addressing such problems as door-to-door sales, debtor protection, telemarketing fraud, and so forth. We will look at only one of those, the so-called **lemon laws,** which address the particularly frustrating problem of a hopelessly defective vehicle.

lemon laws. State statutes providing remedies for those buying vehicles that turn out to be so thoroughly defective that they cannot be repaired after reasonable efforts.

Lemon Laws. Of course, new-car purchases are covered by warranty laws (see Chapter 14 for a discussion of UCC warranty provisions and the federal Magnuson Moss Warranty Act); in addition, all 50 states have some form of law designed to provide recourse for consumers whose new vehicles turn out to be defective such that they cannot be repaired after a reasonable effort. The quarrel, of course, is about when a car is truly a lemon. Lemon laws typically cover new cars for one to two years or 12 to 18 thousand miles after purchase. Typically, state laws provide that the vehicle must have been returned to the manufacturer or dealer three or four times to repair the same defect and that defect must substantially impair the value or safety of the vehicle, *or* the vehicle must have been unavailable to the consumer for a total of at least 30 days. Such a vehicle is a lemon, and the purchaser is entitled to a replacement vehicle or full refund of the purchase price. In some states, used cars may also be treated as lemons. In almost all states, the determination about whether a car is a lemon is handled by an arbitration panel, which in certain states is arranged by the automobile manufacturers; other arrangements, such as a panel provided by the American Arbitration Association, are available in many states. If dissatisfied with the ruling, the consumer may then bring suit.

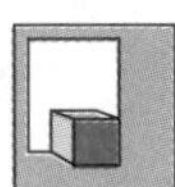

Profile Perspective: Consider again the case of Karen Melvin. Reportedly, water gushed into her minivan during rains. Consumer groups accuse automakers and dealers of passing faulty vehicles like Melvin's to used-car buyers without fully disclosing all they know about the defects. Melvin had received a Chrysler disclosure form indicating that an unspecified water leak had been repaired. The critics also claim those defective vehicles often are moved across state lines to avoid state lemon laws, a practice called *lemon laundering.*

After reading about common law fraud and state lemon laws, do you think that Melvin has a good claim in arbitration or court? Who would she sue?

Some members of Congress, at this writing in 1996, are trying to roll back federal consumer protection laws. A recent *Money* magazine study found many states likewise curbing consumer protection.[4] *Money* surveyed 45 state attorneys general for data about budgets, complaints received, money returned to consumers, and so on. *Money* concluded that 17 states and the District of Columbia are "losing ground" in consumer protection, 9 have made progress, and the balance were essentially unchanged. Washington, DC is so short of cash that in 1995 it simply quit enforcing its consumer protection laws. Forty-four of the consumer protection offices had their budgets reduced during the previous decade even though, as *Money* observed, a well-run office can give consumers a very good return on their tax dollars. For example, in Minnesota, the state's consumer protection division recouped an average of $1.7 million annually for its citizens while operating on a budget of about $520,000.

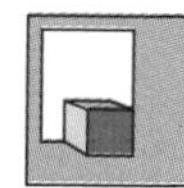

Public Policy Questions

1. If you were a federal or state politician, what arguments would you offer to defend these consumer protection cutbacks?
2. In the dual roles we have asked you to assume as both manager and citizen, how do you feel about those cutbacks? Explain.

B. Federal Laws

The Federal Trade Commission. The Federal Trade Commission was created in 1914 to prevent "unfair methods of competition and unfair or deceptive acts or practices in and affecting commerce." In conducting its business, the FTC performs as a miniature government with extensive and powerful quasi-legislative and quasi-judicial roles.

Rule Making. The primary legislative direction is in issuing **trade regulation rules** to enforce the intent of broadly drawn congressional legislation. That is, the rules specify those particular acts or practices that the commission deems unfair or deceptive.

trade regulation rules. Directives from the Federal Trade Commission interpreting the will of Congress and specifying those practices that the Commission considers unfair or deceptive.

In the same vein, the FTC issued **industry guides,** which are the commission's interpretations of laws it enforces. The guides provide advice to industry and the public about the likely legality of specific marketing practices. For example, in 1992, the FTC issued industry guides to identify forms of environmental or "green" advertising and labeling that might be misleading or unfair. The guides do not have the force of law, but a failure to observe them might result in adjudication.

industry guides. Published advice to industry and the public providing Federal Trade Commission interpretations of the likely legality of specific marketing practices.

The FTC's quasi-legislative role is well illustrated by its ongoing struggle with the telemarketing industry. As required by the 1994 Telemarketing and Consumer Fraud and Abuse Prevention Act, the FTC has written a new set of rules governing fraudulent telemarketing practices, which cost consumers an estimated $40 billion annually. Consider a few of the standards:

- Require callers to quickly reveal the name of the business, the nature of the product, and so on.
- Limit calls to between 8 A.M. and 9 P.M.

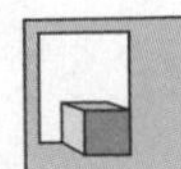

- Ban calls to those who have indicated that they do not want to be called.
- Ban threats, profanity, and repeated calling.[5]

The FTC had originally proposed much tougher standards, but after a period of public comment, including intense opposition from the telemarketing industry, the standards were revised. For example, the original rules would have limited calls to a given individual to once in three months, required contests to start and end within 18 months, and required marketers to secure signed agreements before many phone sales would have become effective.[6] Critics are concerned that the new federal rules will conflict with generally more demanding state rules and leave customers with reduced protection, although the federal program does provide for civil penalties of $10,000 per violation.

On balance, is telemarketing good or bad for America?

Public Policy Questions

Assume your dual role of both manager and responsible citizen. Consider just one of the new rules, that calls are permissible only between 8 A.M. and 9 P.M.

1. Are those hours reasonable? What about weekends?
2. On balance, is telemarketing good or bad for America?

Adjudication. On its own initiative or as a result of a citizen complaint, the FTC may conduct investigations into suspect trade practices. At that point, the FTC may drop the proceeding, settle the matter informally, or issue a formal complaint. An informal settlement normally takes the form of a consent agreement in which the party under investigation voluntarily discontinues the practice in question but is not required to admit guilt.

Profile Perspective: Consumer advocates, in 1995, petitioned the FTC to create an enforcement program to stop the lemon laundering that left Karen Melvin with her faulty van. Basically, the consumer groups want the FTC to use its authority to prevent manufacturers from simply moving their defective vehicles across state lines in order to avoid lemon laws.

Car Rentals. In 1992, Dollar Rent-A-Car and Value Rent-A-Car both agreed to settle FTC charges that they had failed to disclose mandatory "extra" charges when giving price quotations to potential customers. The FTC claimed that ads and telephone quotes failed to reveal extra charges such as required airport surcharges or fees for drivers beneath age 25. Neither company admitted any wrongdoing, and both said the alleged violations occurred under previous owners.[7]

Where an agreement cannot be reached, the FTC may proceed with a formal complaint. In that case, the matter proceeds essentially as a trial conducted before an administrative law judge (see Chapter 8).

The FTC has no authority to impose criminal sanctions. Although it can impose fines, the commission often engages in more creative remedies—for example, ordering corrective advertising to counteract previous, misleading ads or requiring contracts to be altered. In the case of "high-pressure sales," the FTC has allowed the consumer a cooling-off period in which to cancel a contract.

Deceptive Practices. FTC regulatory efforts range across the spectrum of consumer activity. For example, it issued a rule specifying that mail-order sellers are in violation of the Federal Trade Commission Act if they solicit orders through the mail without a reasonable expectation that the goods can be shipped in 30 days or less. The FTC has pursued broad-scale regulatory initiatives against a number of industries, including insurance, used autos, and credit cards; but perhaps the best examples of FTC rule-making and adjudicatory actions lie in the area of advertising, which we discussed in Chapter 11.

The Consumer Product Safety Commission. Perhaps you are an ardent in-line skater? You decide to open your own skate shop as you observe the dramatically increased interest in the sport. Business is booming, with skaters numbering more than 12 million in 1993. Then you read some troublesome data. Head injuries increased from 2,000 to 7,000 from 1993 to 1994, and five people died in skating accidents from August 1992 to summer 1994.[8] How should you respond to these developments? Do you need to warn each customer about the hazards and encourage each to wear safety equipment? If one of your customers was skating without a helmet and suffered a crippling head injury, would you feel responsible? Or can you in good conscience leave this issue to the force of the market and customer responsibility? Should the government intervene and require skaters to use helmets and other safety equipment?

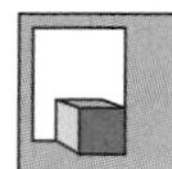

The Consumer Product Safety Commission, charged with government oversight in this area, conducted a study and found nothing defective about in-line skates, but the CPSC did issue a warning in 1994 that skating is dangerous and that skaters should take a variety of safety precautions.

Dangerous Products. The CPSC, created in 1972, is responsible for reducing the risks in using some 15,000 consumer products, including toys, lawn mowers, washing machines, bicycles, portable heaters, and household chemicals. Each year, about 22,000 deaths and 30 million injuries are associated with those products.[9] In 1992, lawn-mower injuries alone sent 50,000 people to hospital emergency rooms and an estimated 135,000 were injured by lawn care products generally.[10]

The CPSC has had some success in fulfilling its mission:

> Thanks to CPSC action, kids now have flame-retardant sleepwear, chain saws are safer, and aerosol cans are less hazardous. Slats on cribs are spaced to prevent babies' strangling to death. Injuries from the blades of rotary lawn mowers, which once stood at about 80,000 a year, are down dramatically after the CPSC ordered design changes.[11]

Nonetheless, the CPSC is a generally benign presence in Washington, DC, after 12 years of cuts that reduced the agency's budget by half. The Reagan and Bush administrations favored greater reliance on voluntary industry standards and counted on market forces to protect the consumer. President Clinton appears more sympathetic to the role of the CPSC.

Firmer Rules. Unhappy with CPSC inactivity, in 1994 Congress and President Clinton approved the Child Safety Protection Act, which among other things, bans the sale of any ball or block smaller than 1.75 inches in diameter and requires choking hazard warnings for small toys, toy parts, latex balloons, and vending machines that sell those things. From January 1, 1993, through September 30, 1994, 22 children died from choking on toys.[12] Similarly, in 1993, as required by Congress, the CPSC developed a new rule governing garage-door openers. It requires safety features to prevent humans and animals from being crushed accidentally by closing doors. The CPSC reported that 54 children were killed by garage doors between 1982 and 1992.[13] The new rule requires one of three safety mechanisms: "a control button that has to be held constantly to make the door close, an electric-eye sensor, or a door-edge sensor like those on elevators." All of the necessary technology is readily available and is expected to add $20 to $25 to the cost of an opener.

Public Policy Questions

1. Given the lives to be saved versus the additional cost for improved garage-door openers, do you support the new rule? Explain.
2. Why did toy manufacturers support the Child Safety Protection Act?

Warning: Do Not Tilt

In response to a Consumer Product Safety Commission voluntary campaign, the nation's seven soda vending machine manufacturers agreed in 1995 to post warnings on their machines saying: "Do not rock or tilt. May cause serious injury or death. Machine will not dispense free product if tipped." The CPSC says 37 people have been killed and 113 injured in such accidents since 1978.

Duties. The CPSC's duties may be summarized as follows.

1. Data collection. The commission conducts research and collects information as a foundation for regulating product safety. Its National Electronic Injury Surveillance System (NEISS) collects data from many hospital emergency rooms across the country.

2. Rule making. The commission, via its rule-making authority, promulgates mandatory consumer product safety, performance, and labeling standards. It invites public comments and suggestions. Industry trade associations have been more active in submitting offers to set standards, but consumers and consumer groups have been encouraged to participate. Standards are processed under traditional due process requirements, including publication in the ***Federal Register,*** notice to the affected parties, and hearings. Affected parties may petition for a judicial reversal of the rules.

Federal Register. Daily publication of federal agency regulations and other legal materials coming from the executive branch of government.

The difficulty in issuing successful rules is well illustrated by the CPSC's 1995 change in child-resistant cap standards originally promulgated in 1972. The change makes the caps easier to open, but ironically it was prompted by continued childhood poisoning. Adults, frustrated by the difficulty of opening the caps, sometimes either leave the caps off or transfer the contents to other packages, making it easier for children to reach and ingest the medicine. The CPSC found that grandparents' medicine was involved in about 20 percent of the poisonings (42 total poisonings of children in 1992 as opposed to 216 the year before the original standard was imposed).[14] Thus, the original rule successfully reduced poisonings, but the 1995 revision is expected to further diminish that total.

Ninety percent of a 100-person panel, composed of people 50 to 70 years old, must be able to open and close the package within five minutes.

"The difficulty in standard-setting is illustrated by the test the CPSC has decided to employ to determine whether packaging is satisfactory: Ninety percent of a 100-person panel, composed of people 50 to 70 years old, must be able to open and close the package within five minutes, then again within one minute," says Eric Rubel, the commission's general counsel. "If more than 20 of 100 children under five years old could open the package in 10 minutes, it would fail."[15]

3. Compliance. The CPSC is empowered to use a variety of strategies in securing compliance. Manufacturers must certify before distribution that products meet federal safety standards. Agents of the commission may inspect manufacturing sites. The commission can mandate specific product safety testing procedures, and businesses other than retailers are required to keep safety records.

4. Enforcement. In cases of severe and imminent hazards, the CPSC may seek an immediate court order to remove a product from the market. In less urgent circumstances, the commission may proceed with its own administrative remedy. Because it prefers to secure voluntary compliance, the commission may urge the company to issue public or private notices of a defect, or it may seek the repair or replacement of defective parts. For example, in 1995, 21 makers of children's clothing agreed to begin replacing drawstrings, blamed for strangulations, with snaps, buttons, and other fastening devices. Where voluntary negotiations fail, the CPSC may proceed with an adjudicative hearing, conducted in the manner of a trial, before an administrative law judge or members of the commission. The decision may be appealed to the full commission and thereafter to the U.S. Court of Appeals. Failure to comply with safety provisions may result in civil or criminal penalties.

Only a few products have actually been banned from the market. For example, in 1988 Congress required the CPSC to ban most lawn darts. The play items had resulted in at least three deaths and several thousand injuries. Most lawn-dart injuries have been suffered by children.

A case—Baby walkers. The American Academy of Pediatrics (AAP) and others believe that baby walkers are unreasonably dangerous, and in 1995, the AAP called for a ban on the walkers. According to the American Medical Association, the walkers are associated with an average of one death annually. In 1991, 29,000 injuries, of which 9,500 were considered severe, were connected to walkers.[16] In 1994, the commission voted to begin a formal rule-making action, but it also continued negotiations directed toward voluntary guidelines.

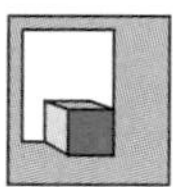

Critics say additional regulation is foolish and that the problem lies principally with poor supervision by parents: "Four out of five walker-related accidents were preventable with baby gates and adult supervision: 77 percent of the infants fell down stairs and 4 percent fell off a porch or out a door."[17]

The critics contend that few injuries associated with walkers are actually the product of the walkers themselves, noting that more than 99 percent of the babies using walkers are not injured.[18]

Public Policy Question

What action would you take in the baby walker controversy? Explain.

III. Debtor/Creditor Law

A. *Secured Transactions*

In building and managing any contemporary business, a key ingredient to success lies in addressing the problem of *credit;* that is, to what extent will you rely on borrowed money to operate your enterprise and to what extent will you allow customers to pay for goods and services at some future date?

collateral. Property pledged as security for satisfaction of a debt.
unsecured. Refers to a loan not backed by some kind of security.
security. As to loans, refers to a lien, promise, mortgage, or the like given by a debtor to assure payment or performance of her or his debt.
surety. A person who promises to perform the same obligation as the principal and is jointly liable with the principal for that performance.
guarantor. A person who promises to perform the same obligation as the principal if the principal should default.
creditor. A person to whom a debt is owed.
real property. Land, buildings, and things permanently attached to land or buildings.
mortgage. An interest in land formalized by a written instrument providing security for the payment of a debt.
mortgagor. One who pledges property for a particular purpose such as security for a debt.
mortgagee. One who receives a mortgage to secure repayment of a debt.
foreclose. To terminate the mortgagor's rights in the property covered by the mortgage.

Assume that you own and operate a video-rental store. Perhaps you start off in a small operation financed, in part, by a $10,000 loan from your parents. Knowing you to be a good, reliable person, they loan you the money on the understanding that you will repay it two years hence. They do not demand **collateral,** for example, your car as a guarantee that they will be able to recover their money. This kind of loan is **unsecured.** You have simply promised to repay. Alternatively, perhaps your family agrees to make the loan only if your provide some **security;** that is, they want to minimize their risk. Broadly, you can provide that security in three ways: (1) You can offer the promise of another (a guarantee) to pay if you do not. (2) You could offer real property as security should you fail to pay. (3) You could offer personal property as security should you fail to pay.

Guarantee. Perhaps your fiancee's mother agrees to provide security for your start-up loan by guaranteeing that she will pay it if you do not. She could become a **surety** for your loan by co-signing with you an agreement providing that you will repay your parents. In a variation on that theme, she might become a **guarantor** of your loan by reaching a separate agreement to repay if you fail to do so. That is, she does not co-sign with you, but rather she strikes a separate understanding with your parents that she will pay the loan if you fail to do so. The critical distinction here is that a surety is *primarily* liable on the loan, whereas a guarantor is *secondarily* liable. Thus, the guarantor (your fiancee's mother) need pay only if the you, the recipient of the loan, fail to do so. If your fiancee's mother takes the role of surety, the **creditor** (in this case your parents) could collect from the surety as soon as the debt is due and without first seeking payment from you.

Real Estate. **Real property** (immovable property, including land, buildings, and unsevered crops) often serves as security for a loan. A **mortgage** is a security interest in real property given by the **mortgagor**/debtor to the **mortgagee**/creditor. If the debtor fails to pay, the creditor can then **foreclose** on the real property. Foreclosure is a legal proceeding that varies somewhat from state to state, but it results in the creditor either taking possession of the real property or forcing its sale to satisfy the debt. Security interests in real property may also arise from a **deed of trust** or a **land contract,** but those will not be discussed here.

Real property also can serve as security for a debt arising out of improvements to that property. For example, in opening your video store, perhaps you contracted with a carpenter to build shelves and counters. If you fail to pay, the carpenter can place a **mechanic's lien** (also called a **materialman's lien**) on the property, assuming you own the building. A **lien** is a claim on property to secure the satisfaction of a debt. Creation and execution of a mechanic's lien are governed by state law, but the general idea is that, after providing proper notice, the lienholder can foreclose against the property to satisfy the debt.

deed of trust. A three-party instrument used to create a security interest in real property in which the legal title to the real property is placed in one or more trustees to secure the repayment of a sum of money or the performance of other conditions.

Personal Property. In opening your video store as your first business, you are unlikely to have real property to offer as security and you may be unable or unwilling to use third parties to guarantee loans for you. In that case, if security is required, you can turn to your personal property. Your car, your household goods, such as a stereo, any stocks you might own, equipment, and many other things, both tangible and intangible, could serve as personal property collateral, that is, security, for your loan. You may already have had the experience of borrowing money from a bank to buy a car, in which case the bank takes a **security interest** (a lien) in the car until the loan is repaid.

From the creditor's (lender) point of view, a security interest in personal property involves an assessment of two key questions: (1) In the event of a **default** (failure to pay) by the debtor, does the creditor have an enforceable interest in the debtor's property? (2) If the creditor has that enforceable interest, will it take priority over the interests of other creditors?

Creation and use of a security interest in personal property is governed by Article 9 of the Uniform Commercial Code. The heart of the creation of a security interest is a two-step process: **attachment** and **perfection.**

Attachment. As provided for by the UCC, the creditor's rights to the collateral attach (in a legal rather than a physical sense) with the completion of three requirements: (1) An agreement (normally in writing) must be achieved in which the debtor grants a security interest to the creditor. (2) The creditor must give value (e.g., lend money) to the debtor. (3) The debtor must have rights (ownership or right to possession) in the collateral. Once those requirements are fulfilled, the creditor's rights attach to the collateral.

Perfection. Once attachment has been achieved, the creditor's concerns turn to any third parties who might then or later have claims to the attached collateral. Perfection is the legal process by which the creditor's claim to the collateral achieves protection against claims by other creditors or those who might purchase the collateral; that is, the creditor is seeking priority over other possible claimants. As provided by the UCC, three principal means of perfection may be employed.

1. *Perfection by public filing*—A **financing statement,** filed normally either in the appropriate county office or with the secretary of state, gives notice that the creditor claims an interest in the debtor's collateral. The financing statement must meet the formal requirements specified by the UCC.
2. *Perfection by possession*—Under the UCC, the change of possession of collateral from the debtor to the creditor operates as a perfection of the creditor's security interest. Since the debtor does not have possession of the collateral, third parties are put on notice of the security interest just as they would be with perfection achieved by public filing.
3. *Automatic perfection*—In this instance, public notice is not required. Perfection is achieved automatically in a variety of ways, most important of which is a credit sale of **consumer goods** such as appliances, furniture, and stereos. If a creditor lends the money needed to buy the goods or if the seller retains a security interest in the goods to assure payment, perfection of the security interest is achieved automatically. The lender or seller has provided the money to make the purchase and thus has, under Article 9, an automatically perfected security interest. These circumstances give the creditor what is labeled a **purchase-money security interest,** thus eliminating the administrative burden of a filing.

B. Enforcing Security Agreements

Suppose you had used your car as collateral for the loan to open your video store, but things went badly for you and you were unable to repay the loan. What happens? In general, Article 9 defines the parties' rights and duties if a security agreement has been breached. The UCC does not define the circumstances under which a default occurs, but normally the agreement between the parties does so. In the event of default, the debtor has the option of (1) repossessing and retaining the collateral (2) repossessing and disposing of the collateral, or (3) ignoring the collateral and suing for the sum due.

land contract. Typically, an installment contract for the sale of land wherein the purchaser receives the deed from the owner on payment of the final installment.

mechanic's lien or materialman's lien. A claim created by law for the purpose of securing a priority of payment of the price or value of work performed and materials furnished in erecting or repairing a structure.

lien. A charge or security or encumbrance on property for payment of some debt.

security interest. A lien given by a debtor to his creditor to secure payment or performance of a debt or obligation.

default. A party fails to pay money when due or when lawfully demanded.

attachment. As to secured transactions, the process by which a security interest in the property of another becomes enforceable.

perfection. Process by which a secured party obtains a priority claim over other possible claimants to certain collateral belonging to a debtor.

financing statement. Document notifying others that the creditor claims an interest in the debtor's collateral. Must be filed as provided for by law in order to perfect a security interest.

consumer goods. Under the UCC, goods used or bought primarily for personal, family, or household purposes.

purchase money security interest. A security interest that is (1) taken or retained by the seller of collateral to secure all or part of its purchase price or (2) taken by a debtor to acquire rights in or the use of the collateral if the value is so used.

C. Government Oversight—Credit Regulations

Perhaps you are selling furniture, appliances, cars, or other consumer goods, and your customers ordinarily do not pay in cash. You may have strong faith in the free market; however, Congress, the state legislatures, and most American people have decided that credit arrangements are so important, so confusing, and so potentially hurtful that they have supplemented the market's powerful messages with specific government rules. In your own life as a consumer and in your career, if you enter consumer sales, you need to understand the general protections that federal and state laws afford to consumers seeking and securing credit. We will take an abbreviated look at several particularly important pieces of federal consumer credit legislation.

Profile Perspective: Think again about Karen Melvin and her waterlogged van. Assume that she, like most consumers, borrowed money to pay for the van. Unlike the frustrations and uncertainties that accompanied her lemon van, the process of borrowing money was probably quite routine and satisfactory. Here, consumer protection seems to be effective. A series of rather specific rules shelter consumers and allow managers to clearly understand what is required of them.

Regulation Z. Rules of the Federal Reserve Board implementing provisions of the Federal Truth-in-Lending Act.

annual percentage rate (APR). The rate of interest charged for borrowing money as expressed in a standardized, yearly manner allowing for comparison among lenders' fees.

open-end loan. Credit arrangement not involving a lump sum but permitting repeated borrowing where payment amounts are not specified.

closed-end loan. Credit arrangement where a specified sum is borrowed and a repayment plan usually is established.

Truth in Lending Act (TILA).[19]

As we increasingly turned to credit financing, consumers often did not understand the full cost of buying on credit. The TILA is part of the Consumer Credit Protection Act of 1968. Having been designed for consumer protection, it does not cover all loans. The following standards determine the TILA's applicability:

1. The debtor must be a "natural person" rather than an organization.
2. The creditor must be regularly engaged in extending credit or arranging for the extension of credit.
3. The purpose of the credit must be "primarily for personal, family, or household purposes" not in excess of $25,000. However, "consumer real property transactions" are covered by the act. Hence, home purchases fall within TILA provisions.
4. The credit must be subject to a finance charge or payable in more than four installments.

Following the enactment of the TILA, the Federal Reserve Board developed **Regulation Z** detailing the specific requirements of the act. The TILA was designed both to protect consumers from credit abuse and to assist them in becoming more informed regarding credit terms and costs so they could engage in comparison shopping. Congress presumed the increased information would stimulate competition in the finance industry. The heart of the act is the required conspicuous disclosure of the finance charge (the actual dollar sum to be paid for credit) and the **annual percentage rate (APR)** (the total cost of the credit expressed at an annual rate). The finance charge includes not just interest but service charges, points, loan fees, carrying charges, and others. TILA disclosure requirements apply to both **open-end** (for example, VISA and MasterCard) and **closed-end loans** (those of a fixed amount for a definite time).

Questions

A health spa sells some memberships for cash and some on an installment basis. The price is the same whether the buyer pays cash or buys on the installment plan. The spa has an arrangement with a financing agency to sell the installment contracts to the agency at a discount (a price lower than the face value of the contract).

1. How would you argue that the installment contract sales are in violation of TILA and Regulation Z?
2. How would you rule on such a case? [See *Joseph* v. *Norman's Health Club, Inc.*, 532 F.2d 86 (8th Cir. 1976).]

Credit and Charge Cards. As an aggressive marketer, you may want to hand out credit cards in your student union, but the TILA provides that credit cards cannot be issued to a consumer unless requested. Cardholder liability for unauthorized use (lost or stolen card) cannot exceed $50, and the cardholder bears no liability after notifying the issuer of the missing card.

The Fair Credit and Charge Card Disclosure Act of 1988 creates extensive disclosure requirements for card issuers. The act requires notification of various cost factors when card issuers solicit applications. Details vary, depending on whether the card application was solicited by mail, telephone, or "take ones" (e.g., a magazine insert). In general, issuers must disclose key cost features, including APR, annual membership fees, minimum finance charges, late payment charges, and so on.

Equal Credit Opportunity ACT (ECOA). In a society historically beset with discrimination, it is hardly surprising that credit was often denied on the basis of prejudices and stereotypes. In 1974, Congress enacted the Equal Credit Opportunity Act to combat bias in lending. Credit cannot be denied to creditworthy applicants because of sex, marital status, age, race, color, religion, national origin, good faith exercise of rights under the Consumer Credit Protection Act, or receipt of public assistance (e.g., food stamps or Aid to Dependent Children). The ECOA was in large part a response to anger over differing treatment of women and men in the financial marketplace. Creditors often would not loan money to married women under the woman's own name. Single, divorced, and widowed women were at a great disadvantage, vis-à-vis their male counterparts, in securing credit; and frequently women who married had to reapply for credit under their husband's name.

In addition to forbidding explicit discrimination in granting credit, the ECOA limits the information a creditor can require in processing an application. In general, the creditor cannot seek information about marital status, income from alimony, child support, birth control practices, child-bearing plans, or other matters that might lead to discrimination.

Fair Credit Reporting Act (FCRA). Dealing with credit problems is a routine ingredient of business life. Before selling consumer goods, selling insurance, hiring an employee, or lending money, you will commonly engage in a credit search. Rather than conduct your own credit investigation, you are likely to turn to the dominant national firms (TRW, Equifax, and Trans Union) or local credit bureaus. You will depend on the accuracy of their reports in making managerial decisions. Similarly, as a consumer you will depend on the accuracy of those reports about your personal credit record. Because the credit-rating business has become so important in our lives, Congress passed legislation imposing detailed standards on credit information providers ("consumer reporting agencies," in the language of the act) and those who use that information. Broadly, the Fair Credit Reporting Act strives to ensure that credit information is accurate, that it is used only for legitimate purposes, and that consumer privacy is not unduly compromised. The key requirements of the FCRA are as follows:

1. *Consumer rights*—If requested, consumer reporting agencies must—with certain exceptions—provide each consumer with the information in his or her file. However, the consumer does not have the right to see the file itself. Inaccurate, obsolete, and unverifiable information must be removed. If the contents of the file remain in dispute, the consumer has the right to include in the file a brief statement of her or his version of the issues in question. If a consumer should be denied employment, credit, or insurance because of an agency report, the user of the report must so inform the consumer, and the consumer must be advised as to the origin of the credit report.

If requested, consumer reporting agencies must—with certain exceptions—provide each consumer with the information in his or her file.

2. *Reporting agency responsibilities*—In brief, agencies are required to follow reasonable procedures to ensure that information is both accurate and up-to-date. Consumer credit reports can be furnished only for the following purposes without the consumer's permission or a court order: (*a*) credit, (*b*) insurance, (*c*) employment, (*d*) obtaining a government benefit, or (*e*) other legitimate business purpose involving a consumer. Inasmuch as protection of privacy is one of the stated purposes of the act, it is interesting that Congress imposed no limitation on the kinds of information that may be included in a file. Hence, sexual practices, political preferences, hair length, friendships, organizational memberships, and the like can lawfully be reported.

3. *User responsibilities*—Those who purchase a consumer credit investigation must inform the consumer in advance of the pending inquiry. When a consumer is denied credit, employment, or insurance, or where financial charges are increased because of an adverse credit report, the consumer must be apprised of the name and address of the consumer reporting agency that provided the information.

4. *Penalties*—Both consumer reporting agencies and users of credit reports may be subject to civil and criminal penalties, including damages, fines, and imprisonment, under the FCRA. The primary enforcement burden lies with the Federal Trade Commission.

Accuracy and Privacy. Perhaps the biggest concern today about credit reporting is the fear that consumers have lost control over how information about them is circulated and used. Grocery store computers track our purchases; we provide personal information when we apply for jobs, insurance, or credit; and some companies buy or search for personal information in workers' compensation hearings, police records, changes of address, and so on. All of that information is then absorbed by the big credit companies, repackaged, and stored for sale. In recent years, the FTC has aggressively pursued the major credit information providers, claiming that they are violating the FCRA accuracy requirements and failing to honor consumers' legitimate privacy expectations. For example, a 1995 Equifax settlement with the FTC required, among others, the following terms:

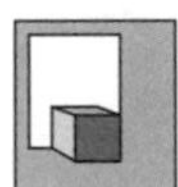

> The settlement requires Equifax to reinvestigate within three days information disputed by a consumer. If Equifax does not verify the information within this time period, it must delete the information until it is verified.
>
> When a consumer provides Equifax with documentation confirming the consumer's version of a dispute, Equifax is required to accept that version unless it has reason to doubt the authenticity of the document.

Equifax will limit the furnishing of consumer reports to those with a permissible purpose under the FCRA.[20]

Public Policy Questions

1. Provide some free market reasoning that supports the credit industry position that evermore detailed government regulation of credit providers is not in the public's best interest.
2. Credit bureaus package and repackage data about consumers and then sell it without permission to banks, retailers, telemarketers, and others who, in turn, ply consumers with phone calls and junk mail. Should credit bureaus be prohibited by law from selling credit information without the consumer's written permission? Explain.

The 1994 case that follows illustrates the courts' treatment of such credit report accuracy disputes.

CASE

HENSON V. CSC CREDIT SERVICES

29 F.3d 287 (7th Cir. 1994)

Facts

[T]he Cosco Federal Credit Union [sued] Greg Henson and his brother Jeff. In that action, the state court clerk erroneously noted in the Judgment Docket that a money judgment had been entered against Greg. Two credit reporting agencies, CSC Credit Services and Trans Union Corporation, relied on the state court Judgment Docket and indicated in Greg's credit report that he owed the money judgment. Greg and Mary Henson [then sued] CSC and Trans Union . . . for violating . . . the Fair Credit Reporting Act . . . The district court dismissed the Hensons' complaint . . .

Background

In June 1986, Greg Henson purchased a 1980 Chevrolet Camaro Z-28 . . . In March 1990, Greg's brother, Jeff, filed a loan application with Cosco so that he could purchase the Camaro from Greg. Cosco loaned Jeff enough money to purchase the car and paid off Greg's note. Soon thereafter, the Camaro was stolen and Jeff stopped making payments to Cosco.

On February 7, 1990, Cosco filed suit against Jeff and Greg . . . Cosco alleged . . . that Jeff had defaulted on his loan obligation. Cosco sought possession of the Camaro and a 1978 Ford Mustang, so that they could be sold and the proceeds applied to Jeff's outstanding loan balance. Cosco stated in the complaint that "Greg Henson, may claim some interest in the 1980 Chevy Camaro Z-28 . . . and he is made a party to this litigation to answer as to any ownership interest in or other claim that he may have to said automobile, if any."

On April 17, 1990, Cosco filed a Motion for Default Judgment and Judgment of Foreclosure against Jeff and Greg. The motion . . . contained proposed findings of fact and law. Cosco proposed the following finding, which the state court adopted: "the Court further finds that the Defendant,

Continued

Continued

Greg Henson, has no ownership of or interest in the 1980 Chevy Camaro Z-28 . . . and the Plaintiff may sell said automobile free and clear of any claim or right of Greg Henson." After Cosco took possession of the Camaro and sold it for $850, it asked the court to render a deficiency judgment against Jeff. The court rendered this judgment against Jeff on July 18, 1990. Shortly thereafter, the Clerk of the Bartholomew Circuit Court incorrectly noted the judgment in the Judgement Docket. The Judgment Docket listed Jeff and Greg together and erroneously indicated that a money judgment was entered against both of them in the amount of $4,075.54.

Greg and his wife, Mary, . . . filed . . . suit, . . . alleg[ing] that CSC and Trans Union violated the FCRA by "erroneously report[ing] in its credit reports that Greg owed a money/civil judgment in the amount of $4,076." . . . The Hensons also allege that they "contacted Trans twice, in writing, to correct the horrible injustice. However, nobody at Trans would correct the injustice." The Hensons' complaint does not allege that they ever contacted CSC . . .

As the result of the defendants' conduct, the complaint states that Greg and Mary suffered "denial of credit, high interest loans, public ridicule and humiliation, and embarrassment." . . .

[The] district court held that "Trans Union's and CSC's reporting of the recorded default judgment was not 'inaccurate' under FCRA" and granted their motions to dismiss . . . The Hensons now appeal.

* * *

Judge Kanne

Duty to Use Reasonable Procedures under the FCRA

Under the FCRA, a consumer reporting agency is required to follow "reasonable procedures to assure maximum possible accuracy" of the information contained in a consumer's credit report. . .

In order to state a claim under [FCRA section 1681e(b)] a consumer must sufficiently allege "that a credit reporting agency prepared a report containing 'inaccurate' information." However, the credit reporting agency is not automatically liable even if the consumer proves that it prepared an inaccurate credit report because the FCRA "does not make reporting agencies strictly liable for all inaccuracies" . . .

The parties initially dispute whether the information contained in Greg's credit report was inaccurate. Greg argues that the information was inaccurate because his credit report indicated that he owed a money judgment in the amount of $4,075.74. Greg has shown that he owes no such money judgment. Trans Union and CSC, on the other hand, state that they simply reported that "a judgment against [Greg] in the amount of $4,076 had been entered in the public records of the Bartholomew Superior Court". . .

Trans Union and CSC argue that the Judgment Docket conclusively establishes that a money judgment was *entered* against Greg. They were wrong.

* * *

The court documents in question conclusively establish that no money judgment was *rendered* against Greg. . . The documents do conclusively establish, however, that the clerk erroneously *noted* in the Judgment Docket that a money judgment had been entered against Greg.

Thus, even if we were to accept CSC and Trans Union's position that they only reported that a money judgment had been *entered* against Greg, we would still conclude that this information was inaccurate. The court documents show that no money judgment was ever *entered* against Greg. Making a notation on the Judgment Docket is not the official act of entering judgment under Indiana law.

Continued

Continued

Our finding that the information contained in Greg's credit report was inaccurate does not end our inquiry. CSC and Trans Union are not liable under the FCRA if they followed "reasonable procedures to assure maximum possible accuracy" of the information reported. CSC and Trans Union argue that they followed "reasonable procedures" by obtaining the information from the Judgment Docket, a presumptively reliable source. We agree and hold that, as a matter of law, a credit reporting agency is not liable under the FCRA for reporting inaccurate information obtained from a court's Judgment Docket, absent prior notice from the consumer that the information may be inaccurate.

A contrary rule of law would require credit reporting agencies to go beyond the face of numerous court records to determine whether they correctly report the outcome of the underlying action. Such a rule would also require credit reporting agencies to engage in background research which would substantially increase the cost of their services.

* * *

The district court correctly dismissed the Hensons' complaint in so far as it alleges that CSC and Trans Union violated section 1681e(b).

Duty to Reinvestigate

In their complaint, the Hensons also allege that "Greg by his wife Mary, contacted, Trans [Union] twice, in writing, to correct the horrible injustice. However, nobody at Trans would correct the injustice."

* * *

Trans Union argues that it did not violate a duty to reinvestigate because it had no duty, as a matter of law, to go beyond the Judgment Docket in conducting its reinvestigation. We disagree. A credit reporting agency that has been notified of potentially inaccurate information in a consumer's credit report is in a very different position than one who has no such notice. As we indicated earlier, a credit reporting agency may initially rely on public court documents, because to require otherwise would be burdensome and inefficient. However, such exclusive reliance may not be justified once the credit reporting agency receives notice that the consumer disputes information contained in his credit report. . .

Accordingly, a credit reporting agency may be required, in certain circumstances, to verify the accuracy of its initial source of information, in this case the Judgment Docket.

* * *

Whether the credit reporting agency has a duty to go beyond the original source will depend, in part, on whether the consumer has alerted the reporting agency to the possibility that the source may be unreliable or the reporting agency itself knows or should know that the source is unreliable. The credit reporting agency's duty will also depend on the cost of verifying the accuracy of the source versus the possible harm inaccurately reported information may cause the consumer.

On remand, the Hensons will have the burden of showing that they brought the alleged error in Greg's credit report to Trans Union's attention.

* * *

Affirmed in part. Reversed in part. Remanded.

Continued

Continued

Questions

1. Why did the Court find that CSC and Trans Union did not violate the FCRA even though they included inaccurate information in Greg Henson's credit reports?
2. Are credit reporting agencies strictly liable for their errors under this Court's reasoning? That is, do they have an absolute duty to avoid errors or pay the consequences if they do err?
3. Grant's application for a Texaco credit card was denied because TRW, a credit reporting company, indicated that a $400 judgment had been entered against Grant in a landlord tenant dispute; but TRW failed to note that Grant had, in turn, recovered $608 from the landlord in the dispute, leaving Grant with a net of $131.90. Grant complained to TRW and received an "Updated Credit Profile" showing a deletion of the $400 judgment. Grant again applied for the credit card and was again denied because the $400 judgment appeared on his credit record. Grant sued, claiming a violation of the FCRA. Decide. Explain. [See *Grant* v. *TRW, Inc.,* 789 F. Supp. 690 (D.Md. 1992).]

Fair Credit Billing Act (FCBA). The FCBA, passed in 1974, provides a mechanism to deal with the billing errors that accompany credit card and certain other credit transactions. A cardholder who receives an erroneous bill must complain in writing to the creditor within 60 days of the receipt of the bill. If so, the creditor must acknowledge receipt of the complaint within 30 days. Then, within two billing cycles but not more than 90 days, the creditor must issue a response either acknowledging or denying the error. If the former, appropriate adjustments must be made. If the latter, the creditor must explain why the bill is correct. After filing its response, the creditor must wait 10 days before reporting the account as delinquent. If the consumer continues to dispute the accuracy of the bill, the creditor must file notice of the continuing dispute with any third party to whom notice of the delinquency is directed. Penalties for a creditor in violation of the act are quite modest. The creditor forfeits the right to collect the amount in question and any accompanying finance charges, but the forfeiture cannot exceed $50 for each charge in dispute.

Truth in Savings Act. Under this federal law, which became effective in 1993 (1994 for credit unions), banks and savings institutions must (among other things) (1) fully disclose the fees and terms of their checking and savings accounts, (2) express interest on deposits in the form of an **annual percentage yield (APY)** that includes compounding, and (3) pay interest on deposits in full on a daily basis. However, as the *Des Moines Register* reported, these protections come at a price:

annual percentage yield (APY). The rate of interest paid on a deposit as expressed in a standardized, yearly manner allowing for comparison of returns among institutions.

> Truth is not cheap.
>
> Nor, when it comes to banking, is it easy.
>
> It takes 166 pages to explain the federal government's new Truth in Savings Act.
>
> Iowa bankers estimate that compliance with the act could cost them more than $20 million a year in mailing charges alone. And there's the cost of new computer hardware and software that many banks will need to buy to comply with the proposed rules.[21]

D. Electronic Fund Transfers

Your future as a manager is almost certain to be marked by our societal transition from checks, bills, and coins to "electronic money." Of course, we are rapidly moving in that direction now with ATMs, point-of-sale machines, electronic deposits, and so forth. The growth of electronic fund transfers caused Congress in 1978 to pass the Electronic Fund Transfer Act. Congress was concerned that established legal principles were not adequate to resolve the many new legal problems arising from electronic transfers. The act defines electronic fund transfers (and hence the act's coverage) as "any transfer of funds other than a transaction originated by check, draft, or similar paper instrument, which is initiated through an electronic terminal, telephonic instrument, computer, or magnetic tape so to order, instruct, or authorize a financial institution to debit or credit an account."

Electronic fund transfer (EFT) systems include:

- Point-of-sale transfers, where a computer is used to immediately transfer funds from a consumer's bank account to that of the merchant from whom the consumer is making a purchase.
- Automatic teller machines.
- Direct bank deposit and withdrawal systems for automatic deposit of checks or automatic payment of a regularly recurring bill.
- Transfers initiated by phone, where consumers call their bank to order payments or transfer funds between accounts.

The act provides remedies for an extended series of problems that may confront the EFT consumer. For example:

- A resolution system is provided when the consumer believes an error has been made in an EFT billing.
- In general, if a consumer's EFT card is lost or stolen, the consumer's liability for unauthorized use is limited to $50, but liability may exceed $50 if the financial institution is not notified of the loss within two days.
- With certain exceptions, the bank is liable for all actual damages sustained by the consumer in situations when the bank failed to transfer funds in a timely manner, following a proper order by the consumer.
- Civil and criminal penalties ranging from $100 (as well as court costs and attorneys' fees) to $5,000 fines and up to one year in prison may be imposed.

E. Debtor Protection

Earlier in this chapter, we asked you to place yourself in the role of a furniture store owner whose sales contracts were challenged on unconscionability grounds. The goal of those contracts was to better protect you in case a customer failed to pay in full, a not unlikely prospect. Dealing with consumer debt is a routine and crucial ingredient of successful business practice. In operating that furniture store you may simply use your personal skills to persuade customers to pay when they have fallen in arrears. More likely, you will employ some kind of debt collection agency. To a merchant, a nonpaying debtor may be a "lazy bum" who fails to meet his or her contractual obligations, but from the government's point of view the debtor is often the victim of excessively zealous collection measures. In 1995, a jury in El Paso, Texas, awarded $11 million to Marianne Driscol, a victim of a heavy-handed collection agency:

Collection agents made numerous profanity-laced phone calls to Driscol's home and office.

Collection agents made numerous profanity-laced phone calls to Driscol's home and office . . making at least one death threat and phoning in a bomb threat to her workplace, according to the lawsuit.[22]

Driscol owed $2,000 on a credit card. The credit card company that hired the bill collection agency has indicated that it will appeal.

Such overzealous practices in company with the humane recognition that many good consumers inevitably suffer economic reverses, particularly in times of recession, caused the government to create protective legislation.

Debt Collection. The Fair Debt Collection Practices Act (FDCPA) of 1977 (amended in 1986) is designed to shield debtors from unfair debt collection tactics by debt collection agencies and attorneys who routinely operate as debt collectors. The act does not extend to creditors who are themselves trying to recover money owed to them. Several thousand debt collection agencies nationwide pursue those who are delinquent in their debts. The agencies are normally paid on a commission basis and are often exceedingly aggressive and imaginative in their efforts.

The FDCPA forbids, among others, the following practices:

- Use of obscene language.
- Contact with third parties other than for the purpose of locating the debtor. (This provision is an attempt to prevent harm to the debtor's reputation.)
- Use of or threats to use physical force.
- Contact with the debtor during "inconvenient" hours. For debtors who are employed during "normal" working hours, the period from 9 P.M. to 8 A.M. would probably be considered inconvenient.
- Repeated phone calls with the intent to harass.
- Contacting the debtor in an unfair, abusive, or deceptive manner.

The Federal Trade Commission is responsible for administering the FDCPA. A wronged debtor may also file a civil action to recover all actual damages (for example, payment for job loss occasioned by wrongful debt collection practices as well as damages for associated embarrassment and suffering). A civil penalty up to $1,000 as well as attorneys' fees and court costs may also be collected.

The case that follows suggests some of the problems in debt collection practices.

CASE

Cortright v. Thompson

812 F. Supp. 772 (N.D. Ill. 1992)

Facts

Plaintiffs, Robert F. Cortright and Janie Cortright, filed a complaint against defendant, James C. Thompson, alleging that defendant violated the Fair Debt Collection Practices Act . . . The complaint alleges that a letter sent by defendant violated the Act by stating differing views of the validity of the debt; namely stating that the debt was due immediately and should be paid within 10 days but later stating that after 30 days the debt would be considered valid. This claim also alleges that the letter misrepresented the "imminence of legal action" and the "existence of 'mandatory court' attendance." . . . Plaintiffs have filed a . . . motion for partial summary judgment as to liability.

Continued

Continued

On April 2, 1991, defendant, a licensed attorney in Illinois, sent plaintiffs a letter notifying them that their account at Rockford Clinic in the amount of $1152.27 was "long past due." . . . The letter was written on defendant's firm's letterhead and stated the following:

CREDITOR—ROCKFORD CLINIC
AMOUNT DUE 1,152.27
REF—192236
300587
CORTRIGHT, JANIE/CHRISTIN
CORTRIGHT ROBERT
5608 BELLVILLE DR
ROCKFORD IL 61108

IT HAS COME TO MY ATTENTION THAT YOUR ACCOUNT WITH THE CREDITOR NAMED ABOVE IS LONG PAST DUE. THEREFORE, IT IS ESSENTIAL THAT THE BALANCE DUE IS PAID IMMEDIATELY, OR IN THE ALTERNATIVE, THAT SATISFACTORY PAYMENT ARRANGEMENTS BE MADE THROUGH MY CLIENT, ROCKFORD MERCANTILE AGENCY. . . . IN THE EVENT THE BALANCE IS NOT PAID IN FULL OR SATISFACTORY PAYMENT ARRANGEMENTS MADE WITHIN TEN DAYS, IT MAY BE NECESSARY TO FILE AT ANY TIME THEREAFTER A LAWSUIT TO RECOVER THE AMOUNT DUE IF SO REQUESTED BY MY CLIENT. I AM CERTAIN THAT YOU REALIZE THAT SUCH ACTION COULD OBLIGATE YOU TO PAY ADDITIONAL SUMS FOR COURT COSTS AND ALSO LEAD TO YOU MISSING TIME FROM WORK TO ATTEND MANDATORY COURT APPEARANCES . . .

Very truly yours,

KOSTANTACOS, TRAUM, REUTERFORS & McWILLIAMS, P.C.

James C. Thompson §

Unless you notify my client at (815) 965-0581 within 30 days of the receipt of this letter that you dispute any portion of this debt, we will assume the debt is valid.

* * *

Judge Reinhard

A two-step process is used to determine if a debt collector violated the Act: first, the court must interpret the statute, and second, the court must determine if defendant violated the Act as interpreted by the court. As defendant concedes, the clear weight of authority for determining if a debt collector violated the Act requires that the court apply the least sophisticated consumer analysis.

The statutory section at issue here is 15 U.S.C. § 1692g(a). This section is commonly referred to as the debt validation notice section. This section of the Act requires a debt collector to send a consumer, either in its initial communication or within five days of its initial communication, a written notice containing: (1) the debt amount; (2) the name of the current creditor; (3) a statement that if the consumer disputes the debt in writing within 30 days, the collector will send verification of the debt to the consumer; (4) a statement that if the consumer does not dispute the debt within 30 days, the collector will assume the debt to be valid; and (5) a statement that the collector will send the name of the original creditor, upon written request within 30 days.

In *Swanson* v. *Southern Oregon Credit Services, Inc.,* the court held that although the communication, a letter, contained the validation notice required by § 1692g, the notice, in small, ordinary typeface at the bottom of the page, was not effective because it was overshadowed and contradicted by the debt collector's boldfaced, underlined statement which said, "IF THIS ACCOUNT IS PAID WITHIN THE NEXT 10 DAYS IT WILL NOT BE RECORDED IN OUR MASTER FILE AS AN UNPAID COLLECTION ITEM. A GOOD CREDIT RATING—IS YOUR MOST VALUABLE ASSET." While this statement visually overshadowed the § 1692g notice, the court

Continued

Continued

also stated, "*More importantly,* the substance of the language stands in threatening contradiction to the text of the debt validation notice." The contradiction is that the notice allows for 30 days, yet harm is threatened if the consumer did not act within 10 days.

Since *Swanson,* several courts have applied this overshadowing and threatening factor to the least sophisticated consumer analysis.

* * *

Viewing defendant's letter in light of the least sophisticated consumer, the letter violates § 1692g(a) because the body of the letter contradicts and overshadows the validation notice. The letter demands that the balance due be paid immediately and that possible legal action would result if the balance due was not paid within 10 days despite the 30 day validation requirement. Although the letter is not as threatening visually as some described in cases finding violations of § 1692g(a), defendant's letter appears on law firm stationery and states that it may be necessary to file a lawsuit at any time after 10 days, and that a lawsuit could obligate plaintiffs to pay for court costs and miss time from work. The least sophisticated consumer reading defendant's letter would not effectively receive the validation notice in standard size print based on the information which contradicts the notice contained in the body of the letter which was in capital letters.

Therefore, plaintiffs' motion for partial summary judgment as to liability is granted.

Questions

1. In what way did Thompson, the defendant/debt collector/lawyer, violate the Fair Debt Collection Practices Act?
2. In your judgment, are we wise to tie debt collection rules to the capabilities of the "least sophisticated consumer"? Explain.
3. Miller owed $2,501.61 to the Star Bank of Cincinnati. Payco attempted to collect the debt by sending a one-page collection form to Miller. The front side of the form included, among other words, in very large capital letters a demand for IMMEDIATE FULL PAYMENT, the words PHONE US TODAY, and the word NOW in white letters nearly two inches tall against a red background. At the bottom of the page in the smallest print on the form was the message: NOTICE: SEE REVERSE SIDE FOR IMPORTANT INFORMATION. The reverse side contained the validation notice required under the FDCPA. Does the form conform to FDCPA requirements? Explain. [See *Miller* v. *Payco-General American Credits, Inc.,* 943 F. 2d 482 (4th Cir. 1991).]

Ethics/Public Policy Question

Why shouldn't debt collectors be able to use aggressive tactics to encourage payment of legitimate bills?

IV. Bankruptcy

In building or managing a business and in life as a consumer, these unpredictable and demanding economic times force us to consider the possibility that we may fail. Perhaps you will open your own business only to see it collapse around you because of hard times or your own errors. Perhaps you will have begun what looks to be a secure and promising management career when your employer goes under and your job vanishes. Perhaps when you lose that job, you are faced with the threat and humiliation of personal bankruptcy.

Perhaps you will have begun what looks to be a secure and promising management career when your employer goes under and your job vanishes.

Even in the hypothetical form presented in this book, these are chilling thoughts because we know them to be increasingly real possibilities.

Our culture encourages indebtedness. In 1995, for the first time we collectively owed over $1 *trillion* in consumer debts, an average of $4,000 per American.[23] The result is that bankruptcies have skyrocketed. In the 12 months ending June 30, 1995, more than 800,000 people sought bankruptcy as compared with 80,000 in 1958.[24] Corporate filings, although up from 10 years ago, have declined a bit since their high in 1987.[25] Some debtors become encumbered beyond reasonable hope of recovery. So to help those debtors make a fresh start and their creditors to recover as much as possible, federal bankruptcy laws provide for the possibility of "forgiveness."

A. THE LAW

Bankruptcy in the United States is governed exclusively by federal law; the states do not have the constitutional authority to enact bankruptcy legislation. Our attention will be limited to the principal federal statute, the Bankruptcy Reform Act of 1978, as amended by the Bankruptcy Reform Act of 1994.

Bankruptcy is an adjudication relieving a debtor of all or part of his or her liabilities. Any person, partnership, or corporation may seek debtor relief. Three forms of bankruptcy action are important to us:

1. **Liquidation** (**Chapter 7** of the Bankruptcy Act), in which all assets except exemptions are distributed to creditors.
2. **Reorganization (Chapter 11),** in which creditors are kept from the debtor's assets while the debtor, under the supervision of the court, works out a plan to continue in business while paying creditors.
3. **Adjustment of debts** of an individual with regular income **(Chapter 13),** in which individuals with limited debts are protected from creditors while paying their debts in installments.

liquidation (Chapter 7). "Straight" bankruptcy action in which all assets except exemptions are distributed to creditors.

reorganization (Chapter 11). A bankruptcy action in which creditors are kept from the debtor's assets while the debtor, under court supervision, works out a repayment plan and continues operations.

adjustment of debts (Chapter 13). Individuals with limited debts are protected from creditors while paying their debts in installments.

Liquidation.

A Chapter 7 liquidation petition can be *voluntarily* filed in federal court by the debtor (individual, partnership, or corporation), or creditors can seek an *involuntary* bankruptcy judgment. A Chapter 7 liquidation is commonly called a "straight" bankruptcy.

In a voluntary action, the debtor files a petition with the appropriate federal court. The court then has jurisdiction to proceed with the liquidation, and the petition becomes the *order for relief.* The debtor need not be insolvent to seek bankruptcy.

An involuntary bankruptcy can be compelled only if the creditors have an individual or aggregate claim of at least $10,000. The debtor may challenge the bankruptcy action. The court will enter an order for relief if it finds the debtor has not been paying his or her debts when due or if most of the debtor's property is under the control of a custodian for the purpose of enforcing a lien against that property.

After the order for relief is granted, voluntary and involuntary actions proceed in a similar manner. Creditors are restrained from reaching the debtor's assets. An interim bankruptcy trustee is appointed by the court. The creditors then hold a meeting, and a permanent trustee is elected. The trustee collects the debtor's property and converts it to money, protects the interests of the debtor and creditors, may manage the debtor's business, and ultimately distributes the estate proceeds to the creditors. Both federal and state laws permit the debtor to keep **exempt property,** which typically includes a car, a homestead, some household or personal items, life insurance, and other "necessities." Normally, a dollar maximum is attached to each. For example, the federal exemptions include a vehicle, not to exceed $2,400 in value, and household goods/personal belongings not to exceed $8,000.

exempt property. Specified classes of property that are unavailable to the creditor upon default of the debtor.

The debtor's nonexempt property is then divided among the creditors according to the priorities prescribed by statute. Secured creditors are paid first. If funds remain, "priority" claims, such as employees' wages and alimony/child support, are paid. Then, funds permitting, general creditors are paid. Each class must be paid in full before a class of lower priority will be compensated. Any remaining funds will return to the debtor.

When distribution is complete, the bankruptcy judge may issue an order discharging (relieving) the debtor of any remaining debts except for certain statutorily specified claims. Those include, for example, taxes and educational loans. The debtor might fail to receive a *discharge* if he or she had received one in the previous six years, if property was concealed from the court, or if good faith in the bankruptcy process was lacking in other respects.

As noted, educational loans normally are not discharged in bankruptcy. In the Chapter 7 bankruptcy case that follows, a married couple seek to be relieved of their student loan responsibilities on the grounds of undue hardship.

CASE

Cheesman and Cheesman v. Tennessee Student Assistance Corporation

25 F.3rd 356 (6th Cir. 1994), cert. denied, 115 S.Ct. 731 (1995)

Facts

In 1983, Margaret Cheesman secured two student loans totaling approximately $5,000. The loans were guaranteed by the Tennessee Student Assistance Corporation (TSAC). In 1984, she earned a bachelor of arts degree from Middle Tennessee State University (MTSU). The loans came due in June 1985. She made only two payments of $50 each. Between 1989 and 1991, she worked intermittently as a teacher's aide and earned an average gross monthly salary of $651. She took maternity leave in 1991, and her former job was no longer available when she reapplied. She then continued to seek work.

In February 1985, Dallas Cheesman received a $3,500 loan to attend MTSU. The loan was guaranteed by TSAC. He withdrew from MTSU to take a second job. He made two $50 payments on his loan. From 1986 through 1990, he worked first as director of an alternative school ($1,538 gross per month) and then as a family worker ($1,632 gross per month). Margaret and Dallas Cheesman filed a Chapter 7 bankruptcy petition in August 1991, at which time Dallas was working at a mental health center for a gross salary of $1,123 per month. He hoped for an early promotion. In 1991, the Cheesmans' gross income was $15,676, leaving them with a net income of $13,720. Their debts totaled approximately $30,000, of which $14,267 was attributable to the student loans. Their monthly living expenses totaled $1,594. They owned a 1988 Chevy Nova valued at $3,000. They owed over $7,000 on the car and made monthly payments of $350.

The Cheesmans petitioned to have their student loans discharged on the grounds of undue hardship as provided for under the United States Bankruptcy Code Section 523(a)(8)(B). The trial court ruled that the loans imposed an undue hardship, but due to the Cheesmans' employment potential, the case was to be reviewed 18 months later. TSAC appealed to the district court, which affirmed the undue hardship ruling. TSAC appealed to the United States Court of Appeals for the 6th Circuit.

* * *

Continued

Continued

Judge Timbers

Undue Hardship

TSAC contends that Dallas and Margaret Cheesman's student loans were not dischargeable pursuant to § 523(a)(8)(B). They assert that the loans did not impose an undue hardship . . .

Section 523(a)(8)(B) provides that an educational loan is not to be discharged unless "excepting such debt from discharge . . . will impose an undue hardship on the debtor and the debtor's dependents." Congress designed this provision "to remedy an abuse by students who, immediately upon graduation, filed petition for bankruptcy and obtained a discharge of their educational loans."

Courts have used a number of tests in determining what constitutes an undue hardship. One test requires the debtor to demonstrate "(1) that the debtor cannot maintain, based on current income and expenses, a 'minimal' standard of living for herself and her dependents if forced to repay the loans; (2) that additional circumstances exist indicating that this state of affairs is likely to persist for a significant portion of the repayment period . . .; and (3) that the debtor has made good faith efforts to repay the loans."

Other tests have focused on " 'whether there would be anything left from the debtor's estimated future income to enable the debtor to make some payment on his/her student loan without reducing what the debtor and his/her dependents need to maintain a minimal standard of living.' "

In its decision, the bankruptcy court did not state which test it used to determine that the Cheesmans' loans imposed an undue hardship. We believe, however, that the loans were dischargeable under any undue hardship test the court may have used in reaching its decision.

First, there was no indication that the Cheesmans were capable of paying the loans while maintaining a minimal standard of living. The Cheesmans' 1992 gross income of $15,676 exceeded by only a slim margin the government's 1992 poverty income guideline of $13,950 for a family of four. The expense chart presented by the Cheesmans demonstrated that they maintained a frugal lifestyle consistent with their low income. Despite this fact, the Cheesmans had a monthly deficit of approximately $400. Under these circumstances, we are satisfied that the Cheesmans could not maintain a minimal standard of living for their family if they were required to repay their loans.

Furthermore, there is no indication that the Cheesmans' financial situation will improve in the foreseeable future. True, Dallas testified that he was hoping for a promotion at his current job, and Margaret testified that she was actively seeking employment. There is no assurance, however, that either will obtain their objectives. Moreover, Margaret's employment history does not indicate that the Cheesmans' financial condition would improve considerably if she obtained a position as a teacher's aide.

* * *

There is no evidence that the Cheesmans did not act in good faith. This is not a case where the petitioner seeks discharge within a month of loans becoming due. The Cheesmans made minimal payments on their loans several years after their loans became due and at least a year before filing for bankruptcy. Furthermore, the Cheesmans chose to work in worthwhile, albeit low-paying, professions. There is no indication that they were attempting to abuse the student loan system by having their loans forgiven before embarking on lucrative careers in the private sector. In light of these considerations, we hold that the Cheesmans' student loans imposed an undue hardship.

[Affirmed.]

Continued

Continued

Judge Guy dissenting

I . . . disagree with the court's finding that requiring the Cheesmans to repay their loans would impose an undue hardship.

* * *

The Cheesmans are not disabled. They are not ill. They are not elderly. They are both college trained. At the time of the bankruptcy hearing, Mr. Cheesman held a job, and he testified that there was the possibility of a promotion with his current employer. Mrs. Cheesman is qualified to tutor or substitute teach, as she did prior to the filing of the Chapter 7 petition.

* * *

The record does not support a finding that the Cheesmans have demonstrated their current adverse financial condition will persist for a significant time.

Moreover, I do not believe the Cheesmans proved they acted in good faith. As discussed in the court's holding, one element considered in evaluating a debtor's good faith is the effort the debtor has made to repay his or her loans. Here, during the six-year period after the loans first became due and payable, the Cheesmans made only two $50 payments on each of their loans. There also is no evidence that the Cheesmans sought the less drastic remedy of a deferment of payments on their debts before attempting to discharge them.

"Undue hardship" is not defined in the Bankruptcy Code. The term "undue hardship," however, indicates that the type of hardship involved in a particular circumstance must be significant. I do not believe the Cheesmans have carried their burden in demonstrating that circumstances will prevent their financial condition from improving in the future or that they have acted in good faith; thus, I would find the undue hardship requirements have not been met . . .

Questions

1. List the three factors that caused the majority to support the discharge.
2. Would you vote with the majority or the dissent? Explain.
3. Mary Lou Baker received educational loans of $6,635. After graduation, her take-home pay was less than $650 and monthly expenses for her and her three children were approximately $925. She had no other income or support. She had medical bills that she was unable to pay. One of her children needed special shoes; another had a reading difficulty. Should she receive a discharge in bankruptcy for her student loans based on the hardship rule? Explain. [See *In re Baker,* 10 B.R. 870 (E.D. Tenn. 1981).]

Ethics/Public Policy Question

Is it in the best interests of the debtor and of society to provide bankrupt Americans with an opportunity for a fresh start?

Reorganization. Chapter 11 is available to individuals and most businesses. The basic thrust of this type of bankruptcy is to allow financially troubled enterprises to continue in operation while debtor adjustments are arranged. Thus, both debtor and creditor may ultimately benefit more than from a straight liquidation. The debtor may voluntarily seek reorganization, or the creditors may petition for an involuntary action. When a reorganization petition is filed with the court and relief is ordered, one or more committees of creditors are appointed to participate in bankruptcy procedures. Typically, the debtor continues to operate the business, although the court may appoint a trustee to replace the debtor if required because of dishonesty, fraud, or extreme mismanagement. The company, its bankers, and suppliers will meet to work out a method for continuing operations. A plan must be developed that will satisfy the creditors that their interests are being served by the reorganization. Perhaps new capital is secured, or perhaps creditors receive some shares in the company. The plan must be approved by the creditors and confirmed by the court. The company is then required to carry out the plan.

The most highly publicized and ironic Chapter 11 in history was filed in May 1995, when the Mitsubishi Estate Co., 80 percent owner of New York's Rockefeller Center, sought protection for its famous property. The Rockefeller family, which had sold that 80 percent share to Mitsubishi, retained a 20 percent stake and failed in its efforts to stop the bankruptcy and prevent a stain on the family name and on the New York City landmark.

Adjustment of Debts. Under Chapter 13, individuals (not partnerships or corporations) can seek the protection of the court to arrange a debt adjustment plan (see Figure 12.1). Chapter 13 permits only voluntary bankruptcies and is restricted to those with steady incomes and somewhat limited debts ($250,000 unsecured, $750,000 secured). The process can begin only with a voluntary petition from the debtor. Creditors are restrained from reaching the debtor's assets. The debtor develops a repayment plan. If creditors' interests are sufficiently satisfied by the plan, the court may confirm it and appoint a trustee to oversee the plan. The debtor may then have three to five years to make the necessary payments.

Bankruptcy Reform Act of 1994. Congress has become concerned that many debtors see bankruptcy as an easy way out of debt problems. Further, the process is often slow, expensive, and ultimately not economically efficient. The Reform Act of 1994 was designed to speed up the entire process and to encourage debtors to follow the Chapter 13 repayment procedure rather than Chapter 7's liquidation approach. Various technical changes were effected toward those ends, basically making it easier to keep one's home if electing Chapter 13 rather than 7 and harder to avoid alimony/child support if electing Chapter 7. The new act also strengthens creditors' rights after some years of what many perceived to be unduly forgiving arrangements for debtors. Under Chapter 11, small businesses are provided with a fast-track procedure that is expected to significantly reduce bankruptcy time and expense and thus save many businesses that might otherwise fail. The act also includes measures designed to combat the filing of bankruptcy as a fraud on creditors.

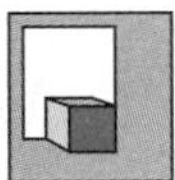

V. Consumer Protection Abroad

Profile Perspective: Consider once more the case of Karen Melvin and her soggy van. Certainly we sympathize with her and with the thousands each year who have similar struggles, but let's think for a moment about how Karen Melvin would have fared had she been living in Hong Kong, Thailand, the Philippines, China, or other foreign countries.

In America, as we have discovered in this chapter, we have a broad and deep assortment of remedies for wronged consumers. As examined in the following article, that kind of protection is substantially undeveloped in many nations of the world.

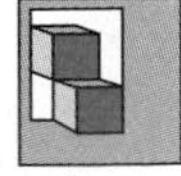

FIGURE 12.1 THE BANKRUPTCY OPTION

Though it is considered the measure of last resort, overwhelmed debtors can turn to bankruptcy as a way out of their debt binds. Below is a primer on personal bankruptcy:

Advantages

- Prevents financial ruin.
- Prevents foreclosure on your house.
- Prevents IRS seizure of property for back taxes.
- Provides fresh start.

Disadvantages

- Harms credit rating.
- Possible loss of assets.
- Certain debts cannot be discharged.
- Social stigma.
- Loss of privacy.

Long-Term Effects

- Credit reporting agencies such as TRW list bankruptcies on personal credit records for up to 10 years.
- Those who have filed bankruptcy may be turned down or have to pay higher interest rates for credit cards and loans.
- Landlords often refuse to rent to those with credit problems.
- Some employers consider an applicant's credit history as criteria for hiring.

Personal Bankruptcy Options

Chapter 13

- Allows debtors to consolidate debts and pay creditors back in full or in part over three to five years.
- Interest on unsecured debt such as credit card borrowing is waived—payment goes entirely to principal.
- Lump-sum payments are made to a court-appointed trustee who supervises the payment plan.
- Protects homeowners from foreclosure by allowing them to make up missed mortgage payments over time.
- $160 filing fee.
- No time limit on repeat filings.
- Typical attorney fee: $800–$1,600.

Chapter 7

- Also called straight bankruptcy.
- Wipes out unsecured debt.
- Debtor has option to return items bought with secured loans, such as a car, and owe nothing, or keep belongings and continue making payments.
- May keep homes and automobiles with a limited amount of equity.
- $175 filing fee.
- Can be filed once every six years.
- Typical attorney fee: $500–$1,000.

The Process

- Debtor files petition in federal court claiming insolvency.
- Within 15 days, debtor must file papers listing all debts, assets, income, living expenses and personal information.
- Case is reviewed by a court-appointed trustee. A notice is sent to each of the filer's creditors.
- Within six weeks of initial filing, an administrative hearing is held by the trustee, the debtor and the debtor's attorney. Creditors may also attend.
- Case is finalized within 90 days of hearing.

Source: *Los Angeles Times,* December 11, 1995, p. D4.

FLEDGLING CONSUMER GROUPS MOBILIZE TO UPGRADE SAFETY STANDARDS

by Sherry Buchanan

Asia's consumer boom may become a bust in terms of safety. Throughout the region, an increasing number of accidents caused by substandard goods are being reported. Among the dangerous products on the market in Asia are faulty electrical plugs and steam irons . . . in Hong Kong, . . . hazardous pesticides in Thailand, and exploding beer bottles in China . . .

All too often, lower consumer awareness and lower legal safety standards than those in the United States or Europe mean that some manufacturers have little incentive to test their products for safety. Others, consumer groups say, dump products deemed unsafe in the West into the less regulated Asian markets.

"If we don't have legislation, Hong Kong will continue to be the dumping ground of other substandard products," says Connie Lau, chief researcher for the government-funded Consumer Council in Hong Kong. "Right now products don't have safety standards in Hong Kong." A new consumer protection law went into force this year, she says, adding "It is better than none but it all depends on how effective the future enforcement of the law will be . . ."

Hong Kong is an interesting case because, even though it is one of the wealthiest of the Asian economies, with an annual per capita income of $15,660, it only passed a consumer safety protection law covering most consumer goods in 1994. (Hong Kong did pass rules regulating toys and other children's products in 1993.)

. . . If business interests have managed to block consumer initiatives in Hong Kong, where the Consumer Council is considered relatively vocal and has some funding from the government, what of places like the Philippines?

"It's pretty hard for Third World countries like us," says Julie Amargo, president of the Philippine Consumers Movement Inc. in Manila. She believes that freer trade under the GATT agreement signed last year . . . will only make the dumping of unsafe goods worse. . . .

Under the GATT accord, the preshipment inspection programs for goods imported into the Philippines, Indonesia, and Pakistan will be internationally recognized. But consumer groups argue that these rules do not protect consumer interests.

* * *

The Consumer Council in Hong Kong estimates that of the 9,492 fires in 1993, 1,240 were electrically related. New safety rules for electrical appliances are being introduced, which will require product testing before products can go on the shelves.

Consumer attitudes, too, have contributed to relatively lax safety and protection rules.

A recent survey by the Consumer Protection Board of Thailand showed that 71 percent of 1,200 Bangkok residents polled thought they were not protected by consumer rights and 95 percent of those surveyed said they felt complaining to legal authorities was useless.

"People in Hong Kong still operate on the principle of Buyer Beware, they don't make an issue of it," says Peter Caldwell, managing director of the Arbitration Center in Hong Kong, who has found little support among business for his proposal to create community mediation services, which would deal with minor consumer complaints. The proposal is based on the British idea that trade associations find it in their interest to participate to get rid of unscrupulous competitors.

In addition to relatively low consumer awareness and little hope of legal redress, quality control in low-wage countries such as China can't always keep pace with growth as enterprises rush to make quick profits from the boom in consumer goods.

The problem of substandard goods in China has become so great that Beijing . . . launched a campaign against substandard goods by enlisting consumers to register complaints . . .

But as with most edicts from Beijing, the problem is convincing the provincial governments, where, as a result of China's new market economy, many governments are in business themselves producing inferior [or] counterfeit goods . . .

Continued

Continued

The China Consumer Association statistics reports that consumer associations and groups in 29 provinces handled a total of 106,791 complaints in the third quarter of 1994, up 41 percent from a year earlier. Complaints ranged from being ripped off by unscrupulous traders injecting water into chickens to increase their weight to 300 complaints about exploding beer bottles, which injured 22 people and blinded nine.

When complaints are resolved in favor of the consumer, awards are often too low to act as a deterrent. . . . In Hong Kong, . . . a recent award for a complaint about unsafe baby pacifiers amounted only to 2,000 Hong Kong dollars ($259) according to the Consumer Council, although under Hong Kong's new rules . . . the maximum fine for a first offense will be 100,000 Hong Kong dollars and 500,000 Hong Kong dollars for a second one.

The average compensation award in China is about $50, the equivalent of one month's wage. That is enough, perhaps, to deter a hawker from injecting chickens with water but hardly enough to work as an incentive for larger enterprises to tighten quality and safety controls.

Source: *International Herald Tribune,* February 20, 1995. Reprinted by permission of The New York Times Syndication Sales Corporation.

Summary

Legal Review. The forepart of this chapter was devoted to the common law, that is, the judge-made law of consumer protection, with particular attention to judicial decisions forbidding fraudulent and unconscionable consumer transactions. Thereafter, we turned our attention to state and federal oversight of consumer affairs as exemplified by lemon laws, as well as the Federal Trade Commission's regulatory initiative to stop unfair and deceptive commercial practices (e.g., abusive telemarketing) and the Consumer Product Safety Commission's strategies for protecting us from dangerous products.

A large portion of this chapter addressed debtor/creditor law, surveying secured transactions and the various federal statutory protections for borrowers, including such government mandates as truth in lending, nondiscrimination in lending, and barriers to overzealous debt collection practices. The chapter included a brief look at consumer protection in Asia.

Ethics/Public Policy Review. Naturally enough, this chapter is suffused with ethical and public policy puzzles. The entire idea of consumer protection law is, after all, an ethical and public policy choice on our part. That is, as a society we decided that close legal oversight was needed to prevent wrongs in parts of our lives that had previously been largely untouched by law and that, as we have seen, remain largely untouched in many other nations. We have decided that contracts can be unconscionable, that cars can be lemons, that telemarketing and debt collection can be too intrusive, that failure to pay one's bills can be forgiven, and so on. These are ethical and public policy choices that we have made with the result that consumers are shielded to some extent but businesses have sacrificed some freedom of operation.

Economics Review. Just as this chapter is suffused with ethics/public policy considerations, so it is, at bottom, an expression of our continuing struggle to find the optimal balance between the free market and government intervention. Obviously, the very existence of consumer protection law represents our judgment that the market (in combination with ethics) does not sufficiently shelter us from wrongdoing. At the same time, we have seen a worldwide explosion of faith in free market principles. We have been significantly deregulating the American economy. Not surprisingly then, those in the forefront of the recent Republican revolution in Washington see some elements of consumer protection as ill-advised. They believe that the market would accomplish much the same results at much reduced cost and without the loss of personal freedom. After reading this chapter, what do you think?

Chapter Questions—Law

1. A door-to-door salesman representing Your Shop at Home Services, Inc., called on Clifton and Cora Jones, who were welfare recipients. The Jones couple decided to buy a freezer from the salesman for $900. Credit charges, insurance, and so on were added to that $900 base so that the total purchase price was $1,439.69. Mr. and Mrs. Jones signed a sales agreement that accurately stipulated the price and its ingredients. The Joneses sued to reform the contract on unconscionability grounds. They had paid $619.88 toward the total purchase price. At trial, the retail value of the new freezer at the time of purchase was set at approximately $300.
   a. What is the issue in this case?
   b. Decide. Explain.
   [See *Jones* v. *Star Credit Corp.*, 298 N.Y.S. 2d 264 (1969).]
2. The plaintiff, a wholesaler, reached an agreement with Philco, a manufacturer, to distribute Philco appliances to retailers. The plaintiff agreed to carry an adequate inventory of Philco parts. The agreement provided that either party could terminate the contract with 90 days' written notice. In the event of termination, the wholesaler agreed on demand to resell and deliver its remaining Philco stock to Philco. The resale price was to be agreed. The agreement was terminated, but Philco declined to exercise its option to repurchase. The wholesaler was unable to sell most of the remaining Philco inventory and demanded that Philco repurchase, but Philco declined. The plaintiff brought suit, claiming the contract was unconscionable. Decide. Explain. [See *W. L. May Co., Inc.* v. *Philco-Ford Corporation,* 543 P.2d 283 (Or. 1975).]
3. Roseman resigned from the John Hancock Insurance Company following allegations of misuse of his expense account. He reimbursed the account. Subsequently, he was denied employment by another insurance firm after that firm read a Retail Credit Company credit report on him. The credit report included accurate information regarding Roseman's resignation. Was Retail Credit in violation of the Fair Credit Reporting Act in circulating information regarding the resignation? Explain. [See *Roseman* v. *Retail Credit Co., Inc.,* 428 F. Supp. 643 (Pa. 1977).]
4. Dun & Bradstreet, Inc., a credit reporting agency, erroneously reported to five subscribers that Greenmoss Builders had filed for voluntary bankruptcy. A correction was subsequently issued. Greenmoss, remaining dissatisfied, filed suit for defamation. The Supreme Court has held—in *New York Times* v. *Sullivan,* 376 U.S. 254 (1964)—that a public official cannot recover damages for defamation in the absence of a showing that the statement was made with "actual malice"—knowledge that it was false or with reckless disregard for whether it was false. Here, the credit report in question was not a matter of public importance. Must the plaintiff, Greenmoss, show actual malice by Dun & Bradstreet? Explain. [See *Dun & Bradstreet, Inc.* v. *Greenmoss Builders, Inc.,* 472 U.S. 749 (1985).]
5. The Fair Debt Collection Practices Act forbids debt collectors from making false or misleading representations or engaging in unfair or abusive practices. The act defines a "debt collector" as one who "regularly collects or attempts to collect, [consumer]

debts owed to another." In 1986, Congress removed language in the act that had excluded lawyers who, through litigation, engage in collecting consumer debts. Congress did not replace that language.

Heintz is a lawyer representing a bank that sued Jenkins to recover the balance due on a defaulted loan. Heintz wrote to Jenkins listing the amount owed, including over $4,000 for insurance. Jenkins argued that she did not owe the insurance money, as specified. Then Jenkins sued Heintz, claiming that his letter violated the act in making a "false representation of the amount of any debt." The district court dismissed Jenkins's suit for failure to state a claim in that, the court ruled, the act does not apply to lawyers collecting debts through litigation. The court of appeals reversed, saying the act does reach litigating lawyers who are acting as debt collectors. The Supreme Court granted certiorari. Does the FDCPA apply to lawyers who are litigating to collect debts? Explain. [See *Heintz* v. *Jenkins,* 63 *Law Week* 4266 (1995).]

Chapter Questions—Economics/Public Policy

1. Once the government decided to intervene in the free market on behalf of consumers, two broad product safety options presented themselves: (*a*) the government could have limited its effort to generating and distributing information to consumers, or (*b*) the government could have set safety standards for all products. Assuming the government were forced to choose one or the other but not elements of both, which option should it choose? Explain.
2. Consumers sometimes abuse sellers. One familiar technique is shoplifting. Of course, shoplifting is a crime. However, the criminal process is cumbersome and often does not result in monetary recoveries for sellers. As a result, at least 43 states now have laws permitting store owners to impose civil fines, the collection of which is usually turned over to a lawyer or collection agency with a threat to sue in civil court, file criminal charges, or both if payment is not forthcoming. Fines may range from $50 to $5,000 or more, depending on the value of the item stolen.
   a. Defense lawyers say this civil fine system is unfair. Why?
   b. On balance, is the civil fine approach to shoplifting a good idea? Explain.
3. In recent years, Congress has considered legislation banning tobacco advertising. Leaving health and legal issues aside, international marketing professor J. J. Boddewyn of the City University of New York argues that an advertising ban would be ill advised. Boddewyn explains that tobacco advertising was banned in five free market countries (Italy, Iceland, Singapore, Norway, and Finland). Per capita tobacco consumption did not decline in those countries following the advertising prohibitions; indeed, it increased by margins ranging from 3 percent in Finland to 68 percent in Italy. A study in five nations found only 1 percent of the 7- to 15-year-old children interviewed pointed to advertising as the most important reason for their decisions to begin smoking. The influence of parents, siblings, and friends was easily the dominant factor as they understood their decisions. And the results of the survey were the same across the five nations, even though one nation actually banned tobacco advertising (Norway), two significantly restricted it (Australia and the United Kingdom), and two employed modest restrictions (Spain and Hong Kong).[26]
   a. What arguments would you raise in favor of a ban on tobacco advertising?
   b. How would you vote on such a bill? Explain.
4. Cite some examples of consumers abusing businesspeople.

5. The Consumer Product Safety Commission reported that in 1992, 39,000 people were injured while using chain saws.[27] Based on these figures, should chain saw sales be banned until a safer product is produced? Would such a ban be effective? Explain.

Notes

1. This account is taken from Associated Press, "Consumer Groups Want Feds to Guard against 'Lemon Laundering,' " *Waterloo Courier,* November 9, 1995, p. B6.
2. *Lindberg Cadillac Co.* v. *Aron,* 371 S.W.2d 651 (1963).
3. See *Williams* v. *Walker-Thomas Furniture Company,* 350 F.2d 445 (C.A.D.C. 1965).
4. "The Cruel Joke of Relying on the States," *Money,* March 1996, p. 104.
5. *Austin American-Statesman,* June 1, 1995, p. D7.
6. Ira Teinowitz, *Advertising Age,* June 5, 1995, p. 8.
7. Michael Katz, "FTC Forces Car Rental Firms to Reveal All," *The Wall Street Journal,* August 8, 1992, p. B4.
8. Michael Janofsky, "In-Line Skating Injuries Soaring," *Des Moines Register,* June 10, 1994, p. 1A.
9. Michael Lemov and Malcolm Woolf, "Underreporting Defects Is Risky," *National Law Journal,* December 14, 1992, p. S6.
10. *Boston Globe,* "Thousands Hurt in Mowing Accidents," *The Montreal Gazette,* June 21, 1993, p. B4.
11. Viveca Novak, "The Grinch That Stole the CPSC," *National Law Journal,* December 19, 1992, p. 2921.
12. Clare Collins, "Toy Safety Comes under Scrutiny," *Des Moines Register,* November 18, 1994, p. 3T.
13. *Washington Post,* "Garage Doors Covered by New Rules," *Waterloo Courier,* January 3, 1993, p. E6.
14. Joe Davidson, "Days of Irksome Childproof Caps Are Numbered," *The Wall Street Journal,* June 14, 1995, p. B1.
15. Ibid.
16. Diana Lundin, "Will Consumer Groups Put the Brakes on Walkers for Babies?" *Des Moines Register,* December 26, 1992, p. T1.
17. Amy Eskind, "Bringing Up Baby," *The Wall Street Journal,* April 13, 1993, p. A14.
18. Ibid.
19. The materials in this section are drawn, in part, from Donald Rothschild and David Carroll, *Consumer Protection Reporting Service* (Owings Mills, MD: National Law Publishing Corporation, 1983).
20. "Equifax, FTC Settle Charges over Privacy of Credit Reports," *Credit Risk Management Report* 5, no. 3 (February 13, 1995).
21. David Elbert, "Dark Side to Reform Measure," *Des Moines Register,* June 14, 1992, p. G1.
22. Associated Press, "Credit Company Must Pay Harassment Tab," *Des Moines Register,* August 25, 1995, p. 4A.
23. "The Other National Debt," *Des Moines Register,* January 11, 1995, p. 6A.
24. Associated Press, "Bankruptcy Loses Its Stigma in U.S.," *Des Moines Register,* November 3, 1995, p. 10S.
25. Kenneth Bacon, "Losses in Bankruptcies Spur Lenders to Strive to Protect Themselves," *The Wall Street Journal,* June 17, 1993, p. A1.
26. J. J. Boddewyn, "Smoking Ads Don't Get People Hooked," *The Wall Street Journal,* November 21, 1986, p. 24.
27. Joanne Ball Artis, "Pattern of Injuries Cited in Wood-Chipper Case," *Boston Globe,* August 19, 1993, p. 34.

CHAPTER

13

BUSINESS TORTS AND CRIMES

READER'S GUIDE

Throughout this text, we have been asking you to think about how the law will influence you in your role as a manager or owner of a business. Hence, we have looked at, among other topics, entering contracts, buying property, hiring employees, raising money, and marketing products or services, and how the law influences each of those operations. Now we turn from the building process to the less happy responsibility of dealing with mistakes and wrongs in business practice. We will examine both **tort** and criminal law. Broadly, a tort is an injury to person or property, not arising from a contract, for which a court will provide a remedy. A **crime** is a public wrong—an act punishable by the state.

tort. An injury to person or property, not arising from a contract, for which a court will provide a remedy.
crime. A public wrong, an act punishable by the state.

PROFILE

In 1995, a conspiracy of more than a decade involving $15 million in bribes and kickbacks came undone and crashed on a group of American Honda executives. At least 18 former executives of American Honda have been convicted or pleaded guilty in the conspiracy. Those executives solicited bribes from dealers in exchange for awarding franchises or for larger allotments of Hondas at a time when the cars were in great demand and short supply and thus could be sold for thousands beyond their sticker prices. Honda policy forbade accepting gifts of more than $50, but the executives solicited and accepted bribes ranging from cars to swimming pools to Rolex watches to envelopes sheltering tens of thousands in cash.[1] One of those executives, Stanley James Cardiges, former senior vice president of sales for American Honda, was accused of accepting some $5 million in cash and gifts, including five Rolex watches, six new cars, and a fur coat.[2] Cardiges pleaded guilty, cooperated with federal prosecutors, and was sentenced to five years in prison and fined $364,000.[3]

A variety of tort and criminal wrongs were alleged in the Honda story. We will look at them from time to time throughout this chapter.

I. TORTS

assault. Placing another in apprehension of an imminent, intentional, unwanted touching.
battery. Intentional, unwanted touching of another without consent or legal excuse.
compensatory damages. Damages that will compensate a party for actual losses due to an injury suffered.

This chapter examines both torts and crimes; thus, at the outset we need to distinguish these two closely related wrongs. As noted, torts are civil wrongs not arising from contracts. Torts involve injuries to particular persons, whereas crimes are regarded as wrongs to all of society (although, of course, they are most commonly directed at a specific person or persons). Crimes are prosecuted by the state; tort actions are initiated by individuals. Criminal law punishes wrongdoers, but the point of tort law is to make whole an injured party. At the same time, there is much overlap between torts and crimes, and many acts can be treated either as a civil wrong (a tort) or as a crime, or both. For example, a physical attack on another can, of course, lead to criminal charges, but it can also produce civil tort claims, most commonly, **assault** and **battery.**

The injured party in a tort litigation can seek **compensatory damages** to make up for the harm suffered. Those damages may consist of medical expenses, lost income, and pain and suffering, among other possibilities. In some cases, **punitive damages** may be awarded in order to punish the wrongdoer and to discourage others from similar behavior. Ordinarily, punitive damages would be available only in cases of intentional torts or strict liability.

punitive damages. Damages designed to punish flagrant wrongdoers and to deter them and others from engaging in similar conduct in the future.

A. *Tort Categories*

Fundamentally, torts are of three kinds: (1) **intentional,** (2) **negligent,** and (3) **strict liability.** Intentional torts involve voluntary acts that harm a protected interest. **Intent** is established by showing the defendant meant to do the act that caused the harm. The plaintiff need not show that the harm itself was intended. The defendant would be liable for all reasonably foreseeable injuries from that intentional act.

To explain, if you run an advertisement defaming a fast-food competitor by saying its food processing does not meet government standards, but you cannot prove the truth of your allegations, you will probably be guilty of the intentional tort of **injurious falsehood** (product disparagement).

Negligence is discussed extensively in Chapter 14, Product Liability, but we will look briefly in this chapter at negligent torts not arising from defective products. These are situations in which harm is caused accidentally. Intent is absent, but because of one party's carelessness, another has suffered injury. Thus, if one of your employees is making a delivery for the printing business you are managing and carelessly runs a red light, striking another car, the employee appears to be guilty of negligent conduct for which both she and your firm may be subject to civil damages. Further, you might bear personal responsibility if, for example, you hired her with knowledge that she had been a careless driver.

Strict liability is, in essence, a no-fault concept where one is responsible for harm without proof of carelessness. Strict liability is limited to "unreasonably dangerous" products and practices about which we have decided, as a matter of social policy, that responsibility for injury will automatically attach without establishing blame. Thus, if one works with dynamite or sells a product that is (1) defective and (2) unreasonably dangerous and someone is hurt, strict (absolute) liability may attach even though fault is not established. (Detailed attention to strict liability appears in Chapter 14.)

intentional tort. Voluntary civil wrong causing harm to a protected interest.

negligent tort. Unintentional, civil wrong causing harm to a protected interest. Injury to another resulting from carelessness.

strict liability. Civil wrong springing from defective and "unreasonably dangerous" products and practices where responsibility automatically attaches without proof of blame or fault.

intent. Conscious and purposeful state of mind.

injurious falsehood. Intentional tort based on a false statement made with malice that disparages the property of another.

II. Tort Law

A. *Selected Intentional Torts against Persons*

Suppose you are warehouse manager for a plumbing supply business, and a subordinate does a poor job with some work, which in turn brings your boss down on you. In your frustration, you call the subordinate into your office where you chastise him and then light up a cigar and casually but pointedly blow smoke in his face. Could he sue you for your insulting behavior? Let's look at the law in this area.

> In your frustration, you light up a cigar and casually but pointedly blow smoke in his face.

Battery. Intentionally touching another in a harmful or offensive way without legal justification or the consent of that person is a battery. Merely touching another's clothing or touching an occupied car may constitute a battery. Assuming no allergic response, our example of cigar smoke in the victim's face may not be physically harmful; but could it constitute a battery, nonetheless, if the touching was offensive? Few such cases have been litigated, but a recent pair of decisions suggests that recipients of smoke may, under some circumstances, be able to successfully raise battery claims. Recently, an Ohio Court of Appeals held that smoking could constitute a battery. In that case, a talk show host had invited an antismoking activist to his show and then allegedly deliberately blew cigar smoke in the guest's face and on his clothing. The trial court dismissed the case, but the appeals court reversed and sent it back for trial, holding that tobacco smoke fit the Ohio Supreme Court's definition of battery.[4] On the other hand, in a crowded world, we cannot expect the law to help us erect a glass cage around ourselves such that we could sue anyone who brushes against us because we find all human contact offensive.

Assault. Intentionally causing another reasonably to believe that he or she is about to be the victim of a battery is an assault. The battery need not occur and the victim need not be frightened; but an assault nonetheless transpires if the victim reasonably anticipated a substantially imminent battery. Thus, raising one's hand as if to strike another even though the blow never transpires constitutes the tort of assault if the victim reasonably thought herself to be in immediate danger.

false imprisonment. Tort of intentionally restricting the freedom of movement of another.
wrongful discharge. Tort of dismissing another from employment in violation of public policy.
malicious prosecution. Criminal prosecution carried on with malice and without probable cause with damages resulting.

False Imprisonment. If you have anticipated a career in retailing, you may have given thought to the problem of shoplifters and strategies for preserving your inventory without yourself violating customers' rights. The statutory and judge-made law of most states now protects store managers and owners from **false imprisonment** claims where they justifiably detain a suspected shoplifter for a reasonable period of time and in a reasonable manner. Broadly, false imprisonment occurs when someone is intentionally confined against his or her will, that is, his or her freedom of movement is restricted. That restriction might include being shut in a room, being bound, being threatened, and so on. Even a moment could conceivably constitute imprisonment, although simply sending a customer, for example, through a more distant store exit would not meet the test. The case that follows examines a commonplace false imprisonment dilemma and provides an introduction to the torts of **wrongful discharge** and **malicious prosecution.**

CASE

Jackson v. Kmart Corp.

851 F. Supp. 469 (M.D. Ga. 1994)

Facts

On December 18, 1991, Rocky Malone, a loss prevention manager working at a Kmart store in Macon, Georgia, noticed two females with shopping carts full of merchandise enter a checkout lane. One of the females was Kathleen Bell. Malone . . . suspected that the two females were involved in a theft scheme . . . Malone observed plaintiff/Debbie Jackson, a cashier/scan several items from Bell's shopping cart into the computer and then void the items off the sale. [Jackson] then placed these items into a shopping cart. As Malone watched these transactions take place, he noticed Kathleen Bell staring at him. Therefore, to avoid arousing suspicion, Malone walked out of the store and . . . positioned himself . . . to observe the transactions through the windows located on the front of the building.

Continued

Continued

Subsequently, as Bell attempted to leave the store with the shopping carts, Malone stopped her and asked to see her receipt. Bell refused. Eventually, Malone recovered the receipt from one of the shopping carts. The receipt indicated that Bell had purchased only one item, which had a value of $4.99. The carts, however, contained merchandise worth $834.86. Consequently, Bell was taken to a private security office in the rear of the store and the police were summoned.

Shortly thereafter, plaintiff [Jackson] was asked to close her register and report to an office at the rear of the store . . . [T]he store manager questioned her about the transactions. Plaintiff, however, denied any knowledge of the attempted theft. The manager then told plaintiff that he could make a pass at [her] and that there would be nothing [she] could do about it. In addition, the manager told plaintiff that he wished she was white, because, according to the manager, shoplifting always involved blacks. The manager also refused to allow plaintiff to use the phone to call her husband and told [her] "that he was going to keep [her] there until [plaintiff told] him . . . the truth."

After being interviewed by the store manager for approximately thirty minutes, plaintiff was taken to the room where Kathleen Bell had been placed. By this time, Officer Jeffrey Lary of the Macon Police Department had arrived. Lary questioned both plaintiff and Bell about the incident. Plaintiff told Lary that although she knew Bell, she had no knowledge of the theft. Bell, however, told the officer that plaintiff was involved in the theft scheme. Subsequently, Lary was instructed by his supervisor to contact Magistrate Pam Rogers for directions. The magistrate advised Lary to make a warrantless arrest of both Bell and plaintiff.

On March 12, 1992, a grand jury indicted Kathleen Bell and plaintiff on charges of theft by deception. Kathleen Bell subsequently plead guilty to the charges . . . Plaintiff was subsequently acquitted.

On October 27, 1992, plaintiff filed suit against Kmart Corporation for wrongful discharge, malicious prosecution, and false imprisonment.

* * *

Chief Judge Owens

I. Wrongful Discharge

Plaintiff does not contest defendant's assertion that plaintiff was an at-will employee. Accordingly, as the law of the State of Georgia does not recognize a cause of action for wrongful discharge by an at-will employee, defendant's motion for summary judgment on this issue is **GRANTED.**

II. Malicious Prosecution Claim

Official Code of Georgia Annotated . . . provides: "A criminal prosecution which is carried on maliciously and without any probable cause and which causes damage to the person prosecuted shall give him a cause of action." The elements of a malicious prosecution claim are: "(1) prosecution for a criminal offense; (2) the prosecution instigated under a valid warrant, accusation, or summons; (3) termination of the prosecution in favor of the plaintiff; (4) malice; (5) want of probable cause; and (6) damage to the plaintiff."

* * *

The central question is whether the officials involved made an "independent decision to arrest or prosecute." Although a Kmart employee may have indicated to Officer Lary a desire to have plaintiff arrested, the record clearly indicates that this was not the "determining factor" in

Continued

Continued

the decision to arrest. Prior to arresting plaintiff, Lary contacted Magistrate Pam Rogers. It was on the magistrate's recommendation that the officer arrested plaintiff; that is, the magistrate made an independent decision that an arrest should take place. Further, the record offers no support to a contention that an employee of Kmart offered the officer false information or exercised an undue influence over the decision to prosecute. Accordingly, because plaintiff has failed to put forward evidence sufficient to establish that defendant "instigated" the prosecution of plaintiff, defendant's motion for summary judgment on the issue of malicious prosecution is **GRANTED.**

* * *

III. False Imprisonment Claim

"False imprisonment is the unlawful detention of the person of another, for any length of time, whereby such person is deprived of his personal liberty." O.C.G.A. § 51–7–20.

* * *

[Under Georgia law], a defendant is required to establish (1) that a reasonable person would have believed that the plaintiff was shoplifting, *and* (2) that the manner and length of the detention were reasonable.

* * *

[T]he court holds that the indictment of plaintiff by the grand jury on charges of theft by deception, in that the indictment was based on the very same facts giving rise to plaintiff's detention, creates a presumption that plaintiff acted in a manner such that a reasonable person would have believed that she was shoplifting. Although the presumption may be rebutted . . . , plaintiff has failed to do so. Accordingly, defendant has satisfied the first requirement of [Georgia law].

The second requirement [has two elements]. First, the manner of the detention must be reasonable. That is, "a person [should not] be subjected to gratuitous and unnecessary indignities during the course of . . . a detention." And second, the length of the detention must be reasonable.

As a general rule, "[t]he determination of whether . . . the manner and length of the detention were reasonable [are] matters for the jury, not the court, to determine." Plaintiff has put forth sufficient evidence to challenge the reasonableness of the manner in which she was detained. A jury could reasonably find that the actions of the store manager subjected plaintiff to "gratuitous and unnecessary indignities." Further, inasmuch as the reasonableness of the length of plaintiff's detention may be impacted by the manner in which she was detained, the court also finds that a genuine issue of fact exists as to the reasonableness of the length of plaintiff's detention. Accordingly, defendant's motion for summary judgment on plaintiff's claim of false imprisonment is **DENIED.**

Questions

1. Why did the plaintiff, Debbie Jackson, fail in her wrongful discharge and malicious prosecution claims?
2. If the court had found that Kmart had, in fact, instigated the prosecution of the plaintiff, Debbie Jackson, what proof would be required for Jackson to win her malicious prosecution claim?
3. What facts arguably supported the plaintiff's false imprisonment claim?

Continued

Continued

4. Burrow selected two lamps at a Georgia Kmart. The salesman put the lamps in two cardboard boxes (not the original containers) with two end flaps up and two down. The salesman carried the boxes to the cashier and quoted the prices. Burrow paid, received a receipt, and proceeded to leave when she was stopped by the store greeter, who, according to her own testimony, said, "May I check your box, please?" According to Burrow, the greeter said she had to search the boxes and "snatched" them from Burrow's hands. Burrow said the greeter talked loudly, the episode was embarrassing, and the manager, when called, failed to help rectify the wrong. Burrow sued for false imprisonment and was awarded $25,000. Kmart appealed. Decide. Explain. [See *Burrow* v. *Kmart Corp.,* 304 S.E.2d 460 (1983).]

Fraud. Intentional misrepresentations of facts, sometimes identified by the formal title of **deceit,** can lead to tort claims. We discuss **fraud** in the criminal law materials that follow in this chapter and in the contracts (Chapter 4), marketing (Chapter 11), and consumer protection (Chapter 12) chapters. For now, simply note the general test for fraud:

1. Misrepresentation of a material fact.
2. The misrepresentation was intentional.
3. The injured party justifiably relied on the misrepresentation.
4. Injury resulted.

deceit. A tort involving intentional misrepresentation to deceive or trick another.

fraud. An intentional misrepresentation of a material fact with intent to deceive where the misrepresentation is justifiably relied on by another and damages result.

Defamation. Assume you are at a company party engaging in the networking that you understand to be essential to success. Still in the management trainee program, you are carefully watching your step. A coworker approaches and, after some casual talk, remarks: "I guess you have been warned about your boss, Smith. You know he can't be trusted. He lies when it serves his purposes." Language of that kind may constitute **slander,** the spoken form of the tort of **defamation. Libel** is defamation in print or some other tangible form such as a picture, movie, or video. Most courts also treat defamatory radio and television statements as forms of libel. The basic test for establishing defamation:

1. A false statement.
2. Harm to the victim's reputation.
3. Publication of the statement. (The statement must reach someone other than the one being defamed.)

The law's interest here is in protecting reputations. Any living person or any organization can be the victim of defamation, although public figures such as politicians or actors face the additional burden of proving **malice** if they are to be successful in a defamation claim. Malice generally requires a showing of actual knowledge of the falsehood or reckless disregard for the truth. Libel or slander about a company's products or property would constitute the tort of injurious falsehood, which is discussed later.

In general, a claim of slander requires a showing of actual harm, such as job loss. However, some statements are so inherently damaging that actual damage need not be shown. Those statements are labeled **slander per se** and include allegations of serious sexual misconduct, commission of a serious crime, professional incompetence, or having a loathsome disease. Similarly, libel, leaving a more permanent stain, generally does not require a showing of actual harm.

slander. Tort of defaming or injuring another's reputation by a published oral expression.

defamation. Tort of disparaging another's reputation by oral or written publication.

libel. Tort of defaming or injuring another's reputation by a published writing.

malice. A required element of proof in a libel or slander claim by a public figure. Proof of a defamatory statement expressed with actual knowledge of its falsity or with reckless disregard for the truth would establish malice.

slander per se. Category of oral defamation not requiring proof of actual harm in order to recover.

absolute privilege. In libel and slander law, situations where a defendant is entirely excused from liability for defamatory statements because of the circumstances under which the statements were made.

qualified privilege. In libel and slander law, situations where a defendant is excused from liability for defamatory statements except where the statements were motivated by malice.

invasion of privacy. Violation of the right to be left alone.

appropriation. Making commercial use of an individual's name or likeness without permission.

intrusion. Wrongfully entering upon or prying into the solitude or property of another.

public disclosure of private facts. Public disclosure of private facts where disclosure of the matter in question would be highly offensive to a reasonable person.

false light. Falsely and publicly attributing certain characteristics, conduct, or beliefs to another such that a reasonable person would be highly offended.

intentional infliction of emotional distress. Intentional tort based on outrageous conduct that causes severe emotional distress in another.

Truth acts as a complete defense to a defamation claim. Hence, if we tell the truth about others, we cannot be guilty of the tort of defamation, regardless of our evil intentions. Further, many statements are protected because of the circumstances in which they are made. We label these either **absolute** or **qualified privileges.** Absolute privileges to defame include, for example, remarks by government officials in the course of their duties or by participants in a trial. Qualified privileges to defame include statements to secure credit or a job. In those instances, the statement will not be treated as defamatory, even though false, unless it was motivated by malice.

Invasion of Privacy. A key ingredient in personal freedom is the right to be left alone. Our courts recognize a right of recovery in tort law when we are the victims of some kind of unconscionable exposure of our private lives. **Invasion of privacy** takes four forms:

1. *Appropriation of a person's name or likeness*—When an individual's name or image is used without permission for commercial purposes, called an **appropriation,** that person probably has a cause of action for invasion of privacy. Typically, this problem involves a company's use of a celebrity's name or picture without permission to imply that he or she has endorsed the product.
2. *Intrusion*—An intentional invasion of a person's solitude is labeled an **intrusion** if it would be highly offensive to a reasonable person. Physical intrusions such as opening an employee's mail or more subtle strategies such as an electronic probe of an employee's bank account are examples of tortious intrusion.
3. *Public disclosure of private facts*—This form of invasion of privacy bears a strong resemblance to defamation. Again, if the disclosure would be highly offensive to a reasonable person, the tort of **public disclosure of private facts** might be invoked. We believe that certain elements of one's life, such as debt payment practices or sexual preferences, are, with rare exceptions, no one else's business. In these cases, truth does *not* constitute a good defense.
4. *False light*—When claims are published about another that have the effect of casting the victim in a **false light** in the public mind, a tort claim may emerge. Such a claim would be much like defamation except that false light involves one's interest in being left alone while defamation involves injury to reputation. Again, the claim would need to be highly offensive to the reasonable person. So, if an employee's office was wrongfully searched, and he was led from the workplace by superiors in full view of other employees and in a manner that suggested that he was engaging in dishonorable conduct, a false light tort claim might be raised. Here, truth would constitute a complete defense.

Intentional Infliction of Emotional Distress. Your managerial career doubtless will feature many unpleasant moments. Perhaps you will need to fire someone. You may feel badly, but worse, you may be sued. In the *Jackson* v. *Kmart* case above, we looked briefly at the tort of wrongful dismissal; but in recent years we have seen increasing use of the tort of **intentional infliction of emotional distress** in dismissals and many other personnel decisions or conflicts. Historically, most courts have been reluctant to recognize this tort, principally because of fears about fraudulent emotional claims. Some continue to require accompanying proof of physical injury, but the emotional distress tort in recent years has added some complexity to the manager's decision-making process. Dismissals, drug tests, and sexual harassment cases have become particularly fertile grounds for emotional distress claims, although it should be understood that the courts have demanded compelling evidence before permitting recovery.

Your managerial career doubtless will feature many unpleasant moments. Perhaps you will need to fire someone. You may feel badly, but worse, you may be sued.

B. Selected Intentional Torts against Property

We will briefly examine four prominent tort claims arising from wrongs to property: trespass, conversion, nuisance, and injurious falsehood.

Trespass to **real property** (land and immovable objects attached to it) occurs with the intentional entry onto the land of another without consent. Trespass to **personal property** (movable property; all property other than real property) involves an intentional interference with a person's right to enjoy his or her personal property, for example, the manager of a parking lot refuses for a day to return a car to its owner in the mistaken belief that the owner has not paid his monthly bill.

trespass Entering the property of another without any right, lawful authority, or invitation.

real property. Land, buildings, and things permanently attached to land or buildings.

personal property. Movable property. All property other than real estate.

conversion. Wrongfully exercising control over the personal property of another.

nuisance. Unreasonable interference with another's right to enjoyment of real property.

More serious and extensive interference with personal property may be labeled a **conversion.** For example, if the parking lot company kept the car for months, and it suffered damage during the impoundment, a conversion probably occurred.

Nuisance is the situation in which enjoyment of one's land is impaired because of some tortious interference. That interference often takes the form of light, noise, smell, or vibration. Here, the owner is not deprived of the land and the land has not been physically invaded, but the full enjoyment of the land cannot be achieved because of the interference. If you opened a beer garden on the open roof of your bar, which is located near residences, you might well be sued by those neighbors on the grounds that the noise or light from the beer garden constitute a nuisance.

Injurious falsehood is a form of defamation that is directed against the property of a person. Thus, to falsely claim that a competitor's product is defective or harmful would likely constitute injurious falsehood. As with defamation, the statement must be false and it must be published. Damages must result. Often, malice must also be shown. In some instances, both injurious falsehood and defamation claims may arise from the same set of facts. Additional torts could be discussed, but this list must suffice.

C. Selected Intentional Tort Defenses

Let's take a brief look at a few of the more significant defenses to the intentional torts that we have been examining.

Consent. Clearly, if you consent to the use of your picture in an advertising campaign and you subsequently feel that your public image has been harmed, you will have difficulty in pursuing a tort claim. Of course, if you gave permission under mistake, fraud, or duress, your consent was not meaningful. Or the picture use may have exceeded the bounds of the consent that you offered.

Mistake. As store security manager, you are radioed by a clerk to "stop the guy in the New York Yankees cap" on suspicion of shoplifting. After stopping someone fitting that description, you later discover that someone else, also wearing a Yankees cap, was the actual suspect. If the store is sued for false imprisonment, can it successfully raise a mistake defense? Unless protected under state statutory law, probably not. Having acted intentionally, you and, by extension, your employer probably will bear responsibility. Of course, false imprisonment does not occur unless the detention was unreasonable.

On the other hand, mistake can be a good defense, particularly in instances in which events happen rapidly. Say, for example, a store's security personnel broke up what looked to be an assault and battery in the mall parking lot, only to discover that the incident was merely horsing around by the parties. A mistake defense might be appropriate here.

Necessity. In what we would broadly label emergency situations, one may intentionally commit a tort and yet be excused under the necessity defense. A case of public necessity might involve, for example, a person's breaking into an unoccupied building late at night because he saw a fire burning inside. An example of a private necessity is when a defendant intrudes on the property of another to save himself only; he might thereafter raise a necessity defense against the tort claim of trespass.

Self-Defense. Suppose your career has taken you into retail management, and you have now decided to buy your own hardware store. You encounter the ups and downs that characterize entrepreneurial life, but you become particularly frustrated by the theft and vandalism that seem so much a part of contemporary small business practice. Finally, in an effort to stop the breaking, entering, and minor theft that has troubled your business, you build a trap in your store. You take up a few floorboards in a rear entryway where vandals have broken in, and you pound nails into those boards. Then you cover the nails with some soft felt so that they are not visible; but when stepped on, the nails will pierce the felt and stab the feet of any intruder. Suppose your trap works, and an intruder is injured. Suppose the intruder then sues you for his injury. Could you cite self-defense of your property as an excuse? What if a police officer stepped on a nail responding to an alarm at your business? The *Katko* case that follows looks at the self-defense theme.

CASE

KATKO V. BRINEY

183 N.W.2d 657 (1971)

Facts

The Brineys, defendants/appellants in this case, owned an unoccupied farm house. During the period from 1957 to 1967, trespassers broke into the house, broke windows, and stole some items. The Brineys boarded windows and erected "no trespassing" signs on the land. On June 11, 1967, the Brineys attached a 20-gauge, loaded shotgun to a bed in the house, pointing the barrel toward the bedroom door. They attached a wire to the trigger and the bedroom door knob so that the gun would fire if the door were opened. At first, Mr. Briney directed the gun so that it would hit an intruder in the stomach, but agreed with Mrs. Briney's suggestion to lower the barrel so that it would strike an intruder's legs. The gun could not be seen from the outside and no warning about it was posted.

Katko, the plaintiff/appellee, worked in an Eddyville, Iowa, gas station. He and a friend, McDonough, had found antiques—old bottles and fruit jars—on their first trip to the Briney house, which Katko considered to be abandoned. On their second trip, they entered the house through a window. Katko opened the bedroom door and was shot in the right leg. Much of that leg, including part of the tibia, was blown away. Katko was hospitalized for 40 days. His leg was in a cast for approximately one year, and he was required to wear a brace for an additional year. His leg was permanently shortened by the trauma.

Katko sued the Brineys and secured a jury verdict of $30,000. The Brineys appealed to the Iowa Supreme Court.

* * *

Continued

Continued

Chief Justice Moore

The primary issue presented here is whether an owner may protect personal property in an unoccupied, boarded-up farm house against trespassers and thieves by a spring gun capable of inflicting death or serious injury.

We are not here concerned with a man's right to protect his home and members of his family. Defendant's home was several miles from the scene of the incident to which we refer.

* * *

Plaintiff testified he knew he had no right to break and enter the house with intent to steal bottles and fruit jars therefrom. He further testified he had entered a plea of guilty to larceny in the nighttime of property of less than $20 value from a private building. He stated he had been fined $50 and costs and paroled during good behavior from a 60-day jail sentence. Other than minor traffic charges this was plaintiff's first brush with the law. . .

The main thrust of the defendants' defense in the trial court and on this appeal is that "the law permits use of a spring gun in a dwelling or warehouse for the purpose of preventing the unlawful entry of a burglar or thief" . . .

In the statement of issues the trial court stated plaintiff and his companion committed a felony when they broke and entered defendant's house. In instruction 2 the court referred to the early case history of the use of spring guns and stated under the law their use was prohibited except to prevent the commission of felonies of violence and where human life is in danger. The instruction included a statement that breaking and entering is not a felony of violence.

Instruction 5 stated: "You are hereby instructed that one may use reasonable force in the protection of his property, but such right is subject to the qualification that one may not use such means of force as will take human life or inflict great bodily injury. Such is the rule even though the injured party is a trespasser and is in violation of the law himself."

Instruction 6 stated: "An owner of premises is prohibited from willfully or intentionally injuring a trespasser by means of force that either takes life or inflicts great bodily injury; and therefore a person owning a premise is prohibited from setting out 'spring guns' and like dangerous devices which will likely take life or inflict great bodily injury, for the purpose of harming trespassers. The fact that the trespasser may be acting in violation of the law does not change the rule. The only time when such conduct of setting a 'spring gun' or a like dangerous device is justified would be when the trespasser was committing a felony of violence or a felony punishable by death, or where the trespasser was endangering human life by his act" . . .

The overwhelming weight of authority, both textbook and case law, supports the trial court's statement of the applicable principles of law.

Prosser on Torts, Third Edition, pages 116–18, states:

> the law has always placed a higher value upon human safety than upon mere rights in property, it is the accepted rule that there is no privilege to use any force calculated to cause death or serious bodily injury to repel the threat to land or chattels, unless there is also such a threat to the defendant's personal safety as to justify a self-defense . . . spring guns and other mankilling devices are not justifiable against a mere trespasser, or even a petty thief. They are privileged only against those upon whom the landowner, if he were present in person would be free to inflict injury of the same kind.

* * *

In *Hooker* v. *Miller,* 37 Iowa 613, we held defendant vineyard owner liable for damages resulting from a spring gun shot although plaintiff was a trespasser and there to steal grapes. At pages 614, 615, this statement is made: "This court has held that a mere trespass against property

Continued

Continued

other than a dwelling is not a sufficient justification to authorize the use of a deadly weapon by the owner in its defense; and that if death results in such a case it will be murder, though the killing be actually necessary to prevent the trespass. . .

In Wisconsin, Oregon, and England the use of spring guns and similar devices is specifically made unlawful by statute.

* * *

Affirmed.

Questions

1. Why did the Iowa Supreme Court rule in favor of the criminal intruder, Katko?
2. What classes of people other than intruders are of concern to the courts in cases like *Katko?*
3. Did the Iowa Supreme Court reach a just verdict? Explain.
4. A businessman in Cordele, Georgia, troubled by small thefts from a cigarette machine in front of his store, allegedly booby-trapped the machine after hours with dynamite. A teenager then died when tampering with the machine. What legal action should be taken? Resolve.

D. Negligence

Profile Perspective: Let's return to the American Honda scandal. In sentencing some of the executives involved in the bribes, Judge Joseph A. DiClerico, Jr., said that American Honda "could well be accused of being negligent," but not criminally culpable.[5] Indeed, at this writing, American Honda is being sued by many of its dealers for fraud, breach of contract, negligence, and other claims. In what sense were American Honda and its executives arguably negligent even though company policy expressly forbade this behavior?

negligence. Failure to do something that a reasonable person would do under the circumstances, or an action that a reasonable and prudent person would not take under the circumstances.

duty of due care. Standard of conduct expected of a reasonable, prudent person under the circumstances.

proximate cause. Occurrences that in a natural sequence, unbroken by potent intervening forces, produce an injury that would not have resulted in the absence of those occurrences.

To answer that question, consider your own managerial duties. If you fail to perform your work in a reasonable manner such that another is injured, you may be liable for a **negligence** claim. In brief, you are accused of being careless. As a manager you have a duty to exhibit care in hiring employees, supervising those employees, and even firing them (see Chapter 6). You must see that records are kept satisfactorily. You must properly maintain your premises. You must provide appropriate security. At every turn, carelessness on your part or on the part of your employees may lead to injury to another and a negligence claim against you. So American Honda's negligence probably depends on the reasonableness of its management practices and policies in the bribery case.

Test. We have examined intentional torts, where one's state of mind is a critical ingredient in the wrong. Negligence, on the other hand, concerns conduct alone; intent is irrelevant. Broadly, the standard is that of the reasonable person. As a manager or owner, you must behave reasonably under the circumstances. As discussed in much greater detail in Chapter 14, Product Liability, a successful negligence claim requires a showing of: (1) **duty of due care,** (2) breach of that duty, (3) that the breach was both the actual and **proximate cause** of the injury, and (4) injury.

Defenses. The primary defenses to a negligence claim are **contributory negligence, comparative negligence,** and **assumption of the risk.**

Historically, most states followed the contributory negligence rule where a plaintiff who contributed in any way to his or her own harm could not recover for the defendant's negligence. The harshness of that rule has led most states to adopt a comparative negligence stance in which the *relative* fault of each party is weighed and damages are assessed accordingly. Actual practice varies from state to state, but in brief, if the plaintiff suffers $10,000 in damages and is 25 percent responsible for his or her own harm, and the defendant is 75 percent responsible, the plaintiff will normally recover $7,500.

Assumption of the risk ordinarily is a complete defense to a negligence claim in that a plaintiff who has voluntarily exposed him- or herself to a known danger cannot recover for any subsequent injury. If you see a clearly marked construction zone ahead of you, proceed into it, and suffer injury, you are unlikely to be able to sue because you assumed the risk.

Negligence Per Se. Sometimes a negligence claim arises from the violation of a statute or regulation. When a statute sets a standard, such as removing ice and snow from one's sidewalk, driving 55 miles per hour, or bartender liability as embodied in the **dramshop law** mentioned in the *Granny's Rocker* case below, that statute may be interpreted as creating a duty for the community. Hence, violation of the statute would constitute breach of the duty of due care. Such situations are labeled **negligence per se;** proof of violating the statute without further evidence conclusively establishes proof of negligence.

Similarly, if a criminal statute is violated, that behavior is presumed to be negligent. In a subsequent civil suit, the court will accept the criminal conviction as sufficient evidence of negligence.

Landowner Duties. Property owners and managers have special duties in protecting those who enter their premises. Historically, the degree of protection required depended on the status of the visitor. An owner in a trespassing situation (see *Katko* above) would be liable only for intentional harm to that **trespasser.**

Unlike a trespasser, a **licensee** enters another's property with express or implied permission but does so to serve the licensee's own interests (e.g., a door-to-door salesperson or a person taking a shortcut while walking). Basically, the owner's duty is to warn about hidden dangers.

An **invitee** is the particular concern of the businessperson because she or he (e.g., customer or delivery person) is on the premises for the purposes of the owner. Invitees are entitled to a high degree of protection, and the ordinary standards of negligence would apply such that the owner would need to employ reasonable care in maintaining safe premises.

Although these distinctions by category probably remain the majority position, the courts are gradually eroding them such that invitees and licensees are viewed much the same in many jurisdictions and even trespassers, especially when they are children, are accorded an increasing degree of protection. The case that follows examines negligence law in the context of maintaining proper security in a crowded bar.

contributory negligence. Defense in a negligence action wherein the defendant attempts to demonstrate that the plaintiff contributed to the harm on which the litigation was based thereby barring the plaintiff's claim.

comparative negligence. Defense in a negligence suit in which the plaintiff's recovery is reduced by an amount equivalent to her contribution to her own injury.

assumption of the risk. Defense in a negligence case in which the defendant seeks to bar recovery by the plaintiff by showing that the plaintiff knowingly and voluntarily exposed himself or herself to the danger that resulted in injury.

dramshop law. State laws imposing liability on the seller of intoxicating liquors when a third party is injured as a result of the intoxication of the buyer where the sale has caused or contributed to that intoxication.

negligence per se. Action violating a public duty, particularly where that duty is specified by statute.

trespasser. A person who enters the property of another without any right, lawful authority, or invitation.

licensee. One who comes on the premises of another for her own purpose but with the occupier's consent.

invitee One who comes on the premises of another by invitation of the owner, in connection with the owner's business, and for the benefit of the owner or for the mutual benefit of the invitee and the owner.

CASE

Loomis v. Granny's Rocker Nite Club

620 N.E.2d 664 (Ill. 1993)

Facts

Soon after Granny's Rocker Nite Club . . . opened in the mid-1980s, it began having a weekly "fanny" contest, which involves male and female volunteer contestants competing for cash prizes by dancing . . . The audience [judges] the contest. While attending the fanny contest on April 4, 1990, plaintiff Jeffrey Loomis got into a fight with another patron . . . Loomis'[s] right ear was bitten and torn . . .

Loomis'[s] claim against Granny's Rocker had two counts, one based on the Illinois Dramshop Act and one based on negligence. The jury found for the defendant on the dramshop count, but it found that Granny's Rocker was negligent in failing to have adequate security to stop a physical altercation on the nights of the fanny contests when it knew or should have known that such contests would result in a large and rowdy group of patrons. Granny's Rocker appeals.

* * *

Judge Chapman

In order to recover under a negligence theory, a plaintiff must offer evidence which establishes that the defendant owed a duty to the plaintiff, that the defendant breached the duty, and that the breach proximately caused the plaintiff's injuries. Whether a duty exists is a question of law to be determined by the court and depends on whether parties stood in such a relationship to one another that the law imposes an obligation on the defendant to act reasonably for the protection of the plaintiff. In determining whether a duty exists in a particular case, a court must weigh the foreseeability of the injury, the likelihood of the injury, the magnitude of the burden of guarding against it, and the consequences of placing that burden on the defendant.

The testimony at trial was as follows. Bob Rollins, owner and manager of Granny's Rocker, testified that the fanny contest has been a weekly event for six years. When asked what the contestants are permitted to do during the fanny contest, he explained: "[They can do] basically whatever they want to do. They cannot—there is no nudity. We don't allow G-strings or that sort of thing. No total nudity. A guy can take off his shirt. Some people will not take off anything. Some people will take off down to their underwear." Rollins testified that the fanny contest is a promotion "to try to create more business during the weekdays." He testified that on the night of the incident Granny's Rocker employed three bartenders, a front door man, a back door man, a disk jockey, and approximately four security guards. Granny's Rocker employs the same number of people on Friday and Saturday nights, but on Tuesdays and Thursdays there are two less bartenders and two less security personnel.

Jeffrey Loomis testified that he was 19 years old at the time of the incident, which was the first time he had been in Granny's Rocker. Loomis and four of his friends were at Granny's Rocker one and one-half hours before the fanny contest, during which time Loomis had a sip of a gin and tonic and a few glasses of beer. He testified that after the winner of the fanny contest was announced, she walked within six feet of him. Loomis testified that everyone in the area was commenting, "We vote for you, number five" and "You're hot." After the girl walked past, Loomis was tapped on the shoulder by an unidentified man who said, "Let my old lady through." Loomis testified that he tried to calm the man, but the man pushed him and then started punching him in the face. The two men continued fighting, and Loomis's ear was bitten in the altercation.

Continued

Continued

* * *

Jeffrey Loomis's friend, Jennifer McFall, testified that . . . [a]fter the fanny contest she heard names being called . . . She . . . turned and saw Jeffrey Loomis thrown against the foosball table and an unidentified man climb on top of him and bite his ear. McFall testified: "I stood there for awhile just shocked, then ran to the back of the bar to grab some help because no one—it took them awhile to get there before I seen [sic] anybody actually come up to help the [sic] fight. I ran to the back of the bar and I yelled at two of the back bouncers to get some help up there, and that had been two, three, maybe four minutes, the fight had been going on, so I finally ran back there and grabbed somebody." She testified that it was so crowded at Granny's Rocker that night that it took her a while to get back and look for the security personnel. She testified that it took three or four security personnel to stop the fight. McFall further testified that before the incident, she frequented Granny's Rocker approximately two or three times a week. She had seen the fanny contest approximately 10 to 15 times. She opined that the crowd at Granny's Rocker was rowdiest by far on Wednesday nights and that the fanny contest seemed to spawn rowdiness.

* * *

Daniel Glavin, another friend of plaintiff's, testified that after the fanny contest one of the contestants walked past them, and Loomis said something like, "We were rooting for you" or "Nice job." Glavin testified that Loomis did not touch the girl. An unidentified man came over to Loomis and said "Leave the girl alone." Loomis put his arm around the man and said, "I don't have a problem with you." The man put his beer down and punched Loomis in the face . . . Glavin testified that from the time the first punch was thrown until the time Loomis headed outside approximately five to seven minutes elapsed. During that time security personnel were not involved in the confrontation.

Denzel Whitehead testified that he and a friend were at Granny's Rocker the night of the incident. He watched a contestant from the fanny contest walk past the plaintiff, and the plaintiff put his arm around her. Whitehead testified: "I seen what was going on so I stood up on a chair and told him not to mess with her because this guy over here is going to hurt you, and by then the other guy was already there and he pushed him, and that's when the other guy grabbed him."

The foregoing review of the record discloses that there was evidence that Wednesday nights at Granny's Rocker are particularly crowded and that a rowdy crowd is attracted to or developed by the fanny contest.

* * *

No evidence was presented as to the placement of security personnel or of any actions taken by personnel once the altercation began. In fact, there was evidence that security never did get involved in stopping the altercation. Consequently, evidence was presented that the altercation was reasonably foreseeable by Granny's Rocker and that defendant could have prevented it or could have at least interfered in the altercation prior to Loomis sustaining the injuries to his ear.

A possessor of land who holds it open to the public is under a duty to the members of the public who enter in response to his invitation to protect them against unreasonable risk of physical harm.

* * *

Granny's Rocker argues that the jury's verdict is against the manifest weight of the evidence. In support of this claim defendant argues that the evidence establishes that it acted reasonably

Continued

Continued

given the circumstances that were known, or should have been known, by the defendant at the time of plaintiff's injury. It is axiomatic that unless a jury verdict is unreasonable, arbitrary, or not supported by the evidence it will not be disturbed on review.

* * *

The fanny contest draws a large and rowdy crowd. . . Moreover, evidence was presented that, given the large crowd, access to security personnel was difficult, and security personnel did not even assist in the altercation until after several minutes had passed. Given the evidence, we have not found . . . any legitimate basis for disturbing the jury's verdict that defendant should be held liable.. . .

Affirmed.

Questions

1. As a matter of law, why was Granny's Rocker adjudged negligent?
2. Does this decision mean that a bar is always liable if a fight breaks out and patrons are injured? Explain.
3. A plaintiff's husband became intoxicated at a floating restaurant on a river. Security personnel escorted the husband to a stool near the ramp exiting the restaurant. Thereafter, the husband fell into the river and drowned. No one observed the incident. The plaintiff claimed that the restaurant failed to provide safe premises. How would you rule on that claim? Explain. [See *Willingham* v. *Speciality Restaurants Corp., Inc.,* Michigan *Lawyers Weekly,* October 18, 1993, p. 21A (unpublished opinion, Michigan Court of Appeals).]

III. Criminal Law

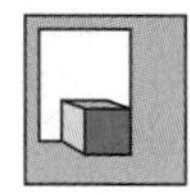

white-collar crime. Law violations by corporations or by managerial and executive personnel in the course of their professional duties.

As you build your managerial career or your own business, you will face the discouraging reality that crime is commonplace in corporate life. Of course, we all understand that shoplifters are a multibillion dollar drag on the bottom line of retailers, and employee theft is routine and very expensive. However, the really big bill to society is in the form of **white-collar crime,** where businesspeople themselves, people generally similar to you and your friends, engage in crime against their organization, competitors, and the general public. Crimes such as embezzlement, theft, and fraud may be committed by employees against their employers. Corporations themselves often become criminals in schemes such as price-fixing, environmental degradation, tax evasion, and securities fraud. Ultimately, the consumer is the victim in all of these wrongs.

White-collar crime is estimated to cost businesses some $50 billion annually.[6] The total cost to society is astronomical. For example, tax fraud losses are estimated to total 10 times our annual bill for all street crimes.[7] Health care fraud alone is estimated to cost every U.S. family about $500 annually.[8] Commercial crime reaches into every corner of our lives. Counterfeit clothing (garments illegally displaying a famous label such as Guess or Disney) from outlaw manufacturers is estimated to earn $70 to $100 billion annually, a figure approximately equal to the amount earned by the legitimate, properly licensed industry.[9]

Tax fraud losses are estimated to total 10 times our annual bill for all street crimes.

Contrary to our widespread fear, street crime apparently has been declining in America since the mid-1970s.

Crime Abroad. Total crime rates in the United States remain the highest in the world, but contrary to our widespread fear, street crime apparently has been declining in America since the mid-1970s. In 1975, one in three houses was personally affected by crime; that figure had fallen to one in four by 1994.[10] Street crime is climbing rapidly in nations where it had previously not been a major problem (e.g., Hungary, Scandinavia, and the United Kingdom).[11] As *USA Today* reports, white-collar crime is blossoming in the United States and many other nations:

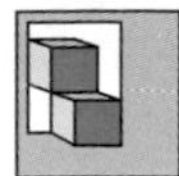

> One group of offenses that appears to be escalating everywhere in the Western world and in high-tech societies elsewhere is white-collar crime—from breach of trust and fraud to computer theft. It is expected to continue unabated in the near future. Few countries have been able to gain a good perspective on types and amounts of these crimes as they are difficult to define, discover, enforce, and adjudicate, and there is little government or public support to place priority on curtailing them. Yet, in Russia, authorities say nearly all businesses in Moscow and other major cities must pay "protection" money to organized groups.[12]

Public Policy Question

How do you explain the dramatic, worldwide rise in crime, both in the streets and in commercial life?

A. FRAUD

Suppose your management career is going well, but you want to achieve greater independence and more money. You hear about a new business opportunity labeled "Hollywood Pop," which promises $6,000 a year in earnings if you invest $6,000 in a flavored-popcorn machine.[13] Many investors did just that, but according to the Federal Trade Commission, they were unable to achieve any profits.[14] The FTC secured a restraining order against the Florida company, but not before Hollywood Pop allegedly had gained several million dollars. In 1995, federal and state regulators, through Project Telesweep, identified about 100 companies that were believed to be engaging in fraudulent business opportunity schemes across the United States.

A fraudulent scheme, such as that alleged in the Hollywood Pop case, can be the subject of both criminal charges and a civil tort action, as mentioned earlier in this chapter. Fraud takes many forms. Telemarketing fraud is said to be America's largest and fastest growing scam, costing Americans about $40 billion annually.[15] Bank fraud and other forms of white-collar bank crimes may cost society $100 for every dollar stolen in conventional bank robberies.[16] The list of fraudulent schemes is limited only by the imagination of clever white-collar criminals.

The Law of Fraud. All states have laws attacking fraud, in either its criminal or civil form, or both. In addition to phony investment schemes, most states forbid the sale of worthless products and such practices as issuing fraudulent checks or short-weighting items for sale. The federal Wire and Mail Fraud Act has been a very powerful weapon in attacking crime that can be construed to involve fraudulent acts and accomplished via the mails or through interstate telephone service.

Profile Perspective: The American Honda bribery prosecution was, in part, an example of mail fraud in that bribes, in some instances, were accomplished through the mails. More generally, American Honda itself argued that it was a victim of fraud in that the company had suffered direct financial losses because of the conspiracy and would suffer long-term injury to its reputation.

B. Bribery

bribe. Anything of value given or taken with the corrupt intent to influence an official in the performance of her or his duties.

What would you do if a **bribe** is part of the price you must pay to secure a business you have sought for years?

Profile Perspective: Georgia realtor Bob Foster was a Honda motorcycle dealer in Athens, Georgia, in 1979. He was hoping to be awarded a Honda auto dealership. Honda's district manager came in one day and, according to Foster, asked to speak in private. According to Foster, the manager said, "Nobody really loves you but your momma, and everybody else got to pay a little cash up front."[17] Uncertain, Foster asked the manager what he meant, and according to Foster, the reply was that a nice location in Athens ought to be worth at least $20,000 and the title to a new, nine-passenger Ford station wagon. Foster says that he then told the manager to get out of his store. The franchise went to someone else. Recently, that same manager was tried in New Hampshire in the Honda bribery trial. Foster was there and, after the sentencing, stopped the manager in the courthouse to say, "You told me one time that nobody loves you but your momma, and everybody else got to pay a little cash up front. Well, this is your cash up front, sir."[18]

Will you do as Foster says he did when taking or giving a bribe might give a big boost to your business career? Broadly, a bribe is intentionally offering or taking anything of value in corrupt payment for the purpose of influencing conduct, that is, a breach of duty in return for a favor. Note that the act of *offering* a bribe, whether accepted or not, constitutes a crime. As illustrated by the Honda case, bribery among businesspeople can be a serious problem, but we have given more attention in recent years to dealing with bribes directed to government officials. The Foreign Corrupt Practices Act specifically forbids bribes to foreign officials to secure business except for minor grease to expedite routine government action. Giving money or gifts to government officials in this country is criminal conduct if the required criminal intent can be established.

Ethics/Public Policy Questions

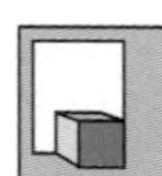

1. How do we distinguish an unlawful bribe from a legitimate business incentive plan?
2. Were your parents guilty of bribery (not, of course, in the criminal sense) if they offered you money for good grades or favors for good behavior, or are you guilty of a bribe if you simply give a gift to your boss? Explain.

C. RICO

RICO. Federal organized crime law making it illegal to acquire or operate an enterprise by a pattern of racketeering behavior.

The Racketeer Influenced and Corrupt Organizations Act (RICO) is perhaps the most highly publicized and controversial of federal criminal statutes. Many states have also passed antiracketeering statutes. The federal act, approved in 1970, was aimed at curbing the influence of organized criminal elements in legitimate business operations. The act was initially directed to organized crime, but lawyers gradually began to stretch RICO across a variety of rather ordinary commercial cases such as fraud, antitrust, and inside trading. [In 1995, the Private Securities Litigation Reform Act (see Chapter 10) expressly eliminated securities fraud from the list of wrongs to which RICO may be applied, although a RICO action can be sought if the securities fraud resulted in a criminal conviction.]

In recent years, RICO has even been applied to cases outside what we think of as commercial activity. The striking reach of RICO was well illustrated in a 1994 Supreme Court decision in which the justices unanimously ruled that abortion-rights activists may use the law against protesters who endeavor to close abortion clinics.[19] Because RICO permits recoveries that triple the actual damages sustained, the decision could open protesters to crippling claims. However, the Court's ruling did not address the substantive question of whether protesters have actually violated RICO in pursuing antiabortion activities.

RICO provides for both criminal and civil actions.

Criminal RICO. The act forbids (1) using income derived from a "pattern of racketeering activity" to establish or operate an interstate enterprise, (2) using a pattern of racketeering activity to acquire or maintain an interest in an interstate enterprise, (3) using a pattern of racketeering activity to conduct or participate in conducting an interstate enterprise, or (4) conspiring to do any of the foregoing.

A pattern of racketeering requires a showing that the defendant committed at least two crimes covered by the act within a 10-year period. The crimes must be related and continuing (or raise the threat of continuing) so that they amount to a pattern. Four categories of crime are covered by RICO: (1) commission of violent acts, including murder, extortion, arson, and so on; (2) provision of illegal goods and services, such as prostitution, pornography, and drugs; (3) corruption in labor relations or in state or federal governments; and (4) commercial fraud. Criminal penalties include imprisonment for up to 20 years and large fines.

Civil RICO. The government can also seek civil penalties under RICO, including dissolving the organization, and individuals can seek treble (triple) damages for their losses. The treble damages provision has encouraged attorneys to find imaginative ways of bringing civil RICO actions. Indeed, the Honda dealers who are suing American Honda (following the huge bribery scandal that we have been examining) strengthened their negligence and breach of contract claims by adding RICO and its treble damages possibilities to their allegations. Thus, under both its criminal and civil provisions, critics argue, the courts have allowed an expansion of RICO from its original organized crime agenda.

D. Regulatory Crimes

Government rules regulating business are the core of this text. Most of our discussion is devoted to the civil side of those laws; but at both the federal and state levels, many government regulation of business statutes also include criminal penalties. Those statutes are discussed throughout the text, but we will merely note here that many environmental statutes, the federal securities laws, the Occupational Safety and Health Act, the Sherman Antitrust Act, and others provide for both civil and criminal penalties. The *Park* case, below, involves an alleged regulatory crime. We should also note that federal prosecutions of businesses under those criminal provisions are not very common. In fiscal year 1994, the federal Justice Department brought just 250 cases where the lead charge alleged serious violations of environmental, job safety, or consumer laws. During that same year the Justice Department brought more than 51,000 other prosecutions, most of them for drug violations.[20]

E. Criminal Liability for Managers and Corporations

Suppose your first job begins with a management training program in which you are learning statistical quality control for a tire manufacturer. You have moved across America, you have college loans to pay, you are a bit homesick, and your boss seems utterly uninterested in your personal problems. In short, you are under stress. Then, in doing tests on a new tire to be supplied to the government, you discover that the tire does not meet contract standards. You tell your boss, who says, "Well, forget what you learned in those books. Make it work. We're way behind on this project. My job is on the line and so is yours. See that this test comes out the way we need it." What would you do?

If you did as instructed by, for example, falsely completing the necessary government forms, and someone was injured because of a defective tire, you might be conscience-stricken for your life. Would you also be a criminal? If you falsified government documents, certainly that would be the case. What if someone died? Would you then be guilty of manslaughter or some such crime? Would your boss? The officers and directors? The corporation itself?

The law is murky in this area, but we are able to say: (1) individuals are liable for their own crimes even if committed at the behest of a boss or an organization, and (2) if a boss initiated a conspiracy as described above, he or she has engaged in criminal conduct.

Increasingly, courts are finding corporations themselves responsible for crimes. The general rule in the federal courts is that a corporation is liable for the criminal acts of all of its employees. However, state law varies considerably. If the act was authorized by a director, officer, or high-level manager, all states are likely to find corporate criminal responsibility. If the act was committed by a subordinate and not authorized, the corporation might still be liable in many states under ***respondeat superior*** (let the master answer) reasoning. If authorization cannot be proven, the prosecution would not be able to establish intent, a critical ingredient in proof of a crime in this country. That is, an individual ordinarily cannot be guilty of a crime unless he or she intended the act in question. Since a corporation has no mind, it cannot have intent (but see our discussion of this issue in Chapter 3, Business Organizations). However, some states have eliminated the intent requirement for certain crimes with broad public welfare implications such as some antitrust and securities violations.

respondeat superior. "Let the master respond." Doctrine holding the employer liable for negligent acts committed by an employee while in the course of employment.

What then about officers and directors? If they commit, abet, authorize, or request the criminal behavior, then they too are criminals. But what if criminal behavior occurs deep in the organization where an officer can scarcely be expected to know about day-to-day activity? Could she or he, nonetheless, be criminally liable for the conduct of subordinates? The next case explores that possibility.

What about officers and directors? If they commit, abet, authorize, or request the criminal behavior, then they are criminals.

CASE

United States v. Park

421 U.S. 658 (1970)

Facts

John R. Park was president of Acme Markets, a national retail food chain with 36,000 employees, 874 stores, and 16 warehouses. Acme, headquartered in Philadelphia, pleaded guilty to numerous violations of the Federal Food, Drug, and Cosmetic Act for failing to maintain sanitary conditions in some of its warehouses. Park pleaded not guilty. Park had received government notice of the problems. Acme's Baltimore division vice president took steps to remedy the situation, but a second inspection found continuing violations. At trial, Park testified that he was responsible for the entire operation of the company but that he left sanitation details to "dependable subordinates." He had conferred with his vice president for legal affairs, was assured that corrective action was underway, and felt that he couldn't improve on what was already being done. He did concede that as CEO he was responsible for "any result which occurs in our company." Park argued that he was not personally responsible for the situation, but he was convicted. His conviction was reversed on appeal and the Supreme Court granted certiorari.

* * *

Chief Justice Burger

I

The question presented by the Government's petition for certiorari in *United States* v. *Dotterweich* and the focus of this Court's opinion, was whether "the manager of a corporation, as well as the corporation itself, may be prosecuted under the Federal Food, Drug, and Cosmetic Act of 1938 for the introduction of misbranded and adulterated articles into interstate commerce."

* * *

[T]his Court looked to the purposes of the Act and noted that they "touch phases of the lives and health of people which, in the circumstances of modern industrialism, are largely beyond self-protection." It observed that the Act is of "a now familiar type" which "dispenses with the conventional requirement for criminal conduct—awareness of some wrongdoing. In the interest of the larger good it puts the burden of acting at hazard upon a person otherwise innocent but standing in responsible relation to a public danger."

Central to the Court's conclusion that individuals other than proprietors are subject to the criminal provisions of the Act was the reality that "the only way in which a corporation can act is through the individuals who act on its behalf."

* * *

At the same time, however, the Court was aware of the concern . . . that literal enforcement "might operate too harshly by sweeping within its condemnation any person however remotely entangled in the proscribed shipment." A limiting principle, in the form of "settled doctrines of criminal law" defining those who "are responsible for the commission of a misdemeanor," was available. In this context, the Court concluded, those doctrines dictated that the offense was committed "by all who . . . have . . . a responsible share in the furtherance of the transaction which the statute outlaws."

* * *

Continued

Continued

II

The rationale of the interpretation given the Act in *Dotterweich,* as holding criminally accountable the persons whose failure to exercise the authority and supervisory responsibility reposed in them by the business organization resulted in the violation complained of, has been confirmed in our subsequent cases. Thus, the Court has reaffirmed the proposition that "the public interest in the purity of its food is so great as to warrant the imposition of the highest standard of care on distributors." . . .

Courts of Appeals have recognized that those corporate agents vested with the responsibility, and power commensurate with that responsibility, to devise whatever measures are necessary to ensure compliance with the Act bear a "responsible relationship" to, or have a "responsible share" in, violations.

Thus *Dotterweich* and the cases which have followed reveal that in providing sanctions which reach and touch the individuals who execute the corporate mission—and this is by no means necessarily confined to a single corporate agent or employee—the Act imposes not only a positive duty to seek out and remedy violations when they occur but also, and primarily, a duty to implement measures that will insure that violations will not occur. The requirements of foresight and vigilance imposed on responsible corporate agents are beyond question demanding, and perhaps onerous, but they are no more stringent than the public has a right to expect of those who voluntarily assume positions of authority in business enterprises whose services and products affect the health and well-being of the public that supports them.

The Act does not, as we observed in *Dotterweich,* make criminal liability turn on "awareness of some wrongdoing" or "conscious fraud." The duty imposed by Congress on responsible corporate agents is, we emphasize, one that requires the highest standard of foresight and vigilance, but the Act, in its criminal aspect, does not require that which is objectively impossible. The theory upon which responsible corporate agents are held criminally accountable for "causing" violations of the Act permits a claim that a defendant was "powerless" to prevent or correct the violation to "be raised defensively at a trial on the merits." If such a claim is made, the defendant has the burden of coming forward with evidence, but this does not alter the Government's ultimate burden of proving beyond a reasonable doubt the defendant's guilt, including his power, in light of the duty imposed by the Act, to prevent or correct the prohibited condition. Congress has seen fit to enforce the accountability of responsible corporate agents dealing with products which may affect the health of consumers by penal sanctions cast in rigorous terms, and the obligation of the courts is to give them effect so long as they do not violate the Constitution.

III

We cannot agree with the Court of Appeals that it was incumbent upon the District Court to instruct the jury that the Government had the burden of establishing "wrongful action" in the sense in which the Court of Appeals used that phrase. The concept of a "responsible relationship" to, or a "responsible share" in, a violation of the Act indeed imports some measure of blameworthiness; but it is equally clear that the Government establishes a prima facie case when it introduces evidence sufficient to warrant a finding by the trier of the facts that the defendant had, by reason of his position in the corporation, responsibility and authority either to prevent in the first instance, or promptly to correct, the violation complained of, and that he failed to do so . . .

Reversed.

Continued

Continued

Questions

1. Why was Park found guilty?
2. Why was the specific standard of proof under the Federal Food, Drug, and Cosmetic Act crucial to the outcome of this case?
3. What defense is afforded to corporate executives under the terms of the Federal Food, Drug, and Cosmetic Act?
4. Butch Stanko started the Cattle King Packing Company in Adams County, Colorado, in 1981. Stanko allegedly instructed employees to circumvent the Federal Meat Inspection Act by such practices as mixing inedible scraps with good meat and reshipping spoiled meat to buyers who had previously rejected that meat. Stanko moved to Scottsbluff, Nebraska, but kept in touch by phone and visits. Was either the company or Stanko liable for criminal violations as provided for under FMIA? Decide. Explain. [See *United States v. Cattle King Packing Co. Inc.*, 793 F.2d 232 (1986).]

Ethics/Public Policy Question

1. Should we expect Park and similarly situated CEOs to be personally responsible for all of the details of company operations at least where they knew or should have known about those operations? Explain.

Indemnification. Liability concerns discourage some people from becoming officers and directors in corporations. Consequently, many companies indemnify them for any losses they might sustain. Often, the costs of **indemnification** (defense expenses and any judgments or settlements) is borne through the purchase of insurance policies by the corporation.

Liability concerns discourage some people from becoming officers and directors in corporations.

indemnification. Corporate policy to compensate officers and directors for losses sustained in defending themselves against litigation associated with their professional duties where those duties were performed with reasonable business judgment.

F. Punishment

Profile Perspective: Throughout this chapter, we have been reflecting on the $15 million bribery case involving American Honda executives. As noted at the beginning of the chapter, perhaps the biggest player in the scheme, Stanley J. Cardiges, who allegedly collected as much as $5 million in cash and gifts, was sentenced to five years in prison and fined $364,000 after pleading guilty and agreeing to testify against other defendants. He could have been sentenced to 35 years in prison and fined $1 million. Was the court too lenient with Cardiges even if his testimony was critical in other prosecutions? The materials that follow explain the federal sentencing process.

Guidelines. At the state level, punishment for white-collar crimes, in theory at least, serves the purposes of removing the criminal from open society, deterring further crime, and providing personal rehabilitation that we hope for in connection with street crime. The much more interesting punishment questions for businesspeople are at the federal level, where Congress authorized **federal sentencing guidelines** to achieve greater predictability and consistency in punishments for both white-collar and street crime. The guidelines, which are binding on federal judges, were developed by the U.S. Sentencing Commission and went into effect in 1987 for individuals and in 1991 for organizations.

federal sentencing guidelines. Standards established by the U.S. Sentencing Commission that rank the seriousness of individual and organizational federal crimes and provide sentences that, with little flexibility, must be applied to those crimes.

The guidelines for individuals use a grid to categorize and rank over 2,000 federal crimes based on their seriousness. Additional factors such as the criminal history of the offender and specific characteristics of the offense (e.g., was a gun used?) are also given weight. By plotting the crime on the grid according to its seriousness, ranking, and the additional factors, the judge determines the range of sentence that must be imposed. Within that limited range (e.g., 21–27 months), the judge has latitude to lower or raise the sentence based on such considerations as community involvement, or special skills used in committing the crime (e.g., electronics knowledge used in theft via an ATM).

The organizational guidelines permit fines up to many millions of dollars. A base fine is computed according to the seriousness of the offense and the money gained or lost as a consequence of the crime. That fine may then be raised or lowered according to a culpability score. That score can be lowered if the corporation has an effective program for preventing and detecting violations, but the corporation can be placed on probation if an effective compliance program is not in place. The guidelines, both individual and corporate, have been vigorously criticized.

Summary

Legal Review. Many kinds of torts and crimes can affect business practice. We began by reviewing the three categories of torts: intentional, negligent, and strict liability. In doing so, we examined a lengthy list of specific tort wrongs, including assault, battery, defamation, nuisance, and trespass, along with the tests and defenses associated with each. Our criminal law survey began with common white-collar crimes, including fraud, bribery, and racketeering. Then we turned to an analysis of the rather murky area of crimes arising from work on the job. We examined some of those circumstances in which managers, officers, directors, and the corporation itself may be guilty of criminal conduct. We closed the chapter by thinking about the federal sentencing rules that establish guidelines for judges' decisions about criminal sentencing. Of course, the entire chapter was built in part on the interesting American Honda bribery case and all of its implications in both tort and criminal law.

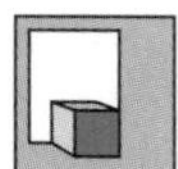

Ethics/Public Policy Review. Tort and criminal law, in and of themselves, represent ethical judgments. By definition, those who commit either a civil or criminal wrong have, in most instances, fallen short of our ethical preferences. Either intentionally or carelessly, they have caused harm to others. So both tort and criminal law, to a considerable extent, reflect our sense that it is simply wrong to defame, mislead, strike, steal, bribe, and so on. In some instances, we provide defenses and excuses, of course, but fundamentally, in designating certain actions as compensable in tort suits or as punishable in criminal suits, we have spoken as a society and said that those behaviors are ethically unacceptable.

Economics Review. The history of 20th century American economic policy is, in good part, a search for the most desirable balance between government intervention and market freedom. Now that we are at the end of the chapter, we should think about that search in the context of tort and criminal law. Should we roll back the clock a bit more closely to the time when the force of the free market and self-regulation (ethics) were the primary constraints on improper business behavior? Do you have the impression that tort and criminal law have harmed our efficiency, innovation, or productivity and caused our personal freedom to be devalued? On the other hand, is the market simply incapable of providing sufficient protection against the kinds of wrongs we have surveyed here?

Chapter Questions—Law

1. Maintaining security and thus avoiding tort injury claims have become an important part of many businesses' agendas.

   Two teenagers were allowed to enter a Canton, Ohio, gun show. The two boys stole several pistols and at least six knives, and one of the boys, then 13 years old, bought ammunition at the show. One of the boys later said that the "guns were just laying around." The boys stole a car and were crushing garbage cans and trashing lawns when chased by two men. In the chase, one of the pursuers was shot and paralyzed from the waist down. He sued the gun show for negligence. How would you rule? Explain. [See *Pavlides* v. *Niles Gun Show,* 637 N.E.2d 404 (1994), for an appellate court review of the law in this case. For a journalistic account of the jury's conclusion, see Milo Geyelin, "Ohio Jury . . . for Injuries from Stolen Weapon," *The Wall Street Journal,* May 18, 1995, p. B4.]
2. At this writing, Hormel Foods is suing Jim Henson Productions because of the use of the name "Spa'am" in a movie, *Muppet Treasure Island.* Hormel makes Spam canned lunch meat. Hormel says that the movie character Spa'am is a "grotesque and noxious appearing wild boar" that is intentionally portrayed as "evil in porcine form." The result, says Hormel, is that Hormel's trademark has been "tarnished" and that Spam has been "falsely disparaged." How would you rule on Hormel's product disparagement claim? Explain.
3. Nadine L. Peterson, a guest at the Palm Springs, California, Marquis Hotel, suffered severe head injuries when she fell while taking a shower in a bathtub. She sued both Kohler, the maker of the tub, and the hotel. She said the tub was defective because it was too slippery and lacked proper safety features such as grab rails. She settled with Kohler for $600,000. Is the hotel liable for the presence of a defective product on its premises? Explain. [For a journalistic account, see Margaret A. Jacobs, "California Supreme Court Finds Flaws in Ruling and Reverses Itself," *The Wall Street Journal,* August 30, 1995, p. B8.]
4. In 1981, students from the State University of New York at Alfred made arrangements with Edwin Clancy, the president of Penn Valley Resorts, for a dinner dance, including an open bar. One of the students, 20-year-old William Edward Frazer, Jr., consumed alcohol such that he was legally intoxicated, staggering, and slurring his speech. He died after the dance when he crashed his car. The state brought criminal charges, and at trial Penn Valley Resorts was found guilty of involuntary manslaughter, reckless endangerment, and two counts of furnishing liquor to minors and visibly intoxicated persons. Clancy knew that most of the students were not of legal drinking age. He served alcohol to Frazer even though Frazer was visibly intoxicated and also after commenting about that intoxication. Penn Valley appealed. Can a corporation be guilty of criminal conduct under these facts? Explain. [See *Commonwealth* v. *Penn Valley Resorts,* 494 A.2d 1139 (1985).]
5. In 1979, Philip and Wendy Kirkham were properly crossing a highway after departing their school bus. A truck owned by the Fortner LP Gas Company failed to stop and struck the children, killing Wendy and injuring Philip. The truck's brakes were determined to be "grossly defective." The Commonwealth of Kentucky prosecuted Fortner Corporation and a grand jury indicted it on manslaughter charges. Fortner moved to dismiss the indictment on the grounds that a corporation cannot commit manslaughter. Decide. Explain. [See *Commonwealth* v. *Fortner LP Gas Co.,* 610 S.W.2d 941 (Ky. 1980).]

6. Defendants O'Brien, Gallup, and Lyon sold underfunded health insurance to employer associations and misrepresented that the health plan was backed by a legitimate insurance carrier. The defendants falsely represented a contract with a nationally recognized insurance carrier to cover all medical claims over $50,000. Defendants diverted company money to personal uses. The defendants were prosecuted by the United States and found guilty of various criminal charges, including conspiracy, mail and wire fraud, and money laundering. At sentencing, the judge enhanced (increased) the defendants' penalties under a provision in the federal sentencing guidelines that permits enhancement when the defendant "should have known" the victim was "unusually vulnerable." A victim can be "unusually vulnerable due to age [or] physical or mental condition." Here, individuals with medical problems could not get their claims paid because of the defendants' fraud.
   a. Explain the defendants' argument that they should not be subject to the enhanced penalty.
   b. Decide whether the enhanced penalty should be applied.
   [See *U.S.* v. *O'Brien,* 50 F.3d 751 (9th Cir. 1995).]

Chapter Questions—Economics/Public Policy

1. The tort reform movement that is at the forefront of many legislators' agendas includes a 1995 Illinois provision limiting noneconomic damages to $500,000.
   a. Explain the proponents' argument that the cap will reduce litigation.
   b. Explain how tort victims may be hurt by the law beyond the fact that their potential recovery is now capped.
2. *a.* How might tort reform measures that eliminate punitive damages, eliminate joint and several liability, set caps on damages, and so forth actually encourage more trials?
   b. Assuming tort reforms are needed, make the argument that they should be accomplished at the federal level rather than by the individual states.
3. The conclusion of a Rand Institute for Civil Justice study: "In sum, emerging data suggest that the tort liability system serves too many people it shouldn't serve, or at least pays them too much, doesn't serve enough of the people it should serve, and doesn't serve many well enough." Comment. [See Martha Middleton, "A Changing Landscape," *ABA Journal* 81 (August 1995), p. 57.]
4. Lawyer Edward Sadowsky argues that "it is virtually impossible to detect discrimination in violation of the ADA" (Americans with Disabilities Act). Therefore, Sadowsky has called for criminal penalties for ADA violations. He says, "How is willful discrimination against persons covered under the ADA significantly different than a securities violation, bank fraud, falsification of loan documents, or other white-collar crime? . . . [I]t is unrealistic to expect broad-based voluntary compliance in the absence of criminal penalties."

   Should discrimination be treated as a crime? Explain. [See Edward Sadowsky, "Strengthening Enforcement of the ADA," *New York Law Journal,* August 15, 1994, p. 2.]
5. Under federal sentencing guidelines for corporations, compliance standards are established in part by the companies themselves. Corporate officers confer to acquire a sense of what other companies believe to be proper compliance in various situations, thus jointly arriving at industry norms for preventing and dealing with criminal behavior.

How might the practice of allowing companies to arrive at industry standards lead to an undercutting of the goals of the guidelines? [See Joe Davidson, "Corporate Sentencing Guidelines Have Snagged Mostly Small Firms," *The Wall Street Journal,* August 28, 1995, p. B5.]

Notes

1. James Bennet, "Four Former Honda Employees Sentenced in Kickback Case," *New York Times,* August 26, 1995, sec. 1, p. 35.
2. John O'Dell, "Ex-Honda Sales Chief Admits Taking Bribes," *Los Angeles Times,* February 8, 1995, p. D1.
3. John O'Dell, "Ex-U.S. Honda Executive Gets 5-Year Term in Bribery Case," *Los Angeles Times,* August 26, 1995, p. D1.
4. See *Leichtman* v. *WLW Jacor Communs., Inc.,* 634 N.E.2d 697 (1994). For a case where the victim suffered an allergic reaction, see *Richardson* v. *Hennly,* 434 S.E. 2d 772 (1993).
5. Bennet, "Four Former Honda Employees," p. 35.
6. Richard Finkel, "Modern Gumshoes Investigate by the Numbers," *Connecticut Law Tribune,* July 24, 1995, p. S4.
7. Gene Stephens, "We Are Facing a Global Crime Wave," *USA Today Magazine* 124 (July 1995), p. 26.
8. Natalie Schrimpf, "Fight against Fraud Packs More Punches: Effort Stepped Up to Stem Billions Lost Yearly," *Crain's Detroit Business,* August 7, 1995, p. 13.
9. Anne O'Connor, "Investigators Wrinkle Plans of Clothing Counterfeiters," *Minneapolis Star Tribune,* August 4, 1995, p. 3B.
10. Stephens, "Global Crime Wave," p. 26.
11. Ibid.
12. Ibid.
13. Jeffrey Tannenbaum, "Undercover Blitz Targets Business-Opportunity Scams," *The Wall Street Journal,* July 19, 1995, p. B2.
14. Ibid.
15. George Kuempel, "State Targets Phone Fraud," *Dallas Morning News,* August 18, 1995, p. 1D.
16. Casey Wian, "Bank Fraud on the Rise in Southern California," *Moneyline,* transcript #1491-4, August 24, 1995.
17. Lindsay Chappell, "Billmyer Sentence Satisfies Ex-Dealer," *Automotive News,* October 9, 1995, p. 6.
18. Ibid.
19. *N.O.W.* v. *Scheidler,* 114 S.Ct. 798 (1994).
20. David Burnham, "The Feeble War on Corporate America," *Los Angeles Times,* December 29, 1995, p. B9.

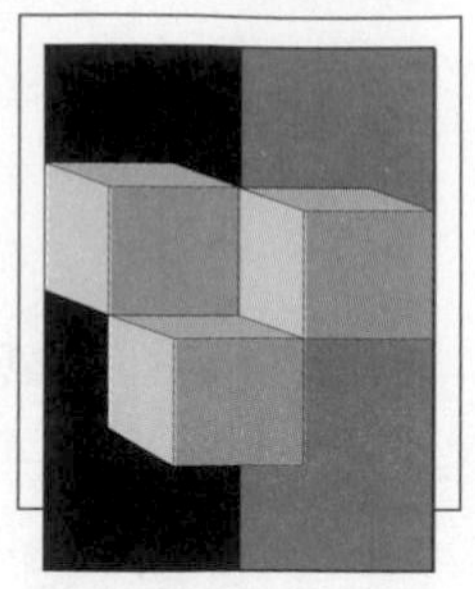

CHAPTER 14

PRODUCT LIABILITY

READER'S GUIDE

The forepart of Chapter 13, Business Torts and Crimes, introduced many of the personal injury claims (torts) that commonly emerge from business practice. Now we turn in this chapter to a subset of tort claims, product liability, that has taken on enormous importance in business strategy in recent years. Here we will survey the law of negligence, warranties, and strict liability, the three principal means of recovery for consumers injured by defective products. Throughout that survey we will consider the public policy implications of product liability law. Critics argue that our liability system requires reform, but consumer advocates and trial lawyers say that aggressive tort claims are necessary to discourage carelessness by the business community.

PROFILE

> The business of making small airplanes is all but dead in this country, wiped out mainly by product liability lawsuits.[1]

That 1991 pronouncement by *The Wall Street Journal* powerfully depicts the influence of product liability laws in the practice of American business. Today a key ingredient in a successful business is a plan for dealing with litigation costs. **Product liability** law addresses all those situations in which injuries result from defective products.

product liability. Refers to legal responsibility of manufacturers and sellers to compensate buyers, users, and, in some cases, bystanders, for harm from defective products.

In the early 1990s, as *The Wall Street Journal* observed, the single-engine plane industry in the United States was largely dead. The major American manufacturer, Cessna Aircraft of Wichita, Kansas, stopped making small planes in 1986. Its chief rival, Piper Aircraft, struggled with bankruptcy. Single-engine aircraft production in the United States fell from a peak of 13,000 units in 1977 to 444 in 1994.[2] For Cessna, employment fell from approximately 14,000 in the early 80s to fewer than 4,000 in 1986 when the company quit making single-engine planes and focused its attention on the business-plane market.[3] The problems were, in part, attributable to overproduction, high fuel costs, and recession, but the *Journal* argued that the chief cause was the legal system:

> [W]hat is happening now, according to practically every constituency except the lawyers, is a clear case of products-liability law eating a sick industry alive.[4]

Particularly troublesome for the small-plane companies is the so-called liability tail that accompanies their products. Airplanes must be built to last for many years, but because product liability claims ordinarily have no time limit, a manufacturer can be pursued for claims decades after the plane has left its control. The result is that insurance fees skyrocket, driving up airplane prices and frightening lenders and investors.[5]

The American Trial Lawyers Association blamed the small-plane industry's problems on poor management. Clearly, poor management did play a role, but ultimately Congress landed on the side of the plane companies by passing, in 1994, the General Aviation Revitalization Act, which offers protection against serious liability claims and limits claims involving planes that are more than 18 years old.[6] Cessna now believes that by 1998 it will be selling 2,000 small planes annually, resulting in 1,500 new jobs.[7] At this writing, Piper Aircraft of Vero Beach, Florida, continues to struggle with bankruptcy but expects to approximately double its production of small planes and increase employment from 410 to 535.[8]

I. NEGLIGENCE

In dangerously simplified terms, **negligence** is a breach of the duty of due care. To paraphrase *Black's Law Dictionary,* a negligent act is the failure to do what a reasonable person, guided by those considerations that ordinarily regulate human affairs, would do or doing what a reasonable person would not do. Thus, a producer or distributor has a duty to exercise reasonable care in the entire stream of events associated with the development and sale of a product. In designing, manufacturing, testing, repairing and warning of potential dangers, those in the chain of production and distribution must meet the standard of the reasonably prudent person. Failure to do so constitutes negligence. Furthermore, rather recent decisions extend potential liability to those situations in which a product is being put to an unintended but reasonably foreseeable *misuse.*

negligence. Failure to do something that a reasonable person would do under the circumstances, or an action that a reasonable and prudent person would not take under the circumstance.

Historically, consumers dealt face to face with producers and could bring breach of contract claims if injured by a defective product. However, the development in the modern era of multilayered production and distribution systems eliminated that contractual relationship between producer and consumer, making it difficult for consumers to sue producers. Then in a famous 1916 New York State decision *(McPherson* v. *Buick Motor Co.)*,[9] brilliant jurist Benjamin Cardozo held that a consumer could bring a negligence claim against the manufacturer of a defective automobile even though the consumer did not purchase the car directly from that manufacturer. Cardozo's view has since been broadly adopted, thus permitting victims of negligence to bring actions against all careless parties in the chain of production and distribution.

To establish a successful negligence claim, the plaintiff must meet each of the following requirements:

1. *Duty*—The plaintiff must establish that the defendant owed a **duty of due care** to the plaintiff. In general, the standard applied is that of the fictitious reasonable man or woman. That reasonable person acts prudently, sensibly, and responsibly. The standard of reasonableness depends, of course, on the circumstances of the situation.

duty of due care. Standard of conduct expected of a reasonable, prudent person under the circumstances.

2. *Breach of duty*—The plaintiff must demonstrate that the defendant breached the duty of due care by engaging in conduct that did not conform to the reasonable person standard. Breach of the duty of due care may result from either the commission of a careless act or the omission of a reasonable, prudent act. Would a reasonable man or woman discharge a firearm in a public park? Would a reasonable person foresee that failure to illuminate one's front entry steps might lead to a broken limb?
3. *Causation*
   a. *Cause in fact*—Did the defendant's breach of the duty of due care actually cause the harm in question? Commonly, the "but for" test is applied to determine cause in fact. For example, but for the defendant's failure to stop at the red light, the plaintiff pedestrian would not have been struck down in the crosswalk.
   b. *Proximate cause*—The plaintiff must establish that the defendant's actions were the **proximate cause** of the injury. As a matter of policy, is the defendant's conduct sufficiently connected to the plaintiff's injury as to justify imposing liability? Many injuries arise from a series of events—some of them wildly improbable. Did the defendant's negligence lead directly to the plaintiff's harm, or did some intervening act break the causal link between the defendant's negligence and the harm? For example, the community's allegedly negligent maintenance resulted in a blocked road, forcing the plaintiff to detour. While on the detour route, the plaintiff's vehicle was struck by a plane attempting to land at a nearby airport. Was the community's negligence the proximate cause of the plaintiff's injury?[10]

proximate cause. Occurrences that in a natural sequence, unbroken by potent intervening forces, produce an injury that would not have resulted in the absence of those occurrences.

4. *Injury*—The plaintiff must have sustained injury, and, due to problems of proof, that injury often must be physical.

Profile Perspective: In building a business involving a hazardous activity like flying, negligence litigation is simply inevitable. Very often, the problem that arises is one of proximate cause. For example, the plaintiff/pilot, having been seriously injured when his small Cessna plane crashed, may claim that the plane was improperly designed for the turbulence that accompanies stormy weather. The manufacturer will deny that claim and argue that both the cause in fact and the proximate cause of the pilot's injury were pilot error, that is, negligence on the part of the pilot. In the case that follows we see how the manufacturer of a seemingly harmless product, a game, can become the defendant in a complex product liability litigation.

CASE

Watters v. TSR, Inc.

904 F.2d 378 (6th Cir. 1990)

Facts

Johnny Burnett, described by his mother, Sheila Watters, as a "devoted" Dungeons & Dragons player, killed himself. (The record did not disclose his age at the time of death.) Mrs. Watters blamed the death on her son's absorption in the game. She claimed that "he lost control of his own independent will and was driven to self-destruction."

Dungeons & Dragons is an adventure game set in an imaginary ancient world; the players assume the roles of various characters as suggested by illustrated booklets. The play is orchestrated by a player labeled the "Dungeon Master." The outcome of the play is determined by using dice in conjunction with tables provided with the game. The game's materials do not mention suicide or guns. More than one million copies of the game have been sold, many to schools where it is used as a learning tool.

In federal district court, Mrs. Watters brought a wrongful death claim against TSR, the manufacturer of Dungeons & Dragons. TSR sought a summary judgment on various grounds, including (1) TSR owed no duty to stop distributing the game or to warn about playing it, and (2) Johnny Burnett's suicide was an intervening or superseding cause of his death. Summary judgment was granted to TSR. Watters appealed.

* * *

Circuit Judge David A. Nelson

III

"Actionable negligence," under Kentucky law, "consists of a duty, a violation thereof, and consequent injury" . . . "Every person owes a duty to every other person to exercise *ordinary care* in his activities to prevent any *foreseeable injury* from occurring to such other person."

* * *

The plaintiff's complaint alleges that the defendant violated its duty of ordinary care in two respects: it disseminated Dungeons & Dragons literature to "mentally fragile persons," and it failed to warn that the "possible consequences" of playing the game might include "loss of control of the mental processes." To submit this case to a jury on either theory, it seems to us, would be to stretch the concepts of foreseeability and ordinary care to lengths that would deprive them of all normal meaning.

Continued

Continued

The defendant cannot be faulted, obviously, for putting its game on the market without attempting to ascertain the mental condition of each and every prospective player. The only practicable way of insuring that the game could never reach a "mentally fragile" individual would be to refrain from selling it at all—and we are confident that the courts of Kentucky would never permit a jury to say that simply by marketing a parlor game, the defendant violated its duty to exercise ordinary care.

As to the supposed breach of a duty to warn, Kentucky law imposes a general duty on manufacturer and suppliers to warn of dangers known to them but not known to persons whose use of the product can reasonably be anticipated . . .

Johnny Burnett was certainly one of the class of people whose use of the game could reasonably have been anticipated, and there is no contention that he or his mother, Mrs. Watters, knew of any danger in using it. (An affidavit executed by Mrs. Watters indicates that she knew the game was often played at the public library; that Johnny and his friends played the game constantly after school and on weekends over a period of several years; and that never, either before or during the period when he and his friends were immersed in the game, did Johnny cause his mother any problems.) But if Johnny's suicide was not foreseeable to his own mother, there is no reason to suppose that it was foreseeable to defendant TSR.

In moving for summary judgment on the breach of duty question, defendant TSR put Mrs. Watters to her proof on foreseeability and knowledge—on whether TSR knew of some danger that made the suicide foreseeable. Mrs. Watters was not free simply to rest on her pleadings; she was required, by affidavits, depositions, answers to interrogatories, or the like, to "designate 'specific facts showing that there [was] a genuine issue for trial'" . . . This she failed to do. Aside from one vague reference to hearsay about the game's "dangerous propensities"—Mrs. Watters' affidavit concluded with a sentence reading, in its entirety, "I have subsequently read in many publications including the *Paducah Sun* of the dangerous propensities of the game Dungeons & Dragons"—the record sets forth no "specific fact" showing that the defendant's game was in fact dangerous or that the defendant had knowledge of any danger when the materials that Johnny and his friends had been using for so many years were manufactured and sold.*

The actual content of the materials in question would hardly have given TSR reason to foresee that players of the game would become more susceptible to murder or suicide than non-players. The materials make it clear that Dungeons & Dragons is a "let's pretend" game, not an incitement to do anything more than exercise the imagination. And the imaginary world referred to in the booklets—a world of magical spells, hidden treasures, and fantastic monsters—does not appear to be a world in which people kill themselves or engage in acts of wanton cruelty toward other people. We are not dealing here with the kind of violence or depravity to which children can be exposed when they watch television, or go to the movies, or read the fairy tales of the Brothers Grimm, for example.

Television, movies, magazines, and books (including comic books) are far more pervasive than the defendant's games. Were the courts of Kentucky prepared to say that works of the imagination can be linked to a foreseeable danger of antisocial behavior, thereby giving rise to a duty

*We have found two decisions, not cited in the briefs, mentioning claims that Dungeons & Dragons has dangerous propensities. In *State* v. *Molitor,* 729 S.W.2d 551 (Mo.Ct.App.1987), where a young woman was tied up and strangled after an all-night houseparty devoted to listening to music, consuming liquor, smoking marijuana and practicing martial arts, the defendent sought to introduce expert testimony suggesting that he had been "desensitized." at some point by playing Dungeons & Dragons. The appellate court sustained exclusion of the testimony on relevance grounds and because the defendant's offer of proof made no showing that he had, in fact, been "desensitized." In *People* v. *Ventiquattro,* 138 App.Div.2d 925, 527 N.Y.S.2d 137 (1988), a 15-year-old boy who killed a companion with a shotgun gave the police several conflicting accounts of how the shooting occurred. In one account he stated he was playing the game Dungeons & Dragons and shot the victim while fantasizing that it was his job to exterminate evil. Whether this particular account was truthful, and whether TSR ever learned of it, we do not know.

Continued

Continued

to warn, one would expect to find Kentucky caselaw to that effect in lawsuits involving television networks, book publishers, or the like. There is no such caselaw. And what little authority exists outside Kentucky favors the defendant, not the plaintiff. See for example, *Zamora* v. *Columbia Broadcasting System,* 480 F.Supp. 199 (S.D.Fla. 1979) (no cause of action stated against three major television networks for allowing the plaintiffs' minor child to become so "intoxicated" by television violence that he was "stimulated, incited and instigated" to shoot and kill an elderly neighbor) [and] *Herceg* v. *Hustler Magazine, Inc.,* 565 F.Supp. 802 (S.D. Texas 1983) (absent an allegation of incitement, no claim stated against magazine for publishing a description of "auto-erotic asphyxiation" that allegedly prompted plaintiffs' decedent to hang himself).

* * *

IV

By itself, moreover, a breach of duty is not enough to warrant recovery; there can be no liability for negligence if the negligence is not shown to have "caused" the injury complained of. And the courts of Kentucky have long recognized that the chain of causation may be broken by "facts [that] are legally sufficient to constitute an intervening cause" . . .

Facts sufficient to constitute an intervening cause "are facts of such 'extraordinary rather than normal,' or 'highly extraordinary,' nature, unforeseeable in character, as to relieve the original wrongdoer of liability to the ultimate victim."

* * *

The fact of Johnny Burnett's suicide is undisputed. The third paragraph of Mrs. Watters' complaint affirmatively avers "[t]hat on the 29th day of September, 1987 the deceased departed this world as a direct and proximate result of a gun shot wound self inflicted by said deceased." Whether that extraordinary and tragic occurrence was or was not a "superseding cause" is thus a legal issue that must be resolved by the court.

Courts have long been rather reluctant to recognize suicide as a proximate consequence of a defendant's wrongful act . . . Generally speaking, it has been said, the act of suicide is viewed as "an independent intervening act which the original tortfeasor could not have reasonably [been] expected to foresee" . . .

There are several exceptions to the general rule. Where a person known to be suicidal is placed in the direct care of a jailer or other custodian, for example, and the custodian negligently fails to take appropriate measures to guard against the person's killing himself, the act of self destruction may be found to have been a direct and proximate consequence of the custodian's breach of duty. *Sudderth* v. *White,* 621 S.W.2d 33 (Ky. App. 1981) . . .

* * *

Johnny was not known to be suicidal, as far as the plaintiff has told us, and he was not placed in the care or custody of defendant TSR. Accordingly, the plaintiff can derive no benefit from cases such as *Sudderth* v. *White* . . . The fact is, unfortunately, that youth is not always proof against the strange waves of despair and hopelessness that sometimes sweep seemingly normal people to suicide, and we have no way of knowing that Johnny would not have committed suicide if he had not played Dungeons & Dragons. Finally, of course, it does not appear that Mrs. Watters can show that Johnny was delirious or psychotic, or that he acted under an irresistible impulse or while incapable of realizing what he was doing.

On the contrary, Mrs. Watters' affidavit shows affirmatively that Johnny Burnett, who lived in her household throughout his life, never caused Mrs. Watters any problems. He went to school regularly, and he took care of a paper route. The record contains no affidavit from a psychiatrist or similar expert

Continued

Continued

suggesting that he suffered from any psychosis. As far as the record discloses, no one had any reason to know that Johnny Burnett was going to take his own life. We cannot tell why he did so or what his mental state was at the time. His death surely was not the fault of his mother, or his school, or his friends, or the manufacturer of the game he and his friends so loved to play. Tragedies such as this simply defy rational explanation, and courts should not pretend otherwise.

Affirmed.

Questions

1. What was the central issue in this case?
2. What test does the court employ in determining whether the defendant, TSR, owed a duty to the deceased?
3. Why did the court conclude that the plaintiff, Watters, had failed to show that TSR had *caused* Johnny Burnett's death?
4. Plaintiff was seven month's pregnant and the mother of 17-month-old James. She was standing on the sidewalk, and James was in the street. A truck being negligently driven bore down on the boy, running him over. The shock caused the mother to miscarry and suffer actual physical and emotional injury. She brought suit against the driver for harm to herself and the infant child.
   a. What is the issue in this case?
   b. Decide the case. Explain.
   [See *Amaya* v. *Home Ice, Fuel & Supply Co.,* 379 P.2d 513 (Cal. S. Ct. 1963). But also see *Dillon* v. *Legg,* 441 P.2d 912 (Cal. S. Ct. 1968).]
5. Is a fireworks manufacturer liable for harm to children who ignited an explosive that had failed to detonate in the town public display the previous day? Explain.
6. The mother of a 12-year-old boy who died in a shooting accident when a gun he was playing with accidentally discharged sued *Boys Life,* a magazine published by the Boy Scouts of America. The mother claimed that the boy was influenced to experiment with a rifle after reading a 16-page firearms advertising section in the magazine.
   a. What product liability claims would the mother raise?
   b. What constitutional defense would the Boy Scouts raise?
   c. Decide. Explain.
   [See *Jan Way* v. *Boy Scouts of America,* 856 S.W.2d 230 (Tex. 1993).]

A. CLASSES OF NEGLIGENCE CLAIMS

Negligence claims emerging from defective products fall into three categories of analysis : (1) manufacturing defects, (2) design defects, and (3) inadequate warnings.

In 1992, then 79-year-old grandmother, Stella Liebeck, ordered breakfast at an Albuquerque, New Mexico, McDonald's and subsequently caused a sensation that made headlines around the world.

Manufacturing Defects. In building a business, it goes without saying that customers must be satisfied. McDonald's sells a billion cups of coffee each year, in part, because its coffee is extremely hot—180 to 190 degrees—which is exactly what its customers prefer and which, McDonald's believes, produces tastier coffee than the 140-145 degrees normally achieved at home. In 1992, then 79-year-old grandmother, Stella Liebeck, ordered breakfast at an Albuquerque, New Mexico, McDonald's and subsequently caused a sensation that made headlines around the world. While trying to get the top off the container, she spilled the coffee on her lap, resulting in severe burns. She was hospitalized and required skin grafts. She sought a settlement with McDonald's, but according to her family, McDonald's offered only $800.[11] Ms. Liebeck sued accusing McDonald's of gross negligence for selling coffee that was "unreasonably dangerous" and "defectively manufactured."[12]

compensatory damages. Damages that will compensate a party for actual losses due to an injury suffered.

punitive damages. Damages designed to punish flagrant wrongdoers and to deter them and others from engaging in similar conduct in the future.

A jury awarded Ms. Liebeck $160,000 in **compensatory** and $2.7 million in **punitive damages.** The jury found Ms. Liebeck 20 percent responsible for her own injury. The judge subsequently reduced the award to $640,000. The parties then settled out of court for an undisclosed amount. According to news reports, the jury awarded Ms. Liebeck $2.7 million in punitive damages because of what it perceived to be McDonald's callous attitude toward the accident and because of the many previous coffee-burn claims that had been filed against McDonald's.[13] The fallout from the case has been enormous. For example, Wendy's said it would temporarily halt the sale of hot chocolate because it might be too hot for children.[14] And, as *Newsweek* expressed it, Ms. Liebeck became a "poster lady" for the tort reform movement.[15]

res ipsa loquitur. "The thing speaks for itself." Rule of evidence establishing a presumption of negligence if the instrumentality causing the injury was in the exclusive control of the defendant, the injury would not ordinarily occur unless someone was negligent, and there is no evidence of other causes.

As we see then with the McDonald's coffee case, *improper manufacturing, handling, or inspection* of products often gives rise to negligence claims. However, the extremely complex process of producing, distributing, and using a product sometimes so obscures the root of the injury in question that proof of fault is nearly impossible to establish. In those circumstances, many courts have adopted the doctrine of ***res ipsa loquitur*** (the thing speaks for itself), which in some cases permits the court to infer the defendant's negligence even though that negligence cannot be proven—that is, the facts suggest that the plaintiff's injury must have resulted from the defendant's negligence, but the circumstances are such that the plaintiff is unable to prove negligence. A showing of *res ipsa loquitur* requires (1) the injury was caused by an instrumentality under the control of the defendant, (2) the accident ordinarily would not happen absent the defendant's negligence, and (3) there is no evidence of other causes for the accident.[16]

Design Defects. From Cessna's single-engine airplanes to five-gallon buckets (which may hold liquid sufficient for a child to drown) to automobile seat belts and on across the spectrum of American products, manufacturers must think about designing products in such a way as to anticipate and avoid consumer injury that might be attributable to defective design. In recent years, the Ford Motor Company has paid more than $110 million to settle 334 injury and death claims springing from accidents involving one of its sport utility vehicles, the Bronco II. The claimants have argued that the Bronco II's high, short, and narrow design makes it unusually susceptible to rolling over. In 1995, an Indiana jury awarded $62.4 million in damages against Ford in a Bronco II case, and a class action against Ford is pending at this writing. Ford intends to appeal the Indiana decision, and it has won several Bronco II litigations. Ford argues that the Bronco II, which was produced from 1983 to 1990, is safe; but its critics say that Ford knew the vehicle was dangerous before it went into production but proceeded without proper adjustments because it was in a race with General Motors for the sport utility market.[17]

risk/utility test. Measure of negligence holding that a product is negligently designed if the benefits of that product's design are outweighed by the risks that accompany that design.

reasonable expectations test. Measure of negligence holding that a product is negligently designed if it is not safe for its intended use and also for any reasonably foreseeable use,

As you will see later in the chapter in reading the *Leichtamer* case, design issues often lead to serious and convincing claims against manufacturers. Two principal lines of analysis have emerged in these cases: (1) The **risk/utility test** holds that a product is negligently designed if the benefits of a product's design are outweighed by the risks that accompany that design. (2) The **reasonable expectations test** imposes on the manufacturer a duty to design its products so that they are safe not only for their intended use but for any reasonably foreseeable use.

At this writing, members of the American Law Institute, a group of legal experts, is drafting the *Restatement (Third) of Torts,* which does not constitute law but represents those experts' best judgment about what the law *should* be. They have given preliminary approval to a design defect standard that supports the risk/utility model and gives much less attention to consumer expectations. Further, a product would be considered defective in design only if its foreseeable risks could have been reduced or avoided by a reasonable alternative design and if failure to include that design makes the product not reasonably safe. That is, plaintiffs apparently would need to show that some better design was available and was not incorporated in the product in question.

Public Policy Questions

1. Professor Kip Viscusi argues that we should exempt companies from liability for design defects where they can show "either compliance with a specific government regulation or the use of a hazard warnings program that is sufficiently effective that it leads to informed market decisions." [See W. Kip Viscusi, *Reforming Products Liability Law* (Cambridge: Harvard University Press, 1991), p. 128. This book was reviewed by Suzanne Lambert, *Michigan Law Review* 90 (May 1992), p. 1634.]
   a. Explain what Viscusi is proposing.
   b. Explain the weaknesses in relying on government regulation as a method of consumer protection.
2. Do you share Viscusi's confidence in the market? Explain.

Inadequate Warnings. Small, plastic signs reading something like "Warning! Coffee is hot!" seem to be popping up all over America in the wake of the aforementioned McDonald's case. Are those warnings necessary? Are they effective either in protecting consumers or in relieving producers of liability? Certainly the law provides that a negligence claim may arise from a supplier's failure to warn of a danger associated with the product. The question is whether the supplier knew or should have known that the product could be dangerous in its foreseeable use. Courts would also consider the feasibility of an effective warning and the probable seriousness of the injury.

CASE

Brown Forman Corp. v. Brune

893 S.W.2d 640 (Tex. App. 1994)

Facts

In 1983, Marie Brinkmeyer and a friend went to a bar to drink. Brinkmeyer was an 18-year-old, first-year college student. The legal drinking age in Texas at the time was 19. Apparently, she was not asked for identification. She drank a 32-ounce pitcher of Hurricanes and an unknown number of White Russians. After leaving the bar, Brinkmeyer illegally bought a bottle of Pepe Lopez tequila, which was produced by Brown-Forman. At a party that evening, Brinkmeyer drank one-half of a glass of tequila unmixed with nonalcoholic beverages; then she began drinking straight from the tequila bottle. After drinking heavily and rapidly, Brinkmeyer lost consciousness. Friends took her to her room, placed her on her bed, and left her. The next morning she was found in her bed having died from ingesting large amounts of ethanol.

Continued

Continued

In 1983, no warning labels were required on liquor containers, but in 1988 a federal law was approved requiring warnings about the general health risks associated with drinking and specific warnings about drinking and driving and drinking while pregnant. That statute expressly precluded state warning laws.

Brinkmeyer's mother, Joyce Brune, sued Brown-Forman on grounds of negligence and strict liability (explained later in this chapter). Brune argued that alcohol is unreasonably dangerous in the absence of a warning. A jury found Brown-Forman guilty of negligence and 35 percent responsible for Brinkmeyer's death. Brune was awarded $535,000. Brown-Forman appealed.

* * *

Justice Yanez

It is fundamental that the existence of a legally cognizable duty is a prerequisite to all tort liability. Whether a legal duty exists under a set of facts is a question of law. Therefore, regardless of whether the theory of liability is based upon strict liability or negligence, the threshold question is whether Brown-Forman had a duty to warn of the risk of death from overconsumption of alcohol in a short period of time. We note that because there existed no federal or state legislation in 1983 regarding warnings on alcoholic beverage containers does not mean that distillers may not be found liable for a failure to warn should courts find such a duty exits . . . [C]onsidering "the creation of new concepts of duty in tort is historically the province of the judiciary."

Therefore, we consider whether a common law duty existed in 1983 for distillers to warn that overconsumption of tequila within a short amount of time may cause death and whether there existed a duty to provide instructions about the safe use of tequila . . . Determining whether a legal duty exists necessarily entails the interpretation and application of legal precedent as well as policy considerations. We consider social, economic, and political questions and their applicability to the facts at hand. Other factors to be considered include the extent of the risk involved, "the foreseeability and likelihood of injury weighed against the social utility of the actor's conduct, the magnitude of the burden of guarding against the injury, and the consequences of placing the burden on the defendant." We note that foreseeability alone is not a sufficient basis for creating a new duty. In a failure to warn case, we consider the extent to which the tort system is capable of devising an adequate warning.

In assessing whether a legal duty exists under the facts before us, we find Justice Kilgarlin's words distinguishing moral and legal duties particularly instructive:

> In spite of a societal dynamic to expand duty, Texas still follows a general rule that Texans do not owe others general amorphous legal duties. The rule in Texas still distinguishes between moral and legal duty. Although one may have a moral duty to prevent a blind person from crossing a busy street against a light, a person has no legal duty to do so unless additional factors exist. These other factors include the existence of familial or voluntary relationships which impose a duty, statutes or ordinances which may legally require action, or special circumstances, such as having placed the blind man in his precarious position in the first place . . .

The common law has long recognized that the alcoholic beverage drinker maintains the ultimate power and thus the obligation to control his own drinking behavior. We believe that the common law should remain focused on the drinker as the person primarily responsible for his behavior.

Though no Texas court has had to decide whether a distiller has a duty to warn of the risk of death from overconsuming alcohol in a short period of time, Texas courts have addressed whether alcoholic beverage manufacturers must warn of other risks and dangers associated with alcoholic beverages. All concluded that the alcoholic beverage manufacturer had no duty to warn of whatever risk or danger was asserted.

* * *

Continued

Continued

When choosing to enter the business of manufacturing alcoholic beverages a manufacturer should make an effort to inform its users about risks and dangers associated with its product. That effort may include a larger public education campaign rather than simply labeling a bottle. In fact, education may be the only remedy we have in preventing binge drinking. Despite education, however, there will always be individuals who, though informed about the dangers associated with the use of alcoholic beverages, choose to misuse the product. The circumstances behind an individual's choice to misuse beverage alcohol are profoundly complex and will not be addressed by placing a few warning words on the outside of a bottle . . . Holding an alcoholic beverage manufacturer financially responsible for the death of an individual who consumed a large quantity of alcohol in a short amount of time does not answer the more direct question about why the individual would consume a known dangerous product in such a quantity.

* * *

The standard for common knowledge is the overall knowledge common to the community that is a basis for determining a duty to warn, not what individual users may or may not know. Many products cannot possibly be made entirely safe for all consumption. The product sold must be dangerous to an extent beyond that which would be contemplated by the ordinary consumer who purchases it, with the ordinary knowledge common to the community as to its characteristics . . . While morally it might appear prudent to require manufacturers of alcoholic beverages to place a warning on alcoholic beverages about the danger of death after ingesting large amounts of alcohol over a short period of time, we find no legal duty to do so.

Considering the extensive involvement of the federal and state government in regulating alcoholic beverages, we conclude that the subject of warnings on alcoholic beverages and placing instructions for use on an alcoholic beverage container should be left to the legislative process. The issues relevant to this case have for so long been political issues we conclude that courts are ill-equipped to develop effective and feasible warnings and instructions . . .

In light of this political judgment, it would seem arbitrary for courts to hold a whiskey distiller liable for the foreseeable injurious effects to some people of whiskey which has standard ingredients and qualities. The political judgment would seem to foreclose a judicial holding that the recognized dangers of whiskey render it unreasonably dangerous . . .

We understand that binge drinking and underage drinking is a problem. However, merely because it is foreseeable that an underage drinker may gain access to alcoholic beverages and misuse them is not a reason to impose a duty to warn about death from overconsumption and impose liability for the drinker's death upon the distiller . . .

Additionally, because of the inability to fashion effective instructions about the proper use of tequila, we conclude that no legal duty exists on the part of Brown-Forman to place instructions for proper use on its containers of tequila.

* * *

Even if a warning could be fashioned, there existed no evidence that Marie would have heeded the warning. The evidence was that Marie had received and disregarded warnings about the abuse of alcoholic beverages generally.

* * *

Finding that Brown-Forman had no legal duty to warn Marie about the dangers of consuming a large amount of tequila over a short time period and no duty to provide instructions about the proper use of tequila, we reverse the trial court's judgment, render judgment for Brown-Forman, and render that Brune take nothing.

Continued

Continued

Questions

1. What was the issue in this case?
2. Why did the court reverse the jury's judgment?
3. George Hacker, director of the alcohol policies project for the Center for Science in the Public Interest: "In terms of acute intoxication, I don't think it's widely known that this is a highly toxic substance when consumed too rapidly—especially among young people who are inexperienced in drinking." Comment. [See Wendy Bounds, "Liquor Firm Liability Verdict Reversed," *The Wall Street Journal* January 6, 1995, p. B2.]
4. Laaperi installed a smoke detector in his bedroom, properly connecting it to his home's electrical system. Six months later, Laaperi's house burned and three of his children were killed. A short circuit, which caused the fire, also deprived the A.C.-powered smoke detector of electricity. Thus the detector did not sound a warning. Laaperi then claimed that Sears, Roebuck, where he purchased the detector, was guilty of negligence for failing to warn him that a fire might disable his smoke detector such that no warning would issue. How would you rule in this case? [See *Laaperi* v. *Sears, Roebuck & Co.*, 787 F.2d 726 (1st Cir. 1986).]
5. The Court in the *Brown-Forman* case favorably cites Justice Kilgarlin's view that legal and moral duties are often not one and the same. In your view, if an act (or a failure to act) is immoral, should it also be illegal? Explain.

B. Negligence Defenses

Even if the plaintiff has established all of the necessary ingredients in a negligence claim, the defendant may still prevail by asserting a good defense. The two most prominent legal defenses in these cases are (1) contributory or comparative negligence and (2) assumption of the risk.

Assume you have enjoyed your first job after college, but you want to be your own boss. You have been saving, perhaps your family chips in a bit, and you manage to scrape together the money to open a small, indoor amusement park/arcade, featuring miniature golf, video games, pool tables, and trampolines. Recognizing the danger associated with the latter, you post warning signs, and you closely monitor the trampolines to prevent use by those who are intoxicated or unduly reckless. Notwithstanding your precautions, what happens if someone is injured? Depending on the extent and nature of your insurance coverage, you may bear a financially devastating loss. Presumably, you would argue that the plaintiff had contributed to his own harm or that he had assumed the risk, a risk that you had warned of. Would you prevail? Consider a recent case.

A trampoline at the Beta Theta Pi fraternity house at the University of Denver led to a broken neck and paralysis when a 20-year-old fraternity member, Oscar Whitlock, unsuccessfully attempted a flip at 10 P.M. in the dark. The student, Whitlock, had extensive experience with trampolines. The day of the accident he had slept until 2 P.M. after drinking that morning until 2 A.M. The trampoline was located in front of the house on university land that was leased by the fraternity. The trampoline had been used over a 10-year period by students and community members. A number of injuries had resulted. The university kept its own trampoline under lock and key because of safety concerns.

A trampoline at the Beta Theta Pi fraternity house at the University of Denver led to a broken neck and paralysis when a 20-year-old fraternity member, Oscar Whitlock, unsuccessfully attempted a flip at 10 P.M. in the dark.

At trial, the jury found the university 72 percent at fault, with the remainder of the blame lying with the plaintiff/student. He recovered 72 percent of $7,300,000 ($5,256,000). On appeal, the judgment was upheld, but the dissent argued that the university had no duty to warn against obvious risks, saying that "no reasonable person could conclude that the plaintiff was not at least as negligent as the defendant." Hence, the dissent was saying, in effect, that the plaintiff had *assumed the risk* and, in any case, was himself arguably more *negligent* than the university. [See *Whitlock* v. *University of Denver,* 712 P.2d 1072 (Col. Ct. App. 1985).

The Colorado State Supreme Court then reviewed the appeals court decision and reversed on the grounds that the university did not maintain a "special relationship" with the plaintiff that would have justified imposing a duty of due care on the university to assure safe use of the trampoline. [See *University of Denver* v. *Whitlock,* 744 P.2d 54 (Col. S. Ct. 1987).]

Questions

1. Would the dissent's reasoning in the court of appeals decision apply to the trampoline in your private, amusement park business? Explain.
2. Would your warning and close supervision protect you from liability under the court of appeals decision? Explain.
3. Would you have the duty of due care for your customers that the Supreme Court said the University of Denver did not have for Whitlock? Explain.

The Rules of Negligence Defenses. Let's look more closely now at the central defenses in negligence cases.

Comparative Negligence. Most states have adopted **comparative negligence** as a defense. It involves weighing the relative negligence of the parties. Though the formula varies from state to state, typically the plaintiff's recovery is reduced by a percentage equal to the percentage of the plaintiff's fault in the case. Assume a plaintiff sustained $10,000 in injuries in an accident. If the plaintiff's own negligence is found to be 20 percent responsible for the injuries, then the plaintiff's recovery will be reduced to $8,000. When the plaintiff's fault actually exceeds that of the defendant, the plaintiff may be barred from recovery.

comparative negligence. Defense in a negligence suit in which the plaintiff's recovery is reduced by an amount equivalent to her contribution to her own injury.

Contributory Negligence. Rather than employing the comparative negligence doctrine, a few states continue to follow the historic rule that any contribution by the plaintiff to his or her own harm constitutes a *complete bar to recovery.* This is called **contributory negligence.** If the plaintiff is found to have contributed in any way to his or her injury, even if that contribution is minuscule, he or she is unable to recover.

contributory negligence. Defense in a negligence action wherein the defendant attempts to demonstrate that the plaintiff contributed to the harm on which the litigation was based, thereby barring the plaintiff's claim.

Assumption of Risk. A plaintiff who willingly enters a dangerous situation and is injured will not be permitted to recover. For example, if a driver sees that the road ahead is flooded, he will not be compensated for the injuries sustained when he loses control as he attempts to drive through the water. His recovery is barred even though the road was flooded due to operator error in opening a floodgate. The requirements for use of the **assumption of risk** defense are (1) knowledge of the risk and (2) voluntary assumption of the risk.

assumption of risk. Defense in a negligence case in which the defendant seeks to bar recovery by the plaintiff by showing that the plaintiff knowingly and voluntarily exposed himself or herself to the danger that resulted in injury.

II. Warranties

warranty. A guarantee or promise by a seller that the goods being sold possess certain qualities.

As explained previously, negligence claims are often difficult to prove. For that reason and others, a wronged consumer may wish to raise a breach of warranty claim in addition to or in place of a negligence action. A **warranty** is simply a guarantee arising out of a contract. If the product does not conform to the standards of the warranty, the contract is violated (breached), and the wronged party is entitled to recovery. Note that a negligence claim arises from breach of the duty of due care, whereas a warranty claim arises from a breach of contract.

Let's return to your indoor amusement park. Assume that after near bankruptcy from litigation expenses and unfavorable publicity you replace the hazardous trampolines with an electronic driving range that permits customers to simulate the experience of driving a golf ball. You sell, at a deep discount, a "Golfing Gizmo" to those who record the longest drive each week. The Golfing Gizmo is, in effect, a golf ball on a tether and is designed to provide practice. The Gizmo package displays the language: Completely safe—ball will not hit player. The package also pictures a player hitting a golf ball. Unfortunately, your bad luck continues, as one of your customers, in using the Gizmo, is hit by the ball and suffers a serious injury . Both you and the manufacturer of the Gizmo are sued for **breach of warranty.** The manufacturer says its duty is to provide a product that is safe when used properly. The manufacturer argues that (1) the Gizmo package pictures a golfer hitting the ball "properly" and (2) the picture acts as a **disclaimer** limiting any warranty that might be claimed from the package language, "completely safe—ball will not hit player." Is the manufacturer liable for breach of warranty? Are you?

breach of warranty. Failure, without legal excuse, to fulfill the terms of the guarantee.

disclaimer. As to warranties, a contract term wherein a party attempts to relieve itself of potential liability under that contract.

The California Supreme Court in hearing a case involving the actual Golfing Gizmo said the manufacturer was liable because the product was expressly designed for "duffers" and because the use of the picture as a disclaimer was impermissible since it directly conflicted with the language—"completely safe—ball will not hit player"—which the court held to be an express warranty. [See *Hauter* v. *Zogarts,* 534 P.2d 377 (Cal. 1975).]

But what about the impact of warranty law in your business practice? Read below to determine the retailer's liability for defective merchandise sold in the ordinary course of business.

A. Express Warranties

express warranty. A guarantee made by affirmation of fact or promise, by description of the goods, or by sample or model.

An **express warranty** exists if a seller of goods affirms a fact or makes a promise regarding the character or quality of the goods. Warranties are governed primarily by the terms of the Uniform Commercial Code. The UCC is designed to codify and standardize the law of commercial practice throughout the United States. Forty-nine states have adopted all or the bulk of the UCC. Louisiana has adopted only portions.

UCC 2–313. Express Warranties by Affirmation, Promise, Description, Sample

1. Express warranties by the seller are created as follows:
   a. Any affirmation of fact or promise made by the seller to the buyer which relates to the goods and becomes part of the basis of the bargain creates an express warranty that the goods shall conform to the affirmation or promise.
   b. Any description of the goods which is made part of the basis of the bargain creates an express warranty that the goods shall conform to the description.
   c. Any sample or model which is made part of the basis of the bargain creates an express warranty that the whole of the goods shall conform to the sample or model.

The philosophy undergirding UCC 2–313 is straightforward. The seller who seeks to enhance the attractiveness of his or her product by offering representations as to the nature or quality of the product must fulfill those representations or fall in breach of contract and be subject to the payment of damages.

Puffing. Perhaps the area of greatest confusion in determining the existence and coverage of an express warranty is distinguishing a seller's promise from a mere expression of opinion. The latter, often referred to as sales talk or **puffing,** does not create an express warranty. The UCC requires an affirmation of fact or promise. Hence, a statement of opinion is not covered by the code. For example, the sales clerk who says, "This is the best TV around," would not be guaranteeing that the television in question is the best available. The salesperson is expressing a view. We, as consumers, seem to be quite patient with sellers' exaggerations. If, on the other hand, the clerk said, "This TV has a solid walnut cabinet," when in fact it was a pine veneer stained to a walnut tone, a breach of warranty action might ultimately be in order. The test to be applied in such situations is one of reasonable expectations. An expression of opinion coming from an expert may well create an express warranty because the buyer should reasonably be able to rely on the expert's affirmations. That would particularly be the case if the buyer is not knowledgeable about the product.

puffing. An expression of opinion by a seller not made as a representation of fact.

At this writing, the National Conference of Commissioners on Uniform State Laws is proposing that the states change their statutory approach to express warranties by treating what we now label puffing as an express warranty or a statement of fact. If sued, advertisers would need to substantiate their claims or show that no reasonable person would rely on the language. The commissioners apparently believe that the market has changed, with buying decisions now more commonly made on the strength of ads than was the case when Article 2 of the UCC was adopted in the late 1950s.

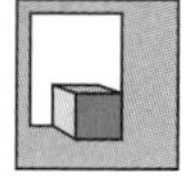

Ethics/Public Policy Questions

1. Frito-Lay says, "You can't eat just one," and BMW calls its cars "the ultimate driving machines."
   a. Should we require those companies to substantiate their claims or refrain from making them?
   b. How does the market protect us from puffing?
2. Professor Ivan Preston of the University of Wisconsin, an expert in this area, says, "Right now, companies can say something is the best without having to base that claim on anything. Under the revisions, advertisers would simply have to use claims more carefully." In your view, has a company behaved unethically if its ads include statements of opinion that cannot be substantiated? Explain. [See Fara Warner, "Code Revisions Would Limit 'Puffery,'" *The Wall Street Journal,* May 17, 1995, p. B8.]

B. Implied Warranties

A seller enters into a contract for the sale of goods and, as a consequence, an implied warranty arises by operation of law. That is, an implied warranty automatically attaches to the sale of goods unless the warranty is disclaimed (disavowed) by the seller.

Two types of implied warranties are provided for:

UCC 2–314. Implied Warranty: Merchantability; Usage of Trade

(1) Unless excluded or modified (Section 2–316), a warranty that the goods shall be merchantable is implied in a contract for their sale if the seller is a merchant with respect to goods of that kind. Under this section the serving for value of food or drink to be consumed either on the premises or elsewhere is a sale.

UCC 2–315. Implied Warranty: Fitness for Particular Purpose

Where the seller at the time of contracting has reason to know any particular purpose for which the goods are required and that the buyer is relying on the seller's skill or judgment to select or furnish suitable goods, there is unless excluded or modified under the next section an implied warranty that the goods shall be fit for such purpose.

implied warranty of merchantability. A warranty that arises by operation of law and promises that the good warranted is at least of average, fair, reasonable quality.

implied warranty of fitness for a particular purpose. A warranty that arises by operation of law and promises that the good warranted is reasonably useful for the buyer's purpose where the buyer was relying on the seller's expertise in making the purchase.

The **implied warranty of merchantability** is a powerful tool for the wronged consumer in that the warranty arises automatically by operation of law. If the seller is a merchant regularly selling goods of the kind in question, the warranty of merchantability simply accompanies the sale unless the warranty is excluded via a disclaimer (explained below). The warranty arises even if the seller made no certification as to the nature or quality of the goods. UCC 2–314 enshrines the consumer's reasonable expectation that only safe goods of at least ordinary quality will appear on the market.

The **implied warranty of fitness for a particular purpose** likewise arises by operation of law, but only when the seller (merchant or not) knows (or has reason to know) that the goods are to be used for a specific purpose, and the seller further knows that the buyer is relying on the seller's judgment. If those conditions obtain, the warranty exists automatically unless disclaimed.

C. Disclaimers

Express warranties may be disclaimed (excluded) or modified only with great difficulty. In any contract displaying both an express warranty and language disclaiming that warranty (for example, sold "as is" or "with all faults"), the warranty will remain effective unless the warranty and the disclaimer can reasonably be read as consistent.

Implied warranties may be excluded or modified by following either of the two patterns explained in UCC sections 2–316(2) and (3)(a).

2. Subject to subjection (3), to exclude or modify the implied warranty of merchantability or any part of it the language must mention merchantability and in case of a writing must be conspicuous, and to exclude or modify any implied warranty of fitness the exclusion must be by a writing and conspicuous. . .
3. Notwithstanding subsection (2)
   a. unless the circumstances indicate otherwise, all implied warranties are excluded by expressions like "as is," "with all faults" or other language which in common understanding calls the buyer's attention to the exclusion of warranties and makes plain that there is no implied warranty . . .

Finally, when a buyer, before entering a contract, inspects the goods (or a sample thereof), or declines to inspect, no implied warranty exists with regard to defects that should have been apparent on inspection [UCC 2–316(3)(b)].

Breach of Warranty? Let's imagine that your legal battles have driven you from the indoor amusement park business, and you turn now to what you presume to be the calm of selling home appliances. Assume that Gloria Crandell discusses buying a clothes dryer that you have conspicuously labeled "Quality Reconditioned Unit," "Tag-Tested," and "Guaranteed." Your salesperson orally promised Ms. Crandell a 90-day guarantee for "workmanship, parts, and labor" with the dryer. Ms. Crandell bought the dryer, and your employee installed it for her. Soon thereafter, Ms. Crandell observed that the dryer had apparently overheated a load of clothing so she turned the heat dial down to a lower setting and continued to use it. A few days later, a blanket caught fire in the dryer, the fire spread through the utility room where the dryer was located, and smoke damaged much of the Crandell home, with damages exceeding $25,000. Crandell now sues you.

Questions

1. List Crandell's warranty claims.
2. Defend your business.
3. Now play the role of judge. Decide the case. Explain.

[See *Crandell* v. *Larkin and Jones Appliance Company,* 334 N.W.2d 31 (S.D. 1983).]

4. A father asks his 11-year-old son to go to the kitchen, open a bottle of beer, and return with it. In opening the beer, the son's hand is cut when the bottle breaks. The father sues the bottler on behalf of his son. The father raises both negligence and breach of warranty claims. At trial, it is established that the son was not negligent. The bottler defends by establishing that the beer was purchased by the father. Decide. Explain.

D. Magnuson-Moss Warranty Act

Although the Uniform Commercial Code embodies our primary expression of warranty rules, Congress has extended and clarified those rules by passing the Magnuson-Moss Warranty Act. Congress approved the act following a study that found widespread abuse of consumers. Warranties were often vague, deceptive, or simply incomprehensible to the average purchaser. The act, administered by the FTC, applies only to consumer products and only to written warranties. It does not require offering an express written warranty, but where such a warranty is offered and the cost of the goods is more than $10, the warranty must be labeled *full* or *limited.* A full warranty requires free repair of any defect. If repair is not achieved within a reasonable time, the buyer may elect either a refund or replacement without charge. If a limited warranty is offered, the limitation must be conspicuously displayed.

If a warranty is offered on goods costing more than $15, the warrantor must "fully and conspicuously disclose in simple and readily understandable language the terms and conditions of the warranty." The FTC has developed various rules to implement the intent of the disclosure requirement. For example, if the warrantor requires return of the completed warranty registration card in order to activate the warranty, that return requirement must be clearly disclosed in the warranty.

The effect of the Magnuson-Moss Act has not been entirely consistent with Congress's hopes. In practice, many sellers may have either offered limited warranties or eliminated them entirely.

III. Strict Liability

Profile Perspective: A key element in the small-plane industry's struggle against product liability claims is the doctrine of **strict liability,** which permits plaintiffs to recover without being required to prove that the manufacturer or others in the chain of distribution were actually at fault. The threat of lawsuits from alleged defective products became one of the dominant considerations in building business plans in the small-plane industry, as it has in many other product lines across the nation.

strict liability. Civil wrong springing from defective and "unreasonably dangerous" products where responsibility automatically attaches without proof of blame or fault.

Particularly frustrating for manufacturers is that sometimes things happen that they can neither prevent nor even explain and yet liability may attach. For example, imagine you are operating a clothing store. A customer enters and decides to try on a pair of slacks. You show her to the dressing room. Soon after, you hear a scream from the room. As it turns out your customer has been bitten by a spider. Not surprisingly, she thinks the blame lies with your store. She sues on product liability grounds, but you win. Her negligence and breach of warranty claims are rejected by the court. (Can you explain why she loses?) Finally, she raises a strict liability in tort argument, but the court denies that claim also. Read the overview of strict liability that follows and think about why the court denied her claim. [See *Flippo* v. *Mode O'Day Frock Shops of Hollywood,* 248 Ark. 1, 449 S.W.2d 692 (1970).]

Imagine you are operating a clothing store. A customer enters and decides to try on a pair of slacks. You show her to the dressing room. Soon after you hear a scream from the room. As it turns out your customer has been bitten by a spider.

A. Strict Liability Overview

Negligence and warranty actions are helpful to the harmed consumer. However, rapid changes in the nature of commercial practice, as well as an increasing societal concern for consumer protection, led the legal community to gradually embrace yet another cause of action. *Strict liability in tort* offers the prospect of holding all of those in the chain of distribution liable for damages from a defective product, rather than imposing the entire burden on the injured consumer. Manufacturers and sellers are best positioned to prevent the distribution of defective products, and they are best able to bear the cost of injury by spreading the loss via pricing policies and insurance coverage.

Strict liability as an independent tort emerged in 1963 in the famous California case of *Greenman* v. *Yuba Power Products, Inc.*[18] In the ensuing two decades, most states, via either their judiciaries or their legislatures, have adopted strict liability in concept. The essence of the strict liability notion is expressed in Section 402A of the *Restatement (Second) of Torts.* In brief, 402A imposes liability where a product is sold in a *defective condition, unreasonably dangerous*[19] to the user. The 402A test:

1. One who sells any product in a defective condition, unreasonably dangerous to the user or consumer or to his property, is subject to liability for physical harm thereby caused to the ultimate user or consumer, or to his property, if
   a. the seller is engaged in the business of selling such a product, and,
   b. it is expected to and does reach the user or consumer without substantial change in the condition in which it is sold.
2. The rule stated in Subsection (1) applies although
   a. the seller has exercised all possible care in the preparation and sale of his product, and
   b. the user or consumer has not bought the product from or entered into any contractual relation with the seller.

B. Coverage

All of those engaged in the preparation and distribution of a defective product may be liable for any harm caused by the defect, regardless of proof of actual fault. Furthermore, the courts have extended strict liability coverage to reach injured bystanders. Coverage generally extends to both personal injuries and property damage, but in some states the latter is excluded. Some states limit strict liability recovery to new goods, and some have limited liability to a designated period (for example, 15 years) after the manufacture or sale of the product.

C. Defenses

Profile Perspective: If a Cessna or Piper plane crashed because the pilot flew close to the ground to wave to friends, was trying stunts, or used the plane for crop dusting even though it was not designed for that purpose, how would the manufacturer defend itself? That is, what defenses are available to those who are sued on strict liability grounds?

Assumption of risk and product misuse are both good defenses and, if factually supported, can act as a complete bar to strict liability recovery. Assumption of the risk involves the plaintiff's decision to proceed to use the product despite obvious dangers associated with that use. Thus, if a pilot decided to fly knowing that the plane's wing flaps were not operating properly, she may well have assumed the risk if she subsequently crashed. When the product is used improperly, or its directions are ignored or it is used in an unforeseeable way, the defendant would raise the misuse defense. Presumably, crop dusting with a plane not designed for that purpose would constitute misuse. Some courts, however, hold those in the chain of distribution liable for foreseeable misuses. Since strict liability is a no-fault theory, contributory negligence ordinarily is not a recognized defense.

The *Leichtamer* case that follows offers an overview of strict liability reasoning.

CASE

Leichtamer v. American Motors Corp.

424 N.E.2d 568 (0hio. 1981)

Facts

Paul Vance and his wife, Cynthia, invited Carl Leichtamer and his sister, Jeanne, to go for a ride in the Vance's Jeep CJ-7 at the Hall of Fame Four-Wheel Club, an off-road recreation facility. The driving course consisted of hills and trails in an abandoned strip mine. Paul Vance drove the Jeep down a 33-degree hill, then across a 70-foot-wide terrace, and was proceeding down over the brow of a 30-degree hill when the rear end of the Jeep raised up and pitched over, with the vehicle landing upside down, the front-end facing back up the hill. Paul Vance and his wife, riding in the front, were killed. Carl Leichtamer sustained a skull fracture, and Jeanne was rendered a paraplegic.

Paul Vance bought his four-wheel-drive Jeep from a factory-authorized dealer, Petty's Jeep & Marine. The Jeep came with a factory-installed roll bar. The entire vehicle was designed and manufactured by Jeep Corporation, a wholly owned subsidiary of American Motors. The vehicle had been manufactured exactly as designed, and it reached Paul Vance in that condition.

Carl and Jeanne Leichtamer sued Jeep and American Motors for "enhanced injuries." They argued that their injuries were causally related to the displacement of the roll bar on the vehicle. They claimed that Paul Vance's negligence caused their injuries but that those injuries were enhanced by the roll bar displacement.

* * *

Continued

Continued

Justice Brown

The speed that the Vance vehicle was traveling at the time of the pitch-over was an issue of dispute. The Leichtamers, who are the only surviving eyewitnesses to the accident, described the vehicle as traveling at a slow speed. Carl Leichtamer described the accident as occurring in this fashion.

> Well, we turned there and went down this trail and got to the top of this first hill . . . And Paul looked back and made sure that everybody had their seat belt fastened. That it was fastened down; and he pulled the automatic lever down in low and he put it in low wheel, four wheel, too . . And then he just let it coast like over the top of this hill and was using the brake on the way down, too. We came to the level-off part. He just coasted up to the top of the second hill, and then the next thing I remember is the back end of the Jeep going over . . . When we got to the top of the second hill, the front end went down like this [demonstrating] and the back end just started raising up like that [demonstrating].

John L. Habberstad, an expert witness for American Motors Corporation, testified that the vehicle had to be traveling between 15 and 20 miles per hour. This conclusion was based on evidence adduced by American Motors that the vehicle landed approximately 10 feet from the bottom of the second slope, having traversed about 47 feet in the air and having fallen approximately 23.5 feet.

* * *

The focus of appellees' case was that the weakness of the sheet metal housing upon which the roll bar had been attached was causally related to the trauma to their bodies. Specifically, when the vehicle landed upside down, the flat sheet metal housing of the rear wheels upon which the roll bar tubing was attached by bolts gave way so that the single, side-to-side bar across the top of the vehicle was displaced to a position 12 inches forward of and 14½ inches lower than its original configuration relative to the chassis. The movement of the position of the intact roll bar resulting from the collapse of the sheet metal housing upon which it was bolted was, therefore, downward and forward. The roll bar tubing did not punch through the sheet metal housing, rather the housing collapsed, taking the intact tubing with it. That this displacement or movement of the intact roll bar is permitted by the thin nature of the sheet metal wheel housing to which it is attached and the propensity of the bar to do so when the vehicle lands upside down is central to the appellees' case.

The appellants' position concerning the roll bar is that, from an engineering point of view, the roll bar was an optional device provided solely as protection for a side-roll.

* * *

The other principal element of appellees' case was that the advertised use of the vehicle involves great risk of forward pitch-overs. The accident occurred at the Hall of Fame Four-Wheel Club, which had been organized, among others, by Norman Petty, the vendor of the Vance vehicle. Petty allowed the club to meet at his Jeep dealership. He showed club members movies of the performance of the Jeep in hilly country. This activity was coupled with a national advertising program of American Motors Sales Corporation, which included a multimillion-dollar television campaign. The television advertising campaign was aimed at encouraging people to buy a Jeep, as follows: "Ever discover the rough, exciting world of mountains, forests, rugged terrain? The original Jeep can get you there, and Jeep guts will bring you back."

The campaign also stressed the ability of the Jeep to drive up and down steep hills. One Jeep CJ-7 television advertisement, for example, challenges a young man, accompanied by his girlfriend: "[Y]ou guys aren't yellow, are you? Is it a steep hill? Yeah, little lady, you could say it is

Continued

Continued

a steep hill. Let's try it. The King of the Hill, is about to discover the new Jeep CJ-7." Moreover, the owner's manual for the Jeep CJ-5/CJ-7 provided instructions as to how "[a] four-wheel-drive vehicle can proceed in safety down a grade which could not be negotiated safely by a conventional two-wheel-drive vehicle." Both appellees testified that they had seen the commercials and that they thought the roll bar would protect them if the vehicle landed on its top.

Appellees offered the expert testimony of Dr. Gene H. Samuelson that all of the physical trauma to the body of Jeanne Leichtamer were causally related to the collapse of the roll bar support. These injuries—fractures of both arms, some ribs, fracture of the dorsal spine, and a relative dislocation of the cervical spine and injury to the spinal cord—were described by Samuelson as permanent. He also testified that the physical trauma to the body of Carl Leichtamer was causally related to the collapse of the roll bar.

Appellants' principal argument was that the roll bar was provided solely for a side-roll. Appellants' only testing of the roll bar was done on a 1969 Jeep CJ-5, a model with a wheel base 10 inches shorter than the Jeep CJ-7. Evidence of the test was offered in evidence and refused. With regard to tests for either side-rolls or pitch-overs on the Jeep CJ-7 appellants responded to interrogatories that no "proving ground," "vibration or shock," or "crash" tests were conducted.

The jury returned a verdict for both appellees. Damages were assessed for Carl Leichtamer at $100,000 compensatory and $100,000 punitive. Damages were assessed for Jeanne Leichtamer at $1 million compensatory and $1 million punitive . . .

I(A)

Appellants' first three propositions of law raise essentially the same issue: that only negligence principles should be applied in a design defect case involving a so-called "second collision." In this ease, appellees seek to hold appellants liable for injuries "enhanced"' by a design defect of the vehicle in which appellees were riding when an accident occurred. This cause of action is to be contrasted with that where the alleged defect causes the accident itself. Here, the "second collision" is that between appellees and the vehicle in which they were riding.

I(B)

. . . [T]he vast weight of authority is in support of allowing an action in strict liability in tort, as well as negligence, for design defects. We see no difficulty in also applying Section 402A [*Restatement* (*Second*) *of Torts*] to design defects. As pointed out by the California Supreme Court, "[a] defect may emerge from the mind of the designer as well as from the hand of the workman." A distinction between defects resulting from manufacturing processes and those resulting from design, and a resultant difference in the burden of proof on the injured party, would only provoke needless questions of defect classification, which would add little to the resolution of the underlying claims. A consumer injured by an unreasonably dangerous design should have the same benefit of freedom from proving fault provided by Section 402A as the consumer injured by a defectively manufactured product which proves unreasonably dangerous.

* * *

Strict liability in tort has been applied to design defect "second collision" cases. While a manufacturer is under no obligation to design a "crash-proof" vehicle, an instruction may be given on the issue of strict liability in tort if the plaintiff adduces sufficient evidence that an unreasonably dangerous product design proximately caused or enhanced plaintiff's injuries in the course of a foreseeable use. Here, appellants produced a vehicle which was capable of off-the-road use. It was advertised for such a use. The only protection provided the user in the case of roll-overs or pitch-overs proved wholly inadequate. A roll bar should be more than mere ornamentation.

Continued

Continued

I(C)

We turn to the question of what constitutes an unreasonably dangerous defective product.

Section 402A subjects to liability one who sells a product in a "defective condition, unreasonably dangerous" which causes physical harm to the ultimate user. Comment *g* defines defective condition as "a condition not contemplated by the ultimate consumer which will be unreasonably dangerous to him." Comment *i* states that for a product to be unreasonably dangerous, "[t]he article sold must be dangerous to an extent beyond that which would be contemplated by the ordinary consumer who purchases it, with the ordinary knowledge common to the community as to its characteristics."

With regard to design defects, the product is considered defective only because it causes or enhances an injury. "In such a case, the defect and the injury cannot be separated, yet clearly a product cannot be considered defective simply because it is capable of producing injury." Rather, in such a case the concept of "unreasonable danger" is essential to establish liability under strict liability in tort principles.

The concept of "unreasonable danger," as found in Section 402A, provides implicitly that a product may be found defective in design if it is more dangerous in use than the ordinary consumer would expect. Another way of phrasing this proposition is that "a product may be found defective in design if the plaintiff demonstrates that the product failed to perform as safely as an ordinary consumer would expect when used in an intended or reasonably foreseeable manner."

* * *

Thus, we hold a cause of action for damages for injuries "enhanced" by a design defect will lie in strict liability in tort. In order to recover, the plaintiff must prove by a preponderance of the evidence that the "enhancement" of the injuries was proximately caused by a defective product unreasonably dangerous to the plaintiff.

* * *

[Part II omitted.]

III

Appellants . . . contend that it was error for the trial court to have admitted in evidence television commercials which advertised the Jeep CJ-7 as a vehicle to "discover the rough, exciting world of mountains, forests, rugged terrain" Appellants further contend that "a jury may not base its verdict upon such television commercials in the absence of a specific representation contained in the commercials as to the quality or merit of the product in question and in the absence from the plaintiff that the use of the product was in reliance upon such representations." [sic]

We hold that a product is unreasonably dangerous if it is dangerous to an extent beyond the expectations of an ordinary consumer when used in an intended or reasonably foreseeable manner. The commercial advertising of a product will be the guiding force upon the expectations of consumers with regard to the safety of a product, and is highly relevant to a formulation of what those expectations might be. The particular manner in which a product is advertised as being used is also relevant to a determination of the intended and reasonably foreseeable uses of the product. Therefore, it was not error to admit the commercial advertising in evidence to establish consumer expectations of safety and intended use.

Affirmed.

Justice Holmes, dissenting

The majority reaches its decision by virtue of the application in a second collision case of the doctrine of strict liability as contained in Section 402A of the Restatement of Torts 2d.

Continued

Continued

I am unable to join in this analysis. In a products liability action based upon an alleged design defect of the product, which allegedly has enhanced the plaintiff's injuries, I feel that the manufacturer should be held liable only when the plaintiff is able to prove that the manufacturer was negligent in adopting his chosen design.

It is my view that the proper rule to be applied in crashworthiness cases is set forth in *Larsen* v. *General Motors Corp.* as follows:

> The manufacturers are not insurers but should be held to a standard of reasonable care in design to provide a reasonably safe vehicle in which to travel.
>
> This duty of reasonable care in design rests on common law negligence that a manufacturer of an article should use reasonable care in the design and manufacture of his product to eliminate any unreasonable risk of foreseeable injury.

There should be no requirements in the law that manufacturers must design their automotive products to withstand extraordinary accidents of unusual circumstance or severity.

* * *

As stated, there was a significant absence of specific proof as to any reliance by these plaintiffs upon the capability of the roll bar in a pitch-over situation or otherwise. Additionally, there was an insufficiency of proof that this type of an accident, involving a pitch-over of a Jeep, was a common accident and one reasonably foreseeable. In fact, the evidence would tend to controvert such a finding in that there was testimony from both plaintiffs and defense witnesses that pitch-overs are rare events which occur infrequently and only if the specific conditions necessary to bring it about exist.

American Motors presented testimony that the roll bars were installed on these Jeeps to aid in the protection of occupants in roll-over situations, not pitch-over accidents as was occasioned here.

* * *

There also was a failure of proof here as to any alternate safer design practicable under the circumstances of a pitch-over rather than a roll-over, and absence of any proof of any lessened or differential injuries that might have been sustained had an alternate design been installed in this jeep.

As stated, in the application of the proper standards here, the manufacturer's duty is to exercise reasonable care in the design of its product to eliminate any reasonable risk of foreseeable injury, but it need not be designed to make the vehicle accident proof.

Questions

1. Many courts now employ what is known as the risk/utility test in deciding design defect cases like *Leichtamer* under a strict liability analysis. The risk/utility test holds that a product is defective if the usefulness of particular elements of the product's design are outweighed by the dangers accompanying those elements. In *Leichtamer,* the court relied on the consumer expectations test.
   a. Explain the consumer expectations test.
   b. Criticize it.
2. The dissent in *Leichtamer* argued for the application of a negligence standard in this case. Had the court adopted that view, rather than relying on strict liability reasoning, would the decision have been different? Explain.
3. *a.* Why did the *Leichtamer* court apply strict liability to this case?
   b. Are you persuaded by the court's reasoning? Explain.

Continued

Continued

4. Does this decision have the effect of requiring the Jeep to be "accident proof" (as argued by the dissent) to avoid liability? Explain.
5. Had Jeep designed the vehicle without a roll bar of any kind, who would have won this case? Explain.
6. The deceased had rented an auto from the Hertz Corporation. A tire blew out, and a fatal crash resulted. The tire was manufactured by Firestone. The estate of the deceased filed suit against Hertz and Firestone. Evidence presented at trial caused the jury to believe that the dangerous condition of the tire arose after its manufacture.
   a. Can the plaintiff successfully raise a strict liability claim against Hertz? Explain.
   b. Against Firestone? Explain.
   [See *Stang* v. *Hertz Corp.*, 83 N.M. 730, 497 P.2d 732 (1972).]
7. Nancy Denny was driving her Ford Bronco II. She swerved to avoid a deer and suffered serious injuries when the Bronco tipped over. She sued on strict liability, negligence, and breach of implied warranty grounds. The jury found for Denny on warranty grounds but rejected the strict liability and negligence claims, finding that the Bronco was not defective. Denny was awarded $3 million. Ford appealed, saying that the jury's findings were inconsistent.
   a. Explain Ford's argument.
   b. Decide. Explain.
   c. The jury found Denny 60 percent responsible for her own harm. Does that finding change the results? Explain.
   [See *Nancy Denny and Robert Denny* v. *Ford Motor Company,* 88-CV-1180, U.S. District Court, Binghamton, New York (1993).]

D. Market Share Liability

market share liability. Product liability action by which plaintiffs may be able to recover against manufacturers of defective products based on those manufacturers' market shares even though proof of causation cannot be established.

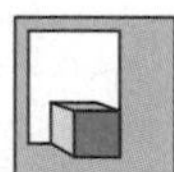

A challenging test for the courts in the product liability area is to determine just how far negligence and strict liability reasoning should be expanded. In recent years, some cases involving multiple defendants have been resolved under a doctrine labeled **market share liability.** That line of cases emerged from litigation involving an FDA-approved prescription drug, DES. In the leading case, *Sindell* v. *Abbott Laboratories.*[20] Sindell's mother had taken DES while pregnant with Sindell in order to prevent a miscarriage. Many years thereafter, the younger Sindell developed cervical cancer that was traced to her mother's use of DES (which had been removed from the market due to its danger). Because of the passage of time and the loss of accurate records, Sindell could not identify which drug manufacturer produced the DES that led to her illness. Those facts caused the court to allow Sindell to sue all manufacturers of DES. Those manufacturers were then required to pay damages in proportion to their share of the DES market unless they could prove that they could not have been responsible. Thus, Sindell was relieved of the duty of proving precisely who caused her injury. Subsequent market share liability decisions have been split. Some jurisdictions have followed the *Sindell* reasoning, some have modified it, and others have rejected the doctrine entirely.[21] In very recent years, courts have ruled that third-generation DES claimants, that is, granddaughters, may not recover on market share grounds.[22]

Ethics/Public Policy Questions

Although strict liability requires proof of a defect, it does not require proof of fault in the conventional sense.

1. How can we justify holding a company responsible without proof that its behavior was negligent in some respect?
2. Does a no-fault policy like strict liability, in any sense, undermine or depreciate our sense of personal responsibility or our conception of right and wrong? Explain.

E. Product Liability: A Summary Case

Service businesses have become a primary employment venue in our increasingly postindustrial American economy. Many students work in restaurants prior to graduation, some enter the giant franchise chains after graduation, and a few open their own establishments. In all of these roles, they are likely to encounter the potential public relations nightmare of foreign matter, for example, a mouse, in foodstuffs. The California case that follows combines negligence, warranty, and strict liability claims by a customer who has been injured while consuming food.

CASE

Mexicali Rose v. The Superior Court of Alameda County and Jack A. Clark, Real Party in Interest

822 P.2d 1292 (Cal. 1992)

Facts

Plaintiff/appellee Jack A. Clark ordered a chicken enchilada at defendant/appellant's restaurant. Clark sustained throat injuries when he swallowed a one-inch bone contained in the enchilada. Clark sued on theories of negligence, breach of implied warranty, and strict liability. He argued that the defendant negligently left the bone in the enchilada, the food was unfit for human consumption, he did not expect to find a bone, and it is not common knowledge that bones may be found in chicken enchiladas.

Chief Justice Lucas

According to plaintiff, defendants could be held (i) liable in negligence for their failure to exercise reasonable care in the preparation of the food, (ii) liable for violating California's statutory implied warranty because a chicken bone in a chicken enchilada renders the latter unfit for human consumption under the implied warranty of merchantability and fitness of California Uniform Commercial Code sections 2314 and 2315, and (iii) strictly liable because the food item was "defective" under the theory of Restatement Second of Torts section 402A, comment i, imposing strict liability when food is "dangerous beyond that which would be contemplated by the ordinary consumer who purchases it, with the ordinary knowledge common to the community as to its characteristics."

The question we address, therefore, is whether a restaurant keeper may be held liable for serving food containing substances natural to the product that, when consumed by the patron, cause injury. As explained below, we agree with plaintiff that a "reasonable expectation"' test is applicable in this context and, in part at least, is consistent with the development of tort law in our jurisdiction. Accordingly, we adopt that test as our own. As we further explain, although we conclude that under a reasonable expectation test plaintiff may not state a cause of action under

Continued

Continued

the theories of strict liability or breach of the implied warranties of merchantability or fitness, we conclude that under the same test, he may state a cause of action in negligence based on defendants' asserted failure to exercise due care in the preparation of the chicken enchilada.

Mix and Its Progeny: The Foreign-Natural Test and the Reasonable Expectations of the Consumer

In *Mix,* the plaintiff swallowed a fragment of chicken bone contained in a chicken pot pie he consumed in the defendant's restaurant . . . We held there could be no liability under either an implied warranty or negligence theory . . . Although we conceded that it is frequently a question for the jury to determine whether an injury-producing substance present in food makes the food unfit for consumption, we maintained that a court in appropriate cases may find as a matter of law that an alleged harmful substance in food does not make the food defective or unfit for consumption. We explained our holding as follows:

> Bones which are natural to the type of meat served cannot legitimately be called a foreign substance, and a consumer who eats meat dishes ought to anticipate and be on his guard against the presence of such bones . . . Certainly no liability would attach to a restaurant keeper for the serving of a T-bone steak, or a beef stew, which contained a bone natural to the type of meat served, or if a fish dish should contain a fish bone, or if a cherry pie should contain a cherry stone—although it be admitted that an ideal cherry pie would be stoneless. We concluded as a matter of law that a chicken pot pie containing chicken bones is reasonably fit for consumption, and there could be no breach of the implied warranty.

* * *

More recently however, courts addressing the foreign-natural distinction have deviated from strict application of *Mix* to conclude that the ultimate issue of liability should not be based on a determination whether the object causing injury was either foreign or natural, but instead should be based on whether the consumer reasonably should have anticipated the natural injury-producing substance in the food.

* * *

In sum, the trend developing in courts recently considering the issue whether a plaintiff may recover for injuries caused by a natural or foreign substance can be summarized as follows: If the injury-producing substance is natural to the preparation of the food served, it can be said that it was reasonably expected by its very nature and the food cannot be determined to be unfit for human consumption or defective.* Thus, a plaintiff in such a case has no cause of action in implied warranty or strict liability. The expectations of the consumer do not, however, negate a defendant's duty to exercise reasonable care in the preparation and service of the food. Therefore, if the presence of the natural substance is due to a defendant's failure to exercise due care in the preparation of the food, an injured plaintiff may state a cause of action in negligence. By contrast, if the substance is foreign to the food served, then a trier of fact additionally must determine whether its presence (i) could reasonably be expected by the average consumer and (ii) rendered the food unfit for human consumption or defective under the theories of the implied warranty of merchantability or strict liability.

* * *

*Unfortunately, both dissents misrepresent the scope and application of our holding. The term "natural" refers to bones and other substances natural to the product served, and does not encompass substances such as mold, botulinus bacteria or other substances (like rat flesh or cow eyes) not natural to the preparation of the product served.

Continued

Continued

Defendants assert that "public policy and good common sense support the *Mix* rule." They contend that allowing a plaintiff to recover even in negligence for an injury caused by a natural substance is unreasonable because, they assert, this would place a burden on all restaurants to remove all bones. Defendants claim the better policy is "to encourage consumers to be careful."

As noted above, we agree with defendants to the extent they reason that a restaurant patron cannot expect a chicken pie to be free of all bones. Such an expectation would be unreasonable and unrealistic to the ordinary consumer and would not conform to either federal or state health and safety standards . . .

On the other hand, we disagree with defendants . . . that we should continue to preclude a plaintiff from attempting to state a cause of action in negligence when a substance natural to the preparation of the food product has caused injury . . .

[W]e believe a patron can reasonably expect that a restaurateur will exercise reasonable care in preparing chicken enchiladas so that any natural substances contained in the food will not be either of such size, shape or quantity to cause injury when consumed. It is reasonably foreseeable that a sizable bone could cause the unsuspecting patron substantial injury if swallowed. Under these principles, we believe it is a question for the trier of fact to determine whether the presence of the injury-producing substance was caused by the failure of the defendants to exercise reasonable care in the preparation of the food, and whether the breach of the duty to exercise such care caused the consumer's injury. In so concluding, we emphasize that restaurateurs have available all the traditional defenses to a negligence cause of action, including comparative negligence.

The strict foreign-natural test of *Mix* should be rejected as the exclusive test for determining liability when a substance natural to food injures a restaurant patron. We conclude instead that in deciding the liability of a restaurateur for injuries caused by harmful substances in food, the proper tests to be used by the trier of fact are as follows:

If the injury-producing substance is natural to the preparation of the food served, it can be said that it was reasonably expected by its very nature and the food cannot be determined unfit or defective. A plaintiff in such a case has no cause of action in strict liability or implied warranty.

If, however, the presence of the natural substance is due to a restaurateur's failure to exercise due care in food preparation, the injured patron may sue under a negligence theory.

If the injury-causing substance is foreign to the food served, then the injured patron may also state a cause of action in implied warranty and strict liability, and the trier of fact will determine whether the substance (i) could be reasonably expected by the average consumer and (ii) rendered the food unfit or defective.

* * *

Based on the foregoing, we affirm the Court of Appeal judgment to the extent it directs the trial court to sustain defendants' demurrers to the implied warranty and strict liability causes of action, and we reverse the judgment directing the demurrer to plaintiff's negligence cause of action be sustained.

[Remanded.]

Justice Mosk, dissenting

The majority hold that processed food containing a sharp, concealed bone is fit for consumption, though no reasonable consumer would anticipate finding the bone. They declare in effect that the bone is natural to the dish, therefore the dish is fit for consumption. The majority never explain why this should be the rule, when it is universally held that in the analogous case of a sharp bit of wire in processed food, liability occurs under both the implied warranty of fitness and the theory of strict liability for defective consumer products.

* * *

Continued

Continued

A nutshell in a scoop of ice cream, a bit of crystalized corn in a serving of corn flakes or a chunk of bone in a hamburger is as harmful and unanticipated from the injured consumer's point of view as a bit of rock, glass or wire in the same food products. For social policy reasons we have long held the restaurateur strictly liable for injuries caused by unwholesome food, and there is no reason to abandon this social policy when the object in food that causes the injury is "natural."

It is a fallacy to assume that all objects which were a natural part of the ingredients of the food at an early stage of preparation are characteristic of the finished product or are anticipated by the consumer of the finished product. The more highly processed the food, the less it is to be anticipated that injurious natural objects such as shells or bones will be present.

* * *

I see no reason to breathe new life into an arbitrary and artificial distinction between natural and foreign defects in food products. This distinction is no longer followed in the majority of jurisdictions that have considered the matter in the last 30 years . . . I agree with the majority that when the consumer is injured by a foreign object, we should determine liability on warranty and strict liability theories on the basis of the reasonable expectation of the consumer. In the interest of public health, I would apply the same standard to so-called natural defects.

Questions

1. How did the court express the central issue in the *Mexicali* case?
2. *a.* In *Mexicali,* did the California Supreme Court adopt the foreign-natural test or the reasonable expectation test?
   b. Explain each.
3. Build a decision tree showing how to apply the *Mexicali* court's test to the question of whether a consumer who broke a tooth when biting a cherry pit in a cherry pie, for example, should be able to recover in negligence, warranty, or strict liability.
4. The plaintiff, born and raised in New England, was eating fish chowder at a restaurant when a fish bone lodged in her throat. The bone was removed and the plaintiff sued the restaurant, claiming a breach of implied warranty under the UCC. Evidence was offered at trial to show that fish chowder recipes commonly did not provide for removal of bones. Decide. Explain. [See *Webster* v. *Blue Ship Tea room, Inc.,* 198 N.E.2d (Mass. 1964).]

IV. Product Liability and Public Policy

Profile Perspective: We have seen that the threat of product liability claims plays an important role in business planning. In part because of the liability tail that followed small planes, sometimes for decades, that industry lost tens of thousands of jobs. The 1994 General Aviation Revitalization Act limited that liability and the light-plane industry now expects as many as 25,000 new jobs by the turn of the century.

Is legal reform that limits liability necessary in other segments of American life? Certainly much of the business community thinks so. Imagine yourself in the place of Bruce Hoegger, the president and owner of a small Minneapolis hydraulic-components company. In one three-month period of 1994, he spent 50 tough hours in depositions and meetings with his lawyers as they dealt with a product liability suit. Hoegger feared that he might lose his business if a large punitive penalty were awarded in the case. Not surprisingly, his 15-year marriage to his wife, Linda, was strained. The case eventually was settled for $25,000, and all of the costs were borne by his insurer.[23]

Bigger firms, too, shape their business strategy to cope with liability risks. Consider the discount retailer, Duckwall-Alco Stores:

> Alco won't sell exercise equipment or child car seats unless the supplier carries as much as $5 million in liability insurance. And the retailer won't buy property unless the owner certifies that any environmental mess has been cleaned up. That is necessary, Alco executives say, because under U.S. law retailers can be sued for problems arising from the goods they sell or the property they buy even if they didn't create the problems.[24]

A. *Reform?*

In owning or managing a business, you must understand product liability law from two perspectives. You must be mindful of the role of the legal system in the practice of business, but at the same time, you must pursue your responsibilities as a citizen; that is, you must encourage the pursuit of justice for all. With these sometimes conflicting expectations in mind, we turn now to the question that Congress has been grappling with for a number of years: Do we need to reform our liability system? The majority of states have done so at least to some extent, but congressional action has been difficult.

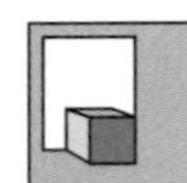

In 1996, Congress passed legislation curbing damage awards in product liability suits, but the bill was vetoed by President Clinton, who felt it cut too sharply into consumer protection. The heart of the bill was a provision that would have limited punitive damages in product liability suits to $250,000 or two times the victim's economic damage, whichever were greater.

The Supreme Court provided some encouragement to the reformers in a 1996 decision striking down a $2 million punitive damages award as "grossly excessive" and thus a violation of the Constitution's due process requirements.[25] In that case, an Alabama jury had awarded $4,000 in compensatory damages to Ira Gore, whose $40,000 BMW 535i had suffered modest paint damage and been repainted before sale without notification to Gore. The jury then awarded Gore $4 million in punitive damages to penalize BMW for the roughly 1,000 new cars it had refinished and sold as new throughout the United States under its policy of notifying buyers of repairs only when the cost exceeded 3 percent of the suggested retail price of the car. The Alabama Supreme Court reduced that award to $2 million.

In striking down Gore's punitive damage recovery, the U.S. Supreme Court did not set a "bright line" by which to identify unconstitutional punitive damages. Rather, the justices pointed to three factors that should be used, on a case-by-case basis, to resolve that question:

1. The "degree of reprehensibility" of the defendant's conduct.
2. The ratio between the punitive award and the actual harm suffered by the plaintiff.
3. The difference between the punitive award and penalties in "comparable cases."

The *BMW* case, while very important, clearly does not settle the punitive damages debate. Many states currently limit punitive damage awards, and the Supreme Court in the *BMW* case appears to have affirmed the responsibilities of state judges and legislators in this area.

Our total annual product liability bill (insurance, legal fees, and actual damages) is about $4 billion.

$4 billion is less than what Americans spend annually on dog food.

The Evidence. Do we need to reform our liability system? We have examined the economic and even emotional pressures that product liability imposes on the business community. Now let's look at the empirical evidence. Our total annual product liability bill (insurance, legal fees, and actual damages) is about $4 billion.[26] As journalist Robert Kuttner remarks, "$4 billion is less than what Americans spend annually on dog food. It is one-fifth of one percent of retail sales."[27] A 1995 study found that only 8 percent of tort awards exceeded $1 million and only 6 percent included any punitive damages. And when punitive damages were awarded, the median recovery was just $50,000.[28]

On the other hand, product liability was estimated to represent about $100 of the cost of a $200 football helmet, $500 of the cost of a new car, and $20 on the cost of a $100 ladder.[29] In any case, jurors seem to be losing sympathy with product liability claims. From 1987 to 1992, plaintiffs' chances of winning those suits declined from 54 to 43 percent.[30] About 75 percent of jurors interviewed in a recent study said jury awards were too large, and two-thirds said we are having too many lawsuits.[31]

A recent study by the well-regarded Rand Institute suggests that product liability laws sometimes work well in protecting consumers and sometimes result in curbing innovation and harming business. Some good products have been withheld from the market, but some unacceptably risky products have departed quickly because of liability pressure. In most cases, liability laws have had negligible effects on pricing. Rand senior economist Steven Garber summed up the situation: "One of the important messages here is that liability is very complex, and it has good and bad effects."[32]

B. A Pair of Examples

Our examination of product liability law as a public policy issue turns now to a pair of highly publicized examples that summarize much of the debate.

The tobacco industry is in a litigation war with consumers.

Tobacco. The tobacco industry is in a litigation war with consumers who claim that tobacco is a defective product and that tobacco advertising is false and misleading. Historically, plaintiffs had no success in claiming that tobacco smoking and chewing leads to cancer and other health problems. Recent developments, however, have produced threatening fissures in the tobacco industry's mighty armor.

In 1996, Liggett Group, the smallest of the five major American tobacco companies, agreed to a settlement of its part of a class-action lawsuit claiming that smoking is addictive and that cigarette makers withheld that information from smokers and manipulated nicotine levels in cigarettes. Liggett, which makes Chesterfield and Eve cigarettes, admitted no wrongdoing but agreed to make payments (a maximum of $50 million per year) for the next 25 years toward smoking cessation. The deal, if approved, would be the first time a tobacco company has paid money to settle a litigation.[33]

The settlement was part of the *Castano* case, a huge class-action lawsuit on behalf of "all nicotine-dependent persons in the United States."[34] The court's definition of those considered nicotine-dependent included any smoker warned by a doctor about the hazards of smoking who, nonetheless, continued smoking. However, the 5th circuit federal court of appeals in 1996 unanimously decertified that class action saying that it would have required a single federal court judge to apply the varying tort laws of the 50 states.[35] Now the nicotine-addiction claims will be litigated, at least initially, as individual trials in the various states.

As part of the settlement, Liggett agreed to pay one million dollars each and a portion of future earnings to Florida, Massachusetts, Mississippi, and West Virginia. Those states and others are suing for reimbursement from the tobacco industry for the states' costs in treating Medicaid (welfare) recipients for ailments related to smoking.

The Liggett settlement also included an agreement by Liggett not to use cartoon characters in tobacco ads and to comply with some other elements of the proposed new FDA rules designed to curb smoking among minors.

Another important case involved Rose Cipollone, who died of cancer in 1984 after having smoked for 40 years. Prior to her death, she brought a product liability claim against three tobacco companies. Her family carried on the litigation for nearly a decade, during which time they were awarded $400,000 (subsequently thrown out on appeal). They won a partial victory in the U.S. Supreme Court, which ruled that smokers can successfully sue tobacco companies despite the federal warnings on cigarette packages where the tobacco companies can be shown to have committed fraud or misrepresentation; that is, where they hid or distorted the health risks of smoking.[36]

In the midst of all this bad news, R. J. Reynolds did weather one storm when the Federal Trade Commission voted by a 3–2 margin against banning Joe Camel ads. Critics say the ads are directed to children, but the FTC was troubled by the First Amendment implications of a ban and by a lack of conclusive evidence against Reynolds.[37]

In the midst of all this bad news, R. J. Reynolds did weather one storm when the Federal Trade Commission voted by a 3–2 margin against banning Joe Camel ads.

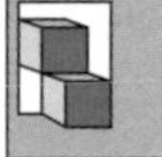

The Dalkon Shield and International Product Liability Claims. The Dalkon Shield, an intrauterine contraceptive device, was manufactured in the United States by A. H. Robins from 1970 to 1974, at which time the product was removed from the market because of multiplying cases of various serious medical problems associated with the shield. Thereafter, over 9,000 U.S. women filed liability claims against Robins, and by mid-1985 the company had paid some $378 million in damages. With further suits pending, Robins sought bankruptcy protection.

One of the troublesome complications of contemporary product liability law is that corporate defendants such as Robins now must learn to manage claims from abroad, including the special problems of language, cultural differences, access to proof, differing economic standards, and so on, that accompany those claims.

Nearly 14,000 foreign women filed claims of injury from the Dalkon Shield, and Robins continued to sell the device abroad for more than a year after it had discontinued domestic sales. The problems associated with those claims are multiple, including the simple difficulty of communicating across many cultures and languages. Medical records are difficult to obtain. And as *The Wall Street Journal* explained, financial/legal complexities abound in these cross-border disputes:

> Should foreign claimants receive the full dollar value of their settlements or should the amounts be adjusted to reflect the value of the dollar where they live? What is the likelihood that a claim against Robins could succeed in a foreign country and should that be considered when deciding how much to pay abroad? Some countries, Sweden for example, don't have tort systems in which to bring negligence or product-liability lawsuits.[38]

Summary

Legal Review. The three causes of action at the core of this chapter are negligence, breach of warranty, and strict liability. Fundamentally, negligence involves breach of the duty of due care, a failure to act in a reasonable manner under the circumstances. Breach of warranty actions arise out of the Uniform Commercial Code's provisions for express warranties (promises) and the two implied warranties of merchantability and fitness for a particular purpose. Strict liability, the most powerful of the three causes of action, requires proof that a product is defective and unreasonably dangerous. Strict liability claims are potentially applicable to all parties in the chain of distribution of the product in question.

Ethics/Public Policy Review. Small planes, the subject of our chapter profile, are particularly susceptible to product liability litigation, but dealing with litigation risks must now be treated as a routine ingredient in all corporate planning. That is not to say that our product liability system is merely an unfair drain on the corporate bottom line. Much publicized problems with tobacco, breast implants, and exploding cars or trucks caution us that consumers need the protection of the legal system. Presumably, the general answer is that we need to achieve some kind of responsible balance so that our economy thrives while justice is yet served. Certainly we do not want the law to discourage honorable businesses such as small-plane manufacturers, but we do want protection for injured consumers. The businessperson's duty is to minimize the hazards and develop a plan for dealing with litigation should it arise.

Economics Review. Now that you have examined the state of product liability law in America, what advice do you have for our corporate, political, and judicial leaders? Have we gone too far in providing remedies for injured consumers? That is, are we relying excessively on the law? Could we count on the free market to protect consumers from dangerous products? Specifically, would we as consumers learn how to better protect ourselves if we knew the law wouldn't be so readily available to us? Would companies that are careless or dishonest in producing products be punished by the market? If they were punished, would those penalties come quickly and sternly enough to offer meaningful protection to the public? Has the market failed such that legal intervention is necessary to achieve justice?

Chapter Questions—Law

1. A bartender, Parrillo, was opening a bottle of grenadine when it exploded, causing injury. Parrillo sued Giroux Company, the producer of the liquor. Giroux packaged the liquor itself after buying bottles from a manufacturer. Giroux visually inspected the bottles and ordinarily found defects in one of very 400 to 500 bottles. The evidence showed that Parrillo did not mishandle the bottle. Decide. Explain. [See *Parrillo* v. *Giroux Co.,* 426 A.2d 1313 (R.I. 1981).]
2. Alejandro Phillips, a young California man, was shot four times in the back at the opening of the movie *Boyz N the Hood,* a depiction of growing up in a dangerous Los Angeles neighborhood dominated by gangs. Phillips was shot during a scuffle involving alleged gang members. According to his lawyers, Phillips himself was not a member of a gang. Dozens of similar violent episodes accompanied the opening of the movie. Phillips's lawyers accuse Columbia Pictures of

negligence in marketing the film. They claim that the movie's advertising concentrated on the relatively minor episodes of violence in the movie and largely ignored the affirmative and pacifist ingredients at the core of the movie. They contend that Columbia should have anticipated violence as a consequence of that advertising approach. Phillips filed suit.

a. Explain Phillips's legal claims.

b. Defend Columbia.

c. Decide. Explain.

[For journalistic accounts, see Joanne Lipman, "Issue of Ads Leading to Violence Is Raised in Suit Tied to Movie," *The Wall Street Journal,* April 27, 1992, p. B10; and "Film Patron Injury," *Entertainment Law Reporter* 15, no. 1, p. 22.]

3. Embs, the plaintiff, was shopping in a self-serve grocery store. A carton of 7UP was on the floor about one foot from where she was standing. She was unaware of the carton. Several of the bottles exploded, severely injuring Embs's leg. Embs brought a strict liability action against the bottler.

   a. Raise a defense against the strict liability claim.

   b. Decide. Explain.

   [See *Embs* v. *Pepsi-Cola Bottling Co. of Lexington. Kentucky, Inc.,* 528 S.W.2d 703 (1975).]

4. Plaintiffs Dr. Arthur Weisz and David and Irene Schwartz bought two paintings at auctions conducted by the defendant, Parke-Bernet Galleries, Inc. The paintings were listed in the auction catalog as those of Raoul Dufy. It was later discovered that the paintings were forgeries. The plaintiffs took legal action to recover their losses. Parke-Bernet defended itself by, among other arguments, asserting that the conditions of sale included a disclaimer providing that all properties were sold "as is." The conditions of sale were 15 numbered paragraphs embracing several pages in the auction catalog. The bulk of the auction catalog was devoted to descriptions of the works of art to be sold, including artists' names, dates of birth and death, and, in some instances, black-and-white reproductions of the paintings. It was established at trial that plaintiff Weisz had not previously entered bids at Parke-Bernet, and he had no awareness of the conditions of sale. Plaintiffs David and Irene Schwartz, however, were generally aware of the conditions of sale. Is the Parke-Bernet disclaimer legally binding on the plaintiffs? Explain. [See *Weisz* v. *Parke-Bernet,* 325 N.Y.S.2d 576 (Civ. Ct. N.Y.C. 1971).]

5. Lisa Mazur, a Philadelphia girl, received a measles vaccination at school in 1982 as part of a mass immunization program. The vaccination caused a fatal neurological disorder. Her parents sued the manufacturer, Merck & Co. Assume the vaccine was produced according to all applicable safety standards but that all such vaccines carry a small degree of risk of side effects or of mimicking the disease itself.

   a. Explain the Mazur family's legal claim.

   b. Decide.

   c. Assume Merck sold the drug through the federal Centers for Disease Control, which was required by contract with Merck to ensure that all patients received information about the potential risks of the vaccine. Would that arrangement change the outcome of the case? Explain.

   [See *Mazur* v. *Merck,* 964 F.2d 1348 (1992).]

6. A child contracted Reye's syndrome after being given aspirin. The aspirin package contained an English language warning regarding a connection between Reye's syndrome and aspirin, but the child's Hispanic mother could not read the warning. Does the manufacturer have a duty to warn in a foreign language? Explain. [See *Ramerez* v. *Plough,* 62 *Law Week* 2383 (1993).]

7. The plaintiff-employee was operating a machine designed to flatten and then curve metal sheets. The metal was shaped by three long rollers. The plaintiff turned off the rollers to remove a piece of slag. He left the power on. In trying to remove the slag, he accidentally brushed a gear lever, which activated the rollers. His hand was drawn into the rollers, and injury resulted. At the time of the machine's manufacture, two safety mechanisms were available to prevent such accidents but the manufacturer of the machine (San Angelo) had not installed those mechanisms. What defense would you offer on behalf of the defendant machine manufacturer? Decide. Explain. [See *Suter* v. *San Angelo Foundry and Machine Co.,* 406 A.2d 140 (N.J. 1979).]
8. On December 29, 1980, a .38 caliber, Saturday night special handgun was used in the attempted robbery of a 7-Eleven store in Dallas, Texas. During the crime, the handgun was used to shoot and kill James Patterson, a clerk at the store. Patterson's mother filed a product liability action against Rohm, the manufacturer of the handgun; R.G. Industries, the distributor of the gun, and R.G. Industries' officers. The plaintiff claimed the gun was defective in design and that it was defectively marketed and distributed. How would you rule on the plaintiff's claim? Explain. [See *Patterson* v. *Rohm Gesellschaft,* 608 F.Supp. 1206 (N.D. Tex. 1985).]

Chapter Questions—Economics/Public Policy

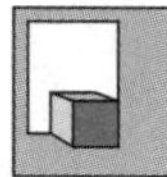

1. Tort claims sometimes arise out of accidents involving strangers, but often those episodes involve people who have some kind of relationship (e.g., buyer-seller or doctor-patient). In the latter set of circumstances, Professor Paul Rubin, among others, suggested that we should allow the parties to establish, in advance, a contract that would resolve the claims if an accident should happen. Thus, a physician and a patient might enter into an agreement in advance of treatment providing that the patient would sue only for limited damages (such as out-of-pocket medical expense and lost wages) in the event of malpractice.
   a. What benefits would consumers derive from such agreements?
   b. Why do the courts ordinarily refuse to enforce such agreements?
   c. Would you favor Rubin's approach to tort reform? Explain.
   [See Paul Rubin, *Tort Reform by Contract* (Washington, DC: The AEI Press, 1993).]
2. In the mid-1980s, the state of Colorado began enacting a series of tort reform measures in hopes of increasing insurance availability, reducing insurance rates, giving business a respite from litigation, and curbing what were believed to be unjustified jury awards. *The Wall Street Journal* summarized some of the measures and their results:

   > State laws here protect ski resorts and dude ranches from lawsuits over accidental injuries. Bars are virtually immune from legal blame for the acts of drunk patrons. Jury awards for pain and suffering top out at $250,000. And defendants can't be forced to ante up more in damages just because they have the deepest pockets.[39]

   After a few years of experience with the Colorado reforms, *The Wall Street Journal* observed that the results have been "quite mixed." Explain that judgment; that is, how is tort reform likely to affect consumers, insurance firms, businesses, and lawyers?

3. A man drowned on a family outing while using equipment rented from a canoe and inner-tube outfitter. His family sued, claiming the outfitter was negligent in failing to properly patrol the river and provide emergency assistance. The family won an $800,000 jury award. The parties later agreed to settle the case out of court. According to expert opinion, a 6-mile canoe trip costing $12 per person would cost more than $87 if lifeguards were to be required along rivers.
   a. In addition to the lack of safety equipment and personnel, what other claims are plaintiffs likely to raise in such situations?
   b. How might states act to protect recreational outfitters such as those who provide canoe, hiking, mountain climbing, and horseback riding?
   c. Some recreational outfitters, summer camps, motels, and others have responded to the threat of litigation by eliminating activities such as horseback riding and implements such as diving boards. The result, plaintiffs' lawyers argue, is increased safety. How do you feel about the reduction of summer recreation in exchange for increased safety? Explain. [See Edward Felsenthal, "Modern Bathing Suits Spoil Summer Fun," *The Wall Street Journal,* June 24, 1993, p. B9.]

Notes

1. Timothy K. Smith, "Liability Costs Drive Small-Plane Business Back into Pilots, Barns," *The Wall Street Journal,* December 11, 1991, p. A1.
2. Mike Clancy, "Cessna Will Once Again Make Small Aircraft," *The Des Moines Register,* March 15, 1995, p. 8S.
3. Barbara Carton, "Cessna Says It Will Make More Small Airplanes," *The Wall Street Journal,* March 14, 1995, p. B1.
4. Smith, "Liability Costs," p. A8.
5. Ibid.
6. Carton, "Cessna Says," p. B1.
7. Ibid.
8. Ibid.
9. 111 N.E. 1050 (N.Y. 1916).
10. *Doss* v. *Town of Big Stone Gap,* 134 S.E. 563 (1926).
11. Aric Press, Ginny Carrol, and Steven Waldman, "Are Lawyers Burning America?" *Newsweek,* March 20, 1995, p. 30.
12. Ibid., p. 34.
13. "McDonald's Settles Lawsuit over Burn from Coffee," *The Wall Street Journal,* December 2, 1994, p. A14.
14. "Wendy's to Interrupt Hot Chocolate Sales to Cool Temperature," *The Wall Street Journal,* November 23, 1994, p. A4.
15. Press, "Are Lawyers Burning America?" p. 30.
16. *Pat Stalter* v. *Coca-Cola Bottling Company of Arkansas and Geyer Springs Food City, Inc.,* 669 S.W.2d 460 (Ark. 1984).
17. Milo Geyelin, "Ford Hit by $62.4 Million Award in Trial of Bronco II Rollover Case," *The Wall Street Journal,* November 1, 1995, p. B7.
18. 27 Cal. Rptr. 697, 377 P.2d 897 (1963).
19. Some states have eliminated the "unreasonably dangerous" standard from their strict liability tests.
20. 163 Cal. Rptr. 132, 607 P.2d 924 (1980), cert. denied, 449 U.S. 912 (1980).
21. See, e.g., *Smith* v. *Eli Lilly & Co.,* 560 N.E.2d 324 (Ill. 1990).
22. For a journalistic account, see Amy Stevens and Christi Harlan, "Third-Generation DES Lawsuit Dismissed by State Appeals Court," *The Wall Street Journal,* February 21, 1991, p. B7.
23. Michael Selz and Jeffrey A. Tannenbaum, "Scared of Lawsuits, Small Businesses Applaud Reform," *The Wall Street Journal,* March 13, 1995, p. B1.
24. Bob Davis, Peter Gumbel, and David Hamilton, "To All U.S. Managers Upset by Regulations: Try Germany or Japan," *The Wall Street Journal,* December 14, 1995, p. A1.
25. *BMW of North America* v. *Gore,* 1996 U.S. Lexis 3390.

26. Robert Kuttner, "Product Liability Reform: You Lose," *Des Moines Register,* June 26, 1994, p. 3C.
27. Ibid.
28. "Timeout in the Tort Reform Wars," *Los Angeles Times,* December 3, 1995, p. M4.
29. Dick Thornburgh, "Fourth Down in Super Bowl of Civil Justice," *Waterloo Courier,* December 28, 1995, p. A6.
30. Edward Felsenthal, "Juries Display Less Sympathy in Injury Claims," *The Wall Street Journal,* March 21, 1994, p. B1.
31. Ibid.
32. Junda Woo and Milo Geyelin, "Rand Liability Study," *The Wall Street Journal,* September 24, 1993, p. B6.
33. Alix M. Freedman, Suein L. Hwang, Steven Lipin, and Milo Geyelin, "Liggett Group Offers First-Ever Settlement of Cigarette Lawsuits," *The Wall Street Journal,* March 13, 1996, p. A1.
34. Suein L. Hwang and Milo Geyelin, "Tobacco Industry, Plaintiffs Square Off as Cigarette Suit Is Ruled Class Action," *The Wall Street Journal,* February 21, 1995, p. A3.
35. *Castano* v. *American Tobacco Co.,* 1996 U.S. App. Lexis 11815.
36. *Cipollone* v. *Liggett Group,* 112 S.Ct. 2608 (1992).
37. Keith H. Hammonds, "Joe Camel Gets to Stick Around," *Business Week,* June 13, 1994, p. 50.
38. Milo Geyelin, "Plaintiffs' Lawyers Move to Preserve Exchange of Data," *The Wall Street Journal,* July 25, 1989, p. B8.
39. Milo Geyelin, "Overhaul of Civil Law in Colorado Produces Quite Mixed Results," *The Wall Street Journal,* March 3, 1992, p. A1.

PART IV

The Business's Relationship with the Community

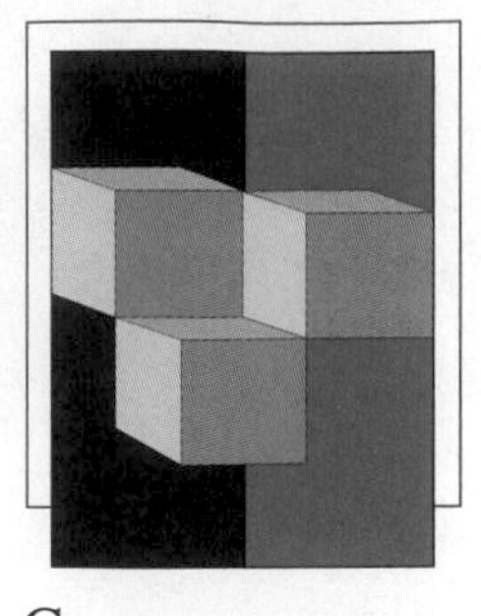

CHAPTER 15

ENVIRONMENTAL LAW: BUILDING AND MANAGING THE FIRM AS PART OF THE WORLD

READER'S GUIDE

As we have seen, firms are regulated in a number of ways for the purposes of protecting consumers, encouraging competition, protecting against fraud, and other reasons. This chapter addresses the role of the firm as an actor in the world, discusses the impact of the firm on the world's environment, and examines how the firm's environmental-related decisions are regulated.

PROFILE

From boat level in the Los Angeles Harbor, the mountains of shredded metal at the Hugo Neu-Proler Co. rise high enough to obscure the sunrise for several minutes each morning.[1]

It is less the unsightly heaps of former cars, washing machines, and iron pipes that concern neighbors and environmentalists, however, than what goes unseen—industrial toxins that have seeped into the soil and washed into the bay during the company's 33 years in the scrap metal business.

The company was aware of contamination problems for years, critics contend, but has done little to correct them, and only now is planning to take action as it negotiates with the Port of Los Angeles for a new 30-year lease. If the port grants the new lease without first making the company clean up its site—a move that appears likely—it would, some say, be rewarding Hugo Neu-Proler for years of inattention.

Any new lease would require cleanup, but environmentalists say that would give Hugo Neu-Proler little incentive to take care of the problem quickly, if at all.

For their part, Hugo Neu-Proler officials contend they have addressed pollution problems as they have come up over the years—though often only after being cited. They have not performed a comprehensive cleanup of the 26.7-acre site because some of the contamination was there when they arrived in 1962, they said. And both company and port officials said that while Hugo would have to clean up whether it leaves or stays, a lease gives the company an incentive to be a good neighbor and do the maximum, rather than fight over pollution it contends it did not create.

The port has a vested interest in seeing the company stick around. Hugo Neu-Proler, which also has operations on the East Coast, is the nation's largest exporter of scrap metal, and is the port's 15th largest money generator, paying $3 million a year in rent, dockage, and wharf fees.

Initially scheduled to be voted on by the Board of Harbor Commissioners in November, the final environmental impact report (EIR) is unlikely to be completed until spring, company officials said.

"We have guaranteed the port that we are going to clean the property" regardless of the final cost, said company president Jeffrey Neu. The $10 million escrow account, he said, was a "gesture of goodwill" rather than the maximum the company would agree to spend.

QUESTIONS

1. Whose responsibility is the cleanup of the Neu-Proler site?
2. Do you believe the firm's contentions that it will have greater incentives to clean the site if it obtains a new lease, or are you instead persuaded by environmentalists who claim that a new lease would encourage the firm to take its time with a cleanup?
3. As the owner or manager of a firm, how would you best avoid the problems presented above?

I. Environmental Concerns of Business

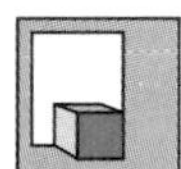

The focus of this text has been on the construction of a business, from a one-person operation to a corporate presence. Why then do we include a chapter on environmental law? Because from the moment a firm begins to produce, service, manufacture, or create, its operations affect the environment. Imagine the small decisions made by a company: Does it pack its glassware in plastic bubbles or corrugated wrapping? Does it publish a catalog once a month or once a year? Is that catalog published on paper or only through the Internet? Does it meet with the community before choosing a disposal system? Each of these decisions will have an impact on our physical world, hence it is critical to understand the law as it relates to the environment and to be aware of the ethics of each decision.

And our decisions affect not only those around us, but others around the world. In 1991, Saddam Hussein corrupted the Persian Gulf with the largest oil spill in history. Exxon has spent an estimated $3.5 billion in trying to clean up after the 1989 tragedy of the Exxon *Valdez* oil spill in Alaska. A considerable expanse of the former Soviet Union will remain uninhabitable for years as a result of the 1986 Chernobyl nuclear power plant accident.

Although the earth is a natural recycler of wastes—a very effective garbage dump—its ability to successfully neutralize the cumulative refuse of modern society is finite. Some concerns about pollution are centuries old, but the upsurge in population and increased industrialization and urbanization in the last 100 years have concentrated ever-increasing amounts of waste matter in small areas and put much greater pressure on the assimilative capabilities of the planet. Further, an improved understanding of the effects of various waste materials on the environment has generated widespread interest and awareness of pollution problems on the parts of both the general public and business decision makers.

A. *Who's to Pay?*

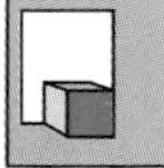

Both of these stakeholders are understandably concerned, however, about who will pay for the costs of environmental awareness. As history has shown, left alone many firms are quite willing to pollute the environment. The additional damage to the environment caused by the acts of one firm may not be severe. Therefore, that one firm may not be persuaded to take action to prevent this damage. The cost of this damage seems outweighed by the cost to ensure that the environment is *not* harmed. In those cases in which the acts of one firm do not have an extreme impact on the environment, but the same acts by a number of firms *would* have an extreme impact, it is arguable that the government must step in to regulate. The government believes that it has no choice but to regulate the operations of businesses to maintain a clean and healthy environment.

Fortune magazine reported on a 1992 Roper poll:

> [N]early two-thirds of those polled believe economic growth and environmental protection can go hand in hand, but if compromises between the two cannot be found, they clearly side with the environment. Americans say they are willing to divert money from other federal programs and make personal financial sacrifices to improve the environment.

For example, without regulation, a firm may consider that dumping its garbage into a canal is no big deal. In fact, perhaps the slight amount of garbage that this firm dumps *is* no big deal. However, if every firm were allowed to dump this amount, the canal would become excessively and irreversibly polluted. This situation may warrant government intervention. Or consider the possibility that we may all prefer less costly though more polluting cars. In this scenario, are the rights of future generations protected? They probably would have preferred that we were more careful so that their air would be cleaner.

Pollution, in this discussion, would be categorized by economists as an "externality." Wilfred Beckerman described the economic analysis as follows:

> [T]he costs of pollution are not always borne fully, if at all, by the polluter. . . Naturally, he has no incentive to economize in the use [of the environment] in the same way that he has for other factors of production that carry a cost, such as labor or capital. . . This defect of the price mechanism needs to be corrected by governmental action in order to eliminate excessive pollution.[2]

In a 1992 national poll, 92 percent of the respondents believed that the government "should be doing more." Favored government initiatives included:

- More regulations on disposal of industrial waste—83 percent.
- Mandatory recycling—80 percent.
- More environmental information—76 percent.[3]

Perhaps more to the point, most Americans are willing to change their lives to aid the environmental cause. Also revealed by the poll: When asked what they are doing to "save the planet," 93 percent said they personally are helping, 89 percent recycle garbage, 78 percent conserve electricity, 65 percent buy environmentally safe products, and 63 percent conserve water.

Table 15.1 summarizes the sacrifices that Americans say they are (and are not) willing to make in the environmental cause. Of course, what we would actually be willing to do when talk turns to action remains to be seen.

B. Business to Blame?

Business certainly is not the sole contributor to the environmental pollution we face. Individual citizens are primarily responsible for particulate matter discharged by wood-burning stoves, indoor pollution from cigarette smoking, and air pollution caused by our national one-worker-per-car commuting habits. Most forms of pollution, however, probably do have some business connection—whether direct or indirect. Thus, this chapter provides an opportunity to review the ethical considerations of business decision making and the overall social responsibility of business.

TABLE 15.1

WHAT AMERICANS WILL DO—AND WON'T

	Favor	*Oppose*
Require people to separate garbage and solid waste for recycling	93%	6%
Ban foam containers used by fast-food chains and other packaging that adds to the solid waste problem	84	14
Require testing and repairs of your car each year for air pollution and emissions	80	19
Ban disposable diapers, reducing the amount of solid waste in landfills	74	23
Require pollution control equipment that would add $600 to the cost of a new car	68	28
In metropolitan areas, require people who drive to work to take public transportation one day a week	57%	41%
Enforce stricter air quality regulations, increasing utility bills $10 per month	57	40
Limit the number of large cars that could be produced	51	44
Add a 20-cent-per-gallon increase to the price of gasoline for cleaner fuels	48	50
Close pollution-producing factories, resulting in a loss of jobs	33	59

Source: Barbara Rosewicz, "Americans Are Willing to Sacrifice to Reduce Pollution," *The Wall Street Journal,* April 20, 1990, p. A12. Reprinted with permission of *The Wall Street Journal,*

Monsanto Co.'s wastewater contains about 36 million pounds of ammonia per year. Recently, it announced that it would pay SRI International $1 million to find out how to recover the ammonia from the water![4]

C. PROBLEMS? WHAT PROBLEMS?

Greenies. The green majority. Tree huggers. Granolas. The environmental left. Liberal lake lovers. Greenpeacemakers. Whatever they are called, individuals who support the protection of the environment have often found themselves in the minority. Others claim that the problems aren't that bad or that there's nothing that we can do about it. To be sure, hearing that there is a hole in the ozone layer is much akin to hearing that the sky is falling. Environmentalists are treated as the Chicken Littles of the 90s. Yet, there is a slight difference. Environmentalists may have something to be worrying about. Consider the following.

Destruction of the Amazon. The following excerpt explains what has been described as "one of the greatest tragedies of history":

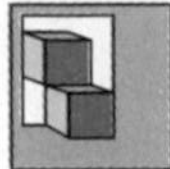

> The skies over western Brazil will soon be dark both day and night. Dark from the smoke of thousands of fires, as farmers and cattle ranchers engage in their annual rite of destruction: clearing land for crops and livestock by burning the rain forests of the Amazon. . . Last year the smoke grew so thick that Porto Velho, the capital of the state of Rondonia, was forced to close its airport for days at a time. An estimated 12,350 sq. mi. of Brazilian rain forest—an area larger than Belgium—was reduced to ashes.
>
> [The destruction of the forests] would be an incalculable catastrophe for the entire planet. Moist tropical forests are distinguished by their canopies of interlocking leaves and branches that shelter creatures below from sun and wind, and by their incredible variety of animal and plant life. If the forests vanish, so will more than 1 million species—a significant part of earth's biological diversity and genetic heritage. Moreover, the burning of the Amazon could have dramatic effects on global weather patterns—for example, heightening the warming trend that may result from the greenhouse effect.
>
> To Brazilians, such pressure amounts to unjustified foreign meddling and a blatant effort by the industrial nations to preserve their economic supremacy at the expense of the developing world.[5]

The Most Polluted Place in the World. One particularly devastated section of the old Soviet Union has assumed the dubious title of dirtiest place on the planet:

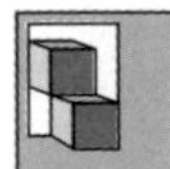

> In the Ust Kamenogorsk region of Soviet Central Asia, site of a nuclear-fuel explosion in September, there are so many chemical plants that sweeping the streets is banned so as not to stir up contaminants.
>
> On the coast of the Baltic republic of Estonia, "gray snow" spewing from a cement factory hardens like mortar on village roofs.
>
> About 30 miles from the 1986 nuclear disaster at Chernobyl, some farmers are told to leave their land and come back when it's safe—in 600 years.
>
> The most polluted place in the world—"no question in my mind"—is a lakeshore in Russia's heavily industrialized Ural Mountains, says Thomas B. Cochran, a physicist at the Natural Resources Defense Council in Washington. "No place else on Earth can you just stand, and get a lethal dose in an hour."
>
> The deadly spot is on the shore of 100-acre Karachay Lake, which in the early 1950s became the repository for radioactive wastes from the nuclear-weapons production complex at Chelyabinsk, 900 miles east of Moscow.
>
> The dose rate near the outlet pipe is "in the hundreds of roentgens per hour," Cochran says. An hour's dose is enough to kill a person within weeks. Surrounded by forest, the lake is cordoned off to everyone except heavily shielded workers stabilizing the contamination.[6]

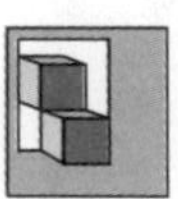

Shifting Society's Pollution. Though Japan and Western Europe have tough environmental standards, anyone who travels the third world quickly discovers it's a fantasy that the industrial countries are the polluted ones. Air quality in Mexico City, New Delhi, or Lagos makes Pasadena at noon seem like a mountain health spa. General pollution in Taiwan, South Korea, Poland, Brazil, Indonesia, and other developing nations far surpasses the West's.

A cold, free market analysis of this situation might conclude that this is acceptable. The environment of the West is worth more, measured by property values, than in the developing world; so why not shift pollution there? Health in the West, measured by the courtroom standard of lifetime-earnings potential in dollars, is worth dramatically more than third world health measured in bahts or rupees. So why not let somebody else get sick while we enjoy cheap products made possible by distant pollution?

Shifting society's pollution to other lands is no more acceptable than exporting uncertified drugs. One of the Bush administration's first acts was a selfless order that U.S. firms not ship toxic wastes to undeveloped countries. Another step in the right direction might be a "pollution tariff"—a levy on products imported from countries not making good-faith steps toward ecological control. The levy may help American industry and pressure foreign governments to protect their own citizens and workers. On the other hand, firms that relied on foreign firms for their materials would suffer from the levies.[7]

The Global Picture. Table 15.2 presents a *Wall Street Journal* summary of the current state of the global environment.

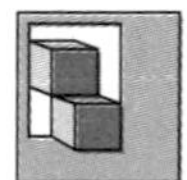

A LAYMAN'S GUIDE TO KEY ENVIRONMENTAL ISSUES

TABLE 15.2

	Description	*Pessimist's View*	*Optimist's View*
Overpopulation	Now at 5.4 billion, the world's population is growing by about 95 million a year. If current trends continue, world population could nearly triple to 14 billion by the latter half of the next century.	Overpopulation worsens poverty, accelerates pollution, jeopardizes food supplies, spreads disease. Failure to curb population growth undermines economic progress and magnifies environmental decline.	Population growth is a natural partner of economic progress. The world's carrying capacity is vast, and natural resources are abundant. Technology and human ingenuity can solve any serious shortages, if they arise.
Biodiversity	Human activities continue to reduce biological diversity. Extinction rates are accelerating. Among the causes: poverty, pollution, excessive exploitation, habitat destruction, and the introduction of alien species.	As economic development spreads, ecosystems are chopped into ever-smaller fragments, able to support fewer species. Genetic materials—for example, specimens of individual species—need to be protected and managed as sovereign resources.	Extinction of species from time to time is part of nature's way. Biotechnology and business need unfettered access to the world's natural resources to support scientific progress and economic growth.

TABLE 15.2 (CONTINUED)

	Description	Pessimist's View	Optimist's View
Deforestation	Forests are reeling from pressures of economic development. Clear-cutting destroys habitat and watersheds, increases erosion, and reduces the world's ability to cope with greenhouse gases.	Deforestation threatens the entire planet. More than 90% of the world's land-dwelling plants and animals inhabit forests. Tropical deforestation is accelerating.	Trees are a renewable resource and the supply is abundant. Selective cutting of the forests brings needed jobs and income, spurring further economic development.
Ocean pollution	The single greatest threat to the world's oceans is pollution from land-based sources, which account for about 70% of all the toxic chemicals, sediment, garbage, and other pollutants at sea.	As toxic algae blooms spread, they deplete oxygen and block sunlight, killing fish and other life forms. Alarming threats are also posed by alien species introduced as cargo ships routinely discharge ballast water in foreign harbors.	The capacity of the oceans to cleanse themselves is enormous. Besides, most ocean pollution from land-based sources can be managed effectively by individual nations and through bilateral and regional arrangements.

Source: David Stipp and Frank Allen, "Forecast for Rio: Scientific Cloudiness," *The Wall Street Journal,* June 3, 1992, p. B1. Reprinted by permission of *The Wall Street Journal,*

D. Why Doesn't the Market Take Care of This?

Are there solutions for these problems that are acceptable to all stakeholders? Most people want a cleaner environment, yet the free market apparently is not of sufficient strength to guide the economy in that direction. The problem is not a failure in pricing theory; rather, the pricing system works to perfection, albeit in the wrong directions. This inconvenience can be traced to what economists call the "externality," "free good," or "commons" problem. Simply stated, producers have used the environment as a free garbage dump. In effect, producers can pollute a river and pass the costs (in the form of dirty water, dead fish, disease, and so forth) onto society as a whole. If a good can be obtained at no cost, an economist or a businessperson would be inclined to use as much of the free good as possible, and producers have done just that. There is no pricing incentive to minimize pollution if pollution has no direct cost to the company; in fact, the incentive is to maximize pollution. In this instance, the welfare of individuals acting in their own private interests does not coincide with the general good.

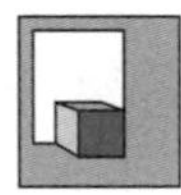

Collective Good. Another way in which an economist might examine the problem is as a *collective good.* If the citizens want a clean environment, the market would presumably reflect that desire by paying nonpolluting companies higher prices for their goods. Unfortunately, the benefits of clean air and water are not restricted to those paying for them through higher prices, because equal benefits are bestowed on those still trading, at lower prices, with polluting companies. Thus, a clean environment benefits everyone equally, regardless of each individual's contribution toward it. A rational utility-maximizing strategy for each person, then, is to patronize cheaper, polluting firms to the exclusion of the more expensive nonpolluters, despite the desire of society for a clean environment. Therefore, industries have no incentive not to pollute. Externalities and collective goods are instances of market failure.

Ethics. Another solution mechanism for conflicts between business and society is letting the individual ethics of decision makers determine which course of action to take. Of course, one of the many problems in relying on individual or corporate conscience to resolve environmental problems lies simply in identifying the right course of action. Even if disposed to do good, how does one choose in the short term between, for example, clean air and jobs?

Patrick Moore, chairman of the Forest Practices Committee, Forest Alliance of British Columbia, framed the ethics issue as follows:

> More than 20 years ago, I was one of a dozen or so activists who founded Greenpeace in the basement of the Unitarian Church in Vancouver. . . . For me, Greenpeace is about ringing an ecological alarm, awakening mass consciousness to the true dimensions of our global predicament, pointing out the problems and defining their nature. Greenpeace doesn't necessarily have the solutions to those problems and certainly isn't equipped to put solutions into practice. That requires the combined efforts of environmentalists, governments, public and private institutions, and corporations. This demands a high degree of cooperation and collaboration. The politics of blame and shame must be replaced with the politics of working together and win-win.[8]

Law. And what of the law? Obviously, international environmental problems cannot be cured merely by passing a new regulation in this country. Increasingly, the nations of the world are reaching understandings about cleansing the globe. In June 1992, environmental concerns drew together in Rio de Janeiro, Brazil, the largest gathering of heads of state in history. That remarkable assemblage for the Earth Summit testifies to the increasing global recognition of environmental problems and their critical role in international economic development and trade. Consider also the 1990 revision to the Montreal Protocol, a global environmental accord: "Driven by disturbing new evidence of a widening hole in the Earth's ozone layer, representatives of 53 nations agreed . . . to ban major ozone-destroying chemicals by the year 2000."[9]

Similarly, in 1994, 64 nations added teeth to the 1990 Basel Convention (curbing transnational toxic waste shipment) by agreeing to immediately stop dumping toxic waste in developing countries. The United States, feeling, among other things, that certain materials such as scrap metal could properly be sent abroad for recycling if the receiving governments agree, has not ratified the Basel Convention.[10]

Profile Perspective: Would the market adequately take care of the Neu-Proler site problem? Where are the incentives for the firm, and where are the incentives for the municipal government?

II. Regulatory Structure of Environmental Law

The United States has developed a wide variety of environmental protection laws and remedies, some of which are discussed in this part. Throughout this discussion, keep in mind the central problem in environmental law—how much are we willing to pay? This is not an easy question to answer. For example, as a society, do we want clean air at any cost? How do we value human life so we can decide how much to spend to reduce the statistical incidence of a particular hazard, thereby saving some estimated number of lives annually? Must we sacrifice short-term economic development to achieve long-term environmental goals? And, if so, who should pay for achieving these goals?

A. The Federal Role

Surprisingly, the federal government has long maintained a role in the protection of the environment, some would argue too great a role. In as early as 1899, Congress enacted a law that required a permit to discharge refuse into navigable waters. As it became apparent that private, state, and local environmental efforts were not adequate to the burgeoning problems, in the early 1970s Congress began to take a number of aggressive legislative initiatives.

National Environmental Policy Act. Requires that the government "use all practicable means" to conduct federal affairs in harmony with the environment.

National Environmental Policy Act (NEPA).

In 1970, President Nixon signed the **National Environmental Policy Act** (NEPA), which established a strong federal presence in the promotion of a clean and healthy environment. NEPA represents a general commitment by the federal government to "use all practicable means" to conduct federal affairs in a fashion that both promotes "the general welfare" and operates in "harmony" with the environment. A portion reads:

Public Law 91-190 (1969), 42 U.S.C. §4331 *et seq.*

PURPOSE

> The purposes of this Act are: To declare a national policy which will encourage productive and enjoyable harmony between man and his environment; to promote efforts which will prevent or eliminate damage to the environment and biosphere and stimulate the health and welfare of man; to enrich the understanding of the ecological systems and natural resources important to the Nation; and to establish a Council on Environmental Quality.

Council on Environmental Quality. Council serves as an advisor to the president in connection with the preparations of the annual Environmental Quality Report.

environmental impact statement (EIS). Statement of the anticipated impact on the environment of legislation or other major federal action, and suggestions for reasonable alternatives.

The **Council on Environmental Quality** (CEQ) serves as an advisor to the president. Specifically, the CEQ must "assist and advise the president in the preparation of the [annual] Environmental Quality Report." The CEQ is a watchdog of sorts. It is required to conduct studies and collect information regarding the state of the environment. The council then develops policy and legislative proposals for the president and Congress.

But NEPA's primary influence results from its **environmental impact statement (EIS)** requirements. With few exceptions, "proposals for legislation and other major federal action significantly affecting the quality of the human environment" must be accompanied by an EIS explaining the impact on the environment and detailing reasonable alternatives. Major federal construction projects (highways, dams, and nuclear reactors) would normally require an EIS; but less visible federal programs (ongoing timber management or the abandonment of a lengthy railway) may also require EIS treatment. Although the focus here is on *federal* actions, thus exempting solely private acts from this scrutiny, a major private-sector action supported by federal funding or by one of several varieties of federal permission may also require an EIS. Hence, private companies receiving federal contracts, funding, licenses, and the like may be parties to the completion of an EIS.

Environmental Protection Agency. Created in 1970 to gather information relating to pollution and to assist in pollution control efforts and sanctions.

Environmental Protection Agency (EPA).

The private sector was not left without regulation or constraint. Also in 1970, Congress created the **Environmental Protection Agency** (EPA) to oversee the public regulation of environmental issues. EPA duties include, among other things, (1) information gathering, particularly in surveying pollution problems, (2) conducting research on pollution problems, (3) assisting state and local pollution control efforts, and (4) administering many of the federal laws directed to environmental concerns.

Congress is considering, as it has for some years, the elevation of the EPA to cabinet-level status. That legislation may not succeed. However, the CEQ has received increased funding from the Clinton administration. The president had originally intended to abolish the CEQ, but after political opposition, the administration changed direction and strengthened the council while also establishing the White House Office on the Environmental Policy. The Clinton CEQ will be responsible for NEPA compliance with general environmental policy being managed by the White House Office.

Profile Perspective: Whose responsibility should it be to oversee sites such as that of Neu-Proler's? Is the state or local government adequately equipped to deal with these problems or, because of their impact on the greater environment, should the oversight be left to federal agencies?

B. Regulation of Air Pollution: Taking a Breath of Fresh . . .

We depend on (indeed, we emotionally embrace) the automobile. In doing so, we have opened vistas of opportunity not previously imagined. However, for the present at least, we also have eliminated clean air. This may seem like an extreme statement, yet we don't think it strange for someone to claim they notice a difference between city and country air. Motor vehicles discharge carbon monoxide, nitrogen oxide, and hydrocarbons as by-products of the combustion of fuel.

Motor vehicles are the major source of air pollution, but industrial production and the combustion of fossil fuels in homes and industry are also significant contributors to the dilemma of dirty air. For most Americans, air pollution is simply an unpleasant fact of life. To the average Los Angeles resident, smog has been more central to daily activity than the area's beaches and mountains.

Progress? These discouraging words are facts of contemporary life; but it is also a fact that our hard work and vast expenditures may succeed in dissipating much of the gloom. As *Newsweek* recently reported, "Most barometers of air quality have been showing positive trends for years."[11] (Airborne levels of lead have fallen by 96 percent, for example.) *Newsweek* attributes much of this salutary trend to the continuing replacement of old, "dirty" cars with newer, environmentally friendly models—1993 models emit only about 1 percent as much pollution as cars of 20 years ago.[12] From 1982 to 1992, overall U.S. smog incidence dropped by 8 percent, such that New York City, for example, fell from 71 "bad" carbon monoxide days in 1985 to 2 days in 1991 and 1 in 1992.[13]

Severe problems remain, however. Approximately 90 million people breathe unhealthy air, and recent improvements in smog conditions have resulted in part from the good fortune of cooler summers (smog is more likely in hotter weather).[14]

Clean Air Act of 1990 (CAA). Early clean air legislation in 1963 and 1965 afforded the government limited authority. The **Clean Air Act** amendments of 1970 and 1977 gave the EPA the power to set air-quality standards and to ensure that those standards were achieved according to a timetable prescribed by the agency. Politics brought clean air to the fore in 1990, and a new Clean Air Act followed. The Clean Air Act of 1990, which is being phased in over a period of years, generally requires tougher auto emission controls, cleaner burning gasoline, and new equipment to capture industrial and

Clean Air Act. Amended in 1990, establishes air-quality standards and enforcement procedures for the standards.

business pollution, all of which work toward the general goal of reducing airborne pollutants by about 50 percent. The act's virtues are summarized in the following remarks from the *Los Angeles Times:*

> Washington has revisited the federal Clean Air Act for the first time since the 1970s, and the winners are:
>
> - Southern California. The law itself will not create clean air. But it provides a framework for the region actually to meet federal health standards one day, something that has never quite been within our reach.
> - Canada. Its lakes and forests will no longer be eaten alive by acid rain. By 1995, power plants in 21 states must reduce by 5 million tons the quantity of sulfuric acid that they now scatter into the atmosphere to mix with clouds and form acid rain. Another 5 million tons must be taken out of the air by 2000.
> - A largely untested theory that market economics can play a role in controlling smog and acid rain. That's if government regulators make it worth something to polluting industries to reduce dirty emissions. A power plant that cuts emissions by, say, 10 percent more than the law requires can sell its "right" to pollute to another plant that needs to add that 10 percent to its own smokestacks to generate more power.[15]

Implementing the CAA. In 1993, a Senate report entitled "Three Years Later: Report Card on the 1990 Clean Air Act Amendments" accorded the government a B-minus in its measurement of progress toward implementing the very prescriptive provisions of the new, 800-page law.[16]

Cost-benefit. The central question is whether big benefits, like those noted above, are worth the cost—in the case of the Clean Air Act, about $25 billion annually. Currently, we are spending over $120 billion annually on total environmental cleanup, and that figure is expected to rise to nearly $180 billion by 2000, which would represent approximately 2.8 percent of the gross domestic product.[17]

Obviously, consumers will bear much of the cost of clean air. For example, new Ford cars are expected to rise in price by an average of $225 in the short term and by as much as $1,125 in the long term due to CAA requirements. Much of the $225 increase is attributable to replacing ozone-depleting chlorofluorocarbons in air conditioners with hydrofluorocarbons, which are believed to be harmless to the atmosphere.[18]

Business, too, will pay. The heavy cost associated with clean air is well illustrated by a corner of the CAA that requires bigger businesses in severe air pollution regions of 11 states to reduce the number of people who drive to work or face penalties. Mass transit, where available, car pools, and company transportation are the likely options. Some estimates place the cost to employers at between $200 and $900 annually for each employee.

The benefits have approached the miraculous in some instances, but the bill is very high. Now our task is to decide where we want to put our money and how much we want to pay for what many scientists believe to be rather trivial advances in air quality. As explained in *Fortune:*

> Take acid rain and ozone depletion. Most scientists agree that acid rain poses only a minor danger to rivers and lakes and no serious threat to human health. By contrast, the number of skin cancer deaths due to ozone depletion could rise from 500 a year currently to 100,000 by 2050. Yet Eileen Clausen, the EPA's director of atmos-

pheric programs, figures the United States will spend about $1 billion annually for the next eight years to fight ozone depletion, and perhaps $4 billion a year "forever" to reduce acid rain.[19]

Passive Smoke. If the subject is clean air, smog immediately comes to mind; but in 1993, the EPA opened a new "indoor" front in its antipollution strategy by declaring that breathing secondhand tobacco smoke increases the risk of illness. As might be expected, this interesting initiative has been greeted with great publicity and a lawsuit from the tobacco industry, which seeks to have the EPA passive-smoke report declared null and void on the grounds that the scientific evidence does not support the EPA conclusion. The EPA report says that evidence conclusively establishes a link between inhaling secondhand tobacco smoke and illness. The report blamed passive smoke for approximately 3,000 lung cancer deaths annually in nonsmokers, and it attributed 150,000 to 300,000 annual cases of bronchitis and pneumonia in young children to that smoke.

Implications. The report put immediate pressure on schools, work sites, restaurants, and other public places to make new arrangements for dealing with this so-called environmental tobacco smoke. Even sports stadiums have begun to ban smoking altogether or to restrict it to limited areas. The report may lead to tighter Occupational Safety and Health Administration regulations on smoke in the workplace. It may influence child custody decisions depending on whether one of the parents smokes; and it is likely that child abuse charges will be brought, in some instances, against parents who smoke around children who suffer from respiratory problems.

Most States Unhappy with New Emissions Testing Program

by Philip Davis, National Public Radio

Daniel Zwerdling, host: One of the downsides of owning a car is the fact that you have to wait in line for an auto emissions test each year, and then you have to pass it. You know the drill. You go to a test center or a nearby gas station; they hook a hose from a machine to your exhaust pipe to make sure your car doesn't pollute the air too much. If you flunk, you have to get what could be an expensive tune-up, or pay a fine. Beginning this year, drivers here in Washington, DC, and in 27 states are scheduled to undergo even tougher testing at centralized sites because, according to standards in the Clean Air Act, air in those places is still dangerously dirty. But NPR's [National Public Radio] Philip Davis reports that angry drivers and state politicians may get the new system killed.

Philip Davis, reporter: One of the first states to put in the new centralized emissions testing program was Maine. Maine's political leaders wanted to get a jump on the new requirements and the tests began last summer.

Mel Leary, reporter: There was a firestorm of protest across the state.

Davis: Mel Leary covers the issue for Maine Public Radio in Augusta. He says the program was a disaster from the start. Maine had never had an auto-testing program before and Leary says the state did a poor job of preparing people for what to expect. People were shocked to see their cars put on a treadmill and the en-

Continued

Continued

gine revved up and down. Leary says the testing program had serious flaws. For example, a computer program failed some cars whether they were polluting or not. Within weeks, there was public uproar.

Leary: When they found out that these people were fiddling around under the hoods, unhooking hoses and hooking them up wrong and causing damage to their cars or their trucks, you got people who were very angry. I remember that the members of the legislature that attended one public hearing said they were fearful that people were going to start throwing things at them.

Davis: As if that wasn't bad enough, Governor John McKernan let it slip that the benefits of the testing program were not going to go to cleaner air, but were going to be converted into air pollution credits that could be used by big companies to pollute more.

Leary: That was probably the biggest political blunder in recent times in Maine politics that really ticked a lot of people off. The feeling was that that kind of a trade-off was simply wrong, that if you're going to do something to clean up the air, then you should do something to clean up the air. It shouldn't be bankable, if you will, as a credit so that it could be used to pollute somewhere else.

Davis: A grassroots rebellion sprang up nearly overnight. In record time, 68,000 people in Maine signed an antitesting ballot initiative. Within weeks, the state moved to put the test on hold. Maine's experience reverberated across the country. States that thought they could easily roll out the new testing program started having second thoughts. Even though it can mean the loss of federal highway funds, politicians in states as conservative as Georgia and as liberal as Massachusetts decided to put their programs on hold, too. Paul Caron is a Massachusetts lawmaker who is involved in that state's decision.

Paul Caron: Nobody, I think, at this point wanted to be out in the forefront of requiring additional requirements of its citizens if other states would not be following suit.

Davis: Massachusetts didn't want to pay for an expansive new network of testing stations if other states didn't have to, too. And politicians didn't want to irritate the politically powerful network of gas station owners who currently had the auto-testing business and who would lose if the new centralized system was put into place. Paul Caron says the Environmental Protection Agency suddenly seemed willing to compromise.

Caron: Amazing what happens when you had a change in Congress down in Washington. It really happened after November, after Newt Gingrich and the Republicans came into power in Washington. All of a sudden, there was a willingness on EPA's part to start talking to states about what might be problematic in implementing the system.

Davis: In state after state, local political realities are making a mishmash of the federal Clean Air program. A number of states are still going ahead with the tests, but only after lots of statehouse wheeling and dealing that leaves the test programs quite different from what the Clean Air Act originally envisioned. Take the way the program developed in Colorado. Big industry supported a centralized testing program there because they did not want more controls slapped on them. But gas stations who had been given all the testing business up till then opposed the centralized program. So when Colorado's testing program went on line in January, it was only half centralized. Old cars could still go to local gas stations for tests while newer cars went to the centralized test facilities. But there have been howls of complaints anyway. . .

It seems like each week brings a new incentive for states not to do the tests. On Capitol Hill, lawmakers are talking of stripping the EPA of money it has budgeted for enforcement of the Clean Air Act, and the head of the EPA has written a letter to the states promising to give states even more time and leeway when it comes to testing. States say they are still committed to clean air, but without tougher testing, the EPA says air pollution will not improve unless more expensive pollution controls are slapped on factories and utilities. And that's something that would bring on yet another set of political battles. This is Philip Davis, in Washington.

Continued

Continued

Questions

1. If the EPA wants the states to comply without "wheeling and dealing," what approach would you recommend? Is there a way for all parties to be happy here?
2. Should enforcement of compliance with something like the emissions standards be voluntary on the part of the states? Recall from the reading that a state's failure to comply (or to ensure that its citizens are in compliance) results in the loss of federal highway funds. Do you consider this a sufficient motivation?
3. Were Maine's intentions improper (converting the efforts into pollution credits for Maine companies)?

Source: National Public Radio, "All Things Considered," April 15, 1995.

Deep Ecology and the Spotted Owl

by Mark Peterson

What deep ecology does is provide a perspective from which to understand our relation to the environment, a "deep" perspective. It also, as a result of this, provides a way to resolve all sorts of theoretical problems in the field of ethics. It can provide these solutions primarily because it is a quasi-dialectical approach to environmental ethics—dialectical in that it asks questions about what we presuppose in ethical questions about nature, and quasi because its proponents are generally not familiar with the technical aspects of dialect.

Deep ecology was devised by Arne Naess as a response to what he saw as a shallow approach to questions of environmental ethics. Typically, we still hear environmental arguments phrased in a way characterized as shallow. Here's an example: we can either log the Pacific Northwest, or we can have spotted owls. If we log at all, we'll lose spotted owls. If we don't log, we'll lose thousands of jobs and the quality of people's lives is damaged. The shorthand way to describe this is to point out that shallow environmental arguments are given using an exclusive "or." This way of phrasing locks us into a very specific set of possible responses. . .

This won't work because we can never figure out a consistent basis for determining what the interests or rights of animals are. I suppose I should go further and tell you that, from my own experience, it is equally impossible to determine, in a consistent way, what the rights of humans are, but that is for a different paper altogether.

In any event, the way this whole issue was phrased conditions the possible answers, and the possible modes of resolution. Naess' insight was that there is a deeper way to ask about spotted owl/human relations. A deep ecological perspective would point out that the problem isn't spotted owls at all, but that humans are using the forests in such a way that the environment as a whole is being affected. The fact that it doesn't affect us right away is irrelevant. The fact that spotted owls may become extinct is a side issue to the larger issue of the overall relation of human being to the environment.

What deep ecology requires is that we simply recognize that we are already deeply implicated not in but with the environment—that our relationship to the environment is not one of a disinterested observer to an externally existent world with which we do not already have an intimate and reciprocal relation. We are, under a deep ecological point of view, *part* of the environment.

[Authors' note: Consider that, in December 1994, a federal judge approved a plan that places a limit on logging levels of 1.1 billion board feet per year (a fourth of the yearly average cut in the 1980s). Environmentalists contend that this plan ignores recent findings that the spotted owl is disappearing at an increased rate, and logging industry representatives claim that the limit is far too low and that logging communities will not be able to survive.]

Source: Mark Peterson, "Deep Ecology: Faculty Colloquium," University of Wisconsin–Washington County, December 8, 1993. Reprinted by permission of the author.

C. Regulation of Water Pollution

You wouldn't want to swim in a wading pool after someone cleaned their outboard motor in it; you wouldn't want to drink water from a fountain into which people have thrown garbage; and you wouldn't want to wash your car with water cloudy from industrial waste deposits. We understand the costs when they arrive at our doorstep, yet often we do not give it a second thought to let cups fall in the water as we enjoy our boats. As with the air, we have displayed a tendency to treat our water resources as free goods. Rather than paying the full cost of producing goods and services, we have simply piped a portion of that cost into the nearest body of water. The waste from production—indeed from the totality of our life experience—has commonly been disposed of in the water at a cost beneath that required to dispose of the waste in an ecologically sound fashion.

The corruption of our water system arose in a variety of ways. We have not always realized what we now know about the danger of wastes and the cleansing limits of our lakes and streams. The Gulf of Mexico provides a particularly alarming example. Industrial wastes, lawn chemicals, farm fertilizers, and household wastewater from all over the eastern two-thirds of the United States flow into the Gulf of Mexico, with the result that a patch of the bottom waters up to 20 meters thick and about the size of New Jersey is effectively dead. Divers found no crab, shrimp, or fish in the dead zone. Nitrates from farm fertilizers encourage massive algae growth that sinks to the Gulf floor, decays, and consumes the available oxygen.[20]

Approximately 10 percent of the freshwater runoff in the United States is used for industrial cooling. Often, the result is water that is inhospitable to aquatic life. Herbicides, pesticides, acid runoff from strip mining, and oil spills are more examples of our assault on the waterways. Although scientists differ on the severity of the problem, we have learned that in recent years, airborne pollutants such as acid rain sometimes damage our water resources as well.

Clean Water Act. Establishes standards for water quality relating to the protection of water life as well as for safe recreation, and the enforcement of those standards.

Federal Policy. The **Clean Water Act** (CWA), designed to "restore and maintain the chemical, physical, and biological integrity of the nation's waters," establishes two national goals: (1) achieving water quality sufficient for the protection and propagation of fish, shellfish, and wildlife and for recreation in and on the water; and (2) eliminating the discharge of pollutants into navigable waters. The states have primary responsibility for enforcing the CWA, but the federal government, via the Environmental Protection Agency, is empowered to assume enforcement authority if necessary.

National Pollutant Discharge Elimination System. Requires that all who discharge pollutants obtain an EPA permit before adding pollutants to a navigable stream.

The goals of the Clean Water Act are to be implemented primarily by imposing limits on the amount of pollutants that may lawfully enter the water of the United States from any "point source" (typically a pipe). The **National Pollutant Discharge Elimination System** (NPDES) requires all pollutant dischargers to secure an EPA permit before pouring effluent into a navigable stream. The permit specifies maximum permissible levels of effluent. Typically, the permit also mandates the use of a particular pollution control process or device and requires the permit holder to monitor its own performance and report on that performance to the state or the EPA, as appropriate.

Nonpoint Pollution. Water runoff from the land commonly carries with it pollutants, including silt, fertilizers, and pesticides. Virtually the entire U.S. coastline, as well as many bays, rivers, lakes, and other waterways, are affected by these nonpoint pollutants. The problems are multiple—for example, fertilizer runoff from agricultural land feeds algae, which spreads to the point that it consumes the oxygen in some inlets and coves, thus eliminating other plant and animal life. Existing legislation has been ineffectual, and nonpoint pollution remains largely unregulated.

One anecdote, however, may explain the problems inherent in the CWA's definitions: *Newsweek* magazine recently reported that both environmentalists and Native American groups were concerned that cattle were contaminating certain rivers and thereby destroying the wild salmon that lived there. The groups filed a lawsuit under the Clean Air Act, claiming that the cattle were a source of "pollution discharge" that robbed the water of oxygen. The suit asks that the farmers be forced to comply with the act and construct miles of fencing and off-stream watering systems.[21] The farmers contend that the cattle are not the type of "polluters" contemplated by the act.

New Directions. Congress is expected to rewrite federal clean water law. The primary initiatives are expected to be (1) an increase in pollution control spending (assuming deficit reduction targets are met) that would add $500 million annually to the existing $2 billion expenditure up to a total of $5 billion in the year 2000, and (2) increased attention to nonpoint pollution such as that from farmlands, streets, and construction sites.[22]

D. Regulation of Land Pollution: The Grass Is Always Greener . . .

Pollution does not fit tidily into the three compartments (air, water, land) used for convenience in this text. Acid rain, as discussed above, debases air and water as well as the fruits of the water and land, such as fish and trees. Similarly, the problems of land pollution addressed in this section often do damage to the fullness of the natural world. For most of recorded history, we felt safe and comfortable in using the Earth as a garbage dump. When we did begin to recognize emerging dangers, our initial concern was simply the problem of disposing of the enormous bulk of our solid wastes.

Garbage. Basically, the problem is that our lifestyles result in mountains of solid waste that grow higher every year. As of 1992, we were spending $30 billion annually for municipal trash collection, a figure that will rise to perhaps $75 billion by 2000.[23] Our total waste stream, which the EPA sought to curb by 25 percent, has in fact increased 13 percent since 1988. Some initiatives by both business and government have sought to control the solid waste problem, but other actions taken are merely cosmetic. For example, McDonald's attempted to educate its customers regarding its use of polystyrene packaging, explaining that it would be able to use recycled materials. However, the public believes polystyrene to be always environmentally harmful, so McDonald's succumbed and switched its packaging to brown paper, thereby requiring the use of more trees.

And the public has become increasingly conscious of waste-generating lifestyles:

> Disposable diaper makers blamed consumer misunderstanding for survey results that show people support a ban on their product. About 16 billion disposables are sold each year. Because of environmental and health issues, bans or taxes are being considered in at least 20 states. A Gallup poll showed 43 percent of people support a ban. Officials say consumers don't realize cloth diapers take more energy to make and need water for cleaning.[24]

But consumer misunderstanding about the environmental impact of cloth and disposable diapers can be traced to conflicting information given by different industry groups. A 1990 study sponsored by the diaper arm of the American Paper Institute showed that "disposables and reusables were, environmentally speaking, equivalent."[25] However, a 1991 study sponsored by the cloth diaper industry found "cloth diapers environmentally superior."[26]

Recycling. Nine states have bottle bills that result, according to industry figures, in recycling about 80 percent of the beverage containers in those states. We dispose of 115 billion beer and pop cans annually. Those containers consume about 5 percent of our landfill space. According to the federal General Accounting Office, 70 percent of Americans favor a nationwide bottle bill, but Congress has never given its approval.

In Germany, manufacturers are required by law to clean up the garbage they produce. As a result, Bavarian Moter Werks (BMW), for example, uses junked BMWs to make plastics, with a goal of recycling 90 percent of each car. In total, the United States reuses about one-third as much of its waste as do Germany and Japan. Of course, recycling is not a cure-all for our waste management problems.

Solid Waste Disposal Act. To attack the massive garbage problem, Congress approved the Solid Waste Disposal Act of 1965. The act, in brief, leaves solid waste problems to states and localities, but the federal government offers research and financial support.

Toxic Substances Control Act (TSCA). Requires chemical manufacturers to report information relating to chemicals that pose a "substantial risk" and allows the EPA to review and limit, or to stop, the introduction of new chemicals.

Resource Conservation and Recovery Act (RCRA). Authorizes the federal government to provide assistance to states and localities in connection with solid waste, to prohibit open dumping, and to establish programs to recover energy and valuable materials from solid waste.

Toxic Substances Control Act (TSCA). In 1976, Congress approved the **Toxic Substances Control Act (TSCA)** to identify toxic chemicals, assess their risks, and control dangerous chemicals. Under the terms of the TSCA, the Environmental Protection Agency requires the chemical industry to report any information it may have suggesting that a chemical poses a "substantial risk." The EPA is empowered to review and limit or stop the introduction of new chemicals.

Resource Conservation and Recovery Act (RCRA). By 1976, the dangers of hazardous substances were becoming apparent to all, and Congress complemented the TSCA with the **Resource Conservation and Recovery Act (RCRA).** The act addresses both solid and hazardous wastes. Its solid waste provisions are more supportive than punitive in tone and approach. The federal government is authorized, among other strategies, to provide technical and financial assistance to states and localities; to prohibit future open dumping; and to establish cooperative federal, state, local, and private-enterprise programs to recover energy and valuable materials from solid waste.

Subtitle C of the RCRA is designed to ensure the safe movement and disposal of hazardous wastes. The generator of the waste must determine if that waste is hazardous under EPA guidelines and, if so, report the waste site and waste activities to the government. The waste generator must then create a manifest to be used in tracking the waste from its creation to its disposal. Along the cradle-to-grave path of the waste, all those with responsibility for it must sign the manifest and safely store and transport the waste. Once the waste reaches a licensed disposal facility, the owner or manager of that site signs the manifest and returns a copy of it to the generator.

Disposal Sites. Owners and operators of hazardous waste disposal sites must obtain government permits to begin operation. Those sites must be operated according to EPA standards, and remedial action must be taken should hazardous wastes escape from the sites.

Through the 1980s, the general thrust of RCRA was to replace land burial of hazardous waste with treatments that destroy those wastes and neutralize their toxicity. Then in 1993, the EPA announced a crackdown on incinerators, which have been widely employed as an alternative to burial in dealing with toxic garbage. Under the new policy, announced in May 1993, the EPA imposed a moratorium of 18 months on all new hazardous waste incinerators, during which time the agency will be overhauling its rules governing hazardous waste burning and will develop strategies to force reduction of waste. The policy applies to incinerators, industrial boilers, industrial furnaces, and cement kilns that burn everything from general garbage to suspected cancer-causing agents such as dioxin. Each year, we burn 5 million tons of hazardous waste, enough to fill tank trucks stretching end to end from Washington, DC, to Los Angeles.[27]

NIMBY. The transportation and disposal of solid and hazardous waste have led citizens' groups and state and local governments to aggressive action under the general banner of "Not in My Backyard" (NIMBY). Citizens are contesting the siting of new landfills, shipments of nuclear waste, the creation of hazardous waste facilities, and the like. Some communities have passed ordinances forbidding the transportation of wastes through their boundaries. In 1992, the Supreme Court struck down Michigan and Alabama NIMBY statutes. The Michigan law prohibited private landfill operators from accepting solid waste from outside the county in question unless explicitly permitted to do so by the county. The Court held that the Michigan law discriminated against interstate commerce. The Court reached a similar conclusion in the Alabama case, in which the state imposed fees on all hazardous waste disposed of within the state but imposed a higher fee on garbage that came from out of state.[28]

Discrimination? For some years, complaints have been raised that government decisions regarding hazardous waste disposal have had the effect of exposing black Americans to greater levels of toxic pollution than whites. For the first time, in 1993 the Clinton administration agreed to investigate those complaints. In ongoing lawsuits aimed at the situation, plaintiffs have argued that they need not prove that states or the federal government *intended* to discriminate in decisions such as choosing sites for hazardous waste disposal; rather, they need only show that the *effect* of the decisions is to disproportionately burden blacks. They believe that would be so even if the decisions were made on the basis of the cost of land, population density, and other conditions unrelated to race.

EPA chief Carol Browner has said, "I don't think that there is any doubt that low-income and minority communities have borne the brunt of our industrial lifestyle."[29] And the data do show dramatic disparities in some cases. For instance, according to the *New York Times,* in Carville, Louisiana, where the population is 70 percent African-American, 353 pounds of toxic material per capita are released, whereas the statewide average per capita is 105 pounds.[30]

The discrimination theme has also played a prominent role in efforts to strengthen pesticide protection rules under the Federal Insecticide, Fungicide, and Rodenticide Act. After beginning the process in 1984, the EPA in 1992 issued new standards that apply to farm workers (farm owners and families are exempt from many of the rules) and employees in nurseries, greenhouses, and forests. To limit exposure to pesticides, which cause an estimated 1,000 fatalities annually, employers must train workers in pesticide safety, post safety information and warnings, use both English and Spanish in giving warnings, and bar workers from recently sprayed fields. Migrant labor advocates, while applauding the new rules, argued that they do not go far enough in training our 1.5 to 2.5 million hired farm workers about pesticide exposure.

NAFTA and Waste. The following article illustrates the nature of hazardous waste problems and suggests that the recent passage of the North American Free Trade Agreement (NAFTA) may lead to significant cross-border waste management progress between Mexico and the United States. Here, California officials alleged that RSR Corp., the world's largest auto battery recycler, hired a California company, Alco Pacifica, to ship battery lead from California to a processing plant in Mexico from which salvageable material was to be returned to California. However, the material was simply abandoned in Mexico, prosecutors charged, with little or no processing.[31]

NAFTA May Get Lift from Pact on Toxic Site

by Bob Davis

[Los Angeles] prosecutor David Eng and Mexican environmental officials [announced] a novel plan to clean up an abandoned lead-recycling plant outside Tijuana, Mexico. . .

Mr. Eng, an environmental prosecutor in the Los Angeles County District Attorney's office, has used a state law classifying lead slag as a hazardous waste to negotiate toxic-waste cleanups south of the border. In the deal, RSR Corp., a privately owned Dallas lead recycler, said it will pay $2.5 million and plead no contest to charges of improperly transporting lead waste from its Los Angeles smelter to Mexico.

$2 Million Cleanup

Of the $2.5 million fine, $2 million will be used to clean up the site, called Alco Pacifico de Mexico, said Los Angeles authorities and the companies involved. Los Angeles District Attorney Gil Garcetti also plans to donate $300,000 of the fine to a foundation that provides medical care for border-area residents. And the Mexican government will use the Alco Pacifico site's recoverable lead, valued at between $100,000 and $200,000, to help pay back wages of workers at the plant, which closed in 1991 after a strike.

The Los Angeles authorities could have prosecuted the case alone, but without the cooperation of the Mexican government the settlement wouldn't have helped clean up the site or provided benefits to people in the area.

* * *

Alco Pacifico has become a grim reminder of Mexico's difficulties in enforcing environmental standards. The 14-acre lead-recycling facility is in the arid hills outside Tijuana, next to dairies that feed the city. The plant has been shut for two years. The rusting furnaces are surrounded by hills of lead ash and slag, open to the wind.

Daniel Muno Garay, who owns one of the nearby dairies, said that over the past decade, 14 cows suddenly keeled over and died. Alco Pacifico managers paid for the losses. "When the animals first started dying, the dairy owner named his price for the animals," Mr. Muno said in an interview last year. "The second time, they would just go over (to Alco Pacifico) for the money."

Occasionally, Mexican regulators visited Alco Pacifico, Mr. Muno said. Plant managers would promise to install new equipment, he said, but the factory would start running at night to avoid the regulators' attention.

* * *

Afterword.

In December 1993, the chief executive of Alco Pacifico, the California company that transported lead slag for RSR from Los Angeles to the Tijuana, Mexico, site, was sentenced to 16 months in jail on three felony counts of unlawful transportation of hazardous wastes to Mexico. That sentence was the sternest such prosecution ever in the United States.[32]

Continued

Continued

Questions

1. *a.* Do you think it is a moral wrong for black communities to be burdened with a disproportionate share of toxic waste?
   b. A legal wrong? Explain.
   c. In shipping wastes to underdeveloped countries, are U.S. firms guilty of racism? Explain.
2. Presumably, most of us bear some responsibility for the hazardous waste problem because our consumption preferences lead to the creation of waste. Because market decisions created the problem, should we let the market resolve it by permitting hazardous waste disposal in the most profitable fashion? Explain.
3. Hazardous waste sites are necessary, but few communities will accept them. Assume government intervention is necessary to manage the hazardous waste problem. Should the federal government pass legislation requiring all states and localities to accept all hazardous waste sites that comply with the federal government's disposal standards? Explain.

Source: *The Wall Street Journal,* June 15, 1993, p. A2. Reprinted by permission of *The Wall Street Journal,*

Superfund—Comprehensive Environmental Response, Compensation, and Liability Act of 1980 (CERCLA). **CERCLA,** known as **Superfund,** is designed to help clean up hazardous dumps and spills. In many instances, those responsible for hazardous dumps and spills cannot afford to pay for cleanup. Other hazardous sites have been abandoned. In both cases, the threat to the public is such that the government created the Superfund to attack those sites that are so dangerous that they have been included on the **National Priorities List** (NPL). The bulk of the fund is drawn from taxes on chemicals and petroleum. Private citizens suffering injury from hazardous wastes do not receive relief under the terms of CERCLA. Rather, they must pursue their claims through the judicial system.

Superfund/CERCLA. Established to help pay for the cleanup of hazardous dumps and spills.

National Priorities List. A list of hazardous dump or spill sites scheduled to be cleaned using CERCLA funds.

Cost. The NPL now includes some 1,245 sites and is expected to eventually grow to more than 3,000. Twelve to 15 years and $25 to $30 million have been required to clean the average site.[33] Total cleanup costs are estimated at $500 billion, and 50 years may be required for the job. Furthermore, some 35,000 additional sites need attention but are currently less threatening than those on the NPL.[34]

All parties responsible for any illegal hazardous waste discharge are strictly liable, with certain limitations, for all costs associated with the necessary cleanup. Unfortunately, many polluters have disappeared or are unable to pay. The result is that the government has been able to secure only about one-fifth of the cleanup costs that potentially could have been recovered from polluters. Particularly frustrating is the sum of money devoted to the legal fees expended in protecting the interests of the many parties who are often involved in a Superfund case. For example:

> One critic recently cited the case of a Long Island, NY, site in which 136 law firms represent potentially responsible parties (PRPs) and another 72 law firms represent the PRPs' 442 insurers. Although the site was reportedly placed on Superfund's priority list more than eight years ago, no cleanup plan has yet been approved.[35]

In testimony before Congress, Du Pont's corporate counsel, Bernard Reilly, argued for greater use of privatization of Superfund cleanups. He pointed to a pair of sites in southern New Jersey: "One landfill is being cleaned up by a chemical industry group at one-third the cost of the EPA-managed site."[36]

President Clinton has proposed a plan for rewriting the Superfund law. He seeks to relax cleanup standards in some instances with the expectation that costs may be reduced by as much as 25 percent. The plan also includes a new tax on commercial insurance companies that would be used to settle lawsuits by polluting businesses against their insurers and an arbitration system designed to remove Superfund cases from the courts. The administration thinks that the combined effect of these measures would be to halve Superfund litigation.

Emergency Planning and Community Right-to-Know act of 1986. Amended Superfund requiring companies to inform the government upon release of any hazardous chemicals into the environment, and to provide to the government an inventory of their hazardous chemicals. The act also requires states to establish emergency procedures for chemical discharges.

Right-to-Know Act. Spurred by the Bhopal, India, chemical plant disaster, which resulted in the deaths of more than 3,000 people, Congress passed the **Emergency Planning and Community Right-to-Know Act of 1986** as an amendment to the Superfund law. The act requires companies to notify the government if they release any extremely hazardous chemicals into the environment, and they must submit an inventory of their hazardous chemicals to the government. Each state must establish emergency response commissions, local emergency planning committees, and emergency plans to deal with chemical discharges. In general, information regarding dangerous chemicals must be released to the public on request. Beyond preparing for chemical release emergencies, the hope behind the law is that its disclosure requirements will enhance community awareness of chemical hazards, thus provoking sufficient community pressure to cause companies to voluntarily reduce their emissions.

Profile Perspective: Which of the regulations cited in this chapter would be most effective against Neu-Proler?

III. Enforcement and Penalties under Federal Law

Because of the risks associated with pollution, environmental protection bodies have been given strong enforcement authority. Very often, violators initially are warned and a compliance schedule is set out. If corrective action is not forthcoming, sterner measures are followed, including an administrative order to comply. Where problems persist or the difficulties are more serious, the government may initiate civil or criminal actions against both firms and managers. Penalties vary with the act in question, but the provisions of the Clean Air Act are typical in that civil fines of $25,000 per day up to a maximum of $200,000 (and higher under some conditions) are provided for. Individuals may be jailed for one year or more and fined. In some instances, an entire operation may be shut down.

Government action has increased over the years, and civil suits have remained the preferred mode of enforcement. "In 1982, according to EPA statistics, 112 civil and 29 criminal cases were referred to [the Justice Department.] In 1991, the numbers were 393 and 81."[37] Figure 15.1 details the pattern of criminal enforcement of environmental laws.

A worrisome dimension of the criminal prosecution record is that small operators are much more likely to go to jail than are managers of big firms. According to a recent study, defendants from large companies who were found guilty had an 18 percent chance of going to jail, compared with a 43 percent chance for those from small businesses.[38]

CRACKING DOWN ON ENVIRONMENTAL CRIME **FIGURE 15.1**

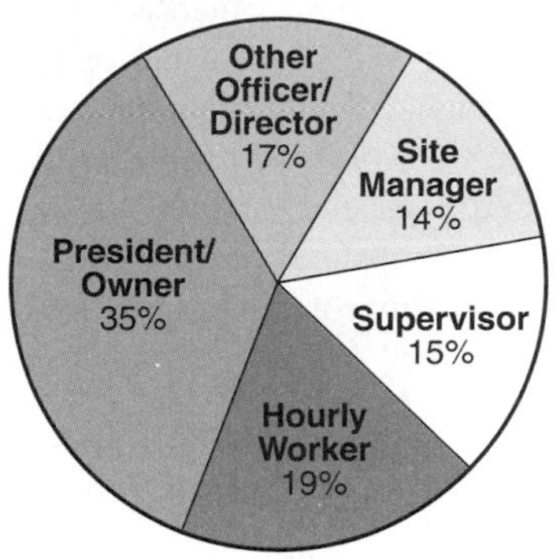

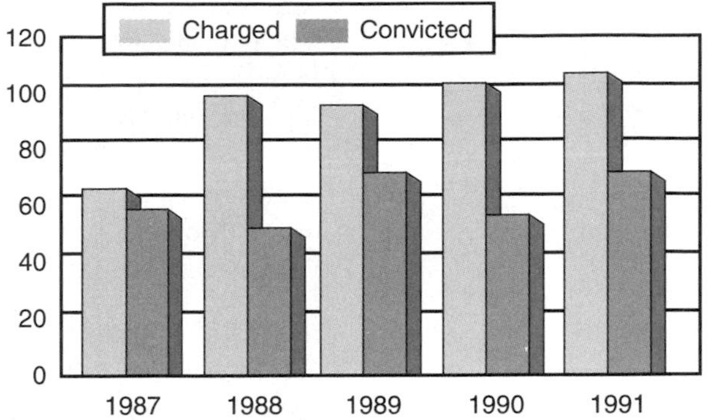

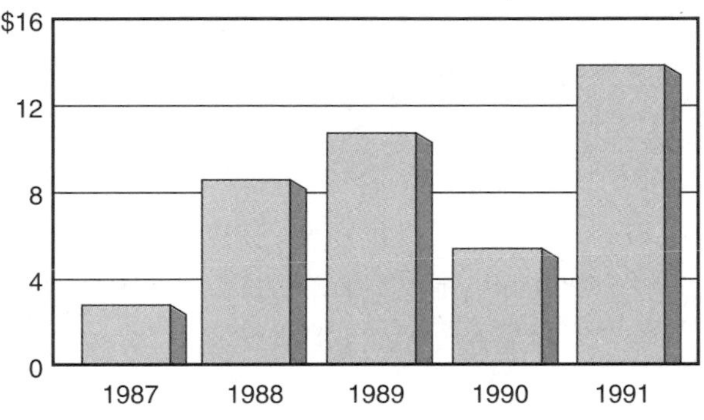

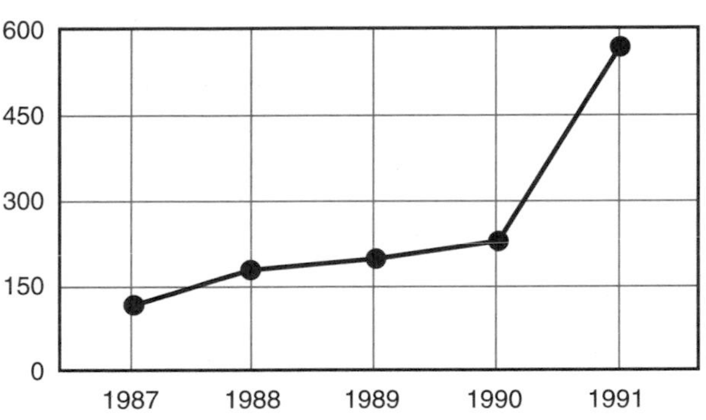

*Data are for fiscal years that ended September 30, 1991.

Source: Frank Allen, "Few Big Firms Get Jail Time for Polluting, *The Wall Street Journal,* December 9, 1991, p. B1. Reprinted by permission of *The Wall Street Journal,* © 1991 Dow Jones & Company, Inc. All rights reserved worldwide.

Enforcement Mechanisms. Many environmental statutes require companies to monitor their own environmental performance and report that information, including violations, to the government. Government agencies generally have broad authority to conduct environmental inspections of both plants and records as necessary, although they will need to seek search warrants if criminal prosecutions are anticipated. Finally, many environmental statutes provide for the possibility of *citizen suits,* wherein an individual is empowered to challenge government environmental decisions such as the granting of a permit and generally to demand both governmental and private-sector compliance with the law.

A. STATE AND LOCAL REGULATION

Under their police powers, state and local governments have the right to impose various controls on citizens to protect and maintain the public health and safety and its general welfare. State and local governments are increasingly acting in the area of environmental protection to do just that. Although rejected by voters by a two-to-one margin, a 1990 California environmental initiative (the so-called Big Green) is reflective of the activism at the state level.

> California's size and its role as an environmental pacesetter often copied by other states made Big Green a closely watched national barometer of how far the public would go for cleaner air, more trees, and fewer pesticides. The initiative would have eventually banned a host of pesticides currently used on food crops. It would have set aside $300 million for buying ancient redwood trees, further strengthened California's already strict limits on air pollutants, permanently banned oil drilling off California's coast, and set up a new elective office of Environmental Advocate empowered to enforce all state environmental laws.[39]

Although California has led the way in environmental activism, most states have now joined the crusade. Ralph Rosenberg, former Iowa state legislator, explained:

> The states have enacted right-to-know legislation to inform the public of hazardous materials. In addition, people are gaining a greater say in the location of hazardous waste facilities. Georgia recently required that the public be notified of applications for hazardous waste facilities.
>
> * * *
>
> States have passed laws aimed at fighting improper hazardous waste management. Indiana, for example, enacted a law that calls for buyers of property to be advised that they might be liable for environmental cleanup costs.
>
> * * *
>
> [T]he Iowa Legislature created a $200 million program to deal with leaking underground storage tanks and assist businesses in meeting federal standards.
>
> These laws exemplify how society is beginning to hold itself environmentally accountable.[40]

IV. Remedies Other than Legislation

A Modest Proposal

One major component of a federal privatization agenda would be to sell off federal enterprises and assets. . . Not national parks and wilderness areas, but supposedly income-producing "commodity lands" administered by the Bureau of Land Management and the U.S. Forest Service. A 1989 Reason Foundation study estimated their value at $160 billion. Environmentalists would go ballistic, but in fact some of the most successful examples of ecologically sensitive resource development occur in privately owned commercial forests and wilderness areas owned by environmental groups. Given the feds' dismal record in managing grazing and timber lands, enlightened environmentalists might see net gains in some form of privatization.

Source: Robert Poole, "The Asset Test: A Privatization Agenda," *Reason Magazine,* February 1995, reprinted in *New York Times,* February 7, 1995.

A. The Common Law

Long before the federal government became actively involved in environmental issues, courts were grappling with the problem. As early as the 1500s, city officials were ordered by a court to keep the streets clean of dung deposited by swine allowed to run loose; the air was said to be "corrupted and infected" by this practice. Legal arguments have typically revolved around the right of a person to use and enjoy private or public property if such usage causes harm to a neighbor's property.

The doctrines of nuisance and trespass are paramount in common law environmental litigation. A private nuisance is a substantial and unreasonable invasion of the private use and enjoyment of one's land; a public nuisance is an unreasonable interference with a right common to the public. Harmful conduct may be both a public and private nuisance simultaneously; the case law distinctions between the two are often blurred. A trespass occurs and liability is imposed with *any* intentional invasion of an individual's right to the exclusive use of his or her own property.

The distinction between trespass and nuisance is fine, and the two may be coextensive. Nuisance and trespass causes of action have been entered for such offenses as fouling a neighbor's water, flooding another's land, or causing excessive noise, smell, or particulate matter on another's property. The remedies available to a successful plaintiff are monetary damages for the harm suffered or an injunction to prevent similar conduct by the defendant in the future, or both.

Negligence and strict liability claims may also arise from pollution cases. For example, a company might well be guilty of negligence if it failed to correct a pollution problem where the technology and necessary resources were available to do so, and that failure caused harm to someone to whom the company owed a duty. In addition, certain activities, such as the use of toxic chemicals, might be so abnormally dangerous as to provoke a strict liability claim.

Common law pollution remedies, although taking a backseat to federal and state laws, remain useful tools in addressing environmental harm. The *Boomer* case that follows is perhaps the most controversial common law treatment of an environmental nuisance.

CASE

Boomer v. Atlantic Cement Co.

26 N.Y.2d 219, 257 N.E.2d 870 (1970)

Facts

The defendant operated a large cement plant near Albany, New York. The case involved actions for injunction and damages by neighboring land owners alleging injury to property from dirt, smoke, and vibration emanating from the plant. A nuisance was found after trial, and temporary damages were allowed but an injunction denied.

* * *

Judge Bergan

It seems apparent that the amelioration of air pollution will depend on technical research in great depth; on a carefully balanced consideration of the economic impact of close regulation; and of the actual effect on public health. It is likely to require massive public expenditure and to demand more than any local community can accomplish and to depend on regional and interstate controls.

Continued

Continued

A court should not try to do this on its own as a by-product of private litigation and it seems manifest that the judicial establishment is neither equipped in the limited nature of any judgment it can pronounce nor prepared to lay down and implement an effective policy for the elimination of air pollution. This is an area beyond the circumference of one private lawsuit. It is a direct responsibility for government and should not thus be undertaken as an incident to solving a dispute between property owners and a single cement plant—one of many—in the Hudson River Valley.

The cement-making operations of defendant have been found by the court at Special Term to have damaged the nearby properties of plaintiffs in these two actions. That court, as it has been noted, accordingly found defendant maintained a nuisance and this has been affirmed at the Appellate Division. The total damage to plaintiff's properties is, however, relatively small in comparison with the value of defendant's operation and with the consequences of the injunction which plaintiffs seek.

The ground for the denial of injunction, notwithstanding the finding both that there is a nuisance and that plaintiffs have been damaged substantially, is the large disparity in economic consequences of the nuisance and of the injunction. This theory cannot, however, be sustained without overruling a doctrine which has been consistently reaffirmed in several leading cases in this court and which has never been disavowed here, namely that where a nuisance has been found and where there has been any substantial damage shown by the party complaining an injunction will be granted.

The rule in New York has been that such a nuisance will be enjoined although marked disparity be shown in economic consequence between the effect of the injunction and the effect of the nuisance.

* * *

[T]o follow the rule literally in these cases would be to close down the plant at once. This court is fully agreed to avoid that immediately drastic remedy; the difference in view is how best to avoid it.

One alternative is to grant the injunction but postpone its effect to a specified future date to give opportunity for technical advances to permit defendant to eliminate the nuisance; another is to grant the injunction conditioned on the payment of permanent damages to plaintiffs, which would compensate them for the total economic loss to their property present and future caused by defendant's operations. For reasons which will be developed the court chooses the latter alternative.

If the injunction were to be granted unless within a short period—e.g., 18 months—the nuisance be abated by improved methods, there would be no assurance that any significant technical improvement would occur.

* * *

Moreover, techniques to eliminate dust and other annoying by-products of cement making are unlikely to be developed by any research the defendant can undertake within any short period, but will depend on the total resources of the cement industry nationwide and throughout the world. The problem is universal wherever cement is made.

For obvious reasons the rate of the research is beyond control of defendant. If at the end of 18 months the whole industry has not found a technical solution, a court would be hard put to close down this one cement plant if due regard be given to equitable principles.

On the other hand, to grant the injunction unless defendant pays plaintiffs such permanent damages as may be fixed by the court seems to do justice between the contending parties. All of the attributions of economic loss to the properties on which plaintiffs' complaints are based will have been redressed.

The nuisance complained of by these plaintiffs may have other public or private consequences, but these particular parties are the only ones who have sought remedies and the judgment proposed will fully redress them. The limitation of relief granted is a limitation only within the four corners of these actions and does not foreclose public health or other public agencies from seeking proper relief in a proper court.

Continued

Continued

It seems reasonable to think that the risk of being required to pay permanent damages to injured property owners by cement plant owners would itself be a reasonably effective spur to research for improved techniques to minimize nuisance.

[Reversed and remanded.]

Questions

1. *a.* The defendant was required to pay a "tax" for the right to continue to pollute. In your opinion, was the court correct in imposing that tax rather than requiring further pollution abatement? Explain.
   b. In a portion of the opinion not reprinted here, the dissenting Judge Jasen argued: "The promotion of the polluting cement company has, in my opinion, no public use or benefit." Do you agree? Explain.
2. In a portion of the opinion not reprinted here, the dissenting Judge Jasen argued that the use of permanent money damages in place of an injunction has been limited to cases in which "the use to which the property was intended to be put was primarily for the public benefit." Why might the denial of the injunction be acceptable in public benefit cases but not in cases of private benefit?
3. Plaintiff Webb developed Sun City, a retirement village near Phoenix, Arizona. At the time, a distance of two and a half to three miles separated the development from defendant Spur Industries' cattle-feeding operation. The feed lot was well managed and clean for a business of that character. Prior to the Sun City project, the area around the feed lot had been largely undeveloped. Sun City and related growth brought large numbers of people in proximity to the cattle lot. As time passed, the two businesses expanded, until at the initiation of the suit, only 500 feet separated the two. The plaintiff filed suit to enjoin the defendant's operation as a nuisance. Decide. Explain. [See *Spur Industries, Inc.* v. *Del E. Webb Development Co.*, 494 P.2d 700 (1972).]

Profile Perspective: Who has standing to file a claim against Neu-Proler for its contamination of the Port of Los Angeles? Who has been affected by the contamination? Do all of those parties have the right to sue?

B. The Free Market

Our steady, even spectacular, strides forward in environmental protection have not dispelled the view, particularly among economists and businesspeople, that legislation is sometimes not the best remedy for environmental problems. To them, pollution control is not so much a matter of law as of economics. They believe that with proper incentives, the market will, in many instances, prove superior to legislation in preventing and correcting environmental problems. For example, 20 years ago, 164 pounds of metal were required to create 1,000 soda cans. In 1995, manufacturers have discovered better, more efficient uses of resources and now use only 35 pounds of metal for the same number of cans. In fact, the Heartland Institute, a conservative think tank based in Chicago, reported that air quality was improving as fast or faster before the Clean Air Act as it has since that time.[41]

The general idea of economic efficiency and proper incentives is also well illustrated by New York City's efforts to deal with its daily production of 385 tons of sludge, which cannot legally be dumped into the ocean and which overwhelms local landfill capacity. Bio Gro Systems of Annapolis, Maryland, ships 100 tons of sludge daily by rail from New York City to Colorado and Arizona, where farmers are now on waiting lists to have the potent fertilizers spread on their land. The city pays Bio Gro, but the sludge is free to farmers, whose reliance on chemical fertilizers has been reduced.[42]

Cost-Benefit. From the free market point of view, environmental legislation very often imposes unacceptable costs. *Fortune* asked, "How much is America overpaying for environmental regulations?"[43] In 1990, our total bill for federal air and water legislation was estimated to be $320 billion, of which $79 billion came in direct costs; the balance was the result of reduced job growth, reduced capital formation, and lower savings.[44] According to economists Michael Hazilla and Raymond Kopp, those costs resulted in a 5.8 percent reduction in the gross national product. Some of these costs appear to be excessive. For example, Brookings fellow Robert Crandall has calculated that solid and toxic waste cleanup regulations cost $5 to $9 billion annually. If that money saves half of the 1,100 annual cancers that the EPA attributes to the waste, the cost per cancer case prevented would be $10 to $18 million.[45]

Firms may reap results in other ways as well. The market may support the efforts of environmentally conscious companies precisely *because* they're environmentally conscious. Consider the progress of Patagonia, Inc., the outerwear manufacturer whose sales increased by 20 percent in its last fiscal year alone. "Its founders and sole owners, Yvon Chouinard and his wife Malinda, are determined to create a business that is successful in ways far different from what any business school will teach young prodigies."[46] Patagonia had a list of five-year environmental goals (dating to 1994), which included the elimination of all solid waste sent to landfills from domestic facilities and the inclusion of environmental costs in accounting and production systems and decisions. Chouinard justified his approach as follows:

> I'm a pessimist about the fate of civilization. Ever since I can remember we've been losing on the environmental front, and all indicators say we are still losing now. Gains we make are wiped out by development or population growth. So, I'm pessimistic and I feel responsible to do all that I can. I figure the best tool I have to help the environment is this company.[47]

So in helping the environment, Chouinard has been able to post earnings unmatched by many other firms.

One possible solution to remedy our environmental balance sheet and return us to a true free market would be to leave the risks of unintended (as well as intended) pollution to the insurance industry. A company could simply insure itself against claims of pollution, and injured parties would sue the offending firm through its insurance company for restitution. In this way, firms that are more likely to suffer claims would have high insurance premiums, thus encouraging them to reduce their polluting behavior. Firms that did not have a history of polluting would have lower insurance premiums, thus awarding to them a benefit for protecting the environment.[48] The government could require a bond from companies that continue to engage in environmentally risky activities, similar to workers' compensation statutes. The end goals of accountability and responsibility would therefore be served.

The article that follows illustrates the particular environmental regulatory burden borne by small businesses.

Small Firms Spend Much Time, Money Complying with Environment Rules

by Eugene Carlson

Someday, William Anderson's costly struggle to rid his auto dealership of five small underground gas and oil tanks will be over for good. Someday, his Dreisbach Buick dealership on the outskirts of Pontiac, Michigan, will be certified environmentally pristine by the state.

Someday—but not yet. Mr. Anderson has spent two years, and more than $100,000, on the task so far. Two holes the size of swimming pools have been dug and filled in the lot behind the dealership building. Consultants have been hired, soil and water tested, and reports filed in numbing detail. The five steel tanks have long since been cut up and sold for scrap. Yet, much remains to be done.

Mr. Anderson isn't some big-time polluter. While gas, oil, and chemicals leaking from underground tanks have fouled water supplies around the United States, there is no suggestion that his dealership's tanks were faulty. Over the years, occasional small oil and gas spills around the mouths of the tanks seeped into the ground, but tests indicate that the oily residue contaminated ground water no more than a few yards from the source. A consultant hired by Mr. Anderson says the threat to drinking-water supplies is nil.

Nor is the 57-year-old car dealer a casualty of a bureaucracy run amok. By most accounts, Michigan is making a good-faith effort to implement a 1988 federal rule aimed at eliminating defective underground storage tanks. To escape liability risks, Mr. Anderson and thousands of other car dealers and service-station operators in the state are replacing their old tanks with new ones.

Rather, Mr. Anderson considers himself the victim of good intentions gone awry. "Ours is just one small business, and we're trying very hard to be a good citizen and comply with environmental regulations. If it wasn't tragic, it'd be comical," Mr. Anderson says.

Avalanche of Paper

Entrepreneurs say that environmental regulation is a particularly fast-growing part of their red-tape burden these days. Many business owners strongly support efforts to clean the nation's air and water and protect workers and consumers from hazardous materials. But they say the "green" movement also has created a growing regulatory labyrinth.

Large corporations typically have in-house experts to guide the company through the maze. But most small businesses lack the staff and resources required to track the avalanche of paper from environmental agencies.

Up to now, small-business managers have typically taken an ad hoc approach to environmental rules, scanning trade association newsletters for hints of rule changes and hiring consultants to explain the seeming gobbledygook. But regulation's lengthening reach is forcing some companies to change tactics. "We now have two employees with engineering degrees who do nothing but track [regulatory] paper," says Earlyn Church, vice president and co-owner of Superior Technical Ceramics Corp., St. Albans, Vermont.

Sardonic Photograph

To demonstrate the magnitude of the problem, an employee at Bernhardt Furniture Co., Lenoir, North Carolina, put all the government forms dealing with disposal of dirty cleaning rags, the company's principal hazardous waste, in a pile and stood beside it for a sardonic photograph.

"He's 6 feet, 2 inches, and the stack of forms is slightly taller than he is," says Alex Bernhardt, the company's president. Mr. Bernhardt says his company "could easily spend twice as much on [environmental] compliance in the next five years as on R&D and new machinery and equipment" combined.

* * *

Mr. Anderson's adventure in digging up his storage tanks reads like an environmental soap opera. Like many states, Michigan has tried to ease the pain of excavation by setting up a trust fund to pay for all but $10,000 of owners' removal costs. The fund, which totaled $41.6 million last April 30, is financed by a fee on wholesale sales of gas and oil.

Continued

Continued

To remain eligible for reimbursement, a tank owner has to follow a strict timetable, spending money at each step. But the reimbursement pipeline is clogged. Mr. Anderson, for instance, says he still hasn't seen a penny from the trust fund.

Among the expenses he says he has incurred since 1990: $500 for registering his tanks with the state; $375 to purchase a state-required surety bond; $1,100 to test the contents of the tanks before excavation; $25,000 to dig up the tanks; $73,000 to fill the holes; and roughly $12,000 in consulting fees.

State law stipulates reimbursement for approved expenses within 90 days. But Sarah Burton, the private consultant supervising Dreisbach Buick's tank-removal project, says payment typically takes "nine months to a year, easily." Meanwhile, she adds, "You have to keep forking out money to stay eligible."

Dreisbach Buick isn't on the ropes. Mr. Anderson says business has "dramatically improved" from last year. But he is angry over a program that requires him to spend large sums with no apparent payoff to his company or to the public. "It's terribly inefficient, and it's a criminal use of capital," he says. "I could take that money and buy 10 used cars and turn those cars in 60 days and make an average $1,000 each."

* * *

But now comes Phase II. Mr. Anderson's consultant says the state will undoubtedly order the car dealer to sink from 4 to 10 shallow wells around the perimeter of the old tank storage area to establish if oily water remains in the soil and, if so, to see how far it has seeped.

This means hiring a drill rig, monitoring the well and, perhaps, capturing the water and removing the pollutants. "A nice Phase II investigation with a report," Ms. Burton says. "We're talking $25,000."

Source: *The Wall Street Journal,* June 15, 1992, p. B1. Reprinted by permission of *The Wall Street Journal,*

Free Market Solutions. Recognizing that forced compliance with standards is only one, albeit necessary, ingredient in the struggle for a clean environment, the federal government has recently been aggressive in finding ways to employ the natural incentives and advantages of market-based reasoning and mechanisms in attacking pollution. The government, in trying to force power generators to cut sulfur dioxide emissions in half by the year 2000, is now employing a free market approach in which pollution rights can be bought and sold. The Clean Air Act provides for pollution allowances putting a ceiling on how much sulfur dioxide utilities can emit. Plants can keep their allowances in order to pollute, or they can install cleaner equipment and sell their allowances on the open market. One result of this approach is that environmental groups can now buy air pollution rights, allow them to expire, and prevent tons of pollution from reaching the air.

A Balance? Of course, unbridled faith in the free market is not likely to be in our long-term best interests. Chile's experience under General Augusto Pinochet from 1973 to 1990 illustrates the risk. Pinochet put his faith in the free market. With privatization and deregulation, he brought Chile the most vibrant economy in South America. However, many argue that Pinochet was also a dictator who failed to respect the individual property rights of his citizens. In addition, now that Pinochet is gone, the environmental price of unregulated growth is becoming apparent. Forests, streams, and valleys have been plundered. The result, as described in *Time* magazine, is most apparent in the smog-enshrouded capital, Santiago:

> A thick layer of contaminants settles almost daily over the city, trapped by cold air and mountains on all sides. The causes of the filth: haphazard development

and an out-of-control bus system that Pinochet began deregulating in 1975. Two-thirds of the smog's harmful elements come from the 11,000 privately owned buses that spew diesel fumes through the city. The government bought out 2,600 of the worst offenders. But pollution still reached lethal levels for two days in July, forcing the government to shut schools and factories and to warn parents to keep their children indoors.[49]

Questions

1. A pollution permit policy often results in shifting pollution from one site to another. Is that policy ethically, or even logically, defensible? Explain.
2. Suggested free market incentives for pollution control include government taxes or fees on pollution and government rules mandating refundable deposits on hazardous materials. Explain how those incentives would work.
3. A *Wall Street Journal* editorial commenting on the market for pollution rights:

> The best news about the introduction of a market for rights to avoid compliance is that the public will finally get a precise measure of the cost of environmental rules. Once that is known, voters can decide if the price is worth the result, or if the law should be changed to comply with what the public is willing to pay.[50]

Are we paying too much for environmental protection? Explain.

V. The Business Response

In 1989, the Exxon *Valdez* oil tanker struck a reef in Prince William Sound, Alaska, and spilled 11 million gallons of oil, the worst such disaster in American history. An estimated 1,500 miles of shoreline were contaminated. More than 500,000 birds and mammals died. Facing 1,990 criminal charges, Exxon paid $100 million in restitution and $150 million in fines. Then, under a 1991 settlement, Exxon agreed to pay $900 million to settle state and federal civil claims for environmental damage. Exxon has also spent an estimated $2 billion in cleanup efforts in Prince William Sound. At this writing in 1994, 14,000 Alaska natives, property owners, and fishermen are suing Exxon for $1.5 to $3 billion in compensatory damages and unspecified punitive damages on the grounds that the oil spill has severely damaged their livelihoods and culture.

Joseph Hazelwood, captain of the Exxon *Valdez,* who was not at the wheel at the time of the accident, was acquitted of charges that he was drunk and reckless but was found guilty of the lesser charge of "negligent discharge of oil," for which he was fined $50,000 and ordered to undertake 1,000 hours of cleanup work at Prince William Sound. That sentence is on appeal.[51]

A. New Climate

The *Valdez* spill established a climate in which the Congress and President Bush agreed on new legislation, the Oil Pollution Act of 1990, to dramatically increase shipowners' liability for spills, to require double hulls in new tankers and phase in double hulls in used tankers, and to establish new cleanup and prevention requirements.

However, the most far-reaching consequence of the spill is a heightened public consciousness of environmental issues, which has in turn forced the business community to embrace a new environmental sensitivity that *Business Week* labeled "The Greening of Corporate America—Sometimes You Find that the Public Has Spoken, and You Get On with It."

Similarly, *Fortune* reported:

> "The 1990s will be the decade of the environment." That's not the chief druid of Greenpeace talking, but rather the new president of the Petroleum Marketers Association of America in a November speech. Mere corporate ecobabble intended to placate the latest group of special-interest loonies? Any company that thinks that way will probably regret it. Exxon provides the obvious if inadvertent example of the bitter costs of seeming unconcerned about the environment. Not long after the March accident in Valdez, Alaska, 41 percent of Americans were angry enough to say they'd seriously consider boycotting the company.[52]

B. The Weight of the Law

Public opinion has been effective in motivating increased corporate environmental concern, but the weight of the law has clearly played an enormous role. A *National Law Journal* survey of 200 corporate general counsels revealed that many corporations felt caught in an ever-tighter legal squeeze of harsher penalties, tighter scrutiny, and more complex laws. Most, however, believed that sound environmental practices improved long-term profitability, and they applauded closer attention to pollution. At the same time, two-thirds admitted that their businesses had operated at least some time in the past year in violation of environmental laws.[53]

The press of the law on corporate operations is evident in these other findings from the survey:

- The environmental workload forced 67 percent of corporations to hire law firms specifically to handle green issues in the last year.
- Only 30 percent of the attorneys believed that full compliance with the matrix of U.S. and state environmental laws was possible.
- Only 14 percent of the general counsels said overregulation was forcing their companies to consider moving operations abroad.
- About 58 percent said their companies had performed voluntary cleanup of hazardous waste sites, costly actions designed to fend off future liabilities.

"Environmental law is no longer a black box you add on at the end" of management decision making, said one general counsel. "It is moving away from mere compliance towards a time when a company that doesn't build environmental safety into its products will no longer be able to compete."[54]

C. Public Opinion

Legislation and a sense of social responsibility have helped shape the business community's approach to environmental issues. However, the most powerful engine behind the 1990's greening of the corporation is public opinion. Corporate America believes that the citizenry is now so serious about the environment that spending decisions will be influenced by environmental considerations. The articles that follow describe some of the strategies businesses are embracing in response to heightened public concern.

INDUSTRIES ENLISTING IN GREEN REVOLUTION

by Dick Rawe

Shoppers buying meat at Kroger grocery stores can choose between foamlike polystyrene trays or butcher paper.

At McDonald's, diners sip through thinner straws, saving a million pounds of plastic annually.

Retail giant Wal-Mart responded to consumer concerns with an ecological plan that seeks products from suppliers that are nonpolluting and biodegradable.

MacConnection, a computer sales firm, has switched from foam peanuts to shredded newsprint as packaging material to protect products during shipment.

The Ban the Box Coalition is fighting to eliminate longboxes used to ship CDs, saying they unnecessarily add to the waste stream.

These are but ripples in the rising tide of consumer-driven changes in packaging and recycling to reduce landfill waste at the source. In short, American business has joined the green revolution.

"There has been a striking change in response of industry to global issues," said Jan Beyea, senior scientist for the nonprofit National Audubon Society. "Business is taking this issue seriously, realizing nobody can escape. Those businesses that have intimate contact with consumers are feeling tremendous pressure from consumers who want fewer environmentally damaging products.

"There are 600 proposed bans on plastics around the United States that have made the chemical industry sit up and take notice. It has forced companies that had been very cavalier about the environment to recognize that their business depends on changing the public image. It's an exciting time because you see public concerns translated into actions, a willingness to sit down and come up with solutions."

Americans produce about 160 million tons of waste annually, the U.S. Environmental Protection Agency estimates. We generate more per person than any other nation—about a pound a day more than the average person in West Germany, for example. Existing landfills are getting full, especially in the East and West Coast states, and resistance to opening new dumps is stiffening because nobody wants one for a neighbor.

"The feckless voyage of the garbage barge" has become a national symbol of America's solid waste dilemma, said the EPA's Agenda for Action report of 1988.

The public perception is that making plastic creates pollution, that plastics never deteriorate in landfills, and that disposable diapers not only fill our landfills but also contribute to groundwater pollution.

In fact, the EPA said plastics constitute but 6.5 percent of landfill waste and disposable diapers less than 2 percent versus 41 percent for paper and 18 percent for lawn waste. And plastics dug up out of landfills after 10 years were found to have deteriorated 50 percent, according to Riley Kinman, a University of Cincinnati professor who has probed and studied landfills for 20 years.

But the widespread perception otherwise has put pressure on companies to reduce plastic and paper in packaging.

"We tend to react with simple solutions," said Geoffrey Place, Procter & Gamble vice president [of] research and development. Sometimes, he added, what seems to be excessive packaging is necessary.

"We have packaging to prevent tampering, to protect food products, and to prevent damage during shipments," he noted. "In some cases, we have regulatory requirements so packaging is not as useless as it is sometimes thought to be. At the same time there is a valid argument that we use more packaging than there needs to be. We need to retain what is vital and useful and eliminate the wasteful part of packaging.

Howard McIlvain, creative director for Libby Perszyk Kathman, a Cincinnati firm that designs packaging for a number of national firms, said environmental impact is a frequent topic during meetings to discuss a new product and packaging.

"Clients ask: Is it an efficient use of material? Is there waste in this packaging? Are we using recyclable material? Are we making sure that designation is clearly printed on the container or overwrap? Are we using thinner, or less material?"

Continued

Continued

He said one client, Valvoline, "clearly has at the top of its thinking" ways of promoting the proper disposal of oil and empty one-quart plastic bottles. Valvoline may eventually switch to gallon jugs to replace four 1-quart bottles, he said.

Here's what some other companies are doing:

- The Kroger Co.: The grocery firm has an 11-point source reduction and recycling program. "Buying meat over the counter just wrapped in butcher paper avoids the polystyrene tray," said Thomas Schlachter, assistant manager–store operations.
- H.J. Heinz Co.: By next year, half of the 400 million bottles of ketchup the company sells worldwide annually will be of recyclable PET (polyethylene terephthalate) plastic. The other half will be of recyclable glass.
- Procter & Gamble: The leader in the $3.8 billion laundry detergent market is expanding U.S. use of its Tide, Cheer, Oxydol, and Gain brands in reformulated compact versions. P&G sells the compacts, which require less packaging, in 20 countries worldwide. P&G's disposable diapers are now only half as thick.
- Fuji Film: Fuji Photo Film U.S.A. Inc. said the company will replace plastic canisters in which film is sold in the United States with moisture-proof paper.
- McDonald's: The world's largest hamburger chain is switching to a tanker system for delivery of concentrates such as Coca Cola and orange juice to eliminate several million pounds of packaging annually.

Questions

1. *a.* Should consumers boycott Exxon because of the *Valdez* oil spill? Explain.
   b. Would you do so? Explain. Would this decision more likely be based on ethical concerns or economic concerns?
2. *a.* Is the greening of the corporation a sincere corporate response to perceived environmental problems or a bottom-line, profit-maximizing response to consumer pressure, or both? Explain.
   b. Does it matter? Explain.
3. How might the government's ever-increasing environmental regulations along with the public's call for a new environmental consciousness favor big-business interests over those of small-business owners?

Source: *Waterloo Courier,* October 21, 1990, p. C8. Reprinted with permission of Scripps Howard News Service.

Consider:

In June 1995, Earth Day 2000, a San Francisco environmental group, offered its "Greenwash" awards to 10 companies. The awards go to the companies that, Earth Day claims, have made misleading or deceptive claims about the environmental benefits of their products or services. Here are a few of the winners (losers?):

- SC Johnson & Sons: Recyclable symbol on its Windex Cleanser misleads because the container can't be recycled in most communities.
- General Motors: Claimed it would plant a tree for each Geo sold. However, to counteract the carbon dioxide produced during the average life of one Geo, 734 trees would need to be planted.
- America's Favorite Chicken Company: Placed a recyclable symbol on its food containers, but could not recycle those containers once soiled. (Also subject of a Federal Trade

Continued

Continued

Commission action that required packaging modification.)

- Nuclear Energy Institute: Claimed that nuclear plants don't pollute the air because they don't burn anything, but failed to explain that the plants do operate with regular releases of radioactive gases.

Source: "This Year's Greenwash Winners Are . . . ," *Business Ethics*, May–June 1995, p. 11.

Summary

Legal Review. For the past century, the federal government has played an important role in the protection of the natural environment. Protection includes statutes relating to land, air, and water, as well as the wildlife contained in those environments. Federal impact on the environment is overseen by the Council on Environmental Quality, and all other areas are administered by the Environmental Protection Agency.

Individual businesses must ensure that their operations comply with the Clean Air Act (through emission controls and other equipment standards), the Clean Water Act (maintenance of standards relating to the discharge of pollutants into the waterways), CERCLA, RCRA, the Solid Waste Disposal and Toxic Substances Control acts (through regulation of industrial substance and hazardous waste disposal), and other state statutes. Penalties for failure to comply with these regulations may result in hefty fines and, possibly, imprisonment.

Ethics Review. Do firms have an ethical or social responsibility to protect the environment? If not, where does the responsibility lie? Threats to environmental health generally come from an aggregate impact, as opposed to the impact of the acts of one firm. As a result, one firm may view its actions as inconsequential to the environment and therefore continue them. Unfortunately, it is because of this type of thinking that problems occur. How can our society encourage businesses to cover the cost of environmental protection without placing an undue, unfair, or unbalanced burden on corporate America?

Economist Robert Solomon cautioned us, however, not to couch the environmental debate in such polarized terms.

> There is the harsh distinction between altruism and self-interest—yielding some fascinating sociobiological arguments but clouding the issue. . . Whatever else it may be, environmentalism need not and should not include a rejection of the human perspective. It should be an appeal to what is best and most human in us, our aesthetic and spiritual sensitivities, our ability to step back from our narrow projects and our prejudices and appreciate, empathize, and cooperate in a world that is bigger and grander than ourselves.[55]

Economics Review. There is no doubt that environmental protection laws cost businesses a portion of their profits. Some economists believe that the free market, if left to its own devices, would balance appropriately the interests of firms and of society. (Recall the sludge example.) Others argue that, given the problem of aggregate impact discussed above, each market player has incomplete information and therefore believes that her or his acts will not have a measurable impact on the environment. Consequently, the incentives would persuade a decision maker *not* to protect the environment, but instead to choose the most profitable solution, without regard to the environmental impact—unless the decision maker is sufficiently educated to realize the aggregate impact of her or his one act on the environment as a whole. Are efforts at such an education effective? Possible?

Chapter Questions

1. What advice would you give a developing country on an appropriate stance on environmental protection? Be realistic in terms of recognizing probable budget and technology constraints.
2. Economist B. Peter Pashigian:

   > It is widely thought that environmental controls are guided by the public-spirited ideal of correcting for "negative externalities"—the pollution costs that spill over from private operations. This view is not wrong by any means. But it is suspiciously incomplete. After all, there are numerous studies of regulatory programs in other fields that show how private interests have used public powers for their own enrichment.[56]

   What forces in addition to correcting for negative externalities might be influencing the course of federal pollution control?
3. William Tucker:

   > [Environmentalism is] essentially aristocratic in its roots and derives from the land- and nature-based ethic that has been championed by upper classes throughout history. Large landowners and titled aristocracies . . . have usually held a set of ideals that stresses 'stewardship' and the husbanding of existing resources over exploration and discovery. This view favors handicrafts over mass production and the inheritance ethic over the business ethic.[57]

   Tucker went on to argue that environmentalism favors the economic and social interests of the well-off. He said people of the upper middle class see their future in universities and the government bureaucracy, with little economic stake in industrial expansion. Indeed, such expansion might threaten their suburban property values. Comment.
4. Professor and business ethics scholar, Norman Bowie:

   > Environmentalists frequently argue that business has special obligations to protect the environment. Although I agree with the environmentalists on this point, I do not agree with them as to where the obligations lie. Business does not have an obligation to protect the environment over and above what is required by law; however, business does have a moral obligation to avoid intervening in the political arena in order to defeat or weaken environmental legislation.[58]

   a. Explain Professor Bowie's reasoning.
   b. Do you agree with him? Explain.

5. Economist Robert Crandall:

> [O]ur best chances for regulatory reform in certain environmental areas, particularly in air pollution policy, come from the states. Probably, responsibility for environmental regulation belongs with the states anyway, and most of it ought to be returned there.[59]

   a. What reasoning supports Crandall's notion that responsibility for environmental regulation belongs with the states?
   b. How might one reason to the contrary?
   c. If the power were yours, would environmental regulation rest primarily at the state or the federal level? Explain.

6. Why do plaintiffs typically experience great difficulty in prevailing in negligence actions alleging injury from toxic substances?
7. The doctrine of strict liability—originally applied to extrahazardous activities and more recently to defective products—could be extended to the area of toxic waste. Jeremy Main commented on that possibility in *Fortune* magazine:

> If strict liability were now extended to toxic wastes, then it would do a company no good to plead that it had obeyed the laws and followed approved procedures when it disposed of its wastes. It would still be liable, even if the hazards are seen only in retrospect.[60]

   Should the strict liability doctrine routinely be extended to toxic waste cases? Explain.

8. The Pennsylvania Coal Company owned coal land in the drainage basin of the Meadow Brook. The company's mining operation released water into the brook, thus polluting it. Sanderson owned land near the stream, and she had been securing water from it. However, the mining operation rendered the stream useless for Sanderson's purposes. Sanderson filed suit against the coal company. In 1886, a final verdict was rendered in the case. Should Sanderson prevail? [See *Pennsylvania Coal Co.* v. *Sanderson and Wife,* 6 A. 453 (1886).]
9. Some critics claim that the current fever for using material suitable for recycling has the effect of focusing an unsound degree of attention on landfill space while ignoring total environmental efficiency:

> Several cities—for example, Portland, Oregon, and Newark, New Jersey—have essentially banned polystyrene food packages, yet a Franklin Associates comparison of polystyrene packaging and its alternative, paperboard containers, showed that the polystyrene hamburger clamshell uses 30 percent less energy than paperboard. Its manufacturing results in 46 percent less air pollution, and 42 percent less water pollution.[61]

   Would fast-food companies exhibit poor judgment if they replaced polystyrene with paperboard? Explain.

10. Lynn Scarlett, solid-waste management authority:

> [T]oo many local governments have failed to charge anything—or anything like the actual costs—for collecting and disposing of garbage. Cities such as Baltimore, Denver, and Los Angeles do not directly charge households for garbage collection. In fact, a study of more than 200 U.S. cities found that 39 percent charge no direct fees at all for garbage service, giving consumers little incentive to

"conserve" on their waste production. Instituting pricing for collection and disposal will remedy that. Seattle's introduction of per-can charges a few years ago encouraged more than 70 percent of all residents to recycle and reduce waste.[62]

Comment.

11. For some time now, the government has been buried in the seemingly insoluble conflict between loggers and environmentalists in the northwest United States. The object of their conflict is a threatened species, the northern spotted owl. At this writing in 1994, the government was struggling with new measures to ease the restrictions on logging in spotted owl territories by shrinking the 2,600-acre "owl circles" around spotted owl nests, a proposal unlikely to satisfy either side.

    The Political Economy Research Center in Bozeman, Montana, proposes a market-based solution: Except for designated wilderness land, the government should put lumber rights up for auction. How would that approach work, and why might it be preferred to government rules about where logging is permitted?
12. The Endangered Species Act provides that all federal agency actions are to be designed such that they do not jeopardize endangered or threatened species. The act had been interpreted to reach to federal agency work or funding in foreign countries, but the federal government changed that interpretation in 1986 to limit the act's reach to the United States and the high seas. A group labeled Defenders of Wildlife filed suit, seeking to reinstate the original interpretation. The case reached the U.S. Supreme Court, where Justice Scalia wrote that Defenders of Wildlife would have to submit evidence showing that at least one of its members would be "directly" affected by the interpretation. In response, one member of Defenders of Wildlife wrote that she had visited Egypt and observed the endangered Nile crocodile and hoped to return to do so again but feared that U.S. aid with the Aswan High Dam would harm the crocodiles.

    a. Why did Scalia call for that evidence?

    b. Decide the case. Explain.

    [See *Lujan* v. *Defenders of Wildlife,* 112 S.Ct. 2130 (1992).]

Notes

1. Profile is taken from Eric Slater, "Harboring Doubts," *Los Angeles Times,* January 8, 1996, p. B1.
2. Wilfred Beckerman, "Public Utilities Fortnightly," cited in Robert Solomon, *The New World of Business* (Lanham, MD: Rowman & Littlefield, 1994), p. 319.
3. Mark Clements, "How Much Do We Care?" *Parade,* June 14, 1992, p. 16.
4. "This Year's Greenwash Winners Are. . . ," *Business Ethics,* May–June 1995, p. 10.
5. Eugene Linden, "Playing with Fire," *Time,* September 18, 1989, p. 76. Copyright © 1989, The Time Inc. Magazine Company. Reprinted by permission.
6. Joy Aschenbach, "Damaged Soviet Ecology Finally Out in the Open," *Waterloo Courier,* October 30, 1990, p. C9.
7. Gregg Easterbrook, "Cleaning Up," *Newsweek,* July 24, 1989, pp. 26, 33. © Newsweek, Inc. All rights reserved. Reprinted by permission.
8. Patrick Moore, "Hard Choices: Environmentalists and the Forests," Heartland Policy Study no. 65, ISSN #0889-8014 (April 7, 1995), p. 2.
9. Larry Stammer, "53 Nations Pledge to Ban Ozone Destroyers by 2000," *Los Angeles Times,* June 30, 1990, p. A1.
10. Catherine Bolgar, "Toxic Waste Exports Banned," *The Wall Street Journal,* March 28, 1994, p. B17.

11. Gregg Easterbrook, "Winning the War on Smog," *Newsweek,* August 23, 1993, p. 29.
12. Ibid.
13. Ibid.
14. Ibid.
15. "Something Special in the Wind," *Los Angeles Times,* October 31, 1990, p. B6.
16. "Implementation of Clean Air Act Brings B-Minus for EPA," *Waterloo Courier,* November 15, 1993, p. A2.
17. Faye Rice, "Next Steps for the Environment," *Fortune* 126, no. 8 (October 19, 1992), p. 98.
18. Timothy Noah, "Clear Benefits of Clean Air Act Come at a Cost," *The Wall Street Journal,* November 15, 1993, p. B1.
19. Rice, "Next Steps," p. 98.
20. Associated Press, "Midwest Flooding Doubled Gulf's 'Dead Zone,'" *Waterloo Courier,* November 19, 1993, p. A3.
21. "Fish Tale," *Newsweek,* May 1, 1995, p. 6.
22. Janet Hook and the *Congressional Quarterly* staff, "Clinton Controls Fall Agenda, although Not Its Results," *Congressional Quarterly,* September 4, 1993, pp. 2295 & 2315.
23. Rice, "Next Steps," p. 100.
24. Kathleen Lavey, "Nationline," *USA Today,* June 14, 1990, p. 3A. Copyright © 1990, *USA Today.* Reprinted with permission.
25. Cynthia Crossan, "How Tactical Research Muddied Diaper Debate," *The Wall Street Journal,* May 17, 1994, pp. B1, B7.
26. Ibid.
27. Bureau of National Affairs, "Hazardous Waste, EPA Issues New Strategy, Freeze on Hazardous Waste Incineration," *Daily Report for Executives,* May 19, 1993, p. 95.
28. 61 *Law Week* 3105 (August 18, 1992).
29. John Cushman, "U.S. to Weigh Blacks' Complaints about Pollution," *New York Times,* November 19, 1993, p. A16.
30. Ibid.
31. Andrea Ford, "Firm Agrees to Clean Up Tijuana Site," *Los Angeles Times,* June 16, 1993, p. A3.
32. Dianne Solis, "Jail Term Given in Cross-Border Pollution Case," *The Wall Street Journal,* December 16, 1993, p. A13.
33. Peter Prestley, "The Future of Superfund," *ABA Journal,* August 1993, p. 62.
34. Ibid.
35. Ibid., p. 65.
36. Rice, "Next Steps," p. 100.
37. Henry Reske, "Record EPA Prosecutions," *ABA Journal,* March 1992, p. 25.
38. Frank Edward Allen, "Few Big Firms Get Jail Time for Polluting," *The Wall Street Journal,* December 9, 1991, p. B1.
39. Charles McCoy, "Environmental Initiative Rejected in California," *The Wall Street Journal,* October 8, 1990, p. A12.
40. Ralph Rosenberg, "No Free Lunch in Nature's Cafe," *State Government News* 33, no. 1 (January 1990), p. 24.
41. Heartland Institute, "Environment: Private Property Rights," document no. 2366001, p. 2.
42. Frank Edward Allen, "Western Farmers Love New York Sludge," *The Wall Street Journal,* November 24, 1992, p. B1.
43. Louis Richman, "How Zealous Greens Hurt Growth," *Fortune* 125, no. 6 (March 23, 1992), p. 26.
44. Ibid.
45. Ibid.
46. Mary Scott, "Interview: Yvon Chouinard," *Business Ethics,* May–June 1995, pp. 31–34.
47. Ibid.
48. Heartland Institute, "The Free Market and the Environment," document no. 2317401, p. 6.
49. Brooke Larmer, "The Greening of Santiago," *Newsweek,* August 10, 1992, p. 41.
50. "Efficient-Markets Pollution," *The Wall Street Journal,* March 2, 1992, p. A12.
51. *State of Alaska* v. *Joseph J. Hazelwood,* 866 P.2d 827 (1993).
52. David Kirkpatrick, "Environmentalism: The New Crusade," *Fortune* 121, no. 4 (February 12, 1990), p. 44. © 1990 Time Inc. Magazine Company. All rights reserved.
53. Marianne Lavelle, "Environment Vise: Law, Compliance," *National Law Journal,* August 30, 1993, p. S1.
54. Ibid., p. S2.
55. Solomon, *The New World of Business,* p. 272.
56. B. Peter Pashigian, "How Large and Small Plants Fare under Environmental Regulation," *Regulation,* March–April 1983, p. 19.

57. "Tucker Contra Sierra," *Regulation,* March–April 1983, pp. 48–49.
58. Norman Bowie, with Kenneth Goodpaster, "Corporate Conscience, Money and Motorcars," in *Business Ethics Report, Highlights of Bentley College's Eighth National Conference on Business Ethics,* ed. Peter Kent, 1989, pp. 4, 6.
59. Robert Crandall, "The Environment," in "Regulation—The First Year," *Regulation,* January–February 1982, pp. 19, 29, 31.
60. Jeremy Main, "The Hazards of Helping Toxic Waste Victims," *Fortune* 108, no. 9 (October 31, 1983), pp. 158, 166.
61. Lynn Scarlett, "Make Your Environment Dirtier—Recycle," *The Wall Street Journal,* January 14, 1991, p. A12.
62. Ibid.

International Business: Building and Managing a Business as It Goes Global

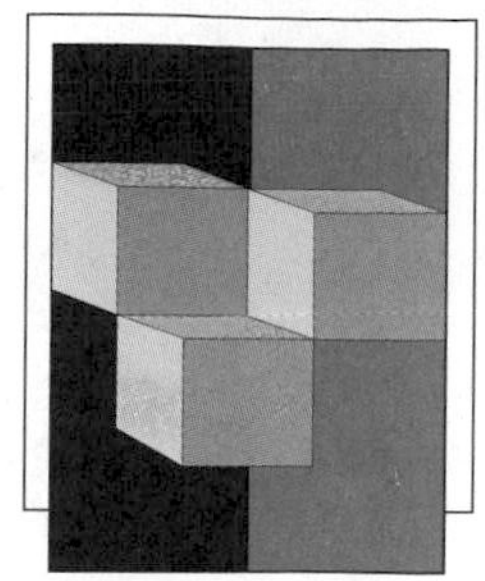

Chapter 16

Reader's Guide

Your business is growing and you seek to explore new markets. You have complied with U.S. regulations and are ready to expand your visibility throughout the world. This chapter enumerates the various issues you will face as you take the first steps toward global operations.

P R O F I L E

Martina Zeleski's parents arrived in the United States from Poland nearly 25 years ago, and Martina, now a junior in college, returns to Poland quite frequently. Each time Zeleski returns, she is keenly aware of the great differences between the two countries. She also sees a business opportunity:

> I see an emerging market in Poland for American goods, clothing in particular! My father is a clothing manufacturer who specializes in sportswear such as college sweatshirts and other cotton items. The Poles love this stuff because it has the American look and feel. I've decided to market these items in Poland but I don't know where to begin my planning process.

Questions

1. How will Zeleski do business in Poland? What form of business?
2. What problems might she run into doing business in a newly established economy?
3. How can she protect her interests from the United States?

I. Why Go Global?

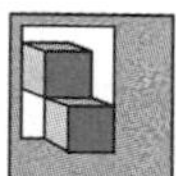

The preceding chapters have addressed general concepts of American law. Today, many companies expand not only within their domestic borders, but across continents and seas. It is critical that these companies understand the economics, ethics, and law across borders as well as those at home. Unless a firm continues to meet the demands of worldwide constituents (clients, customers, consumers), it may be left behind without the means to effectively challenge its competitors.

Unless a firm continues to meet the demands of worldwide constituents (clients, customers, consumers), it may be left behind without the means to effectively challenge its competitors.

In becoming a global operation, a firm can have more efficient access to resources, reduce tariffs paid, and take advantage of the geographical area that provides the best return for its investment. And companies are not alone in this effort to globalize; many governments have entered into agreements with other countries to facilitate the process. For instance, in the fall of 1993,

Canada, the United States, and Mexico joined in the North American Free Trade Agreement, which opened the trade borders of North America, allowing easier access and growth opportunities for affected firms.

But what are the implications of this expansion around the globe? To what laws are companies subject if they cannot even determine what is their home country? What happens when one country's ethics conflict with those of another? Do rules of supply and demand translate between countries? As firms become companies of the world, rather than of one nation, conflicts that might otherwise have been easily settled can become legal quagmires.

II. The Changing Environment of International Business: What's It Like Out There?

Since Adam Smith, many have argued that a decrease in trade barriers between any two or more countries will stimulate the world economy, not simply those of the countries involved in the specific trade agreement. Accordingly, NAFTA was successful in the United States Congress because the legislators believed that a stimulation of the Mexican and Canadian economies would lead to a boost in the American economy. During the national debate on NAFTA, labor leaders contended that with a lowering of trade barriers, U.S. firms would immediately take advantage of lower-cost labor locations in Mexico and thus sacrifice American jobs. This, however, is seen by some as a short-term setback to the American economy in trade for long-term gains by the creation of more robust markets for American goods.

The desire to reach some common legal ground in international business is not new. As explained later in the *Sumitomo* case, the United States negotiated commercial treaties as early as 1778 that regulated shipping and trading rights and rules between individuals of different countries. However, with the advent of the multinational enterprise, these early international treaties became outmoded. With new agreements come new concerns.

As is evidenced by the NAFTA debate, countervailing forces are at work in the global economy. On the one hand, consider the practically unprecedented expansion of world trade through agreements such as NAFTA, the General Agreement on Tariffs and Trade (GATT), the MERCOSUR Common Market (created by Argentina, Brazil, Paraguay, and Uruguay), and the East African Community (created by Kenya, Tanzania, and Uganda), among others. These alliances represent not only legislative victories, but also resistance to a growing isolationist tendency in the United States and elsewhere.

For example, despite the support of every living president in the United States, as well as Nobel Prize–winning economists, almost half of the American public opposed NAFTA. The alliance that will expand trade across the North American continent was passed in Congress by only a slight margin. In addition, after years of negotiation the current round of GATT was finally successfully concluded in December 1993, eliminating many tariff barriers between and among most countries worldwide. Economists believe that "within the mind-numbing text of GATT lies an enormous stimulus to the world economy as tariffs are reduced and new markets are opened."[1]

Trade Pact with U.S. Tantalizing Europeans

by B. C. Longworth

After NAFTA, here comes TAFTA.

The Trans-Atlantic Free Trade Agreement, that is: a tariff-free common market uniting the world's two mightiest economic areas, North America and the European Union.

So far, TAFTA is only a gleam in the eyes of statesmen, mostly European and Canadian, who fear the United States may be jilting its old allies in favor of Japan and other booming Asian nations.

The United States itself remains cool. But the idea, little mentioned before last year, has benefited from international drum-beating in recent months, with a surprising amount of the talk taking place here in Chicago this spring.

TAFTA "must be our target . . . our objective," British Foreign Secretary Douglas Hurd said here Thursday, echoing German Foreign Minister Klaus Kinkel's speech to the Chicago Council on Foreign Relations in April.

The free-trade zone, Kinkel said, should be a part of "a trans-Atlantic zone of close political, economic, and military cooperation [that] is the logic of our common history."

* * *

All this advocacy seems to have caught the Clinton administration by surprise. In one of the administration's few public comments, Assistant Secretary of State Richard Holbrooke called TAFTA "an idea whose time has not yet come."

Part of the administration's reluctance stems from the fear that yet another free-trade pact, coming after the debates on the North American Free Trade Agreement and the General Agreement on Tariffs and Trade (GATT) world trade pact, would be a very hard sell in Congress.

* * *

[The Commerce Department] doubts that the European enthusiasm is more than stargazing. It wonders if the EU is ready to make real concessions in areas—farming, aircraft, textiles, and entertainment—that have bedeviled trans-Atlantic trade relations for years.

* * *

Ironically, the fact that Europe and North America already have such wide and deep economic relations makes setting up a free-trade area that much harder.

The United States joined with Japan and other Asian nations last year to set up the Asia-Pacific Economic Cooperation Forum (APEC) and agreed to make free trade and open investment a reality among its 18 members by the year 2020.

This agreement symbolized America's tilt toward the Pacific and generated alarm among Europeans that has led to their enthusiasm for TAFTA.

Questions

1. If the direction of all industrialized nations is to open trade barriers and to allow free movement of goods and services, what stops countries from removing all remaining barriers? Why continue to negotiate one by one with each country to have these cooperative agreements?
2. What would be the result if there were no trade agreements, including GATT?
3. What would happen to the one country that refused to participate in any of these agreements?

Source: *Chicago Tribune,* May 21, 1995, section 7, pp. 1, 7.

Countervailing Forces. Contrary to the above article, there are forces that in effect limit the globalization of world business. First, the European Union is painfully mired in several issues that do not seem to be easily resolved. The EU's aims have been retarded since the failure of the Maastricht Conference, which sought to establish a common currency for member-countries. Financial and immigration concerns, as well as power struggles, have characterized the debate on this topic, slowing efforts at trade expansion. Second, the former Soviet Union is experiencing growing pains that have frustrated Russian leader Boris Yeltsin's original timeline for reform and a free market economy. In December 1993, Yeltsin had to deal with the election of a number of right-wing legislators who opposed the swiftness and direction of his reforms. Consequently, he was forced to decelerate the privatization process, which in turn accelerated inflation and removed the nation, for the time being, from the international trading place. Finally, China too is experiencing rampant inflation as it endures growth at a pace of 13 percent per year and resulting "demand pull" inflation. There are too many yuan chasing too few goods, and the consequence could be reduced exports and imports. Again, a potentially enormous market player may be delayed in playing the game.

The following article illustrates the dramatic recent changes in the European trading market.

Europe's Borders Fade and People and Goods Can Move More Freely

by Tony Horwitz

Barry Cotter is the unlikely face of the new Europe. A florid, beer-bellied Englishman, he speaks no foreign languages and jokes about "cloggies" (the Dutch) and "Kermits" (as in "frogs," or Frenchmen). But as he steers his 18-wheel tanker through the Pyrenees between Spain and France, he assumes a less provincial role: a European [Union] passport holder, driving for a German transport firm and hauling Spanish-made chemicals to Italy.

Not that anyone at the border cares. On January 1, 1993, officials here—as at many borders in Europe—stopped making passport, customs, and other checks that used to delay Mr. Cotter for hours, even days. "On most trips, I made worse time than Hannibal," he says, referring to the Carthaginian general who crossed this same mountain pass with elephants in 218 B.C. Now, Mr. Cotter speeds across a border without so much as a glance from a lone, idle guard. With the traditional delays vanishing across Europe, he can span the Continent in three days, against four or more just six months ago. "In this business, time is money," he says, "and these days I've got a lot more of both."

His glee contrasts sharply with the gloom in European capitals. There, the conventional wisdom holds that the dream of a United States of Europe is evaporating amid recession, political bickering, and paralysis over Bosnia. But viewed from the ground, reports of the new Europe's demise appear greatly exaggerated. A visit to the borders of seven nations finds a quiet revolution under way as people vote with their feet and wallets against high taxes and heavy revolution.

Frontier regions have become laboratories of new Europe, a place where shoppers, smugglers, entrepreneurs, and savers hunting for the best bank are testing the bounds of a much heralded but still novel entity: a border-free market of 12 nations and 345 million consumers.

* * *

The Danish border shows how the new Europe spells doom for uncompetitive tax rates and prices. Already, a traditional and rather surreal tax dodge—driving to Germany to buy Danish beer at supermarkets

Continued

Continued

with Danish-speaking staff and Tuborg-lined aisles—has forced Copenhagen to lower its beer tax. Now, a bizarre scheme devised by Fleggaard, a household goods company, may force down Denmark's hefty value-added tax as well.

At Fleggaard outlets across Denmark, shoppers simply ask to pay the German VAT of 15 percent rather than the 25 percent Danish rate. Fleggaard prints out an invoice at a small office just across the border in Germany, loads an appliance at a warehouse on the Danish side, and drives across the frontier. Then the truck turns around and delivers the machine to the Danish buyer. The invoice and short trip make Germany the point of sale, and of taxation. Fleggaard says its sales so far this year have more than doubled, with over five million kroners ($800,000) going into German tax coffers.

* * *

Such tactics wouldn't be possible without the freeing-up of cross-border transport, once a clotted and corrupt sector that exemplified Europe's economic stagnation, its "Eurosclerosis." Until recently, differing fees and inspections at each border stalled truckers and inflated their costs. Some nations limited how much diesel fuel truckers could carry, forcing them to buy it at that country's pumps. Others required obscure checks to boost employment and tax revenue. Bribes were routine, particularly in Italy.

* * *

But it is the Spanish border town of La Jonquera that drivers regard as a shrine to the *ancien regime.* Here, paperwork that took 10 minutes in Denmark and Germany typically required a day. The procedures were so tangled that truckers hired middlemen to fill out forms and get them stamped while they themselves waited in the town's shops, bars and brothels. Once a desolate, windblown town of 2,500, known only for its arsenic mines, La Jonquera became a bustling place where even clerks could earn 300,000 pesetas (about $2,500) a month—not counting rake-offs.

Now 35 percent of La Jonquera's workforce is unemployed, and shops that had enjoyed a captive market of bored truckers are silent. "Paperwork is finished as a career," Pere Brugat, the town's mayor, says wistfully as the 4,000 or so trucks that once stopped here daily now whiz past on the highway outside his window.

He and other officials concede that the red tape was largely unnecessary. But they fear that without it [EU] states such as Spain and Portugal can't compete with the countries like Germany.

"Bureaucracy helped equalize things," says Jose Guanter, a reference librarian for the few remaining customs agents. His computer is turned off, his shelves filled with dusty tomes of defunct regulations. "Without all this," he adds, "we are in Darwin's world, where only the strong ones survive."

La Jonquera, at least, is evolving. Having once thrived as a gatekeeper, it now hopes to become a gateway instead. The town is turning a vast parking lot where trucks waited out the delays into an industrial park, and it is offering free land to companies that relocate there. Its offer—advertised with glossy brochures titled "A Doorway to Europe"—has already lured a few Spanish and French concerns, which plan to open distribution warehouses.

"From here, you can move quickly to anywhere in France or Spain, without bureaucracy," says Mr. Brugat, smiling at the irony of his boast.

Questions

1. *a.* What is your reaction to La Jonquera Mayor Pere Brugat's concern that Spain and Portugal will not be able to compete with countries like Germany?
   b. How would you feel if you were a business owner in Lisbon, Portugal?
2. *a.* What other ideas could you offer Brugat in connection with the revitalization of his town? Imagine that you lived there and had similar concerns.
   b. Would you advocate government intervention in this situation?
3. *a.* Why do you believe that it has taken until now to open borders?
   b. What incentives did countries have to maintain tighter border controls?
   c. Do you feel that it is an ethically acceptable form of patriotism to prevent foreigners from doing business in your country?

Source: *The Wall Street Journal,* May 18, 1993, p. A1.

III. The International Regulatory Environment

A. Foundations of International Law

Profile Perspective: Consider a problem that arises when Zeleski sends her products to a distributor in Warsaw. The distributor later sends to Zeleski a payment that is apparently half of what she believes she is due. What law covers this issue? Polish? American? Where would she go to litigate this dispute, if it came to that?

Or consider instead that a firm with manufacturing plants in Argentina and Thailand, and corporate headquarters in Bangkok, enters into a contract with a French firm to distribute its products produced in the Argentinean plant. The French firm is not satisfied with the quality of the products being sent. What law would apply to this situation? Argentinean? Thai? French? The answer to this question is not simple, even for seasoned lawyers; yet the firms involved will be greatly affected by the decision, since contract law varies from country to country. Consider also what would be the effect on international negotiations if there were no common body of law considered "international law," no customs surrounding global contracts, and no common understanding regarding the enforcement of these contracts.

private law. Individually determined agreement of the parties relating to choice of laws, where disagreements shall be settled, and the language of the transactions.

jurisdiction. The power of a court to hear and to decide a case; the location of a court empowered to hear and to decide a case.

choice of law rule. A rule of law in each jurisdiction that determines which jurisdiction's laws will be applied to a case. For instance, one state may have a choice of laws rule that says that the law of the jurisdiction where the contract was signed shall govern any disputes; while another state may apply a different rule.

The source of law applicable to an international issue depends on the issue involved. In general, private parties such as business owners are free to form agreements in whatever manner they wish. This may cause ethical and legal problems, however, across country borders. As a result of the multitude of sources of international law, the answer to this concern is not so easily found.

Because they are powerful, the multinationals possess formidable moral responsibilities. These are not simply responsibilities to bend obediently to regulation. No matter how vehemently we may believe that nation-states must regulate corporate activities, the international regulation of business is feeble.

Source: Thomas Donaldson, "Can Multinationals Stage a Universal Morality Play?" *Business and Society Review* 81 (Spring 1992), p. 51.

Whenever the parties to a transaction are from different jurisdictions and are involved in a lawsuit, the court will look to the agreement of the parties to resolve these issues.

The parties to an agreement can determine which nation's law shall govern the contract, where disagreements in connection with the contract shall be settled, and even in which language the transactions shall be made. This is considered **private law.** Whenever the parties to a transaction are from different **jurisdictions** and are involved in a lawsuit, the court will look to the agreement of the parties to resolve these issues. Otherwise, where the contract is silent as to the choice of law, jurisdiction, and other questions, the court must decide. Generally, the **choice of law rule** of the jurisdiction in which the transaction occurred is applied. If the transaction is done by mail, as are many international trade negotiations, most often the law of the jurisdiction of the seller's place of business applies. Recall, however, that the parties to the contract may always reach an agreement on the law to be applied.

Public law, on the other hand, includes those rules of each nation that regulate the contractual agreement between the parties; for instance, import and export taxes, packaging requirements, and safety standards. In addition, public law regulates the relationships between nations. A business owner would be affected by public law in its impact on business operations. For instance, it would be important for a person opening a plant in France to first understand the safety requirements under French law and human resource regulations, such as vacation time required to be given (which, in fact, is a great deal more than United States regulations require).

public law. Rules of national law that regulate transactions between parties, as well as the relationships between nations.

Public law derives from a number of sources. The most familiar source of public law is a **treaty or convention** (a contract between nations). For example, the United States, Canada, and Mexico have NAFTA, a convention regarding free trade between those countries. Public law is also found in *international custom* or *generally accepted principles of law.* These terms refer to those practices that are accepted as appropriate for business between "civilized" nations, generally meaning Western, free market economies. For instance, sovereign immunity is an accepted principle of international law. A custom is derived from consistent behavior over time and is accepted as binding by the countries that engage in that behavior.

treaty or convention. A contract between nations.

The Development of Customs. One might understand the concept of custom better if it is analogized to the law of sales in the United States. For years, merchants would follow certain accepted customs or principles in connection with the sale of goods. These customs or manners of dealing between merchants were later codified in the Uniform Commercial Code, which regulates the sale of goods and has certain provisions specifically related to the sale of goods between merchants. In this way, customs or practices traditionally followed by merchants have become accepted principles of law.

On the other hand, in the international legal arena, customary practices are not stagnant; the development of custom as a guide for behavior or decision making is constantly evolving. For instance, it has always been the custom that personal information flow freely between countries to encourage the free flow of information in the business world. Recently, however, the European Union began to examine the potential for invasions of privacy and has now proposed minimum standards that must be maintained by a country receiving information from an EU country.

Two factors are used to determine whether a custom exists: (1) consistency and repetition of the action or decision, and (2) recognition by nations that this custom is binding. The first merely holds that the action or decision must be accepted by a number of nations for a time long enough to establish uniformity of application. The second dictates that the custom be accepted as binding by nations observing it. If the custom is accepted as merely persuasive, it does not rise to the level of a generally accepted principle of law. Through persistent objections, any nation may ensure that certain customs are not applied to cases in which it is involved.

Courts seldom agree as to what constitutes customary law. In fact, the International Court of Justice has warned against imposing the customs of one country on another. In one case, *Fisheries Jurisdiction, United Kingdom and Northern Ireland* v. *Iceland* (July 25, 1974), the court considered the claim that it was "customary" international law that a country had exclusive fishing rights for 12 miles from its shore. In discussing the requirements for establishing a practice as a custom, the court stated: "Uniformity is good only when it is convenient, that is to say when it simplifies the task at hand; it is bad when it results from an artificial assimilation of dissimilar cases. The nature of international society does not merely make it difficult to develop rules of international law of general application, it sometimes makes them undesirable."

As the fisheries case shows, even when there are laws purportedly claiming to cover arguments between countries, custom may prevail to dictate action. The following story, reported on National Public Radio, relates to an escalating argument over fishing rights between Spain and Canada.

Spain and Canada Clash over Fishing Rights

by Andy Bowers, National Public Radio

Andy Bowers, reporter: In a story reminiscent of old pirate novels, Canadian and Spanish vessels have been confronting each other on the open seas for several months. But who's playing the pirate role in this drama depends on which side you ask. Canada claims Spanish fisherman are the villains, mercilessly overfishing the area between Newfoundland and Greenland and threatening to wipe out the halibut, or turbot as it's also known. Canada's high commissioner to Britain, Brice Fritz, says his country is simply trying to protect dwindling fish stocks from unscrupulous mariners.

Brice Fritz: It's a global problem, it's a worldwide problem—conservation and the enforcement of conservation principles.

Bowers: But from Spain's point of view, it's Canada that has adopted Bluebeard's tactics. To stop the Spanish trawlers, even though they were operating in international waters, the Canadian Coast Guard seized one ship briefly and tried to sever the fishing nets of others. The Spanish fisheries minister, Luis Atienza, complains that Canada wants to dictate who can fish, even beyond the 200-mile exclusion zone along the Canadian coast.

Luis Atienza: We are for the 200 miles, and not for the enlargement of the 200 miles. We are against violence and against the use of violence to get an engagement, a compromise—and I think that the European Union cannot accept a compromise which is dictated.

Bowers: As a member of the European Union, Spain has been negotiating with Canada under the auspices of the EU, but Canada has some sympathy among other EU members, especially Great Britain. Last year, several British fishing boats were themselves attacked by Spanish vessels, who claimed that the British were using illegal nets. In addition, because the EU is supposed to be one big open market, the aggressive Spanish fleet will soon be allowed access to waters once reserved for English and Irish fishermen. Indeed, boats in English ports have begun flying Canadian flags to show their solidarity, so much so that stores ran out of Maple Leaf banners. This morning, high commissioner Brice Fritz went to Cornwall, England, to meet the supportive anglers in person.

Fritz: The first thing I am going to say is "thank you." I'm going to thank them for all the support they have given us, and this is a very important thing, important to us, important to our negotiators, but a great emotional experience.

Bowers: Spain has fought back by introducing visa requirements for Canadians wanting to visit the country. At a meeting of EU foreign ministers yesterday, Spain refused to approve a draft resolution of the conflict that would have allowed it to catch less than half the amount of halibut it caught last year. Canada is now threatening to take action again if Spain doesn't agree by tomorrow and, in the meantime, two Spanish fishermen will appear in court today in another EU country, Ireland, where they're accused of illegal fishing. I'm Andy Bowers in London.

Questions

1. What would you do if you were deciding Canadian policy here? Would you encourage the Bluebeard tactics taken by some Canadians?
2. Do you believe that the European Union is the appropriate entity to resolve this dispute, given its in-fighting and coalitions as discussed in the program?
3. Is it appropriate for Spain to fight back in other areas, such as with visa requirements? What else could it do?

Source: National Public Radio, "Morning Edition," April 11, 1995.

Courts. Public international law is also found in *judicial decisions.* The only court that is devoted entirely to hearing cases of public law is the International Court of Justice (ICJ) in the United Nations. The ICJ is made up of 15 judges from 15 different member-countries. The ICJ may issue two types of decisions depending on its jurisdiction. The court has **advisory jurisdiction,** where the UN asks it for an opinion on a matter of international law. These opinions are merely advisory and do not bind any party. The ICJ may also have **contentious jurisdiction.** This exists only where two or more nations (not individual parties) have consented to the jurisdiction of the court and have requested an opinion. In this case, the opinion would be considered binding on the parties involved. The court, however, is not bound by its own earlier decisions as precedent.

advisory jurisdiction. Power of the ICJ to hear a dispute and to render an advisory opinion on the matter. The opinion is not binding on any party.

contentious jurisdiction. Power of the ICJ to hear a dispute and to render a binding opinion on the issue and the parties involved. All parties must give prior consent to contentious jurisdiction.

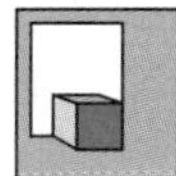

B. Comity

The unique aspect of public international law is that countries are generally not subject to law in the international arena unless they consent to such jurisdiction. For instance, a country is not bound by a treaty unless it has signed that treaty. A country is not bound by international custom unless it has traditionally participated in that custom. And prior judicial decisions are only persuasive if a country accepts them as precedent. In fact, perhaps the most critical element in understanding international law is knowing that it is not actually what we generally consider to be law. Countries are not bound to abide by it except through **comity,** the concept that countries *should* abide by international custom, treaties, and other sources of international direction because that is the civil way to engage in relationships. To have effective relationships, nations must respect each other and accept some basic principles of dealing with each other.

comity. A concept holding that countries *should* abide by international agreements.

It may be helpful to analogize the concept of comity with a deontological ethical theory suggesting that there are certain universal principles of a civilized society to which all involved should be subject. This type of reasoning assumes that there are certain acts that are right and certain acts that are wrong, no matter where you are or where you are from. The belief that countries *should* abide by international agreements would be a universal principle that is arguably right according to comity, no matter what situation is proposed.

Although some believe that the origins of law are in religion and its commandments, others have argued that law derives from a natural tendency to prevent chaos. International law is an attempt to prevent chaos in the international marketplace through the application of universal principles, and comity is the means by which it is encouraged.

IV. Regulatory Law Affecting Today's Global Firms

As explained above, there is no such thing as one body of international law per se that regulates international contracts and trade. Instead, contracts between firms in different countries may be subject to the laws of one country or the other, depending on (1) whether it is a sales contract subject to the UN Convention on the International Sale of Goods (discussed later), (2) whether the contract itself stipulates the applicable law and forum in which a dispute will be heard, and (3) the rules regarding conflict of laws in each jurisdiction. Consequently, a business owner may actually decide to market a good in one country over another simply because of that country's laws relating to the particular good or commercial contracts in general.

On the other hand, many countries have domestic laws that regulate business conducted within their borders, or by their domestic firms outside of their borders. These laws govern the areas of employment-related activities, discrimination, product liability, intellectual property, antitrust and trade practices, and import taxes, to name a few. Consider the effect of a change in these domestic laws or agreements between nations on the economy of the host country. If laws are modified to make the country more hospitable or desirable to foreign businesses, more businesses will locate there and the economy will get a boost in employment and production. If laws are modified to make that country less welcoming of foreign businesses, employment rates may decrease, trade imbalances may result, and inflation may surge (as a result of greater imports than exports).

The concept of extraterritorial application of national laws, that is, application of those laws beyond the borders of the country imposing them, may pose ethical dilemmas. For instance, if the culture of one country believes that it is unethical for a woman to work, the extraterritorial application of America's antidiscrimination laws may pose an ethical dilemma to an American manager in that foreign country. Does the manager abide by American law or by the business ethics of that foreign country? The same may be true in connection with the abhorrence of bribes in American business. If a business is in another country where a bribe is required to conduct business, does the businessperson break the American law and make the bribe or follow American business ethics but fail in business in that country?

A. Employment-Related Regulations

When the U.S. Congress passed the Civil Rights Act of 1991, it expressly provided for extraterritorial application of Title VII's antidiscrimination provisions. In doing so, Congress extended American firms' liability for discrimination against their American employees to situations outside of the United States. For instance, if a firm conducts operations in Saudi Arabia, where women are not expected to hold certain management positions, that firm is still held to Title VII's prohibition against gender discrimination in connection with American citizens who work there. Similarly, if an American firm does business in Taiwan, but prefers to have American workers *of Anglo-Saxon origin* serve in management positions, as opposed to American workers *of Asian origin,* unsuccessful applicants might have a claim for national origin discrimination under Title VII, even though that office of the firm is not located in the United States.

Other U.S. employment-related statutes also survive the trip across borders and oceans. For instance, the Occupational Safety and Health Act and the Employee Retirement Income Security Act do not distinguish between workers for American firms who work in the United States and those who work in other parts of the world. Moreover, labor regulations of other countries may differ to a large extent from those in the United States, and an American firm doing business in another country may be responsible for complying with those regulations. For instance, Italy requires that employees receive the benefit of the government pension plan, a staff medical scheme, a relocation allowance, insurance coverage to reimburse medical expenses, and scholarships for their children. In Spain, companies with more than 100 workers must have a committee in charge of all matters relating to health and safety at work; and all employees are statutorily entitled to an appropriate health and safety policy at work.

Declaration on the Elimination of Violence Against Women

Concerned that violence against women is an obstacle to the achievement of equality, development and peace, as recognized in the Nairobi Forward-looking Strategies for the Advancement of Women, in which a set of measures to combat violence against women was recommended, and to the full implementation of the Convention on the Elimination of All Forms of Discrimination Against Women . . .

[We] solemnly proclaim the following Declaration on the Elimination of Violence Against Women and urge that every effort be made so that it becomes generally known and respected:

* * *

Article 3

Women are entitled to the equal enjoyment and protection of all human rights and fundamental freedoms in the political, social, cultural, civil, or any other field. These rights include, inter alia:

a. The right to life.
b. The right to equality.
c. The right to liberty and security of person.
d. The right to equal protection under the law.
e. The right to be free from all forms of discrimination.
f. The right to the highest standard attainable of physical and mental health.
g. The right to just and favorable conditions of work.
h. The right not to be subjected to torture, or other cruel, inhuma, or degrading treatment or punishment.

Questions

1. *a.* How are these rights different, if at all, for the rights afforded under the American Bill of Rights?
   b. Why do you think they might be slightly different?
2. Do you notice any right that should be included, in your opinion, but is not?

Source: UNz General Assembly Resolution 48/104, February 23, 1994.

B. Product Liability Statutes

Product liability (see Chapter 14) refers to the legal responsibility of a manufacturer for any harm that results from the ordinary use of its products. In the United States, for instance, if a person drinks from a pop can, swallows a shard of glass, and suffers physical harm, the manufacturer of that beverage will likely be held responsible, no matter how careful it was in preventing that harm (i.e., even if the firm's quality inspection program is the best in the country).

In general, a product is considered defective if it is unreasonably dangerous in ordinary use. This is a test that is easily met in most cases, and almost automatic if injury has occurred.

Profile Perspective If someone in Poland is harmed because Zeleski's shirts are made of fabric that is unusually flammable, is Zeleski liable for this injury?

Liability laws differ from country to country, as do damage awards and and requirements of proof. If Poland eventually joins the European Union, it will have a product liability standard that is similar to that in the United States. The following article addresses some of the problems that might arise from a system that differs from our own.

In Japan, Lax Liability Laws Shroud Blame

by Merrill Goozner

Last fall, a major drug company here introduced a new drug to combat skin disease. Within a month, 14 patients died, victims of the drug's fatal reaction with an anti-cancer medication they also were taking. The government hastily withdrew the drug from the market.

Had that happened in the United States, attorneys for the victims' families would be tripping over each other in their race to the courthouse. That's not what happened here.

According to Nippon Shoji Kaisha, Ltd., the Osaka-based pharmaceutical company that codeveloped, manufactured, and sold the anti-shingles drug Sorivudine, not a single suit has been filed against the company.

Shocking press accounts of Japan's "most deadly drug debut ever" have shrouded blame for the incident in a mystery. The company, which refused to discuss details of the case, put the drug on the market even though it knew a cancer patient died during clinical trials.

In its application for government approval of the new drug, Nippon Shoji told the Ministry of Health and Welfare that it was "unknown" if a reaction between Sorivudine and that patient's anti-cancer medication led to the death.

Last September, its approval in hand, the company began shipping the drug to doctors and hospitals. It included a warning that it shouldn't be taken in combination with cancer-treatment drugs. But the warning never said it could result in serious injury or death.

* * *

For consumer activists and Japan's tiny legal community, the Sorivudine disaster has dramatized the need for stronger product liability laws. Over the years, Japan has endured its share of major and minor product mishaps, a natural byproduct of its national obsession with promoting export industries and a lax regulatory structure overseeing domestic business activities.

But consumers here have had little recourse when something goes horribly wrong, as it did in the Sorivudine case. Since World War II, there have been only 160 successful lawsuits against manufacturers because of unsafe products.

* * *

Business concerns here echo the complaints frequently heard from industry in the United States—that an overly liberal product liability system will sap Japan of its competitiveness and inhibit product innovation. They also fear a rash of expensive lawsuits.

"Many industrial groups feel if we change the product liability system too much, we will become like the United States—a litigious society," said Yashiro Kawaguchi, deputy director of the consumer affairs division of the Economic Planning Agency.

* * *

The Japanese court system doesn't allow for trials by juries, which might be sympathetic to an injured consumer. All product liability cases are heard by judges who narrowly interpret laws that define who is to blame for manufacturing defective products. . . Once the case is filed, Japanese lawyers do not have the right to discovery, which is considered indispensable by U.S. attorneys trying to determine if a company knew that its product might cause harm. Consumers in Japan seeking to prove that a product is unsafe usually have to pay for their own laboratory tests.

* * *

On top of all the structural barriers to court access, Japanese society frowns on open displays of disharmony like a court suit. Ritual apologies and discreet payments to those who have suffered grievous harm are the norm.

Questions

1. In the United States, a consumer must prove that the manufacturer's product was responsible

Continued

Continued

for the harm suffered. What would be the potential problems for a plaintiff under the American system in the above case?

2. *a.* Are you persuaded by the argument that product liability laws may sap industry of its competitiveness and inhibit product innovation?
   b. What are the ethical and economic ramifications of your argument? Explain.
   c. What would be the effect on safety and price if there were no laws protecting consumers, such as product liability?
3. *a.* What is the benefit to businesses and consumers of Japan's tendency to downplay conflict and resolve it in ways distinct from the traditional American way of handling a conflict?
   b. How would you expect this to affect the price of products in Japan?

Source: *Chicago Tribune,* January 9, 1994, section 7, p. 1.

C. *Intellectual Property Regulations*

Intellectual property generally refers to copyrights, patents, and trademarks, as opposed to real property such as land, real estate, and personal property, that is, all other tangible items. Here, we briefly discuss the application of international law in protecting intellectual property.

Trademarks. A trademark is that which identifies a product, whether it is a trade name, packaging, logo, or other distinguishing mark. When the law protects a trademark, it grants to the holder of the mark a limited monopoly: no one else may use that mark without the holder's permission. Under Section 526 of the Tariff Act of 1930, it is unlawful to import goods bearing a trademark registered with the Patent Office that is "owned by a citizen of, or by a corporation or association . . . organized within the United States" without the permission of the mark holder.

This provision regulates the import of goods that would infringe on a trademark holder's rights in the United States. But what about an American company that wants to obtain trademark protection in other countries?

Profile Perspective: What if Zeleski wanted to trademark the logo of her father's company in Poland?

Each country has distinct trademark regulations, and each offers different levels of protection to marks registered in other countries.

Paris Convention. In 1883, several countries entered into an agreement called the International Convention for the Protection of Intellectual Property, which was revised in 1971. As of 1988, 98 countries, including the United States, were parties to the agreement, now called the Paris Convention. In short, member-countries ensure trademark protection to marks registered in other member-countries. The Paris Convention also provides for *national treatment,* which requires that any individual claiming infringement will have the same protections as would a national of that country. A member-country may not favor its own nationals over foreigners. The Madrid Agreement, established after the Paris Convention, was an attempt to create an international trademark system. If a holder registers a trademark with the World Intellectual Property Organization in Switzerland, that mark is protected in all member-countries requested by the holder. The United States has yet to adopt the Madrid Agreement.

Inventions. A *patent* is a monopoly on a product, process, or device; the item or process claimed is an innovation, unique and inventive, and useful. The Paris Convention refers to patents, as well as trademarks; however, it does not establish a worldwide network of protection. Instead, it requires that member-countries follow simplified procedures for registration. The most important provision provides the *right of priority,* which grants the first person to obtain a patent in any member-country priority over other individuals seeking to register the same patent. In addition, since a patent must be original to be registered in any country, many countries hold that patents previously awarded in other countries automatically preclude additional patent registration. The European Patent Convention was established in 1978 to create an international registration procedure for patents. Individuals who obtain patents through the European Patent Office have valid patents in each member-country.

Authors/Artists. A *copyright* is a government grant giving the copyright holder exclusive control over the reproduction of a literary, musical, or artistic work. For example, Zeleski's father may choose to copyright a certain image that is represented on his sweat clothes. Most developed nations provide copyright protection within their borders, but many also belong to international copyright protection pacts. The Berne Convention of 1886 and the Universal Copyright Convention (UCC) of 1952 both provide a measure of international protection against the unauthorized reproduction of one's original books, photos, drawings, movies, and the like. Copyright protection extends for a period provided by national law; for example, in the United States, a copyright spans the author's life plus 50 years. The United States is a party to the UCC but not to the Berne Convention.

Broadly, we should recognize that we have not succeeded in establishing a solid international system of protection for intellectual property. As the following case illustrates, those who believe their rights are infringed must rely on national legal systems for protection, and proof of intellectual property infringements is very difficult, indeed.

CASE

Comité Interprofessionel du Vin de Champagne v. Wineworths Group, Ltd.

2 N.Z.L.R. 432 (1991), High Court of Wellington, New Zealand

Facts

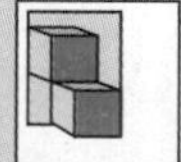

An Australian company sought to sell Australian sparkling wine, made from Australian grapes, in the New Zealand market. The Australian company wanted to use the word *champagne* on the bottle labels. A group of French champagne producers (the Comité Interprofessionel du Vin de Champagne) sought an injunction against the Australian company's use of the word *champagne.* The French producers argued that the Australians were, in effect, "passing off" Australian wine as though it had been produced in the famous Champagne region of France.

* * *

Continued

Continued

Judge Jeffries

These proceedings are brought by the plaintiffs to protect their claimed property right in the word "Champagne." As an editorial policy in this judgment I am using the word champagne with a capital when it refers to the district and the wine from the district. The plaintiffs seek in effect to prevent the defendant from importing into New Zealand sparkling wine from Australia labelled champagne.

The *Comité Interprofessionel du Vin de Champagne* (hereafter referred to by the acronym CIVC) is . . . a semi-official body . . . whose purposes include the protection of the name Champagne for the sparkling wine produced in Champagne, a district of France, from grapes grown in that district.

In essence French wine interests are disputing with Australian wine interests the New Zealand market for sparkling wines which Australian manufacturers and exporters to this country seek to label and sell as champagne. The plaintiffs say according to the law of New Zealand they cannot do that for it constitutes deceptive conduct because the wine [labeled] champagne was made in Australia from grapes grown there.

Champagne as we know it is relatively new, having its origin in time at the end of the seventeenth century but its final development was a nineteenth century phenomenon. Dom Perignon of the Benedictine Abbey of Hautvillers near Epernay in the Champagne district is credited with its beginning. There are four generally acknowledged ingredients of Champagne being its wine type, the grapes used, most importantly the location of a sparkling wine, usually but not always, white in [color]. The two features of Champagne of prime importance for its uniqueness are the soil and climate in which the grapes are grown, and the method of manufacture by skilled personnel. The first of those elements cannot be exactly duplicated anywhere in the world, but the second can.

For the production of grapes for Champagne there are strict geographical limitations imposed by law. On July 22, 1927, a law strictly delimited the boundaries of the vine growing Champagne area. Within those boundaries, and in each village, the soil suitable for planting vines has been meticulously indexed. By law the wine allowed to carry the appellation Champagne must be produced exclusively within precise zones.

* * *

New Zealand has . . . no history of material consumption, or manufacture, of sparkling wine prior to 1980. Today several wine producers here market a wine using the methode champenoise process. One demands special mention. In about 1981 Montana Wines, Ltd., which is New Zealand's largest maker, launched a sparkling wine produced by methode champenoise and [labeled] it "Lindauer New Zealand Champagne." There were two other New Zealand makers who followed suit . . . [T]here had been a tiny importation of Australian wines calling themselves champagne through the 1960s and 1970s which did not provoke a response from the CIVC.

Proceedings were issued in 1982 against Montana and after four years were settled by a consent order of the Court issuing an injunction generally restraining the use of the word champagne on that defendant's products. Over about the last four years all New Zealand makers have observed that order and all leading wine importers have declined to import Australian sparkling wine [labeled] champagne. Absenting the events now to be described New Zealand, judged by the attitude of markers and importers, conceded to the plaintiffs their legal proprietary right in the appellation champagne.

Indigenous wine making and consumption were much more a part of Australian life than they were in New Zealand until about 30 years ago. Australia has a record of well over a century of making acceptable wines of great variety and styles which have been consumed by its people. Sparkling wine calling itself champagne made from grapes grown in Australia by the methode champenoise, and by other methods, has been entirely accepted and without direct

Continued

Continued

challenge from the CIVC. The plaintiffs recognize, and although reluctantly accept, for Australia, like Canada and the United States of America, there is no legal protection available to them over the use of the appellation champagne.

The sparkling wine market in New Zealand changed dramatically with the introduction here from Australia in 1986 of Yalumba Angas Brut Champagne. The wine was of good quality and reasonably priced. It was a stunning success and other wine importers began a serious search in Australia for competitors.

It is appropriate now to focus directly on the acts of Australia's wine maker, Penfolds Wine Pty., Ltd. (hereafter referred to as Penfolds), which brought about these proceedings. In August 1987 Penfolds reached agreement with the defendant Wineworths Group, Ltd., to export into New Zealand a sparkling wine made by its wholly owned subsidiary Seaview Winery Pty., Ltd., bearing the label "Australian Champagne." Before this arrangement Penfolds through another agent in 1986 had sold a Seaview wine [labeled] "Brut Champagne."

It is appropriate here to emphasize the plaintiffs' view of what makes the product and therefore the name of Champagne so special. First, Champagne as a product is a unique wine which must be elaborated from particular grape varieties, grown in conducive soil and climate, and made into wine by an exceptional technique performed by highly skilled persons. The product is a quality one and by virtue of the cost of manufacture it is necessarily expensive, which is part of its exclusivity. From the quality product the reputation has developed, which reflects the specialness of the wine itself arising from factors outlined above . . .

The particular attraction of Seaview was that its champagne was made by methode champenoise. . . .

The Court thinks a deliberate choice was made by Penfolds to test the New Zealand law with a middle- to upper-bracket sparkling wine made by methode champenoise rather than a wine made by the [inferior] transfer method, and specifically [labeled] it "Australian Champagne." That action by Penfolds set up these proceedings.

[The court discusses the dilution of the word *champagne* in the Australian and United States markets.] . . . Apparently there is some evidence of the change in the United States as well. That trend clearly suggests that the word champagne has been so devalued in the market in Australia that the public now needs a word, or words, that will convey the excitement and quality surrounding the word champagne say in New Zealand or the United Kingdom. It was a point consistently made by the plaintiffs' wine writers and experts that it is for the public's good in New Zealand to maintain the legitimate pretensions of the word champagne.

This defendant, of course, does not deny the origin of the name champagne, or that the wine made in the Champagne district is a fine and special wine having the attributes claimed for it. What the defendant does say is that the word champagne has in New Zealand lost its distinctive significance so as to be properly defined now as a generic term having generic use within the wine market. It is in the same category as many other words whose origins are almost identical such as sherry, port, burgundy, graves, and chablis.

No case was cited to the Court how it should go about making a decision on a fact of that nature. To decide whether a word has become (for there is no doubt it once was not) a generic word is not a how, when, where fact. The task of the Court is to decide how the adult population of New Zealand as a group perceives the word. One has only to frame the task in that way to demonstrate its immense difficulty.

Market research is a powerful source of information but its value is not always consistent. There were two studies performed in New Zealand, one in 1987 for the defendant and one in 1989 for the plaintiffs.

The Court holds both studies supported the contention that there is significant evidence that champagne is not a generic word by usage in New Zealand. The evidence of the plaintiffs' survey in 1989 shows about 43 percent link champagne with France as the country of origin. The defendant's survey of 1987 less directly confirmed the link between the word and France.

* * *

Continued

Continued

Notwithstanding some interesting and persuasive evidence to the contrary, the Court's decision is that the word champagne in New Zealand is not generically used to describe any white sparkling wine.

The word champagne does in my view, have a special impact or impression on ordinary, average New Zealanders for whom wine drinking generally plays no significant part in their lives. This non-expert, phlegmatic, even uninterested representative New Zealander does have a definite response to the word champagne over and above noting it to be a white sparkling wine, or one with bubbles in it . . . Finally, I think the whole case of the defendant is that it well understands that the word champagne is one invested with considerable commercial charm and does not rank with sherry, port, or chablis as was argued to the Court.

* * *

The plaintiffs in this case must establish sufficient reputation or goodwill in the name of Champagne.

In this Court's view that has been established by the evidence. The plaintiffs have had a presence in this country now for 150 years approximately. There has already been a finding that the word champagne retains a distinctive reputation and goodwill and it has not become a generic word.

The question for the Court is whether importation into New Zealand as aforesaid by the defendant advertising and selling Seaview Champagne, is deceptive in the way complained of by the plaintiffs. The Court's decision is that it is deceptive . . .

In short the Court says the word champagne is distinctive in New Zealand for the French product and it would be deceptive for other traders, foreign or domestic, to seek to attach themselves to that reputation by using the word champagne to describe sparkling wine made out of Champagne, France.

[For the plaintiffs.]

Questions

1. *a.* Does it matter to your impression of this case whether Penfolds intended to pass off the wine as a product of the French Champagne region or merely intended to use the moniker to describe generically the type of wine?
   b. Is there anything that Penfolds could have done to use the word *champagne* in such a way as to emphasize a more generic meaning, rather than its geographical usage?
   c. Was Penfolds's action unethical?
2. How does CIVC protect its mark, "champagne"?
3. Would the result in this case have been different if it were brought in Australia? The United States? Explain.

D. *Antitrust and Trade Regulations*

Fair trade, argue proponents of antitrust regulation, is possible only with market restrictions and regulations. However, as James Bovard claimed, "in America, as elsewhere, protectionists are wrapping themselves in a cloak of fairness and proclaiming that fair trade requires the creation of endless new restrictions on people's freedom of contract. Unfortunately, fair trade is a delusion that could be leading to economic catastrophe."[2] Bovard argued that trade barriers are anything but fair. On the other hand, proponents of barriers claim that these restrictions are reasonable and serve to foster a more competitive market.

Trade is regulated in the United States, in part, by the Sherman Antitrust Act, which prohibits (1) any contract that unreasonably restrains trade and (2) any action that tends to lessen competition or to create a monopoly. The purpose of the act is to preserve competition for the benefit of American consumers. So, how does this relate to multinational businesses? The act applies to all conduct that has a direct and substantial effect on U.S. commerce, domestic consumers, or export opportunities of domestic firms.

For example, the Sherman Act prohibits two retailers from agreeing on the price they will both charge for a certain item. The act also prohibits those two retailers eliminating competition between themselves by agreeing on territories that each would serve. Predatory pricing is prohibited; this occurs when a seller prices items at below cost in order to oust others from the market, only to raise prices after it has the market all to itself.

If actions such as these are conducted outside the U.S. borders, but have a substantial and direct effect on U.S. commerce, the Sherman Act would apply. On the other hand, if few or no U.S. interests are at stake, courts are less likely to intervene. Take, for instance, the case of *Montreal Trading* v. *Amax, Inc,*[3] in which Canadian subsidiaries of American firms refused to sell Canadian potash to a Canadian company because that company was going to resell it to North Korean buyers. The court determined that there was an insignificant and remote effect on U.S. commerce and, as a result, held that it lacked jurisdiction to hear the case.

Certain corporate activities are considered per se illegal by the courts, no matter the motivation. If the purpose of an agreement, for instance, is to fix prices, courts do not look to the effect on the market, but instead presume that this activity will have a negative effect and will hold the parties in violation of the Sherman Act. In connection with international business operations, courts allow a certain amount of latitude and instead will generally apply the rule of reason; in other words, the courts will look to whether the procompetitive effect of the activity outweighs the anticompetitive effect.

Trade is also regulated by the Clayton Act, which prohibits mergers of firms that may substantially lessen competition. For example, a proposed merger between Coca-Cola and PepsiCo. would be prohibited by the Clayton Act because of its potential to lessen competition in the soda-pop industry. To determine whether a merger is in violation of the Clayton Act, courts will look to not only the size and competitive position of the merging firms, but also to the barriers to entry in that market, the market's definition, and the degree of concentration in that market. The European Union Commission performs a similar analysis.

Although most small, start-up or emerging firms have little concern regarding antitrust regulation because of the pervasive requirement of market power or a significant effect on the market, there are certain situations in which a start-up firm may have cause for attention to these laws. For instance, if a firm produces a good that is unique, the first of its kind, there is the potential for the growth of a monopoly relating to that good. Of course, the determination would depend on the ability of the good to command a market response.

E. Imports

General Agreement on Tariffs and Trade. Establishes and regulates import duties among signatory countries.

The **General Agreement on Tariffs and Trade** (GATT), now called the World Trade Organization (WTO), regulates import duties among signatory countries to reduce barriers to trade and to ensure fair treatment. Without the WTO, it is argued, countries with stronger markets would be able to wrestle better deals on imports than would other countries. In addition, countries with strong market economies could use the threat of higher import taxes as a bargaining chip in other negotiations. There are several important components of the WTO that affect decisions about where a company may conduct operations and to which country that company may export its products.

To promote fair trade, the WTO prohibits two practices in its member-countries. The first is called *dumping*. Dumping occurs when a manufacturer sells its goods in a foreign country for less than their normal value. If this practice causes or threatens material injury to a domestic or established foreign manufacturer in the foreign country, the act is prohibited. The price is considered less than normal value if it is less than the price charged in the producer's home country. A firm may want to dump its goods in a foreign market for two reasons. First, its home market may be saturated and can not support any further supply. Second, in an effort to establish itself and perhaps drive other firms out of the market, the firm may sell its goods in a foreign market at a price below other competitors and support that price with higher prices in its home country. In this way, its competitors may be forced from the market, and the producer may then raise prices to the normal level or above.

Provisional Antidumping Duty on Imports of Aspartame Originating in Japan and the United States

The European [Union] considered a claim that U.S. and Japanese producers of Aspartame (known in the United States by the brand name Nutrasweet) were dumping in the Dutch market. The following is its consideration of the appropriate comparison price to determine whether dumping existed.

(a)(1) Procedure—The Commission received a complaint lodged by the Holland sweetener company HSC, the sole producer of Aspartame in the [European Union]. The complaint contained evidence of dumping of this product originating in Japan and the United States of America and of material injury resulting therefrom, which was considered sufficient to justify initiation of this proceeding.

(c)(12) Dumping—The United States of America—Normal Value

The U.S. exporter and Nutrasweet, the related company, argued that there were differences in the price elasticity of Aspartame between the U.S. and the [EU] markets because of a higher degree of health awareness, and therefore preference for Aspartame in the United States. In addition, the [EU] market for Aspartame developed later than the U.S. market and the product would therefore be less known by [EU] consumers. Consequently, domestic prices in the United States would not permit a proper comparison and should not be used to determine normal value.

(16) The Commission accepts that, in general, there must be a difference in price elasticity between the U.S. and the [EU] market since a difference in price could not otherwise exist. Since difference in price elasticity is indeed a prerequisite for price differentiation and if adjustments had to be made for it, dumping could never be sanctioned.

(17) The exporter also claimed that, since it sold under patent on the U.S. market, while on the [EU] market the patents had lapsed, no protective measures should be taken on the basis of a normal value based on domestic prices, since these prices would not allow a proper comparison.

(18) The Commission cannot accept this claim as justified. Injurious price discrimination is condemned by the [EU] and by international law irrespective of the reasons and motives underlying such discrimination. The patent in the United States does not determine the domestic price level. If the exporter uses its position as patent holder to practice higher prices domestically than for export sales, such a practice results from his free commercial decision. There is no reason why this price differentiation, to the extent that it leads to material injury to the [EU] industry, should escape the application of antidumping rules.

* * *

Continued

Continued

(61) Having considered the various arguments of the exporters, the Commission concludes that it is in the [EU's] general interest to eliminate the injurious effects of the dumped imports and that the benefits of such protection clearly outweigh any short-term effects, particularly on price.

(62) In order to eliminate the injury suffered by the [EU] industry, and to guarantee its survival, it is necessary that the measures taken allow the industry concerned to obtain a normal profit which it has been deprived of through the effects of imports at dumped prices.

[The Commission therefore applied a duty to imports of Aspartame to allow for a "reasonable" profit margin for the [EU] industry.]

Questions

1. What is the relevance of the U.S. patent protection of Aspartame?
2. Can you make an argument that this type of Commission decision is anything but protectionism in favor of [EU] industries? Is there any benefit to the world market?
3. *a.* If the answer to question 2 is in the negative, is the Commission's action unethical?
   b. Were the actions of the exporters unethical or wrong, in your opinion?

Source: European Community Commission Resolution no. 3241/90, November 16, 1990.

Profile Perspective: If Zeleski charges more for her sweat clothes in a WTO member-country than in America, she may be accused of dumping in the American market. She would be subject to liability if it could be shown that the sales of her sweat clothes at these below normal prices caused material injury to a domestic or established foreign clothes manufacturer. The domestic manufacturer may show that it is unable to match Zeleski's prices because they are so far below the price of production.

The WTO also prohibits the payment of **unfair subsidies** by governments. This occurs where a government, in an effort to encourage growth in a certain industry, offers subsidies to producers in that industry. The producers are therefore able to sell their goods at prices lower than those of their worldwide competitors. Subsidies are considered unfair if they are used by the governments to promote export trade that harms another country. If unfair subsidization or dumping has been found to occur in the United States, the U.S. Department of Commerce may impose **countervailing duties** on those products in an amount sufficient to counteract the effect of the subsidy or the decreased price.

International trade barriers are discussed during trade "rounds" in which a number of countries negotiate duties and other agreements. One negotiation principle is called **most favored nation** (MFN) **status.** If the United States has MFN status with France, the United States has the right to the lowest applicable tariff on its goods imported by France. If France negotiates a lower tariff with Korea, the United States is entitled to a reduction in its tariff rates as well. In fact, all nations having MFN status with France would be entitled to that lower tariff rate. A second negotiating principle is called **national treatment.** This concept dictates that once goods have been imported into a country, they must be treated as if they were domestic goods. Consequently, the only place where a tariff may be felt is at the border.

unfair subsidies. Subsidies offered to producers in a certain industry by a government in order to spur growth in that industry. These subsidies are considered unfair if they are used to promote export trade that harms another country.

countervailing duties. Duties imposed by a government against the products of another government who has offered subsidies to its own producers.

most favored nation status. Preferential status offered to certain countries under the GATT that allows the MFN country to obtain the lowest applicable tariff on goods.

national treatment. Concept that requires that, once goods have been imported into a country, they must be treated as if they were domestic goods (i.e., no tariff may be imposed other than that at the border).

Import Duties. The tariff treatment that the United States imposes on an imported product often depends on such considerations as whether the product was made with American raw materials and whether the product was actually fabricated abroad or simply assembled abroad using American-made components. The case that follows examines the question of the appropriate duty for Samsonite luggage imported from Mexico.

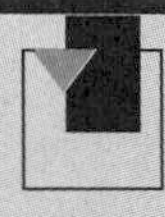

CASE

SAMSONITE CORPORATION v. UNITED STATES

889 F.2d 1074 (Fed. Cir. 1989)

Facts

Samsonite assembles luggage in Mexico and imports the completed bags into the United States. Samsonite shipped steel strips from the United States to Mexico to use them in the assembly of the bags. The steel pieces were shipped as five-inch, oil-coated strips with a value of between 95 cents and $1.26. Once in Mexico, the strips were cleaned, bent into a baggage-handle form, covered with vinyl, riveted to a plastic frame, then attached to vinyl bags to form soft-sided luggage. When the luggage was later imported to the United States, the Customs Service assessed a duty on the entire bag, including the value of the steel strips, at a rate of 20 percent ad valorem. The Court of International Trade upheld the Customs Service's decision that the steel strips were not "exported in a condition ready for assembly." Samsonite appealed.

* * *

Senior Circuit Judge Friedman

To obtain a deduction for American-fabricated articles assembled abroad, the components (*a*) must have been exported from the United States "in condition ready for assembly without further fabrication," (*b*) not have lost their physical identity in the articles by change in form, shape, or otherwise, and (*c*) not have been advanced in value or improved in condition "except by being assembled" and except "by operations incidental to the assembly process such as cleaning, lubricating, and painting." As the Court of International Trade correctly pointed out, since the "foregoing three conditions for a deduction are set forth in the conjunctive . . . each must be satisfied before a component can qualify for duty-free treatment." We agree with that court that the steel strips involved in this case did not meet those conditions.

The critical inquiry is whether the bending and shaping that the strips underwent constituted "fabrication" or mere assembly and operations incidental to the assembly process. We hold that what was done to the strips in Mexico was fabrication and not mere assembly.

When the steel strips were exported from the United States, they were just that: five-inch strips that could not serve as the frame of the luggage without undergoing a complete change in shape. Prior to assembling the luggage, the strips were bent by machine into a carefully and specially configured rectangular shape that was necessary before the original strip would serve its ultimate function as part of the frame of the luggage.

In short, what emerged after the bending operation was a different object from that which left the United States. The latter was a steel strip, the former was a metal frame for a piece of luggage. The transformation of the strip in this manner into a luggage frame was a fabrication. The strips therefore had not been exported from the United States "in condition ready for assembly without further fabrication."

Continued

Continued

Samsonite contends, however, that prior decisions of the Court of Customs and Patent Appeals require a contrary conclusion. It relies particularly on *General Instrument Corp.* v. *United States,* 499 F.2d 1318 (CCPA 1974). That case involved wire wound on spools that had been exported from the United States to Taiwan. There the wire was removed from the spools, formed into a horizontal coil by a winding machine, taped to prevent unraveling, dipped in cement, dried, precision shaped, removed from the spools, and wound around a core. The end product made from the wire was a component of a television set that was imported into the United States.

The Court of Customs and Patent Appeals held that: "The steps performed upon the wire after is exportation to Taiwan are not 'further fabrication' steps, but rather assembly steps within the meaning of [the statute]."

Samsonite argues that far more was done to the wire in *General Instrument* than was done to the steel strips in this case. It argues that if the processing the wire underwent in *General Instrument* was not "fabrication," a fortiori "the one simple-minded act of bending a straight frame into a 'C' was neither 'a further fabrication' nor 'a nonincidental operation."

The critical inquiry in determining whether fabrication rather than mere assembly took place here is not the amount of processing that occurred in the two cases, but its nature. In *General Instrument,* the wire, when it left the United States and when it returned as part of a finished product, was a coil. The wire was taken directly from the supply spool on which it was wound and, after processing, was used in assembling the TV set components. The wire underwent no basic change in connection with its incorporation into the television set component.

In contrast, in the present case the steel strips had to undergo a significant change in shape before the actual assembly of luggage could begin. Until the steel strips had been made into "C" shapes they could not be used as a part of the luggage. Unlike the "assembly" that the court in *General Instrument* held the processing of the wire involved, here "further fabrication" of the steel strips was required in order to change them into frames for luggage, before the assembly of the luggage could take place.

[Affirmed.]

Questions

1. *a.* Do you agree with the court's distinction of the *General Instrument Corp.* case?
   b. Aren't the steps performed on the steel strips in this case merely "assembly steps within the meaning of the statute"? Explain.
2. *a.* If Samsonite wanted to continue its practice of importing steel strips to be used in the assembly process in Mexico, is there a way in which it could alter its process to avoid the higher duty? Explain.
   b. Would there be any effect on the price of the luggage?

F. Exports

While imports are regulated to protect American businesses, exports by these businesses may also be regulated. Export regulation serves several purposes, articulated in the Export Administration Act of 1979:

> It is the policy of the United States to use export controls only after full consideration of the import on the economy of the United States and only to the extent necessary

(*a*) to restrict the export of goods and technology that would make a significant contribution to the military potential of any other country . . . which could prove detrimental to the national security of the United States;

(*b*) to restrict the export of goods and technology where necessary to further significantly the foreign policy of the United States or to fulfill its declared international obligations; and

(*c*) to restrict the export of goods where necessary to protect the domestic economy from the excessive drain of scarce materials and to reduce the serious inflationary impact of foreign demand.

Therefore, regulations may exist to restrict the free market flow of certain goods and technology out of the United States. This restriction on the free market is purportedly justified by the above concerns. What would be the result if this form of regulation did not exist?

Under the act, anyone wishing to export any type of good or technology from the United States to a foreign country must obtain a license. Violations of the licensing requirement bring imprisonment of up to 10 years and a fine of $250,000, or five times the value of the export or $1 million, whichever is higher.

There are two types of licenses available, *general* or *validated* licenses. It is the shipper's responsibility to determine which type is required. A commodity control list is published that specifies which goods are controlled and for which countries a validated license is required. Otherwise, a general license is available if no specific export license is required. To obtain a general license, the shipper must merely fill out a declaration form at the time of shipping. A validated license is required when a firm exports certain goods or technology to specified controlled countries. Firms must apply for the license at the Office of Export Administration in the Department of Commerce prior to shipping.

In determining whether to award a license, the Department of Commerce will look to several factors, including the type and amount of the exported good, the importing country, the good's use or purpose, the unrestricted availability of the same or comparable item in the importing country, and the intended market in the importing country.

Exports may be prevented for other reasons as well. For instance, in early 1981, President Jimmy Carter signed an executive order that limited the export of products banned or restricted from sale in the United States. But, 33 days later, once Ronald Reagan filled the office chair that Carter left vacant, Reagan revoked the order. Reagan claimed that it would put America at a competitive disadvantage. One observer cited an example of the result of Reagan's act: "With a laissez-faire policy giving them wide latitude, U.S.-based pharmaceutical and pesticide companies, or their foreign subsidiaries, continue to sell developing countries drugs and bug killers that are banned or severely restricted in the United States because of health hazards."[4] On the other hand, President Clinton recently expressed U.S. support for an international code to end deceptive marketing of infant formula, an issue that has plagued American companies and others for over 20 years. Thus, export regulation may be imposed to effectuate U.S. policy toward protectionism or, to the contrary, toward free market capitalism.

China Reasserts Control over Exports, Causing Problems for Foreign Concerns

by Kathy Chen

Just when it is trying to open its economy and join the world trading system, China has reasserted what some critics see as central control over some exports, causing big headaches for foreign trading companies.

Beijing, citing a need to bring order to the country's chaotic export trade, has quietly started requiring trading companies to bid for the rights to export certain products. The rights are then handed out as quotas.

China's new quota-bidding system may be a case of good intentions gone awry. Tang Wei, a division chief at the Ministry of Foreign Trade and Economic Cooperation, says the bidding process aims to replace China's former system of handing out export quotas based on family or political connections or other arbitrary methods. The government wants to stop price wars being waged among Chinese trading companies and maximize Chinese earnings on exports. Higher prices also would head off foreign allegations of dumping, he says. Dumping refers to selling goods abroad at below cost to gain market share.

* * *

Mr. Tang says the new system should help China meet standards set by the World Trade Organization, scheduled to soon replace the General Agreement on Tariffs and Trade, to which China is seeking reentry. Though China's export quota system is self-imposed, Mr. Tang says it is consistent with GATT: "It's fair, open, transparent and prevents favoritism."

* * *

But the bidding system is also wreaking havoc on China's trading system, other traders say. Chinese trading companies that fail to win export quotas are backing out of contracts they signed before the new system was implemented. Some of these that win them, though, are demanding to renegotiate contracts to cover the unexpected costs of bidding for quotas.

Questions

1. Do you consider the intentions cited above "good" ones "gone awry?"
2. *a.* Is it appropriate for a government to designate the amount of goods its domestic firms may export? Why or why not?
   b. What is the impact of such a restriction on the economy of that country?
3. How do you believe American companies would react to a similar restriction?

Source: *The Wall Street Journal,* Dec. 14, 1994, p. A11. Reprinted by permission of *The Wall Street Journal.*

V. Doing Business in a Foreign Country: Where to Begin

Profile Perspective: What law governs the contracts that Zeleski will enter into when she begins to sell her sweat clothes in Poland? The UN Convention on Contracts for the International Sale of Goods provides a good foundation on which to answer this question.

A. UN Convention on Contracts for the International Sale of Goods

In 1988, 10 nations (including the United States) signed and became bound by the UN Convention on Contracts for the International Sale of Goods (CISG). As of 1995, 44 nations had signed it. The CISG applies to contracts and provides uniform rules for the sale of goods between parties of different countries that have signed it. The CISG may also apply when the parties to a contract are in nonsignatory countries but performance would be in a contracting country.

The CISG contains rules regarding the interpretation of contracts and negotiations and the form of contracts. Many obligations of the parties are enunciated by the CISG. For instance, the seller is required to deliver the goods and any documents relating to the goods, as well as make sure that the goods are in conformance with the contract terms. The buyer, on the other hand, is required to pay the contract price and to accept delivery of the goods. The CISG, however, does not answer all questions that may arise in the course of a transaction. For instance, it leaves to national law questions of a contract's validity. Under American law, a contract requires four elements:

- *Capacity* to enter the contract.
- *Offer and acceptance* of the terms of the contract.
- *Consideration* for the promises in the contract.
- *Legality* of purpose of the contract.

As is discussed in Chapter 4, capacity refers to the parties' ability to understand the nature and consequences of the contract. For example, an individual who is under the influence of alcohol might not have capacity to enter into a contract. The offer and acceptance must evidence a meeting of the minds between the parties, that is, there must be a mutual understanding regarding the terms of the contract.

Consideration means that something of value (whether monetary or otherwise) has passed between the parties. For example, one party agrees to pay money, and the other party agrees to deliver the goods requested. Countries that are not based in the common law, but instead in civil law systems, do not require consideration for a contract. The final element requires that the contract's purpose be legal. For instance, under American law, if a company agreed to pay money to import certain goods to a country where those goods are not allowed, that agreement would not be enforceable.

Generally, once a contract has been created, it is enforceable according to its terms by all parties to the contract. As the following case highlights, however, one party may rescind or modify a contract on the basis that performance of the contract's terms is not impossible but commercially impracticable.

CASE

Transatlantic Financing Corporation v. United States

363 F.2d 312 (D.C. Cir. 1966)

Facts

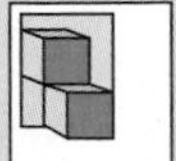

In 1956, Transatlantic Financing, a steamship operator, contracted with the United States to ship wheat from Texas to Iran. Six days after the ship left port for Iran, the Egyptian government was at war with Israel and blocked the Suez Canal to shipping. The steamer therefore was forced to sail around the Cape of Good Hope. Transatlantic accordingly sued the United States for its added expenses as a result of this change of circumstances. Transatlantic contended that it had contracted only to travel the "usual and customary" route to Iran and that the United States had received a greater benefit than that for which it contracted. The district court held for the United States; Transatlantic appealed.

* * *

Continued

Continued

Judge Skelly Wright

Transatlantic's claim is based on the following train of argument. The charter was a contract for a voyage from a Gulf port to Iran. Admiralty principles and practices, especially stemming from the doctrine of deviation, require us to [infer] into the contract the term that the voyage was to be performed by the "usual and customary" route. The usual and customary route from Texas to Iran was, at the time of contract, via Suez, so the contract was for a voyage from Texas to Iran via Suez. When Suez was closed this contract became impossible to perform. Consequently, appellant's argument continues, when Transatlantic delivered the cargo by going around the Cape of Good Hope, in compliance with the Government's demand under claim of right, it conferred a benefit upon the United States for which it should be paid on quantum meruit.

The contract in this case does not expressly condition performance upon availability of the Suez route. Nor does it specify "via Suez" or, on the other hand, "via Suez or Cape of Good Hope." Nor are there provisions in the contract from which we may properly [infer] that the continued availability of Suez was a condition of performance. Nor is there anything in custom or trade usage, or in the surrounding circumstances generally, which would support our constructing a condition of performance. The numerous cases requiring performance around the Cape when Suez was closed indicate that the Cape route is generally regarded as an alternative means of performance. So the implied expectation that the route would be via Suez is hardly adequate proof of an allocation to the promise of the risk of closure. In some cases, even an express expectation may not amount to a condition of performance. The doctrine of deviation supports our assumption that parties normally expect performance by the usual and customary route, but it adds nothing beyond this that is probative of an allocation of the risk.

If anything, the circumstances surrounding this contract indicate that the risk of the Canal's closure may be deemed to have been allocated to Transatlantic. We know or may safely assume that the parties were aware, as were most commercial men with interest affected by the Suez situation, that the Canal might become a dangerous area. No doubt the tension affected freight rates, and it is arguable that the risk of closure became part of the dickered terms. We do not deem the risk of closure so allocated, however. Foreseeability or even recognition of a risk does not necessarily prove its allocation. Parties to a contract are not always able to provide for all the possibilities of which they are aware, sometimes because they cannot agree, often simply because they are too busy. Moreover, that some abnormal risk was contemplated is probative but does not necessarily establish an allocation of the risk of the contingency which actually occurs. In this case, for example, nationalization by Egypt of the Canal Corporation and formation of the Suez Users Group did not necessarily indicate that the Canal would be blocked even if a confrontation resulted. The surrounding circumstances do indicate, however, a willingness by Transatlantic to assume abnormal risks, and this fact should legitimately cause us to judge the impracticability of performance by an alternative route in stricter terms than we would were the contingency unforeseen.

We turn then to the question whether occurrence of the contingency rendered performance commercially impracticable under the circumstances of this case. The goods shipped were not subject to harm from the longer, less temperate Southern route. The vessel and crew were fit to proceed around the Cape. Transatlantic was no less able than the United States to purchase insurance to cover the contingency's occurrence. If anything, it is more reasonable to expect owner-operators of vessels to insure against the hazards of war. They are in the best position to calculate the cost of performance by alternative routes (and therefore to estimate the amount of insurance required), and are undoubtedly sensitive to international troubles which uniquely affect the demand for and cost of their services. The only factor operating here in appellant's favor is the added expense, allegedly $43,972.00 above and beyond the contract price of $305,842.92, of extending a 10,000 mile voyage by approximately 3,000 miles. While it may be

Continued

Continued

an overstatement to say that increased cost and difficulty of performance never constitute impracticability, to justify relief there must be more of a variation between expected cost and the cost of performing by an available alternative than is present in this case, where the promisor can legitimately be presumed to have accepted some degree of abnormal risk, and where impracticability is urged on the basis of added expense alone.

We conclude, therefore, as have most other courts considering related issues arising out of the Suez closure, that performance of this contract was not rendered legally impossible.

Affirmed.

Questions

1. Would there be a different result in this case if the shipment had been tomatoes as opposed to wheat? Explain. Would there be a different result in this case if the United States and Transatlantic agreed by contract that shipment was to arrive in Iran within a period of time that was only possible if the shipper used the canal route? Explain.
2. What do you think it would take for a court to render a contract commercially impracticable? In this case, the shipper was forced to spend almost $44,000 more than it had expected to spend in performing the $305,000 contract. What if the added cost had amounted to $100,000? Would you be persuaded that the contract was then commercially impracticable? What if the closing of the canal doubled the price of the contract? How might this change the supply and demand for these goods?
3. What would you do in a similar situation if you were in the position of the United States in this case? Would you hold a company to a contract no matter the cost to that firm to fulfill the contract? Even if these costs were not anticipated at the time of contract? Is it ethical to simply say, "you should have known," or "sorry, but we *do* have a contract"?

As stated above, questions of a contract's validity are left to national law. Contract law does vary from country to country. For instance, in a number of countries, contract law developed not through precedent and judicial interpretation but instead through the institution of a civil code. Note that the United States has adopted the Uniform Commercial Code (See Appendix B) in connection with the interpretation and enforcement of contracts, but even it was based in large part on prior legal decisions.

> Questions of a contract's validity are left to national law. Contract law does vary from country to country.

Germany is a country that relies on its civil code for the interpretation of contracts. The civil code in Germany provides for several differences from those rules applied in the United States. For instance, an offer must be held open for a reasonable period of time if no time is specified. In the United States, an offer may be withdrawn at any time prior to acceptance, unless someone has paid to keep it open.

Second, consideration is not required for there to be a contract under the German civil code. In other words, a mere promise by one party that is accepted by the other is enforceable. The same holds true in Japan. In America, this would not be the case in most circumstances.

Third, while an acceptance is valid in the United States once it is dispatched, and therefore the offer can no longer be withdrawn, an acceptance under German civil law is valid only when it is received. Consequently, since the rules vary significantly from country to country, a businessperson would be wise to investigate the national rules of each country in addition to becoming familiar with the common rules of the CISG.

The Caux Round Table Principles for Business

The Caux Round Table was established 10 years ago to bring together global corporate leaders for the purpose of reducing trade tensions. Created in 1994, the principles form an international code of ethical conduct for global firms and were created through collaboration with business leaders in Europe, Japan, and the United States.

These principles are rooted in two basic ideals: kyosei and human dignity. The Japanese concept of kyosei means living and working together for the common good—enabling cooperation and mutual prosperity to coexist with healthy and fair competition. Human dignity refers to the sacredness or value of each person as an end, not simply as a means to the fulfillment of other's purposes or even majority prescription.

* * *

Section 2. General Principles

Principle 1. The responsibilities of business: beyond shareholders to stakeholders.

Principle 2. The economic and social impact of business: toward innovation, justice and world community.

Principle 3. Business behavior: beyond the letter of law toward a spirit of trust.

Principle 4. Respect for rules.

Principle 5. Support for multilateral trade.

Principle 6. Respect for the environment.

Principle 7. Avoidance of illicit operations.

Source: Joe Skelly, "The Rise of International Ethics," *Business Ethics* (May–June 1995), p. 24.

B. Different Forms of Global Expansion

Profile Perspective: Zeleski's primary concern is the form of business through which to sell her sweats in Poland. Should she market these clothes through a distributor, an agent, a licensing agreement? What are the benefits or risks associated with each form?

multinational enterprise. A company that conducts business in more than one country.

Multinational Enterprise (MNE).

The term **multinational enterprise** traditionally refers to a company that conducts business in more than one country. Any of the following operations, except for a direct contract with a foreign purchaser, may qualify a company as a MNE.

Direct Contract. A firm may expand its business across territorial borders using a variety of methods. The most simplified, from a contractual perspective, occurs when a firm in one country enters into an agreement with a firm or individual in another country. For example, a firm might decide to sell its product to a purchaser in another country through a basic contractual agreement. This is called a *direct sale* to a foreign purchaser. In this situation, the parties shall agree on the terms of the sale and shall record them in the contract.

American Society of International Law Interest Group on International Economic Law, Document III-B, Commission on Transnational Corporations, "United Nations ECOSOC Draft Code of Conduct on Transnational Corporations" (1989)

48. Transnational corporations should receive fair and equitable and nondiscriminatory treatment in accordance with the laws, regulations and administrative practices of the countries in which they operate, as well as intergovernmental obligations to which the governments of these countries have freely subscribed consistent with international law.

Questions

1. Is there any reason why transnational corporations should *not* be accorded treatment by a country similar to that of a domestic corporation?
2. What do you think would be the natural market reaction to transnational corporations if there were no regulations requiring equal treatment?

If the contract is silent as to a term of the sale, the law specified in the contract will apply in connection with the missing term; if none is specified, the applicable law will depend on the country in which the court is located. Some courts will apply the *vesting of rights doctrine,* where the applicable law is the law of the jurisdiction in which the rights in the contract vested. Other courts may apply the *most significant relationship doctrine,* where the applicable law is that of the jurisdiction that has the most significant relationship to the contract and the parties. Finally, some courts will apply the *governmental interest doctrine,* where the court will either apply the law of its own jurisdiction or that which has the greatest interest in the outcome of the issue. It is evidently a more efficient and beneficial business objective to identify all relevant terms and articulate all agreements in the contract itself. Of course, one can never anticipate all possible circumstances.

One of the most complicated issues pertaining to direct sales is that of *payment.* The seller should and usually does require an *irrevocable letter of credit,* which the buyer obtains from a bank after paying that amount to the bank (or securing that amount of credit). The bank then promises to pay the seller the amount of the contract after conforming goods have been shipped. The "irrevocable" component is that the bank may not revoke the letter of credit without the consent of both the buyer and the seller. In this way, the seller is protected because the buyer already has come up with adequate funds for the purchase, confirmed by a bank. The buyer is protected because the funds are not turned over to the seller until it has been determined that the goods conform to the contract. It is important to the buyer, however, that the letter of credit be specific as to the conformance of the goods, as the bank will only ensure that the goods conform to the letter of credit and not to the contract itself (see Figure 16.1).

Foreign Representation. A second type of foreign expansion is a sale through a representative in the foreign country, whether it is through a distributor, agent, or other type of representative. In this way, the firm has some representation in the foreign country and, depending on the type of representation, someone with experience dealing with that country's customs and regulations. For example, Zeleski may choose to hire a distributor to sell her sweat clothes in Poland because that person may be more familiar with Polish regulations and customs than Zeleski.

FIGURE 16.1 IRREVOCABLE LETTER OF CREDIT

FORM 5-10
Irrevocable Letter of Credit

THE FIRST NATIONAL BANK OF BOSTON
INTERNATIONAL DIVISION
BOSTON, MASSACHUSETTS, U.S.A.

LETTER OF CREDIT NO. DATE

GENTLEMEN:

WE HEREBY OPEN OUR IRREVOCABLE LETTER OF CREDIT IN YOUR FAVOR AVAILABLE BY YOUR DRAFTS DRAWN ON

AT SIGHT FOR ANY SUM OR SUMS NOT EXCEEDING IN TOTAL

FOR ACCOUNT OF
FOR INVOICE COST OF

TO BE SHIPPED FROM TO
INSURANCE TO BE EFFECTED BY
DRAFTS WHEN PRESENTED FOR NEGOTIATION MUST BE ACCOMPANIED BY:

- INVOICES
- SPECIAL CUSTOMS INVOICES
- INSURANCE POLICIES OR CERTIFICATES IN DUPLICATE COVERING NOT LESS THAN INVOICE COST (THESE DOCUMENTS ARE REQUIRED ONLY IF INSURANCE IS TO BE EFFECTED BY SHIPPER)
- A FULL SET OF CLEAN ON BOARD OCEAN BILLS OF LADING, MADE TO THE ORDER OF

BILLS OF LADING MUST BE DATED ON OR BEFORE AND DRAFTS MUST BE NEGOTIATED ON OR BEFORE . EACH DRAFT HEREUNDER MUST BE ENDORSED ON THE REVERSE OF THIS LETTER OF CREDIT AND MUST BEAR UPON ITS FACE "DRAWN UNDER LETTER OF CREDIT NO. DATED OF THE FIRST NATIONAL BANK OF BOSTON, BOSTON, MASSACHUSETTS.
EXCEPT SO FAR AS OTHERWISE EXPRESSLY STATED HEREIN, THIS LETTER OF CREDIT IS SUBJECT TO THE "UNIFORM CUSTOMS AND PRACTICE FOR DOCUMENTARY CREDITS (1962 REVISION), INTERNATIONAL CHAMBER OF COMMERCE BROCHURE NO. 222".
WE HEREBY AGREE WITH THE DRAWERS, ENDORSERS, AND BONA FIDE HOLDERS OF BILLS DRAWN AND NEGOTIATED IN COMPLIANCE WITH THE TERMS OF THIS LETTER OF CREDIT THAT SAID BILLS WILL BE DULY HONORED ON PRESENTATION AT THE COUNTER OF THE ABOVE MENTIONED DRAWEE BANK.

VERY TRULY YOURS

AUTHORIZED OFFICIAL AUTHORIZED OFFICIAL

D-1181

(UCC F&P Art. 5)

(concluded) **Figure 16.1A**

¶ 52.31 LETTERS OF CREDIT 5-106

Form 5-1C

(Reverse Side)

ENDORSEMENTS OF DRAFTS DRAWN:

DATE	NEGOTIATED BY	AMOUNT IN WORDS	AMOUNT IN FIGURES

THIS LETTER OF CREDIT SHOULD BE CANCELLED AND ATTACHED TO THE LAST DRAFT

A firm may decide to sell through an *agent,* an individual who will remain permanently in the foreign country, negotiate contracts, and assist in the performance of the contracts. The agent would be compensated on a commission basis. On the other hand, the firm may act through a *representative* who may solicit and take orders but, unlike an agent, may not enter into contracts on behalf of the firm. *Distributors* purchase the goods from the seller, then negotiate sales to foreign purchasers on their own behalf. In doing so, a distributor may be more likely to invest resources to develop the foreign market for the good.

exclusive dealing agreements. An agreement by which the distributor agrees to sell the goods of only one manufacturer and the manufacturer agrees to sell only to that distributor in that area.

It is important to note that **exclusive dealing agreements** with a distributor, where the distributor agrees to sell only the goods of one manufacturer and the manufacturer agrees to sell only to that distributor in that area, generally are not allowed in many countries. The antitrust laws of the United States are more lax in this area, but foreign antitrust laws such as those in the European Union consider this a restrictive trade practice that unreasonably restrains trade. The effect of an exclusive dealing agreement is to constrain the supply of a certain good.

Profile Perspective: What if Zeleski chose to market her sweats through one exclusive Polish dealer? The benefit to the dealer would be that it would be the only place in Poland where her goods are available (allowing it to raise prices as a result of a monopolized supply) and Zeleski has one distributor who is focusing on her product.

Export trading companies are firms that specialize in acting as the intermediary between businesses and purchasers in foreign countries. The firm will take title to the good being sold and then proceed to complete the sale in the foreign country. *Export management companies,* on the other hand, merely manage the sale but do not take title to the goods, and consequently do not share in any of the risk associated with the sale.

Joint Venture. A firm may decide to expand globally through an agreement of a joint venture between two or more parties. This type of agreement is usually for one or several specific projects and in effect for a specified period of time. For instance, several Japanese automobile manufacturers have entered into joint ventures with American firms to manufacture some or all of certain models in America. For instance, Mitsubishi entered into a joint venture with Chrysler Corporation in connection with the Eclipse and Eagle Talon models. In this way, companies such as Mitsubishi can market certain models by claiming that they were made in America, using American parts and labor.

Profile Perspective: Zeleski may decide that manufacturing the goods in Poland would be more desirable. In that case, she may enter into a joint venture with a Polish or other manufacturing firm.

Branch Office or Subsidiary. A branch office is a wholly owned extension of a corporate entity in a foreign country. A subsidiary is a separate corporation formed in a foreign country and owned in whole or in part by the parent company. For example, an Indian paper company may open a branch office in London to market and sell its products. That office would be a mere extension of the offices established already in India. On the other hand, the Indian firm may create a separate subsidiary to handle its British orders, which might then have an office in London. A subsidiary or branch office relationship may also come about through an acquisition of an existing firm in the foreign country.

Profile Perspective: Zeleski's father may decide to merely open a branch of his manufacturing company in Poland and run it as a wholly owned extension of his present manufacturing operations. In this way, he would maintain complete control over the operations and marketing of the sweat clothes.

The primary difference between branch offices and subsidiaries comes into play with the question of liability. In most situations when a subsidiary is sued, the parent company is not liable. To the contrary, however, the liabilities of a branch office immediately become the liabilities of the main office. In addition, the income of a branch office is considered income to the parent firm and must be reported on that firm's income tax return. Income to a subsidiary remains on the balance sheet of the subsidiary. On the other hand, there is a benefit to opening a branch office. The branch office is considered by all dealing with it as merely an arm of the parent firm. In this respect, loans and insurance may be easier to obtain for a branch as opposed to a subsidiary.

The following case addresses the complicated issue of which country's laws apply to a subsidiary, those of the country in which it is located or those of the country in which the parent is located.

CASE

Sumitomo Shoji America, Inc. v. Avagliano

102 S.Ct. 2374 (1982)

Facts

Sumitomo is a New York corporation that is a wholly owned subsidiary of Sumitomo Shoji Kabushiki Kaisha, a Japanese trading company. Female secretarial employees of Sumitomo brought an action against their employer based on its policy that it would only hire male Japanese citizens to fill executive, managerial, and sales positions. The corporation moved to dismiss the complaint, claiming that the issue was subject to the Friendship, Commerce, and Navigation Treaty between the United States and Japan. The lower court held that, because the subsidiary was a New York corporation, it was not subject to the Treaty. The Court of Appeals reversed the decision and the Supreme Court held that the Treaty provided no defense to a Title VII employment discrimination action since an American subsidiary is not a Japanese company and thus not covered by the Treaty.

* * *

Chief Justice Burger

Interpretation of the Friendship, Commerce, and Navigation Treaty between Japan and the United States must, of course, begin with the language of the Treaty itself. The clear import of treaty language controls unless "application of the words of the treaty according to their obvious meaning effects a result inconsistent with the intent or expectations of its signatories."

Article VIII(1) of the Treaty provides in pertinent part:

"[C]ompanies of either Party shall be permitted to engage, within the territories of the other Party, accountants and other technical experts, executive personnel, attorneys, agents and other specialists of their choice."

* * *

Continued

Continued

Clearly Article VIII(1) only applies to companies of one of the Treaty countries operating in the other country. Sumitomo contends that it is a company of Japan, and that Article VIII(1) of the Treaty grants it very broad discretion to fill its executive, managerial, and sales positions exclusively with male Japanese citizens.

Article VIII(1) does not define any of its terms; the definitional section of the Treaty is contained in Article XXII. Article XXII(3) provides:

> As used in the present Treaty, the term "companies" means corporations, partnerships, companies and other associations, whether or not with limited liability and whether or not for pecuniary profit. Companies constituted under the applicable laws and regulations within the territories of either Party shall be deemed companies thereof and shall have their juridical status recognized within the territories of the other Party.

Sumitomo is "constituted under the applicable laws and regulations" of New York; based on Article XXII(3), it is a company of the United States, not a company of Japan. As a company of the United States operating in the United States, under the literal language of Article XXII(3) of the Treaty, Sumitomo cannot invoke the rights provided in Article VIII(1), which are available only to companies of Japan operating in the United States and to companies of the United States operating in Japan.

The Governments of Japan and the United States support this interpretation of the Treaty. Both the Ministry of Foreign Affairs of Japan and the United States Department of State agree that a United States corporation, even when wholly owned by a Japanese company, is not a company of Japan under the Treaty and is therefore not covered by Article VIII(1).

* * *

Our role is limited to giving effect to the intent of the Treaty parties. When the parties to a treaty both agree as to the meaning of a treaty provision, and that interpretation follows from the clear treaty language, we must, absent extraordinarily strong contrary evidence, defer to that interpretation.

Sumitomo maintains that although the literal language of the Treaty supports the contrary interpretation, the intent of Japan and the United States was to cover subsidiaries regardless of their place of incorporation. We disagree.

Contrary to the view of the Court of Appeals and the claims of Sumitomo, adherence to the language of the Treaty would not "overlook the purpose of the Treaty." The Friendship, Commerce, and Navigation Treaty between Japan and the United States is but one of a series of similar commercial agreements negotiated after World War II. The primary purpose of the corporation provisions of the Treaties was to give corporations of each signatory legal status in the territory of the other party, and to allow them to conduct business in the other country on a comparable basis with domestic firms. Although the United States negotiated commercial treaties as early as 1778, and thereafter throughout the 19th century and early 20th century, these early commercial treaties were primarily concerned with the trade and shipping rights of individuals. Until the 20th century, international commerce was much more an individual than a corporate affair.

As corporate involvement in international trade expanded in this century, old commercial treaties became outmoded. Because "corporation[s] can have no legal existence out of the boundaries of the sovereignty by which [they are] created," it became necessary to negotiate new treaties granting corporations legal status and the right to function abroad. A series of Treaties negotiated before World War II gave corporations legal status and access to foreign courts, but it was not until the postwar Friendship, Commerce, and Navigation Treaties that United States corporations gained the right to conduct business in other countries. The purpose of the Treaties was not to give foreign corporations greater rights than domestic companies, but instead to assure them the right to conduct business on an equal basis without suffering discrimination based on their alienage.

Continued

Continued

The Treaties accomplished their purpose by granting foreign corporations "national treatment" in most respects and by allowing foreign individuals and companies to form locally incorporated subsidiaries. These local subsidiaries are considered for purposes of the Treaty to be companies of the country in which they are incorporated; they are entitled to the rights, and subject to the responsibilities of other domestic corporations. By treating these subsidiaries as domestic companies, the purpose of the Treaty provisions—to assure that corporations of one Treaty party have the right to conduct business within the territory of the other party without suffering discrimination as an alien entity—is fully met.

We are persuaded, as both signatories agree, that under the literal language of Article XXII(3) of the Treaty, Sumitomo is a company of the United States; we discern no reason to depart from the plain meaning of the Treaty language. Accordingly, we hold that Sumitomo is not a company of Japan and is thus not covered by Article VIII(1) of the Treaty. The judgment of the Court of Appeals is vacated, and the case is remanded for further proceedings consistent with this opinion.

Questions

1. In your opinion, is it fair or ethical to hold an American subsidiary of a Japanese company to the laws of the United States? Can you think of a reason it would not be fair? Do you believe that foreign companies *should* have rights equal to those of domestic firms to conduct business in the United States?
2. Under what method of doing business in the United States could Sumitomo have avoided problems such as those presented in the above case?
3. What is the economic effect or impact on international trade of holding an American subsidiary of a Japanese company to the laws of the United States?

Licensing. If a company has no interest in commencing operations in a foreign country, but instead merely wants to have its product or name in the market there, it may decide to license the rights to the name or to manufacturing the product to another company. For instance, assume an American firm owns the rights to the name, "Wash 'n Dry" car-wash service. This firm manufactures and operates car-washing machines for instant washes. A firm in Italy may license the right to use the name, product, and process in Italy in exchange for a royalty fee and would then be responsible for all aspects of the business operation.

The benefit to this type of relationship is that the licensor (holder of the right) has the opportunity to enter the foreign market, while the licensee assumes all of the obligations of running the business. In addition, the foreign government may be more hospitable to a domestic company's operations than a foreign firm's. On the other hand, it is critical in a licensing situation that the license contract be particular as to the quality of the good produced or service provided. Imagine the problems that could arise if a firm licenses the right to use its name on something that is of a much lower quality than the original good.

Profile Perspective: What if Zeleski's father allowed a Polish manufacturer to use his logo and trademark in producing and selling similar items? The Polish firm may desire to do this because of the marketability of American-named goods; but Zeleski's father may have a concern about losing control, and therefore consistency, of the manufacturing of the clothes.

Franchising. In a franchise agreement, the franchisee pays the franchisor for a license to use trademarks, formulas, and other trade secrets. A franchise agreement may be made up of a number of licensing arrangements and other obligations. For instance, in a typical franchise agreement for a fast-food franchise, the franchisor will license to the franchisee the right to use its trademark, name, logo, recipes, menus, and other recognized resources. The agreement may also include a commitment from the franchisor to lease a space for the franchisee or to provide advertising or training; or it may include a commitment from the franchisee to comply not only with quality standards, but also with hours of operation, marketing, and sales programs.

VI. Foreign Businesses in the United States

Foreign firms may wish to establish operations in the United States in that Americans are more inclined to buy goods made in this country. As we have seen, foreign car companies have built manufacturing plants in the United States and consequently have used as a marketing theme the fact that many of their cars sold in America are now also made in America. On the other hand, doing business in the United States brings with it the requirement that these foreign businesses comply with U.S. laws and regulations. As a result of a growing foreign trade deficit in the United States, the U.S. government has been more diligent in enforcing regulations against unfair trade practices of foreign businesses. The Department of Justice has been actively enforcing antidumping and countervailing duty laws, as well as requiring that certain countries (e.g., Japan) open their markets to U.S. exports if that country engages in voluminous exports to the United States.

VII. The Multicultural Environment: Ethics Across International Borders

A. *Consistency in Behavior*

Do ethical concepts and standards cross borders? If it is ethical to act in a certain way in one country, is it similarly ethical to do so in another? Many ethical dilemmas have arisen due to variances between cultures and the claim by some ethicists that companies engage in a convenient cultural relativism: do what's considered right in the country in which you find yourself because there is no objective right or wrong. In addition, is there any general standard of moral conduct expected from a global firm?

It might be a firm's general practice to conform to the legal standards in any country in which it does business, but this does not mean that the firm is acting consistently ethically. For example, the United States requires that cigarette companies place labels on all products and product advertisements warning of the hazardous effects of smoking. Such warning labels are not required worldwide. Consequently, cigarette manufacturers place labels on their products sold in the United States and generally not on products marketed in countries that do not require the labeling. If putting a label on the product has been deemed ethical behavior by American society, are the companies acting unethically by not doing so in other countries? Economic theory would explain that there is a demand for cigarettes in both

It might be a firm's general practice to conform to the legal standards in any country in which it does business, but this does not mean that the firm is acting consistently ethically.

the United States and elsewhere; however, the United States places additional requirements on firms that wish to take advantage of the American market (warning labels). Some other countries do not impose this additional requirement. If the addition of a warning label imposes a cost on the manufacturer, it is unlikely that the manufacturer will add a warning label in those markets that do not require it. Is there any identifiable economic *gain* to a manufacturer that chooses to add a label where none is required?

A second approach adopted by some firms is to maintain consistent standards without regard to the country in which they are doing business, rather than conforming their behavior only to that required by the country. The problem with this approach is that maintaining standards that are higher than those required in the host country may impose higher costs on the firm, raising the cost of doing business and, consequently, prices to consumers. The firm would be hurt competitively because other firms would not have this additional cost. On the other hand, there is also an economic benefit to maintaining consistency throughout the firm in that it need only produce one label, for instance, and not separate labels for each country.

American firms also claim that their opportunity to compete has been hampered by the U.S. government. Our government has attempted to encourage Vietnam to recognize a code of human rights and to turn over information regarding MIAs. Because Vietnam is extremely interested in economic ties with the United States, we have been able to use trade as a bargaining chip for our interests in human rights. However, American industry does not want to be foreclosed from the very promising Vietnamese market.

In his book, *Ethics in the Global Market,* ethicist Thomas Donaldson identified 10 rights that both multinational and domestic companies are bound to respect in their dealings with each other, their employees, and their clients and customers:[5]

1. The right to freedom of physical movement.
2. The right to ownership of property.
3. The right to freedom from torture.
4. The right to a fair trial.
5. The right to nondiscriminatory treatment.
6. The right to physical security.
7. The right to freedom of speech and association.
8. The right to minimal education.
9. The right to political participation.
10. The right to subsistence.

The relevance of these rights to corporate behavior includes consideration of retraining obligations, protection from deprivation, the refusal to hire children if it would deprive them of minimal educational opportunities, antidiscrimination provisions, and so on. These rights or obligations, ethicists would argue, represent "hypernorms," those norms that make up the foundations of human interaction and therefore have relevance across cultures. When a conflict arises between cultural norms, one might look to the hypernorm to determine the ethical resolution of the conflict.

Profile Perspective: As Zeleski begins to investigate her options for marketing her sweatshirts and other clothes in the Polish market, she will need to take a look at the impact of her clothes on that market. Although sweats may not seem to present complicated issues, imagine a book publisher that begins to distribute books originally banned in that country. Does the book manufacturer have an obligation to refrain from selling those books or to sell them in a certain manner in that country? Or consider the concerns of certain

French government ministers related to the marketing of American items in France. The ministers were concerned that France was becoming too much like the United States and not preserving enough of its own character. The ministers even proposed a ban on the use of American words (such as *weekend* or even *french fry*) in store names and newspaper headlines.

B. The Foreign Corrupt Practices Act (FCPA)

Recall from Chapter 13 (Business Torts and Crimes) that the Foreign Corrupt Practices Act prohibits U.S. companies and some joint ventures from making certain payments or gifts to government officials for the purpose of influencing business decisions. Although the FCPA appears to be well motivated, some critics argue that it is inappropriate for the United States to "unilaterally attempt to legislate morality in foreign trade."[6] In addition, others argue that the FCPA unduly restricts American companies operating in other countries and prevents them from effectively competing with other firms.

C. Social Responsibility to Host Country

If a firm is involved in business abroad, does it have social duties to the host country beyond those required by the market and the law? This issue has arisen most recently in connection with the environment. For instance, are firms that engage in business that may result in a depletion of the rain forests responsible for protecting the forests, even if there are no laws requiring them to do so?

Power companies AES Corporation and New England Electric System evidently believed that they were responsible. When they learned that the carbon dioxide emissions from fossil-fueled power plants in the United States were dangerous to trees in the rain forests, they engaged in a voluntary program to replant the forest with new trees to offset the effects of their industry.[7] On the other hand, Chiquita, Dole, and Del Monte have all been cited as companies that have engaged in harmful practices. These companies have expanded their banana plantations in Central and South America, increasing the amount of pesticides used in those areas, which has then led to extreme deforestation.

Business for the International Common Good?

Philosophe/ethicist Manuel Velasquez addressed an important question:

> Can we say that businesses operating in a competitive international environment have any moral obligations to contribute to the international common good, particularly in light of realist objections? Unfortunately, my answer to this question will be in the negative.

Velasquez defined his conception of the common good, taken from another philosopher, Jeremy Bentham:

> The interest of the community then is—what? The sum of the interests of the several members who compose it. . . It is vain to talk of the interest of the community, without understanding what is the interest of the individual. A thing is said to promote the interest or to be for the interest

Continued

Continued

of an individual when it tends to add to the sum total of his pleasure; or what comes to the same thing, to diminish the sum total of his pains.

Velasquez explained that in the absence of an international authority that can force all businesspeople to contribute to the global common good, we cannot expect any one businessperson to sense an obligation. He was not claiming that no moral obligation exists, but instead that certain agents, under certain limited conditions, seem to have no obligations.

This is not an argument, however, for complete despair. What the argument points to is the need to establish an effective international authority capable of forcing all agents to contribute their part toward the global common good.

Do you think that this is a possibility? A good idea? What type of authority do you envision? What type of regulations might that authority issue and who would be subject to them?

Source: Manuel Velasquez, "International Business: Morality and the Common Good," *Business Ethics Quarterly* 2 (1992), pp. 27–49.

D. Social Responsibility to Home Country

Notwithstanding a potential responsibility to the countries in which a firm does business, does that firm have any special obligation back to its home country? In 1993, the federal government had prohibited American firms from participating in an embargo of Israel imposed by Arab countries, including Iraq, Kuwait, Libya, Yemen, Saudi Arabia, and Syria. The Arab countries refused to do business not only with Israel, but also with any firm that did business with Israel.

Baxter Pharmaceuticals allegedly cooperated with the Arab embargo by refusing to do business with Israel because it wanted to maintain certain lucrative Arab contracts. Vernon Loucks, Baxter's CEO, was called on the carpet by Baxter's institutional stockholders and was at risk of losing his position because of this decision. In fact, when Loucks introduced himself as the CEO at Baxter's annual meeting, he was met with a response of "Not for long!" from one of the shareholders. Although Loucks kept his job (he did step down from his position on the board of Yale University as a result of student protests regarding his involvement in the Arab boycott), Baxter suffered gravely in the U.S. press and paid $6.5 million in fines. In addition, one month after the fines were imposed, the Defense Department banned Baxter from new business contracts with the Department.

Baxter, in this situation, argued that it should be able to contract with whomever it chooses, that it owes no obligation to the foreign policy matters of the U.S. government. In this case, the firm was in violation of U.S. law; in other cases, the line may not be so clearly drawn. For instance, McDonnell Douglas, after years of defense contracts with the U.S. government, was faced with similar allegiance questions when it proposed a sale of a portion of its manufacturing interests to Taiwan Aerospace. Opponents of the plan were concerned that privileged information regarding America's defense would fall into the wrong hands. They contended that McDonnell Douglas had a duty to the United States to maintain the confidentiality of this information within America's borders. McDonnell Douglas, on the other hand, argued that it was a private company and could sell its assets to the highest bidder, which was Taiwan by a wide margin. U.S. law did not prohibit the sale in this instance, and McDonnell Douglas was faced with the prospect of violating the wishes of its home government in order to stay afloat, or complying with the government's request to stop the sale, and perhaps sacrificing the survival of the company.

U.S. Suffering from Embarrassing Morality Gap

by John McCarron

The topic of this Sunday's sermon shall be, ahem, morality. Or more precisely, America's growing morality gap.

It's a risky subject because nobody likes to be lectured on the difference between right and wrong. At least not during income tax season, when even the saints among us tend to lean on the pencil when itemizing deductions on Schedule A.

But this isn't about how much you claimed on those suits you gave to the Salvation Army, or that bogus office-in-the-home. That's peanuts. Nor am I talking about Bill Clinton's Whitewater troubles, his wife's early success with cattle futures, or even Newt Gingrich's million-dollar book deal. That's popcorn.

This is about big stuff. Because last week, while we Americans were feeling guilty about unreported income and angry about Commerce Secretary Ron Brown's side deals, the rest of the world was running amok, skating immoral circles around the good old U.S. of A.

Ladies and gentlemen, the missile gap ended with the Cold War. The morality gap has just begun. How are we supposed to keep up with stuff like this:

- In Mexico, the new government of Ernesto Zedillo Ponce de Leon arrested Raul Salinas de Gortari, brother of the former president, Carlos Salinas de Gortari, on charges that he masterminded the assassination of the chief of the long-dominant PRI political party. Insiders say that Raul may have wanted to silence the victim's protests about corruption in the PRI.
- In Russia, the nation's top TV news anchorman was shot dead mob-style (close up and with a silencer), most likely by underworld types who want to control advertising revenues in the newly privatized television industry.
- In Italy, former Premier Giulio Andreotti, perhaps the country's leading post-war statesman, was indicted on charges of consorting with the Mafia. Andreotti allegedly broke a long-standing deal under which the Mafia delivered the Sicilian vote for the Christian Democrats, who in return gave the mob a wink and a nod.
- In France, the top leader of the Socialist party went on trial for gross violation of that country's campaign financing laws. It is alleged that government contractors were told to hire certain consultants, who in turn kicked back millions of francs to funds controlled by Henri Emmanuelli.
- In South Africa, police raided the posh homestead of President Nelson Mandela's estranged wife, Winnie, in search of evidence that she has been shaking down builders of subsidized housing.
- The Clinton administration issued a report saying that the [Columbian] government acts disinterested in curbing the cocaine trade.

All this happened in the last seven days. Just one week!

Questions:

1. Are you persuaded that America's moral standards are higher than those in other countries? Give examples.
2. Look at today's newspaper. Do you feel numb to the atrocities going on in the world around you, or are you instead constantly upset by events reported? Is there a balance?

Source: *Chicago Tribune,* March 5, 1995, section 7, p. 2.

VIII. International Dispute Resolution: What Does a Business Owner Do when the Problems Begin?

As we have seen to this point, international ethical/legal relationships are highly complex. Disputes are inevitable. Resolution of these international disputes often faces several roadblocks. First, as mentioned above, the interpretation of contract terms, the language of the contract, the law applicable to the resolution of the conflict, and the appropriate jurisdiction in which to resolve the dispute all raise dilemmas that are not easily dismissed. Moreover, two doctrines, accepted as general principles of international law, also pose quandaries to the courts and barriers to judicial enforcement of rights: the **act of state doctrine** and the **doctrine of sovereign immunity.**

act of state doctrine. Principle that a court in one country does not have the authority to challenge the acts of another country within that country's borders.

doctrine of sovereign immunity. Principle that a foreign nation may not be sued in American courts, with certain exceptions.

A. *Act of State Doctrine*

It is generally accepted that a country has absolute rule over what occurs within its borders. Consequently, the act of state doctrine holds that a judge in one country does not have the authority to examine or challenge the acts of another country within that country's borders. For instance, a point that might concern Zeleski, an American court may not declare the acts of the Polish government invalid because it is presumed that the Polish government acted legally within its own territory.

One area that has caused a great deal of dispute in connection with the act of state doctrine is **expropriation.** Expropriation is the taking by a national government of property or rights of a foreign firm within its borders. The United States contends that international law dictates that an individual or firm be compensated for the taking by the government. Not all governments agree with this statement of law. On the other hand, if a government expropriates property or rights without offering just compensation, the foreign government of the firm affected may retaliate economically or otherwise. The following case concerns expropriation.

expropriation. The taking of property and/or rights of a foreign firm by a national government within its borders.

CASE

Banco Nacional de Cuba v. Sabbatino, Receiver, et al.

376 U.S. 398 (1963)

Facts

Farr, Whitlock, an American commodities broker, contracted with a Cuban firm, Compania Azucarera Vertientes (CAV) to buy Cuban sugar. After the United States reduced the Cuban sugar quota, the Cuban government expropriated the firm's property and rights, including the sugar scheduled to be shipped to Farr. Farr then entered into a new contract to buy the sugar from the Cuban government. After Farr later received payment for the sugar from its clients, it turned the proceeds over to CAV instead of Banco Nacional. Banco Nacional sued Farr, as well as Sabbatino (temporary receiver for CAV) to prevent it from disposing of the money given to it by Farr. Farr argued that the title to the sugar never passed to the government because the expropriation violated international law. Banco Nacional responded that the act of state doctrine prohibited the U.S. courts from determining the legality of the expropriation.

Continued

Continued

Justice Harlan

While acknowledging the continuing vitality of the Act of State doctrine, [the District Court] believed it inapplicable when the questioned foreign act is in violation of international law. Proceeding on the basis that a taking invalid under international law does not convey good title, the District Court found the Cuban expropriation decree to violate such law in three separate respects. It was motivated by a retaliatory and not a public purpose; it discriminated against American nationals; and it failed to provide adequate compensation.

* * *

That international law does not require application of the doctrine is evidenced by the practice of nations. Most of the countries rendering decisions on the subject fail to follow the rule rigidly. No international arbitral or judicial decision discovered suggests that international law prescribes recognition of sovereign acts of foreign governments and apparently no claim has ever been raised before an international tribunal that failure to apply the Act of State doctrine constitutes a breach of international obligation. If international law does not prescribe use of the doctrine, neither does it forbid application of the rule even if it is claimed that the act of state in question violated international law. The traditional view of international law is that it establishes substantive principles for determining whether one country has wronged another. Because of its peculiar nation-to-nation character the usual method for an individual to seek relief is to exhaust local remedies and then repair to the executive authorities of his own state to persuade them to champion his claim in diplomacy or before an international tribunal. Although it is, of course, true that the United States courts apply international law as a part of our own in appropriate circumstances, the public law of nations can hardly dictate to a country which is in theory wronged how to treat that wrong within its domestic borders.

* * *

There are few if any issues in international law today on which opinion seems to be so divided as the limitations on a state's power to expropriate the property of aliens. There is, of course, authority, in international judicial and arbitral decisions, in the expressions of national governments, and among commentators for the view that a taking is improper under international law if it is not for a public purpose, is discriminatory or is without provision for prompt, adequate, and effective compensation. However, Communist countries, although they have in fact provided a degree of compensation after diplomatic efforts, commonly recognize no obligation on the part of the taking country. Certain representatives of the newly independent and underdeveloped countries have questioned whether rules of state responsibility toward aliens can bind nations that have not consented to them and it is argued that the traditionally articulated standards governing expropriation of property reflect "imperialist" interests and are appropriate to the circumstances of emergent states.

* * *

When we consider the prospect of the courts characterizing foreign expropriations, however justifiably, as invalid under international law and ineffective to pass title, the wisdom of precedents is confirmed. While each of the leading cases in this court may be argued to be distinguishable on its facts from this one . . . the plain implication in all of these opinions, and the import of express statements in [other cases] is that the Act of State doctrine is applicable even if international law has been violated. . .

The possible adverse consequences of a conclusion to the contrary of that implicit in these cases is highlighted by contrasting the practices of the political branch with the limitations of the judicial process in matters of this kind. Following an expropriation of any significance, the

Continued

Continued

Executive engages in diplomacy to assure that United States citizens who are harmed are compensated fairly. Judicial determinations of invalidity of title can, on the other hand, have only an occasional impact, since they depend on the fortuitous circumstance of the property in question being brought in this country. Such decisions would, if the acts involved were declared invalid, often be likely to give offense to the expropriating country; since the concept of territorial sovereignty is so deep seated, any state may resent the refusal of another sovereign to accord validity to acts within its territorial borders. Piecemeal dispositions of this sort involving the probability of affront to another state could seriously interfere with negotiations being carried on by the Executive Branch and might prevent or render less favorable the terms of an agreement that could otherwise be reached. Relations with third countries which have engaged in similar expropriations would not be immune from effect.

* * *

Another serious consequence of the exception pressed by respondents would be to render uncertain titles in foreign commerce, with the possible consequence of altering the flow of international trade. If the attitude of the United States courts were unclear, one buying expropriated goods would not know if he could safely import them into this country. Even were takings known to be invalid, one would have difficulty determining after goods had changed hands several times whether the particular articles in question were the product of an ineffective state act.

* * *

However offensive to the public policy of this country and its constituent states an expropriation of this kind may be, we conclude that both the national interest and progress toward the goal of establishing the rule of law among nations are best served by maintaining intact the Act of State doctrine in this realm of its application.

Questions

1. *a.* Do you agree with the reasoning of the court?
   b. Should the likelihood of favorable negotiations between the United States and other countries affect the court's decision regarding this specific case? Explain.
2. What did the court mean by "relations with third countries which have engaged in similar expropriations would not be immune from effect"?
3. What is the impact of the potential for expropriation on the economic stability of a firm?

B. Doctrine of Sovereign Immunity

The doctrine of sovereign immunity is based on the concept that "the king can do no wrong." In other words, if the king makes the rules, how could the king ever be wrong? As Chief Justice Marshall explained in *The Schooner Exchange* v. *McFaddon,*[8]

> The jurisdiction of the nation within its own territory is necessarily exclusive and absolute. It is susceptible of no limitation not imposed by itself; deriving validity from an external source would imply a diminution of its sovereignty to the extent of the restriction, and an investment of that sovereignty to the same extent in that power which could impose such restriction.

The doctrine has been codified in the United States by the Foreign Sovereign Immunities Act of 1976 (FSIA), which provides that foreign countries may not be sued in American courts, subject to several exceptions. Accordingly, it would not be possible for a U.S. citizen to sue Britain in the U.S. courts. A foreign country may be sued in American courts if the claim falls into one of the following FSIA exceptions:

1. The case involves a foreign country that has waived its immunity (that is, consented to be sued in another country's courts).
2. The legal action is based on a foreign country's *commercial activity* in the United States or outside of but having a direct effect in the United States.

Therefore, a country that conducts a commercial activity in a foreign country may not hide behind sovereign immunity if sued, but a country acting on its own behalf and not for a commercial purpose would be able to avail itself of the protection. This "restrictive theory of immunity" is to be contrasted with the policies of some countries that contend that immunity is absolute, that is, no exceptions exist.

C. Arbitration

In light of the difficulty of obtaining jurisdiction and the choice of laws, language, and forum issues, parties to an international contract may prefer to insert a clause that calls for international arbitration in case of a dispute. Arbitration is a nonjudicial means to settle a conflict whereby the parties agree to a hearing in front of a third party who will issue a binding award decision (see Chapter 2). The arbitration clause will specify the identity of the third party (or the association from which the parties will seek a third party), the place of arbitration, and in many cases, the laws that will apply.

Although arbitration is considered binding on the parties consenting to it, there are times when a losing party may opt not to satisfy the award to the other party. In that case, the successful party must petition a court of law to enforce the award. In that regard, the United Nations Convention on the Recognition and Enforcement of Foreign Arbitral Awards provides that the successful party obtain possession of the property of the losing party located in any signatory country for the purpose of satisfying the debt.

The following case illustrates the problems that may arise, even when an arbitration clause is apparently clear.

CASE

Mitsubishi Motors v. Soler Chrysler-Plymouth

473 U.S. 614 (1985)

Facts

Soler Chrysler-Plymouth distributed Plymouth automobiles in Puerto Rico for CISA, a Swiss subsidiary of Chrysler. CISA and Mitsubishi Heavy Industries, Inc., entered into a joint venture called Mitsubishi Motors. CISA, Soler, and Mistubishi Motors entered into an agreement stating that all disputes that arose in connection with the agreement would be settled by arbitration in Japan in accordance with the rules of the Japan Commercial Arbitration Association. After several years, Mitsubishi requested arbitration in Tokyo and filed a federal district court action to compel arbitration

Continued

Continued

under the agreement. Soler argued that antitrust and other violations were involved in the dispute and that these issues were not appropriate for arbitration. The District Court ordered arbitration; the Court of Appeals reversed the decision regarding the arbitration of the antitrust matters. Mitsubishi appealed to the Supreme Court.

* * *

Justice Blackmun

. . . We also reject the proposition that an arbitration panel will pose too great a danger of innate hostility to the constraints on business conduct that antitrust law imposes. International arbitrators frequently are drawn from the legal as well as the business community; where the dispute has an important legal component, the parties and the arbitral body with whose assistance they have agreed to settle their dispute can be expected to select arbitrators accordingly. We decline to indulge the presumption that the parties and arbitral body conducting a proceeding will be unable or unwilling to retain competent, conscientious, and impartial arbitrators . . .

There is no reason to assume at the outset of the dispute that international arbitration will not provide an adequate mechanism. To be sure, the international arbitral tribunal owes no prior allegiance to the legal norms of particular states; hence, it has no direct obligation to vindicate their statutory dictates. The tribunal, however, is bound to effectuate the intentions of the parties. Where the parties have agreed that the arbitral body is to decide a defined set of claims which includes, as in these cases, those arising from the application of American antitrust law, the tribunal therefore should be bound to decide that dispute in accord with the national law giving rise to the claim . . .

Having permitted the arbitration to go forward, the national courts of the United States will have the opportunity at the award-enforcement stage to ensure that the legitimate interest in the enforcement of the antitrust laws has been addressed. The Convention reserves to each signatory country the right to refuse enforcement of an award where the "recognition or enforcement of the award would be contrary to the public policy of that country." While the efficacy of the arbitral process requires that substantive review at the award-enforcement stage remain minimal, it would not require intrusive inquiry to ascertain that the tribunal took cognizance of the antitrust claims and actually decided them.

As international trade has expanded in recent decades, so too has the use of international arbitration to resolve disputes arising in the course of that trade. The controversies that international arbitral institutions are called upon to resole have increased in diversity as well as in complexity. Yet the potential of these tribunals for efficient disposition of legal disagreements arising from commercial relations has not yet been tested. If they are to take a central place in the international legal order, national courts will need to "shake off the old judicial hostility to arbitration," and also their customary and understandable unwillingness to cede jurisdiction of a claim arising under domestic law to a foreign or transnational tribunal. To this extent, at least, it will be necessary for national courts to subordinate domestic notions of arbitrability to the international policy favoring commercial arbitration.

[Affirmed in part, reversed in part.]

Questions

1. What were the bases for Soler's contention that matters such as antitrust should not be submitted to arbitration?
2. How does the court propose that Soler's concerns will be addressed?
3. *a.* If the legal system is overloaded with cases and litigation may take up to a decade to reach resolution, is there really any downside to arbitration?
   b. Do you consider arbitration an ethical form of conflict resolution?
   c. If arbitration did not exist as an option, do you believe the market would create it?

Summary

Legal Review. Recall that there is actually no true body of law called *international law*. Instead, the resolution of international disputes may involve a variety of conclusions that are derived by looking to customs, domestic laws of the countries involved, treaties or conventions between the countries involved, International Court of Justice decisions, or comity. Firms doing business globally must be aware, however, of the impact of certain laws of the host country on their operations. For instance, employers must be concerned about complying with employment-related statutes; marketing managers must be aware of antitrust regulations; manufacturing operations must be conscious of the differences in product liability laws worldwide, import and export rules and regulations, and other laws affecting global commerce.

When expanding globally, firms have a number of options of forms of business growth. The reasons for expansion, benefits and costs of each form of expansion, and type of business a firm engages in may all govern the response to this issue.

Ethics Review. Acceptable customs of doing business may change from country to country. Do the acceptable standards within an organization change depending on the country in which it is doing business? A firm cannot escape answering this question as it determines the standards of operation throughout the company. We have all heard the comparisons between the United States and other countries: in some circumstances, the United States has a great deal of regulation where other countries have little, and in others, the situation is reversed. To whom does a firm answer? If not to itself, then perhaps its operating standards are flexible. Or a firm may have an internal code or standard that permeates the business no matter its global environment.

Further, does a global firm have a patriotic obligation to its home country? Does a firm have a duty not to ameliorate the economic system of another country when it might harm that of the home country? Does a firm have an obligation to keep important technological advances only within the reach of its government, or could such information be sold to the highest bidder? Answering these questions by looking only to the bottom line may be shortsighted and unaccountable. However, considering only the impact on one's conscience may not take into account the firm's duty to its shareholders.

Economics Review. Law in the global environment is one of those circumstances in which there remains a rather free market. In fact, there is little legislation or regulation that is binding on private parties to an agreement. In that regard, the international market remains open and relatively pure. On the other hand, many would argue that the intrusion of national interests and governmental policies to the market is an impediment to the true freedom that is still possible in this relatively new marketplace.

Chapter Questions

1. What are the relative advantages and disadvantages of each form of doing business in a foreign country? Why would a firm choose one form over another?
2. What economic argument can one make in favor of broadening a firm's market to include the global marketplace?
3. If you were advising a global firm regarding a legal issue, what sources of law would you look to for answers? Where would you look first?

4. Assume that you are interested in importing silk blouses from Bangkok to France. What facts might persuade you to enter into an agency agreement with the Thai blouse manufacturer rather than a distributorship and vice versa?
5. Nigeria contracted to purchase large quantities of cement from Portland Cement to support its rapidly expanding infrastructure. Nigeria overpurchased the cement, and the country's harbors became clogged with ships waiting to unload. Imports of other goods ground to a halt as well. Nigeria consequently repudiated its contracts with those shippers, who then filed suits to enforce the contracts. Nigeria responded that it is immune from prosecution in connection with these contracts under the Foreign Sovereign Immunities Act, claiming that its contracts were governmental and not of a commercial nature. Decide. [See *Texas Trading and Milling Corp.* v. *Federal Republic of Nigeria,* 647 F.2d 300 (2d Cir. 1981).]
6. Prior to 1941, Kalmich owned a business in Yugoslavia. In 1941, the Nazis confiscated his property as a result of Kalmich's Jewish heritage and faith. Bruno purchased the business from the Nazis in 1942 without knowledge of the potential unlawful conversion. Kalmich contends that since the confiscation was in violation of well-defined principals of international law prior to the German occupation, the transfer to Bruno was ineffective. Kalmich seeks to apply a 1946 Yugoslavian statute called "Law Concerning the Treatment of Property Taken Away from the Owner." That law provides that if property is taken from its owners, the owner may bring an action against "responsible persons" for recovery. Does the act of state doctrine apply here? If not, what is the result in an American court? [See *Kalmich* v. *Bruno,* 450 F. Supp. 227 (N.D. Ill. 1978).]
7. Bandes owned and managed 73 percent of the shares of Industria Nacional de Clavos y Alambres (INCA), a Nicaraguan corporation. In 1978, INCA paid $460,000 to Harlow & Jones, Inc. (H&J), a U.S. company, for steel billets. However, the events of the Nicaraguan civil war prevented INCA from taking delivery of the goods after they had been paid for and caused Bandes to flee the country. Decree no. 10, enacted by the new Nicaraguan government, gave the state the right to intervene in any business that had been abandoned. In 1979, the Nicaraguan government confiscated the shares held by others in the company and stripped Bandes of all power to represent INCA. In February 1980, the government issued another decree that stated that all individuals who lost rights under the prior decree no. 10 must appear in Nicaragua within 10 days to contest the taking; otherwise the property would belong to the state with no further right to contest. Bandes did not appear because his act of abandonment would have been considered a crime under the decree, but later filed suit in the U.S. district courts seeking to get back from H&J the money INCA had paid to it, which Bandes believed he was rightly due.

   Does the act of state doctrine apply here? Are the acts of the Nicaraguan government in line with U.S. law and policies? Does it make a difference that the funds sought by Bandes are located in the United States? [See *Bandes* v. *Harlow & Jones, Inc.,* 852 F.2d 661 (1988).]
8. Lee Bun entered Hong Kong illegally by boat from China. He sought to claim refugee status on the basis that he had been involved in political protests in China and feared persecution if he returned. After judicial review of deportation orders was dismissed, Lee Bun claimed that he had been denied the right to a fair hearing, guaranteed by the Geneva Convention. The Department of Immigration responded that, although Britain had ratified the Convention, it had not been extended to Hong Kong and was not, therefore, part of the law of Hong Kong. What ethical or legal arguments could Lee Bun make in his favor, supporting the application of the Geneva Convention or his right to a fair hearing? [See *Lee Bun* v. *Dir. of Immigration,* 2 HKLR 466 (1990).]

9. Zedan received a telephone call from a Saudi Arabian organization offering him an engineering position at a construction project in Saudi Arabia. The Ministry of Communications, an agency of the government, guaranteed payment to Zedan for any work he performed there, whether for the government or for a nonsovereign third party. After three years, Zedan left the country without being fully paid. After he returned to the United States, he filed an action in federal court seeking to enforce the Ministry's guarantee. The Ministry argued that it was protected under the Foreign Sovereign Immunities Act. Was Zedan's recruitment in the United States a commercial activity as required by the act? Did this action have a direct effect in the United States as required by the act? [See *Zedan* v. *Kingdom of Saudi Arabia,* 849 F.2d 1511 (1988).]
10. *a.* Sonia is employed as an operations manager for a large midwestern manufacturing firm and has worked at the firm for 10 years. She is aware that there is an opening for someone with her abilities at the company's plant in the Middle East. The firm does not offer her the position, claiming that women are not treated well as managers in that area and that she would not have the respect that she deserves in that position. They are concerned that she, therefore, would not be able to adequately perform her functions. Sonia is upset and considers filing a complaint with the EEOC. What guidance would you offer to her?

    b. Consider a slight change to the above scenario. Sonia is the assistant operations manager for the Middle East plant and resides in that area. She is told that if she wants a higher position, she should either move back to the States or consider a different company. The firm cites the reasons mentioned above for this conclusion. Does Sonia have rights under Title VII?
11. Must a rule be universal to be considered customary international law? For instance, if a majority of states consider the limit of one country's territorial waters to be 10 miles out from each point along the coast, but a number of states do not follow this basic rule, can it be said that the rule is still a custom of international law?
12. Camel Manufacturing imported nylon tents to the United States. The tents held nine people and weighed over 30 pounds. The tents' floors ranged from 8 feet by 10 feet to 10 feet by 14 feet. The tents were to be used as shelter during camping. The importer categorized the goods as "sports equipment," which carried a 10 percent import duty; but the U.S. Customs Service considered the tents "textile articles not specifically provided for" with a duty of $.25 per pound plus 15 percent import duty. The importer appealed the decision. Decide. [See *Camel Manufacturing Co.* v. *United States,* 686 F.Supp. 912 (C.I.T. 1988).]

Notes

1. Michael Elliot, "Dining on Goose, Talking Turkey," *Newsweek,* December 20, 1993, p. 40.
2. James Bovard, "Trade Barriers vs. International Property," *World Capitalism Review* 2, (1994). p. 17.
3. 661 F.2d 864 (10th Cir. 1981).
4. Michael Zuckoff, "Using U.S. Exports Can Be Risky," *The Boston Globe,* July 11, 1994, pp. 1, 6.
5. Thomas Donaldson, *Ethics of International Business* (New York, Oxford Univ. Press, 1989), p. 81.
6. Mark Bader and Bill Shaw, "Amendment of the Foreign Corrupt Practices Act," *Journal of International Law and Policy* 15 (1983), pp. 627, 628.
7. Desda Moss, "Report: Companies Help Rain Forests Breathe a Little Easier," *USA Today,* September 15, 1993, p. 5A.
8. 11 U.S. (7 Cranch) 116 (1812).

APPENDIX A

THE CONSTITUTION OF THE UNITED STATES OF AMERICA

Preamble

We the People of the United States, in Order to form a more perfect Union, establish Justice, insure domestic Tranquility, provide for the common defence, promote the general Welfare, and secure the Blessings of Liberty to ourselves and our Posterity, do ordain and establish this Constitution for the United States of America.

Article I

Section 1. All legislative Powers herein granted shall be vested in a Congress of the United States, which shall consist of a Senate and House of Representatives.

Section 2. (1) The House of Representatives shall be composed of Members chosen every second Year by the People of the several States, and the Electors in each State shall have the Qualifications requisite for Electors of the most numerous Branch of the State Legislature.

(2) No Person shall be a Representative who shall not have attained to the Age of twenty five Years, and been seven Years a Citizen of the United States, and who shall not, when elected, be an Inhabitant of that State in which he shall be chosen.

(3) Representatives and direct Taxes shall be apportioned among the several States which may be included within this Union, according to their respective Numbers, which shall be determined by adding to the whole Number of free Persons, including those bound to Service for a Term of Years, and excluding Indians not taxed, three fifths of all other Persons.[1] The actual Enumeration shall be made within three Years after the first Meeting of the Congress of the United States, and within every subsequent Term of ten Years, in such Manner as they shall by Law direct. The number of Representatives shall not exceed one for every thirty Thousand, but each State shall have at Least one Representative; and until such enumeration shall be made, the State of New Hampshire shall be entitled to chuse three, Massachusetts eight, Rhode-Island and Providence Plantations one, Connecticut five, New-York six, New Jersey four, Pennsylvania eight, Delaware one, Maryland six, Virginia ten, North Carolina five, South Carolina five, and Georgia three.

(4) When vacancies happen in the Representation from any State, the Executive Authority thereof shall issue Writs of Election to fill such Vacancies.

(5) The House of Representatives shall chuse their Speaker and other Officers; and shall have the sole Power of Impeachment.

Section 3. (1) The Senate of the United States shall be composed of two Senators from each State, chosen by the Legislature thereof,[2] for six Years; and each Senator shall have one Vote.

(2) Immediately after they shall be assembled in Consequence of the first Election, they shall be divided as equally as may be into three Classes. The Seats of the Senators of

[1]Refer to the Fourteenth Amendment.

[2]Refer to the Seventeenth Amendment.

the first Class shall be vacated at the Expiration of the second Year, of the second Class at the Expiration of the fourth Year, and of the third Class at the Expiration of the sixth Year, so that one third may be chosen every second Year; and if Vacancies happen by Resignation, or otherwise, during the Recess of the Legislature of any State, the Executive thereof may make temporary Appointments until the next Meeting of the Legislature, which shall then fill such Vacancies.[3]

(3) No Person shall be a Senator who shall not have attained to the Age of thirty Years, and been nine Years a Citizen of the United States, and who shall not, when elected, be an Inhabitant of that State for which he shall be chosen.

(4) The Vice President of the United States shall be President of the Senate, but shall have no Vote, unless they be equally divided.

(5) The Senate shall chuse their other Officers, and also a President pro tempore, in the Absence of the Vice President, or when he shall exercise the Office of President of the United States.

(6) The Senate shall have the sole Power to try all Impeachments. When sitting for that Purpose, they shall be on Oath or Affirmation. When the President of the United States is tried, the Chief Justice shall preside: And no Person shall be convicted without the Concurrence of two thirds of the Members present.

(7) Judgment in Cases of Impeachment shall not extend further than to removal from Office, and disqualification to hold and enjoy any Office of honor, Trust or Profit under the United States: but the Party convicted shall nevertheless be liable and subject to Indictment, Trial, Judgment and Punishment, according to Law.

Section 4. (1) The Times, Places and Manner of holding Elections for Senators and Representatives, shall be prescribed in each State by the Legislature thereof; but the Congress may at any time by Law make or alter such Regulations, except as to the Places of chusing Senators.

(2) The Congress shall assemble at least once in every year, and such Meeting shall be on the first Monday in December, unless they shall by Law appoint a different Day.[4]

Section 5. (1) Each House shall be the Judge of the Elections, Returns and Qualifications of its own Members, and a Majority of each shall constitute a Quorum to do Business; but a smaller Number may adjourn from day to day, and may be authorized to compel the Attendance of absent Members, in such Manner, and under such Penalties as each House may provide.

(2) Each House may determine the Rules of its Proceedings, punish its Members for disorderly Behaviour, and, with the Concurrence of two thirds, expel a Member.

(3) Each House shall keep a Journal of its Proceedings, and from time to time publish the same, excepting such Parts as may in their Judgment require Secrecy; and the Yeas and Nays of the Members of either House on any question shall, at the Desire of one fifth of those Present, be entered on the Journal.

(4) Neither House, during the Session of Congress, shall, without the Consent of the other, adjourn for more than three days, nor to any other Place than that in which the two Houses shall be sitting.

Section 6. (1) The Senators and Representatives shall receive a Compensation for their Services, to be ascertained by Law, and paid out of the Treasury of the United States.

[3]Ibid.

[4]Refer to the Twentieth Amendment.

They shall in all Cases, except Treason, Felony and Breach of the Peace, be privileged from Arrest during their Attendance at the Session of their respective Houses, and in going to and returning from the same; and for any Speech or Debate in either House, they shall not be questioned in any other Place.

(2) No Senator or Representative shall, during the Time for which he was elected, be appointed to any civil Office under the Authority of the United States, which shall have been created, or the Emoluments whereof shall have been encreased during such time; and no Person holding any Office under the United States, shall be a Member of either House during his Continuance in Office.

Section 7. (1) All Bills for raising Revenue shall originate in the House of Representatives; but the Senate may propose or concur with Amendments as on other Bills.

(2) Every Bill which shall have passed the House of Representatives and the Senate, shall, before it becomes a Law, be presented to the President of the United States; if he approve he shall sign it, but if not he shall return it, with his Objections to that House in which it shall have originated, who shall enter the Objections at large on their Journal, and proceed to reconsider it. If after such Reconsideration two thirds of that House shall agree to pass the Bill, it shall be sent, together with the Objections, to the other House, by which it shall likewise be reconsidered, and if approved by two thirds of that House, it shall become a Law. But in all such Cases the Votes of both Houses shall be determined by yeas and Nays, and the Names of the Persons voting for and against the Bill shall be entered on the Journal of such House respectively. If any Bill shall not be returned by the President within ten Days (Sundays excepted) after it shall have been presented to him, the Same shall be a Law, in like Manner as if he had signed it, unless the Congress by their Adjournment prevent its Return in which Case it shall not be a Law.

(3) Every Order, Resolution, or Vote to which the Concurrence of the Senate and House of Representatives may be necessary (except on a question of Adjournment) shall be presented to the President of the United States; and before the Same shall take Effect, shall be approved by him, or being disapproved by him, shall be repassed by two thirds of the Senate and House of Representatives, according to the Rules and Limitations prescribed in the Case of a Bill.

Section 8. (1) The Congress shall have Power To lay and collect Taxes, Duties, Imposts and Excises, to pay the Debts and provide for the common Defence and general Welfare of the United States; but all Duties, Imposts and Excises shall be uniform throughout the United States;

(2) To borrow Money on the credit of the United States;

(3) To regulate Commerce with foreign Nations, and among the several States, and with the Indian Tribes;

(4) To establish an uniform Rule of Naturalization, and uniform Laws on the subject of Bankruptcies throughout the United States;

(5) To coin Money, regulate the Value thereof, and of foreign Coin, and fix the Standard of Weights and Measures;

(6) To provide for the Punishment of counterfeiting the Securities and current Coin of the United States;

(7) To establish Post Offices and post Roads;

(8) To promote the Progress of Science and useful Arts, by securing for limited Times to Authors and Inventors the exclusive Right to their respective Writings and Discoveries;

(9) To constitute Tribunals inferior to the supreme Court;

(10) To define and punish Piracies and Felonies committed on the high Seas, and Offenses against the Law of Nations;

(11) To declare War, grant Letters of Marque and Reprisal, and make Rules concerning Captures on Land and Water;

(12) To raise and support Armies, but no Appropriation of Money to that Use shall be for a longer Term than two Years;

(13) To provide and maintain a Navy;

(14) To make Rules for the Government and Regulation of the land and naval Forces;

(15) To provide for calling forth the Militia to execute the Laws of the Union, suppress Insurrections and repel Invasions;

(16) To provide for organizing, arming, and disciplining, the Militia, and for governing such Part of them as may be employed in the Service of the United States, reserving to the States respectively, the Appointment of the Officers, and the Authority of training the Militia according to the discipline prescribed by Congress;

(17) To exercise exclusive Legislation in all Cases whatsoever, over such District (not exceeding ten Miles square) as may, by Cession of particular States, and the Acceptance of Congress, become the Seat of the Government of the United States, and to exercise like Authority over all Places purchased by the Consent of the Legislature of the State in which the Same shall be, for the Election of Forts, Magazines, Arsenals, dock-Yards and other needful Buildings;—And

(18) To make all Laws which shall be necessary and proper for carrying into Execution the foregoing Powers, and all other Powers vested by this Constitution in the Government of the United States, or in any Department or Officer thereof.

Section 9. (1) The Migration or Importation of Such Persons as any of the States now existing shall think proper to admit, shall not be prohibited by the Congress prior to the Year one thousand eight hundred and eight, but a Tax or duty may be imposed on such Importation, not exceeding ten dollars for each Person.

(2) The privilege of the Writ of Habeas Corpus shall not be suspended, unless when in Cases of Rebellion or Invasion the public Safety may require it.

(3) No Bill of Attainder or ex post facto Law shall be passed.

(4) No Capitation, or other direct, Tax shall be laid, unless in Proportion to the Census or Enumeration herein before directed to be taken.[5]

(5) No Tax or Duty shall be laid on Articles exported from any state.

(6) No Preference shall be given by the Regulation of Commerce or Revenue to the Ports of one State over those of another: nor shall Vessels bound to, or from, one State, be obliged to enter, clear, or pay Duties in another.

(7) No Money shall be drawn from the Treasury, but in Consequence of Appropriations made by Law; and a regular Statement and Account of the Receipts and Expenditures of all public Money shall be published from time to time.

(8) No Title of Nobility shall be granted by the United States: And no Person holding any Office of Profit or Trust under them, shall, without the Consent of the Congress, accept of any present, Emolument, Office, or Title, of any kind whatever, from any King, Prince, or foreign State.

Section 10. (1) No State shall enter into any Treaty, Alliance, or Confederation; grant Letters of Marque and Reprisal; coin Money; emit Bills of Credit; make any Thing but gold and silver Coin a Tender in Payment of Debts; pass any Bill of Attainder, ex post facto Law, or Law impairing the Obligation of Contracts, or grant any Title of Nobility.

[5]Refer to the Sixteenth Amendment.

(2) No State shall, without the Consent of the Congress, lay any Imposts or Duties on Imports or Exports, except what may be absolutely necessary for executing its inspection Laws; and the net Produce of all Duties and Imposts, laid by any State on Imports or Exports, shall be for the Use of the Treasury of the United States; and all such Laws shall be subject to the Revision and Controul of the Congress.

(3) No State shall, without the Consent of Congress, lay any Duty of Tonnage, keep Troops, or Ships of War in time of Peace, enter into any Agreement or Compact with another State, or with a foreign Power, or engage in War, unless actually invaded, or in such imminent Danger as will not admit of delay.

Article II

Section 1. (1) The executive Power shall be vested in a President of the United States of America. He shall hold his Office during the Term of four Years, and, together with the Vice President, chosen for the same Term, be elected, as follows:

(2) Each State shall appoint, in such Manner as the Legislature thereof may direct, a Number of Electors, equal to the whole Number of Senators and Representatives to which the State may be entitled in the Congress: but no Senator or Representative, or Person holding an Office of Trust or Profit under the United States, shall be appointed an Elector.

(3) The Electors shall meet in their respective States, and vote by Ballot for two Persons, of whom one at least shall not be an Inhabitant of the same State with themselves. And they shall make a list of all the Persons voted for, and of the Number of Votes for each; which List they shall sign and certify, and transmit sealed to the Seat of the Government of the United States, directed to the President of the Senate. The President of the Senate shall, in the Presence of the Senate and House of Representatives, open all the Certificates, and the Votes shall then be counted. The Person having the greatest Number of Votes shall be the President, if such Number be a Majority of the whole Number of Electors appointed; and if there be more than one who have such Majority, and have an equal Number of Votes, then the House of Representatives shall immediately chuse by Ballot one of them for President; and if no Person have a Majority, then from the five highest on the List the said House shall in like Manner chuse the President. But in chusing the President, the Votes shall be taken by States, the Representation from each State having one Vote; A quorum for this Purpose shall consist of a Member or Members from two thirds of the States, and a Majority of all the States shall be necessary to a Choice. In every Case, after the Choice of President, the Person having the greatest Number of Votes of the Electors shall be the Vice President. But if there should remain two or more who have equal Votes, the Senate shall chuse from them by Ballot the Vice President.[6]

(4) The Congress may determine the Time of chusing the Electors, and the Day on which they shall give their Votes; which Day shall be the same throughout the United States.

(5) No person except a natural born Citizen, or a Citizen of the United States, at the time of the Adoption of this Constitution, shall be eligible to the Office of President; neither shall any person be eligible to that Office who shall not have attained to the Age of thirty-five Years, and been fourteen Years a Resident within the United States.

(6) In Case of the Removal of the President from Office, or of his Death, Resignation, or Inability to discharge the Powers and Duties of the said Office, the Same shall devolve on the Vice President, and the Congress may by Law provide for the Case of Removal,

[6]Refer to the Twelfth Amendment.

Death, Resignation or Inability, both of the President and Vice President, declaring what Officer shall then act as President, and such Officer shall act accordingly, until the Disability be removed, or a President shall be elected.[7]

(7) The President shall, at stated Times, receive for his Services, a Compensation, which shall neither be increased nor diminished during the Period for which he shall have been elected, and he shall not receive within that Period any other Emolument from the United States, or any of them.

(8) Before he enter on the Execution of his Office, he shall take the following Oath or Affirmation:—"I do solemnly swear (or affirm) that I will faithfully execute the Office of President of the United States, and will to the best of my Ability, preserve, protect and defend the Constitution of the United States."

Section 2. (1) The President shall be Commander in Chief of the Army and Navy of the United States, and of the Militia of the several States, when called into the actual Service of the United States; he may require the Opinion, in writing, of the principal Officer in each of the executive Departments, upon any Subject relating to the Duties of their respective Offices, and he shall have Power to grant Reprieves and Pardons for Offenses against the United States, except in Cases of Impeachment.

(2) He shall have Power, by and with the Advice and Consent of the Senate, to make Treaties, provided two thirds of the Senators present concur; and he shall nominate, and by and with the Advice and Consent of the Senate, shall appoint Ambassadors, other public Ministers and Consuls, Judges of the supreme Court, and all other Officers of the United States, whose Appointments are not herein otherwise provided for, and which shall be established by Law: but the Congress may by Law vest the Appointment of such inferior Officers, as they think proper, in the President alone, in the Courts of Law, or in the Heads of Departments.

(3) The President shall have Power to fill up all Vacancies that may happen during the Recess of the Senate, by granting Commissions which shall expire at the End of their next Session.

Section 3. He shall from time to time give to the Congress Information of the State of the Union, and recommend to their Consideration such Measures as he shall judge necessary and expedient; he may, on extraordinary Occasions, convene both Houses, or either of them, and in Case of Disagreement between them, with Respect to the Time of Adjournment, he may adjourn them to such Time as he shall think proper; he shall receive Ambassadors and other public Ministers; he shall take Care that the Laws be faithfully executed, and shall Commission all the Officers of the United States.

Section 4. The President, Vice President and all civil Officers of the United States, shall be removed from Office on Impeachment for, and Conviction of, Treason, Bribery, or other high Crimes and Misdemeanors.

Article III

Section 1. The judicial Power of the United States, shall be vested in one supreme Court, and in such inferior Courts as the Congress may from time to time ordain and establish. The Judges, both of the supreme and inferior Courts, shall hold their Offices during good

[7]Refer to the Twenty-Fifth Amendment.

Behaviour, and shall, at stated Times, receive for their Services, a Compensation, which shall not be diminished during their Continuance in Office.

Section 2. (1) The judicial Power shall extend to all Cases, in Law and Equity, arising under this Constitution, the Laws of the United States, and Treaties made, or which shall be made, under their Authority;—to all Cases affecting Ambassadors, other public Ministers and Consuls;—to all Cases of admiralty and maritime Jurisdiction;—to Controversies to which the United States shall be a Party;—to Controversies between two or more States;—between a State and Citizens of another State;[8]—between Citizens of different states—between Citizens of the same State claiming Lands under the Grants of different States, and between a State, or the Citizens thereof, and foreign States, Citizens or Subjects.

(2) In all Cases affecting Ambassadors, other public Ministers and Consuls, and those in which a State shall be Party, the supreme Court shall have original Jurisdiction. In all the other Cases before mentioned, the supreme Court shall have appellate Jurisdiction, both as to Law and Fact, with such Exceptions, and under such Regulations as the Congress shall make.

(3) The Trial of all Crimes, except in Cases of Impeachment, shall be by Jury; and such Trial shall be held in the State where the said Crimes shall have been committed; but when not committed within any State, the Trial shall be at such Place or Places as the Congress may by Law have directed.

Section 3. (1) Treason against the United States, shall consist only in levying War against them, or, in adhering to their Enemies, giving them Aid and Comfort. No Person shall be convicted of Treason unless on the Testimony of two Witnesses to the same overt Act, or on Confession in open Court.

(2) The Congress shall have Power to declare the Punishment of Treason, but no Attainder of Treason shall work Corruption of Blood, or Forfeiture except during the Life of the Person attainted.

Article IV

Section 1. Full Faith and Credit shall be given in each State to the public Acts, Records, and judicial Proceedings of every other State; And the Congress may by general Laws prescribe the Manner in which such Acts, Records and Proceedings shall be proved, and the Effect thereof.

Section 2. (1) The Citizens of each State shall be entitled to all Privileges and Immunities of Citizens in the several States.

(2) A Person charged in any State with Treason, Felony, or other Crime, who shall flee from Justice, and be found in another State, shall on Demand of the executive Authority of the State from which he fled, be delivered up, to be removed to the State having Jurisdiction of the Crime.

(3) No Person held to Service or Labour in one State, under the Laws thereof, escaping into another, shall, in Consequence of any Law or Regulation therein, be discharged from such Service or Labour, but shall be delivered up on Claim of the Party to whom such Service or Labour may be due.[9]

---

[8]Refer to the Eleventh Amendment.

[9]Refer to the Thirteenth Amendment.

Section 3. (1) New States may be admitted by the Congress into this Union; but no new State shall be formed or erected within the Jurisdiction of any other State; nor any State be formed by the Junction of two or more States, or Parts of States, without the Consent of the Legislatures of the States concerned as well as of the Congress.

(2) The Congress shall have Power to dispose of and make all needful Rules and Regulations respecting the Territory or other Property belonging to the United States; and nothing in this Constitution shall be so construed as to Prejudice any Claims of the United States, or of any particular State.

Section 4. The United States shall guarantee to every State in this Union a Republican Form of Government, and shall protect each of them against Invasion; and on Application of the Legislature, or of the Executive (when the Legislature cannot be convened) against domestic Violence.

Article V

The Congress, whenever two thirds of both Houses shall deem it necessary, shall propose Amendments to this Constitution, or, on the Application of the Legislatures of two thirds of the several States, shall call a Convention for proposing Amendments, which, in either Case, shall be valid to all Intents and Purposes, as Part of this Constitution, when ratified by the Legislatures of three fourths of the several States, or by Conventions in three fourths thereof, as the one or the other Mode of Ratification may be proposed by the Congress; Provided that no Amendment which may be made prior to the Year One thousand eight hundred and eight shall in any Manner affect the first and fourth Clauses in the Ninth Section of the first Article; and that no State, without its Consent, shall be deprived of its equal Suffrage in the Senate.

Article VI

(1) All Debts contracted and Engagements entered into, before the Adoption of this Constitution, shall be as valid against the United States under this Constitution, as under the Confederation.

(2) This Constitution, and the Laws of the United States which shall be made in Pursuance thereof; and all Treaties made, or which shall be made, under the Authority of the United States, shall be the supreme Law of the Land; and the Judges in every State shall be bound thereby, any Thing in the Constitution or Laws of any State to the Contrary notwithstanding.

(3) The Senators and Representatives before mentioned, and the Members of the several State Legislatures, and all executive and judicial Officers, both of the United States and of the several States, shall be bound by Oath or Affirmation, to support this Constitution; but no religious Test shall ever be required as a Qualification to any Office or public Trust under the United States.

Article VII

The Ratification of the Conventions of nine States, shall be sufficient for the Establishment of this Constitution between the States so ratifying the Same.

[Amendments 1–10, the Bill of Rights, were ratified in 1791.]

Amendment I

Congress shall make no law respecting an establishment of religion, or prohibiting the free exercise thereof; or abridging the freedom of speech, or of the press, or the right of the people peaceably to assemble, and to petition the Government for a redress of grievances.

Amendment II

A well regulated Militia, being necessary to the security of a free State, the right of the people to keep and bear Arms, shall not be infringed.

Amendment III

No Soldier shall, in time of peace be quartered in any house, without the consent of the Owner, nor in time of war, but in a manner to be prescribed by law.

Amendment IV

The right of the people to be secure in their persons, houses, papers, and effects, against unreasonable searches and seizures, shall not be violated, and no Warrants shall issue, but upon probable cause, supported by Oath or affirmation, and particularly describing the place to be searched, and the persons or things to be seized.

Amendment V

No person shall be held to answer for a capital, or otherwise infamous crime, unless on a presentment or indictment of a Grand Jury, except in cases arising in the land or naval forces, or in the Militia, when in actual service in time of War or public danger; nor shall any person be subject for the same offence to be twice put in jeopardy of life or limb, nor shall be compelled in any criminal case to be a witness against himself, nor be deprived of life, liberty, or property, without due process of law; nor shall private property be taken for public use without just compensation.

Amendment VI

In all criminal prosecutions, the accused shall enjoy the right to a speedy and public trial, by an impartial jury of the State and district wherein the crime shall have been committed; which district shall have been previously ascertained by law, and to be informed of the nature and cause of the accusation; to be confronted with the witnesses against him; to have compulsory process for obtaining witnesses in his favor, and to have the assistance of counsel for his defence.

Amendment VII

In Suits at common law, where the value in controversy shall exceed twenty dollars, the right of trial by jury shall be preserved, and no fact tried by jury shall be otherwise re-examined in any Court of the United States, than according to the rules of the common law.

Amendment VIII

Excessive bail shall not be required, nor excessive fines imposed, nor cruel and unusual punishments inflicted.

Amendment IX

The enumeration in the Constitution of certain rights shall not be construed to deny or disparage others retained by the people.

Amendment X

The powers not delegated to the United States by the Constitution, nor prohibited by it to the States, are reserved to the States respectively, or to the people.

Amendment XI [1795]

The Judicial power of the United States shall not be construed to extend to any suit in law or equity, commenced or prosecuted against one of the United States by Citizens of another State, or by Citizens or Subjects of any Foreign State.

Amendment XII [1804]

The Electors shall meet in their respective states, and vote by ballot for President and Vice President, one of whom, at least, shall not be an inhabitant of the same state with themselves; they shall name in their ballots the person voted for as President, and in distinct ballots the person voted for as Vice-President, and they shall make distinct lists of all persons voted for as President, and of all persons voted for as Vice-President, and of the number of votes for each, which lists they shall sign and certify, and transmit sealed to the seat of the government of the United States, directed to the President of the Senate;—The President of the Senate shall, in the presence of the Senate and House of Representatives, open all the certificates and the votes shall then be counted;—The person having the greatest number of votes for President, shall be the President, if such number be a majority of the whole number of Electors appointed; and if no person have such majority, then from the persons having the highest numbers not exceeding three on the list of those voted for as President, the House of Representatives shall choose immediately, by ballot, the President. But in choosing the President, the votes shall be taken by states, the representation from each state having one vote; a quorum for this purpose shall consist of a member or members from two-thirds of the states, and a majority of all the states shall be necessary to a choice. And if the House of Representatives shall not choose a President whenever the right of choice shall devolve upon them before the fourth day of March next following, then the Vice-President shall act as President, as in the case of the death or other constitutional disability of the President.[10]—The person having the greatest number of votes as Vice-President, shall be the Vice-President, if such number be a majority of the whole number of Electors appointed, and if no person have a majority, then from the two highest numbers on the list, the Senate shall choose the Vice-President; a quorum for the purpose shall consist of two-thirds of the whole number of Senators, and a majority of the whole number shall be necessary to a choice. But no person constitutionally ineligible to the office of President shall be eligible to that of Vice-President of the United States.

Amendment XIII [1865]

Section 1. Neither slavery nor involuntary servitude, except as a punishment for crime whereof the party shall have been duly convicted, shall exist within the United States, or any place subject to their jurisdiction.

Section 2. Congress shall have power to enforce this article by appropriate legislation.

Amendment XIV [1868]

Section 1. All persons born or naturalized in the United States and subject to the jurisdiction thereof, are citizens of the United States and of the State wherein they reside. No State shall make or enforce any law which shall abridge the privileges or immunities of

[10]Refer to the Twentieth Amendment.

citizens of the United States; nor shall any State deprive any person of life, liberty, or property, without due process of law; nor deny to any person within its jurisdiction the equal protection of the laws.

Section 2. Representatives shall be apportioned among the several States according to their respective numbers, counting the whole number of persons in each State, excluding Indians not taxed. But when the right to vote at any election for the choice of electors for President and Vice President of the United States, Representatives in Congress, the Executive and Judicial officers of a State, or the members of the Legislature thereof, is denied to any of the male inhabitants of such State, being twenty-one years of age,[11] and citizens of the United States, or in any way abridged, except for participation in rebellion, or other crime, the basis of representation therein shall be reduced in the proportion which the number of such male citizens shall bear to the whole number of male citizens twenty-one years of age in such State.

Section 3. No person shall be a Senator or Representative in Congress, or elector of President and Vice President, or hold any office, civil or military, under the United States, or under any State, who, having previously taken an oath, as a member of Congress, or as an officer of the United States, or as a member of any State legislature, or as an executive or judicial officer of any State, to support the Constitution of the United States, shall have engaged in insurrection or rebellion against the same, or given aid or comfort to the enemies thereof. But Congress may by a vote of two-thirds of each House, remove such disability.

Section 4. The validity of the public debt of the United States, authorized by law, including debts incurred for payment of pensions and bounties for services in suppressing insurrection or rebellion, shall not be questioned. But neither the United States nor any State shall assume or pay any debt or obligation incurred in aid of insurrection or rebellion against the United States, or any claim for the loss or emancipation of any slave; but all such debts, obligations and claims shall be held illegal and void.

Section 5. The Congress shall have power to enforce, by appropriate legislation, the provisions of this article.

Amendment XV [1870]

Section 1. The right of citizens of the United States to vote shall not be denied or abridged by the United States or by any State on account of race, color, or previous condition of servitude.

Section 2. The Congress shall have power to enforce this article by appropriate legislation.

Amendment XVI [1913]

The Congress shall have power to lay and collect taxes on incomes, from whatever source derived, without apportionment among the several States, and without regard to any census or enumeration.

Amendment XVII [1913]

(1) The Senate of the United States shall be composed of two Senators from each State, elected by the people thereof, for six years; and each Senator shall have one vote. The electors in each State shall have the qualifications requisite for electors of the most numerous branch of the State legislatures.

[11]Refer to the Twenty-Sixth Amendment.

(2) When vacancies happen in the representation of any State in the Senate, the executive authority of such State shall issue writs of election to fill such vacancies: *Provided,* That the legislature of any State may empower the executive thereof to make temporary appointments until the people fill the vacancies by election as the legislature may direct.

(3) This amendment shall not be so construed as to affect the election or term of any Senator chosen before it becomes valid as part of the Constitution.

Amendment XVIII [1919]

Section 1. After one year from the ratification of this article the manufacture, sale, or transportation of intoxicating liquors within, the importation thereof into, or the exportation thereof from the United States and all territory subject to the jurisdiction thereof for beverage purposes is hereby prohibited.

Section 2. The Congress and the several States shall have concurrent power to enforce this article by appropriate legislation.

Section 3. This article shall be inoperative unless it shall have been ratified as an amendment to the Constitution by the legislatures of the several States, as provided in the Constitution, within seven years from the date of the submission hereof to the States by the Congress.[12]

Amendment XIX [1920]

(1) The right of citizens of the United States to vote shall not be denied or abridged by the United States or by any State on account of sex.

(2) Congress shall have power to enforce this article by appropriate legislation.

Amendment XX [1933]

Section 1. The terms of the President and Vice President shall end at noon on the 20th day of January, and the terms of Senators and Representatives at noon on the 3d day of January, of the years in which such terms would have ended if this article had not been ratified; and the terms of their successors shall then begin.

Section 2. The Congress shall assemble at least once in every year, and such meeting shall begin at noon on the 3d day of January, unless they shall by law appoint a different day.

Section 3. If, at the time fixed for the beginning of the term of the President, the President elect shall have died, the Vice President elect shall become President. If the President shall not have been chosen before the time fixed for the beginning of his term, or if the President elect shall have failed to qualify, then the Vice President elect shall act as President until a President shall have qualified; and the Congress may by law provide for the case wherein neither a President elect nor a Vice President elect shall have qualified, declaring who shall then act as President, or the manner in which one is to act shall be selected, and such person shall act accordingly until a President or Vice President shall have qualified.

---

[12]Refer to the Twenty-First Amendment.

Section 4. The Congress may by law provide for the case of the death of any of the persons from whom the House of Representatives may choose a President whenever the right of choice shall have devolved upon them, and for the case of the death of any of the persons from whom the Senate may choose a Vice President whenever the right of choice shall have devolved upon them.

Section 5. Sections 1 and 2 shall take effect on the 15th day of October following the ratification of this article.

Section 6. This article shall be inoperative unless it shall have been ratified as an amendment to the Constitution by the legislatures of three-fourths of the several States within seven years from the date of its submission.

Amendment XXI [1933]

Section 1. The eighteenth article of amendment to the Constitution of the United States is hereby repealed.

Section 2. The transportation or importation into any State, Territory, or possession of the United States for delivery or use therein of intoxicating liquors, in violation of the laws thereof, is hereby prohibited.

Section 3. This article shall be inoperative unless it shall have been ratified as an amendment to the Constitution by conventions in the several States, as provided in the Constitution, within seven years from the date of the submission hereof to the States by the Congress.

Amendment XXII [1951]

Section 1. No person shall be elected to the officer of the President more than twice, and no person who has held the office of President, or acted as President, for more than two years of a term to which some other person was elected President shall be elected to the office of President more than once. But this Article shall not apply to any person holding the office of President when this Article was proposed by the Congress, and shall not prevent any person who may be holding the office of President, or acting as President, during the term within which this Article becomes operative from holding the office of President or acting as President during the remainder of such term.

Section 2. This article shall be inoperative unless it shall have been ratified as an amendment to the Constitution by the legislatures of three-fourths of the several States within seven years from the date of its submission to the States by the Congress.

Amendment XXIII [1961]

Section 1. The District constituting the seat of Government of the United States shall appoint in such manner as the Congress may direct:

> A number of electors of President and Vice President equal to the whole number of Senators and Representatives in Congress to which the District would be entitled if it were a State, but in no event more than the least populous state; they shall be in addition to those appointed by the states, but they shall be considered, for the purposes of the election of President and Vice President, to be electors appointed by a State; and they shall meet in the District and perform such duties as provided by the twelfth article of amendment.

Section 2. The Congress shall have power to enforce this article by appropriate legislation.

Amendment XXIV [1964]

Section 1. The right of citizens of the United States to vote in any primary or other election for President or Vice President, for electors for President or Vice President, or for Senator or Representative in Congress, shall not be denied or abridged by the United States or any State by reason of failure to pay any poll tax or other tax.

Section 2. The Congress shall have power to enforce this article by appropriate legislation.

Amendment XXV [1967]

Section 1. In case of the removal of the President from office or of his death or resignation, the Vice President shall become President.

Section 2. Whenever there is a vacancy in the office of the Vice President, the President shall nominate a Vice President who shall take office upon confirmation by a majority vote of both Houses of Congress.

Section 3. Whenever the President transmits to the President pro tempore of the Senate and the Speaker of the House of Representatives his written declaration that he is unable to discharge the powers and duties of his office, and until he transmits to them a written declaration to the contrary, such powers and duties shall be discharged by the Vice President as Acting President.

Section 4. Whenever the Vice President and a majority of either the principal officers of the executive departments or of such other body as Congress may by law provide, transmit to the President pro tempore of the Senate and the Speaker of the House of Representatives their written declaration that the President is unable to discharge the powers and duties of his office, the Vice President shall immediately assume the powers and duties of the office as Acting President.

Thereafter, when the President transmits to the President pro tempore of the Senate and the Speaker of the House of Representatives his written declaration that no inability exists, he shall resume the powers and duties of his office unless the Vice President and a majority of either the principal officers of the executive departments or of such other body as Congress may by law provide, transmit within four days to the President pro tempore of the Senate and the Speaker of the House of Representatives their written declaration that the President is unable to discharge the powers and duties of his office. Thereupon Congress shall decide the issue, assembling within forty-eight hours for that purpose if not in session. If the Congress, within twenty-one days after receipt of the latter written declaration, or, if Congress is not in session, within twenty-one days after Congress is required to assemble, determines by two-thirds vote of both Houses that the President is unable to discharge the powers and duties of his office, the Vice President shall continue to discharge the same as Acting President; otherwise, the President shall resume the powers and duties of his office.

Amendment XXVI [1971]

Section 1. The right of citizens of the United States, who are eighteen years of age or older, to vote shall not be denied or abridged by the United States or by any State on account of age.

Section 2. The Congress shall have power to enforce this article by appropriate legislation.

APPENDIX B

UNIFORM COMMERCIAL CODE (EXCERPTS FROM THE OFFICIAL TEXT—1990)*

ARTICLE 2 SALES

PART 1 SHORT TITLE, GENERAL CONSTRUCTION AND SUBJECT MATTER

§ 2–101. Short Title

This Article shall be known and may be cited as Uniform Commercial Code—Sales.

§ 2–102. Scope; Certain Security and Other Transactions Excluded From This Article

Unless the context otherwise requires, this Article applies to transactions in goods; it does not apply to any transaction which although in the form of an unconditional contract to sell or present sale is intended to operate only as a security transaction nor does this Article impair or repeal any statute regulating sales to consumers, farmers or other specified classes of buyers.

§ 2–103. Definitions and Index of Definitions

(1) In this Article unless the context otherwise requires

(a) "Buyer" means a person who buys or contracts to buy goods.

(b) "Good faith" in the case of a merchant means honesty in fact and the observance of reasonable commercial standards of fair dealing in the trade.

(c) "Receipt" of goods means taking physical possession of them.

(d) "Seller" means a person who sells or contracts to sell goods.

(2) Other definitions applying to this Article or to specified Parts thereof, and the sections in which they appear are:

"Acceptance." Section 2–606.
"Banker's credit." Section 2–325.
"Between merchants." Section 2–104.
"Cancellation." Section 2–106(4).
"Commercial unit." Section 2–105.
"Confirmed credit." Section 2–325.
"Conforming to contract." Section 2–106.
"Contract for sale." Section 2–106.

"Cover." Section 2–712.
"Entrusting." Section 2–403.
"Financing agency." Section 2–104.
"Future goods." Section 2–105.
"Goods." Section 2–105.
"Identification." Section 2–501.
"Installment contract." Section 2–612.
"Letter of Credit." Section 2–325.
"Lot." Section 2–105.
"Merchant." Section 2–104.
"Overseas." Section 2–323.
"Person in position of seller." Section 2–707.
"Present sale." Section 2–106.
"Sale." Section 2–106.
"Sale on approval." Section 2–326.
"Sale or return." Section 2–326.
"Termination." Section 2–106.

(3) The following definitions in other Articles apply to this Article:
"Check." Section 3–104.
"Consignee." Section 7–102.
"Consignor." Section 7–102.
"Consumer goods." Section 9–109.
"Dishonor." Section 3–507.
"Draft." Section 3–104.

(4) In addition Article 1 contains general definitions and principles of construction and interpretation applicable throughout this Article.

§ 2–104. Definitions: "Merchant"; "Between Merchants"; "Financing Agency"

(1) "Merchant" means a person who deals in goods of the kind or otherwise by his occupation holds himself out as having knowledge or skill peculiar to the practices or goods involved in the transaction or to whom such knowledge or skill may be attributed by his employment of an agent or broker or other intermediary who by his occupation holds himself out as having such knowledge or skill.

(2) "Financing agency" means a bank, finance company or other person who in the ordinary course of business makes advances against goods or documents of title or who by arrangement with either the seller or the buyer intervenes in ordinary course to make or collect payment due or claimed under the contract for sale, as by purchasing or paying the seller's draft or making advances against it or by merely taking it for collection whether or not documents of title accompany the draft. "Financing agency" includes also a bank or other person who similarly intervenes between persons who are in the position of seller and buyer in respect to the goods (Section 2–707).

(3) "Between merchants" means in any transaction with respect to which both parties are chargeable with the knowledge or skill of merchants.

§2–105. Definitions: Transferability; "Goods"; "Future Goods"; "Lot"; "Commercial Unit"

(1) "Goods" means all things (including specially manufactured goods) which are moveable at the time of identification to the contract for sale other than the money in which the

price is to be paid, investment securities (Article 8) and things in action. "Goods" also includes the unborn young of animals and growing crops and other identified things attached to realty as described in the section on goods to be severed from realty (Section 2–107).

(2) Goods must be both existing and identified before any interest in them can pass. Goods which are not both existing and identified are "future" goods. A purported present sale of future goods or of any interest therein operates as a contract to sell.

(3) There may be a sale of a part interest in existing identified goods.

(4) An undivided share in an identified bulk of fungible goods is sufficiently identified to be sold although the quantity of the bulk is not determined. Any agreed proportion of such a bulk or any quantity thereof agreed upon by number, weight or other measure may to the extent of the seller's interest in the bulk be sold to the buyer who then becomes an owner in common.

(5) "Lot" means a parcel or a single article which is the subject matter of a separate sale or delivery, whether or not it is sufficient to perform the contract.

(6) "Commercial unit" means such a unit of goods as by commercial usage is a single whole for purposes of sale and division of which materially impairs its character or value on the market or in use. A commercial unit may be a single article (as a machine) or a set of articles (as a suite of furniture or an assortment of sizes) or a quantity (as a bale, gross, or carload) or any other unit treated in use or in the relevant market as a single whole.

§ 2–106. Definitions: "Contract"; "Agreement"; "Contract for Sale"; "Sale"; "Present Sale"; "Conforming to Contract"; "Termination"; "Cancellation"

(1) In this Article unless the context otherwise requires "contract" and "agreement" are limited to those relating to the present or future sale of goods. "Contract for sale" includes both a present sale of goods and a contract to sell goods at a future time. A "sale" consists in the passing of title from the seller to the buyer for a price (Section 2–401). A "present sale" means a sale which is accomplished by the making of the contract.

(2) Goods or conduct including any part of a performance are "conforming" or conform to the contract when they are in accordance with the obligations under the contract.

(3) "Termination" occurs when either party pursuant to a power created by agreement or law puts an end to the contract otherwise than for its breach. On "termination" all obligations which are still executory on both sides are discharged but any right based on prior breach or performance survives.

(4) "Cancellation" occurs when either party puts an end to the contract for breach by the other and its effect is the same as that of "termination" except that the cancelling party also retains any remedy for breach of the whole contract or any unperformed balance.

§ 2–107. Goods to Be Severed From Realty: Recording

(1) A contract for the sale of minerals or the like (including oil and gas) or a structure or its materials to be removed from realty is a contract for the sale of goods within this Article if they are to be severed by the seller but until severance a purported present sale thereof which is not effective as a transfer of an interest in land is effective only as a contract to sell.

(2) A contract for the sale apart from the land of growing crops or other things attached to realty and capable of severance without material harm thereto but not described in subsection (1) or of timber to be cut is a contract for the sale of goods within this Article whether the subject matter is to be severed by the buyer or by the seller even though it forms part of the realty at the time of contracting, and the parties can by identification effect a present sale before severance.

(3) The provisions of this section are subject to any third party rights provided by the law relating to realty records, and the contract for sale may be executed and recorded as a document transferring an interest in land and shall then constitute notice to third parties of the buyer's rights under the contract for sale.

Part 2 Form, Formation and Readjustment of Contract

§ 2–201. Formal Requirements; Statute of Frauds

(1) Except as otherwise provided in this section a contract for the sale of goods for the price of $500 or more is not enforceable by way of action or defense unless there is some writing sufficient to indicate that a contract for sale has been made between the parties and signed by the party against whom enforcement is sought or by his authorized agent or broker. A writing is not insufficient because it omits or incorrectly states a term agreed upon but the contract is not enforceable under this paragraph beyond the quantity of goods shown in such writing.

(2) Between merchants if within a reasonable time a writing in confirmation of the contract and sufficient against the sender is received and the party receiving it has reason to know its contents, it satisfies the requirements of subsection (1) against such party unless written notice of objection to its contents is given within 10 days after it is received.

(3) A contract which does not satisfy the requirements of subsection (1) but which is valid in other respects is enforceable

(a) if the goods are to be specially manufactured for the buyer and are not suitable for sale to others in the ordinary course of the seller's business and the seller, before notice of repudiation is received and under circumstances which reasonably indicate that the goods are for the buyer, has made either a substantial beginning of their manufacture or commitments for their procurement; or

(b) if the party against whom enforcement is sought admits in his pleading, testimony or otherwise in court that a contract for sale was made, but the contract is not enforceable under this provision beyond the quantity of goods admitted; or

(c) with espect to goods for which payment has been made and accepted or which have been received and accepted (Section 2–606).

§ 2–202. Final Written Expression: Parol or Extrinsic Evidence

Terms with respect to which the confirmatory memoranda of the parties agree or which are otherwise set forth in a writing intended by the parties as a final expression of their agreement with respect to such terms as are included therein may not be contradicted by evidence of any prior agreement or of a contemporaneous oral agreement but may be explained or supplemented

(a) by course of dealing or usage of trade (Section 1–205) or by course of performance (Section 2–208); and

(b) by evidence of consistent additional terms unless the court finds the writing to have been intended also as a complete and exclusive statement of the terms of the agreement.

§ 2–203. Seals Inoperative

The affixing of a seal to a writing evidencing a contract for sale or an offer to buy or sell goods does not constitute the writing of a sealed instrument and the law with respect to sealed instruments does not apply to such a contract or offer.

§ 2–204. Formation in General

(1) A contract for sale of goods may be made in any manner sufficient to show agreement, including conduct by both parties which recognizes the existence of such a contract.

(2) An agreement sufficient to constitute a contract for sale may be found even though the moment of its making is undetermined.

(3) Even though one or more terms are left open a contract for sale does not fail for indefiniteness if the parties have intended to make a contract and there is a reasonably certain basis for giving an appropriate remedy.

§ 2–205. Firm Offers

An offer by a merchant to buy or sell goods in a signed writing which by its terms gives assurance that it will be held open is not revocable, for lack of consideration, during the time stated or if no time is stated for a reasonable time, but in no event may such period of irrevocability exceed three months; but any such term of assurance on a form supplied by the offeree must be separately signed by the offeror.

§ 2–206. Offer and Acceptance in Formation of Contract

(1) Unless otherwise unambiguously indicated by the language or circumstances

(a) an offer to make a contract shall be construed as inviting acceptance in any manner and by any medium reasonable in the circumstances;

(b) an order or other offer to buy goods for prompt or current shipment shall be construed as inviting acceptance either by a prompt promise to ship or by the prompt or current shipment of conforming or nonconforming goods, but such a shipment of nonconforming goods does not constitute an acceptance if the seller seasonably notifies the buyer that the shipment is offered only as an accommodation to the buyer.

(2) Where the beginning of a requested performance is a reasonable mode of acceptance an offeror who is not notified of acceptance within a reasonable time may treat the offer as having lapsed before acceptance.

§ 2–207. Additional Terms in Acceptance or Confirmation

(1) A definite and seasonable expression of acceptance or a written confirmation which is sent within a reasonable time operates as an acceptance even though it states terms additional to or different from those offered or agreed upon, unless acceptance is expressly made conditional on assent to the additional or different terms.

(2) The additional terms are to be construed as proposals for addition to the contract. Between merchants such terms become part of the contract unless:

(a) the offer expressly limits acceptance to the terms of the offer;

(b) they materially alter it; or

(c) notification of objection to them has already been given or is given within a reasonable time after notice of them is received.

(3) Conduct by both parties which recognizes the existence of a contract is sufficient to establish a contract for sale although the writings of the parties do not otherwise establish a contract. In such case the terms of the particular contract consist of those terms on which the writings of the parties agree, together with any supplementary terms incorporated under any other provisions of this Act.

§ 2–208. Course of Performance or Practical Construction

(1) Where the contract for sale involves repeated occasions for performance by either party with knowledge of the nature of the performance and opportunity for objection to it by the other, any course of performance accepted or acquiesced in without objection shall be relevant to determine the meaning of the agreement.

(2) The express terms of the agreement and any such course of performance, as well as any course of dealing and usage of trade, shall be construed whenever reasonable as consistent with each other; but when such construction is unreasonable, express terms shall control course of performance and course of performance shall control both course of dealing and usage of trade (Section 1–205).

(3) Subject to the provisions of the next section on modification and waiver, such course of performance shall be relevant to show a waiver or modification of any term inconsistent with such course of performance.

§ 2–209. Modification, Rescission and Waiver

(1) An agreement modifying a contract within this Article needs no consideration to be binding.

(2) A signed agreement which excludes modification or rescission except by a signed writing cannot be otherwise modified or rescinded, but except as between merchants such a requirement on a form supplied by the merchant must be separately signed by the other party.

(3) The requirements of the statue of frauds section of this Article (Section 2–201) must be satisfied if the contract as modified is within its provisions.

(4) Although an attempt at modification or rescission does not satisfy the requirements of subsection (2) or (3) it can operate as a waiver.

(5) A party who has made a waiver affecting an executory portion of the contract may retract the waiver by reasonable notification received by the other party that strict performance will be required of any term waived, unless the retraction would be unjust in view of a material change of position in reliance on the waiver.

§ 2–210. Delegation of Performance; Assignment of Rights

(1) A party may perform his duty through a delegate unless otherwise agreed or unless the other party has a substantial interest in having his original promisor perform or control the acts required by the contract. No delegation of performance relieves the party delegating of any duty to perform or any liability for breach.

(2) Unless otherwise agreed all rights of either seller or buyer can be assigned except where the assignment would materially change the duty of the other party, or increase materially the burden or risk imposed on him by his contract, or impair materially his chance of obtaining return performance. A right to damages for breach of the whole contract or a right arising out of the assignor's due performance of his entire obligation can be assigned despite agreement otherwise.

(3) Unless the circumstances indicate the contrary a prohibition of assignment of "the contract" is to be construed as barring only the delegation to the assignee of the assignor's performance.

(4) An assignment of "the contract" or of "all my rights under the contract" or an assignment in similar general terms is an assignment of rights and unless the language or the circumstances (as in an assignment for security) indicate the contrary, it is a delegation of performance of the duties of the assignor and its acceptance by the assignee constitutes a promise by him to perform those duties. This promise is enforceable by either the assignor or the other party to the original contract.

(5) The other party may treat any assignment which delegates performance as creating reasonable grounds for insecurity and may without prejudice to his rights against the assignor demand assurance from the assignee (Section 2–609).

PART 3 GENERAL OBLIGATION AND CONSTRUCTION OF CONTRACT

§ 2–301. General Obligations of Parties

The obligation of the seller is to transfer and deliver and that of the buyer is to accept and pay in accordance with the contract.

§ 2–302. Unconscionable Contract or Clause

(1) If the court as a matter of law finds the contract or any clause of the contract to have been unconscionable at the time it was made the court may refuse to enforce the contract, or it may enforce the remainder of the contract without the unconscionable clause, or it may so limit the application of any unconscionable clause as to avoid any unconscionable result.

(2) When it is claimed or appears to the court that the contract or any clause thereof may be unconscionable the parties shall be afforded a reasonable opportunity to present evidence as to its commercial setting, purpose and effect to aid the court in making the determination.

§ 2–303. Allocation or Division of Risks

Where this Article allocates a risk or a burden as between the parties "unless otherwise agreed," the agreement may not only shift the allocation but may also divide the risk or burden.

§ 2–304. Price Payable in Money, Goods, Realty, or Otherwise

(1) The price can be made payable in money or otherwise. If it is payable in whole or in part in goods each party is a seller of the goods which he is to transfer.

(2) Even though all or part of the price is payable in an interest in realty the transfer of the goods and the seller's obligations with reference to them are subject to this Article, but not the transfer of the interest in realty or the transferor's obligations in connection therewith.

§ 2–305. Open Price Term

(1) The parties if they so intend can conclude a contract for sale even though the price is not settled. In such case the price is a reasonable price at the time for delivery if

(a) nothing is said as to price; or

(b) the price is left to be agreed by the parties and they fail to agree; or

(c) the price is to be fixed in terms of some agreed market or other standard as set or recorded by a third person or agency and it is not so set or recorded.

(2) A price to be fixed by the seller or by the buyer means a price for him to fix in good faith.

(3) When a price left to be fixed otherwise than by agreement of the parties fails to be fixed through fault of one party the other may at his option treat the contract as cancelled or himself fix a reasonable price.

(4) Where, however, the parties intend not to be bound unless the price be fixed or agreed and it is not fixed or agreed there is no contract. In such a case the buyer must return any goods already received or if unable so to do must pay their reasonable value at the time of delivery and the seller must return any portion of the price paid on account.

§ 2–306. Output, Requirements and Exclusive Dealings

(1) A term which measures the quantity by the output of the seller or the requirements of the buyer means such actual output or requirements as may occur in good faith, except that no quantity unreasonably disproportionate to any stated estimate or in the absence of a stated estimate to any normal or otherwise comparable prior output or requirements may be tendered or demanded.

(2) A lawful agreement by either the seller or the buyer for exclusive dealing in the kind of goods concerned imposes unless otherwise agreed an obligation by the seller to use best efforts to supply the goods and by the buyer to use best efforts to promote their sale.

§ 2–307. Delivery in Single Lot or Several Lots

Unless otherwise agreed all goods called for by a contract for sale must be tendered in a single delivery and payment is due only on such tender but where the circumstances give either party the right to make or demand delivery in lots the price if it can be apportioned may be demanded for each lot.

§ 2–308. Absence of Specified Place for Delivery

Unless otherwise agreed

(a) the place for delivery of goods is the seller's place of business or if he has none his residence; but

(b) in a contract for sale of identified goods which to the knowledge of the parties at the time of contracting are in some other place, that place is the place for their delivery; and

(c) documents of title may be delivered through customary banking channels.

§ 2–309. Absence of Specific Time Provisions; Notice of Termination

(1) The time for shipment or delivery or any other action under a contract if not provided in this Article or agreed upon shall be a reasonable time.

(2) Where the contract provides for successive performances but is indefinite in duration it is valid for a reasonable time but unless otherwise agreed may be terminated at any time by either party.

(3) Termination of a contract by one party except on the happening of an agreed event requires that reasonable notification be received by the other party and an agreement dispensing with notification is invalid if its operation would be unconscionable.

§ 2–310. Open Time for Payment or Running of Credit: Authority to Ship Under Reservation

Unless otherwise agreed

(a) payment is due at the time and place at which the buyer is to receive the goods even though the place of shipment is the place of delivery; and

(b) if the seller is authorized to send the goods he may ship them under reservation, and may tender the documents of title, but the buyer may inspect the goods after their arrival before payment is due unless such inspection is inconsistent with the terms of the contract (Section 2–513); and

(c) if delivery is authorized and made by way of documents of title otherwise than by subsection (b) then payment is due at the time and place at which the buyer is to receive the documents regardless of where the goods are to be received; and

(d) where the seller is required or authorized to ship the goods on credit the credit period runs from the time of shipment but post-dating the invoice or delaying its dispatch will correspondingly delay the starting of the credit period.

§ 2–311. Options and Cooperation Respecting Performance

(1) An agreement for sale which is otherwise sufficiently definite (subsection (3) of Section 2–204) to be a contract is not made invalid by the fact that it leaves particulars of performance to be specified by one of the parties. Any such specification must be made in good faith and within limits set by commercial reasonableness.

(2) Unless otherwise agreed specifications relating to assortment of the goods are at the buyer's option and except as otherwise provided in subsection[s] (1)(c) and (3) of Section 2–319 specifications or arrangements relating to shipment are at the seller's option.

(3) Where such specification would materially affect the other party's performance but is not seasonably made or where one party's cooperation is necessary to the agreed performance of the other but is not seasonably forthcoming, the other party in addition to all other remedies

(a) is excused for any resulting delay in his own performance; and

(b) may also either proceed to perform in any reasonable manner or after the time for a material part of his own performance treat the failure to specify or to cooperate as a breach by failure to deliver or accept the goods.

§ 2–312. Warranty of Title and Against Infringement; Buyer's Obligation Against Infringement

(1) Subject to subsection (2) there is in a contract for sale a warranty by the seller that

(a) the title conveyed shall be good, and its transfer rightful; and

(b) the goods shall be delivered free from any security interest or other lien or encumbrance of which the buyer at the time of contracting has no knowledge.

(2) A warranty under subsection (1) will be excluded or modified only by specific language or by circumstances which give the buyer reason to know that the person selling does not claim title in himself or that he is purporting to sell only such right or title as he or a third person may have.

(3) Unless otherwise agreed a seller who is a merchant regularly dealing in goods of the kind warrants that the goods shall be delivered free of the rightful claim of any third person by way of infringement or the like but a buyer who furnishes specifications to the seller must hold the seller harmless against any such claim which arises out of compliance with the specifications.

§ 2–313. Express Warranties by Affirmation, Promise, Description, Sample

(1) Express warranties by the seller are created as follows:

(a) Any affirmation of fact or promise made by the seller to the buyer which relates to the goods and becomes part of the basis of the bargain creates an express warranty that the goods shall conform to the affirmation or promise.

(b) Any description of the goods which is made part of the basis of the bargain creates an express warranty that the goods shall conform to the description.

(c) Any sample or model which is made part of the basis of the bargain creates an express warranty that the whole of the goods shall conform to the sample or model.

(2) It is not necessary to the creation of an express warranty that the seller use formal words such as "warrant" or "guarantee" or that he have a specific intention to make a warranty, but an affirmation merely of the value of the goods or a statement purporting to be merely the seller's opinion or commendation of the goods does not create a warranty.

§ 2–314. Implied Warranty: Merchantability; Usage of Trade

(1) Unless excluded or modified (Section 2–316), a warranty that the goods shall be merchantable is implied in a contract for their sale if the seller is a merchant with respect to goods of that kind. Under this section the serving for value of food or drink to be consumed either on the premises or elsewhere is a sale.

(2) Goods to be merchantable must be at least such as

(a) pass without objection in the trade under the contract description; and

(b) in the case of fungible goods, are of fair average quality within the description; and

(c) are fit for the ordinary purposes for which such goods are used; and

(d) run, within the variations permitted by the agreement, of even kind, quality and quantity within each unit and among all units involved; and

(e) are adequately contained, packaged, and labeled as the agreement may require; and

(f) conform to the promises or affirmations of fact made on the container or label if any.

(3) Unless excluded or modified (Section 2–316) other implied warranties may arise from course of dealing or usage of trade.

§ 2–315. Implied Warranty: Fitness for Particular Purpose

Where the seller at the time of contracting has reason to know any particular purpose for which the goods are required and that the buyer is relying on the seller's skill or judgment to select or furnish suitable goods, there is unless excluded or modified under the next section an implied warranty that the goods shall be fit for such purpose.

§ 2–316. Exclusion or Modification of Warranties

(1) Words or conduct relevant to the creation of an express warranty and words or conduct tending to negate or limit warranty shall be construed wherever reasonable as consistent with each other; but subject to the provisions of this Article on parol or extrinsic evidence (Section 2–202) negation or limitation is inoperative to the extent that such construction is unreasonable.

(2) Subject to subsection (3), to exclude or modify the implied warranty of merchantability or any part of it the language must mention merchantability and in case of a writing must be conspicuous, and to exclude or modify any implied warranty of fitness the exclusion must be by a writing and conspicuous. Language to exclude all implied warranties of fitness is sufficient if it states, for example, that "There are no warranties which extend beyond the description on the face hereof."

(3) Notwithstanding subsection (2)

(a) unless the circumstances indicate otherwise, all implied warranties are excluded by expressions like "as is," "with all faults" or languages which in common understanding calls the buyer's attention to the exclusion of warranties and makes plain that there is no implied warranty; and

(b) when the buyer before entering into the contract has examined the goods or the sample or model as fully as he desired or has refused to examine the goods there is no implied warranty with regard to defects which an examination ought in the circumstances to have revealed to him; and

(c) an implied warranty can also be excluded or modified by course of dealing or course of performance or usage of trade.

(4) Remedies for breach of warranty can be limited in accordance with the provisions of this Article on liquidation or limitation of damages and on contractual modification of remedy (Section[s] 2–718 and 2–719).

§ 2–317. Cumulation and Conflict of Warranties Express or Implied

Warranties whether express or implied shall be construed as consistent with each other and as cumulative, but if such construction is unreasonable the intention of the parties shall determine which warranty is dominant. In ascertaining that intention the following rules apply:

(a) Exact or technical specifications displace an inconsistent sample or model or general language of description.

(b) A sample from an existing bulk displaces inconsistent general language of description.

(c) Express warranties displace inconsistent implied warranties other than an implied warranty of fitness for a particular purpose.

§ 2–318. Third Party Beneficiaries of Warranties Express or Implied

Note: *If this Act is introduced in the Congress of the United States this Section should be omitted. (States to select one alternative.*

Alternative A. A seller's warranty whether express or implied extends to any natural person who is in the family or household of his buyer or who is a guest in his home if it is reasonable to expect that such person may use, consume or be affected by the goods and who is injured in person by breach of the warranty. A seller may not exclude or limit the operation of this section.

Alternative B. A seller's warranty whether express or implied extends to any natural person who may reasonably be expected to use, consume or be affected by the goods and who is injured in person by breach of the warranty. A seller may not exclude or limit the operation of this section.

Alternative C. A seller's warranty whether express or implied extends to any person who may reasonably be expected to use, consume or be affected by the goods and who is injured by breach of the warranty. A seller may not exclude or limit the operation of this section with respect to injury to the person of an individual to whom the warranty extends.

§2–319. F.O.B. and F.A.S. Terms

(1) Unless otherwise agreed the term F.O.B. (which means "free on board") at a named place, even though used only in connection with the stated price, is a delivery term under which

(a) when the term is F.O.B. the place of shipment, the seller must at the place ship the goods in the manner provided in this Article (Section 2–504) and bear the expense and risk of putting them into the possession of the carrier; or

(b) when the term is F.O.B. the place of destination, the seller must at his own expense and risk transport the goods to that place and there tender delivery of them in the manner provided in this Article (Section 2–503);

(c) when under either (a) or (b) the term is also F.O.B. vessel, car or other vehicle, the seller must in addition at his own expense and risk load the goods on board. If the term is F.O.B. vessel the buyer must name the vessel and in an appropriate case the seller must comply with the provisions of this Article on the form of bill of lading (Section 2–323).

(2) Unless otherwise agreed the term F.A.S. vessel (which means "free alongside") at a named port, even though used only in connection with the stated price, is a delivery term under which the seller must

(a) at his own expense and risk deliver the goods alongside the vessel in the manner usual in that port or on a dock designated and provided by the buyer; and

(b) obtain and tender a receipt for the goods in exchange for which the carrier is under a duty to issue a bill of lading.

(3) Unless otherwise agreed in any case falling within subsection (1)(a) or (c) or subsection (2) the buyer must seasonably give any needed instructions for making delivery, including when the term is F.A.S. or F.O.B. the loading berth of the vessel and in an appropriate case its name and sailing date. The seller may treat the failure of needed instructions as a failure of cooperation under this Article (Section 2–311). He may also at his option move the goods in any reasonable manner preparatory to delivery or shipment.

(4) Under the term F.O.B. vessel or F.A.S. unless otherwise agreed the buyer must make payment against tender of the required documents and the seller may not tender nor the buyer demand delivery of the goods in substitution for the documents.

§ 2–320. C.I.F. and C. & F. Terms

(1) The term C.I.F. means that the price includes in a lump sum the cost of the goods and the insurance and freight to the named destination. The term C. & F. or C.F. means that the price so includes cost and freight to the named destination.

(2) Unless otherwise agreed and even though used only in connection with the stated price and destination, the term C.I.F. destination or its equivalent requires the seller at his own expense and risk to

(a) put the goods into the possession of a carrier at the port for shipment and obtain a negotiable bill or bills of lading covering the entire transportation to the named destination; and

(b) load the goods and obtain a receipt from the carrier (which may be contained in the bill of lading) showing that the freight has been paid or provided for; and

(c) obtain a policy or certificate of insurance, including any war risk insurance, of a kind and on terms then current at the port of shipment in the usual amount, in the currency of the contract, shown to cover the same goods covered by the bill of lading and providing for payment of loss to the order of the buyer or for the account of whom it may concern; but the seller may add to the price the amount of the premium for any such war risk insurance; and

(d) prepare an invoice of the goods and procure any other documents required to effect shipment or to comply with the contract; and

(e) forward and tender with commercial promptness all the documents in due form and with any indorsement necessary to perfect the buyer's rights.

(3) Unless otherwise agreed the term C. & F. or its equivalent has the same effect and imposes upon the seller the same obligations and risks as a C.I.F. term except the obligation as to insurance.

(4) Under the term C.I.F. and C. & F. unless otherwise agreed the buyer must make payment against tender of the required documents and the seller may not tender nor the buyer demand delivery of the goods in substitution for the documents.

§ 2–321. C.I.F. or C. & F.: "Net Landed Weights"; "Payment on Arrival"; Warranty of Condition on Arrival

Under a contract containing a term C.I.F. or C. & F.

(1) Where the price is based on or is to be adjusted according to "net landed weights," "delivered weights," "out turn" quantity or quality or the like, unless otherwise agreed the seller must reasonably estimate the price. The payment due on tender of the documents called for by the contract is the amount so estimated, but after final adjustment of the price a settlement must be made with commercial promptness.

(2) An agreement described in subsection (1) or any warranty of quality or condition of the goods on arrival places upon the seller the risk of ordinary deterioration, shrinkage and the like in transportation but has no effect on the place or time of identification to the contract for sale or delivery or on the passing of the risk of loss.

(3) Unless otherwise agreed where the contract provides for payment on or after arrival of the goods the seller must before payment allow such preliminary inspection as is feasible; but if the goods are lost delivery of the documents and payment are due when the goods should have arrived.

§ 2–322. Delivery "Ex-Ship"

(1) Unless otherwise agreed a term for delivery of goods "ex-ship" (which means from the carrying vessel) or in equivalent language is not restricted to a particular ship and requires delivery from a ship which has reached a place at the named port of destination where goods of the kind are usually discharged.

(2) Under such a term unless otherwise agreed

(a) the seller must discharge all liens arising out of the carriage and furnish the buyer with a direction which puts the carrier under a duty to deliver the goods; and

(b) the risk of loss does not pass to the buyer until the goods leave the ship's tackle or are otherwise properly unloaded.

§ 2–323. Form of Bill of Lading Required in Overseas Shipment; "Overseas"

(1) Where the contract contemplates overseas shipment and contains a term C.I.F. or C. & F. or F.O.B. vessel, the seller unless otherwise agreed must obtain a negotiable bill of lading stating that the goods have been loaded on board or, in the case of a term C.I.F. or C. & F., received for shipment.

(2) Where in a case within subsection (1) a bill of lading has been issued in a set of parts, unless otherwise agreed if the documents are not to be sent from abroad the buyer may demand tender of the full set; otherwise only one part of the bill of lading need be tendered. Even if the agreement expressly requires a full set

(a) due tender of a single part is acceptable within the provisions of this Article on cure of improper delivery (subsection (1) of Section 2–508); and

(b) even though the full set is demanded, if the documents are sent from abroad the person tendering an incomplete set may nevertheless require payment upon furnishing an indemnity which the buyer in good faith deems adequate.

(3) A shipment by water or by air or a contract contemplating such shipment is "overseas" insofar as by usage of trade or agreement it is subject to the commercial, financing or shipping practices characteristic of international deep water commerce.

§ 2–324. "No Arrival, No Sale" Term

Under a term "no arrival, no sale" or terms of like meaning, unless otherwise agreed,

(a) the seller must properly ship conforming goods and if they arrive by any means he must tender them on arrival but he assumes no obligation that the goods will arrive unless he has caused the nonarrival; and

(b) where without fault of the seller the goods are in part lost or have so deteriorated as no longer to conform to the contract or arrive after the contract time, the buyer may proceed as if there had been casualty to identified goods (Section 2–613).

§ 2–325. "Letter of Credit" Term; "Confirmed Credit"

(1) Failure of the buyer seasonably to furnish an agreed letter of credit is a breach of the contract for sale.

(2) The delivery to seller of a proper letter of credit suspends the buyer's obligation to pay. If the letter of credit is dishonored, the seller may on seasonable notification to the buyer require payment directly from him.

(3) Unless otherwise agreed the term "letter of credit" or "banker's credit" in a contract for sale means an irrevocable credit issued by a financing agency of good repute and, where the shipment is overseas, of good international repute. The term "confirmed credit" means that the credit must also carry the direct obligation of such an agency which does business in the seller's financial market.

§ 2–326. Sale on Approval and Sale or Return; Consignment Sales and Rights of Creditors

(1) Unless otherwise agreed, if delivered goods may be returned by the buyer even though they conform to the contract, the transaction is

(a) a "sale on approval" if the goods are delivered primarily for use, and

(b) a "sale or return" if the goods are delivered primarily for resale.

(2) Except as provided in subsection (3), goods held on approval are not subject to the claims of the buyer's creditors until acceptance; goods held on sale or return are subject to such claims while in the buyer's possession.

(3) Where goods are delivered to a person for sale and such person maintains a place of business at which he deals in goods of the kind involved, under a name other than the name of the person making delivery, then with respect to claims of creditors of the person conducting the business the goods are deemed to be on sale or return. The provisions of

this subsection are applicable even though an agreement purports to reserve title to the person making delivery until payment or resale or uses such words as "on consignment" or "on memorandum." However, this subsection is not applicable if the person making delivery

(a) complies with an applicable law providing for a consignor's interest or the like to be evidenced by a sign or

(b) establishes that the person conducting the business is generally known by his creditors to be substantially engaged in selling the goods of others, or

(c) complies with the filing provisions of the Article on Secured Transactions (Article 9).

(4) Any "or return" term of a contract for sale is to be treated as a separate contract for sale within the statute of frauds section of this Article (Section 2–201) and as contradicting the sale aspect of the contract within the provisions of this Article on parol or extrinsic evidence (Section 2–202).

§ 2–327. Special Incidents of Sale on Approval and Sale or Return

(1) Under a sale on approval unless otherwise agreed

(a) although the goods are identified to the contract the risk of loss and the title do not pass to the buyer until acceptance; and

(b) use of the goods consistent with the purpose of trial is not acceptance but failure seasonably to notify the seller of election to return the goods is acceptance, and if the goods conform to the contract acceptance of any part is acceptance of the whole; and

(c) after due notification of election to return, the return is at the seller's risk and expense but a merchant buyer must follow any reasonable instructions.

(2) Under a sale or return unless otherwise agreed

(a) the option to return extends to the whole or any commercial unit of the goods while in substantially their original condition, but must be exercised seasonably; and

(b) the return is at the buyer's risk and expense.

§ 2–328. Sale by Auction

(1) In a sale by auction if goods are put up in lots each lot is the subject of a separate sale.

(2) A sale by auction is complete when the auctioneer so announces by the fall of the hammer or in other customary manner. Where a bid is made while the hammer is falling in acceptance of a prior bid the auctioneer may in his discretion reopen the bidding or declare the goods sold under the bid on which the hammer was falling.

(3) Such a sale is with reserve unless the goods are in explicit terms put up without reserve. In an auction with reserve the auctioneer may withdraw the goods at any time until he announces completion of the sale. In an auction without reserve, after the auctioneer calls for bids on an article or lot, that article or lot cannot be withdrawn unless no bid is made within a reasonable time. In either case a bidder may retract his bid until the auctioneer's announcement of completion of sale, but a bidder's retraction does not revive any previous bid.

(4) If the auctioneer knowingly receives a bid on the seller's behalf or the seller makes or procures such a bid, and notice has not been given that liberty for such bidding is reserved, the buyer may at his option avoid the sale or take the goods at the price of the last good faith bid prior to the completion of the sale. This subsection shall not apply to any bid at a forced sale.

Part 4 Title, Creditors and Good Faith Purchasers

§ 2–401. Passing of Title; Reservation for Security; Limited Application of This Section

Each provision of this Article with regard to the rights, obligations and remedies of the seller, the buyer, purchasers or other third parties applies irrespective of title to the goods except where the provision refers to such title. Insofar as situations are not covered by the other provisions of this Article and matters concerning title become material the following rules apply:

(1) Title to goods cannot pass under a contract for sale prior to their identification to the contract (Section 2–501), and unless otherwise explicitly agreed the buyer acquires by their identification a special property as limited by this Act. Any retention or reservation by the seller of the title (property) in goods shipped or delivered to the buyer is limited in effect to a reservation of a security interest. Subject to these provisions and to the provisions of the Article on Secured Transactions (Article 9), title to goods passes from the seller to the buyer in any manner and on any conditions explicitly agreed on by the parties.

(2) Unless otherwise explicitly agreed title passes to the buyer at the time and place at which the seller completes his performance with reference to the physical delivery of the goods, despite any reservation of a security interest and even though a document of title is to be delivered at a different time or place; and in particular and despite any reservation of a security interest by the bill of lading

(a) if the contract requires or authorizes the seller to send the goods to the buyer but does not require him to deliver them at destination, title passes to the buyer at the time and place of shipment; but

(b) if the contract requires delivery at destination, title passes on tender there.

(3) Unless otherwise explicitly agreed where delivery is to be made without moving the goods,

(a) if the seller is to deliver a document of title, title passes at the time when and the place where he delivers such documents; or

(b) if the goods are at the time of contracting already identified and no documents are to be delivered, title passes at the time and place of contracting.

(4) A rejection or other refusal by the buyer to receive or retain the goods, whether or not justified, or a justified revocation of acceptance revests title to the goods in the seller. Such revesting occurs by operation of law and is not a "sale."

§ 2–402. Rights of Seller's Creditors Against Sold Goods

(1) Except as provided in subsections (2) and (3), rights of unsecured creditors of the seller with respect to goods which have been identified to a contract for sale are subject to the buyer's rights to recover the goods under this Article (Section 2–502 and 2–716).

(2) A creditor of the seller may treat a sale or an identification of goods to a contract for sale as void if as against him a retention of possession by the seller is fraudulent under any rule of law of the state where the goods are situated, except that retention of possession in good faith and current course of trade by a merchant-seller for a commercially reasonable time after a sale or identification is not fraudulent.

(3) Nothing in this Article shall be deemed to impair the rights of creditors of the seller

(a) under the provisions of the Article on Secured Transactions (Article 9); or

(b) where identification to the contract or delivery is made not in current course of trade but in satisfaction of or as security for a pre-existing claim for money, security or the like and is made under circumstances which under any rule of law of the state where the goods are situated would apart from this Article constitute the transaction a fraudulent transfer or voidable preference.

§ 2–403. Power to Transfer; Good Faith Purchase of Goods; "Entrusting"

(1) A purchaser of goods acquires all title which his transferor had or had power to transfer except that a purchaser of a limited interest acquires rights only to the extent of the interest purchased. A person with voidable title has power to transfer a good title to a good faith purchaser for value. When goods have been delivered under a transaction of purchase the purchaser has such power even though

(a) the transferor was deceived as to the identity of the purchaser, or

(b) the delivery was in exchange for a check which is later dishonored, or

(c) it was agreed that the transaction was to be a "cash sale," or

(d) the delivery was procured through fraud punishable as larcenous under the criminal law.

(2) Any entrusting of possession of goods to a merchant who deals in goods of that kind gives him power to transfer all rights of the entruster to a buyer in ordinary course of business.

(3) "Entrusting" includes any delivery and any acquiescence in retention of possession regardless of any condition expressed between the parties to the delivery or acquiescence and regardless of whether the procurement of the entrusting or the possessor's disposition of the goods have been such as to be larcenous under the criminal law.

(4) The rights of other purchasers of goods and of lien creditors are governed by the Articles of Secured Transactions (Article 9), Bulk Transfers (Article 6) and Documents of Title (Article 7).

Part 5 Performance

§ 2–501. Insurable Interest in Goods; Manner of Identification of Goods

(1) The buyer obtains a special property and an insurable interest in goods by identification of existing goods as goods to which the contract refers even though the goods so identified are nonconforming and he has an option to return or reject them. Such identification can be made at any time and in any manner explicitly agreed to by the parties. In the absence of explicit agreement identification occurs

(a) when the contract is made if it is for the sale of goods already existing and identified;

(b) if the contract is for the sale of future goods other than those described in paragraph (c), when goods are shipped, marked or otherwise designated by the seller as goods to which the contract refers;

(c) when the crops are planted or otherwise become growing crops or the young are conceived if the contract is for the sale of unborn young to be born within twelve months after contracting or for the sale of crops to be harvested within twelve months or the next normal harvest season after contracting whichever is longer.

(2) The seller retains an insurable interest in goods so long as title to or any security interest in the goods remains in him and where the identification is by the seller alone he may until default or insolvency or notification to the buyer that the identification is final substitute other goods for those identified.

(3) Nothing in this section impairs any insurable interest recognized under any other statute or rule or law.

§ 2–502. Buyer's Right to Goods on Seller's Insolvency

(1) Subject to subsection (2) and even though the goods have not been shipped a buyer who has paid a part or all of the price of goods in which he has a special property under the provisions of the immediately preceding section may on making and keeping good a tender of any unpaid portion of their price recover them from the seller if the seller becomes insolvent within ten days after receipt of the first installment on their price.

(2) If the identification creating his special property has been made by the buyer he acquires the right to recover the goods only if they conform to the contract for sale.

§ 2–503. Manner of Seller's Tender of Delivery

(1) Tender of delivery requires that the seller put and hold conforming goods at the buyer's disposition and give the buyer any notification reasonably necessary to enable him to take delivery. The manner, time and place for tender are determined by the agreement and this Article, and in particular

(a) tender must be at a reasonable hour, and if it is of goods they must be kept available for the period reasonably necessary to enable the buyer to take possession; but

(b) unless otherwise agreed the buyer must furnish facilities reasonably suited to the receipt of the goods.

(2) Where the case is within the next section respecting shipment tender requires that the seller comply with its provisions.

(3) Where the seller is required to deliver at a particular destination tender requires that he comply with subsection (1) and also in any appropriate case tender documents as described in subsections (4) and (5) of this section.

(4) Where goods are in the possession of a bailee and are to be delivered without being moved

(a) tender requires that the seller either tender a negotiable document of title covering such goods or procure acknowledgment by the bailee of the buyer's right to possession of the goods; but

(b) tender to the buyer of a non-negotiable document of title or of a written direction to the bailee to deliver is sufficient tender unless the buyer seasonably objects, and receipt by the bailee of notification of the buyer's rights fixes those rights as against the bailee and all third persons; but risk of loss of the goods and of any failure by the bailee to honor the non-negotiable document of title or to obey the direction remains on the seller until the buyer has had a reasonable time to present the document or direction, and a refusal by the bailee to honor the document or to obey the direction defeats the tender.

(5) Where the contract requires the seller to deliver documents

(a) he must tender all such documents in correct form, except as provided in this Article with respect to bills of lading in a set (subsection (2) of Section 2–323); and

(b) tender through customary banking channels is sufficient and dishonor of a draft accompanying the documents constitutes non-acceptance or rejection.

§ 2–504. Shipment by Seller

Where the seller is required or authorized to send the goods to the buyer and the contract does not require him to deliver them at a particular destination, then unless otherwise agreed he must

(a) put the goods in the possession of such a carrier and make such a contract for their transportation as may be reasonable having regard to the nature of the goods and other circumstances of the case; and

(b) obtain and promptly deliver or tender in due form any document necessary to enable the buyer to obtain possession of the goods or otherwise required by the agreement or by usage of trade; and

(c) promptly notify the buyer of the shipment. Failure to notify the buyer under paragraph (c) or to make a proper contract under paragraph (a) is a ground for rejection only if material delay or loss ensues.

§ 2–505. Seller's Shipment Under Reservation

(1) Where the seller has identified goods to the contract by or before shipment:

(a) his procurement of a negotiable bill of lading to his own order or otherwise reserves in him a security interest in the goods. His procurement of the bill to the order of a financing agency or of the buyer indicates in addition only the seller's expectation of transferring that interest to the person named.

(b) a non-negotiable bill of lading to himself or his nominee reserves possession of the goods as security but except in a case of conditional delivery (subsection (2) of section 2–507) a non-negotiable bill of lading naming the buyer as consignee reserves no security interest even though the seller retains possession of the bill of lading.

(2) When shipment by the seller with reservation of a security interest is in violation of the contract for sale it constitutes an improper contract for transportation within the preceding section but impairs neither the rights given to the buyer by shipment and identification of the goods to the contract nor the seller's powers as a holder of a negotiable document.

§ 2–506. Rights of Financing Agency

(1) A financing agency by paying or purchasing for value a draft which relates to a shipment of goods acquires to the extent of the payment or purchase and in addition to its own rights under the draft and any document of title securing it any rights of the shipper in the goods including the right to stop delivery and the shipper's right to have the draft honored by the buyer.

(2) The right to reimbursement of a financing agency which has in good faith honored or purchased the draft under commitment to or authority from the buyer is not impaired by subsequent discovery of defects with reference to any relevant document which was apparently regular on its face.

§ 2–507. Effect of Seller's Tender; Delivery on Condition

(1) Tender of delivery is a condition to the buyer's duty to accept the goods and, unless otherwise agreed, to his duty to pay for them. Tender entitles the seller to acceptance of the goods and to payment according to the contract.

(2) Where payment is due and demanded on the delivery to the buyer of goods or documents of title, his right as against the seller to retain or dispose of them is conditional upon his making the payment due.

§ 2–508. Cure by Seller of Improper Tender or Delivery; Replacement

(1) Where any tender or delivery by the seller is rejected because non-conforming and the time for performance has not yet expired, the seller may seasonably notify the buyer of his intention to cure and may then within the contract time make a conforming delivery.

(2) Where the buyer rejects a non-conforming tender which the seller had reasonable grounds to believe would be acceptable with or without money allowance the seller may if he seasonably notifies the buyer have a further reasonable time to substitute a conforming tender.

§ 2–509. Risk of Loss in the Absence of Breach

(1) Where the contract requires or authorizes the seller to ship the good by carrier

(a) if it does not require him to deliver them at a particular destination, the risk of loss passes to the buyer when the goods are duly delivered to the carrier even though the shipment is under reservation (Section 2–505); but

(b) if it does require him to deliver them at a particular destination and the goods are there duly tendered while in the possession of the carrier, the risk of loss passes to the buyer when the goods are there duly so tendered as to enable the buyer to take delivery.

(2) Where the goods are held by a bailee to be delivered without being moved, the risk of loss passes to the buyer.

(a) on his receipt of a negotiable document of title covering the goods; or

(b) on acknowledgment by the bailee of the buyer's right to possession of the goods; or

(c) after his receipt of a non-negotiable document of title or other written direction to deliver, as provided in subsection (4)(b) of Section 2–503.

(3) In any case not within subsection (1) or (2), the risk of loss passes to the buyer on his receipt of the goods if the seller is a merchant; otherwise the risk passes to the buyer on tender of delivery.

(4) The provisions of this section are subject to contrary agreement of the parties and to the provisions of this Article on sale on approval (Section 2–327) and on effect of breach on risk of loss (Section 2–510).

§ 2–510. Effect of Breach on Risk of Loss

(1) Where a tender or delivery of goods so fails to conform to the contract as to give a right of rejection the risk of their loss remains on the seller until cure or acceptance.

(2) Where the buyer rightfully revokes acceptance he may to the extent of any deficiency in his effective insurance coverage treat the risk of loss as having rested on the seller from the beginning.

(3) Where the buyer as to conforming goods already identified to the contract for sale repudiates or is otherwise in breach before risk of their loss has passed to him, the seller may to the extent of any deficiency in his effective insurance coverage treat the risk of loss as resting on the buyer for a commercially reasonable time.

§ 2–511. Tender of Payment by Buyer; Payment by Check

(1) Unless otherwise agreed tender of payment is a condition to the seller's duty to tender and complete any delivery.

(2) Tender of payment is sufficient when made by any means or in any manner current in the ordinary course of business unless the seller demands payment in legal tender and gives any extension of time reasonably necessary to procure it.

(3) Subject to the provisions of this Act on the effect of an instrument on an obligation (Section 3–802), payment by check is conditional and is defeated as between the parties by dishonor of the check on due presentment.

§ 2–512. Payment by Buyer Before Inspection

(1) Where the contract requires payment before inspection non-conformity of the goods does not excuse the buyer from so making payment unless

(a) the non-conformity appears without inspection; or

(b) despite tender of the required documents the circumstances would justify injection against honor under the provisions of this Act (Section 5–114).

(2) Payment pursuant to subsection (1) does not constitute an acceptance of goods or impair the buyer's right to inspect or any of his remedies.

§ 2–513. Buyer's Right to Inspection of Goods

(1) Unless otherwise agreed and subject to subsection (3), where goods are tendered or delivered or identified to the contract for sale, the buyer has a right before payment or acceptance to inspect them at any reasonable place and time and in any reasonable manner. When the seller is required and authorized to send the goods to the buyer, the inspection may be after their arrival.

(2) Expenses of inspection must be borne by the buyer but may be recovered from the seller if the goods do not conform and are rejected.

(3) Unless otherwise agreed and subject to the provisions of this Article on C.I.F. contracts (subsection (3) of Section 2–321), the buyer is not entitled to inspect the goods before payment of the price when the contract provides

(a) for delivery "C.O.D." or on other like terms; or

(b) for payment against documents of title, except where such payment is due only after the goods are to become available for inspection.

(4) A place or method of inspection fixed by the parties is presumed to be exclusive but unless otherwise expressly agreed it does not postpone identification or shift the place for delivery or for passing the risk of loss. If compliance becomes impossible, inspection shall be as provided in this section unless the place or method fixed was clearly intended as an indispensable condition failure of which avoids the contract.

§ 2–514. When Documents Deliverable on Acceptance; When on Payment

Unless otherwise agreed documents against which a draft is drawn are to be delivered to the drawee on acceptance of the draft if it is payable more than three days after presentment; otherwise, only on payment.

§ 2–515. Preserving Evidence of Goods in Dispute

In furtherance of the adjustment of any claim or dispute

(a) either party on reasonable notification to the other and for the purpose of ascertaining the facts and preserving evidence has the right to inspect, test and sample the goods including such of them as may be in the possession or control of the other; and

(b) the parties may agree to a third party inspection or survey to determine the conformity or condition of the goods and may agree that the findings shall be binding upon them in any subsequent litigation or adjustment.

Part 6 Breach, Repudiation and Excuse

§ 2–601. Buyer's Rights on Improper Delivery

Subject to the provisions of this Article on breach in installment contracts (Section 2–612) and unless otherwise agreed under the sections on contractual limitations of remedy (Sections 2–718 and 2–719), if the goods or the tender of delivery fail in any respect to conform to the contract, the buyer may

(a) reject the whole; or
(b) accept the whole; or
(c) accept any commercial unit or units and reject the rest.

§ 2–602. Manner and Effect of Rightful Rejection

(1) Rejection of goods must be within a reasonable time after their delivery or tender. It is ineffective unless the buyer seasonably notifies the seller.

(2) Subject to the provisions of the two following sections on rejected goods (Sections 2–603 and 2–604),

(a) after rejection any exercise of ownership by the buyer with respect to any commercial unit is wrongful as against the seller; and

(b) if the buyer has before rejection taken physical possession of goods in which he does not have a security interest under the provisions of this Article (subsection (3) of Section 2–711), he is under a duty after rejection to hold them with reasonable care at the seller's disposition for a time sufficient to permit the seller to remove them; but

(c) the buyer has no further obligations with regard to goods rightfully rejected.

(3) The seller's rights with respect to goods wrongfully rejected are governed by the provisions of this Article on Seller's remedies in general (Section 2–703).

§ 2–603. Merchant Buyer's Duties as to Rightfully Rejected Goods

(1) Subject to any security interest in the buyer (subsection (3) of Section 2–711), when the seller has no agent or place of business at the market of rejection a merchant buyer is under a duty after rejection of goods in his possession or control to follow any reasonable instructions received from the seller with respect to the goods and in the absence of such instructions to make reasonable efforts to sell them for the seller's account if they are perishable or threaten to decline in value speedily. Instructions are not reasonable if on demand indemnity for expense is not forthcoming.

(2) When the buyer sells goods under subsection (1), he is entitled to reimbursement from the seller or out of the proceeds for reasonable expenses of caring for and selling them, and if the expenses include no selling commission then to such commission as is usual in the trade or if there is none to a reasonable sum not exceeding ten per cent on the gross proceeds.

(3) In complying with this section the buyer is held only to good faith and good faith conduct hereunder is neither acceptance nor conversion nor the basis of an action for damages.

§ 2–604. Buyer's Options as to Salvage of Rightfully Rejected Goods

Subject to the provisions of the immediately preceding section on perishables if the seller gives no instructions within a reasonable time after notification of rejection the buyer may store the rejected goods for the seller's account or reship them to him or resell them for the seller's account with reimbursement as provided in the preceding section. Such action is not acceptance or conversion.

§ 2–605. Waiver of Buyer's Objections by Failure to Particularize

(1) The buyer's failure to state in connection with rejection a particular defect which is ascertainable by reasonable inspection precludes him from relying on the unstated defect to justify rejection or to establish breach

(a) where the seller could have cured it if stated seasonably; or

(b) between merchants when the seller has after rejection made a request in writing for a full and final written statement of all defects on which the buyer proposes to rely.

(2) Payment against documents made without reservation of rights precludes recovery of the payment for defects apparent on the face of the documents.

§ 2–606. What Constitutes Acceptance of Goods

(1) Acceptance of goods occurs when the buyer

(a) after a reasonable opportunity to inspect the goods signifies to the seller that the goods are conforming or that he will take or retain them in spite of their non-conformity; or

(b) fails to make an effective rejection (subsection (1) of Section 2–602), but such acceptance does not occur until the buyer has had a reasonable opportunity to inspect them; or

(c) does not act inconsistent with the seller's ownership; but if such act is wrongful as against the seller it is an acceptance only if ratified by him.

(2) Acceptance of a part of any commercial unit is acceptance of that entire unit.

§ 2–607. Effect of Acceptance; Notice of Breach; Burden of Establishing Breach After Acceptance; Notice of Claim or Litigation to Person Answerable Over

(1) The buyer must pay at the contract rate for any goods accepted.

(2) Acceptance of goods by the buyer precludes rejection of the goods accepted and if made with knowledge of a nonconformity cannot be revoked because of it unless the acceptance was on the reasonable assumption that the non-conformity would be seasonably cured but acceptance does not of itself impair any other remedy provided by this Article for non-conformity.

(3) Where a tender has been accepted

(a) the buyer must within a reasonable time after he discovers or should have discovered any breach notify the seller of breach or be barred from any remedy; and

(b) if the claim is one for infringement or the like (subsection (3) of Section 2–312) and the buyer is sued as a result of such a breach he must so notify the seller within a reasonable time after he receives notice of the litigation or be barred from any remedy over for liability established by the litigation.

(4) The burden is on the buyer to establish any breach with respect to the goods accepted.

(5) Where the buyer is sued for breach of a warranty or other obligation for which his seller is answerable over

(a) he may give his seller written notice of the litigation. If the notice states that the seller may come in and defend and that if the seller does not do so he will be bound in any action against him by his buyer by any determination of fact common to the two litigations, then unless the seller after seasonable receipt of the notice does come in and defend he is so bound.

(b) if the claim is one for infringement or the like (subsection (3) of Section 2–312) the original seller may demand in writing that his buyer turn over to him control of the litigation including settlement or else be barred from any remedy over and if he also agrees to bear all expense and to satisfy any adverse judgment, then unless the buyer after seasonable receipt of the demand does turn over control the buyer is so barred.

(6) The provisions of subsections (3), (4), and (5) apply to any obligation of a buyer to hold the seller harmless against infringement or the like (subsection (3) of Section 2–312).

§ 2–608. Revocation of Acceptance in Whole or in Part

(1) The buyer may revoke his acceptance of a lot or commercial unit whose non-conformity substantially impairs its value to him if he has accepted it

(a) on the reasonable assumption that its non-conformity would be cured and it has not been seasonably cured; or

(b) without discovery of such non-conformity if his acceptance was reasonably induced either by the difficulty of discovery before acceptance or by the seller's assurances.

(2) Revocation of acceptance must occur within a reasonable time after the buyer discovers or should have discovered the ground for it and before any substantial change in condition of the goods which is not caused by their own defects. It is not effective until the buyer notifies the seller of it.

(3) A buyer who so revokes has the same rights and duties with regard to the goods involved as if he had rejected them.

§ 2–609. Right to Adequate Assurance of Performance

(1) A contract for sale imposes an obligation on each party that the other's expectation of receiving due performance will not be impaired. When reasonable grounds for insecurity arise with respect to the performance of either party the other may in writing demand adequate assurance of due performance and until he receives such assurance may if commercially reasonable suspend any performance for which he has not already received the agreed return.

(2) Between merchants the reasonableness of grounds for insecurity and the adequacy of any assurance offered shall be determined according to commercial standards.

(3) Acceptance of any improper delivery or payment does not prejudice the aggrieved party's right to demand adequate assurance of future performance.

(4) After receipt of a justified demand failure to provide within a reasonable time not exceeding thirty days such assurance of due performance as is adequate under the circumstances of the particular case is a repudiation of the contract.

§ 2–610. Anticipatory Repudiation

When either party repudiates the contract with respect to a performance not yet due the loss of which will substantially impair the value of the contract to the other, the aggrieved party may

(a) for a commercially reasonable time await performance by the repudiating party; or

(b) resort to any remedy for breach (Section 2–703 or Section 2–711), even though he has notified the repudiating party that he would await the latter's performance and has urged retraction; and

(c) in either case suspend his own performance or proceed in accordance with the provisions of this Article on the seller's right to identify goods to the contract notwithstanding breach or to salvage unfinished goods (Section 2–704).

§ 2–611. Retraction of Anticipatory Repudiation

(1) Until the repudiating party's next performance is due he can retract his repudiation unless the aggrieved party has since the repudiation cancelled or materially changed his position or otherwise indicated that he considers the repudiation final.

(2) Retraction may be by any method which clearly indicates to the aggrieved party that the repudiating party intends to perform, but must include any assurance justifiably demanded under the provisions of this Article (Section 2–609).

(3) Retraction reinstates the repudiating party's right under the contract with due excuse and allowance to the aggrieved party for any delay occasioned by the repudiation.

§ 2–612. "Installment Contract"; Breach

(1) An "installment contract" is one which requires or authorizes the delivery of goods in separate lots to be separately accepted, even though the contract contains a clause "each delivery is a separate contract" or its equivalent.

(2) The buyer may reject any installment which is non-conforming if the non-conformity substantially impairs the value of that installment and cannot be cured or if the non-conformity is a defect in the required documents; but if the non-conformity does not fall within subsection (3) and the seller gives adequate assurance of its cure the buyer must accept that installment.

(3) Whenever non-conformity or default with respect to one or more installments substantially impairs the value of the whole contract there is a breach of the whole. But the aggrieved party reinstates the contract if he accepts a non-conforming installment without seasonably notifying of cancellation or if he brings an action with respect only to past installments or demands performance as to future installments.

§ 2–613. Casualty to Identified Goods

Where the contract requires for its performance goods identified when the contract is made, and the goods suffer casualty without fault of either party before the risk of loss passes to the buyer, or in a proper case under a "no arrival, no sale" term (Section 2–324) then

(a) if the loss is total the contract is avoided; and

(b) if the loss is partial or the goods have so deteriorated as no longer to conform to the contract the buyer may nevertheless demand inspection and at his option either treat the contract as avoided or accept the goods with due allowance from the contract price for the deterioration or the deficiency in quantity but without further right against the seller.

§ 2–614. Substituted Performance

(1) Where without fault of either party the agreed berthing, loading, or unloading facilities fail or an agreed type of carrier becomes unavailable or the agreed manner of delivery otherwise becomes commercially impracticable but a commercially reasonable substitute is available, such substitute performance must be tendered and accepted.

(2) If the agreed means or manner of payment fails because of domestic or foreign governmental regulation, the seller may withhold or stop delivery unless the buyer provides a means or manner of payment which is commercially a substantial equivalent. If delivery has already been taken, payment by the means or in the manner provided by the regulation discharges the buyer's obligation unless the regulation is discriminatory, oppressive or predatory.

§ 2–615. Excuse by Failure of Presupposed Conditions

Except so far as a seller may have assumed a greater obligation and subject to the preceding section on substituted performance:

(a) Delay in delivery or non-delivery in whole or in part by a seller who complies with paragraphs (b) and (c) is not a breach of his duty under a contract for sale if performance as agreed has been made impracticable by the occurrence of a contingency the nonoccurrence of which was a basic assumption on which the contract was made or by compliance in good faith with any applicable foreign or domestic governmental regulation or order whether or not it later proves to be invalid.

(b) Where the causes mentioned in paragraph (a) affect only a part of the seller's capacity to perform, he must allocate production and deliveries among his customers but may at his option include regular customers not then under contract as well as his own requirements for further manufacture. He may so allocate in any manner which is fair and reasonable.

(c) The seller must notify the buyer seasonably that there will be delay or non-delivery and, when allocation is required under paragraph (b), of the estimated quota thus made available for the buyer.

§ 2–616. Procedure on Notice Claiming Excuse

(1) Where the buyer receives notification of a material or indefinite delay or an allocation justified under the preceding section he may by written notification to the seller as to any delivery concerned, and where the prospective deficiency substantially impairs the value of the whole contract under the provisions of this Article relating to breach of installment contracts (Section 2–612), then also as to the whole,

(a) terminate and thereby discharge any unexecuted portion of the contract; or

(b) modify the contract by agreeing to take his available quota in substitution.

(2) If after receipt of such notification from the seller the buyer fails so to modify the contract within a reasonable time not exceeding thirty days the contract lapses with respect to any deliveries affected.

(3) The provisions of this section may not be negated by agreement except in so far as the seller has assumed a greater obligation under the preceding section.

PART 7 REMEDIES

§ 2–701. Remedies for Breach of Collateral Contracts Not Impaired

Remedies for breach of any obligation or promise collateral or ancillary to a contract for sale are not impaired by the provisions of this Article.

§ 2–702. Seller's Remedies on Discovery of Buyer's Insolvency

(1) Where the seller discovers the buyer to be insolvent he may refuse delivery except for cash including payment for all goods theretofore delivered under the contract, and stop delivery under this Article (Section 2–705).

(2) Where the seller discovers that the buyer has received goods on credit while insolvent he may reclaim the goods upon demand made within ten days after the receipt, but if misrepresentation of solvency has been made to the particular seller in writing within three months before delivery the ten day limitation does not apply. Except as provided in this subsection the seller may not base a right to reclaim goods on the buyer's fraudulent or innocent misrepresentation of solvency or of intent to pay.

(3) The seller's right to reclaim under subsection (2) is subject to the rights of a buyer in ordinary course or other good faith purchaser under this Article (Section 2–403). Successful reclamation of goods excludes all other remedies with respect to them.

§ 2–703. Seller's Remedies in General

Where the buyer wrongfully rejects or revokes acceptance of goods or fails to make a payment due on or before delivery or repudiates with respect to a part or the whole, then with respect to any goods directly affected and, if the breach is of the whole contract (Section 2–612), then also with respect to the whole undelivered balance, the aggrieved seller may

(a) withhold delivery of such goods;
(b) stop delivery by any bailee as hereafter provided (Section 2–705);
(c) proceed under the next section respecting goods still unidentified to the contract;
(d) resell and recover damages as hereafter provided (Section 2–706).
(e) recover damages for non-acceptance (Section 2–708) or in a proper case the price (Section 2–709);
(f) cancel.

§ 2–704. Seller's Right to Identify Goods to the Contract Notwithstanding Breach or to Salvage Unfinished Goods

(1) An aggrievated seller under the preceding section may

(a) identify to the contract conforming goods not already identified if at the time he learned of the breach they are in his possession or control;
(b) treat as the subject of resale goods which have demonstrably been intended for the particular contract even though those goods are unfinished.

(2) Where the goods are unfinished an aggrieved seller may in the exercise of reasonable commercial judgment for the purposes of avoiding loss and of effective realization either complete the manufacture and wholly identify the goods to the contract or cease manufacture and resell for scrap or salvage value or proceed in any other reasonable manner.

§ 2–705. Seller's Stoppage of Delivery in Transit or Otherwise

(1) The seller may stop delivery of goods in the possession of a carrier or other bailee when he discovers the buyer to be insolvent (Section 2–702) and may stop delivery of carload, truckload, planeload or larger shipments of express or freight when the buyer repudiates or fails to make a payment due before delivery or if for any other reason the seller has a right to withhold or reclaim the goods.

(2) As against such buyer the seller may stop delivery until

(a) receipt of the goods by the buyer; or

(b) acknowledgment to the buyer by any bailee of the goods except a carrier that the bailee holds the goods for the buyer; or

(c) such acknowledgment to the buyer by a carrier by reshipment or as warehouseman; or

(d) negotiation to the buyer of any negotiable document of title covering the goods.

(3)(a) To stop delivery the seller must so notify as to enable the bailee by reasonable diligence to prevent delivery of the goods.

(b) After such notification the bailee must hold and deliver the goods according to the directions of the seller but the seller is liable to the bailee for any ensuing charges or damages.

(c) If a negotiable document of title has been issued for goods the bailee is not obliged to obey a notification to stop until surrender of the document.

(d) A carrier who has issued a non-negotiable bill of lading is not obliged to obey a notification to stop received from a person other than the consignor.

§ 2–706. Seller's Resale Including Contract for Resale

(1) Under the conditions stated in Section 2–703 on seller's remedies, the seller may resell the goods concerned or the undelivered balance thereof. Where the resale is made in good faith and in a commercially reasonable manner the seller may recover the difference between the resale price and the contract price together with any incidental damages allowed under the provisions of this Article (Section 2–710), but less expenses saved in consequence of the buyer's breach.

(2) Except as otherwise provided in subsection (3) or unless otherwise agreed resale may be at public or private sale including sale by way of one or more contracts to sell or of identification to an existing contract of the seller. Sale may be as a unit or in parcels and at any time and place and on any terms but every aspect of the sale including the method, manner, time, place and terms must be commercially reasonable. The resale must be reasonably identified as referring to the broken contract, but it is not necessary that the goods be in existence or that any or all of them have been identified to the contract before the breach.

(3) Where the resale is at private sale the seller must give the buyer reasonable notification of his intention to resell.

(4) Where the resale is at public sale

(a) only identified goods can be sold except where there is a recognized market for a public sale of futures in goods of the kind; and

(b) it must be made at a usual place or market for public sale if one is reasonably available and except in the case of goods which are perishable or threaten to decline in value speedily the seller must give the buyer reasonable notice of the time and place of the resale; and

(c) if the goods are not to be within the view of those attending the sale the notification of sale must state the place where the goods are located and provide for their reasonable inspection by prospective bidders; and

(d) the seller may buy.

(5) A purchaser who buys in good faith at a resale takes the goods free of any rights of the original buyer even though the seller fails to comply with one or more of the requirements of this section.

(6) The seller is not accountable to the buyer for any profit made on any resale. A person in the position of a seller (Section 2–707) or a buyer who has rightfully rejected or justifiably revoked acceptance must account for any excess over the amount of his security interest, as hereinafter defined (subsection (3) of Section 2–711).

§ 2–707. "Person in the Position of a Seller"

(1) A "person in the position of a seller" includes as against a principal an agent who has paid or become responsible for the price of goods on behalf of his principal or anyone who otherwise holds a security interest or other right in goods similar to that of a seller.

(2) A person in the position of a seller may as provided in this Article withhold or stop delivery (Section 2–706) and recover incidental damages (Section 2–710).

§ 2–708. Seller's Damages for Non-Acceptance or Repudiation

(1) Subject to subsection (2) and to the provisions of this Article with respect to proof of market price (Section 2–723), the measure of damages for non-acceptance or repudiation by the buyer is the difference between the market price at the time and place for tender and the unpaid contract price together with any incidental damages provided in this Article (Section 2–710), but less expenses saved in consequence of the buyer's breach.

(2) If the measure of damages provided in subsection (1) is inadequate to put the seller in as good a position as performance would have done then the measure of damages is the profit (including reasonable overhead) which the seller would have made from full performance by the buyer, together with any incidental damages provided in this Article (Section 2–710), due allowance for costs reasonably incurred and due credit for payments or proceeds of resale.

§ 2–709. Action for the Price

(1) When the buyer fails to pay the price as it becomes due the seller may recover, together with any incidental damages under the next section, the price

(a) of goods accepted or of conforming goods lost or damaged within a commercially reasonable time after risk of their loss has passed to the buyer; and

(b) of goods identified to the contract if the seller is unable after reasonable effort to resell them at a reasonable price or the circumstances reasonably indicate that such effort will be unavailing.

(2) Where the seller sues for the price he must hold for the buyer any goods which have been identified to the contract and are still in his control except that if resale becomes possible he may resell them at any time prior to the collection of the judgment. The net proceeds of any such resale must be credited to the buyer and payment of the judgment entitles him to any goods not resold.

(3) After the buyer has wrongfully rejected or revoked acceptance of the goods or has failed to make a payment due or has repudiated (Section 2–610), a seller who is held not entitled to the price under this section shall nevertheless be awarded damages for non-acceptance under the preceding section.

§ 2–710. Seller's Incidental Damages

Incidental damages to an aggrieved seller include any commercially reasonable charges, expenses or commissions incurred in stopping delivery, in the transportation, care and custody of goods after the buyer's breach, in connection with return or resale of the goods or otherwise resulting from the breach.

§ 2–711. Buyer's Remedies in General; Buyer's Security Interest in Rejected Goods

(1) Where the seller fails to make delivery or repudiates or the buyer rightfully rejects or justifiably revokes acceptance then with respect to any goods involved, and with respect to the whole if the breach goes to the whole contract (Section 2–612), the buyer may cancel and whether or not he has done so may in addition to recovering so much of the price as has been paid

(a) "cover" and have damages under the next section as to all the goods affected whether or not they have been identified to the contract; or

(b) recover damages for non-delivery as provided in this Article (Section 2–713).

(2) Where the seller fails to deliver or repudiates the buyer may also

(a) if the goods have been identified recover them as provided in this Article (Section 2–502); or

(b) in a proper case obtain specific performance or replevy the goods as provided in this Article (Section 2–716).

(3) On rightful rejection or justifiable revocation of acceptance a buyer has a security interest in goods in his possession or control for any payments made on their price and any expenses reasonably incurred in their inspection, receipt, transportation, care and custody and may hold such goods and resell them in like manner as an aggrieved seller (Section 2–706).

§ 2–712. "Cover"; Buyer's Procurement of Substitute Goods

(1) After a breach within the preceding section the buyer may "cover" by making in good faith and without unreasonable delay any reasonable purchase of or contract to purchase goods in substitution for those due from the seller.

(2) The buyer may recover from the seller as damages the difference between the cost of cover and the contract price together with any incidental or consequential damages as hereinafter defined (Section 2–715), but less expenses saved in consequence of the seller's breach.

(3) Failure of the buyer to effect cover within this section does not bar him from any other remedy.

§ 2–713. Buyer's Damages for Non-Delivery or Repudiation

(1) Subject to the provisions of this Article with respect to proof of market price (Section 2–723), the measure of damages for non-delivery or repudiation by the seller is the difference between the market price at the time when the buyer learned of the

breach and the contract price together with any incidental and consequential damages provided in this Article (Section 2–715), but less expenses saved in consequence of the seller's breach.

(2) Market price is to be determined as of the place for tender or, in cases of rejection after arrival or revocation of acceptance, as of the place of arrival.

§ 2–714. Buyer's Damages for Breach in Regard to Accepted Goods

(1) Where the buyer has accepted goods and given notification (subsection (3) of Section 2–607) he may recover as damages for any non-conformity of tender the loss resulting in the ordinary course of events from the seller's breach as determined in any manner which is reasonable.

(2) The measure of damages for breach of warranty is the difference at the time and place of acceptance between the value of the goods accepted and the value they would have had if they had been as warranted, unless special circumstances show proximate damages of a different amount.

(3) In a proper case any incidental and consequential damages under the next section may also be recovered.

§ 2–715. Buyer's Incidental and Consequential Damages

(1) Incidental damages resulting from the seller's breach include expenses reasonably incurred in inspection, receipt, transportation and care and custody of goods rightfully rejected, any commercially reasonable charges, expenses or commissions in connection with effecting cover and any other reasonable expense incident to the delay or other breach.

(2) Consequential damages resulting from the seller's breach include

(a) any loss resulting from general or particular requirements and needs of which the seller at the time of contracting had reason to know and which could not reasonably be prevented by cover or otherwise; and

(b) injury to person or property proximately resulting from any breach of warranty.

§ 2–716. Buyer's Right to Specific Performance or Replevin

(1) Specific performance may be decreed where the goods are unique or in other proper circumstances.

(2) The decree for specific performance may include such terms and conditions as to payment of the price, damages, or other relief as the court may deem just.

(3) The buyer has a right of replevin for goods identified to the contract if after reasonable effort he is unable to effect cover for such goods or the circumstances reasonably indicate that such effort will be unavailing or if the goods have been shipped under reservation and satisfaction of the security interest in them has been made or tendered.

§ 2–717. Deduction of Damages From the Price

The buyer on notifying the seller of his intention to do so may deduct all or any part of the damages resulting from any breach of the contract from any part of the price still due under the same contract.

§ 2–718. Liquidation or Limitation of Damages; Deposits

(1) Damages for breach by either party may be liquidated in the agreement but only at an amount which is reasonable in the light of the anticipated or actual harm caused by the

breach, the difficulties of proof of loss, and the inconvenience or nonfeasibility of otherwise obtaining an adequate remedy. A term fixing unreasonably large liquidated damages is void as a penalty.

(2) Where the seller justifiably withholds delivery of goods because of the buyer's breach, the buyer is entitled to restitution of any amount by which the sum of his payments exceeds.

(a) the amount to which the seller is entitled by virtue of terms liquidating the seller's damages in accordance with subsection (1), or

(b) in the absence of such terms, twenty percent of the value of the total performance for which the buyer is obligated under the contract or $500, whichever is smaller.

(3) The buyer's right to restitution under subsection (2) is subject to offset to the extent that the seller establishes

(a) a right to recover damages under the provisions of this Article other than subsection (1), and

(b) the amount of value of any benefits received by the buyer directly or indirectly by reason of the contract.

(4) Where a seller has received payment in goods their reasonable value or the proceeds of their resale shall be treated as payments for the purposes of subsection (2); but if the seller has notice of the buyer's breach before reselling goods received in part performance, his resale is subject to the conditions laid down in this Article on resale by an aggrieved seller (Section 2–706).

§ 2–719. Contractual Modification or Limitation of Remedy

(1) Subject to the provisions of subsections (2) and (3) of this section and of the preceding section on liquidation and limitation of damages,

(a) the agreement may provide for remedies in addition to or in substitution for those provided in this Article and may limit or alter the measure of damages recoverable under this Article, as by limiting the buyer's remedies to return of the goods and repayment of the price or to repair and replacement of non-conforming goods or parts; and

(b) resort to a remedy as provided is optional unless the remedy is expressly agreed to be exclusive, in which case it is the sole remedy.

(2) Where circumstances cause an exclusive or limited remedy to fail of its essential purpose, remedy may be had as provided in this Act.

(3) Consequential damages may be limited or excluded unless the limitation or exclusion is unconscionable. Limitation of consequential damages for injury to the person in the case of consumer goods is prima facie unconscionable but limitation of damages where the loss is commercial is not.

§ 2–720. Effect of "Cancellation" or "Rescission" on Claims for Antecedent Breach

Unless the contrary intention clearly appears, expressions of "cancellation" or "rescission" of the contract or the like shall not be construed as a renunciation or discharge of any claim in damages for an antecedent breach.

§ 2–721. Remedies for Fraud

Remedies for material misrepresentation or fraud include all remedies available under this Article for nonfraudulent breach. Neither rescission or a claim for rescission of the contract for sale nor rejection or return of the goods shall bar or be deemed inconsistent with a claim for damages or other remedy.

§ 2–722. Who Can Sue Third Parties for Injury to Goods

Where a third party so deals with goods which have been identified to a contract for sale as to cause actionable injury to a party to that contract

(a) a right of action against a third party is in either party to the contract for sale who has title to or a security interest or a special property or an insurable interest in the goods; and if the goods have been destroyed or converted a right of action is also in the party who either bore the risk of loss under the contract for sale or has since the injury assumed that risk as against the other;

(b) if at the time of the injury the party plaintiff did not bear the risk of loss as against the other party to the contract for sale and there is no arrangement between them for disposition of the recovery, his suit or settlement is, subject to his own interest, as a fiduciary for the other party to the contract;

(c) either party may with the consent of the other sue for the benefit of whom it may concern.

§ 2–723. Proof of Market Price: Time and Place

(1) If an action based on anticipatory repudiation comes to trial before the time for performance with respect to some or all of the goods, any damages based on market price (Section 2–708 or Section 2–713) shall be determined according to the price of such goods prevailing at the time when the aggrieved party learned of the repudiation.

(2) If evidence of a price prevailing at the times or places described in this Article is not readily available the price prevailing within any reasonable time before or after the time described or at any other place which in commercial judgment or under usage of trade would serve as a reasonable substitute for the one described may be used, making any proper allowance for the cost of transporting the goods to or from such other place.

(3) Evidence of a relevant price prevailing at a time or place other than the one described in this Article offered by one party is not admissable unless and until he has given the other party such notice as the court finds sufficient to prevent unfair surprise.

§ 2–724. Admissibility of Market Quotations

Whenever the prevailing price or value of any goods regularly bought and sold in any established commodity market is in issue, reports in official publications or trade journals or in newspapers or periodicals of general circulation published as the reports of such market shall be admissible in evidence. The circumstances of the preparation of such a report may be shown to affect its weight but not its admissibility.

§ 2–725. Statute of Limitations in Contracts for Sale

(1) An action for breach of any contract for sale must be commenced within four years after the cause of action has accrued. By the original agreement the parties may reduce the period of limitation to not less than one year but may not extend it.

(2) A cause of action accrues when the breach occurs, regardless of the aggrieved party's lack of knowledge of the breach. A breach of warranty occurs when tender of delivery is made, except that where a warranty explicitly extends to future performance of the goods and discovery of the breach must await the time of such performance the cause of action accrues when the breach is or should have been discovered.

(3) Where an action commenced within the time limited by subsection (1) is so terminated as to leave available a remedy by another action for the same breach such other action may be commenced after the expiration of the time limited and within six months after the termination of the first action unless the termination resulted from voluntary discontinuance or from dismissal for failure or neglect to prosecute.

(4) This section does not alter the law on tolling of the statute of limitations nor does it apply to causes of action which have accrued before this Act becomes effective.

Article 2A Leases

Part 1 General Provisions

§ 2A–101. Short Title

This Article shall be known and may be cited as the Uniform Commercial Code—Leases.

§ 2A–102. Scope

This Article applies to any transaction, regardless of form, that creates a lease.

§ 2A–103. Definitions and Index of Definitions

(1) In this Article unless the context otherwise requires:

(a) "Buyer in ordinary course of business" means a person who in good faith and without knowledge that the sale to him [or her] is in violation of the ownership rights or security interest or leasehold interest of a third party in the goods buys in ordinary course from a person in the business of selling goods of that kind but does not include a pawnbroker. "Buying" may be for cash or by exchange of other property or on secured or unsecured credit and includes receiving goods or documents of title under a pre-existing contract for sale but does not include a transfer in bulk or as security for or in total or partial satisfaction of a money debt.

(b) "Cancellation" occurs when either party puts an end to the lease contract for default by the other party.

(c) "Commercial unit" means such a unit of goods as by commercial usage is a single whole for purposes of lease and division of which materially impairs its character or value on the market or in use. A commercial unit may be a single article, as a machine, or a set of articles, as a suite of furniture or a line of machinery, or a quantity, as a gross or carload, or any other unit treated in use or in the relevant market as a single whole.

(d) "Conforming" goods or performance under a lease contract means goods or performance that are in accordance with the obligations under the lease contract.

(e) "Consumer lease" means a lease that a lessor regularly engaged in the business of leasing or selling makes to a lessee who is an individual and who takes under the lease primarily for a personal, family, or household purpose [if the total payments to be made under the lease contract, excluding payments for options to renew or buy, do not exceed $______].

(f) "Fault" means wrongful act, omission, breach, or default.

(g) "Finance lease" means a lease with respect to which:

(i) the lessor does not select, manufacture, or supply the goods;

(ii) the lessor acquires the goods or the right to possession and use of the goods in connection with the lease; and

(iii) one of the following occurs:

(A) the lessee receives a copy of the contract by which the lessor acquired the goods or the right to possession and use of the goods before signing the lease contract;

(B) the lessee's approval of the contract by which the lessor acquired the goods or the right to possession and use of the goods is a condition to effectiveness of the lease contract;

(C) the lessee, before signing the lease contract, receives an accurate and complete statement designating the promises and warranties, and any disclaimers of warranties, limitations or modifications of remedies, or liquidated damages, including those of a third party, such as the manufacturer of the goods, provided to the lessor by the person supplying the goods in connection with or as part of the contract by which the lessor acquired the goods or the right to possession and use of the goods; or

(D) if the lease is not a consumer lease, the lessor, before the lessee signs the lease contract, informs the lessee in writing (a) of the identity of the person supplying the goods to the lessor, unless the lessee has selected that person and directed the lessor to acquire the goods or the right to possession and use of the goods from that person, (b) that the lessee is entitled under this Article to the promises and warranties, including those of any third party, provided to the lessor by the person supplying the goods in connection with or as part of the contract by which the lessor acquired the goods or the right to possession and use of the goods, and (c) that the lessee may communicate with the person supplying the goods to the lessor and receive an accurate and complete statement of those promises and warranties, including any disclaimers and limitations of them or of remedies.

(h) "Goods" means all things that are movable at the time of identification to the lease contract, or are fixtures (Section 2A–309), but the term does not include money, documents, instruments, accounts, chattel paper, general intangibles, or minerals or the like, including oil and gas, before extraction. The term also includes the unborn young of animals.

(i) "Installment lease contract" means a lease contract that authorizes or requires the delivery of goods in separate lots to be separately accepted, even though the lease contract contains a clause "each delivery is a separate lease" or its equivalent.

(j) "Lease" means a transfer of the right to possession and use of goods for a term in return for consideration, but a sale, including a sale on approval or a sale or return, or retention or creation of a security interest is not a lease. Unless the context clearly indicates otherwise, the term includes a sublease.

(k) "Lease agreement" means the bargain, with respect to the lease, of the lessor and the lessee in fact as found in their language or by implication from other circumstances including course of dealing or usage of trade or course of performance as provided in this Article. Unless the context clearly indicates otherwise, the term includes a sublease agreement.

(l) "Lease contract" means the total legal obligation that results from the lease agreement as affected by this Article and any other applicable rules of law. Unless the context clearly indicates otherwise, the term includes a sublease contract.

(m) "Leasehold interest" means the interest of the lessor or the lessee under a lease contract.

(n) "Lessee" means a person who acquires the right to possession and use of goods under a lease. Unless the context clearly indicates otherwise, the term includes a sublessee.

(o) "Lessee in ordinary course of business" means a person who in good faith and without knowledge that the lease to him [or her] is in violation of the ownership rights or security interest or leasehold interest of a third party in the goods, leases in ordinary course from a person in the business of selling or leasing goods of that kind but does not include a pawnbroker. "Leasing" may be for cash or by exchange of other property or on secured or unsecured credit and includes receiving goods or documents of title under a pre-existing lease contract but does not include a transfer in bulk or as security for or in total or partial satisfaction of a money debt.

(p) "Lessor" means a person who transfers the right to possession and use of goods under a lease. Unless the context clearly indicates otherwise, the term includes a sublessor.

(q) "Lessor's residual interest" means the lessor's interest in the goods after expiration, termination, or cancellation of the lease contract.

(r) "Lien" means a charge against or interest in goods to secure payment of a debt or performance of an obligation, but the term does not include a security interest.

(s) "Lot" means a parcel or a single article that is the subject matter of a separate lease or delivery, whether or not it is sufficient to perform the lease contract.

(t) "Merchant lessee" means a lessee that is a merchant with respect to goods of the kind subject to the lease.

(u) "Present value" means the amount as of a date certain of one or more sums payable in the future, discounted to the date certain. The discount is determined by the interest rate specified by the parties if the rate was not manifestly unreasonable at the time the transaction was entered into; otherwise, the discount is determined by a commercially reasonable rate that takes into account the facts and circumstances of each case at the time the transaction was entered into.

(v) "Purchase" includes taking by sale, lease, mortgage, security interest, pledge, gift, or any other voluntary transaction creating an interest in goods.

(w) "Sublease" means a lease of goods the right to possession and use of which was acquired by the lessor as a lessee under an existing lease.

(x) "Supplier" means a person from whom a lessor buys or leases goods to be leased under a finance lease.

(y) "Supply contract" means a contract under which a lessor buys or leases goods to be leased.

(z) "Termination" occurs when either party pursuant to a power created by agreement or law puts an end to the lease contract otherwise than for default.

(2) Other definitions applying to this Article and the sections in which they appear are :
"Accessions." Section 2A–310(1).
"Construction mortgage." Section 2A–309(1)(d).
"Encumbrance." Section 2A–309(1)(e).
"Fixtures." Section 2A–309(1)(a).

"Fixture filing." Section 2A–309(1)(b).
"Purchase money lease." Section 2A–309(1)(c).

(3) The following definitions in other Articles apply to this Article:
"Account." Section 9–106.
"Between merchants." Section 2–104(3).
"Buyer." Section 2–103(1)(a).
"Chattel paper." Section 9–105(1)(b).
"Consumer goods." Section 9–109(1).
"Document." Section 9–105(1)(f).
"Entrusting." Section 2–403(3).
"General intangibles." Section 9–106.
"Good faith." Section 2–103(1)(b).
"Instrument." Section 9–105(1)(i).
"Merchant." Section 2–104(1).
"Mortgage." Section 9–105(1)(j).
"Pursuant to commitment." Section 9–105(1)(k).
"Receipt." Section 2–103(1)(c).
"Sale." Section 2–106(1).
"Sale on approval." Section 2–326.
"Sale or return." Section 2–326.
"Seller." Section 2–103(1)(d).

(4) In addition Article 1 contains general definitions and principles of construction and interpretations applicable throughout this Article.

As amended in 1990.

§ 2A–104. Leases Subject to Other Law

(1) A lease, although subject to this Article, is also subject to any applicable:

(a) certificate of title statute of this State: (list any certificate of title statutes covering automobiles, trailers, mobile hones, boats, farm tractors, and the like);

(b) certificate of title statute of another jurisdiction (Section 2A–105); or

(c) consumer prediction statute of this State, or final consumer protection decision of a court of this State existing on the effective date of this Article.

(2) In case of conflict between this Article, other than Sections 2A–105, 2A–304(3), and 2A–305(3), and a statute or decision referred to in subsection (1), the statute or decision controls.

(3) Failure to comply with an applicable law has only the effect specified therein.

As amended in 1990.

§ 2A–105. Territorial Application of Article to Goods Covered by Certificate of Title

Subject to the provisions of Sections 2A–304(3) and 2A–305(3), with respect to goods covered by a certificate of title issued under a statute of this State or of another jurisdiction, compliance and the effect of compliance or noncompliance with a certificate of title statute are governed by the law (including the conflict of laws rules) of the jurisdiction issuing the certificate until the earlier of (a) surrender of the certificate, or (b) four months after the goods are removed from that jurisdiction and thereafter until a new certificate of title is issued by another jurisdiction.

§ 2A–106. Limitation on Power of Parties to Consumer Lease to Choose Applicable Law and Judicial Forum

(1) If the law chosen by the parties to a consumer lease is that of a jurisdiction other than a jurisdiction in which the lessee resides at the time the lease agreement becomes enforceable or within 30 days thereafter or in which the goods are to be used, the choice is not enforceable.

(2) If the judicial forum chosen by the parties to a consumer lease is a forum that would not otherwise have jurisdiction over the lessee, the choice is not enforceable.

§ 2A–107. Waiver or Renunciation of Claim or Right after Default

Any claim or right arising out of an alleged default or breach of warranty may be discharged in whole or in part without consideration by a written waiver or renunciation signed and delivered by the aggrieved party.

§ 2A–108. Unconscionability

(1) If the court as a matter of law finds a lease contract or any clause of a lease contract to have been unconscionable at the time it was made the court may refuse to enforce the lease contract, or it may enforce the remainder of the lease contract without the unconscionable clause, or it may so limit the application of any unconscionable clause as to avoid any unconscionable result.

(2) With respect to a consumer lease, if the court as a matter of law finds that a lease contract or any clause of a lease contract has been induced by unconscionable conduct or that unconscionable conduct has occurred in the collection of a claim arising from a lease contract, the court may grant appropriate relief.

(3) Before making a finding of unconscionability under subsection (1) or (2), the court, on its own motion or that of a party, shall afford the parties a reasonable opportunity to present evidence as to the setting, purpose, and effect of the lease contract or clause thereof, or of the conduct.

(4) In an action in which the lessee claims unconscionability with respect to a consumer lease:

(a) If the court finds unconscionability under subsection (1) or (2), the court shall award reasonable attorney's fees to the lessee.

(b) If the court does not find unconscionability and the lessee claiming unconscionability has brought or maintained an action he [or she] knew to be groundless, the court shall award reasonable attorney's fees to the party against whom the claim is made.

(c) In determining attorney's fees, the amount of the recovery on behalf of the claimant under subsections (1) and (2) is not controlling.

§ 2A–109. Option to Accelerate at Will

(1) A term providing that one party or his [or her] successor in interest may accelerate payment or performance or require collateral or additional collateral "at will" or "when he [or she] deems himself [or herself] insecure" or in words of similar import must be construed to mean that he [or she] has power to do so only if he [or she] in good faith believes that the prospect of payment or performance is impaired.

(2) With respect to a consumer lease, the burden of establishing good faith under subsection (1) is on the party who exercised the power; otherwise the burden of establishing lack of good faith is on the party against whom the power has been exercised.

Part 2 Formation and Construction of Lease Contract

§ 2A–201. Statute of Frauds

(1) A lease contract is not enforceable by way of action or defense unless:

(a) the total payments to be made under the lease contract, excluding payments for options to renew or buy, are less than $1,000; or

(b) there is a writing, signed by the party against whom enforcement is sought or by that party's authorized agent, sufficient to indicate that a lease contract has been made between the parties and to describe the goods leased and the lease term.

(2) Any description of leased goods or of the lease term is sufficient and satisfies subsection (1)(b), whether or not it is specific, if it reasonably identifies what is described.

(3) A writing is not insufficient because it omits or incorrectly states a term agreed upon, but the lease contract is not enforceable under subsection (1)(b) beyond the lease term and the quantity of goods shown in the writing.

(4) A lease contract that does not satisfy the requirements of subsection (1), but which is valid in other respects, is enforceable:

(a) if the goods are to be specially manufactured or obtained for the lessee and are not suitable for lease or sale to others in the ordinary course of the lessor's business, and the lessor, before notice of repudiation is received and under circumstances that reasonably indicate that the goods are for the lessee, has made either a substantial beginning of their manufacture or commitments for their procurement;

(b) if the party against whom enforcement is sought admits in that party's pleading, testimony or otherwise in court that a lease contract was made, but the lease contract is not enforceable under this provision beyond the quantity of goods admitted; or

(c) with respect to goods that have been received and accepted by the lessee.

(5) The lease term under a lease contract referred to in subsection (4) is:

(a) if there is a writing signed by the party against whom enforcement is sought or by that party's authorized agent specifying the lease term, the term so specified;

(b) if the party against whom enforcement is sought admits in that party's pleading, testimony, or otherwise in court a lease term, the term so admitted; or

(c) a reasonable lease term.

§ 2A–202. Final Written Expression: Parol or Extrinsic Evidence

Terms with respect to which the confirmatory memoranda of the parties agree or which are otherwise set forth in a writing intended by the parties as a final expression of their agreement with respect to such terms as are included therein may not be contradicted by evidence of any prior agreement or of a contemporaneous oral agreement but may be explained or supplemented:

(a) by course of dealing or usage of trade or by course of performance; and

(b) by evidence of consistent additional terms unless the court finds the writing to have been intended also as a complete and exclusive statement of the terms of the agreement.

§ 2A–203. Seals Inoperative

The affixing of a seal to a writing evidencing a lease contract or an offer to enter into a lease contract does not render the writing a sealed instrument and the law with respect to sealed instruments does not apply to the lease contract or offer.

§ 2A–204. Formation in General

(1) A lease contract may be made in any manner sufficient to show agreement, including conduct by both parties which recognizes the existence of a lease contract.

(2) An agreement sufficient to constitute a lease contract may be found although the moment of its making is undetermined.

(3) Although one or more terms are left open, a lease contract does not fail for indefiniteness if the parties have intended to make a lease contract and there is a reasonably certain basis for giving an appropriate remedy.

§ 2A–205. Firm Offers

An offer by a merchant to lease goods to or from another person in a signed writing that by its terms gives assurance it will be held open is not revocable, for lack of consideration, during the time stated or, if no time is stated, for a reasonable time, but in no event may the period of irrevocability exceed 3 months. Any such term of assurance on a form supplied by the offeree must be separately signed by the offeror.

§ 2A–206. Offer and Acceptance in Formation of Lease Contract

(1) Unless otherwise unambiguously indicated by the language or circumstances, an offer to make a lease contract must be construed as inviting acceptance in any manner and by any medium reasonable in the circumstances.

(2) If the beginning of a requested performance is a reasonable mode of acceptance, an offeror who is not notified of acceptance within a reasonable time may treat the offer as having lapsed before acceptance.

§ 2A–207. Course of Performance or Practical Construction

(1) If a lease contract involves repeated occasions for performance by either party with knowledge of the nature of the performance and opportunity for objection to it by the other, any course of performance accepted or acquiesced in without objection is relevant to determine the meaning of the lease agreement.

(2) The express terms of a lease agreement and any course of performance, as well as any course of dealing and usage of trade, must be construed whenever reasonable as consistent with each other; but if that construction is unreasonable, express terms control course of performance, course of performance controls both course of dealing and usage of trade, and course of dealing controls usage of trade.

(3) Subject to the provisions of Section 2A–208 on modification and waiver, course of performance is relevant to show a waiver or modification of any term inconsistent with the course of performance.

§ 2A–208. Modification, Rescission and Waiver

(1) An agreement modifying a lease contract needs no consideration to be binding.

(2) A signed lease agreement that excludes modification or rescission except by a signed writing may not be otherwise modified or rescinded, but, except as between

merchants, such a requirement on a form supplied by a merchant must be separately signed by the other party.

(3) Although an attempt at modification or rescission does not satisfy the requirements of subsection (2), it may operate as a waiver.

(4) A party who has made a waiver affecting an executory portion of a lease contract may retract the waiver by reasonable notification received by the other party that strict performance will be required of any term waived, unless the retraction would be unjust in view of a material change of position in reliance on the waiver.

§ 2A–209. Lessee Under Finance Lease as Beneficiary of Supply Contract

(1) The benefit of a supplier's promises to the lessor under the supply contract and of all warranties, whether express or implied, including those of any third party provided in connection with or as part of the supply contract, extends to the lessee to the extent of the lessee's leasehold interest under a finance lease related to the supply contract, but is subject to the terms of the warranty and of the supply contract and all defenses or claims arising therefrom.

(2) The extension of the benefit of a supplier's promises and of warranties to the lessee (Section 2A–209(1)) does not: (i) modify the rights and obligations of the parties to the supply contract, whether arising therefrom or otherwise, or (ii) impose any duty or liability under the supply contract on the lessee.

(3) Any modification or rescission of the supply contract by the supplier and the lessor is effective between the supplier and the lessee unless, before the modification or rescission, the supplier has received notice that the lessee has entered into a finance lease related to the supply contract. If the modification or rescission is effective between the supplier and the lessee, the lessor is deemed to have assumed, in addition to the obligations of the lessor to the lessee under the lease contract, promises of the supplier to the lessor and warranties that were so modified or rescinded as they existed and were available to the lessee before modification or rescission.

(4) In addition to the extension of the benefit of the supplier's promises and of warranties to the lessee under subsection (1), the lessee retains all rights that the lessee may have against the supplier which arise from an agreement between the lessee and the supplier or under other law.

As amended in 1990.

§ 2A–210. Express Warranties

(1) Express warranties by the lessor are created as follows:

(a) Any affirmation of fact or promise made by the lessor to the lessee which relates to the goods and becomes part of the basis of the bargain creates an express warranty that the goods will conform to the affirmation or promise.

(b) Any description of the goods which is made part of the basis of the bargain creates an express warranty that the goods will conform to the description.

(c) Any sample or model that is made part of the basis of the bargain creates an express warranty that the whole of the goods will conform to the sample or model.

(2) It is not necessary to the creation of an express warranty that the lessor use formal words, such as "warrant" or "guarantee," or that the lessor have a specific intention to make a warranty, but an affirmation merely of the value of the goods or a statement purporting to be merely the lessor's opinion or commendation of the goods does not create a warranty.

§ 2A–211. Warranties Against Interference and Against Infringement; Lessee's Obligation Against Infringement

(1) There is in a lease contract a warranty that for the lease term no person holds a claim to or interest in the goods that arose from an act or omission of the lessor, other than a claim by way of infringement or the like, which will interfere with the lessee's enjoyment of its leasehold interest.

(2) Except in a finance lease there is in a lease contract by a lessor who is a merchant regularly dealing in goods of the kind a warranty that the goods are delivered free of the rightful claim of any person by way of infringement or the like.

(3) A lessee who furnishes specifications to a lessor or a supplier shall hold the lessor and the supplier harmless against any claim by way of infringement or the like that arises out of compliance with the specifications.

§ 2A–212. Implied Warranty of Merchantability

(1) Except in a finance lease, a warranty that the goods will be merchantable is implied in a lease contract if the lessor is a merchant with respect to goods of that kind.

(2) Goods to be merchantable must be at least such as

(a) pass without objection in the trade under the description in the lease agreement;

(b) in the case of fungible goods, are of fair average quality within the description;

(c) are fit for the ordinary purposes for which goods of that type are used;

(d) run, within the variation permitted by the lease agreement, of even kind, quality, and quantity within each unit and among all units involved;

(e) are adequately contained, packaged, and labeled as the lease agreement may require; and

(f) conform to any promises or affirmations of fact made on the container or label.

(3) Other implied warranties may arise from course of dealing or usage of trade.

§ 2A–213. Implied Warranty of Fitness for Particular Purpose

Except in a finance lease, if the lessor at the time the lease contract is made has reason to know of any particular purpose for which the goods are required and that the lessee is relying on the lessor's skill or judgment to select or furnish suitable goods, there is in the lease contract an implied warranty that the goods will be fit for that purpose.

§ 2A–214. Exclusion or Modification of Warranties

(1) Words or conduct relevant to the creation of an express warranty and words or conduct tending to negate or limit a warranty must be construed wherever reasonable as consistent with each other; but, subject to the provisions of Section 2A–202 on parol or extrinsic evidence, negation or limitation is inoperative to the extent that the construction is unreasonable.

(2) Subject to subsection (3), to exclude or modify the implied warranty of merchantability or any part of it the language must mention "merchantability," be by a writing, and be conspicuous. Subject to subsection (3), to exclude or modify any implied warranty of fitness the exclusion must be by a writing and be conspicuous. Language to exclude all implied warranties of fitness is sufficient if it is in writing, is conspicuous and states, for example, "There is no warranty that the goods will be fit for a particular purpose".

(3) Notwithstanding subsection (2), but subject to subsection (4),

(a) unless the circumstances indicate otherwise, all implied warranties are excluded by expressions like "as is," or "with all faults," or by other language that in common understanding calls the lessee's attention to the exclusion of warranties and makes plain that there is no implied warranty, if in writing and conspicuous;

(b) if the lessee before entering into the lease contract has examined the goods or the sample or model as fully as desired or has refused to examine the goods, there is no implied warranty with regard to defects that an examination ought in the circumstances to have revealed; and

(c) an implied warranty may also be excluded or modified by course of dealing, course of performance, or usage of trade.

(4) To exclude or modify a warranty against interference or against infringement (Section 2A–211) or any part of it, the language must be specific, be by a writing, and be conspicuous, unless the circumstances, including course of performance, course of dealing, or usage of trade, give the lessee reason to know that the goods are being leased subject to a claim or interest of any person.

§ 2A–215. Cumulation and Conflict of Warranties Express or Implied

Warranties, whether express or implied, must be construed as consistent with each other and as cumulative, but if that construction is unreasonable, the intention of the parties determines which warranty is dominant. In ascertaining that intention the following rules apply:

(a) Exact or technical specifications displace an inconsistent sample or model or general language of description.

(b) A sample from an existing bulk displaces inconsistent general language of description.

(c) Express warranties displace inconsistent implied warranties other than an implied warranty of fitness for a particular purpose.

§ 2A–216. Third-Party Beneficiaries of Express and Implied Warranties

Alternative A. A warranty to or for the benefit of a lessee under this Article, whether express or implied, extends to any natural person who is in the family or household of the lessee or who is a guest in the lessee's home if it is reasonable to expect that such person may use, consume, or be affected by the goods and who is injured in person by breach of the warranty. This section does not displace principles of law and equity that extend a warranty to or for the benefit of a lessee to other persons. The operation of this section may not be excluded, modified, or limited, but an exclusion, modification, or limitation of the warranty, including any with respect to rights and remedies, effective against the lessee is also effective against any beneficiary designated under this section.

Alternative B. A warranty to or for the benefit of a lessee under this Article, whether express or implied, extends to any natural person who may reasonably be expected to use, consume, or be affected by the goods and who is injured in person by breach of the warranty. This section does not displace principles of law and equity that extend a warranty to or for the benefit of a lessee to other persons. The operation of this section may not be excluded, modified, or limited, but an exclusion, modification, or limitation of the warranty, including any with respect to rights and remedies, effective against the lessee is also effective against the beneficiary designated under this section.

Alternative C. A warranty to or for the benefit of a lessee under this Article, whether express or implied, extends to any person who may reasonably be expected to use, consume, or be affected by the goods and who is injured by breach of the warranty. The operation of this section may not be excluded, modified, or limited with respect to injury to the person of an individual to whom the warranty extends, but an exclusion, modification, or limitation of the warranty, including any with respect to rights and remedies, effective against the lessee is also effective against the beneficiary designated under this section.

§ 2A–217. Identification

Identification of goods as goods to which a lease contract refers may be made at any time and in any manner explicitly agreed to by the parties. In the absence of explicit agreement, identification occurs:

(a) when the lease contract is made if the lease contract is for a lease of goods that are existing and identified;

(b) when the goods are shipped, marked, or otherwise designated by the lessor as goods to which the lease contract refers, if the lease contract is for a lease of goods that are not existing and identified; or

(c) when the young are conceived, if the lease contract is for a lease of unborn young of animals.

§ 2A–218. Insurance and Proceeds

(1) A lessee obtains an insurable interest when existing goods are identified to the lease contract even though the goods identified are nonconforming and the lessee has an option to reject them.

(2) If a lessee has an insurable interest only by reason of the lessor's identification of the goods, the lessor, until default or insolvency or notification to the lessee that identification is final, may substitute other goods for those identified.

(3) Notwithstanding a lessee's insurable interest under subsections (1) and (2), the lessor retains an insurable interest until an option to buy has been exercised by the lessee and risk of loss has passed to the lessee.

(4) Nothing in this section impairs any insurable interest recognized under any other statute or rule of law.

(5) The parties by agreement may determine that one or more parties have an obligation to obtain and pay for insurance covering the goods and by agreement may determine the beneficiary of the proceeds of the insurance.

§ 2A–219. Risk of Loss

(1) Except in the case of a finance lease, risk of loss is retained by the lessor and does not pass to the lessee. In the case of a finance lease, risk of loss passes to the lessee.

(2) Subject to the provisions of this Article on the effect of default on risk of loss (Section 2A–220), if risk of loss is to pass to the lessee and the time of passage is not stated, the following rules apply:

(a) If the lease contract requires or authorizes the goods to be shipped by carrier

(i) and it does not require delivery at a particular destination, the risk of loss passes to the lessee when the goods are duly delivered to the carrier; but

(ii) if it does require delivery at a particular destination and the goods are there duly tendered while in the possession of the carrier, the risk of loss passes to the lessee when the goods are there duly so tendered as to enable the lessee to take delivery.

(b) If the goods are held by a bailee to be delivered without being moved, the risk of loss passes to the lessee on acknowledgment by the bailee of the lessee's right to possession of the goods.

(c) In any case not within subsection (a) or (b), the risk of loss passes to the lessee on the lessee's receipt of the goods if the lessor, or, in the case of a finance lease, the supplier, is a merchant; otherwise the risk passes to the lessee on tender of delivery.

§ 2A–220. Effect of Default on Risk of Loss

(1) Where risk of loss is to pass to the lessee and the time of passage is not stated:

(a) If a tender or delivery of goods so fails to conform to the lease contract as to give a right of rejection, the risk of their loss remains with the lessor, or, in the case of a finance lease, the supplier, until cure or acceptance.

(b) If the lessee rightfully revokes acceptance, he [or she], to the extent of any deficiency in his [or her] effective insurance coverage, may treat the risk of loss as having remained with the lessor from the beginning.

(2) Whether or not risk of loss is to pass to the lessee, if the lessee as to conforming goods already identified to a lease contract repudiates or is otherwise in default under the lease contract, the lessor, or, in the case of a finance lease, the supplier, to the extent of any deficiency in his [or her] effective insurance coverage may treat the risk of loss as resting on the lessee for a commercially reasonable time.

§ 2A–221. Casualty to Identified Goods

If a lease contract requires goods identified when the lease contract is made, and the goods suffer casualty without fault of the lessee, the lessor or the supplier before delivery, or the goods suffer casualty before risk of loss passes to the lessee pursuant to the lease agreement or Section 2A–219, then:

(a) if the loss is total, the lease contract is avoided; and

(b) if the loss is partial or the goods have so deteriorated as to no longer conform to the lease contract, the lessee may nevertheless demand inspection and at his [or her] option either treat the lease contract as avoided or, except in a finance lease that is not a consumer lease, accept the goods with due allowance from the rent payable for the balance of the lease term for the deterioration or the deficiency in quantity but without further right against the lessor.

Part 3 Effect of Lease Contract

§ 2A–301. Enforceability of Lease Contract

Except as otherwise provided in this Article, a lease contract is effective and enforceable according to its terms between the parties, against purchasers of the goods and against creditors of the parties.

§ 2A–302. Title to and Possession of Goods

Except as otherwise provided in this Article, each provision of this Article applies whether the lessor or a third party has title to the goods, and whether the lessor, the lessee, or a third party has possession of the goods, notwithstanding any statute or rule of law that possession or the absence of possession is fraudulent.

§ 2A–303. Alienability of Party's Interest Under Lease Contract or of Lessor's Residual Interest in Goods; Delegation of Performance; Transfer of Rights

(1) As used in this section, "creation of a security interest" includes the sale of a lease contract that is subject to Article 9, Secured Transactions, by reason of Section 9–102(1)(b).

(2) Except as provided in subsections (3) and (4), a provision in a lease agreement which (i) prohibits the voluntary or involuntary transfer, including a transfer by sale, sublease, creation or enforcement of a security interest, or attachment, levy, or other judicial process, of an interest of a party under the lease contract or of the lessor's residual interest in the goods, or (ii) makes such a transfer an event of default, gives rise to the rights and remedies provided in subsection (5), but a transfer that is prohibited or is an event of default under the lease agreement is otherwise effective.

(3) A provision in a lease agreement which (i) prohibits the creation or enforcement of a security interest in an interest of a party under the lease contract or in the lessor's residual interest in the goods, or (ii) makes such a transfer an event of default, is not enforceable unless, and then only to the extent that, there is an actual transfer by the lessee of the lessee's right of possession or use of the goods in violation of the provision or an actual delegation of a material performance of either party to the lease contract in violation of the provision. Neither the granting nor the enforcement of a security interest in (i) the lessor's interest under the lease contract or (ii) the lessor's residual interest in the goods is a transfer that materially impairs the prospect of obtaining return performance by, materially changes the duty of, or materially increases the burden or risk imposed on, the lessee within the purview of subsection (5) unless, and then only to the extent that, there is an actual delegation of a material performance of the lessor.

(4) A provision in a lease agreement which (i) prohibits a transfer of a right to damages for default with respect to the whole lease contract or of a right to payment arising out of the transferor's due performance of the transferor's entire obligation, or (ii) makes such a transfer an event of default, is not enforceable, and such a transfer is not a transfer that materially impairs the prospect of obtaining return performance by, materially changes the duty of, or materially increases the burden or risk imposed on, the other party to the lease contract within the purview of subsection (5).

(5) Subject to subsection [A] (3) and (4):

(a) if a transfer is made which is made an event of default under a lease agreement, the party to the lease contract not making the transfer, unless that party waives the default or otherwise agrees, has the rights and remedies described in Section 2A–501(2);

(b) if paragraph (a) is not applicable and if a transfer is made that (i) is prohibited under a lease agreement or (ii) materially impairs the prospect of obtaining return performance by, materially changes the duty of, or materially increases the burden or risk imposed on, the other party to the lease contract, unless the party not making the transfer agrees at any time to the transfer in the lease contract or otherwise, then, except as limited by contract, (i) the transferor is liable to the party not making the transfer for damages caused by the transfer to the extent that the damages could not reasonably be prevented by the party not making the transfer and (ii) a court having jurisdiction may grant other appropriate relief, including cancellation of the lease contract or an injunction against the transfer.

(6) A transfer of "the lease" or of "all my rights under the lease," or a transfer in similar general terms, is a transfer of rights and, unless the language or the circumstances, as in a transfer for security, indicate the contrary, the transfer is a delegation of duties by the

transferor to the transferee. Acceptance by the transferee constitutes a promise by the transferee to perform those duties. The promise is enforceable by either the transferor or the other party to the lease contract.

(7) Unless otherwise agreed by the lessor and the lessee, a delegation of performance does not relieve the transferor as against the other party of any duty to perform or of any liability for default.

(8) In a consumer lease, to prohibit the transfer of an interest of a party under the lease contract or to make a transfer an event of default, the language must be specific, by a writing, and conspicuous.

As amended in 1990.

§ 2A–304. Subsequent Lease of Goods by Lessor

(1) Subject to Section 2A–303, a subsequent lessee from a lessor of goods under an existing lease contract obtains, to the extent of the leasehold interest transferred, the leasehold interest in the goods that the lessor had or had power to transfer, and except as provided in subsection (2) and Section 2A–527(4), takes subject to the existing lease contract. A lessor with voidable title has power to transfer a good leasehold interest to a good faith subsequent lessee for value, but only to the extent set forth in the preceding sentence. If goods have been delivered under a transaction of purchase, the lessor has that power even though:

(a) the lessor's transferor was deceived as to the identity of the lessor;

(b) the delivery was in exchange for a check which is later dishonored;

(c) it was agreed that the transaction was to be a "cash sale"; or

(d) the delivery was procured through fraud punishable as larcenous under the criminal law.

(2) A subsequent lessee in the ordinary course of business from a lessor who is a merchant dealing in goods of that kind to whom the goods were entrusted by the existing lessee of that lessor before the interest of the subsequent lessee became enforceable against that lessor obtains, to the extent of the leasehold interest transferred, all of that lessor's and the existing lessee's rights to the goods, and takes free of the existing lease contract.

(3) A subsequent lessee from the lessor of goods that are subject to an existing lease contract and are covered by a certificate of title issued under a statute of this State or of another jurisdiction takes no greater rights than those provided both by this section and by the certification of title statute.

As amended in 1990.

§ 2A–305. Sale or Sublease of Goods by Lessee

(1) Subject to the provisions of Section 2A–303, a buyer or sublessee from the lessee of goods under an existing lease contract obtains, to the extent of the interest transferred, the leasehold interest in the goods that the lessee had or had power to transfer, and except as provided in subsection (2) and Section 2A–511(4), takes subject to the existing lease contract. A lessee with a voidable leasehold interest has power to transfer a good leasehold interest to a good faith buyer for value or a good faith sublessee for value, but only to the extent set forth in the preceding sentence. When goods have been delivered under a transaction of lease the lessee has that power even though:

(a) the lessor was deceived as to the identity of the lessee;

(b) the delivery was in exchange for a check which is later dishonored; or

(c) the delivery was procured through fraud punishable as larcenous under the criminal law.

(2) A buyer in the ordinary course of business or a sublessee in the ordinary course of business from a lessee who is a merchant dealing in goods of that kind to whom the goods were entrusted by the lessor obtains, to the extent of the interest transferred, all of the lessor's and lessee's rights to the goods, and takes free of the existing lease contract.

(3) A buyer or sublessee from the lessee of goods that are subject to an existing lease contract and are covered by a certificate of title issued under a statute of this State or of another jurisdiction takes no greater rights than those provided both by this section and by the certificate of title statute.

§ 2A–306. Priority of Certain Liens Arising by Operation of Law

If a person in the ordinary course of his [or her] business furnishes services or materials with respect to goods subject to a lease contract, a lien upon those goods in the possession of that person given by statute or rule of law for those materials or services takes priority over any interest of the lessor or lessee under the lease contract or this Article unless the lien is created by statute and the statute provides otherwise or unless the lien is created by rule of law and the rule of law provides otherwise.

§ 2A–307. Priority of Liens Arising by Attachment of Levy on, Security Interests in, and Other Claims to Goods

(1) Except as otherwise provided in Section 2A–306, a creditor of a lessee takes subject to the lease contract.

(2) Except as otherwise provided in subsections (3) and (4) and in Sections 2A–306 and 2A–308, a creditor of a lessor takes subject to the lease contract unless:

(a) the creditor holds a lien that attached to the goods before the lease contract became enforceable,

(b) the creditor holds a security interest in the goods and the lessee did not give value and receive delivery of the goods without knowledge of the security interest; or

(c) the creditor holds a security interest in the goods which was perfected (Section 9–303) before the lease contract became enforceable.

(3) A lessee in the ordinary course of business takes the leasehold interest free of a security interest in the goods created by the lessor even though the security interest is perfected (Section 9–303) and the lessee knows of its existence.

(4) A lessee other than a lessee in the ordinary course of business takes the leasehold interest free of a security interest to the extent that it secures future advances made after the secured party acquires knowledge of the lease or more than 45 days after the lease contract becomes enforceable, whichever first occurs, unless the future advances are made pursuant to a commitment entered into without knowledge of the lease and before the expiration of the 45-day period.

As amended in 1990.

§ 2A–308. Special Rights of Creditors

(1) A creditor of a lessor in possession of goods subject to a lease contract may treat the lease contract as void if as against the creditor retention of possession by the lessor is fraudulent under any statute or rule of law, but retention of possession in good faith and current course of trade by the lessor for a commercially reasonable time after the lease contract becomes enforceable is not fraudulent.

(2) Nothing in this Article impairs the rights of creditors of a lessor if the lease contract (a) becomes enforceable, not in current course of trade but in satisfaction of or as security for a pre-existing claim for money, security, or the like, and (b) is made under circumstances which under any statute or rule of law apart from this Article would constitute the transaction a fraudulent transfer or voidable preference.

(3) A creditor of a seller may treat a sale or an identification of goods to a contract for sale as void if as against the creditor retention of possession by the seller is fraudulent under any statute or rule of law, but retention of possession of the goods pursuant to a lease contract entered into by the seller as lessee and the buyer as lessor in connection with the sale or identification of the goods is not fraudulent if the buyer bought for value and in good faith.

§ 2A–309. Lessor's and Lessee's Rights When Goods Become Fixtures

(1) In this section:

(a) goods are "fixtures" when they become so related to particular real estate that an interest in them arises under real estate law;

(b) a "fixture filing" is the filing, in the office where a mortgage on the real estate would be filed or recorded, of a financing statement covering goods that are or are to become fixtures and conforming to the requirements of Section 9–402(5);

(c) a lease is a "purchase money lease" unless the lessee has possession or use of the goods or the right to possession or use of the goods before the lease agreement is enforceable;

(d) a mortgage is a "construction mortgage" to the extent it secures an obligation incurred for the construction of an improvement on land including the acquisition cost of the land, if the recorded writing so indicates; and

(e) "encumbrance" includes real estate mortgages and other liens on real estate and all other rights in real estate that are not ownership interests.

(2) Under this Article a lease may be of goods that are fixtures or may continue in goods that become fixtures, but no lease exists under this Article of ordinary building materials incorporated into an improvement on land.

(3) This Article does not prevent creation of a lease of fixtures pursuant to real estate law.

(4) The perfected interest of a lessor of fixtures has priority over a conflicting interest of an encumbrancer or owner of the real estate if:

(a) the lease is a purchase money lease, the conflicting interest of the encumbrancer or owner arises before the goods become fixtures, the interest of the lessor is perfected by a fixture filing before the goods become fixtures or within ten days thereafter, and the lessee has an interest of record in the real estate or is in possession of the real estate; or

(b) the interest of the lessor is perfected by a fixture filing before the interest of the encumbrancer or owner is of record, the lessor's interest has priority over any conflicting interest of a predecessor in title of the encumbrancer or owner, and the lessee has an interest of record in the real estate or is in possession of the real estate.

(5) The interest of a lessor of fixtures, whether or not perfected, has priority over the conflicting interest of an encumbrancer or owner of the real estate if:

(a) the fixtures are readily removable factory or office machines, readily removable equipment that is not primarily used or leased for use in the operation of the real estate, or readily removable replacements of domestic appliances that are goods subject to a consumer lease, and before the goods become fixtures the lease contract is enforceable; or

(b) the conflicting interest is a lien on the real estate obtained by legal or equitable proceedings after the lease contract is enforceable; or

(c) the encumbrancer or owner has consented in writing to the lease or has disclaimed an interest in the goods as fixtures; or

(d) the lessee has a right to remove the goods as against the encumbrancer or owner. If the lessee's right to remove terminates, the priority of the interest of the lessor continues for a reasonable time.

(6) Notwithstanding subsection (4)(a) but otherwise subject to subsections (4) and (5), the interest of a lessor of fixtures, including the lessor's residual interest, is subordinate to the conflicting interest of an encumbrancer of the real estate under a construction mortgage recorded before the goods become fixtures if the goods become fixtures before the completion of the construction. To the extent given to refinance a construction mortgage, the conflicting interest of an encumbrancer of the real estate under a mortgage has this priority to the same extent as the encumbrancer of the real estate under the construction mortgage.

(7) In cases not within the preceding subsections, priority between the interest of a lessor of fixtures, including the lessor's residual interest, and the conflicting interest of an encumbrancer or owner of the real estate who is not the lessee is determined by the priority rules governing conflicting interests in real estate.

(8) If the interest of a lessor of fixtures, including the lessor's residual interest, has priority over all conflicting interests of all owners and encumbrancers of the real estate, the lessor or the lessee may (i) on default, expiration, termination, or cancellation of the lease agreement but subject to the agreement and this Article, or (ii) if necessary to enforce other rights and remedies of the lessor or lessee under this Article, remove the goods from the real estate, free and clear of all conflicting interests of all owners and encumbrancers of the real estate, but the lessor or lessee must reimburse any encumbrancer or owner of the real estate who is not the lessee and who has not otherwise agreed for the cost of repair of any physical injury, but not for any diminution in value of the real estate caused by the absence of the goods removed or by any necessity of replacing them. A person entitled to reimbursement may refuse permission to remove until the party seeking removal gives adequate security for the performance of this obligation.

(9) Even though the lease agreement does not create a security interest, the interest of a lessor of fixtures, including the lessor's residual interest, is perfected by filing a financing statement as a fixture filing for leased goods that are or are to become fixtures in accordance with the relevant provisions of the Article on Secured Transactions (Article 9).

As amended in 1990.

§ 2A–310. Lessor's and Lessee's Rights When Goods Become Accessions

(1) Goods are "accessions" when they are installed in or affixed to other goods.

(2) The interest of a lessor or a lessee under a lease contract entered into before the goods became accessions is superior to all interests in the whole except as stated in subsection (4).

(3) The interest of a lessor or a lessee under a lease contract entered into at the time or after the goods became accessions is superior to all subsequently acquired interests in the whole except as stated in subsection (4) but is subordinate to interests in the whole existing at the time the lease contract was made unless the holders of such interests in the whole have in writing consented to the lease or disclaimed an interest in the goods as part of the whole.

(4) The interest of a lessor or a lessee under a lease contract described in subsection (2) or (3) is subordinate to the interest of

(a) a buyer in the ordinary course of business or a lessee in the ordinary course of business of any interest in the whole acquired after the goods became accessions; or

(b) a creditor with a security interest in the whole perfected before the lease contract was made to the extent that the creditor makes subsequent advances without knowledge of the lease contract.

(5) When under subsections (2) or (3) and (4) a lessor or a lessee of accessions holds an interest that is superior to all interests in the whole, the lessor or the lessee may (a) on default, expiration, termination, or cancellation of the lease contract by the other party but subject to the provisions of the lease contract and this Article, or (b) if necessary to enforce his [or her] other rights and remedies under this Article, remove the goods from the whole, free and clear of all interests in the whole, but he [or she] must reimburse any holder of an interest in the whole who is not the lessee and who has not otherwise agreed for the cost of repair of any physical injury but not for any diminution in value of the whole caused by the absence of the goods removed or by an necessity for replacing them. A person entitled to reimbursement may refuse permission to remove until the party seeking removal gives adequate security for the performance of this obligation.

§ 2A–311. Priority Subject to Subordination

Nothing in this Article prevents subordination by agreement by any person entitled to priority.

As added in 1990.

Part 4 Performance of Lease Contract: Repudiated, Substituted and Excused

§ 2A–401. Insecurity: Adequate Assurance of Performance

(1) A lease contract imposes an obligation on each party that the other's expectation of receiving due performance will not be impaired.

(2) If reasonable grounds for insecurity arise with respect to the performance of either party, the insecure party may demand in writing adequate assurance of due performance. Until the insecure party receives that assurance, if commercially reasonable the insecure party may suspend any performance for which he [or she] has not already received the agreed return.

(3) A repudiation of the lease contract occurs if assurance of due performance adequate under the circumstances of the particular case is not provided to the insecure party within a reasonable time, not to exceed 30 days after receipt of a demand by the other party.

(4) Between merchants, the reasonableness of grounds for insecurity and the adequacy of any assurance offered must be determined according to commercial standards.

(5) Acceptance of any nonconforming delivery or payment does not prejudice the aggrieved party's right to demand adequate assurance of future performance.

§ 2A–402. Anticipatory Repudiation

If either party repudiates a lease contract with respect to a performance not yet due under the lease contract, the loss of which performance will substantially impair the value of the lease contract to the other, the aggrieved party may:

(a) for a commercially reasonable time, await retraction of repudiation and performance by the repudiating party;

(b) make demand pursuant to Section 2A–401 and await assurance of future performance adequate under the circumstances of the particular case; or

(c) resort to any right or remedy upon default under the lease contract or this Article, even though the aggrieved party has notified the repudiating party that the aggrieved party would await the repudiating party's performance and assurance and has urged retraction. In addition, whether or not the aggrieved party is pursuing one of the foregoing remedies, the aggrieved party may suspend performance or, if the aggrieved party is the lessor, proceed in accordance with the provisions of this Article on the lessor's right to identify goods to the lease contract notwithstanding default or to salvage unfinished goods (Section 2A–524).

§ 2A–403. Retraction of Anticipatory Repudiation

(1) Until the repudiating party's next performance is due, the repudiating party can retract the repudiation unless, since the repudiation, the aggrieved party has canceled the lease contract or materially changed the aggrieved party's position or otherwise indicated that the aggrieved party considers the repudiation final.

(2) Retraction may be by any method that clearly indicates to the aggrieved party that the repudiating party intends to perform under the lease contract and includes any assurance demanded under Section 2A–401.

(3) Retraction reinstates a repudiating party's rights under a lease contract with due excuse and allowance to the aggrieved party for any delay occasioned by the repudiation.

§ 2A–404. Substituted Performance

(1) If without fault of the lessee, the lessor and the supplier, the agreed berthing, loading, or unloading facilities fail or the agreed type of carrier becomes unavailable or the agreed manner of delivery otherwise becomes commercially impracticable, but a commercially reasonable substitute is available, the substitute performance must be tendered and accepted.

(2) If the agreed means or manner of payment fails because of domestic or foreign governmental regulation:

(a) the lessor may withhold or stop delivery or cause the supplier to withhold or stop delivery unless the lessee provides a means or manner of payment that is commercially a substantial equivalent; and

(b) if delivery has already been taken, payment by the means or in the manner provided by the regulation discharges the lessee's obligation unless the regulation is discriminatory, oppressive, or predatory.

§ 2A–405. Excused Performance

Subject to Section 2A–404 on substituted performance, the following rules apply:

(a) Delay in delivery or nondelivery in whole or in part by a lessor or a supplier who complies with paragraphs (b) and (c) is not a default under the lease contract if performance as agreed has been made impracticable by the occurrence of a contingency the nonoccurrence of which was a basic assumption on which the lease contract was made or by compliance in good faith with any applicable foreign or domestic governmental regulation or order, whether or not the regulation or order later proves to be invalid.

(b) If the causes mentioned in paragraph (a) affect only part of the lessor's or the supplier's capacity to perform, he [or she] shall allocate production and deliveries among his [or her] customers but at his [or her] option may include regular customers not then under contract for sale or lease as well as his [or her] own requirements for further manufacture. He [or she] may so allocate in any manner that is fair and reasonable.

(c) The lessor seasonably shall notify the lessee and in the case of a finance lease the supplier seasonably shall notify the lessor and the lessee, if known, that there will be delay or nondelivery and, if allocation is required under paragraph (b), of the estimated quota thus made available for the lessee.

§ 2A–406. Procedure on Excused Performance

(1) If the lessee receives notification of a material or indefinite delay or an allocation justified under Section 2A–405, the lessee may by written notification to the lessor as to any goods involved, and with respect to all of the goods if under an installment lease contract the value of the whole lease contract is substantially impaired (Section 2A–510):

(a) terminate the lease contract (Section 2A–505(2)); or

(b) except in a finance lease that is not a consumer lease, modify the lease contract by accepting the available quota in substitution, with due allowance from the rent payable for the balance of the lease term for the deficiency but without further right against the lessor.

(2) If, after receipt of a notification from the lessor under Section 2A–405, the lessee fails so to modify the lease agreement within a reasonable time not exceeding 30 days, the lease contract lapses with respect to any deliveries affected.

§ 2A–407. Irrevocable Promises: Finance Leases

(1) In the case of a finance lease that is not a consumer lease the lessee's promises under the lease contract become irrevocable and independent upon the lessee's acceptance of goods.

(2) A promise that has become irrevocable and independent under subsection (1):

(a) is effective and enforceable between the parties, and by or against third parties including assignees of the parties; and

(b) is not subject to cancellation, termination, modification, repudiation, excuse, or substitution without the consent of the party to whom the promise runs.

(3) This section does not affect the validity under any other law of a covenant in any lease contract making the lessee's promises irrevocable and independent upon the lessee's acceptance of the goods.

As amended in 1990.

Part 5 Default

A. In General

§ 2A–501. Default: Procedure

(1) Whether the lessor or the lessee is in default under a lease contract is determined by the lease agreement and this Article.

(2) If the lessor or the lessee is in default under the lease contract, the party seeking enforcement has rights and remedies as provided in this Article and, except as limited by this Article, as provided in the lease agreement.

(3) If the lessor or the lessee is in default under the lease contract, the party seeking enforcement may reduce the party's claim to judgment, or otherwise enforce the lease contract by self-help or any available judicial procedure or nonjudicial procedure, including administrative proceeding, arbitration, or the like, in accordance with this Article.

(4) Except as otherwise provided in Section 1–106(1) or this Article or the lease agreement, the rights and remedies referred to in subsections (2) and (3) are cumulative.

(5) If the lease agreement covers both real property and goods, the party seeking enforcement may proceed under this Part as to the goods, or under other applicable law as to both the real property and the goods in accordance with that party's rights and remedies in respect of the real property, in which case this Part does not apply.

As amended in 1990.

§ 2A–502. Notice after Default

Except as otherwise provided in this Article or the lease agreement, the lessor or lessee in default under the lease contract is not entitled to notice of default or notice of enforcement from the other party to the lease agreement.

§ 2A–503. Modification or Impairment of Rights and Remedies

(1) Except as otherwise provided in this Article, the lease agreement may include rights and remedies for default in addition to or in substitution for those provided in this Article and may limit or alter the measure of damages recoverable under this Article.

(2) Resort to a remedy provided under this Article or in the lease agreement is optional unless the remedy is expressly agreed to be exclusive. If circumstances cause an exclusive or limited remedy to fail of its essential purpose, or provision for an exclusive remedy is unconscionable, remedy may be had as provided in this Article.

(3) Consequential damages may be liquidated under Section 2A–504, or may otherwise be limited, altered, or excluded unless the limitation, alteration, or exclusion is unconscionable. Limitation, alteration, or exclusion of consequential damages for injury to the person in the case of consumer goods is prima facie unconscionable but limitation, alteration, or exclusion of damages where the loss is commercial is not prima facie unconscionable.

(4) Rights and remedies on default by the lessor or the lessee with respect to any obligation or promise collateral or ancillary to the lease contract are not impaired by this Article.

As amended in 1990.

§ 2A–504. Liquidation of Damages

(1) Damages payable by either party for default, or any other act or omission, including indemnity for loss or diminution of anticipated tax benefits or loss or damage to lessor's residual interest, may be liquidated in the lease agreement but only at an amount or by a formula that is reasonable in light of the then anticipated harm caused by the default or other act or omission.

(2) If the lease agreement provides for liquidation of damages, and such provision does not comply with subsection (1), or such provision is an exclusive or limited remedy that circumstances cause to fail of its essential purpose, remedy may be had as provided in this Article.

(3) If the lessor justifiably withholds or stops delivery of goods because of the lessee's default or insolvency (Section 2A–525 or 2A–526), the lessee is entitled to restitution of any amount by which the sum of his [or her] payment exceeds:

(a) the amount to which the lessor is entitled by virtue of terms liquidating the lessor's damages in accordance with subsection (1); or

(b) in the absence of those terms, 20 percent of the then present value of the total rent the lessee was obligated to pay for the balance of the lease term, or, in the case of a consumer lease, the lesser of such amount or $500.

(4) A lessee's right to restitution under subsection (3) is subject to offset to the extent the lessor establishes:

(a) a right to recover damages under the provisions of this Article other than subsection (1); and

(b) the amount or value of any benefits received by the lessee directly or indirectly by reason of the lease contract.

§ 2A–505. Cancellation and Termination and Effect of Cancellation, Termination, Rescission, or Fraud on Rights and Remedies

(1) On cancellation of the lease contract, all obligations that are still executory on both sides are discharged, but any right based on prior default or performance survives, and the cancelling party also retains any remedy for default of the whole lease contract or any unperformed balance.

(2) On termination of the lease contract, all obligations that are still executory on both sides are discharged but any right based on prior default or performance survives.

(3) Unless the contrary intention clearly appears, expressions of "cancellation," "rescission," or the like of the lease contract may not be construed as a renunciation or discharge of any claim in damages for an antecedent default.

(4) Rights and remedies for material misrepresentation or fraud include all rights and remedies available under this Article for default.

(5) Neither rescission nor a claim for rescission of the lease contract nor rejection or return of the goods may bar or be deemed inconsistent with a claim for damages or other right or remedy.

§ 2A–506. Statute of Limitations

(1) An action for default under a lease contract, including breach of warranty or indemnity, must be commenced within 4 years after the cause of action accrued. By the original lease contract the parties may reduce the period of limitation to not less than one year.

(2) A cause of action for default accrues when the act or omission on which the default or breach of warranty is based is or should have been discovered by the aggrieved party, or when the default occurs, whichever is later. A cause of action for indemnity accrues when the act or omission on which the claim for indemnity is based is or should have been discovered by the indemnified party, whichever is later.

(3) If an action commenced within the time limited by subsection (1) is so terminated as to leave available a remedy by another action for the same default or breach of warranty or indemnity, the other action may be commenced after the expiration of the time limited and within 6 months after the termination of the first action unless the termination resulted from voluntary discontinuance or from dismissal for failure or neglect to prosecute.

(4) This section does not alter the law on tolling of the statute of limitations nor does it apply to causes of action that have accrued before this Article becomes effective.

§ 2A–507. Proof of Market Rent: Time and Place

(1) Damages based on market rent (Section 2A–519 or 2A–528) are determined according to the rent for the use of the goods concerned for a lease term identical to the remaining lease term of the original lease agreement and prevailing at the times specified in Sections 2A–519 and 2A–528.

(2) If evidence of rent for the use of the goods concerned for a lease term identical to the remaining lease term of the original lease agreement and prevailing at the times or places described in this Article is not readily available, the rent prevailing within any reasonable time before or after the time described or at any other place or for a different lease term which in commercial judgment or under usage of trade would serve as a reasonable substitute for the one described may be used, making any proper allowance for the difference, including the cost of transporting the goods to or from the other place.

(3) Evidence of a relevant rent prevailing at a time or place or for a lease term other than the one described in this Article offered by one party is not admissible unless and until he [or she] has given the other party notice the court finds sufficient to prevent unfair surprise.

(4) If the prevailing rent or value of any goods regularly leased in any established market is in issue, reports in official publications or trade journals or in newspapers or periodicals of general circulation published as the reports of that market are admissible in evidence. The circumstances of the preparation of the report may be shown to affect its weight but not its admissibility.

As amended in 1990.

B. Default by Lessor

§ 2A–508. Lessee's Remedies

(1) If a lessor fails to deliver the goods in conformity to the lease contract (Section 2A–509) or repudiates the lease contract (Section 2A–402), or a lessee rightfully rejects the goods (Section 2A–509) or justifiably revokes acceptance of the goods (Section 2A–517), then with respect to any goods involved, and with respect to all of the goods if under an installment lease contract the value of the whole lease contract is substantially impaired (Section 2A–510), the lessor is in default under the lease contract and the lessee may:

(a) cancel the lease contract (Section 2A–505(1));

(b) recover so much of the rent and security as has been paid and is just under the circumstances;

(c) cover and recover damages as to all goods affected whether or not they have been identified to the lease contract (Sections 2A–518 and 2A–520), or recover damages for nondelivery (Sections 2A–519 and 2A–520);

(d) exercise any other rights or pursue any other remedies provided in the lease contract.

(2) If a lessor fails to deliver the goods in conformity to the lease contract or repudiates the lease contract, the lessee may also:

(a) if the goods have been identified, recover them (Section 2A–522); or

(b) in a proper case, obtain specific performance or replevy the goods (Section 2A–521).

(3) If a lessor is otherwise in default under a lease contract, the lessee may exercise the rights and pursue the remedies provided in the lease contract, which may include a right to cancel the lease, and in Section 2A–519(3).

(4) If a lessor has breached a warranty, whether express or implied, the lessee may recover damages (Section 2A–519(4)).

(5) On rightful rejection or justifiable revocation of acceptance, a lessee has a security interest in goods in the lessee's possession or control for any rent and security that has been paid and any expenses reasonably incurred in their inspection, receipt, transportation, and care and custody and may hold those goods and dispose of them in good faith and in a commercially reasonable manner, subject to Section 2A–527(5).

(6) Subject to the provisions of Section 2A–407, a lessee, on notifying the lessor of the lessee's intention to do so, may deduct all or any part of the damages resulting from any default under the lease contract from any part of the rent still due under the same lease contract.

As amended in 1990.

§ 2A–509. Lessee's Rights on Improper Delivery; Rightful Rejection

(1) Subject to the provisions of Section 2A–510 on default in installment lease contracts, if the goods or the tender or delivery fail in any respect to conform to the lease contract, the lessee may reject or accept the goods or accept any commercial unit or units and reject the rest of the goods.

(2) Rejection of goods is ineffective unless it is within a reasonable time after tender or delivery of the goods and the lessee seasonably notifies the lessor.

§ 2A–510. Installment Lease Contracts: Rejection and Default

(1) Under an installment lease contract a lessee may reject any delivery that is nonconforming if the nonconformity substantially impairs the value of that delivery and cannot be cured or the nonconformity is a defect in the required documents; but if the nonconformity does not fall within subsection (2) and the lessor or the supplier gives adequate assurance of its cure, the lessee must accept that delivery.

(2) Whenever nonconformity or default with respect to one or more deliveries substantially impairs the value of the installment lease contract as a whole there is a default with respect to the whole. But, the aggrieved party reinstates the installment lease contract as a whole if the aggrieved party accepts a nonconforming delivery without seasonably notifying of cancellation or brings an action with respect only to past deliveries or demands performance as to future deliveries.

§ 2A–511. Merchant Lessee's Duties as to Rightfully Rejected Goods

(1) Subject to any security interest of a lessee (Section 2A–508(5)), if a lessor or a supplier has no agent or place of business at the market of rejection, a merchant lessee, after rejection of goods in his [or her] possession or control, shall follow any reasonable instructions received from the lessor or the supplier with respect to the goods. In the absence of those instructions, a merchant lessee shall make reasonable efforts to sell, lease, or otherwise dispose of the goods for the lessor's account if they threaten to decline in value speedily. Instructions are not reasonable if on demand indemnity for expenses is not forthcoming.

(2) If a merchants lessee (subsection (1)) or any other lessee (Section 2A–512) disposes of goods, he [or she] is entitled to reimbursement either from the lessor or the supplier or out of the proceeds for reasonable expenses of caring for and disposing of the

goods and, if the expenses include no disposition commission, to such commission as is usual in the trade, or if there is none, to a reasonable sum not exceeding 10 percent of the gross proceeds.

(3) In complying with this Section 2A–512, the lessee is held only to good faith. Good faith conduct hereunder is neither acceptance or conversion nor the basis of an action for damages.

(4) A purchaser who purchases in good faith from a lessee pursuant to this section or Section 2A–512 takes the goods free of any rights of the lessor and the supplier even though the lessee fails to comply with one or more of the requirements of this Article.

§ 2A–512. Lessee's Duties as to Rightfully Rejected Goods

(1) Except as otherwise provided with respect to goods that threaten to decline in value speedily (Section 2A–511) and subject to any security interest of a lessee (Section 2A–508(5)):

(a) the lessee, after rejection of goods in the lessee's possession, shall hold them with reasonable care at the lessor's or the supplier's disposition for a reasonable time after the lessee's seasonable notification of rejection;

(b) if the lessor or the supplier gives no instructions within a reasonable time after notification of rejection, the lessee may store the rejected goods for the lessor's or the supplier's account or ship them to the lessor or the supplier or dispose of them for the lessor's or the supplier's account with reimbursement in the manner provided in Section 2A–511; but

(c) The lessee has no further obligations with regard to goods rightfully rejected.

(2) Action by the lessee pursuant to subsection (1) is not acceptance or conversion.

§ 2A–513. Cure by Lessor of Improper Tender or Delivery; Replacement

(1) If any tender or delivery by the lessor or the supplier is rejected because nonconforming and the time for performance has not yet expired, the lessor or the supplier may seasonably notify the lessee of the lessor's or the supplier's intention to cure and may then make a conforming delivery within the time provided in the lease contract.

(2) If the lessee rejects a nonconforming tender that the lessor or the supplier had reasonable grounds to believe would be acceptable with or without money allowance, the lessor or the supplier may have a further reasonable time to substitute a conforming tender if he [or she] seasonably notifies the lessee.

§ 2A–514. Waiver of Lessee's Objections

(1) In rejecting goods, a lessee's failure to state a particular defect that is ascertainable by reasonable inspection precludes the lessee from relying on the defect to justify rejection or to establish default:

(a) if, stated seasonably, the lessor or the supplier could have cured it (Section 2A–513); or

(b) between merchants if the lessor or the supplier after rejection has made a request in writing for a full and final written statement of all defects on which the lessee proposes to rely.

(2) A lessee's failure to reserve rights when paying rent or other consideration against documents precludes recovery of the payment for defects apparent on the face of the documents.

§ 2A–515. Acceptance of Goods

(1) Acceptance of goods occurs after the lessee has had a reasonable opportunity to inspect the goods and

(a) the lessee signifies or acts with respect to the goods in a manner that signifies to the lessor or the supplier that the goods are conforming or that the lessee will take or retain them in spite of their nonconformity; or

(b) the lessee fails to make an effective rejection of the goods (Section 2A–509(2)).

(2) Acceptance of a part of any commercial unit is acceptance of that entire unit.

§ 2A–516. Effect of Acceptance of Goods; Notice of Default; Burden of Establishing Default After Acceptance; Notice of Claim or Litigation to Person Answerable Over

(1) A lessee must pay rent for any goods accepted in accordance with the lease contract, with due allowance for goods rightfully rejected or not delivered.

(2) A lessee's acceptance of goods precludes rejection of the goods accepted. In the case of a finance lease, if made with knowledge of a nonconformity, acceptance cannot be revoked because of it. In any other case, if made with knowledge of a nonconformity, acceptance cannot be revoked because of it unless the acceptance was on the reasonable assumption that the nonconformity would be seasonably cured. Acceptance does not of itself impair any other remedy provided by this Article or the lease agreement for nonconformity.

(3) If a tender has been accepted:

(a) within a reasonable time after the lessee discovers or should have discovered any default, the lessee shall notify the lessor and the supplier, if any, or be barred from any remedy against the party not notified;

(b) except in the case of a consumer lease, within a reasonable time after the lessee receives notice of litigation for infringement or the like (Section 2A–211) the lessee shall notify the lessor or be barred from any remedy over for liability established by the litigation; and

(c) the burden is on the lessee to establish any default.

(4) If a lessee is sued for breach of a warranty or other obligation for which a lessor or a supplier is answerable over the following apply:

(a) The lessee may give the lessor or the supplier, or both, written notice of the litigation. If the notice states that the person notified may come in and defend and that if the person notified does not do so that person will be bound in any action against that person by the lessee by any determination of fact common to the two litigations, then unless the person notified after seasonable receipt of the notice does come in and defend that person is so bound.

(b) The lessor or the supplier may demand in writing that the lessee turn over control of the litigation including settlement if the claim is one for infringement or the like (Section 2A–211) or else be barred from any remedy over. If the demand states that the lessor or the supplier agrees to bear all expense and to satisfy any adverse judgment, then unless the lessee after seasonable receipt of the demand does turn over control the lessee is so barred.

(5) Subsection (3) and (4) apply to any obligation of a lessee to hold the lessor or the supplier harmless against infringement or the like (Section 2A–211).

As amended in 1990.

§ 2A–517. Revocation of Acceptance of Goods

(1) A lessee may revoke acceptance of a lot or commercial unit whose nonconformity substantially impairs its value to the lessee if the lessee has accepted it:

(a) except in the case of a finance lease, on the reasonable assumption that its nonconformity would be cured and it has not been seasonably cured; or

(b) without discovery of the nonconformity if the lessee's acceptance was reasonably induced either by the lessor's assurances or, except in the case of a finance lease, by the difficulty of discovery before acceptance.

(2) Except in the case of a finance lease that is not a consumer lease, a lessee may revoke acceptance of a lot or commercial unit if the lessor defaults under the lease contract and the default substantially impairs the value of that lot or commercial unit to the lessee.

(3) If the lease agreement so provides, the lessee may revoke acceptance of a lot or commercial unit because of other defaults by the lessor.

(4) Revocation of acceptance must occur within a reasonable time after the lessee discovers or should have discovered the ground for it and before any substantial change in condition of the goods which is not caused by the nonconformity. Revocation is not effective until the lessee notifies the lessor.

(5) A lessee who so revokes has the same rights and duties with regard to the goods involved as if the lessee had rejected them.

As amended in 1990.

§ 2A–518. Cover; Substitute Goods

(1) After a default by a lessor under the lease contract of the type described in Section 2A–508(1), or, if agreed, after other default by the lessor, the lessee may cover by making any purchase or lease of or contract to purchase or lease goods in substitution for those due from the lessor.

(2) Except as otherwise provided with respect to damages liquidated in the lease agreement (Section 2A–504) or otherwise determined pursuant to agreement of the parties (Sections 1–102(3) and 2A–503), if a lessee's cover is by a lease agreement substantially similar to the original lease agreement and the new lease agreement is made in good faith and in a commercially reasonable manner, the lessee may recover from the lessor as damages (i) the present value, as of the date of the commencement of the term of the new lease agreement, of the rent under the new lease agreement applicable to that period of the new lease term which is comparable to the then remaining term of the original lease agreement minus the present value as of the same date of the total rent for the then remaining lease term of the original lease agreement, and (ii) any incidental or consequential damages, less expenses saved in consequence of the lessor's default.

(3) If a lessee's cover is by lease agreement that for any reason does not qualify for treatment under subsection (2), or is by purchase or otherwise, the lessee may recover from the lessor as if the lessee had elected not to cover and Section 2A–519 governs.

As amended in 1990.

§ 2A–519. Lessee's Damages for Non-delivery, Repudiation, Default, and Breach of Warranty in Regard to Accepted Goods

(1) Except as otherwise provided with respect to damages liquidated in the lease agreement (Section 2A–504) or otherwise determined pursuant to agreement of the parties (Sections 1–102(3) and 2A–503), if a lessee elects not to cover or a lessee elects to cover and the cover is by lease agreement that for any reason does not qualify for treatment under Section 2A–518(2), or is by purchase or otherwise, the measure of damages for non-delivery or repudiation by the lessor or for rejection or revocation of acceptance by the lessee is the present value, as of the date of default, of the then market rent minus the present value as of the same date of the original rent, computed for the remaining lease term of the original lease agreement, together with incidental and consequential damages, less expenses saved in consequence of the lessor's default.

(2) Market rent is to be determined as of the place for tender or, in cases of rejection after arrival or revocation of acceptance, as of the place of arrival.

(3) Except as otherwise agreed, if the lessee has accepted goods and given notification (Section 2A–516(3)), the measure of damages for nonconforming tender or delivery or other default by a lessor is the loss resulting in the ordinary course of events from the lessor's default as determined in any manner that is reasonable together with incidental and consequential damages, less expenses saved in consequence of the lessor's default.

(4) Except as otherwise agreed, the measure of damages for breach of warranty is the present value at the time and place of acceptance of the difference between the value of the use of the goods accepted and the value if they had been as warranted for the lease term, unless special circumstances show proximate damages of a different amount, together with incidental and consequential damages, less expenses saved in consequence of the lessor's default or breach of warranty.

As amended in 1990.

§ 2A–520. Lessee's Incidental and Consequential Damages

(1) Incidental damages resulting from a lessor's default include expenses reasonably incurred in inspection, receipt, transportation, and care and custody of goods rightfully rejected or goods the acceptance of which is justifiably revoked, any commercially reasonable charges, expenses or commissions in connection with effecting cover, and any other reasonable expense incident to the default.

(2) Consequential damages resulting from a lessor's default include:

(a) any loss resulting from general or particular requirements and needs of which the lessor at the time of contracting had reason to know and which could not reasonably be prevented by cover or otherwise; and

(b) injury to person or property proximately resulting from any breach of warranty.

§ 2A–521. Lessee's Right to Specific Performance or Replevin

(1) Specific performance may be decreed if the goods are unique or in other proper circumstances.

(2) A decree for specific performance may include any terms and conditions as to payment of the rent, damages, or other relief that the court deems just.

(3) A lessee has a right of replevin, detinue, sequestration, claim and delivery, or the like for goods identified to the lease contract if after reasonable effort the lessee is unable to effect cover for those goods or the circumstances reasonably indicate that the effort will be unavailing.

§ 2A–522. Lessee's Right to Goods on Lessor's Insolvency

(1) Subject to subsection (2) and even though the goods have not been shipped, a lessee who has paid a part or all of the rent and security for goods identified to a lease contract (Section 2A–217) on making and keeping good a tender of any unpaid portion of the rent and security due under the lease contract may recover the goods identified from the lessor if the lessor becomes insolvent within 10 days after receipt of the first installment of rent and security.

(2) A lessee acquires the right to recover goods identified to a lease contract only if they conform to the lease contract.

C. Default by Lessee

§ 2A–523. Lessor's Remedies

(1) If a lessee wrongfully rejects or revokes acceptance of goods or fails to make a payment when due or repudiates with respect to a part or the whole, then, with respect to any goods involved, and with respect to all of the goods if under an installment lease contract the value of the whole lease contract is substantially impaired (Section 2A–510), the lessee is in default under the lease contract and the lessor may:

(a) cancel the lease contract (Section 2A–505(1));

(b) proceed respecting goods not identified to the lease contract (Section 2A–524);

(c) withhold delivery of the goods and take possession of goods previously delivered (Section 2A–525);

(d) stop delivery of the goods by any bailee (Section 2A–526);

(e) dispose of the goods and recover damages (Section 2A–527), or retain the goods and recover damages (Section 2A–528), or in a proper case recover rent (Section 2A–529).

(f) exercise any other rights or pursue any other remedies provided in the lease contract.

(2) If a lessor does not fully exercise a right or obtain a remedy to which the lessor is entitled under subsection (1), the lessor may recover the loss resulting in the ordinary course of events from the lessee's default as determined in any reasonable manner, together with incidental damages, less expenses saved in consequence of the lessee's default.

(3) If a lessee is otherwise in default under a lease contract, the lessor may exercise the rights and pursue the remedies provided in the lease contract, which may include a right to cancel the lease. In addition, unless otherwise provided in the lease contract:

(a) if the default substantially impairs the value of the lease contract to the lessor, the lessor may exercise the rights and pursue the remedies provided in subsections (1) or (2); or

(b) if the default does not substantially impair the value of the lease contract to the lessor, the lessor may recover as provided in subsection (2).

As amended in 1990.

§ 2A–524. Lessor's Right to Identify Goods to Lease Contract

(1) After default by the lessee under the lease contract of the type described in Section 2A–523(1) or 2A–523(3)(a) or, if agreed, after other default by the lessee, the lessor may:

(a) identify to the lease contract conforming goods not already identified if at the time the lessor learned of the default they were in the lessor's or the supplier's possession or control; and

(b) dispose of goods (Section 2A–527(1)) that demonstrably have been intended for the particular lease contract even though those goods are unfinished.

(2) If the goods are unfinished, in the exercise of reasonable commercial judgment for the purposes of avoiding loss and of effective realization, an aggrieved lessor or the supplier may either complete manufacture and wholly identify the goods to the lease contract or cease manufacture and lease, sell, or otherwise dispose of the goods for scrap or salvage value or proceed in any other reasonable manner.

As amended in 1990.

§ 2A–525. Lessor's Right to Possession of Goods

(1) If a lessor discovers the lessee to be insolvent, the lessor may refuse to deliver the goods.

(2) After a default by the lessee under the lease contract of the type described in Section 2A–523(1) or 2A–523(3)(a) or, if agreed, after other default by the lessee, the lessor has the right to take possession of the goods. If the lease contract so provides, the lessor may require the lessee to assemble the goods and make them available to the lessor at a place to be designated by the lessor which is reasonably convenient to both parties. Without removal, the lessor may render unusable any goods employed in trade or business, and may dispose of goods on the lessee's premises (Section 2A–527).

(3) The lessor may proceed under subsection (2) without judicial process if it can be done without breach of the peace or the lessor may proceed by action.

As amended in 1990.

§ 2A–526. Lessor's Stoppage of Delivery in Transit or Otherwise

(1) A lessor may stop delivery of goods in the possession of a carrier or other bailee if the lessor discovers the lessee to be insolvent and may stop delivery of carload, truckload, planeload, or larger shipments of express or freight if the lessee repudiates or fails to make a payment due before delivery, whether for rent, security or otherwise under the lease contract, or for any other reason the lessor has a right to withhold or take possession of the goods.

(2) In pursing its remedies under subsection (1), the lessor may stop delivery until

(a) receipt of the goods by the lessee;

(b) acknowledgment to the lessee by any bailee of the goods, except a carrier, that the bailee holds the goods for the lessee; or

(c) such an acknowledgment to the lessee by a carrier via reshipment or as warehouseman.

(3)(a) To stop delivery, a lessor shall so notify as to enable the bailee by reasonable diligence to prevent delivery of the goods.

(b) After notification, the bailee shall hold and deliver the goods according to the directions of the lessor, but the lessor is liable to the bailee for any ensuing charges or damages.

(c) A carrier who has issued a nonnegotiable bill of lading is not obliged to obey a notification to stop received from a person other than the consignor.

§ 2A–527. Lessor's Rights to Dispose of Goods

(1) After a default by a lessee under the lease contract of the type described in Section 2A–523(1) or 2A–523(3)(a) or after the lessor refuses to deliver or take possession of goods (Section 2A–525 or 2A–526), or, if agreed, after other default by a lessee, the lessor may dispose of the goods concerned or the undelivered balance thereof by lease, sale, or otherwise.

(2) Except as otherwise provided with respect to damages liquidated in the lease agreement (Section 2A–504) or otherwise determined pursuant to agreement of the parties (Sections 1–102(3) and 2A–503), if the disposition is by lease agreement substantially similar to the original lease agreement and the new lease agreement is made in good faith and in a commercially reasonable manner, the lessor may recover from the lessee as damages (i) accrued and unpaid rent as of the date of the commencement of the term of the new lease agreement, (ii) the present value, as of the same date, of the total rent for the then remaining lease term of the original lease agreement minus the present value, as of the same date, of the rent under the new lease agreement applicable to that period of the new lease term which is comparable to the then remaining term of the original lease agreement, and (iii) any incidental damages allowed under Section 2A–530, less expenses saved in consequence of the lessee's default.

(3) If the lessor's disposition is by lease agreement that for any reason does not qualify for treatment under subsection (2), or is by sale or otherwise, the lessor may recover from the lessee as if the lessor had elected not to dispose of the goods and Section 2A–528 governs.

(4) A subsequent buyer or lessee who buys or leases from the lessor in good faith for value as a result of a disposition under this section takes the goods free of the original lease contract and any rights of the original lessee even though the lessor fails to comply with one or more of the requirements of this Article.

(5) The lessor is not accountable to the lessee for any profit made on any disposition. A lessee who has rightfully rejected or justifiably revoked acceptance shall account to the lessor for any excess over the amount of the lessee's security interest (Section 2A–508(5)).

As amended in 1990.

§ 2A–528. Lessor's Damages for Non-acceptance, Failure to Pay, Repudiation, or Other Default

(1) Except as otherwise provided with respect to damages liquidated in the lease agreement (Section 2A–504) or otherwise determined pursuant to agreement of the parties (Sections 1–102(3) and 2A–503), if a lessor elects to retain the goods or a lessor elects to dispose of the goods and the disposition is by lease agreement that for any reason does not qualify for treatment under Section 2A–527(2), or is by sale or otherwise, the lessor may recover from the lessee as damages for a default of the type described in Section 2A–523(1) or 2A–523(3)(a), or, if agreed, for other default of the lessee, (i) accrued and unpaid rent as of the date of the default if the lessee has never taken possession of the goods, or, if the lessee has taken possession of the goods, as of the date the lessor repossesses the goods or an earlier date on which the lessee makes a tender of the goods to the lessor, (ii) the present value as of the date determined under clause (i) of the total rent for the then remaining lease term of the original lease agreement minus the present value as

of the same date of the market rent at the place where the goods are located computed for the same lease term, and (iii) any incidental damages allowed under Section 2A–530, less expenses saved in consequence of the lessee's default.

(2) If the measure of damages provided in subsection (1) is inadequate to put a lessor in as good a position as performance would have, the measure of damages is the present value of the profit, including reasonable overhead, the lessor would have made from full performance by the lessee, together with any incidental damages allowed under Section 2A–530, due allowance for costs reasonably incurred and due credit for payments or proceeds of disposition.

As amended in 1990.

§ 2A–529. Lessor's Action for the Rent

(1) After default by the lessee under the lease contract of the type described in Section 2A–523(1) or 2A–523(3)(a) or, if agreed, after other default by the lessee, if the lessor complies with subsection (2), the lessor may recover from the lessee as damages:

(a) for goods accepted by the lessee and not repossessed by or tendered to the lessor, and for conforming goods lost or damaged within a commercially reasonable time after risk of loss passes to the lessee (Section 2A–219), (i) accrued and unpaid rent as of the date of entry of judgment in favor of the lessor, (ii) the present value as of the same date of the rent for the then remaining lease term of the lease agreement, and (iii) any incidental damages allowed under Section 2A–530, less expenses saved in consequence of the lessee's default; and

(b) for goods identified to the lease contract if the lessor is unable after reasonable effort to dispose of them at a reasonable price or the circumstances reasonably indicate that effort will be unavailing, (i) accrued and unpaid rent as of the date of entry of judgment in favor of the lessor, (ii) the present value as of the same date of the rent for the then remaining lease term of the lease agreement, and (iii) any incidental damages allowed under Section 2A–530, less expenses saved in consequence of the lessee's default.

(2) Except as provided in subsection (3), the lessor shall hold for the lessee for the remaining lease term of the lease agreement any goods that have been identified to the lease contract and are in the lessor's control.

(3) The lessor may dispose of goods at any time before collection of the judgment for damages obtained pursuant to subsection (1). If the disposition is before the end of the remaining lease term of the lease agreement, the lessor's recovery against the lessee for damages is governed by Section 2A–527 or Section 2A–528, and the lessor will cause an appropriate credit to be provided against a judgment for damages to the extent that the amount of the judgment exceeds the recovery available pursuant to Section 2A–527 or 2A–528.

(4) Payment of the judgment for damages obtained pursuant to subsection (1) entitles the lessee to the use and possession of the goods not then disposed of for the remaining lease term of and in accordance with the lease agreement.

(5) After default by the lessee under the lease contract of the type described in Section 2A–523(1) or Section 2A–523(3)(a) or, if agreed, after other default by the lessee, a lessor who is held not entitled to rent under this section must nevertheless be awarded damages for non-acceptance under Section 2A–527 or Section 2A–528.

As amended in 1990.

§ 2A–530. Lessor's Incidental Damages

Incidental damages to an aggrieved lessor include any commercially reasonable charges, expenses, or commissions incurred in stopping delivery, in the transportation, care and custody of goods after the lessee's default, in connection with return or disposition of the goods, or otherwise resulting from the default.

§ 2A–531. Standing to Sue Third Parties for Injury to Goods

(1) If a third party so deals with goods that have been identified to a lease contract as to cause actionable injury to a party to the lease contract (a) the lessor has a right of action against the third party, and (b) the lessee also has a right of action against the third party if the lessee:

(i) has a security in the goods;
(ii) has an insurable interest in the goods; or
(iii) bears the risk of loss under the lease contract or has since the injury assumed that risk as against the lessor and the goods have been converted or destroyed.

(2) If at the time of the injury the party plaintiff did not bear the risk of loss as against the other party to the lease contract and there is no arrangement between them for disposition of the recovery, his [or her] suit or settlement, subject to his [or her] own interest, is as a fiduciary for the other party to the lease contract.

(3) Either party with the consent of the other may sue for the benefit of whom it may concern.

§ 2A–532. Lessor's Rights to Residual Interest

In addition to any other recovery permitted by this Article or other law, the lessor may recover from the lessee an amount that will fully compensate the lessor for any loss of or damage to the lessor's residual interest in the goods caused by the default of the lessee.

As added in 1990.

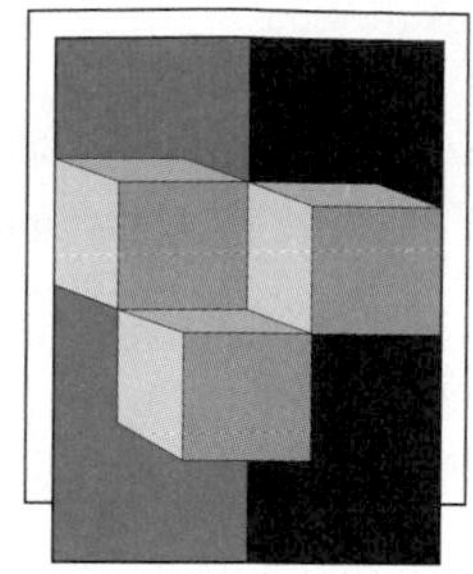

Glossary of Legal Terms

absolute privilege In libel and slander law, situations where a defendant is entirely excused from liability for defamatory statements because of the circumstances under which the statements were made.

acceptance The actual or implied receipt and retention of that which is tendered or offered.

accord and satisfaction A legally binding agreement to settle a disputed claim for a definite amount.

accredited investors Financially sophisticated and/or wealthy individuals and institutions who understand and can withstand the risk associated with securities investments.

act of state doctrine The view that a judge in the United States or another country does not have the authority to challenge the legality of acts by a foreign government within that foreign government's own borders.

actus reus Wrongful act or omission.

ad substantiation Under Federal Trade commission policy, product claims for which reasonable evidentiary support does not exist. Constitute unfair and deceptive trade practices.

ad valorem According to value. Hence, an ad valorem tax would be based upon the value of the item in question rather than, for example, a fixed rate for all such items.

adjudication The formal pronouncement of a judgement in a legal proceeding.

adjustment of debts (Chapter 13) Individuals with limited debts are protected from creditors while paying their debts in installments.

administrative agency An agency of the government charged with administering particular legislation.

administrative law That branch of public law addressing the operation of the government's various agencies and commissions. Also the rules and regulations established by those agencies and commissions.

administrative law judge An officer who presides at the initial hearing on matters litigated before an administrative agency. He or she is independent of the agency staff.

Administrative Procedure Act A federal statute specifying the procedural rules under which the government's agencies and commissions conduct their business.

adverse impact An employee may make a prima facie case for adverse impact where the employer's facially neutral rule may result in a different impact on one protected group than on another.

adverse possession Open and notorious possession of real property over a given length of time that denies ownership in any other claimant.

advisory jurisdiction Power of the ICJ to hear a dispute and to render an advisory opinion on the matter. The opinion is not binding on any party.

affidavit A written statement sworn to by a person officially empowered to administer an oath.

affirmative action A government/private sector program, springing from the civil rights movement, designed to *actively promote* the employment or educational opportunities of protected classes rather than merely forbidding discrimination.

affirmative defense A portion of a defendant's answer to a complaint in which the defendant presents contentions that, if proved true, will relieve the defendant of liability even if the assertions in the complaint are correct.

agent A person entrusted by a principal to act on behalf of that principal; one who is authorized to carry out the business of another.

agreement A meeting of the minds based upon an offer by one party and acceptance by another.

alternate dispute resolution The growing practice of employing strategies other than conventional litigation to solve conflicts. Those strategies include negotiation, arbitration, and mediation with variations like "minitrials" and "rent-a-judge" arrangements.

amicus curiae A "friend of the court" who, though not a party to the case, files a brief because of a strong interest in the litigation.

annual percentage rate (APR) The rate of interest charged for borrowing money as expressed in a standardized, yearly manner allowing for comparison among lenders' fees.

annual percentage yield (APY) The rate of interest paid on a deposit as expressed in a standardized, yearly manner allowing for comparison of returns among institutions.

answer The defendant's first pleading in a lawsuit, in which the defendant responds to the allegations raised in the plaintiff's complaint.

anticipatory breach A contracting party's indication before the time for performance that he cannot or will not perform the contract. Same as anticipatory repudiation.

appeal The judicial process by which a party petitions a higher court to review the decisions of a lower court agency in order to correct errors.

appellant The party filing an appeal.

appellee The party against whom an appeal is filed.

appraisal Assessment of the value of property by one with appropriate qualifications for the task.

appropriation Making commercial use of an individual's name or likeness without permission.

arbitrary trademark A trademark that is a new word or a common word that bears no relation to the product to which it is applied.

arbitration An extrajudicial process in which a dispute is submitted to a mutually agreeable third party for a decision.

arraignment A criminal law proceeding in which a defendant is brought before a judge to be informed of the charges and to file a plea.

assault A show of force that would cause the reasonable person to believe that they are about to receive an intentional unwanted harmful physical touching.

assignee A person to whom an assignment is made.

assignment A transfer of property, or some right or interest therein, from one person to another.

assignor The maker of an assignment.

assumption of risk An affirmative defense in a negligence case in which the defendant seeks to bar recovery by the plaintiff by showing that the plaintiff knowingly exposed himself or herself to the danger that resulted in injury.

attachment As to secured transactions, the process by which a security interest in the property of another becomes enforceable.

at-will employee An individual not under contract for a specified term and therefore, under the general rule, subject to discharge by the employer at any time and for any reason.

bait-and-switch advertising An unlawful sales tactic in which the seller attracts buyer interest by insincerely advertising a product at a dramatically reduced price while holding no genuine intent to sell the product at that price. The seller then disparages the "bait" and diverts the buyer's attention to a higher-priced product (the switch), which was the sales goal from the first.

barriers to entry Economic or technological conditions in a market making entry by a new competitor very difficult.

battery An intentional, unwanted, harmful physical touching.

beyond a reasonable doubt The level of proof required for conviction in a criminal case.

bilateral contract A contract formed by an offer requiring a reciprocal promise.

blacklists Lists of union organizers or participants in labor activities circulated to companies in order to dissuade the companies from hiring the listed individuals.

blue laws Laws forbidding certain kinds of business on Sundays.

blue sky laws Statutes regulating the sale of stocks and other securities to prevent consumer fraud.

bona fide In good faith; honestly.

bona fide occupational qualification (BFOQ) A defense in a discrimination claim where the employer argues that a particular religion, sex, or national origin is a necessary qualification for a particular job.

boycott A confederation or conspiracy involving a refusal to do business with another or an attempt by the confederation to stop others from doing business with the target person or organization.

breach of contract Failure, without legal excuse, to perform any promise that forms the whole or part of a contract.

breach of warranty Failure, without legal excuse, to fulfill the terms of the guarantee.

bribe Anything of value given or taken with the corrupt intent to influence an official in the performance of her or his duties.

brief A written document setting out for the court the facts, the law, and the argument of a party to the lawsuit.

burden of proof The party with the burden of proof (normally the plaintiff in a civil suit and the state in a criminal case) is required to prove the truth of a claim or lose on that issue.

business judgment rule A rule protecting business managers from liability for making bad decisions when they have acted prudently and in good faith.

bylaws A document that governs the maintenance and operation of a condominium building.

capacity The ability to incur legal obligations and acquire legal rights.

capitalism Private ownership of the means of production with a largely unrestricted marketplace in goods and services.

cause in fact The actual cause of an event. One of the required elements in a negligence claim.

cause of action Facts sufficient to support a valid civil lawsuit.

caveat emptor Let the buyer beware.

cease and desist order An instruction from an agency instructing a party to refrain from a specified goal.

certificate of incorporation An instrument from the State bestowing the right to do business under the corporate form of organization. Same as charter.

certiorari A legal procedure affording an appellate court the opportunity to review a lower court decision. Also a writ asking the lower court for the record of the case.

choice of law rule A rule of law in each jurisdiction that determines which jurisdiction's laws will be applied to a case. For instance, one state may have a choice of law rule that says that the law of the jurisdiction where the contract was signed shall govern any disputes; while another state may apply a different rule.

civil law The branch of law dealing with private rights. Contrast with criminal law.

class action A legal action brought by one on behalf of himself or herself and all others similarly situated.

Clean Air Act Amended in 1990, establishes air-quality standards and enforcement procedures for the standards.

Clean Water Act Establishes standards for water quality relating to the protection of water life as well as for safe recreation, and the enforcement of those standards.

closed-end loan Credit arrangement where a specified sum is borrowed and a repayment plan usually is established.

closing date The date on which a transfer of property is made.

Code of Federal Regulations A compilation of final federal agency rules.

codetermination German corporate governance and labor law system in which board representation by labor unions is required.

Colgate doctrine Sellers may lawfully engage in resale price maintenance if they do nothing more than specify prices at which their products are to be resold and unilaterally refuse to deal with anyone who does not adhere to those prices.

collateral Property pledged as security for satisfaction of a debt.

comity Courtesy. Nations often recognize the laws of other nations not because they must do so but because of the tradition of comity; that is, goodwill and mutual respect.

Commerce Clause That portion of the United States Constitution that provides for federal regulation of foreign and interstate trade.

commercial impracticability The standard used by the UCC to relieve a party of his or her contract obligations because of the occurrence of unforeseeable, external events beyond his or her control.

commercial speech Speech directed toward a business purpose. Advertising is an example of commercial speech. Such speech is protected by the First Amendment, but not to the degree that we protect other varieties of speech.

Commodity Futures Trading Commission (CFTC) Federal regulatory agency responsible for overseeing futures trading.

common law Judge-made law. To be distinguished from statutory law as created by legislative bodies.

common shares Most universal type of corporate stock.

community property Property acquired during marriage through the labor or skill of either spouse.

comparable worth The legal theory that all employees should be paid the same wages for work requiring comparable skills, effort, and responsibility and having comparable worth to the employer.

comparative negligence Defense in a negligence suit in which the plaintiff's recovery is reduced by an amount equivalent to her contribution to her own injury.

compensatory damages Damages that will compensate a party for actual losses due to an injury suffered.

complaint The first pleading filed by the plaintiff in a civil lawsuit.

concerted activity Organizing, forming, joining, or assisting labor organizations, bargaining collectively through representatives of the employees' choosing, or other activities taken for the purpose of collective bargaining or other mutual aid or protection.

concurrent conditions When each party's obligation to perform under a contract is dependent on the other party's performance.

condemning To appropriate land for public use.

conditions precedent Conditions that operate to give rise to a contracting party's duty to perform.

conditions subsequent Conditions that operate to discharge one from an obligation under a contract.

condominium or cooperative ownership An interest in property where owners retain individual control and specific ownership over a precise segment of real estate, but own common areas as tenants in common.

confession of judgment clause A clause stipulating that the lessee grants judgment in any action on the contract to the landlord without the formality of an ordinary proceeding.

conglomerate merger A merger between firms operating in separate markets and having neither buyer–seller nor competitive relationships with each other.

conscious parallelism Conduct by competitors that is very similar or identical but that is not the product of a conspiracy and thus is not, in and of itself, illegal.

consent decree A settlement of a lawsuit arrived at by agreement of the parties. Effectively, an admission by the parties that the decree is a just determination of their rights.

consent order The order administrative agencies issue when approving the settlement of an administrative action against some party.

consequential damages Damages that do not flow directly and immediately from an act but rather flow from the results of the act.

consideration A required element in an enforceable contract. The thing of value passing between the parties which results in a benefit to the one making the promise or a detriment to the one receiving the promise.

conspiracy An agreement between two or more persons to commit an unlawful act.

constructive eviction A breach of duty by the landlord that makes the property uninhabitable or otherwise deprives the tenant of the benefit of the lease and gives rise to the tenant's right to vacate the property and to terminate the lease.

consumer goods Under the UCC, goods used or bought primarily for personal, family, or household purposes.

contentious jurisdiction Power of the ICJ to hear a dispute and to render a binding opinion on the issue and the parties involved. All parties must give prior consent to contentious jurisdiction.

contingent fee An arrangement wherein an attorney is compensated for his or her services by receiving a percentage of the award in a lawsuit rather than receiving an hourly wage or specified fee.

contract An agreement that is legally enforceable by the courts.

contract bar rule The NLRB prohibits an election during the term of a collective bargaining agreement, for a maximum of three years.

contributory negligence A defense in a negligence action wherein the defendant attempts to demonstrate that the plaintiff contributed to the harm on which the litigation was based. Contrast with competitive negligence.

conversion Wrongfully exercising control over the personal property of another.

copyright The creator's (artist, author, etc.) right to control the copying and distribution of his or her work for a period of time specified by statute.

corporate opportunity A doctrine that prevents corporate officials from personally appropriating an opportunity that belongs to the corporation.

corporation A form of business organization that is owned by *shareholders* who have no inherent right to manage the business, and is managed by a board of directors elected by the shareholders.

Council on Environmental Quality Council serves as an advisor to the president in connection with the preparation of the annual Environmental Quality Report.

counterclaim A cause of action filed by the defendant in a lawsuit against the plaintiff in the same suit.

counteroffer Response by the offeree that, in its legal effect, constitutes a rejection of the original offer and proposes a new offer to the offeror.

countervailing duties Duties imposed by a government against the products of another government who has offered subsidies to its own producers.

covered disabilities A physical or mental impairment that substantially limits one or more major life activities of an individual; a record of such impairment or being regarded as having such impairment.

creditor A person to whom a debt is owed.

creditor beneficiary Person who has given consideration, who is an intended beneficiary of a contract though not a party, and thus is entitled to enforce the contract.

crime A public wrong, an act punishable by the state.

criminal law Wrongs against society that the state has seen fit to label crimes and that may result in penalties against the perpetrator(s). Contrast with civil law.

cumulative voting A procedure for voting for directors that permits a shareholder to multiply the number of shares he or she owns by the number of directors to be elected and to cast the resulting total of votes for one or more directors.

curtesy interest The right of a husband upon the death of his wife to receive all of the wife's real property as long as the two had a child between them.

d.b.a. Doing business as.

de facto In fact. Actually. As *de facto* school segregation, which is caused by social and economic conditions rather than by government act.

de jure Legitimate. Lawful. Of right. As *de jure* school segregation, which is caused by government order and thus is legally correct even if morally wrong.

debenture Any long-term debt instrument, such as a bond, issued by a company or institution, secured only by the general assets of the issuer.

deceit A tort involving intentional misrepresentation to deceive or trick another.

deception Trade claim which is either false or likely to mislead the reasonable consumer and which is material to the consumer's decision making.

deceptive advertising Advertising practices likely to mislead the reasonable consumer where the practice in question is material in that it affected consumer choice.

declaration A document that defines the rights, responsibilities, and powers of property owners in a condominium.

declaratory judgment or order A judicial or agency action expressing an opinion or articulating the rights of the parties without actually requiring that anything be done.

deed An instrument transferring title to property.

deed of trust A three-party instrument used to create a security interest in real property in which the legal title to the real property is placed in one or more trustees to secure the repayment of a sum of money or the performance of other conditions.

defamation A false and intentional verbal or written expression that damages the reputation of another.

default A party fails to pay money when due or when lawfully demanded.

defeasible fee simple A title to property that is open to attack, that might be defeated by the performance of some act, or that is subject to conditions.

defendant The party in a civil suit against whom the cause of action was brought and, in a criminal case, the party against whom charges have been filed.

delegatee The one to whom a duty is delegated.

delegator The one who delegates a duty.

deposition A discovery procedure wherein a witness's sworn testimony is taken out of court, prior to trial, for subsequent use at trial.

deregulation Returning authority to the free market by shrinking government bureaucracies and reducing government rules.

derivative suit A lawsuit by a stockholder on behalf of the corporation where the corporation declines to act to protect the organization's rights against the conduct of an officer, director, or outsider.

derivatives Specialized trading contracts tied to underlying assets such as bonds or currencies.

descriptive mark A trademark that is merely descriptive of the product or its qualities.

dicta Statements in a judicial opinion that are merely the views of the judge(s) and are not necessary for the resolution of the case.

directed verdict Party to a lawsuit makes a motion asking the judge to instruct the injury to reach a particular decision because reasonable minds could not differ about the correct outcome of the case.

discharged Released from liability.

disclaimer As to warranties, a contract term wherein a party attempts to relieve itself of potential liability under that contract.

discovery Legal procedures by which one party to a litigation may obtain information from the other party. Depositions and interrogatories are examples of discovery procedures.

disparate impact Employment discrimination theory in which a facially neutral employment practice (such as requiring a high school diploma for new hires) results in an unfair and adverse impact on a protected class.

disparate treatment Theory of employment discrimination wherein an individual or group is intentionally disfavored via actual discriminatory policies and practices.

dissolution In partnership law, the change in the relation of the partners caused by any partner ceasing to be associated with the carrying on of the business.

diversity of citizenship One standard by which federal courts may gain jurisdiction over a lawsuit. Plaintiffs and defendants must be from different states and more than $50,000 must be at issue.

divestiture In antitrust law, a remedy wherein the court orders a defendant to dispose of specified assets.

dividend A shareholder's earnings from his or her stock in a corporation.

doctrine of sovereign immunity Principle that a foreign nation may not be sued in American courts, with certain exceptions.

dominant estate The property accessed through an easement appurtenant or implied easement.

donee beneficiary Person who has not given consideration, but is an intended beneficiary of a contract, though not a party, and is entitled to enforce the contract.

double jeopardy The United States Constitution provides that the same individual may not be tried twice in the same tribunal for the same criminal offense.

dower interest The right of a wife upon the death of her husband to receive a life estate in one-third of her husband's real property.

dramshop law State laws imposing liability on the seller of intoxicating liquors when a third party is injured as a result of the intoxication of the buyer where the sale has caused or contributed to that intoxication.

due care and diligence Corporate officers and directors must act in good faith and in a prudent manner.

due diligence A defense against a securities violation claim where the defendant used ordinary prudence and still failed to find an error or omission in the registration statement.

due process A constitutional principle requiring fairness in judicial proceedings and that government laws and conduct be free of arbitrariness and capriciousness.

dumping The commercial practice of selling goods in a foreign market at a price substantially beneath that charged in the domestic market.

duress Overpowering of the will of a person by force or fear.

duty of due care Standard of conduct expected of a reasonable, prudent person under the circumstances.

easement The right to use property without taking anything away from the property.

easement or profit appurtenant The right of an owner of adjacent land to enter or to enter and take away from property next to it.

economies of scale Expansion of a firm or industry's productive category resulting in a decline in long-run average costs of production.

efficiencies A defense to an otherwise unlawful merger in which costs of production are reduced because of the merger.

election year or certification year bar NLRB prohibits an election for 12 months following a prior election.

elective share Legislative mandate that a spouse receive a specific percentage interest in a deceased spouse's estate.

embargo Government order prohibiting importation of some or all products from a particular country.

embezzlement The fraudulent and unauthorized taking of the money of another while charged with the care of that money.

Emergency Planning and Community Right-To-Know Act of 1986 Amended Superfund requiring companies to inform the government upon release of any hazardous chemicals into the environment, and to provide to the government an inventory of their hazardous chemicals. The Act also requires states to establish emergency procedures for chemical discharges.

eminent domain The state's power to take private property for public use.

employer identification number Number issued to employer by federal and state governments for the purpose of record keeping associated with income and social security tax collections.

en banc All of the judges hearing a case as a group rather than individually or in panels.

enabling legislation Law that establishes an administrative agency and grants power to that agency.

enjoin To require. A court issues an injunction requiring a certain act or ordering a party to refrain from a certain act.

enterprise law Legal doctrine treating all companies in a corporate group as one giant organization rather than a collection of smaller, independent units.

entity law Legal doctrine treating each company in a corporate group as a separate, independent unit.

environmental impact statement Statement of the anticipated impact on the environment of legislation or other major federal action, and suggestions for reasonable alternatives.

Environmental Protection Agency Created in 1970 to gather information relating to pollution and to assist in pollution control efforts and sanctions.

equal protection The Fourteenth Amendment to the United States Constitution provides that all similarly situated individuals are entitled to the same advantages and must bear the same burdens under the law.

equitable remedies Injunction, specific performance, restraining orders, and the like, as opposed to money damages.

equity Fairness; a system of courts that developed in England. A chancellor presided to mete out fairness in cases that were not traditionally assigned to the law courts headed by the king.

essential functions of a position Those tasks that are fundamental, as opposed to marginal or unnecessary, to the fulfillment of the position's objectives.

establishment clause The First Amendment to the United States Constitution forbids the United States government from creating a government-supported church or religion.

estate An interest in land or property owned by a decedent at the time of her or his death.

estate per *autre vie* A life estate that is measured by the life of someone other than the possessor.

estoppel A legal doctrine providing that one may not assert facts that are in conflict with one's own previous acts or deeds.

eviction Depriving the tenant of the possession of the leased premises.

excise taxes Taxes imposed at both the state and federal levels on the sale of particular commodities, especially, alcohol, tobacco, and gasoline.

exclusive dealing Agreement to deal only with a particular buyer or a particular seller.

exculpatory clause Portion of a contract that seeks to relieve one of the parties to the contract from any liability for breach of duty under that contract.

executed In contract law, full performance of the terms of the bargain.

executed contract Performances are complete.

executory contract Not yet fully performed, completed.

exemplary damages Same as punitive damages.

exempt property Specified classes of property which are unavailable to the creditor upon default of the debtor.

exempt security Certain kinds of securities and certain transactions involving securities are not required to meet federal registration requirements under the 1933 Act.

existentialism A philosophy emphasizing the individual's responsibility to make herself what she is to become. Existence precedes essence.

express authority Corporate officers' powers as expressed in the bylaws or conferred by the board of directors.

express authorization In contract law, offeror specifies a means of communication by which the offeree can accept.

express conditions Conditions within contracts that are clear from the language.

express contract Contract whose terms are clear from the language.

express warranty A guarantee made by affirmation of fact or promise, by description of the goods, or by sample or model.

expropriation A government's taking of a business's assets, such as a manufacturing facility, usually without just compensation.

extraterritoriality The application of United States laws on persons, rights, or relations beyond the geographic limits of this country and even though the parties involved are not American citizens.

failing company doctrine A defense to an otherwise unlawful merger in which the acquired firm is going out of business and no other purchaser is available.

fair use A doctrine that permits the use of copyrighted works for purposes such as criticism, news reporting, training, or research.

false imprisonment Tort of intentionally restricting the freedom of movement of another.

false light Falsely and publicly attributing certain characteristics, conduct, or beliefs to another such that a reasonable person would be highly offended.

featherbedding A labor law term describing the practice where workers were paid even though they did not perform any work. Featherbedding is a violation of federal labor law.

federal question Litigation involving the federal constitution, statutes, and treaties. The federal courts have jurisdiction over cases involving federal questions.

Federal Register Daily publication of federal agency regulations and other legal materials coming from the executive branch of government.

Federal Sentencing Guidelines Standards established by the U.S. Sentencing Commission that rank the seriousness of individual and organizational federal crimes and provide sentences that, with little flexibility, must be applied to those crimes.

Federal Trade Commission Agency of the federal government responsible for promoting fair trade practices in interstate commerce.

federalism The division of authority between the federal government and the states to maintain workable cooperation while diffusing political power.

fee simple A form of land ownership that gives the owner the right to possess and to use the land for an unlimited period of time, subject only to governmental or private restrictions, and unconditional power to dispose of the property during his or her lifetime or upon death.

felony A crime of a serious nature ordinarily involving punishment by death or imprisonment in a penitentiary.

fiduciary One who holds a relationship of trust with another and has an obligation to act in the best interests of the other; as one who manages property on behalf of another.

fiduciary duty The responsibility of one in a position of trust with another to act in the best interests of the other.

financing statement Document notifying others that the creditor claims an interest in the debtor's collateral. Must be filed as provided for by law in order to perfect a security interest.

firm offer Under the Uniform Commercial Code, a signed, written offer by a merchant containing assurances that it will be held open, and which is not revocable for the time stated in the offer, or for a reasonable time if no such time is stated.

fixture A thing that was originally personal property and that has actually or constructively affixed to the soil itself or to some structure legally a part of the land.

foreclose To terminate the mortgagor's rights in the property covered by the mortgage.

franchise A marketing arrangement in which the franchisor permits the franchisee to produce, distribute, or sell the franchisor's product using the franchisor's name or trademark.

franchisee A holder of a franchise.

franchisor A party granting a franchise.

fraud An intentional misrepresentation of a material fact with intent to deceive where the misrepresentation is justifiably relied on by another and damages result.

fraud-on-the-market theory Misleading statements distort the market and thus defraud a securities buyer whether the buyer actually relies on the misstatement or not. Based on the assumption that the price of a stock reflects all of the available information about that stock.

Free Exercise Clause First Amendment provision guaranteeing all Americans the right to pursue their religious beliefs free of government intervention (with limited exceptions).

free riders Those who lawfully benefit from goods or services without paying a share of the cost of those goods or services.

Full Faith and Credit Clause Provision of the United States Constitution requiring each state to recognize the laws and judicial decisions of all other states.

futures Contracts to deliver or take delivery of specified quantities of commodities at a previously specified price.

G7 An association embracing seven of the world's leading industrial powers (Canada, France, Italy, Germany, Japan, the United Kingdom, and the United States) designed to improve worldwide economic and political conditions.

garnishment Action by a creditor to secure the property of a debtor where that property is held by a third party.

General Agreement on Tariffs and Trade Establishes and regulates import duties among signatory countries.

general duty An OSHA provision requiring that employers furnish to each employee a place of employment free from recognized hazards that cause or are likely to cause death or serious physical harm to the employee.

general warranty deed A deed that carries with it certain warranties or guarantees.

generic mark A trademark employing a common descriptive name for a product.

genuineness of assent In contract law, the parties knowingly agreed to the same thing.

going public Selling shares in a company on the open market.

good faith Honesty; an absence of intent to take advantage of another.

goods All things that are movable at the time of identification to the contract for sale except the money in which the price is to be paid, investment securities, and so forth.

grand jury A body of people convened by the state to determine whether the evidence is sufficient to bring a criminal indictment (formal accusation) against a party.

grant deed A deed that does not have the warranties contained in a warranty deed.

gray market Transactions conducted outside the usual supplier-approved channels of distribution. These transactions (unlike *black market* sales) are lawful but are often discouraged by suppliers. The gray market operates parallel to the "officially" authorized chain of distribution.

grease Payments to low-ranking authorities for the purpose of facilitating business in another nation. Not forbidden by the Foreign Corrupt Practices Act if legal in the host nation.

greenmail Takeover defense involving the target corporation's repurchase of a takeover raider's stock at a premium not offered to other shareholders.

group boycott An agreement among traders to refuse to deal with one or more other traders.

guarantor A person who promises to perform the same obligation as the principal if the principal should default.

Herfindahl-Hirschman Index (HHI) Calculation used by the Justice Department to determine the degree of economic concentration in a particular market and to determine the degree to which a proposed horizontal merger would further concentrate that market. Computed by squaring the market share of each firm in a market and summing those totals.

holdover lease The tenancy that exists where a tenant subject to a term lease is allowed to remain on the premises after the term has expired.

horizontal divisions of the market Competitors agree to share their market geographically or to allocate customers or products among themselves.

horizontal merger Acquisition by one company of another company competing in the same product and geographic markets.

hostile takeover The acquisition of a formerly independent business where the acquired business resists the union.

Immigration Reform and Control Act (IRCA) Enacted by Congress, IRCA's purpose is to eliminate work opportunities that attract illegal aliens to the United States.

implied authority Corporate officers' powers to take actions that are reasonably necessary to achieve their express duties.

implied authorization In contract law, where the offeror's behavior or previous dealings with the offeree suggest an agreeable means of communicating an acceptance.

implied easement Also called easement by prescription or way of necessity. An interest created where someone has openly used an adjoining piece of property for access with no complaint from the owner for a statutorily determined period of time.

implied warranty of fitness for a particular purpose A warranty that arises by operation of law and promises that the good warranted is reasonably useful for the buyer's purpose where the buyer was relying on the seller's expertise in making the purchase.

implied warranty of habitability Implied warranty arising in lease or sale of residential real estate that the property will be fit for human habitability.

implied warranty of merchantability A warranty that arises by operation of law and promises that the good warranted is at least of average, fair, reasonable quality.

implied-in-fact conditions Conditions derived from the parties' conduct and the circumstances of the bargain.

implied-in-law conditions or constructive conditions Conditions imposed by the court to avoid unfairness.

implied-in-fact contract Contract whose terms are implicitly understood based on the behavior of the parties.

in personam jurisdiction The power of the court over a person.

incidental beneficiary Person who is not a party to a contract, who benefits indirectly from the contract, who was not contemplated by the parties, and who may not enforce the contract.

incidental damages Collateral damages that are incurred because of a breach; damages that compensate a person injured by a breach of contract for reasonable costs incurred in an attempt to avoid further loss.

incorporators Those who initiate a new corporation.

indemnification Corporate policy to compensate officers and directors for losses sustained in defending themselves against litigation associated with their professional duties where those duties were performed with reasonable business judgment.

indemnify Reimburse one who has suffered a loss.

indenture Agreement governing the conditions under which bonds are issued.

indenture trustee Person or institution holding legal title to trust property and charged with carrying out the terms of the indenture.

independent contractor A person who contracts with a principal to perform some task according to his or her own methods, and who is not under the principal's control regarding the physical details of the work.

indictment A grand jury's formal accusation of a crime.

Industry Guides Published advice to industry and the public providing Federal Trade Commission interpretations of the likely legality of specific marketing practices.

information A prosecutor's formal accusation of a crime.

initial public offering (IPO) A security offered for sale to the public for the first time.

injunction A court order commanding a person or organization to do or not do a specified action.

injurious falsehood Intentional tort based on a false statement made with malice that disparages the property of another.

innocent misrepresentation An unintentional misrepresentation of material fact where the misrepresentation is justifiably relied on by another and damages result.

insider In securities law, anyone who has knowledge of facts not available to the general public.

insider trading Trading securities while in possession of material nonpublic information, in violation of a fiduciary duty.

intellectual property Intangible personal property.

intent A conscious and purposeful state of mind.

intentional infliction of emotional distress Intentional tort based on outrageous conduct that causes severe emotional distress in another.

intentional tort Voluntary civil wrong causing harm to a protected interest.

interference with contractual relations Improperly causing a third party to breach or fail to perform its contract with another.

interference with prospective advantage Improperly causing a third party not to enter a prospective contractual relationship.

interpretive rules In administrative law, an agency's formally enacted rules that have the effect of law.

interrogatories An ingredient in the discovery process wherein one party in a lawsuit directs written questions to another party in the lawsuit.

intrastate offerings Registration exemption for securities sold only to residents of the state in which the issuer is organized and doing business.

intrusion Wrongfully entering upon or prying into the solitude or property of another.

invasion of privacy Violation of the right to be left alone.

invitee One who comes on the premises of another by invitation of the owner, in connection with the owner's business, and for the benefit of the owner or for the mutual benefit of the invitee and the owner.

joint and several liability Liability of a group of persons in which the plaintiff may sue all members of the group collectively or one or more individuals for the entire amount.

joint liability Liability of a group of persons in which, if one of these persons is sued, he can insist that the other liable parties be joined to the suit as codefendants, so that all must be sued collectively.

joint tenancy An estate held by two or more jointly with an equal right in all to share in the enjoyment of the land during their lives.

joint venture A form of business organization essentially identical to a partnership, except that it is engaged in a single project, not carrying on a business.

judgment notwithstanding the verdict (judgment n.o.v.) A judge's decision overruling the finding of the jury.

judgment proof Describes those against whom money judgments will have no effect because they are insolvent or their assets are beyond the reach of the court.

judicial review A court's authority to review statutes and, if appropriate, declare them unconstitutional. Also refers to appeals from administrative agencies.

jurisdiction The power of a judicial body to adjudicate a dispute. Also the geographical area within which that judicial body has authority to operate.

jurisprudence The philosophy and science of law.

jury instructions A judge's directions to the jury explaining the law that must be applied in the case at hand.

keiretsu Japanese cartels of vertically related firms working together in a collaborative fashion.

land contract Typically, an installment contract for the sale of land wherein the purchaser receives the deed from the owner on payment of the final installment.

landlord/lessor A party to a lease contract who allows a tenant to possess and to use his or her property in return for rent payments.

latent defects Imperfections that are not readily apparent upon reasonable inspection.

lease A contract for the possession and use of land or other property, including goods, on one side, and a recompense of rent or other income on the other.

leasehold estate A right to occupy and to use land pursuant to a lease or contract.

legal detriment Any act or forbearance by a promisee.

legal impossibility A party to a contract is relieved of his or her duty to perform when that performance has become objectively impossible because of the occurrence of an event unforeseen at the time of contracting.

legality of purpose The object of the contract does not violate law or public policy.

legitimate nondiscriminatory reason (LNDR) An employer's justification for taking adverse action against an employee or applicant where the basis for the action is something other than the individual's membership in a protected class (such as termination for dishonesty or theft).

lemon laws State statutes providing remedies for those buying vehicles which turn out to be so thoroughly defective that they cannot be repaired after reasonable efforts.

letter of credit A statement from a financial institution such as a bank guaranteeing that it will pay the financial obligations of a particular party.

libel Tort of defaming or injuring another's reputation by a published writing.

license A contractual right to use property in a certain manner.

licensee A person lawfully on land in possession of another for purposes unconnected with business interests of the possessor.

licenses Government-granted privileges to do some act or series of acts. Authorization to do what, without a license, would be unlawful. Same as *permits.*

lien A claim against a piece of property in satisfaction of a debt. The financial interest of the lienholder in the property as a result of a debt or other obligation of the landowner.

life estate A property interest that gives a person the right to possess and to use property for a time that is measured by her or his lifetime or that of another person.

life tenant The possessor of a life estate interest.

limited liability Maximum loss normally limited to the amount invested in the firm.

limited liability company (LLC) Hybrid of limited partnership and corporation receiving partnership tax treatment with the operating advantages of a corporation.

limited liability partnership A special partnership form providing some of the advantages of limited liability.

limited partnership A form of business organization that has one or more general partners who manage the business and have unlimited liability for the obligations of the business and one or more limited partners who do not manage and have limited liability.

liquidated damages Damages made certain by the prior agreement of the parties.

liquidation (Chapter 7) "Straight" bankruptcy action in which all assets except exemptions are distributed to creditors.

lockout defense Takeover defense where the target company manipulates its assets, shares, etc. in order to make the company unattractive as a takeover candidate.

lockouts Where employees are kept from the workplace by the employer. Where the landlord deprives the tenant of the possession of the premises by changing the locks on the property.

long-arm statute A state enactment that accords the courts of that state the authority to claim jurisdiction over people and property beyond the borders of the state so long as certain "minimum contacts" exist between the state and the people or property.

mail box rule Rule holding that a mailed acceptance is effective upon dispatch when the offeror has used the mail to invite acceptance; the rule has been expanded to include the use of any reasonable manner of acceptance.

malice A required element of proof in a libel or slander claim by a public figure. Proof of a defamatory statement expressed with actual knowledge of its falsity or with reckless disregard for the truth would establish malice.

malicious prosecution Criminal prosecution carried on with malice and without probable cause with damages resulting.

malpractice Improper or negligent conduct in the performance of duties by a professional such as a doctor or lawyer.

market failure Economic theory arguing that the free market works imperfectly because of certain allegedly inherent defects such as monopoly, public goods, and so forth.

market foreclosure In vertical mergers, the concern that the newly- combined firm will close its doors to potential suppliers and purchasers such that competition will be harmed.

market share liability Product liability action by which plaintiffs may be able to recover against manufacturers of defective products based on those manufacturers' market shares even though proof of causation cannot be established.

material breach In contract law, performance that falls beneath substantial performance and does not have a lawful excuse.

mechanic's lien or materialman's lien A claim created by law for the purpose of securing a priority of payment of the price or value of work performed and materials furnished in erecting or repairing a structure.

mediation An extrajudicial proceeding in which a third party (the mediator) attempts to assist disputing parties to reach an agreeable, voluntary resolution of their differences.

mens rea Evil intent.

merger The union of two or more business organizations wherein all of the assets, rights, and liabilities of one are blended into the other with only one firm remaining.

misappropriation In securities law, taking material, nonpublic information and engaging in insider trading in violation of a fiduciary duty.

misdemeanor A criminal offense less serious than a felony normally requiring a fine or less than a year in a jail other than a penitentiary.

misrepresentation The innocent assertion of a fact that is not in accord with the truth.

mitigation Obligation of a person who has been injured by a breach of a contract to attempt to reduce the damages.

Model Business Corporation Act (MBCA) Drafted by legal experts, the MBCA is designed to improve corporate law and to serve as a model for state legislatures in drafting their corporate laws.

mommy track An employment track, whether formally or informally instituted, in some firms that allows for slower upward mobility for mothers who must divide their attention between their positions and their families.

monopoly Market power permitting the holder to fix prices or exclude competition.

moot An issue no longer requiring attention or resolution because it has ceased to be in dispute.

mortgage An interest in land formalized by a written instrument providing security for the payment of a debt.

mortgagee One who receives a mortgage to secure repayment of a debt.

mortgagor One who pledges property for a particular purpose such as security for a debt.

most favored nation status (MFN) Preferential status offered to certain countries under the GATT which allows the MFN country to obtain the lowest applicable tariff on goods.

motion A request to a court seeking an order or action in favor of the party entering the motion.

motion for a directed verdict A request by a party to a lawsuit arguing that the other party has failed to prove facts sufficient to establish a claim and that the judge must, therefore, enter a verdict in favor of the moving party.

multinational enterprise A company that conducts business in more than one country.

mutual mistake Where both parties to the contract are in error about a material fact.

National Environmental Policy Act Requires that the government "use all practicable means" to conduct federal affairs in harmony with the environment.

National Pollutant Discharge Elimination System Requires that all who discharge pollutants obtain an EPA permit before adding pollutants to a navigable stream.

National Priorities List A list of hazardous dump or spill sites scheduled to be cleaned using CERCLA funds.

national treatment Concept that requires that, once goods have been imported into a country, they must be treated as if they were domestic goods. (i.e., no tariff may be imposed other than that at the border).

nationalization A country taking over a private business often without adequate compensation to the ex-owners.

necessaries That which is reasonably necessary for a minor's proper and suitable maintenance.

negative externality A spillover in which all the costs of a good or service are not fully absorbed by the producer and thus fall on others.

negligence Failure to do something that a reasonable person would do under the circumstances, or an action that a reasonable and prudent person would not take under the circumstances.

negligence per se Action violating a public duty, particularly where that duty is specified by statute.

negligent tort Unintentional, civil wrong causing harm to a protected interest. Injury to another resulting from carelessness.

nolo contendere A no-contest plea in a criminal case in which the defendant does not admit guilt but does submit to such punishment as the court may accord.

nominal damages Small damages, oftentimes $1, awarded to show that there was a legal wrong even though the damages were very slight or nonexistent.

noncompetition clause Employee agrees not to go into business in competition with employer.

nonpossessory interest An interest in real property that is not sufficient to be an ownership or possessory interest.

nonprice restraints Resale limitations imposed by manufacturers on distributors or retailers in any of several forms (such as territorial or customer restraints) that do not directly affect price.

nonreversionary interest The interest held by the remainderman. It is called nonreversionary because it does not revert to the original grantor.

nonvoting stock Owners of nonvoting stock participate in firm profits and dividends but may not vote at shareholder meetings.

novation A mutual agreement between all parties concerned for the discharge of a valid existing obligation by the substitution of a new valid obligation on the part of the debtor or another, or a like agreement for the discharge of a lessee to a landlord by the substitution of a new lessee.

nuisance A class of wrongs that arises from the unreasonable, unwarrantable, or unlawful use by a person of his or her property that produces material annoyance, inconvenience, discomfort, or hurt.

obligor A person who is bound by a promise or other obligation; a promisor.

offer A proposal by one person to another that is intended to create legal relations on acceptance by the person to whom it is made.

oligopoly An economic condition in which the market for a particular good or service is controlled by a small number of producers or distributors.

open-end loan Credit arrangement not involving a lump sum but permitting repeated borrowing where payment amounts are not specified.

option contract A separate contract in which an offeror agrees not to revoke her or his offer for a stated period of time in exchange for some valuable consideration.

ordinance A law, rule, or regulation enacted by a local unit of government (e.g., a town or city).

output restriction An agreement to limit production which is a per se violation of the Sherman Act and may have the effect of artificially stabilizing or raising prices.

over-the-counter securities Those stocks, bonds, and like instruments sold directly from broker to customer rather than passing through a stock exchange.

parole evidence When the written document is intended as the parties' final expression of their contract, parole evidence of prior agreements or representations cannot be used to vary the terms of the document.

partial ownership interest An interest that may revert back to the original grantor.

partition A legal proceeding that enables joint tenants or tenants in common to put an end to the tenancy and to vest in each tenant a sole estate in specific property or an allotment of the lands and buildings. If division is impossible, the estate may have to be sold and the proceeds divided.

partnership An association of two or more persons where they agree to work together in a business designed to earn a profit.

past consideration Performance that is not bargained for and was not given in exchange for the promise.

patent A right conferred by the federal government allowing the holder to restrict the manufacture, distribution, and sale of the holder's invention or discovery.

patent defects Imperfections that are visible and obvious.

per curiam By the court. Refers to legal opinions offered by the court as a whole rather than those instances where an individual judge authors the opinion.

per se By itself; inherently.

per se doctrine Certain antitrust violations are considered so harmful to competition that they are always unlawful and no proof of actual harm is required.

peremptory challenge At trial, an attorney's authority to dismiss prospective members of the jury without offering any justification for that dismissal.

perfection Process by which a secured party obtains a priority claim over other possible claimants to certain collateral belonging to a debtor.

periodic tenancy The tenancy that exists when the landlord and tenant agree that the rent will be paid in regular successive intervals until notice to terminate is given but do not agree on a specific duration of the lease.

personal property Movable property. All property other than real estate.

piercing the corporate veil Holding a shareholder responsible for acts of a corporation due to a shareholder's domination and improper use of the corporation.

plaintiff One who initiates a lawsuit.

pleadings The formal entry of written statements by which the parties to a lawsuit set out their contentions and thereby formulate the issues on which the litigation will be based.

police power The government's inherent authority to enact rules to provide for the health, safety, and general welfare of the citizenry.

political action committee A legally defined lobbying group that uses funds and activities to support certain political views.

possibility of reverter An interest that is uncertain or may arise only upon the occurrence of a condition.

precedent A decision in a previously decided lawsuit that may be looked to as an authoritative statement for resolving current lawsuits involving similar questions of law.

predatory pricing Selling of goods below cost for the purpose of harming competition.

preemption doctrine Constitutional doctrine providing that the federal government "preempts the field" where it passes laws in an area thus denying the states the right to pass conflicting laws or, in some cases, denying the states the right to pass any laws in that area.

preemptive right A shareholder's option to purchase new issuances of shares in proportion to the shareholder's current ownership of the corporation.

preexisting duty Prior legal obligation or commitment, performance of which does not constitute consideration for a new agreement.

preferred shares Shares having dividend and liquidation preferences over other classes of shares.

pretext After an employee has established a prima facie case of discrimination and the employer has articulated a BFOQ or LNDR, the employee must show that the proffered defense is pretextual, that is, that the BFOQ is not actually bona fide (or not applied in all situations) or that the LNDR has been applied differently to this individual compared to another.

price discrimination Selling goods of like grade and quality to different buyers at different prices without justification where competitive harm results.

price-fixing An agreement among competitors to charge a specified price for a particular product or service. Also any agreement that prevents a seller from independently setting a price or from independently establishing the quantity to be produced.

prima facie case A litigating party may be presumed to have built a prima facie case when the evidence is such that it is legally sufficient unless contradicted or overcome by other evidence.

principal In agency law, one under whose direction an agent acts and for whose benefit that agent acts.

private law Individually determined agreement of the parties relating to choice of laws, where disagreements shall be settled, and the language of the transactions.

private placements Securities sold without a public offering thus excusing them from SEC registration requirements.

privatization The many strategies for shifting public-sector activities back to private enterprise. Those strategies include contracting out government work to private parties, raising the user fees charged for public services, selling state-owned property and enterprises, and returning government services such as garbage collection to the private sector.

privity of contract The legal connection that arises when two or more parties enter a contract.

procedural due process Constitutional principle requiring that the government assure fundamental fairness to all in the execution of our system of laws.

procedural rules In administrative law, an agency's internal operating structure and methods.

product liability Refers to legal responsibility of manufacturers and sellers to compensate buyers, users, and, in some cases, bystanders for harm from defective products.

profit à prendre The right to enter property and to take something away from it, such as crops.

promisee The person to whom a promise is made.

promisor A person who makes a promise to another.

promissory estoppel An equitable doctrine that protects those who foreseeably and reasonably rely on the promises of others by enforcing such promises when enforcement is necessary to avoid injustice.

promoter A person who incorporates a business, organizes its initial management, and raises its initial capital.

prospectus A communication, usually in the form of a pamphlet, offering a security for sale and summarizing the information needed for a prospective buyer to evaluate the security.

proximate cause Occurrences that in a natural sequence, unbroken by potent intervening forces, produce an injury that would not have resulted in the absence of those occurrences.

proxy Written permission from a shareholder to others to vote his or her share at a stockholders' meeting.

public disclosure of private facts Public disclosure of private facts where disclosure of the matter in question would be highly offensive to a reasonable person.

public goods Goods or services usually provided by government when underproduced by markets.

public law Rules of national law that regulate transactions between parties, as well as the relationships between nations.

public policy That which is good for the general public, as gleaned from a state's constitution, statutes, and case law.

puffing An expression of opinion by a seller not made as a representation of fact.

punitive damages Damages designed to punish flagrant wrongdoers and to deter them and others from engaging in similar conduct in the future.

purchase money security interest A security interest that is (1) taken or retained by the seller of collateral to secure all or part of its purchase price or (2) taken by a debtor to acquire rights in or the use of the collateral if the value is so used.

qualified person with a disability An individual with a covered disability who can perform the essential functions of her or his position, with or without reasonable accommodation.

qualified privilege In libel and slander law, situations where a defendant is excused from liability for defamatory statements except where the statements were motivated by malice.

quantum meruit As much as he deserves. Describes a plea for recovery under a contract implied by law. Fair payment for work performed.

quasi-contract The doctrine by which courts imply, as a matter of law, a promise to pay the reasonable value of goods or services when the party receiving such goods or services has knowingly done so under circumstances that make it unfair to retain them without paying for them.

quid pro quo Exchanging one thing of value for another. In sexual harassment law, quid pro quo cases are those where employment benefits are conditioned on the subordinate's submission to sexual advances.

quitclaim deed A deed conveying only the right, title, and interest of the grantor in the property described, as distinguished from a deed conveying the property itself.

ratified The adoption or affirmance by a person of a prior act that did not previously bind her or him.

ratify Adopting or affirming a prior, nonbinding act.

real property Land, buildings, and things permanently attached to land or buildings.

real property or real estate The earth's crust and all things firmly attached to it.

reasonable accommodation An accommodation to an individual's disability or religion that does not place an undue burden on the employer, which may be determined by looking to the size of the employer, the cost to the employer, the type of employer, and the impact of the accommodation on the employer's operations.

reasonable expectations test Measure of negligence holding that a product is negligently designed if it is not safe for its intended use and also for any reasonably foreseeable use.

reasonable person Fictitious being the law constructs to determine whether a person's behavior falls short of what a "reasonable person" would do under the circumstances.

red herring A preliminary securities prospectus which provides information but does not constitute an offer to sell.

redlining Most commonly, the practice of refusing to make loans in economically unstable areas with the result that minorities are sometimes discriminated against in securing credit.

reformation An equitable remedy in which a court effectively rewrites the terms of a contract.

registration statement Document filed with the SEC upon issuance of a new security detailing the information investors need to evaluate that security.

Regulation Z Rules of the Federal Reserve Board implementing provisions of the Federal Truth-in-Lending Act.

release Agreement to relinquish a right or a claim. Sometimes labeled a "waiver" or a "hold harmless" clause.

remainderman One who is entitled to the remainder of the estate after a particular estate carved out of it has expired.

remand To send back. For example, a higher court sends a case back to the lower court from which it came.

rent The consideration paid by a lessee to a lessor in exchange for the right to possess and to use property.

rent-strike statutes Legislation that allows a tenant to deduct from the rent payment the cost of property repairs that are otherwise the responsibility of the landlord.

reorganization (Chapter 11) A bankruptcy action in which creditors are kept from the debtor's assets while the debtor, under court supervision, works out a re-payment plan and continues operations.

res A thing, object, or status.

res ipsa loquitur The thing speaks for itself. Rule of evidence establishing a presumption of negligence if the instrumentality causing the injury was in the exclusive control of the defendant, the injury would not ordinarily occur unless someone was negligent, and there is no evidence of other causes.

res judicata A thing decided. A doctrine of legal procedure preventing the retrial of issues already conclusively adjudicated.

resale price maintenance Manufacturer's effort to restrict the price at which its product is resold.

rescission Cancelling a contract; its effect is to restore the parties to their original position.

Resource Conservation and Recovery Act Authorizes the federal government to provide assistance to states and localities in connection with solid waste, to prohibit open dumping, and to establish programs to recover energy and valuable materials from solid waste.

respondeat superior Let the master respond. Doctrine holding the employer liable for negligent acts committed by an employee while in the course of employment.

Restatement of Contracts A collection of the rules of contract law created by the American Law Institute to provide guidance to lawyers and judges.

restitution A remedy whereby one is able to obtain the return of that which he has given the other party, or an equivalent amount of money.

restraints of trade Contracts, combinations, or conspiracies resulting in obstructions of the marketplace, including monopoly, artificially inflated prices, artificially reduced supplies, or other impediments to the natural flow of commerce.

restrictive covenant An agreement restricting use of real property.

reverse Overturn the decision of a court.

RICO Federal organized crime law making it illegal to acquire or operate an enterprise by a pattern of racketeering behavior.

right of survivorship A feature of a joint tenancy that causes a co-owner's interest in property to be transferred on her or his death to the surviving co-owner(s).

right-of-way Where an easement appurtenant refers to the right to physically cross property.

right-to-know laws Federal and state laws and regulations requiring employers to assume the affirmative responsibility of acquainting employees with hazardous substances and conditions in the workplace.

risk/utility test Measure of negligence holding that a product is negligently designed if the benefits of that product's design are outweighed by the risks that accompany that design.

rule of reason For antitrust purposes, reviewing an agreement in its specific factual setting, considering its pro- and anticompetitive features, to determine if it is harmful to competition.

scienter Intent to commit a legal wrong. Guilty knowledge.

scope of employment Limitation on master's liability to only those torts that a servant commits while "about the master's business."

scorched earth defense Takeover defense where the target corporation takes on new debt, sells assets, and so on in an effort to make itself a less attractive target.

secondary boycott Typically a union strategy that places pressure not on the employer with whom the union has a dispute but rather with a supplier or customer of that employer in the hope that the object of the boycott will persuade the employer to meet the union's expectations.

Securities and Exchange Commission (SEC) Federal regulatory agency responsible for overseeing the securities markets.

security A stock, bond, note, or other investment interest in an enterprise designed for profit and operated by one other than the investor.

As to loans, refers to lien, promise, mortgage or the like given by a debtor to assure payment or performance of her debt.

security interest A lien given by a debtor or his creditor to secure payment or performance of a debt or obligation.

self-employment tax A social security tax on people who are self-employed.

separate property Property held by either spouse at the time of marriage or property received by either spouse through a gift or inheritance.

separation of powers The strategy of dividing government into separate and independent executive, legislative, and judicial branches, each of which acts as a check on the power of the others.

service mark A word, mark, symbol, design, picture, or combination thereof that identifies a service provider.

servient estate The property subject to an easement appurtenant or implied easement.

sexual harassment Unwelcome sexual advances, requests for sexual favors, and other unwanted physical or verbal conduct of a sexual nature.

shareholder One holding stock in a corporation.

shark repellant Various kinds of corporate behaviors designed to make a company unattractive to potential acquirers.

shelf registration IPO registration which permits the issuer to hold the securities for sale until favorable market conditions emerge or the issuer needs the proceeds.

short-swing profits Profits made by an insider through sale/purchase of company stock within six months of acquisition.

slander A defamatory statement orally communicated to at least one third party.

slander per se Category of oral defamation not requiring proof of actual harm in order to recover.

small claims courts Courts of limited powers designed to hear cases involving modest sums of money (often limited to about $1,000) in hearings free of many of the formalities and burdens associated with the more conventional judicial process.

small issues Registration exemption for securities issued in small amounts.

sole proprietorship A form of business under which one person owns and controls the business.

sovereign immunity The government's right to exclude itself from being sued for damages in all but those situations where it consents to be sued. In international law, sovereign immunity permits a nation to decline to be sued in the courts of other nations.

specific performance A contract remedy whereby the defendant is ordered to perform precisely according to the terms of his contract.

standing A stake in a dispute sufficient to afford a party the legal right to bring or join a litigation exploring the subject of the dispute.

stare decisis Let the decision stand. A doctrine of judicial procedure expecting a court to follow precedent in all cases involving substantially similar issues unless extremely compelling circumstances dictate a change in judicial direction.

state action Situation of a sufficiently close relationship between the state and the action in question that the action can reasonably be treated as that of the state itself.

statute A legislative enactment.

statute of frauds A statute specifying that certain contracts must be in writing to be enforceable.

statute of limitations A statute requiring that certain classes of lawsuits must be brought within defined limits of time after the right to begin them accrued or the right is lost.

straight voting A form of voting for directors that ordinarily permits a shareholder to cast a number of votes equal to the number of shares he or she owns for as many nominees as there are directors to be elected.

strict liability Civil wrong springing from defective and "unreasonably dangerous" products where responsibility automatically attaches without proof of blame or fault.

sub S corporation A close corporation whose shareholders have elected to be taxed essentially like partners are taxed under federal income tax law.

sublease A transfer of some but not all of a tenant's remaining right to possess property under a lease.

subpoena An order from a court or administrative agency commanding that an individual appear to give testimony or produce specified documents.

substantial performance Performance with minor, unimportant, and unintentional deviation.

substantive due process Due Process Clause of the Constitution requires that a statute be fair and reasonably related to a legitimate government purpose so that persons are not improperly deprived of their property rights.

suggestive mark A trademark that suggests the product or its qualities, more than merely descriptive.

summary judgment A judicial determination prior to holding that no factual dispute exists between the parties and that, as a matter of law, one of the parties is entitled to a favorable judgment.

summons A document originating in a court and delivered to a party or organization indicating that a lawsuit has been commenced against him, her, or it. The summons constitutes notice that the defendant is expected to appear in court to answer the plaintiff's allegations.

sunset legislation A statute providing that a particular government agency will automatically cease to exist as of a specified date unless the legislative body affirmatively acts to extend the life of the agency.

Superfund/CERCLA Established to help pay for the cleanup of hazardous dumps and spills.

Supremacy Clause An element of the U.S. Constitution providing that all constitutionally valid federal laws are the paramount law of the land and, as such, are superior to any conflicting state and local laws.

surety A person who promises to perform the same obligation as the principal and is jointly liable with the principal for that performance.

suretyship A third party agrees to answer for the debt of another.

takeover bid A tender offer designed to assume control of a corporation.

teleological ethical systems Systems that assume that everything has a purpose.

tenancy at sufferance The leasehold interest that occurs when a tenant remains in possession of property after the expiration of a lease.

tenancy at will A leasehold interest that occurs when a property is leased for an indefinite period of time and is terminable at the will of either party to the lease.

tenancy by the entirety A form of co-ownership of property by a married couple that gives the owners a right of survivorship.

tenancy in partnership The manner in which partners co-own partnership property, much like tenancy in common, except that partners have a right of survivorship.

tenant/lessee A party to a lease contract who pays rent in return for the right to possess and to use property.

tenants in common Co-owners of real property who have undivided interests in the property and equal rights to possess it.

tender offer A public bid to the shareholders of a firm offering to buy shares at a specified price for a defined period of time.

term tenancy The tenancy that exists where a landlord and tenant have agreed to the terms of the lease period and a specific termination date for the lease.

test of nonobviousness Determines whether the development described in a patent application would have been obvious to an ordinary skilled worker in the art at the time the invention was made.

third-party beneficiaries People who are not parties to a contract but who have the right to enforce it because the contract was made with the intent to benefit them.

thrust upon Company holds a monopoly innocently because of superior performance, the failure of competition, or changing market conditions.

tippee In securities law, one who receives inside information from another.

tipper In securities law, one who conveys inside information to another.

tombstone ad A securities advertisement that does not constitute an offer and that usually appears in the financial press set inside heavy black borders suggestive of a tombstone.

tort A civil wrong not arising from a contract.

totalitarianism A rigid, undemocratic government according power to a particular political group and excluding all others from access to political influence. The Soviet Union, Nazi Germany, and Fascist Italy were totalitarian states.

Toxic Substances Control Act Requires chemical manufacturers to report information relating to chemicals that pose a "substantial risk" and allows the EPA to review and limit, or to stop, the introduction of new chemicals.

Trade Regulation Rules Directives from the Federal Trade Commission interpreting the will of Congress and specifying those practices that the Commission considers unfair or deceptive.

trademark A word, name, or other distinctive symbol registered with the government and used exclusively by the owner to identify its product.

trademark infringement Unauthorized use of the trademark of another.

treaty or convention A contract between nations.

treble damages An award of damages totaling three times the amount of actual damages, authorized by some statutes in an effort to discourage further wrongful conduct.

trespass Entering the property of another without any right, lawful authority, or invitation.

trespasser A person who enters the property of another without any right, lawful authority, or invitation.

tying arrangement Dealer agrees to sell or lease a product (the tying product) only on the conditions that the buyer also purchases or leases another product (the tied product).

ultra vires Corporate conduct beyond the scope of activities provided for under the terms of incorporation.

unconscionable A contract so one-sided and oppressive as to be unfair.

underwriter Professional who helps sell new securities or buys those securities for the purpose of resale.

undivided share A share of the interest in property that is not subject to division into parts.

undue hardship A burden imposed on an employer by accommodating an individual's disability or religion that would be too onerous for the employer to bear. [See *reasonable accommodation.*]

undue influence Dominion that results in a right to rescind a contract.

unemployment taxes Federal and state (most) taxes paid by employers as a percentage of the total payroll for the purpose of funding benefits for those who have lost their jobs.

unenforceable contract Meets basic requirements, but remains faulty.

unfair labor practice Activities identified by Congress that employers might use to thwart workers' attempts to unionize and to undermine the economic power that would come from the workers' right to concerted activities and to unionize.

unfair subsidies Subsidies offered to producers in a certain industry by a government in order to spur growth in that industry. These subsidies are considered unfair if they are used to promote export trade that harms another country.

Uniform Partnership Act (UPA) Original uniform act for creation and operation of partnerships.

unilateral contract A contract wherein the only acceptance of the offer that is necessary is the performance of the act.

unilateral mistake Where one party to a contract is in error about a material fact.

union shop In labor law, the situation where all employees of a company must join a union in order to retain employment. Forbidden in right-to-work states.

unjust enrichment An unearned benefit knowingly accepted.

unsecured Refers to a loan not backed by some kind of security.

use taxes Normally, taxes imposed on the use, storage, or consumption of tangible personal property bought outside of the state imposing the taxes.

usury Charging an interest rate exceeding the legally permissible maximum.

venture capital funds Organizations designed to invest in new and often risky business enterprises.

venue The specific geographic location in which a court holding jurisdiction should properly hear a case, given the convenience of the parties and other relevant considerations.

verdict The jury's decision as to who wins the litigation.

vertical merger A union between two firms at different levels of the same channel of distribution.

vesting rights The right of an individual to a present or future fixed benefit.

voidable contract Capable of being made void; enforceable but can be cancelled.

voir dire The portion of a trial in which prospective jurors are questioned to determine their qualifications, including absence of bias, to sit in judgment in the case.

voting stock Owners of voting stock have the right to vote at shareholder meetings.

waiver Relinquishing a legal right—as the situation where one agrees not to sue if injured while participating in a particular activity, such as attending a baseball game.

warranty Any promise, expressed or implied, that the facts are true as specified. For example, in consumer law, the warranty of merchantability is a guaranty that the product is reasonably fit for the general purpose for which it was sold.

watered stock Inadequate consideration received for stock.

white-collar crime Law violations by corporations or by managerial and executive personnel in the course of their professional duties.

white knight In a takeover battle, a friendly company that rescues the target company from a hostile takeover. Often the rescue is accomplished by a merger between the target and the white knight.

winding up In partnership and corporation law, the orderly liquidation of the business's assets.

without reserve At an auction advertised as "without reserve," the seller is not free to withdraw an item before the high bid is accepted.

workers' compensation laws State statutes providing fixed recoveries for injuries and illnesses sustained in the course of employment. Under those statutes, workers need not establish fault on the part of the employer.

wrongful discharge Tort of dismissing another from employment in violation of public policy.

yellow dog contract An employment agreement by an employee not to become a member of a union.

zoning Restriction on the use of land as a result of public land use regulation.

zoning ordinances Dividing a city or a county into geographical areas of restriction—for example, only residential housing would be permitted in an area zoned R.

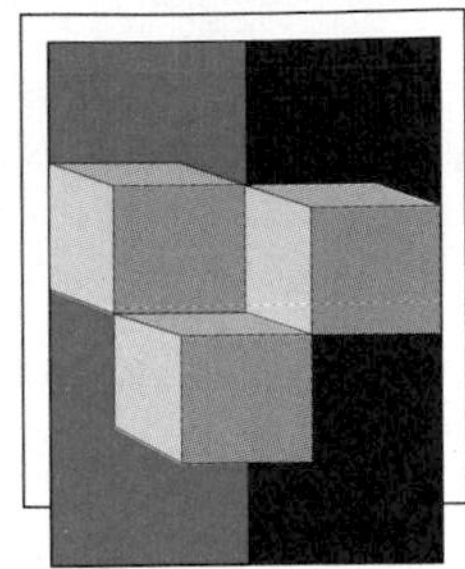

Case Index

Capital letters indicate cases excerpted in text.

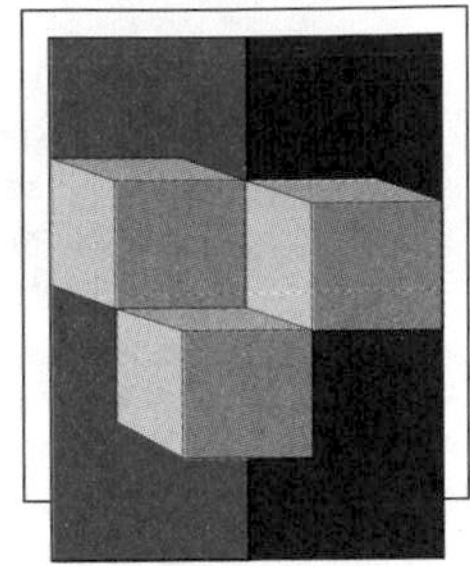

General Index

F